Freedom on My Mind

A History of African Americans with Documents

SECOND EDITION

Deborah Gray White
Rutgers University

Mia Bay
Rutgers University

Waldo E. Martin Jr.
University of California, Berkeley

bedford/st.martin's
Macmillan Learning
Boston | New York

FOR BEDFORD/ST. MARTIN'S

Vice President, Editorial, Macmillan Learning Humanities: Edwin Hill
Publisher for History: Michael Rosenberg
Senior Executive Editor for History: William J. Lombardo
Director of Development for History: Jane Knetzger
Developmental Editor: Jennifer Jovin
Editorial Assistant: Lexi DeConti
Senior Production Editor: Rosemary Jaffe
Media Producer: Michelle Camisa
Production Supervisor: Robert Cherry
History Marketing Manager: Melissa Famiglietti
Copy Editor: Arthur Johnson
Indexer: Leoni Z. McVey
Cartography: Mapping Specialists, Ltd.
Photo Editor: Cecilia Varas
Photo Researcher: Bruce Carson
Permissions Editor: Eve Lehmann
Senior Art Director: Anna Palchik
Text Design: Boynton Hue Studio
Cover Design: John Callahan
Cover Photos: Top to bottom: *Olaudah Equiano: Portrait of an African,* c. 1757–1760 (oil on canvas), Ramsay, Allan (1713–1784) (attr. to)/Royal Albert Memorial Museum, Exeter, Devon, UK/Bridgeman Images; Harriet Tubman: Lindsley, H. B., photographer (*Harriet Tubman, full-length portrait, standing with hands on back of a chair*) between c. 1860 and 1875. Retrieved from the Library of Congress, https://www.loc.gov/item/2003674596; Madame C. J. Walker: The Granger Collection, New York; Shirley Chisholm: © Everett Collection Historical/Alamy Stock Photo; U.S. President Barack Obama: Andrew Harrer/Bloomberg via Getty Images.
Composition: Jouve
Printing and Binding: King Printing Co., Inc.

For information, write: Bedford/St. Martin's, 75 Arlington Street, Boston, MA 02116   (617-399-4000)

ISBN 978-1-319-02133-7 (Combined Edition)
ISBN 978-1-319-06052-7 (Volume 1)
ISBN 978-1-319-06053-4 (Volume 2)

ACKNOWLEDGMENTS

Preface for Instructors

Why This Book This Way

"Freedom is never voluntarily given by the oppressor; it must be demanded by the oppressed," wrote Martin Luther King Jr. in his "Letter from Birmingham City Jail." Written in April 1963 while he was incarcerated for participating in a nonviolent protest against racial segregation, King's letter was a rebuttal to white religious leaders who condemned such protests as unwise and untimely. King's understanding of freedom also summarizes the remarkable history of the many generations of African Americans whose experiences are chronicled in this book. Involuntary migrants to America, the Africans who became African Americans achieved freedom from slavery only after centuries of struggle, protest, and outright revolt. Prior to the Civil War, most were unfree inhabitants of a democratic republic that took shape around the ideals of "life, liberty, and the pursuit of happiness." Although largely exempted from these ideals, African Americans fought for them.

Writing of these enslaved noncitizens in the first chapter of *The Souls of Black Folk* (1903), black historian W. E. B. Du Bois proclaimed, "Few men ever worshipped Freedom with half such unquestioning faith as did the American Negro." Du Bois saw a similar spirit among his contemporaries: He was certain that "there are to-day no truer exponents of the pure human spirit of the Declaration of Independence than the American Negroes." Yet Du Bois lived in an era when freedom was still the "unattained ideal." Segregated and disfranchised in the South, and subject to racial exploitation and discrimination throughout the nation, black people still sought "the freedom of life and limb, the freedom to work and think, the freedom to love and aspire." Moreover, as long as black people were not free, America could not be the world's beacon of liberty. The black freedom struggle would continue, remaking the nation as a whole.

Our Approach

Like Du Bois, we, the authors of *Freedom on My Mind*, take African Americans' quest for freedom as the central theme of African American history and explore all dimensions of that quest, situated as it must be in the context of American history. Our perspective is that African American history complicates American history rather than diverging from it. This idea is woven into our narrative, which records the paradoxical experiences of a group of people at once the most American of Americans — in terms of their long history in America, their vital role in the American economy, and their enormous impact on American culture — and at the same time the Americans most consistently excluded from the American dream. Juxtaposed against American history as a whole, this is a study of a group of Americans who have had to fight too hard for freedom yet have been systematically excluded from many of the opportunities that allowed other groups to experience the United States as a land of opportunity. This text encourages students to think critically and analytically about African American history and the historical realities behind the American dream.

The following themes and emphases are central to our approach:

The principal role of the black freedom struggle in the development of the American state. Our approach necessitates a study of the troubled relationship between African Americans and the American democratic state. *Freedom on My Mind* underscores the disturbing fact that our democracy arose within the context of a slaveholding society, though it ultimately gave way to the democratic forces unleashed by the Revolution that founded the new nation and the Civil War that reaffirmed federal sovereignty. Exempt from the universalist language of the Declaration of Independence — "all men are created equal" — African Americans have been, as Du Bois insightfully noted, "a concrete test of the underlying principles of the great republic." Most vividly illustrated during the political upheavals of Reconstruction and the civil rights movement — which is often called America's second Reconstruction — African American activism has been crucial to the evolution of American democratic institutions.

The diversity of African Americans and the African American experience. Any study of the African American freedom struggle must recognize the wide diversity of African Americans who participated in it, whether they did so through open rebellion and visible social protest; through more covert means of defiance, disobedience, and dissent; or simply by surviving and persevering in the face of overwhelming odds. Complicating any conceptions students might have of a single-minded, monolithic African American collective, *Freedom on My Mind* is mindful of black diversity and the ways and means that gender, class, and ethnicity — as well as region, culture, and politics — shaped the black experience and the struggle for freedom. The book explores African Americans' search for freedom in slave rebellions, everyday resistance to slavery, the abolitionist movement, Reconstruction politics, post-emancipation labor struggles, the great migration, military service, civil rights activism, and the black power movement. It shows how American democracy was shaped by African Americans' search for, as Du Bois put it, "human opportunity" — and the myriad forms and characters that this search assumed.

An emphasis on culture as a vital force in black history. *Freedom on My Mind* also illuminates the rich and self-affirming culture blacks established in response to their exclusion from and often adversarial relationship with American institutions — the life Du Bois metaphorically characterized as "behind the veil." The rhythms and structure of black social and religious life, the contours of black educational struggles, the music Du Bois described as the "greatest gift of the Negro people" to the American nation, the parallel institutions built as a means of self-affirmation and self-defense — all of these are examined in the context of African Americans' quest for freedom, escape from degradation, and inclusion in the nation's body politic.

A synthesis that makes black history's texture and complexity clear. While culture is central to *Freedom on My Mind*, we offer an analytical approach to African American culture that enables students to see it as a central force that both shaped and reflected other historical developments, rather than as a phenomenon in a vacuum. How do we process black art — poetry, music, paintings, novels, sculptures, quilts — without understanding the political, economic, and social conditions that these pieces express? When spirituals, jazz, the blues, and rap flow from the economic and social conditions experienced by multitudes of blacks, how can we not understand black music as political? Indeed, African American culture, politics, and identity are inextricably entwined in ways that call for an approach to this subject that blends social, political, economic, religious, and cultural history. Such distinctions often seem arbitrary in American history as a whole and are impossible in chronicling the experiences of African Americans. How can we separate the religious and political history of people whose church leaders have often led their communities from the pulpit and the political stump? Therefore, *Freedom on My Mind* sidesteps such divisions in favor of a synthesis that privileges the sustained interplay among culture, politics, economics, religion, and social forces in the African American experience.

Twenty-first-century scholarship for today's classroom. Each chapter offers a synthesis of the most up-to-date historiography and historiographical debates in a clear narrative style. So much has changed since Du Bois pioneered the field of African American history. Once relegated to black historians and the oral tradition, African American history as a scholarly endeavor flowered with the social history revolt of the 1960s, when the events of the civil rights movement drew new attention to the African American past and the social upheaval of the 1960s inspired historians to recover the voices of the voiceless. Women's history also became a subject of serious study during this era, and as a result of all of these changes, we now survey an American history that has been reconstituted by nearly a half century of sustained attention to race, class, and gender.

Drawing on the most recent scholarship, this text not only will deepen students' understanding of the interconnectedness of African American and American history but also will link African American struggles for political and civil rights, individual autonomy, religious freedom, economic equity, and racial justice to other Americans: white, red, yellow, and brown. As Americans, these groups shared a world subject to similar structural forces, such as environmental changes, demographic forces, white supremacy, and the devastating effects of world events on the American economy in times of global economic upheaval or war. Sometimes blacks bonded with other groups, and sometimes their interests clashed. Often the experiences of other Americans ran parallel to the African American experience, and sometimes African American resistance served as a template for the resistance of others. *Freedom on My Mind* recounts this complex historical interaction. Although more than a century has unfolded since Du Bois wrote *Souls*, we have tried to remain true to the spirit of that text and write, with "loving emphasis," the history of African Americans.

The Docutext Format

We believe that the primary goals of our book — to highlight the deep connections between black history and the development of American democracy, illustrate the diversity of black experience, emphasize the centrality of black culture, and document the inextricable connections among black culture, politics, economics, and social and religious life — could not be realized to their fullest extent through narrative alone. Thus *Freedom on My Mind*'s unique docutext structure combines a brief narrative with rich, **themed sets of textual and visual primary documents**, reimagining the relationship between the narrative and the historical actors who form it. The narrative portion of each chapter is followed by a set of primary sources focused on a particular chapter topic. Each set is clearly cross-referenced within the narrative so that students can connect it to and interpret it in terms of what they've learned. Carefully developed pedagogical elements — including substantive introductions, document headnotes, and Questions for Analysis at the close of each set — help students learn to analyze primary documents and practice "doing" history.

These visuals and documents showcase and examine a rich variety of African American cultural elements and underscore the abiding connections among African American political activism, religious beliefs, economic philosophies, musical genres, and literary and fine art expression. A host of pictorial source types — from artifacts, photographs, paintings, and sculpture to cartoons and propaganda — and documentary sources ranging from personal letters, memoirs, and poetry to public petitions and newspaper accounts illuminate the primary evidence that underpins and complicates the history students learn. Taken together, documents and images as varied as slave captivity narratives, early American visual portrayals of black freedom fighters, the writings of free blacks like Absalom Jones and James Forten, scenes of everyday realities in the 1930s, accounts from Tuskegee Syphilis Study participants, the narratives of the civil rights era, reflections on redefining community in a diverse black America, and the responses of #BlackLivesMatter protesters and the police to the deaths of young black men all provide students with a vivid and appealing illustration of the interplay of societal forces and the centrality of African American culture to American culture. By placing these historical actors in conversation with one another, we enable students to witness firsthand the myriad variations of and nuances within individual and collective black experiences and to appreciate the points at which African Americans have diverged, as well as those at which they have agreed. Together with a narrative that presents and analyzes their context, these documents facilitate students' comprehension of the textured, complicated story that is the history of African America.

Support for Students

Freedom on My Mind includes a variety of carefully crafted pedagogical features to help students grasp, assimilate, analyze, and recall what they've learned. Each chapter opens with a **thematic vignette** illustrating the issues confronting African Americans of that time period and then transitions to an informative **introduction** that sets out the thesis and takeaway points of the chapter. A **chapter timeline** highlights the most significant events of both African American history and general United States history during that time period, providing a quick reference for students. At the end of each chapter's narrative, a **Conclusion** allows students to retrace their steps through the chapter and previews the chapter that follows. A **Chapter Review** section provides a list of key terms — all of which are bolded when first defined in the narrative and listed with their definitions in a **Glossary of Key Terms** at the end of the book — as well as three to five **Review Questions** encouraging students to think critically about the deeper implications of each chapter section and the connections between sections.

In addition to the visual sources in the document sets, the narrative is enhanced by the inclusion of **over 160 images** and **35 maps and By the Numbers graphs**, each with a substantive caption that helps students relate what they're seeing to what they've read and analyze quantitative data.

To facilitate further research and study, we have included extensive **Notes** and section-specific lists of **Suggested References** at the close of every chapter. Finally, we have provided an **Introduction for Students** that introduces students to the work of the historian and the practice of primary source analysis, and two **Appendices** that include a wide variety of tables, charts, and vital documents, many of them annotated to provide a deeper reference tool. We are confident that these elements will be useful not only for students but also for instructors who wish to introduce students to the practice of history and provide the resources their students will need for research projects, further reading, and reference.

Support for Instructors

We structured this book with the instructor in mind as well as the student: We believe that the book's docutext format provides the convenience and flexibility of a textbook and source reader in one, allowing instructors a unique opportunity to incorporate primary readings and visuals seamlessly into their classes and introduce students to primary-source analysis and the practice of history. The **Document Projects** and the pedagogy that supports them can be used in many ways — from in-class discussion prompts to take-home writing assignments or essay questions on exams. An **Instructor's Resource Manual** for *Freedom on My Mind* provides a variety of creative suggestions for making the best use of the documents program and for incorporating rich multimedia resources into the course. *The Bedford Lecture Kit* and **online test bank** provide additional instructional support. For more information on available student and instructor resources and the wide range of books that can be packaged with this text at a discount, see the Versions and Supplements section on pages x–xii.

New to the Second Edition

Based on reviewer feedback to the first edition, we decided to consolidate the written and visual primary sources at the ends of the chapters into mixed-source Document Projects. As a result, we were able to expand the number and types of documents offered on a particular topic, such as those on the Middle Passage (chapter 1), debt peonage (chapter 9), lynching (chapter 9), and the Tuskegee experiments during World War II (chapter 11). The new edition also gave us the opportunity to add wholly new document sets on the codification of slavery in the seventeenth and eighteenth centuries (chapter 2) and the Black Lives Matter movement (chapter 15).

Outside of the Document Projects, we expanded coverage of key topics in both African American and general U.S. history. In the eighteenth century, we further explore the impact of the Great Awakening on slaves' lives (chapter 3) and go into more depth about the significance of Crispus Attucks to American Revolutionary history (chapter 3). We examine African Americans' roles in the War of 1812, both as members of the nation's military forces and as free black civilians (chapter 4). We added to our examination of the evolution of race relations over the last one hundred years by discussing racial discrimination in labor unions (chapter 10), white backlash against affirmative action in the late 1960s and early 1970s (chapter 14), increased tension among blacks and other racial groups that also felt marginalized and oppressed (chapter 14), and the relationship between the black community and law enforcement (chapter 15). Finally, we updated the last chapter to include an analysis of President Obama's second term.

Acknowledgments

In completing this book, we owe thanks to the many talented and generous friends, colleagues, and editors who have provided us with suggestions, critiques, and much careful reading along the way.

Foremost among them is the hardworking group of scholar-teachers who reviewed the first edition for us. We are deeply grateful to them for their insights and suggestions, and we hope we do them justice in the second edition. We thank Luther Adams, *University of Washington Tacoma*; Ezrah Aharone, *Delaware State University*; Jacqueline Akins, *Community College of Philadelphia*; Okey P. Akubeze, *University of Wisconsin–Milwaukee*; Lauren K. Anderson, *Luther College*; Scott Barton, *East Central University*; Diane L. Beers, *Holyoke Community College*; Dan Berger, *University of Washington Bothell*; Christopher Bonner, *University of Maryland*; Susan Bragg, *Georgia Southwestern State University*; Lester Brooks, *Anne Arundel Community College*; E. Tsekani Browne, *Montgomery College*; Monica L. Butler, *Seminole State College of Florida*; Thomas L. Bynum, *Middle Tennessee State University*; Erin D. Chapman, *George Washington University*; Meredith Clark-Wiltz, *Franklin College*; Alexandra Cornelius, *Florida International University*; Julie Davis, *Cerritos College*; John Kyle Day, *University of Arkansas at Monticello*; Dorothy Drinkard-Hawkshawe, *East Tennessee State University*; Nancy J. Duke, *Daytona State College, Daytona Beach*; Reginald K. Ellis, *Florida A&M University*; Keona K. Ervin, *University of Missouri–Columbia*; Joshua David Farrington, *Eastern Kentucky University*; Marvin Fletcher, *Ohio University*; Amy Forss, *Metropolitan Community College*; Delia C. Gillis, *University of Central Missouri*; Kevin D. Greene, *The University of Southern Mississippi*; LaVerne Gyant, *Northern Illinois University*; Timothy Hack, *Middlesex County College*; Kenneth M. Hamilton, *Southern Methodist University*; Martin Hardeman, *Eastern Illinois University*; Jarvis Hargrove, *North Carolina Central University*; Jim C. Harper II, *North Carolina Central University*; Margaret Harris, *Southern New Hampshire University*; Patricia Herb, *North Central State College*; Elizabeth Herbin-Triant, *University of Massachusetts Lowell*; Pippa Holloway, *Middle Tennessee State University*; Marilyn Howard, *Columbus State Community College*; Carol Sue Humphrey, *Oklahoma Baptist University*; Bryan Jack, *Southern Illinois University Edwardsville*; Jerry Rafiki Jenkins, *Palomar College*; Karen J. Johns, *University of Nebraska at Omaha*; Winifred M. Johnson, *Bethune-Cookman University*; Gary Jones, *American International College*; Ishmael Kimbrough III, *Bakersfield College*; Michelle Kuhl, *University of Wisconsin Oshkosh*; Lynda Lamarre, *Georgia Military College*; Renee Lansley, *Framingham State University*; Talitha LeFlouria, *University of Virginia*; Monroe Little, *Indiana University–Purdue University Indianapolis*; Margaret A. Lowe, *Bridgewater State University*; Vince Lowery, *University of Wisconsin–Green Bay*; Robert Luckett, *Jackson State University*; Steven Lurenz, *Mesa Community College*; Peggy Macdonald, *Florida Polytechnic University*; Bruce Mactavish, *Washburn University*; Gerald McCarthy, *St. Thomas Aquinas College*; Suzanne McCormack, *Community College of Rhode Island*; Anthony Merritt, *San Diego State University*; Karen K. Miller, *Boston College*; Steven Millner, *San Jose State University*; Billie J. Moore, *El Camino Compton Center*; Maggi M. Morehouse, *Coastal Carolina University*; Lynda Morgan, *Mount Holyoke College*; Earl Mulderink, *Southern Utah University*; Cassandra Newby-Alexander, *Norfolk State University*; Victor D. Padilla Jr., *Wright College*; N. Josiah Pamoja, *Georgia Military College, Fairburn*; Leslie Patrick, *Bucknell University*; Abigail Perkiss, *Kean University*; Alex Peshkoff, *Cosumnes River College*; Melvin Pritchard, *West Valley College*; Margaret Reed, *Northern Virginia Community College, Annandale Campus*; Stephanie Richmond, *Norfolk State University*; John Riedl, *Montgomery College*; Natalie J. Ring, *University of Texas at Dallas*; Maria Teresa Romero, *Saddleback College*; Tara Ross, *Onondaga Community College*; Selena Sanderfer, *Western Kentucky University*; Jonathan D. Sassi, *CUNY–College of*

Staten Island; Gerald Schumacher, *Nunez Community College*; Gary Shea, *Center for Advanced Studies and the Arts*; Tobin Shearer, *University of Montana*; John Howard Smith, *Texas A&M University–Commerce*; Solomon Smith, *Georgia Southern University*; Pamela A. Smoot, *Southern Illinois University Carbondale*; Karen Sotiropoulos, *Cleveland State University*; Melissa M. Soto-Schwartz, *Cuyahoga Community College*; Idris Kabir Syed, *Kent State University*; Linda D. Tomlinson, *Fayetteville State University*; Felicia A. Viator, *University of California, Berkeley*; Eric M. Washington, *Calvin College*; and Joanne G. Woodard, *University of North Texas*.

Our debt to the many brilliant editors at Bedford/St. Martin's is equally immeasurable. We are grateful to publisher Michael Rosenberg, senior executive editor William J. Lombardo, director of development Jane Knetzger, history marketing manager Melissa Famiglietti, editorial assistant Lexi DeConti, and the other members of Bedford's outstanding history team for guiding the development of this second edition. We also thank Bruce Carson and Cecilia Varas for researching and clearing the book's photographs, Kalina Ingham and Eve Lehmann for clearing the text permissions, Arthur Johnson for copyediting the manuscript, Roberta Sobotka and Linda McLatchie for proofreading, Leoni Z. McVey for indexing, Cia Boynton for her design of the book's interior, and John Callahan for his design of the cover. We also want to acknowledge Rosemary Jaffe, our production editor for both the first and second editions, who coordinated the work of copyediting, proofreading, and illustrating this book with amazing grace, good humor, and attention to detail. Finally, we would like to thank Jennifer Jovin, whose careful editing of the second edition helped streamline and fine-tune the original text. Letting go of carefully crafted paragraphs and sections is always difficult, but Jennifer's insight, patience, and gentle nudging made it easier than usual. Without her guidance we would not have been able to reimagine the book. We thank them all for making the writing of this book such a pleasant experience.

In writing this book we have also relied on a large number of talented scholars and friends within the academy to supply us with guidance, editorial expertise, bright ideas, research assistance, and many other forms of support, and we would like to thank them here. The enormous — but by no means comprehensive — list of colleagues, friends, students, and former students to whom we are indebted includes Isra Ali, Marsha Barrett, Rachel Bernard, Melissa Cooper, John Day, Jeff Dowd, Joseph L. Duong, Ann Fabian, Jared Farmer, Larissa Fergeson, Krystal Frazier, Raymond Gavins, Sharon Harley, Nancy Hewitt, Martha Jones, Stephanie Jones-Rogers, Mia Kissil, Christopher Lehman, Thomas Lekan, Emily Lieb, Leon F. Litwack, Julie Livingston, David Lucander, Catherine L. Macklin, Jaime Martinez, Story Matkin-Rawn, Gregory Mixon, Donna Murch, Kimberly Phillips, Alicia Rodriguez, David Schoebun, Karcheik Sims-Alvarado, Jason Sokol, Melissa Stein, Ellen Stroud, Melissa Stuckey, Anantha Sudakar, Patricia Sullivan, Keith Wailoo, Dara Walker, and Wendy Wright. Deborah would especially like to thank Maya White Pascual for her invaluable assistance with many of the documents in the last third of the book. Her insight, skill, and talent were absolutely indispensable.

Finally, all three of us are grateful to our families and loved ones for the support and forbearance that they showed us during our work on this book.

Deborah Gray White
Mia Bay
Waldo E. Martin Jr.

Versions and Supplements

Adopters of *Freedom on My Mind* and their students have access to abundant resources, including documents, presentation and testing materials, volumes in the acclaimed Bedford Series in History and Culture, and much more.

To Learn More

For more information on the offerings described below, visit the book's catalog site at **macmillanlearning.com**, or contact your local Bedford/St. Martin's sales representative.

Get the Right Version for Your Class

To accommodate different course lengths and course budgets, *Freedom on My Mind* is available in several different formats, including e-Books, which are available at a substantial discount.

- Combined edition (chapters 1–15) — available in paperback and e-Book formats
- Volume 1: To 1885 (chapters 1–8) — available in paperback and e-Book formats
- Volume 2: Since 1865 (chapters 8–15) — available in paperback and e-Book formats

Students can find PDF versions of the e-Book at our publishing partners' sites, such as VitalSource, Barnes & Noble NookStudy, RedShelf, Kno, CafeScribe, and Chegg. As noted below, any of these volumes can be packaged with additional titles for a discount. To get ISBNs for discount packages, visit **macmillanlearning.com** or contact your Bedford/St. Martin's sales representative.

Take Advantage of Instructor Resources

Bedford/St. Martin's has developed a rich array of teaching resources for this book and for this course. They range from lecture and presentation materials to course management options. Most can be downloaded at **macmillanlearning.com**.

Bedford Coursepack for Blackboard, Canvas, Brightspace by D2L, or Moodle. We can help you integrate our rich content into your course management system. Registered instructors can download coursepacks that include our popular free resources and book-specific content for *Freedom on My Mind*. Visit **macmillanlearning.com** to find your version or download your coursepack.

Instructor's Resource Manual. The instructor's manual offers both experienced and first-time instructors tools for preparing lectures and running discussions. It includes content learning objectives, annotated chapter outlines, and strategies for teaching with the textbook, plus a survival guide for first-time teaching assistants.

Guide to Changing Editions. Designed to facilitate an instructor's transition from the previous edition of *Freedom on My Mind* to this new edition, this guide presents an overview of major changes as well as changes within each chapter.

Online Test Bank. The test bank includes a mix of fresh and carefully crafted multiple-choice, matching, short-answer, and essay questions for each chapter, along with volume-based essay questions. Many of the multiple-choice questions feature a map, an image, or a primary-source excerpt as the prompt. All questions appear in easy-to-use test bank software that allows instructors to add, edit, re-sequence, and print questions and answers. Instructors can also export questions into a variety of course management systems.

The Bedford Lecture Kit: **Maps, Images, and Lecture Outlines.** Be effective and save time with *The Bedford Lecture Kit*. These presentation materials are downloadable individually from the Instructor Resources tab at **macmillanlearning.com**. They include fully customizable multimedia presentations built around chapter outlines that are embedded with maps, figures, and images from the textbook and are supplemented by more detailed instructor notes on key points and concepts.

America in Motion: **Video Clips for U.S. History.** Set history in motion with *America in Motion*, an instructor DVD containing dozens of short movie files of events in twentieth-century American history. *America in Motion* engages students with dynamic scenes from key events and challenges them to think critically. All files are classroom-ready, edited for brevity, and easily integrated with presentation slides or other software for electronic lectures or assignments. An accompanying guide provides each clip's historical context, ideas for use, and suggested questions.

Print, Digital, and Custom Options for More Choice and Value

For information on free packages and discounts up to 50%, visit **macmillanlearning.com** or contact your local Bedford/St. Martin's sales representative.

New! Bedford Custom Tutorials for History. Designed to customize textbooks with resources relevant to individual courses, this collection of brief units, each of which is 16 pages long and loaded with examples, guides students through basic skills such as using historical evidence effectively, working with primary sources, taking effective notes, avoiding plagiarism and citing sources, and more. Up to two tutorials can be added to a Bedford/St. Martin's history survey title at no additional charge, freeing you to spend your class time focusing on content and interpretation. For more information, visit **macmillanlearning.com/historytutorials**.

New! The Bedford Digital Collections for African American History. This source collection provides a flexible and affordable online repository of discovery-oriented primary-source projects ready to assign. Each curated project — written by a historian about a favorite topic — poses a historical question and guides students step-by-step through analysis of primary sources. African American history projects include "Convict Labor and the Building of Modern America" by Talitha L. LeFlouria, "War Stories: African American Soldiers and the Long Civil Rights Movement" by Maggi M. Morehouse, "Organization and Protest in the Civil Rights–Era South: The Montgomery Bus Boycott" by Paul Harvey, and "The Challenge of Liberal Reform: School Desegregation, North and South" by Joseph Crespino. For more information, visit **macmillanlearning.com/bdcafricanamerican/catalog**. Available free when packaged.

New! Bedford Digital Collections Custom Print Modules. Choose one or two document projects from the source collection (see above) and add them in print to a Bedford/St. Martin's title, or select several projects to be bound together in a custom reader created specifically for your course. Either way, the modules are affordably priced. For more information, contact your Bedford/St. Martin's sales representative.

The Bedford Series in History and Culture. More than 100 titles in this highly praised series combine first-rate scholarship, historical narrative, and important primary documents for undergraduate courses. Each book is brief, inexpensive, and focused on a specific topic or period. New or recently revised titles include *The Interesting Narrative of the Life of Olaudah Equiano, Written by Himself, with Related Documents,* Third Edition, edited with an introduction by Robert J. Allison; *The Confessions of Nat Turner, with Related Documents,* Second Edition, edited with an introduction by Kenneth S. Greenberg; *Narrative of the Life of Frederick Douglass, an American Slave, Written by Himself, with Related Documents,* Third Edition, edited with an introduction by David W. Blight; *Dred Scott v. Sandford: A Brief History with Documents,* Second Edition, by Paul Finkelman; *Southern Horrors and Other Writings: The Anti-Lynching Campaign of Ida B. Wells, 1892–1900,* Second Edition, edited with an introduction by Jacqueline Jones Royster; and *Freedom Summer: A Brief History with Documents,* by John Dittmer, Jeffrey Kolnick, and Leslie Burl McLemore. For a complete list of titles, visit **macmillanlearning.com**. Package discounts are available.

Rand McNally Atlas of American History. This collection of over 80 full-color maps illustrates key events and eras in American history, from early exploration, settlement, expansion, and immigration to U.S. involvement in wars abroad and on U.S. soil. Introductory pages for each section include a brief overview, timelines, graphs, and photos to quickly establish a historical context. Free when packaged.

The Bedford Glossary for U.S. History. This handy supplement gives students historically contextualized definitions for hundreds of terms — from *abolitionism* to *zoot suit* — that they will encounter in lectures, reading, and exams. Free when packaged.

Trade Books. Titles published by sister companies Hill and Wang; Farrar, Straus and Giroux; Henry Holt and Company; St. Martin's Press; Picador; and Palgrave Macmillan are available at a 50% discount when packaged with Bedford/St. Martin's textbooks. For more information, visit **macmillanlearning.com**.

A Pocket Guide to Writing in History. This portable and affordable reference tool by Mary Lynn Rampolla provides reading, writing, and research advice useful to students in all history courses. Concise yet comprehensive advice on approaching typical history assignments, developing critical reading skills, writing effective history papers, conducting research, using and documenting sources, and avoiding plagiarism — enhanced with practical tips and examples throughout — has made this slim reference a best seller. Package discounts available.

A Student's Guide to History. This complete guide to success in any history course provides the practical help students need to be effective. In addition to introducing students to the nature of the discipline, author Jules Benjamin teaches a wide range of skills, from preparing for exams to approaching common writing assignments, and explains the research and documentation process with plentiful examples. Package discounts available.

Brief Contents

Contents

CHAPTER 1
From Africa to America, 1441–1808
2

Color engraving, 1850, based on a
French engraving from the 1830s/
Photo © CCI/Bridgeman Images.

CHAPTER 4
Slavery and Freedom in the New Republic, 1775–1820   *130*

CHAPTER 5
Black Life in the Slave South, 1820–1860

172

© North Wind Picture Archives/Alamy Stock Photo.

CHAPTER 9

Black Life and Culture during the Nadir, 1880–1915

342

ITE SUPREMACY!

ttention, White Men!

d Torch-Light Procession

At JACKSON,

On the Night of the

The Granger Collection, New York.

CHAPTER 10
The New Negro Comes of Age, 1915–1940

390

Chicago History Museum/ Getty Images.

CHAPTER 13 Multiple Meanings of Freedom: The Movement Broadens, 1961–1976   *524*

© *George Ballis/Take Stock/ The Image Works.*

CHAPTER 14 · Racial Progress in an Era of Backlash and Change, 1967–2000 · 570

Don Hogan Charles/Archive Photos/Getty Images.

CHAPTER 15 · African Americans and the New Century, 2000–Present · 614

© *David M. Grossman/Image Works.*

Maps and Figures

Introduction for Students

It is a joy to offer *Freedom on My Mind* to enhance your knowledge of both African American history and the craft of history. For us, the authors, history has never been just a series of dates and names. It is not just memorizable facts, consumed only to pass a test or complete an assignment. For us, history is adventure; it's a puzzle that must be both unraveled and put together. Being a historian is like being a time-traveling detective. To be able to use our sleuthing skills to unveil the history of African Americans, a history that for too long was dismissed but tells us so much about American democracy, is not just a delight but a serious responsibility.

The History of African American History

Although black Americans first came to North America in 1619, before the *Mayflower* brought New England Pilgrims, the history of African American history has a relatively recent past. For most of American history black history was ignored, overlooked, exploited, demeaned, discounted, or ridiculed — much as African Americans were. Worse yet, history was often used to justify the mistreatment of African Americans: The history of Africans was used to justify slavery, and the history of slavery was used to justify the subsequent disfranchisement, discrimination, rape, and lynching of African Americans.

American blacks understood this connection between a history that misrepresented them and their citizenship, and they fought not only to free themselves from bondage but also to create a legacy that future generations could be proud of: a legacy that championed their self-inspired "uplift" and that countered the negative images and history that prevailed in American society. Take just one example: D. W. Griffith's film *The Birth of a Nation* (1915) used revolutionary cinematography to disseminate a history that represented slaves as happy and race relations as rosy, until the Civil War and Reconstruction unleashed black criminals and sexual predators on an innocent South. Many used Griffith's film to justify the lynching of black men and the segregation of the races. Indeed, President Woodrow Wilson, the historian who as president introduced segregation into the government offices of Washington, D.C., premiered the film in the White House and praised its historical accuracy.

The same year that *The Birth of a Nation* premiered, Harvard-trained black historian Carter G. Woodson founded the Association for the Study of Negro Life and History (ASNLH). Woodson's ASNLH was the culmination of what has become known as the New Negro history movement, begun in the late nineteenth century. The organization's goal was to counter Griffith-type images by resurrecting a positive black history and recounting all that African Americans had done for themselves and for America. Because professional American historical journals generally did not publish black history, the ASNLH, with Woodson as editor, issued the *Journal of Negro History* and the *Negro History Bulletin*. During the 1920s, the *Journal of Negro History* and the ASNLH focused much of their attention on proving Griffith wrong. Professionally researched articles and scholarly convention panels demonstrated that black people were not criminals or sexually dangerous. Black scholars wrote a history that showed how blacks, despite being mercilessly degraded, had in the one generation after slavery's end become a mostly literate people who voted responsibly and elected representatives who practiced fiscal responsibility and pursued educational and democratic reforms. Because black history was excluded from public school curricula, the ASNLH also spearheaded the movement that brought about Negro History Week (later to be a month), observed first in African American communities and then in the nation at large. The second week of February was chosen because it marked the birthdays of the Great Emancipator, Abraham Lincoln, and the great black freedom fighter, Frederick Douglass. Black leaders believed that a celebration of the lives of Lincoln and Douglass would evolve into the study of African Americans in general.

Black scholars did this because they understood the connection between their history and their status in America. The preeminent twentieth-century black historian W. E. B. Du Bois sternly warned against the erasure and/or distortion of the role played by African Americans in the building of the American nation. "We the darker ones come . . . not altogether empty-handed," he said.[1] African Americans had much to offer this country, much to teach America about humanitarianism and morality, and thus Du Bois pleaded for the study of black history and its inclusion in the national consciousness. Black history was even more important to African Americans, he instructed. Black people needed to know their history "for positive advance, . . . for negative defense," and to have "implicit trust in our ability and worth." "No people that laughs at itself, and ridicules itself, and wishes to God it was anything but itself ever wrote its name in history," counseled Du Bois at the turn of the twentieth century.[2] For him, black history, black freedom, and American democracy were all of a piece.

It should come as no surprise that when the freedom struggle moved onto the national stage in the mid-twentieth century, African American history became a central focus. Both black and white activists demanded not just an end to white terrorism, desegregation in all areas of American life, equality in the job market, voting rights, and the freedom to marry regardless of race, but also that non-distorted African American history and studies be included in elementary through high school public school curricula and textbooks, as well as in college courses. They insisted that colleges and universities offer degrees in African American studies and that traditional disciplines offer courses that treated black subjects as legitimate areas of study. In the 1960s, demands were made to extend Negro History Week to a full month, and in 1976, Woodson's organization, by then renamed the Association for the Study of African American Life and History (1972), designated February as Black History Month — a move acknowledged and approved by the federal government.

Debating African American History and Its Sources

Historians rely on documents written in the past. Before we can analyze a period, we must locate and unearth our sources. Primary sources originate during the period under study. Some are official or unofficial documents issued by public and private institutions; items as varied as church records, government census records, newspapers and magazines, probate records, court transcripts, and schoolbooks are

---

1. W. E. B. Du Bois, *The Souls of Black Folk: Essays and Sketches* (Chicago: A. C. McClurg, 1903), 11.
2. W. E. B. Du Bois, "The Conservation of Races," in *W. E. B. Du Bois: A Reader*, ed. David Levering Lewis (New York: Henry Holt, 1995), 25.

exceptionally revelatory of the past. Other records come from individuals. Personal letters and diaries, bank statements, photographs, and even gravestone inscriptions help historians figure out what happened during a particular time period. Once we assemble all of our documents, we write history based on our examination and analysis of them. Our histories become part of a body of secondary sources for the period under study — secondary because they originate from someone who has secondarily written an account that relied on first, or primary, sources.

Researching African American history has always presented a challenge for scholars. During their almost 250 years of enslavement, Africans and African Americans had few belongings they could call their own; thus they left few of the personal records that historians depend on to write history. Added to this obstacle is the fact that during slavery black literacy was outlawed. Schools for free blacks were regularly destroyed, and anyone teaching a slave to read could be arrested, fined, whipped, or jailed for corrupting a labor force that was considered most efficient when it was illiterate. Black Americans, therefore, developed a rich oral tradition. Certainly, as you will see from the sources presented in this book, some blacks, mostly those who were not enslaved, wrote letters, gave speeches, kept diaries, or wrote narratives of their experiences. However, most black communication and communion took place through personal interaction and via the spoken word. Before black history was committed to paper, it was committed to memory and passed down through folklore, art, and secular and religious music. This continued long into the twentieth century as segregation, disfranchisement, and attacks on black education forced African Americans to depend on their oral tradition.

For historians, who rely heavily on written sources, this presented a problem — as did the fact that the struggle for black freedom was often manifested in a struggle over who could and/or should write black history. This overlapped the problem of sources, because many thought it unfair to write black history using only those sources emanating from the very people and institutions responsible for the African American's second-class citizenship. For example, in his 1935 post–Civil War history, *Black Reconstruction*, Du Bois, a Harvard-trained historian, railed against the professional historians who had written about the period using only the sources that came from the defeated South. It was to be expected, argued Du Bois, that these historians, who were mostly white, male, and southern, would find fault with the freedmen; their sources were those of defeated slave owners and others who had a stake in painting ex-slaves as unworthy of freedom. "The chief witness in Reconstruction, the emancipated slave himself, has been almost barred from court," argued Du Bois.[3] In presenting a case for using the written records of black representatives, which included the few biographies of black leaders and the unedited debates of the Reconstruction conventions, Du Bois called for true fairness: "If history is going to be scientific, if the record of human action is going to be set down with that accuracy and faithfulness of detail which will allow its use as a measuring rod and guidepost for the future of nations, there must be set some standards of ethics in research and interpretation."[4] In other words, history could not be written from just one point of view, or with sources that were highly prejudicial or

---

3. W. E. B. Du Bois, *Black Reconstruction in America, 1860–1880* (1935; repr., New York: Free Press, 1998), 721.
4. Ibid., 714.

exclusionary. But who was to say which sources were best, and who was best qualified to write African American history? Could not those sympathetic to black causes also use history for their own purposes and bend it to their needs? And given that so many African American sources were oral and not preserved in archives, or were personal artifacts packed away in family storage, how could the existing sources be accessed to produce written history?

These issues were hotly debated during the mid-twentieth-century freedom struggle, and out of that debate came a new consensus about African American history and history in general. For as African Americans, traditionally the lowest in the American social strata, demonstrated how important their history was to them and to the nation, other Americans followed suit. Women, workers, and members of America's many ethnic groups expanded the study of their pasts and insisted on inclusion in the narrative of American history. Rather than focusing on presidents, or the nation's wars, or the institutions at the top of America's political, economic, and social systems, ordinary American citizens called for a study of America from the "bottom up." Everyone made history, these advocates argued. The daily lives of average Americans were as important for historians as the decisions made by heads of state. It was not just the rich and famous, not just men, not just whites, not just Anglo-Saxon Protestants, and not just heterosexuals who made history. As women, Native Americans, Asian Americans, Hispanic Americans, and gay, lesbian, bisexual, and transgendered citizens demanded equal inclusion in American society, they demanded that their history be included as well. Scholars picked up the gauntlet thrown down by these groups and began to change their research methods by including different kinds of sources and asking different kinds of questions; consequently, their histories changed. The midcentury rights movements birthed not just new and expanded citizenship rights but also a new way of thinking about and doing history. Sometimes history from the "bottom up" looks very different from "top-down" history. Sometimes the differences are reconcilable, but often they are not. Adding sources from rank-and-file Americans made a difference in how the past was written and understood.

The Craft of African American History

Historians of slavery pioneered the "new" African American history in the 1970s. Following the advice of Du Bois, they ceased barring the "chief witness" from their studies, integrating the experiences of former slaves into their work and writing some histories from the slave's point of view. This necessitated using different kinds of sources, which, not surprisingly, were oral interviews conducted after slavery or oral testimony given to the Freedmen's Bureau, the government agency established to aid freedpeople in their transition from slavery to freedom. Because black testimony differed significantly from most white testimony, historians were now tasked with recounting a history that looked at slavery from different vantage points.

Once historians added African American testimony, it changed the way many interpreted seemingly objective sources like census and probate records, court cases, and congressional debates. For example, Harriet Brent Jacobs's account of her master's attempt at rape and her recounting of the sexual exploitation of female slaves changed the way some historians looked at plantation lists that showed a preponderance of single females with children. This was once assumed to indicate the promiscuity of black women, but historians now had to consider the sexual profligacy of white men. Plantation records were also combed to trace black family lineages, a laborious process that revealed, for example, that not all slaves took the last names of their masters. Additionally, though the law did not recognize slave marriages, these records showed that many slaves partnered carefully and with intention — not in a willy-nilly fashion, as had previously been assumed. In the 1970s, historians studied previously excluded black folktales and black music and art as a way to discern slaves' belief systems and culture. The new sources stimulated different answers to age-old questions and prompted serious reconsideration of previously held historical assumptions. Whereas slave owners had maintained that blacks were happy under slavery and unfit for freedom, black-originated sources spoke of ever-present black resistance to slavery. Whereas most white-originated sources gave Abraham Lincoln and other whites credit for black emancipation, black-originated sources showed how African Americans stole themselves from slavery, joined Union armies, and fought for their own freedom and for the Union cause. These new sources showed how a people who were once African became African American, and how and why a people so excluded embraced American democratic principles.

African American sources opened a window not just on slavery and, more broadly, the African American experience but on the entire American experience. They allowed historians to present a total history: not just one that looked at black oppression and race relations, but a rich history that included nearly four hundred years of black cultural production, black faith and religious communion, black family history, black politics, and connections to the African diaspora — that is, the dispersal and movement of peoples of African descent to different parts of the world. In the 1970s, as other groups demanded the inclusion of their own sources in the historical record, their histories grew into fields of study that challenged historians to integrate race, class, gender, and sexuality into American history. Soon, African Americans at the intersection of many of these groups — for example, African American women — also insisted that sources illuminating their history be examined and that their particular history be told. Today, many Americans object to what they see as the fractionalization of American history, preferring a more unified history that downplays difference and emphasizes the unity of the American people and the development of a unique American character. Others are comfortable with an American history that is complicated and revealing of Americans' diverse experiences.

Freedom on My Mind: History and Documents

Freedom on My Mind offers a balance between a top-down and a bottom-up approach to history. Using both primary and secondary sources, we have written a narrative of African American history that is presented in the context of American history and the evolution of American democracy. Our narrative includes the voices of blacks and whites, of leaders as well as followers, of men as well as women, and of the well-to-do, the middle classes, and the poor. In creating this narrative, we have used both primary sources that originate in American and African American institutions and primary sources from individuals. We have used secondary sources that present the latest research and analysis of the African American past. We have shown how African Americans were represented by others and how they represented themselves. When enabled by our sources, we have noted the different experiences and perspectives of native-born African Americans, Caribbean and African blacks, and blacks in the lesbian, gay, bisexual, and transgender (LGBT) community.

Equal to our narrative in importance are the Document Projects that allow you, the student, to be a time-traveling detective and "do" history. We've offered our analysis of the sources, but we want you to be more than passive recipients of the secondary source that is this book — we want you to participate. We want you to investigate primary sources and create a narrative of your own, as if you, too, were a historian.

As you will discover, sleuthing the past is complicated. Take, for example, the narrative of Olaudah Equiano, a prominent eighteenth-century abolitionist and former slave. As a child, Equiano was stolen from Africa and enslaved, but through a unique set of circumstances, he became a free and outspoken opponent of slavery. Reading his narrative will provide you with insight into what it must have been like to be an eighteenth-century West African and allow you to empathize with those who were involuntarily separated from all that they knew and understood about life. However, you will quickly realize that being a historian requires much more than empathy. Questions will arise, such as "What does Equiano's narrative tell us about his region of Africa, and how did things change over time?" You may also ask questions like "Was Equiano typical?" or "Might Equiano have fabricated or embellished his story to gain support for abolitionism?"

Invariably, one question and answer leads to others. If you pursue your inquiry, and we encourage you to do so, you will find yourself needing additional sources, both primary and secondary. Gradually, a picture of West Africa and the slave trade will emerge — one that you have created from the sources you unearthed. If you decide to compare your study with the secondary works produced by others, you might find differences in approach and perspective. Perhaps you focused on the everyday lives of enslaved eighteenth-century Africans and wrote a "bottom-up" history, while others focused on the leaders of the abolitionist movement and used a more "top-down" approach. One thing you will note is that two historians seldom write the same exact history. This will become apparent when you and your classmates compare your answers to the questions that accompany the sources in *Freedom on My Mind*. Your stations in life, your personal identities, the time period you live in — all of these factors influence the questions you ask and the way you interpret the sources you read.

Freedom on My Mind includes a wide variety of sources to enable you to practice history while learning about African Americans and American democracy. This is what we think makes this text special. Although we have included many events and the names of many people and places, we have tried not to overwhelm you with such information; rather, we have included sources that allow you to reach conclusions on your own and thereby analyze the conclusions we have drawn. This is what excites us about our text, and we invite you to explore and get excited with us.

Freedom on My Mind

A History of African Americans with Documents

SECOND EDITION

From Africa to America

1441–1808

CHRONOLOGY *Events specific to African American history are in purple. General United States history events are in black.*

c. 830–1230	Ghana empire rules western and central Africa
c. 1230–1500	Mali empire rules western and central Africa
1325	Aztecs set up capital at Tenochtitlán
1418–1470s	Portuguese launch exploratory expeditions
1441	Expedition sponsored by Prince Henry the Navigator picks up ten slaves on African coast
1444	Portuguese expedition returns from Africa carrying 235 slaves; Atlantic slave trade begins
1452	Pope Nicholas V issues proclamation sanctioning African slavery
1488	Portuguese explorer Bartolomeu Dias rounds Cape of Good Hope
1492	Christopher Columbus lands on island of Hispaniola
1493	Columbus makes second voyage to New World
1494	Treaty of Tordesillas gives Portuguese control of early transatlantic slave trade
1497	Italian explorer John Cabot lands in Newfoundland, searches for Northwest Passage
1498	Portuguese explorer Vasco da Gama lands in India
1500–1591	Songhai empire rules western and central Africa; region splits into independent kingdoms following collapse
Early 1500s	Direct trade between Africa and New World colonies begins under *asiento* system
1502	Spanish soldier Nicolás de Ovando brings ten black slaves to Hispaniola
1508	Juan Ponce de León employs armed Africans in invasion of Puerto Rico

1511–1512	Diego Velázquez employs black auxiliaries in conquest of Cuba
1513	Ponce de León lands in Florida
1516	Bartolomé de Las Casas encourages Spanish to replace Indian slaves with Africans
1518	First Africans arrive in Mexico with Hernán Cortés
1519	Ferdinand Magellan sets off to sail around world
1519–1521	Cortés conquers Aztecs
1532–1535	Francisco Pizarro conquers Peru, vanquishes Incas
1539	Hernando de Soto explores southeastern North America
1540	Francisco Vásquez de Coronado explores Southwest and Great Plains
1542	Spanish government bans enslavement of Indian peoples within its territories
1550	First slave ship lands in Brazil
1565	Spanish Florida founded
1587	Sir Walter Raleigh establishes Roanoke, first English settlement in New World
1608	French explorer Samuel de Champlain establishes Quebec
1756	Olaudah Equiano kidnapped and sold into slavery
1788	British government restricts number of slaves British ships may carry
1797	Slave women steal weapons in insurrection aboard British ship *Thomas*
1808	United States withdraws from international slave trade

Prince Henry's African Captives

In the summer of 1441, a Portuguese vessel under the command of Antam Goncalvez acquired ten slaves in Mauritania, a Berber kingdom on the coast of North Africa. Commissioned to explore the African coast by the Portuguese monarch Prince Henry the Navigator, Goncalvez and his crew arrived there eager to bring home captives that would satisfy the prince's curiosity about the "other dwellers of the land." After they attacked and enslaved three local "Moors," the captives, who themselves owned slaves, offered to buy their own freedom by giving the Europeans a larger group of enslaved Africans. Goncalvez agreed, receiving in payment ten Africans, male and female, from several different places in West Africa. These slaves, whom Goncalvez described as "black moors," were not only more numerous than his original captives but also of greater potential value to his mission. In particular, he hoped they would "give him news of a land much more distant," which would be of significant interest to the man who had sponsored the voyage.

Prince Henry thus opened Europe's age of exploration by sponsoring a series of voyages down the West African coast, setting the stage for Columbus's first expedition across the Atlantic in 1492. Like Columbus, Henry sought not slaves but gold, other profitable merchandise, and a passage to the Orient. Goncalvez's voyage did not achieve these goals, but it did inaugurate a lucrative trade in people. The Atlantic slave trade began only three years later when, with Henry's permission, a Portuguese merchant-adventurer dispatched another expedition to the African coast, this time specifically in search of slaves.

On August 8, 1444, the 235 enslaved Africans captured on the expedition arrived in the maritime town of Lagos, Portugal, where they were met by a crowd that included Prince Henry. Mounted on horseback, the prince looked on as the leader of the expedition paraded the captives from the docks to the town gates. The men, women, and children of all complexions and colors were distressed and disoriented as they walked through the streets of Lagos. "Some kept their heads low, and their faces [were] bathed with tears, looking upon one another," noted Henry's court chronicler, while others were "looking up to the heavens and crying out loudly, as if asking for help from the Father of nature." The spectacle ended with an auction that moved even the chronicler, a steadfast admirer of his monarch, to pity. Before their sale, the captives were divided into lots in order to help the merchants split the proceeds of their voyage — and to pay Henry the required 20 percent royal tax. The separation was bound to "increase their suffering still more," the chronicler noted, since it parted "fathers from sons, husbands from wives, brothers from brothers. No respect was shown either to friends or relations, but each fell where his lot took him."[1]

The scene marked the beginning of an African **diaspora**, or mass dispersion of a people from their homeland, that would carry millions of Africans across the ocean in slavery under European and Euro-American masters. Although Goncalvez's captives would land in Portugal, most of this slave trade's captives ended up much farther away. With European settlement of the New World in the 1500s, a highly profitable exchange of goods and enslaved labor began to take shape between Europe, Africa, and the New World. Now known as the transatlantic slave trade, this expansive commercial enterprise involved a triangle trade: European merchants exchanged manufactured goods for enslaved Africans, shipped the slaves to the Americas to exchange for New World commodities, and used those materials to manufacture more European goods.

This immensely lucrative trade transformed both Africa and the American colonies. Although a long-standing internal slave trade had existed in West Africa prior to the arrival of Europeans, the new triangle trade both exploited and expanded it, ultimately leaving many parts of the region depopulated. Moreover, the transatlantic slave trade forever changed the lives of the millions of Africans it dispersed. Most captives hailed from vibrant West African communities that had had little contact with Europe prior to the rise of the slave trade, and most were enslaved before they ever left Africa. Once early European slave traders began to meet with armed resistance from the peoples who lived on the West African coast, they quickly turned to African traders to supply them with slaves.

Although the men, women, and children they purchased were not free in Africa, once they were swept into the transatlantic slave trade, these diasporic Africans would encounter a new kind of slavery. Crowded aboard slave ships for the long and often lethal voyage to the New World, the Africans who ended up in the Americas entered a system of bondage unlike anything that existed in Africa. Whereas slavery in Africa was often temporary and rarely heritable, in the Americas slavery was lifelong and passed from parent to child. Thus for those who survived, the transatlantic voyage marked the beginning of a captivity that would pass from one generation to the next.

Dispersed across the Americas, these slaves set about rebuilding their lives and creating new communities. As members of many different ethnic and linguistic groups, the slave trade's victims came from a variety of villages and kingdoms. Few, if any, thought of themselves as *Africans* when they first boarded the slave ships. Only in the Americas would they take on a collective identity imposed on them by slavery, forced migration, and the strange new world in which they found themselves.

African Origins

The ancestry of African Americans can be traced to the beginning of human history. Scientists believe that Africa was home to the ancient ancestors of all human beings, who first originated in East Africa more than a million years ago. Africa's long history witnessed the emergence of human agriculture and the rise and fall of vast civilizations in ancient Egypt, Ethiopia, and Nubia, as well as the development of a variety of states thereafter. In the fifteenth century, when the peoples of West Africa first came into sustained contact with the explorers, merchants, and traders who launched the European settlement of the New World, their region of the African continent was largely divided into small village states and kingdoms. Consequently, they spoke many different languages, belonged to a variety of ethnic groups, and would bring to America a rich heritage of customs and cultures.

One institution these societies shared, however, was the practice of slavery. They had well-established slave trading networks, which the seafaring European traders who began doing business along Africa's Atlantic coast were quick to exploit. Out of this exploitation would come a new form of slavery that was transatlantic in scope and brutal in nature, and that forever separated millions of enslaved Africans from their homelands.

The History of West Africa

Three times the size of Europe and almost double that of the United States, Africa, at well over 11 million square miles, is the second-largest continent on earth, after Asia. Its landmass spans four hemispheres and links the rich cultural worlds of the Mediterranean, the Middle East, and sub-Saharan Africa. Throughout the ages, Africa has been populated by a diverse array of peoples, whose cultural, ethnic, and sociological differences have been shaped by the continent's varied landscape. The world's largest desert and the world's most impenetrable rain forest, as well as nearly every other kind of natural environment, are located in Africa. The prime meridian and the equator run through the continent, which encompasses climates that range from tropical to glacial and vary dramatically even within the various regions.

Not surprisingly, given its great diversity of physical environments and long history of human settlement, Africa has been home to many different societies. Ghana, the first West African state of which there is any record, sustained a powerful empire between approximately 830 and 1230. West Africa's first great trading empire, Ghana was situated between the Sahara and the headwaters of the Senegal and Niger Rivers, in an area now occupied by southeastern Mauritania and western Mali. From within a region rich in gold, Ghana's merchants engaged in a lucrative trans-Saharan trade with the Muslim countries of the Middle East, which supplied Ghana with salt and other Mediterranean goods. This trade allowed Ghana's Soninke kings to control a large army and rule over many African tribes.

After Ghana's collapse in the face of invading forces and internal divisions, Mali, a state within Ghana, emerged as an imperial power and controlled a large portion of western and central Africa between roughly 1230 and 1500. Mali's most important ruler was Mansa Musa (r. 1312–1337), a devout Muslim who became well known throughout Europe and the Middle East as a result of his 1324 pilgrimage to Mecca. He made the four-thousand-mile journey with an opulent personal caravan that included

Facsimile of the Catalan Atlas *Showing the King of Mali Holding a Gold Nugget, 1375*
Largely devoid of geographic detail, this Spanish nautical map of the known world is adorned with pictures, including sketches of camels, as well as a large and lavish illustration of an African ruler identified as "Muse Melley," "lord of the Negroes of Guinea." This illustration likely refers to Mansa Musa, who ruled the Mali empire between 1312 and 1337, although his placement on the map is closer to North Africa than to West Africa. A devout Muslim, Musa caught the attention of the Islamic and European worlds in 1324, when he made a pilgrimage to Mecca. His caravan included twelve hundred servants and eighty camels carrying two tons of gold, which he distributed to the needy along his route. Not soon forgotten, Musa was depicted in several fourteenth-century maps of the world.
Bibliothèque Nationale, Paris, France /Erich Lessing/Art Resource, NY.

twelve hundred servants and eighty camels carrying two tons of gold, which he distributed to the needy along his route. Not soon forgotten, Musa was thereafter pictured in several European maps of the world, which emphasized his wealth by depicting him wearing a large gold crown and holding a gold nugget and scepter. Not surprisingly, stories of Musa's wealth helped inspire Portuguese explorations of Africa's west coast.

Musa's legend outlived his empire. In the century following his rule, his sons proved unable to maintain control over their many subjects. Mali's imperial power was largely displaced by the rise of the Songhai empire, a small kingdom that broke away from Mali in 1320. Home to flourishing economies and an active international trade, Songhai reached its peak in the late 1400s and became the last of western and central Africa's three successive empires.

Like West Africa's previous rulers, the Songhai derived much of their wealth and power from the trans-Saharan trade. They also controlled the city of Timbuktu, an important commercial center that gained widespread prominence as a center of Islamic culture under Songhai ruler Askia al-Hajj Muhammad (r. 1493–1528). Home to three of Africa's oldest mosques, as well as several universities, the city attracted scholars from throughout the Muslim world. But the Songhai lost control of both Timbuktu and their empire in 1591, when a civil war divided their kingdom, opening it up to foreign invasion. That year, Morocco captured and sacked Timbuktu and other Songhai seats of power, causing the once-powerful empire to collapse. But Morocco never secured dominion over the vast territories once controlled by the Songhai, and with their retreat, the region split into many small, independent kingdoms (Map 1.1).

By the sixteenth century, when the transatlantic slave trade first took shape, most of Africa was populated by many small societies of people who spoke different languages, worshipped different deities, and had diverse cultures. These West African peoples generally practiced one of a variety of polytheistic religions that recognized many deities and spirits, as well as a more remote, all-powerful creator. Adherents of these religions saw the force of God in all things and often invoked the spirits of their ancestors, as well as a spirit world associated with their natural surroundings. But these similar beliefs did not lead West Africans to unite around a single church or religious doctrine. West Africa was also home to a small Muslim population, which rejected these indigenous beliefs and embraced a strictly monotheistic idea of God. Islam had been brought to West Africa in the tenth and eleventh centuries by traders from North Africa and the Middle East, but prior to the eighteenth and nineteenth centuries, its followers came mainly from the region's small commercial elite.

Despite their religious and regional diversity, the West African societies that supplied the transatlantic slave trade had a number of features in common. They tended to be of modest size: Only about 30 percent of the African continent was ruled by organized states of any size; the rest was occupied by small groups of people. Moreover, the peoples who lived on Africa's west coast had a very different relationship to the Atlantic Ocean than did the seafaring Europeans who arrived on their shores in the 1400s. Unlike Europe's west coast, West Africa's treacherous coast had never been conducive

MAP 1.1   Africa's Diverse States and Geography, 900–1800

The world's second-largest continent after Asia, Africa is bisected by the equator and subject to a variety of very different climates. This map divides the continent into eight climatic regions that range in temperature from desert to tropical rain forest to chilly highlands. The map also illustrates the geographic location of precolonial Africa's most important empires or kingdoms, many of which extended over several of the continent's climatic zones.

to long-distance trade and travel. A mixture of coastal swamps and rocky promonto-
ries, the coastline had few natural harbors that could accommodate large boats. African
maritime tradition was largely limited to the use of dugout canoes that could be carried
into the water. These shallow vessels, usually carved from a single tree trunk, required
no docks and were used for fishing expeditions and other trips just outside the rough
surf that made the coast so hazardous. They were better suited to inland travel on the
Niger, Senegal, and Gambia Rivers than to the open seas. As a result, West Africa's
inland waterways sustained extensive trade networks, with canoes carrying agricultural products, lumber, fish, and slaves.

Most of the peoples along the coast lived in villages or kingdoms united by common ancestors. Property and political leadership usually passed from generation to
generation along matrilineal or patrilineal lines — from mother to daughter or father to
son. The governance of larger African polities such as the kingdoms of the West African
interior, which tended to be ruled by confederacies of royal families, also were based on
kinship affiliations. Thus the power of African rulers was often local and limited, much
of it being derived from the network of kinship ties that bound individuals to their
communities. The African proverb "I am because we are, and because we are therefore
I am" expresses the collective nature of African social identity.[2]

African systems of landownership were also collective rather than individual. Villages held common land whose use was administered by a local official known as the
grand master of the ground. People were entitled to cultivate their ancestral homelands, but they did not own them and could not pass them on to their descendants. As
a result, African societies tended to figure wealth and power not in land, but in people.
In these small kinship-based societies, an abundance of people helped make ruling
families powerful, as did institutions that gave rulers power over people, such as
slavery.

Slavery in West Africa

In both Europe and Africa, slavery was often a by-product of war. On both continents,
slave status was traditionally assigned to war captives. Conquering peoples who
enslaved their enemies acquired a valuable source of labor, concubines, and trade
revenues — the last of which they could accrue by selling off their most dangerous
enemies to distant lands where they would no longer pose a threat. Military conflicts
could foster other types of enslavement as well. European serfs, for example, acquired
their unfree status during the war-torn Middle Ages, when they placed themselves voluntarily under the control of powerful warriors who offered them protection in return
for their service.

But war was not the only route to enslavement. In many West African societies,
slave status was assigned to those convicted of serious crimes such as adultery, murder,
or sorcery. These people not only were reduced to slavery but were usually sold away
from their families as well — a harsh punishment in these kinship-based societies.

Debtors were also enslaved. Some were pawns, debtors who voluntarily submitted to temporary slavery in order to pay off their debts.

Members of most of these groups could move in and out of slavery, although not all of them succeeded in doing so. Pawns, for example, could work off their debts, while female captives of war frequently became members of their owners' families via concubinage — a form of sexual slavery that typically ended in freedom if the concubine bore a freeman's child. Two other routes out of slavery were assimilation into an owner's kinship network by marriage, and manumission — a legal process that slave owners could initiate to grant freedom to a favored slave.

Within West Africa, since slave status was rarely inherited, slavery did not create a permanent class of slaves or slave owners. Indeed, prior to the arrival of Europeans in the 1440s, slave ownership and slave trading were relatively modest sources of wealth in West African societies. West Africans sold their surplus slaves to Arab slave traders who transported them across the Sahara to North Africa, for resale in the Arab world. But the expansion of slavery within West Africa was limited by the decentralized character of the region's political regimes and its lack of commerce in slave-produced goods. Agriculture was a collective pursuit dedicated to subsistence rather than trade and did not require the harsh work regimes that would come to characterize slave labor in the New World.

Slaves in African societies were socially marginal and powerless, but there were limits to their subjugation. They were generally employed in the same agricultural and domestic work that occupied other members of the community. They also retained a number of civic rights and privileges. In most African communities, slaves were permitted to educate themselves and were generally free to marry and raise children. Slavery also varied across the region, sometimes taking the form of domestic servitude, in which female slaves predominated. Larger West African polities such as Songhai employed slave soldiers and bureaucrats, whose slave status did not keep them from becoming wealthy and powerful servants of the state.

However different African slavery was from the slavery that developed in the Americas, the fact that it was an entrenched and dynamic institution would have tragic and far-reaching consequences. The European trade with sub-Saharan Africa, which began shortly before Europeans first arrived in the New World, would create a new kind of slave trade to supply the workers needed to exploit these new lands.

The Rise of the Transatlantic Slave Trade

Although Europeans and West Africans lived on neighboring continents separated only by the societies of the Middle East, they were virtual strangers prior to the fifteenth century. Small numbers of people and small quantities of goods had moved between the two continents via overland trade networks for centuries, and North African Arabs had maintained a long-standing presence in the Middle East. But prior to the expeditions pioneered by Prince Henry, Europe and West Africa were largely sealed off from each other by massive natural barriers. The Sahara desert made over-land travel between the two regions difficult and dangerous, while the powerful winds and currents off the Saharan coast had long prevented sea travel between Europe and Africa. Separated by desert and sea, West Africa and western Europe were home to two distinct societies that came together abruptly in the fifteenth century — with tragic consequences. Their encounters would foster a transatlantic trade in African peoples that would last for several hundred years and depopulate many regions of West Africa.

Europe in the Age of the Slave Trade

When the Portuguese first began raiding West Africa's sub-Saharan coast, Europe was not yet the conglomeration of powerful empires it would later become. Ruled by a variety of monarchs, city-states, and feuding nobles, European societies were larger, more far-flung, and more economically interconnected than most precolonial West African societies. But they were also divided and socially unstable. European rulers, such as the Portuguese royal family, were still in the process of inventing powerful nation-states that could maintain social order — a development that would be greatly facilitated by the exploitation of Africa and the New World.

Europeans reached these regions at a time of dramatic social and political upheaval within Europe. Powerful monarchies had risen to replace Europe's feuding nobility, and Muslim incursions into eastern Europe and the Iberian Peninsula during the Crusades had allowed ambitious monarchs to expand their influence by defending Christendom and offering their subjects a more secure and politically stable social order. These rulers created royalty-based nation-states in England, France, and Iberia, securing their influence by building powerful bureaucracies and establishing standing armies and navies. But these new state powers were expensive to maintain and difficult to protect, and to sustain their influence, rulers soon needed to explore and exploit new lands.

In Africa, European monarchs such as Prince Henry hoped to find sources of gold and other luxury goods they could use to enrich their treasuries, pay their armies, and increase the commercial power of their nations. Europeans were unfamiliar with the African coast south of Cape Bojador, a headland west of the Sahara marked by treach-erous winds that prevented European sailors from traveling farther down the coast. But they hoped that in crossing the unknown lands that lay south of the Cape, they would find a direct route to the riches of the Far East.

Portugal, one of Europe's earliest nation-states, pioneered the navigation of the West African coast. As the most accomplished shipbuilders in Europe, the Portuguese were the first to develop oceangoing vessels suitable for long exploratory voyages. Called **carracks** and **caravels**, these small sailing ships had two or three masts and were powered by both triangular and square sails. An innovation borrowed from the Arab dhow, the triangular sails that graced Portuguese ships allowed them to brave strong winds and travel faster and farther than any other vessels of their day. In particular, they allowed Portuguese mariners to cut through the dangerous northeasterly winds blowing off Cape Bojador.

Between 1418 and the 1470s, the Portuguese launched a series of exploratory expeditions that remapped the oceans south of Portugal, charting new territories that one explorer described as "oceans where none had ever sailed before."[3] They also discovered several uninhabited islands only a few hundred miles off Africa's west coast, which they began to settle and cultivate. These islands — christened Madeira, the Azores, Arguin, the Cape Verde Islands, and São Tomé and Príncipe — provided the Portuguese a stepping-off point for expeditions farther down the coast, allowing them to reach the Cape of Good Hope in 1487.

The Atlantic slave trade first took shape in conjunction with these expeditions, as Portuguese seamen began to bring back enslaved Africans to sell both in Portugal and in its Atlantic islands. Spain was also active in this early trade and established its own Atlantic colony in the Canary Islands during the fifteenth century. Located off the northwest coast of Africa, the ten islands that make up the Canaries were not as easily settled as the uninhabited islands claimed by Portugal. They were home to an indigenous people known as the **Guanches**, whose ancestors likely originated among the Berber peoples of North Africa. The Guanches fought off the Spanish from 1402, when the first Spanish expedition arrived, to the 1490s, when the last of the Guanches were finally conquered. Even before that, however, the Spanish began exploiting the islands' fertile soil and temperate weather by planting sugarcane, wheat, and other crops. The Canaries proved ideal for the production of sugar, which also flourished on the Portuguese islands of Madeira and São Tomé.

Sugarcane, a valuable crop previously grown primarily in Cyprus, Sicily, and parts of southern Spain, demanded far more labor than the islands' small Guanche population could provide. First cultivated in the Pacific Rim more than 10,000 years ago, sugar was introduced to Europe in the eleventh century and became an immediate hit. It was in demand among cooks as a spice, sweetener, and preservative and was used by physicians and pharmacists as a remedy for disorders of the blood, stomach, and lungs. As a crop requiring both warm weather and intensive labor, however, sugar was in short supply in Europe. In the Mediterranean, sugarcane was cultivated on large plantations by enslaved workers from Russia and the Balkans — traditional sources of European forced labor. But with the emergence of Portuguese and Spanish colonies in the Atlantic, this plantation system moved offshore and became increasingly dependent on the labor of enslaved Africans. By the 1490s, Madeira was the largest European sugar producer. In the sixteenth century, sugar production boomed in the Azores, the Canaries, Cape Verde, and São Tomé — all of which required imported laborers.

Despite the successful slave raids that took place on some of the earliest Portuguese expeditions to Africa, kidnappings would not remain the means by which the Portuguese secured these laborers. After the early raids, West African rulers quickly organized to defend their coast. By the 1450s, Portuguese slaving expeditions along the Senegambian and Gambian coast were driven offshore by fleets of African canoe men

African Slave Traders Seizing Captives in Guinea, 1789

This engraving of a painting by the artist Richard Westall is titled *A View Taken near Bain on the Coast of Guinea in West Africa. Dedicated to the FEELING HEARTS in All Civilized Nations.* Westall was inspired by the work of Carl Bernhard Wadström, a Swedish industrialist who toured the coast of West Africa in 1787 and 1788 and sketched what he saw there. During his visit, Wadström witnessed firsthand the slave raiding and warfare caused by the slave trade and became an abolitionist as a result of this experience. A View Taken near Bain, on the Coast of Guinea in Africa, *engraved by Catherine Prestell, based on sketches made on location by C. B. Wadström, published by J. Phillips, London, 1789/Private Collection/© Michael Graham-Stewart/Bridgeman Images.*

armed with arrows and javelins. Although these African canoes lacked the firepower of the caravels, which were equipped with cannons, they could easily outmaneuver the much larger European vessels, and the canoe men could use their weapons to pick off Europeans who attempted to land. After 1456, the Portuguese crown began negotiating commercial treaties with West African rulers, who agreed to supply the Portuguese with slaves in return for European goods. Thus the slave trade first emerged as a commercial relationship between coastal peoples: African merchants tapped the internal slave trade, which had existed in Africa since ancient times, to supply European traders with thousands of slaves per year.

The Enslavement of Indigenous Peoples

If the Portuguese trade in African slaves had served only Europe, the Atlantic slave trade might well have been short-lived. Europe's population boomed in the second half of the fifteenth century, making labor abundant and slave imports unnecessary. But the cultivation of Europe's Atlantic colonies created an additional labor market, which was soon complemented by similar markets in the Americas. Indeed, the first Africans arrived in the Americas either with or shortly after Columbus, who may have employed African seamen on some of his voyages. As Spaniards began to populate Hispaniola — the colony Columbus established in 1492 on the island that is now divided between Haiti and the Dominican Republic — African slaves joined them. Nicolás de Ovando, a Spanish soldier who replaced Columbus as governor of Hispaniola in 1502, brought several Iberian-born black slaves, who he hoped would both provide labor and help subdue Hispaniola's indigenous population. His hopes evidently disappointed, Ovando banned the further importation of blacks shortly thereafter, "on the grounds that they incited native rebellion."[4] But Spain's New World colonies would prove far too hungry for labor for any such ban to persist.

African workers were first used in the copper and gold mines of Hispaniola, which resumed importing them in 1505. These workers were needed because Spanish attempts to exploit the labor of the island's native inhabitants, the **Taino Indians**, had met with limited success. During the first few decades of Spanish settlement, the conquistadors were able to extract forced labor from the Indians under the *encomienda* system, which permitted the Spaniards to collect tribute — in the form of labor, gold, or other goods — from the native peoples they controlled. The colonists demanded both labor and gold from the Tainos, whom they put to work mining the island's rivers and streams. But the Indians did not flourish under Spanish rule.

Some resisted working for the Spaniards and were slaughtered by them, while many more succumbed to the Old World diseases that the Spanish interlopers carried with them. Not having been exposed to common European illnesses such as influenza, smallpox, chicken pox, mumps, and measles, the Tainos possessed no resistance to these diseases and began to die in droves. By the first decade of the sixteenth century, their population had dropped from 500,000 to 60,000; by 1514 it was down to 28,000; and by 1542 there were only a few hundred Tainos left on the island.

The rapid decline of the native population in Hispaniola was repeated throughout the Americas and set the stage for the development of the transatlantic slave trade. With their settlements triggering large population losses among the hemisphere's indigenous peoples, European colonists had to look elsewhere for workers. Not surprisingly, they turned to the African slave trade to supply their needs. African slavery was already an established enterprise, offered an almost limitless supply of workers, and had several advantages over Indian slavery. Most important among them was that African peoples, who lived in the same hemisphere as the Europeans, had some immunity to Old World diseases. Moreover, African laborers were strangers to the New

World, which made them more manageable than the region's native populations. Unfamiliar with the local peoples and surrounding terrain, they could not easily escape their confinement.

African slavery was also sanctioned by the Catholic Church, while the enslavement of Indians was more controversial. The Old World practice of African enslavement had received explicit license in a papal bull (formal proclamation) issued by Pope Nicholas V in 1452. Titled *Dum Diversas*, this proclamation granted the kings of Spain and Portugal permission "to invade, search out, capture, vanquish, and subdue all the Saracens [Muslims] and pagans . . . and other enemies of Christ wheresoever placed," as well as "their kingdoms, duchies, counties, principalities, [and other] possessions . . . and to reduce their persons into perpetual slavery."[5]

Issued before Columbus's voyages, *Dum Diversas* was designed to sanction European attacks on the Islamic societies of North Africa and the Middle East. It did not address the Spanish enslavement of indigenous peoples of the Americas. Troubled by Spanish mistreatment of these peoples, Dominican missionaries were quick to challenge the legitimacy of Native American slavery. "Tell me by what right of justice do you hold these Indians in such a cruel and horrible servitude?" Antonio de Montesinos, a Dominican priest stationed on Hispaniola, asked in a sermon delivered in 1511. "Why do you keep them so oppressed and exhausted, without giving them enough to eat or curing them of the sicknesses they incur from the excessive labor you give them, and they die, or rather you kill them, in order to extract and acquire gold every day?"[6] His critique was taken up by other Dominicans, most notably Bartolomé de Las Casas, who pressured both the Spanish crown and the pope to protect the Indians. Concerned about their rapidly declining populations, Las Casas, starting in 1516, encouraged the Spanish to replace Indian slaves with those imported from Africa — a position he later came to regret. He was not then aware, he explained in 1560, of "how unjustly and tyrannically Africans were taken as slaves, in the same fashion as Indians."[7]

How much Las Casas could have done to curb African slavery had he come to this realization earlier remains an open question. But as it was, his campaign put Indian rather than African slavery under contention. In 1537, Pope Paul III issued another papal bull declaring that the Indians were rational beings who should be converted rather than enslaved, and in 1542 the Spanish government banned the enslavement of Indians within its territories. Although both rulings were largely ignored by colonists and ineffective in curbing the abuses of the encomienda system, they facilitated the transatlantic slave trade's expansion, which took shape alongside European settlement of the New World and displacement of the region's indigenous peoples.

The First Africans in the Americas

Roughly 300,000 Africans landed in the Americas before 1620. Most came after 1550, when their numbers began to exceed those of Portuguese and Spanish migrants. By then, the Spanish conquest of the Americas had extended to include the islands of

Puerto Rico, Cuba, Guadeloupe, Trinidad, and Jamaica, as well as the mainland regions of Mexico and Peru, while the Portuguese had laid claim to Brazil. Enslaved Africans supplied labor for all these colonies. The Africans' presence expanded outward from Hispaniola, which served as the staging ground for further Spanish incursions into the New World. There they worked on sugar plantations after the island's small store of precious metals had been tapped out and accompanied the Spanish on military expeditions. The Spanish explorer Juan Ponce de León employed armed Africans to supplement his forces when he invaded Puerto Rico in 1508, while Diego Velázquez used black auxiliaries in his 1511–1512 conquest of Cuba. Likewise, the first Africans to arrive in Mexico accompanied Hernán Cortés, who in 1519–1521 conquered the Aztecs with a force that included Juan Garrido, a free black conquistador who had fought with Ponce de León.

Like Juan Garrido, many of the earliest Africans in the New World were *ladinos*, latinized blacks who hailed from Spain or Portugal, or from those countries' Atlantic or American colonies. Already acculturated to European ways, ladinos spoke Spanish or Portuguese and had no sympathy with the indigenous peoples of the Americas. Such attributes made them useful as domestic servants as well. Many European migrants to New Spain and Brazil brought black or mulatto (mixed-race) servants with them when they first settled these regions. The Spanish colonists began replacing their declining supply of indigenous laborers with slaves imported directly from Africa as early as 1518, and the first slave ship arrived in Portuguese Brazil in 1550.

Known in New Spain as *bozales*, these African-born slaves quickly accounted for the majority of the New World's slaves. They were also the most downtrodden, forced to do the dirtiest, most dangerous, and most demanding work. Employed to extract the silver and gold the Spanish found in Mexico and Peru, they toiled in underground tunnels that sometimes collapsed on top of them and acquired lung disease from the toxic mineral dust. Diving for pearls off the coast of Veracruz, Mexico, Africans drowned in such numbers that their bodies attracted sharks. Some worked on sugar plantations, typically laboring from dawn until dusk planting, harvesting, and refining sugar. In particular, they suffered high mortality rates due to the long hours and hazards involved in boiling the cane at high temperatures to produce sugar. The cultivation of sugarcane, one of the earliest slave-grown crops, was first introduced on Hispaniola and eventually spread throughout the Caribbean. But the largest sixteenth-century sugar producers were Brazil and Mexico, which imported tens of thousands of Africans to plant and process sugar during this period.

The demand for such labor would only increase over time, giving rise to an international slave trade that would last more than three centuries and carry approximately 12.5 million slaves to the New World. The African American population of the Americas took shape around these forced migrations.

Black Conquistadors

Some of the first Africans in the Americas arrived with Spanish military expeditions. In Mexico, Africans initially came with Hernán Cortés, whose forces included the free black conquistador Juan Garrido. In this illustration from a sixteenth-century manuscript, Cortés is depicted meeting the Indians of the Tlaxcala region. Garrido is pictured at the far left.

From History of Indians, *by Diego Duran (1537–1588)/Biblioteca Nacional, Madrid, Spain/De Agostini Picture Library/ Gianni Dagli Orti/Bridgeman Images.*

The Business of Slave Trading

By the beginning of the seventeenth century, the Spanish and Portuguese had begun to lose their monopoly of the exploration and settlement of the New World. Drawn by the riches that their predecessors had extracted from these lands, other European powers such as the Dutch, English, and French began to claim territory in the Americas. They also followed the example set by the Spanish and Portuguese when it came to importing enslaved Africans to help build and sustain their New World settlements.

As a result, the transatlantic slave trade expanded rapidly. Average annual slave exports from Africa increased from a little over ten thousand slaves at the beginning of the seventeenth century to nearly sixty thousand by the eighteenth century. The transatlantic trade exploited and expanded on the existing internal slave trade in Africa, pitting African leaders against one another and making the capture and enslavement of prisoners of war more profitable than ever before. Europeans also expanded the trade by traversing larger stretches of the African coast. Whereas early European traders sought their cargo largely along the Senegambian coast, the trade eventually extended south to include Guinea-Bissau, the Gold Coast, Benin, Kongo, and Angola. Some traders even did business with the East African country of Mozambique. The captives brought to these places were drawn from an expansive interior trade that extended into west-central Africa and as far east as Madagascar (Map 1.2).

For Europeans, the slave trade remained a coastal exchange that took place largely in their West African trading centers. The earliest such center was the **Elmina Castle** on the southern coast of present-day Ghana. Built as a Portuguese trading post in 1482, Elmina — the first of several forts the European powers established on the West African coast — began, by the early seventeenth century, to serve a far more enduring trade in human beings. Like later European trading forts, it had been erected with the agreement or license of local rulers in exchange for access to European commodities and military support. The castles on present-day Ghana's Gold Coast offered European merchants a secure harbor for their vessels and access to African markets trading in goods as well as people. Controlled by the Dutch after 1637, the Elmina Castle remained an active slave trading post until the Dutch withdrew from the trade in 1814.

The Portuguese controlled the early transatlantic slave trade by virtue of the 1494 Treaty of Tordesillas — an agreement between Spain and Portugal granting the Western Hemisphere to Spain, and Africa and Asia to Portugal. The earliest African slaves were shipped to the New World from Lisbon and other European ports, but direct trade between Africa and European colonies in the New World began in the early 1500s under Spain's *asiento* system. Initially, the Spanish crown both regulated the slave trade and secured a portion of its profits by selling asientos (agreements) permitting individual Portuguese merchants to sell slaves in Spain's New World colonies. But as the Portuguese trade with New Spain expanded, so too did the asiento system. In 1595 Spain issued a new kind of asiento, which gave Portugal a monopoly over the transatlantic slave trade and authorized Portuguese merchants to ship enslaved Africans directly from Africa to New Spain. After Spain and Portugal became enemies in the 1640s, the Spanish transferred their business first to the Dutch and then to the British, who dominated the eighteenth-century transatlantic trade.

European slave ships carried on a **triangle trade** that began with the transport of European copper, beads, guns, ammunition, textiles, and other manufactured goods to the West African coast. After these goods were exchanged for slaves, the second leg of

MAP 1.2   Slave Origins and Destinations, 1501–1867

This map of the transatlantic slave trade illustrates the many routes that slave traders used to carry millions of enslaved Africans to the Americas between 1501 and 1867. It also documents the trading routes that took much smaller numbers of African captives to Europe and the Middle East during this period.

the triangle trade — which slave traders called the Middle Passage — began. During this most infamous and dangerous phase, slave ships transported enslaved blacks from the West African coast to the slave ports of the New World. The ships then returned to their European ports of origin laden with profitable slave-grown crops, including sugar, tobacco, rice, indigo, and later cotton (Map 1.3). This trade fueled the economic development of Europe, supplying much of the raw material and capital that propelled European powers into the industrial age. The trade was equally crucial to the economic growth of the Americas, supplying European colonists with much of the labor they needed to make the New World settlements profitable.

For Africans, however, the trade was largely tragic. Although the African rulers, merchants, and middlemen who participated in the trade profited from it, most of the continent's inhabitants did not. By the early nineteenth century, Britain and other imperial powers had begun to withdraw from the slave trade — a process that started with Britain's ban on the trade in 1807 and the United States' Act to Prohibit the Importation of Slaves, which took effect in 1808. Nevertheless, several hundred years of forced migration had taken a severe toll on Africa and its peoples. Generations of young people had been lost, many of them perishing as a result of the trade. The transatlantic slave trade also imposed almost unimaginable suffering on the millions of individual Africans who survived their capture and sale. (See Document Project: Firsthand Accounts of the Slave Trade, pp. 34–44.)

The Long Middle Passage

For African captives, the journey into slavery began long before they saw a European ship. Most of them came from regions outside the West African coast. The African communities that surrounded the European slave trading settlements rarely sold their own people into slavery. The trade was an African enterprise until it reached the coast; only in Angola were Europeans ever really involved in capturing slaves themselves. Instead, African traders acquired slaves by way of an increasingly far-flung network that extended through much of western and west-central Africa.

Separated from their families and cultures, captives endured a long trek to the coast, where they were often imprisoned for months before embarking on the horrifying transatlantic voyage. Underfed and brutally treated throughout their journey, some captives died before ever leaving Africa. Still more perished aboard the slave ships, where they were confined in filthy, overcrowded conditions. But others survived, and some even resisted their circumstances by engaging in revolts and other subversive acts on board ship. Whatever the circumstances, the transatlantic slave trade had tragic consequences and lasting effects for both the Africans who remained at home and those who endured the forced migration abroad.

MAP 1.3   The Triangle Trade

The transatlantic slave trade is known as a triangle trade because it took shape around an exchange of goods that involved ports in three different parts of the world. As illustrated in this map, the first leg of the trade took traders from Europe to Africa, where they exchanged manufactured goods such as cloth, copper, beads, guns, and ammunition for enslaved Africans, whom they then sold to buyers in American ports in return for commodities such as sugar, tobacco, and cotton.

Capture and Confinement

The transatlantic slave trade was a dirty and dangerous business for everyone involved. It began in the interior of Africa, where African traders purchased slaves and marched them to the coast. In addition to prisoners of war, the enslaved Africans included individuals who were kidnapped from their homes by African slave raiders. Children were especially vulnerable to such raids, as illustrated in the story of Olaudah Equiano. Born around 1745, Equiano was eleven years old when he and his sister were taken from their family compound by "robbers," who carried them off on a journey that lasted many days.[8] The children of an Igbo village leader in the kingdom of Benin, Equiano and his sister were separated long before they reached the West African coast. Like many enslaved Africans, Equiano was sold several times by African traders before he ended up in the hands of European traders on the coast.

Equiano and other African captives reached the coast by way of a long overland trek of up to a thousand miles, which often took them through parts of Africa they had never seen. Usually poorly fed and harshly treated during the journey, they marched in **coffles**, or chained groups, bound together to prevent escape. The slave traders secured the coffles using a variety of brutal restraints that included sets of iron collars and chains that strung the slaves together, as well as interconnected wooden yokes that served a similar purpose. In addition to wearing these restraints, members of the coffles were often forced to work as porters for the traders, carrying loads of food and other goods. Those who were not up to the rigors of the journey were whipped and dragged along, and captives too weak to continue were left to die by the road.

As many as one in ten of the captured Africans died before they reached the coast, where new dangers awaited the survivors. On the final leg of the forced march, many captives saw the ocean for the first time and had to brace themselves for a journey into the unknown. Thirteen-year-old Samuel Ajayi Crowther, who was kidnapped from his Oyo County home (in modern-day Nigeria) nearly a century after Olaudah Equiano entered the trade, had never seen a river before reaching the inland tributary where his captors loaded him on a canoe bound for Lagos, Nigeria, which was then a major slave trading port. He had originally planned to drown himself rather be sold to the Portuguese, but he was far too frightened of the river to do so. "I had never seen anything like it in my life," he later recalled. "Nothing now terrified me more than the river and the thought of going into another world. . . . During the whole night's voyage on the canoe, not a single thought of leaping into the river had entered my mind, but on the contrary the fear of the river occupied my thoughts."[9]

New terrors confronted the African prisoners when they reached the coast, where they were held in **barracoons**, or temporary barracks. Some barracoons were little more than exposed pens built near the European trading forts, while others were sturdier structures deep inside the forts themselves. Debilitated by the long journey, some captives succumbed to infections they developed after being exposed to European diseases for the first time. Whether confined in pens or in the dank dungeons below one of the coastal castles, the captives who survived were then put on display before

Chaine d'esclaves venant de l'intérieure.

Slave Coffles and Leg Irons

In the top engraving, traders lead a slave coffle to the West African coast. The slaves are nude and bound together at the neck. Armed, fully clothed traders are positioned at the head and the end of the coffle. The bottom photograph depicts some eighteenth- and nineteenth-century slave fetters and shackles. Made of iron, these brutal restraints provided a variety of ways to secure captives and prevent escapes or rebellions during the long trek to the coast.

Top: From L'Afrique, by R. Geoffrey, 1814/Bibliothèque de L'Arsenal, Paris, France/Archives Charmet/Bridgeman Images; Bottom: The Granger Collection, New York.

African and European traders, who stripped them naked and inspected every inch of their bodies. The Portuguese were especially picky buyers, sometimes spending up to four hours scrutinizing the captives. They would sniff each captive's throat and make each one laugh and sing to ensure that his or her lungs were sound. They also would attempt to guess each male captive's age by licking or rubbing his chin to measure the amount of facial hair.

These inspections determined which captives would be marketed to the European and American slave ships that cruised the West African coast. Certain types of slaves were unlikely to attract European buyers and were resold on the African market instead. John Barbot, an agent for the French Royal Africa Company, noted that European traders were usually willing to buy only young and relatively healthy slaves: They "rejected those above thirty-five years of age, or defective in their limbs, eyes or teeth; or grown grey, or that have the venereal disease, or any other imperfection." According to Barbot, captives who were unlucky enough to meet these requirements were "marked on the breast, with a red-hot iron, imprinting the mark of the French, English, or Dutch companies, that so each nation may distinguish their own, and to prevent their being chang'd by the natives for worse, as they are apt enough to do. In this particular, care is taken that the women, as tenderest, be not burnt too hard."[10]

Life in the barracoons was another horror of the long Middle Passage. Fed only enough to keep them alive, the captives were typically confined on the coast for several months as the traders awaited European buyers. Often stripped of their clothes, they lived in quarters that became ever more crowded as the traders accumulated potential cargo. Those in the outdoor pens escaped the elements only at night, when they were locked in filthy cells, without even a fire for warmth. The barracoons had no toilets or other facilities for human waste, so the captives also had to live with their own excrement, which covered the ground of the pens.

The slaves confined in the underground dungeons of the slave castles suffered a different but equally horrifying confinement. The imposing Cape Coast Castle — a magnificent triangular fortress, protected and adorned by elegantly designed turrets and other fortifications — housed the British merchants who lived and worked in the airy chambers located on the castle's upper floors. All but invisible (then and now) were the castle's slave quarters, which were located beneath the ground — and barely above the water. This dank "slave hole," divided into three vaulted cellars, was used to house as many as one thousand captives at a time. Carved into the rocky cliffs that supplied the castle's foundation, the slave hole was designed to protect the rest of the garrison from slave insurrections and to prepare the captives for the darkness into which they would descend once they boarded the slave ships. Shackled and confined underground, the victims were cut off from the world just as they would be in the slave ships' holds. Packed in dark, windowless rooms that received air only through narrow vents cut into the ceilings, they had little to do but listen to the ocean's waves crash against the rocks and anticipate the next stage of their journey.

The overland trek and the harsh living conditions in the barracoons killed as many as 10 percent of the captives — a figure often left unmentioned in mortality statistics. In 1684, one official at the Cape Coast Castle matter-of-factly noted that "Sundry of our slaves being lately dead and others falling sick daily makes me get to think that they are to[o] much crowded in their lodging and besides have not the benefit of Air."[11]

If they were healthy enough to do so, some captives tried to escape, but their attempts met with limited success. By the time they reached the barracoons, most of them were already far from home and could not rely on local people to shelter them even if they somehow managed to escape confinement. The towns that grew up around European settlements such as the Elmina Castle and Cape Coast Castle were populated by Africans who made their living off the slave trade and would likely return runaways to their European owners for a small fee. Fugitives who eluded immediate capture risked being reenslaved and even resold by other coastal Africans, who saw them as commodities rather than countrymen.

On the Slave Coast

The slave castles and barracoons offered little hope for successful escape. Once purchased, the slaves in the barracoons usually parted company with the African middlemen and were paddled out to new prisons aboard the slave ships. Those confined in slave castles such as Elmina, the home of the famous "door of no return," exited their dungeons through doors that opened to the sea. Olaudah Equiano was terrified when he boarded the slave ship and saw its captain and crew, who he thought might have "no country, but . . . this *hollow* place." The white men and their vessel were unlike anything he had seen before, and he was convinced that he "had gotten into a world of bad spirits, and that they were going to kill me."[12]

Although Equiano was only eleven when he was kidnapped, this fear and confusion struck captives of all ages. A Muslim ironworker named Mahommah G. Baquaqua, who was kidnapped from his home as an adult in Benin almost a century later, was equally disoriented. "I had never seen a ship before," he recalled, and "my idea of it was that it was some sort of object of worship of the white man. I imagined that we were all to be slaughtered, and were being led there for that purpose."[13]

With no knowledge of the New World or the brutal **cash crop** agriculture that drove white men to travel the West African coast in search of slaves, many African captives suspected the slave traders of being cannibals who had already consumed their own people and were in search of more human flesh. African fears of cannibalism were so widespread that Portuguese slave ship owners instructed their captains to avoid letting the captives see the large metal cauldrons used to cook food, lest the Africans become convinced that they were to be boiled alive. Such fears were an expression of traditional African anxieties about dangerous foreign peoples, which often centered on fears of cannibalism. But they also speak to the social dislocation resulting from the slave trade, which produced suffering so great that some Africans associated the trade

Slaves on the Coast

In this eighteenth-century engraving, anguished Africans prepare to board a slave ship. Europeans were relieved to leave the coast and the many dangers it held, but their captives found themselves in a terrifying, alien world. Africans who had never before seen a ship did not know what to make of it, or of their strange new captors and the conditions under which they had been torn from their communities and their homelands. Many African slaves who left personal narratives, such as Olaudah Equiano, recalled the moment pictured here—as slaves catch their first glimpse of the imposing ship—as one filled with panic. They could not know the new horrors, psychological and physical, that awaited them on board.   © Roger-Viollet/The Image Works.

with man-eating witches or sorcerers. What else, they thought, could account for the social and physical traumas of the barracoons, or the mysterious and demoralizing future that faced the captives once they boarded the slave ships?

The ships' captains and crews had their own reasons to feel uneasy as long as their ships lingered on the West African coast. Although the captains were sometimes under instructions to bring back cargoes of slaves from specific areas, or specific proportions of men and women, they were anxious to load their ships with a full complement of marketable slaves healthy enough to survive the ocean voyage. Unless they could secure a complete cargo of salable slaves at the first barracoon they visited—which was often not the case—they had to travel from port to port for several weeks, collecting human cargo along the way.

For the slave ships' largely European seamen, these sojourns along the coast were among the most dangerous phases of the triangle trade. Exposed to tropical fevers, they worried about falling sick, especially since their proximity to the coast created other hazards that required strength and awareness. While anchored in the deep waters off the coast, slave ships were targets for marauding pirates and the naval ships of hostile European powers. Slave ships anchored close to shore were sometimes attacked by African forces that accused them of kidnapping free Africans.

But internal mutiny was the slave traders' paramount concern. As long as the mainland remained in view, their terrified captives had one last hope of escape. During the dangerous days and weeks of travel along the coast, slave resistance had to be contained through the use of physical restraints that kept the captives all but immobilized in the holds of the ships. "There is put aboard . . . 30 paire of shackles and boults for such of your negers as are rebellious and we pray you be veary careful to keepe them under . . . that they ryse not against you as they have done in other ships," the Guinea Company advised the slave trader Bartholomew Hayward in 1651.[14]

Iron hand and leg cuffs known as **bilboes**, among the central tools of the trade, were always in short supply. Used primarily on male slaves, bilboes consisted of two iron shackles locked on a post and usually fastened around the ankles of two men. Joined in this way, the captives were hobbled like competitors in some macabre three-legged race. In the packed hold of a slave ship, the bilboes' heavy iron bars all but immobilized both men, making any attempt to rebel or swim to shore impossible — although they did not prevent some captives from throwing themselves overboard, shackles and all. Similarly, throughout the voyage, the captives required careful supervision, since suicides and other deaths caused by depression were not uncommon.

Inside the Slave Ship

Once they had gathered their cargo and caught favorable winds, the slave ship's captain and crew were happy to leave the African coast behind. The journey from Guinea to Caribbean island ports, which were generally the first stop for slave ships bound for North America, lasted fifty to ninety days. Portuguese slave ships could traverse the ocean between Angola and Brazil in thirty to sixty days. Sailing times varied based on weather, ocean currents, and the size of the ship. Advances in shipbuilding and navigation resulted in shorter crossing times.

The worst part of the long Middle Passage began as men, women, and children were packed, nearly naked, into ships designed to accommodate the maximum number of slaves in the least amount of space. Slave ships varied in size from 11-ton sloops that could accommodate only thirty slaves to 566-ton behemoths that carried up to seven hundred captives.[15] Throughout the slave trade's history, these were the most crowded oceangoing vessels in the Atlantic world.[16] By the time they were fully loaded, most ships were overflowing with naked Africans. There was some debate among shipowners over the virtues of **tight packing**, to maximize profits by packing the ship to capacity, versus "loose packing," in hopes that a slightly smaller cargo would reduce the death rate. However, prior to 1788, when the British government restricted the number of slaves British ships could carry, slave traders generally loaded as many slaves as they could fit on their ships.

The Middle Passage
Slaves belowdecks lived for months in conditions of squalor and indescribable horror. Ill health and impossibly close quarters were a perfect breeding ground for contagious diseases. Mortality rates were high, and death made conditions belowdecks even worse. Although the corpses of the dead were eventually thrown overboard, crew members avoided the ship's hold, so slaves who had succumbed to sickness were not always discovered immediately. Living slaves could remain shackled to the dead for hours and sometimes days. *The Art Archive at Art Resource, NY.*

Throughout the slave trade, men outnumbered women by a ratio of roughly 2:1, while children under age fifteen became increasingly common over time, probably as a result of changes in the internal African slave trade. Before 1700, children accounted for roughly 12 percent of slave ships' cargo, but by 1810 the proportion had risen to an average of 46 percent. The women and children on board slave ships did not constitute family groupings. As was the case with Olaudah Equiano and his sister, enslaved family members were often separated long before they boarded the ships, and once aboard the captives were segregated by gender.

Male slaves were generally kept in the ship's hold, where they experienced the worst of the crowding. They were shackled together during much of the voyage and were often accommodated one on top of another on crudely constructed bunks, like "rows of books on shelves."[17] The captives stationed on the floor beneath low-lying bunks could barely move and spent much of the voyage pinned to the floorboards, which could, over time, wear the skin on their elbows down to the bone.

The men belowdecks were the biggest worry. Mutinies were not uncommon aboard slave ships, and male slaves were most likely to mutiny when they were on deck. To protect themselves from their cargo, crews were often twice as large as usual. Armed crew members closely watched the shackled men whenever they were brought on deck, which was normally for only a few hours each day, primarily for meals, exercise, makeshift saltwater baths, and medical inspections. During rough or rainy weather, they stayed below all day.

During their time on deck, the captives often received exercise through a practice called "dancing the slaves." The crew forced the slaves, under close supervision, to jump or dance as best they could in their leg irons, while one of them played a drum or an African banjo, or a sailor played the bagpipes. Exercise was not optional. "If they go about it reluctantly or do not move with agility," one eighteenth-century ship's surgeon observed, "they are flogged; a person standing by them all the time with a cat-o'-nine-tails in his hands for the purpose."[18]

Danse de Nègres
Captives aboard slave ships were brought on deck for daily exercise in fair weather. Sometimes still in chains, they were often forced to exert themselves by dancing. In this engraving from a book titled *La France maritime, fondée et dirigée par Amédée Gréhan . . .* (Paris: Postel, 1837–1842), three slaves are spurred into a reluctant, cowering dance by two sailors holding whips. *Color engraving, 1850, based on a French engraving from the 1830s/Photo © CCI/ Bridgeman Images.*

Women and children, by contrast, were usually housed in rooms set apart from the main hold — sometimes together, sometimes separately. Generally indifferent to family ties, the slave traders honored only the relationship between infants and nursing mothers, whom they rarely separated. Regardless of where they slept, women and children — considered less dangerous than men, though they sometimes aided in slave revolts — were usually allowed to move about the ship more freely.

These arrangements also gave the seamen easy access to enslaved women, which the men regarded as one of the perks of the trade. One seaman noted that "on board some ships, the common sailors are allowed to have intercourse with such black women whose consent they can procure."[19] Other witnesses described the sexual violence inherent in such exchanges in more explicit terms. The eighteenth-century British slave trader turned abolitionist John Newton maintained that enslaved women were often "exposed to the wanton rudeness of white savages." "Naked, trembling, terrified and perhaps already exhausted with fatigue and hunger," he wrote, "the poor creatures cannot understand the language they hear, but the looks are sufficient. . . . The prey is provided on the spot and reserved till opportunity offers."[20] Though presented in an antislavery publication, Newton's description does not seem exaggerated. In a more prosaic diary entry written when he was still working in the trade, Newton recorded a sexual assault he witnessed in matter-of-fact terms: "William Cooney seduced a woman slave down into the room and lay with her brutelike in view of the whole quarter deck. . . . If anything happens to her I shall impute to him, for she is big with child. Her number is 83."[21] Likewise, witnesses such as the ex-slave Ottobah Cugoano recalled that "it was common for the dirty filthy sailors to take African women and lie upon their bodies."[22]

Such practices must have infuriated and demoralized the enslaved men confined belowdecks, as Cugoano's bitter comment suggests. But the segregation of the sexes during the Middle Passage limited interaction between African men and women. Far more mobile than men, enslaved women had better access to information on the ship's crew, fortifications, and daily routine, but little opportunity to communicate this to the men confined in the ship's hold. On the rare occasions that captive women did find ways to contact their male counterparts, they often played important roles in slave revolts. Women, for example, instigated a 1797 insurrection aboard the British ship *Thomas* by stealing weapons and passing them to the men below, and they engaged in hand-to-hand combat with slave ship crews during several other revolts.

Hardship and Misery on Board

Suicides were common both during the Middle Passage and after the captives arrived in the New World. (See Document Project: Firsthand Accounts of the Slave Trade, pp. 34–44.) One observer noted that captives were often "so willful and loth to leave their own country that, they have often leap'd out of canoes, boat and ship, into the sea, and kept under water till they were drowned."[23] Many were fueled by the

West African religious belief that the dead join the spirits of their ancestors — a formulation that led some slave ship captains to mutilate their charges on the basis of the conviction that "many of the Blacks believe that if they are put to death and not dismembered, they shall return again to their own country, after they are thrown overboard."[24]

Suicidal thoughts among captives were no doubt influenced by depression as much as by any hope for a happier afterlife. During the ocean passage, many captives were either unwilling or unable to eat enough to stay alive, and they resisted their captors' attempts to force-feed them. The slave trader John Barbot, who considered himself "naturally compassionate," noted that he was "necessitated sometimes to cause the teeth of those wretches to be broken, because they would not open their mouths, or be prevailed upon by any entreaties to feed themselves; and thus have forced some sustenance into their throats."[25] Traders also forced slaves to exercise, which they mistakenly thought would prevent both melancholy and scurvy (a disease caused by vitamin C deficiency).

The greatest cause of death during the Middle Passage, however, was disease. Estimates of average mortality on slave ships, which rest on scholarly calculations drawn from a slave ship database that is not yet complete, currently range from 15 to 20 percent. Such figures, however, obscure the wide variation in mortality rates seen on different ships. Rates ranged from 4 percent to 55 percent, but could be even higher. In 1773, for example, the Dutch slave ship *Nooitgedacht* lost 89 percent of its 157 slaves to scurvy.[26]

The single biggest killer was dysentery, a gastrointestinal disorder that routinely swept through the packed holds. An inflammation of the intestines caused by a bacterial infection, dysentery was more evocatively known in the trade as the "bloody flux." Slaves boarded ships already malnourished and weakened by the forced march to the West African coast and their time in the barracoons, making them highly susceptible to this infection, which could also be caused or aggravated by the poor food and water on board. Highly contagious, dysentery was one of the great horrors of the voyage, even among those who survived its ravages. The holds of the slave ships had no toilets, bathing areas, or facilities set aside for the sick, so the African captives who came down with the infection had to endure the acute cramping and diarrhea caused by it while shackled to one another in airless confinement. Cooped up in these unsanitary conditions, captives also died from outbreaks of other communicable diseases, including smallpox, measles, and ophthalmia (a blinding eye infection). Any of these diseases could decimate crews and cargoes, which is one reason mortality rates on ships varied so widely.

The holds were so filthy by the time the ships docked that they gave off a stench that could be detected from the shore. The smell must have made life belowdecks even more unendurable — as did the deaths that took place there. Since the crews avoided the pestilence below as much as possible, even death did not always separate the living from the dead. Some slaves were forced to spend hours or even days chained to a dead companion. Indeed, death was an overwhelming and ubiquitous presence during the ocean voyage. Confined in close quarters, the captives watched their shipmates die in increasing numbers as the voyage progressed. High mortality rates were so common, even on voyages that escaped any major influx of disease, that contemporaries considered any slave voyage on which less than 20 percent of the slaves died to be a financial success.

The historian Stephanie Smallwood has suggested that the high mortality rates on slave ships produced "an extraordinary social crisis" among the captives because the deaths took place outside any social context that might allow the living to understand and make peace with them. The Akan captives imported to the Americas from the Gold Coast, for example, believed that mortuary rites were essential for a complete death. How could they make sense of the spiritual fate of shipmates, or even kinfolk, who perished and were summarily tossed overboard by the crew? To the Akan, their shipmates' deaths were spiritually incomplete. Surrounded by death and powerless to protect the dead, the Akan and other African captives faced what Smallwood has described as a "dual crisis: the trauma of death, and also of the inability to respond appropriately to death."[27]

The dying did not end with landfall. Even after the ships landed in Barbados, which was often their first stop, the slaves who disembarked there and at other New World ports continued to die despite the traders' attempts to revive them with fresh food and water. In the New World, the survivors of the long Middle Passage encountered more new diseases, which killed as many as 30 percent of them after they arrived. Estimates of how many Africans boarded slave ships vary, but current research suggests that upwards of twelve million were dispatched from Africa on more than forty thousand voyages that killed almost two million people.[28] Taking into account the deaths that occurred on the overland trek to the West African coast and in the barracoons — up to 10 percent of the captives — some scholars estimate that only half of the Africans destined for New World slavery survived.

CONCLUSION
The Slave Trade's Diaspora

Between the sixteenth century and the nineteenth century, when the slave trade finally ended, more than twelve million black captives departed Africa for the New World. Most came from West Africa, where they were captured or purchased by West African slave traders who sold them to European traders operating along the coast. Although the early trade was dominated by the Spanish and Portuguese, by the 1600s Dutch, French, English, Danish, Swedish, and other European traders were all visiting Africa's west coast. After 1730, traders based in North America also began to participate in the transatlantic trade. The slave trade did not take shape overnight, but instead grew in conjunction with European settlement of the New World. Approximately 3 percent of

African captives arrived in the Americas before 1600; about 16 percent came in the seventeenth century, more than 50 percent in the eighteenth century, and about 30 percent in the nineteenth century.

The number of enslaved Africans in the New World began to increase in the seventeenth century as other European powers joined the Spanish and Portuguese in establishing settlements there. Intent on exploiting the hemisphere's rich resources, these newcomers depended on enslaved Africans for much of the labor they needed to sustain their colonies.

The forced migration of Africans to the Americas lasted for generations and created enduring African American communities throughout the hemisphere. Brought to the Americas in chains, slave trade survivors took on new identities in the New World. Whether of Igbo, Akan, Wolof, Mandinka, or other descent, slave captives were initially separated by barriers of national affiliation, ethnic group, and language. Once in the Americas, through shared experience, they would forge a collective identity as Africans — and, eventually, as African Americans.

First imported to what is now the United States to clear and cultivate early English and Dutch settlements in Virginia and New York, enslaved Africans were central to the survival and success of these early settlements. They would continue to play vital roles in many other colonies throughout the region in the coming years.

CHAPTER 1 **REVIEW**

KEY TERMS

diaspora p. 4

carracks/caravels p. 11

Guanches p. 12

Taino Indians p. 14

encomienda p. 14

ladinos p. 16

bozales p. 16

Elmina Castle p. 18

asiento p. 18

triangle trade p. 18

coffles p. 22

barracoons p. 22

cash crop p. 25

bilboes p. 27

tight packing p. 27

REVIEW QUESTIONS

1. In what ways were African social identity, politics, and economics kinship based and collective in nature? Why might the transatlantic slave trade have been especially damaging to societies structured in this way?

2. To what factors can we attribute the initial development and eventual expansion of African slavery in Europe's New World colonies? How would you describe this progression?

3. How did traditional West African beliefs — about death, foreigners, and cannibalism, for example — serve to shape African slaves' experience of the Middle Passage?

4. Why did the diasporic Africans brought to the New World not consider themselves members of the same group? How might their shared experience have helped them form a new, collective African American identity?

5. Provide several examples of Africans' resistance to European intrusions in the early slave trade. How did Africans fight back, both individually and collectively, against slave raids, kidnappings, and their own captivity?

Firsthand Accounts of the Slave Trade

The slave trade was a grueling and often lethal business that left behind a historical record consisting largely of logs kept by slave ship captains and business records documenting profits and losses. However, some firsthand accounts of the Middle Passage do exist. They include accounts of slave trade voyages written by Europeans who worked aboard the slave ships, as well as a handful of narratives that record the experiences of the African captives who made the journey largely belowdecks.

The following documents provide examples of these different sources. Two of the written sources record the Middle Passage experiences of two eighteenth-century Africans who were captured and sold into the transatlantic slave trade as children. They include a vivid account of the long journey into slavery endured by Olaudah Equiano, an ex-slave who authored one of the first slave narratives, and a brief account of the captivity and terrifying transatlantic voyage of a Massachusetts slave known only as Belinda, who shared her story in a petition addressed to the Massachusetts legislature. Another pair of documents records life aboard the slave ships from the perspective of two men who worked in the slave trade: James Barbot Jr., who served as a ship's officer aboard several slave ships, and Alexander Falconbridge, a British surgeon who took part in four slave trade voyages between 1780 and 1787. All four written documents contain discussions of the Middle Passage that are filtered through memory and were recorded to support their authors' ambitions. Nonetheless, they offer enormously valuable accounts of life inside the trade.

Also useful to understanding just how dangerous these voyages were for all concerned are visual sources. Included here is an artist's depiction of a slave revolt aboard ship, as well as two pages taken from a slave ship's logbook. Kept by the captain for the ship's owners, the ship's account book provided a daily record of the important events that took place during each voyage, documenting where the ship traveled, where it picked up cargo, and what it carried, and any illnesses or other casualties that occurred aboard ship. On the slave ships, death was a routine matter, as can be seen in the pages from the brig *Sally's* log, which enumerate the deaths that took place during a particular voyage.

Olaudah Equiano | *The Interesting Narrative of the Life of Olaudah Equiano, or Gustavus Vassa, the African, 1789*

Born in what is today southeast Nigeria, OLAUDAH EQUIANO (1745–1797) was the youngest son of an Igbo village leader in the kingdom of Benin. Kidnapped into slavery at age eleven, he was resold several times by African masters during his six-month journey to the African coast, where he was sold to a slave trader who carried him to the West Indies and into slavery in Virginia. Written after Equiano purchased his own freedom and became active in the British antislavery movement, *The Interesting Narrative of the Life of Olaudah Equiano* has long been considered the best African account of enslavement, the Middle Passage, and eighteenth-century life in an African village — although one scholar has recently suggested that Equiano's description of his African past is fictional.[29]

One day, when all our people were gone out to their works as usual, and only I and my dear sister were left to mind the house, two men and a woman got over our walls, and in a moment seized us both; and, without giving us time to cry out, or make resistance, they stopped our mouths, tied our hands, and ran off with us into the nearest wood. . . . At the end of six or seven months after I had been kidnapped, I arrived at the sea coast. . . .

The first object which saluted my eyes when I arrived on the coast was the sea, and a slave-ship, which was then riding at anchor, and waiting for its cargo. These filled me with astonishment, which was soon converted into terror. . . . When I was carried on board I was immediately handled, and tossed up, to see if I were sound, by some of the crew; and I was now persuaded that I had got into a world of bad spirits, and that they were going to kill me. Their complexions too differing so much from ours, their long hair, and the language they spoke, which was very different from any I had ever heard, united to confirm me in this belief. Indeed, such were the horrors of my views and fears at the moment, that, if ten thousand worlds had been my own, I would have freely parted with them all to have exchanged my condition with that of the meanest slave in my own country. When I looked round the ship too, and saw a large furnace of copper boiling, and a multitude of black people of every description chained together, every one of their countenances expressing dejection and sorrow, I no longer doubted of my fate, and, quite overpowered with horror and anguish, I fell motionless on the deck and fainted. When I recovered a little, I found some black people about me, who I believed were some of those who brought me on board, and had been receiving their pay; they talked to me in order to cheer me, but all in vain. I asked them if we were not to be eaten by those white men with horrible looks, red faces, and long hair? They told me I was not; and one of the crew brought me a small portion of spirituous liquor in a wine glass; but, being afraid of him, I would not take it out of his hand. One of the blacks therefore took it from him and gave it to me, and I took a little down my palate, which, instead of reviving me, as they thought it would, threw me into the greatest consternation at the strange feeling it produced having never tasted any such liquor before. Soon after this, the blacks who brought me on board went off, and left me abandoned to despair. I now saw myself deprived of all chance of returning to my native country, or even the least glimpse of hope of gaining the shore, which I now considered as friendly: and even wished for my former slavery, in preference to my present situation, which was filled with horrors of every kind, still heightened by my ignorance of what I was to undergo. I was not long suffered to indulge my grief; I was soon put down under the decks, and there I received such a salutation in my nostrils as I had never experienced in my life: so that with the loathsomeness of the stench, and crying together, I became so sick and low that I was not able to eat, nor had I the least desire to taste any thing. I now wished for the last friend, Death, to relieve me; but soon, to my grief, two of the white men offered me eatables; and, on my refusing to eat, one of them held me fast by the hands, and laid me across, I think, the windlass, and tied my feet, while the other flogged me severely. I had never experienced any thing of this kind before; and although not being used to the water, I naturally feared that element the first time I saw it; yet, nevertheless, could I have got over the nettings, I would have jumped over the side; but I could not; and, besides, the crew used to watch us very closely who were not chained down to the decks, lest we should leap into the water; and I have seen some of these poor African prisoners most severely cut for attempting to do so, and hourly whipped for not eating. This indeed was often the case with myself. In a little time after, amongst the poor chained men, I found some of my own nation, which in a small degree gave ease to my mind.

SOURCE: Olaudah Equiano, *The Interesting Narrative of the Life of Olaudah Equiano, or Gustavus Vassa, the African. Written by Himself.* (London: printed for the author, 1789), 32, 45, 46–50, 51–53, 54–55, 56.

I inquired of them what was to be done with us? they gave me to understand we were to be carried to these white people's country to work for them. I then was a little revived, and thought, if it were no worse than working, my situation was not so desperate: but still I feared I should be put to death, the white people looked and acted, as I thought, in so savage a manner; for I had never seen among any people such instances of brutal cruelty; and this not only shewn towards us blacks, but also to some of the whites themselves. One white man in particular I saw, when we were permitted to be on deck, flogged so unmercifully with a large rope near the foremast, that he died in consequence of it; and they tossed him over the side as they would have done a brute. This made me fear these people the more; and I expected nothing less than to be treated in the same manner. I could not help expressing my fears and apprehensions to some of my countrymen: I asked them if these people had no country, but lived in this hollow place the ship? they told me they did not, but came from a distant one. "Then," said I, "how comes it in all our country we never heard of them?" They told me, because they lived so very far off. I then asked, where were their women? had they any like themselves? I was told they had: "And why," said I, "do we not see them?" they answered, because they were left behind. I asked how the vessel could go? they told me they could not tell; but that there were cloth put upon the masts by the help of the ropes I saw, and then the vessel went on; and the white men had some spell or magic they put in the water when they liked in order to stop the vessel. I was exceedingly amazed at this account, and really thought they were spirits. I therefore wished much to be from amongst them, for I expected they would sacrifice me: but my wishes were vain; for we were so quartered that it was impossible for any of us to make our escape. . . . At last, when the ship we were in had got in all her cargo, they made ready with many fearful noises, and we were all put under deck, so that we could not see how they managed the vessel. But this disappointment was the least of my sorrow. The stench of the hold while we were on the coast was so intolerably loathsome, that it was dangerous to remain there for any time, and some of us had been permitted to stay on the deck for the fresh air; but now that the whole ship's cargo were confined together, it became absolutely pestilential. The closeness of the place, and the heat of the climate, added to the number in the ship, which was so crouded that each had scarcely room to turn himself, almost suffocated us. This produced copious perspirations, so that the air soon became unfit for respiration, from a variety of loathsome smells, and brought on a sickness amongst the slaves, of which many died, thus falling victims to the improvident avarice, as I may call it, of their purchasers. This wretched situation was again aggravated by the galling of the chains, now become insupportable; and the filth of the necessary tubs, into which the children often fell, and were almost suffocated. The shrieks of the women, and the groans of the dying, rendered the whole a scene of horror almost inconceiveable. Happily perhaps for myself I was soon reduced so low here that it was thought necessary to keep me almost always on deck; and from my extreme youth I was not put in fetters. In this situation I expected every hour to share the fate of my companions, some of whom were almost daily brought upon deck at the point of death, which I began to hope would soon put an end to my miseries. Often did I think many of the inhabitants of the deep much more happy than myself; I envied them the freedom they enjoyed, and as often wished I could change my condition for theirs. Every circumstance I met with served only to render my state more painful, and heighten my apprehensions and my opinion of the cruelty of the whites. One day they had taken a number of fishes; and when they had killed and satisfied themselves with as many as they thought fit, to our astonishment who were on the deck, rather than give any of them to us to eat, as we expected, they tossed the remaining fish into the sea again, although we begged and prayed for some as well as we could, but in vain; and some of my countrymen, being pressed by hunger, took an opportunity, when they thought no one saw them, of trying to get a little privately; but they were discovered, and the attempt procured them some very severe floggings.

One day, when we had a smooth sea, and moderate wind, two of my wearied countrymen, who were chained together (I was near them at the time), preferring death to such a life of misery, somehow made through the nettings, and jumped into the sea; immediately another quite dejected fellow, who, on account of his illness, was suffered to be out of irons, also followed their example; and I believe many more would very soon have done the same, if they had not been prevented by the ship's crew, who were instantly alarmed. . . . At last, we came in sight of the island of Barbadoes, at which the whites on board gave a great shout, and made many signs of joy to us. We did not know what to think of this; but, as the vessel drew nearer, we plainly saw the harbour, and other ships of different kinds and sizes: and we soon anchored amongst them off Bridge Town. Many merchants and planters now came on board, though it was in the evening. They put us in separate parcels, and examined us attentively. They also made us jump, and pointed

to the land, signifying we were to go there. We thought by this we should be eaten by these ugly men, as they appeared to us; and when, soon after we were all put down under the deck again, there was much dread and trembling among us, and nothing but bitter cries to be heard all the night from these apprehensions, insomuch that at last the white people got some old slaves from the land to pacify us. They told us we were not to be eaten, but to work, and were soon to go on land, where we should see many of our country people. This report eased us much; and sure enough, soon after we landed, there came to us Africans of all languages. . . . We were not many days in the merchant's custody before we were sold after their usual manner, which is this: — On a signal given, (as the beat of a drum), the buyers rush at once into the yard where the slaves are confined, and make choice of that parcel they like best. The noise and clamour with which this is attended, and the eagerness visible in the countenances of the buyers, serve not a little to increase the apprehension of the terrified Africans, who may well be supposed to consider them as the ministers of that destruction to which they think themselves devoted. In this manner, without scruple, are relations and friends separated, most of them never to see each other again.

Belinda | *The Petition of Belinda, 1782*

The following account of an African childhood interrupted by enslavement appears in a petition to the Massachusetts legislature written on behalf of an African-born slave known only as BELINDA. Captured and enslaved in the 1720s, she spent much of her life as the property of Isaac Royall, a Medford, Massachusetts, resident and British loyalist during the Revolutionary War. Royall fled the colony and died in 1781. Freed after her master's death, Belinda petitioned the new state's new government for an "allowance" from the estate of her former master. Composed when she was over seventy years old, Belinda's petition was signed with an *X*, indicating that she was illiterate. No record of who wrote the text exists. What arguments does Belinda make on her own behalf? How does she relate slavery to current events?

To the honourable the senate and house of representatives, in general court assembled:
The petition of Belinda, an African,

Humbly shews,

That seventy years have rolled away, since she, on the banks of the Rio de Valta, received her existence. The mountains, covered with spicy forests — the vallies, loaded with the richest fruits, spontaneously produced — joined to that happy temperature of air, which excludes excess, would have yielded her the most complete felicity, had not her mind received early impressions of the cruelty of men, whose faces were like the moon, and whose bows and arrows were like the thunder and the lightning of the clouds. The idea of these, the most dreadful of all enemies, filled her infant slumbers with horror, and her noon-tide moments with cruel apprehensions! But her affrighted imagination, in its most alarming extension, never represented distresses equal to what she has since really experienced: for before she had twelve years enjoyed the fragrance of her native groves, and ere she realized that Europeans placed their happiness in the yellow dust, which she carelessly marked with her infant footsteps — even when she, in a sacred grove, with each hand in that of a tender parent, was paying her devotion to the great Orisa, who made all things, an armed band of white men, driving many of her countrymen in chains, rushed into the hallowed shades! Could the tears, the sighs, and supplications, bursted from the tortured parental affection, have blunted the keen edge of avarice, she might have been rescued from agony, which many of her country's children have felt, but which none have ever described. In vain she lifted her supplicating voice to an insulted father, and her guiltless hands to a dishonoured deity! She was ravished from the bosom of her country, from the arms of her friends, while the advanced age of her parents, rendering them unfit for servitude, cruelly separated her from them for ever.

Scenes which her imagination had never conceived of, a floating world, the sporting monsters of the deep, and the familiar meetings of billows and clouds, strove, but in vain, to divert her attention from three hundred Africans in chains, suffering the most excruciating torment; and some of them rejoicing that the pangs of death came like a balm to their wounds.

Once more her eyes were blest with a continent: but alas! how unlike the land where she received her being! How all things appeared unpropitious. She learned to catch the ideas, marked by the sounds of language, only to know that her doom was slavery, from which death alone was to emancipate her. What did it avail her, that the walls of her lord were hung with splendor, and that the dust trodden under foot in her native country, crouded his gates with sordid worshippers! The laws rendered her incapable of receiving property: and though she was a free moral agent, accountable for her own actions, yet never had she a moment at her own disposal! Fifty years her faithful hands have been compelled to ignoble servitude for the benefit of an Isaac Royall, until, as if nations must be agitated, and the world convulsed, for the preservation of that freedom, which the Almighty Father intended for all the human race, the present war commenced. The terrors of men, armed in the cause of freedom, compelled her master to fly, and to breathe away his life in a land, where lawless dominion sits enthroned, pouring blood and vengeance on all who dare to be free.

The face of your petitioner is now marked with the furrows of time, and her frame feebly bending under the oppression of years, while she, by the laws of the land, is denied the enjoyment of one morsel of that immense wealth, a part whereof hath been accumulated by her own industry, and the whole augmented by her servitude.

SOURCE: "Petition of an African Slave, to the Legislature of Massachusetts," *The American Museum, or Repository of Ancient and Modern Fugitive Pieces, Prose and Poetical* 1, no. 6 (June 1787): 538–40.

Wherefore, casting herself at the feet of your honours, as to a body of men, formed for the extirpation of vassalage, for the reward of virtue, and the just returns of honest industry — she prays that such allowance may be made her, out of the estate of colonel Royall, as will prevent her, and her more infirm daughter, from misery in the greatest extreme, and scatter comfort over the short and downward path of their lives: and she will ever pray.

BELINDA.
Boston, February, 1782.

James Barbot Jr. | *General Observations on the Management of Slaves, 1700*

The son and nephew of slave traders, JAMES BARBOT JR. worked aboard slave ships for much of his life and recorded his experiences in several published works. Employed on the *Don Carlos* as the supercargo (officer) in charge of the slaves' purchase and sale, Barbot wrote the following description of how best to manage the captives on board. Despite the precautions described here, an onboard rebellion took place on the ship's first day at sea. At least twenty-eight captives were "lost" — either killed in battle or through suicide by drowning. Judging from this document, what did Barbot view as the most important measures to take to prevent slave insurrections?

As to the management of our slaves aboard, we lodge the two sexes apart, by means of a strong partition at the main mast; the forepart is for men, the other behind the mast for the women. If it be in large ships carrying five or six hundred slaves, the deck in such ships ought to be at least five and a half or six foot high, which is very requisite for driving a continual trade of slaves: for the greater height it has, the more airy and convenient it is for such a considerable number of human creatures; and consequently far the more healthy for them, and fitter to look after them. We build a sort of half-decks along the sides with deals and spars° provided for that purpose in *Europe*, that half-deck extending no farther than the sides of our scuttles, and so the slaves lie in two rows, one above the other, and as close together as they can be crouded. . . .

. . . The planks, or deals, contract some dampness more or less, either from the deck being so often wash'd to keep it clean and sweet, or from the rain that gets in now and then through the scuttles or other openings, and even from the very sweat of the slaves; which being so crouded in a low place, is perpetual, and occasions many distempers, or at best great inconveniences dangerous to their health. . . .

It has been observ'd before, that some slaves fancy they are carry'd to be eaten, which makes them desperate; and others are so on account of their captivity: so that if care be not taken, they will mutiny and destroy the ship's crew in hopes to get away.

To prevent such misfortunes, we use to visit them daily, narrowly searching every corner between decks, to see whether they have not found means, to gather any pieces of iron, or wood, or knives, about the ship, notwithstanding the great care we take not to leave any tools or nails, or other things in the way: which, however, cannot be always so exactly observ'd, where so many people are in the narrow compass of a ship.

We cause as many of our men as is convenient to lie in the quarter-deck and gun-room, and our

SOURCE: James Barbot Jr., "An Abstract of a Voyage to Congo River, or the Zair, and to Cabinde, in the Year 1700," in *A Collection of Voyages and Travels*, ed. Awnsham Churchill and John Churchill (London: J. Walthoe, 1732), 5:546–48.

° Deals and spars are planks and poles.

principal officers in the great cabbin, where we keep all our small arms in a readiness, with sentinels constantly at the door and avenues to it; being thus ready to disappoint any attempts our slaves might make on a sudden.

These precautions contribute very much to keep them in awe; and if all those who carry slaves duly observ'd them, we should not hear of so many revolts as have happen'd. Where I was concern'd, we always kept our slaves in such order, that we did not perceive the least inclination in any of them to revolt, or mutiny, and lost very few of our number in the voyage.

It is true, we allow'd them much more liberty, and us'd them with more tenderness than most other *Europeans* would think prudent to do; as, to have them all upon deck every day in good weather; to take their meals twice a-day, at fix'd hours, that is, at ten in the morning, and at five at night; which being ended, we made the men go down again between decks; for the women were almost entirely at their own discretion, to be upon deck as long as they pleas'd, nay even many of the males had the same liberty by turns, successively; few or none being fetter'd or kept in shackles, and that only on account of some disturbances, or injuries, offer'd to their fellow captives, as will unavoidably happen among a numerous croud of such savage people. Besides, we allow'd each of them betwixt their meals a handful of *Indian* wheat and *Mandioca*, and now and then short pipes and tobacco to smoak upon deck by turns, and some cocoa-nuts; and to the women a piece of coarse cloth to cover them, and the same to many of the men, which we took care they did wash from time to time, to prevent vermin, which they are very subject to; and because it look'd sweeter and more agreeable. Towards the evening they diverted themselves on the deck, as they thought fit, some conversing together, others dancing, singing, and sporting after their manner, which pleased them highly, and often made us pastime; especially the female sex, who being a-part from the males, on the quarter-deck, and many of them young sprightly maidens, full of jollity and good-humour, afforded us abundance of recreation; as did several little fine boys, which we mostly kept to attend on us about the ship. . . .

Much more might be said relating to the preservation and maintenance of slaves in such voyages, which I leave to the prudence of the officers that govern aboard, if they value their own reputation and their owners advantage; and shall only add these few particulars, that tho' we ought to be circumspect in watching the slaves narrowly, to prevent or disappoint their ill designs for our own conservation, yet must we not be too severe and haughty with them, but on the contrary, caress and humour them in every reasonable thing. Some commanders, of a morose peevish temper are perpetually beating and curbing them, even without the least offence, and will not suffer any upon deck but when unavoidable necessity to ease themselves does require; under pretence it hinders the work of the ship and sailors, and that they are troublesome by their nasty nauseous stench, or their noise; which makes those poor wretches desperate, and besides their falling into distempers thro' melancholy, often is the occasion of their destroying themselves.

Such officers should consider, those unfortunate creatures are men as well as themselves, tho' of a different colour, and pagans; and that they ought to do to others as they would be done by in like circumstances.

A Slave in Revolt

This image of a slave in chains on the deck of a ship first appeared in a 1793 edition of Thomas Day's antislavery poem *The Dying Negro*. Whereas many antislavery portraits of Africans depicted their subjects kneeling and praying for mercy, this unusual image features a black man standing and holding a dagger. It is not clear whether he is contemplating rebellion or suicide, although Day's poem was inspired by an incident in which a slave who had escaped from slavery in the West Indies, only to be recaptured and confined aboard a slave ship bound for America, shot himself rather than be returned to slavery.

Engraving with the poem, The Dying Negro, *by Thomas Day, 1793/© National Maritime Museum, London/The Image Works.*

Alexander Falconbridge | An Account of the Slave Trade on the Coast of Africa, 1788

The British surgeon ALEXANDER FALCONBRIDGE (d. 1792) served as a ship's surgeon on four slave trade voyages between 1780 and 1787 before rejecting the slave trade and becoming an abolitionist. He wrote *An Account of the Slave Trade on the Coast of Africa* in 1788, after his conversion. It provides an unflinching account of the brutality of the transatlantic trade.

When the ships arrive in the West-Indies, (the chief mart for this inhuman merchandize), the slaves are disposed of, as I have before observed, by different methods. Sometimes the mode of disposal, is that of selling them by what is termed a *scramble*; and a day is soon fixed for that purpose. But previously thereto, the sick, or refuse slaves, of which there are frequently many, are usually conveyed on shore, and sold at a tavern by . . . public auction. These, in general, are purchased . . . upon speculation, at so low a price as five or six dollars a head. I was informed by a mulatto woman, that she purchased a sick slave at Grenada, upon speculation, for the small sum of one dollar, as the poor wretch was apparently dying of the flux. It seldom happens that any, who are carried ashore in the emaciated state to which they are generally reduced by that disorder, long survive their landing. I once saw sixteen conveyed on shore, and sold in the foregoing manner, the whole of whom died before I left the island, which was within a short time after. Sometimes the captains march their slaves through the town at which they intend to dispose of them; and then place them in rows where they are examined and purchased.

The mode of selling them by scramble having fallen under my observation the oftenest, I shal[l] be more particular in describing it. Being some years ago, at one of the islands in the West-Indies, I was witness to a sale by scramble. . . .

On a day appointed, the negroes were landed, and placed altogether in a large yard, belonging to the merchants to whom the ship was consigned. As soon as the hour agreed on arrived, the doors of the yard were suddenly thrown open, and in rushed a considerable number of purchasers, with all the ferocity of brutes. Some instantly seized such of the negroes as they could conveniently lay hold of with their hands. Others, being prepared with several handkerchiefs tied together, encircled with these as many as they were able. While others, by means of a rope, effected the same purpose. It is scarcely possible to describe the confusion of which this mode of selling is productive. It likewise causes much animosity among the purchasers, who, not unfrequently upon these occasions, fall out and quarrel with each other. The poor astonished negroes were so much terrified by these proceedings, that several of them, through fear, climbed over the walls of the court yard, and ran wild about the town; but were soon hunted down and retaken. . . .

Various are the deceptions made use of in the disposal of sick slaves; and many of these, such as must excite in every humane mind, the liveliest sensations of horror. I have been well informed, that a Liverpool captain boasted of his having cheated some Jews by the following stratagem: A lot of slaves, afflicted with the flux, being about to be landed for sale, he directed the surgeon to stop the anus of each of them with oakum. Thus prepared, they were landed, and taken to the accustomed place of sale; where, being unable to stand but for a very short time, they are usually permitted to sit. The Jews, when they examine them, oblige them to stand up, in order to see if there be any discharge; and when they do not perceive this appearance, they consider it as a symptom of recovery. In the present instance, such an appearance being prevented, the bargain was struck, and they were accordingly sold. But it was not long before a discovery ensued. The excruciating pain which the prevention of a discharge of

SOURCE: Alexander Falconbridge, *An Account of the Slave Trade on the Coast of Africa* (London: J. Phillips, 1788), 33–36.

such an acrimonious nature occasioned, not being to be borne by the poor wretches, the temporary obstruction was removed, and the deluded purchasers were speedily convinced of the imposition.

The Brig Sally's Log

These pages are drawn from an account book kept by Esek Hopkins, the captain of a hundred-ton brigantine called *Sally*, which left Providence, Rhode Island, for West Africa on a slaving voyage on September 11, 1764. The *Sally* reached the coast of what is today Guinea-Bissau one month later and spent many months anchored there, acquiring goods and slaves. Not until August 20, 1765, more than nine months after reaching Africa, was the *Sally* finally ready to return. All told, Hopkins secured 196 slaves, but he sold off 29 of them to other traders before ever leaving Africa. Some 19 captives died before the ship left the coast, and another captive was left for dead on the day the *Sally* set sail, reducing Hopkins's remaining human cargo to about 147 people. An additional 68 Africans perished during *Sally*'s transatlantic voyage; twenty more died shortly after the ship docked in the West Indies in October 1765, and the *Sally* lost one last slave between the West Indies and Providence, bringing the death toll among her cargo to 109. Hopkins's log records these deaths and also notes the dates on which they took place.

1765

Date	Entry	No
august 21	1 garle Slave Dyed	21
25	1 boye Slave Dyed	22
27	1 woman & 1 boye Dyed	23 24
28	Slaves Rose on us Was obliged fire on them Destroyed 8 and Several more Wounded badly 1 thye & ones thy broke	25 to 32
30	1 boye & 1 garle Slaves Dyed	33 34
31	1 woman Slave Dyed	35
Septe 1	1 woman & 1 garle Slaves Dyed	36 37
2	1 woman Slave Dyed	38
3	1 boy Slave Dyed	39
4	1 boye Slave Dyed	40
6	1 man Slave Dyed	41
7	3 boys & 1 garle Dyed	42 43 44 45
8	2 women and 2 boys Dyed	46 47 48 49
9	1 woman & 1 garle Slave Dyed	50 51
11	1 boye Slave Dyed	52
12	1 boye Slave Dyed	53
14	1 garle Slave Dyed	54
15	1 garle Slave Dyed	55
16	1 woman Slave Dyed	56
19	1 man Slave Dyed of his wounds on the Ribs when Slaves Rose	57
20	1 boye Slave Dyed	58
22	1 woman Slave Dyed	59
23	2 women & 1 garle Slaves Dyed	60 61 62
25	1 man & 1 woman Slaves Dyed	63 64
26	2 men & 1 garle Slaves Dyed	65 66 67

1765

Date	Entry	No
Sept 27	2 men & 1 woman Slaves dyed	68 69 70
29	1 woman & 1 garle Slaves dyed	71 72
30	2 woman & 1 boy Slave Dyed	73 74 75
octor 1	3 woman Slaves dyed	76 77 78
2	3 men Slaves and 2 woman Slaves Dyed	79 80 81 82 83
3	1 garle Slave Dyed	84
5	1 man Slave Dyed	85
6	1 man & 1 woman Slaves dyed	86 87
8	1 man Slave Dyed	88
11	3 woman & 1 man Slave Dyed	89 90 91 92
14	1 boy Slave Dyed and 1 man Slave Dyed of his wound in the thy Rec when Slaves Rose	93 94
15	1 woman Slave Dyed	95
17	1 woman Slave Dyed	96
20	1 man Slave Dyed	97
23	1 man and 1 woman Slaves Dyed	98 99
25	1 woman Slave Dyed	100
27	1 boy Slave Dyed	101
30	1 woman Slave Dyed	102
Nov 3	1 man boy Dyed	103
5	1 woman Slave Dyed	104
10	1 yong man Slave Dyed	105
11	1 man boy Slave Dyed	106
12	1 woman Slave Dyed	107
15	1 man Slave Dyed	108
Jun 20	1 man Slave Dyed	109

Courtesy of the John Carter Brown Library at Brown University.

QUESTIONS FOR ANALYSIS

1. Most of the few available African accounts of the Middle Passage relate experiences of being captured and enslaved as children but were recorded many years later. How might age and the passage of time have affected Belinda's and Olaudah Equiano's recollections of the slave trade?

2. The literary scholar Vincent Carretta has argued that Equiano was born in South Carolina rather than Africa.[30] Two British documents — a Royal Navy muster roll from 1773 and a baptismal record from 1759 — list Equiano's birthplace as Carolina, leading Carretta to speculate that Equiano fabricated the story of his capture and forced migration from Africa to make his narrative a more effective critique of the slave trade. But historians of Africa such as Paul Lovejoy contend that Equiano's detailed knowledge of Igbo culture and language make it unlikely that he invented the story of his early childhood. They also question the importance and accuracy of the records cited by Carretta.[31] Draw on the information contained in the documents in this set to assess the accuracy of Equiano's account of his transatlantic voyage.

3. The slave trade involved both European and African rulers, merchants, and middlemen. Using these documents, describe and analyze the various roles Europeans and Africans played in perpetuating the trade. Did one group predominate? What evidence do you have to indicate this?

4. Draw on your reading of the documents in this set to answer the following questions: What can slave trade records such as James Barbot's and Alexander Falconbridge's descriptions of what they witnessed aboard slave ships and the record of slave deaths from the *Sally*'s account book tell us about the African experience of the Middle Passage? What are the limitations of such evidence?

NOTES

1. Gomes Eannes de Azurara, *The Chronicle of the Discovery and Conquest of Guinea* (c. 1453), trans. C. Raymond Beazley and Edgar Prestage, in *Documents Illustrative of the History of the Slave Trade to America*, ed. Elizabeth Donnan (Washington, DC: Carnegie Institution, 1930), 1:28.

2. John S. Mbiti, *African Religions and Philosophy* (New York: Praeger, 1969), 108.

3. Luis de Camões, *Os Lusíadas*, quoted in Luis Madureira, "The Accident of America: Marginal Notes on the European Conquest of the World," *CR: The New Centennial Review* 2, no. 1 (2002): 145.

4. Matthew Restall, "Black Conquistadors: Armed Africans in Early Spanish America," *Americas* 57, no. 2 (October 2000): 176.

5. *Dum Diversas* as summarized in the bull *Romanus Pontifex* (January 8, 1455), translated and reprinted in *European Treaties Bearing on the History of the United States and Its Dependencies to 1648*, ed. Frances Gardiner Davenport (Washington, DC: Carnegie Institution, 1917), 23.

6. Quoted in George Sanderlin, trans. and ed., *Bartolomé de Las Casas: A Selection of His Writings* (New York: Knopf, 1971), 81.

7. Quoted in Lawrence Clayton, "Bartolomé de las Casas and the African Slave Trade," *History Compass* 7, no. 6 (September 2009): 1528.

8. Olaudah Equiano, *The Interesting Narrative of the Life of Olaudah Equiano, or Gustavus Vassa, the African* (London: printed for the author, 1789), 49, 51.

9. Samuel Ajayi Crowther, "Narrative of the Events in the Life of a Liberated Negro," *The Missionary Register* (London: Seeley, Jackson, & Halliday, 1837), 436.

10. John Barbot, "A Description of the Coasts of North and South-Guinea," in *A Collection of Voyages and Travels*, ed. Awnsham Churchill and John Churchill (London: J. Walthoe, 1732), 5:326.

11. Quoted in Stephanie E. Smallwood, *Saltwater Slavery: A Middle Passage from Africa to American Diaspora* (Cambridge: Harvard University Press, 2007), 119.

12. Equiano, *Interesting Narrative*, 76, 70.

13. Mahommah Gardo Baquaqua and Samuel Moore, *Biography of Mahommah G. Baquaqua, a Native of Zoogoo, in the Interior of Africa* (Detroit: Geo. E. Pomeroy, 1854), 41.

14. Quoted in Michael A. Gomez, *Exchanging Our Country Marks: The Transformation of African Identities in the Colonial and Antebellum South* (Chapel Hill: University of North Carolina Press, 1998), 158.
15. Marcus Rediker, *The Slave Ship: A Human History* (New York: Viking, 2007), 63.
16. Herbert S. Klein, Stanley L. Engerman, Robin Haines, and Ralph Shlomowitz, "Transoceanic Mortality: The Slave Trade in Comparative Perspective," *William and Mary Quarterly*, 3rd ser., 58, no. 1 (2001): 93–118.
17. Thomas Clarkson, *The History of the Rise, Progress, and Accomplishment of the Abolition of the African Slave-Trade by the British Parliament* (London: R. Taylor, 1808), 197.
18. Alexander Falconbridge, *An Account of the Slave Trade on the Coast of Africa* (London: J. Phillips, 1788), 23.
19. Ibid., 24–25.
20. John Newton, *Thoughts upon the African Slave Trade* (1788), in *The Works of Reverend John Newton* (New York: J. Seymour, 1811), 6:532.
21. John Newton, *Journal of a Slave Trader*, ed. Bernard Martin and Mark Spurrell (London: Epworth Press, 1962), 75.
22. Ottobah Cugoano, *Narrative of the Enslavement of Ottobah Cugoano, a Native of Africa; Published by Himself, in the Year 1787*, reprinted in Thomas Fisher, "The Negro's Memorial, or, Abolitionist's Catechism; by an Abolitionist" (London: printed for the author, 1825), 124.
23. Thomas Phillips, *A Journal of a Voyage Made in the Hannibal of London, Ann. 1693, 1694*, in *A Collection of Voyages and Travels*, ed. Awnsham Churchill and John Churchill (London: J. Walthoe, 1732), 6:235.
24. Captain Thomas Snelgrave, quoted in Hugh Thomas, *The Slave Trade: The Story of the Atlantic Slave Trade, 1440–1870* (New York: Simon & Schuster, 1999), 427.
25. Barbot, "Coasts of North and South-Guinea," 272.
26. Neta Crawford, *Argument and Change in World Politics* (Cambridge: Cambridge University Press, 2002), 64.
27. Smallwood, *Saltwater Slavery*, 152.
28. Rediker, *Slave Ship*, 5.
29. Vincent Carretta, *Equiano, the African: Biography of a Self-Made Man* (Athens: University of Georgia Press, 2005).
30. Vincent Carretta, "Olaudah Equiano or Gustavus Vassa? New Light on an Eighteenth-Century Question of Identity," *Slavery and Abolition* 20, no. 3 (December 1999): 96–105.
31. Paul E. Lovejoy, "Autobiography and Memory: Gustavus Vassa, Alias Olaudah Equiano, the African," *Slavery and Abolition* 27, no. 3 (December 2006): 317–47.

SUGGESTED REFERENCES

African Origins

Curtin, Philip D. *Africa Remembered: Narratives by West Africans from the Era of the Slave Trade*. Prospect Heights, IL: Waveland Press, 1997.

Davis, David Brion. *The Problem of Slavery in Western Culture*. New York: Oxford University Press, 1988.

Gomez, Michael. *Diasporic Africa: A Reader*. New York: New York University Press, 2006.

Iliffe, John. *Africans: The History of a Continent*. Cambridge: Cambridge University Press, 2007.

Mbiti, John S. *African Religions and Philosophy*. New York: Praeger, 1969.

Northrup, David. *Africa's Discovery of Europe, 1450–1850*. New York: Oxford University Press, 2002.

Patterson, Orlando. *Slavery and Social Death: A Comparative Study*. Cambridge: Harvard University Press, 2007.

The Rise of the Transatlantic Slave Trade

Eltis, David. *The Rise of African Slavery in the Americas*. Cambridge: Cambridge University Press, 1999.

Green, Toby. *The Rise of the Trans-Atlantic Slave Trade in Western Africa, 1300–1589*. New York: Cambridge University Press, 2011.

Heywood, Linda M., and John K. Thornton. *Central Africans, Atlantic Creoles, and the Foundation of the Americas, 1585–1660*. New York: Cambridge University Press, 2007.

Lovejoy, Paul E. *Transformations in Slavery: A History of Slavery in Africa*. Cambridge: Cambridge University Press, 2000.

Schwartz, Stuart B. *Tropical Babylons: Sugar and the Making of the Atlantic World, 1450–1680*. Chapel Hill: University of North Carolina Press, 2004.

Thornton, John. *Africa and Africans in the Making of the Atlantic World, 1400–1800*. Cambridge: Cambridge University Press, 1998.

The Long Middle Passage

Berlin, Ira. *Many Thousands Gone: The First Two Centuries of Slavery in North America*. Cambridge: Belknap Press of Harvard University Press, 2000.

Christopher, Emma. *Slave Ship Sailors and Their Captive Cargoes, 1730–1807*. Cambridge: Cambridge University Press, 2006.

Eltis, David, and David Richardson. *Atlas of the Transatlantic Slave Trade*. New Haven, CT: Yale University Press, 2010.

Inikori, Joseph E., and Stanley L. Engerman, eds. *The Atlantic Slave Trade: Effects on Economies, Societies, and Peoples in Africa, the Americas, and Europe*. Durham, NC: Duke University Press, 1992.

Klein, Herbert S. *The Atlantic Slave Trade*. Cambridge: Cambridge University Press, 1999.

Rediker, Marcus. *The Slave Ship: A Human History*. New York: Viking, 2007.

Restall, Matthew. "Black Conquistadors: Armed Africans in Early Spanish America." *Americas* 57, no. 2 (October 2000).

Smallwood, Stephanie E. *Saltwater Slavery: A Middle Passage from Africa to American Diaspora*. Cambridge: Harvard University Press, 2007.

St Clair, William. *The Door of No Return: The History of Cape Coast Castle and the Atlantic Slave Trade*. New York: BlueBridge, 2007.

Taylor, Eric Robert. *If We Must Die: Shipboard Insurrections in the Era of the Atlantic Slave Trade*. Baton Rouge: LSU Press, 2006.

African Slavery in North America

1619–1740

CHRONOLOGY *Events specific to African American history are in purple. General United States history events are in black.*

1606	Virginia Company receives royal charter
1607	English found Jamestown colony
1611	Jamestown settlers begin cultivating tobacco
1614	Dutch claim New Netherland
	English settler John Rolfe marries Pocahontas, daughter of Powhatan
1619	First enslaved Africans arrive in English North American colonies
1620	Pilgrims found Plymouth colony
1622	Opechancanough, chief of Powhatan's confederacy, leads Indian uprising against Virginia colonists
1624	Virginia becomes royal colony
1625	Dutch West India Company establishes North American headquarters on island of Manhattan
1626	Dutch begin importing slaves to New Netherland
1630	Massachusetts Bay colony founded
1634	Settlers arrive in Maryland
1635–1664	Blacks in New Netherland petition for freedom, win half-freedom
1636	Rhode Island and Connecticut colonies established
1641	Massachusetts becomes first North American colony to legally recognize slavery
1643	Plymouth, Connecticut, and New Haven colonies legally recognize slavery
1644	Opechancanough leads second uprising against English colonists
1656	Quakers arrive in Massachusetts
1660	Royal African Company established; English enter slave trade
1662	Virginia pronounces slavery to be heritable through mother
1663	Carolina becomes royal colony

1664	English seize New Netherland from Dutch, rename it New York
1676	Nathaniel Bacon leads attack on Virginia's government in Bacon's Rebellion
1681	William Penn founds Pennsylvania
1685	Louis XIV issues Code Noir
1686	Dominion of New England created
1687	First runaway slaves arrive in Spanish Florida
1688	Germantown Quakers issue first American antislavery petition
1689–1713	England, France, and Spain at war
1690	South Carolina adopts harsh Barbadian slave code
1691	Virginia restricts marriage between blacks and whites
1692–1693	Salem witch trials
1693	Spain grants liberty to all fugitive slaves who convert to Catholicism
1700	Samuel Sewall issues first New England antislavery tract
1705	Massachusetts outlaws marriage between blacks and whites
1729–1730	Natchez uprising against French; blacks fight on both sides
1730	Three hundred slaves in Virginia organize mass escape
	Approximately four hundred slaves in Louisiana conspire to kill French and seize colony
1732	Georgia colony founded
1739	Stono rebellion
1739–1748	British war with Spain in Caribbean, with France in Canada and Europe
1740	South Carolina passes Negro Act

"20. and Odd Negroes": The Story of Virginia's First African Americans

Late in August 1619, the Dutch warship *White Lion* docked in Jamestown, Virginia, with a cargo of "20. and odd negroes."[1] These Africans had begun their transatlantic journey in Luanda, a slave trading port in the Portuguese colony of Angola, where they were loaded onto the slave ship *São João Bautista* with more than three hundred other slaves. They survived the harrowing Middle Passage, with illness killing almost a third of the ship's human cargo before they reached the New World. When the ship docked briefly in Jamaica to buy medicine and supplies, Captain Manuel Mendes da Cunha paused to report that he still "had many sick aboard" before hurrying on to the Mexican port of Veracruz, his final destination.[2] But the *Bautista*'s long journey was interrupted when, less than five hundred miles from Veracruz, it was captured by the *Treasurer* and the *White Lion*, two English ships sailing under the Dutch flag. Both ships were heavily armed privateers. Privateers were private warships commissioned by European powers to attack their enemies' ships and seize their cargo. Such piracy could be highly profitable; Spanish ships, for example, often carried gold. But the *Bautista* carried only African captives, so the privateers had to content themselves with seizing as many healthy slaves as they could carry.

Among them were the twenty slaves that the *White Lion*'s captain would exchange for provisions when he docked in Jamestown. The seventeen men and three women who arrived in the Chesapeake in 1619, as the first of many generations of African captives to land in English North America, have largely disappeared into history. They likely hailed from one of the African kingdoms along Angola's borders — which included Kongo, Ndongo, and Benguela — before being sold in Angola, a small coastal colony where Portuguese traders exported slaves purchased elsewhere.[3] But their exact origins are difficult to reconstruct, because the Virginia colonists who noted their arrival did not record the names or histories of the region's first black settlers. The lives they led in Virginia are also largely undocumented.

Colonial records do reveal that Virginia governor George Yeardley and a prominent merchant named Abraham Pierson purchased all twenty slaves in exchange for corn and other supplies. Both men owned large plantations, where they put their new Africans to work growing tobacco and other crops. Less clear, however, is whether all twenty of these involuntary migrants remained enslaved for life. They had landed in one of the few New World colonies where slavery had yet to take root, and individual Africans could still move from slavery to freedom with relative ease.

Slavery took several decades to develop in Virginia. The English migrants who settled there initially preferred to hire white servants, who were more familiar to them. But white laborers were not always available and often proved unwilling to work as servants for any great length of time. African slaves, who could be held in bondage for life, presented no such limitations. By the end of the seventeenth century, slave labor had become crucial to southern colonies such as Virginia and common in European settlements throughout North America.

Enslaved workers were already living in Spanish Florida when the English first arrived. They had come with the Spanish explorer Pedro Menéndez de Avilés, who imported five hundred African slaves to construct the town of St. Augustine in 1565. The Dutch entrepreneurs who settled New Netherland starting in 1625 brought in enslaved workers to clear land and help build their roads and towns, as did the French in Louisiana after 1719. European immigrants to North America were never plentiful enough to meet the colonies' labor needs, so colonists throughout the region imported enslaved Africans to provide additional labor.

With few rights under European law, African workers could be far more brutally exploited than European immigrants and were often used to perform the most grueling tasks. Once the European colonies began to take shape, slaves continued to provide much of the backbreaking labor needed to make these settlements profitable, especially in the plantation colonies that developed in the South. Meanwhile, their presence shaped the character of the communities in which they lived, creating multicultural societies in which European colonists assigned enslaved Africans a distinct and inferior legal and political status.

The character of North American slavery changed dramatically between 1619 and 1740. As African captives arrived in ever-larger numbers and racial slavery became more entrenched, it became increasingly difficult for slaves to secure their freedom or cast off the growing stigma that blackness and slavery held among the English colonists. Nevertheless, African people throughout the region slowly became African Americans. They developed a distinctive culture forged by the cross-cultural exchanges and biological intermixture that took place among Africans, Europeans, and Native Americans; by the legal and social barriers that defined their caste; and by the experience of enslavement.

Slavery and Freedom in Early English North America

Seventeenth-century English colonists did not arrive in the New World expecting to people their settlements with enslaved Africans. In fact, they hailed from a nation where slavery was no longer practiced. "As for slaves and bondmen we have none," one English historian boasted in the 1570s. "Nay, such is the privilege of our country . . . that if any come hither from other realms, so soon as they set foot on land they become so free . . . all note of servile bondage is utterly removed from them."[4] Although enslaved Africans were not unknown in England, this claim was correct in underscoring that English common law recognized no form of slavery. Villenage, an English form of serfdom, was extinct by the 1600s and would not be revived in the English colonies.

Instead, the earliest slaveholders in the colonies adopted a new system of racial slavery that took several decades to emerge and still longer to give rise to the plantation societies that ultimately became established in the colonial South. For much of the 1600s, Africans who arrived in these colonies entered societies where servitude was far more common than slavery, and slaves and servants occupied a similar status. But by the beginning of the eighteenth century, enslaved Africans, who had proved to be more profitable, more plentiful, and far easier to exploit than white servants, predominated in the Chesapeake colonies of Virginia and Maryland. Meanwhile, slavery appeared in New England, where the Puritans and Pilgrims held small numbers of slaves, and fueled the growth of a plantation economy in colonial Carolina.

Settlers, Servants, and Slaves in the Chesapeake

England's first successful permanent settlement in North America was founded in 1607 on Jamestown Island, about thirty miles from the mouth of Chesapeake Bay. Financed by the Virginia Company, a joint-stock company chartered by King James I in 1606 to establish an English settlement in the New World, Jamestown was not established with slavery in mind. The company's investors hoped to earn a profit on their shares, while the king hoped to expand England's imperial power.

Indeed, advocates of English colonization, such as the explorer Sir Francis Drake and the writer and armchair traveler Richard Hakluyt, had long maintained that English settlement of the New World could help rescue both blacks and Indians from the "Spanish tyranny" described by Bartolomé de Las Casas. Drake, who spent much of his career raiding the Spanish colonies for gold, undermined slavery whenever he could. For instance, he allied with a community of escaped slaves, or **maroons**, in his attack on the Spanish at Panama in 1572, and he liberated slaves when he sacked the Spanish town of St. Augustine in 1586.

The first English colonists, not unlike Drake, hoped to live off the riches of the New World. Known as "adventurers," they consisted largely of gentlemen and soldiers. But they would find no precious metals or valuable commodities in Virginia. Instead, they could barely feed themselves. Jamestown was surrounded by a fertile environment full of game and fish, but the colonists were unprepared to fend for themselves in Virginia's alien landscape. Inexperienced in hunting, fishing, or farming, they initially relied on local Indians to supply them with corn. As a result, they soon wore out their welcome among the indigenous inhabitants.

On the verge of extinction by 1611, the colony was revived by the development of a lucrative cash crop that also created a new market for labor. The colonists experimented with planting a type of tobacco imported from South America. The experiment proved so successful that when Captain Samuel Argall arrived to take over Virginia's governorship in 1617, he found "the market-place, and streets, and all other spare places planted with Tobacco."[5] Tobacco requires constant care throughout its long growing season and must be cleaned, rolled, and dried after it is harvested. But whereas the Spanish had been able to force the Aztecs, Incas, and other indigenous populations to work for them, the English never managed to subjugate the Eastern Woodlands Indians in Powhatan's confederacy. Other Chesapeake tribes also resisted English rule and enslavement, although the colonists did acquire small numbers of Indian slaves from other regions. After 1619, they began to purchase African slaves as well, but even enslaved Africans were in short supply during the colony's early years (Map 2.1).

White servitude, rather than black or Indian slavery, initially predominated in colonial Virginia and its close neighbor Maryland, which English colonists founded in 1634. Both colonies were established at a time when England had an oversupply of

Engraving of a Virginia Tobacco Farm, 1725

This engraving shows several slaves working in a tobacco shed. Tobacco leaves, which must be cured, or dried, before processing, hang above them, and the slaves prepare these dried leaves for the market. At the far end of the shed, a slave woman and child are pulling down the tobacco leaves. In the foreground, another woman strips the leaves off the stems. Behind her, a man rolls the leaves flat for shipping. To his left, another man cuts pieces of rope to tie up the leaves. Was the omission of a white overseer or supervisor deliberate on the part of the artist? *Pierre Pomet, A Complete History of Drugs, London, 1725 edition/Image Select/Art Resource, NY.*

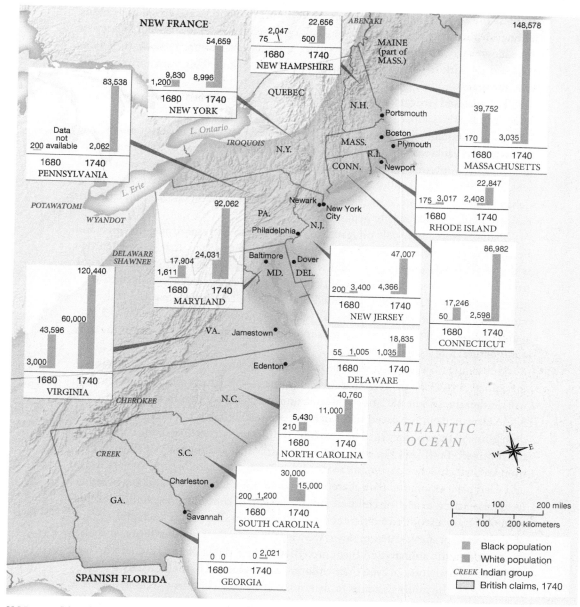

MAP 2.1   Distribution of Blacks and Whites, 1680 and 1740

This map shows the distribution of blacks and whites in British North America in 1680 and 1740. While there were black people living throughout the colonies by 1740, the vast majority of the black population lived in the southern colonies of Virginia, Maryland, and the Carolinas.

landless rural laborers and urban paupers. Impoverished and unemployed, thousands of English and Scots-Irish servants were willing to travel abroad to cultivate tobacco in the Chesapeake. Most arrived in Virginia as **indentured servants**. As such, they were required to work for four to seven years to pay the cost of their transportation and maintenance.

The enslaved Africans who ended up in the Chesapeake arrived no more than a few dozen at a time aboard privateers and other small boats. By all evidence, these early arrivals were initially incorporated into a labor force that was at least nominally free. Slaves and servants worked and lived alongside one another, ran away together, cohabited, and even intermarried. Early colonial documents list both groups as servants, which has long made the legal status of slavery in the early Chesapeake a matter of debate. During this time, enslaved Africans moved from slavery to freedom far more easily than they would in later generations.

Planters were not legally obligated to release blacks from servitude, however, and by 1640 Virginia courts had at least tacitly recognized this fact. That year, when two white servants and one black servant were captured in Maryland after running away from a Virginia farmer, they received dramatically different sentences. All three were sentenced to thirty lashes and extended terms of service. But whereas the white servants were assigned only an additional year of servitude, the black servant — a man named John Punch — was ordered to "serve his said master or his assigns for the time of his natural Life here or elsewhere."[6]

Subsequent laws suggest that blacks began to acquire a uniquely inferior status in the colony. A 1643 law decreed that African women — who were often assigned to field work rather than domestic labor — would, unlike English women, be taxed as laborers. A 1662 law made the enslaved status of black women heritable, decreeing that "all children borne in this country shall be held bond or free only according to the condition of the mother."[7] Both laws ran contrary to the patriarchal assumptions of English common law, which defined women's work as domestic, and therefore not subject to tax, and used paternity rather than maternity to determine inheritance and assign fathers legal jurisdiction over their children. But the system of **chattel slavery** under development in Virginia required a different set of assumptions. Purchased as chattel, or movable personal property, African slaves were legally equivalent to other forms of chattel, such as domestic animals and furniture. They had no rights of any kind and no legal authority over anyone — even their children, who belonged to their owners.

By using the mother's status to determine whether a child would be slave or free, Virginia legislators also resolved a number of practical questions. For instance, English law required servant women who became pregnant to work extra time to compensate their masters for the loss of their labor and expenses associated with the birth — sanctions that could not be imposed on slave women, who were already enslaved for life. Moreover, in making slavery heritable through the mother, the legislators prevented slave women from seeking liberty for their children by claiming freemen as the fathers, and they shielded white men from paternity claims. Finally, the new legislation clarified the legal status of slave women's children, which had previously been ambiguous. This ambiguity is evident in the case of Elizabeth Key, the illegitimate daughter of an enslaved mother and English father who petitioned for her freedom in 1656. Several courts ruled on her case, handing down different verdicts. She gained her freedom only after she married her English lawyer, who won her case before the colony's general assembly.

By the early 1690s, both Key's victory and her marriage would have been impossible. In addition to passing the 1662 law that made slave status heritable through the mother, Virginia lawmakers in 1691 all but outlawed interracial marriage. The new law decreed that any white person who married a "negroe, mulatto, or Indian" would be forever banished from the colony "within three months of such marriage." Ironically, though expressly designed to prevent "that abominable mixture and spurious issue which hereafter may encrease in this dominion," this measure attacked legitimate unions between the races rather than race mixture.[8] Intermarriage became a crime, but white men were neither barred nor discouraged from entering into sexual relationships with slave women.

As lawmakers created new laws, they also eliminated legal uncertainties that the colony's first generation of black residents had used to seek freedom in the courts. As late as the 1660s, for example, Chesapeake courts remained undecided about the compatibility between slavery and Christianity. Black and Indian converts became Christians with baptism, which gave them legal standing in colonial courts. But Christianity lost any further association with freedom in 1667, when the Virginia legislature passed an act explicitly exempting slaves from the freedoms normally extended to Christians. The "blessed sacrament of baptisme," the act noted, "doth not alter the condition of the person as to his bondage or freedome." (See Document Project: Making Slaves, pp. 78–85.)

As Virginia lawmakers solidified the legal status of slavery, forces outside the colony gave the institution new economic advantages. By midcentury, Virginia's supply of white servants was declining. The colony's reputation for exploiting and abusing servants had made it increasingly unappealing to immigrants, who were also in short supply as a result of the English Civil Wars, which diverted large numbers of Englishmen into military service. Meanwhile, local supplies of enslaved Africans were slowly increasing. The Dutch, who had established settlements on the Middle Atlantic coast starting in the 1620s, took advantage of shipping disruptions caused by the English Civil Wars to secure new commercial markets in the English colonies. They began to supply slaves to the Chesapeake, where the black population soared from a few hundred in 1650 to four thousand in 1680. The English themselves entered the slave trade with the 1660 establishment of the Royal African Company, which held a monopoly over English trade with Africa until 1698, transporting between 90,000 and 100,000 slaves to English colonies in the New World. The rise of the Royal African Company and of other English entities after 1698 offered English colonists a steady and affordable supply of slaves.

Chattel slavery also offered a variety of noneconomic advantages. Both slaves and servants ran away, but enslaved Africans were far easier to recover. Once they escaped

Sex, Power, and Slavery in Virginia
Painted on the back of another painting by an anonymous artist, this piece of art is unusual in its frank depiction of the two kinds of power white slaveholders wielded over their slaves. On the left is an image of sexual power, which shows a well-dressed slave owner embracing a female slave. On the right is an illustration of physical, brute power, seen as an owner or overseer prepares to whip a male slave's bare back. Although Virginia prohibited marriage between whites and blacks and fined white women who gave birth to mulatto children, it did not discourage sexual relationships between white men and black women, leaving much room for slaveholders to take advantage of female slaves. Why did the artist title the painting *Virginian Luxuries*? Virginian Luxuries, c. 1825/The Colonial Williamsburg Foundation, Museum Purchase.

beyond neighborhoods where they were known, white English-speaking servants could easily blend in with other European settlers and live as free people. By contrast, black runaways' color marked them as likely slaves, making them easy to recapture. One newly arrived African discovered this in 1739 when he was committed to the James City County Jail. According to the *Virginia Gazette*, he was "a new Negro" who could not "speak English; his Name is understood to be Tom." He was soon picked up by local authorities, who "suppos'd [him] to be a Runaway," and imprisoned to ensure that his "Owner may have him again."[9]

Enslaved Africans offered significant long-term advantages over servant laborers. Their bondage was permanent and hereditary, which allowed slave owners to invest in a labor supply that could reproduce itself. Slaves also were subject to far stricter social controls than freemen, which made them appealing to white planters intent on maintaining their power. In contrast, by the 1670s landless white ex-servants had become a disruptive force in the Chesapeake. Largely male, young, and discontented, they competed with more established colonists for land and often drifted from county to county, challenging colonial authorities, encouraging slaves to run away, and antagonizing local Indian populations by encroaching on their land.

The dangers posed by ex-servants and their allies were vividly illustrated in a 1676 upheaval in Virginia known as Bacon's Rebellion. Led by Nathaniel Bacon, a wealthy colonist who commanded the support of an army largely made up of landless freemen, servants, and slaves, the rebellion pitted land-hungry colonists against the royal authority of Governor William Berkeley. At issue was the colony's Indian policy, which was not aggressive enough to suit the many landless men who rallied around Bacon to make war on "Indians in generall," and especially nearby Native American allies.[10] Charged with treason after an attack on several such groups, Bacon and his makeshift army attacked the colony's royal government, managing to capture Jamestown and set it on fire before English troops arrived to crush the rebellion.

Bacon's Rebellion underscored the dangers of importing thousands of white male servants into a colony that held few opportunities for them. The fact that Bacon had managed to mobilize both poor whites and black bondmen also left officials worried about the common grievances uniting these two groups. Virginia's colonial government thus moved to forestall further challenges to its authority by sharpening the distinctions between servants and slaves. The legislature enacted harsh new laws allowing slave owners to kill rebellious slaves with impunity. At the same time, it curbed planters' power over white servants and freedmen by limiting the years of service that could be imposed on white servants and lowering the poll taxes that kept poor whites from voting. By empowering whites and subjecting blacks to ever-stricter systems of control, the colonial legislature took significant steps toward deepening the racial divide and creating an entrenched system of racial slavery.

The Expansion of Slavery in the Chesapeake

"They import so Many Negroes hither," the Virginia planter William Byrd wrote in 1736, "that I fear this Colony will some time or other be confirmed by the name of New Guinea."[11] Byrd's statement reflects an extraordinary demographic shift in the eighteenth-century Chesapeake. In 1680, blacks constituted approximately 7 percent of Virginia's population, but by 1750 the colony's population was 44 percent black. Maryland's black population likewise increased from 9 percent to 30 percent during the same time span. (See By the Numbers: Black and White Populations in the Seventeenth-Century Chesapeake.) Both colonies, although initially populated largely by white servants, had built plantation economies that revolved around black slavery.

BY THE NUMBERS   Black and White Populations in the Seventeenth-Century Chesapeake

This graph underscores the fact that blacks remained rare in the Chesapeake prior to the 1660s. While the number of blacks increased steadily over the decades, this region's black population nevertheless grew more slowly than its white population throughout most of the seventeenth century.

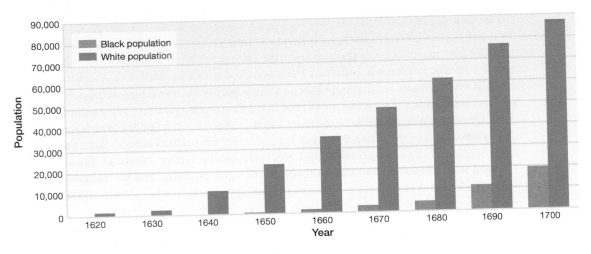

The Africans who flooded the Chesapeake after 1680 had few of the opportunities afforded to early arrivals. Not many would achieve freedom, own property, or establish families. Increasingly drawn from the interior of Africa, the "new Negroes," as they were known, arrived by the boatload and were sold in small lots at numerous riverside wharfs bordering the Chesapeake. The region's farming was dispersed; even large land-holders generally owned several small plantations, and few employed more than ten slaves on any single holding. Their slaves were thus widely dispersed as well, and plant-ers usually assigned new arrivals to unskilled labor on their most remote upcountry holdings. The newcomers, who were not yet conversant in English or trained to do other work, cleared land and cultivated tobacco and other crops under the supervision of white overseers. Still ravaged by the transatlantic journey, one-quarter died within a year of arrival, and few managed to reproduce. In addition, two-thirds of the new arriv-als were men, and many planters assigned their slaves to sex-segregated quarters where they had little chance to form family ties.

Drawn from different parts of Africa, the newcomers could not always converse with more acculturated slaves — or even with each other. The young Olaudah Equiano, who was shipped to Virginia in the 1750s, ended up in complete linguistic isolation. Most of his countrymen had been sold in Barbados, and he and his remaining ship-mates landed in a part of Virginia where "we saw few or none of our native Africans, and not one soul who could talk to me."[12] Often the only English words the newcomers knew were the names assigned to them by their owners. They received no other instruc-tion in the language.

Linguistically isolated, subjected to a harsh work regime, and forced to abandon even the names that tied them to their homelands, the newcomers struggled but somehow managed to survive. They forged a common language, which one Anglican minister described as "a wild confused medley of negro and corrupt English." These Americanized, or **creole**, forms of communication probably represented a blend of English and several African languages. Newcomers also formed close bonds within their quarters. African-born slaves were far less likely to run away than American-born ones, and they rarely ran away alone. Instead, they fled with other Africans, sometimes with the goal of creating their own communities on the frontier.

Groups of African-born slaves sometimes conspired to revolt and escape together. When word of planned revolts in 1710 and 1722 reached the colonists, they arrested and executed the conspirators before the rebellions could take place. But one Sunday in the fall of 1730, when most plantation owners were in church, more than three hundred slaves organized into military groups and left their plantations for the Dismal Swamp — a coastal plain on Virginia's southeastern border. Taking shelter on the frontier, the runaways "did a great deal of Mischief in that Province [of Virginia]," a visitor to the colony reported, before the colonists recruited some Pasquotank Indians to hunt them down.[13]

The slaves' defiance affected the colony's free people of color, who were often suspected of fostering slave rebellions. Virginia's small free black population, mostly descended from the slaves who had secured their freedom during the colony's early years, also included **mulatto**, or mixed-race, descendants of unions between slaves and whites — some of whom had been born to a white mother and a slave father. Regardless of their origins, all lost some of their freedoms as a result of the slave unrest of the early 1700s, which led white colonists to define all blacks as dangerous. The laws that Virginia passed in the 1720s disarming and disfranchising free blacks and mulattoes reflected this conviction. With such laws, Virginia transformed a society once overrun by discontented white servants into a racially divided democracy in which only white men could be fully free.

The Creation of the Carolinas

Unlike the Chesapeake settlers, the planters who in 1663 established the colony of Carolina — which would split into the separate colonies of North and South Carolina in 1729 — arrived with plans to use a workforce of enslaved Africans to clear and cultivate their settlement. About half of these settlers hailed from the English colony of Barbados, where slavery was already an established institution. By the mid-seventeenth century, this Caribbean island was dominated by sugar plantations, where wealthy planters used slave labor to grow and harvest the demanding crop. The whites emigrating from Barbados to Carolina came in search of new land to plant and brought slaves with them. The major challenge for them was finding a suitable staple crop.

Rice cultivation, long popular in West Africa, flourished in South Carolina largely as a result of the slaves' expertise. The crop was unfamiliar to most English planters, who nonetheless saw its potential and consulted their slaves on the possibility of growing it in Virginia as early as 1648. "The ground and Climate is very proper for it [rice] as our *Negroes* affirme," one colonist reported that year, explaining that "in their Country [it] is most of their food."[14] Experiments in rice cultivation foundered in Virginia but were far more successful in Carolina, which by the 1720s had begun to export nearly ten million pounds of rice a year. Drawing on their own expertise, slaves grew, harvested, and processed the crop with the same equipment and techniques used in their homelands.

TO BE SOLD on board the Ship *Bance-Yland*, on tuefday the 6th of *May* next, at *Afhley-Ferry* ; a choice cargo of about 250 fine healthy **NEGROES,** juft arrived from the Windward & Rice Coaft. —The utmoft care has already been taken, and fhall be continued, to keep them free from the leaft danger of being infected with the SMALL-POX, no boat having been on board, and all other communication with people from *Charles-Town* prevented.
Auftin, Laurens, & Appleby.

N. B. Full one Half of the above Negroes have had the SMALL-POX in their own Country.

Slaves and Rice Cultivation in Carolina
Carolina planters relied on African slaves' knowledge of and experience with cultivating rice to grow this challenging and lucrative crop. The extent to which the planters valued African expertise is illustrated in advertisements placed by slave traders promoting the fact that the slaves on a particular ship came from rice-cultivating regions of Africa. This advertisement, which appeared in an eighteenth-century newspaper during a smallpox epidemic, also assured potential buyers that careful measures had been taken to keep the slaves free of the disease. *The Granger Collection, New York.*

Rice plantation slaves worked under a **task system,** which involved minimal white supervision. Unlike slaveholders in the Chesapeake, Carolina rice planters did not employ white overseers to direct gangs of slave laborers. Instead, low-country slaves worked largely under their own direction, completing daily tasks laid out by a black **driver** — a bondman chosen to oversee the work of other slaves. Used only in rice-growing regions, the task system reflected Carolina planters' reliance on slaves' knowledge of African cultivation methods. This reliance is also evident in planters' demand for slaves from rice-growing parts of Africa, such as the Upper Guinea coast, Senegambia, and the Windward Coast. In response, slave traders promoted shipments from these regions, advertising "choice cargo[s] of Windward and Gold Coast Negroes, who have been accustomed to the planting of rice."[15]

Under the task system, slaves were required to carry out specific agricultural tasks each day, after which they were free to work on their own behalf. This small measure of independence, used as an incentive for slaves to complete their daily work quickly, was a mixed blessing. Slaves were permitted to farm small allotments of land where they could raise livestock and grow provisions to feed themselves. But with the adoption of rice culture, the practice grew increasingly exploitative. Rather than supplying rations to their slaves, planters expected them to provision themselves during whatever time they had left after completing their grueling tasks in the rice fields. While whites observed the Sabbath, most enslaved people needed to work on Sundays just to survive.

As in the Chesapeake, Carolina slave owners had little interest in providing their slaves with religious instruction. Frustrated missionaries dispatched by the Anglican Church routinely proclaimed that the slaves' seven-day workweek made conversion "scarcely possible." "The slaves have not time to be instructed by the minister but on the Lord's Day," reported the minister Gideon Johnston in 1713, who noted the additional difficulty of gathering slaves when "the plantations are so many and so remote and distant from one another." But he was also not sure that such gatherings would be wise, given that they would provide slaves an "opportunity of knowing their own strength and superiority in point of number" and make them "tempted to recover their liberty."[16] Slave owners shared Johnston's worries and often discouraged missionary work among their slaves as a result.

Carolina slaves remained isolated and numerous enough to create a distinctly African world of their own. Many lived in self-contained slave communities on plantations that housed as many as one hundred slaves. Responsible for building their own quarters, they crafted mud-walled homes with palmetto roofs using techniques and materials that were common in sub-Saharan Africa. They cooked their food in hand-made earthenware pots, similar to those used in Africa, which they either made themselves or purchased from the Indians. Predominantly African-born until the 1760s, some also bore physical marks of their heritage. These included facial scars known as **country marks,** which members of some African ethnic groups received at puberty to mark their origins, and filed or clipped teeth, which often served a similar purpose. African in their speech as well as their appearance, low-country slaves rarely mastered standard English.

Carolina slaves also retained African religious traditions, although their new environment may have reshaped some of their beliefs. The religious practices of early black Carolinians are difficult to reconstruct in detail, since most white observers simply dismissed the slaves as pagans "who knew nothing of the true God."[17] Slaves often believed in magic and the existence of conjurers, who could heal the sick and kill their enemies. Such figures served as "Negro doctors" among the slaves, dispensing medicine, charms, and sometimes even poison. Conjurers were powerful figures, respected and feared even by whites, who when they fell ill sometimes accused black conjurers of having caused their illnesses.

But other beliefs accorded with those of white Christians. One Anglican missionary reported that "our negro-pagans have a notion of God and of a Devil" and interviewed a "negro-pagan woman" who described her God as an omnipotent being who controlled "all things."[18] Such a God was a feature of many West African religions, which usually recognized a multitude of lesser gods and powerful ancestral spirits as well, but slaves in the New World may have placed an increasing emphasis on the idea of a single Supreme Being. Far from their villages and sacred places, with few priests to guide them, African-born slaves and their descendants did not hold the same religious beliefs as their ancestors. Instead, they developed new, communal belief systems shaped by their experiences of exile, forced migration, and enslavement.

A brutal labor regime also shaped the character of the Carolina slave community. In Barbados, where many of the colony's slaveholding planters originated, slaves began "work as soon as the day is light, or sometimes two hours before," and did not stop until sunset. Worked literally to death, the slaves who labored on Barbados's sugar plantations often died young and rarely left children behind. Subject to grueling labor clearing land and cultivating crops in swamps, African-born slaves in Carolina experienced similarly high mortality rates. Throughout much of the eighteenth century, slave deaths in the colony routinely outnumbered births. But low-country blacks, like their counterparts in both Barbados and Virginia, did not always submit to their subjugation. Enslaved Carolinians sometimes escaped alone or with others to live in maroon communities on the colony's frontiers. By the early decades of the eighteenth century, however, the expansion of white settlement into North Carolina and Georgia made it increasingly difficult to avoid detection. As in Virginia, Carolina planters paid Indian slave catchers to capture and return runaways. Planters also instituted measures intended to prevent runaways or rebellions. In 1690, South Carolina adopted the Barbadian slave code, which provided that slaves who ran away or defied their masters more than once could be whipped, slit through the nose, and branded with a hot iron. Three-time offenders could be castrated or hamstrung (have their leg tendons cut). Such punishments were not uncommon, according to one Huguenot missionary, who noted that South Carolina slaves were often crippled or disfigured for "small faults."[19]

Africans in New England

The New England colonies, first settled in the 1620s and 1630s, never became home to a large number of slaves or relied on slave labor to sustain their economies. The region's cold climate and short growing season prohibited the cultivation of labor-intensive crops such as sugar, tobacco, and rice, resulting in little need for enslaved workers. Instead, most New England agriculture took the form of small family farms dedicated to the production of crops and livestock that could be tended by household members. Prior to 1700, blacks constituted less than 1 percent of the region's population (or fewer than one thousand people), and they never amounted to more than 3 percent.

Indeed, these limits to slavery's growth in New England were more a result of geography than of antislavery measures. The Pilgrims and Puritans who established the New England colonies came to the Americas to escape religious persecution in Europe, but their religious ideals did not preclude slave ownership. They looked to the Bible for guidance in establishing exemplary Protestant communities and accepted the slavery of both prisoners of war and foreign peoples as practices sanctioned by the Scriptures.

Accordingly, the Puritans and Pilgrims, who were frequently at odds with their Indian neighbors, enslaved Native Americans whenever they could. Early New England communities, which comprised a collection of coastal settlements, were also drawn into African slavery as a result of their commercial relationships with slaveholding colonies in the Caribbean. New Englanders shipped provisions such as wheat, beef, butter, fish, and cheese to these island colonies and received molasses, sugar, indigo, and other slave-grown goods in return. Occasionally, they purchased slaves as well.

In addition, New England colonists also acquired black slaves in exchange for Native American prisoners of war, whom they often shipped off to slavery in the Caribbean. These exchanges required New Englanders to address slavery's legality earlier than other English colonists. Massachusetts became the first North American colony to legally recognize chattel slavery, which was sanctioned in the Body of Liberties the colonists compiled in 1641. This document, an enumeration of colonists' rights, permitted them to enslave "Captives taken in just warres" and purchase "such strangers as willingly selle themselves or are sold to us." With the formation of the New England Confederation in 1643, the Plymouth, Connecticut, and New Haven colonies legally recognized slavery as well. New Hampshire, under the legal jurisdiction of Massachusetts until 1679, also began importing small numbers of slaves. Only Rhode Island, founded as a haven for religious dissenters in 1636, hesitated. Rhode Island colonists initially rejected permanent bondage, passing a law that limited the servitude of both blacks and whites to ten years. But the law was never enforced, and Rhode Island went on to import more slaves per capita than any other New England colony.

By the beginning of the eighteenth century, Boston's slave population had grown large enough to trouble some Puritans. "Numerousness of Slaves at this day in the Province, and the Uneasiness of them under their Slavery, hath put many upon thinking whether the Foundation of it be firmly and well laid," wrote the wealthy Boston merchant and judge Samuel Sewall, who had presided over the Salem witch trials in 1692–1693. The only one of three Salem judges to publicly regret his role in the conviction and execution of nineteen accused witches, Sewall issued a formal apology in 1697. But after quieting his conscience on that score, he became increasingly uneasy with himself for having "long neglected doing anything" about slavery.[20] In 1700, he issued the first antislavery tract published in New England, a pamphlet entitled *The Selling of Joseph: A Memorial*, which questioned the morality of slavery.

Sewall's pamphlet may have been inspired by the freedom struggles of a slave named Adam, who belonged to John Saffin, a New England merchant and politician. Saffin had pledged to free Adam after he completed a seven-year term of servitude, but Saffin later reneged on his promise, forcing Adam to petition for his freedom and inspiring white Bostonians to circulate a petition on his behalf. Sewall's antislavery tract did not take up Adam's case, however. Instead, it questioned the legitimacy of slavery as an institution by invoking the biblical tale of Joseph, who was sold into slavery by his jealous brothers. Joseph's enslavement was not lawful, natural, or just, wrote Sewall, who suggested that African slavery might be equally illegitimate. New England slave owners had no reason to believe that their bondmen and bondwomen were captured in just wars, Sewall maintained: "Every War is upon one side Unjust." Moreover, given the central role that European slave traders played in "forcing the *Africans* to become Slaves amongst our selves," slavery as practiced in the Americas was little more than manstealing, with African men and women being abducted from their homes and shipped abroad to enrich those who participated in the trade. Sewall argued that, though Africans might look different from Europeans, as "Sons of Adam" they should have full title to the rights of other men, including an "equal Right unto Liberty, and all other outward Comforts of Life."

Sewall's challenge to the religious morality of slavery fell on deaf ears. Saffin spoke out in his own defense, issuing a pamphlet entitled *A Brief and Candid Answer to a Late Printed Sheet, Entitled, The Selling of Joseph* (1701) that insisted that the Bible sanctioned "different Orders and Degrees of Men in the World." Blacks shared few of Joseph's virtues, Saffin maintained; they were "*Cowardly and cruel . . . Libidinous, Deceitful, False and Rude.*" Saffin's invective provides an early example of the racist attacks on the character of black people that whites frequently invoked to justify slavery. But most of Sewall's contemporaries did not even bother to respond to his argument that slavery was immoral and unchristian: They simply ignored his pamphlet.

The colonists saw slavery as a time-honored institution, that had spiritual sanction. Even the colony's Puritan clergy were confident that Massachusetts provided slaves "all the liberties and Christian usages which the law of god established in Israell concerning such persons doeth morally require." Though subject to some forms of segregation, enslaved Africans were permitted to legally marry, were entitled to a trial by jury when accused of a crime, and were welcome to join New England churches. The influential Puritan minister Cotton Mather claimed that as long as slave owners were conscientious about providing religious instruction to slaves, Christianity "wonderfully Dulcifies, and Mollifies, and Moderates the Circumstances of [slavery]." A slave owner himself, Mather supplied special catechisms that other slave owners could use to guide enslaved Africans toward salvation and told them to promise their slaves that "*if they Serve God patiently and cheerfully in the Condition which he orders for them*," they will be rewarded with "*Eternal Happiness*" in heaven. Mather also took pains to reassure slave owners that the "*Law of Christianity*" did not set the "*Baptised slave at Liberty.*"[21]

Though sanctioned by spiritual authorities such as Mather, the practice of slave-holding grew only modestly in New England. Few slaves were imported into the region by New England slave merchants, who typically delivered their shipments to the lucra-tive slave markets of the Caribbean or the American South rather than to northern slave trading ports. Instead, New England remained a secondary market for slaves, where traders disposed of a small number of blacks who were too young, old, or sick to be sold elsewhere. Known in the trade as "refuse slaves," most of them arrived in the region after their shipmates had been sold in the Caribbean.

Venture Smith, a native of Guinea who was captured and sold into slavery at age eight, was imported to Barbados with approximately 260 other African captives, only 200 of whom survived after smallpox broke out on board ship. All but four of the sur-vivors attracted West Indian buyers; the rest sailed on to Rhode Island. Purchased and employed by the steward of the slave ship that brought him there, Smith was typical of the slaves who ended up in New England: He was too young to appeal to planters in the West Indies or in Britain's southern colonies, who sought brawny adult laborers for plantation work. Bought for four gallons of rum and a piece of calico, he was a specula-tive investment on the part of the ship's steward, who named him Venture and sent him home to his family to work as a domestic servant.

Young slaves such as Venture Smith, who were more affordable than adults, were welcome in northern markets. Buyers sometimes expressed a preference for young slaves — "the younger the better if not quite children," one buyer specified.[22] These slaves were often trained to perform domestic service and skilled work. Young Africans were in a better position to learn English, achieve a measure of acculturation, and mas-ter domestic tasks and other new skills than were the adult field hands the planters preferred. Young Venture's masters put him to work carding wool and pounding dried corn into meal until he grew old enough for farmwork; then he switched to working both in and out of doors.

Venture Smith grew up to be a strong, healthy, and hardworking man who mar-ried, fathered three children, and ultimately managed to purchase his own and his fam-ily's freedom. But many blacks in New England did not share his fate. Mortality rates were high and birthrates low among the region's black population during the eigh-teenth century. Those who survived had trouble finding partners and establishing fami-lies, because most were male, and they tended to be employed by different households scattered across the region, which limited their contact with other blacks.

Even slaves who were lucky enough to marry each other often lived in different households and may have hesitated to have children because they could not raise a

A Young Domestic Slave
Young slaves often assumed domestic roles, sometimes tending to children in a planter's household. In this painting, Henry Darnall III, the young son of a wealthy Maryland planter, is shown with a black boy about the same age as he. Darnall stands in front of a balustrade, holding a bow and arrow; his young servant stands behind it, holding a dead bird. Notice the differences in the two figures' dress, positions, and activities. What does this tell us about the training of young slaves and their relationships with the members of their masters' households, including the children? *Portrait, Henry Darnall III, 1702–c. 1787, oil on canvas by Justus Engelhardt Kühn, c. 1710. Museum Department/ Courtesy of the Maryland Historical Society, image ID 1912.1.3.*

family together. Slave children were not prized by northern masters, whose households were rarely large enough to accommodate slave families. Enslaved women were sometimes sold because of their reproductive potential, as one Connecticut ad for a sixteen-year-old girl indicates. Her owner wished to dispose of her "for no other fault but because she is like[ly] to be a good breeder."[23] Although some black men found African or Indian spouses, marriage between blacks and whites was outlawed in Massachusetts in 1705 and discouraged virtually everywhere else.

Slavery in the Middle Atlantic Colonies

The settlement of North America's Middle Atlantic coast was pioneered by the Dutch, who began importing slave workers to the region in 1626, just a few years after the first white settlers arrived. Known as New Netherland, the region the Dutch settled included large portions of present-day New York, Connecticut, Delaware, and New Jersey, as well as parts of Pennsylvania. This land remained under Dutch rule only until 1664, when England, at war with the Dutch throughout much of the seventeenth century, seized the colony and opened the region to English settlement. Slavery continued and became more repressive under English rule.

Slavery and Half-Freedom in New Netherland

The Dutch colonization of New Netherland was led by the West India Company, a group of Dutch merchants who held a royal monopoly over Dutch trade in the Caribbean and the Americas, as well as dominion over Dutch participation in the African slave trade. Chartered in 1621, the West India Company established its North American headquarters on the island of Manhattan in 1625. The settlement, known as New Amsterdam, was designed as a fur trading center that also supplied timber for Dutch ships and developed farms to feed Dutch settlers and sell food to the Netherlands. Anxious to reduce their tiny nation's need to import food from other European powers, the company's directors hoped that Dutch farmers would lead the agricultural settlement of New Netherland. But such hopes were dashed when the colony attracted only itinerant fur traders. In 1626, the West India Company began importing slaves to build New Amsterdam, the colony's capital. Owned by the company, the enslaved laborers were drawn from various Dutch slave trading regions and included individuals from Angola, Kongo, the Caribbean, and Brazil.

These laborers were crucial to New Netherland's survival. They cleared land and built New Amsterdam's fort, church, warehouses, sawmills, and farms. Unable to attract European migrants willing to clear, cultivate, and occupy their colony, the company's directors soon resolved that "Negroes would accomplish more work for their masters and at less expense, than farm servants, who must be bribed to go thither by a great deal of money and promises."[24] After 1629, the company's attempts to attract white immigrants included a promise "to supply the colonists with as many Blacks as they conveniently can."[25] The offer encouraged slaveholding settlers to fan out throughout the lower Hudson Valley, creating settlements in what would later become Manhattan's five boroughs and moving across the river to present-day New Jersey as well. Slavery was even adopted by the Swedish colonists who established settlements along Delaware Bay in 1638. New Netherland's widely dispersed slave population grew steadily, rising to approximately 25 percent of the colony's population by midcentury.

That many of the colony's slaves were the property of the West India Company rather than of individual owners complicated the slaves' status under Dutch law and left the terms of their service open to challenge. Company slaves were quick to take advantage of this ambiguity and began petitioning for wages and suing for their freedom as early as the 1630s. Their litigation had mixed results: It won them wages but not freedom, and it further confused the legal status of slavery in the colony. But their efforts did establish that enslaved blacks had the right to petition colonial authorities and gain access to Dutch courts. Between 1635 and 1664, black colonists in New Netherland took legal action to allow them to earn money, buy land, and petition for freedom.

In the 1640s, such petitions led to a status called **half-freedom**. Primarily allotted to blacks who had helped defend the colony against Indian attacks, half-freedom liberated adult slaves but not their children. These adults maintained obligations to the West India Company and were required to serve as wage laborers for the company

Nieu Amsterdam, c. 1642–1643
Enslaved workers constructed roads and buildings in early colonial urban settlements such as New Amsterdam, which would later become New York City. Though rarely mentioned in modern-day histories of Manhattan, black laborers can be seen in this depiction of early New Amsterdam. The central figures in this engraving are a Dutch woman, who appears to be holding a tray of fruits and vegetables, and a Dutch man holding a sheaf of tobacco. But behind them are several busy black figures, as well as a view of the city's harbor. *New York Public Library, USA/Bridgeman Images.*

when needed, but they were free to work for themselves at all other times, provided they paid a yearly tribute of "one hog, 23 bushels of corn, wampum, or fur pelts worth 20 guilders" to the company.[26]

Half-freedom was exploitative in that it exempted the Dutch West India Company from having to take responsibility for the adult slaves it freed, while retaining the labor of their children and requiring slave families to pay corporate tribute. But it ultimately enhanced black liberty in the Middle Atlantic region, because many half-free blacks successfully petitioned the company for full freedom shortly before the English took over New Netherland in 1664. Anxious to retain their allegiance, the company freed the blacks' children and removed all other restrictions on their liberty. Some petitioners even received small plots of farmland. The legacy of half-freedom enabled one in five New Netherland blacks to claim freedom when the Dutch surrendered the colony to the English.

Slavery in England's Middle Colonies

In 1664, the English seized New Netherland from the Dutch, laying permanent claim to New York, New Jersey, Delaware, and land that would later be incorporated into Pennsylvania. Since slavery was already well established in Dutch America, this acquisition greatly expanded the geographic and demographic scope of slavery throughout England's northern colonies. New Netherland was home to approximately 300 slaves and 75 free blacks, who altogether constituted around 25 percent of the colony's 1,500 inhabitants. When the English took over, they continued to rely on enslaved Africans to supply much of the region's labor. King Charles II granted control of the colony to his brother James, Duke of York, renaming the colony New York in James's honor.

Eager to develop New York as a market for slaves, James — who held a controlling interest in the Royal African Company — developed policies that favored the purchase of slaves from the company, such as the abolition of any property tax on slaves and the imposition of tariffs on domestic slave imports. James also put the colony under the control of English administrators, who made few efforts to attract European workers and permitted the Royal African Company to sell large cargoes of African slaves directly to New Yorkers at fixed prices. When New Yorkers proved to be more interested in buying seasoned and acculturated slaves from the West Indies, the company accommodated their preferences by exchanging locally grown provisions for Caribbean slaves. New York's slave population grew steadily as a result of these measures, increasing at a faster pace than the colony's white population between 1698 and 1738.

Slavery in the other Middle Atlantic colonies developed along much the same lines. New Jersey and Delaware had slave populations when the English arrived and continued to import slaves thereafter. New Jersey, which was initially controlled by English proprietors appointed by Charles II, sought to encourage the settlement and cultivation of farmland by offering sixty acres per slave to any colonist who imported slaves. New Jersey maintained a similar policy even after it became a formal colony in 1702. At this time, England's Queen Anne, who saw slavery as crucial to the success of the North American colonies, instructed the royal governors of all the colonies to make sure that the colonists had access to "a constant and sufficient supply of Merchantable Negroes at moderate prices."[27]

New York, New Jersey, Delaware, and Pennsylvania, which was founded by the Quaker leader William Penn in 1681, all contained agricultural areas where Dutch and English farmers used a mixture of slave and servant workers to grow a variety of crops. Farms throughout the region were small and largely dedicated to the production of wheat, corn, and other provisions, rather than tobacco, rice, or any of the other labor-intensive crops that predominated in the slave South. Even in Delaware, where tobacco

A Parcel of young able bodied Negro Men, one of whom is a Cooper by Trade, two Negroes Wenches, and likewife two Girls, one of 12 Years old, and the other 16, the latter a good Seemſtreſs, and can be well recommended.

Northern Slave Markets
Britain's Middle Atlantic colonies became lucrative markets for slaves in the eighteenth century. Northern slaves proliferated in port cities, where they performed a variety of skilled and unskilled jobs. They also played an important role in developing and cultivating the region's agricultural areas. This advertisement for a New York slave auction, which was published in the *New York Journal or General Advertiser*, announces the availability of five slaves, one a cooper by trade and another a seamstress. *The Granger, Collection, New York.*

production flourished during the late seventeenth and early eighteenth centuries, large slaveholders remained rare. Most of the colony's tobacco was grown by small farmers who owned only a few slaves.

In addition to working in the fields, Middle Atlantic slaves cleared land; tended livestock; chopped wood; pressed cider; maintained fences, buildings, and grounds; and served as domestic workers as needed. Like the indentured servants with whom they often worked, they did not have their own quarters, but were relegated to the household's back rooms, attics, closets, kitchens, and outbuildings. Slaves usually occupied the least appealing spaces, as noted in a 1742 advertisement for a Long Island estate whose farmhouse included "a room of 14 by 16 foot for white servants, over it lodging rooms and a back stairs; behind it a kitchen with a room fit for negroes."[28] Despite the importance of slave labor in these agricultural areas, port cities remained the largest slaveholding communities in both the Middle Atlantic and New England colonies.

Founded in 1681 with the establishment of the Commonwealth of Pennsylvania, Philadelphia is a case in point. Both the city and the commonwealth were the brainchild of William Penn, an English-born **Quaker**, or member of the egalitarian English Protestant sect also known as the Religious Society of Friends. Penn and other Quakers embraced religious freedom as one of the commonwealth's founding principles. But they were slower to embrace other universal freedoms, so slave laborers soon proliferated in the port city of Philadelphia, which was home to a lively trade with England's Caribbean colonies. Among the many Philadelphia Quakers who owned and employed slaves was Penn himself, who noted that he preferred black slaves to white indentured servants, "for *then a man has them while they live*."[29]

But slavery became controversial among the Quakers even during Penn's lifetime, which may help explain why Penn, who died in 1718, freed his slaves in his will. A group of Germantown Quakers issued the first American antislavery petition in 1688. Its authors were four Dutch-speaking Quakers who had left Europe to escape religious persecution. Dismayed to hear that some of their Quaker neighbors had decided to use slave labor, they drafted a petition deploring what they called "the traffik of men-body." "Is there any that would be done or handled at this manner?" they wrote in a document that displayed remarkable empathy for the slaves. "We should do to all men like as we will be done ourselves; making no difference of what generation, descent, or colour they are. . . . To bring men hither [to America], or to rob and sell them against their will, we stand against. In Europe there are many oppressed for conscience-sake; and here there are those oppressed which are of a black colour."[30]

This early petition did not gain a broad audience or wide support. Instead, slavery continued to flourish in Philadelphia, where many Quaker merchants owned slaves, and imports of enslaved Africans helped sustain Pennsylvania's economic growth during periods when European wars curtailed white immigration.

Frontiers and Forced Labor

In the early eighteenth century, slavery began to extend farther west and south into the frontier colonies located on the periphery of European settlement. These colonies, which included French Louisiana and Spanish Florida, were short of labor but too isolated and sparsely settled to maintain a secure slave labor force. Between 1717 and 1731, thousands of slaves were imported into the Mississippi valley, where the French had claimed a vast stretch of land known as Louisiana. But Louisiana planters were neither numerous enough nor powerful enough to establish a well-regulated plantation society, and they struggled to maintain control of their slaves.

Colonists in Spanish Florida, founded in 1565, took a less ambitious approach by permitting slavery but never establishing plantations. The colony was instead founded as a military outpost to defend Spain's New World empire, and by the eighteenth century it had also become a haven for fugitive slaves from Carolina. The Spanish permitted these maroons to establish free black communities; in return, the runaways joined the colony's militia and helped protect its borders.

The British colony of Georgia, founded in 1732, was likewise founded to protect Britain's New World colonies and initially prohibited slavery for that reason. Georgia was meant to serve as a buffer zone between Carolina and Spanish Florida, and its crown-appointed trustees believed that slavery would threaten its military security. They banned slavery until 1750, when they reversed the ban in response to a sustained campaign among the colonists to legalize slavery.

The early history of slavery in these three frontier settlements illustrates the immense importance of enslaved African laborers in the settlement of the American South, as well as the security risks such workers posed.

Slavery in French Louisiana

France's Louisiana colony, situated on the western frontier of most European settlements in the New World, extended from the Gulf of Mexico to the Canadian border. Claimed by the French explorer Robert de La Salle, who traveled down the Mississippi River in 1682, the colony attracted few European immigrants, but it facilitated a lucrative fur trade with the region's Indian nations. By 1700, French investors and the French crown were eager to set up plantation settlements. They had established profitable sugar colonies on the West Indian islands of Guadeloupe, Martinique, and Saint Domingue during the seventeenth century and hoped to grow lucrative crops in Louisiana as well.

At this time, however, Louisiana lacked the manpower to sustain commercial agriculture. As of 1706, the colony had fewer than one hundred French and Canadian inhabitants, most of whom were fur traders and soldiers. The Company of the West Indies, which was granted a trade monopoly in the colony by France's King Louis XV in 1719, needed workers to clear land; build fortifications, roads, levees, and irrigation works; and cultivate the plantations that the company hoped to establish. But few French men and women were willing to immigrate to this frontier outpost. Virtually the only white migrants to the region were a few thousand convicts exiled from France for serious crimes, but even with these new additions, the colony's white population remained well under two thousand throughout the 1720s. Mortality rates among the immigrants were high, and those who survived often fled. Meanwhile, experiments with Native American labor were disappointing. The Indians of the region, who maintained an indigenous slave trade of their own, supplied Louisiana with more than two hundred slaves during its early years. But the Indian slaves provided "very little service," a French official complained in a 1709 letter to the French Ministry of the Colonies, adding that "they are not appropriate for hard labor like the blacks."[31]

With the colony teetering on the brink of collapse, France responded to the colonists' complaints by sending them shiploads of slaves directly from Africa. Most of the ships originated in Senegal, where the French controlled the slave trade, and they delivered almost six thousand slaves to Louisiana between 1719 and 1731. These forced migrants were crucial to the colony's survival. Approximately two-thirds came from Senegambia, where they had cultivated many of the same crops they would be required to grow in Louisiana. Officials from the Company of the West Indies were aware that rice cultivation was practiced in Africa, and they capitalized on the slaves' expertise in this regard. They instructed the captains who delivered the colony's first shiploads of slaves to deliver several barrels of rice seed as well and to make sure their human cargo included captives who knew how to grow rice. Within a year, rice was growing along large stretches of the Mississippi River.

Slaves from Senegambia were also likely crucial to the success of Louisiana's indigo and tobacco plantations. Whereas the French were unfamiliar with the cultivation of these crops, in Senegambia and other regions of West Africa, as one European traveler observed, "tobacco is planted about every man's house."[32] Most Senegambians knew how to plant and grow tobacco seedlings, which they cultivated alongside corn and beans, as was also customary among Native Americans. Louisiana's indigo production was even more dependent on African expertise. A powerful blue textile dye most famously used for coloring denim, indigo is the product of a leafy subtropical shrub that originated in India but was grown in Africa during the era of the slave trade. Indigo plants could be cultivated and harvested by unskilled field hands, but transforming indigo into dye required skilled workers. Slaves in Louisiana and in other French colonies such as Saint Domingue, Guadeloupe, and Martinique pioneered the New World production of indigo dye in the seventeenth century, using techniques similar to those used in Africa.

Despite the success of the colony's slave-grown crops, the future of Louisiana remained far from secure. Nearly one-third of the Africans imported to the colony died, and the remainder proved hard to control. Louisiana's black majority outnumbered the colonists by a ratio of 2:1 and never fully accepted French rule. Some ran away and formed fugitive communities in Louisiana's dense woods and tidal wetlands; others sought refuge among their Natchez Indian neighbors, who were hostile to the French. Blacks fought on both sides of the Natchez uprising against the French in 1729–1730, and they plotted their own uprising shortly after the French defeated the Natchez. In 1730, a group of approximately four hundred Bambara slaves (members of a Malinke-speaking people whose homeland was on the northern banks of the Senegal River) conspired to kill the French and take over the colony, but their plot was discovered. Even after the leaders of the conspiracy were publicly executed, however, slavery in Louisiana remained a disturbing force. Slave imports all but ceased after 1731, when the Company of the West Indies resigned its monopoly over the region. The colony's slave population eroded further when colonists established a free black militia to secure the colony from slave uprisings and Indian attacks.

Thus, instead of becoming a lucrative plantation society, French Louisiana remained a chaotic frontier settlement. Consequently, its racial hierarchies remained somewhat fluid. As a French colony, Louisiana had strict slave laws known as the **Code Noir**, or "Black Code," which had been issued in 1685 by Louis XIV for use throughout France's empire. Under the code, slaves who ran away three times were subject to capital punishment, but the French colonists were too few and too poor to kill off their workers — or even capture their slaves when they ran away. Many fugitives ended up living out their lives in Bas du Fleuve, a maroon community located on the outskirts of New Orleans. One of the colony's fastest-growing settlements, Bas du Fleuve housed almost a third of Louisiana's slaves by 1763. These fugitives, subservient to no one, made their living farming and supplying lumber to New Orleans sawmills.

Black Society in Spanish Florida

Like French Louisiana, Spanish Florida never developed large-scale plantation agriculture. The thinly populated military outpost had been established with the help of slaves supplied by the Spanish crown, but its enslaved population remained small after that. Given its military purpose, Spanish Florida needed soldiers more than field hands. Slaves constructed and maintained the region's forts, grew their own food, were assigned tasks as needed, and served in the colony's militia, which also enlisted free blacks. But free blacks and slaves alike had a high degree of autonomy in Spanish Florida, which made the colony an attractive destination for runaway slaves from Carolina. The first arrived in 1687, just a few decades after Carolina was founded. That year, eight men, two women, and a nursing child made their way to St. Augustine in a stolen canoe, requesting baptism in the "true faith" of the Catholic Church.

These fugitives successfully appealed to the church, which claimed religious authority over the lives of all its members, both free and enslaved. The Spanish governor Diego de Quiroga y Losada welcomed them and refused to return them to their English owners, maintaining that they were religious refugees and even offering to buy them from the Carolina official who traveled to St. Augustine to reclaim them. When word of these negotiations spread to slaves back in Carolina, they began making their way to the Spanish colony in greater numbers. In 1690, Carolina's governor complained to the Spanish that his colony's slaves ran off "dayly to your towns."[33] He received little satisfaction. Intent on defending their own colony, and more than willing to undermine English colonies in the New World, the Spanish continued to welcome the refugees. In 1693, Spain's King Charles II issued a royal proclamation granting liberty to all fugitive slaves who wished to convert to Catholicism. Not surprisingly, this policy infuriated English officials in Carolina, who launched military assaults on St. Augustine in 1702 and 1728. The Spanish colony was able to draw on its growing population of fugitives to rebuff these attacks and to retaliate against the English.

Runaways from Carolina also joined and sometimes even led raids on their former owners, whose slaves they freed and brought back to St. Augustine. They also fought for their own freedom and autonomy in Florida. Fugitives were initially subject to reenslavement by Spanish colonists who ignored the king's promise to free slaves seeking religious sanctuary. After petitioning colonial officials for decades, the runaways finally received a grant of unconditional freedom in 1738. That year, they also established their own settlement, the town of Gracia Real de Santa Teresa de Mose, which became known as Fort Mose. Located two miles outside St. Augustine, this settlement was the first free black town within the present-day borders of the United States. Founded by a population of about a hundred runaways, it served the interests of its inhabitants as well as those of the Spanish crown. The town was strategically situated to warn St. Augustine residents of any foreign attack, and it offered the refugees a comfortable home on land where they could support themselves. Surrounded by fertile fields and forests, Fort Mose was bisected by a saltwater river with an abundant supply of fish and shellfish. The ex-slave sanctuary would not survive for long,

Slaves in St. Augustine
This 1673 engraving shows black slaves engaged in a variety of tasks, including escorting the Spanish to their ships. A little over a decade later, the first recorded runaway slaves from Carolina would successfully seek sanctuary in Spanish Florida, where they were welcomed by Spanish officials. Spanish authorities refused to return such fugitives to the English, which made St. Augustine a prime destination for those fleeing slavery. *Private Collection/Peter Newark American Pictures/Bridgeman Images.*

however. Captured and destroyed by the British in 1739 during the War of Jenkins's Ear — a dispute between Britain and Spain over land claims — the fort was resettled only briefly in the 1750s.

Slavery and Servitude in Early Georgia

Just north of Spanish Florida lay yet another frontier colony designed to act as a buffer and protect its founders' imperial interests. Georgia's colonization was led by a group of British trustees who envisioned a colony populated by lower-class whites. Indentured servants were welcome, but slaves were not, since they could not be expected to defend the colony against its Indian and Spanish enemies. If slavery was permitted in Georgia, one of the colony's founders noted in 1732, "there would not be 50 out of 500 remain[ing] in two months time, for they would fly to the Spaniards [in Florida]."[34] Royal officials agreed, instituting a ban on slavery. But few of Georgia's early settlers ended up supporting the ban. No whites could be found to perform the backbreaking work required to clear Georgia's land for production. Even the indentured servants fled to South Carolina and other British colonies rather than serve out their terms in Georgia. Meanwhile, the settlers who stayed lobbied relentlessly to end the ban on slave labor.

Other than the trustees, the only colonists in favor of maintaining the ban were the Salzburgers, a group of approximately three hundred German-speaking Protestants who migrated to Georgia in 1734. The Salzburgers hailed from the Catholic principality of Salzburg, Austria, which expelled its Protestant population in 1731. This small, hardworking community of friends and relatives, who came to Georgia with the support of the region's trustees, saw no reason to object to the ban even after their British neighbors told them that it was "impossible and dangerous for White People to plant and manufacture any rice, being a Work only for Negroes."[35] Instead, to prove that the colony could prosper without forced labor, they planted rice and soon mastered its cultivation to the point of producing a surplus.

Their opposition to slavery, however, was more practical than moral. They worried that it would weaken their close-knit sect by scattering its members across large plantations. They were also alarmed by reports of black uprisings in the West Indies, which convinced them that slavery was a dangerous institution. Shortly after the Salzburgers arrived in America, their pastor, Johann Martin Bolzius, heard that slaves on St. John in the Virgin Islands had massacred "all the white people that were their masters," and he wondered whether the "great convenience" of slave labor was not offset by the dangers that it posed. His worries were compounded a few weeks later when one of the Salzburgers' supporters in South Carolina lent them a dozen slaves to help them clear land and build roads in their settlement of Ebenezer, Georgia. Bolzius was dismayed by the violent conflicts between the slaves and the white overseer who was sent to supervise them. He objected when the overseer whipped several slaves and was still more horrified when one slave threatened the overseer with an ax. "The departure of the Negroes has deprived us of some advantage," Bolzius wrote after the slaves returned to South Carolina, "but it has also freed us of much disquietude and worry."[36] Similar anxieties colored the Salzburgers' antislavery petitions. They knew "by Experience," they told the Georgia trustees, "that Houses and Gardens will be robbed always by them, and White People are in Danger of Life because of them."[37]

The Stono Rebellion

In 1739, the Salzburgers' fears were borne out by a slave uprising that began near the Stono River in St. Paul's Parish, South Carolina, and took the lives of about twenty whites and more than forty African Americans. On the morning of Sunday, September 9, approximately twenty slaves gathered on the banks of the Stono. They broke into a nearby store that sold guns and ammunition, killed the shopkeepers, and armed themselves with guns, axes, and clubs. They then headed south, killing the whites they encountered and burning their homes to the ground. The rebels spared the life of a local tavern owner who was known to be kind to his slaves and overlooked one planter who was hidden by his slaves, but they were otherwise merciless, massacring entire families. Joined by other slaves as they marched, the rebels were approximately sixty strong and ten miles from home when they were finally tracked down by a hastily assembled patrol of armed whites late that afternoon. More than forty slaves were killed before the **Stono rebellion** was finally suppressed. Most of those who escaped were eventually captured or killed.

The rebels, who were executed without trial, left little evidence of what had inspired the largest slave uprising in the British colonies. The rebellion occurred at the end of a long, hot summer marked by a malaria epidemic in Charleston, and amid heightened political tensions between Britain and Spain. Exhausted by the heat, depleted by the epidemic, and apprehensive about a possible war with Spain, the colony's white population was unusually troubled, which may have influenced the timing of the rebellion. The early eighteenth century's traffic in black Christians from Kongo also could have played a role. The kingdom of Kongo, once ruled by a Catholic king and his son, had collapsed by the 1710s, leaving many Catholic converts in its wake. Slaves brought to South Carolina from this region would have been alert to Spanish proclamations offering freedom and sanctuary to Catholics. The rebels also may have seized on colonial troubles as an opportunity to fight their way to refuge in St. Augustine. Few made it that far, but their rebellion was a wake-up call to white colonists across the South. "Evil brought home to us, within our very Doors, awaken'd the Attention of the most Unthinking," a committee of South Carolina legislators noted, summarizing the impact of the rebellion.[38]

However, the colonists' commitment to slavery remained unshaken. Colonial officials were convinced that "the *Negroes* would not have made this Insurrection had they not depended on *St. Augustine* for a Place of Reception afterwards," which allowed them to blame the Spanish. The officials moved quickly to pass a slave code to discourage further uprisings.[39] South Carolina's 1740 Negro Act was designed to keep slaves in "due subjection and obedience" and underscored that whites were free to kill rebellious slaves without a trial. It also allowed colonists to keep slaves under constant surveillance by empowering all whites to police slaves' movements. After 1740, slaves could no longer travel beyond the boundaries of their masters' plantations without a ticket or pass granting permission. All whites were authorized to investigate and whip slaves caught without a pass and could "lawfully" kill any slave who physically resisted interrogation or punishment.[40] Moreover, the colony's governor also enlisted the help of local Indian tribes to retrieve slaves who did manage to escape, instituting a system of rewards that encouraged Chickasaw and Catawba Indians to hunt down slave runaways.[41]

Despite these precautions, the Stono rebellion was not British America's first slave revolt, nor would it be the last. "Freedom wears a cap that Can without a Tongue, Call together those who wish to shake of[f] the fetters of slavery," Lieutenant Governor Alexander Spotswood warned Virginia planters in 1710 after they hanged, quartered, and decapitated two slaves who had conspired to revolt. The planters divided the miscreants' corpses over several counties to ensure that their body parts were on display in all of the "most publick places" — reserving the head of one rebel for exhibition in the colony's capital. Their goal was to "inspire such a terror in the other Negroes, as will keep them from forming such designs for the future," but Spotswood was not convinced that violence alone could secure the safety of the colonists. After all, even the "Babel of Languages" spoken among African slaves had not prevented them from conspiring to revolt. The colonists must suppress all "consultations" among black people, Spotswood argued, lest they come together around a common love of liberty.[42]

CONCLUSION

Regional Variations of Early American Slavery

The first half of the eighteenth century saw slavery become ever more entrenched in British America. Though unfamiliar to the continent's earliest English settlers, slavery was eventually adopted by colonists from New England to Georgia, who employed slaves to perform many different kinds of work. Slave labor was most vital to sustaining the settlement and growth of the southern colonies, where slave owning landowners built a plantation economy dedicated to the production of lucrative **cash crops**. Colonists farther north were less dependent on slave labor, but slaves were common in the region's port cities and in its most productive agricultural areas.

Africans in early America led lives that were shaped by the regional economies in which they found themselves. Culturally isolated New England slaves were more likely to learn English and adopt European ways than their counterparts in Georgia and South Carolina, who often lived in African enclaves on remote plantations and retained many of their West African cultural practices and beliefs. Most slaves in the southern colonies worked as field hands, while those in New England and the Middle Atlantic were as likely to perform domestic service as farmwork.

Regardless of region, however, slave life remained a struggle. Male slaves predominated in many areas, and not all of them were able to find mates or establish families. New shipments of captive Africans became increasingly common in the southern colonies, bringing in men and women for whom the traumas of the Middle Passage were still fresh. Moreover, both recent arrivals and native-born slaves were increasingly subjected to harsh discipline and careful surveillance. Faced with a growing slave population, colonial legislatures across British America enacted strict slave codes that outlawed slave gatherings, punished slave rebellions, and instituted armed slave patrols. Only in sparsely populated frontier settlements such as French Louisiana and Spanish Florida, where whites relied on people of color to help them defend their borders, did slaves and free blacks retain some degree of freedom.

Even so, throughout the colonies, enslaved Africans proved difficult to control. The strict slave codes introduced in Carolina and other British colonies did little to suppress slave resistance. Instead, during the second half of the eighteenth century, freedom would only become more alluring to African Americans. As the social and political turmoil of the Revolutionary era disrupted slavery and the slave trade, it offered large numbers of individual bondmen and bondwomen opportunities to escape their condition. The era's debates over slavery, liberty, and the rights of man would supply enslaved Africans throughout the colonies with an even more dangerous weapon: a revolutionary rhetoric that could be mobilized against all forms of tyranny, including slavery.

CHAPTER 2 **REVIEW**

KEY TERMS

maroons p. 49

indentured servants p. 52

chattel slavery p. 52

creole p. 57

mulatto p. 57

task system p. 59

driver p. 59

country marks p. 59

half-freedom p. 65

Quaker p. 68

Code Noir p. 71

Stono rebellion (1739) p. 75

cash crops p. 76

REVIEW QUESTIONS

1. Describe the regional variations of slavery throughout Britain's North American colonies. How did the development of and attitudes toward the institution differ in each area?

2. How and why did the nature of slavery change in the Middle Atlantic colonies after the English seized the region from the Dutch?

3. What tactics did slaves in the frontier colonies use to win their freedom? Why were the slaves in these regions more difficult for slaveholders and colonial governments to control?

4. How did the character of slavery change throughout colonial North America between 1619 and 1739? What factors were responsible for these changes?

Making Slaves

To transform African captives into chattel slaves, the English colonists developed legal codes that regulated who could be enslaved and assigned both slaves and free blacks a distinctive legal status. Virginia, one of the first colonies to codify slavery, led the way by passing laws determining how slavery would pass from parent to child and establishing that enslaved Africans who converted to Christianity would not be entitled to the same freedoms as other Christians. The colony's law books also include several rulings that some historians have read as clear evidence that the English colonists always disapproved of interracial sex. Other scholars have suggested that cases such as the 1630 ruling sanctioning Hugh Davis for "lying with a negro" might have been judgments against extramarital sex or homosexuality. Since the legal proceedings were not recorded, the specific circumstances they addressed remain unknown. How much definitive information can we draw from such legal cases?

Meanwhile, the Massachusetts Bay colony's Puritan rulers also addressed slavery in their laws. Slaves were not numerous in early Massachusetts, but the colony's first legal code did authorize the enslavement of "Captives taken in just warres, and such strangers as willingly selle themselves or are sold to us." Slave owners, this code further stipulated, should follow biblical precepts on the "Christian usages" of slaves.

In the long run, however, slavery would require far more complicated legal relations and generate laws regulating every aspect of slave behavior. These laws governed the behavior of whites as well and typically included sanctions against interracial marriage, measures prohibiting whites from sheltering runaway slaves, and provisions requiring slave owners to supply food and clothing to slaves. Though frequently disregarded by both masters and slaves, the legal codes regulating slavery gave slave owners license to govern their slaves and almost unlimited powers of discipline.

The following documents include excerpts from laws developed by English colonists to regulate the slave systems in Virginia, Massachusetts, New Jersey, and South Carolina, as well as an image illustrating the legal Code Noir — or Black Code — used to regulate slavery in France's colonies. The documents also show the cover of one of America's first antislavery tracts: Samuel Sewall's *The Selling of Joseph*, which challenged the legitimacy of all such laws.

The Codification of Slavery and Race in Seventeenth-Century Virginia, 1630–1680

Determining the legal status of blacks in early Virginia remains controversial because laws regulating slavery do not appear in the colony's legal statutes until the 1660s — more than forty years after the first African slaves arrived. However, cases prosecuted in Virginia in 1630 and 1640 suggest that Africans may not have received equal justice even before then, while excerpts from laws passed in the 1660s and beyond are clearly discriminatory. The relatively gradual appearance of such laws has led some historians to argue that racial prejudice was crucial to the development of black slavery.

[1630]
September 17th, 1630. Hugh Davis to be soundly whipped, before an assembly of Negroes and others for abusing himself to the dishonor of God and shame of Christians, by defiling his body in lying with a negro; which fault he is to acknowledge next Sabbath day.

[1640]
October 17, 1640. *Whereas Robert Sweat* hath begotten with child a negro woman servant belonging unto Lieutenant *Sheppard, the court hath therefore ordered* that the said negro woman shall be whipt at the whipping post and the said *Sweat* shall tomorrow in the forenoon do public penance for his offence at *James City* church in the time of divine service according to the laws of *England* in that case provided.

[1662]
WHEREAS some doubts have arisen whether children got by any Englishman upon a negro woman should be slave or free, *Be it therefore enacted and declared by this present grand assembly*, that all children borne in this country shall be held bond or free only according to the condition of the mother, *And* that if any christian shall commit fornication with a negro man or woman, he or she so offending shall pay double the fines imposed by the former act.

[1667]
WHEREAS some doubts have risen whether children that are slaves by birth, and by the charity and piety of their owners made pertakers of the blessed sacrament of baptisme, should by vertue of their baptisme be made free; *It is enacted and declared by this grand assembly, and the authority thereof*, that the conferring of baptisme doth not alter the condition of the person as to his

SOURCE: William Waller Hening, ed., *The Statutes at Large; Being a Collection of All the Laws of Virginia* (Richmond, VA: Samuel Pleasants, 1810), 1:146, 552; 2:170, 260, 267, 270, 280–81.

bondage or freedome; that diverse masters, freed from this doubt, may more carefully endeavour the propagation of christianity by permitting children, though slaves, or those of greater growth if capable to be admitted to that sacrament.

[1668]
WHEREAS some doubts, have arisen whether negro women set free were still to be accompted [accounted] tithable according to a former act, *It is declared by this grand assembly* that negro women, though permitted to enjoy their freedome yet ought not in all respects to be admitted to a full fruition of the exemptions and impunities of the English, and are still lyable to payment of taxes.

[1669]
WHEREAS the only law in force for the punishment of refractory servants (*a*) resisting their master, mistris or overseer cannot be inflicted upon negroes, nor the obstinacy of many of them by other then [than] violent meanes supprest, *Be it enacted and declared by this grand assembly*, if any slave resist his master (or other by his masters order correcting him) and by the extremity of the correction should chance to die, that his death shall not be accompted [accounted] felony, but the master (or that other person appointed by the master to punish him) be acquit from molestation, since it cannot be presumed that prepensed malice (which alone makes murther felony) should induce any man to destroy his owne estate.

[June 1670]
WHEREAS it hath beene questioned whither Indians or negroes manumited, or otherwise free, could be capable of purchasing christian servants, *It is enacted* that noe negroe or Indian though baptised and enjoyned their owne freedome shall be capable of any such purchase of christians, but yet not debarred from buying any of their owne nation.

The Massachusetts Body of Liberties, 1641

Adopted in 1641, the Massachusetts Body of Liberties was New England's first legal code. Drafted by the Puritan lawyer Nathan Ward of Ipswich, it drew on both English common law and biblical law to define the rights of the region's European colonists. Enslaved "Forreiners and Strangers," however, were not entitled to freedom under the Body of Liberties.

LIBERTIES OF FORREINERS AND STRANGERS.

89. If any people of other Nations professing the true Christian Religion shall flee to us from the Tiranny or oppression of their persecutors, or from famyne, warres, or the like necessary and

compulsorie cause, They shall be entertayned and succoured amongst us, according to that power and prudence, god shall give us.

90. If any ships or other vessels, be it freind or enemy, shall suffer shipwrack upon our Coast, there shall be no violence or wrong offerred to their persons or goods. But their persons shall be harboured, and relieved, and their goods preserved in safety till Authoritie may be certified thereof, and shall take further order therein.

91. There shall never be any bond slaverie, villinage or Captivitie amongst us unles[s] it be lawfull Captives taken in just warres, and such strangers as willingly selle themselves or are sold to us. And these shall have all the liberties and Christian usages which the law of god established in Israell concerning such persons doeth morally require. This exempts none from servitude who shall be Judged thereto by Authoritie.

SOURCE: Charles W. Eliot, ed., *American Historical Documents, 1000–1904,* The Harvard Classics (New York: P. F. Collier & Son, 1910), 43:83–84.

An Act for Regulating of Slaves in New Jersey, 1713–1714

Colonial statutes regulated the status of individual slaves and the workings of the slave system as a whole. New Jersey legislators enacted the following law to prohibit the colony's citizens from engaging in any kind of commercial transaction with slaves without first securing the permission of the slave's owner. It also prohibited citizens from sheltering slaves who might be fugitives or from freeing their own slaves without pledging "security" funds to the colony should the former slaves ever require public support.

[§1] *Be it Enacted by the Governour, Council and General Assembly, and by the Authority of the same,* That all and every Person or Persons within this Province, who shall at any time after Publication hereof, buy, sell, barter, trade or traffick with any *Negro, Indian* or *Mullatto Slave,* for any Rum, Wine, Beer, Syder, or other strong Drink, or any other Chattels, Goods, Wares or Commodities whatsoever, unless it be by the consent of his, her or their Master or Mistress, or the person under whose care they are, shall pay for the first Offence *Twenty Shillings,* and for the second and every other Offence, *forty Shillings,* Money according to the Queens Proclamation, the one half to the Informer, the other half to the use of the Poor of that Place where the Fact is committed, to be recovered by Action of Debt before any one of Her Majesties Justices of the Peace.

SOURCE: "An Act for Regulating of Slaves," in *The Law of Slavery in New Jersey,* comp. Paul Axel-Lute, rev. October 8, 2009, New Jersey Digital Legal Library, http://njlegallib.rutgers.edu/slavery/acts/A13.html.

[§2] *And be it further Enacted by the Authority aforesaid*, That all and every Person or Persons within this Province, who shall find or take up any Negro, Indian or Mullato Slave or Slaves, five Miles from his, her or their Master or Mistresses habitation, who hath not leave in writing from his, her or their Master or Mistress, or are not known to be on their service, he, she or they, so taken up, shall be Whipt by the party that takes them up, or by his order, on the bare back, not exceeding Twenty Lashes; and the Taker up shall have for his reward Five Shillings, Money aforesaid, for every one taken up as aforesaid, with reasonable Charges for carrying him, her or them home, paid him by the Master or Mistress of the Slave or Slaves so taken up; and if above the said five Miles, *six pence per Mile* for every Mile over and above, to be recovered before any one Justice of the Peace, if it exceeds not Forty Shillings, and if more, by Action of Debt in the Court of Common Pleas in the County where the fact shall arise. . . .

[§12] *Be it further Enacted by the Authority aforesaid*, That no Person or Persons whatsoever shall hereafter imploy, harbour, Conceal or entertain other Peoples Slaves at their Houses, Out-Houses or Plantation, without the consent of their Master or Mistress, either signified to them Verbally, or by Certificate in writing under the said Master or Mistresses Hand, excepting in Distress of Weather, or other extraordinary Occasions, upon the forfeiture of *Forty Shillings* for every Time they are so entertained and concealed, to be paid to the Master or Mistress of such Slave or Slaves (so that the Penalty for entertaining such Slave exceeds not the Value of the said Slave) And if any Person or Persons whatsoever shall be found guilty [of] so harbouring, entertaining or concealing of any Slave, or assisting to the conveying them away, if such Slave shall happen to be lost, Dead, or otherways rendered Unserviceable, such Person or Persons so harbouring, entertaining, concealing, assisting or conveying them away, shall be also liable to pay the value of such Slave to the Master or Mistress, to be recovered by Action of Debt in any Court of Record within this Province. . . .

[§14] *And Whereas* it is found by experience, that Free Negroes are an Idle Sloathful People, and prove very often a charge to the Place where they are,

Be it therefore further Enacted by the Authority aforesaid, That any Master or Mistress, manumitting and setting at Liberty any Negro or Mullatto Slave, shall enter into sufficient Security unto Her Majesty, Her Heirs and Successors, with two Sureties, in the Sum of *Two Hundred Pounds*, to pay yearly and every year to such Negro or Mullatto Slave, during their Lives, the Sum of *Twenty Pounds*. And if such Negro or Mullatto Slave shall be made Free by the Will and Testament of any Person deceased, that then the Executors of such Person shall enter into Security, as above, immediately upon proving the said Will and Testament, which if refused to be given, the said Manumission to be void, and of none Effect.

The South Carolina Slave Code, 1740

Punishment was another important function of slave law. In the aftermath of the Stono rebellion, the South Carolina legislature strengthened its already severe code of slave punishment by passing the following legislation. How did this statute attempt to safeguard against future rebellions?

SOURCE: Joseph Brevard, *An Alphabetical Digest of the Public Statute Law of South-Carolina* (Charleston, SC: John Hoff, 1816), 2:229–31, 233, 238, 240–41, 243.

An Act for the Better Ordering and Governing [of] Negroes and Other Slaves in This Province

4. *Whereas* in his majesty's plantations in America, slavery has been introduced and allowed; and the people commonly called negroes, Indians, mulattoes and mestizos, have been deemed absolute slaves, and the subjects of property in the hands of particular persons; the extent of whose power over such slaves, ought to be settled and limited by positive laws, so that the slaves may be kept in due subjection and obedience, and the owners and other persons having the care and government of slaves, may be restrained from exercising too great rigour and cruelty over them; and that the public peace and order of this province may be preserved.

* * *

7. *Provided*, that in any action or suit to be brought in pursuance of the direction of this act, the burthen of the proof shall lay upon the plaintiff, and it shall be always presumed, that every negro, Indian, mulatto and mestizo, is a slave, unless the contrary can be made appear. (The Indians in amity with this government excepted) in which case the burthen of the proof shall lie on the defendant.

* * *

12. If any slave, who shall be out of the house or plantation where such slave shall live or shall be usually employed, or without some white person in company with such slave, shall refuse to submit to or undergo the examination of any white person, it shall be lawful for any such white person to pursue, apprehend and moderately correct such slave; and if such slave shall assault and strike such white person, such slave may be lawfully killed.

* * *

20. . . . *Be it therefore enacted*, that the several crimes and offences herein after particularly enumerated, are hereby declared to be felony without the benefit of the clergy, *that is to say*, if any slave, free negro, mulatto, Indian or mestizo, shall wilfully and maliciously burn or destroy any stack of rice, corn or other grain, of the product, growth or manufacture of this province; or shall wilfully and maliciously set fire to, burn or destroy any tar kiln, barrels of pitch, tar, turpentine or rosin, or any other [of] the goods or commodities of the growth, produce or manufacture of this province; or shall feloniously steal, take or carry away any slave, being the property of another, with intent to carry such slave out of this province; or shall wilfully and maliciously poison, or administer any poison to any person, freeman, woman, servant or slave; every such slave, free negro, mulatto, Indian, (except as before excepted) and mestizo, shall suffer death as a felon.

21. Any slave who shall be guilty of homicide of any sort, upon any white person, except by misadventure, or in defence of his master or other person under whose care and government such slave shall be, shall upon conviction thereof as aforesaid suffer death.

22. And every slave who shall raise or attempt to raise an insurrection in this province, *or shall endeavour to delude or entice any slave to run away and leave this province; every such slave and slaves, and his and their accomplices, aiders and abettors, shall upon conviction as aforesaid suffer death.*

* * *

35. *And whereas* several owners of slaves do suffer their slaves to go and work where they please, upon conditions of paying to their owners certain sums of money agreed upon between the owner and slave; which practice has occasioned such slaves to pilfer and steal, to raise money for their owners, as well as to maintain themselves in drunkenness and evil courses; for prevention of which practices for the future, *Be it enacted*, That no owner, master or mistress of any slave, after the passing of this act, shall permit or suffer any of his, her or their slaves to go and work out of their respective houses or families, without a ticket in

writing, under pain of forfeiting the sum of ten pounds, current money, for every such offence.

* * *

41. And for that as it is absolutely necessary to the safety of this province, that all due care be taken to restrain the wanderings and meetings of negroes and other slaves, at all times, and more especially on Saturday nights, Sundays and other holidays, and their using and carrying wooden swords, and other mischievous and dangerous weapons, or using or keeping of drums, horns, or other loud instruments, which may call together or give sign or notice to one another of their wicked designs and purposes; and that all masters, overseers and others may be enjoined diligently and carefully to prevent the same:

42. *Be it enacted*, That it shall be lawful for all masters, overseers and other persons whomsoever, to apprehend and take up any negro or other slave that shall be found out of the plantation of his or their master or owner, at any time, especially on Saturday nights, Sundays or other holidays, not being on lawful business, and with a letter from their master or a ticket, or not having a white person with them, and the said negro or other slave or slaves correct by a moderate whipping. . . .

43. *And whereas* cruelty is not only highly unbecoming those who profess themselves Christians, but is odious in the eyes of all men who have any sense of virtue or humanity; therefore to restrain and prevent barbarity being exercised towards slaves, *Be it enacted*, That if any person or persons whosoever, shall wilfully murder his own slave, or the slave of any other person, every such person shall upon conviction thereof, forfeit and pay the sum of seven hundred pounds current money, and shall be rendered, and is hereby declared altogether and for ever incapable of holding, exercising, enjoying or receiving the profits of any office, place or employment civil or military within this province. . . .

* * *

45. And if any person shall, on a sudden heat [of] passion, or by undue correction, kill his own slave or the slave of any other person, he shall forfeit the sum of three hundred and fifty pounds current money. And in case any person or persons shall wilfully cut out the tongue, put out the eye, castrate, or cruelly scald, burn, or deprive any slave of any limb or member, or shall inflict any other cruel punishment, other than by whipping or beating with a horse-whip, cow-skin, switch or small stick, or by putting irons on, or confining or imprisoning such slave; every such person shall for every such offence, forfeit the sum of one hundred pounds current money.

46. That in case any person in this province, who shall be owner, or who shall have the care, government or charge of any slave or slaves shall deny, neglect or refuse to allow such slave or slaves under his or her charge, sufficient cloathing, covering or food, it shall and may be lawful for any person or persons, on behalf of such slave or slaves, to make complaint to the next neighbouring justice in the parish where such slave or slaves live or are usually employed; . . . and shall and may set and impose a fine or penalty on any person who shall offend in the premises, in any sum not exceeding twenty pounds current money, for each offence.

* * *

52. *And whereas* many owners of slaves, and others who have the care, management and overseeing of slaves, do confine them so closely to hard labour, that they have not sufficient time for natural rest; *Be it therefore enacted*, That if any owner of slaves, or other person who shall have the care, management or overseeing of any slaves, shall work or put any such slave or slaves to labour, more than fifteen hours in twenty-four hours, from the twenty-fifth day of March to the twenty-fifth day of September, or more than fourteen hours in twenty-four hours, from the twenty-fifth day of September to the twenty-fifth day of March; every such person shall forfeit any sum not exceeding twenty pounds, nor under five pounds current money, for every time he,

she or they shall offend herein, at the discretion of the justice before whom the complaint shall be made.

53. *And whereas* the having of slaves taught to write, or suffering them to be employed in writing, may be attended with great inconveniencies; *Be it enacted,* That all and every person and persons whatsoever, who shall hereafter teach, or cause any slave or slaves to be taught to write, or shall use or employ any slave as a scribe in any manner of writing whatsoever, hereafter taught to write; every such person and persons shall, for every such offence, forfeit the sum of one hundred pounds current money.

Samuel Sewall | *The Selling of Joseph, 1700*

Published in Boston in 1700, *The Selling of Joseph* was the first antislavery tract published in New England. Its author, SAMUEL SEWALL (1652–1730), was a judge, businessman, and printer who questioned the morality of both the transatlantic slave trade and the institution of slavery in North America. Sewall's challenge to his era's justifications for slavery was grounded in Scripture and used the story of Joseph, a biblical figure who was sold into slavery by his own brothers, to argue that slavery was a sin.

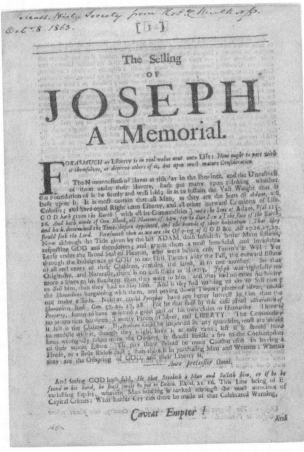

Samuel Sewall, *The Selling of Joseph: A Memorial.* (*Boston: The Massachusetts Bay Colony. Printed by Bartholomew Green and John Allen, June 24, 1700*). © Massachusetts Historical Society, Boston, Massachusetts, USA/Gift from Robert C. Winthrop, 1863/Bridgeman Images.

The Code Noir

The Code Noir, or "Black Code," originated with a decree issued by the French king Louis XIV in 1685. Like the slave codes adopted in the British colonies, the Code Noir regulated the legal status of slaves and free blacks, as well as the relationship between slaves and slave owners. Slaveholders were given almost unlimited physical control over their slaves but were also obliged to make sure their slaves were baptized and permitted to practice the Roman Catholic faith.

The British Library, London, UK/akg-images.

QUESTIONS FOR ANALYSIS

1. Describe the legal foundations of slavery in Massachusetts and Virginia. Could anyone be enslaved, or was slavery limited to peoples of African descent?

2. What powers of punishment and control did Virginia, Massachusetts, New Jersey, and South Carolina slave laws give to white colonists? To what extent did slave regulations vary over time and place?

3. What kind of legal obligations did colonial slave statutes impose on whites in South Carolina? Why might these have been viewed as important in preventing future slave insurrections?

4. How does religion figure in the documents and images included here?

NOTES

1. John Rolfe, "A Letter to Sir Edwin Sandys, January 1619/20," in *The Records of the Virginia Company of London*, ed. Susan Myra Kingsbury (Washington, DC: Government Printing Office, 1933), 3:243.

2. Tim Hawshaw, *The Birth of Black America: The First African Americans and the Pursuit of Freedom at Jamestown* (New York: Carroll and Graf, 2007), 69.

3. John Thornton, "The African Experience of the '20. and Odd Negroes' Arriving in Virginia in 1619," *William and Mary Quarterly* 55, no. 3 (1998): 421–24.

4. Raphael Holinshed, William Harrison, and others, *Holinshed's Chronicles of England, Scotland, and Ireland* (1587; repr., London: J. Johnson, 1807), 1:275.

5. Quoted in Anthony S. Parent Jr., *Foul Means: The Formation of a Slave Society in Virginia, 1660–1740* (Chapel Hill: University of North Carolina Press, 2003), 16.

6. Meeting minutes, July 9, 1640, in *Minutes of the Council and General Court of Colonial Virginia* (Richmond, VA: Colonial Press, 1924), 466.

7. William Waller Hening, ed., *The Statutes at Large; Being a Collection of All the Laws of Virginia* (Richmond, VA: Samuel Pleasants, 1810), 2:170.

8. William Waller Hening, ed., *The Statutes at Large; Being a Collection of All the Laws of Virginia from the First Session of the Legislature, in the Year 1619* (New York: R. & W. & G. Bartow, 1823), 3:87.

9. *Virginia Gazette* (Williamsburg), November 2, 1739.

10. "Bacon's 'Manifesto,'" *Virginia Magazine of History and Biography* 1 (1893), quoted in Warren Billings, ed., *The Old Dominion in the Seventeenth Century: A Documentary History of Virginia, 1606–1689* (Chapel Hill: University of North Carolina Press, 1975), 277–79.

11. William Byrd to John Perceval, Earl of Egmont, July 12, 1736, in *Documents Illustrative of the History of the Slave Trade to America*, ed. Elizabeth Donnan (Washington, DC: Carnegie Institution, 1930), 4:131–32.

12. Olaudah Equiano, *The Interesting Narrative of the Life of Olaudah Equiano, or Gustavus Vassa, the African* (London: printed for the author, 1789), 90.

13. John Brickell, *The Natural History of North-Carolina* (1737), quoted in Parent, *Foul Means*, 161.

14. Quoted in Daniel Littlefield, *Rice and Slaves: Ethnicity and the Slave Trade in Colonial South Carolina* (Baton Rouge: LSU Press, 1981), 100.

15. Advertisement, *Charleston Evening Gazette*, July 11, 1785, quoted in Judith Ann Carney, *Black Rice: The African Origins of Rice Cultivation in the Americas* (Cambridge: Harvard University Press, 2001), 90.

16. Gideon Johnston, "Instructions of the Clergy of South Carolina Given to Mr. Johnston" (1713), in *Carolina Chronicle: The Papers of Commissary Gideon Johnston, 1707–1716*, ed. Frank J. Klingberg, University of California Publications, vol. 35 (Berkeley: University of California Press, 1946), 123, 124.

17. Henry Melchior Muhlenberg, *The Journals of Henry Melchior Muhlenberg*, trans. Theodore G. Tappert and John W. Doberstein (Philadelphia: Muhlenberg Press, 1942), 1:58.

18. Quoted in Albert J. Raboteau, *Slave Religion: The "Invisible Institution" in the Antebellum South* (New York: Oxford University Press, 1978), 122.

19. Francis Le Jau, *The Carolina Chronicle of Dr. Francis Le Jau, 1706–1717* (Berkeley: University of California Press, 1980).

20. Samuel Sewall, *Diary of Samuel Sewall*, June 19, 1700, Collections of the Massachusetts Historical Society, vol. 6 (Boston: Published by the Society, 1878), 16.

21. Cotton Mather, *The Negro Christianized. An Essay to Excite and Assist That Good Work, the Instruction of Negro-Servants in Christianity* (1706), ed. Paul Royster, Electronic Texts in American Studies, paper 28, UNL DigitalCommons@University of Nebraska-Lincoln, 16, 20, http://digitalcommons.unl.edu/cgi/viewcontent.cgi?article=1028&context=etas.

22. Quoted in William Dillon Piersen, *Black Yankees: The Development of an Afro-American Subculture in Eighteenth-Century New England* (Amherst: University of Massachusetts Press, 1988), 5.

23. *Connecticut Courant*, February 23, 1733.

24. Quoted in Thelma Wills Foote, *Black and White Manhattan: The History of Racial Formation in Colonial New York City* (New York: Oxford University Press, 2004), 36.

25. "Freedoms and Exemptions Granted by the Board of the Nineteen of the Incorporated West India Company, to All Patroons, Masters or Private Persons Who Will Plant Colonies in New Netherland" (1630), in *Documents Relative to the Colonial History of the State of New-York*, ed. Edmund B. O'Callaghan (Albany: Weed, Parsons and Company, 1858), 2:557.

26. Foote, *Black and White Manhattan*, 39.

27. See, for example, "Draft of Instructions for Robert Hunter, Governor of New-York" (1709), in *Documents Relative to the Colonial History of the State of New-York*, ed. Edmund B. O'Callaghan (Albany: Weed, Parsons and Company, 1855), 5:136.

28. *New-York Weekly Journal*, June 21, 1742.

29. William Penn quoted in Samuel McPherson Janney, *The Life of William Penn; With Selections from His Correspondence and Auto-biography* (Philadelphia: Hogan, Perkins and Company, 1852), 422.

30. The Germantown Protest (1688), quoted in David Brion Davis, "Slavery and Emancipation in Western Culture," in *Slavery and Freedom in American History and Memory*, Gilder Lehrman Center for the Study of Slavery, Resistance, and Abolition, Yale University, http://www.yale.edu/glc/aces/germantown.htm.

31. Nicolas de la Salle to the French Ministry of the Colonies, Fort Louis, 29 August 1709, trans. and quoted in Gwendolyn Midlo Hall, *Africans in Colonial Louisiana: The Development of Afro-Creole Culture in the Eighteenth Century* (Baton Rouge: LSU Press, 1995), 57.

32. William Finch, a British merchant who visited Sierra Leone in 1607, quoted in Alexander Peter Kup, *A History of Sierra Leone, 1400–1787* (New York: Cambridge University Press, 1961), 160.

33. Quoted in Jane Landers, *Black Society in Spanish Florida* (Urbana: University of Illinois Press, 1999), 25.
34. Quoted in Patrick Riordan, "Finding Freedom in Florida: Native Peoples, African Americans, and Colonists, 1670–1816," *Florida Historical Quarterly* 75, no. 1 (1996): 30–31.
35. Salzburger Petition 91739, quoted in James Van Horn Melton, "From Alpine Miner to Low-Country Yeoman: The Transatlantic Worlds of a Georgia Salzburger, 1693–1761," *Past and Present* 201, no. 1 (2008): 125.
36. Johann Martin Bolzius, quoted in Melton, "From Alpine Miner," 126, 127.
37. "Protest of the Salzburgers," in Charles Colcock Jones Jr., *The History of Georgia* (Boston: Houghton, Mifflin, 1883), 1:307.
38. "Statements Made in the Introduction to the Report on General Oglethorpe's Expedition to St. Augustine" (1741), in *Historical Collections of South Carolina*, ed. Bartholomew Rivers Carroll (New York: Harper & Bros., 1836), 2:359.
39. "Report of the Committee Appointed to Enquire into the Causes of the Disappointment of Success in the Late Expedition against St. Augustine" (1741), in *Stono: Documenting and Interpreting a Southern Slave Revolt*, ed. Mark Michael Smith (Columbia: University of South Carolina Press, 2005), 28.
40. Joseph Brevard, *An Alphabetical Digest of the Public Statute Law of South-Carolina* (Charleston: John Hoff, 1816), 229, 231.
41. William Bull to the Royal Council, October 5, 1739, South Carolina Department of Archives and History, Columbia.
42. Quoted in Parent, *Foul Means*, 155, 153, 154.

SUGGESTED REFERENCES

Slavery and Freedom in Early English North America

Berlin, Ira. *Generations of Captivity: A History of African-American Slaves.* Cambridge: Belknap Press of Harvard University Press, 2003.

Breen, T. H., and Stephen Innes. *"Myne Owne Ground": Race and Freedom on Virginia's Eastern Shore, 1640–1676.* New York: Oxford University Press, 1982.

Brown, Kathleen M. *Good Wives, Nasty Wenches, and Anxious Patriarchs: Gender, Race, and Power in Colonial Virginia.* Chapel Hill: University of North Carolina, 1996.

Carney, Judith Ann. *Black Rice: The African Origins of Rice Cultivation in the Americas.* Cambridge: Harvard University Press, 2001.

Gomez, Michael A. *Exchanging Our Country Marks: The Transformation of African Identities in the Colonial and Antebellum South.* Chapel Hill: University of North Carolina Press, 1998.

Greene, Lorenzo Johnston. *The Negro in Colonial New England, 1620–1776.* Bowie, MD: Heritage Books, 1998.

Knight, Frederick. *Working the Diaspora: The Impact of African Labor on the Anglo-American World, 1650–1850.* New York: New York University Press, 2010.

Morgan, Jennifer L. *Laboring Women: Reproduction and Gender in New World Slavery.* Philadelphia: University of Pennsylvania Press, 2004.

Morgan, Philip D. *Slave Counterpoint: Black Culture in the Eighteenth-Century Chesapeake and Lowcountry.* Chapel Hill: University of North Carolina Press, 1998.

Parent, Anthony S., Jr. *Foul Means: The Formation of a Slave Society in Virginia, 1660–1740.* Chapel Hill: University of North Carolina Press, 2003.

Wood, Peter H. *Black Majority: Negroes in Colonial South Carolina from 1670 through the Stono Rebellion.* New York: Norton, 1996.

Slavery in the Middle Atlantic Colonies

Berlin, Ira, and Leslie Harris, eds. *Slavery in New York.* New York: New Press, 2005.

Essah, Patience. *A House Divided: Slavery and Emancipation in Delaware, 1638–1865.* Charlottesville: University of Virginia Press, 1996.

Foote, Thelma Wills. *Black and White Manhattan: The History of Racial Formation in Colonial New York City.* New York: Oxford University Press, 2004.

Harris, Leslie M. *In the Shadow of Slavery: African Americans in New York City, 1626–1863.* Chicago: University of Chicago Press, 2004.

Hodges, Graham Russell. *Root and Branch: African Americans in New York and East Jersey, 1613–1863.* Chapel Hill: University of North Carolina Press, 1999.

———. *Slavery and Freedom in the Rural North: African Americans in Monmouth County, New Jersey, 1665–1865.* Lanham, MD: Rowman & Littlefield Publishers, 1997.

Williams, Oscar. *African Americans and Colonial Legislation in the Middle Colonies.* London: Routledge, 1998.

Williams, William H. *Slavery and Freedom in Delaware, 1639–1865.* Lanham, MD: Rowman & Littlefield Publishers, 1999.

Frontiers and Forced Labor

Deagan, Kathleen A., and Darcie A. MacMahon. *Fort Mose: Colonial America's Black Fortress of Freedom.* Gainesville: University Press of Florida, 1995.

Hall, Gwendolyn Midlo. *Africans in Colonial Louisiana: The Development of Afro-Creole Culture in the Eighteenth Century.* Baton Rouge: LSU Press, 1995.

Hoffer, Peter Charles. *Cry Liberty: The Great Stono River Slave Rebellion of 1739.* New York: Oxford University Press, 2010.

Landers, Jane. *Black Society in Spanish Florida.* Urbana: University of Illinois Press, 1999.

Smith, Mark Michael, ed. *Stono: Documenting and Interpreting a Southern Slave Revolt.* Columbia: University of South Carolina Press, 2005.

Usner, Daniel H., Jr. "From African Captivity to American Slavery: The Introduction of Black Laborers to Colonial Louisiana." *Louisiana History* 20, no. 1 (1979).

Wood, Betty. *Slavery in Colonial Georgia, 1730–1775.* Athens: University of Georgia Press, 2007.

Young, Jeffrey Robert. *Domesticating Slavery: The Master Class in Georgia and South Carolina, 1670–1837.* Chapel Hill: University of North Carolina Press, 1999.

African Americans in the Age of Revolution

1741–1783

CHRONOLOGY *Events specific to African American history are in purple. General United States history events are in black.*

1720 Britain eliminates duties on slaves imported directly from Africa

Mid-1730s–1740s Great Awakening begins, then spreads south

1741 Series of fires in New York prompts slave conspiracy trials

1750 Georgia lifts ban on slave imports

1754–1763 French and Indian War (called Seven Years' War in Europe)

1765 Britain passes Stamp Act

1770 Boston Massacre

Crispus Attucks becomes first casualty of American Revolution

1772 Somerset case inspires challenges to slavery throughout British empire

1773 Boston Tea Party

1774 Britain passes Intolerable Acts

First Continental Congress

1775 British and colonists engage in battles at Lexington and Concord, Massachusetts

Second Continental Congress

George Washington appointed commander in chief of Continental army, bans enlistment of black men

1775 *Continued*
Lord Dunmore offers freedom to slaves who will join British forces

Continental army reverses position and declares blacks eligible for service

1776 Thomas Paine publishes *Common Sense*, arguing for independence

Continental Congress adopts Declaration of Independence

1777–1820s Northern states begin to abolish slavery

1778 British adopt southern strategy

1779 Philipsburg Proclamation promises to free slaves serving Britain in any capacity

1781 Colonists adopt Articles of Confederation

British surrender at Yorktown, Virginia

1783 United States and Great Britain sign Treaty of Paris

Virginia law directs attorney general to seek manumission for all slave soldiers still held in bondage

Massachusetts Supreme Court rules that slavery is incompatible with state constitution

The New York Slave Plot of 1741

During the winter of 1741, British colonists were quick to blame a series of fires that swept lower Manhattan on a massive slave conspiracy. In the wake of a recent maroon war in Jamaica and slave revolts in Antigua and South Carolina (the Stono rebellion; see chapter 2), white New Yorkers were nervous about the two thousand slaves who made up one-fifth of the city's population. New York slaves had good reason to be discontented during that unusually cold winter, when food and fuel were scarce. The first fire took place inside Fort George, which contained Lieutenant Governor George Clarke's mansion. Soldiers stationed there rescued Clarke and his family, and citizens gathered with buckets to douse the flames. But onlookers were disturbed to note that although some blacks pitched in to help, not all of them tried to fight the fire. One slave confided to another that he "wished the governor had been burnt in the middle of it," while a slave named Cuffee danced as the fire spread.[1]

The Fort George fire was only the first in a series of conflagrations. One week later, flames scorched a nearby house, and a week after that a warehouse burned to the ground. The first week of April saw seven fires, one next to the house of Captain Jacob Sarly. The captain owned a slave named Juan de la Silva, who along with several of his shipmates had been captured and sold into slavery after an attack on a Spanish ship. All of the men swore that they were sailors rather than slaves and "free subjects of Spain" as well. They had also publicly threatened to roast John Lush, the privateer who had captured their ship, like "a piece of beef." Moreover, de la Silva had vowed to burn Sarly's house as well. After the fire at Sarly's neighbor's house broke out, some New Yorkers assumed that de la Silva and his shipmates had started all the fires in a plot to "ruin the city." A cry swept through the city: "Take up the Spanish negroes."[2] But even as de la Silva and his compatriots were rounded up and dragged off to City Hall, another fire broke out in a warehouse on New Street. Cuffee, the slave who had danced while Fort George burned, was seen leaving the building. A huge mob chased him down and carried him to the city jail, shouting, "The Negroes are rising!"[3]

More than 100 blacks and several whites were arrested and imprisoned as authorities investigated the alleged conspiracy, coercing confessions from the men and women they tried and convicted. By the end of the trials, 17 blacks and 4 whites had been hanged, 13 blacks had been burned at the stake, and 70 blacks and 7 whites had been banished from the colony. How many of them were guilty of arson — or anything else — remains an open question. The trials took place at a moment when New Yorkers were alert to the dangers of slave rebellion, embroiled in an imperial war with Spain, and suffering the economic effects of a deep recession. One witness reported that blacks planned "to burn the town, kill the white men, and take their wives and daughters as mistresses." Others maintained that the fires had been set by blacks and poor whites who had united against the wealthier classes. But once the hysteria of the trials died down, many New Yorkers wondered whether they had been caught in "the merciless Flames of an Imaginary Plot."[4]

Planned or not, the fires provoked fears that illuminated the dangers of slavery, as well as the dangers of interracial freedom struggles in colonial America. Trial testimony reveals a world of discontented slaves, servants, and white workers, whose grievances could easily swell into outright rebellion. Most of the accused were men and women who worked on New York's racially mixed waterfront, where they socialized together, slept together, and shared a common resentment toward more prosperous New Yorkers and the city's social order. But such allegiances did not prevent blacks from becoming the primary scapegoats. Some of the alleged ringleaders, such as the dancing Cuffee, were criminals whose traffic in stolen goods may have made them easy targets of property owners. Others, such as the hapless "Spanish Negroes," were men who were primarily focused on securing their own freedom.

As the eighteenth century progressed and American colonists battled for independence from Britain, freedom-seeking blacks would become important foot soldiers in what one historian has described as "the motley crew" of the American Revolution.[5] Discontented blacks, with no property or privileges to preserve, saw the Revolution as an opportunity to win their own freedom. They fought on both sides of the conflict and participated in all of the Revolution's major battles. White patriots were initially reluctant to enlist black soldiers, fearing a slave revolt, but after the British began enlisting slaves in 1775, most of the colonies followed suit. While securing black freedom was not among the colonists' Revolutionary goals, they and the British usually freed slaves who served in their armed forces. African Americans on both sides of the conflict were quick to embrace these opportunities.

The Revolutionary era offered African Americans other routes to freedom as well. The religious revivals of the Great Awakening fostered a spirit of egalitarianism that was appealing to both blacks and whites. Moreover, as white Americans struggled to free themselves from British domination, many began to question the legitimacy of slavery. Whites manumitted, or freed, more than twenty thousand slaves during the final decades of the eighteenth century. Some were inspired to do so by their religious convictions, while others were influenced by the Revolution's democratic ideals.

Thus the American Revolution fueled the freedom dreams of African Americans, who took advantage of the war's social and political dislocation to join the patriot or British forces, run away, or challenge the terms of their enslavement in court. Their actions helped to erode slavery in America, resulting in a new nation where slavery was permitted in some states but not in others.

African American Life in Eighteenth-Century North America

During the 1741 slave trials, New York chief justice Daniel Horsmanden warned slaveholders that they had "enemies of their own household," who should be replaced and "replenished with white people."[6] But New York slaveholders proved no more willing to relinquish their slaves than had their counterparts in South Carolina, even in the wake of the bloody Stono rebellion. As the supply of white workers shrank, North America's British colonies imported even more captive Africans. Sixty percent of all the African-born slaves imported into the American colonies, most of whom ended up in the South, arrived between the 1720s and the 1780s. In the North, the newcomers joined an existing black population in which American-born blacks predominated. English-speaking and comfortable living among whites, many American-born black northerners had become Christians as well. During these years, African Americans forged a distinct and evolving identity, combining the contributions of the continuous flow of African newcomers with those of the large population of American-born blacks.

Slaves and Free Blacks across the Colonies

By the mid-eighteenth century, white laborers were in short supply throughout the colonies, especially after Europe's Seven Years' War of 1756–1763 reduced the flow of European indentured servants and increased the rate of military enlistment in Europe. This shortage led colonists to embrace slavery with greater enthusiasm than ever before. Whereas the total number of slaves shipped from Africa to North America between 1700 and 1720 was roughly 20,000, colonists imported more than 50,000 captives per decade in the 1740s and 1750s and maintained similar rates, with only a slight drop-off, in the years immediately preceding the Revolution. Most of these newcomers ended up in the southern colonies, but slave imports in the North increased as well, enlarging and Africanizing the region's small black population.

In the South, the newcomers populated an expanding plantation frontier. Georgia, which was founded with a ban of slave imports, was home to only 500 slaves in 1750. That year, however, its trustees agreed to lift the ban as of January 1, 1751, and after that, the colony quickly became a slave society. Its slave population soared, reaching 18,000 in 1775. South Carolina also resumed massive imports of slaves in the 1750s, bringing in 56,000 between 1751 and 1775, even as the colony's slave population began to expand by natural increase. Only in the Chesapeake, which was already home to almost half a million people of African descent, did slave imports slow. As a result of robust rates of natural increase, most Chesapeake planters could expect slave families to grow on their own. Planters did continue to bring enslaved Africans to recently settled areas, such as the Virginia Piedmont and western Maryland, but those imports declined over time and amounted to less than one thousand per year by the 1770s.

By contrast, the enslaved population in the northern colonies was never self-sustaining. Northern employers had to import slaves to meet their labor needs. Scattered across the region, northern slaves were rarely able to find partners, so their numbers were not replenished by reproduction. Although the slave population in the North remained modest in comparison to that in the South, between 1732 and 1754 slaves made up a third of all immigrants (voluntary or involuntary) entering New York City, and black New Yorkers accounted for almost 20 percent of the city's population. Likewise, one in five Philadelphia laborers and one in ten of all Bostonians were enslaved by midcentury. Massachusetts as a whole saw its black population increase by 50 percent during each decade between 1700 and 1750.

During the mid-eighteenth century, the use of enslaved labor expanded into new occupational sectors in New England and the middle colonies. Slaves had long been common in northern port cities such as New York, Boston, and Philadelphia, where they served as domestic and maritime workers. But urban artisans who had traditionally employed white apprentices now began to train black slaves to work in their shops. Increasing numbers of enslaved Africans were also employed in agriculture, both in southern New England and in the grain-producing regions of the middle colonies, areas that had previously relied on white immigrant workers. Landowners in slave owning regions such as Narragansett County, Rhode Island, became more dependent on slave labor, while farmers in Pennsylvania, northern New Jersey, the Hudson Valley, and Long Island began to import large numbers of enslaved Africans for the first time.

As slaves became integral to the northern labor force, both American and African American society changed. Since slave birthrates remained extremely low in the North, slavery there was sustained by "a continual supply . . . from Africa," as Benjamin Franklin noted.[7] As his observation indicates, by the 1740s northern merchants had begun to import boatloads of West African slaves. Prior to 1741, 70 percent of the slaves shipped to New York originated in the Caribbean, and only 30 percent came directly from Africa. After 1741, the proportions were reversed.[8] Changes in both demand and supply shaped this shift in the composition of slave imports. As the demand for slaves rose in northern cities, the slave market there could no longer rely on the small-scale trade in "refuse slaves" from the West Indies. At the same time, in 1720 the British crown eliminated duties on slaves imported directly from Africa, making it easier for American merchants to buy shiploads of African slaves.

As slavery expanded in eighteenth-century America, black freedom contracted. Both the northern and southern colonies had long been home to small numbers of free blacks, whose populations were increasingly dwarfed by the steady influx of enslaved migrants. By 1775, one observer recalled, "the number of free negroes [in Virginia] was so small that they were seldom to be met with."[9] Free blacks were even scarcer in South Carolina. Laws discouraging manumission and requiring African Americans who did gain freedom to leave the state also limited the free black population in the South. Free blacks were somewhat more common in the North, where such restrictions were rare, but as of 1760 they still totaled only 10 percent of the region's small black population — or a few thousand people.

Shaping an African American Culture

The steady importation of thousands of West African captives ensured that African culture shaped the lives of blacks throughout the colonies, even as the American-born black population also increased. The cultural impact of these migrants varied by region: It was most striking in areas where American- and Caribbean-born blacks predominated, such as the Northeast, and weakest in the colonies of the Lower South, where African-born slaves had long formed a majority.

African American communities in the North were transformed when shiploads of Africans began docking in northeastern port cities in the 1740s. The newcomers infused African culture into these increasingly acculturated black communities, made up of English-speaking slaves who had long lived and worked among whites and maintained only limited ties to their African roots. But northern blacks were sufficiently set apart from the white world to enjoy their own evolving culture. Both African and American, they welcomed the new migrants and embraced their African traditions. By midcentury, blacks across the North began to adopt a self-consciously African identity, which shaped the naming of early black organizations such as the African Lodge No. 1, a black Masonic lodge founded in 1776.

During this period, Africans and African Americans in the North united across cultural and linguistic divides in a boisterous annual celebration known as **Negro Election Day**. Largely a New England phenomenon, Negro Election Day combined the Puritan tradition of an election day holiday with African rituals of festive role reversals, in which the powerless temporarily played the role of the powerful. This holiday saw black New Englanders elect their own kings and governors in elaborate ceremonies that included royal processions, political parades, and inaugural parties. Those ceremonies, which partly spoofed white behavior on official election days, were often regarded with amused disdain by whites, who tended not to grasp the extent to which Negro Election Day parodied its white counterpart. In fact, white municipal authorities sanctioned the festivities. On this day, one white observer noted, "all the various languages of Africa, mixed with broken and ludicrous English, filled the air, accompanied with the music of the fiddle, tambourine, the banjo, drum, etc."[10]

But the elections were at least semiserious in their public recognition of local black leaders' authority. Black governors and kings were often African-born men of royal lineage, and many had the added distinction of serving wealthy and powerful white men, who supplied them with the food, liquor, and elegant clothing required to compete for these offices. Although these were primarily ceremonial positions, some black governors and kings were authorized to speak on behalf of their communities and were called on to preside over informal trials of slaves accused of petty crimes.

Black northerners also came together for African-influenced funeral ceremonies, which struck white observers as alarmingly pagan. Drawing on West African mortuary rites that celebrated the dead with music and song designed to ease their journey into the spirit world, black funerals confounded white New Englanders. "They did not express so much sorrow at the funeral," a white observer named William Bentley wrote of a black funeral in Salem, Massachusetts, "as real gratification at appearing so well, a greater sympathy with living happily than the bereaved."[11] Such celebrations made far more sense to the black men and women who participated in them. Bentley's comments suggest that, while white northerners found African religious traditions alien, black northerners did not. Instead, such traditions were a shared point of connection between African newcomers and blacks who had spent many years in America.

The brisk slave trade in the Chesapeake ensured that slaves there, like their northern counterparts, did not become wholly estranged from their African cultural heritage. At midcentury, blacks who lived in the Chesapeake tended to be highly acculturated as a result of sustained contact with whites, with whom they shared modest-sized plantations and urban dwellings. Between 1720 and the 1770s, however, the planters who settled in the Virginia Piedmont imported approximately fifteen thousand African captives. Most of these settlers came from the tidewater region on Virginia's eastern coast, where decades of tobacco production had exhausted the soil, forcing planters to seek more fertile land farther west. As the settlers fanned out, they carved new plantations out of the wilderness using the labor of both American blacks and recent African migrants, who worked and lived together. The African-born slaves helped sustain African cultural practices and beliefs among the American-born blacks throughout the region. In turn, the American blacks helped the newcomers assimilate. Over time, the two groups blended and intermixed, creating a slave culture that was simultaneously African and American.

This blended culture was also evident in linguistic patterns that developed in the Upper South, where blacks spoke English but also continued to use African idioms and syntax. According to John Smyth, an Englishman who immigrated to Virginia shortly before the Revolution, these cultural hybrids spoke "a mixed dialect between the Guinea and English."[12] Local whites, who in turn adopted some of the black idioms, called the regional variation of English spoken by Chesapeake blacks "Virginian," a term that recognized the influence of the blend of African and American culture on the region as a whole.

African cultural beliefs and customs also remained common in the Upper South. Like northern blacks, even highly acculturated southern blacks often insisted on honoring the dead by singing, dancing, and rejoicing at funerals. They also honored traditional African beliefs in the power of **conjure**. Rooted in West African religious traditions and rituals recognizing the existence of magic and the influence of ancestral spirits and other occult powers in daily life (see chapter 2), conjure was also influenced by the surroundings in which it took shape in North America, drawing on Native American knowledge of natural remedies. Conjurers, who could be men or women, were also known as "root doctors" or "Negro doctors" and were often skilled in the use of botanical medicines. Black and white southerners alike consulted them to heal the sick with spells and charms as well as roots and herbs. Conjurers also created love potions and were thought to be able to predict the future. On a more sinister note, many people believed that they poisoned their enemies.

Conjure and other African traditions were most entrenched in the Lower South, where acculturation was minimal. Most blacks in eighteenth-century South Carolina, for example, lived in an increasingly Africanized world. Slave birthrates remained low there for much of the century, forcing the colony's planters to import thousands of West African slaves each year to meet the needs of the growing plantation economy. The new arrivals reinforced African cultural practices and spiritual beliefs among low-country slaves, even after the number of American-born blacks in the region slowly began to increase.

The Creation of an African American Culture

This late-eighteenth-century painting, *The Old Plantation*, depicts a group of slaves on a South Carolina plantation. The slaves' activities strongly suggest the persistence of West African cultural traditions and practices in the Lower South. This painting may depict a wedding, which sometimes featured the tradition of "jumping the broom," or it may depict a dance. Many of the participants' accoutrements — the women's head ties and the players' instruments, for example — are West African in origin. But the other garments shown are typical of American working-class attire during this period, and the slave cabins and other plantation buildings remind us of the setting in which this distinctly African American culture was taking shape. *The Old Plantation, attributed to John Rose, Beaufort County, South Carolina, c. 1785–1790/The Colonial Williamsburg Foundation, Gift of Abby Aldrich Rockefeller.*

Many low-country blacks never mastered the English language. Isolated on large plantations and put to work under the supervision of black drivers, they had little contact with English speakers. As a result, even the region's native-born blacks often spoke a creole language known as **Gullah**, which whites found difficult to understand. Gullah speakers mixed English with West African syntax and words. For instance, using a term from the Efik-Ibibio language spoken by many people in what is today southeastern Nigeria, they referred to white people as "backra" or "buckra," meaning "he who surrounds or governs."[13]

The Slaves' Great Awakening

The enduring influence of African traditions and beliefs and the influx of new arrivals limited the spread of Christianity among African Americans in the eighteenth century. So, too, did the lack of enthusiasm that many slave owners expressed toward slave conversion. But the period also saw the slow beginnings of Afro-Christianity in both the North and the South, inspired by the **Great Awakening**, a wave of religious revivals that began in New England in the mid-1730s and spread south during the Revolutionary era. This multidenominational movement was led by evangelical ministers from various Protestant sects, attracting Presbyterian, Congregationalist, Baptist, and Methodist participants, as well as members of German and Dutch Reformed churches. These ministers, known as **New Lights**, rejected Protestantism's traditional emphasis on doctrine and ritual in favor of emotional sermons that urged listeners to repent and find spiritual salvation in Christ. New Lights did not seek out black converts, but they welcomed black and Indian congregants, and their emotional preaching drew spectators of all colors and faiths.

Their message was also appealing. New Light ministers stressed that the liberating effects of faith were open to all. "You that are servants," Benjamin Colman of Boston's Brattle Street Church told his congregants in 1740, "and the meanest of our Household Servants, even our poor Negroes, chuse you the Service of CHRIST; He will make you his Freemen; The SON OF GOD, shall make you free, and you shall be free indeed."[14] At revival meetings, ministers encouraged blacks and women to relate their conversion experiences and serve as religious examples for other worshippers, opening up new religious roles for both groups. Moreover, Baptist churches allowed blacks to serve as exhorters, deacons, or even elders (church leaders). While few black worshippers ever achieved these leadership roles, their growing prominence in church affairs did not go unnoticed. "Women and girls; yea, Negroes, have taken it upon them to do the business of preachers," one hostile observer complained in 1743.[15]

The Great Awakening's egalitarian spirit fostered the education, conversion, and eventual manumission of several notable black northerners, including the famous poet Phillis Wheatley. Wheatley, who was seven or eight years old when she was sold into slavery in the Senegal/Gambia region, was converted and educated by the devout family who purchased her from a slave ship in 1761. Her pious mistress, Susannah Wheatley, loved the "spellbinding sermon[s]" of evangelical leaders and took their message to heart, encouraging her daughter, Mary, to teach their young slave to read, write, and commit much of the Bible to memory. Phillis Wheatley began writing poetry in her teens, publishing her first book of poems in London when she was twenty years old. *Poems on Various Subjects, Religious and Moral* won her a following among British anti-slavery activists and also helped her win her own freedom. Later that year, Wheatley's owner freed her "at the desire of [his] friends in England."[16] (See Document Project: Black Freedom Fighters, pp. 121–27.)

Likewise, the Nigerian-born James Albert Ukawsaw Gronniosaw's road to religious awakening began when he was purchased by Theodore Frelinghuysen, one of New Jersey's leading New Light ministers, who sent Gronniosaw to school to learn to read. Initially reluctant to accept Frelinghuysen's notion of a divine father, Gronniosaw told the minister that "my father liv'd at Bournou, and that I wanted very much to see

Phillis Wheatley
Poet and antislavery activist Phillis Wheatley published her first book of poems, *Poems on Various Subjects, Religious and Moral,* in 1773 at age twenty. The title page and frontispiece, shown here, feature an engraving of a dignified, intellectual Wheatley engaged in her craft. The frame around her portrait identifies her as "Phillis Wheatley, Negro Servant to Mr. John Wheatley, of Boston." Later that year, John Wheatley would free her. *Title page and frontispiece to Poems on Various Subjects, Religious and Moral by Phillis Wheatley (1753–1784), published in London, 1773 (engraving)/ © Massachusetts Historical Society, Boston, MA, USA/Bridgeman Images.*

him, and likewise my dear mother, and sister, and I wish'd he would be so good as to send me home to them."[17]

But once he learned to read English, Gronniosaw proved more receptive to Frelinghuysen's instruction. He devoured spiritual classics such as John Bunyan's *The Pilgrim's Progress* and embraced the evangelical wisdom of Richard Baxter's fire-and-brimstone *A Call to the Unconverted*. Meanwhile, Gronniosaw's master seems to have also embraced evangelicalism's liberatory message. Convinced that "the largest portion of the faithful have been poor and of little account," Frelinghuysen freed Gronniosaw in his will, leaving his former slave ten pounds to support himself as he continued his spiritual journey.[18]

Wheatley and Gronniosaw were not the only slaves to find a religious path to freedom. As the Great Awakening moved south, it inspired thousands of slaveholders to take a new interest in slaves' religious education and triggered a wave of manumissions among devout masters. But the revival movement posed only a limited challenge to slavery as an institution. Although New Light ministers welcomed black worshippers, few challenged slavery. In fact, the movement's leading luminaries, the Connecticut Congregationalist Jonathan Edwards and George Whitefield, an itinerant Anglican minister from Gloucester, England, both owned slaves themselves.

These evangelical leaders had little trouble reconciling slavery with their religious faith. Edwards, who owned several domestic slaves, criticized slave owners who mistreated their slaves, but he also maintained that slaves flourished under the guidance of a good Christian master. Whitefield, once he moved from England to preach in Savannah, Georgia, developed similar convictions. Although he openly chided some Georgia slave owners who abused their slaves, calling them "Monsters of Barbarity,"[19] he also remained convinced that slavery was compatible with Christianity as long as slave owners were careful to attend to their slaves' spiritual needs. He seems to have been terrified by the prospect of a slave revolt, having traveled through South Carolina shortly after the Stono rebellion in 1739. Whitefield encouraged enslaved blacks to "stay in your calling at all costs . . . [and] give up the thought of seeking freedom from your masters." He also "pray[ed] God, they may never be permitted to get the upper hand."[20]

Whitefield was not alone in worrying that religion might overturn the South's social order. Indeed, in South Carolina his message of slave conversion was largely suppressed after it moved two of his most enthusiastic converts to flout the colony's long-standing ban on slave gatherings. Wealthy siblings Hugh and Jonathan Bryan, who owned plantations in St. Helena's Parish, South Carolina, took to heart Whitefield's critique of masters who failed to offer religious instruction to slaves. But when the Bryan brothers resolved to organize a Negro school, they were soon investigated for calling together "great numbers of Negroes and other slaves." A committee assembled by the South Carolina Commons House of Assembly in 1742 concluded that, "however commendable" it may be for planters to instruct slaves on the "Principles of Religion or Morality, in their own Plantations," anyone who encouraged slaves from different plantations to congregate was endangering the "Safety of the Province."[21] Fined and threatened with arrest, the Bryan brothers repented and thereafter confined their religious proselytizing to their own slaves.

In the Chesapeake, where white colonists outnumbered black slaves, there was less opposition to black participation in the revivals. Virginia and Maryland slaves, who were primarily native-born and spoke English, had no trouble understanding the evangelical movement's message and were drawn to its emotional style of worship. Evangelical revival services, which often took place in tent encampments, usually included songs and testimonials as well as prayer. They were more lively and open to innovation than the highly ritualized services offered in the Chesapeake's traditional churches, and they provided black participants with opportunities to incorporate African music and styles of expression. Although some white ministers deplored the "groans, cries, screams, and agonies" heard from blacks and other enthusiastic worshippers, most welcomed such congregants. "Ethiopia has . . . stretched forth her hands to God," the Presbyterian revivalist Samuel Davies declared after more than a hundred African Americans attended a revival he held in Hanover County, Virginia, in 1751. Anxious to instruct slaves in the Christian faith, Davies distributed Bibles and other religious literature at his revivals. Many of his slave congregants, hungry for literacy as well as salvation, spent "every leisure hour" learning to read.[22]

By the late eighteenth century, black lay preachers were leading conversions of their own. Many kept their calling largely silent and led congregations that met in secret. Slave preachers and their followers were members of a multidenominational black church that one historian has called the "invisible institution."[23] The product of an era when slaves were generally forbidden to hold public gatherings, slave congregations often met only under the veil of night. As a result, the activities of enslaved preachers are not well documented.

Even free black preachers were often forbidden to lead public forms of worship, as the Virginia-born John Marrant found out. A lay preacher, he was eager to share his religious faith with the slaves on the Charleston, South Carolina, plantation where he worked as a carpenter, but the plantation's mistress objected. She insisted that Christianity would only result in "negroes ruined," Marrant later recalled. He defied her wishes by leading covert prayer meetings, until her husband launched a surprise raid on one such meeting, bringing in neighbors and employees who helped him flog the congregants until "blood ran from their backs and sides to the floor to make them leave off praying." Thereafter, Marrant's followers prayed only in secret.[24]

Despite white opposition, African Americans' "invisible institution" flourished, offering worshippers a buffer against the white racism they faced on a daily basis. Whereas the South's white evangelicals hoped that Christianity would school blacks in obedience and submission to make them better slaves, black converts took other lessons from their newfound faith. Drawn in by the egalitarian spirit of the evangelical movement, they embraced Christianity's message that all men and women are equal before God, and they saw in the Bible's promises of spiritual deliverance some hope of eventually achieving freedom on earth as well as in heaven. In doing so, they crafted a distinctly Afro-Christian religious faith that helped them survive slavery while praying for freedom.

Johann Valentine Haidt, **The First Fruits, 1747**
The Moravians who established settlements in Pennsylvania and North Carolina during the eighteenth century were ambivalent about the moral correctness of slavery and welcomed both black and Indian converts as full brothers and sisters in Christ. This painting by German-born artist Johann Valentine Haidt, who was also a deacon in the Moravian Church, dramatizes the racial egalitarianism of this Protestant sect. It depicts a diverse group of Moravian converts from many different nations gathered around the throne of Christ in heaven. The angel on the right side of the picture holds a sign that describes these redeemed converts as "first fruits of God and the Lamb" (Revelation 14:4). *Moravian Archives, Bethlehem, Pennsylvania.*

The African American Revolution

The Revolutionary era was a time of remarkable ideological ferment among African Americans. The Great Awakening offered both a new religious faith and educational opportunities to many black converts, who often found a critique of slavery in the revivalists' message of religious equality. African Americans found the egalitarian principles on which the colonists based their struggles against the British to be equally liberating. The American Revolution took place during the Enlightenment, a time when thinkers throughout the Americas and western Europe questioned traditional institutions, customs, and morals. The discontented colonists framed their complaints in terms of philosophical principles with far-reaching implications.

The colonists' rift with Britain took shape over the taxes, import duties, and other obligations the British Parliament imposed on the American colonies. But the colonists went beyond financial disputes to insist that all men had a natural right to self-government. In doing so, they opened up new questions about the legitimacy of slavery. The Revolutionary leader James Otis Jr. maintained that "the colonists are by the law of nature freeborn, as indeed all men are, white or black," and many of Otis's fellow patriots opposed American participation in the African slave trade.[25] But the Revolution's leaders avoided direct attacks on American slavery for fear that internal controversies might derail their attempts to unite the colonies in the common cause. African Americans did not share these fears and approached the Revolution as an antislavery struggle from the outset. They drew on both Revolutionary ideology and the social and political chaos of war to challenge slavery by petitioning for freedom, running away, and fighting for their own liberty on both sides of the conflict.

The Road to Independence

The American colonists' discontent with British rule began in the early 1760s, when the British Parliament levied a new series of taxes on the colonies. The taxes, designed to raise money to pay off British debts incurred during the French and Indian War (1754–1763), when British troops were deployed to protect the colonists' land, were not excessive. But they represented a shift from Britain's previous policy of benign neglect toward the colonies. Colonists had long controlled their own affairs and paid only local taxes. They also had no say in British imperial policy and no political representation in Parliament, which they felt entitled to as British subjects. In particular, they insisted that they should not be subject to "taxation without representation." Taxes imposed on the colonies by Parliament, the rebellious colonists maintained, deprived them of their property without their consent, making them little better than slaves.

African Americans were largely unaffected by British taxes because most blacks were either enslaved or impoverished, and therefore had little access to the goods that were taxed. But colonists' protests against British tyranny nonetheless held a powerful appeal for African Americans. White patriots cast their opposition to British authority as a struggle for freedom, denouncing the "vile, ignominious slavery" imposed on them by Britain's new policies.[26] Their protests drew on the natural rights philosophy articulated by thinkers such as Britain's own John Locke, who maintained that "men being . . . by nature all free, equal, and independent, no one can be put out of this estate and subjected to the political power of another without his own consent."[27]

Though rarely intended to challenge slavery, white colonists' rhetoric gave slaves a powerful new political language with which to address their own condition. When white colonists in Charleston protested passage of the Stamp Act of 1765 — which required colonists to print most documents on a special stamped paper that was issued and taxed by the British government — with chants of "Liberty! Liberty and stamp'd paper," local slaves also called for "Liberty, liberty," much to the horror of white observers. A South Carolina politician, recording the incident, dismissed the slaves' chant as "a thoughtless imitation" of whites.[28] But slave unrest mounted throughout the years leading up to the Revolution, as the conflict inspired African Americans to stage freedom struggles of their own.

In the pre-Revolution years, as American colonists boycotted British goods; protested taxes on stamped documents, sugar, and tea; and scuffled with British soldiers stationed on American soil, slaves across the colonies took advantage of the unrest to escape from their owners. In Georgia and South Carolina, they fled to swamplands and other unsettled frontier areas to form maroon communities. In the more densely populated North, they often headed for urban areas. According to Boston patriot John Adams, some of the slaves already living in northern cities took advantage of the social disorder to free themselves. As the colonies moved toward declaring their independence, he later recalled, Boston slaves pushed for their own freedom by becoming "lazy, idle, proud, vicious and at length wholly useless to their masters, to such a degree that the abolition of slavery became a measure of economy."[29]

Other black northerners publicly embraced the Revolutionary struggle. In 1772, while still a slave herself, Phillis Wheatley wrote a poem dedicated to the Earl of Dartmouth, the British king's newly appointed secretary of state for North America — and a man who the colonists hoped might remedy their discontent. In verses linking the patriots' tribulations with those of the black slaves, Wheatley heralded Dartmouth's appointment as a sign that New England would once more see "Freedom's charms unfold." She went on to explain that having been "young in life" when she was "snatch'd from Afric's fancy'd happy seat," she knew the pain of slavery all too well and could "but pray / Others may never feel tyrannic sway." After her emancipation, Wheatley continued publicly to question how the colonists could reconcile their "cry of liberty" with "the exercise of oppressive power over others." (See Document Project: Black Freedom Fighters, pp. 121–27.)

Most of Wheatley's black contemporaries did not possess her writing skills, but some managed to take such questions to the courts by initiating **freedom suits** that challenged local magistrates and colonial legislatures to recognize their natural rights.

"Attended Court; heard the trial of an action of trespass, brought by a mulatto woman, for damages, for restraining her of her liberty," John Adams wrote in his diary in 1766 after witnessing a freedom suit brought by Jenny Slew of Ipswich, Massachusetts. "This is called suing for liberty; the first action that ever I knew of the sort, though I have heard there have been many."[30] As the daughter of a free white woman, Slew claimed her liberty as a birthright, but later slave litigants claimed freedom as a natural right, sometimes winning their liberty as a result.

Some of the impetus for the freedom suits came from events in Britain rather than America. The **Somerset case**, which freed an American slave named James Somerset in 1772, inspired new challenges to slavery throughout the British empire. Somerset was born in Africa and sold into slavery in Virginia, where he lived until his owner, Charles Stewart, brought him to London while traveling on business. Somerset ran away but was caught and imprisoned on a ship bound for Jamaica, where Stewart planned to sell him. The British antislavery activist Granville Sharp, a municipal official, hired lawyers who issued a writ of **habeas corpus** challenging Stewart's right to detain Somerset. Designed to prevent false imprisonment, writs of habeas corpus (Latin for "you should have the body") request the legal review of prisoners detained without trial. The Somerset case ended up in the court of Britain's lord chief justice William Murray, Earl of Mansfield, who was aware that it could challenge the legal status of British slavery. He nonetheless ruled in favor of freeing Somerset, although his ruling was carefully worded to apply only to Somerset's case.

The Somerset case did not make slavery illegal in Britain or even address its status anywhere else, but when British antislavery activists celebrated Somerset's release, slaves in Britain and the Americas drew on the case to make their own claims to liberty. In January 1773, Massachusetts blacks collectively petitioned the colony's governor and legislature for the first time. Signed by one author, Felix [Holbrook], but written on behalf of slaves throughout Massachusetts, the document appealed to legislators to relieve the "unhappy state and condition" of the enslaved. Invoking the Somerset case as a precedent for their own emancipation, petitioners noted that "men of Great note and Influence . . . have pleaded our cause with arguments which we hope will have their weight with this honorable court."[31] Meanwhile, in Virginia, news of the Somerset case may have prompted a slave named Bacchus to begin a long journey to England in 1774. Bacchus's owner, a Virginia lawyer named Gabriel Jones, certainly suspected as much. The runaway slave advertisement that Jones submitted to the *Virginia Gazette* on June 18, 1774, described the appearance of the thirty-year-old runaway and predicted that "he will probably endeavour to pass for a Freeman by the Name of *John Christian*, and attempt to get on Board some Vessel bound for *Great Britain*, from the Knowledge he has of the late Determination of *Somerset*'s Case."[32]

What became of Bacchus is unknown, but the Massachusetts legislature tabled Felix's petition. They received another petition a month later. The new petition listed several authors: Peter Bestes, Sambo Freeman, Felix Holbrook, and Chester Joie. It also bypassed the colony's unpopular governor to speak directly to the patriots in the rebellious house of representatives. "We expect great things from men who have made such a noble stand against the designs of their *fellow-men* to enslave them," they wrote, before requesting the representatives' "assistance in our peaceable and lawful attempts to gain our freedom . . . which, *as men*, we have a natural right to."[33] Framed in the Revolutionary rhetoric of the day, the petitioners' request echoed the expansive natural rights philosophy celebrated by Massachusetts patriots such as James Otis Jr. But Otis never even freed his own slave manservant, and Massachusetts legislators proved equally unwilling to link the petitioners' freedom struggles to their own. They ignored the second petition and several subsequent appeals.

Black Patriots

Despite such disappointments, many black northerners joined the patriot cause. Once the conflict began, fugitives could often secure their freedom through military service. More than five thousand African Americans are estimated to have fought alongside American forces during the Revolution, while other blacks sided with the patriots without actually enlisting. Among the best known of these unofficial patriots is Crispus Attucks, a black seaman who was in all likelihood a fugitive slave. Attucks was the American Revolution's first casualty.

The son of an African father and a Natick Indian mother, Attucks was likely born into slavery in Framingham, Massachusetts, sometime in the early 1720s, and fled a farm there in 1750. After his escape, Attucks may have kept a low profile to avoid capture. But as a sailor and dockworker who lived and worked on the Boston waterfront when he was not at sea, Attucks was among the many Bostonians who resented the growing British military presence in New England's premier port city. The British "redcoats" were especially unpopular among men in Attucks's profession, because they often supplemented their meager military salaries by working part-time at lower wages than American workers were willing to accept. The soldiers' presence on the docks also discouraged the brisk business in smuggled goods that had long allowed colonial shippers to avoid British taxes. Finally, the British troops threatened the liberty of American sailors and dockworkers, who were often impressed or forced into service in the British navy. These discontented American workers figured prominently in igniting what became known as the Boston Massacre.

The conflict took place on the afternoon of March 5, 1770, beginning in a tavern on Boston's waterfront, where a group of men that one observer described as a "motley rabble of saucy boys, Negroes and mulattoes, Irish teagues [a derogatory term for Catholics] and outlandish jacktars [sailors]" encountered a British soldier who came in to inquire about part-time work.[34] Later that day, outraged by this intrusion onto their turf, more than thirty men from the bar gathered outside the port's customhouse to taunt and heckle the British soldiers stationed outside. The scuffle ended only when the redcoats fired on the crowd, killing five men and wounding eleven more.

The first to die was Attucks, who was forty-seven years old at the time of his death. More than six feet tall and powerfully built, Attucks was one of the mob's leaders. He may not have been fighting for freedom, but as a member of a close-knit community of workingmen, he was willing to defend his livelihood and died a hero as a result. Attucks and the massacre's other martyrs were honored with a funeral procession that attracted ten thousand mourners, and they were buried together in a common grave.

Attucks was widely celebrated as the "first to defy, the first to die," but his race was rarely noted in Revolutionary-era commemorations of the Boston Massacre.[35] As a man of color who was probably a fugitive slave, Attucks embodied contradictions that might divide the former colonists as they fought to establish a slaveholding republic. Accordingly, the famous silversmith and engraver Paul Revere chose not to include Attucks in his popular engraving of the conflict. Even the color prints of the engraving created by Christian Remick — the artist Revere employed to colorize his broadside — feature British soldiers shooting into a crowd of white patriots. As one nineteenth-century black abolitionist would later put it, white Americans were not ready to acknowledge that "but for the blow struck at the right time by a black man, the United States, with all that it of right and justice boasts, might not have been an independent republic."[36]

The Boston Massacre rallied men and women across the thirteen colonies to the patriot cause. In Boston, it set the stage for the Boston Tea Party in 1773. In an open rebellion against the British Tea Act, colonists dressed as Indians boarded British ships and dumped boxes of tea into Boston harbor. The conflict escalated when Britain passed a series of laws known as the Intolerable Acts. These included the Massachusetts Government Act and the Administration of Justice Act, which curtailed the colonial government's power; the Boston Port Act, which closed Boston's port until its citizens reimbursed British officials for the tea they had destroyed; and the Quartering Act, which stationed British troops in Boston. The British hoped that this punitive legislation would isolate the Massachusetts rebels, but instead it united the American colonists in outrage. In 1774, they organized the First Continental Congress to lobby Britain for the reversal of the Intolerable Acts. The congress threatened to boycott British goods if the acts were not repealed and pledged to support Massachusetts in the event of a British attack, which was not long in coming. On April 19, 1775, the British marched on the towns of Lexington and Concord in a surprise attack designed to subdue the rebellious colony's leaders. Instead, it started a war.

Black northerners were among the patriots who rallied against the British, often joining the struggle in hopes of encouraging the colonists to reject African slavery as well as British tyranny. For instance, a free black resident of Massachusetts named Lemuel Haynes joined the Granville minutemen and fought in several battles before he fell ill. Horrified when the British invaded Lexington and Concord, the twenty-two-year-old Haynes had recently been freed from indentured servitude and saw the Battle of Lexington as a fight between "tyrants" and the "Liberty [for which] each freeman

Paul Revere, The Bloody Massacre, 1770
A man of mixed Indian and African ancestry who may have been a fugitive slave, Crispus Attucks was an unlikely hero whose race was not mentioned in most Revolutionary-era commemorations of the Boston Massacre. Most notably, Paul Revere chose to omit Attucks from his popular engraving depicting the event. The engraving captures the first casualty of the conflict, but the figure lying in the foreground is white. *Library of Congress, Prints and Photographs Division, Washington, D.C., LC-DIG-ppmsca-01657.*

strives."[37] He also wished to expand the boundaries of that freedom. Although the Declaration of Independence, issued in 1776, maintained that "all men are created equal," it did not free the slaves, an omission that inspired the studious Haynes, who became a Congregationalist minister, to write his own addendum to it later that year. Titled "Liberty Further Extended," Haynes's unpublished manuscript called for the abolition of slavery in the American colonies. (See Document Project: Black Freedom Fighters, pp. 121–27.)

As Haynes's actions illustrate, even before the Second Continental Congress met in May 1775 to organize the war effort, colonial militias mobilized all over New England, enlisting blacks as well as whites. The Massachusetts Safety Committee, formed in the summer of 1774 to protect citizens from British tyranny, had initially barred slave enlistment as "inconsistent with the principles [of freedom] that are to be supported."[38] But bans had little practical effect after the British marched on Lexington. As the redcoats approached, Peter Salem, a local slave, was freed to help defend the town. Salem went on to become one of the approximately one hundred patriots of color who served during the Battle of Bunker Hill, where he was widely credited with firing the shot that killed the unpopular British leader Major John Pitcairn.[39] Many of the Revolution's black soldiers probably entered the patriot forces on similar terms. Militia rosters across New England listed men such as "Joshua Boylston's Prince" and "Isaac Gardner's Adam," whose names suggest that they, too, had only recently been freed from slavery.[40]

LA DESTRUCTION DE LA STATUE ROYALE A NOUVELLE YORCK.

Die Zerstorung der Koniglichen Bild Saule zu Neu Yorck | *La Destruction de la Statue royale a Nouvelle Yorck*

African Americans in the Revolution

On July 9, 1776, a group of New York patriots pulled down and destroyed an equestrian statue of Britain's King George III. This French print shows one artist's attempt to depict the event. Although the image has some flaws — rather than being mounted on horseback as he was in the actual statue, for example, the king is shown standing in the print — it is significant in its portrayal of the patriots, most of whom appear to be slaves. Black northerners, free and slave, were a vital force in the patriot struggle. They hoped that in casting off British rule, the colonists would also renounce African slavery. *La Destruction de la statue royale à Nouvelle Yorck/Die Zerstorung der Koniglichen Bild Saule zu Neu Yorck, published in Paris, 1777/Library of Congress, Prints and Photographs Division, Washington, D.C., LC-USZC4-1476.*

Haynes hoped that military service would win black Americans their "*undeniable right to . . . liberty,*" and many slave combatants clearly shared his hope.[41] Slaves enlisted in large numbers after northern colonies from Rhode Island to New York passed legislation pledging to free blacks willing to serve for the duration of the conflict. Shortly before the war, the Connecticut slave Boyrereau Brinch, whose autobiography later recorded his ambivalence about fighting "to liberate freemen, my tyrants," was drafted into the Sixth Connecticut Regiment while still enslaved. He fought for five years before finally receiving his freedom.[42]

For other black northerners, military service brought immediate freedom. In Rhode Island, where slavery was entrenched, the promise of freedom prompted blacks to enlist at twice the rate of whites — despite their owners' warnings that the British would ship them off to the West Indies if they were captured. Undeterred, slaves abandoned their masters to enlist until the state began offering masters up to 120 pounds for each slave they liberated for military service. In addition to paying for slave soldiers, northern states encouraged slave enlistments by allowing owners to send slave substitutes into battle rather than fight themselves.

Black patriots were far less common in the South, where widespread opposition to slave soldiers prohibited black enlistments during the early years of the conflict. As the war began, white southerners understandably questioned slaves' loyalty to the cause. As early as 1774, slaves in Virginia had conspired to run away in groups when British troops arrived, convincing slave owners that the slaves would side with the British. "If America & Britain come to a hostile rupture," Virginian James Madison worried, "an Insurrection among the slaves may and will be promoted."[43]

Appointed commander in chief of the newly established Continental army on June 15, 1775, General George Washington shared Madison's sentiments. When he traveled to Cambridge, Massachusetts, to assume command of the patriot forces, he was horrified to find armed black men among them. He issued general orders barring their enlistment, which he renewed in December. But there is little evidence that Washington's prohibitions, which he later reversed, had a significant effect on blacks' service. Many New England troops were integrated from the start of the conflict, and after 1776 other colonies used slave soldiers to fill enlistment quotas. Only South Carolina and Georgia never mobilized their black populations.

The slaveholding colonists who resisted the use of black soldiers feared slave insurrections and were also afraid of losing their human property. As the Revolution spread south, both outcomes quickly became real possibilities. In 1775, long before the southern colonies had begun to enlist enslaved blacks, the British organized their first regiment of runaway slaves. They also encouraged runaways to join their armies throughout the conflict. In doing so, they created thousands of black **loyalists**, as those who remained loyal to the British were called. In this war, African Americans sought freedom on both sides of the conflict (Map 3.1).

Black Loyalists

Approximately fifteen thousand black loyalists served with the British. They first entered the war early at the request of Virginia's royal governor John Murray, the Earl of Dunmore, whom patriot forces had driven out in June 1775. Determined to recapture the colony, Dunmore took refuge on a British ship patrolling the waters outside Yorktown. With only three hundred men at his disposal, he desperately needed reinforcements. On November 7, he reached out to local allies by issuing what became known as **Lord Dunmore's Proclamation**. This published broadside offered freedom to all "indentured Servants, Negroes, or others, (appertaining to Rebels) . . . able and willing to bear Arms" for the British.

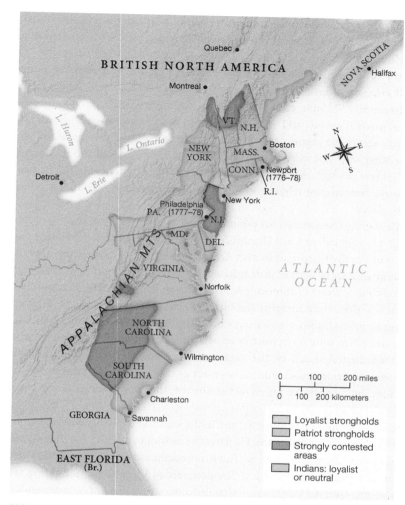

MAP 3.1   Patriots and Loyalists

The American Revolution divided the eastern seaboard's inhabitants into loyalists and patriots, whose sympathies varied from place to place. Patriots were in the majority in most of the colonies; loyalists were widely dispersed, but their strongholds were limited. These political allegiances were hard to track and shifted often, making it difficult to pinpoint the exact numbers of patriots and loyalists at any given point.

Like other British officials, Dunmore realized that many blacks would serve on whichever side would allow them to fight for their own freedom. He had begun receiving slave volunteers as early as April 1775 — many months before he issued his proclamation. He knew that by enlisting slaves, he would also deprive rebellious planters of their workers — and send some rebel soldiers scurrying home to guard their slaves.

But he still hesitated to enlist enslaved soldiers for fear of alienating loyal colonists. By November, he had no choice and issued the carefully worded proclamation, designed to recruit only slaves belonging to rebels.

But his message may have reached a larger audience. Lord Dunmore's Proclamation unleashed a massive tide of slave unrest that fundamentally reshaped the character of the war. Between late 1775 and early 1776, some eight hundred male slaves and many of their families made their way to Dunmore's floating headquarters, while thousands more fanned out across the swamplands in an effort to reach Dunmore or seize their freedom some other way. The wave of runaways disrupted slave agriculture and forced Virginia slaveholders to wage a war on two fronts: In addition to defeating the British, they had to battle armed slave rebels and devote additional manpower to patrolling their remaining slaves.

Meanwhile, Dunmore secured his position by organizing the fittest of the fugitives into a military unit called Lord Dunmore's Ethiopian Regiment — possibly the first black regiment in the history of British America. Members of the regiment were rumored to wear uniforms with sashes reading "Liberty for Slaves," although this rumor was likely false, since Dunmore could barely outfit his existing troops. The men spent much of their time foraging for supplies. They also saw battle, making up half of Dunmore's forces in his victory over the Virginia militia at Kemp's Landing on November 16, 1775, only to be nearly wiped out less than a month later when patriot forces decimated much of the regiment. Replenished with new fugitive slaves, black troops accompanied Dunmore's men as they retreated to the shores of Chesapeake Bay, but smallpox killed off many of the new recruits and their families.

Dunmore failed to hold on to Virginia, and in the summer of 1776, just as the Continental Congress began circulating the Declaration of Independence, he abandoned Virginia to join British forces in New York. But his proclamation had an important and enduring effect on patriot military policy. The prospect of Virginia slaves fighting for the British convinced General Washington that the outcome of the war now depended on "which side can arm the Negroes faster," and with his support, the congress declared all blacks eligible for service in the Continental army a week after Dunmore issued his proclamation.[44]

Lord Dunmore's Proclamation also attracted freedom-seeking black loyalists from as far away as New York and New Jersey. One was a twenty-two-year-old slave named Titus, who ran away from a farmer in Monmouth County, New Jersey, to join the Ethiopian Regiment. He was shipped out when Dunmore retreated to New York and soon ended up less than a hundred miles from his home. Undeterred, Titus joined New Jersey's loyalist troops and fought in the Battle of Monmouth County in June 1778, capturing the head of the Monmouth militia. Although he was never officially commissioned as an officer, Titus earned the name "Colonel Tye" for his successful raids. He organized his own commando unit, known as the Black Brigade, with New Jersey blacks who knew the countryside well. The brigade raided the homes of slaveholding farmers, making off with their cattle, horses, and slaves. Tye and his men turned their captives over to the British and sold the British the food and supplies that they seized. By the spring of 1780, Tye had New Jersey patriots so terrified that they prevailed on their governor to declare martial law — to little avail. Tye's men continued to terrorize New Jersey until the fall of that year, when Tye died after being wounded in battle.

Lord Dunmore's Proclamation had its most significant impact in the South. Most of the blacks who served with loyalist forces were southerners, and the proclamation also triggered a mass exodus of fugitive slaves, who escaped their plantations by crossing British lines. Historians estimate that 80,000 to 100,000 southern slaves fled their masters during the Revolution. Not all remained with the British, however. Some freed themselves and headed to places where they were likely to remain free, such as cities and towns with large free black populations or frontier areas where slavery had yet to take hold. Moreover, the British did not offer shelter to all the runaways who crossed their lines. British officers were obliged to return any fugitives who had escaped from loyalist owners, and some British officers sold slaves who had escaped from patriot owners.

Despite such risks, the chance to find freedom with the British appealed to African Americans throughout the war. Most refugees did not end up in British uniforms, because British commanders had little time to train new troops and were often unable to supply their black volunteers with food and shelter, let alone arms. So they put the refugees to work foraging for food and supplies. Although such duties frequently required the fugitives to carry arms and fight any patriots they encountered, they did so without recognition or military pay. Refugees worked behind the lines as well, building fortifications, transporting munitions, cooking for troops, and doing their laundry. British commanders also employed refugees as domestic servants, often supplying their officers with an entire staff of black domestics.

Black refugees were entitled to a "certificate of freedom" for their work but received few other benefits and often had to provide food and shelter for themselves. They also faced other dangers. Not only were food and clean water often in short supply, but disease remained endemic in the British camps. Thousands escaped slavery only to die of smallpox and what contemporaries called "camp fever," which was likely typhus. Despite these harrowing conditions, many African Americans took their chances with the British, who offered them their only opportunity to achieve freedom.

The service of these runaways was crucial to Britain's war effort and helped reshape British military strategy — and not a moment too soon. In 1778, after three years' worth of military action in the North, the British had yet to win a decisive victory. Worse still for the British, after patriot forces defeated General John Burgoyne's army at Saratoga, New York, in 1777, the French entered the war on the side of the Americans, raising fears that Spain would join their cause as well. France and Spain were Britain's chief imperial rivals, and both countries saw the American rebellion as a chance to challenge Britain's power in America and the Caribbean. With an increasingly international war now under way, Britain's military resources were overextended. Even the mighty British navy could not defend the Caribbean as long as Britain devoted most of its military resources to subduing the die-hard patriots.

Slaves, Soldiers, and the Outcome of the Revolution

As the Revolutionary War dragged on, Britain's decision to free slaves in exchange for service angered slave owners and weakened loyalist support in the South. When the British abandoned the American colonies in defeat, they also abandoned many black allies who had fought valiantly in hopes of gaining their freedom. The American Revolution set the northern states on a path to ending slavery — immediately (1777) in some states and more gradually in others, until it was almost entirely eliminated by the 1820s. The free black population of both the North and the Chesapeake increased significantly throughout this period. Only elsewhere in the South did slavery remain entrenched.

American Victory, British Defeat

Toward the end of 1778, the British Parliament adopted a new battle plan known as the **southern strategy**. Its goal was to crush the rebellion by retaking the South, which was home to far more loyalists than the Northeast and would therefore, the British hoped, be far easier to conquer. The plan depended partly on enlisting help from the region's slaves, whose loyalties lay with the British rather than the patriots. Moving the war south also allowed the British to monitor French and Spanish activities in the Caribbean, as well as to blockade southern ports to prevent the delivery of French aid to the patriots.

Britain's southern strategy initially paid off. British troops captured Savannah in 1778 and Charleston in 1779. Black loyalists were crucial to their efforts from the start. In Georgia, a black sailor named Samson guided the British fleet over shoals at the mouth of the Savannah River. When British troops disembarked, they discovered that the patriots had destroyed a bridge leading to the city and guarded the only remaining road. An elderly slave named Quamino Dolly approached a lieutenant colonel with his plans for an alternative approach and showed troops a route through a nearby swamp, which allowed the British to stage a surprise attack and capture Savannah.

Sir Henry Clinton, who became commander in chief of the British forces later that year, was eager to enlist similar slave support. In June 1779, as he prepared for an assault on Charleston, he issued the Philipsburg Proclamation. It expanded Lord Dunmore's Proclamation by promising to free all slaves willing to serve in any capacity, rather than just those who joined the fighting. It also recognized the growing importance of African American patriot combatants by declaring that any blacks found serving the patriots would be sold for the benefit of the crown.

In the end, however, Britain's southern strategy failed. The vast geographic scope of the southern states ensured that the British would never have enough manpower to defend the areas they conquered, while the loyalist support they had hoped for failed to materialize. Instead of finding allies among the former colonists, the British were thwarted by determined opposition from patriot forces. In addition, the embattled new nation had no crucial center of power that British forces could capture and subdue. Even though the British twice seized Philadelphia, the new nation's original capital, they could not derail the Americans.

Moreover, the growing presence of black soldiers in the Continental army often undermined British attempts to use the patriots' own slaves against them. In the summer of 1781, for example, a black patriot spy double-crossed the British by infiltrating their headquarters on behalf of the Marquis de Lafayette, a French volunteer who became a general in George Washington's army. Lafayette was desperate to drive the British general Charles Cornwallis out of Virginia and had been trying for months, without success, to gain advance information about his troop movements. He finally succeeded when he dispatched an ex-slave named James Armistead, who easily infiltrated Cornwallis's camp at Yorktown by posing as a refugee looking for work. Armistead won the trust of Cornwallis, who invited him to spy for the British, at which point Armistead became a double agent. He supplied true information to the Americans and false information to the British, remaining undiscovered until the day the defeated Cornwallis encountered Armistead in Lafayette's camp and realized that he had been duped.

Still more fatal to Britain's southern strategy was the distinctly mixed success of the British policy of freeing the rebels' slaves. Although the British desperately needed manpower, by enlisting slave support, both Dunmore and Clinton eroded their loyalist support in the South and stiffened the resolve of southern patriots. Many southerners were ambivalent about independence when the fighting began, but after Dunmore issued his proclamation, the British never commanded the widespread southern support they envisioned. Clinton's Philipsburg Proclamation only compounded the problem. In the Carolinas and Georgia especially, where most whites owned slaves, loyalists were regarded as traitors to public safety and patriots were as dedicated to protecting slavery as they were to achieving independence. With support for the war wavering at home, the British abandoned America to the patriots rather than continue the fight. Cornwallis's 1781 surrender at Yorktown was the beginning of the war's end and set the stage for a military retreat that largely devastated Britain's black allies.

The Fate of Black Loyalists

At the siege of Yorktown, Britain's first major defeat, Cornwallis provided no protection for the thousands of African Americans serving in his forces. Under a sustained assault from French and American forces that began in late September 1781, his headquarters were crowded, ravaged by smallpox, and cut off from British supply lines.

Black Patriots and Loyalists

African Americans served valiantly on both sides of the Revolution, often allying themselves with the side they felt provided the best opportunity for securing their own freedom. The black soldier-musician in the image on the right is a member of a French expeditionary corps that fought with the patriots. The woodcutter in the image below is a loyalist who sought refuge in Canada after the war. When the British retreated, black loyalists scrambled to avoid reenslavement. Many resettled in British colonies in Canada, Jamaica, the Bahamas, South Africa, and Australia.

Right: Gouache by Nicolas Hoffmann, 1780/The Granger Collection, New York; Below: William Booth, A Black Wood Cutter at Shelburne, 1788. Library and Archives Canada/W. H. Coverdale Collection of Canadiana/ e008438313.

Desperately short of food by mid-October, Cornwallis first slaughtered his horses to prevent them from starving and then issued orders expelling his African American allies to fend for themselves. "It is not to be done," mourned the senior British officer who took the orders and was all too aware that the refugees would be reenslaved. "We drove back to the enemy all of our black friends," another soldier later reflected. "We had used them to good advantage and set them free and now, with fear and trembling they had to face the reward of their cruel masters."[45] The British surrendered a week later, evacuating their troops and leaving their black allies behind. As the British boarded their boats, American troops patrolled the banks of the York River to ensure that no African Americans escaped.

Other loyalist troops held their positions as late as 1783. In 1782, Lord Dunmore and other "fight-to-the-end" generals who still hoped to reverse the Yorktown defeat made desperate appeals for ten thousand black troops. But Britain's military leaders remained unwilling to make full use of their black allies, even as defeat stared them in the face. Parliament had never intended to abolish American slavery — or to compromise Britain's multimillion-dollar investment in the slave trade and its West Indian sugar colonies. Profits from the slave trade and the export of manufactured goods to Britain's slave colonies were crucial to Britain's prosperity and economic growth during the eighteenth century. British statesman Edmund Burke warned Parliament that freeing the slaves to fight might unleash a conflict even more ruinous than the American bid for independence. For example, as of 1775 the British West Indies was home to 450,000 slaves, who might revolt if given a chance to do so. Once slaves were armed, Burke maintained, they would keep fighting until they "made themselves masters of the houses, goods, wives, and daughters of their murdered lords."[46] Unable to win the war and unwilling to jeopardize British investments, the House of Commons voted to begin peace talks with the former colonists in the spring of 1782.

The retreat of the British dealt a cruel blow to their black allies. The Royal Navy eventually managed to evacuate fifteen thousand black loyalists, whom they transported to England or resettled in Britain's remaining colonies in Canada, Jamaica, the Bahamas, South Africa, and Australia. But at least as many were left behind. In Charleston, the navy had to ship out thousands of slaves belonging to white loyalists — who were unwilling to leave their human property behind — and at the same time find room for the ex-slaves whose service entitled them to freedom.

Unable to accommodate all the refugees, the British left behind the families of many slave allies, who faced reenslavement. As the British fleet filled up, African Americans dove into Charleston harbor and swam out to longboats loading the navy's vessels in desperate hopes of securing a berth. Most were beaten back with cutlasses by the British soldiers who manned the boats. Some clung to the boats until their fingers were sliced off their hands. Even the blacks who made it aboard faced an uncertain future. Many former slaves were resold into slavery in Jamaica and other British colonies, while some free fugitives found themselves claimed as property by unscrupulous British soldiers and subject to reenslavement or sale.

For most refugees, the prospect of returning to slavery in the South was more fearsome than the uncertainties of relocation. When the British evacuation of New York in 1783 inspired rumors that the slaves who fought with the British would be returned to their masters, ex-slaves were terrified. As Boston King, a fugitive slave from South Carolina who fought with the British in New York, later recalled, "Many of the slaves had very cruel masters, so that the thoughts of returning home with them embittered life to us. For some days, we lost our appetite for food, and sleep departed from our eyes."[47] To King's great relief, loyalists in New York offered more generous shelter than their southern counterparts: Between three thousand and four thousand blacks accompanied the British troops when they left. (See Document Project: Black Freedom Fighters, pp. 121–27.)

Other black loyalists continued to defend their territory in the low-country swamps as late as 1786 — three years after the Treaty of Paris, the agreement that formally ended the war and recognized the United States. On Bear Creek, which runs through the Savannah River marshes that once divided South Carolina and Georgia along the coast, fugitive slaves built a fortified village one mile long and four hundred feet wide. From there, they raided nearby plantations in both states until May 1789, when the South Carolina governor dispatched a coalition of troops from South Carolina and Georgia, as well as some Catawba Indians, to destroy the settlement. Vanquished after a four-day battle, the Bear Creek settlers, who called themselves "the King of England's Soldiers," were branded a gang of common criminals by the governor.[48]

Closer to Freedom

Despite the crushing losses suffered by black loyalists, the American Revolution brought African Americans closer to freedom. Most of the five thousand blacks who served among the American forces ended up free, although some struggled to achieve their freedom. James Armistead, the double agent who spied for Lafayette, was briefly reenslaved after the British left. Despite supplying invaluable intelligence, he never held an official position in the patriot forces and did not qualify for manumission. He was not freed until 1786, after Lafayette wrote a letter of commendation for him that he used to secure his freedom. Black patriots on the muster rolls were not generally subject to reenslavement, even in the southern states — with the notable exception of Virginia, where some slaveholders tried to retain the slave substitutes who had fought for them during the war. This caused a public outcry and inspired a 1783 legislative decree that declared the actions of such slaveholders "contrary to principles of justice and to their own solemn promise" and directed the state's attorney general to seek manumission for any enslaved former soldiers.[49]

Black veterans formed only part of the greatly enlarged free black community that emerged in the decades following the war. Concentrated largely in the North and the Upper South, free blacks, who had numbered only a few thousand in 1760, reached 60,000 in 1790 and 110,000 in 1800 (Map 3.2). These remarkable increases reflect a

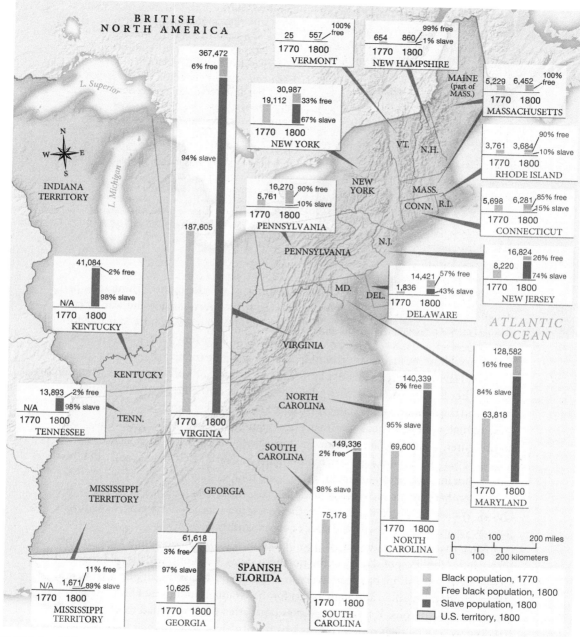

MAP 3.2 **African Americans across the Developing Nation, 1770 and 1800**

This map illustrates the varying regional distribution of the new nation's black population. The gold bars show each state's black population in 1770. The red and pink bars show each state's slave population and free black population in 1800. The bar graphs underscore the rapid expansion of the slave populations in the southern states during these years, as well as the increasing predominance of free blacks in the North.

Freedom Suits

After suffering ongoing physical abuse as a slave, Mum Bett, depicted here, worked with lawyer Theodore Sedgwick to win her freedom in a 1781 court case. Between 1781 and 1783, her case served as a precedent for a series of cases involving a slave named Quock Walker. Adjudicated by the Massachusetts Supreme Court in 1783, the final Quock Walker case ruled that slavery was incompatible with the state's new constitution.

Portrait of Elizabeth "Mumbet" Freeman (c. 1742–1829), watercolor on ivory, Sedgwick, Susan Anne Livingston Ridley III (f. 1811)/© Massachusetts Historical Society, Boston, MA, USA/Bridgeman Images.

number of developments. Thousands had seized their liberty during the war by running away or pursuing successful freedom suits. In 1780, Mum Bett, a slave in Sheffield, Massachusetts, filed a suit that helped push her state toward abandoning slavery for good. Having endured years of physical abuse at the hands of her master's wife, she sued for her freedom after hearing public discussions of the Declaration of Independence and the Massachusetts state constitution. "I heard that paper read yesterday that says, all men are born equal, and that every man has a right to freedom. I am not a dumb critter; won't the law give me my freedom?" Bett asked a local lawyer named Theodore Sedgwick, who agreed to represent her in court.[50] Bett's successful suit transformed her into Elizabeth Freeman, a name she took as a symbol of her liberty. Three years later, her lawsuit provided a precedent for the state's final freedom suit — the Quock Walker case of 1783, in which the Massachusetts Supreme Court ruled that slavery was incompatible with the state's new constitution.

After the war, the number of free blacks in the new nation increased steadily through the abolition of slavery in the northern states. Vermont, which had never had a large slave population, banned slavery in 1777. Pennsylvania began planning to end slavery shortly thereafter, although its Act for the Gradual Abolition of Slavery of 1780 was far from generous. It freed only slaves born after 1780, who had to pay for their freedom by serving their owners for the first twenty-eight years of their lives. Still, this groundbreaking law advanced the cause of freedom in the new nation and set the stage for gradual abolition in other northern states, which was largely complete by the 1820s.

The free black population in the South also increased dramatically, largely as a result of manumissions in the Upper South between the 1750s and 1790s. The Great

Awakening, combined with antislavery sentiments inspired by the American Revolution, prompted slaveholders across the region to free large numbers of slaves. American Quakers abandoned slavery during this period, and they encouraged non-Quakers to do so as well. Manumissions were also facilitated by the declining profitability of plantation agriculture in the Chesapeake during the second half of the eighteenth century, which reduced the profits to be gained from slave labor. Whereas free blacks had constituted a tiny percentage of the region's black population for much of the century, by the 1790s about 10 percent of Chesapeake blacks were free. Only in the Lower South did free blacks remain a rarity (see Map 3.2).

Free black communities across the nation gained strength after the Revolution. Although free blacks continued to be persecuted in the South, their swelling numbers provided more allies and stronger claims to a status separate from that of their enslaved brethren. In the North, the abolition of slavery allowed blacks to live in free territory for the first time in American history. To be sure, newly freed blacks were poor and subject to racial discrimination, but once emancipated, they could form autonomous families and communities for the first time in their history.

The Revolution was only one step toward black freedom, however. The majority of African Americans were still permanently enslaved in regions where no end to slavery was in sight. African American slaves constituted 92 percent of the nation's black population in 1790. The slave population continued to increase in the decades that followed due to slave imports and high rates of reproduction. By the start of the Civil War in 1861, the United States would be home to millions of slaves.

CONCLUSION

The American Revolution's Mixed Results for Blacks

The American Revolution was a watershed in African American history, but it produced mixed results for blacks. On one hand, the gradual demise of slavery across the northern states and the expansion of black freedom in the Upper South marked a great victory for blacks in these regions. Few white Americans were willing to make the abolition of slavery a central goal, but black northerners sought to make the American rebellion against British rule an end to the tyranny of slavery as well, and they were largely successful in doing so — at least in the North. On the other hand, the Revolution's outcome was far less rewarding for black southerners, who faced longer odds and gained much less ground. Most sided with the loyalists, suffering great hardships during the war for little compensation. Some achieved freedom by enlisting with the patriots, escaping to the North, or leaving the country with the British, but the majority remained trapped in a region still deeply committed to slavery.

African Americans continued to fight for freedom long after the war ended. Among slaves, freedom remained a goal even as plantation slavery expanded across the South. Among free blacks, the persistence of southern slavery marked the limits of the freedom that they had achieved and the battles that still lay ahead. Many of their friends, relatives, and countrymen remained enslaved, and in the years to come, free blacks would struggle to emancipate their enslaved brothers and sisters, while also fighting to fully secure their own freedom.

In these struggles, blacks throughout America would continue to embrace the egalitarian principles of both the Great Awakening and the patriot cause. In the years to come, slaves and free blacks continued to join evangelical churches and embrace an Afro-Christian faith that stressed the equality of all men and women before God. Free black communities established their own churches, which became central to the anti-slavery movement that took shape among northern free blacks. So, too, did the democratic principles of the American Revolution, as post-Revolutionary African American leaders stressed that their "fathers fought, bled and died for liberty which neither they nor their children have yet received."[51]

CHAPTER 3 REVIEW

KEY TERMS

Negro Election Day p. 93

conjure p. 94

Gullah p. 96

Great Awakening p. 96

New Lights p. 96

freedom suits p. 102

Somerset case (1772) p. 103

habeas corpus p. 103

loyalists p. 108

Lord Dunmore's Proclamation (1775) p. 108

southern strategy p. 112

REVIEW QUESTIONS

1. What role did religion — both traditional West African beliefs and practices and Christianity — play in the shaping of an African American culture during the eighteenth century?

2. How did African Americans on both the patriot and loyalist sides use the Revolution to pursue and secure their own freedom? How did they draw on the conflict's ideology to do so? Choose several examples from the chapter to support your argument.

3. Overall, how would you assess African Americans' gains and losses during the Revolutionary era? Consider the outcomes for patriots and loyalists, northerners and southerners, and free blacks and slaves. Who benefited the most and the least? What factors were responsible for these results?

4. How did African Americans' participation on both sides of the war change its course? How might the progression or outcome of the conflict have been different had blacks been barred from service?

Black Freedom Fighters

African Americans fought for their own freedom with the pen and the sword during the American Revolution. Black soldiers joined both the patriot and loyalist forces, and both free blacks and slaves were drawn into the natural rights debates engendered by the Revolution. Slaves who petitioned for freedom in patriot courts articulated claims to the "Natural and Unaliable [inalienable] Right to that freedom which the Grat Parent of the Unavers hath Bestowed equalley on all menkind," but black loyalists also fought for freedom.[52] The following documents present black perspectives from both sides of the conflict. They include writings by the poet Phillis Wheatley and the free black soldier Lemuel Haynes, both of whom supported the patriots; an excerpt from the memoirs of Boston King, a black loyalist; and artwork depicting Revolutionary-era African American soldiers.

Born around 1753 and freed in 1773, the poet Phillis Wheatley was still very young when the war was beginning to take shape, but she kept a close eye on the Revolution's ideological conflicts. In 1772, a year before she was emancipated, she wrote a poem addressed to King George's secretary of state for North America, the Earl of Dartmouth, in which she supported the patriot cause while also mourning the freedom that blacks had not yet won. Two year later, she expressed similar sentiments as a free woman in a letter written to the Indian leader Samson Occom. Both pieces are included here.

Wheatley's compositions are followed by an essay by Lemuel Haynes, a free black who was born in Connecticut and raised in Massachusetts and who served with both the minutemen and the Continental army. Although he fought with the patriots, Haynes was dissatisfied with the new nation's political principles and called for Americans to extend liberty to blacks as well as whites.

A slave in South Carolina when the British invaded Charleston, Boston King had a very different perspective on the Revolution than either Wheatley or Haynes. He was a discontented slave whose only chance of liberty lay in joining the English forces. His memoirs, written nearly twenty years after the Revolution, describes his wartime thoughts and experiences.

Sketched by a French officer who fought with the patriots, the image *Soldiers in Uniform* illustrates the American opponents that King might have confronted, including French soldiers, former slaves, state militiamen, and frontier fighters, while the painting *The Death of Major Peirson* depicts a black loyalist fighting among British forces.

Phillis Wheatley | *A Poem to the Earl of Dartmouth, 1772*

Born in Gambia, PHILLIS WHEATLEY (c. 1753–1784) was only seven or eight years old when she was sold into slavery. Her masters encouraged her to learn how to read and write and were so impressed by her intelligence that they permitted her to devote her time largely to her education and to develop her gift for poetry. Wheatley wrote and published her first poems as a teenager, attracting attention and controversy as an early black author who spoke on behalf of a people whom many whites saw as illiterate by nature. What was Wheatley trying to accomplish with this poem, addressed to Britain's secretary of state for North America? How does she go about it in the poem?

TO THE RIGHT HONORABLE WILLIAM, EARL OF DARTMOUTH.
His Majesty's Principal Secretary of State for North America, etc.

Hail, happy day, when smiling like the morn,
Fair Freedom *rose New England to adorn;*
The northern clime beneath her genial ray,
Dartmouth *congratulates thy blissful sway;*
Elate with hope her race no longer mourns,
Each soul expands, each grateful bosom burns,
While in thine hand with pleasure we behold
The silken reins, and Freedom's charms unfold.
Long lost to realms beneath the northern skies
She shines supreme, while hated faction dies;
Soon as appeared the Goddess long desir'd,
Sick at the view, she languish'd and expir'd;
Thus from the splendor of the morning light
The owl in sadness seeks the caves of night.

No more America, *in mournful strain*
Of wrongs, and grievance unredress'd complain,
No longer shall thou dread the iron chain,
Which wanton Tyranny with lawless hand
Had made, and with it meant to enslave the land.
Should you, my lord, while you peruse my song,

Wonder from whence my love of Freedom *sprung,*
Whence flow these wishes for the common good,
By feeling hearts alone best understood,
I, young in life, by seeming cruel fate
Was snatch'd from Afric's fancy'd happy seat;
What pangs excruciatingly must molest,
What sorrows labour in my parent's breast?
Steel'd was that soul and by no misery mov'd
That from a father seized his babe belov'd;
Such, such my case. And can I then but pray
Others may never feel tyrannic sway?

For favors past, great Sir, our thanks are due,
And thee we ask thy favors to renew,
Since in thy pow'r, as in thy will before,
To sooth the griefs, which thou didst once deplore.
May heav'nly grace the sacred sanction give
To all thy works, and thou forever live
Not only on the wings of fleeting Fame,
Though praise immortal crowns the patriot's name,
But to conduct to heav'n's refulgent fane
May fiery coursers sweep th' etherial plain,
And bear thee upwards to the blest abode,
Where, like the prophet, thou shalt find thy God.

SOURCE: Phillis Wheatley, *Poems on Various Subjects, Religious and Moral* (1773; repr., Denver: W. H. Lawrence, 1887), 66–68.

Phillis Wheatley | *Letter to the Reverend Samson Occom, 1774*

PHILLIS WHEATLEY's letter to the Reverend Samson Occom, a Mohegan Indian and ordained minister with whom she had a correspondence, was in response to a piece that Occom had written in condemnation of Christian ministers who owned slaves. It was first printed in the *Connecticut Gazette* on March 11, 1774. What sort of a future does Wheatley foresee for slavery in the letter? What justifications does she offer for her views?

Boston, February 11th, 1774.

Rever'd & Honoured Sir,

I this day received your kind obliging epistle, and am greatly satisfied with your reasons respecting the Negroes, and think highly reasonable what you offer in vindication of their natural

SOURCE: *Connecticut Gazette*, March 11, 1774, 188.

rights. Those that invade them cannot be insensible that the divine light is insensibly chasing away the thick darkness which broods over the land of Africa, and the chaos which has reigned so long is converting into beautiful order, and reveals more and more clearly the glorious dispensation of civil and religious liberty, which are so inseparably united, that there is little or no enjoyment of one without the other; otherwise the Israelites had been less solicitous for their freedom from Egyptian slavery. I do not say they would have been contented without it — by no means: for in every human breast God has implanted a principle which we call, love of freedom. It is impatient of oppression, and pants for deliverance; and, by the leave of our modern Egyptians, I will assert that the principle lives in us — God grant deliverance in his own way and time, and get him honour upon all those whose avarice compels them to countenance and help forward the calamities of their fellow creatures. This I desire not for the hurt, but to convince them of the strange absurdities of their conduct whose words and actions are so diametrically opposite. How well the cry of liberty and the reverse disposition for the exercise of oppressive power over others agree, I humbly think it does not require the penetration of a philosopher to determine.

Lemuel Haynes | *Liberty Further Extended, 1776*

Born in Connecticut, LEMUEL HAYNES (1753–1833) was abandoned by his white mother and African father. He grew up in Massachusetts, where he was bound out as an indentured servant at the age of six months. He joined the Granville minutemen and fought with patriot forces until 1776, when he caught typhus and had to return home. That year, he wrote the following unpublished and recently discovered manuscript. Probably composed shortly after the publication of the Declaration of Independence, it expands on that document by calling for an antislavery revolution. Haynes was self-educated and became ordained as a Congregationalist minister. How does he use the principles of the Declaration of Independence to argue his point here?

We hold these truths to be self-Evident, that all men are created Equal, that they are Endowed By their Creator with Ceartain unalienable rights, that among these are Life, Liberty, and the pursuit of happyness.

Congress.

The Preface [of the Declaration of Independence]. As *tyrony* had its Origin from the infernal regions: so it is the Deuty, and honner of Every son of freedom to repel her first motions. But while we are Engaged in the important struggle, it cannot Be tho't impertiment for us to turn one Eye into our own Breast, for a little moment, and See, whether thro' some inadvertency, or a self-contracted Spirit, we Do not find the monster Lurking in our own Bosom; that now while we are inspir'd with so noble a Spirit and Becoming Zeal, we may Be Disposed to tear her from us. If the following would produce such an Effect the auther should rejoice. . . .

Liberty, & freedom, is an innate principle, which is unmovebly placed in the human Species; and to see a man aspire after it, is not Enigmatical, seeing he acts no ways incompatible with his own Nature; consequently, he that would infring upon a mans Liberty may reasonably Expect to meet with oposition, seeing the Defendant cannot Comply to Non-resistance, unless he Counter-acts the very Laws of nature.

Liberty is a Jewel which was handed Down to man from the cabinet of heaven, and is Coaeval [originated at the same time] with his Existance.

SOURCE: Ruth Bogin, "'Liberty Further Extended': A 1776 Antislavery Manuscript by Lemuel Haynes," *William and Mary Quarterly*, 3rd ser., 40, no. 1 (1983): 94–96.

And as it proceed from the Supreme Legislature of the univers, so it is he which hath a sole right to take away; therefore, he that would take away a mans Liberty assumes a prerogative that Belongs to another, and acts out of his own domain.

One man may bost a superorety above another in point of Natural previledg; yet if he can produse no convincive arguments in vindication of this preheeminence his hypothesis is to Be Suspected. To affirm, that an Englishman has a right to his Liberty, is a truth which has Been so clearly Evinced, Especially of Late, that to spend time in illustrating this, would be But Superfluous tautology. But I query, whether Liberty is so contracted a principle as to be Confin'd to any nation under Heaven; nay, I think it not hyperbolical to affirm, that Even an african, has Equally as good a right to his Liberty in common with Englishmen.

I know that those that are concerned in the Slave-trade, Do pretend to Bring arguments in vindication of their practise; yet if we give them a candid Examination, we shall find them (Even those of the most cogent kind) to be Essencially Deficient. We live in a day wherein *Liberty & freedom* is the subject of many millions Concern; and the important Struggle hath alread caused great Effusion of Blood; men seem to manifest the most sanguine resolution not to Let their natural rights go without their Lives go with them; a resolution, one would think Every one that has the Least Love to his country, or futer posterity, would fully confide in, yet while we are

so zelous to maintain, and foster our own invaded rights, it cannot be tho't impertinent for us Candidly to reflect on our own conduct, and I doubt not But that we shall find that subsisting in the midst of us, that may with propriety be stiled *Opression*, nay, much greater opression, than that which Englishmen seem so much to spurn at. I mean an oppression which they, themselves, impose upon others. . . .

. . . There is Not the Least precept, or practise, in the Sacred Scriptures, that constitutes a Black man a Slave, any more than a white one.

Shall a mans Couler Be the Decisive Criterion whereby to Judg of his natural right? or Becaus a man is not of the same couler with his Neighbour, shall he Be Deprived of those things that Distuingsheth [Distinguisheth] him from the Beasts of the field?

I would ask, whence is it that an Englishman is so far Distinguished from an Affrican in point of Natural privilege? Did he recieve it in his origenal constitution? or By Some Subsequent grant? Or Does he Bost of some hygher Descent that gives him this pre-heminance? for my part I can find no such revelation. It is a Lamantable consequence of the fall, that mankind, have an insatiable thurst after Superorety one over another: So that however common or prevalent the practise may be, it Does not amount, Even to a Surcomstance, that the practise is ~~Legal~~° warrentable.

° The strikethrough is part of the original document.

Jean Baptiste Antoine de Verger | *Soldiers in Uniform, 1781*

The following watercolor sketch by French sub-lieutenant JEAN BAPTISTE ANTOINE DE VERGER (1762–1851) documents the diversity of the troops in George Washington's colonial forces at the siege of Yorktown. It depicts (left to right) a black soldier of the First Rhode Island Regiment, a New England militiaman, a frontier rifleman, and a French officer. Why do you think de Verger chose to sketch this group of soldiers? Based on your reading of the chapter, how common do you think it was for an African American to serve alongside a white soldier?

Jean Baptiste Antoine de Verger (1762–1851)/Brown University Library, Providence, Rhode Island, USA/Bridgeman Images.

Boston King | *Memoirs of a Black Loyalist, 1798*

Born on a plantation near Charleston, South Carolina, BOSTON KING (c. 1760–1802) joined the loyalists rather than return to the carpenter to whom his master had apprenticed him and who beat him brutally. The following excerpt describes King's experiences with British and American forces in South Carolina.

To escape [my master's] cruelty, I determined to go to Charles-Town, and throw myself into the hands of the English. They received me readily, and I began to feel the happiness of liberty, of which I knew nothing before, altho' I was much grieved at first, to be obliged to leave my friends, and reside among strangers. In this situation

SOURCE: "Memoirs of the Life of Boston King, a Black Preacher," *Methodist Magazine*, March 1798, 107–8.

I was seized with the small-pox, and suffered great hardships; for all the Blacks affected with that disease, were ordered to be carried a mile from the camp, lest the soldiers should be infected, and disabled from marching. This was a grievous circumstance to me and many others. We lay sometimes a whole day without any thing to eat or drink; but Providence sent a man, who belonged to the York volunteers whom I was acquainted with, to my relief. He brought me such things as I stood in need of; and by the blessing of the Lord I began to recover.

By this time, the English left the place; but as I was unable to march with the army, I expected to be taken by the enemy. However when they came, and understood that we were ill of the small-pox, they precipitately left us for fear of the infection. Two days after, the waggons were sent to convey us to the English Army, and we were put into a little cottage, (being 25 in number) about a quarter of a mile from the Hospital.

Being recovered, I marched with the army to Chamblem [Camden, New Jersey]. . . . Upon returning to the camp, to my great astonishment, I found all the English were gone, and had left only a few [loyalist] militia. I felt my mind greatly alarmed, but Captain Lewes, who commanded the militia, said, "You need not be uneasy, for you will see your regiment before 7 o'clock to-night." This satisfied me for the present, and in two hours we set off. As we were on the march, the Captain asked, "How will you like me to be your master?" I answered that I was Captain Grey's servant. "Yes," said he; "but I expect they are all taken prisoners before now; and I have been long enough in the English service, and am determined to leave them." These words roused my indignation, and I spoke some sharp things to him. But he calmly replied, "If you do not behave well, I will put you in irons, and give you a dozen stripes every morning." I now perceived that my case was desperate, and that I had nothing to trust to, but to wait the first opportunity for making my escape. The next morning, I was sent with a little boy over the river to an island to fetch the Captain some horses. When we came to the Island we found about fifty of the English horses, that Captain Lewes had stolen from them at different times while they were at Rockmount [Rocky Mount]. Upon our return to the Captain with the horses we were sent for, he immediately set off by himself. I stayed till about 10 o'clock and then resolved to go to the English army.

John Singleton Copley | *The Death of Major Peirson, 1782–1784*

Massachusetts loyalist JOHN SINGLETON COPLEY (1738–1815) included a black loyalist soldier in his painting *The Death of Major Peirson*, which portrays the death of fellow loyalist Major Francis Peirson, who was killed at the Battle of Jersey in the Channel Islands. A British island off the coast of Normandy, Jersey was far from the Revolution's main theater of operations, but it became part of the conflict in 1781, when France invaded the island in the hope of limiting the British naval threat to French and American shipping. France failed to gain control of Jersey, which was defended by loyalist forces led by Peirson. In the painting, the death of Peirson, a British army officer who served in the Revolutionary War, is avenged by his servant Pompey, an armed black loyalist. Whether or not Pompey actually existed is not known, but Copley's painting is perhaps the only Revolutionary-era portrait of a black loyalist. The black figure wears the colors of the Royal Ethiopian Regiment organized by Lord Dunmore in Virginia, suggesting that Copley imagined him as one of the African American loyalists evacuated by British forces.

Detail, The Death of Major Peirson, *1782–1784, by John Singleton Copley (1738–1815)/Universal Images Group/Getty Images.*

QUESTIONS FOR ANALYSIS

1. What do these documents reveal about their authors' hopes for the war's outcome?

2. What role does religion play in the antislavery arguments made by Wheatley and Haynes?

3. What actions did King take to secure and preserve his own freedom?

4. Compare and contrast the various historical images of soldiers featured in this document set. Can black patriots or black loyalists be associated with any specific type of imagery?

NOTES

1. Daniel Horsmanden, *The New York Conspiracy, or a History of the Negro Plot, with the Journal of the Proceedings against the Conspirators at New-York in the Years 1741–2* (New York: Southwick and Pelsue, 1810), 181.
2. Ibid., 28, 155, 160, 161.
3. Quoted in Jill Lepore, *New York Burning: Liberty, Slavery, and Conspiracy in Eighteenth-Century Manhattan* (New York: Knopf, 2005), 50, 51.
4. Leopold S. Launitz-Schurer Jr., "Slave Resistance in Colonial New York: An Interpretation of Daniel Horsmanden's New York Conspiracy," *Phylon* 41, no. 2 (1980): 137–52.
5. Marcus Rediker, "A Motley Crew of Rebels: Sailors, Slaves, and the Coming of the American Revolution," in *The Transforming Hand of Revolution: Reconsidering the American Revolution as a Social Movement*, ed. Ronald Hoffman and Peter J. Albert (Charlottesville: University Press of Virginia, 1995), 155.
6. Quoted in Thelma Wills Foote, *Black and White Manhattan: The History of Racial Formation in Colonial New York City* (New York: Oxford University Press, 2004), 46.
7. Quoted in Gary B. Nash and Jean R. Soderlund, *Freedom by Degrees: Emancipation in Pennsylvania and Its Aftermath* (New York: Oxford University Press, 1991), xii.
8. Leslie M. Harris, *In the Shadow of Slavery: African Americans in New York City, 1626–1863* (Chicago: University of Chicago Press, 2003), 47.
9. Quoted in Philip D. Morgan, *Slave Counterpoint: Black Culture in the Eighteenth-Century Chesapeake and Lowcountry* (Chapel Hill: University of North Carolina Press, 1998), 490.
10. Quoted in William Dillon Piersen, *Black Yankees: The Development of an Afro-American Subculture in Eighteenth-Century New England* (Amherst: University of Massachusetts Press, 1988), 121.
11. Quoted ibid., 77.
12. Quoted in Morgan, *Slave Counterpoint*, 572.
13. Morgan, *Slave Counterpoint*, 567.
14. Quoted in Thomas S. Kidd, *The Great Awakening: The Roots of Evangelical Christianity in Colonial America* (New Haven: Yale University Press, 2007), 215–16.
15. Charles Chauncy, *Seasonable Thoughts on the State of Religion in New-England* (Boston: Rogers and Fowle, 1743), 226.
16. Mukhtar Ali Isani, "Phillis Wheatley in London: An Unpublished Letter to David Wooster," *American Literature* 51, no. 2 (1979): 257.
17. James Albert Ukawsaw Gronniosaw, *A Narrative of the Most Remarkable Particulars in the Life of James Albert Ukawsaw Gronniosaw, An African Prince, as Related by Himself* (Bath: Printed by W. Gye, 1770), 12.
18. Quoted in Timothy L. Hall, *American Religious Leaders* (New York: Facts on File, 2003), 137.
19. Quoted in Stephen J. Stein, "George Whitefield on Slavery: Some New Evidence," *Church History* 42, no. 2 (1973): 243–56.
20. George Whitefield, *The Works of the Reverend George Whitefield, M.A.* (London: printed for Edward and Charles Dilly, 1771), 4:38.
21. Quoted in Allan Gallay, "The Origins of Slaveholders' Paternalism: George Whitefield, the Bryan Family, and the Great Awakening in the South," *Journal of Southern History* 53, no. 3 (1987): 386.
22. "Davies' Account of the Negroes" (1756), reprinted in William Henry Foote, *Sketches of Virginia, Historical and Biographical* (Philadelphia: W. S. Martien, 1850), 290.
23. Albert J. Raboteau, *Slave Religion: The "Invisible Institution" in the Antebellum South* (New York: Oxford University Press, 2004).
24. John Marrant, *A Narrative of the Lord's Wonderful Dealings with John Marrant, a Black, (Now Going to Preach the Gospel in Nova-Scotia) Born in New-York, in North-America* (London: R. Hawes, 1785), 30–33.
25. James Otis, *The Rights of the British Colonists, Asserted and Proved* (1761), reprinted in *Pamphlets of the American Revolution, 1750–1776*, ed. Bernard Bailyn (Cambridge: Harvard University Press, 1965), 444.
26. Quoted in Patricia Bradley, *Slavery, Propaganda, and the American Revolution* (Jackson: University Press of Mississippi, 1999), 3.
27. John Locke, *The Second Treatise of Civil Government* (1689; repr., Amherst, NY: Prometheus Books, 1986), 54.
28. Quoted in Sylvia R. Frey, *Water from the Rock: Black Resistance in a Revolutionary Age* (Princeton, NJ: Princeton University Press, 1993), 15.
29. Quoted in John Wood Sweet, *Bodies Politic: Negotiating Race in the American North, 1730–1830* (Philadelphia: University of Pennsylvania Press, 2006), 253.
30. John Adams, *The Works of John Adams, Second President of the United States: With a Life of the Author, Notes and Illustrations* (Boston: Charles C. Little and James Brown, 1850), 2:200.
31. "Felix" [Holbrook], "The humble PETITION of many Slaves" in *A Documentary History of the Negro People in the United States*, ed. Herbert Aptheker (New York: Citadel Press, 1951), 6.
32. *Virginia Gazette* (Williamsburg, VA), June 30, 1774.
33. Quoted in Aptheker, *A Documentary History of the Negro People in the United States*, 7, 8.
34. Quoted in David McCullough, *John Adams* (New York: Simon and Schuster, 2008), 67.
35. The quote is from a poem by John Boyle O'Reilly that appears on the Crispus Attucks Memorial on Boston Common.
36. George T. Downing to William Cooper Nell, 3 March 1860, in *William Cooper Nell, Nineteenth-Century African American Abolitionist, Historian, Integrationist: Selected Writings from 1832–1874*, ed. Dorothy Porter Wesley and Constance Porter Uzelac (Baltimore: Black Classic Press, 2002), 581.
37. Ruth Bogin, "'The Battle of Lexington': A Patriotic Ballad by Lemuel Haynes," *William and Mary Quarterly*, 3rd ser., 42, no. 4 (1985): 501, 503.
38. Quoted in Michael Stephenson, *Patriot Battles: How the War of Independence Was Fought* (New York: HarperCollins, 2008), 184.
39. Benjamin Quarles, *The Negro in the American Revolution* (Chapel Hill: University of North Carolina Press, 1996), 10–11.

40. Margaret Elizabeth May, *Brookline in the Revolution*, Publications of the Brookline Historical Publication Society, 1st ser., no. 3 (Brookline, MA: Riverdale Press, 1897), 30.

41. Ruth Bogin, "'Liberty Further Extended': A 1776 Antislavery Manuscript by Lemuel Haynes," *William and Mary Quarterly*, 3rd ser., 40, no. 1 (1983): 92.

42. Boyrereau Brinch, *The Blind African Slave, or Memoirs of Boyrereau Brinch* (St. Albans, VT: Harry Whitney, 1810), 156.

43. Quoted in Sidney Kaplan and Emma Nogrady Kaplan, *The Black Presence in the Era of the American Revolution* (Amherst: University of Massachusetts Press, 1989), 254.

44. Quoted in Robin Blackburn, *The Overthrow of Colonial Slavery, 1776–1848* (New York: Verso, 1988), 112–13.

45. Quoted in Simon Schama, *Rough Crossings: The Slaves, the British, and the American Revolution* (New York: HarperCollins, 2007), 123.

46. Quoted in Peter A. Dorsey, *Common Bondage: Slavery as Metaphor in Revolutionary America* (Knoxville: University of Tennessee Press, 2009): 131.

47. "Memoirs of the Life of Boston King, a Black Preacher," *Methodist Magazine*, April 1798, 15.

48. Schama, *Rough Crossings*, 127.

49. Quoted in Henry Wiencek, *An Imperfect God: George Washington, His Slaves, and the Creation of America* (New York: Macmillan, 2004), 248.

50. Quoted in Catharine Maria Sedgwick, "Slavery in New England," *Bentley's Miscellany* 34 (1853), 424.

51. Jeremiah Asher, *Incidents in the Life of the Reverend J. Asher* (1850; repr., Freeport, NY: Books for Libraries Press, 1971), 18.

52. "Petition for Freedom to the Massachusetts Council and the House of Representatives" (January 1777), in *Collections of the Massachusetts Historical Society*, 5th ser. (Boston: The Massachusetts Historical Society, 1877), 3:436.

SUGGESTED REFERENCES

African American Life in Eighteenth-Century North America

Gomez, Michael A. *Exchanging Our Country Marks: The Transformation of African Identities in the Colonial and Antebellum South.* Chapel Hill: University of North Carolina Press, 1998.

Hodges, Graham Russell. *Root and Branch: African Americans in New York and East Jersey, 1613–1863.* Chapel Hill: University of North Carolina Press, 1999.

Lepore, Jill. *New York Burning: Liberty, Slavery, and Conspiracy in Eighteenth-Century Manhattan.* New York: Knopf, 2005.

Morgan, Philip D. *Slave Counterpoint: Black Culture in the Eighteenth-Century Chesapeake and Lowcountry.* Chapel Hill: University of North Carolina Press, 1998.

Olwell, Robert. *Masters, Slaves, and Subjects: The Culture of Power in the South Carolina Low Country, 1740–1790.* Ithaca, NY: Cornell University Press, 1998.

Piersen, William Dillon. *Black Yankees: The Development of an Afro-American Subculture in Eighteenth-Century New England.* Amherst: University of Massachusetts Press, 1988.

Sidbury, James. *Becoming African in America: Race and Nation in the Early Black Atlantic.* New York: Oxford University Press, 2009.

Sweet, John Wood. *Bodies Politic: Negotiating Race in the American North, 1730–1830.* Philadelphia: University of Pennsylvania Press, 2006.

The African American Revolution

Bradley, Patricia. *Slavery, Propaganda, and the American Revolution.* Jackson: University Press of Mississippi, 1999.

Countryman, Edward. *Enjoy the Same Liberty: Black Americans and the Revolutionary Era.* Lanham, MD: Rowman & Littlefield Publishers, 2012.

Egerton, Douglas R. *Death or Liberty: African Americans and Revolutionary America.* New York: Oxford University Press, 2009.

Gates, Henry Louis, Jr. *The Trials of Phillis Wheatley: America's First Black Poet and Her Encounters with the Founding Fathers.* New York: Basic Civitas Books, 2003.

Holton, Woody. *Black Americans in the Revolutionary Era: A Brief History with Documents.* Boston: Bedford/St. Martin's, 2009.

Kaplan, Sidney, and Emma Nogrady Kaplan. *The Black Presence in the Era of the American Revolution.* Amherst: University of Massachusetts Press, 1989.

Nash, Gary B. *The Forgotten Fifth: African Americans in the Age of Revolution.* Cambridge: Harvard University Press, 2006.

———. *The Unknown American Revolution: The Unruly Birth of Democracy and the Struggle to Create America.* New York: Penguin, 2006.

Saillant, John. *Black Puritan, Black Republican: The Life and Thought of Lemuel Haynes, 1753–1833.* New York: Oxford University Press, 2002.

Wiencek, Henry. *An Imperfect God: George Washington, His Slaves, and the Creation of America.* New York: Macmillan, 2004.

Slaves, Soldiers, and the Outcome of the Revolution

Frey, Sylvia R. *Water from the Rock: Black Resistance in a Revolutionary Age.* Princeton, NJ: Princeton University Press, 1993.

Gilbert, Alan. *Black Patriots and Loyalists: Fighting for Emancipation in the War for Independence.* Chicago: University of Chicago Press, 2012.

Hochschild, Adam. *Bury the Chains: Prophets and Rebels in the Fight to Free an Empire's Slaves.* New York: Mariner Books, 2006.

Jasanoff, Maya. *Liberty's Exiles: American Loyalists in the Revolutionary World.* New York: Knopf, 2011.

Piecuch, Jim. *Three Peoples, One King: Loyalists, Indians, and Slaves in the Revolutionary South, 1775–1782.* Columbia: University of South Carolina Press, 2008.

Pulis, John W., ed. *Moving On: Black Loyalists in the Afro-Atlantic World.* London: Routledge, 1999.

Pybus, Cassandra. *Epic Journeys of Freedom: Runaway Slaves of the American Revolution and Their Global Quest for Liberty.* Boston: Beacon Press, 2007.

Quarles, Benjamin. *The Negro in the American Revolution.* Chapel Hill: University of North Carolina Press, 1996.

Schama, Simon. *Rough Crossings: The Slaves, the British, and the American Revolution.* New York: HarperCollins, 2007.

Slavery and Freedom in the New Republic

1775–1820

CHRONOLOGY *Events specific to African American history are in purple. General United States history events are in black.*

1775	Nation's first antislavery organization founded in Pennsylvania	**1791–1804**	Haitian Revolution
1776–1787	Ten states ban importation of slaves from outside United States	**1792–1821**	New slave states established: Kentucky, Tennessee, Louisiana, Mississippi, Alabama, and Missouri
1780–1804	Pennsylvania, Connecticut, Rhode Island, New York, and New Jersey enact gradual emancipation laws	**1793**	Fugitive Slave Act establishes legal mechanisms for capture and return of escaped slaves
1785	Thomas Jefferson writes *Notes on the State of Virginia*, positing black inferiority		Eli Whitney invents cotton gin
1786–1787	Armed militia of farmers seeks economic reform in Shays's Rebellion	**1794**	African Methodist Episcopal (AME) Church established
1787	Absalom Jones and Richard Allen found Free African Society	**1798**	Alien and Sedition Acts tighten restrictions on aliens in United States, limit speech criticizing government
	Constitutional Convention meets in Philadelphia	**1800**	Gabriel's rebellion
	Northwest Ordinance bans slavery north of Ohio River and east of Mississippi River	**1803**	Louisiana Purchase doubles size of United States
	New York Manumission Society founds New York African Free School	**1804**	Ohio passes black laws
1789	George Washington inaugurated as first U.S. president	**1806**	Virginia imposes new restrictions on manumission
	First U.S. Congress meets	**1808**	International slave trade ends
1790s	Southern planters begin cultivating sugar and cotton	**1812–1815**	War of 1812
	Naturalization Act of 1790, first U.S. immigration law, passed	**1815**	Paul Cuffe takes thirty-eight black Bostonians to Sierra Leone
1791	Vermont becomes state	**1816**	American Colonization Society (ACS) first meets in Washington, D.C.
	Bill of Rights ratified	**1817**	Free blacks reject colonization at a mass meeting in Philadelphia

Benjamin Banneker Questions Thomas Jefferson about Slavery in the New Republic

In 1791, a fifty-nine-year-old black man named Benjamin Banneker composed a carefully worded letter to Thomas Jefferson, the new nation's first secretary of state. Born free, Banneker owned a small farm just outside Baltimore, where he made his living growing fruit and raising cattle and bees. He was also a self-educated scientist, inventor, and author who had recently published an almanac, which he sent to Jefferson along with his letter. Although he enjoyed "those blessings which proceed from that free and unequalled liberty," Banneker told Jefferson, he was well aware that most of his fellow black Americans remained enslaved. After winning a war dedicated to protecting their own liberties, white Americans had offered few rights to blacks. Instead, they dismissed them, Banneker complained, as "a race of beings" more "brutish than human, and scarcely capable of mental endowments." Banneker appealed to Jefferson to help African Americans "eradicate that train of absurd and false ideas and opinions, which so generally prevails with respect to us."[1]

As a Virginia planter who owned hundreds of slaves, Jefferson might seem to have been an unlikely choice of correspondents. But Banneker addressed Jefferson as a revolutionary rather than a planter, reminding him that he had once had reservations about the injustices of slavery. Indeed, when faced with the "arms and tyranny of the British crown," Banneker wrote, Jefferson had composed the Declaration of Independence, asserting that "all men are created equal, and that they are endowed by their creator with certain inalienable rights, that among these are life, liberty, and the pursuit of happiness."[2]

Jefferson's brief reply to Banneker was courteous but noncommittal. "Nobody wishes more than I do," he wrote, "to see such proofs as you exhibit, that nature has given to our black brethren, talents equal to those of the other colors of men, and that the appearance of a want of them is owing merely to the degraded condition of their existence, both in Africa and America." He even forwarded Banneker's almanac to the French Academy of Sciences as evidence of one black man's accomplishments.[3] But Jefferson did not address Banneker's critique of his support for slavery. The Virginia planter had never managed to reconcile slavery with the egalitarian ideals that he articulated in the Declaration of Independence, so he had good reason to ignore Banneker's charges against him.

Instead, Jefferson's reply centered on the question of black racial inferiority, which would become a central issue in the post-Revolutionary debate over slavery, liberty, and equal rights. He told Banneker that while he, too, hoped to see conditions for blacks improve, he remained unsure that the race could rise very far. In *Notes on the State of Virginia* (1785), Jefferson advanced the "suspicion" that blacks were "inferior to the whites in the endowments both of body and mind," and he would never admit otherwise.[4] In a private letter written to a friend in 1809, Jefferson even questioned Banneker's intellect, writing, "I have a long letter from Banneker, which shows him to have had a mind of very common stature indeed."[5]

Both Banneker's 1791 letter and Jefferson's response speak to the limits of black freedom in the new nation. The Revolution marked the beginning of slavery's abolition in the northern states and provided many African Americans throughout the country with the possibility of freedom through military service, manumission, or escape. But slavery still persisted throughout the South. Fueled by the production of cotton and sugar, the region's plantation economy expanded west and south into new territories. As Jefferson's guarded response to Banneker indicates, although he and other slaveholders of his era often deplored slavery, they were even more opposed to emancipation and questioned whether blacks were fit for freedom. For example, Jefferson's friend and fellow Founding Father James Madison, who deemed slavery "the most oppressive dominion ever exercised by man over man," nevertheless considered blacks "degraded" and abolition impractical.[6]

Not all Americans agreed with Jefferson and Madison. In the aftermath of the Revolution, thousands of white southerners liberated their slaves, while white northerners began eliminating slavery altogether. Massachusetts and Vermont abolished slavery during the Revolution, and

New Hampshire had fewer than fifty slaves by 1786. The citizens of Pennsylvania, Connecticut, Rhode Island, New York, and New Jersey also

Cover of Benjamin Banneker's Almanac, 1795
The cover of the 1795 edition of Benjamin Banneker's almanac, shown above, features a woodcut portraying the sixty-four-year-old author. Created by an unknown artist, the portrait depicts Banneker as a dignified figure dressed in simple black-and-white clothing. Although never a Quaker himself, Banneker was closely associated with the antislavery sect, and like many Quakers he avoided clothing colored with indigo and other dye stuffs, which were often produced by slaves. *Manuscript by Benjamin Banneker. Printed and sold by John Fisher, Stationer, Baltimore. Special Collections/Courtesy of the Maryland Historical Society, image ID MS2700.*

enacted gradual emancipation laws between 1780 and 1804. These laws dictated an emancipation process that was far from swift, however. They freed only those born after the laws were passed, and these slaves were emancipated only after they had served their masters for decades.

Moreover, free blacks in the North and the South did not have the same liberties as whites. Once the political idealism that ran high during the Revolution died down, many whites proved unwilling to embrace free blacks as their political or social equals. Whites, as citizens of a republic in which most free blacks were ex-slaves and hundreds of thousands of African Americans were still in slavery, tended to associate blackness with slavery and degradation.

To combat these prejudices, free blacks established separate black churches, schools, and social organizations and focused their efforts on building their own communities.

Both prejudice and slavery persisted in the Republic, calling into question whether blacks would ever be granted the liberties enshrined in the Declaration of Independence. This question remained largely unresolved during the Republic's early decades, which saw both black slavery and black freedom expand and the Founders adopt a Constitution that neither endorsed nor outlawed slavery. The result left African Americans, both slave and free, on the fringes of American democracy.

The Limits of Democracy

The circumscribed nature of black freedom in the post-Revolutionary era was bitterly disappointing to African Americans, who during and immediately after the Revolution had some reason to hope that slavery might collapse. Between 1776 and 1787, all but three of the new nation's thirteen states banned the importation of slaves from outside the United States — although South Carolina only suspended the trade for three years. Among the three states that did not ban the trade, only Georgia, which had suffered massive slave losses during the war, resumed the trade uninterrupted. North Carolina, which also had no ban, nevertheless discouraged participation in the slave trade by putting prohibitive duties on slave imports. New Hampshire had no ban because it did not import enough slaves to need one.

Yet the politicians who met to draft the U.S. Constitution in 1787 extended both slavery and the slave trade by agreeing that the United States would not withdraw from the international slave trade prior to 1808 and by creating few checks on the institution within the United States. Slavery quickly rebounded in Georgia and South Carolina and expanded rapidly across the Lower South starting in the 1790s, as planters developed lucrative new **cash crops**. The expansion of slavery was also facilitated by a vast expanse of new land that the United States acquired when it bought Louisiana from the French in 1803.

The Status of Slavery in the New Nation

In the decade following the Revolution, even the new nation's federal government seemed willing to take action to prohibit slavery's growth. When the Congress of the Confederation, which served as the country's governing body prior to the ratification of the Constitution in 1790, met in July 1787 to organize the U.S. territories northwest of the Ohio River into prospective states (and auction off some of the land to pay its debts), leaders from across the nation agreed to ban slavery in these territories, which included the present-day states of Illinois, Indiana, Michigan, Ohio, and Wisconsin, as well as part of Minnesota. The congress approved the resulting legislation, known as the **Northwest Ordinance**, when it met to draft the Constitution a month later. But the Northwest Ordinance was not an antislavery triumph. It lent tacit approval to slavery south of the Ohio River, giving the institution license to expand there and specifying that slaves who escaped to those territories should be "lawfully reclaimed and conveyed" to their owners (Map 4.1).

MAP 4.1   The Northwest Ordinance

Passed by the Congress of the Confederation on July 13, 1787, the Northwest Ordinance organized U.S. lands north and west of the Ohio River and east of the Mississippi River into a region known as the Northwest Territory. The Northwest Ordinance also prohibited slavery in this region.

Moreover, the Constitutional Convention put no further constraints on slavery. The framers of the Constitution left slavery's status within the existing states under the jurisdiction of the state legislatures. The fifty-five delegates were charged with strengthening the new nation's first system of government rather than addressing the issue of slavery, and they were willing to compromise on divisive issues in order to form a viable federal union. Accordingly, they rejected Pennsylvania delegate Gouverneur Morris's suggestion for a compensated gradual emancipation, which would have required owners to free their slaves after a set number of years and used federal funding to reimburse them for the loss of their property. With Georgia's and South Carolina's delegates threatening to leave the Union if the Constitution included such a measure, the delegates crafted a document that made no explicit reference to slaves or slavery and included several measures to preserve both.

The Founders protected the interests of the slave states with a clause forbidding all states to shelter or emancipate fugitive slaves — or, as termed in the Constitution, "Person[s] held to Service or Labour." This **fugitive slave clause** was later reinforced by the Fugitive Slave Act of 1793, which established the legal mechanisms by which escaped slaves could be seized and returned. The Constitution also offered slaveholders federal aid to subdue slave rebellions in a clause providing federal protection against "domestic violence" within a state's borders.

The delegates balanced the opposing interests of slaveholding and nonslaveholding states when it came to the thorny issue of how slaves would be counted toward each state's federal representation and tax burden. Would slaves be enumerated in the tallies that determined the number of political representatives allotted to each state? Would slaves be taxed? Representatives from slave states wanted their slaves counted for the purposes of representation but left untaxed; delegates from the other states wanted slaves to be taxed but not represented. The **Three-Fifths Compromise** split the difference: Three-fifths of each state's slave population would be counted in determining each state's tax burden and representation in the House of Representatives. The compromise was spelled out in the three-fifths clause of the Constitution.

The result was more generous to the southern states than the Founders had intended. In the decades following the Constitutional Convention, southern congressional representation soared as the region's slave population increased. The number of slaves in the United States grew from 694,207 in 1790 to 3,953,760 in 1860 — almost all of whom lived in the South. As a result, southerners dominated the House of Representatives and controlled the presidency and the Supreme Court for much of the antebellum era (the period before the Civil War). But most of the delegates who met in 1787 did not foresee the long-term consequences of the three-fifths clause.

When the Founders met in Philadelphia, the future of slavery was far from certain. A wave of manumissions had swept through the Upper South during the Revolutionary era, increasing the number of free blacks and underscoring the declining economic viability of slavery in the region. By the 1780s, tobacco production was declining in Virginia and Maryland, two of the largest slave states, and many Chesapeake planters were beginning to grow wheat, which required fewer full-time workers. The slackening demand for slaves was one reason Constitutional Convention delegates agreed to set a twenty-year limit on states participating in the foreign slave trade. This potentially controversial measure had the support of Upper South delegates, such as James Madison, who claimed to oppose the slave trade on humanitarian principles but who was also aware that his region did not need more slaves. Among the thirteen states that ratified the Constitution, only Georgia and South Carolina had expanding slave economies.

Slavery's Cotton Frontiers

Although slavery seemed to be shrinking in 1787, the southern economy was soon transformed in ways the Founders could not have anticipated. In the 1790s, southern planters developed two new cash crops, sugar and cotton, that secured the future of slavery and turned the South into a growing Slave Power. As Florida and Louisiana came under U.S. control, American planters expanded into those regions, which became the nation's primary sugar-producing areas. But these developments were really fueled by the 1793 invention of Eli Whitney's cotton gin, a machine that facilitated the processing of cotton. Cotton became the most widely cultivated slave-grown crop, flourishing throughout the lower Mississippi valley and beyond and leading to the establishment of new slave states, including Kentucky (1792), Tennessee (1796), Louisiana (1812), Mississippi (1817), Alabama (1819), Missouri (1821), and Arkansas (1836).

The cultivation of cotton was not new to the Lower South. During the first half of the eighteenth century, Carolina's early proprietors and Georgia's colonial trustees had encouraged the colonists to diversify the emerging plantation economy by growing cotton, hemp, flax, and foodstuffs, rather than producing only cash crops such as rice and indigo. But most planters took little interest in what was then a garden crop rather than an export staple. Slaves and small farmers tended small cotton patches, but the fibrous cotton bolls, or seedpods, that they yielded took much of the winter to clean, card, and spin. Only slaves and whites too poor to buy ready-made British textiles bothered to produce homespun cotton fabric. Cotton farming had little commercial appeal because salable cotton required far too much work to be cost-effective.

Southern landowners became more interested in producing cotton and other textiles in the years leading up to the Revolution. As the conflict took shape, rebellious colonists began to boycott British goods. Once a badge of poverty, homespun clothing became a symbol of patriotism. It was a necessity during the war, when British imports were no longer available and British warships blockaded the southern colonies, cutting off most of their exports of rice, tobacco, and indigo. Cotton thus became more marketable and useful than ever before, expanding even before Whitney patented his famous gin and soaring thereafter.

The commercial cultivation of cotton first took hold in the Sea Islands of coastal Georgia and South Carolina, where the weather was consistently warm enough to support the cultivation of long-staple, or long-fibered, cotton — an easily cleaned,

Slaves Processing Cotton

This image depicts early-nineteenth-century slaves picking, baling, and ginning cotton. Cotton, and the invention of the cotton gin, transformed the American South and rendered its economy ever more dependent on slave labor. As you examine this image, consider what the artist chose to depict and how he or she chose to depict it. What is included, and what has been left out? What is the general feeling of the image, and where do its accuracies and/or inaccuracies lie?

© North Wind Picture Archives/Alamy Stock Photo.

premium variety. But only a short-staple variety known as "upland cotton," whose fuzzy green seeds had to be carefully combed out, flourished on the mainland. The cotton gin, which used wire spikes, brushes, and a pair of rollers to separate the cotton from its seeds, revolutionized cotton production by transforming mainland cotton into a commercial crop. Whereas cleaning a pound or two of cotton had once taken a full day, the cotton gin allowed a single worker to clean as many as fifty pounds in that time. Upland cotton was also a hardy plant that could be grown throughout much of the South, and as a labor-intensive, profitable crop with a long growing season, it quickly proved to be an ideal crop for slave labor.

The South's upland cotton production skyrocketed from 150,000 pounds a year in 1793 to 6.5 million pounds in 1795, and by 1815 the region was producing well over

100 million pounds annually. Because its cultivation depended on slave labor, cotton sustained slavery as well, creating an enduring demand for slaves throughout the Lower South. The quest for cotton profits drove slaveholding settlers farther south and west in search of new land, creating an expanding frontier where forced labor predominated. Between 1790 and 1820, more than 250,000 white migrants from Virginia and Maryland settled in the backcountry regions of South Carolina and Georgia and on the frontiers of Alabama, Mississippi, Louisiana, and Missouri. The wealthiest settlers brought hundreds of slaves with them; others used the profits from growing cotton to buy foreign and domestic slaves. (See By the Numbers: The Growth of Slavery and Cotton, 1820–1860.)

As the cotton boom began, slaves were especially in demand in Georgia and South Carolina, which had both been short of slaves even before the boom. Georgia had lost two-thirds of its slave population during the Revolutionary War, while South Carolina may have lost up to one-quarter. To recoup their losses, planters in these states tracked

BY THE NUMBERS   The Growth of Slavery and Cotton, 1820–1860

Slave laborers played a crucial role in the production of U.S. cotton crops. As this figure indicates, cotton production expanded tremendously as the slave population grew. As slavery fostered the growth of cotton, cotton also promoted the expansion of slavery: The demanding crop required forced labor to clear the land and plant, cultivate, and prepare the cotton for sale. White migrants to the expanding cotton frontiers brought slaves with them and purchased both foreign and domestic slaves to meet their growing needs.

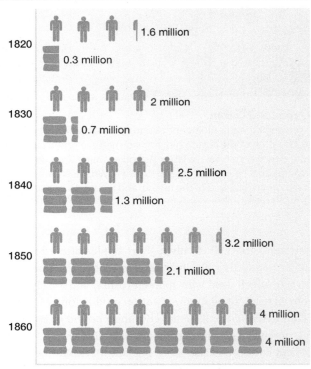

1820   1.6 million / 0.3 million
1830   2 million / 0.7 million
1840   2.5 million / 1.3 million
1850   3.2 million / 2.1 million
1860   4 million / 4 million

Number of slaves/
Annual production of cotton

0.5 million slaves   0.5 million cotton bales

down wartime fugitives who had escaped to other states and used their militias and Native American slave catchers to hunt down maroon communities living in the region's backwoods and most inaccessible swamps. Before 1808, when the United States withdrew from the international slave trade, planters in the Lower South imported most of the new slaves they purchased from Africa and the Caribbean. But as the international slave trade came to an end, such buyers increasingly sought slaves in the Chesapeake and the North, where many slave owners were anxious to unload their slaves while slavery was still legal in their states. Between 1790 and 1820, nearly 170,000 slaves were transferred to frontier plantations in an internal migration that continued to increase thereafter.

The cotton frontier provided planters in the Upper South, whose slaves were multiplying rapidly as a result of robust birthrates, with a profitable market for slaves, who increasingly exceeded the labor needs of the region. Cotton also enriched the nation as a whole, fueling the growth of northern industry and quickly becoming the country's premier export crop. Cotton's impact on African Americans in the South was equally far-reaching but also far more tragic. As the cotton frontier expanded west, families were scattered in slave sales that forever separated siblings, husbands and wives, and children and parents. For African Americans consigned to the cotton fields, slave labor grew more mind-numbing than ever.

Unlike other skilled or seasonal work, tending cotton crops demanded unremitting menial labor. Clearing new land was backbreaking, and planting and raising cotton was nearly as arduous. Cotton has a 180- to 200-day growing season, and once the plants matured, slaves spent several more months picking the cotton, carefully ginning it, and pressing it into bales. By the time they finished, it was almost time to return to the cotton fields and beat down the stems of the old plants to prepare the new crop. Cotton planters typically planted and harvested corn during breaks in the cotton-growing season, which ensured that slaves worked all year round.

This unrelenting regime left little time for slaves to cultivate their own food or take care of their families. Thus, while their official workday ended at nightfall, their labors continued long afterward. On returning home, the average slave, one observer noted, "does not lose his time. He goes to work at a bit of the land which he has planted with provisions for his own use, while his companion, if he has one, busies herself in preparing [some food] for him, herself, and their children."[7]

Between sundown and sunrise, plantation slaves also had to build new communities. Newly imported African- and Caribbean-born slaves were far from home, and American-born slaves from the Upper South or the North had little hope of reconnecting with their kin. Planters who migrated to the new cotton frontiers sometimes brought all the slaves they owned, but they were usually more selective and often ended up separating married couples and breaking up families. Planter migrants needed strong slaves who could clear their new land and survive the rigors of the long trip south, often made on foot. As a result, planters favored young adults over their parents and grandparents, and left young children and nursing mothers behind.

Slave families in the Upper South also were broken up by slave sales. One example is the family of Charles Ball, who lived in Calvert County, Maryland, until age four. After his master died in the 1780s, his mother and all of his siblings were sold to separate purchasers, including a Georgia trader who drove Ball's mother away from him with a rawhide whip. Ball survived his childhood and went on to have a family of his own. But in 1805, he, too, was sold to a slave trader without warning and never saw his wife and children again. As he was dragged away from his former master's home, Ball begged to "be allowed to go to see my wife and children" one last time, but the trader told Ball that he "would be able to get another wife."[8] Ball ended up in Georgia, along with numerous other slaves who had left behind families in the Chesapeake. He eventually escaped from slavery and settled in Pennsylvania, where he wrote his memoir and remained "fearful, at this day, to let my place of residence be known."[9]

Slavery and Empire

For most of the eighteenth century the United States' westward expansion was limited by Spanish, French, and Native American claims to much of the continent's interior. At the turn of the century, the new nation took advantage of imperial conflicts in Europe and the Caribbean to expand its national boundaries. The most notable of these conflicts was the Haitian Revolution in the French colony of Saint Domingue, which had far-reaching effects for France's New World empire. This massive slave rebellion scared slaveholders across the hemispheres and provided African American populations with an enduring vision of political freedom. It also reshaped the New World's commodity markets and imperial borders in ways that helped expand slavery in the United States.

The Haitian Revolution (1791–1804) took place in the wake of the French Revolution (1789), when France's grasp on its colonies was already weakened by internal turmoil. Slave rebels, who numbered 100,000, burned their plantations, executed their owners, and shut down sugar production in Haiti, then one of the world's largest sugar producers. Their actions reverberated across the Atlantic world, with sugar in short supply and whites fleeing Haiti. Many of Haiti's sugar planters took refuge in the lower Mississippi valley and began to cultivate sugar there. Meanwhile, France never regained control of Haiti. The powerful French general Napoleon Bonaparte, who unseated France's revolutionary leaders at the beginning of the nineteenth century, tried to reenslave Haiti's former slaves. But even after he captured their leader, Toussaint-Louverture, who died in a French jail in 1803, Haiti's black population resisted reenslavement and declared the country's independence in 1804. The loss of this most lucrative New World colony caused Napoleon to reevaluate how many colonies France could maintain. He decided to sell off some of its least valuable assets, including Louisiana.

Thomas Jefferson, elected president in 1800, profited from France's shrinking imperial ambitions. In 1802, Jefferson dispatched James Monroe to France to offer to buy the port city of New Orleans, which was vital to U.S. trade. Jefferson authorized Monroe to pay $10 million for the city, along with as much land west of the Mississippi

Incendie du Cap

Revolte générale des Nègres. Massacre des Blancs.

SAINT-DOMINGUE,

OU

HISTOIRE

DE SES RÉVOLUTIONS;

CONTENANT

*Le récit effroyable des divisions, des
troubles, des ravages, des meurtres,
des incendies, des dévastations et des
massacres qui eurent lieu dans cette
île, depuis 1789 jusqu'à la perte de la
colonie.*

A PARIS,

Chez TIGER, IMPRIMEUR-LIBRAIRE,
rue du Petit-Pont St-Jacques, n. 10.

Au Pilier littéraire.

The Haitian Revolution

The Haitian Revolution (1791–1804) in the French colony of Saint Domingue inspired slaves internationally and terrified their owners. The frontispiece of this 1815 history of the revolution conveys slaveholders' greatest fears, depicting white men, women, and children running helplessly from armed blacks. Note, in particular, how the women are portrayed. There are many mothers with small children, a wife mourning her collapsed husband, an elderly woman with a cane, and a young woman who appears to be partially naked from the waist up. How is white womanhood used here to illustrate the dangers of a slave revolt and perhaps to justify slaves' bondage? *Schomburg Center, NYPL/Art Resource, NY.*

River as the French government could be persuaded to surrender. When Monroe arrived in France, he found Napoleon's foreign minister willing to sell all of Louisiana for the bargain price of $15 million. "They ask for only one town of Louisiana," Napoleon said, "but I consider the whole colony as completely lost."[10] Monroe was quick to agree, for the purchase would give the United States dominion over a vast section of North America's interior, extending from the Gulf of Mexico to the Canadian border and including large swaths of land on the western banks of the Mississippi River.

The **Louisiana Purchase** (1803) doubled the size of the United States, adding 828,000 square miles of land, and fostered the spread of slavery in what Jefferson called the "empire for liberty." It included territory that would later become the slave states of Arkansas and Missouri, as well as present-day Oklahoma and portions of Texas (Map 4.2). This new land was well suited to the cultivation of cotton, adding millions of acres to the South's growing cotton frontier. Southeastern Louisiana contained land suitable for the cultivation of sugar, an even more profitable cash crop. This purchase spurred new waves of westward migration among the planters of the Upper South and

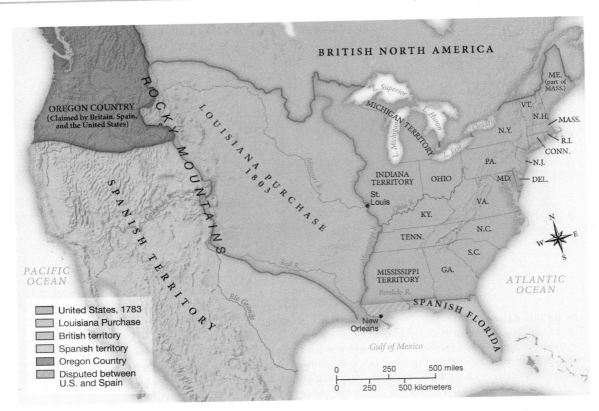

MAP 4.2   The Louisiana Purchase

The 828,000 square miles of land that the United States purchased from France in 1803 extended from the Gulf of Mexico to Canada and included all of present-day Arkansas, Missouri, Iowa, Oklahoma, Kansas, and Nebraska, most of North and South Dakota, and parts of Minnesota, New Mexico, Texas, Colorado, and Louisiana. The acquisition, which doubled the size of the United States, also had a tremendous impact on slavery: It opened new lands for the cultivation of slave-grown cotton and sugar crops and sparked a westward migration of planters, facilitating the growth of the slave trade.

offered lucrative new markets for the domestic slave trade, adding to the thirty thousand slaves already living in Louisiana. New Orleans quickly became a principal port for the resale of African slaves. (To evade the congressional ban on importing foreign slaves into New Orleans, traders first sold the slaves in South Carolina, then resold them in New Orleans.)

Slavery and Freedom outside the Plantation South

If cotton gave slavery a new lease on life in the plantation South, the status of slavery elsewhere was more mixed. In southern cities, slavery first expanded and then contracted after the Revolution. The acquisition of New Orleans greatly enlarged the South's enslaved urban population, as did the rapid growth of other urban areas.

Thriving markets for cotton and other slave-grown crops fueled the growth of these cities, which shipped the commodities out of their harbors. Urban businessmen employed slaves to haul, load, and unload goods and to build the barrels, crates, and storehouses that contained them. Slaves also worked in port cities as tradesmen's assistants and domestics.

But slavery never became as entrenched in urban areas as it did in the countryside, and over time the use of free black workers became increasingly common in southern cities. Urban slaves were more expensive to maintain than free workers and potentially more dangerous. They often achieved a greater degree of independence than plantation slaves, which made southerners uneasy — especially in the wake of Gabriel's rebellion, an abortive slave plot that took place in Richmond, Virginia, in 1800.

Meanwhile, in the North, slavery was outlawed in every state in the decades following the Revolution. But slavery was slow to die, because several states adopted gradual emancipation laws that kept African Americans enslaved well into the early decades of the nineteenth century. Moreover, not all slave owners honored these laws, and some slaves were forced to seek their freedom in court.

Urban Slavery and Southern Free Blacks

The slave population in most nineteenth-century southern cities either declined or leveled off over time. Most of the slaves who passed through the commercial hubs and major slave trading centers such as New Orleans and Charleston were sold to rural slave owners. Southern cities tended to be sites of exchange rather than industry, and did not require a large population of enslaved laborers. One major exception was Richmond, which became Virginia's state capital in 1780 and produced a variety of manufactured goods. The success of industrial slavery in Richmond was widespread enough to sustain a growing population of enslaved laborers, but the city was unusual in this regard.

Blacks did not disappear from such cities, however. Instead, in cities where slave populations declined, the number of free blacks usually increased. In Baltimore, which saw the earliest and most dramatic shift of this kind, slavery boomed in the decades immediately after the Revolution and declined after 1810. But the city's free black population soared thereafter.

During the Revolution, Baltimore expanded when Maryland planters abandoned tobacco, which no longer fetched high prices, in favor of wheat and other grains. The city profited enormously from this shift and became a center for milling grain into flour. Baltimore workers also produced the barrels used to store the flour and supplied the labor needed to transport, package, and ship all of Maryland's agricultural exports, as well as to construct roads, warehouses, and other buildings. Between 1790 and 1810, the city's slave population expanded rapidly as a result of these developments. "Surplus" slaves brought in from the surrounding countryside were cheap and plentiful in a region where tobacco no longer occupied most of the labor force, and they initially supplied much of the labor needed to sustain the city's economic growth. But the rise of cotton, combined with the closing of the international slave trade in 1808, soon made such slaves increasingly expensive. Maryland planters with surplus slaves began selling them to planters on the cotton frontier rather than to local buyers, and Baltimore's slave population shrank.

Meanwhile, free blacks flocked to Baltimore. The city's growing free black population, like its economic growth, was a product of forces in the countryside. The declining labor needs of Maryland's planters inspired a wave of manumissions, especially among Baptist and Methodist planters. Many still chose to sell rather than free their surplus slaves, however, and the fear of being sold inspired some slaves to free themselves — either by working to purchase their freedom or by escaping. Fugitive slaves and free blacks alike migrated to Baltimore, where jobs were plentiful and the large free black population could provide a community for freemen and shelter runaways. Maryland slave masters often suspected that missing slaves were in Baltimore passing as free blacks. In 1789, one owner ran a newspaper ad seeking the whereabouts of a missing slave named Charity. His ad maintained that he was all but certain she "is in or near Baltimore-town, passes for a free woman, practices midwifery, and goes by the name of Sarah Dorsey, or Dawson, the Granny."[11]

The economics of slavery in urban areas were never as clear-cut as they were in the rural South. On one hand, the rise of the domestic slave trade after 1808 ensured that urban slaves commanded a good price, which encouraged owners to retain their slaves as investments. On the other hand, urban slaves tended to be less productive than their agricultural counterparts. Whether they worked as domestic laborers or served under tradesmen, city slaves were rarely subjected to the unremitting labor regime that prevailed in the countryside. Moreover, urban slaves could become a drain on their owners' finances if they were not fully employed, because they were more expensive to clothe, house, and feed in the city than on the plantation.

Thus a system of **hiring out** was developed to exploit urban slaves' labor, allowing some owners to make a good living by contracting out their slaves. The practice allowed businessmen who could not afford to buy slaves or needed their labor for only a short time to employ enslaved workers for anywhere from one day to one year. Unlike slave owners, these employers had no obligation to house their workers or supervise them after they left work. Although slaves who were hired out for domestic jobs might live in their employers' homes, many others lived independently. They were allowed to keep a portion of their earnings to cover their room and board and were given the freedom to find their own lodging. This practice, known as **living out**, evolved because many urban employers had no place to house slave workers.

The hiring-out system gave slaves a degree of freedom that often worried white southerners, who enacted but rarely enforced laws banning the system. Slaves who were hired out in southern cities typically made their own work arrangements, remained largely unsupervised, and were often in close contact with free blacks. This could reduce their value, as one slave owner discovered when he tried to sell a slave family he had long hired out. His slaves attracted no offers because other owners were

Receipt for the Hire of a Slave
Dated January 1, 1834, this receipt for the hire of a slave in Virginia is written in a standardized legal form that lists the expenses and obligations involved in renting human property. Slave hiring was a popular practice that allowed slave owners who did not need to use their slaves to profit from the slaves' labor, and supplied slave labor to those who could not afford slaves or who needed slave labor for only a limited time period. *Private Collection/© Michael Graham-Steward/ Bridgeman Images.*

wary of purchasing slaves who had known independence. By contrast, this autonomy benefited enslaved men and women, who sometimes accumulated enough money to buy their freedom by living cheaply and working extra hours. It could also tempt them to free themselves by either running away or rebelling.

Gabriel's Rebellion

Although city life offered some degree of freedom, it was not enough for an urban slave known as Prosser's Gabriel, who led a plot to overturn slavery in Richmond in the summer of 1800. Gabriel's rebellion testified to slaves' abiding discontent, but it was also inspired by recent events. At a time when the memory of the American Revolution was very much alive, the more recent Haitian Revolution underscored the possibility that an enslaved people could overthrow their oppressors. Gabriel was among the black Virginians who embraced this possibility. An enslaved blacksmith, he lived outside Richmond with his brothers, Solomon and Martin, on a tobacco plantation belonging to his owner, Thomas Prosser. Aware that divisions among the French had helped set the stage for the Haitian Revolution, Gabriel hoped that Virginia's slaves could exploit the social and political tensions among whites in their state, which were then running high in anticipation of the election of 1800.

With the aid of his brothers and other enslaved confederates, Gabriel planned to enlist about a thousand slaves to attack Richmond's wealthy citizens, while sparing the city's poor whites. He hoped that these discontented Virginians, as well as antislavery whites such as the city's Methodists and Quakers, would join the rebels and help them take control of the state. Most of Gabriel's slave recruits worked in or around Richmond and were American-born and highly acculturated. Many were artisans whose labor was not closely supervised. They saw themselves as workingmen united around a cause, much as the colonists had been a quarter century earlier. Gabriel even planned to carry a flag reading "Death or liberty," evoking well-known Revolutionary-era language. Gabriel and his followers took advantage of their freedom of movement to hold secret planning meetings in local taverns and shops and even traveled to the countryside to recruit rural followers at barbecues and revival meetings. They were also able to amass a small cache of weapons, which they hoped to use to seize more weapons in Richmond.

In the end, Gabriel's plot collapsed. As word of the revolt spread to hundreds of slaves across the Virginia countryside, two disclosed the plot to their master, who alerted Virginia governor James Monroe. Between this betrayal and a torrential storm that delayed implementation of the plan, the rebellion failed. Six of the ringleaders were captured immediately, and a militia assembled by the governor tracked down the remaining twenty. Among the last to surrender was Gabriel, who eluded the militia for almost three weeks before he was captured and taken back to Richmond in chains. There he was tried and executed along with the twenty-five others. More slaves also were indicted, but by mid-October a state law requiring Virginia to compensate owners of slaves convicted of capital crimes made the executions prohibitively expensive. The state had paid $8,899.91 to the owners of the condemned men, and many more suspects awaited trial. Governor Monroe suspended the executions after Thomas Jefferson suggested that the rebels might instead be sold outside the United States.

Even though Gabriel's rebellion failed, white Virginians lived in fear of an uprising, especially after another slave plot was uncovered in 1802. Some members of the Virginia General Assembly even contemplated abandoning slavery completely, commissioning the governor to confer with President Jefferson about locating a place where "such negroes or mulattoes, as may be emancipated, may be sent or choose to remove as a place of asylum."[12] Instead, most slave owners called for laws that would discourage slave revolts.

Virginia authorities responded by eliminating much of the independence and mobility that urban blacks enjoyed. In Richmond, Monroe secured the state capital's arsenals and public buildings by instituting a nightly police patrol. The officers were responsible for rounding up any slaves caught on the street after nine o'clock. According to the law, these slaves would receive "as many stripes" as the officer "might see proper to inflict."[13] In addition, African American laborers were regulated much more carefully than before. Although it was already illegal, slaves' hiring out of their own time was outlawed once more, and this time the legislature mandated stiff fines for slave owners and severe whippings for slaves who broke the law. The general assembly also cracked down on the "unlawful assemblages" of slaves who gathered to relax after work or on Sundays, ordering the state's justices of the peace to break up all such gatherings and to punish slaves who participated in them. Even attending church became difficult, because slaves could no longer go anywhere without a written pass from their masters, who were often unwilling to supply one.

Free blacks found themselves more confined in the aftermath of Gabriel's rebellion as well. Although none were implicated, free blacks were suspected of helping the rebels promote their plot and steal from their owners. Moreover, many white Virginians were convinced that free blacks' very existence endangered slavery. "If blacks see all their color as slaves," one lawmaker explained, "it will seem to them a disposition of Providence, and they will be content. But if they see others like themselves free, and enjoying the rights they are deprived of, they will repine."[14] So when the state assembly clamped down on the network of black boatmen who had helped spread word of the planned revolts of 1800 and 1802, it targeted both free blacks and slaves. An 1802 law banned any "negro or mulatto" from obtaining a ship pilot's license, and black pilots whose licenses were issued prior to the law were confined to their boats as they traveled through Virginia. As slave patrols proliferated, free blacks came under scrutiny in their own neighborhoods. They could no longer survive without papers and had to register with their towns as "Free Negroes & Mulattoes."[15]

In the wake of Gabriel's rebellion, opportunities to pass from slavery to freedom began to decrease across the South. In 1806, Virginia legislators reversed the liberal manumission law the state had adopted during the Revolutionary era, which made manumission a private matter, and replaced it with a new law that made manumission very difficult. The law also required newly emancipated slaves to leave the state within twelve months or forfeit their freedom and become subject to reenslavement and sale. Newly freed blacks and their owners could petition the legislature to exempt individuals from the law, but self-purchase and manumission no longer offered Virginia slaves a direct route to lasting freedom. Unless they could secure permission from the legislature to remain in state, newly freed slaves now had to migrate north and forever separate themselves from their enslaved family and friends. Not surprisingly, many were unwilling to leave on these terms. By 1815, the state legislature was so overwhelmed by petitions from free blacks who wanted to remain in Virginia that they authorized the county courts to permit any black freed for "extraordinary merit" to stay.[16]

Achieving Emancipation in the North

In addition to expanding the boundaries of America's slave South, the Louisiana Purchase added more land to the free territory of the Old Northwest. The Northwest Ordinance had banned slavery in U.S. territories north of the Ohio River and east of the Mississippi River. In the short term, the ban did not prevent some early settlers from keeping slaves in those areas: It did not apply to slaves already living there and did not keep some settlers from importing more. But the gradual emancipation of slaves in the northern states discouraged such imports, paving the way for the creation of other free states throughout the region.

By 1804, every northern state had either abolished slavery outright or passed a plan to eliminate slavery over time, and the new states that emerged in the Old Northwest followed suit. But black freedom was not easily gained or maintained in these states. In Indiana Territory, which included much of the upper Mississippi valley, gradual emancipation meant brutal forms of indentured servitude for up to thirty years before slaves became free. To avoid becoming a haven for fugitive slaves, Ohio, which became a free state in 1803, policed the border along the Ohio River between the slave South and the free North. In 1804, Ohio passed **black laws** requiring all free blacks to supply legal proof of their free status and to post a $500 bond to guarantee their good behavior. Indiana, which became a state in 1816, and Illinois, which gained statehood in 1818, also entered the Union as free states with similar laws. Though not uniformly enforced, such laws were common in the western states and imposed bond requirements for free blacks that eventually reached $1,000 — a sum well beyond the reach of most African Americans.

Federal legislation passed during the early national period also solidified the limits on black freedom. The nation's first immigration law, the **Naturalization Act of 1790**, instituted residence and racial requirements for potential citizens. Naturalization was available to "free white person[s]" who had been in the United States for at least two years. Free blacks, by contrast, were not classified as full citizens under the laws of the Republic: They were barred from joining the national militia, carrying federal mail, or holding elected office in the District of Columbia. Moreover, the Constitution did not protect blacks from racially discriminatory laws imposed by individual states. Emancipation would not bring full freedom for black northerners, and just achieving emancipation was a struggle for many blacks.

Throughout the North, former slaves were liberated on terms that were neither swift nor generous. Slavery was outlawed in Massachusetts and Vermont during the Revolution, and abolished by means of gradual emancipation laws in the other northern states — with the exception of New Hampshire, which passed no abolition law and instead let its tiny slave population dwindle to nothing through manumission and attrition. The first state to adopt a gradual emancipation law was Pennsylvania. Passed in 1780, Pennsylvania's Act for the Gradual Abolition of Slavery provided a model for similar laws in Connecticut and Rhode Island in 1784, New York in 1799, and New Jersey in 1804. These laws applied only to slaves born after the legislation was passed — those born before then generally remained enslaved for life — and specified that slaves were to be freed in their mid- to late twenties, after they had labored long enough, in effect, to pay for their own freedom. As a result, despite their efforts to speed the application of these laws, thousands of black northerners remained in bondage through the 1820s.

Many slave owners were reluctant to emancipate slaves even after they had completed the terms of service required. Isabella Baumfree, who later renamed herself Sojourner Truth, was one of many black northerners who struggled to achieve the freedom promised her by law. Born in upstate New York in 1797, two years too early to qualify for gradual emancipation, Baumfree had little hope of ever obtaining her freedom until 1817, when the New York legislature revised state law, setting July 4, 1827, as the date by which all New York slaves would achieve freedom regardless of birth date. This revision did not release slave children born before that date from their service obligation, but it reduced the term to twenty-one years. Baumfree, who endured several abusive owners and many hardships as a slave, was understandably eager to be freed, and she no doubt welcomed the law's reduction of her five children's terms of service. As 1827 approached, she even managed to get her owner, John Dumont, to agree to release her a year early if she behaved well and served him faithfully. But July 4, 1827, came and went, and Baumfree remained enslaved. Dumont insisted that Baumfree owed him more time because she had worked less than usual that year due to a "badly diseased hand."[17]

That fall, Baumfree freed herself by sneaking out of Dumont's house early one morning with a baby in one arm and her clothing in the other. She left behind her husband, whom Dumont had picked for her, and the rest of her children, who still owed Dumont many years of labor. But she did not travel far from her family. She took refuge with two antislavery neighbors, Maria and Isaac Van Wagenen, who sheltered Baumfree despite her owner's objections. When Dumont tried to drag Baumfree and her baby back to his home, Isaac Van Wagenen told his neighbor that even though he had "never been in the practice of buying and selling slaves; [and] he did not believe in slavery," he would buy out the remainder of Baumfree's time rather than see her return. Dumont accepted his offer of $20 for Baumfree's freedom and $5 for her baby's. Baumfree, who could hardly believe her good fortune, initially assumed that she had changed hands once more. Only after Van Wagenen assured her that "there is but *one* master; and he who is *your* master is *my* master" did she believe that she was free.[18] Baumfree still had to fight to free her other children, who remained with Dumont, and even took him to court to achieve that end.

Gradual emancipation laws gave northern slaveholders many years to devise ways to sell their slaves out of state rather than set them free. Unscrupulous owners sold thousands of black northerners illegally in the South. Northern blacks resisted such sales and sought the support of antislavery whites in recovering friends and family members who had been sold illegally. In Pennsylvania, reports of illegal slave sales helped inspire the birth of the nation's first antislavery organization. Founded in 1775 by French-born abolitionist Anthony Benezet, the Society for the Relief of Free

Negroes Unlawfully Held in Bondage, which was later reorganized as the Pennsylvania Society for Promoting the Abolition of Slavery and for the Relief of Free Negroes Unlawfully Held in Bondage, was a white organization with a predominantly Quaker membership. The American revolutionary Thomas Paine was also a founding member, and Benjamin Franklin joined the organization in the mid-1780s and for a time served as its president. The New York Manumission Society, founded in 1785 by American statesman and Founding Father John Jay, took shape around similar concerns. Its members protested the kidnapping of blacks, both slave and free, in the years immediately following the Revolution and pushed the legislature to prevent New Yorkers from evading gradual emancipation by exporting their slaves. But such practices were difficult to police.

Over time, however, the illegal sale and exportation of northern slaves ended along with slavery itself. Although some slave owners managed to evade gradual emancipation, northern emancipation statutes also provided many of the region's slaves with unprecedented opportunities for negotiation. Slave owners were most willing to offer early emancipation to very young and very old slaves, who were their least profitable workers, but eventually they had to free all their slaves and were sometimes willing to free them early. The region was home to almost 50,000 slaves in 1770, but that number declined rapidly thereafter. By 1820, fewer than 20,000 slaves, most of whom lived in New York and New Jersey, remained in the North. By 1840, the North was home to more than 1,000 slaves.

Free Black Life in the New Republic

As northern blacks achieved emancipation, free black communities took shape across the region. Whereas free blacks in the North never numbered more than a few thousand during the colonial era, by 1810 there were 50,000 of them. That number doubled by 1820 and reached 170,728 in 1840. Most were located in port cities, which had had large black communities even during the colonial era. No longer bound to rural masters, the ex-slave population congregated in major northern cities such as New York, Philadelphia, and Boston, all of which attracted fugitive slaves as well. City life offered safety in numbers to escaped slaves and also held significant advantages for free blacks, including greater opportunities for independence and employment. With their new freedom, African Americans sought to build their own households and sustain larger black communities that could support churches, schools, and social organizations.

Free Black Organizations

Black life in the larger northern cities was not without promise for ambitious ex-slaves such as Absalom Jones and Richard Allen. Both were born in Delaware, a state where slavery declined to very low levels after the Revolution but was never formally abolished.

The two men, both Methodist converts owned by evangelical masters who allowed them to purchase their freedom in the early 1780s, met in Philadelphia and became life-long friends and allies. They also prospered in business: Jones was a shoemaker, and Allen owned a chimney-sweeping business. They became prominent members of Phila-delphia's rapidly growing free black community and founded the city's first black **mutual aid society** in 1787. Members of the Free African Society pledged to support one another "in sickness, and for the benefit of their widows and fatherless children."[19]

The Free African Society was one of several similar free black organizations estab-lished during the late eighteenth and early nineteenth centuries. Others included the African Union Society of Providence, Rhode Island, established in 1780; the Brown Fellowship Society of Charleston, South Carolina, founded in 1790; Boston's African Society, organized in 1796; New York's African Society for Mutual Relief, established in 1808; and the Resolute Beneficial Society of Washington, D.C., founded in 1818. All of these organizations were funded by dues and other fees collected from members, which they used to provide a social safety net for their community. The specific bene-fits offered varied by organization, but they typically included sickness and disability benefits, burial insurance, and pensions to widows and orphans. Mutual aid societies also helped free blacks establish other institutions that proved crucial to their commu-nity's well-being. Most notable among these were black churches.

Absalom Jones, 1810
Painted by Philadelphia artist Raphaelle Peale, this portrait depicts one of black Philadelphia's most important leaders. Absalom Jones escaped from slavery to become a founding member of the city's Free African Society, as well as the nation's first black priest of the Episcopal denomination. Peale's depiction of Jones is respectful and underscores Jones's status as a man of God by por-traying him in ecclesiastical robes, with Bible in hand. *Absalom Jones, 1810 (oil on paper), by Raphaelle Peale (1774–1825)/Delaware Art Museum, Wilmington, Delaware, USA/Gift of Absalom Jones School/ Bridgeman Images.*

Although many early members of the black mutual aid societies initially belonged to white churches, they often ended up establishing their own — a move usually inspired by the prejudices they encountered. Richard Allen, Absalom Jones, and other early members of Philadelphia's Free African Society, for example, attended St. George's Methodist Church. Allen, who was a gifted preacher, even led special services for African Americans there. But as Allen's sermons drew more black worshippers to St. George's, these congregants became increasingly unwelcome. White leaders began to segregate them, asking them first to sit along the walls, then moving them to seats in the balcony. "You must not kneel here," a church trustee told Absalom Jones when he and several others defied this segregated seating plan, claiming seats on the first floor and kneeling to join the rest of the congregation in prayer one Sunday morning in 1792.[20] Heads still bowed, Jones and his followers refused to move until the prayer was over, at which point the trustee summoned several white men to help him force the black congregants to the balcony. Disgusted, St. George's black members got up and walked out of the church.

"We never entered it again!" remembered Allen, who had been soliciting funds for the creation of a separate black church in Philadelphia even before the walkout.[21] The group worshipped in a rented storefront until July 29, 1794, when the African Methodist Episcopal (AME) Church — led by Allen and later renamed the Bethel AME Church — finally opened its doors. Bethel AME joined several other black Methodist churches to form an independent AME denomination in 1816, at which point the new denomination's congregants elected Allen to serve as the AME's first bishop. But not all African Americans who had attended St. George's joined Bethel AME. Some abandoned Methodism altogether, registering a permanent protest against the segregationist policies of white Methodists. Among them was Absalom Jones, who with help from Allen and other members of the Free African Society founded the African Episcopal Church of St. Thomas, the nation's first African American Episcopal church, and became an ordained Episcopal minister in 1804.

Black churches, most of them Methodist or Baptist, proliferated in other cities as well during the early 1800s. Many were funded and built with help from black mutual aid societies, with which the churches often remained closely affiliated. Boston's first black Baptist church, the African Meeting House, was founded in 1805 with the help of Boston's African Society and the city's oldest black fraternal order, the Prince Hall Masonic Lodge. Early black churches hosted mutual aid society meetings, public lectures, protest meetings, and other gatherings and served the needs of newly freed men and women who came in search of educational opportunities and economic assistance as well as Sunday services. Virtually all early black churches also served as schools at various points in their history. Richard Allen founded the nation's first black Sunday school in his church in 1795, and he opened a night school for adults a few years later. Meanwhile, the African Union Society of Providence built its African Union Meeting House in 1821 to serve as both a school and a Baptist church.

Bethel AME Church

Black churches such as the Bethel AME Church in Philadelphia provided far more than church services. They met a variety of needs for their communities and congregations, also serving as schools, meetinghouses, clubhouses, lecture halls, and sites for social and political gatherings. Black churches flourished in northern cities during the early nineteenth century, serving both African Americans who were already well established and the recently arrived migrants and newly freed slaves who came in need of education, work, and community support. *Lithograph by William L. Breton, printed by Kennedy and Luca's Lithography, 1829/Library Company of Philadelphia, Pennsylvania/Bridgeman Images.*

BETHEL AFRICAN METHODIST EPISCOPAL CHURCH, PHILAD?

Free Black Education and Employment

Black northerners emerged from slavery eager to support themselves, and the difficulties they often faced in finding work made them doubly anxious to educate their children. The gradual emancipation acts passed in Pennsylvania, Connecticut, Rhode Island, New York, and New Jersey freed slaves only after they had devoted many of their most productive years to working without pay and without any opportunity to educate themselves or acquire property. In an era when most people started working in their teens and did not live much past forty, these ex-slaves began their lives as free adults far poorer than even the poor whites beside whom they often worked. Some ex-slaves became destitute and swelled the rolls of northern poorhouses.

Even young and healthy free blacks had great difficulty finding anything but low-paying menial jobs. Whereas slaves had once been used in a variety of occupations, the slow progress of gradual emancipation allowed former slave owners and working-class whites time to craft racially discriminatory statutes and practices designed to keep blacks at the bottom of the northern labor market. As slaves, black northerners had not competed directly with white workers for paying jobs. Now white workers saw them as a threat. Many whites were unwilling to work alongside blacks, and many white employers were reluctant to hire former slaves for anything other than menial labor, so even highly skilled ex-slaves had difficulty securing well-paying jobs. Instead, free blacks were welcome only in service trades that were closely associated with slavery. Black women worked as washerwomen, seamstresses, and cooks, while black men were employed as laborers, mariners, barbers, coachmen, porters, and bootblacks.

Northern whites were quick to blame free blacks' poverty and low occupational status on inherent racial inferiority rather than social forces, which only compounded the discrimination that free blacks faced.

Still, black northerners remained hopeful that education would improve the status of their race and help their children to succeed in life, and they worked hard to create educational opportunities for their offspring. Most northern municipalities did not have public schools until the 1830s, however, and the ones that existed were not always welcoming to black children. Boston established a public school system as early as the 1790s, but the African Americans who attended were treated poorly. The black minister Hosea Easton, who attended school in Boston in the early 1800s, later recalled his teachers' blatant racism. Pupils who misbehaved, black or white, were banished to the "nigger seat," while those who did not complete their lessons were deemed as "poor or ignorant as a *nigger*" or as having "no more credit than a *nigger*." According to Easton, this training had a "disastrous [effect] upon the mind of the community; having been instructed from youth to look upon a black man in no other light than a slave." It also drove black parents in Boston to establish their own African School in 1798.[22]

In Philadelphia, African Americans who wished to educate their children faced different obstacles. The city had no public schools prior to 1818, and although the Pennsylvania Society for Promoting the Abolition of Slavery (PAS), a white philanthropic organization, founded a private school for black children at the beginning of the nineteenth century, many parents could not afford to pay the tuition. The fact that PAS leaders decided not to fund schools taught by black teachers — withdrawing the support they had once provided to Richard Allen's church — may have alienated black parents as well, and many continued to send their children to Allen's church to be educated.

In New York, the New York Manumission Society (NYMS) established the New York African Free School in 1787, creating perhaps the most successful early black school established by white reformers. Its distinguished graduates included Ira Aldridge, who became a renowned black actor, and James McCune Smith, the first African American to receive a medical degree. But the NYMS's ideas about education were not always in accord with those of black parents and teachers, and they highlighted the divisions separating early-nineteenth-century blacks from their white allies.

The NYMS, an exclusively white organization founded by some of New York's wealthiest men, had relatively modest antislavery goals. It supported the education and careful supervision of New York's free black population in the hope of fostering public support for abolition. The organization's members resolved to "keep a watchful eye over the conduct of such Negroes as have been or may be liberated; and . . . to prevent them from running into immorality or sinking into idleness." In 1788, they even established the Committee for Preventing Irregular Conduct Among Free Negroes. The New York African Free School set similar goals for both its pupils and

The New York African Free School

The New York African Free School, established in 1787 by the New York Manumission Society, began as a one-room schoolhouse with forty students, most of whose parents were slaves. In 1835, it was incorporated into the New York City public school system. The African Free School had by then graduated more than fourteen hundred students, many of whom went on to achieve distinction in a variety of professions and to advance the cause of abolitionism. The building depicted here is most likely the replacement for the original schoolhouse, which was destroyed in a fire in 1814. *Drawing of the Exterior of the New York African Free School with Penmanship.* Manuscripts Penmanship and Drawing Book, AFS, 1822, vol. 4, p. 6, negative #59134/ Collection of the New-York Historical Society.

their parents, to the point where school administrators reserved the right to place former pupils in jobs or apprenticeships rather than letting them "waste their time in idleness . . . [or] mingle in bad company" once they left school.[23]

Even in cities with black schools, securing an education remained a challenge. These schools were chronically underfunded and short of books and supplies. In addition, not all black parents could afford to send their children to school. Many black youngsters had to work to support their families, while others stayed home because their parents had no money for school clothing or shoes.

Education was a double-edged sword even for those black northerners lucky enough to attend school. Subject to the same racial prejudices as other African Americans, educated blacks were shut out of most jobs, both skilled and unskilled. "What are my prospects?" the valedictorian of the New York African Free School's class of 1819 asked rhetorically when he addressed his fellow classmates. "Shall I be a mechanic? No one will employ me; white boys won't work with me. Shall I be a merchant? No one will have me in his office; white clerks won't associate with me."[24] But education would nevertheless be crucial. During the early decades of the nineteenth century, black schools educated important black leaders whose speeches and publications helped sustain their community's struggle for abolition and civil rights. (See Document Project: Free Black Activism, pp. 162–69.)

White Hostility Rises, Yet Blacks Are Still Called to Serve in the War of 1812

Ironically, African Americans faced more rather than less racial hostility as they moved from slavery to freedom at the turn of the nineteenth century. Many whites continued to see blacks as an economic threat and a social menace. Emancipated blacks, concentrated in urban areas and often impoverished, formed a highly visible underclass in northern cities, where they performed much of the noisiest, dirtiest work. White New Yorkers complained that the "army of black sweeps" left the city filled with dust, that black street vendors were the source of New York's most hideous and outlandish crimes, and that the black tubmen who emptied New York's privies left the houses they passed "filled with stinking stench."[25] Even the activities of more prosperous blacks made many northern whites nervous. Blacks' establishment of their own institutions, as well as the public events they staged to celebrate emancipation, suggested that blacks were beginning to succeed in raising their social status. Consequently, whites regarded free blacks with alarm and subjected them to relentless hostility, mockery, and violence.

Blacks met "daily insults . . . in the streets of Boston," the Revolutionary War veteran Prince Hall complained in 1797. This harassment only escalated on "public days of recreation," when drunken white ruffians celebrated special occasions such as Independence Day by beating black men and stripping "helpless old women."[26] Such actions finally forced African Americans to move their own Independence Day celebrations from July 4 to July 5. Racial violence increased in the early nineteenth century, as white troublemakers and mobs began targeting black institutions, disrupting services at black churches, and sometimes even attacking black congregations. They also began to mock emancipation itself. Racist broadsides made fun of black gatherings to commemorate the abolition of slavery by calling these events **Bobalition** (a deliberate garbling of *abolition*) celebrations.

Northern free blacks and their white allies did not always agree on how best to combat growing prejudice and the persistence of slavery elsewhere in the nation. Members of early white antislavery organizations such as the PAS and NYMS, convinced that prejudice could be addressed only by reforming African Americans, sponsored schools dedicated to young blacks' moral and religious education and urged African Americans to avoid any behavior that might offend whites. Moreover, these white reformers remained cautious about challenging other Americans' property rights and condemned slavery without calling for slaveholders to free their slaves. Instead, they supported the United States' withdrawal from the international slave trade and gradual emancipation within their home states.

By contrast, as early as the 1790s, black activists appealed to Congress to end what one petition called slavery's "unconstitutional bondage."[27] Although ignored by Congress, such petitions articulated a vision of American citizenship in which African Americans qualified for the same federal protection offered to all other Americans. African American leaders also parted company with white antislavery reformers in identifying white racism as one of the greatest obstacles facing the antislavery movement.

Racism and White Hostility

Like many other racist broadsides that appeared in the early nineteenth century, *Dreadful Riot on Negro Hill!* parodies free blacks' speech, activities, and attempts to achieve success in the North. This document, which is billed as a "copy of an intercepted letter from PHILLIS, to her sister in the country," describes a riot in a black urban neighborhood. The text, written in unflattering poetic verse, and the name "Phillis" (which appeared in a number of broadsides) are meant to mock the poet Phillis Wheatley. Consider this image alongside the engraving of Wheatley in chapter 3 (p. 97). How does this portrayal speak to that one? *1827 Broadside/Library of Congress, LC-USZ62-34025.*

Richard Allen and Absalom Jones addressed this issue in a 1794 protest pamphlet, condemning the racist arguments that whites used to justify slavery. "Will you . . . plead our incapacity for freedom, and our contented condition under oppression, as a sufficient cause for keeping us under the grievous yoke?" they asked.[28]

As the egalitarian spirit of the Revolutionary era waned at the beginning of the nineteenth century, African American civil rights contracted, and black leaders had reason to fear that racism would undermine black freedom even in the North. However, black soldiers who served in the War of 1812 hoped that their patriotism would help them win full citizenship. Celebrated by many Americans as the "second war of Independence," the War of 1812 (1812–1815) was caused by conflicts between the United States and Britain over trade rights, the U.S. expansion into British and Indian lands in the Northwest, and Britain's practice of forcibly conscripting American sailors into the British Royal Navy. The war came at a time when the United States had all but eliminated black soldiers from its army. Not only did Congress restrict militia service to "free, able-bodied white male citizens," but most states' militias had similar restrictions, as did the Marine Corps, which was established in 1798.

But the War of 1812 was largely a naval war, and the new nation's navy was too short of personnel to turn away experienced sailors of any color. Instead, African Americans, who had long been one of the shipping industry's major sources of manpower, made up 10 to 20 percent of the crews that defended America's coasts and Great Lakes, and often fought with notable valor. Assigned to reclaim Lake Erie from the British, American commodore Oliver Hazard Perry initially expressed little confidence in some 150 reinforcements sent by his superior officer, Commodore Isaac Chauncey, complaining that they were "a motley set, blacks, Soldiers, and boys." He later changed his appraisal of the African American sailors, however, and reported to Chauncey that he was impressed by the "bravery and good conduct of the negroes," who formed a considerable part of his crew. Captain Isaac Hull, commander of the USS *Constitution*, expressed similar sentiments, albeit in language that underscored that black military service did not always diminish white racial prejudices. "I never had any better fighters than those niggers," Hull later recalled; "they stripped to the waist and fought like devils."[29]

Free black civilians also supported the war effort. In Philadelphia, a Committee of Defense composed of 2,500 black volunteers built fortifications designed to secure the city from British naval attack. Moreover, African Americans joined the war as combatants at the Battle of New Orleans, the war's final conflict. In the fall of 1814, with one of the nation's most important seaports under siege, General Andrew Jackson issued a call to arms to free blacks, appealing for their support as "fellow citizens." The more than 500 free blacks who responded to his call fought in a segregated regiment that formed one-twelfth of the general's forces.

But despite the many contributions of African Americans to the war effort, their civil rights continued to erode. New Jersey blacks lost the right to vote in 1807, even before the war. Blacks also were disfranchised in Connecticut in 1814 and in Pennsylvania in 1838. Even in states where free blacks retained the franchise, they faced voter discrimination. New York, for example, imposed prohibitively high property requirements on black voters, even after abolishing all such requirements for white voters in 1821.

The Colonization Debate

Given the abiding prejudices that African Americans faced during the post-Revolutionary era, some members of both races began to question blacks' long-term prospects for success in the United States. Fearing they would never achieve full citizenship, blacks occasionally contemplated abandoning the United States altogether. Some whites expressed great enthusiasm for their departure, proposing **colonization** schemes designed to send African Americans back to Africa.

During the late eighteenth century, when many blacks were still relatively recent arrivals, some were eager to return to the land of their ancestors. In 1787, a group of Massachusetts blacks petitioned the state legislature to help them migrate to Africa. They asked for help in raising money to "procure lands to settle upon; and to obtain a passage for us and our families."[30] Their petition was never answered, but the idea resurfaced in 1815, when a wealthy black businessman and ship captain named Paul Cuffe, or Cuffee, took thirty-eight black Bostonians to the West African colony of Sierra Leone.

Sierra Leone, founded in 1787 by British reformer Granville Sharp as a refuge for some of London's black poor, was also home to approximately twelve hundred black loyalists from Nova Scotia, many of whom had fled slavery in the United States. Although the main intent of the colony was the repatriation of former slaves to West Africa, it was of interest to Cuffe because his father, Cuffe Slocum, had been born in West Africa. After visiting Sierra Leone in 1811, Cuffe began to consider taking "to Africa some Sober Stedy habited peopel of Colour in order to incourage Soberiety and industry and to interduce culteriantion and Commersce."[31] Cuffe knew a number of African-born men and women who wished to return to the continent, and in 1812 he began to make arrangements to transport a group of them to the colony.

Cuffe's voyage in 1815, however, was not a success. His commercial plans were foiled by British officials who refused to allow him to unload the cargo he had hoped to sell to finance the trip, leaving him $1,700 in debt. He had never planned to lead a mass movement of blacks back to Africa and vowed not to travel there again without assurances that British officials would be more cooperative in the future. He also cautioned other colonization supporters that Sierra Leone was unlikely to welcome large numbers of American expatriates. Cuffe himself never returned to Sierra Leone; he became sick in the summer of 1817 and died that fall.

Although Cuffe's expedition had the support of black leaders such as Absalom Jones, it did not foster a colonization movement among American blacks. Instead, it captured the imagination of white reformers, whose enthusiasm soon had free black communities across the North worried about a forced migration. Reform-minded whites had long "indulge[d] a hope that . . . free people of color be removed to the coast of Africa with their own consent," the Presbyterian minister Robert Finley wrote Cuffe in 1816, appealing to the ship captain to help him plan a mass migration.[32] With Cuffe's voyage standing as testimony to colonization's practical possibility, Finley founded a national organization to promote the colonization of free blacks.

The American Society for Colonizing the Free People of Color of the United States, more popularly known as the American Colonization Society (ACS), first met in Washington, D.C., in 1816. Made up of prominent white clergymen, lawyers, financiers, and politicians—including Speaker of the House Henry Clay—the ACS appealed to both slaveholders and those opposed to slavery. Although Finley hoped colonization would eventually bring an end to slavery, the ACS planned to colonize free blacks only. Its members agreed to avoid the "delicate question" of emancipation, instead assuring southerners that colonization would help secure their slave property by ridding the region of free blacks.[33] Meanwhile, antislavery advocates believed that colonization would facilitate manumissions, allowing planters to free their slaves without enlarging the region's already unpopular free black population or violating the states' manumission laws. By 1819, the ACS's influential white supporters included President James Monroe, who helped the organization secure a congressional appropriation of $100,000 for its cause. In 1821, the ACS used the money to establish the colony of Liberia on the west coast of Africa and to recruit potential migrants.

Most of the blacks the ACS shipped to Liberia were former slaves liberated by the organization in order to allow their emigration. Although the ACS was eager to recruit free blacks, most were both unwilling to move and deeply suspicious. Less than a month after the first ACS meeting in 1816, three thousand free blacks gathered in Richard Allen's Philadelphia church to adopt a set of resolutions denouncing colonization as an "unmerited stigma attempted to be cast upon the reputation of the free people of color." Many of those gathered were American-born blacks with few ties to Africa, and many suspected that colonization was merely a plan to prop up slavery by shipping America's free blacks out of the United States. They issued a statement saying, "We never will separate ourselves voluntarily from the slave population in this country."[34] Although the black leader James Forten, who presided over the meeting and recorded the resolutions, had previously supported Cuffe's voyage to Sierra Leone on the grounds that black Americans would "never become a people untell they com[e] out from amongst the white people," black Philadelphians' mass opposition to the ACS changed his mind.[35]

Most African Americans remained suspicious of colonization throughout the antebellum era. But white enthusiasm for the idea did not depend on black support, and the American Colonization Society continued to attract white members.

CONCLUSION

African American Freedom in Black and White

Faced with the threat of forced removal, northern free blacks saw the idea of colonization as an assault on their community. Like Benjamin Banneker several decades earlier, they were convinced that African Americans were entitled to the rights and freedoms that Americans had defended during the Revolution, and they believed that immediate emancipation was the only way to end slavery in the United States.

After 1817, northern free blacks drew on the network of mutual aid societies and churches they had founded as they fought their way out of slavery. The anticolonization campaign that they mounted linked the future of all African Americans, both slave and free, to a freedom struggle that would not end until slavery was abolished throughout the United States. Laying new and stronger claims to the United States as "the land of our nativity," northern blacks drew on their own recent history to insist that slavery could be defeated. "Every year, many of us have restored to us by the gradual, but certain march of the cause of abolition—Parents from whom we have long been separated—Wives and Children whom we had left in servitude—and Brothers, in blood as well as in early sufferings, from whom we had long been parted," Philadelphia's anticolonizationist blacks maintained.[36]

The new Republic's black southerners, by contrast, had much less cause for optimism. Although free black communities expanded in some parts of the South during the nation's early decades, slavery experienced more spectacular gains with the growth of plantation agriculture. Slavery was protected by federal laws mandating the return of fugitive slaves and sanctioned in the Constitution, which gave slaveholders additional political representation under the three-fifths clause. With the acquisition of Louisiana from France, the United States further guaranteed slavery's institutional strength by acquiring vast new territories that would soon become home to slaveholding settlers. As slavery's cotton frontier expanded into Louisiana, Mississippi, and Alabama during the first half of the nineteenth century, the expansion of plantation agriculture brought wealth and power to the region's slaveholders and tremendous anguish to the slaves. Once the United States ceased importing slaves from Africa in 1808, most of the slaves who cleared the land and cultivated the crops in these new states were American-born. The majority hailed from the Chesapeake or the northern states and had to leave behind families, friends, and neighbors as they embarked on the forced migration to plantations in the deep South.

CHAPTER 4 **REVIEW**

KEY TERMS

cash crops p. 133
Northwest Ordinance (1787) p. 134
fugitive slave clause p. 135
Three-Fifths Compromise p. 135
Louisiana Purchase (1803) p. 141
hiring out p. 144
living out p. 144
black laws p. 148
Naturalization Act of 1790 p. 148
mutual aid society p. 151
Bobalition p. 156
colonization p. 158

REVIEW QUESTIONS

1. Describe the fate of slavery in the post-Revolutionary years and the various factors — political, social, and economic — that contributed to this state of affairs. Would it have been possible to predict in 1783 that things would turn out this way? Why or why not? How might things have been different if political, social, or economic circumstances had been different?

2. Describe the various freedoms allowed, and the restrictions placed on, urban slaves, southern free blacks, northern slaves, and newly emancipated northern free blacks. What limits to their freedom and mobility did each group experience? Which groups were the most and the least restricted and why?

3. Why did whites grow increasingly hostile toward African Americans as they moved from slavery to freedom? How did the proliferation of free black organizations help African Americans combat this hostility?

4. How did the colonization effort change from a small, black-led initiative to a large, white-led movement? What initial appeal did colonization have for its black supporters? How was this different from the appeal it held for whites, both slaveholders and abolitionists?

Free Black Activism

While the American Revolution greatly enlarged the size of the free black population, the rights that free blacks obtained were never secure. Free blacks could not testify on their own behalf in southern courts, which meant that they had no legal means to free themselves if they were abducted by slave traders, and even in northern states such as Pennsylvania, they were required to document their freedom. By the early nineteenth century, many whites had begun to embrace colonization rather than civil rights as a remedy for the discrimination that free blacks faced, forcing free blacks to fight for a place in the United States.

The following documents include a 1799 petition to Congress composed by the Philadelphia clergyman Absalom Jones, which protested the fact that the federal government's fugitive slave law made free blacks vulnerable to illegal enslavement; a selection from an 1813 pamphlet condemning a discriminatory bill under consideration in Pennsylvania; a list of resolutions opposing colonization from a meeting of free blacks in 1817; and an editorial introducing the inaugural issue of the nation's first black newspaper. They are supplemented by an abolitionist engraving illustrating the kidnapping of a free black woman and child and a racist cartoon mocking African American celebrations of the "Bobalition" of slavery. Taken together, these documents show free blacks' efforts to secure their status by expressing their views on slavery, racial discrimination, and African American civil rights, as well as portraying some of the physical and psychological dangers they faced.

Absalom Jones and Others | Petition to Congress on the Fugitive Slave Act, 1799

The following petition is one of the earliest surviving free black petitions to the U.S. Congress. Written by ABSALOM JONES (1746–1818) and signed by more than seventy others, it was submitted on December 30, 1799. Its authors contend that the Fugitive Slave Act of 1793, which was passed to enforce the Constitution's fugitive slave clause and allowed slave catchers to detain slaves and free blacks, threatened the lives and welfare of African Americans. The petitioners sought protection for free blacks abducted by slave catchers and challenged the constitutional basis of slavery. Congress ignored their appeal. How do the petitioners use the Constitution to make their argument?

To the President, Senate, and House of Representatives.

The Petition of the People of Colour, free men, within the City and Suburbs of Philadelphia, humbly sheweth,

That, thankful to God, our Creator, and to the Government under which we live, for the blessings and benefits granted to us in the enjoyment of our natural right to liberty, and the protection of our persons and property, from the oppression

SOURCE: Petition of Absalom Jones and others, December 30, 1799, *Records of the U.S. House of Representatives*, Record Group 233 (4~HR6A-F4.2. Jan. 2, 1800), National Archives, Washington, DC.

and violence which so great a number of like colour and national descent are subject to, we feel ourselves bound, from a sense of these blessings, to continue in our respective allotments, and to lead honest and peaceable lives, rendering due submission unto the laws, and exciting and encouraging each other thereto, agreeable to the uniform advice of our friends, of every denomination; yet while we feel impressed with grateful sensations for the Providential favour we ourselves enjoy, we cannot be insensible of the condition of our afflicted brethren, suffering under various circumstances, in different parts of these states; but deeply sympathizing with them, are incited by a sense of social duty, and humbly conceive ourselves authorized to address and petition you on their behalf, believing them to be objects of your representation in your public councils, in common with ourselves and every other class of citizens within the jurisdiction of the United States, according to the design of the present Constitution, formed by the General Convention, and ratified in the different states, as set forth in the preamble thereto in the following words, viz. "We, the people of the United States, in order to form a more perfect union, establish justice, insure domestic tranquillity, provide for the common defence, and to secure the blessings of liberty to ourselves and posterity, do ordain, &c." We apprehend this solemn compact is violated, by a trade carried on in a clandestine manner, to the coast of Guinea, and another equally wicked, practised openly by citizens of some of the southern states, upon the waters of Maryland and Delaware; men sufficiently callous to qualify them for the brutal purpose, are employed in kidnapping those of our brethren that are free, and purchasing others of such as claim a property in them: thus, those poor helpless victims, like droves of cattle, are seized, fettered, and hurried into places provided for this most horrid traffic, such as dark cellars and garrets, as is notorious at Northwest-fork, Chestertown, Eastown, and divers other places. After a sufficient number is obtained, they are forced on board vessels, crouded under hatches, without the least commiseration, left to deplore the sad separation of the dearest ties in nature, husband from wife, and parents from children; thus packed together, they are transported to Georgia and other places, and there inhumanly exposed to sale. Can any commerce, trade, or transaction, so detestably shock the feeling of man, or degrade the dignity of his nature equal to this? And how increasingly is the evil aggravated, when practised in a land high in profession of the benign doctrines of our Blessed Lord, who taught his followers to do unto others as they would they should do unto them. Your petitioners desire not to enlarge, though volumes might be filled with the sufferings of this grossly abused part of the human species, seven hundred thousand of whom, it is said, are now in unconditional bondage in these states: but conscious of the rectitude of our motives in a concern so nearly affecting us, and so effectually interesting to the welfare of this country, we cannot but address you as guardians of our rights, and patrons of equal and national liberties, hoping you will view the subject in an impartial, unprejudiced light. We do not ask for an immediate emancipation of all, knowing that the degraded state of many, and their want of education, would greatly disqualify for such a change; yet, humbly desire you may exert every means in your power to undo the heavy burdens, and prepare the way for the oppressed to go free, that every yoke may be broken. The law not long since enacted by Congress, called the Fugitive Bill, is in its execution found to be attended with circumstances peculiarly hard and distressing; for many of our afflicted brethren, in order to avoid the barbarities wantonly exercised upon them, or through fear of being carried off by those men-stealers, being forced to seek refuge by flight, they are then, by armed men, under colour of this law, cruelly treated, or brought back in chains to those that have no claim upon them. In the Constitution and the Fugitive Bill, no mention is made of black people, or slaves;

therefore, if the Bill of Rights, or the Declaration of Congress are of any validity, we beseech, that as we are men, we may be admitted to partake of the liberties and unalienable rights therein held forth; firmly believing that the extending of justice and equity to all classes, would be a means of drawing down the blessing of Heaven upon this land, for the peace and prosperity of which, and the real happiness of every member of the community, we fervently pray.

James Forten | *Letters from a Man of Colour, 1813*

Published anonymously in 1813, the pamphlet *Letters from a Man of Colour* was written by JAMES FORTEN (1766–1842), a prosperous black businessman. It contained a series of letters condemning a bill then under consideration before the Pennsylvania Senate that would have required all blacks who entered Pennsylvania to register with the state. Proposed at a time when antiblack hostility was on the rise throughout the North, the bill, which did not pass, aimed to make it more difficult for both fugitive slaves and free blacks to settle in Pennsylvania. As the following letter makes clear, Forten was outraged by the bill. What was the source of his outrage?

We hold this truth to be self-evident, that GOD created all men equal, and is one of the most prominent features in the Declaration of Independence, and in that glorious fabrick of collected wisdom, our noble Constitution. This idea embraces the Indian and the European, the Savage and the Saint, the Peruvian and the Laplander, the white Man and the African, and whatever measures are adopted subversive of this inestimable privilege, are in direct violation of the letter and the spirit of our Constitution, and become subject to the animadversion of all, particularly those who are deeply interested in the measure.

These thoughts were suggested by the promulgation of a late bill, before the Senate of Pennsylvania, to prevent the emigration of people of colour into this state. It was not passed into a law at this session and must in consequence lay over until the next, before when we sincerely hope, the white men, whom we should look upon as our protectors, will have become convinced of the inhumanity and impolicy of such a measure, and forbear to deprive us of those inestimable treasures, Liberty and Independence. This is almost the only state in the Union wherein the African race have justly boasted of rational liberty and the protection of the laws, and shall it now be said they have been deprived of that liberty, and publickly exposed for sale to the highest bidder? Shall colonial inhumanity that has marked many of us with shameful stripes, become the practice of the people of Pennsylvania, while Mercy stands weeping at the miserable spectacle? People of Pennsylvania, descendants of the immortal Penn, doom us not to the unhappy fate of thousands of our countrymen in the Southern States and the West Indies; despise the traffick in blood, and the blessing of the African will for ever be around you. Many of us are men of property, for the security of which, we have hitherto looked to the laws of our blessed state, but should this become a law, our property is jeopardized, since the same power which can expose to sale an unfortunate fellow creature, can wrest from him those estates, which years of honest industry have accumulated. Where shall the poor African look for protection, should the people of Pennsylvania

SOURCE: [James Forten], *Letters from a Man of Colour, on a Late Bill before the Senate of Pennsylvania* (Pennsylvania: n.p., 1813), 1–3.

consent to oppress him? We grant there are a number of worthless men belonging to our colour, but there are laws of sufficient rigour for their punishment, if properly and duly enforced. We wish not to screen the guilty from punishment, but with the guilty do not permit the innocent to suffer. If there are worthless men, there are also men of merit among the African race, who are useful members of Society. The truth of this let their benevolent institutions and the numbers clothed and fed by them witness. Punish the guilty man of colour to the utmost limit of the laws, but sell him not slavery! If he is in danger of becoming a publick charge prevent him! If he is too indolent to labour for his own subsistence, compel him to do so; but sell him not to slavery. By selling him you do not make him better, but commit a wrong, without benefitting the object of it or society at large. Many of our ancestors were brought here more than one hundred years ago; many of our fathers, many of ourselves, have fought and bled for the Independence of our country. Do not then expose us to sale. Let not the spirit of the father behold the son robbed of that Liberty which he died to establish, but let the motto of our legislators, be: "The Law knows no distinction."

Sentiments of the People of Color, 1817

In January 1817, free blacks gathered at Richard Allen's Bethel AME Church in Philadelphia to voice their opposition to colonization and to articulate their claims to a permanent place in the United States. The meeting adopted the following resolutions.

Whereas our ancestors (not of choice) were the first successful cultivators of the wilds of America, we their descendants feel ourselves entitled to participate in the blessings of her luxuriant soil, which their blood and sweat manured; and that any measure or system of measures, having a tendency to banish us from her bosom, would not only be cruel, but in direct violation of those principles, which have been the boast of this republic.

Resolved, That we view with deep abhorrence the unmerited stigma attempted to be cast upon the reputation of the free people of color, by the promoters of this measure, "that they are a dangerous and useless part of the community," when in the state of disfranchisement in which they live, in the hour of danger they ceased to remember their wrongs, and rallied around the standard of their country.

Resolved, That we never will separate ourselves voluntarily from the slave population in this country; they are our brethren by the ties of consanguinity, of suffering, and of wrong; and we feel that there is more virtue in suffering privations with them, than fancied advantages for a season.

Resolved, That without arts, without science, without a proper knowledge of government, to cast into the savage wilds of Africa the free people of color, seems to us the circuitous route through which they must return to perpetual bondage.

Resolved, That having the strongest confidence in the justice of God, and philanthropy of the free states, we cheerfully submit our destinies to the guidance of Him who suffers not a sparrow to fall, without his special providence.

Resolved, That a committee of eleven persons be appointed to open a correspondence with the honorable Joseph Hopkinson, member of Congress from this city, and likewise to inform him of the sentiments of this meeting, and that the

SOURCE: "Sentiments of the People of Color" (1817), reprinted in William Lloyd Garrison, *Thoughts on African Colonization*, Part II (Boston: Garrison and Knapp, 1832), 9–10.

following named persons constitute the committee, and that they have power to call a general meeting, when they in their judgment may deem it proper.

Rev. Absalom Jones, Rev. Richard Allen, James Forten, Robert Douglass, Francis Perkins,

Rev. John Gloucester, Robert Gorden, James Johnson, Quamoney Clarkson, John Summersett, Randall Shepherd.

JAMES FORTEN, Chairman.
Russell Parrott, Secretary.

Samuel E. Cornish and John Brown Russwurm | *An Editorial from* Freedom's Journal, 1827

Freedom's Journal, the nation's first African American–owned and–operated newspaper, was founded in New York City in 1827 by Episcopal priest Peter J. Williams (1786–1840) and several other prominent black New Yorkers. The paper's founders selected SAMUEL E. CORNISH (1795–1858), a Presbyterian minister, and JOHN BROWN RUSSWURM (1799–1851), a recent graduate of Bowdoin and one of the first African Americans to graduate from an American college, to serve as the paper's editors. Written by Cornish and Russwurm and featured in the paper's inaugural issue, the editorial excerpted here outlines the new publication's goals.

TO OUR PATRONS.

. . . We wish to plead our own cause. Too long have others spoken for us. Too long has the publick been deceived by misrepresentations, in things which concern us dearly, though in the estimation of some mere trifles; for though there are many in society who exercise towards us benevolent feelings; still (with sorrow we confess it) there are others who make it their business to enlarge upon the least trifle, which tends to the discredit of any person of colour; and pronounce anathemas and denounce our whole body for the misconduct of this guilty one. We are aware that there are many instances of vice among us, but we avow that it is because no one has taught its subjects to be virtuous: many instances of poverty, because no sufficient efforts accommodated to minds contracted by slavery, and deprived of early education have been made, to teach them how to husband their hard earnings, and to secure to themselves comforts.

Education being an object of the highest importance to the welfare of society, we shall endeavour to present just and adequate views of it, and to urge upon our brethren the necessity and expediency of training their children, while young, to habits of industry, and thus forming them for becoming useful members of society. . . .

Though not desiring of dictating, we shall feel it our incumbent duty to dwell occasionally upon the general principles and rules of economy. The world has grown too enlightened, to estimate any man's character by his personal appearance. Though all men acknowledge the excellency of Franklin's maxims, yet comparatively few practise upon them. We may deplore when it is too late, the neglect of these self-evident truths, but it avails little to mourn. Ours will be the task of admonishing our brethren on these points.

The civil rights of a people being of the greatest value, it shall ever be our duty to vindicate our brethren, when oppressed, and to lay the case

---

SOURCE: *Freedom's Journal*, March 16, 1827.

before the publick. We shall also urge upon our brethren, (who are qualified by the laws of the different states) the expediency of using their elective franchise; and of making an independent use of the same. We wish them not to become the tools of party. . . .

It is our earnest wish to make our Journal a medium of intercourse between our brethren in the different states of this great confederacy: that through its columns an expression of our sentiments, on many interesting subjects which concern us, may be offered to the publick: that plans which apparently are beneficial may be candidly discussed and properly weighed; if worthy, receive our cordial approbation; if not, our marked disapprobation.

Useful knowledge of every kind, and every thing that relates to Africa, shall find a ready admission into our columns; and as that vast continent becomes daily more known, we trust that many things will come to light, proving that the natives of it are neither so ignorant nor stupid as they have generally been supposed to be.

And while these important subjects shall occupy the columns of the FREEDOM'S JOURNAL, we would not be unmindful of our brethren who are still in the iron fetters of bondage. They are our kindred by all the ties of nature; and though but little can be effected by us, still let our sympathies be poured forth, and our prayers in their behalf, ascend to Him who is able to succour them. . . .

THE EDITORS

Kidnapping of an African American Mother and Child, c. 1840

This engraving from an abolitionist publication dramatizes the kidnapping of a free black mother and child. Known as "blackbirding," this sinister practice was a threat to the liberties of all northern free blacks. Blackbirders could earn easy money by abducting free blacks and selling them to slave traders. Children were a particularly popular target, since they could easily be overpowered.

Culver Pictures/The Art Archive at Art Resource, NY.

Edward Williams Clay | *Bobalition, 1833*

In the 1820s Philadelphia-born artist EDWARD WILLIAMS Clay produced a series of cartoons under the title *Life in Philadelphia* in which he made fun of the city's African American population. The cartoon on page 169, entitled "Grand Celebration ob de Bobalition ob African Slabery," satirizes black celebrations of the prohibition of the international slave trade. Bobalition cartoons and other documents that were also common in Massachusetts lampooned the manners, speech, and political aspirations of northern free blacks. In "Grand Celebration," a group of drunken black men make absurd toasts:

"De day we Celumbrate! Who he no come sooner? Guess de hard fros & de backward Spring put um back. 29 pop gun & 2 grin."

"De Orator ob de day — When I jus hear him begin he discourse, tink he no great ting, but when he come to de end ob um, I tink he like de scorch cat more better dan he look — Moosick — Possum up de Gum tree"

"White man — mighty anxuius to send nigger, to de place dey stole him from, now he got no furder use for him."

"Gubner Eustas — Cleber old sole as eber wore nee buckle in de shoe — 99 cheer an tree quarter."

"De Genuis de Merica — He invent great many curious ting: wonder who fus invent eating & drinking. 30 cheer & ober."

"De Sun — Wonder why he no shine in de night putting nigger to dispense ob de candle."

"Joe Gales — He ax massa Adams 'if he be in health my brudder' and den he cut he guts out."

"King Edwards — Guess he no great tings no more nor udder people all he cut such a swell."

© Hulton-Deutsch Collection/Corbis.

QUESTIONS FOR ANALYSIS

1. What were the specific goals of the free blacks represented in these images and documents? What common problems did they share, and what solutions did they seek?

2. To what communities and authorities did the petitioners, letter writers, and abolitionist artist represented here appeal in their quest for racial justice?

3. What did *Freedom's Journal* hope to achieve? Was the newspaper in dialogue with the Bobalition cartoon and with other white depictions of black people?

4. How might the regions in which these petitioners, letter writers, and artists lived have influenced their outlooks?

NOTES

1. Benjamin Banneker to Thomas Jefferson, 19 August 1791, reprinted in John H. B. Latrobe, "Memoir of Benjamin Banneker," *African Repository, and Colonial Journal* 21 (November 1845): 330.
2. Ibid.
3. Jefferson to Benjamin Banneker, 30 August 1791, in *The Works of Thomas Jefferson*, ed. Paul Leicester Ford, vol. 6 (New York: G. P. Putnam's Sons, 1904), 309–10.
4. Thomas Jefferson, *Notes on the State of Virginia* (London: printed for John Stockdale, 1787), 239.
5. Thomas Jefferson to Joel Barlow, 8 October 1809, in *The Works of Thomas Jefferson*, ed. Paul Leicester Ford, vol. 11 (New York: G. P. Putnam's Sons, 1905), 121.
6. James Madison, speech, Constitutional Convention, June 1787, in *The Debates in the Several State Conventions on the Adoption of the Federal Constitution*, ed. Jonathan Elliott (New York: Lippincott, 1876), 5:162.
7. Quoted in Ira Berlin, *Generations of Captivity: A History of African-American Slaves* (Cambridge: Belknap Press of Harvard University Press, 2003), 151.
8. Charles Ball, *Fifty Years in Chains; or, The Life of an American Slave* (New York: H. Dayton, 1859), 29.
9. Ibid., 430.
10. Quoted in Thomas J. Fleming, *The Louisiana Purchase* (Hoboken, NJ: John Wiley and Sons, 2003), 110.
11. Quoted in Seth Rockman, *Scraping By: Wage Labor, Slavery, and Survival in Early Baltimore* (Baltimore: Johns Hopkins University Press, 2008), 36.
12. "Proceedings of the Virginia Legislature on the Subject of African Colonization," *African Repository, and Colonial Journal* 8, no. 4 (June 1832): 104.
13. Douglas R. Egerton, *Gabriel's Rebellion: The Virginia Slave Conspiracies of 1800 and 1802* (Chapel Hill: University of North Carolina Press, 1993), 164.
14. Quoted in Ira Berlin, *Slaves without Masters: The Free Negro in the Antebellum South* (New York: New Press, 2007), 89.
15. Revisors of the Laws, Virginia, *Draughts of Such Bills as Have Been Prepared by the Revisors of the Laws* (Richmond: Ritchie, Trueheart & Du-Val, and Shepherd & Pollard, 1817), 263.
16. Berlin, *Slaves without Masters*, 147.
17. Sojourner Truth, *Narrative of Sojourner Truth*, ed. Olive Gilbert (Boston: printed for the author, 1850), 39.
18. Ibid., 43.
19. "Preamble of the Free African Society," in William Douglass, *Annals of the First African Church, in the United States of America, Now Styled the African Episcopal Church of St. Thomas, Philadelphia* (Philadelphia: King & Baird, 1862), 15.
20. Quoted in Richard Newman, *Freedom's Prophet: Bishop Richard Allen, the AME Church, and the Black Founding Fathers* (New York: New York University Press, 2008), 64.
21. Ibid., 67.
22. Hosea Easton, *A Treatise on the Intellectual Character, and Civil and Political Condition of the Colored People of the U. States* (Boston: Isaac Knapp, 1837), 41, 43.
23. New York Manumission Society, *An Address to the Parents and Guardians of the Children Belonging to the New York African Free School, by the Trustees of the Institution* (New York: Samuel Wood and Sons, 1818), 20–21.
24. Quoted in Charles C. Andrews, *The History of the New-York African Free-Schools* (New York: Mahlon Day, 1830), 132.
25. *New York Evening Post*, September 22, 1826.
26. Quoted in *Proceedings of the One Hundredth Anniversary of the Granting of Warrant 459 to African Lodge, at Boston* (Boston: Franklin Press, 1885), 15.
27. *Annals of the Congress of the United States*, 4th Cong., 2nd sess. [March 1795–March 1797] (Washington, DC: Gales and Seaton, 1849), 6:2015–18.
28. Absalom Jones and Richard Allen, *A Narrative of the Proceedings of the Black People, During the Late Awful Calamity in Philadelphia, in the Year 1793: and a Refutation of Some Censures, Thrown upon Them in Some Late Publications* (Philadelphia: printed for the authors by William W. Woodward, 1794), 25.
29. Gerald T. Altoff, *Amongst My Best Men: African-Americans and the War of 1812* (Put-in-Bay, OH: Perry Group, 1996), 36, 40, 23.
30. Prince Hall and African Lodge No. 1, "Petition for Repatriation to Africa" (1787), in *The African American Experience: Black History and Culture through Speeches, Letters, Editorials, Poems, Songs, and Stories*, ed. Kai Wright (New York: Black Dog, 2009), 101.
31. Paul Cuffe to Nathan G. M. Senter, 1 March 1814, in *Captain Paul Cuffe's Logs and Letters, 1808–1817: A Black Quaker's "Voice from within the Veil,"* ed. Rosalind Cobb Wiggins (Washington, DC: Howard University Press, 1996), 276.
32. Quoted in Julie Winch, *A Gentleman of Color: The Life of James Forten* (New York: Oxford University Press, 2002), 188.
33. Prince Hall and African Lodge No. 1, "Petition for Repatriation to Africa," 101.
34. Resolution of Assembled Free Blacks, Bethel AME Church, Philadelphia, January 15, 1817, reprinted in William Lloyd Garrison, *Thoughts on African Colonization*, Part II (Boston: Garrison and Knapp, 1832), 9–10.
35. James Forten to Paul Cuffe, 25 January 1817, Cuffe Papers, quoted in Winch, *A Gentleman of Color*, 191.
36. American Convention for Promoting the Abolition of Slavery and Improving the Condition of the African Race, *Minutes of the Proceedings of a Special Meeting of the Fifteenth American Convention for Promoting the Abolition of Slavery and Improving the Condition of the African Race, Assembled at Philadelphia on the Tenth Day of December, 1818* (Philadelphia: printed for the convention by Hall & Atkinson, 1818), 70.

SUGGESTED REFERENCES

The Limits of Democracy

Berlin, Ira. *Generations of Captivity: A History of African-American Slaves.* Cambridge: Belknap Press of Harvard University Press, 2003.

Dain, Bruce. *A Hideous Monster of the Mind: American Race Theory in the Early Republic.* Cambridge: Harvard University Press, 2003.

Fischer, Sibylle. *Modernity Disavowed: Haiti and the Cultures of Slavery in the Age of Revolution.* Durham, NC: Duke University Press, 2004.

Kornblith, Gary J. *Slavery and Sectional Strife in the Early American Republic, 1776–1821.* Lanham, MD: Rowman & Littlefield, 2009.

Mason, Matthew. *Slavery and Politics in the Early American Republic.* Chapel Hill: University of North Carolina Press, 2008.

Morrison, Michael A., and James Brewer Stewart, eds. *Race and the Early Republic: Racial Consciousness and Nation-Building in the Early Republic.* Lanham, MD: Rowman & Littlefield, 2002.

Rothman, Adam. *Slave Country: American Expansion and the Origins of the Deep South.* Cambridge: Harvard University Press, 2005.

Van Cleve, George William. *A Slaveholders' Union: Slavery, Politics, and the Constitution in the Early American Republic.* Chicago: University of Chicago Press, 2010.

Waldstreicher, David. *Slavery's Constitution: From Revolution to Ratification.* New York: Hill and Wang, 2009.

Slavery and Freedom outside the Plantation South

Berlin, Ira. *Slaves without Masters: The Free Negro in the Antebellum South.* New York: New Press, 2007.

Curry, Leonard P. *The Free Black in Urban America, 1800–1850: The Shadow of the Dream.* Chicago: University of Chicago Press, 1986.

Egerton, Douglas R. *Gabriel's Rebellion: The Virginia Slave Conspiracies of 1800 and 1802.* Chapel Hill: University of North Carolina Press, 1993.

Horton, James Oliver, and Lois E. Horton. *Black Bostonians: Family Life and Community Struggle in the Antebellum North.* Rev. ed. New York: Holmes & Meier, 2000.

King, Wilma. *The Essence of Liberty: Free Black Women during the Slave Era.* Columbia: University of Missouri Press, 2006.

Litwack, Leon F. *North of Slavery: The Negro in the Free States, 1790–1860.* Chicago: University of Chicago Press, 1961.

Melish, Joanne Pope. *Disowning Slavery: Gradual Emancipation and "Race" in New England, 1780–1860.* Ithaca, NY: Cornell University Press, 2000.

Painter, Nell Irvin. *Sojourner Truth: A Life, a Symbol.* New York: Norton, 1996.

Rockman, Seth. *Scraping By: Wage Labor, Slavery, and Survival in Early Baltimore.* Baltimore: Johns Hopkins University Press, 2008.

Wade, Richard C. *Slavery in the Cities: The South, 1820–1860.* New York: Oxford University Press, 1967.

Zilversmit, Arthur. *The First Emancipation: The Abolition of Slavery in the North.* 3rd ed. Chicago: University of Chicago Press, 1969.

Free Black Life in the New Republic

Alexander, Leslie M. *African or American? Black Identity and Political Activism in New York City, 1784–1861.* Urbana: University of Illinois Press, 2008.

Dunbar, Erica Armstrong. *A Fragile Freedom: African American Women and Emancipation in the Antebellum City.* New Haven, CT: Yale University Press, 2008.

Horton, James Oliver, and Lois E. Horton. *In Hope of Liberty: Culture, Community, and Protest among Northern Free Blacks, 1700–1860.* New York: Oxford University Press, 1997.

Nash, Gary B. *Forging Freedom: The Formation of Philadelphia's Black Community, 1720–1840.* Cambridge: Harvard University Press, 1991.

Newman, Richard S. *Freedom's Prophet: Bishop Richard Allen, the AME Church, and the Black Founding Fathers.* New York: New York University Press, 2008.

———. *The Transformation of American Abolitionism: Fighting Slavery in the Early Republic.* Chapel Hill: University of North Carolina Press, 2002.

Sweet, John Wood. *Bodies Politic: Negotiating Race in the American North, 1730–1830.* Philadelphia: University of Pennsylvania Press, 2006.

White, Shane. *Stories of Freedom in Black New York.* Cambridge: Harvard University Press, 2007.

Winch, Julie. *A Gentleman of Color: The Life of James Forten.* New York: Oxford University Press, 2002.

CHAPTER 5

Black Life in the Slave South

1820–1860

William Wells Brown and Growing Up in the Slave South

William Wells Brown was born into slavery on a Kentucky plantation in 1814. His early experiences as a slave were varied and painful. Until he was twelve, he lived in rural Missouri, where his master, Dr. Young, moved his household of forty slaves shortly after Brown was born. Young employed Brown's mother and four older siblings on a tobacco and hemp plantation outside St. Louis, where Brown observed the brutal discipline imposed on plantation field hands. As an infant, he often rode on his mother's back while she worked in the fields because she was not allowed to leave the fields to nurse. As a young boy, he was routinely awakened by the sounds of the whippings that Young's overseer gave field hands — including Brown's mother and siblings — who were not at work by 4:30 a.m. He was close enough to the fields to "hear every crack of the whip, and every groan and cry," and he wept at the sounds.[1] More sorrow lay ahead after Young sold Brown's mother and siblings but kept Brown himself because he was the son of Young's cousin and fellow planter George Higgins.

Young hired the boy out to a variety of masters, leaving him with a broad understanding of enslaved life and labor in the antebellum South. His first employer, a tavern owner named Major Freeland, was short-tempered, unstable, and prone to lashing out at his slaves

without warning. To punish disobedient slaves, Freeland employed a technique he had learned in his home state of Virginia. Brown recalled that "he would tie them up in the smokehouse, and whip them; after which, he would cause a fire to be made of tobacco stems, and smoke them. This he called '*Virginia play.*'"[2] Brown was so terrified of Freeland that he ran away and hid in the woods, where another local slaveholder who kept a pack of bloodhounds for this purpose recaptured him. On his return to Freeland's tavern, Brown, too, was whipped and smoked.

After Freeland's business failed, Brown was promptly hired out again. He ended up working as a steward for a slave trader named Mr. Walker, who employed Brown to tend to the slave cargo he shipped from St. Louis to New Orleans. Brown's twelve months in Walker's employ, which he called "the longest year I ever lived," left him with a renewed determination to escape. On the journey south, Brown worried that he would be sold himself once the boat reached New Orleans, and he loathed his duties, which included preventing Walker's slaves from escaping whenever the boat stopped. One woman who had been sold away from her husband and children committed suicide by flinging herself into the Mississippi River. Brown was also in charge of doling out rations during the journey and preparing the slaves for market once the boat docked. After shaving the old men and blackening their whiskers to make them look younger, Brown had to have them all "dressed and driven out into the yard," where "some were set to dancing, some to jumping, some to singing, and some to playing cards" to make them appear cheerful and happy.[3] Brown eventually escaped from Walker, but he was forever haunted by what he had witnessed and became an abolitionist who fought to end slavery.

Brown was a captive spectator to the rapid expansion of a system built around the brutal forced migration and sale of enslaved blacks. With the closing of the international slave trade in 1808, American slaves became a predominantly U.S.-born population. They maintained a robust rate of reproduction, growing in number from a little over 1.5 million in 1820 to almost 4 million in 1860. And they continued to be bought and sold in an expanding domestic slave trade that supplied black workers to the new slave states and territories taking shape in the South.

Slave labor predominated throughout the South, which maintained a largely agricultural economy even as industrialization moved many northern workers from fields to factories. As a result, the North and South became increasingly distinct and divided by the 1820s, especially with regard to the expansion of slavery. But strong economic ties also connected the regions. The South was crucial to American industrialization: Enslaved African Americans cultivated and harvested many of the raw materials used in northern factories. Likewise, the South depended on the North for textiles and manufactured goods — and provided the North with a lucrative market for those goods.

Enslaved African Americans rarely profited from their labor. In addition to working for their masters from sunup to sundown, they had to sustain themselves and their families. They also nurtured their communities and forged a distinctive culture within the confines of an oppressive system of bondage. Successful escapes were rare, and slave uprisings still more so. Slaves fought back by means of truancy, malingering, theft, and outright defiance under the watchful eyes of their owners and overseers. They also followed the sectional debates that divided the slave and free states. Those debates encouraged them to pray for freedom and hope that northern opposition would help topple the slave system. But until that day came, they would have to settle for survival.

The Expansion and Consolidation of Slavery

By 1820, slavery was all but dead in the North and banned throughout the Old Northwest. But it never came close to dying out completely, as many of the Founding Fathers had once predicted it would. Instead, the rise of cotton cultivation in the 1790s fostered the steady expansion of southern plantation agriculture. Moreover, during the first half of the nineteenth century, the Louisiana Purchase, Spain's cession of Spanish Florida, and the annexation of Texas opened new territory to American settlement and expanded the region within which slavery could be practiced. The expansion of the southern states took place at the expense of the Indian inhabitants of the Southeast, whom white settlers pushed off their land. As white settlers moved into this territory, southern slavery became more entrenched.

The domestic slave trade expanded as the Upper South sold its surplus slaves in the Lower South, displacing hundreds of thousands of African Americans and tearing apart black families and communities. The South's most lucrative crops required a large supply of enslaved workers, which strengthened white southerners' commitment to slavery in an era when many northerners were increasingly committed to free labor. These regional differences became a source of major sectional conflict during the late 1810s, when Missouri's petition for statehood threatened to upset the balance between slaveholding and nonslaveholding states, and they remained divisive throughout the antebellum era.

Slavery, Cotton, and American Industrialization

By the 1820s, stark regional differences were emerging between the North and South. Although these years saw the start of a transportation revolution that would link both regions to a shared national market, the new railroads, turnpikes, and shipping routes connected two increasingly distinct societies. With gradual emancipation all but complete, the North was committed to free labor, while the South's investment in slavery only increased over time. Both regions expanded steadily, adding new people and new territory. Whereas population growth in the South relied primarily on natural increase, however, growth in the North also resulted from immigration. Between 1815 and 1860, more than five million Europeans immigrated to the United States, but less than one-eighth of them settled in southern slave states.

Slavery itself discouraged immigration to the South, because there were few jobs for white immigrants. Although a majority of white southerners did not own slaves, nonslaveholding whites were largely small farmers with no employees. The region's major employers and wealthiest men were planters who favored slaves over white workers. In addition to the labor they provided, slaves were a profitable investment: Their prices rose steadily throughout the antebellum era, as did the return that slave owners could expect when slaves reproduced. Slaves also could be forced to do any type of work, including the grueling year-round labor needed to produce the South's lucrative **cash crops**.

The production of tobacco, rice, sugar, hemp, and above all cotton sustained the South's economy. By 1850, 55 percent of the South's slaves worked on cotton plantations, where they grew 75 percent of the world's supply of cotton (Map 5.1). Their labor enriched both the South and the nation as a whole: That year, cotton constituted more than 50 percent of all U.S. exports. Sugar, produced primarily in Louisiana, was another highly profitable crop. Used throughout the United States, Louisiana sugar was also exported, making up as much as one-quarter of the world's sugar production during years when the crop flourished.

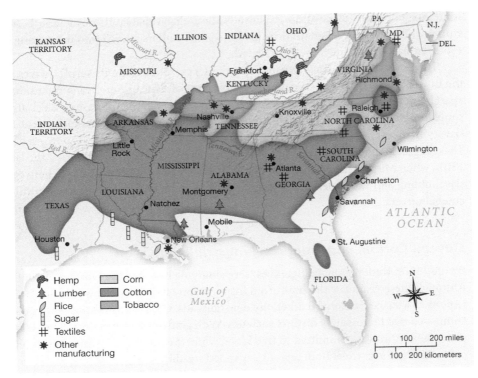

MAP 5.1 **Agriculture and Industry in the Slave South, 1860**

The antebellum South's economy was dominated by cotton production, but southern plant-ers also cultivated corn and tobacco in the Upper South, sugar in parts of Louisiana and Texas, and rice along the coasts of North and South Carolina, Georgia, and Louisiana. In addition, southern workers also produced hemp, lumber, textiles, and small quantities of other kinds of manufactured goods.

Southern businessmen used slave labor in the region's small industrial sector as well. Enslaved workers produced chewing tobacco in Richmond and Petersburg, Virginia; salt in western Virginia; and iron in a variety of ironworks located along Virginia's and Maryland's waterways. They also staffed lumber camps in forests and swamps across the South.

The North, by contrast, was home to a much larger nonagricultural sector. The first half of the nineteenth century saw northern farmers adopt new machinery that allowed them to increase production while reducing the number of workers they employed. Moreover, they took advantage of the reduced transportation costs and increased shipping speeds resulting from the transportation revolution to expand their markets. Food no longer had to be grown locally. Instead, large commercial farms in the Mid-west began to monopolize the North's agricultural sector, while other parts of the region industrialized. Major manufacturing centers emerged in Boston, New York, and

Philadelphia, and factory towns sprang up across the Northeast. Wages were high enough in these industrial areas to attract European immigrants, providing the northern states with a rapidly expanding free white labor force.

The different regional economies that emerged in the North and South were by no means autonomous. Southerners produced few manufactured goods and relied on the North — and, to a lesser extent, Europe — to supply them with furniture, tools, clothing, shoes, and other products. Likewise, northern industrialists imported raw materials such as cotton and indigo from the South. They used these materials to produce textiles, including fabrics manufactured specifically for the southern market, such as "negro cloth," a coarse cotton fabric used for slaves' clothing. Northern manufacturers also imported other crucial raw materials from the South. The most important was lumber, which factories used to make furniture, paper, buttons, bobbins, and many other household items and supplies that were then shipped to the South as finished products.

Despite such ties, the North and South had different economic and political interests. As the regions' economies diverged, northerners favored government measures designed to support American industrial production, such as protective tariffs on manufactured goods. Southerners, who produced few manufactured goods and imported many from abroad, opposed tariffs. Underlying such divergent interests were even deeper divisions over slavery.

The Missouri Compromise Crisis

With Alabama already scheduled for admission to the Union as a slave state in 1819, the nation was made up of eleven free states and eleven slave states. The admission of Missouri threatened to upset the balance. Missouri Territory had no restrictions on slavery, and some of its most fertile farmland had been settled by slaveholders such as William Wells Brown's owner. By 1818, when Missouri applied for statehood, the territory was home to more than two thousand slaves. Nevertheless, northern congressmen were reluctant to admit Missouri as a slave state. The admission of another slave state would increase the South's power in Congress at a time when northern politicians had already begun to regret the Constitution's Three-Fifths Compromise (see chapter 4).

Although more than 60 percent of white Americans lived in the North, by 1818 northern representatives held only a slim majority of congressional seats. The additional political representation allotted to the South as a result of the Three-Fifths Compromise gave southerners many more seats in the House of Representatives than they would have had if the number of representatives had been based on just the free population. Moreover, since each state had two Senate seats, Missouri's admission as a slave state would result in more southern than northern senators.

Many northern legislators also had misgivings about the westward expansion of slavery. One of them was New York representative James Tallmadge, who proposed a radical amendment to Missouri's statehood bill: banning slavery in Missouri and requiring that all slaves already in the region be freed by age twenty-five. Tallmadge's amendment set off a storm of sectional controversy that the elderly Thomas Jefferson likened to a "fire bell in the night," because it raised alarming new questions about whether the United States would remain united.[4]

The "Missouri question" inspired the nation's first extended debate over the expansion of slavery, which engaged both black and white Americans. Anxious to see whether Congress would take action against slavery, free blacks living in Washington, D.C., crowded the galleries of the House and Senate, while white southerners threatened to secede from the Union, and northern politicians embraced federal action against slavery for the first time.

Tallmadge's amendment was narrowly approved in the House of Representatives, but it stalled in the Senate. The question went unresolved until 1820, when a group led by Kentucky senator Henry Clay embraced a compromise in which Missouri would be admitted as a slave state alongside the new free state of Maine, which had split off from Massachusetts to form an independent territory in 1819. The **Missouri Compromise**, as it became known, retained the balance of power between the regions, but it also included a major concession to antislavery northerners: Congress agreed that slavery throughout the rest of the Louisiana Purchase would be prohibited north of latitude 36°30', which runs along Missouri's southern border (Map 5.2). Slavery would not travel north, as many northern whites feared. But the Missouri Compromise was deeply disappointing to African Americans in both regions. It stopped the southward progression of gradual emancipation at Missouri's southern border and shored up slavery in the South.

Slavery Expands into Indian Territory

The relentless expansion of the slave South also had a devastating effect on the region's Native American peoples. White settlers and federal officials used a combination of treaties, warfare, and forced migration to drive the Cherokee, Creek, Choctaw, Chickasaw, and Seminole tribes from their homelands. Known among whites as the Five Civilized Tribes, because they had adopted European institutions in an attempt to live peacefully alongside their white neighbors, these tribes occupied large amounts of land that became increasingly appealing to settlers as the South's plantation economy expanded. The conflicts that white encroachment created culminated in the federal government's passage of the **Indian Removal Act** in 1830, which forced Indians living east of the Mississippi River to relocate to Indian Territory (present-day Oklahoma).

This act came on the heels of several decades of conflict, most of which involved disputes over the Indians' traditional homelands, which were coveted by white settlers. But the Seminole tribe, which lived in northern Florida, also clashed with state and federal authorities on the issue of slavery. Although the Seminoles owned slaves, their system of bondage differed dramatically from that of the other four tribes, whose slave owning

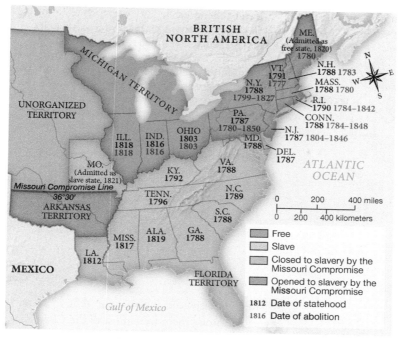

MAP 5.2 **The Missouri Compromise**

Passed in 1820, the Missouri Compromise prohibited slavery north of the parallel 36°30′ north, except within the boundaries of the state of Missouri. As this map shows, the passage of the Missouri Compromise solidified the sectional divide between the slaveholding states of the South and the free states of the North, which had all passed abolition laws well before 1820. The year in which these laws were passed is also indicated, along with the year in which slavery actually ended in states that used gradual emancipation laws to abolish slavery.

practices resembled those of southern whites. Seminole slaves were adopted as kin: They could not be sold to whites, and they rarely passed their enslaved status on to their children. The tribe also allied with runaway slaves and sheltered entire communities of fugitives. Known today as Black Seminoles, the members of these maroon communities remained free by paying their Seminole hosts an annual tribute in livestock or crops, and they helped the Seminoles defend their land from white squatters.

By the late 1820s, however, all five tribes were having trouble holding on to their land. As white settlers proliferated, they drove the Indians out by squatting on their territory, stealing their livestock, and burning their towns. The Indians complained to both state and federal officials, who resolved the conflict by dispossessing the Indians. The Indian Removal Act of 1830 was designed by Andrew Jackson, who had been elected president in 1828, and called for the Five Civilized Tribes to sign treaties giving up their homelands in the Southeast in return for payments and new land in the West. The army

Black Seminoles
Slaves and maroons played a vital role in helping the Seminole tribe to resist the incursions of U.S. troops. Black Seminole leaders such as John Horse, pictured here, gathered recruits and spearheaded efforts to drive the troops out of Florida. In the years immediately following his relocation to Oklahoma, Horse continued to work on behalf of the Seminoles and served as an interpreter. In 1849, he emigrated to Mexico and became a captain in the Mexican army. This engraving, titled *Gopher John, Seminole Interpreter,* first appeared in an 1848 history of the Second Seminole War. *University of Florida, Smathers Library Special and Area Studies Collections, Rare Books Collections.*

forcibly displaced Indians who refused to relocate. Among them were most of the Cherokees, who remained on their land until 1838, when federal troops marched them west on a brutal journey known as the Trail of Tears. As the tribes moved west, they took their slaves with them.

The Seminoles were the only tribe to resist with force. Their slave and maroon allies helped them repel the U.S. troops who arrived to drive them out of Florida in 1835. The Seminoles themselves numbered only 4,000, but they had 800 Black Seminole allies who fiercely opposed relocation. Some of the Black Seminoles were runaways who knew they would be returned to their owners if the tribe agreed to move. Others feared that relocation would reenslave all Black Seminoles. Black Seminole leaders such as John Horse, fighting alongside Seminole leaders such as Osceola, enlisted several hundred rebellious plantation slaves to join the Seminole cause. When Osceola's forces were defeated in the spring of 1838, Horse was forced west along with most of his Seminole allies. Several hundred Seminoles remained behind in the Florida swamps, however, and they waged another war to resist displacement between 1855 and 1858.

The Domestic Slave Trade

Most enslaved African Americans were owned by white southerners. Louisiana and Alabama joined the Union in 1812 and 1819, respectively, further expanding the South's cotton belt. Cotton planters migrated into the territories of Arkansas and Missouri and also established settlements in Spanish Florida, which Spain ceded to the United States in the 1819 Adams-Onís Treaty. (The agreement took effect two years later, in 1821.) Slave-holding settlers also began arriving in Texas as early as the 1820s, when the region still belonged to Mexico, which had abolished slavery. They supported Texas's war for independence in the 1830s and the U.S. annexation of Texas in 1845, which brought Texas into the Union as a slave state. As the last of the four new slave states to enter the Union between 1820 and 1860, Texas followed Missouri (1821), Arkansas (1836), and Florida (1845).

Slavery was most important in the Lower South. Between 1820 and 1860, 1.2 million African Americans moved from the Upper South to the Lower South in a mass migration that relocated almost half of the region's slave population. Approximately one-third of these involuntary migrants belonged to Upper South slaveholders who took their slaves with them as they migrated west and south to establish new plantations in South Carolina, Georgia, Alabama, Mississippi, Louisiana, Florida, Arkansas, and Texas. The remaining two-thirds were bought, transported, and resold in the Lower South by slave traders (Map 5.3).

Most slaves made the grueling journey on foot, in coffles that could contain anywhere from thirty to three hundred men, women, and children. The men were usually chained together in handcuffed pairs, while the women and children trailed behind them or were carried in wagons. Traders on horseback, with whips and guns, accompanied the coffles. After walking twenty to twenty-five miles during the day, the slaves often slept outdoors, sometimes under tents or just huddled together on the ground. As the South's transportation network improved, some traders began to ship their slaves south on steamships that chugged down the Mississippi or on oceangoing ships that docked in New Orleans. By the 1850s, transporting slaves by rail was also common. Lyman Abbott, a northerner who visited the region in 1856, found that "every train going south has . . . slaves on board, twenty or more, and a 'nigger car,' which is very generally also the smoking-car, and sometimes the baggage-car."[5]

Regardless of how the slave migrants traveled, the journey represented a new Middle Passage for them. Slaves dreaded being "sold down the river" to the Lower South, knowing, above all, that such sales usually meant permanent separation from their families and friends. The majority of slaves who entered the trade were under thirty; most left their parents behind, although very young children were usually sold with their mothers. The trade also split up many young slave couples, disrupting one in five slave marriages in the Upper South, and divided siblings, extended families, and friends. These losses were all the more devastating because they came without warning: Owners usually sold slaves in secret to avoid giving them a chance to object. Charity Bowery's mistress, for example, made sure that Bowery was out running errands when she sold Bowery's twelve-year-old son. "She didn't want to be troubled with our cries," Bowery later remembered.[6] Slave owners routinely used the ever-present threat of sale to control their slaves and suppress dissent. According to one slave, his master would threaten "that if we didn't suit him, he would put us in his pocket quick — meaning he would sell us."[7]

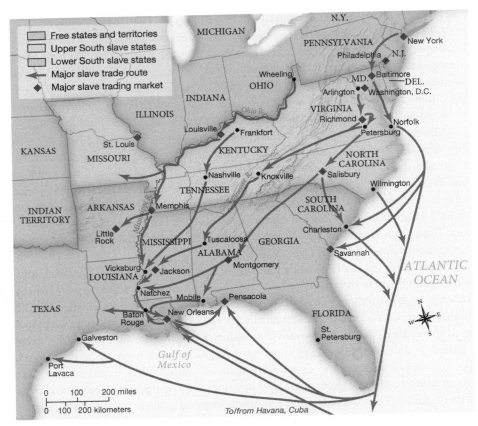

MAP 5.3 The Domestic Slave Trade, 1808–1865

With the termination of the international slave trade in 1808, an extensive domestic slave trade developed to transfer slaves from the North and Upper South, where free labor was increasingly predominant, to the Lower South's ever-expanding plantation frontier. This map illustrates the various routes by which the forced migrants traveled south: Some were carried in railroad cars, while others were loaded onto riverboats and oceangoing vessels and shipped to slave ports such as New Orleans. Many more made the long journey on foot, marching south under the supervision of armed slave traders. DATA SOURCE: *The Atlas of African-American History and Politics: From the Slave Trade to Modern Times*, by Arwin Smallwood and Jeffrey Elliot. Copyright © 1998 The McGraw-Hill Companies, Inc.

Once in the Lower South, slaves faced new traumas. On arrival, they were marketed at auction houses and slave trading centers across the region. Prospective buyers appraised them as if they were farm animals, inspecting their bodies for signs of illness or other physical weakness and for scars from frequent whippings, which might indicate a rebellious nature. Virtually all buyers were men, since even widowed white women often bought their slaves through male intermediaries rather than entering into the trade themselves. Prospective buyers subjected slaves to a level of scrutiny considered too indelicate for white women to witness. Men examined slaves' teeth to determine their

Slave Auction

Slaves experienced tremendous degradation in the process of their auction and sale. Potential buyers, almost all of whom were white men, inspected them bodily and subjected them to questioning. Slave couples and parents of slave children were burdened with the additional fear of having their families torn asunder. In this painting of a slave auction, one woman stands on the auction block before a group of bidders, while potential buyers question and examine the other slaves, most of whom are women and small children.

The Slave Market, *19th-century painting by Friedrich Schulz (1823–1875), oil on canvas/Hirshhorn Museum and Sculpture Garden, Washington, D.C., USA/Bridgeman Images.*

age and pushed back their clothes to look at their muscles. They also "felt all over the women folks," one ex-slave recalled, to try to determine whether they were fertile.[8] Not surprisingly, slaves found the whole procedure deeply degrading. But some also tried to shape its outcome. Henry Bibb, whose Kentucky master punished him for being a chronic runaway by selling his entire family to a slave trader, was so intent on keeping his family together that he told a prospective buyer he had run away only once.

Black Challenges to Slavery

As slavery expanded, black discontent heightened. In 1820, the disappointing outcome of the Missouri crisis helped inspire a free black named Denmark Vesey to denounce slavery and exhort South Carolina slaves to rebel. Divine inspiration, alternatively, moved a slave preacher named Nat Turner to lead a bloody attack on slavery in Southampton,

Virginia, in 1831. Neither of these men's actions succeeded in overturning slavery, but both had an enduring impact. Within the region, Vesey and Turner inspired new repressive measures to forestall any future rebellions. Outside the South, their actions fueled black abolitionist critiques of slavery. In particular, David Walker, a free black man who fled the South after Vesey's planned revolt was suppressed, insisted that slave rebels were heroes and called for others to follow in their footsteps.

Denmark Vesey's Plot

Originally named Telemarque, Denmark Vesey hailed from St. Thomas in the Danish West Indies. As a teenager, he relocated to Charleston, South Carolina, with his owner in 1793. Fluent in both French and English, the young slave had taught himself to read and write by the time he reached Charleston, where his owner employed him as a clerk and domestic servant. As a highly skilled and valuable slave, Vesey might have remained in bondage all his life but for an extraordinary stroke of good luck in 1799. That year, he purchased a lottery ticket — likely with money earned from taking on extra work during his free hours — and won the princely sum of $1,500. He used $600 of it to purchase his own freedom and the remainder to move out of his master's house and establish a carpentry business.

Vesey continued to socialize and identify with slaves, and he became increasingly eager to see all of his enslaved friends set free. In 1819, when congressional debates over the status of Missouri appeared in the Charleston newspapers, Vesey was delighted to see slavery under attack. His plot took at least some inspiration from these debates, the news of which reached black communities across the country. As one Charleston slaveholder complained, "By the Missouri question, our slaves thought, there was a charter of liberties granted them by Congress."9

By 1820, with the help of several enslaved friends, Vesey had begun planning a rebellion. They spent more than a year recruiting other men. Armed with stolen guns and knives, they planned to raid Charleston's Meeting Street Arsenal and a nearby shop to gather additional weapons for their supporters, whom they expected to number in the thousands. Vesey was a lay preacher in Charleston's African Methodist Episcopal (AME) church, and he reviewed the details of the plot at religious classes held in his home, in which he likened the planned rebellion to the delivery of the children of Israel from Egyptian slavery.

The conspirators dreamed of freeing themselves and sailing off to Haiti, but more than a month before the scheduled rebellion, two Charleston slaves divulged the plan to their owners. Local authorities swiftly suppressed the uprising. Over the next month, officials arrested 131 slaves and free blacks, 72 of whom were tried, convicted, and sentenced to death. More died in custody, and 27 were ultimately released. Vesey was hanged on July 2, 1822, with 5 other men in a public spectacle that drew thousands of black and white Charlestonians. The event was followed by several other mass hangings that month.

An Official Report of the Trials of Sundry Negroes . . . , *1822*

In the aftermath of Denmark Vesey's failed attempt to lead a slave uprising in Charleston, South Carolina, in the summer of 1822, the city's Court of Magistrates and Freeholders tried over one hundred accused rebels in a series of closed sessions. Interrogated and tortured, many of the accused conspirators were found guilty: Thirty-five were sentenced to death, and nearly forty were transported outside the United States. The Court's *Official Report* of these proceedings identified Denmark Vesey, a free black resident of Charleston, as "the author and original instigator of this diabolical plot." *Courtesy Everett Collection.*

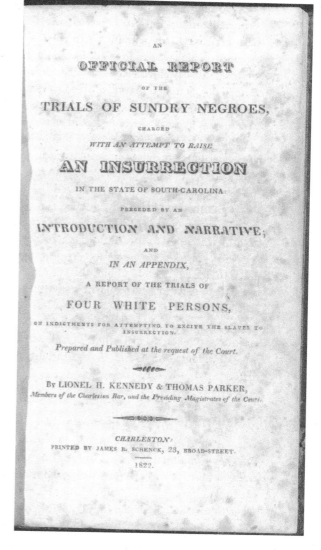

The rebels were deliberately denied funerals or proper burials. Aware that Africans and African Americans cherished funeral rites as a way to free the spirit of the deceased, Charleston authorities had the rebels cut down and dismembered after they were hanged. As the death toll mounted, however, it became clear that the costly executions could not proceed indefinitely. The loss of slave property and labor imposed a severe economic burden on both the slaves' owners and the state. By late July, Carolinians were ready to see the hangings come to an end. As a lawyer told one of Charleston's magistrates, "You must take care and save negroes enough for the Rice crop."[10] The remaining 37 rebels were transported to slave societies outside the United States at their owners' expense.

Neither death nor deportation could erase the memory of Vesey's plot, however, and like Richmond whites in the aftermath of Gabriel's rebellion in 1800 (see chapter 4), white South Carolinians moved quickly to limit the mobility and autonomy of their slaves. State officials banned slaves from hiring themselves out, and they forbade free blacks to hire slaves. The City of Charleston took the additional precaution of hiring a permanent force of 150 guardsmen to patrol the city around the clock. Any slave caught on the street after 9 p.m. without a written pass could be arrested and whipped or, worse, assigned to walk on a prison treadmill installed at the Charleston jail in 1823. The treadmill consisted of a wheel with steps, which was propelled by a group of manacled slaves, who climbed the rotating steps under the supervision of a driver brandishing a cat-o'-nine-tails. The mill was used to grind corn sold to offset the jail's daily expenses, but even when there was no grain to grind, prisoners could be assigned to hard labor on the treadmill.

Bitterly aware that Vesey and most of his key collaborators could read and write, South Carolina officials reinforced existing laws against teaching slaves to read, and the state legislature adopted new legislation forbidding free black education. In the fall of 1822, municipal authorities also razed the AME church where Vesey had preached, although they could find no evidence that church leaders had participated in the plot. As one nineteenth-century commentator later noted, the church was threatening because it "tended to spread the dangerous infection of the alphabet."[11]

Free blacks were also subject to new legislation and surveillance designed to make them feel unwelcome in the state. One law required all free black males over age fifteen to find white guardians willing to post bonds for their good behavior, and another barred free blacks who left the state from returning. The state also began to require free black sailors who worked on ships that docked in South Carolina to be jailed until their vessels left the state. The City of Charleston levied a $50 annual tax on its free black residents, who also had to register with municipal officials twice a year.

David Walker's Exile

Even as Charleston whites moved to ensure that no new Vesey would threaten their safety, Vesey's memory lived on. Among the free blacks who fled Charleston in the wake of the plot was David Walker, who moved north and made a name for himself as the most militant black abolitionist of his era. The rising hostility toward free blacks in Charleston had convinced him that "if I remain in this bloody land . . . I will not live long."[12] By 1825, the forty-year-old Walker had resettled in Boston, where he ran a used clothing store near the harbor, outfitting the sailors and other mariners who passed through the city. In Boston, Walker found a lively black community, married, and joined the African Lodge of the Honorable Society of Free and Accepted Masons. Members included local leaders such as the Reverend Thomas Paul, the minister of Boston's First African Baptist Church.

But moving to Massachusetts did not allow Walker to escape white oppression. He found most African American northerners "ignorant and poor" and unable "to obtain the comforts of life, but by cleaning their [white people's] boots and shoes, old clothes, [and] waiting on them." He also found African Americans hard-pressed to secure their position in the face of the American Colonization Society's plans.[13]

The American Colonization Society (ACS), though opposed by blacks, had become steadily more popular among whites. At their most polite, ACS members continued to champion colonization as a step toward the eradication of slavery. But after founding the West African colony of Liberia in 1821 (see chapter 4), they began to focus their attention on free blacks. While many blacks were not opposed to emigration in theory, they questioned the motives of the ACS and believed that the organization's propaganda hurt black prospects for freedom in America. ACS members rejected the views of an earlier generation of antislavery whites who embraced black education as the road to self-improvement. Instead, colonizationists such as ACS secretary Elias Caldwell contended that improving the condition of African Americans would only give them more "relish for those privileges which they can never attain."[14]

David Walker was appalled by the ACS, viewing colonization as a doctrine designed to perpetuate slavery by banishing free blacks. Walker advocated abolition instead of emigration and denounced colonization as a proslavery plot. Convinced that all blacks should fight for freedom within the United States, he sheltered fugitive slaves in his home and became a contributor to the nation's first black newspaper, *Freedom's Journal* (founded in 1827), which opposed both colonization and slavery. Like the *Journal*'s editors, Walker was convinced that African Americans could not defeat slavery and racism without pleading their own cause. This conviction inspired him to publish an abolitionist manifesto of his own in 1829, titled *Walker's Appeal . . . to the Coloured Citizens of the World*. A fiery protest against slavery and colonization, *Walker's Appeal* lambasted white people for enslaving and oppressing people of color, while it also critiqued blacks for acquiescing to white domination. "Are we MEN!! — I ask you, O my brethren! Are we MEN?" asked Walker, addressing his fellow blacks. "How we could be so *submissive* to a gang of men, . . . I never could conceive." But he reserved his harshest critique for American slaveholders, whom he described as "tyrants and devils."[15]

Walker's controversial pamphlet was influential on several counts. It galvanized a new generation of radical blacks who would lobby for abolition and civil rights for many years to come (see chapter 6). Among whites, it helped shift the focus of the antislavery movement from colonization to emancipation. Walker's call for slave violence was widely condemned by white abolitionists, most of whom were political moderates who supported the ACS, but these reformers proved more open to his critique of colonization. The influential white abolitionist William Lloyd Garrison, who still held moderate views when he first encountered Walker's pamphlet, criticized "the spirit and tendency of this *Appeal*" but also acknowledged that it contained many "valuable truths."[16] Shortly after its publication, Garrison renounced colonization and dedicated himself to the immediate abolition of slavery.

In the South, *Walker's Appeal* made whites even more determined to suppress black dissent. By 1830, the pamphlet had reached Virginia, North Carolina, Georgia,

Frontispiece and Title Page of Walker's Appeal*, 1830*
Printed from an engraving by an unknown artist, the frontispiece for the second edition
of *Walker's Appeal* shows a slave standing on top of a mountain, his hands raised toward
a piece of paper that floats directly above him. Inscribed on the paper are the Latin words
libertas justitia — liberty and justice. *Library of Congress, Prints and Photographs Division, Washington, D.C.,*
LC-USZ62-63775.

Louisiana, and Alabama, where whites discovered copies in the hands of black seamen
and slaves. Terrified by its message, they offered a $3,000 bounty for Walker's death
and a $10,000 reward for anyone willing to kidnap Walker and deliver him alive. His
pamphlet was the subject of special meetings of several southern state legislatures, and
it inspired new laws restricting the rights of slaves and free blacks in Georgia and North
Carolina.

In the midst of this controversy, Walker was found dead in the doorway of his
home in June 1830, just after the publication of the third edition of his *Appeal*. He probably succumbed to tuberculosis, which was rampant in nineteenth-century Boston.
But given the size of the reward that Walker's enemies offered to see him dead, many
free blacks were convinced that he was the victim of foul play. Either way, Walker's
death did not end his influence. His pamphlet had shown that slavery had enemies
throughout the nation.

Nat Turner's Rebellion, the Amistad Case, and the Creole Insurrection

Walker's message received additional support just a few years later when an enslaved lay preacher named Nat Turner led one of the bloodiest slave rebellions in American history. Born in 1800, Turner was a lifelong resident of Southampton County, Virginia, and grew up during a time when many blacks and whites in the Upper South were embracing evangelical Christianity. The first few decades of the nineteenth century saw the **Second Great Awakening**, similar to the Great Awakening of the eighteenth century. Once again, a wave of Baptist and Methodist revivals swept through the nation. But black and white congregants often understood the message of religious equality quite differently, especially in the South.

Raised in a Methodist household, Turner was a pious young man who spent much of his spare time praying and fasting. He experienced powerful religious visions, which eventually convinced him that "the great day of judgment" was at hand. Turner bided his time for years, waiting for "signs in the heavens that it would make known to me when I should commence the great work." On the evening of August 21, 1831, he struck, accompanied by a small band of fellow slaves who shared his vision of "slay[ing] my enemies with their own weapons."[17]

Armed with axes and hatchets, Turner and his men began by murdering Turner's owner, Joseph Travis, and his family and stealing their small cache of guns. They then moved from plantation to plantation freeing slaves; killing white men, women, and children; and gathering more weapons and recruits. Turner's force grew to more than 50 slaves and free blacks, who managed to kill 60 whites before a Virginia militia tracked them down two days later. The rebels scattered but were pursued by a growing force of armed whites, who went on a killing spree that lasted more than two weeks and resulted in the deaths of more than 100 blacks—all of whom died without trial. An additional 48 suspects were captured, tried, and executed by the state, including Turner himself, who managed to evade capture for three months until a white farmer discovered him in hiding.

Turner's rebellion terrified whites across the South. Turner was soon rumored to have an army of 1,200 coconspirators located as far away as North Carolina. In Virginia, as one plantation mistress put it, fears of revolt were "agonizing." Virginia legislators were even willing to consider the abolition of slavery rather than continue to contemplate "the horrors of servile war which will not end until . . . the slaves or the whites are totally exterminated."[18] They debated a gradual emancipation plan but quickly decided that emancipation was not the solution.

Convinced that Turner's uprising was caused by the abolitionist agitation of men such as David Walker, Virginia's leaders instead revised the state's legal code to bar slaves and free blacks from preaching or even attending religious meetings without white supervision. Virginia legislators also targeted free blacks with a colonization bill, which allocated new funding to remove them, and a police bill that denied free blacks trial by jury and made any free blacks convicted of a crime subject to sale and relocation.

Lawmakers also took precautions that were unprecedented in scope. In 1835, southern legislators silenced congressional debates over slavery for almost a decade by passing a **gag rule** prohibiting the reading of antislavery petitions in Congress. Former president John Quincy Adams, now a representative from Massachusetts, tirelessly opposed this rule, believing that it imposed unconstitutional limitations on petitioners' freedom of speech. He also saw congressional support for the rule as evidence that the nation was falling under the control of a dangerous "slavocracy" led by wealthy southern slaveholders. Known as "Old Man Eloquent" for his rhetorical skills, Adams called for rescinding the gag rule every year until 1844, when he finally prevailed.

Still, no gag rule or law could fully suppress black dissent. Instead, in the years following Nat Turner's rebellion, two slave insurrections at sea intensified whites' fears and called the security of the slave system into question. In 1839, a group of Africans who had just been kidnapped and enslaved seized control of the Spanish slave ship *Amistad* in international waters near Cuba. The U.S. navy captured the ship and made the rebels prisoners of the U.S. government, at which point Spain demanded their return. But the rebels' enslavement violated treaties prohibiting the international slave trade, so their status had to be determined in court. The *Amistad* **case** became a widely publicized abolitionist cause and ultimately reached the U.S. Supreme Court, which freed the rebels in 1841.

A similar revolt in 1841 had a comparable outcome. Led by Madison Washington, slaves aboard the *Creole*, an American ship engaged in the internal slave trade, seized the vessel, sailed to British waters, and declared themselves free. The British accepted the slaves' emancipation declaration, enabling them to go free in the Bahamas. Speaking for the U.S. government, Secretary of State Daniel Webster honored the rebels' claims to freedom in the *Creole* **insurrection** but insisted unsuccessfully that the British government compensate the slaves' owners for their lost property.

Although both incidents took place at sea, the *Amistad* and *Creole* revolts reinforced the insecurity that southern slaveholders felt. Like the actions of Denmark Vesey, David Walker, and Nat Turner, these slaves' endeavors suggested that black dissent could never be fully subdued. Moreover, the fact that the *Amistad* rebels went on to win their freedom in U.S. courts underscored the limited support slavery enjoyed outside the South.

Everyday Resistance to Slavery

Both external and internal opposition to slavery unnerved white southerners, whose control over their slave population was precarious and hard-won. Although they used repressive slave codes, vigilant slave patrols, brutal punishments, and the threat of sale to keep their bondmen and bondwomen subdued, they could never eradicate black resistance to slavery. Instead, individual resistance was nearly an everyday occurrence. Organized rebellions became rare in the wake of Nat Turner's revolt, but slave discontent remained ubiquitous. Enslaved African Americans protested their condition in many ways, including stealing plantation property, feigning illness, refusing to work, defying their owners, and running away.

Disobedience and Defiance

Theft was perhaps the most common form of disobedience, although few slaves regarded it as a crime. "Po' nigger had to steal back dar in slav'y eben to git 'nuf t'eat. . . . Ef it hadn't been fo' dem [whites], nigger wouldn't know nothin' 'bout stealin'," explained one ex-slave from Virginia. The former South Carolina slave Rosa Barnwell reported that her owners expected slaves to survive on a weekly allowance of approximately eight quarts of corn and four quarts of sweet potatoes. Given no meat, they sometimes took "a hog on their own account." Louisa Gause, who was also enslaved in South Carolina, concluded, "If [a slave] did [steal], he never take nothin, but what been belong to him."[19]

Slaves also feigned illness to avoid unpleasant work assignments. Planters often complained of slaves who were "lazy . . . and affected to be sick," and some even employed doctors to determine whether their slaves were "really ill or merely 'playing possum.'"[20] Such determinations were not always possible, however, and some ex-laves reported success by refusing to eat for days and pretending to be too weak to stand up.

Slaves also defied their owners by running away and hiding to avoid punishment or other harsh measures. Mostly temporary, such escapes were often propelled by despair and fear rather than being carefully planned. Araminta "Minty" Ross, who later renamed herself Harriet Tubman, fled her mistress in terror at age seven after stealing a lump of sugar. Miss Susan, the brutal mistress for whom Tubman worked as a nursemaid, was a merciless taskmaster who beat Tubman every day, lashing out at the girl every time the baby she tended cried. Caught in the act of stealing, Tubman was afraid to face whatever punishment this far graver transgression might bring. When she saw her mistress grab her rawhide whip, she ran as far as she could and then took shelter in a pigpen, where she hid for five days, braving the muck of the pen and competing with the pigs for scraps to eat. She stayed there until hunger and her increasing fear of the adult pigs drove her to return home and face the wrath of her mistress. Not until 1849, two decades later, did she finally manage to escape permanently.

In escaping from slavery only temporarily, the seven-year-old Tubman became what slaveholders deemed a **truant**—a slave who absconded for a matter of days, weeks, or sometimes months. Although truants were generally adults, many were like Tubman in that they fled to avoid punishment. Others sought to escape especially onerous work assignments or abusive treatment, and they would sometimes agree to return after negotiating better conditions with their owners. Truants often hid in local swamps or woods—a form of resistance also known as **lying out**. In many cases, such runaways received support from other slaves who brought them food and supplies, and sometimes even hid

Harriet Tubman
Harriet Tubman, born Araminta "Minty" Ross, endured a brutal childhood and young adulthood in slavery. Following her final, permanent escape in 1849, she helped many more slaves — including members of her own family — escape to freedom and spoke out against the horrors of the institution. During the Civil War, she served the Union as a cook, nurse, teacher, scout, and spy. *Library of Congress, Prints and Photographs Division, Washington, D.C., LC-USZ62-7816.*

the truants in their homes. But truants also included more short-term escapees, who left to visit loved ones or attend religious meetings, dances, or other social events.

Some slaves countered harsh treatment with outright resistance. The famous fugitive Frederick Douglass almost lost his life at age sixteen when he physically resisted a whipping from a particularly brutal master. Born on a Maryland plantation, Douglass spent much of his youth in Baltimore working as a house servant. But when he became an unruly teenager, Douglass's owner sent him out of the city to work for a poor white farmer named Mr. Covey, who was known for his ability to subdue even the most recalcitrant slaves. Covey subjected Douglass to a brutal work regime and terrible weekly beatings that left Douglass feeling utterly "broken in body, soul, and spirit." One day, however, he found himself fighting back against his tormentor. "From whence came the spirit I don't know," Douglass later recalled. The two men exchanged blows until both were exhausted, and thereafter Douglass recovered his "long-crushed spirit." He took no more beatings from Covey and "let it be known . . . that the white man who expected to succeed in whipping, must also succeed in killing me."[21]

Douglass was lucky to survive this resolution, given that slaves who physically resisted risked death. They had no right to self-defense under southern law, which gave white people uncontrolled authority over slaves' bodies. Even whites who supervised rather than owned slaves had this authority, as the North Carolina Supreme Court justice Thomas Ruffin ruled in the influential 1829 case *State v. Mann.* Ruffin overturned the slave owning widow Elizabeth Jones's attempt to impose criminal sanctions on John Mann, to whom she had hired out her slave Lydia. When Lydia disobeyed Jones, he whipped her, and when she tried to escape, he shot and killed her. Jones's acquittal shored up the power of southern whites who employed or even supervised slaves. Subsequent rulings across the South reinforced these principles. Georgia's Supreme Court ruled in *John v. State* (1854) that any slave accused of killing a white person had to be charged with murder, even if he or she had acted in self-defense (an act that would normally carry a manslaughter charge).[22]

Runaways Who Escaped from Slavery

Successful permanent escapes were rare. Whites patrolled plantation districts on a nightly basis, severely punishing slaves who left their quarters. "Run Nigger, run, Patty Roller will catch you . . . I'll shoot you with my flintlock gun," enslaved African Americans would sing, sometimes in an effort to warn others that patrollers were nearby.[23] Some of slavery's successful fugitives, such as Frederick Douglass, William Wells Brown, and Harriet Tubman, went on to provide eloquent testimony about the brutality of slavery and become among the nation's most influential antislavery activists. Although most runaways were caught before they made it out of the South, even unsuccessful escape attempts had an impact on the slave system, because they cost slave owners time and money and reminded southern whites that African Americans were held in bondage against their will.

One difficulty of permanent escape was that although runaways could hide in nearby woods or swamps with relative ease, they could not travel on roads without a pass. A few exceptionally enterprising fugitives learned to read and write so that they could forge their own passes, but even procuring paper and ink could be a challenge. Solomon Northup, a free black man from New York, learned this firsthand when he was kidnapped and sold into slavery in 1841. Northup was drugged and ended up in a slave pen after traveling to Washington, D.C., with two white men who had offered him a job as a musician. The men sold him to a slave trader, who believed, despite Northup's protests to the contrary, that he was a runaway slave from Georgia. Neither the trader nor any of Northup's subsequent owners had any incentive to believe that he was free, and he was eventually sold as far south as Louisiana, where he toiled on cotton plantations for many years.

Literate and legally free, Northup had white friends in New York who could vouch for his identity, but plantation life made it almost impossible for him to write or mail a letter. He explained his difficulty in his autobiography, *Twelve Years a Slave*: "In the first place, I was deprived of pen, ink, and paper. In the second place, a slave cannot leave his plantation without a pass, nor will a post-master mail a letter for one without written instructions from his owner. I was in slavery nine years, and always watchful and on the alert, before I met with the good fortune of obtaining a sheet of paper." Even after that, Northup had to figure out how to make ink to write his letter and find a white man he trusted to mail it.[24]

Geographic distance created another obstacle. Slaves who lived in Texas sometimes managed to escape to Mexico, but fugitives from other regions generally made their way north. Those who attempted to leave the Lower South faced a trek of hundreds of miles and had to navigate their way through vast expanses of strange territory without getting lost. Uneducated and for the most part illiterate, fugitive slaves had no maps and had to hide during the day and travel at night, guided only by the **North Star**.

Skilled slaves had slightly better opportunities to escape. They could blend in with free blacks more easily in southern cities than could scantily dressed field hands, which gave them opportunities to travel north by boat or train. Although steamboats were often inspected for runaways, and blacks on trains had to carry passes or papers documenting their free status, successful fugitives, such as the slave couple Ellen and William Craft, found ingenious ways to evade detection. The Crafts, who left a plantation in Macon, Georgia, in 1848, escaped by passing the light-skinned Ellen off as a sickly young slave master traveling north to seek medical attention. Her husband played the role of the young invalid's faithful attendant. With Ellen swathed in bandages and pretending to be too ill to speak, the couple rode by train to Savannah, where they boarded a steamship bound for Philadelphia. A year later, the enslaved tobacco factory worker Henry "Box" Brown made an equally daring escape from Richmond. With help from a sympathetic white shopkeeper, Brown had himself shipped to Philadelphia in a large wooden crate, which traveled by steamboat, rail, ferry, and delivery wagon before finally arriving at its destination twenty-seven hours later. Such escapes were well publicized, leaving white southerners ever more vigilant.

Slaves who lived in or traveled through border states and territories had the best chance to escape because of their proximity to free soil. Slaves in Kentucky could cross the Ohio River to seek freedom to the north, while those in Missouri could try their luck in Iowa or Illinois. These slaves were also much closer to the **underground railroad**, a network of black and white antislavery activists who routinely sheltered escaped slaves. But to contact the underground railroad, slaves first had to elude patrollers, slave catchers, and the hunting dogs white southerners used to track them down.

Moreover, family ties kept many slaves from attempting escape. Most successful fugitives were young men from the Upper South and border states who, in addition to being strong enough to withstand the trek, were either childless or already separated from their families due to sale or migration. They also had a better chance of traveling undetected, because planters typically employed young male slaves to run errands. Women, by contrast, were far less likely to be given jobs that took them away from their owners' property. Childbearing and motherhood limited their options even further. Slave women bore an average of seven children, beginning in their late teens, and spent much of their twenties and thirties either pregnant or nursing. They maintained close ties with their children through to adulthood and frequently cared for grandchildren when they became too old to work in the fields. Few women were willing to escape without their offspring, and few fugitives made it far when accompanied by children. Female fugitives who traveled with children could not "walk so far or so fast as scores of *men* that are constantly leaving," one underground railroad volunteer observed, while another estimated that such women were three times more likely to be caught than men who traveled alone.[25]

THE RESURRECTION OF HENRY BOX BROWN AT PHILADELPHIA
Who escaped from Richmond Va in a Box 3 feet long 2½ ft deep and 2 ft wide

Henry "Box" Brown
The Virginia slave Henry "Box" Brown's daring escape, in which he had himself shipped to Philadelphia in a crate, serves as one of the more creative and surprising examples of slaves' determination to be free. After winning his freedom, Brown published an autobiography and became a popular abolitionist speaker and entertainer. Some abolitionists, however, including Frederick Douglass, disapproved of Brown's disclosure of his escape method, feeling that it prevented other slaves from escaping by similar means. *Library of Congress, Prints and Photographs Division, Washington, D.C., LC-USZCN4-225.*

Survival, Community, and Culture

Since permanent escape was not a viable option for most slaves, they increasingly turned to Christianity to help them bear slavery's hardships. They also counted on fellow slaves. Most nineteenth-century slaves lived and worked on holdings large enough to sustain small slave communities. As of 1850, 73.4 percent of all slaves were owned by planters who owned ten or more slaves, and 51.6 percent belonged to planters owning more than twenty. Work took up much of their time and fostered bonds among enslaved laborers, who often worked in gender-segregated work gangs. Meanwhile, even though African American families were often scattered by sale, kinship remained central to slaves' cultural and social life, and family ties were extensive and resilient. Slaves sustained loving relationships with relatives and created new connections with nonrelatives to endure life under slavery and seek refuge from complete domination by their owners.

Slave Religion

By the early 1800s, many enslaved communities had embraced evangelical Christianity, but young slaves received much of their religious education in the slave quarters rather than in church. Drawn to the emotional forms of worship common in Baptist and Methodist revivals and churches, African Americans continued to favor these denominations over Presbyterian and Episcopal churches, where Sunday services tended to be more restrained. They rarely relied solely on white religious leaders for guidance, however. In rural areas, many blacks lacked access to religious services, and even in areas where churches were more plentiful, slave owners did not always permit slaves to attend church. (See Document Project: Slave Testimony, pp. 206–11.)

Even blacks who worshipped alongside whites or received religious instruction from their masters tended to distrust white Christianity. Relegated to segregated pews or sometimes required to listen to the minister's sermon from outside the church, African Americans had few opportunities to worship on equal terms. In the "white folks' church," one former slave remembered, the slaves "couldn't do nuthin' — jes sit dere. Dey could sing, an' take de sacrement; but didn't have no voice — jes like animals!"[26] The character of the religious instruction that slaves received made matters worse. White ministers often stressed obedience and humility, with popular teachings centering on scriptural passages such as "Servants be obedient to their masters" and "Let as many servants as are under the yoke count their own masters worthy of all honor." Slaves understood the obvious self-interest animating such teachings. As the ex-slave Wes Brady recalled, "You ought to have heard that 'Hellish' preaching. . . . 'Obey your Master and Mistress, don't steal chickens, don't steal eggs and meat,' and nary word 'bout having a soul to save."[27]

Rather than accepting this instruction, enslaved blacks across the South often belonged to what historians have termed the **invisible church**. Slave Christianity stressed the equality of all men under God, drawing on the Bible as inspiration for spirituals that expressed slaves' own humanity, capacity for freedom, and hope of justice for an oppressed people. Slaves also embraced scriptural stories that held out the promise of liberation under a just God. Their favorite was the Old Testament's book of Exodus, which tells of how Moses freed the children of Israel from slavery in Egypt. This story was celebrated in slave spirituals such as "Go Down, Moses," which drew a direct parallel between the enslavement of African Americans and the enslavement of the Israelites. "Go down, Moses," its chorus commanded, "Away down to Egypt's land, / And tell King Pharaoh / To let my people go."

Slaves gathered in their homes to hold their own religious ceremonies or assembled in secret "hush harbors" in the woods. Often led by slave elders, these ceremonies might incorporate African spiritual practices such as juju and voodoo. Most common was the **ring shout**, often known simply as the "shout." In this form of worship, congregants formed a circle and moved counterclockwise while shuffling their feet, clapping, singing, calling out, or praying aloud. Practiced in both the West Indies and North America, the ring shout combined West African–based music and dance traditions with the passionate Protestantism of the Second Great Awakening to create a powerful new ritual that offered emotional and physical release. The former slave Mose Hursey, who witnessed these ceremonies as a child in Red River, Texas, recalled, "I heard them [slaves] get up with a powerful force of spirit, clappin' they hands and walking around the place. They'd shout, 'I got the glory. I got the old time religion in my heart.'"[28] The expressive, rhythmic music produced during the shouts lives on today in musical genres such as the blues and gospel.

Ring Shout
An artist's depiction of a prayer meeting at a contraband camp, this 1862 engraving shows black worshippers participating in a ring shout. A religious ritual in which participants shuffled their feet, clapped, and often prayed or sang while moving in a circle, the ring shout probably had roots in West African traditions that combined dance, music, and prayer.
Engraving by J. J. Cade after an original by William Ludlow Sheppard/New York Public Library, USA/Bridgeman Images.

Gender, Age, and Work

In communities forbidden any form of formal education, family structures allowed slaves to pass on wisdom, knowledge, and skills from one generation to the next. Slave elders usually played a vital role in schooling their communities. Few could teach their young people to read or write, because slave literacy was discouraged or banned in the southern states. But elderly slaves passed on other valuable lessons to youngsters, such as how to handle their owners, negotiate with overseers and other white authorities, and resolve disputes within their quarters. Generally respected for their extensive life experience, many served as the spiritual leaders of their communities as well.

Older slaves taught younger ones the agricultural techniques used to cultivate the planters' crops and the gardens that sustained slave families. They also helped young people master other survival skills. Adult men taught young boys how to fish, hunt, and forage for food, while women taught girls how to cook, sew, clean, take care of children, and even help deliver babies. These tasks were not strictly divided by gender. Frederick Douglass recalled that his grandmother was not only a skilled nurse but also "a capital hand at making nets for catching shad and herring" and equally good at using her nets to catch these fish.[29] Children of both sexes performed housework and took care of other children. But once they were old enough for adult labor, typically at puberty, girls and boys often worked separately and learned different tasks.

Although slave men and women both worked in the fields on plantations, tasks were commonly divided by gender. Field hands were usually split into sex-segregated work gangs and assigned different work regimes. Women were classified as three-quarters of a hand (rather than as a full hand), and on plantations with sufficient male workers, women were spared some of the most physically taxing labor. During planting season, women hoed while men plowed, and when slave workers erected fences, the men split the rails while the women assembled the fences.

When additional labor was needed, however, female slaves might be assigned to any task. On Louisiana sugar plantations, for example, female work gangs toiled alongside male gangs. They worked sixty to seventy hours per week under conditions that compromised their capacity to conceive, deliver, and nurture healthy children. Whereas slave populations grew swiftly throughout the rest of the South, in southeastern Louisiana the natural growth rate among slaves declined by 13 percent per decade. During the grinding season, when slaves of both sexes worked almost around the clock cutting cane for the sugar mills, and during planting, which involved hand-planting thousands of seed cane stems, women had trouble conceiving and carrying babies to term. In addition, the cane workers' spare diet of salt pork, molasses, and corn bread did not supply women with enough calories or vitamins to have healthy babies or, in some cases, even sustain their fertility. Stillborns and miscarriages were common, and many infants died.

Such losses were psychologically devastating for slave women, whose numerous pregnancies and miscarriages also taxed their physical health. One woman named

Rachel, who worked on Joseph Kleinpeter's Variety Plantation in Louisiana, gave birth to nine children between 1836 and 1849, only four of whom survived. "My ma died 'bout three hours after I was born," noted the former slave Edward De Bieuw. She was hoeing cane when she went into labor, he explained, and "she told the driver she was sick; he told her to just hoe-right-on. Soon, I was born, and my ma die[d] a few minutes after dey brung her to the house."[30]

Wealthy Louisiana sugar planters could afford to purchase new slaves when theirs did not reproduce, but planters elsewhere generally had a vested interest in encouraging slave reproduction. Some slaveholders reduced the daily work required of pregnant and nursing women, reclassifying them as one-half hands rather than three-quarter ones and assigning them to lighter tasks. Generous masters also increased their food allotment. Such measures helped maintain a robust rate of reproduction throughout much of the antebellum South.

Many slave owners and overseers were convinced that black women were naturally immune to the rigors of pregnancy, which often kept white women confined to their beds for months. One Mississippi planter told a northern visitor that the exercise that black women received performing field work spared them "the difficulty, danger, and pain which attended women of the better classes in giving birth to their offspring." Such beliefs often made masters quick to suspect pregnant slaves and nursing mothers of faking or "playing the lady" when they complained of pain or fatigue.[31] Some even whipped pregnant slaves, and such whippings were common enough that owners developed a special method for administering them. According to one former slave, pregnant slaves were made to "lie face down in a specially dug depression in the ground," which protected the fetus while the mother was abused.[32]

Sent back to work shortly after giving birth, slave women then had to juggle infant care and the grueling labor regime. Some field workers, such as William Wells Brown's mother, were allowed no time to nurse and thus forced to carry their infants with them in the fields. Even when pregnant or nurturing newborns, slave women faced many hours of domestic work upon returning home, where they had to feed their families, take care of their children, and tend to domestic tasks such as sewing and housecleaning. Slave men often supplemented their families' meager diets by catching game and fish, raising vegetables, and keeping domestic animals such as pigs and chickens. But women performed much of the domestic labor in the slave quarters.

Slave women shouldered their burdens by taking care of one another and developing a sense of independence that made them more similar to their husbands than were most antebellum wives. Whereas freemen of that era had considerable power over their wives' behavior and possessions, enslaved men had virtually no authority over slave women. Slave men were not breadwinners and often performed the same kind of work as their wives. Gender norms in the quarters, therefore, tended to recognize black men and women as equal partners with similar abilities.

Marriage and Family

Southern courts never recognized slave marriages because, according to slave codes, chattel slaves were " 'not ranked among sentient beings, but among things,' and things are not married."[33] In practice, however, slaves courted, loved, and formed lasting unions. Enslaved couples came together and remained together largely at the discretion of their owners, many of whom had little interest in their happiness. Owners were anxious for female slaves to reproduce and for male slaves to be tied down by family loyalties, and they generally encouraged their slaves to marry informally, often conducting the ceremonies themselves.

"The marsters married the slaves without any papers," an ex-slave named John Bectom remembered. "All they did was to say . . . 'Frank, I pronounce you and Jane man and wife.' "[34] Some slave owners hosted big slave weddings, even hiring preachers to lead the ceremonies. Such weddings were popular among the slaves, who regarded them as occasions for celebration. Many years after slavery ended, the ex-slave Richard Moring still had good memories of the weddings held on his master's North Carolina plantation. "When dere wus a weddin' dar wus fun fer all," he recalled. "Dey wus all dressed up in new clothes, an' marster's dinin' room wus decorated wid flowers fer de 'casion. . . . De preacher married 'em up good an' tight jist lak he done de white folks."[35] But wedding ceremonies were not always officiated by slaveholders, and some took place within the slave quarters.[36]

However they were celebrated, slave unions lacked the sanctity, and sometimes even the consensual character, of marriages among whites. Sexual partners could be imposed on slaves in appallingly brutal ways. Louisa Everett's marriage began when her owner came into her cabin with a male slave named Sam and forced Sam to undress. According to Louisa, her owner then asked her, " 'Do you think you can stand this big nigger?' He had that old bull whip flung acrost his shoulder, and Lawd, that man could hit so hard! So I jes said 'yassur, I guess so,' and tried to hide my face so I couldn't see Sam's nakedness, but he made me look at him anyhow. Well he told us what we must git busy and do in his presence, and we had to do it. After that we were considered man and wife. Me and Sam was a healthy pair and had fine, big babies, so I never had another man forced on me, thank God. Sam was kind to me and I learnt to love him."[37] Of course, not all slave women could say the same. When Rose Williams was sixteen, she was told to share a cabin occupied by a slave named Rufus, whose sexual advances she did not welcome. When she complained to her master, he threatened to beat her if she did not have sex with Rufus. He paid "big money" for her, he said, "cause I wants you to raise me childrens."[38]

Moreover, all enslaved women, single or married, were vulnerable to sexual abuse, and slave men could offer them little protection from white men's sexual advances. "WHY does the slave ever love?" wrote the fugitive slave Harriet Jacobs when she learned that, in order to keep her as his mistress, her master had rebuffed the free black carpenter who wished to marry her and buy her freedom.[39] Such abuses were so common that one critic of slavery charged that "one of the reasons why wicked men in the

Broomstick Wedding Ceremony
This image of an African American wedding was created by an eyewitness sometime before the Civil War. It shows a young couple preparing to join themselves in marriage by jumping over a broomstick. A substitute for formal marriage, the practice of jumping the broom was a folk tradition in Europe, and may have had parallels in West Africa as well. Recognized as a form of marriage by both blacks and whites, the practice was widely used to commemorate the unions of enslaved couples in the American South, where slave men and women had no legal right to marry. © *North Wind Picture Archives/Alamy Stock Photo.*

South uphold slavery is the facility which it affords for a licentious life."[40] These violations also complicated the family ties between slave couples and their children. Slave men ended up with children who were not their own, and fatherless children were all too common. Henry Bibb never knew his father, Kentucky state senator James Bibb, but he grew up knowing that he and his seven brothers were all children of slaveholders, none of whom prevented any of them from being bought and sold.

Not all slave families were the products of an owner's coercion, however. The prevalence of marriages between slaves on different plantations, known as **abroad marriages**, suggests that many owners allowed slaves to choose their own partners. Though never particularly popular with slave owners, such marriages may have accounted for as many as a third of all slave marriages in mid-nineteenth-century South Carolina.[41] Abroad marriages required a strong commitment, because enslaved men had to secure their masters' permission to visit their wives and then brave the slave patrols en route. "My pa would have to git a pass to come see my mammy. He sometimes come without a pass," recalled the ex-slave Millie Barbie.[42] But these marriages had the advantage of sheltering spouses from witnessing their loved ones' harsh treatment. Newly married Henry Bibb was initially happy to be purchased by Mr. Gatewood, who owned his wife, Malinda, but he soon found himself "much dissatisfied," because "to live where I must be eye witness to her insults, scourgings and abuses, such as are common to be inflicted upon slaves, was more than I could bear."[43]

Parenthood posed similar dilemmas for slaves, whose children could be disciplined or brutalized by their owners. The abuse of Bibb's daughter Mary Frances made his family life under slavery still more unbearable. Once the child grew old enough to be weaned, her parents were no longer permitted to look after her during the day. Instead, they had to work in the fields, leaving their little girl in the home of a cruel and impatient plantation mistress who would often "slap with her hand the face of little Frances, for crying after her mother, until her little face was left black and blue." As much as he loved his daughter, Bibb also regretted fatherhood, stating that he "could never look upon the dear child without being filled with sorrow and fearful apprehensions . . . because she was a slave, regarded as property."[44]

Although adult slaves had little control over the actions of their owners, they did their best to shield their children from abuse. Some subjected their family's children to physical punishment at home, in the hopes of mitigating any punishment administered by the owner, as Eliza Adams found out when she sought out her grandmother after a conflict with her owner. Believing that her grandmother might protect her from punishment, Adams was surprised to receive a whipping from her instead. Enslaved adults also tried to protect children by teaching them to stay out of trouble. Children learned to obey their owners at an early age and received careful instruction on the intricacies of their region's racial etiquette, like stepping aside for white people and not doing anything that might irritate or alarm them. Aware that children are naturally curious, slave parents taught their offspring never to be caught staring at whites or, worse still, eavesdropping on their conversations. But slave children, who were barely noticed by whites, could also amass valuable information — so their elders instructed them in the fine art of "listenin widout no ears en seein widout no eyes," as the ex-slave Julia Woodberry put it.[45]

Enslaved children also received protection and advice from slaves who did not have the opportunity to raise their own children. Although African American family members were frequently scattered by sale, family units remained important even when

A Slave Family in a Georgia Cotton Field, c. 1860
This black-and-white photograph was taken shortly before the Civil
War and shows a slave family picking cotton on a plantation outside
Savannah. Cotton picking typically required the labor of the entire
family, including young children. *Private Collection/Peter Newark American Pictures/*
Bridgeman Images.

their members were not united by blood. African Americans who lost their kinfolk to
sale or migration often created new family connections by embracing nonrelatives as
fictive kin. Orphaned children were taken in by nonrelatives, as young Laura Clark
learned when she and her mother were sold to different owners. Although bereft at the
loss of her daughter, Laura's mother acted quickly to secure a substitute parent. According to Laura, her mother asked a woman who had been sold to the same owner to "take
kier of my baby Chile . . . and if fen I never sees her no mo' raise her for God."[46] Young
migrant teenagers likewise claimed older slaves as foster parents and grandparents.

When such migrants had children of their own, they named them after both the family members they had left behind and their adopted relatives. These new family ties eased, but did not erase, the pain felt by slaves separated from their families by sale.

CONCLUSION

Surviving Slavery

Whether a matter of blood or otherwise, families helped African Americans survive and endure slavery. These powerful social ties united an enslaved people who had originated in many different West African societies and survived the Middle Passage, only to form new communities that also fell prey to slavery and sale. As one prominent scholar has put it, throughout "generations of captivity," African Americans endured by building communities strong enough to overcome these adversities.[47] Slave communities nurtured their children, cherished their elders, passed down African traditions, and provided members with a supportive environment.

No amount of community, however, could spare enslaved blacks from slavery's worst sorrows. Slave families lived in constant fear of separation by sale. Most slaves faced terrible hardships on a daily basis, working long hours under grueling conditions. They were subjected to brutal corporal punishment meted out not only by their owners but also by other whites, such as overseers and employers. Enslaved parents could not protect their children from such punishment or other forms of mistreatment, and enslaved spouses could not defend each other in the face of whippings and sexual abuse.

Slaves often resisted such abuses, but their resistance was usually covert. Slave rebels who offered direct physical opposition to their oppressors rarely survived their confrontations. Truancy as well as more serious escape attempts were common, as were stealing and avoiding work. Supervised by their owners and overseers during the day, and watched by armed patrollers at night, most slaves had few opportunities to plan any form of organized resistance, and those who attempted it were often caught in the act. Still, African American resistance to slavery could never be completely suppressed. Successful slave insurrections or advanced plots, when they did occur, further illuminated the impossibility of completely silencing black dissent.

Antebellum slave communities sustained their hopes for freedom by embracing an egalitarian form of Christianity that assured them that all men were equal under God. In addition to providing spiritual comfort and emotional release, slave religion nourished freedom dreams by emphasizing biblical texts such as the book of Exodus. As sectional struggles increasingly pitted the free North against the slave South, enslaved African Americans began to cherish more secular hopes for freedom as well. Joined by a growing cadre of black abolitionists in the North, they kept a close, hopeful watch on the widening rift between white northerners and southerners, and they stood ready to cast off their chains should freedom ever come.

CHAPTER 5 **REVIEW**

KEY TERMS

REVIEW QUESTIONS

1. Discuss the deepening political, economic, social, and slavery-related divisions between the North and South in the years 1820–1860. How was each region becoming more distinctive, and how were the two regions becoming more opposed to each other? In what ways did the two regions remain linked in spite of the growing divide between them?

2. How did the actions of Denmark Vesey, Nat Turner, David Walker, and the slaves aboard the *Amistad* and the *Creole* resonate throughout the country? Compare the effects of their actions in the North and South, and the implications for slaves and free blacks. What does this tell you about the state of the nation during this period?

3. Discuss the various types of slave resistance. How did individual slaves' circumstances — their age, gender, location, or skill level, for example — make it more or less difficult to defy their masters or escape permanently?

4. How did gender affect slaves' experiences? In what ways were slave women's hardships different from slave men's? In what ways were slave women and men arguably more equal than white women and men of this period?

Slave Testimony

Enslaved African Americans had few opportunities to express their views on slavery. Rarely permitted to learn to read or write, they were usually unable to record their stories even after slavery was abolished. Some former slaves, such as William Wells Brown and Frederick Douglass, published autobiographies known as fugitive slave narratives. Often written with the help of white editors, these book-length works constitute some of the richest testimony we have about the slave experience. Such narratives must, however, be read with caution, always keeping in mind what influence white editors might have had on the black authors.

Similar interpretive issues relate to shorter documents that shed light on the slave experience. The first document excerpted here is fugitive slave James Curry's account of his life. Composed shortly after Curry escaped from slavery in North Carolina, this short memoir was likely written with the assistance of one of the white abolitionists who helped Curry secure his freedom. "Slave Punishment" provides a visual representation of the brutal treatment depicted in Curry's account. Lewis Clarke's questions and answers about slavery follow. A fugitive slave from Kentucky, Clarke describes slavery from his personal experience. The last document is an excerpt from an interview with the ex-slave Mary Reynolds, one of more than 2,300 former slaves interviewed between 1936 and 1938 under the Federal Writers' Project. Part of the federally funded Works Progress Administration (WPA), this Great Depression–era initiative employed mostly white writers and journalists, whom the elderly former slaves often regarded with suspicion. Even so, the interviews provide a crucial record of more than two thousand individuals' perspectives on slavery.

James Curry | *Narrative of James Curry, a Fugitive Slave, 1840*

JAMES CURRY (1815–?) was born into slavery in North Carolina in 1815. After his escape in 1837, he produced a brief account of his life. Curry's memoir was published in an abolitionist magazine and was likely written with the assistance of the antislavery activist Elizabeth Buffum Chace.

My mother was cook in the house for about twenty-two years. She cooked for from twenty-five to thirty-five, taking the family and the slaves together. The slaves ate in the kitchen. After my mistress's death, my mother was the

SOURCE: *The Liberator*, January 10, 1840.

only woman kept in the house. She took care of my master's children, some of whom were then quite small, and brought them up. One of the most trying scenes I ever passed through, when I would have laid down my life to protect her if I had dared, was this: after she had raised my master's children, one of his daughters, a young girl, came into the kitchen one day, and for some trifle about the dinner, she struck my mother, who pushed her away, and she fell on the floor. Her father was not at home. When he came, which was while the slaves were eating in the kitchen, she told him about it. He came down, called my mother out, and, with a hickory rod, he beat her fifteen or twenty strokes, and then called his daughter and told her to take her satisfaction of her, and she did beat her until she was satisfied. Oh! it was dreadful, to see the girl whom my poor mother had taken care of from her childhood, thus beating her, and I must stand there, and did not dare to crook my finger in her defence. My mother's labor was very hard. She would go to the house in the morning, take her pail upon her head, and go away to the cow-pen, and milk fourteen cows. She then put on the bread for the family breakfast, and got the cream ready for churning, and set a little child to churn it, she having the care of from ten to fifteen children, whose mothers worked in the field. After clearing away the family breakfast, she got breakfast for the slaves; which consisted of warm corn bread and buttermilk, and was taken at twelve o'clock. In the meantime, she had beds to make, rooms to sweep, &c. Then she cooked the family dinner, which was simply plain meat, vegetables and bread. Then the slaves' dinner was to be ready at from eight to nine o'clock in the evening. It consisted of corn bread, or potatoes, and the meat which remained of the master's dinner, or one herring apiece. At night she had the cows to milk again. There was little ceremony about the master's supper, unless there was company. This was her work day by day. Then in the course of the week, she had the washing and ironing to do for her master's family, (who, however, were clothed very simply,) and for her husband, seven children and herself. . . .

After I was sixteen, I was put into the field to work in the spring and summer, and in the autumn and winter, I worked in the hatter's shop with my uncle. We raised on the plantation, principally, tobacco, some cotton, and some grain. We commenced work as soon as we could see in the morning, and worked from that time until 12 o'clock before breakfast, and then until dark, when we had our dinner, and hastened to our night-work for ourselves. We were not driven as field slaves generally are, and yet when I hear people here say they work as hard as the slaves, I can tell them from experience, they know nothing about it. And even if they did work as hard, there is one striking difference. When they go home at night, they carry to their families the wages of their daily labor; and then they have the night for rest and sleep. Whereas, the slave carries to his family at night, only a weary body and a sick mind, and all he can do for them is done during the hours allowed him for sleep. A slave, who was hired during one summer by Thomas Maguhee, a rich slaveholder in our neighborhood, soon after his return, passed with me, one day, near a field on his plantation. Pointing to it, he said, "I never saw blood flow any where as I've seen it flow in that field. It flows there like water. When I went there to work, I was *a man*, but now, I am *a boy*. I could then carry several bushels on my shoulder, but now I cannot lift one to it." So very hard had he been worked. When arranging the slaves for hoeing in the field, the overseer takes them, one at a time, and tries their speed, and places them accordingly in the row, the swiftest first, and so on. Then they commence, and all must keep up with the foremost. This Thomas Maguhee used to walk into his field, with his hat close down on his head, and holding his cane over his shoulder. When he came up to the poor slaves, as they were tugging at their hoes, he would call out, "boys!" Then they must all raise their hats and reply simultaneously, "Sir." "Move your hoes." They would spring forward and strive to increase their speed to the utmost; but presently he would call out again, "boys!" Again the hats were raised as they answered, "Sir." "I told you to move your hoes, and you hav'nt moved them yet. I have twice to threat and once to fall." (That is, if you do not move faster, I shall knock you down.) Now the poor creatures must make their last effort, and when he saw that their every power, was exerted, he would set his hat on the top of his head, taking down his cane, set his arms akimbo and strut through the field.

Slave Punishment

Slaves of all ages, male and female, endured a wide range of horrific abuses. Difficult as these were to bear individually, they were made all the worse when slaves had to witness the cruel treatment of their loved ones. This early-nineteenth-century engraving depicts a group of slaves of all ages enduring different kinds of physical abuse, suffering alone as well as witnessing others' pain. At the far right, a young man tries to shield two children from the whip, attempting to halt their tormentor with a gesture.

Snark/Art Resource, NY.

Lewis Clarke | *Questions and Answers about Slavery, 1845*

Born into slavery in Kentucky, LEWIS GARRARD CLARKE (1815–1897) escaped to Canada in 1841 and eventually resettled in Ohio. He became an antislavery lecturer, sharing the story of his life under slavery with audiences across the Northeast. Clarke also published his autobiography, and in one of the book's appendices, he supplemented his life story with a series of answers to the questions that audiences most frequently asked him about slavery.

The following questions are often asked me, when I meet the people in public, and I have thought it would be well to put down the answers here.

How many holidays in a year do the slaves in Kentucky have? — They usually have six days at Christmas, and two or three others in the course of the year. Public opinion generally seems to require this much of slaveholders; a few give more, some less; some *none*, not a day nor an hour.

How do slaves spend the Sabbath? — Every way the master pleases. There are certain kinds of work which are respectable for Sabbath day. Slaves are often sent out to salt the cattle, collect and count the pigs and sheep, mend fences, drive the stock from one pasture to another. Breaking young horses and mules, to send them to market, yoking young oxen, and training them, is proper Sabbath work; piling and burning brush, on the back part of the lot, grubbing brier patches that are out of the way, and where they will not be seen. Sometimes corn must be shelled in the corn-crib; hemp is baled in the hemp-house. The still-house must be attended on the Sabbath. In these, and various other such like employments, the more avaricious slaveholders keep their slaves busy a good part of every Sabbath. It is a great day for visiting and

SOURCE: Lewis Garrard Clarke, *Narratives of the Sufferings of Lewis and Milton Clarke, Sons of a Soldier of the Revolution, during a Captivity of More Than Twenty Years among the Slaveholders of Kentucky, One of the So Called Christian States of North America* (Boston: Bela Marsh, 1846), 103–5.

eating, and the house servants often have more to do on that than on any other day. . . .

What proportion of slaves attend church on the Sabbath? — In the country, not *more* than *one in ten* on an average.

How many slaves have you ever known that could read? — I never saw more than three or four that could properly read at all. I never saw but one that could write.

What do slaves know about the Bible? — They generally believe there is somewhere a real Bible, that came from God; but they frequently say the Bible now used is master's Bible; most that they hear from it being, "Servants, obey your masters."

Are families often separated? How many such cases have you personally known? — I never knew a whole family to live together till all were grown up, in my life. There is almost always, in every family, some one or more keen and bright, or else sullen and stubborn slave, whose influence they are afraid of on the rest of the family, and such a one must take a walking ticket to the south.

There are other causes of separation. The death of a large owner is the occasion usually of many families being broken up. Bankruptcy is another cause of separation, and the hard-heartedness of a majority of slaveholders another and a more fruitful cause than either or all the rest. *Generally* there is but little more scruple about separating families than there is with a man who keeps sheep in selling off the lambs in the fall.

Mary Reynolds | *The Days of Slavery, 1937*

The daughter of a free black father and an enslaved mother, MARY REYNOLDS grew up on the Kilpatrick family plantation in Black River, Louisiana. Although her father was willing to buy Reynolds's mother and children, their owner refused to sell them, so the family remained enslaved until the Union army took control of Louisiana during the Civil War. Reynolds told her story in the mid-1930s to a writer working for the Federal Writers' Project of the Works Progress Administration. Interviewed in the Dallas County (Texas) Convalescent Home, she claimed to be over one hundred years old, and although she appeared feeble and frail, Reynolds was still lively and alert and able to describe her early life in striking detail.

Massa Kilpatrick wasn't no piddlin' man. He was a man of plenty. He had a big house with no more style to it than a crib, but it could room plenty people. He was a medicine doctor and they was rooms in the second story for sick folks what come to lay in. It would take two days to go all over the land he owned. He had cattle and stock and sheep and more'n a hundred slaves and more besides. He bought the bes' of niggers near every time the spec'lators come that way. He'd make a swap of the old ones and give money for young ones what could work.

He raised corn and cotton and cane and 'taters and goobers,° 'sides the peas and other feedin' for the niggers. I 'member I helt a hoe handle mighty onsteady when they put a old woman to larn me and some other chillun to scrape the fields. That old woman would be in a frantic. She'd show me and then turn 'bout to show some other li'l nigger, and I'd have the young corn cut clean as the grass. She say, "For the love of Gawd, you better larn it right, or Solomon will beat the breath out you body." Old man Solomon was the nigger driver.

Slavery was the worst days was ever seed in the world. They was things past tellin', but I got the scars on my old body to show to this day. I seed worse than what happened to me. I seed them put the men and women in the stock with they hands screwed down through holes in the board and they feets tied together and they naked behinds to the world. Solomon the overseer beat them with a big whip and massa look on. The niggers better not stop in the fields when they hear them yellin'. They cut the flesh most to the bones and some they was when they taken them out of stock and put them on the beds, they never got up again. . . .

The times I hated most was pickin' cotton when the frost was on the bolls. My hands git sore and crack open and bleed. We'd have a li'l fire in the fields and iffen the ones with tender hands couldn't stand it no longer, we'd run and warm our hands a li'l bit. When I could steal a 'tater, I used to slip it in the ashes and when I'd run to the fire I'd take it out and eat it on the sly.

In the cabins it was nice and warm. They was built of pine boardin' and they was one long rom [room] of them up the hill back of the big house. Near one side of the cabins was a fireplace. They'd

Mary Reynolds, Age 105, at the Dallas County Convalescent Home, Texas, c. 1937
Mary Reynolds was one of more than 2,300 ex-slaves interviewed by the Federal Writers' Project, a New Deal agency sponsored by the federal government's Works Progress Administration during the 1930s. Despite her advanced age, her memories of slavery were vivid. *Library of Congress, Manuscript Division. WPA Slave Narrative Project (Texas Narratives, vol. 16, part 3), Federal Writers' Project, U.S. Works Progress Administration (USWPA).*

° 'Taters and goobers are potatoes and peanuts. The word *goober* probably comes from *n-guba*, a Kongolese or Kimbundu term for "peanut."

Source: Ex-slave Stories (Texas): Mary Reynolds, in *Born in Slavery: Slave Narratives from the Federal Writers' Project, 1936–1938*, American Memory, Library of Congress, 238–40, http://lcweb2.loc.gov/cgi-bin/query/S?ammem/mesnbib :@field(AUTHOR+@od1(Reynolds,+Mary)).

bring in two, three big logs and put on the fire and they'd last near a week. The beds was made out of puncheons [wooden posts] fitted in holes bored in the wall, and planks laid 'cross them poles. We had tickin' mattresses filled with corn shucks. Sometimes the men build chairs at night. We didn't know much 'bout havin' nothin', though. . . .

Once in a while they'd give us a li'l piece of Sat'day evenin' to wash out clothes. . . . When they'd git through with the clothes . . . the niggers which sold they goobers and 'taters brung fiddles and guitars and come out and play. The others clap they hands and stomp they feet. . . .

We was scart of Solomon and his whip, though, and he didn't like frolickin'. He didn't like for us niggers to pray, either. We never heared of no church, but us have prayin' in the cabins. We'd set on the floor and pray with our heads down low and sing low, but if Solomon heared he'd come and beat on the wall with the stock of his whip. He'd say, "I'll come in there and tear the hide off you backs." But some [of] the old niggers tell us we got to pray to Gawd that he don't think different of the blacks and the whites. I know that Solomon is burnin' in hell today, and it pleasures me to know it.

QUESTIONS FOR ANALYSIS

1. All three of these accounts raise a variety of questions about slaves' views of their owners and of other white people. How do white people figure into the accounts of slavery given by James Curry, Lewis Clarke, and Mary Reynolds? How do these three ex-slaves describe the relationship between slave and slave owner?

2. The documents describing the experiences of Curry and Clarke date to the antebellum era, whereas Reynolds remembers slavery many years after emancipation. How might slaves' and ex-slaves' perspectives on the institution of slavery have changed over time, and why might this have been the case?

3. Most slave testimony, including Curry's memoir and Reynolds's interview, was not written by the slaves themselves. Instead, slaves' stories were recorded by white interlocutors who often guided and reshaped their statements. And even Lewis Clarke framed some of his testimony in the form of answers to questions that were often asked by his antislavery audiences. To what extent do any of these accounts seem to be direct transcriptions of these individuals' own thoughts about slavery? How and where can you detect the presence of another person?

4. What can we learn from these visual and written documents about the experiences of slave children and slave parents?

NOTES

1. William Wells Brown, *Narrative of William W. Brown, a Fugitive Slave. Written by Himself*, 2nd ed. (Boston: Anti-Slavery Office, 1848), 15.

2. Ibid., 20.

3. Ibid., 61, 44.

4. Thomas Jefferson to John Holmes, 22 April 1820, in *Thomas Jefferson: Writings*, ed. Merrill D. Peterson (New York: Library of America, 1984), 1433–35.

5. Lyman Abbott, *Reminiscences* (New York: Houghton Mifflin, 1915), 102.

6. Interview with Charity Bowery, in *Slave Testimony: Two Centuries of Letters, Speeches, Interviews, and Autobiographies*, ed. John W. Blassingame (Baton Rouge: LSU Press, 1977), 265.

7. William Johnson, quoted in Benjamin Drew, ed., *Refugees from Slavery* (Mineola, NY: Dover, 2004), 19.

8. Interview with Carrie E. Davis, in *The WPA Oklahoma Slave Narratives*, ed. T. Lindsay Baker and Julie P. Baker (Norman: University of Oklahoma Press, 1996), 102.

9. Robert James Turnbull [Brutus], *The Crisis: or, Essays on the Usurpations of the Federal Government*, no. 26 (Charleston, SC: A. E. Miller, 1827), 133.

10. Quoted in Douglas R. Egerton, *He Shall Go Out Free: The Lives of Denmark Vesey* (Madison, WI: Madison House, 1999), 198.

11. Thomas Wentworth Higginson, "Denmark Vesey," *Atlantic*, June 1861, 735.

12. David Walker, *Walker's Appeal, in Four Articles; Together with a Preamble, to the Coloured Citizens of the World, but in Particular, and Very Expressly, to Those of the United States of America, Written in Boston, State of Massachusetts, September 28, 1829*, rev. ed (Boston: published by the author, 1830), 5.

13. Ibid., 41.

14. Quoted ibid., 63.

15. Ibid., 19–20, 35.

16. William Lloyd Garrison, "Walker's Appeal," *Liberator*, January 8, 1831, 1; William Lloyd Garrison, "Walker's Pamphlet," *Liberator*, January 29, 1831, 4.

17. Nat Turner, *The Confessions of Nat Turner, the Leader of the Late Insurrection in Southampton, Va.* (Baltimore: Thomas R. Gray, 1831), 10, 11.

18. Both quoted in Kenneth S. Greenberg, ed., *Nat Turner: A Slave Rebellion in History and Memory* (New York: Oxford University Press, 2003), 154, 156.

19. Interview with May Satterfield, in *Weevils in the Wheat: Interviews with Virginia Ex-Slaves*, ed. Charles L. Perdue Jr., Thomas E. Barden, and Robert K. Phillips (Charlottesville: University of Virginia Press, 1976), 244–45; Rosa Barnwell, quoted in Blassingame, *Slave Testimony*, 698; Louisa Gause, quoted in Federal Writers' Project, *Slave Narratives: A Folk History of Slavery in the United States from Interviews with Former Slaves*, vol. 14, *South Carolina Narratives*, part 2 (Washington, DC: 1941), 110.

20. Cozzins v. Whitacker (1833), quoted in Ariela Gross, "Pandora's Box: Slave Character on Trial in the Antebellum Deep South," *Yale Journal of Law & the Humanities* 7, no. 2 (1995): 308; James Stirling, *Letters from the Slave States* (London: John W. Parker and Son, 1857), quoted in Robert Vaughan,

"Epilogue on Books — English Literature," *British Quarterly Review* 26 (July and October 1857): 517.

21. Frederick Douglass, *Narrative of the Life of Frederick Douglass, an American Slave, Written by Himself* (Boston: Anti-Slavery Office, 1845), 63, 71, 73.

22. John v. State, 16 GA 203 (1854).

23. Quoted in Sally E. Hadden, *Slave Patrols: Law and Violence in Virginia and the Carolinas* (Cambridge: Harvard University Press, 2001), 120.

24. Solomon Northup, *Twelve Years a Slave: Narrative of Solomon Northup, a Citizen of New-York, Kidnapped in Washington City in 1841, and Rescued in 1853* (Auburn, NY: Derby and Miller, 1853), 230.

25. Quoted in Deborah Gray White, *Ar'n't I a Woman? Female Slaves in the Plantation South*, rev. ed. (New York: Norton, 1999), 72.

26. Interview with Anna Morgan, in *The American Slave: A Composite Autobiography, North Carolina and South Carolina Narratives*, ed. George P. Rawick, suppl., 1st ser., vol. 11, part 1 (Westport, CT: Greenwood Press, 1978), 149.

27. Interview with Wes Brady, in *The American Slave: A Composite Autobiography, Texas Narratives*, ed. George P. Rawick, suppl., 2nd ser., vol. 2, part 1 (Westport, CT: Greenwood Press, 1979), 401.

28. Interview with Mose Hursey, in *The American Slave: A Composite Autobiography, Texas Narratives*, ed. George P. Rawick, suppl., 2nd ser., vol. 4, part 2 (Westport, CT: Greenwood Press, 1979), 170–71.

29. Frederick Douglass, *My Bondage and My Freedom* (New York: Miller, Orton & Mulligan, 1855), 35.

30. Quoted in Richard Follett, "Heat, Sex, and Sugar: Pregnancy and Childbearing in the Slave Quarters," *Journal of Family History* 28 (October 2003): 528.

31. White, *Ar'n't I a Woman?*, 112.

32. Paul D. Escott, *Slavery Remembered* (Chapel Hill: University of North Carolina Press, 1979), 43.

33. William Goodell, *The American Slave Code in Theory and Practice* (New York: American and Foreign Anti-Slavery Society, 1853), 105.

34. Quoted in Rebecca J. Fraser, *Courtship and Love among the Enslaved in North Carolina* (Jackson: University Press of Mississippi, 2007), 89.

35. Quoted in Thomas E. Will, "Weddings on Contested Grounds: Slave Marriage in the Antebellum South," *Historian* 62, no. 1 (1999): 111.

36. Ibid., 110.

37. Interview with Louisa Everett, in *Far More Terrible for Women: Personal Accounts of Women in Slavery*, ed. Patrick Neal Minges (Winston-Salem, NC: John F. Blair, 2006), 16–17.

38. Quoted in White, *Ar'n't I a Woman?*, 102.

39. Harriet Ann Jacobs, *Incidents in the Life of a Slave Girl* (Boston: printed for the author, 1861), 58.

40. Quoted in Edward D. C. Campbell Jr. and Kim S. Rice, *Before Freedom Came: African-American Life in the Antebellum South* (Charlottesville: University of Virginia Press, 1997), 62.

41. Emily West, "The Debate on the Strength of Slave Families: South Carolina and the Importance of Cross-Plantation Marriages," *Journal of American Studies* 33, no. 2 (1999): 225.

42. Interview with Millie Barbie, in *The American Slave: A Composite Autobiography, South Carolina Narratives*, ed. George P. Rawick, vol. 2, part 1 (Westport, CT: Greenwood Press, 1973), 39.

43. Henry Bibb, *Narrative of the Life and Adventures of Henry Bibb, an American Slave, Written by Himself* (New York: published by the author, 1849), 42.

44. Ibid., 43, 44.

45. Interview with Julia Woodberry, in *The American Slave: A Composite Autobiography, South Carolina Narratives*, ed. George P. Rawick, 1st ser., vol. 3, part 4 (Westport, CT: Greenwood Press, 1972), 95–96.

46. Quoted in Ira Berlin, *The Making of African America: The Four Great Migrations* (New York: Penguin, 2010), 119.

47. This phrase is drawn from the title of Ira Berlin's *Generations of Captivity: A History of African-American Slaves* (Cambridge: Belknap Press of Harvard University Press, 2004).

SUGGESTED REFERENCES

The Expansion and Consolidation of Slavery

Baptist, Edward E. *Creating an Old South: Middle Florida's Plantation Frontier before the Civil War.* Chapel Hill: University of North Carolina Press, 2002.

Campbell, Randolph B. *An Empire for Slavery: The Peculiar Institution in Texas, 1821–1865.* Baton Rouge: LSU Press, 1991.

Deyle, Steven. *Carry Me Back: The Domestic Slave Trade in American Life.* New York: Oxford University Press, 2006.

Follett, Richard. *The Sugar Masters: Planters and Slaves in Louisiana's Cane World, 1820–1860.* Baton Rouge: LSU Press, 2007.

Forbes, Robert Pierce. *The Missouri Compromise and Its Aftermath: Slavery and the Meaning of America.* Chapel Hill: University of North Carolina Press, 2009.

Johnson, Walter. *Soul by Soul: Life inside the Antebellum Slave Market.* Cambridge: Harvard University Press, 1999.

Morrison, Michael A. *Slavery and the American West: The Eclipse of Manifest Destiny.* Chapel Hill: University of North Carolina Press, 1997.

Rothman, Adam. *Slave Country: American Expansion and the Origins of the Deep South.* Cambridge: Harvard University Press, 2005.

Black Challenges to Slavery

Aptheker, Herbert. *American Negro Slave Revolts.* 5th ed. New York: International Publishers, 1983.

Dillon, Merton L. *Slavery Attacked: Southern States and Their Allies, 1619–1865.* Baton Rouge: LSU Press, 1991.

Egerton, Douglas R. *He Shall Go Out Free: The Lives of Denmark Vesey.* Lanham, MD: Rowman & Littlefield, 2004.

Greenberg, Kenneth S., ed. *Nat Turner: A Slave Rebellion in History and Memory.* New York: Oxford University Press, 2003.

Hinks, Peter P. *To Awaken My Afflicted Brethren: David Walker and the Problem of Antebellum Slave Resistance.* University Park: Pennsylvania State University Press, 1997.

Jones, Howard. *Mutiny on the Amistad: The Saga of a Slave Revolt and Its Impact on American Abolition, Law, and Diplomacy.* New York: Oxford University Press, 1997.

Kly, Y. N., ed. *The Invisible War: The African American Anti-Slavery Resistance from the Stono Rebellion through the Seminole Wars.* Atlanta: Clarity Press, 2006.

Rucker, Walter C. *The River Flows On: Black Resistance, Culture, and Identity Formation in Early America.* Baton Rouge: LSU Press, 2006.

Everyday Resistance to Slavery

Berry, Daina Ramey. *"Swing the Sickle for the Harvest Is Ripe": Gender and Slavery in Antebellum Georgia.* Urbana: University of Illinois Press, 2007.

Camp, Stephanie M. H. *Closer to Freedom: Enslaved Women and Everyday Resistance in the Plantation South.* Chapel Hill: University of North Carolina Press, 2004.

Franklin, John Hope, and Loren Schweninger. *Runaway Slaves: Rebels on the Plantation.* New York: Oxford University Press, 1999.

Glymph, Thavolia. *Out of the House of Bondage: The Transformation of the Plantation Household.* Cambridge: Cambridge University Press, 2008.

Jones, Norrece T., Jr. *Born a Child of Freedom, Yet a Slave: Mechanisms of Control and Strategies of Resistance in Antebellum South Carolina.* Hanover, NH: University Press of New England / Wesleyan University Press, 1990.

McLaurin, Melton A. *Celia, a Slave.* New York: Avon, 1999.

Rivers, Larry Eugene. *Rebels and Runaways: Slave Resistance in Nineteenth-Century Florida.* Urbana: University of Illinois Press, 2012.

Schermerhorn, Calvin. *Money over Mastery, Family over Freedom: Slavery in the Antebellum Upper South.* Baltimore: Johns Hopkins University Press, 2011.

Webber, Thomas L. *Deep like the Rivers: Education in the Slave Quarter Community, 1831–1865.* New York: Norton, 1978.

Survival, Community, and Culture

Blassingame, John W. *The Slave Community: Plantation Life in the Antebellum South.* Rev. ed. New York: Oxford University Press, 1979.

Fett, Sharla M. *Working Cures: Healing, Health, and Power on Southern Slave Plantations.* Chapel Hill: University of North Carolina Press, 2002.

Irons, Charles F. *The Origins of Proslavery Christianity: White and Black Evangelicals in Colonial and Antebellum Virginia.* Chapel Hill: University of North Carolina Press, 2008.

Kaye, Anthony E. *Joining Places: Slave Neighborhoods in the Old South.* Chapel Hill: University of North Carolina Press, 2009.

Levine, Lawrence W. *Black Culture and Black Consciousness: Afro-American Folk Thought from Slavery to Freedom.* New York: Oxford University Press, 1978.

Raboteau, Albert J. *Slave Religion: The "Invisible Institution" in the Antebellum South.* New York: Oxford University Press, 1978.

Schwartz, Marie Jenkins. *Born in Bondage: Growing Up Enslaved in the Antebellum South.* Cambridge: Harvard University Press, 2001.

West, Emily. *Chains of Love: Slave Couples in Antebellum South Carolina.* Urbana: University of Illinois Press, 2004.

White, Deborah Gray. *Ar'n't I a Woman? Female Slaves in the Plantation South.* Rev. ed. New York: Norton, 1999.

The Northern Black Freedom Struggle and the Coming of the Civil War

1830–1860

CHRONOLOGY *Events specific to African American history are in purple. General United States history events are in black.*

1829	Riots in Cincinnati drive out half the black population
1830	First National Negro Convention
1831	Maria Stewart begins writing and speaking on black moral reform
1833	American Anti-Slavery Society established
	Philadelphia Female Anti-Slavery Society established
	Great Britain enacts compensated emancipation of all slaves in its empire
1836	American Moral Reform Society established
1837	White mob burns abolitionist print shop in Alton, Illinois, and murders editor
1838	White mob destroys Philadelphia's Pennsylvania Hall
1840	Liberty Party founded
1841	Frederick Douglass begins career as abolitionist lecturer
1842	*Prigg v. Pennsylvania* finds personal liberty laws unconstitutional
1843	Henry Highland Garnet calls on slaves to revolt
	Sojourner Truth begins career as abolitionist lecturer
1845	Frederick Douglass's first autobiography published
1846	American Missionary Association established
1846–1848	Mexican-American War
1847	Douglass begins publishing the *North Star*
1848	Douglass attends women's rights convention in Seneca Falls, New York

1849	*Roberts v. City of Boston* upholds segregated schools in Massachusetts
1850	Compromise of 1850
	Fugitive Slave Act
1851	Christiana Resistance
	Mary Ann Shadd emigrates to Canada
1852	Harriet Beecher Stowe's *Uncle Tom's Cabin* published
	Martin Delany advocates establishing black nation outside United States
1854	Elizabeth Jennings sues New York streetcar company to end segregated seating
	Kansas-Nebraska Act
	Republican Party founded
	Fugitive slave Anthony Burns captured and returned to slavery
1855	Massachusetts becomes first state to prohibit segregation by race in public schools
1856	Violence erupts in Kansas between proslavery and antislavery settlers
1857	Black community of Seneca Village razed to make way for Central Park in New York City
	Dred Scott v. Sandford decision denies African American citizenship
1859	Delany begins search for site of African American emigrant settlement in Africa
	John Brown's raid on Harpers Ferry, Virginia
1860	Abraham Lincoln elected president
	South Carolina secedes from Union

Mary Ann Shadd and the Black Liberation Struggle before the Civil War

In January 1849, twenty-five-year-old Mary Ann Shadd weighed in on the enduring debate among free blacks in the North about how best to advance their cause. A veteran schoolteacher who had benefited from her private education and her family's political activism, Shadd spoke in a self-confident and independent voice. She was also impatient. "We have been holding conventions for years — have been assembling together and whining over our difficulties and afflictions, passing resolutions on resolutions . . . but it does really seem that we have made but little progress, considering our resolves." Her solution was clear and pointed: "We should do more, and talk less."[1]

Shadd was both a doer and a talker. Despairing of African American prospects in the United States, she left her teaching job in New York City in 1851 and moved to Canada. In Windsor, Ontario, where African Americans had already formed a small community, she took another teaching job and soon also became cofounder and editor of the *Provincial Freeman,* a weekly black newspaper whose masthead announced its devotion "to anti-slavery, temperance, and general literature." Attending the 1855 National Negro Convention in Philadelphia as one of only two female delegates, she gave a speech that electrified the audience. An observer described it as "one of the most convincing and telling speeches in favor of Canadian emigration I ever heard."[2]

Teacher, journalist, abolitionist, proponent of emigration to Canada, and women's rights activist, Mary Ann Shadd (later Cary) represents many of the different liberation paths that African Americans pursued after 1830. In the 1830s and 1840s, free blacks in northern cities focused on building their own communities and on promoting moral reform, education, and black unity to beat back anti-black prejudice and discrimination. Increasingly, leading men and women formed organizations to accomplish the paired goals of securing equal rights in the North and ending slavery in the South. They met in local, regional, and national conventions to debate their goals and strategies, and they established and wrote for black newspapers that linked communities and ideas throughout the North. The former fugitives among them described the horrors of slavery to persuade whites to join their efforts. Some black activists mounted legal challenges to the discrimination they endured even in states that had abolished slavery. Some participated in petition campaigns and, though generally barred from voting, joined new political parties that aimed to prohibit the spread of slavery to new territories in the West.

Black activists pushed abolition onto the national agenda, and in the 1840s and 1850s the issue of slavery in the territories increasingly threatened to tear the nation apart. Activists deliberately disobeyed a strict new fugitive slave law, continuing to shepherd fugitive slaves to freedom by way of the underground railroad. Increasingly, that meant fleeing to Canada, as in the 1850s a growing number of free blacks came to believe there was no place for them in the United States. Others chose to stay and to confront injustice directly, a few through violent resistance and even insurrection. By 1860, black activism had helped force a catastrophic national showdown over slavery. As the states of the slave South and the free North grew increasingly discontented, each side convinced that the other was conspiring to take over the federal government, the sectional struggle descended into disunion and civil war.

The Boundaries of Freedom

In the three decades before the Civil War, free blacks in the North sought to make viable lives for themselves and their children while their communities fought against increasing white hostility. Prejudice, law, and custom increasingly limited black opportunities for participation in the political, economic, and social life of the American Republic. As a consequence, black communities turned inward to focus on building attitudes and institutions that would make them self-reliant. Yet their very success often provoked an angry, even violent response among whites. More and more, free blacks in the North saw their struggle for self-improvement and full citizenship as inseparable from the struggle of enslaved blacks to end their bondage.

Racial Discrimination in the Era of the Common Man

By 1830, slavery existed almost exclusively in the South. Starting in the 1780s, northern states had abolished slavery, primarily through gradual emancipation laws that freed slaves after they reached a certain age. In 1830, New Jersey was the only northern state with a significant number of slaves: 2,254. By 1850, that number was 236, and slavery in the North was fast becoming a distant memory.

Yet the end of slavery brought an increase, not a decrease, in antiblack prejudice, discrimination, and violence. After visiting the United States in 1831, the French writer Alexis de Tocqueville noted that "the prejudice of race appears to be stronger in the states that have abolished slavery than in those where it still exists; and nowhere is it so intolerant as in those states where servitude has never been known."[3] There are several explanations for this intensification of racial hostility. Tocqueville was ignorant of the fact that slavery had existed previously throughout the North. Indeed, the legacy of black enslavement and its associated racism shaped northern black life. Whites created structures of discrimination and repression to enforce black submission. Increasingly, they viewed blacks as racially inferior, and studies in the emerging social sciences investigating human origins reinforced their views. In the 1820s and 1830s, Dr. Samuel G. Morton of Philadelphia collected human skulls from all over the world and classified them according to race. Measuring skull cavities, he proposed in *Crania Americana* (1839) that Europeans had the most brain capacity, Africans the least. His studies in craniology claimed to prove racial hierarchies popularized in studies such as *Types of Mankind, or Ethnological Researches* (1854) by Josiah Clark Nott and George Robins Gliddon, with a contribution by Louis Agassiz. Agassiz, a Swiss zoologist and geologist who taught at Harvard, lectured widely on the separate origins of the races and their distinctive characteristics.

Throughout the nineteenth century, leading scholars in Europe and America investigated and debated racial origins and character. For American slaveholders, these early studies in the field that would become anthropology helped justify the enslavement of African Americans. For white northerners, these ideas fed notions of white supremacy and suggested reasons to view free blacks as a problem population. Many favored schemes to remove the problem by colonizing African Americans outside the United States, but the American Colonization Society's efforts to sponsor the emigration of free blacks to Liberia were largely unsuccessful. Most free blacks opposed the idea of colonization, as they believed that the United States was their home. A group of Rochester blacks asserted, "We do not consider Africa to be our home, any more than the present whites do England, Scotland, or Ireland."[4]

Unable to pressure or force free blacks to leave the country, whites circumscribed African Americans' freedom and undermined their impact through segregation and exclusion. Black laws discouraged or forbade blacks from entering or settling in Ohio, Indiana, and Illinois — free states bordering on slave states — as well as in Wisconsin and the slave state of Missouri. By law and by custom, whites severely restricted blacks' access to jobs, public institutions and accommodations, and white neighborhoods. Black passengers on stagecoaches, steamboats, trains, streetcars, and omnibuses were required to sit in separate sections or relegated to separate cars.

The legal system, too, discriminated against blacks. Law enforcement officers routinely left black life, liberty, and property unprotected, and blacks had little redress in the courts. A white Cincinnati lawyer admitted to Tocqueville that the lack of legal protection for local blacks often led to "the most revolting injustices."[5] Blacks were also imprisoned at far higher rates than whites for all kinds of offenses — real and imagined, minor and major — in part because of racist views that held them prone to criminality. Because blacks could not serve on juries or function as witnesses or lawyers, blacks accused of crimes were more likely to be convicted and sentenced than whites similarly accused. Not until the late 1850s were blacks permitted to serve on juries, and then only in Massachusetts.

For whites, this was the era of the common man. Universal white male suffrage became the norm after 1830, while black men lost the right to vote. In 1837, Pennsylvania disfranchised black men, and every state that entered the Union after 1819, except Maine, prohibited black suffrage. In 1860, black men could vote only in Maine,

New Hampshire, Vermont, Massachusetts, and Rhode Island. Blacks constituted just 6 percent of the population in these five states.

Black political exclusion solidified white male supremacy. Fearing that voting by allegedly ignorant and untrustworthy black men would pollute the political system, white men and state laws effectively removed black interests from political representation. Whites degraded the status of blacks and then punished them for it. Excluding blacks from political life also had the effect of marginalizing them in the nation's economic life. Thrown into competition with American-born working-class whites and new white immigrants looking to establish themselves, free blacks were often the targets of a hostility that flared into violence. Racially motivated riots were almost commonplace in northern cities, as white mobs attacked black neighborhoods with much loss of property and even loss of life.

A series of riots in Cincinnati offers an example. Directly across the Ohio River from the slave state of Kentucky, Cincinnati was where southern blacks who had been emancipated or had purchased their freedom often relocated. It was also a common destination for fugitive slaves and, in time, a key stop along the underground railroad. The city's black population grew so rapidly as to alarm its white population, and in late June 1829 local officials announced that they would rigorously apply Ohio's black laws. As the city's blacks began to investigate the possibility of resettling in Canada, white mobs attacked them. Over the summer, half the black population was driven from the city. Some two hundred eventually settled in Upper Canada, where they named their new community Wilberforce, after the British abolitionist William Wilberforce, who led the effort to end slavery in Britain's colonies. His goal was accomplished in 1833 when Parliament passed a compensated emancipation law that applied to the entire British empire.

But the violence was not over in Cincinnati. In 1836, white mobs destroyed the shop that printed an abolitionist newspaper and moved on to destroy houses and churches belonging to African Americans. In 1841, fights between unemployed black and white dockworkers escalated into a battle in which blacks mobilized to protect their neighborhood. After police and militiamen disarmed these blacks, the whites returned, leading to more loss of life and more devastation of property.

Boston, New York, and Providence, Rhode Island, also experienced antiblack riots, but no city had more than Philadelphia, which, not coincidentally, had the largest black population. Riots rocked the city in 1820, 1829, 1834, 1835, 1838, 1842, and 1849. During the 1834 riot, both prosperous and poor blacks were attacked; many died, and hundreds fled the city. Roving white mobs vandalized the African Presbyterian Church and devastated a black Methodist church, while also attacking white supporters of black rights. In 1838, a mob assaulted black and white abolitionists meeting in Philadelphia's Pennsylvania Hall, which had just been dedicated to the cause of abolitionism, and burned the building to the ground. The year before, proslavery activists in Alton, Illinois, hurled the printing presses of a white antislavery newspaper into the Mississippi River, burned the print shop, and murdered the editor, Elijah P. Lovejoy. These race riots, which targeted white abolitionists as well as blacks, formed part of a larger pattern of racial and ethnic hostility that was also evident in politics. During the 1840s and

Destruction by Fire of Pennsylvania Hall,
On the night of the 17th May, 1838

The Destruction of Pennsylvania Hall

Arson has historically been a common form of antiproperty violence, one often associated with frenzied mobs. In May 1838, arsonists torched Philadelphia's Pennsylvania Hall, a building tied to abolitionism and the elevation of free blacks. The primitive state of fire prevention and firefighting at this time typically meant that arson exacted a heavy toll in lives lost and property destroyed. *Hand-colored lithograph by J. C. Wild, 1838/The Library Company of Philadelphia, Pennsylvania, USA/Bridgeman Images.*

1850s, anti-immigrant, anti-Catholic Know-Nothings, so-called for the secret nature of their party organization, won local and state offices in New England, New York, and Pennsylvania. The era of the common man was also an era of intense nativism that defined the United States as Anglo-Saxon and Protestant, a land in which free black people had no place.

The Growth of Free Black Communities in the North

Racial hostility, economic discrimination, political exclusion, and violence had severe consequences for black communities in the North in the decades after 1830. These forces constrained the efforts of northern free blacks to make a living and improve themselves and

"Notice to Colored People"

During the 1850s, free blacks in the South and in parts of the North bordering on the South experienced growing restrictions on their movements between cities, as did the enslaved. These restrictions reflected heightened antiblack racism and racial tensions that stemmed from white anxieties about how best to control blacks in a period of intensifying regional conflict over slavery, as well as from white concern about the place of blacks in a country increasingly seen by whites as a white nation. The 1850 Fugitive Slave Act epitomized the national commitment to constraining slave mobility and solidifying slavery (see p. 237). This 1858 poster declares that all blacks traveling on the Philadelphia, Wilmington and Baltimore Railroad must have a bond posted by a white Baltimorean. White passengers traveling with black slaves are notified to have papers ready for their "servants" as well. Philadelphia and Wilmington were key stops along the underground railroad, which spirited runaway slaves to freedom. The poster is a graphic illustration of the increasing surveillance and repression of enslaved and free blacks in the Upper South and free blacks in the North on the eve of the Civil War. *Spencer Collection, New York Public Library, USA/Bridgeman Images.*

undermined their communities. The jobs available to black people were primarily unskilled and paid the lowest wages. Often the work was seasonal, with periods of unemployment. Between 1820 and 1860, the percentages and relative numbers of black men in skilled and semiskilled jobs actually declined, as these jobs increasingly went to native-born whites and the growing numbers of white immigrants. Between 1830 and 1860, the U.S. population increased from 13 million to 32 million, almost 5 million of whom were immigrants. Most newcomers settled in the cities of the North, where their numbers increased competition for scarce jobs. Serious economic downturns in each decade between 1830 and 1860 further eroded the already declining economic status of northern blacks.

Black women formed a little more than half the population in urban black communities. The shorter life expectancy of black males — owing to disease as well as both overwork and poverty from lack of work — and the consistently high demand for black women as domestic servants help explain their greater numbers. There were more widows than widowers in the black communities in Philadelphia, Boston, and Cincinnati, and the number of female-headed households grew. These households were generally poorer than dual-headed households.

Blacks had shorter life expectancies and higher death rates than whites due to accidents, disease, and a lack of adequate health care. They had higher infant mortality rates and fewer children. After 1840, urban black families in the North were smaller in size than rural black families in the North and southern black families. In the short term, smaller families had a positive impact, as that meant fewer demands on limited family budgets. In the longer term, smaller families had a more negative impact, for there were fewer young people to contribute to the family income.

Yet overall, the number of free blacks in the North continued to grow through natural increase, the migration of free blacks from the South, and the arrival of fugitives from slavery. By 1860, half the nation's free black population (226,152) lived in cities in the North. In 1860, Boston had 2,261 blacks, New York 12,472, and Philadelphia 22,185. As a proportion of the population, however, these black communities were shrinking, for the white population was rising more rapidly due to the influx of immigrants, especially from Ireland, which suffered from widespread famine in the 1840s. Increasingly, the newer cities of the West, such as Pittsburgh and St. Louis, also had large black populations. Cincinnati, for example, counted 3,737 blacks in 1860.[6] (See By the Numbers: Percent Change in Free Black Population, 1830–1860.)

In northern cities, black neighborhoods evolved close to, but mostly separate from, white neighborhoods. Cities were still small and densely settled, and blacks, as one observer noted, found themselves "crammed into lofts, garrets and cellars, in blind alleys and narrow courts." Some neighborhoods were racially diverse, with blacks living among poor and working-class whites, especially recent immigrants. The inhabitants of New York City's Five Points district in lower Manhattan were made up "of all colors, white, yellow, brown and ebony black."[7] Some affluent blacks lived in predominantly white areas, but more white neighborhoods were closed to them. Where the black population was larger, as in "Nigger Hill," on the lower slopes of Boston's Beacon Hill, clusters of white households developed within largely black areas. Black neighborhoods almost everywhere were crowded and lacked clean streets and public services such as police and fire protection. Poor sanitation was one reason life expectancies were shorter for blacks than for whites.

Although the economic and physical security of black communities generally declined from 1830 to 1860, some individuals and families succeeded in pulling themselves out of poverty, primarily by establishing small businesses that grew into larger enterprises. The Forten family of Philadelphia is one example. At the end of the eighteenth century, James Forten, a second-generation free black, purchased a sail loft from the man with whom he had apprenticed. By the 1830s, his sail-making business was highly respected and prosperous, with twenty to thirty employees.[8] Forten was a wealthy man who was able to give his daughters and granddaughters a good education. Most became teachers, and all were active abolitionists and strong advocates of free black **uplift**: the idea, especially popular among the elite, that black self-help, leadership, and autonomy were necessary to elevate the race as a whole. Like Forten,

BY THE NUMBERS   Percent Change in Free Black Population, 1830–1860

As this figure illustrates, the free black population rose significantly in the vast majority of northern states during the period from 1830 to 1860. Despite these increases, however, free black representation in the general population decreased during this same period, owing largely to the influx of white European immigrants to the United States. While the northern slave population became statistically insignificant during these years, it is important to remember that most blacks remained enslaved — and that most free blacks still lived in the South.

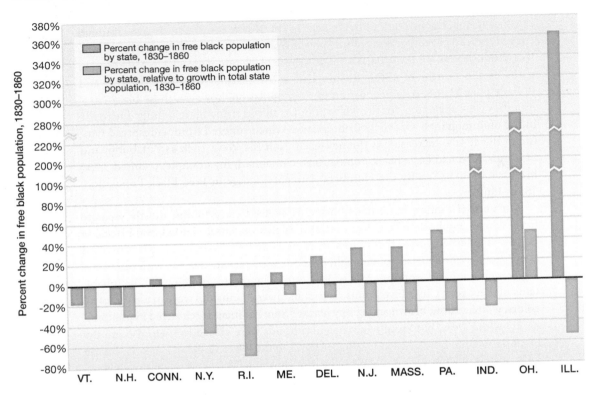

the free blacks who prospered usually came from families that had been free for more than one generation.

Ironically, the very success of black entrepreneurs attracted the animosity of whites, and successful communities were often victims of violence. Seneca Village, in upper Manhattan, was a thriving black community in the 1830s and 1840s, with churches, schools, businesses, cemeteries, and various community institutions. Wealthy blacks invested in it because of its promise; poorer blacks lived there because of its affordability and welcoming atmosphere. Community gardens, with "cabbage, and melon-patches, with hills of corn and cucumbers, and beds of beets, [and] parsnips,"[9] sustained those who lived there. Known as a haven for runaway slaves, Seneca Village was also a center of abolitionism and growing agitation for black rights. In 1857, city officials razed it to make way for Central Park.

FIVE POINTS, 1827.

Five Points

This notorious neighborhood in lower Manhattan featured a racially diverse population, with a sizable number of blacks. It also included a significant number of poor and working-class residents. The interracial socializing in Five Points, especially in its taverns and bawdy houses, was a cause for alarm among whites, including city officials and travelers. High rates of crime and disease marred the community. For these reasons, Five Points was seen as dangerous and immoral. *The Five Points, Junction of Baxter, Worth and Park Streets, New York, hand-colored engraving by George Catlin (1796–1872), © Museum of the City of New York, USA/Bridgeman Images.*

Black Self-Help in an Era of Moral Reform

The day-to-day struggles of northern blacks to overcome oppression created an internal focus on self-improvement and community building. Excluded from the political, economic, and social worlds of whites, blacks looked to one another for emotional and spiritual support as well as for material and institutional resources. Their sense of racial unity built on a growing commitment to self-help — the belief that they themselves must take responsibility for their destinies, regardless of external forces. As the influential black journalist, doctor, and writer Martin R. Delany observed in 1852, "Our elevation must be the result of self-efforts, and work of our own hands. No other human power can accomplish it. If we but determine it shall be so, it will be so."[10]

Mutual aid societies, independent black churches, and black schools knit black communities together. A range of benevolent institutions for women and men, including male lodges and fraternal orders, as well as their women's auxiliaries, helped individuals look out for one another. Female benevolent societies aimed especially to assist the many widows in black communities. By 1840, there were more than sixty such societies in Philadelphia alone. Black orphanages took care of children whose parents had died or could not support them. In New York City, the Colored Orphan Asylum, set up by white Quaker women in 1836, quickly became an important black community institution that provided education, apprenticeships, and job opportunities. In 1846, James McCune Smith was appointed its medical director. Denied admission to American colleges, he had received his medical training in Scotland but had returned to the United States to serve African Americans. His commitment was typical of the way privileged black men and women helped support their communities.

Independent black churches sustained their communities with a range of services. Philadelphia's Mother Bethel AME Church was among the most active. Like other black churches, Mother Bethel sponsored schools in the belief that education would both improve the lives of future generations and decrease white hostility. "If we ever expect to see the influence of prejudice decrease, and ourselves respected," maintained one spokesman in 1832, "it must be by the blessings of an enlightened education."[11] Attending schools with white children was rarely an option, as white families, associating integrated schools with abolition and racial mixing, vigorously opposed them. Sunday schools, which enhanced religious education with basic training in reading, writing, and arithmetic, helped advance black literacy and numeracy.

Northern black communities pushed for separate black public schools and created private schools, often with the assistance of supportive whites, especially Quakers and abolitionists. Yet even white assistance brought little assurance of success. In 1832, when Prudence Crandall, a young Quaker teacher in Canterbury, Connecticut, admitted an African American girl to her female academy, white parents withdrew their students. Crandall responded by closing her school, then reopening it for black girls only. Local opposition escalated, and Connecticut passed a law that made the school illegal. Crandall was arrested, and her school was vandalized and eventually burned. Under pressure from abolitionists, Connecticut repealed the law, but Miss Crandall's School for Young Ladies and Little Misses of Color never reopened.

Though appreciative of the commitment of white teachers, blacks increasingly sought to establish their own schools, with black teachers who could more closely identify with their students. By the 1830s, the New York African Free School had more than fourteen hundred students. Yet most black schools were poorly equipped, lacking books and unable to pay teachers the salaries white teachers received. An assessment in 1848 concluded that the state of black education "has been shamefully limited."[12] Slowly, however, the spread of the common school movement — the effort to create public schools open to all — and court challenges to discrimination in education opened some public schools to African Americans. In Cincinnati, for example, blacks created a community-based black high school in the face of extreme white opposition. The city later built a black public high school.

To meet the expanding need for teachers, northern black secondary education focused on teacher training. The Institute for Colored Youth in Philadelphia trained teachers, as did Charles Avery's Allegheny Institute, established near Pittsburgh in 1849. Avery's school emphasized vocational training, but in the 1850s two new black colleges focused on the arts and sciences. In Chester County, Pennsylvania, the Ashmun Institute opened in 1854 to provide a higher education "for male youth of African descent"; it was renamed Lincoln University after the Civil War. In Ohio in 1856, the Methodist Church founded Wilberforce University, named for the British abolitionist. Also in Ohio, Oberlin College, founded by abolitionists and a major stop along the underground railroad, was committed to progressive causes and had been open to both African Americans and women for twenty years by the mid-1850s.

Teaching attracted many of the most talented black women of the era precisely because it was one of the few professions open to women. Sarah Mapps Douglass, for example, born into a comfortable black Philadelphia family and educated by private tutors, founded a high school for girls that included training in science, atypical of education for girls in the period. In 1853, Douglass began running the girls' department of the Institute for Colored Youth. After taking classes at the Female Medical College of Pennsylvania and Penn Medical University in the late 1850s, she began a series of medical education classes for women in her home.

Douglass was committed to black uplift, and her uplift activities are representative of educated black women. Such women were generally deeply religious and were deeply engaged in the reform spirit of the antebellum era, seeking to remake and perfect society by promoting virtuous living. Using women's role as guardian of the family and home, these women argued for temperance to end the abuses of alcoholism. They also called for an end to prostitution and for more humane treatment of prisoners and the mentally ill. For black women, social reform had the particular aim of improving black communities and elevating the status of blacks.

Among the first to articulate this message of uplift was Maria W. Stewart, who, in Boston in the early 1830s, was the first American woman, white or black, to speak before a mixed audience of men and women — at the time a brave and highly controversial act. She had been influenced by David Walker (see chapter 5), who encouraged her brief but electrifying public speaking career. Intensely religious, Stewart rejected Walker's call for violence, promoting the moral reform of the black community instead. Beginning in 1831, in speeches, essays, and editorials she stressed the importance of education, especially that of girls, and black elevation generally. "How long shall the fair daughters of Africa be compelled to bury their minds and talents beneath a load of iron pots and kettles?" she asked. She also urged African American women to understand their duty as mothers to "create in the minds of your little girls and boys a thirst for knowledge." She implored men to "flee from the gambling board and the dance-hall; for we are poor, and have no money to throw away. . . . Let our money, instead . . . be appropriated for schools and seminaries of learning for our children and youth."[13]

Stewart believed that black moral and intellectual improvement would decrease white prejudice,[14] and other black leaders made similar arguments. Writing in the *Colored American*, the Pittsburgh AME minister and educator Lewis Woodson expressed the commonly held belief that deportment and dress reflect inner character: "Every one must agree that the moral effect of mean dress is, to degrade us in our own eyes and in the eyes of all who behold us." Articulating a particular concern among black women and men, Woodson maintained that "colored females should be extremely attentive to cleanliness and neatness of dress" because "of the prejudices which exist against them in the community in which they live; and they should consider how imprudent it is, by neglecting their personal appearance, to heighten and aggravate that prejudice."[15]

But black leaders recognized that it was not only black people who needed improving. In 1836, James Forten and others founded the Christian-inspired American Moral Reform Society. The society was dedicated to the equality of all, including blacks, whites, and women, and promoted various initiatives — such as public education, peace activism, and temperance — to elevate all Americans regardless of race. They proposed to advance African Americans' struggle as a way of "improving the condition of mankind."[16] Thus they sought an end to slavery and urged members to boycott goods produced by slave labor. The society's program was indicative not only of antebellum reform generally, but also of the difficult situation of a free people striving to work with white allies to achieve respect and dignity in a nation that sanctioned black enslavement.

Forging a Black Freedom Struggle

The far-reaching commitment of northern black communities to self-improvement and moral reform was linked to the abolition of slavery. Free blacks recognized that they could not elevate their own people unless all black people were free. This core belief necessitated black activism, as blacks and their leaders increasingly worked together both within and outside their communities. Only a concerted and widespread effort could bring about fundamental change in the nation's racial conscience, laws, and practices. Through speeches, meetings, annual conventions, and newspapers, black leaders formed networks that connected their communities and sharpened their message of moral reform to address the nation's moral conscience as a means to advance their people's cause. Casting slavery as an evil institution, they wrote and lectured on the ways it debased individual lives and corrupted the nation as a whole. They argued for the importance of equal rights, not only for blacks but often also for women, and they challenged blacks' status in the courts. The arrival of fugitive slaves brought new and powerful voices to strengthen their ranks. Black activists participated in and supported the white abolitionist organizations founded in this era, but they also operated independently. Although largely disfranchised, they engaged in political actions to advance the uplift of free blacks as well as the cause of abolitionism.

Building a National Black Community: The Black Convention Movement and the Black Press

In September 1830, Bishop Richard Allen called black clergy and other leaders to gather at Philadelphia's Mother Bethel AME Church to consider the issues that were of primary concern to their communities, including abolitionism. Some forty responded, from nine states, including the slave states of Delaware, Maryland, and Virginia. The First National Negro Convention was the first in a series of gatherings that constituted the **black convention movement**. In national meetings called annually through 1835 and occasionally thereafter, and especially in a far more prolific series of state and local conventions, black leaders built networks. They discussed and debated the state of their communities and what they could do to improve them. They framed resolutions and undertook projects that sought to elevate the status of free blacks and to promote abolitionism. Many were ministers, and their proposals reflected Christian values and the importance of an upright moral character.

The 1830 convention set an agenda for future meetings. In light of the recent Cincinnati riots, migration to Canada was under discussion, as was black education, especially black vocational schools. At the early conventions, attendees expressed support for programs that enhanced blacks' job prospects and looked for ways to move blacks from menial to vocational jobs, although a proposal for a manual labor school for black boys never materialized. They went on record as promoting cooperative economic enterprises, such as black businesses and mutual savings banks. They also promoted the moral virtue of farm life. In fact, churchgoing and righteous living — including temperance, sexual morality, and thrift — would, they argued, ensure the social and moral reform of individual lives that would benefit the community as a whole.

In the 1840s, conventions met in other cities, including Cleveland, New York City, and Rochester and Troy in upstate New York. Discussions were increasingly political and militant. A new generation of leaders was emerging, men and women who had formerly been slaves and whose frank descriptions of slave life riveted audiences and won converts to abolition among reform-minded white men and women. Speaking at the 1843 convention in Buffalo, New York, were two former slaves from Maryland. Henry Highland Garnet, minister of the Liberty Street Presbyterian Church in Troy, called openly for a slave rebellion, while Frederick Douglass, a lecturer on the abolitionist circuit, advocated a more tempered response, believing it would be better to appeal to the conscience of the nation and to end slavery peaceably. (See Document Project: Forging an African American Nation — Slave and Free, North and South, pp. 248–57.)

These black conventions, especially the national ones, helped create a sense of African Americans as a distinct people. Although debates were often spirited and proposals ranged from conservative to radical, they strengthened black identity through a unity of purpose. These conventions amounted to a significant and alternative black political movement with a core agenda that united free black uplift and abolition. Meeting in Cleveland in 1848, one convention stressed this powerful sense of

African American peoplehood: "We are as a people, chained together. We are one people — one in general complexion, one in a common degradation, one in popular estimation. As one rises, all must rise, and as one falls all must fall."[17]

The black press was also a vital element in the growing network of black leaders and institutions with a unified purpose. In 1827, Samuel Cornish and John Russwurm began publishing *Freedom's Journal*, the nation's first African American newspaper. It was, the first issue announced, "devoted to the dissemination of useful knowledge among our brethren, and to their moral and religious improvement." The *Journal* continued, "We wish to plead our own cause. Too long have others spoken for us."[18] The paper lasted only two years, and in 1829 Cornish began publishing *The Rights of All*, primarily to argue against colonization. This paper, too, was short-lived, its brief run indicative of how difficult it was to sustain any newspaper at this time, but especially a black one. Agents were required to distribute copies and enlist subscribers. Owing to the small base of black subscribers, black papers survived long-term only with the help of wealthy patrons and the support of white subscribers.

Nevertheless, between 1830 and 1860, more than forty black newspapers provided a weekly or monthly perspective on current events and a forum for discussing the fight for abolition as well as issues relevant to free black uplift, such as suffrage, jobs, housing, schools, and fair treatment on public transportation. Because copies were passed from one person to another, the papers had a widespread influence. Stories in one were reprinted in others, building a sense of black unity and contributing to the emergence of a powerful national black press tradition.

The most influential newspaper was published by Frederick Douglass. In 1847 he launched the *North Star* as an explicitly abolitionist paper aiming to "attack slavery in all its forms and aspects; advocate universal emancipation; exalt the standard of public morality; promote the moral and intellectual improvement of the colored people; and hasten the day of freedom to the three millions of our enslaved fellow countrymen."[19] The *North Star* attracted white readers as well as black. In 1851, it merged with the *Liberty Party Paper* to become *Frederick Douglass' Paper*, which continued publication until 1863. Its longevity both derived from and contributed to Douglass's stature as the preeminent black leader of his day. The paper also published contributions from well-known correspondents, such as James McCune Smith, who in 1855 argued vigorously for race pride. "We must learn to love, respect and glory in our Negro nature," he asserted.[20]

Growing Black Activism in Literature, Politics, and the Justice System

In addition to the influential role Frederick Douglass played in the newspaper business, he was a powerful lecturer who captivated white audiences by recounting the realities of his life as a slave. He had escaped from slavery in 1838 and settled in New Bedford, Massachusetts, where he worked as a day laborer. In 1841, while attending an antislavery meeting in Nantucket, he agreed to say a few words. The audience was riveted, and the meeting's organizers urged him to begin lecturing regularly for the abolitionist cause. One of these organizers was the prominent white abolitionist William Lloyd Garrison, who soon encouraged Douglass to make lecturing a career and to publish the story of his life.

In 1845, Douglass published *Narrative of the Life of Frederick Douglass, an American Slave*. It sold more than 30,000 copies in its first five years in print, and in 1855 he published an expanded version, *My Bondage and My Freedom*. Douglass's books reached a wide range of readers and today exemplify the whole genre of slave narratives that emerged as this era's most original and significant form of African American literary expression. Addressed largely to white audiences, these narratives charted individual yet representative journeys from southern slave to free black person. By revealing the details of what it meant to be a slave, they affirmed the humanity of enslaved African Americans. Notable narratives of slavery and escape were written by William Wells Brown, Henry "Box" Brown, and Henry Bibb (see chapter 5). Equally noteworthy was Harriet Jacobs's *Incidents in the Life of a Slave Girl* (published in 1861), which treated explicitly the sexual exploitation of slave women by white masters.[21]

This outpouring of African American literature was in a real sense a renaissance. Jarena Lee, a member of Mother Bethel, wrote a spiritual autobiography (originally published in 1836; expanded and updated in 1849) that recorded her struggles in the male-dominated world of preaching. Frances Ellen Watkins (later Harper) published

Frederick Douglass

This engraving of a smartly dressed young Douglass vividly captures his self-confidence and middle-class bearing. Douglass's emergence as the preeminent black leader and black abolitionist of his era owed significantly to his intelligence, hard work, and ambition. His rise to prominence also owed to his uncanny ability to articulate not only his people's cause but also how that cause shaped America's past, present, and future. As a social reformer dedicated to a wide range of issues, including woman suffrage, Douglass helped bring people together across barriers of race, gender, and class. *From* Narrative of the Life of Frederick Douglass, *1846/ The British Library, London, UK/© British Library Board. All Rights Reserved/Bridgeman Images.*

Poems on Miscellaneous Subjects (1854), a collection that included "The Slave Mother," which examined the unique pain enslaved mothers endured. Frederick Douglass and Martin Delany published novels with plots centered on slave insurrections, while William Wells Brown's novel *Clotel* (1853) helped establish the character type of the "tragic mulatta," a white-looking black woman whose mixed-race identity typically led to tragedy. Both Clotel, allegedly Thomas Jefferson's daughter, and her mother, Currer, Jefferson's alleged mistress, were tragic mulattas. In *Our Nig, or Sketches from the Life of a Free Black* (1859), Harriet E. Wilson explored prejudice in the North through a coming-of-age narrative remarkably like her own life story. James W. C. Pennington wrote both a slave narrative and a study of the history of black people in the United States, while William Cooper Nell recorded the contributions of black soldiers to the nation's wars. Hosea Easton published his challenge to racism in *A Treatise on the Intellectual Character, and Civil and Political Condition of the Colored People of the U. States* (1837).

These works exhibited significantly less of the deference to white leadership that had marked the writings of the first post-Revolutionary generation. Pioneering this increasing black militancy, David Walker's *Appeal* (1829; see chapter 5) had called on slaves to revolt, and Robert Alexander Young's pamphlet *The Ethiopian Manifesto* (1829) had warned slave owners of a terrible punishment from God unless they freed their slaves and sought God's forgiveness. The new generation of black leaders carried forward this militant approach. They sought to reform not only the black community but also the nation. Their strategy of **moral suasion** aimed to convince the white majority that slavery and the oppression of free blacks were immoral, offensive to God, and contrary to the nation's ideals.

Frederick Douglass was certainly the most well-known African American speaker on the abolitionist lecture circuit, but Sojourner Truth may have been the most compelling. Born a slave named Isabella Baumfree, she had achieved freedom and secured custody of her son, who had been sold illegally, through a lawsuit (see chapter 4). In 1843, she transformed herself by taking a new name and occupation. As a lecturer-spiritualist-preacher, she was both outspoken and plainspoken, powerful and fearless. In 1847, before a packed audience in Boston's Faneuil Hall, she challenged even Douglass, who had despaired of God's ability to bring about a peaceful end to slavery. Truth stood up and asked, "Frederick, is God dead?" The audience enthusiastically shouted support for her position.[22]

For Truth, as for many of her religiously motivated reform colleagues, the abolition of slavery was both part of God's divine plan and necessary for America to realize its democratic ideals. But as a woman, Truth also argued for women's rights. In an 1851 speech in Akron, Ohio, she made a powerful case for women's equality: "I have plowed and reaped and husked and chopped and mowed. . . . I can carry as much as any man, and can eat as much too, if I can get it."[23] Truth did not present herself as a respectable middle-class reformer who argued for abolition and equality in the abstract. Her words grew out of her own experience as a slave, a wage earner, and a mother. Her directness won both followers and detractors. In an 1858 speech in a small Indiana town, when

Sojourner Truth

One of the most famous and influential black women of the nineteenth century, Sojourner Truth (born Isabella Baumfree) both embodied and spoke powerfully to the intersection of the struggles of blacks, women, and the dispossessed. Truth's wide-ranging influence and popularity owed heavily to her piercing intelligence, Christian spirituality, striking speaking ability, and commanding sense of self. Notwithstanding her illiteracy, Truth's voice resonated with insight and the power of personal witness. This image was printed on a small card. The caption underneath it, "I Sell the Shadow to Support the Substance," illustrates her willingness to help support herself however she could. *Library of Congress, Prints and Photographs Division, Washington, D.C., LC-USZC4-6165.*

I Sell the Shadow to Support the Substance.
SOJOURNER TRUTH.

hecklers questioned whether so forceful a speaker could actually be a woman, Truth bared her breast.[24]

The experience and approach of Sarah Parker Remond was entirely different. She was born into an affluent free black family in Salem, Massachusetts, but when she was barred from attending a girls' academy there, her family moved to Newport, Rhode Island, where she received an education. She chose a career as an antislavery lecturer, speaking locally, then nationally, and eventually traveling to England to push forward a global campaign against slavery. Remond and other female abolitionist speakers braved strong opposition to women speaking in public. Their perseverance is testimony to their commitment to the abolitionist crusade and offers insight into their support for women's rights.

Elizabeth Jennings, a teacher in New York City's black schools who had also lectured on behalf of black women, took her activism to a new level when, in 1854, she was forcibly removed from a streetcar on her way to church. The Third Avenue Railroad, she was told, had separate cars for black customers. With the support of her congregation, she sued the railroad company, claiming that as public conveyances, streetcars could not refuse to serve passengers on the basis of race. The jury ruled in her favor and awarded her damages. The Third Avenue Railroad stopped segregating its cars, and the case, reported in *Frederick Douglass' Paper*, received considerable attention.[25]

Jennings's case, and a few others in the 1840s and early 1850s, seemed to signal that free blacks could use the courts to end discrimination. Benjamin Roberts initiated one of the most important legal cases. In 1848, Roberts sued the city of Boston on behalf of his daughter Sarah, who was forced to attend a mediocre all-black school when there was a better all-white school closer to the family's home. Robert Morris, one of the nation's first black lawyers, and the white lawyer Charles Sumner, later a U.S. senator, argued the *Roberts* case. In *Roberts v. City of Boston* (1849), the Massachusetts Supreme Court upheld Boston's public school statute requiring racially segregated schools. But the argument presented by Sumner, that "a school, exclusively devoted to one class, must differ essentially, in its spirit and character, from that public school . . . where all classes meet together in equality,"[26] did not go unheeded. Boston blacks organized the Equal School Rights Committee to continue the fight for integrated public schools locally and statewide, and in 1855 Massachusetts became the first state to prohibit segregation of public schools on the basis of race.

Abolitionism: Moral Suasion, Political Action, Race, and Gender

Black abolitionists were innumerable and varied and often operated independently of any organization. From many different perspectives — female and male, former slave and freeborn — they urged their own communities and Americans in general to reform themselves and to better society by ensuring equal rights and ending slavery. Some cooperated with sympathetic white men and women who also organized against slavery. Some broke away from white organizations. Regardless, the agendas of black activists helped shape the growing **abolitionist movement**, which increasingly commanded the attention of white citizens, politicians, and the national government.

In the 1830s, the momentum of abolitionism shifted away from groups advocating gradual emancipation, the compensation of slaveholders for freeing their slaves, and the colonization of blacks outside the United States. The new abolitionist movement sought to end slavery immediately rather than gradually, and without compensation, through moral suasion and **political action** — working within the political system. Despite their exclusion from political life, black activists supported the latter approach as well as the former. Indeed, blacks continued to mount a vigorous and widespread opposition to slavery, working within their own organizations as well as within more influential and better-funded (and mostly white) abolitionist groups.

William Lloyd Garrison led the moral suasion wing of the abolitionist movement, while the wealthy brothers Arthur and Lewis Tappan led the political action wing. Together the three men founded the American Anti-Slavery Society in 1833. Among the sixty-three delegates from eleven states at the society's first meeting in Philadelphia were three African Americans: Robert Purvis, James McCrummell, and James G. Barbadoes. The delegates framed two goals: "the entire abolition of slavery in the United States" and the elevation of "the character and condition of the people of color."[27]

Fugitive Slave Law Convention
This group portrait taken at the Fugitive Slave Law Convention in Cazenovia, New York, in August 1850 captures the diversity of the participants. At center are Frederick Douglass and pioneering women's rights activist and abolitionist Angelina Grimké. *The Art Archive at Art Resource, NY.*

Garrison's moral suasion approach had been shaped by the arguments of black abolitionists, and in 1831, with their support, he began publishing the *Liberator*, the most famous antislavery newspaper of the era. James Forten signed up subscribers in Philadelphia and sent Garrison's Boston office an advance payment on their subscriptions. Writing as "A Colored Philadelphian," he was also a frequent contributor to the paper's early issues.[28] Garrison worked well with black activists and counted them among his friends. He published Maria Stewart's speeches in the *Liberator* and promoted the speaking career of Frederick Douglass, writing a preface to Douglass's slave narrative.

In the pages of the *Liberator*, Garrison condemned slavery as immoral and contrary to Christian principles, and he called for immediate, uncompensated emancipation.

He stated his opposition to colonization, and he promoted many of the era's reforms, including women's rights, prison reform, and temperance. Garrison believed that slavery could be ended and society perfected through a change in the human heart, not through political action. In fact, he perceived the Constitution as a proslavery document and the federal government as fouled by its proslavery connections.

The Tappan brothers, by contrast, saw the Constitution as an antislavery document. Consequently, they fought to end slavery through political action, including electing antislavery candidates and creating antislavery political parties. They believed it best to work within the political system to build a climate favorable to abolition. Political abolitionists gained growing influence as increasing numbers of northern politicians took a stand against slavery. Their strong support for the antislavery wing of the national Whig Party enhanced their impact, and they were actively involved in two antislavery parties — the Liberty Party, founded in 1840, and the Free-Soil Party, which absorbed the Liberty Party upon its founding in 1848.

Although black men and all women were excluded from the nation's political life, they were active in abolitionist organizations. Women worked through women's auxiliaries of the American Anti-Slavery Society, which set up numerous regional affiliates, and also formed separate organizations. In 1833, the white Quaker abolitionist Lucretia Mott founded the Philadelphia Female Anti-Slavery Society; among its members were the black activist Grace Douglass and her daughter Sarah Mapps Douglass, as well as women from the Forten family. There was also a Female Anti-Slavery Society in Boston. Women in these organizations signed petitions, distributed literature, sponsored bazaars to raise money, and vigilantly supported the cause of fugitive slaves. Many participated in the free produce movement, which encouraged boycotting goods produced by slave labor. Female abolitionists often felt a special empathy for slave families torn apart by slave sales, and their concern for the plight of slave women, especially slave mothers, informed their antislavery arguments.

Women's participation in the abolitionist movement contributed significantly to the emergence of the women's rights movement. As women organized petition campaigns and formulated antislavery arguments, they gained confidence in their ability to work in the public arena and felt more keenly the limitations male abolitionist organizers placed on their participation. Women were usually prohibited from speaking in public and routinely denied leadership positions.

The issue of women's role in the abolitionist movement became so contentious that in 1840, when Garrison appointed a woman to the executive committee of the American Anti-Slavery Society, the organization split in two. The Tappans and a group of black ministers, including Henry Highland Garnet, founded the rival American and Foreign Anti-Slavery Society (AFAS), which was committed to political abolitionism and to male leadership at the top levels. At an international meeting of abolitionist organizations in London in June 1840, the AFAS joined with like-minded British abolitionists to prohibit women from participating in policymaking. Lucretia Mott, representing the Philadelphia Female Anti-Slavery Society, had to observe the proceedings from a railed-off space reserved for women.

Eight years later, in Seneca Falls, New York, Mott and Elizabeth Cady Stanton organized the nation's first women's rights convention. Frederick Douglass was in attendance, and some black male activists, including the former slave Jermain W. Loguen, lent their support to women's rights, notably woman suffrage.

By this time, the abolitionist movement was further divided by a split between Garrison and Douglass, who came to agree with Garnet that political action was the most effective means of mobilizing public opposition to slavery. Douglass's decision in 1847 to publish his own newspaper, the *North Star*, also indicated his increasing independence from his mentor. Even the most zealous white abolitionists, including Garrison, did not always treat black activists as equals. Many seemed more committed to freeing slaves than to securing equal rights for free blacks.

Though fraught with divisions, the abolitionist movement won converts to its cause, especially among white evangelical northerners. For many, Christian principles seemed synonymous with concern for the slave. In the 1830s and 1840s, the Baptist, Methodist, and Presbyterian Churches forbade their members to own slaves, and the issue caused proslavery southern churches to withdraw from these denominations and organize separately. In 1846, several white abolitionist missionary societies merged with the black Union Missionary Society to form the **American Missionary Association**. With widespread support from black leaders and members, including Samuel Cornish, Henry Highland Garnet, Jermain Loguen, James Pennington, and Mary Ann Shadd, it promoted not only abolition but Christian education for African Americans as well. The abolitionist movement also succeeded in pushing slavery onto the national political agenda. In 1846, when war with Mexico began, the contest over whether slaves should be allowed in the West intensified, giving the slavery issue an urgent and decidedly political cast.

Slavery and the Coming of the Civil War

What to do about the existence of slavery in a democratic nation that professed freedom and equality was a question that would not go away. Delegates at the Constitutional Convention in 1787 had devised a series of compromises that protected slavery even as some states took steps to end it. As the nation expanded, another compromise in 1820 protected slavery in territories south of Missouri's southern border while prohibiting it to the north. A few decades later, the Compromise of 1850 sought to hold the increasingly disaffected North and South together. But as a consequence, the Missouri Compromise was undone, first by popular sovereignty, a new plan for letting the people themselves decide whether the territory in which they lived would be slave or free, and then by a U.S. Supreme Court ruling that Congress did not have and had never had the authority to prohibit slavery in the territories. Northerners feared that a vast southern slaveholder, or "Slave Power," conspiracy had triumphed, taking away their rights and allowing the detested slave system to undercut their free labor system. With the election of Abraham Lincoln as president in 1860, southerners feared that the incoming Republican administration would implement a vast northern conspiracy to end the slave system. Politics and compromise could no longer hold the Union together. African Americans had more than a political stake in the tumultuous events of the 1850s, as their rights and protections increasingly eroded. Some responded with resistance, even violence. Some saw emigration as the only solution. And some hoped that war, if it came, would end slavery altogether.

Westward Expansion and Slavery in the Territories

Between 1830 and 1860, hundreds of thousands of Americans moved west, including black slaves and Native Americans who were forcibly relocated (see chapter 5). While the Missouri Compromise had, for the Louisiana Territory, settled the issue of which regions would permit slavery and which would not, American incursions into Mexican territory raised the issue anew. By 1830, the more than 20,000 Americans who had settled in Mexican Texas had reintroduced slavery — and 2,000 slaves — into an area where Mexico had formally abolished it. In 1836, these proslavery Americans seceded from Mexico, declared themselves the Lone Star Republic, and sought annexation to the United States. They were at first refused, but in 1845 Texas was admitted to the Union as a slave state. Northerners' opposition to a move they perceived as growing evidence of a Slave Power conspiracy invigorated the Liberty Party, which in 1844 received nearly nine times the number of votes it had in 1840 — 62,000 of the more than 2.5 million votes cast.

By this time, many Americans enthusiastically supported the notion that it was the "manifest destiny" of the nation to rule the continent from the Atlantic to the Pacific. The Oregon Treaty of 1846 between the United States and Great Britain settled a boundary dispute in the Oregon Country, clearing the way for official territorial recognition by the United States. Still, congressional factions wrangled over whether to forbid slavery in the territory, as the Oregon provisional government had already done in 1844, before finally voting to establish the Oregon Territory as a free territory in 1848.

Northern and southern politicians closely watched the number of potential slave and free states, lest one section dominate the other in Congress. Even before the Oregon negotiation with Great Britain was settled, however, the United States was at war with Mexico, following a failed attempt to purchase the Mexican provinces of Upper California and New Mexico. The prospect that these areas would become U.S. possessions ignited the issue of slavery in the territories once again. In the House of Representatives, Pennsylvania Democrat David Wilmot introduced a proviso that "neither slavery nor involuntary servitude shall ever exist in any part" of any territory gained from the Mexican-American War. Wilmot was against slavery, but he was not pro-black. He aimed to keep slavery out of the territories so that free white labor would have a chance to thrive there, and to prevent blacks from coming into the area. The **Wilmot Proviso** failed to pass the Senate, but the angry debate it sparked intensified tensions between the North and South.

In 1848, the Treaty of Guadalupe Hidalgo sealed the U.S. victory over Mexico. In the treaty, Mexico ceded what became the territories of California, New Mexico, and Utah, as well as all of Texas north of the Rio Grande. Meanwhile, the discovery of gold in California drew so many prospectors to that territory (including more than four thousand free blacks) that in 1850 it applied for admission to the Union as a free state. If admitted, California would tip the balance in the Senate to the free states.

The vote on California statehood was one of the issues finally settled by the **Compromise of 1850**, which consisted of a series of separate bills. Neither side got all it wanted. Antislavery northerners succeeded in abolishing the slave trade in the District of Columbia, while southerners prevented the abolition of slavery there. California entered the Union as a free state, but the decision of whether slavery would be allowed in the territories of New Mexico and Utah was left to the people living in those areas, a policy known as **popular sovereignty**. The federal government assumed the debt contracted by the Lone Star Republic, and, as a concession to the South, a new fugitive slave law was enacted.

The **Fugitive Slave Act** of 1850 made it easier for fugitive slaves to be captured and returned to their owners by strengthening federal authority over the capture and return of runaway slaves. Many northerners had long objected to the actions of slave catchers, and some northern states had passed **personal liberty laws** forbidding the kidnapping and forced return of fugitives. These laws were ruled unconstitutional in *Prigg v. Pennsylvania* (1842), but in that decision the U.S. Supreme Court also affirmed that the return of fugitives was a federal matter, in which state officials could not be required to assist. Northern states had then passed new personal liberty laws that forbade state officials to assist in fugitive cases and prohibited the use of state courts and jails for alleged fugitives. Under the Fugitive Slave Act of 1850, federal marshals were required to pursue alleged runaway slaves, and federal commissioners were appointed to oversee runaway cases. The fees these officials received — $10 for a runaway returned to the claimant, $5 for a runaway set free — reflected the law's bias. But it was the authorizing of federal marshals to call on citizen bystanders to aid in the capture of alleged runaways that especially angered northerners. Citizens who refused or who in any way aided an alleged fugitive could be fined $1,000 and sent to prison for six months. Many in the North who had not given much thought to slavery now felt that the federal government had far exceeded its powers. They perceived the federal effort to protect slave property as an attack on their own personal liberty, forcing them to act against their conscience. Wisconsin challenged the constitutionality of the law, and a Massachusetts statute sought to nullify it.

For black Americans, however, the implications of the law were far more menacing. Those who had escaped slavery, even years before, were no longer safe in the North. They were subject to arrest, denied jury trials, and forbidden to testify on their own behalf. A statement by an owner making a claim, together with an identification of the runaway, was all that was needed to return a person to slavery. A growing number of former fugitives left the United States for Canada, Mexico, Europe, and elsewhere. Given the provisions of the law, free blacks were also at risk, as there was little to prevent slave hunters from seizing and enslaving them. An unknowable number of free blacks as well as fugitive slaves suffered enslavement or reenslavement at the hands of slave hunters. During the 1850s, 296 of 330 fugitives formally arrested, or 90 percent, suffered reenslavement.[29]

The Fugitive Slave Crisis and Civil Disobedience

Northern black communities, where many fugitives lived, responded to the Fugitive Slave Act of 1850 with protest meetings, resolutions, and petitions. Blacks and their white allies demanded repeal of the act and mounted vigorous resistance against it. Jermain Loguen, born a slave in Tennessee, proclaimed, "I will not live a slave, and if force is employed to reenslave me, I shall make preparations to meet the crisis as becomes a man."[30]

As a young man, Loguen had escaped to freedom on the underground railroad (Map 6.1). In the North, **vigilance committees**, an aboveground arm of the underground railroad, assisted arriving fugitives by providing temporary shelter, food, clothing, and sometimes legal assistance and jobs. The black printer David Ruggles led the New York Vigilance Committee, which was widely admired for its militancy and effectiveness. Abolitionist Quakers joined the effort, but in the 1830s and 1840s vigilance committees consisted primarily of blacks. After the Fugitive Slave Act was passed in 1850, however, northern white support for the underground railroad grew, and vigilance committees became increasingly interracial. They expanded the networks of cellars, attics, church basements, and other safe spaces where fugitives could take refuge before being shepherded to freedom, often in Canada. Although their operations were of necessity covert, because they were illegal, they helped an untold number of people. For example, the Boston Vigilance Committee acknowledged helping sixty-nine fugitives to escape in 1851 alone.

The best-known "agent" on the underground railroad was William Still. As head of the Philadelphia Vigilance Committee, he kept records on the fugitive slaves he assisted and later published their stories in *The Underground Rail Road* (1872). The most famous "conductor" was Harriet Tubman, who escaped from slavery in 1849. She returned to the South at least fourteen times to lead, directly and indirectly, some 130 slaves to freedom. She was known for her strict discipline and carefully developed plans and reputedly never lost a fugitive. Deeply revered in northern abolitionist circles, where she was hailed as "the Moses of Her People," Tubman was intensely hated in the South, where there was a $40,000 bounty (more than $1 million today) for her capture.[31]

Those who aided fugitive slaves or refused to help in their capture engaged in **civil disobedience** — refusal to obey a law that one considers unjust — a form of protest with a long history among African Americans. Their resolve was soon tested.

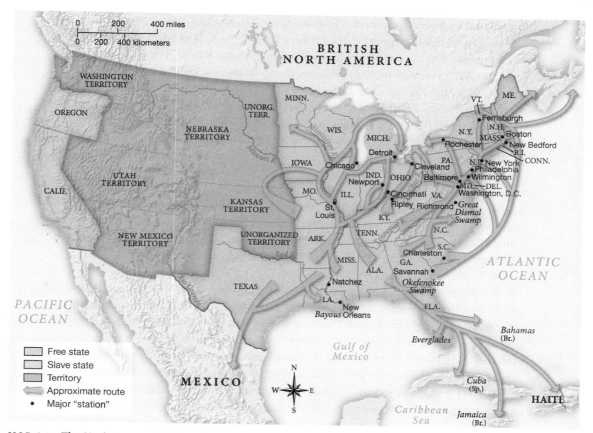

MAP 6.1 The Underground Railroad

As this map illustrates, the reach of the underground railroad was extensive and international in scope. Although these locations remained secret at the time, we now know that the underground railroad consisted of an intricate network of people, routes, and safe places that allowed thousands of slaves to achieve freedom. After 1850, the growing number of organizations and individuals committed to abolitionism caused an increase in the number of fugitive slaves that continued through the Civil War. Escaping from slavery required the utmost secrecy, organization, and coordination, and freedom fighters such as Harriet Tubman placed themselves — and their own freedom — at great risk to help others reach the North.

On September 11, 1851, William Parker, an escaped slave who lived with his wife, Eliza, also an escaped slave, near Christiana, Pennsylvania, refused to allow a U.S. marshal and a party of Maryland slaveholders led by Edward Gorsuch to search the Parker home for recent fugitives from Gorsuch's plantation. Eliza sounded a large dinner horn, summoning more than seventy-five local supporters. In the fight that followed, Gorsuch was killed and his son wounded. The Parkers and the other fugitive slaves they were hiding escaped to Canada, but in the wake of what became known as the Christiana Resistance, thirty-five blacks and three white Quakers were arrested for treason and conspiracy under the Fugitive Slave Act of 1850. Their cause attracted nationwide attention. Support came from as far away as Columbus, Ohio, where a meeting of free blacks adopted a resolution praising "the victorious heroes at the battle of Christiana."[32] Pennsylvania congressman Thaddeus Stevens assisted in their defense, and eventually the charges were dropped.

Boston became a hotbed of resistance to the hated law. In early 1851, slave hunters seized Shadrach Minkins (also known as Frederick Wilkins), an escaped slave working at a coffeehouse, and dragged him to a federal courthouse. Almost instantly, the Boston Vigilance Committee mobilized, and a crowd surrounded the courthouse while a group of black men liberated Minkins and sent him on to freedom in Canada. In late May 1854, a similar effort to save Anthony Burns, another local African American who had been seized and jailed as a fugitive slave, failed. President Franklin Pierce sent federal troops to Boston, and as they escorted Burns to the wharf for his return to slavery, some 50,000 protesters lined the streets and draped Boston's buildings in black. Although Burns was returned to slavery, Boston abolitionists eventually raised enough money to purchase his freedom.

The fugitive slave crisis intensified the conflict between the North and South over slavery. Southerners perceived the confrontations as part of a well-orchestrated northern campaign to defy the law and destroy slavery and the southern way of life that depended on it. For northerners, the confrontations forced an awareness of the reality of slavery and its impact on their lives. So did publication of the best-selling novel *Uncle Tom's Cabin* in 1852. Its white evangelical author, Harriet Beecher Stowe, crafted a sentimental yet graphic depiction of slavery's devastating effects on families, building empathy with slavery's victims in order to increase support for abolition.

Confrontations in "Bleeding Kansas" and the Courts

In 1854, Illinois senator Stephen A. Douglas, who had engineered passage of the Compromise of 1850, reopened the issue of slavery in the territories by promoting popular sovereignty for Kansas and Nebraska. By the terms of the **Kansas-Nebraska Act** (1854), the people who settled those territories would vote to determine whether, as states, they would be slave or free (Map 6.2). The result was a series of violent confrontations between proslavery and antislavery settlers. In May 1856, when proslavery forces from Missouri attacked the antislavery town of Lawrence, Kansas, John Brown, the self-appointed "captain" of antislavery forces, took revenge by murdering five proslavery settlers at Pottawatomie Creek. The furor over "Bleeding Kansas" also brought violence to the floor of the Senate when South Carolina representative Preston S. Brooks beat Massachusetts senator Charles Sumner into unconsciousness at his desk. Brooks claimed to be upholding the honor of his kinsman, South Carolina senator Andrew P. Butler, whom Sumner had singled out for insult in an earlier speech on "The Crime against Kansas."

Anthony Burns

This moving poster centers on an amiable portrait of the young fugitive slave Anthony Burns, surrounded by scenes that feature his tragic reenslavement in Boston in 1854.

Library of Congress, Prints and Photographs Division, Washington, D.C., LC-USZ62-90750.

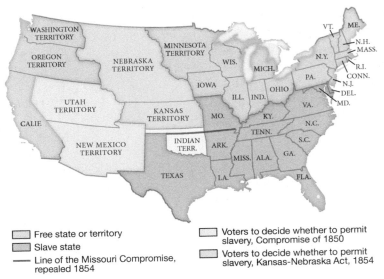

Free state or territory

Slave state

Line of the Missouri Compromise, repealed 1854

Voters to decide whether to permit slavery, Compromise of 1850

Voters to decide whether to permit slavery, Kansas-Nebraska Act, 1854

MAP 6.2   The Kansas-Nebraska Act, 1854

This map shows the free and slave states following the passage of the Kansas-Nebraska Act, as well as the areas where both this act and the Compromise of 1850 allowed popular sovereignty to rule the day. As the map indicates, the Kansas-Nebraska Act promoted the increasingly stark sectional divide between the slave South and the free North. From this point forward, maintaining a balance between the number of free and slave states proved no less essential to preserving the Union than under the Missouri Compromise of 1820, which the act superseded.

The national political system and the methods of civil debate, negotiation, and compromise proved increasingly ineffective in managing the slavery question. The issue eventually split the Whig Party, and it disintegrated. After 1856, the Democratic Party, ever more wedded to proslavery interests, was the only national political party left. Meanwhile, a number of sectional parties related to the slavery issue had merged. The abolitionist Liberty Party, formed in 1840, had called for an end to slavery in the District of Columbia and to the domestic slave trade. In 1848, it became part of the Free-Soil Party, founded that year. With the motto "Free Soil, Free Speech, Free Labor, Free Men," this party announced its opposition to the extension of slavery into the territories. To discourage the spread of plantation agriculture, the party also supported a homestead law that would distribute federal land in small plots to settlers (preferably whites) who would actually farm it, rather than to speculators. Although the party's motivations were often racist and many members were not abolitionists, it did attract influential abolitionist politicians and supporters of civil rights for free blacks, such as Charles Sumner. Free-Soilers, black and white, helped Massachusetts blacks in their successful battles against discrimination in schools and transportation and in overturning state laws prohibiting interracial marriage.

In 1854, Free-Soilers joined with northern opponents of the Kansas-Nebraska Act and others opposed to the spread of slavery to form the Republican Party. Like the Liberty and Free-Soil Parties, the Republican Party was solely a northern party, with no southern support. Its 1856 presidential election slogan, "Free Soil, Free Labor, Free Speech, Free Men, Frémont" (for Republican presidential candidate John Frémont), highlighted Republicans' opposition to the extension of slavery into the territories, but the party made no commitment to end slavery itself. Nevertheless, Frederick Douglass and a growing number of blacks joined the party, believing it could energize the abolitionist crusade. Through the Republican Party, the northern black political struggle connected with the national political system. White southerners, observing black support for the Republicans, feared that the party was conspiring to destroy slavery.

Meanwhile, a case making its way through the courts addressed the issue of slavery in the territories head-on. In 1846, slaves Dred and Harriet Scott sued for their freedom because they had lived with their master in Wisconsin Territory, where slavery was forbidden, before he moved them back to the slave state of Missouri. After a series of technical issues and split decisions in the Missouri courts, the U.S. Supreme Court took the case and in 1857 rendered its decision. In *Dred Scott v. Sandford*, the Court ruled against Scott, and by extension his wife, Harriet. First, said the Court, Scott was not entitled to sue in the courts of Missouri because he was not a citizen. No person of African descent could be a citizen of the United States. Further, from the time of the nation's founding, "negroes of the African race" had been "regarded as beings of an inferior order, and altogether unfit to associate with the white race, either in social or political relations; and so far inferior, that they had no rights which the white man was bound to respect."[33] Slaves were legally protected property, and under the Constitution, Congress had no authority to deny the right of property. Thus it could not forbid slaveholding anywhere. All laws that forbade slavery in the territories were unconstitutional, including the Missouri Compromise of 1820.

Emigration and John Brown's Raid on Harpers Ferry

The effect of the *Dred Scott* decision was instantaneous and inflammatory. Not only abolitionists but also many northerners generally saw the decision as more evidence of a massive Slave Power conspiracy, now authorized by the courts, to extend slavery into new territories. For many northerners, there appeared to be nothing to prevent southern slave labor from undermining northern free labor. Like the Fugitive Slave Act of 1850, *Dred Scott* turned an increasing number of northerners, even whites opposed to abolition and black civil rights, against the Supreme Court's position on slavery, which they saw as eroding their personal liberties.

For black men and women, the decision was devastating. Their citizenship denied and their status declared inferior, they began to question more seriously their ties to the nation in which they lived. Robert Purvis declared that he owed no allegiance to a nation in which black men possessed no rights that whites must respect. Frederick Douglass blasted the decision as "judicial wolfishness." Speaking to African Americans from Canada, Mary Ann Shadd Cary exclaimed, "Your national ship is rotten and sinking, why not leave it?"[34]

The *Dred Scott* decision clearly diminished blacks' prospects for a viable life and meaningful future in the United States. They also had more reason than ever to fear for their personal safety. Many decided to leave the country, with most going to Canada. By 1860, several thousand former African Americans lived in communities there. Proponents of emigration to Canada included H. Ford Douglas, a prominent black leader from Ohio, and Mary Ann Shadd Cary, who had emigrated shortly after Congress passed the Fugitive Slave Act of 1850. Also residing in Canada in the late 1850s was the family of Martin R. Delany.

Thoroughly disillusioned with the United States, Delany became the era's most prominent champion of emigration. He spoke for a loose-knit yet committed group that promoted emigration to Canada, Central and South America, the West Indies, and West Africa. In a series of national emigration conventions, the first and most important of which occurred in Cleveland in 1854, Delany tapped into an emigrationist sentiment that grew stronger and more vocal by the end of the 1850s. In speeches and especially in his influential book *The Condition, Elevation, Emigration, and Destiny of the Colored People of the United States* (1852), he explained how black self-reliance demanded black self-determination, proposing the establishment of a black nation outside the United States. In this regard, he can be considered a father of **black nationalism**: the belief that African Americans were a nation within a nation that required self-determination.

Toward the end of the decade, Delany focused on the prospects for black emigration to West Africa, where he hoped to establish an unnamed though "thriving and prosperous Republic." Africa was "the native home of the African race," he argued, "and there he can enjoy the dignity of manhood, the rights of citizenship, and all the advantages of civilization and freedom."[35] In 1859 and 1860, joined by Robert Campbell, a Jamaican chemist, Delany explored the Niger River valley in search of a site for a black American emigrant settlement. Like most such efforts, the enormous financial, political, and logistical difficulties of this plan led to its failure, and Delany returned to the United States.

Interest in emigration remained widespread, however. In the 1850s, the white-dominated American Colonization Society sponsored the migration of several thousand blacks to Liberia (see chapter 4), while the black press featured a vigorous debate on Liberia's benefits and drawbacks. Proponents stressed black self-rule; opponents stressed Liberia's high mortality rate and inefficient government. Henry Highland Garnet came out in favor of emigration and worked on a plan — ultimately unsuccessful — to establish an emigrant black American colony in West Africa funded by whites. The Episcopal priest and missionary James Theodore Holly promoted emigration to Haiti, and in 1861 he led a group of 101 people to an ill-fated and short-lived settlement there. But most northern blacks remained in the United States. Despite the intensification of racial hostility and legal exclusion, they dared to hope that, as William Still expressed it, "great evils must be consummated that good might come."[36]

Some were not content to wait. In 1859, upon learning that John Brown secretly planned to incite a slave insurrection, five black men joined his effort. Brown's plan was to seize arms and ammunition at the federal arsenal at Harpers Ferry, Virginia, thereby inspiring local slaves to join in an uprising that would trigger a series of slave revolts throughout the South and destroy the institution. On the night of October 16, Brown and his band of twenty-one men slipped into Harpers Ferry from a nearby farm, where they had been hiding out and planning. Poorly conceived, the plan unraveled as quickly as it unfolded. In the federal troops' hastily organized counterattack, ten of Brown's comrades were killed, including two of his sons. Five others escaped; seven, including Brown, were captured.

News of **John Brown's raid** on Harpers Ferry inflamed the conspiratorial views that the slave South and free North increasingly had of each other. Proslavery forces saw Brown as a madman. They perceived the botched though frightful insurrection as evidence of a "Black Republican Conspiracy" bent on destroying slavery and the southern way of life. Yet abolitionists, particularly black abolitionists — even those opposed to violence as a means of emancipation — viewed Brown and his comrades as martyrs. Frances Ellen Watkins called Brown "the hero of the nineteenth century." Frederick Douglass praised him as "a human soul illuminated with divine qualities." A group of Providence blacks applauded him as an "unflinching champion of liberty."[37]

Yet at the time, most Americans supported the restoration of order, swift and harsh justice for the guilty, and renewed efforts to moderate the slavery crisis. Thus Brown's speedy trial and treason conviction were, for them, a relief. On December 2, he went calmly to his hanging death, but not before he handed a note to a jail guard, offering this prediction:

Charlestown, Va. 2nd, December, 1859.

I John Brown am now quite certain that the crimes of this guilty, land: will never be purged away; but with Blood. I had as I now think: vainly flattered myself that without verry [sic] much bloodshed; it might be done.[38]

The next year, when Republican Abraham Lincoln won the presidency, the slavery question seemed less likely than ever to be resolved. Lincoln's appeal was clearly sectional: All his electoral votes came from the free states of the North and West. Most of the electorate voted against him. In a four-way race, with northern and southern wings of the Democratic Party running separate candidates and a hastily organized Constitutional Union Party offering yet another choice, Lincoln won just 39 percent of the popular vote. Although he repeatedly stated that neither he as president nor the Republican Party would disturb slavery where it already existed, the slave states of the South made plans to withdraw from the Union.

CONCLUSION

Whose Country Is It?

Who belongs in the United States of America? When the contest over slavery reached a crisis with the election of Abraham Lincoln, the slave states believed they no longer belonged. But northern free blacks had persistently debated that question throughout the preceding three decades. Most felt they were Americans, and they resisted efforts by white advocates of colonization to resettle them in Africa. But they also struggled to maintain their allegiance to a nation that circumscribed and excluded them.

At the beginning of the 1830s, northern black communities turned inward. In the face of racial prejudice that cast them as inferiors, they sought to be self-reliant. They cared for one another through mutual aid societies; they built independent churches and supported black schools. Black leaders promoted moral reform, arguing that Christian ideals and virtuous living would strengthen their communities and win the approval of whites. But these efforts were to no avail.

Blacks also turned outward, dedicating themselves to abolition. Only by freeing the enslaved, they concluded, could the free elevate themselves. At conventions, they debated strategies. Through newspapers, they built networks. They formed organizations. They boycotted goods produced by slave labor. The arrival of fugitive slaves magnified the voices of black abolitionists and emboldened them. They asserted that white attitudes and practices toward blacks urgently needed to be reformed. They lectured and wrote books. They petitioned the government and sued for equal treatment in schools and on public conveyances. Still, they continued to be hemmed in by laws and practices that denied them representation in the nation's political life and pushed them to the margins of its economic life. Segregation and black exclusion from white circles was the social norm. Studies in the emerging social sciences outlined racial hierarchies that placed blacks at the bottom. Most whites avoided blacks, fearing contamination.

In the 1850s, black prospects for a future in the United States narrowed further. A new law meant that fugitive slaves could not be secure in the free states, and a U.S. Supreme Court ruling asserted that African Americans could not be, and never had been, citizens of the land of their birth. Many concluded that they no longer belonged in such a nation, and some emigrated — to Canada, Africa, Haiti, and elsewhere.

Yet black claims to equality and freedom had pushed the slavery issue onto the national agenda, and the very crisis that undermined their allegiance to the nation also split the nation apart. Following the election of a president whose support was entirely in the North, the states of the South began to withdraw. The coming civil war would prove that African Americans, as free people, indeed belonged in the United States. In fact, that war would redefine the very nature of the nation. Frederick Douglass understood this. In 1849, he wrote, "We deem it a settled point that the destiny of the colored man is bound up with that of the white people of this country. . . . *We are here*, and here we are likely to be. . . . This is *our* country; and the question for the philosophers and statesmen of the land ought to be, What principles should dictate the policy of the action toward us?"[39] That question would not, however, be settled by the war. It would continue to be asked, again and again.

CHAPTER 6 REVIEW

KEY TERMS

uplift p. 221

black convention movement p. 227

moral suasion p. 230

abolitionist movement p. 232

political action p. 232

American Missionary Association p. 235

Wilmot Proviso (1846) p. 236

Compromise of 1850 p. 237

popular sovereignty p. 237

Fugitive Slave Act (1850) p. 237

personal liberty laws p. 237

vigilance committees p. 238

civil disobedience p. 238

Uncle Tom's Cabin **(1852)** p. 240

Kansas-Nebraska Act (1854) p. 240

Dred Scott v. Sandford **(1857)** p. 243

black nationalism p. 244

John Brown's raid (1859) p. 245

REVIEW QUESTIONS

1. In what ways did the end of slavery in the North bring about an increase in antiblack prejudice? What strategies did free black northerners develop to combat discrimination and fortify their communities?

2. How did free black northerners begin to link their plight to that of enslaved southerners?

3. What techniques did free blacks employ, and what organizations and institutions did they found, to advance the developing black freedom movement?

4. Describe the various legal and political battles surrounding slavery during the years 1850–1860. How did black northerners respond? What impact did these events have on the black freedom struggle?

5. How did the events of 1830–1860 fuel the mounting tensions between the North and South?

Forging an African American Nation— Slave and Free, North and South

In antebellum America, African Americans — North and South, slave and free — built over time and place the powerful bonds that united them as a people, a community, and a "nation within a nation." These bonds were neither natural nor God-given; rather, African Americans' shared origins and their shared experiences in America helped solidify their ties to each other. These deep-seated connections intensified over time as subsequent generations of African-descended peoples, enslaved and free, increasingly identified with one another, enabling them to forge fundamental social, cultural, political, and economic networks — such as churches, schools, and mutual benefit societies — that unified them as a singular people. Primary to this evolving sense of African American identity were the core beliefs, commitments, and actions of African Americans themselves. Secondary but still crucial factors that often influenced this evolving racial identification were black enslavement and antiblack repression.

The following documents testify to African Americans' deepening sense of unity as a people, regardless of their location or status, in the middle decades of the nineteenth century. The written documents are from northern blacks, who were relatively more at liberty than their southern brothers and sisters, whether free or enslaved, to express themselves and to mount an open liberation struggle. The excerpt from a speech by Sarah Mapps Douglass, an elite northern free black woman, describes the evolution of her identification with enslaved southern blacks. The African American liberation struggle required both this identification and various liberation strategies and tactics. The speech by Henry Highland Garnet, a former slave who as a child escaped to Pennsylvania with his family, underscores the profound tie between enslaved and free African Americans. It also issues a revolutionary and highly controversial call for armed slave insurrection to emancipate the enslaved. Like Garnet, Frederick Douglass also escaped slavery as a young man, though he later purchased his freedom with the help of English abolitionists. Douglass's speech is a scorching condemnation of the rank hypocrisy of black enslavement in an America wedded to freedom, equality, and democracy.

Similarly, the visual documents highlight important aspects of the developing antebellum African American liberation struggle, which in large part grew out of blacks' evolving identification as an African American people. "Escaping Slavery via the Underground Railroad" illustrates the centrality of active grassroots resistance to slavery. The portraits of Dred and Harriet Scott speak to the significance of fighting within the system to undermine slavery and antiblack repression — in the Scotts' case, by mobilizing the law and the courts in the abolitionist campaign. The depiction of "Jim Crow" vividly represents the racist stereotypes that African Americans continually fought on the cultural battle-front of their freedom struggle.

Sarah Mapps Douglass | *To Make the Slaves' Cause Our Own, 1832*

The majority of black women in the antebellum North were poor, working class, and illiterate; thus firsthand written accounts of their attitudes and experiences are rare. It is possible, however, to learn something of the attitudes and experiences of black women in this era from the few who were well educated and whose family backgrounds and opportunities afforded them elite status. SARAH MAPPS DOUGLASS (1806–1882) was a founding member of the Female Literary Society of Philadelphia and the Philadelphia Female Anti-Slavery Society. A well-regarded lecturer and political essayist, she also established a high school for black girls and taught at the Institute for Colored Youth. Her life and activism reflected her deep commitment to Quakerism. In the speech excerpted here, which she gave at one of the first meetings of the Female Literary Society, she describes the awakening of her compassion for enslaved blacks.

My friends — my sisters: How important is the occasion for which we have assembled ourselves together this evening, to hold a feast, to feed our never-dying minds, to excite each other to deeds of mercy, words of peace; to stir up in the bosom of each, gratitude to God for his increasing goodness, and feeling of deep sympathy for our brethren and sisters, who are in this land of christian light and liberty held in bondage the most cruel and degrading — to make their cause our own!

An English writer has said, "We must feel deeply before we can act rightly; from that absorbing, heart-rendering [*sic*] compassion for ourselves springs a deeper sympathy for others, and from a sense of our weakness and our own upbraidings arises a disposition to be indulgent, to forbear, to forgive." This is my experience. One short year ago, how different were my feelings on the subject of slavery! It is true, the wail of the captive sometimes came to my ear in the midst of my happiness, and caused my heart to bleed for his wrongs; but, alas! the impression was as evanescent as the early cloud and morning dew. I had formed a little world of my own, and cared not to move beyond its precincts. But how was the scene changed when I beheld the oppressor° lurking on the border of my own peaceful home! I saw his iron hand stretched forth to seize me as his prey, and the cause of the slave became my own. I started up, and with one mighty effort threw from me the lethargy which had covered me as a mantle for years; and determined, by the help of the Almighty, to use every exertion in my power to elevate the character of my wronged and neglected race. One year ago, I detested the slaveholder; now I can pity and pray for him. Has not this been your experience, my sisters? Have you not felt as I have felt upon this thrilling subject? My heart assures me some of you have.

SOURCE: C. Peter Ripley, ed., *The Black Abolitionist Papers* (Chapel Hill: University of North Carolina Press, 1991), 3:122–23.

° Douglass may be referring to a slave hunter or to discussions in the Pennsylvania legislature regarding the return of fugitives.

Henry Highland Garnet | An Address to the Slaves of the United States of America, 1843

At the time he delivered this speech, HENRY HIGHLAND GARNET (1815–1882) had been involved in abolitionist activities for more than ten years. He had studied theology at the Oneida Institute in Whitesboro, New York, where he sharpened his intellectual and rhetorical skills. As a pastor, he mastered public speaking. In 1843, he was one of seventy delegates from twelve states who attended the National Negro Convention in Buffalo, New York. There he gave a controversial speech that called on slaves to revolt. Notice a crucial rhetorical technique: He addressed his speech to slaves, although of course no slaves were present.

Brethren and fellow citizens: Your brethren of the North, East and West have been accustomed to meet together in national conventions, to sympathize with each other, and to weep over your unhappy condition. In these meetings we have addressed all classes of the free, but we have never, until this time, sent a word of consolation and advice to you. We have been contented in sitting still and mourning over your sorrows, earnestly hoping that before this day your sacred liberties would have been restored. But we have hoped in vain. Years have rolled on, and tens of thousands have been borne on streams of blood and tears to the shores of eternity. While you have been oppressed, we have also been partakers with you; nor can we be free while you are enslaved. We, therefore, write to you as being bound with you.

Many of you are bound to us, not only by the ties of a common humanity, but we are connected by the more tender relations of parents, wives, husbands and sisters and friends. As such we most affectionately address you. . . .

Two hundred and twenty-seven years ago the first of our injured race were brought to the shores of America. They came not with glad spirits to select their homes in the New World. They came not with their own consent, to find an unmolested enjoyment of the blessings of this fruitful soil. The first dealings they had with men calling themselves Christians exhibited to them the worst features of corrupt and sordid hearts, and convinced them that no cruelty is too great, no villainy and no robbery too abhorrent for even enlightened men to perform, when influenced by avarice and lust. Neither did they come flying upon the wings of Liberty to a land of freedom. But they came with broken hearts from their beloved native land and were doomed to unrequited toil and deep degradation. Nor did the evil of their bondage end at their emancipation by death. Succeeding generations inherited their chains, and millions have come from eternity into time, and have returned again to the world of spirits, cursed and ruined by American Slavery.

The propagators of the system, or their immediate successors, very soon discovered its growing evil and its tremendous wickedness, and secret promises were made to destroy it. The gross inconsistency of a people holding slaves, who had themselves "ferried o'er the wave" for freedom's sake, was too apparent to be entirely overlooked. The voice of Freedom cried, "Emancipate your slaves." . . . But all was [in] vain. Slavery had stretched its dark wings of death over the land, the Church stood silently by, the priests prophesied falsely, and the people loved to have it so. Its throne is established, and now it reigns triumphantly.

Nearly three millions of your fellow citizens are prohibited by law and public opinion (which in this country is stronger than law) from reading the Book of Life. Your intellect has been destroyed as much as possible, and every ray of light they have attempted to shut out from your minds. The oppressors themselves have become involved in the ruin. They have become weak, sensual and rapacious; they have cursed you; they have cursed themselves; they have cursed the earth which they have trod. . . .

SOURCE: Philip S. Foner and Robert James Branham, eds., *Lift Every Voice: African American Oratory, 1787–1900* (Tuscaloosa: University of Alabama Press, 1998), 198–202, 204–5.

Brethren, it is as wrong for your lordly oppressors to keep you in slavery as it was for the man thief to steal our ancestors from the coast of Africa. You should therefore now use the same manner of resistance as would have been just in our ancestors when the bloody footprints of the first remorseless soul thief was placed upon the shores of our fatherland. The humblest peasant is as free in the sight of God as the proudest monarch that ever swayed a scepter. Liberty is a spirit sent out from God and, like its great Author, is no respecter of persons.

Brethren, the time has come when you must act for yourselves. It is an old and true saying that, "if hereditary bondsmen would be free, they must themselves strike the blow."° You can plead your own cause and do the work of emancipation better than any others. The nations of the Old World are moving in the great cause of universal freedom, and some of them at least will, ere long, do you justice. The combined powers of Europe have placed their broad seal of disapprobation upon the African slave trade. But in the slaveholding parts of the United States the trade is as brisk as ever. They buy and sell you as though you were brute beasts. The North has done much; her opinion of slavery in the abstract is known. But in regard to the South, we adopt the opinion of the *New York Evangelist* — "We have advanced so far, that the cause apparently waits for a more effectual door to be thrown open than has been yet." We are about to point you to that more effectual door. Look around you and behold the bosoms of your loving wives heaving with untold agonies! Hear the cries of your poor children! Remember the stripes your fathers bore. Think of the torture and disgrace of your noble mothers. Think of your wretched sisters, loving virtue and purity, as they are driven into concubinage and are exposed to the unbridled lusts of incarnate devils. Think of the undying glory that hangs around the ancient name of Africa — and forget not that you are native-born American citizens, and as such you are justly entitled to all the rights that are granted to the

freest. Think how many tears you have poured out upon the soil which you have cultivated with unrequited toil and enriched with your blood; and then go to your lordly enslavers and tell them plainly that you *are determined to be free.* Appeal to their sense of justice and tell them that they have no more right to oppress you than you have to enslave them. Entreat them to remove the grievous burdens which they have imposed upon you, and to remunerate you for your labor. Promise them renewed diligence in the cultivation of the soil, if they will render to you an equivalent for your services. Point them to the increase of happiness and prosperity in the British West Indies since the Act of Emancipation.° Tell them, in language which they cannot misunderstand, of the exceeding sinfulness of slavery and of a future judgment and of the righteous retributions of an indignant God. Inform them that all you desire is freedom, and that nothing else will suffice. Do this, and forever after cease to toil for the heartless tyrants, who give you no other reward but stripes and abuse. If they then commence the work of death, they, and not you, will be responsible for the consequences. You had far better all die — *die immediately* — than live slaves and entail your wretchedness upon your posterity. If you would be free in this generation, here is your only hope. However much you and all of us may desire it, there is not much hope of redemption without the shedding of blood. If you must bleed, let it all come at once — rather *die freemen than live to be slaves.* . . .

Brethren, arise, arise! Strike for your lives and liberties. Now is the day and the hour. Let every slave throughout the land do this, and the days of slavery are numbered. You cannot be more oppressed than you have been; you cannot suffer greater cruelties than you have already. *Rather die freemen than live to be slaves.* Remember that you are three *millions! . . .*

Let your motto be Resistance! *Resistance!* RESISTANCE! No oppressed people have ever secured their liberty without resistance.

° Paraphrased from Lord Byron, *Childe Harold's Pilgrimage* (1818).

° Slavery had been abolished in the British West Indies by an act of Parliament in 1833.

DOCUMENT PROJECT

Frederick Douglass | *What to the Slave Is the Fourth of July?*, 1852

In 1843, when FREDERICK DOUGLASS (1818–1895) opposed Henry Highland Garnet's call for an armed slave revolt to overthrow slavery, he was relatively new to abolitionist organizing — he had been on the lecture circuit for only two years and a freeman for five. Less than a decade later, he was as seasoned a speaker as Garnet and was better known and more influential. On July 5, 1852, Douglass delivered one of his most famous speeches, to the Ladies' Anti-Slavery Society of Rochester, New York, which had invited him to address an Independence Day celebration in Corinthian Hall. Some five hundred to six hundred people each paid 12½ cents to hear the renowned abolitionist. As with many community celebrations at the time, this event began with a prayer and a reading of the Declaration of Independence. Douglass made the most of the occasion to drive home his message. The audience, the local press reported, reacted with much applause.

Fellow-Citizens — Pardon me, and allow me to ask, why am I called upon to speak here to-day? What have I, or those I represent, to do with your national independence? Are the great principles of political freedom and of natural justice, embodied in that Declaration of Independence, extended to us? and am I, therefore, called upon to bring our humble offering to the national altar, and to confess the benefits, and express devout gratitude for the blessings, resulting from your independence to us?

Would to God, both for your sakes and ours, that an affirmative answer could be truthfully returned to these questions! . . .

But, such is not the state of the case. I say it with a sad sense of the disparity between us. I am not included within the pale of this glorious anniversary! Your high independence only reveals the immeasurable distance between us. The blessings in which you this day rejoice, are not enjoyed in common. The rich inheritance of justice, liberty, prosperity, and independence, bequeathed by your fathers, is shared by you, not by me. The sunlight that brought life and healing to you, has brought stripes and death to me. This Fourth of July is *yours*, not *mine*. *You* may rejoice, *I* must mourn. To drag a man in fetters into the grand illuminated temple of liberty, and call upon him to join you in joyous anthems, were inhuman mockery and sacrilegious irony. Do you mean, citizens, to mock me, by asking me to speak to-day? . . .

Fellow-citizens, above your national, tumultuous joy, I hear the mournful wail of millions, whose chains, heavy and grievous yesterday, are to-day rendered more intolerable by the jubilant shouts that reach them. If I do forget, if I do not faithfully remember those bleeding children of sorrow this day, "may my right hand forget her cunning, and may my tongue cleave to the roof of my mouth!" To forget them, to pass lightly over their wrongs, and to chime in with the popular theme, would be treason most scandalous and shocking, and would make me a reproach before God and the world. My subject, then, fellow-citizens, is AMERICAN SLAVERY. I shall see this day and its popular characteristics from the slave's point of view. Standing here, identified with the American bondman, making his wrongs mine, I do not hesitate to declare, with all my soul, that the character and conduct of this nation never looked blacker to me than on this Fourth of July. Whether we turn to the declarations of the past, or to the professions of the present, the conduct of the nation seems equally hideous and revolting. America is false to the past, false to the present, and solemnly binds herself to be false to the future. Standing with God and the crushed and bleeding slave on this occasion, I will, in the name of humanity

SOURCE: Frederick Douglass, *My Bondage and My Freedom*, Ebony Classics (Chicago: Johnson, 1970), 349–53.

which is outraged, in the name of liberty which is fettered, in the name of the constitution and the bible, which are disregarded and trampled upon, dare to call in question and to denounce, with all the emphasis I can command, everything that serves to perpetuate slavery — the great sin and shame of America! "I will not equivocate; I will not excuse"; I will use the severest language I can command; and yet not one word shall escape me that any man, whose judgment is not blinded by prejudice, or who is not at heart a slaveholder, shall not confess to be right and just.

But I fancy I hear some of my audience say, it is just in this circumstance that you and your brother abolitionists fail to make a favorable impression on the public mind. Would you argue more, and denounce less, would you persuade more and rebuke less, your cause would be much more likely to succeed. But, I submit, where all is plain there is nothing to be argued. . . .

For the present, it is enough to affirm the equal manhood of the Negro race. Is it not astonishing that, while we are plowing, planting, and reaping, using all kinds of mechanical tools, erecting houses, constructing bridges, building ships, working in metals of brass, iron, copper, silver, and gold; that, while we are reading, writing, and cyphering, acting as clerks, merchants, and secretaries, having among us lawyers, doctors, ministers, poets, authors, editors, orators, and teachers; that, while we are engaged in all manner of enterprises common to other men — digging gold in California, capturing the whale in the Pacific, feeding sheep and cattle on the hillside, living, moving, acting, thinking, planning, living in families as husbands, wives, and children, and, above all, confessing and worshiping the Christian's God, and looking hopefully for life and immortality beyond the grave — we are called upon to prove that we are men!

Would you have me argue that man is entitled to liberty? that he is the rightful owner of his own body? You have already declared it. Must I argue the wrongfulness of slavery? Is that a question for republicans? . . . There is not a man

beneath the canopy of heaven that does not know that slavery is wrong *for him*.

What! am I to argue that it is wrong to make men brutes, to rob them of their liberty, to work them without wages, to keep them ignorant of their relations to their fellow-men, to beat them with sticks, to flay their flesh with the lash, to load their limbs with irons, to hunt them with dogs, to sell them at auction, to sunder their families, to knock out their teeth, to burn their flesh, to starve them into obedience and submission to their masters? Must I argue that a system, thus marked with blood and stained with pollution, is wrong? No; I will not. I have better employment for my time and strength than such arguments would imply.

What, then, remains to be argued? Is it that slavery is not divine; that God did not establish it; that our doctors of divinity are mistaken? There is blasphemy in the thought. That which is inhuman cannot be divine. Who can reason on such a proposition! They that can, may! I cannot. The time for such argument is past.

At a time like this, scorching irony, not convincing argument, is needed. Oh! had I the ability, and could I reach the nation's ear, I would to-day pour out a fiery stream of biting ridicule, blasting reproach, withering sarcasm, and stern rebuke. For it is not light that is needed, but fire; it is not the gentle shower, but thunder. We need the storm, the whirlwind, and the earthquake. The feeling of the nation must be quickened; the conscience of the nation must be roused; the propriety of the nation must be startled; the hypocrisy of the nation must be exposed; and its crimes against God and man must be proclaimed and denounced.

What to the American slave is your Fourth of July? I answer, a day that reveals to him, more than all other days in the year, the gross injustice and cruelty to which he is the constant victim. To him, your celebration is a sham; your boasted liberty, an unholy license; your national greatness, swelling vanity; your sounds of rejoicing are empty and heartless; your denunciations of tyrants, brass-fronted impudence; your shouts of liberty and equality, hollow mockery; your prayers and hymns, your sermons and thanksgivings, with all your religious parade and solemnity, are to him mere bombast, fraud, deception, impiety, and hypocrisy — a thin veil to cover up crimes which would disgrace a nation of savages. There is not a nation on the earth guilty of practices more shocking and bloody, than are the people of these United States, at this very hour.

Escaping Slavery via the Underground Railroad

The underground railroad was a network of individuals and groups throughout the South and North who secretly assisted runaway slaves in making their way to freedom. In this engraving, taken from a text discussed earlier in this chapter, William Still's *The Underground Rail Road* (1872) (see p. 238), a group of exhausted slaves, including a mother and infant, arrive at League Island, Philadelphia, from Norfolk, Virginia. Carriages stand by as volunteers help them up the hill to safety. The engraving is a compelling illustration of slave resistance: the lengths to which the slaves themselves went in their quest for freedom. It also shows their committed and courageous allies in the struggle against slavery. Indeed, the underground railroad has come to symbolize the extraordinary difficulties of the fight for both human rights and black freedom.

HEAVY WEIGHTS—ARRIVAL OF A PARTY AT LEAGUE ISLAND.

(Fifteen escaped in this Schooner.)

Newberry Library, Chicago, Illinois, USA/Bridgeman Images.

Dred and Harriet Scott

Harriet and Dred Scott, the enslaved plaintiffs in *Dred Scott v. Sandford* (1857), met and married around 1836. Shortly thereafter, they had two daughters, Eliza and Lizzie. In 1846, they filed separate petitions for freedom in the St. Louis circuit court, which the court subsequently combined, with Dred as the plaintiff. In fact, the U.S. Supreme Court's ruling in the case applied to all the Scotts, including the girls. In its 1857 decision, the Court determined that the Scotts and other African Americans were not citizens of the United States and did not share the same rights that whites enjoyed. Although they were freed almost immediately after the Court announced its decision, Dred died of tuberculosis a year later. Harriet died in 1876.

Library of Congress, Prints and Photographs Division, Washington, D.C., LC-USZ62-79305.

Jim Crow

White blackface minstrelsy, which caricatured and denigrated blacks, grew out of 1820s urban street entertainments in which young black and white men performed for coins and food in public places such as wharves, markets, street corners, and parks. T. D. (Thomas Dartmouth) "Daddy" Rice, the white traveling actor most closely associated with early minstrelsy, developed blackface routines that featured singing, dancing, and humor. His most famous black character was a slave dressed in rags named Jim Crow, who, Rice claimed, was inspired by the dance of a disabled black man. The Jim Crow character made Rice famous, and in time "Jim Crow" became a common racial epithet. By the late nineteenth century, the term was used to refer to the whole range of laws and customs related to racial segregation.

© Collection of the New-York Historical Society, USA/Bridgeman Images.

QUESTIONS FOR ANALYSIS

1. When considered both separately and together, what light do these documents shed on the evolving antebellum African American freedom struggle?

2. Do Sarah Mapps Douglass's racial, class, and gender identities influence her identification with the enslaved? Explain.

3. Compare and contrast the rhetorical techniques used by Henry Highland Garnet and Frederick Douglass. Which speaker and which technique(s) do you find most persuasive? Explain.

4. Compare and contrast the forms of resistance to slavery represented by "Escaping Slavery via the Underground Railroad" and the portraits of Dred and Harriet Scott. Which do you think is the more effective form of resistance, and why?

5. Many have argued that the explicit racism of stereotypes such as "Jim Crow" and cultural forms such as blackface minstrelsy have had a strong impact on American popular culture from the antebellum era to the present day. Do you agree? What specific evidence and broader cultural developments can you use to support your position? Do you see any evidence of the persistence of Jim Crow stereotypes and blackface minstrelsy in contemporary American popular culture?

DOCUMENT PROJECT

NOTES

1. *North Star*, March 23, 1849, quoted in Jane Rhodes, *Mary Ann Shadd Cary: The Black Press and Protest in the Nineteenth Century* (Bloomington: Indiana University Press, 1998), 21.

2. *Frederick Douglass' Paper*, November 9, 1855, quoted ibid., 109.

3. Alexis de Tocqueville, *Democracy in America*, ed. Phillips Bradley (New York: Knopf, 1945), 1:359–60.

4. Quoted in Patrick Rael, *Black Identity and Black Protest in the Antebellum North* (Chapel Hill: University of North Carolina Press, 2002), 262.

5. George Wilson Pierson, *Tocqueville and Beaumont in America* (New York: Oxford University Press, 1938), 565.

6. James O. Horton and Lois E. Horton, *Black Bostonians: Family Life and Community Struggle in the Antebellum North* (New York: Holmes & Meier, 1979), 2; Ira Berlin, *Slaves without Masters: The Free Negro in the Antebellum South* (New York: New Press, 2007), 176.

7. George Foster, "Philadelphia in Slices" (1848–1849), quoted in Leonard P. Curry, *The Free Black in Urban America, 1800–1850: The Shadow of the Dream* (Chicago: University of Chicago Press, 1986), 49; George Foster, "New York in Slices" (1849), quoted ibid., 78.

8. Julie Winch, *A Gentleman of Color: The Life of James Forten* (New York: Oxford University Press, 2003), 84–85.

9. Leslie M. Alexander, *African or American? Black Identity and Political Activism in New York City, 1784–1861* (Urbana: University of Illinois Press, 2008), 158.

10. Martin R. Delany, *The Condition, Elevation, Emigration, and Destiny of the Colored People of the United States* (1852; repr., New York: Arno Press, 1969), 45–46.

11. *Minutes and Proceedings of the Second Annual Convention, for the Improvement of the Free People of Color in These United States* (Philadelphia: published by order of the convention, 1832), 34.

12. *Proceedings of the National Convention of Colored People and Their Friends, Held in Troy, N.Y., on the 6th, 7th, 8th, and 9th October, 1847*, quoted in Leon Litwack, *North of Slavery: The Negro in the Free States, 1790–1860* (Chicago: University of Chicago Press, 1961), 135.

13. *Maria W. Stewart, America's First Black Woman Political Writer: Essays and Speeches*, ed. Marilyn Richardson (Bloomington: Indiana University Press, 1987), 21, 35, 59–60.

14. Ibid., 46.

15. Lewis Woodson [Augustine], "Moral Work for Colored Men," *Colored American*, August 12, 1837.

16. Howard H. Bell, "The American Moral Reform Society, 1836–1841," *Journal of Negro Education* 27, no. 1 (Winter 1958): 34–40; *Minutes and Proceedings of the First Annual Meeting of the American Moral Reform Society* (1837), quoted in Litwack, *North of Slavery*, 238.

17. *Report of the Proceedings of the Colored National Convention, Held at Cleveland, Ohio, on Wednesday, September 6, 1848* (Rochester, NY: John Dick, 1848), 18.

18. *Freedom's Journal*, March 16, 1827.

19. Quoted in Ronald L. F. Davis and B. J. Krekorian, "The Black Press in Antebellum America," Slavery in America, http://www.slaveryinamerica.org/history/hs_es_press.htm.

20. *Frederick Douglass' Paper*, March 9, 1855, quoted in Benjamin Quarles, *Black Abolitionists* (New York: Oxford University Press, 1969), 86.

21. In spite of several early positive reviews, Jacobs's text languished in obscurity, its authenticity questioned, until Jean Fagan Yellin convincingly demonstrated its authenticity in the 1980s. Jean Fagan Yellin, *Harriet Jacobs: A Life* (New York: Basic Civitas Books, 2004).

22. Nell Irvin Painter, *Sojourner Truth: A Life, a Symbol* (New York: Norton, 1996), 160.

23. Quoted ibid., 125.

24. Ibid.

25. "Legal Rights Vindicated," *Frederick Douglass' Paper*, March 2, 1855.

26. Charles Sumner, *Argument . . . against the Constitutionality of Separate Colored Schools, in the Case of Sarah C. Roberts vs. the City of Boston. Before the Supreme Court of Mass., Dec. 4, 1849*, quoted in Litwack, *North of Slavery*, 147.

27. Quoted in Quarles, *Black Abolitionists*, 23.

28. Winch, *A Gentleman of Color*, 241–42.

29. Lois E. Horton, "Kidnapping and Resistance: Antislavery Direct Action in the 1850s," in *Passages to Freedom: The Underground Railroad in History and Memory*, ed. David W. Blight (Washington, DC: Smithsonian Books, 2004), 166.

30. Quoted in Milton C. Sernett, "Jermain Wesley Loguen," in *African American Lives*, ed. Henry Louis Gates Jr. and Evelyn Brooks Higginbotham (New York: Oxford University Press, 2004), 542.

31. This information is drawn largely from Sarah H. Bradford's nineteenth-century biography *Harriet Tubman: The Moses of Her People* (New York: printed for the author by G. R. Lockwood and Son, 1886). Recently, however, scholars have challenged several aspects of this text. For an overview of the debate, see Milton Sernett, *Harriet Tubman: Myth, Memory, and History* (Durham, NC: Duke University Press, 2007), 55–66.

32. Quoted in Quarles, *Black Abolitionists*, 212.

33. Taney, C. J., Opinion of the Court, Scott v. Sandford 60 U.S. 393 (1857).

34. All quoted in Quarles, *Black Abolitionists*, 231.

35. Martin R. Delany, *Official Report of the Niger Valley Exploring Party*, in *Search for a Place: Black Separatism and Africa*, ed. Howard H. Bell (1861; repr., Ann Arbor: University of Michigan Press, 1969), 35.

36. Quoted in Quarles, *Black Abolitionists*, 231.

37. Quoted ibid., 240, 241.

38. Quoted in David S. Reynolds, *John Brown, Abolitionist: The Man Who Killed Slavery, Sparked the Civil War, and Seeded Civil Rights* (New York: Knopf, 2005), 395.

39. "The Destiny of Colored Americans," *North Star*, November 16, 1849.

SUGGESTED REFERENCES

The Boundaries of Freedom

Alexander, Leslie M. *African or American? Black Identity and Political Activism in New York City, 1784–1861*. Urbana: University of Illinois Press, 2008.

Curry, Leonard P. *The Free Black in Urban America, 1800–1850: The Shadow of the Dream*. Chicago: University of Chicago Press, 1986.

Harris, Leslie M. *In the Shadow of Slavery: African Americans in New York City, 1626–1863*. Chicago: University of Chicago Press, 2003.

Hodges, Graham Russell. *Root and Branch: African Americans in New York and East Jersey, 1613–1863*. Chapel Hill: University of North Carolina Press, 1999.

Horton, James O., and Lois E. Horton. *Black Bostonians: Family Life and Community Struggle in the Antebellum North*. New York: Holmes & Meier, 1979.

———. *In Hope of Liberty: Culture, Community, and Protest among Northern Free Blacks, 1700–1860*. New York: Oxford University Press, 1997.

Litwack, Leon. *North of Slavery: The Negro in the Free States, 1790–1860*. Chicago: University of Chicago Press, 1961.

Melish, Joanne Pope. *Disowning Slavery: Gradual Emancipation and "Race" in New England, 1780–1860*. Ithaca, NY: Cornell University Press, 1998.

Forging a Black Freedom Struggle

Bell, Howard H. *A Survey of the Negro Convention Movement, 1830–1861*. New York: Arno Press, 1969.

Blackett, Richard. *Building an Antislavery Wall: Black Americans in the Atlantic Abolitionist Movement, 1830–1860*. Ithaca, NY: Cornell University Press, 1989.

Hall, Stephen G. *A Faithful Account of the Race: African American Historical Writing in Nineteenth-Century America*. Chapel Hill: University of North Carolina Press, 2009.

McCarthy, Timothy Patrick, and John Stauffer, eds. *Prophets of Protest: Reconsidering the History of American Abolitionism*. New York: New Press, 2006.

Painter, Nell Irvin. *Sojourner Truth: A Life, a Symbol*. New York: Norton, 1996.

Pease, Jane H., and William H. Pease. *They Who Would Be Free: Blacks' Search for Freedom, 1830–1861*. New York: Atheneum, 1974.

Quarles, Benjamin. *Black Abolitionists*. New York: Oxford University Press, 1969.

Rael, Patrick. *Black Identity and Black Protest in the Antebellum North*. Chapel Hill: University of North Carolina Press, 2002.

Rhodes, Jane. *Mary Ann Shadd Cary: The Black Press and Protest in the Nineteenth Century*. Bloomington: Indiana University Press, 1998.

Winch, Julie. *Philadelphia's Black Elite: Activism, Accommodation, and the Struggle for Autonomy, 1787–1848*. Philadelphia: Temple University Press, 1988.

Yee, Shirley. *Black Women Abolitionists: A Study in Activism, 1828–1860*. Knoxville: University of Tennessee Press, 1992.

Slavery and the Coming of the Civil War

Bordewich, Fergus. *Bound for Canaan: The Underground Railroad and the War for the Soul of America*. New York: Amistad, 2005.

Fehrenbacher, Don. *The Dred Scott Case: Its Significance in American Law and Politics*. New York: Oxford University Press, 1978.

Finkelman, Paul. *Dred Scott v. Sandford: A Brief History with Documents*. Boston: Bedford/St. Martin's, 1997.

Foner, Eric. *Free Soil, Free Labor, Free Men: The Ideology of the Republican Party before the Civil War*. New York: Oxford University Press, 1995.

Holt, Michael F. *The Fate of Their Country: Politicians, Slavery Extension, and the Coming of the Civil War*. New York: Hill and Wang, 2004.

McPherson, James M. *Battle Cry of Freedom: The Civil War Era*. New York: Oxford University Press, 1988.

Miller, Floyd J. *The Search for a Black Nationality: Black Emigration and Colonization, 1787–1863*. Urbana: University of Illinois Press, 1975.

Slaughter, Thomas P. *Bloody Dawn: The Christiana Riot and Racial Violence in the Antebellum North*. New York: Oxford University Press, 1991.

Still, William. *The Underground Rail Road*. 1872. Reprint, Chicago: Johnson, 1970.

Taylor, Quintard. *In Search of the Racial Frontier: African Americans in the American West, 1528–1990*. New York: Norton, 1998.

Freedom Rising: The Civil War

1861–1865

Robert Smalls and the African American Freedom Struggle during the Civil War

Around three o'clock in the morning on May 13, 1862, the *Planter*, a Confederate steamer loaded with supplies for nearby Confederate outposts, made its way up Charleston harbor with the slave pilot Robert Smalls at the helm. Confederate lookouts, accustomed to seeing black pilots, took little note of the fact that there were no white men on deck.

Once outside the harbor, Smalls revved up the steamer's engine and sped in the direction of the Union blockade. Hoisting a white flag of surrender, he hoped the Union navy would permit the *Planter* to enter Union lines as a fugitive vessel and, more important, that his family members and friends on board would be protected as fugitive slaves. After several tense moments, the Union sailors turned their guns and cannons away, receiving the surrender of the *Planter* and welcoming the fugitives as free men and women.

Smalls had devised a cunning plan to secure his own and his family's freedom. Smalls and those around him had heard that Union forces were using fugitive slaves to help fight the Confederacy. Once behind Union lines, he provided the Union navy with important information about Confederate units in Charleston harbor. Before long, he was piloting the *Planter* for the Union navy, transporting men and supplies within the Union zone. Not long afterward,

Congress gave Smalls and his band of freedom fighters a financial reward for surrendering the *Planter* to Union forces.

The story of Smalls's daring escape captured the attention of African Americans and the northern white press. In October 1862, a meeting of blacks at New York City's Shiloh Baptist Church, pastored by the Reverend Henry Highland Garnet (see chapter 6), welcomed him "with deafening cheers." A resolution adopted by the meeting claimed that Smalls's bold action demonstrated "a faithful devotedness to the cause of the American union."[1] For blacks and their allies, the exploit became one of the most celebrated events of the Civil War. It is also just one instance in what turned out to be a massive defection of slaves from the Confederacy to Union lines. The ever-growing number of slave men, women, and children who seized their freedom by joining the Union cause ultimately contributed to the collapse of the Confederacy.

The Civil War began as a southern war for Confederate independence and a northern war to defeat the Confederate rebellion and restore the Union. At the outset, neither side thought that the war would last very long or eventually lead to the destruction of slavery. The Confederacy was founded to protect slavery. The Union was willing to accept slavery where it already existed, opposing only the extension of slavery into the territories.

The transformation of the Union cause from a war to restore the Union to a war with the additional aim of abolishing slavery owed much to the actions of the slaves themselves. Their escape from slavery and their presence behind Union lines, together with the advocacy of northern free blacks and their white abolitionist allies, put pressure on the Lincoln administration and the U.S. Congress for policy changes and new laws that would address the issue of slavery directly and end it. The Union victory also owed much to the black men — both free and recently freed — who served in the Union army and navy, as well as to the many black men and women who worked alongside the troops and, as civilians, supported the Union cause. Their dedication and service, they believed, would earn them the rights of U.S. citizens. But as free blacks in the North and South had known for decades, freedom did not mean fair treatment and equality, and it was apparent at the war's end that the black freedom struggle was far from over.

The Coming of War and the Seizing of Freedom, 1861–1862

In hindsight, the Civil War seems to have been inevitable, but following the election of Abraham Lincoln as president in November 1860, the war came in a series of small steps, the consequences of which were not fully apparent at the time. As the states of the Confederacy withdrew from the Union to protect slavery, northern free blacks and their allies increasingly expressed the hope that if war came, it would be a war to end slavery everywhere. That was not the Union's initial war aim, but when slaves began pressing the issue by fleeing to Union lines, Union commanders were forced to respond, and in time they moved to protect the refugees' freedom. Slowly, Lincoln and Congress, too, were forced to respond by putting in place policies and practices that pointed toward a general emancipation.

War Aims and Battlefield Realities

With the election of Abraham Lincoln, sectional tensions over slavery reached a point of crisis. Believing they owed no loyalty to a Union that could elect a president without any southern support, the slave states made plans to withdraw. On November 10, 1860, South Carolina called a secession convention, and on December 20 it declared that "the union now subsisting between South Carolina and other States, under the name of the 'United States of America' is hereby dissolved." Four days later, the convention passed a declaration listing the causes justifying secession: the North's interference with slavery; repeated northern condemnations of slavery as sinful; northern support for abolitionism; northerners' aiding and abetting the escape of southern fugitive slaves; northern promotion of slave insurrections through "emissaries, books, and pictures"; and the election of Lincoln, a leader "whose opinions and purposes are hostile to slavery."[2]

South Carolina's secession ordinance declared the state independent, but already a movement was under way for the formation of a confederacy of slave states. By February 1, 1861, Mississippi, Florida, Alabama, Georgia, Louisiana, and Texas also had seceded, and on February 4, delegates from these states met in Montgomery, Alabama, to create the **Confederate States of America**. They wrote a constitution that read much like the U.S. Constitution, with the key difference being that it explicitly protected the right to hold slaves as property within its domain. Setting up a provisional government, they elected Mississippi senator Jefferson Davis as president.

Even as the Confederacy formed, there were two attempts to avert disunion. In Congress, Kentucky senator John J. Crittenden proposed to reinstate the 1820 Missouri Compromise and thus guarantee the protection of slavery in territories south of the southern border of Missouri. After a U.S. Senate committee failed to reach agreement on the proposal, the Virginia legislature called a peace convention. But the delegates in attendance, representing both free and slave states, also failed to find a compromise that would hold the Union together.

While some still hoped for peace, the Confederate States of America prepared for war. They began organizing an army and a navy, and state militias seized federal forts, arsenals, and post offices. Most military posts in the South came under Confederate command. In Charleston, Union major Robert Anderson withdrew from Fort Moultrie to the more easily protected Fort Sumter, on an island in the harbor, and waited for provisions.

On March 4, 1861, Lincoln delivered his inaugural address to a fractured Union. Speaking directly to "the Southern States," he reaffirmed, "I have no purpose, directly or indirectly, to interfere with the institution of slavery in the States where it exists. I believe I have no lawful right to do so, and I have no inclination to do so." At the same time, Lincoln asserted that the Union was a binding and "perpetual" compact. Furthermore, he explained, "no State, upon its own mere motion, can lawfully get out of the Union." He concluded, "Acts of violence, within any State or States, against the authority of the United States, are insurrectionary or revolutionary." Precisely because it was unlawful and thus intolerable, Lincoln believed that secession must be overturned. It was his position that the Union had to be respected and maintained.[3]

In his first cabinet meeting, Lincoln raised the issue of provisioning Fort Sumter, and the matter was discussed often in the following weeks. Eventually, the president determined that the fort should be resupplied, and he informed the governor of South Carolina of this intention. In turn, South Carolina demanded the fort's surrender. When Major Anderson refused, Confederate shore batteries opened fire early on the morning of April 12. The next day, Anderson surrendered. The Civil War had begun.

Anticipating that Anderson was ready to evacuate the fort, Confederate officials did not think their actions would lead to hostilities. After all, back in January, fire from Charleston's shore batteries had forced the withdrawal of a provision ship without further incident. But they miscalculated. On April 15, Lincoln called for 75,000 militia to put down the insurrection and "to repossess the forts, places, and property which have been seized from the Union."[4]

Virginia refused to answer the call. Its first secession convention had rejected leaving the Union, but now a second convention voted for it. By May 20, Arkansas, Tennessee, and North Carolina had also joined the Confederacy, making for a total of eleven Confederate states. The slave states of Delaware, Maryland, Kentucky, and Missouri, known as the border states, remained in the Union, but not without strife. Federal troops occupied Baltimore; guerrilla fighting ravaged Missouri; and a provisional Confederate government was formed in Kentucky, although the state officially declared its neutrality. Even as Virginia's state capital, Richmond, was selected as the new Confederate capital, the state's western counties seceded from Virginia and organized a Unionist government.

Patriotic fervor pervaded both North and South. Each side felt that its cause was just and it would soon prevail. Lincoln's call for volunteers had anticipated a three-month commitment. With their superior economic, material, military, and manpower resources (close to two to one), northerners believed that the Confederate rebellion would be quickly put down. With fierce determination and confidence in their formidable military abilities, southerners believed that they would succeed in establishing the Confederate States of America as an independent nation. They would be defending their homeland, while the Union would be forced to take the war into the Confederate states.

Three months into the war, Union forces marched thirty miles into Virginia. On July 21, 1861, along a creek called Bull Run, the Confederates turned them back. Union officials had miscalculated. It was clear that the Confederacy would not back down in the face of Union advantages on and off the battlefield. It was also clear that the war would not be over soon.

Union Policy on Black Soldiers and Black Freedom

Free black men responded enthusiastically to Lincoln's call for volunteers. In Pittsburgh, the Hannibal Guards, a local black militia, pledged support for the Union cause: "As we consider ourselves American citizens . . . although deprived of all our political rights, we yet wish the government of the United States to be sustained against the tyranny of slavery, and are willing to assist in any honorable way . . . to sustain the present administration."[5] In Albany, Ohio, free blacks organized the Attucks Guards, naming their regiment after Crispus Attucks, the fugitive slave who was the first person to die in the American Revolution (see chapter 3). Albany's black women gave the volunteer company a handsome homemade flag. And at Boston's Twelfth Baptist Church, those assembled unanimously resolved that "we are ready to stand by and defend the Government with 'our lives, our fortunes, and our sacred honor.'" They resolved further that "the colored women could go as nurses, seamstresses, and warriors if need be."[6]

But in all cases, military service by black men was rejected. For many whites, black men serving in the Union forces evoked thoughts of slave insurrections and violated notions of white male superiority. When black men in Cincinnati met to organize a

Regimental and Confederate Flags

At left, the remnant of a handsome flag made by the Colored Ladies of Baltimore for the Fourth Regiment U.S. Colored Troops showcases black patriotism. This regimental flag vividly illustrates the strong black civilian support for the Union war effort. Even more impressively, it illustrates African Americans' deep pride in and zealous support for black Union troops during and after the war. This support was particularly strong among women with male relatives and friends serving in the military. Juxtaposed with this emblem of black Union patriotism is the flag of the Confederacy, which symbolizes both slavery and the Confederate cause. The Confederate flag simultaneously represents two vexing dilemmas that continue to make it intensely controversial, down to the present day: It represents the inherent tension between slavery and freedom, as well as the inherent tension between Confederate patriotism and the treason of Confederate rebellion against the Union.

Regimental flag: Silk mounted on a wooden pole (with the eagle missing). Museum Department, Courtesy of the Maryland Historical Society, image ID 2004.22. Confederate flag: Battle flag of the 21st Tennessee Fifth Confederate Regiment used in the Atlanta campaign/© Don Troiani/Corbis.

home guard to protect the city, white opposition was fierce. Instead of gratitude, these volunteers received "insults . . . for this simple offer." In Cincinnati, as throughout the North, blacks encountered a persistent refrain: "We want you d——d niggers to keep out of this; this is a white man's war."[7] In September 1862, President Lincoln observed that if the Union accepted black troops, he feared "that in a few weeks the arms would be in the hands of the rebels."[8] Despite the service of black men in the American Revolution and the War of 1812, the U.S. army had generally excluded black soldiers, and they were barred from state militias as well.[9]

Nevertheless, from the outset, northern blacks and abolitionists engaged in a vigorous debate about the purposes, possible consequences, and larger meanings of the war. Many worked hard to make emancipation a central war goal. Shortly after the surrender of Fort Sumter, the *Anglo-African Magazine* prophesied that "out of this strife will come freedom, though the methods are not yet clearly apparent." "Justice to the slave," the magazine argued, was "the sure and permanent basis of 'a more perfect Union.'"[10] Frederick Douglass expressed a similarly hopeful vision in May 1861: "Any attempt now to separate the freedom of the slave from the victory of the Government . . . any attempt to secure peace to the whites while leaving the blacks in chains . . . will be labor lost. The American people and the Government at Washington may refuse to recognize it for a time; but the 'inexorable logic of events' will force it upon them in the end; that the war now being waged in this land is a war for and against slavery."[11] (See Document Project: Wartime and Emancipation, pp. 288–95.)

Nevertheless, Lincoln continued to frame the conflict as a rebellion that must be put down so the Union could be preserved. As president and commander in chief, he refused to acknowledge slavery as the cause of the war, or abolition as its goal. He knew he could not afford to alienate the border states, where slavery still existed. The loyalty of Maryland — to the north of Washington, D.C. — was especially important to secure. Without it, the nation's capital would be surrounded by hostile territory. And Maryland's loyalty was uncertain. In Baltimore, federal troops had been shot at as they marched through the city. As riots and civil disorder continued, Lincoln suspended habeas corpus on April 27, 1861. Those suspected of disloyal acts could be taken into custody without the right to have a judge rule on the lawfulness of their imprisonment. In other words, they could be held in jail indefinitely without the authorities showing cause.

To help further secure the border states' loyalty, Lincoln developed a plan for gradual, compensated slave emancipation that allowed the states, not the federal government, to take the initiative. He especially hoped that Delaware, with fewer than 2,000 slaves, would view such a plan favorably. But none of the border states adopted emancipation plans. Congress, however, passed legislation to end slavery in the District of Columbia, and on April 16, 1862, Lincoln signed the act into law. It gave slave owners who could prove their loyalty to the Union up to $300 for each slave freed, and it gave each freed slave who chose emigration to Haiti, Liberia, or any country outside the United States up to $100. Nearly 3,000 slaves were freed by this act, and several hundred chose to accept payment to relocate to Haiti. In June, Congress ended slavery in U.S. territories — those areas west of the Mississippi River not yet organized as states. For the Union, this crucial action settled once and for all an extremely divisive issue that had caused zealous discord between the South and North before the war and that persisted as a fundamental disagreement between the Confederacy and the Union. For the Confederacy, it suggested the Union's ultimate goal was to end southern slavery.

The District of Columbia Emancipation Act showed Lincoln's two-pronged approach to the problem of slavery — compensation and colonization — but it did not prove to be the model that Lincoln had hoped for. In the spring and summer of 1862, the war was not going well for the Union. Despite a massive effort, Union attempts to advance on Richmond failed, and by fall the Confederate Army of Northern Virginia was on the offensive. Calls for a general emancipation proliferated, but in a famous exchange with the journalist Horace Greeley of the *New York Tribune*, who urged Lincoln to commit himself to end slavery, Lincoln replied: "My paramount object in this struggle is to save the Union, and is not either to save or to destroy slavery. . . . What I do about slavery, and the colored race, I do because I believe it helps to save the Union. . . . I have here stated my purpose according to my view of official duty; and I intend no modification of my oft-expressed personal wish that all men every where could be free."[12]

Refugee Slaves and Freedpeople

Pressure to address emancipation directly mounted because some slaves had already freed themselves. Taking advantage of the unsettled conditions of wartime, slaves fled to Union lines and Union-controlled territory, where their presence forced military commanders to determine their status. The first to seize freedom in this way were Frank Baker, James Townsend, and Shepard Mallory, who, just after the hostilities began, had been sent by their owner to build Confederate fortifications in Hampton, Virginia. In the middle of the night on May 23, 1861, they commandeered a skiff and crossed the waters of Hampton Roads to Fortress Monroe, which was still in Union hands. There they received protection from the commander, General Benjamin F. Butler, who refused to return them to their owners. Instead, using the South's definition of slaves as property, Butler designated them **contraband** of war, or confiscated Confederate property. These three men were the first of thousands of fugitive slaves — men, women, and children — who would swell the population at Fortress Monroe. By July 1861, there were 900 refugees there, and by August 1862 there were 3,000. By the end of the war, in April 1865, some 10,000 former slaves lived in camps at Hampton, the village across from the fortress, which had been burned to the ground by retreating Confederates in August 1861.

In military terms, "contraband" designated nonhuman property and goods. Butler's use of it for refugee slaves was unconventional, but it shaped subsequent Union policy. It also implied subordinate status, as the former slaves were not yet fully emancipated. Butler put them to work as diggers and dockworkers, as servants and laundresses and cooks. They received army rations and eventually wages — $8 a month for males, $4 for females. These refugees deprived the Confederacy of a vital labor source that increasingly contributed to the Union cause.

Butler was not the only Union officer to be perplexed by the question of what to do with refugee slaves who fled to Union lines. In early August 1861, Congress sought to clarify the situation through the **First Confiscation Act**, which authorized the confiscation of slaves as Confederate property. This act voided masters' claims to slaves who — like the three who sought refuge at Fortress Monroe — had been working directly for

STAMPEDE AMONG THE NEGROES IN VIRGINIA—THEIR ARRIVAL AT FORTRESS MONROE—FROM SKETCHES BY OUR SPECIAL ARTIST IN FORTRESS MONROE.—SEE PAGE 66.

Slave Contrabands

Enslaved blacks contributed to their emancipation by running away and seeking refuge at Union strongholds such as Fortress Monroe in Virginia, shown here. Union military policies and practices helped shape the freedom journey for tens of thousands of refugee slaves. By redefining fugitive slaves' status as "contraband of war," thus making them subject to seizure by the Union, military officials helped lay the groundwork for employing refugees as non-slave workers, further spurring the transition from slavery to freedom. *Library of Congress, Prints and Photographs Division, Washington, D.C., LC-USZ62-31165.*

the Confederate military. Later that same month, John C. Frémont, the major general in charge of the Department of the West and an outspoken abolitionist, cited civil disorder in Missouri as his rationale for declaring martial law and freeing the slaves of all disloyal owners. Lincoln, concerned about securing the loyalty of the border states, voided the order.

Nevertheless, African Americans, by running from slavery to freedom, were already shaping three related developments: the decisions of individual commanders about what to do with the refugees, Union military policy as a whole, and growing acceptance in the North of former slaves as laborers for the Union military. In March 1862,

Congress passed an additional article of war that prohibited Union navy and army officers from returning fugitives to slavery. Even before that, however, Union officers in recaptured coastal South Carolina were developing their own innovative policies. Port Royal and the Sea Islands had been taken by Union troops in November 1861, as the Union naval blockade of the South proved increasingly successful. Fleeing plantation owners abandoned their land and some 10,000 slaves, who remembered November 7 as "the day of the big gun-shoot."[13]

In what came to be known as the **Port Royal Experiment**, these former slaves were designated contrabands and began working the abandoned cotton plantations under the supervision of Union military officials. They organized their own time and labor, received wages, and sold surplus crops. A few were able to purchase plots of abandoned land when U.S. Treasury officials auctioned it off, but most of the land went to northern businessmen, who hired the contrabands to farm it. The former slaves' success in this endeavor could have been a model for the transition from slavery to freedom.

Assisting the contrabands were a group of idealistic missionaries and teachers sent by northern religious and charitable organizations such as the American Missionary Association. Most of the teachers were white women who saw themselves as civilizing and Christianizing a primitive and inferior people. Sea Island blacks may have resented the women's condescension and racial prejudice, but they were eager to be educated. At makeshift schools in churches and on outdoor benches, they learned to read and write, to understand the Bible and Christian principles, and to master the responsibilities of freedom. One who traveled to the Sea Islands to teach former slaves was Charlotte Forten, the granddaughter of the successful African American businessman James Forten. An abolitionist, writer, poet, and teacher, she subsequently published a revealing narrative of her experiences that showed her empathy and sympathy for the Sea Island freedpeople as well as the class and cultural distance between her and them.

Even as the Port Royal contrabands were building independent lives, their status was uncertain. On May 19, 1862, the Union commander General David Hunter issued a proclamation freeing all the slaves in Florida, Georgia, and South Carolina, but Lincoln again voided the order. Hunter set about organizing the freedmen into a regiment until the War Department forced him to abandon this plan. Finally, on July 17, 1862, Congress clarified the status of refugee slaves. The **Second Confiscation Act** declared freedom for all slaves employed in the rebellion and for refugee slaves able to make it to Union-controlled territory. It thereby freed all slaves who had been deserted by Confederate owners, as well as all those who took refuge behind Union lines or were captured, if their owners were waging war against the Union. Slavery in the border states, however, was protected. The act also empowered the federal government to seize and sell all other Confederate property. Finally, it gave the president the power to authorize the use of "persons of African descent" in any way he deemed necessary to put down the rebellion and "to make provision for the transportation, colonization, and settlement, in some tropical country beyond the limits of the United States, of such persons of the African race, made free by the provisions of this act, as may be willing to emigrate."[14]

Union forces in the West were more successful than those in the East, and by mid-1862 they had captured New Orleans and were moving up the Mississippi River. In Louisiana, as elsewhere, slaves fled to Union lines. Thousands of refugees arrived from the low-lying rice plantations near New Orleans, the cotton plantations around Baton Rouge, and the sugar plantations along the river and west of New Orleans. General Butler, now the military governor of New Orleans, initially followed a two-pronged policy: He welcomed the slaves of masters who were disloyal to the Union, but he returned the runaway slaves of pro-Union planters — some of whom had only recently sworn loyalty to the Union and were looking to Butler to protect their property. In the confusion of wartime conditions, however, it became increasingly difficult, if not impractical, to distinguish between the refugee slaves of loyal and disloyal masters. Butler's solution was to arrange for runaway slaves to provide wage labor for allegedly loyal plantation owners who sought the help, thus avoiding the question of the fugitives' status, which was neither slave nor free.

A growing body of refugee slaves took over and worked abandoned land and carved out hidden runaway settlements in the bayous. The widening slave exodus alarmed southern whites, who increasingly feared slave insurrections. As Union forces gained firmer control of the region, however, they instituted systems of labor that, like the Port Royal Experiment, allowed the former slaves to work the surrounding plantations as independent laborers under the supervision of Union officials.[15]

Turning Points, 1862–1863

In more than a year of fighting, neither side had achieved its aims. Union forces had secured some coastal areas of the Confederacy, but advances on the capital of Richmond had been checked. Fugitive slaves were creating turmoil for Union military officers and forcing the issue of freedom on a cautious Lincoln. But events began to take a decisive turn in the summer of 1862. Within the next twelve months, a military order by the president would decree formal emancipation for slaves under Confederate control and authorize black men to serve in the Union army. Following this change of policy, the use of black units would contribute to the Union's success, as significant military victories in the summer of 1863 marked a turning point in the war.

The Emancipation Proclamation

Abraham Lincoln fully understood the military and political advantages that freeing fugitive slaves and employing them as military labor and support personnel gave the Union cause. He was also aware that recasting the war as a fight against slavery could have diplomatic benefits. In Great Britain especially, where antislavery sentiment was strong, a war aim of ending slavery would enhance the political and moral weight of the Union's cause. It would also seriously undercut the Confederacy's push for diplomatic recognition in Europe.

Through the middle of 1862, Lincoln publicly continued his cautious, pragmatic approach to the question of slavery and the status of refugee slaves. Yet he was privately making plans to take a bolder step. On July 22, he surprised his cabinet by announcing his intention to free all the slaves of those in rebellion against the Union. This act would be a military proclamation issued under his authority as commander in chief. At the suggestion of one of his cabinet members, however, Lincoln agreed to withhold the announcement until after a Union victory on the battlefield, so as not to appear desperate or beholden in any way to the fugitive slaves or to abolitionist pressure.

The Union victory on September 17, 1862, at Antietam Creek, near Sharpsburg, Maryland, gave Lincoln the occasion he needed. Union forces repelled a Confederate offensive, and General Robert E. Lee's army retreated back into Virginia. The victory proved significant, not only for reversing Union military fortunes but also for dissuading Britain from recognizing the Confederacy. Five days later, on September 22, 1862, Lincoln issued the **preliminary Emancipation Proclamation**.

This proclamation gave the Confederates one hundred days — until January 1, 1863 — to cease their rebellion. If they did not, all their slaves would be freed on that date. The proclamation drew its authority from the additional article of war approved in March 1862 and the Second Confiscation Act. The proclamation maintained Lincoln's two-pronged approach to the problem of slavery — compensation and colonization. It recommended that Congress offer loyal slave states monetary assistance to enable them to adopt gradual or immediate emancipation plans. It also offered continued support for the colonization of freedpeople outside the United States.

The Confederacy scorned the preliminary Emancipation Proclamation, and no person or state ceased its rebellion. On January 1, 1863, Lincoln signed the final **Emancipation Proclamation** (see Appendix). This proclamation referenced the preliminary one, with its determination to free the slaves in states or parts of states still in rebellion against the United States as of January 1, and then listed the regions in which the slaves "shall be then, thenceforward, and forever free." Consistent with Lincoln's cautious and pragmatic approach to the war and his strenuous efforts to maintain the loyalty of those within the Union who still had slaves, the Emancipation Proclamation had clear and functional limits. It did not free the enslaved in places that the Union had actual control over: the border states, pro-Union areas within the Confederacy, and former Confederate areas under Union control.

Furthermore, the proclamation said nothing about compensation or colonization, only that military and naval authorities would recognize and maintain the freedom of "said persons," who were urged "to abstain from all violence" and to "labor faithfully for reasonable wages." Finally, it declared that "such persons of suitable condition" were to be "received into the armed service." Lincoln ended the proclamation with an invocation: "Upon this act, sincerely believed to be an act of justice, warranted by the Constitution, upon military necessity, I invoke the considerate judgment of mankind, and the gracious favor of Almighty God." The war to save the Union thus officially became a war also to free the slaves. It was clear that now, when the Union was restored, it would be a nation of free people, a nation in which slavery would not exist.

In the North, blacks and their allies ardently embraced the Emancipation Proclamation. At the grand celebration on January 1, 1863, at the Israel Bethel AME Church in Washington, D.C., Pastor Henry McNeal Turner witnessed a community overcome with joy: "Men squealed, women fainted, dogs barked, white and colored people shook hands, songs were sung. . . . Great processions of colored and white men marched to and fro and passed in front of the White House and congratulated President Lincoln on his proclamation. . . . It was indeed a time of times, and a half time, nothing like it will ever be seen again in this life."[16]

For blacks in captured Confederate territory now under Union control, Emancipation Proclamation celebrations also were widespread, joyous, and hopeful. In Hampton, Virginia, members of the large free black community that had grown up around Fortress Monroe gathered for a reading of the proclamation. They met under a large tree — now known as the Emancipation Oak and still standing on the campus of Hampton University — where a school for former slaves had been conducted since 1861 by Mary S. Peake. In the South Carolina Sea Islands, the high point of the long celebration was unplanned. Colonel Thomas Wentworth Higginson, an abolitionist from Massachusetts and commander of the First Regiment of South Carolina Volunteers, received a Union flag for his unit, which was composed of former slaves. As he received the flag, the freedpeople burst into a spontaneous rendition of "My Country, 'Tis of Thee." "It was a touching and beautiful incident, and sent a thrill through all our hearts," recalled Charlotte Forten.[17]

Slaves under Confederate control who got word of the Emancipation Proclamation kept their responses secret so as not to enrage Confederates and provoke retaliation. Many masters worked hard to prevent word of the proclamation from reaching their slaves, some even relocating their operations to more isolated or more secure Confederate areas, where plantation life continued as usual. The former Texas slave Felix Haywood recalled, "The War didn't change nothin'." In fact, he said, "sometimes you didn't knowed it was goin' on. It was the endin' of it that made the difference."[18]

Nevertheless, news of emancipation continued to spread as Union forces advanced. While the proclamation did not immediately free any slaves still under Confederate control, it transformed the conflict by making emancipation a central war aim, linking emancipation with Union victory. Outside the United States, emancipation was applauded in Britain and France, and it ended Confederate hopes for European diplomatic recognition.

The U.S. Colored Troops

At the beginning of the war, black men and black militia units had been officially excluded from service in the Union army, but some Union commanders in the field had seen the merit of turning contrabands into soldiers. In August 1862, General Hunter finally received permission to recruit freedmen in the Sea Islands, and one hundred signed up to become the First South Carolina Volunteers (later the Thirty-Third U.S. Colored

Troops). In September, General Butler organized the First Louisiana by converting the Louisiana Native Guards—a unit of free blacks in New Orleans that had formed to serve in the Confederate army but had been refused—into a federal unit. Neither regiment saw action until after the Emancipation Proclamation officially declared that blacks would be received into the Union army and the War Department, on May 22, 1863, created a bureau to oversee the new **U.S. Colored Troops.**

In the North, recruitment of free blacks was slow at first. While some black men had already organized militia units, believing that wartime service would help promote emancipation and substantiate their claims to full citizenship, others were less confident. The *Liberator* reported that a well-attended recruitment meeting on April 27, 1863, in New York City's Shiloh Baptist Church had produced only one recruit, despite stirring speeches by Henry Highland Garnet and Frederick Douglass. One audience member explained that the problem "was not cowardice . . . but a proper respect for their own manhood. If the Government wanted their services, let it guarantee to them all the rights of citizens and soldiers, and, instead of one man, he would insure them 5,000 men in twenty days."[19] That summer, Douglass stepped up his efforts to promote black military service, emphasizing its links with citizenship. "Once let the black man get upon his person the brass letters U.S.," he announced, "let him get an eagle on his button, and a musket on his shoulder, and bullets in his pocket, and there is no power on earth or under the earth which can deny that he has earned the right of citizenship in the United States."[20]

Ultimately, 179,000 black men enlisted in the U.S. Colored Troops, almost 10 percent of all who served in the Union army. A few, such as Martin R. Delany, were commissioned officers; 7,122 were noncommissioned officers. Another 29,500 black men served in the Union navy. Among them was Robert Smalls, who by the end of 1863 was captain of a Union vessel. In one estimate, blacks participated in almost 250 battles. They suffered more than 37,000 casualties. Seventeen black soldiers and four black sailors received the Congressional Medal of Honor. (See By the Numbers: African Americans in the Union Military.)

This distinguished record of black military wartime service evolved within the limits imposed by racial prejudice. The military hierarchy reinforced the racial hierarchy of American society. Black units were invariably led by white officers; the idea of black officers leading troops, especially white troops, was totally unacceptable. The white officers who led black troops varied in motivation, quality, and effectiveness, but most barely tolerated their black subordinates. One exception was Robert Gould Shaw, colonel of the Fifty-Fourth Massachusetts Volunteer Infantry Regiment, a unit raised by abolitionists. The first such black unit to be organized, it included two of Frederick Douglass's sons.

Black soldiers fighting for the Union endured many inequities. White officers, many of whom questioned the fitness and bravery of black soldiers, assigned them to the most difficult noncombat duties, such as building fortifications and manning supply lines. These officers often mismanaged their troops, resulting in inept battlefield

BY THE NUMBERS   African Americans in the Union Military

African Americans had a distinguished record of military service and played a significant role in Union victory. Of those who served in the Union army, 33,000 were free blacks from Union states; 42,000 were former slaves and free men from border states; 99,000 were former slaves from Confederate states; and the rest were most likely southern free blacks. Another 29,500 black men served in the Union navy. Black troops accounted for 10 percent of the Union army and nearly 25 percent of the navy.

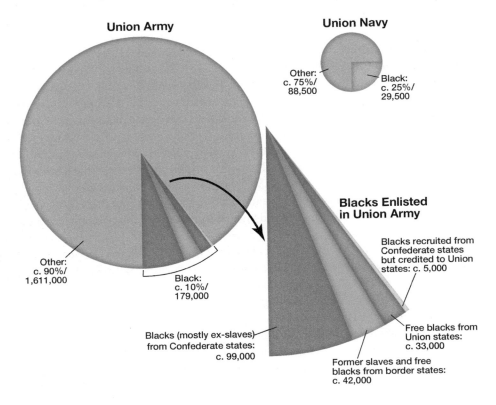

Union Army

Other:
c. 90%/
1,611,000

Black:
c. 10%/
179,000

Union Navy

Other:
c. 75%/
88,500

Black:
c. 25%/
29,500

**Blacks Enlisted
in Union Army**

Blacks recruited from
Confederate states
but credited to Union
states: c. 5,000

Blacks (mostly ex-slaves)
from Confederate states:
c. 99,000

Former slaves and free
blacks from border states:
c. 42,000

Free blacks from
Union states:
c. 33,000

maneuvers and excessive casualty rates. Lack of good training and equipment also contributed to the high number of black fatalities.

Black troops were also at greater risk than white troops because of Confederate policy, which regarded black Union soldiers as instigators of slave insurrections. As such, they were subject to enslavement or execution upon capture. At Fort Pillow, Tennessee, the killing of scores of black prisoners of war by their Confederate captors on April 12, 1864, sparked much controversy. The Confederates denied the incident, but the northern press called it a massacre and used it as propaganda to promote the war effort. The threat of capture and possible enslavement, torture, or murder at the hands of Confederates made black enlistment in the Union army itself an act of courage.

Finally, pay inequities caused considerable resentment. Black soldiers received $10 a month, with $3 deducted for food and clothing, regardless of rank. By contrast,

Martin R. Delany

This hand-colored lithograph features the talented and ambitious Delany in full regalia as the Union military's highest-ranking African American. Toward the end of the war, Delany was appointed field commander and commissioned as a major in the 104th Regiment U.S. Colored Troops. Delany had been active in the northern campaign to recruit black soldiers, and in an earlier, less hopeful moment, he had advocated emigration to Africa. After the war, Delany became a prominent Reconstruction politician in South Carolina.

Martin Robinson Delany (1812–1885), Union army officer. c. 1865. Hand-colored lithograph, 55.2 x 43.8 cm (21¾ in. x 17¼ in.). National Portrait Gallery, Smithsonian Institution, Washington, D.C., USA/Art Resource, NY.

MAJOR MARTIN R. DELANY, U.S.A.

white privates received $13 and free food and clothing, and their pay increased with promotions. So strong was the resentment among the soldiers of the Fifty-Fourth Massachusetts Regiment that they refused to accept any pay at all until the pay for whites and blacks was equalized. In one black regiment in Jacksonville, Florida, the issue of pay inequity sparked a mutiny in which the leader, Sergeant William Walker, a former refugee slave, was executed. On June 15, 1864, Congress passed legislation that equalized the pay of black and white soldiers and offered back pay to all those who had been underpaid or had refused pay in protest. Following this remedy, the recruitment of black soldiers picked up significantly.

African Americans in the Major Battles of 1863

The U.S. Colored Troops helped the Union meet its mounting manpower needs, and when given the opportunity to fight, they fought heroically. The first black units in combat were the former Louisiana Native Guards, fighting for the Union as the African Brigade and soon designated the First Louisiana. Augmented by contrabands, the unit was assigned to the Mississippi River campaign that aimed to split the Confederacy in two. On May 27, these black soldiers participated in the assault on Port Hudson, Louisiana, where they proved they were as courageous as any white soldiers. "The undaunted heroism, and the great endurance of the negro, as exhibited that day," the former slave William Wells Brown later wrote, "created a new chapter in American history for the colored man."[21] On June 7, armed only with old muskets, they defended the Union outpost at Milliken's Bend, Louisiana, causing Charles Dana, assistant secretary of war, to observe, "The bravery of the blacks in the battle at Milliken's Bend completely revolutionized the sentiment of the army with regard to the employment of negro troops. I heard prominent officers who . . . had sneered at the idea of the negroes fighting express themselves after that as heartily in favor of it."[22] Nevertheless, the battle at Milliken's Bend also revealed the risks black troops faced, as several who were captured by Confederates were sold as slaves, and a few were rumored to have been murdered.[23] On July 4, Vicksburg, Mississippi, the last major Confederate stronghold on the Mississippi River, surrendered to General Ulysses S. Grant, and a few days later Lincoln announced that the Mississippi River, now entirely in Union hands, "again goes unvexed to the sea."[24]

Lincoln had much to rejoice about on that Fourth of July. Just days before, Union armies had turned back another Confederate invasion. General Lee's march into Maryland and Pennsylvania was stopped at Gettysburg, where a three-day battle, on July 1–3, resulted in a decisive Union victory. No soldiers of the U.S. Colored Troops participated in the battle, and the services of black units organized in Philadelphia and Harrisburg by Octavius Catto and Thomas Morris Chester, respectively, were rejected. Nevertheless, large numbers of contrabands and free blacks aided the Army of the Potomac. Fearing capture and enslavement, hundreds of Pennsylvania free blacks fled in advance of Lee's march north, but a few were seized and sold.

The most notable battle that July for the U.S. Colored Troops took place in South Carolina. On July 18, the Fifty-Fourth Massachusetts led a second assault on Fort Wagner in Charleston harbor. Despite heavy losses, including the death of their commander, Colonel Shaw, the men of the Fifty-Fourth showed uncommon valor, charging the Confederate batteries in waves. Lewis Douglass, one of Frederick Douglass's sons, wrote to his wife, "I wish we had a hundred thousand colored troops," because then "we would put an end to this war."[25] The bravery of the Fifty-Fourth excited the northern imagination. The unit's performance, said the *New York Tribune*, "made Fort Wagner such a name to the colored race as Bunker Hill has been for ninety years to the white Yankees"[26] (Map 7.1).

In November, Lincoln traveled to Gettysburg to dedicate a national cemetery honoring the fallen soldiers buried there. His short speech, delivered on November 19, 1863, is one of the best-known and most cherished speeches in American history. By announcing "a new birth of freedom" for an American nation "conceived in Liberty, and dedicated to the proposition that all men are created equal,"[27] it fixed forever the noblest goal of the war. Originally aimed to suppress a rebellion and preserve the Union, it was now being fought to preserve democracy and abolish slavery.

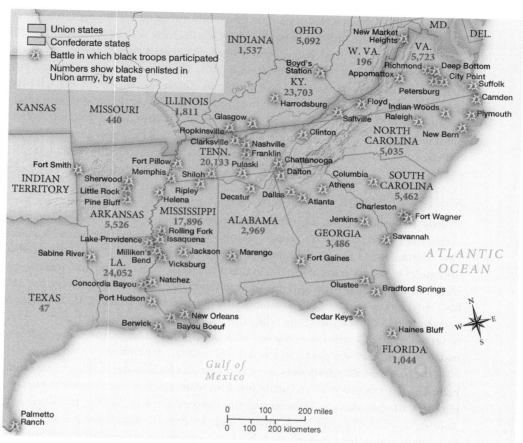

MAP 7.1   African Americans in Battle

Black troops played a pivotal role in the Union war effort, enlisting in the army and navy in significant numbers and participating in close to forty major battles. Their valiant efforts inspired black civilians to intensify their support for the Union cause. The impressive wartime service of black troops also sustained their claims and those of their people for full freedom and full U.S. citizenship. DATA SOURCE: *The Atlas of African-American History and Politics: From the Slave Trade to Modern Times,* by Arwin Smallwood and Jeffrey Elliot. Copyright © 1998 The McGraw-Hill Companies, Inc.

Home Fronts and War's End, 1863–1865

Lincoln's words in the Gettysburg Address reassured many African Americans, but not all were convinced that this change in rhetoric would dramatically change the quality of their lives. Northern Democrats objected to making emancipation a war goal, and in some areas of the North support for the war faltered. As civilians and resources were increasingly mobilized for the war effort, war-weariness set in, and opposition to Lincoln's conduct of the war grew. Congress tried to block his plans for reintegrating former Confederate areas and people into the Union. At the same time, deaths, desertions, and declining numbers of white volunteers forced the imposition of a military draft, despite the addition of new black troops. In New York City, resistance to the draft turned violent, and roving mobs of white men targeted black neighborhoods and institutions. It was clear that any restoration of the Union would need to address civil rights and equality in the North as well as the end of slavery in the South. Black leaders renewed their efforts, recognizing that the freedom struggle would not end with emancipation. In 1865, Union victory and the passage of a constitutional amendment forbidding slavery ensured freedom for all slaves. But for northern and southern blacks, both free and newly freed, the fight for citizenship and human dignity continued.

Riots and Restoration of the Union

Shortly after the Union's decisive victories at Gettysburg and Vicksburg, and just before the assault on Fort Wagner, Union troops were hastily transferred to New York City to put down a riot. A military draft instituted on March 3, 1863, had proved so unpopular in various parts of the North that it triggered violence. The draft was unpopular not only because many did not want to fight a war to end black slavery but also because they saw the draft as inequitable. The prosperous could pay $300 to purchase an exemption or hire a substitute, while the poor and working-class had no choice but to serve. On July 13, when newspapers published the names of the first draftees, chosen by lottery, a mob of white men attacked the Manhattan draft office.

The **New York City draft riots** spread quickly, and for four days roving white mobs, including large numbers of criminals and Irish working-class men, turned to ransacking black neighborhoods. They burned the Colored Orphan Asylum to the ground. Thousands of blacks were left homeless and destitute. Dozens were lynched; some were murdered in their homes. By July 15, as more federal troops arrived in the city, some directly from Gettysburg, the violence subsided.

The causes were deep-seated. Emancipation may have become a war aim, but for many whites it was not welcome. Many white soldiers resented being asked to fight and die to free the slaves. Many white working-class men and women feared that emancipation would mean a flood of black laborers coming north to take their jobs and undercut their wages and status.

The racist language of northern white Democratic politicians and the Democratic press inflamed these fears and tensions. Lincoln was denounced as a tyrant and the Emancipation Proclamation as unconstitutional. Democratic legislatures in Indiana, Illinois, and New Jersey raised formal objections to the war and passed peace resolutions. The language of the Illinois resolution revealed northern fears. After questioning the president's authority to proclaim emancipation, it argued that "the sudden, unconditional and violent liberation of 3,000,000 negro slaves" would have consequences that "cannot be contemplated without the most dismal foreboding of horror and dismay."[28]

The disturbances in New York City were not the only antiblack riots in the North during the war years. In 1862 and 1863, antiblack riots also rocked Brooklyn, New York — then a separate city — and Detroit. But the New York City riots were the worst, and black outrage was intense and widespread. "A gloom of infamy and shame will hang over New York for centuries," prophesied the AME Church's *Christian Recorder*.[29] After blasting local and state authorities for their failure to protect black people and black property, James W. C. Pennington called on blacks not to back down, but to redouble their efforts for full citizenship rights.[30] Events in New York City and elsewhere made it clear that emancipation would not mean racial equality.

These events also made it clear that the war's end would not mean harmony or even peace. Nevertheless, on December 8, 1863, Lincoln formally began to lay the groundwork for reuniting the Confederate and Union states in a stable postwar nation by issuing his **Proclamation of Amnesty and Reconstruction.** By this time, Louisiana, large stretches along the Mississippi River, and areas of Tennessee and Arkansas were in Union hands. To allow the former Confederate states to form pro-Union governments and reenter the Union, Lincoln officially pardoned all except high-ranking Confederate civil and military officials and decreed that their property should be restored to them, "except as to slaves." The proclamation directed that when voters equal to 10 percent of the votes cast in the 1860 election swore an oath of loyalty to the Union, they would be permitted to reestablish a state government. It also expressed the hope that the new state governments would recognize the needs of former slaves as "a laboring, landless, and homeless class" and would provide for their education.[31] This plan guided the reorganization of defeated Confederate areas until Lincoln's death sixteen months later.

Black Civilians at Work for the War

The Union's 1863 military draft made it clear that the initial enthusiasm for the war was over. Even earlier, in April 1862, the Confederate army had sought to solve its manpower shortage through conscription. The war had gone on much longer than anyone had expected, and shortages in military manpower meant that civilians, too, had to be mobilized for the war effort. Resources were strained on both sides, but especially in the South. From the beginning, black labor — free and slave — had been vital to the Confederate war effort. Blacks grew most of the food for Confederate troops. They loaded and carted goods and supplies. Through coercion and impressment, as well as slave hiring and assignment, they worked for the military by building roads, entrenchments, and fortifications. Blacks served as personal servants, cooks, foragers, and spies for Confederate soldiers and officers. But as increasing numbers of slaves fled to the Union lines and Union troops controlled increasing amounts of Confederate territory, the Confederacy weakened. By mid-1864, roughly 400,000 slaves, or almost 10 percent of the slave population, were no longer under Confederate control, and many were laboring for the Union.

To stop slave flight and solidify the slave system, southern whites strengthened slave patrols, clamped down on slave and free black mobility, and moved their slaves away from nearby war zones and Union-controlled areas. At the same time, to quell slave unrest and defections, particularly in places near Union-held areas, masters often yielded to slave demands. These included continuing, or even expanding, previous understandings that allowed slaves to farm their own plots and market their own crops.

African Americans Laboring for the Union
Here African American men are building a stockade in Alexandria, Virginia, to defend the Union Railroad Depot there and thus strengthen the defense of nearby Washington, D.C., against Confederate attack. Building such fortifications was essential to the Union war effort. In the Confederacy as well as the Union, African American civilians, both women and men, were an indispensable element of the labor force that performed such vital work as feeding and serving troops and building encampments and roads. *Photo by Andrew J. Russell/* *© Medford Historical Society Collection/Corbis.*

Some masters and slaves made arrangements such as dividing or sharing harvests, trading wages for labor, and renting land and houses.

As most runaway slaves, at least early on, were males and wartime conditions further cut into the availability of male slave labor, the work of female slaves became increasingly important. Many shouldered additional field work in addition to the domestic work they traditionally performed. More than ever, they were responsible for sustaining their households. Like all slaves who remained under Confederate control, they weighed their options and waited for their chances. Especially toward the end of the war, increasing numbers of slave women, with their children, also began to seek freedom behind Union lines. Elizabeth Botume, a northern teacher sent to the Sea Islands by the New England Freedmen's Aid Society, remembered seeing a refugee mother "striding along with her hominy pot, in which was a live chicken, poised on her head. One child was on her back, with its arms tightly clasped around her neck, and its feet about her waist, and under each arm was a smaller child."[32] In refugee camps, women tried to hold families together.

As an increasing number of slaves fled the Confederacy, their contributions to the Union war effort grew. Not only black soldiers and sailors but also another 200,000 black women and men ultimately traveled with the Union armies over the course of the war and labored in nonmilitary capacities. Both men and women served as servants and spies; men served primarily as road builders, carpenters, wagon drivers, livestock tenders, and foragers; women served primarily as cooks, laundresses, teachers, and nurses. Many individuals often filled many roles at once, working in various capacities depending on what was needed. For example, Harriet Tubman was a scout, spy, teacher, and nurse during the war, even as she continued to assist slaves escaping to freedom. The former slave Susie King Taylor started a school in the Sea Islands and served as a teacher, nurse, and laundress for the all-black Thirty-Third U.S. Colored Troops. In the Confederate White House in Richmond, Mary Elizabeth Bowser worked undercover as a house servant and spied for the Union. Before she escaped toward the end of the war, she tried — unsuccessfully — to burn down the Confederate White House. In the Lincoln White House in Washington, Elizabeth Keckley served as the First Lady's dressmaker and confidante.

In 1862, Keckley used her connections to establish a charitable organization for assisting the contrabands who crowded into the Union capital. This Contraband Relief Association was supported by many prominent abolitionists, including Henry Highland Garnet, Frederick Douglass, and Sojourner Truth, who also raised food and money for black regiments. A report of the association explained, "Our work has been to provide shelter, food, clothing, medicines and nourishments for them, we have also buried their dead, and in fact, done all we could . . . to alleviate their sufferings, and help them on towards a higher plane of civilization."[33] Black women were prominent in the work of northern freedpeople's aid societies as well, such as the Contraband Committee of the Mother Bethel AME Church in Philadelphia and the Freedmen's Friend Society in Brooklyn. From the battlefields and war-torn plantations of the South to the military hospitals and contraband camps in the North, it was often the unpaid work of black women that alleviated suffering and provided humanitarian aid.

Union Victory, Slave Emancipation, and the Renewed Struggle for Equality

Despite the Union's battlefield successes in 1864, Lincoln's reelection was by no means assured. Congressional opposition to the leniency of his "10 percent plan" for the reintegration of former Confederates and Confederate regions into the Union had culminated in the passage on July 2, 1864, of the **Wade-Davis Bill**, which challenged the president's authority. This bill required that before a state government could be reestablished, a majority of the state's white male citizens had to take an ironclad oath that they had never supported the Confederacy. After Lincoln refused to sign the bill, its sponsors published a manifesto that signaled a looming constitutional crisis between the executive and legislative branches over what came to be called Reconstruction.

During the summer of 1864, opposition to the war and to Lincoln's conduct of it grew. Large numbers of Democrats pushed to end the war immediately. Within Lincoln's

Elizabeth Keckley
Best known as First Lady Mary Todd Lincoln's seamstress and confidante from 1861 to 1868, Elizabeth Keckley was born into slavery but achieved economic success and respectability as a dressmaker for elite white women, a group of whom loaned her the money to buy her freedom. Keckley was an abolitionist, the founder and leader of the Washington, D.C.–based Contraband Relief Association, a member of Washington's black elite, and a noted memoirist. Her *Behind the Scenes: or, Thirty Years a Slave, and Four Years in the White House* (1868) is an illuminating look at her fascinating life, notably her rise from slavery to freedom and her intimate interactions with the Lincoln family. *Picture History/Newscom.*

own Republican Party, John C. Frémont, who had been relieved of his command in Missouri, strenuously criticized the president for his overly cautious prosecution of the war. Frémont ran against Lincoln as a Radical Republican, splitting the party until withdrawing from the race in favor of Lincoln in September 1864. To gain Democratic and border state support, Lincoln chose as his vice presidential running mate the former Democratic senator and military governor of Tennessee, Andrew Johnson. In opposition to the Radical Republicans, Lincoln's faction of the Republican Party renamed itself the National Union Party. The Democratic candidate was former Union general George B. McClellan. Lincoln and Johnson won by only 400,000 votes out of 4 million cast. General William Tecumseh Sherman's victories as he marched through Georgia contributed to Lincoln's slim margin of victory.

At Lincoln's second inauguration, on March 4, 1865, the proud black regiments that marched in front of him underscored how much had changed in four years of war. In his address, Lincoln acknowledged that slavery had been the cause of the war, which he cast as God's punishment for the national sin of slavery. Yet he ended with a vision of reconciliation: "With malice toward none, with charity for all, with firmness in the right as God gives us to see the right, let us strive on to finish the work we are in, to bind up the nation's wounds, . . . to do all which may achieve and cherish a just and lasting peace among ourselves and with all nations."[34]

While Lincoln's approach to former Confederates was conciliatory, allowing for pardons and the return of property, it was already being countermanded by his generals in the field. On January 16, 1865, General Sherman issued **Special Field Order 15**, which granted confiscated and abandoned Confederate land to former slaves. Each head of household could receive up to forty acres of land along the Florida, Georgia, and South

Carolina coast, and later a few freedpeople received army mules for working the land. These arrangements granted the freedpeople possessory titles to the land until Congress ruled on the validity of the titles. These arrangements also aimed to facilitate the transition of the freedpeople to independent livelihoods by providing them with farms and a stable economic basis to sustain their freedom.

The same concerns moved Congress, in March 1865, to establish the **Freedmen's Bureau**, a new government agency charged with enabling the former slaves' transition to freedom, assisting them with food, clothing, and shelter. Ultimately, the bureau also supervised and enforced labor contracts, settled disputes, helped establish schools, and set up courts to protect ex-slaves' civil rights.[35]

Meanwhile, the Confederacy tried to avoid the defeat that now seemed inevitable by considering a plan to emancipate and arm slaves. Debate over the plan recognized the tremendous military advantage the Union had gained by arming fugitive slaves. President Davis initially resisted the idea, but General Robert E. Lee endorsed it. On March 13, the Confederate Congress passed the measure and Davis signed it, but by then the war was nearly over. On April 9, Lee surrendered to Grant at Appomattox Court House, Virginia, and other Confederate commanders soon followed suit. Before the Confederates' final capitulation, however, President Lincoln was shot on April 14 by Confederate sympathizer John Wilkes Booth and died the next morning. For a nation ravaged by four years of war, peace and reconciliation without a strong national leader would be even more difficult than it would have been with Lincoln at the helm.

With the Confederate surrender, slaves in the Confederate states were ostensibly freed, but many remained in bondage until Union soldiers reached them to enforce the terms of the Emancipation Proclamation. In Texas, slaves did not receive the news of freedom until June 19, 1865, now commemorated as the African American holiday Juneteenth. The former slaves' responses ran the gamut, from joyous celebrations to fear of the unknown. Texan Richard Carruthers recalled, "That the day I shouted," and fellow Texan Felix Haywood remembered that "everybody went wild." Many former slaves interpreted the moment of emancipation as evidence of God's deliverance. A Virginia woman claimed, "De Lord can make Heaven out of Hell any time, I do believe."[36] But mixed emotions, uncertainty, confusion, and anxiety were common. One former slave in Mississippi said, "Dey all had diffe'nt ways o' thinkin' 'bout it. Mos'ly though dey jus' lak me, dey didn't know zackly what it meant." A former slave in South Carolina remembered that "some were sorry, some hurt, but a few were silent and glad."[37] Some preferred the comfort of the familiar, even the patterns of mutual dependency between whites and blacks that slavery bred. "I was a-farin' pretty well in de kitchen," Texan Aleck Trimble said. "I didn't tink I eber see better times dan what dem was, and I ain't." But most freedpeople agreed with the Texas woman who concluded that "in slavery I owns nothin' and never owns nothin'. In freedom I's own de home and raise de family. All dat cause worriment and in slavery I have no worriment, but I takes de freedom."[38]

Between September 1864 and February 1865, new state constitutions in Louisiana, Maryland, Missouri, and Tennessee abolished slavery. In February, Congress approved the **Thirteenth Amendment**, which abolished slavery everywhere in the Union, and sent

Colored Troops under General Wild, Liberating Slaves in North Carolina, 1864
Amid the tumult of the Civil War, the enslaved experienced emancipation in various ways. An especially moving moment transpired whenever black troops, functioning as a black liberation army, helped free their enslaved brethren. This illustration shows a black soldier shaking the hand of a newly freed slave. The image projects happiness, thanksgiving, and racial solidarity. *The Granger Collection, New York.*

it to the states for ratification. When the amendment was ratified on December 18, 1865, slaves in Kentucky and Delaware were finally free (Map 7.2). The amendment was the culmination of a war initially undertaken to preserve the Union before being transformed into a war to end slavery.

But freedom did not mean equality. Free African Americans living in the North had struggled for civil rights for generations, and their efforts had continued during the war. In Philadelphia, for example, Octavius Catto launched a campaign to desegregate the streetcars, which finally succeeded in 1867. Black activism took place at the state and national levels as well. In California, blacks organized a petition campaign against a state law that prohibited them from testifying against whites in court. Similar laws existed in Oregon, Indiana, Illinois, and Iowa. This overtly discriminatory prohibition allowed unscrupulous whites to take advantage of blacks in shady court dealings. The California petition drive succeeded in 1863, when the state legislature voided the law.

In Illinois, blacks challenged an 1853 law that required African Americans settling in the state to pay a heavy fine. If they failed to do so, they were subject to arrest

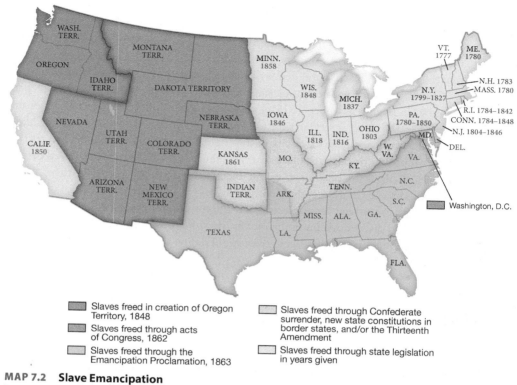

Slaves freed in creation of Oregon Territory, 1848

Slaves freed through acts of Congress, 1862

Slaves freed through the Emancipation Proclamation, 1863

Slaves freed through Confederate surrender, new state constitutions in border states, and/or the Thirteenth Amendment

Slaves freed through state legislation in years given

MAP 7.2 Slave Emancipation

The role of the federal government in the abolition of slavery was neither simple nor straightforward. This map illustrates key steps in the complex process of national state-sponsored emancipation as it unfolded between 1848 and 1865. In those states with gradual emancipation laws, the date spans show the year in which the initial emancipation statutes were passed followed by the year in which slavery actually ended.

and forced labor for the highest bidder in order to pay the fine. Until 1863, the law was seldom enforced. That year, however, eight blacks were arrested under it, and seven were incarcerated and then further victimized as forced laborers. In response, the Repeal Association led by John Jones, the wealthiest black man in Chicago, mounted a vigorous campaign to have the law overturned. The campaign collected more than 11,000 signatures, and in February 1865 the Illinois legislature repealed the law.

At the national level, the National Convention of Colored Men, held in Syracuse, New York, in October 1864, revived the black convention movement. Frederick Douglass served as president of the Syracuse convention, but other black leaders, such as John S. Rock and John Mercer Langston, also made their presence felt. The 145 delegates, from both northern and southern states, endorsed emancipation, legal equality without regard to race, and black male suffrage. They also created the **National Equal Rights League** to advocate for these goals. Like the free black organizations of the antebellum era, the league emphasized moral reform and self-help, aiming "to encourage sound morality, education, temperance, frugality, industry, and promote everything that pertains to a well-ordered and dignified life."[39] To increase the league's influence, black leaders quickly formed state and local auxiliaries that attracted many members. The war correspondent Thomas Morris Chester, for example, was able to join the society in Harrisburg, Pennsylvania, directly upon his return from the front.

The U.S. government also took steps to reverse some inequities. The State Department began issuing passports to blacks, ignoring the nullification of black citizenship asserted in the *Dred Scott* decision (1857). In 1865, Massachusetts senator Charles Sumner, a staunch ally of black citizenship rights, led the successful effort to end the forty-year prohibition against blacks carrying the U.S. mail. Sumner also paved the way for John S. Rock to become the first black man accepted to argue cases before the U.S. Supreme Court in early 1865.

Though important, these piecemeal triumphs did not dramatically alter antiblack prejudice and discrimination in the North. They did, however, solidify black commitment to the long freedom struggle that would define the next generations of African Americans, both north and south.

CONCLUSION

Emancipation and Equality

On New Year's Eve 1862, Frederick Douglass gathered with more than three thousand people at the Tremont Temple in Boston, and later at the Twelfth Baptist Church, to celebrate the Emancipation Proclamation. Speaking at Tremont, he called the gathering a "worthy celebration of the first step on the part of the nation in its departure from the thraldom of the ages."[40] As evidenced by this lukewarm statement, many abolitionists were disappointed in the proclamation, for several reasons. It had been too long in coming; it pertained only to slaves in regions under Confederate control and so freed almost no one; and it seemed more a military necessity than an affirmation of moral right, the intent being to harm slaveholders more than to help slaves. Yet others rejoiced that it made emancipation a war aim and held out hope for the future.[41]

At the beginning of the war, Lincoln avoided addressing slavery directly. He had to move cautiously to retain the loyalty of the border states, where slavery still existed. Although he pressured them to end slavery, none did so. Congress, however, acted to end slavery in all U.S. territories and in the District of Columbia, where Lincoln's preference for the compensation of slave owners and the colonization of slaves was written into the legislation.

Yet even as Lincoln moved cautiously, slaves were themselves forcing the issue of emancipation. By taking advantage of wartime conditions to flee to Union lines in ever-increasing numbers, they compelled Union commanders to make decisions regarding their status. Weeks after the war began, General Benjamin Butler declared that the slaves who had fled to Fortress Monroe for protection were "contraband of war" and refused to return them to their owners. Other commanders made similar decisions.

In the Sea Islands of coastal South Carolina and Georgia, Union commanders oversaw what came to be called the Port Royal Experiment, a system whereby contrabands worked the plantations abandoned by their former owners. Teachers and missionaries from the North helped the ex-slaves make the transition to independent livelihoods. General David Hunter organized black fighting units that were eventually recognized by the War Department, and General Butler did the same in Louisiana.

The Emancipation Proclamation authorized the military recruitment of black men, and eventually black units constituted one-tenth of the U.S. army. Although they gained distinction for their battlefield successes, many black soldiers were assigned to work duties rather than to combat, and only when they protested did they receive the same pay as white troops. Nearly 40,000 African American men died for the Union; disease or infection killed 30,000, or three-fourths of those who died. This ultimate sacrifice, the brave wartime service of black troops, and strong black civilian support proved crucial to the Union victory and strengthened African American claims for full citizenship.

The Confederate defeat and the Thirteenth Amendment to the Constitution ended slavery forever. But as Frederick Douglass pointed out, emancipation was just "the first step"; it did not mean equality. African Americans intensified their efforts to achieve civil rights and citizenship. The fractured nation had to be reconstructed, and they were determined that it would incorporate them as equals.

CHAPTER 7 **REVIEW**

KEY TERMS

REVIEW QUESTIONS

1. Describe the attitudes and approaches of President Abraham Lincoln, Congress, and the Union military toward slavery and slave refugees in the early years of the war. How were their evolving policies and practices shaped by blacks' actions?

2. How did the war's aims shift from the defeat of the rebellion and the preservation of the Union to include emancipation? How might things have been different had the Confederate states responded differently to the preliminary Emancipation Proclamation?

3. How did the enlistment of black soldiers both challenge and reinforce existing racial hierarchies?

4. How did the Emancipation Proclamation promote black equality? In what ways did it fall short?

5. Describe the various contributions of African Americans to the Union war effort — both in the military and on the home front. How did their efforts further the war's aims and their own hopes of achieving freedom and citizenship rights?

Wartime and Emancipation

Wars often bring about huge and unintended social changes, and for African Americans, the outbreak of the Civil War in 1861 was fraught with both opportunities and dilemmas. The central role of slavery in the crises that led to hostilities gave hope to many that the war would end that institution. Yet the uncertainty surrounding the status of slaves who sought freedom by running to Union lines, and the Union's official policy through 1862 of refusing military service by African Americans presented free blacks with dilemmas about how best to respond to, or even take charge of, events that had the potential to be revolutionary.

The speeches excerpted here were two responses heard in Philadelphia, a city with a large and vigorous free black community. Alfred M. Green acknowledges that black men have not been recognized as citizens, yet he urges them to support the Union cause and to respond to President Lincoln's call for volunteers. When Green spoke in April 1861, it was not yet clear that black units would not be accepted in the Union army. Later in 1861, as black volunteers were rejected in what was described by many, white and black, as "a white man's war," Green continued to urge black men to fight for the right to serve. Some black men agreed with him, but others questioned the wisdom of seeking to serve in a military that did not want them and considered them more fit for labor than for combat. Isaiah C. Wears addresses the status of free black men in the American Republic more directly by challenging Lincoln's insinuations about black people as the cause of the war as well as the president's fondness for colonization schemes.

While some blacks debated the opportunities and dilemmas of the war, black women often responded to its uncertainties and demands by assuming new and expanded roles. In the South, as growing numbers of black men, particularly slaves and contrabands, joined the military and the war effort, black women, particularly slaves and contrabands, were called on to do more to keep households and plantations running and to keep their families together. Some used new responsibilities to gain greater control over their lives. Slave women who fled to Union lines took on new roles, too, working in a variety of ways to aid the Union cause. Similarly, free black women in the North strongly supported the war effort on the home front. Susie King Taylor, a slave and then a contraband, served a black military unit in the Sea Islands as a teacher and a nurse. Like many black women during the Civil War, Taylor took on a new, expanded, and empowering set of wartime roles even as she continued to perform the traditional woman's role of serving the needs of others.

The moment of emancipation continues to live on in visual memory. The moment of emancipation was not the same as its meaning, however. What freedom actually meant was much more complicated, emerging only as it was lived in the months and years after slaves were emancipated. The images included in this Document Project offer insights into both the moment and the meaning of emancipation. An especially signifi- cant moment of freedom in black memory — though it actually affected only a small number of slaves — was New Year's Day 1863, when the Emancipation Proclamation went into effect. In *Watch Meeting — Dec. 31st — Waiting for the Hour* (also called *The*

Hour of Emancipation), the New England painter William Tolman Carlton (1816–1888) envisions how slaves or contrabands might have looked as they waited for midnight, when the new year would begin and slaves (at least in theory) would be freed. Two photographs showing Private Hubbard Pryor before and after enlisting in the U.S. Colored Troops suggest that enlistment helped free him. *Freedmen's Memorial* is one of the most famous artistic representations of Abraham Lincoln as the "Great Emancipator."

Alfred M. Green | *Let Us . . . Take Up the Sword, 1861*

ALFRED M. GREEN, a Philadelphia schoolteacher, gave this speech to an assembly of black men in Philadelphia on April 20, 1861, just a few days after Lincoln's call for 75,000 volunteers to put down the insurrection. Green urges an enthusiastic response, pointing to the patriotism of black men who fought in previous wars, despite "past grievances." What other arguments does he give in support of black military service?

The time has arrived in the history of the great Republic when we may again give evidence to the world of the bravery and patriotism of a race, in whose hearts burns the love of country, of freedom, and of civil and religious toleration. It is these grand principles that enable men, however proscribed, when possessed of true patriotism, to say: "My country, right or wrong, I love thee still!"

It is true, the brave deeds of our fathers, sworn and subscribed to by the immortal Washington of the Revolution of 1776, and of Jackson and others in the War of 1812, have failed to bring us into recognition as citizens, enjoying those rights so dearly bought by those noble and patriotic sires.

It is true, that our injuries in many respects are great; fugitive-slave laws, Dred Scott decisions, indictments for treason, and long and dreary months of imprisonment. . . .

Our duty, brethren, is not to cavil over past grievances. Let us not be derelict to duty in the time of need. While we remember the past, and regret that our present position in the country is

not such as to create within us that burning zeal and enthusiasm for the field of battle, which inspires other men in the full enjoyment of every civil and religious emolument, yet let us endeavor to hope for the future, and improve the present auspicious moment for creating anew our claims upon the justice and honor of the Republic; and, above all, let not the honor and glory achieved by our fathers be blasted or sullied by a want of true heroism among their sons. Let us, then, take up the sword, trusting in God, who will defend the right, remembering that these are other days than those of yore — that the world to-day is on the side of freedom and universal political equality.

That the war-cry of the howling leaders of Secession and treason is, let us drive back the advance guard of civil and religious freedom; let us have more slave territory; let us build stronger the tyrant system of slavery in the great American Republic. Remember, too, that your very presence among the troops of the North would inspire your oppressed brethren of the South with zeal for the overthrow of the tyrant system, and confidence in the armies of the living God — the God of truth, justice, and equality to all men.

SOURCE: *Philadelphia Press*, April 22, 1861, in *Letters and Discussions on the Formation of Colored Regiments*, by Alfred M. Green (1862; repr., Philadelphia: Rhistoric Publications, 1969), 3–4.

Isaiah C. Wears | *The Evil Injustice of Colonization, 1862*

Lincoln's own racism and his keen awareness of the pervasiveness of white racism made him unable to envision a multiracial society. These realities shaped his views on emancipation. Until the Emancipation Proclamation of January 1863, his emancipation plans always involved promoting colonization. Meeting with black leaders on August 14, 1862, Lincoln stated, "But for your race among us there could not be war, although many men engaged on either side do not care for you one way or the other. Nevertheless, I repeat, without the institution of Slavery and the colored race as a basis, the war could not have an existence. It is better for us both, therefore, to be separated."[42] The next day, at a meeting of the Statistical Association of the Colored People of Philadelphia, the group's president, ISAIAH C. WEARS (1822–1900), challenged Lincoln's ideas. What reasons does Wears give for arguing that Lincoln is in error?

To be asked, after so many years of oppression and wrong have been inflicted in a land and by a people who have been so largely enriched by the black man's toil, to pull up stakes in a civilized and Christian nation and to go to an uncivilized and barbarous nation, simply to gratify an unnatural wicked prejudice emanating from slavery, is unreasonable and anti-Christian in the extreme.

How unaccountably strange it seems, that wise men familiar with the history of this country, with the history of slavery, with the rebellion and its merciless outrages, yet are apparently totally ignorant of the true cause of the war — or, if not ignorant, afraid or ashamed to charge the guilt where it belongs. . . .

Says the President: The colored race are the cause of the war. So were the children of Israel the cause of the troubles of Egypt. So was Christ the cause of great commotions in Judea, in this same sense; and those identified with Him were considered of the baser sort, and really unfit for citizenship.

But surely the President did not mean to say that our race was the cause of the war, but the occasion thereof.

If black men are here in the way of white men, they did not come here of their own accord. Their presence is traceable to the white man's lust for power, love of oppression and disregard of the plain teachings of the Lord Jesus Christ, whose rule enjoins upon all men to "do unto others as they would be done by." . . .

But it is not the Negro that is the cause of the war; it is the unwillingness on the part of the American people to do the race simple justice. It is not social equality to be made the equal of the white man, to have kind masters to provide for him, or to find for him congenial homes in Africa or Central America that he needs, but he desires not to be robbed of his labor — to be deprived of his God-given rights.

The effect of this scheme of colonization, we fear, will be to arouse prejudice and to increase enmity against us, without bringing with it the remedy proposed or designed.

Repentance is more needed on the part of our oppressors than anything else. . . .

. . . And it seems reasonable to infer that the nation shall not again have peace and prosperity until prejudice, selfishness and slavery are sorely punished in the nation.

SOURCE: Philip S. Foner and Robert James Branham, eds., *Lift Every Voice: African American Oratory, 1787–1900* (Tuscaloosa: University of Alabama Press, 1998), 375–77.

Susie King Taylor | *Reminiscences of My Life in Camp, 1902*

SUSIE KING TAYLOR (1848–1912) was a Georgia slave who in 1862 ran away with her cousins and uncles to a contraband camp in the Sea Islands. Mature, well spoken, and literate, she organized a school for contrabands. After she married Edward King, a black noncommissioned officer in the Thirty-Third U.S. Colored Troops, she was attached to the unit as a laundress. She also taught and nursed the soldiers. The following excerpt is from Taylor's memoir, published in 1902, which is the only published account of its kind. What did Taylor do for the soldiers and why?

When we arrived in Beaufort, Captain Trowbridge and the men he had enlisted went to camp at Old Fort, which they named "Camp Saxton." I was enrolled as laundress.

The first suits worn by the boys were red coats and pants, which they disliked very much, for, they said, "The rebels see us, miles away."

The first colored troops did not receive any pay for eighteen months, and the men had to depend wholly on what they received from the commissary, established by General Saxton. A great many of these men had large families, and as they had no money to give them, their wives were obliged to support themselves and children by washing for the officers of the gunboats and the soldiers, and making cakes and pies which they sold to the boys in camp. Finally, in 1863, the government decided to give them half pay, but the men would not accept this. They wanted "full pay" or nothing. They preferred rather to give their services to the state, which they did until 1864, when the government granted them full pay, with all the back pay due. . . .

On the first of January, 1863, we held services for the purpose of listening to the reading of President Lincoln's proclamation by Dr. W. H. Brisbane, and the presentation of two beautiful stands of colors, one from a lady in Connecticut, and the other from Rev. Mr. Cheever. The presentation speech was made by Chaplain French. It was a glorious day for us all, and we enjoyed every minute of it, and as a fitting close and the crowning event of this occasion we had a grand barbecue. A number of oxen were roasted whole, and we had a fine feast. Although not served as tastily or correctly as it would have been at home, yet it was enjoyed with keen appetites and relish. The soldiers had a good time. They sang or shouted "Hurrah!" all through the camp, and seemed overflowing with fun and frolic until taps were sounded, when many, no doubt, dreamt of this memorable day. . . .

I taught a great many of the comrades in Company E to read and write, when they were off duty. Nearly all were anxious to learn. My husband taught some also when it was convenient for him. I was very happy to know my efforts were successful in camp, and also felt grateful for the appreciation of my services. I gave my services willingly for four years and three months without receiving a dollar. I was glad, however, to be allowed to go with the regiment, to care for the sick and afflicted comrades. . . .

I learned to handle a musket very well while in the regiment, and could shoot straight and often hit the target. I assisted in cleaning the guns and used to fire them off, to see if the cartridges were dry, before cleaning and reloading, each day. I thought this great fun. I was also able to take a gun all apart, and put it together again. . . .

Fort Wagner being only a mile from our camp, I went there two or three times a week, and would go up on the ramparts to watch the gunners send their shells into Charleston (which they did every fifteen minutes), and had a full view of the city from that point. Outside of the fort were many skulls lying about; I have often moved them one side out of the path. The

SOURCE: Susie King Taylor, *Reminiscences of My Life in Camp: An African American Woman's Civil War Memoir*, ed. Catherine Clinton (Athens: University of Georgia Press, 2006), 15–16, 18, 21, 26, 31–32, 34–35.

comrades and I would have quite a debate as to which side the men fought on. Some thought they were the skulls of our boys; others thought they were the enemy's; but as there was no definite way to know, it was never decided which could lay claim to them. They were a gruesome sight, those fleshless heads and grinning jaws, but by this time I had become accustomed to worse things and did not feel as I might have earlier in my camp life.

It seems strange how our aversion to seeing suffering is overcome in war, — how we are able to see the most sickening sights, such as men with their limbs blown off and mangled by the deadly shells, without a shudder; and instead of turning away, how we hurry to assist in alleviating their pain, bind up their wounds, and press the cool water to their parched lips, with feelings only of sympathy and pity. . . .

Finally orders were received for the boys to prepare to take Fort Gregg. . . . I helped as many as I could to pack haversacks and cartridge boxes. . . .

About four o'clock, July 2, the charge was made. The firing could be plainly heard in camp. I hastened down to the landing and remained there until eight o'clock that morning. When the wounded arrived, or rather began to arrive, the first one brought in was Samuel Anderson of our company. He was badly wounded. Then others of our boys, some with their legs off, arm gone, foot off, and wounds of all kinds imaginable. They had to wade through creeks and marshes, as they were discovered by the enemy and shelled very badly. A number of the men were lost, some got fastened in the mud and had to cut off the legs of their pants, to free themselves. . . .

My work now began. I gave my assistance to try to alleviate their sufferings. I asked the doctor at the hospital what I could get for them to eat. They wanted soup, but that I could not get; but I had a few cans of condensed milk and some turtle eggs, so I thought I would try to make some custard. I had doubts as to my success, for cooking with turtle eggs was something new to me, but the adage has it, "Nothing ventured, nothing done," so I made a venture and the result was a very delicious custard. This I carried to the men, who enjoyed it very much. My services were given at all times for the comfort of these men. I was on hand to assist whenever needed. I was enrolled as company laundress, but I did very little of it, because I was always busy doing other things through camp, and was employed all the time doing something for the officers and comrades.

William Tolman Carlton | Watch Meeting — Dec. 31st — Waiting for the Hour, 1863

In *Watch Meeting — Dec. 31st — Waiting for the Hour* (also called *The Hour of Emancipation*), the white painter WILLIAM TOLMAN CARLTON depicts a watch night congregation of slaves or contrabands located in a barn or an outbuilding. About a dozen figures are gathered around a huge pocket watch illuminated by a flaring torch; the watch says five minutes to twelve. Notice the postures of those who have gathered. What are they doing? What emotions do their expressions convey? There is one white woman present. Who is she, and why did the painter place her in the scene? The painting is full of symbols. What book is the central figure looking at? What document is nailed to the wall? How do you interpret the figure of the torch holder with the coffle iron around his neck? After locating the cross in the upper left rafters, find a flag and a banjo. What do these objects symbolize? Although we can use this painting to understand the moment and meaning of emancipation as a New England abolitionist envisioned it,[43] how might the real moment for slaves and contrabands have been different?

The Hour of Emancipation, 1863, by William Tolman Carlton (1816–1888), oil on canvas. Private Collection/Photo © Christie's Images/ Bridgeman Images.

Private Hubbard Pryor, before and after Enlisting in the U.S. Colored Troops, 1864

The following side-by-side photographs show Private Hubbard Pryor literally transformed by his enlistment in the U.S. Colored Troops. Compare the two images, especially taking note of Pryor's dress, facial expression, and posture in each photo.

DOCUMENT PROJECT

Keep in mind that it was not yet a convention to smile for the camera. These paired portraits were consciously staged. Who might have staged them, and what was their purpose? What effect might they have had on those who viewed them?

Courtesy of the National Archives, Records of the Adjutant General's Office, c. 1775–c. 1928, ARC identifiers #849127 and #849136.

Freedmen's Memorial, 1876

Titled *Emancipation* but also known as *Freedmen's Memorial*, this sculpture stands in Lincoln Park on Capitol Hill in Washington, D.C. Created by THOMAS BALL (1819–1911), a white American artist best known for his monumental sculptures of American heroes, *Freedmen's Memorial* was erected with contributions from African Americans, beginning with $5 entrusted to a former master by a former slave to build a monument to the martyred president.[44] Significantly, it portrays Lincoln as "the Great Emancipator," holding out his hand over a kneeling, nearly naked freedman. Is Lincoln offering the freedman a blessing? Is he urging him to rise? A twenty-first-century critic has said, "It looks as if the 16th president is about to pet the man." What do you think? The monument has long been controversial. Frederick Douglass, who spoke at the dedication, was reported by one observer to have said that it "showed the Negro on his knees, when a more manly attitude would have been more indicative of freedom."[45]

The George F. Landegger Collection of District of Columbia Photographs in Carol M. Highsmith's America, Library of Congress, Prints and Photographs Division, Washington, D.C., LC-DIG-highsm-10341.

QUESTIONS FOR ANALYSIS

1. In 1861 and 1862, what choices did the Civil War offer free black men in the North? Why did Green and Wears argue the positions they did? By the end of the war, how had those choices changed, and how might the positions of Green and Wears have shifted?

2. What does Susie King Taylor's account reveal about the wartime labor of black women for the Union cause? What type of work did these women do? How are such tasks handled in the U.S. army today?

3. What does Taylor's account reveal about contraband camps and black military units in the South?

4. What do the watch meeting painting and the Hubbard Pryor photos tell us about similarities and differences in how the freedpeople themselves experienced emancipation and how others imagined emancipation?

5. *Freedmen's Memorial* depicts "the kneeling slave," a common convention in American art from the late eighteenth through the nineteenth century. What does the kneeling posture suggest?

NOTES

1. *New York Times*, October 3, 1862.

2. South Carolina Ordinance of Secession, December 20, 1860, in *Documents of American History*, ed. Henry Steele Commager and Milton Cantor (Englewood Cliffs, NJ: Prentice-Hall, 1988), 1:372; Declaration of the Immediate Causes Which Induce and Justify the Secession of South Carolina from the Federal Union, December 24, 1860, in ibid., 1:372–74.

3. Abraham Lincoln, First Inaugural Address, March 4, 1861, in ibid., 385–88.

4. Quoted in Roy C. Basler, ed., *The Collected Works of Abraham Lincoln* (New Brunswick, NJ: Rutgers University Press, 1953), 4:331–32.

5. Letter from Hannibal Guards to General James S. Negley, *Pittsburgh Gazette*, April 18, 1861, quoted in James M. McPherson, *The Negro's Civil War: How American Negroes Felt and Acted during the War for the Union* (New York: Pantheon, 1965), 19–20.

6. Benjamin Quarles, *The Negro in the Civil War* (Boston: Little, Brown, 1953), 28.

7. Peter H. Clark, *The Black Brigade of Cincinnati* (Cincinnati, 1864), 4–5.

8. Quoted in Basler, *Collected Works of Abraham Lincoln*, 5:423.

9. James M. McPherson, *Battle Cry of Freedom: The Civil War Era* (New York: Oxford University Press, 1988), 563.

10. *Anglo-African Magazine*, April 20–27, 1861.

11. *Douglass' Monthly*, May 1861, 45–52.

12. Quoted in Basler, *Collected Works of Abraham Lincoln*, 5:388–89.

13. Quoted in Willie Lee Rose, *Rehearsal for Reconstruction: The Port Royal Experiment* (Indianapolis: Bobbs-Merrill, 1964), xiii.

14. Second Confiscation Act, July 17, 1862, Freedmen and Southern Society Project, http://www.history.umd.edu/Freedmen/conact2.htm.

15. Ira Berlin et al., eds., *Freedom: A Documentary History of Emancipation, 1861–1867*, 1st ser., vol. 1, *The Destruction of Slavery* (New York: Cambridge University Press, 1985), 103–14, 187–99.

16. Henry M. Turner, *The Negro in Slavery, War and Peace* (Philadelphia: A.M.E. Book Concern, 1913), 6–7.

17. Charlotte Forten, "Life on the Sea Islands," *Atlantic Monthly*, June 1864, 4.

18. Interview with Felix Haywood, in *The American Slave: A Composite Autobiography, Texas Narratives*, ed. George P. Rawick, 2nd ser., vol. 4, part 2 (Westport, CT: Greenwood Press, 1972–1973), 131.

19. *Liberator*, May 22, 1863.

20. *Douglass' Monthly*, August 1863. Douglass said this in an address to a meeting for the promotion of colored enlistments on July 6, 1863.

21. William Wells Brown, *The Negro in the American Rebellion* (Boston: Lee and Shepard, 1867), 172.

22. McPherson, *Battle Cry of Freedom*, 634; Charles A. Dana, *Recollections of the Civil War* (New York: D. Appleton, 1899), 86.

23. McPherson, *Battle Cry of Freedom*, 634.

24. Quoted ibid., 638.

25. Lewis Douglass to Amelia Loguen, 20 July 1863, quoted in McPherson, *The Negro's Civil War*, 190–91.

26. *New York Tribune*, September 8, 1865.

27. Abraham Lincoln, Gettysburg Address, November 19, 1863, in Commager and Cantor, *Documents of American History*, 1:428–29.

28. Resolutions of the Illinois State Legislature, January 7, 1863, in ibid., 1:421–22. See also New Jersey Peace Resolutions, March 18, 1863, in ibid., 1:427–28, and McPherson, *Battle Cry of Freedom*, 595–96.

29. *Christian Recorder*, July 25, 1863, quoted in McPherson, *The Negro's Civil War*, 74.

30. J. W. C. Pennington, "The Position and Duties of the Colored People," cited in Philip S. Foner and Robert James Branham, eds., *Lift Every Voice: African American Oratory, 1787–1900* (Tuscaloosa: University of Alabama Press, 1998), 397–407, 406, 401.

31. Abraham Lincoln, Proclamation of Amnesty and Reconstruction, December 8, 1863, in Commager and Cantor, *Documents of American History*, 1:429–31.

32. Elizabeth Botume, *First Days amongst the Contrabands* (New York: Lee and Shepard, 1893; repr., New York: Arno Press, 1968), 15.

33. *Second Annual Report of the Freedmen and Soldiers Relief Association (Late Contraband Relief Association), Organized August 12, 1862*, quoted in McPherson, *The Negro's Civil War*, 139.

34. Abraham Lincoln, Second Inaugural Address, March 4, 1865, in Commager and Cantor, *Documents of American History*, 1:442–43.

35. For information on the Freedmen's Bureau, see Mary Farmer-Kaiser, *Freedwomen and the Freedmen's Bureau: Race, Gender, and Public Policy in the Age of Emancipation* (New York: Fordham University Press, 2010).

36. Interview with Richard Carruthers, in *The American Slave: A Composite Autobiography, Texas Narratives*, ed. George P. Rawick, vol. 4, part 1 (Westport, CT: Greenwood Press, 1972–1973), 200; Haywood interview, in ibid., 133; interview with Virginia woman, in Virginia Writers Project, *The Negro in Virginia* (New York: Hastings House, 1940), 210.

37. Interview with a former Mississippi slave, in *The American Slave: A Composite Autobiography, Oklahoma and Mississippi Narratives*, ed. George P. Rawick, vol. 7 (Westport, CT: Greenwood Press, 1971), 94; interview with a former South Carolina slave, in *The American Slave: A Composite Autobiography, South Carolina Narratives*, ed. George P. Rawick, vols. 2–3 (Westport, CT: Greenwood Press, 1972), 54.

38. Interview with Aleck Trimble, in *The American Slave: A Composite Autobiography, Texas Narratives*, ed. George P. Rawick, vol. 5, part 4 (Westport, CT: Greenwood Press, 1972), 109; Texas woman, quoted in Edward D. C. Campbell Jr., with Kym S. Rice, eds., *Before Freedom Came: African-American Life in the Antebellum South* (Charlottesville: University of Virginia Press, 1991), xiii.

39. Thomas Morris Chester, *Black Civil War Correspondent: His Dispatches from the Virginia Front*, ed. R. J. M. Blackett (Baton

Rouge: LSU Press, 1989), 46. See also Hugh Davis, *"We Will Be Satisfied with Nothing Less": The African American Struggle for Equal Rights in the North during Reconstruction* (Ithaca, NY: Cornell University Press, 2011), 17–26.

40. Quoted in John Hope Franklin, "The Emancipation Proclamation: An Act of Justice," *Prologue* 25, no. 2 (Summer 1993): 3.
41. Davis, *"We Will Be Satisfied,"* 11–12.
42. Quoted in Basler, *Collected Works of Abraham Lincoln,* 5:370–75.
43. William Kloss and Doreen Bolger, *Art in the White House: A Nation's Pride,* 2nd ed. (Washington, DC: White House Historical Association, 2008), 158–59, 302–3.
44. Kirk Savage, *Standing Soldiers, Kneeling Slaves: Race, War, and Monument in Nineteenth-Century America* (Princeton, NJ: Princeton University Press, 1997), 90.
45. Aaron Lloyd, "Statue of Limitations: Why Does D.C. Celebrate Emancipation in Front of a Statue That Celebrates 19th-Century Racism?" *Washington City Paper,* April 28, 2000; John W. Cromwell, quoted in Freeman H. M. Murray, *Emancipation and the Freed in American Sculpture: A Study in Interpretation* (Washington, DC: published by the author, 1916), 199.

SUGGESTED REFERENCES

The Coming of War and the Seizing of Freedom, 1861–1862

Berlin, Ira, Barbara J. Fields, Thavolia Glymph, Joseph P. Reidy, and Leslie S. Rowland, eds. *Freedom: A Documentary History of Emancipation, 1861–1867.* 1st ser., vol. 1, *The Destruction of Slavery.* New York: Cambridge University Press, 1985.

Gerteis, Louis. *From Contraband to Freedman: Federal Policy toward Southern Blacks, 1861–1865.* Greenwood, CT: Greenwood Press, 1973.

Litwack, Leon F. *Been in the Storm So Long: The Aftermath of Slavery.* New York: Knopf, 1979.

McPherson, James M. *The Negro's Civil War: How American Blacks Felt and Acted during the War for the Union.* 1965. Reprint, New York: Vintage, 2003.

Mohr, Clarence L. *On the Threshold of Freedom: Masters and Slaves in Civil War Georgia.* Baton Rouge: LSU Press, 2001.

Nieman, Donald G. *The Day of the Jubilee: The Civil War Experience of Black Southerners.* New York: Garland, 1994.

Quarles, Benjamin. *The Negro in the Civil War.* Boston: Little, Brown, 1953.

Robinson, Armstead. *Bitter Fruits of Bondage: The Demise of Slavery and the Collapse of the Confederacy, 1861–1865.* Charlottesville: University of Virginia Press, 2005.

Rose, Willie Lee. *Rehearsal for Reconstruction: The Port Royal Experiment.* Indianapolis: Bobbs-Merrill, 1964.

Ward, Andrew. *The Slaves' War: The Civil War in the Words of Former Slaves.* Boston: Houghton Mifflin, 2008.

Turning Points, 1862–1863

Berlin, Ira, Joseph P. Reidy, and Leslie S. Rowland, eds. *Freedom: A Documentary History of Emancipation, 1861–1867.* 2nd ser., *The Black Military Experience.* New York: Cambridge University Press, 1982.

Bernstein, Iver. *The New York City Draft Riots: Their Significance for American Society and Politics in the Age of the Civil War.* New York: Oxford University Press, 1990.

Cornish, Dudley Taylor. *The Sable Arm: Negro Troops in the Union Army, 1861–1865.* New York: Longmans, Green, 1956.

Franklin, John Hope. *The Emancipation Proclamation.* Garden City, NY: Doubleday, 1963.

Glatthaar, Joseph T. *Forged in Battle: The Civil War Alliance of Black Soldiers and White Officers.* Baton Rouge: LSU Press, 1990.

Redkey, Edwin S., ed. *A Grand Army of Black Men: Letters from African American Soldiers in the Union Army, 1861–1865.* New York: Cambridge University Press, 1992.

Smith, John David, ed. *Black Soldiers in Blue: African American Troops in the Civil War Era.* Chapel Hill: University of North Carolina Press, 2002.

Trudeau, Noah Andre. *Like Men of War: Black Troops in the Civil War, 1862–1865.* Boston: Little, Brown, 1998.

Home Fronts and War's End, 1863–1865

Bercaw, Nancy. *Gendered Freedoms: Race, Rights, and the Politics of Household in the Delta, 1861–1875.* Gainesville: University Press of Florida, 2003.

Berlin, Ira, and Leslie S. Rowland, eds. *Families and Freedom: A Documentary History of African-American Kinship in the Civil War Era.* New York: New Press, 1997.

Forbes, Ella. *African American Women during the Civil War.* New York: Garland, 1998.

Frankel, Noralee. *Freedom's Women: Black Women and Families in Civil War Era Mississippi.* Bloomington: Indiana University Press, 1999.

Jordan, Ervin L., Jr. *Black Confederates and Afro-Yankees in Civil War Virginia.* Charlottesville: University of Virginia Press, 1995.

Levine, Bruce. *Confederate Emancipation: Southern Plans to Free and Arm Slaves during the Civil War.* New York: Oxford University Press, 2006.

Schwalm, Leslie A. *A Hard Fight for We: Women's Transition from Slavery to Freedom in South Carolina.* Urbana: University of Illinois Press, 1997.

Williams, Heather Andrea. *Self-Taught: African American Education in Slavery and Freedom.* Chapel Hill: University of North Carolina Press, 2005.

Reconstruction: The Making and Unmaking of a Revolution

1865–1885

CHRONOLOGY *Events specific to African American history are in purple. General United States history events are in black.*

1865	Freedmen's Bureau founded
	Freedman's Savings and Trust Company founded
	Southern states pass black codes
	Ku Klux Klan founded
1866	Civil Rights Act defines U.S. citizenship and overturns black codes
	Congress reauthorizes Freedmen's Bureau with expanded powers
	Southern Homestead Act
	Two black cavalry regiments and two black infantry regiments established
	American Equal Rights Association founded
1867–1868	Reconstruction Acts
1868	President Andrew Johnson impeached; Senate fails to convict him
	Fourteenth Amendment defines and guarantees equal citizenship
	Radical Republican Thaddeus Stevens dies
1869	National Woman Suffrage Association founded
	American Woman Suffrage Association founded
	Knights of Labor founded
	Isaac Myers helps found Colored National Labor Union
1870	Fifteenth Amendment guarantees black male suffrage
	Force Act gives federal troops authority to put down racial disorder
	Hiram Revels becomes first African American U.S. senator

1872	Fisk Jubilee Singers perform at White House
	Freedmen's Bureau disbanded
1873	Colfax Massacre
	Slaughterhouse Cases; U.S. Supreme Court limits Fourteenth Amendment
1874	Freedman's Savings and Trust Company fails
	Radical Republican Charles Sumner dies
	Robert Smalls elected to U.S. House of Representatives
1875	Civil Rights Act requires equal treatment of whites and blacks in public accommodations and on public conveyances
1876	Hamburg Massacre
	Presidential election disputed
1877	Disputed election resolved; deal results in federal troops being withdrawn from South
	Henry O. Flipper becomes first black West Point graduate
1879	More than 6,000 Exodusters leave South for Kansas
1883	*Civil Rights Cases*; U.S. Supreme Court overturns Civil Rights Act of 1875

Jourdon and Mandy Anderson Find Security in Freedom after Slavery

In the summer after the Civil War ended, freedman Jourdon Anderson of Dayton, Ohio, thought hard about the postwar prospects for himself and his wife, Mandy, and their three children. Colonel P. H. Anderson, their "Old Master" in Big Spring, Tennessee, "promising to do better for me than anybody else can," had asked Jourdon and his family to return to the "old home" to work for him. Free since 1864, Jourdon and Mandy had made a nice life for themselves and their family in Dayton. "I get $25 a month, with victuals and clothing; have a comfortable home for Mandy . . . and the children," Jourdon explained in his formal response to Colonel Anderson's invitation. Recalling that Anderson had more than once tried to shoot him, Jourdon demanded "some proof that you are sincerely disposed to treat us justly and kindly" as a condition of return. The terms Jourdon and Mandy laid out were clear and precise.

> We have concluded to test your sincerity by asking you to send us our wages for the time we served you. This will make us forget and forgive old scores, and rely on your justice and friendship in the future. I served you faithfully for thirty-two years and Mandy twenty years. At $25 a month for me, and $2 a week for Mandy, our earnings would amount to $11,680. Add to this the interest for the time our wages has been kept back and deduct what you paid for our clothing and three doctor's visits to me, and pulling a tooth for Mandy, and the balance will show what we are in justice entitled to. Please send the money by Adams Express, in care of V. Winters, esq., Dayton, Ohio. If you fail to pay us for faithful labors in the past we can have little faith in your promises in the future. We trust the good Maker has opened your eyes to the wrongs which you and your fathers have done to me and my fathers, in making us toil for you for generations without recompense.

Besides making sure that their economic situation would be solid, Jourdon and Mandy wanted to know that their domestic and social lives as free people would be protected and dignified. The old patterns of white dominance and black subordination were unacceptable. Jourdon observed that when "the folks here" talk to Mandy, they "call her Mrs. Anderson." Jourdon and Mandy demanded that their daughters Milly and Jane, "now grown up and both good-looking girls," be safe from rape and sexual exploitation at the hands of white men. "I would rather stay here and starve and die if it comes to that than have my girls brought to shame by the violence and wickedness of their young masters." Mandy and Jourdon were also very proud of their son Grundy, whose teacher had told them that Grundy "has a head for a preacher." They made certain their children attended Sunday school and church, as well as grammar school. Committed to a good education for their children, they asked Colonel Anderson "if there has been any schools opened for the colored children in your neighborhood." Jourdon explained, "The great desire of my life now is to give my children an education, and have them form virtuous habits."[1]

Jourdon Anderson's extraordinary response to his former master's request that he and his family come back to work on the old homestead pointedly reveals the concerns of African Americans as they built new lives for themselves in freedom. Family ties, church and community, dignified labor with fair compensation, and education for their children were top priorities. But these were neither safe nor protected in the immediate aftermath of the Civil War, as many white landowners sought to ensure that former slaves continued working the land and remained bound by white rules. The tension between black assertiveness and white racism made interracial conflict inevitable. Freedom brought a revolution in black economic, social, and political life, but it did not bring equality. As President Andrew Johnson and the Radical Republicans in Congress battled over executive and legislative power, the fate of the freedpeople hung in the balance. When Congress proved more powerful, laws and constitutional amendments sought to ensure African American civil and voting rights. For about a decade from 1867 to 1877, African Americans in the South, even more than in the North, actively and responsibly participated in public life. Intense, often violent, southern white opposition, coupled with a dwindling national concern for freedpeople as the country turned to economic development, undermined the revolutionary period of interracial democracy and the political gains black people had made during Reconstruction. Some left the South for other regions of the country, but wherever they tried to put down roots — in the U.S. military, in new all-black towns in Kansas and Oklahoma, and in northern and midwestern cities where they sought jobs in factories — they struggled to achieve equal rights and independent lives.

A Social Revolution

For the four million African Americans who had been enslaved, freedom brought new goals and responsibilities. Foremost for many was reuniting with family members from whom they had been separated. Economic independence wrought immediate changes in family structure and shifting gender roles for men and women, as well as hope for the future. Extended families and community structures such as new schools and independent black churches provided services and support in the new environment of freedom. Labor arrangements had to be renegotiated, even though for most freedpeople, the nature of their work — field work and domestic service — remained largely the same. In freedom, black people had the right to learn to read and write, and they eagerly pursued education. For those who had been enslaved, the first years of freedom involved a transition — from slave households to independent households and from slave labor to free labor — that constituted a social revolution.

Freedom and Family

Freedpeople's struggles to create independent and functional families gave meaning to their freedom. Under slavery, masters had exercised significant control over slave families. With freedom, black people gained control over their families, even as they tried to remake them. Often the first step was to reunite those who had been separated before the war. One government official observed that "the work of emancipation was incomplete until the families which had been dispersed by slavery were reunited."[2] The war itself also had separated families. As individuals fled to Union lines and traveled with Union armies or enlisted in the U.S. Colored Troops, they lost touch with parents, spouses, children, and relatives who were themselves sometimes scattered. A Missouri official reported that after black men had enlisted in the military, their wives and children had been "driven from their masters['] homes," and court records indicate that women separated from children sought help to get them back.[3] In short, wartime conditions had made it increasingly hard to hold black families together.

After the war, thousands of freedpeople traveled great distances at significant material and emotional costs seeking lost and displaced family members. One middle-aged North Carolina freedman who had been sold away from his wife and children traveled almost six hundred miles on foot to try to find them.[4] People inquired for missing relatives at former plantation homes, contraband camps, churches, and government agencies. Others wrote letters, with those who were not literate asking for help from teachers, preachers, missionaries, and government officials. Many took out ads in black newspapers.

Most searches were unsuccessful, owing to time and distance, death, and difficulties that were simply insurmountable given the lack of records. Family members who did find one another expressed relief and joy. Reunited after having been sold apart twenty years earlier, husband and wife Ben and Betty Dodson embraced, and Ben shouted, "Glory! glory! hallelujah." In some cases, people did not recognize one another after such a long absence. One former slave woman, sold away as a child, could identify the woman standing before her as her mother only by a distinctive facial scar.[5]

Sometimes new family ties had replaced old ones. Many forcibly separated partners and spouses over time had come to believe they would never see each other again, and they formed new attachments. For them, reunions were heartrending. Some chose their former spouse; others, the new one. One woman gave each of her two husbands a two-week test run before settling on one. Many men stayed with and supported one wife while continuing to support the other.[6] Others remained torn between two loves. One freedman wrote to his first wife, "I thinks of you and my children every day of my life. . . . I do love you the same. My love to you have never failed. . . . I have got another wife, and I am very sorry. . . . You feels and seems to me as much like my dear loving wife, as you ever did."[7]

The tensions following from troubled reunions often proved overwhelming. Many spouses who accused their partners of infidelity or desertion now sought relief through the courts. The number of wives seeking support for their children and themselves from negligent fathers and husbands increased, as did the number of divorce cases and custody battles over children. Battles between birth parents and the adults who had raised their children were confusing and painful for all involved. During slavery, some white mistresses had taken young slaves from their mothers to be raised in the big house as part of the domestic staff. After emancipation, these children were reclaimed. As one freed mother told her former mistress, "You took her away from me an' didn' pay no mind to my cryin', so now I'se takin' her back home. We's free now, Mis' Polly, we ain't gwine be slaves no more to nobody."[8]

Legalizing slave marriages was a critical step in confirming freedpeople's new identities. Some viewed marriage as a moral and a Christian responsibility; some saw it as a means for legitimating children and becoming eligible for Union veterans' pensions. Preachers, missionaries, and public officials supported marriage as a way to anchor black families and enhance their moral foundation. The rites themselves varied widely, from traditional "jumping the broom" ceremonies, common under slavery, to church weddings. One freedwoman recalled that while she and her husband had had a broomstick ceremony as slaves, once freed they "had a real sho' nuff weddin' wid a preacher. Dat cost a dollar."[9] Mass weddings featuring as many as seventy couples were common. In 1866, seventeen North Carolina counties registered 9,000 marriages of freedpeople; four Virginia counties registered 3,000. Yet some couples remained together without formalizing their marriages, being accepted in their local communities as husband and wife.

Many former slaves took new names to recognize family ties and to symbolize their independence and their desire for a new life characterized by dignity and respect. In slavery, "we hardly knowed our names," one ex-slave recalled. "We was cussed for so many bitches and sons of bitches and bloody bitches, and blood of bitches. We never heard our names scarcely at all."[10] Masters had often assigned first names, such as Pompey and Caesar, and refused to recognize the surnames used within slave communities. Now, as independent people, former slaves legally claimed first and last names of their own choosing.

In form, freed families were flexible and adaptive. Although the most common organization was the nuclear family — two parents and their children — families often included extended kin and nonrelated members. Ties of affection and economic need made extended families, as well as fictive kin (see chapter 5), important. Pooling resources and working collectively sustained these families. Even when dispersed in different households, families tended to live in communities among relatives. Close-knit communities defined women's and men's social and cultural worlds, nurturing a cooperative spirit and a communal folk culture.

Most newly freed families had to meet their household needs with very limited resources, and poverty rendered them fragile. Every person had to work. Immediately after emancipation, large numbers of freedwomen withdrew from field labor and domestic service to manage their own households, but most were soon forced to work outside the home for wages. Although traditional notions of women's and men's roles prevailed—woman as caretaker and homemaker; man as breadwinner and protector—black men rarely earned enough to support their families. One consequence was that black women who were contributing to the family income also participated more fully in family decision making. In addition, black women felt freer to leave dysfunctional relationships and to divorce or simply live apart from their husbands. But female-headed households were almost always poorer than dual-headed households. Moreover, as legal protectors and guarantors of their wives and children, freedmen exercised the rights of contract and child custody. Men typically made and signed labor contracts on behalf of their wives, and they held the upper hand in child custody disputes.

Church and Community

The explosive growth of independent black churches in the South during this period reflects freedpeople's desire for dignity, autonomy, and self-expression. With emancipation, they rejected white Christianity and exited white churches by the thousands to form congregations of their own. As Matthew Gilbert, a Tennessee Baptist minister, noted, "The emancipation of the colored people made the colored churches and ministry a necessity, both by virtue of the prejudice existing against us and of our essential manhood before the laws of the land."[11] Often with the assistance of missionaries from churches in the North, the major black denominations — Baptist, African Methodist Episcopal (AME), and African Methodist Episcopal Zion (AME Zion) —became established in the South. By 1880, nationwide there were more than 500,000 people in the Baptist Church, 400,000 in the AME Church, and 250,000 in the AME Zion Church. By 1890, more than half of those belonging to an independent black church were Baptists.[12]

Next to the family, the black church provided the most important institutional support in the transition from slavery to freedom. Joining a church was an act of physical and spiritual emancipation, and black churches united black communities. They also empowered blacks because they operated outside of white control. Men dominated church leadership, but women constituted most of the members and regular attendees and did most of what was called church work. Women gave and raised money, taught Sunday school, ran women's auxiliaries, welcomed visitors, and led social welfare programs for the needy, sick, and elderly. They were also prominent in domestic and foreign missionary activities. One grateful minister consistently offered "great praise" to the church sisters for all their hard work.[13]

Women derived their authority in churches from their roles as Christian wives, mothers, and homemakers. As "church mothers," they exercised informal yet significant influence in church affairs, including matters of governance typically reserved for male

The Black Church

This 1876 sketch is an evocative presentation of a black church scene in which serious and well-dressed women, men, and children appear to be engaged in serious reflection on a biblical passage. While the preacher and his assistant are clearly leading the Bible study, the multiple settings within the scene enable us to focus on the congregants. The individuals and groupings — indeed, the collective image — convey authentic black Christian propriety.

American Sketches: A Negro Congregation at Washington, *from* The Illustrated London News, *18 November 1876/Private Collection/ Bridgeman Images.*

members, such as the selection of preachers and the allocation of church funds. Although women were not allowed to become preachers, many preached nevertheless, under titles such as "evangelist."

Black women were also leaders in and practitioners of African-derived forms of popular, or folk, religion — such as conjure (see chapter 3) and voodoo, or hoodoo (see chapter 5) — which had evolved during slavery and continued after emancipation. Focusing on magic and the supernatural, they involved healing and harming beliefs and practices. One celebrated voodoo "priestess" was Marie Laveau of New Orleans. Not surprisingly, black church leaders railed against folk religion as an ignorant and idolatrous relic of slavery. Still, these beliefs and practices were common, especially among rural people, but even in towns and cities and among Christians.

In black urban neighborhoods, church networks and resources helped fuel institutional growth, including hospitals, clinics, asylums for orphans and the mentally ill, mutual aid societies, lodges, and unions. Churches led black community efforts to deal with the epidemics of cholera, smallpox, and yellow fever that swept through the South after the war, especially as blacks who had never traveled much before became more exposed to lethal diseases. With help from the Medical Division of the Freedmen's Bureau, former wartime army hospitals were converted into hospitals to serve African Americans. In Washington, D.C., Freedmen's Hospital was established during the war. In New Orleans and Richmond, Virginia, the existing black hospitals expanded. By the late 1860s, segregated asylums and hospitals served black communities in a number of southern cities.

In addition, black churches, northern white churches, and the American Missionary Association (AMA) founded black grade schools and high schools during this period. They also established colleges and teacher training institutes, known as normal schools (see Appendix). These **historically black colleges and universities** reflected their founders' goals, giving great emphasis to religious instruction, Christian morality, and hard work, as well as academic and vocational training.

Through their networks and resources, black churches generated a range of economic organizations. Each church operated as an economic enterprise, undertaking fund-raising, buying and maintaining buildings and real estate, promoting businesses, and supporting social programs for the needy. Mutual aid societies rooted in churches evolved into black insurance companies and banks in the late nineteenth and early twentieth centuries. Church social circles provided ready consumer bases for black products and services. Some churches sold Christian products, such as Bibles and religious pamphlets and lithographs. Black ministers served on the boards of black companies. Churches sponsored business expositions featuring products such as furniture, medicines, and handicrafts to showcase African Americans' economic progress since emancipation.

The church was also the hub of black political life. At all levels — from within the church to local, state, and national politics — it functioned as the key forum for political debate and action. It was vital to black political education and activism, including participation in black community politics and the white-dominated political mainstream. Among black ministers' many roles, that of political leader proved central. Preacher-politicians saw themselves both as faithful servants to their congregations and as representatives of their people to white politicians. They believed that their Christian-based leadership would improve the morality of both the political system and secular society. In the 1870s, the Reverend James Poindexter of the Second Baptist Church in Columbus, Ohio, explained that "all the help the preachers and all other good and worthy citizens can give by taking hold of politics is needed in order to keep the government out of bad hands and secure the ends for which governments are formed."[14]

Land and Labor

Landownership was fundamental to former slaves' aspirations for economic independence. Rebuilding families as independent households required land. Speaking for his people, particularly former slaves, in the summer of 1864, the AME missionary and minister Richard Cain explained, "We must possess the soil, be the owner of lands and become independent."[15] This message was repeated in January 1865, when several hundred blacks in the Sea Islands told General William T. Sherman, "We want to be placed on land until we are able to buy it, and make it our own."[16] Sherman settled more than 40,000 former slaves in coastal areas that had been abandoned by Confederate plantation owners, but what was known as Sherman's Reserve did not last. The Reconstruction plans of President Abraham Lincoln and his successor, Andrew Johnson, directed that former Confederates who swore allegiance to the United States would regain their land, and unclaimed land was auctioned to the highest bidder. Many former slaves were already working this land under federal supervision; others had simply squatted on abandoned land and worked it to sustain themselves. They were all evicted. Although the Freedmen's Bureau was able to help some enter into contracts to rent the land they were already farming, the bureau was not able to help them purchase land. Few freedpeople or free blacks possessed the capital or credit to buy land, and as a result, they lost out to returning ex-Confederate plantation owners and northern and southern investors. The Southern Homestead Act, passed by Congress in 1866, made public land available to freedmen, but it had little impact and was repealed a decade later. In the end, most land in the former Confederacy was returned to white control, often to the original owners. The rest went to northern white investors, former army officers, and Freedmen's Bureau officials.

This "landless emancipation" devastated freedpeople. "Damm such freedom as that," one angry freedman exclaimed, expressing the frustration of many.[17] Freedmen believed that they had earned the right to own the land they and their ancestors had worked as slaves. They argued that freedom without provision for self-sufficiency was a shocking violation of the federal government's economic and moral responsibility. A group of Mississippi blacks called it "a breach of faith on the part of the government."[18] Some simply refused to leave the property they now considered their own. The former slaves on the Taylor farm in Norfolk County, Virginia, mounted an armed resistance when their former owners returned to reclaim their prewar property, but to no avail. Forced evictions of freedpeople from land and farms they assumed now belonged to them were common.

Lacking the means to own land, most freedpeople were forced into tenancy. They rented and worked land that belonged to white landowners under terms that favored the owners. Black male heads of household entered into contracts with landowners that spelled out the paid labor, as opposed to slave labor, relationship. For their part, freedpeople sought fair compensation for their labor, work organized along family lines, and an end to physical punishment and gang-style labor with overseers. They also wanted guaranteed leisure time and the right to hunt, fish, gather wild food plants, raise farm animals, and cultivate designated plots for their own use. For white landowners, the aim of these contracts was to ensure a steady supply of farm labor so that their land-holdings, planted in cash crops, would make a profit. That meant limiting wages, for-bidding worker mobility, and suppressing competition. Labor contracts were difficult to break, and because most freedmen could neither read nor write, many relied on Freedmen's Bureau officials to look out for their best interests. The struggles between freedpeople and landowners were at times bitter and divisive, but in the end, the land-owners were far more powerful, and labor contracts generally favored their interests.

Despite their landholdings, whites operated within cash-strapped southern economies after the war. Instead of paying farmworkers in cash, most negotiated **sharecropping** arrangements under which farmers worked the land for a "share" of the crop, typically one-third or one-half. Often the landowner supplied the cabin or house in which the family lived, as well as seed, work animals, and tools. If a "cropper" had his own mule and plow, he might warrant a larger share of the crop. This he would "sell" to the plantation owner or a local merchant — often the same person — following the harvest. But instead of cash changing hands, the sharecropper would get credit to use for buying food and clothing — or whatever his family might need — from the merchant. At the end of the year, when accounts were settled on "countin' day," the sharecropper usually got no more than a bill showing how much he still owed the landowner or merchant.

All too often, owners and merchants cheated workers, forcing them into a pattern of cyclical debt. Even many black farmers who owned their own land were forced into debt. For example, in a system known as **crop lien**, they had to borrow against antici-pated harvests for seed and supplies. Most black households were thus reduced to a form of coerced labor, a kind of partial slavery, tied to the land they farmed as the only means they had to work off their debt, which every year grew larger instead of smaller. Debtors were also subject to imprisonment, and prisoners were subject to another form of coerced labor, as states contracted out their labor to landowners or businesses in need of a labor force. This **convict lease** system generated income for southern states, but it forced prisoners to work under conditions that blatantly disregarded their human rights.

Immediately after the war, the main goal for white southerners was to reassert con-trol over blacks. State legislatures passed **black codes** that enforced the labor contracts that once again bound freedpeople, who had few other options, to the land. The codes mandated strict obedience to white employers and set work hours, usually sunup to sundown. Although the codes allowed freedpeople to legalize their marriages, own property, make contracts, and access the courts, their aim was to perpetuate a slavelike labor force in conditions of freedom. Thus vagrancy provisions were especially oppres-sive. Individuals without labor contracts who were unable to prove that they were employed risked fines, imprisonment, and forced labor, as did those who left a job before a contract ended or who were unruly or simply lost. In Mississippi, freedpeople were prohibited from renting urban property, helping to ensure that they would stay on plantations and work in agriculture. In Florida, breaking a labor contract often resulted in physical punishment, such as a whipping, or being hired out for a year to a planter. As one southern white pointedly observed in November 1865, the purpose behind black codes and vagrancy laws was to "teach the negro that if he goes to work, keeps his place, and behaves himself, he will be protected by *our* white laws."[19]

Black codes also permitted the courts to order apprenticeships that removed children from black families and bound them to white employers, often without their parents' or guardians' consent. In *Adeline Brown v. State* (1865), the Maryland Court of Appeals upheld the state's black apprentice law. Two years later, however, the case *In re Turner* (1867) overturned the law as unconstitutional because its educational provisions for black youths were different from those for white youths.

The Hope of Education

To operate as free and independent men and women, former slaves — more than 90 percent of whom were illiterate at the moment of emancipation — recognized that they had to learn to read and write, and they did so eagerly. Some began their schooling in the Union military or in contraband camps, where they were sometimes taught by former slaves, such as Susie King Taylor, or by northern black women, such as Charlotte Forten, who went to the Sea Islands to teach (see chapter 7). After the war, makeshift classrooms grew into permanent institutions. On St. Helena Island, so many teachers were from Pennsylvania that the school was named the Penn School, and it expanded to accommodate 1,700 students on a campus that served black children into the 1940s. In Hampton, Virginia, where thousands of contrabands set up their own community soon after the Civil War began, the teacher was a free black woman named Mary S. Peake. Under the sponsorship of the American Missionary Association (AMA), she began her school under a tree later known as the Emancipation Oak. After she died of tuberculosis, General Benjamin Butler stepped in to build the Butler School for Negro Children, again with the assistance of the AMA. In her poem "Learning to Read," Frances Ellen Watkins Harper, who before the war had lectured on behalf of abolition and black education, captured the excitement and sense of independence that came with achieving literacy.

Northern teachers, missionaries, and philanthropists helped found hundreds of schools for black children and adults. Some of these schools were set up in churches and homes. In other cases, freedpeople pooled their resources to buy land, build schoolhouses, and hire teachers. The Freedmen's Bureau assisted by renting facilities, providing books, and transporting teachers, while the AMA helped fund schools and hire teachers, white and black. The Pennsylvania Branch of the American Freedmen's Union Commission sent out 1,400 teachers to serve 150,000 students. In addition to these privately sponsored organizations, Reconstruction state governments, often led by black officials, began to establish public school systems — new for the South — that

Frances Ellen Watkins Harper

Freeborn Frances Ellen Watkins Harper was an influential abolitionist and women's rights advocate, a poet and novelist, and an orator. Her well-received *Poems on Miscellaneous Subjects* (1854) treated gender equality as well as abolitionism. *Minnie's Sacrifice* (1869), a serial novel; *Sketches of Southern Life* (1872), a book of poetry; and her most famous work, the novel *Iola Leroy, or Shadows Uplifted* (1892), all address Reconstruction. Harper's life and work reflect a profound belief in and active commitment to both gender and racial equality. In particular, her activism on behalf of both women's rights and black rights led her to become a founding vice president of the National Association of Colored Women in 1896. *The Granger Collection, New York.*

gave black children access to education, largely in segregated schools that operated only during the winter months, when children were not needed for planting and harvesting. By 1880 black illiteracy had declined to 70 percent, and by 1910 it was down to 30 percent.[20]

In all these schools, the standard New England curriculum prevailed. The three Rs — reading, writing, and arithmetic — were emphasized. In the best schools, instruction in history, geography, spelling, grammar, and music might also be available. Colleges offered a classical liberal curriculum that included math, science, Latin, and Greek. Given the pressing need for teachers, they usually emphasized teacher training, instructing young people in teaching methods and theory as well as diction, geometry, algebra, and map reading.

By 1868, more than half the teachers in black schools in the South were black, and most were women. For them, teaching was a calling, not just a job. "I am myself a colored woman," noted Sarah G. Stanley, "bound to that ignorant, degraded, long enslaved race, by the ties of love and consanguinity; they are socially, and politically, 'my people.'"[21] The increasing preponderance of black teachers reflected a growing race consciousness and commitment to self-reliance. Despite the fact that white teachers may have had better training and more experience, black communities preferred black teachers. The Reverend Richard Cain observed that white "teachers and preachers have feelings, but not as we feel for our kindred."[22] In 1869, a group of blacks in Petersburg, Virginia, petitioned the school board to replace white teachers with black ones, asserting, "We do not want our children to be trained to think or feel that they are inferior."[23] Black female teachers became important community leaders and inspirational role models. Like black schools, they helped build racial solidarity and community identity.

Although the historically black colleges and universities emphasized teacher training, early on they took two different curricular paths that reflected the different expectations freedpeople had for themselves in light of their opportunities. Schools such as Fisk University in Nashville, Tennessee, founded in 1866, embraced the classical liberal arts model, whereas schools such as Hampton Institute in Hampton, Virginia, founded in 1868, adopted the vocational-industrial model. When Booker T. Washington helped found Tuskegee Institute in 1881, he modeled it on Hampton, where he had been a student and teacher. In 1871, Alcorn Agricultural and Mechanical College (Alcorn A&M) opened as Alcorn University in Claiborne County, Mississippi. Alcorn was both the nation's first state-supported college for blacks and the first federal land-grant black college (see Appendix).

Fisk offered a well-rounded academic program to prepare the best and the brightest of the race for citizenship, leadership, and a wide range of careers. The school boldly aimed for "the highest standards, not of Negro education, but of American education at its best."[24] Within six years, however, Fisk faced a serious financial crisis that threatened its survival. In an effort to raise money, George L. White, school treasurer and music professor, organized a choral ensemble to go on a fund-raising tour. Modeling their performances on European presentation styles, but singing slave songs and spirituals little known to white audiences, the Fisk Jubilee Singers were soon famous. In 1872, they performed for President Ulysses S. Grant at the White House, and the next year, while on a European tour, they sang for Britain's Queen Victoria. The money they raised saved the school from bankruptcy and enabled Fisk to build its first permanent building, Jubilee Hall, today a National Historic Landmark. Their performances built worldwide respect and admiration for African American music and culture and inspired other black colleges to create similar groups.

Hampton Institute had a different mission: "to train selected Negro youth who should go out and teach and lead their people first by example, by getting land and homes; . . . to teach respect for labor, . . . and in this way to build up an industrial system for the sake not only of self-support and intelligent labor, but also for the sake of character."[25] Samuel Chapman Armstrong, Hampton's white founder and Booker T. Washington's mentor, believed that training young people in skilled trades, rather than teaching a classical liberal arts curriculum, would best enable poverty-stricken former slaves to pull themselves up by their bootstraps. As skilled laborers and highly trained domestic servants, they would earn adequate wages, build self-respect, and win the admiration of whites. Students at Hampton paid their way by

The Fisk Jubilee Singers
This 1880 photograph illustrates the middle-class refinement of the Fisk Jubilee Singers. This sense of middle-class respectability also revealed their commitment to racial uplift: the presentation of positive images of blacks as a way to enhance their freedom struggle. As former slaves and the children of former slaves, the Jubilee Singers pioneered an African American music tradition that relied on polished versions of slave spirituals. Their noble presentation of this black religious folk music provided a critical counterpoint and challenge to negative stereotypes of blacks resulting from the minstrel tradition (see chapter 6). Over time, the Jubilee Singers' performances for audiences around the world enhanced black and white respect for blacks and their culture. *The Granger Collection, New York.*

working on campus, all the while learning the occupational skills that would qualify them for jobs after graduation. Many learned to teach trade skills such as carpentry and sewing, and they practice-taught at the successor to the Butler School for Negro Children. The Hampton model of vocational training was akin to that of training schools for poor white children and immigrants at the time, but some black leaders feared that it would perpetuate black subordination. The *Louisianian*, a black newspaper, complained that Armstrong "seems to think that we should only know enough to make good servants."[26] The debate over vocational training versus liberal arts intensified toward the end of the century, and at its center was Washington, the preeminent black leader of his day.

A Short-Lived Political Revolution

Even as black men and women built independent lives, they sought a place in American public life, and for a short period known as **Black Reconstruction**, black men were able to vote in the South and to participate in politics. Radical Republicans in Congress had taken charge of Reconstruction and forced the former Confederate states to hold democratically elected constitutional conventions, which wrote new state constitutions that protected black suffrage. The consequences were revolutionary. Nowhere else in the world had an emancipated people been integrated into the political system so quickly. Black men elected or appointed to state and local offices proved able and moderate and demonstrated their interest in compromise and progressive reforms such as public schools. But Black Reconstruction was short-lived. Outraged southern whites mobilized a violent and racist counterrevolution that restored white political dominance by 1877. Congress and the Republican Party abandoned black interests, and the U.S. Supreme Court reversed gains made by Reconstruction laws and amendments. In its retreat from Black Reconstruction, the national government reflected the expanding white opposition to the evolving black freedom struggle.

The Political Contest over Reconstruction

Andrew Johnson, who became president after Abraham Lincoln was assassinated, continued Lincoln's lenient policies toward former Confederates. Like Lincoln, Johnson insisted that the war was an insurrection, that the southern states were never out of the Union, and that the organization of a new civil authority in these states was an executive, not a legislative, function. His rapid restoration of civil government in the former Confederate states, amnesty for former Confederates, and lack of interest in protecting the civil rights of freedpeople angered the Radical Republicans in Congress. This faction, led by Representative Thaddeus Stevens and Senator Charles Sumner, had pressed for more aggressive military campaigns during the war and a quicker end to slavery. Challenging Lincoln, it had run John C. Frémont against him for the presidency in 1864 and passed the Wade-Davis Bill aiming to reverse Lincoln's proposed leniency toward Confederates (see chapter 7). In December 1865, when Johnson declared that the Union had been restored and it looked as though representatives and senators from former Confederate states would be reseated in Congress, the Radical Republicans balked. Concerned for the civil rights of the freedpeople, they quickly appointed a joint committee to examine issues of suffrage and representation for the former Confederate states. The struggle between the president and Congress escalated in early 1866 when Congress passed two bills over Johnson's veto — the reauthorization of the Freedmen's Bureau and the Civil Rights Act.

Established in March 1865, the Freedmen's Bureau aimed to help freedpeople in their economic, social, and political transition to freedom. To prevent them from becoming wards of the state and the bureau from becoming a permanent guardian, it remained a temporary agency that Congress had to renew annually. In reauthorizing the Freedmen's Bureau in February 1866, Congress expanded its powers by establishing military commissions to hear cases of civil rights abuses — of which there were many. The bureau heard shocking reports of whites violently beating and abusing blacks (even murdering them), cheating them out of their wages, shortchanging them on purchased goods, and stealing their crop shares. In September 1865, for example, the head of the Freedmen's Bureau in Mississippi reported, "Men, who are honorable in their dealings with their white neighbors, will cheat a negro without feeling a single twinge of their honor; to kill a negro they do not deem murder; to debauch a negro woman they do not think fornication; to take property away from a negro they do not deem robbery. . . . They still have the ingrained feeling that the black people at large belong to the whites at large."[27] When Johnson vetoed the reauthorization bill, stating that the military commissions were unconstitutional, Congress passed the bill over his veto. The bureau experienced severe cutbacks in 1869, however, and its reach and effectiveness seriously declined before it was finally ended in 1872.

To further protect the civil rights of freedpeople, Congress passed the **Civil Rights Act of 1866**, again over Johnson's veto. This act defined U.S. citizenship for the first time and affirmed that all citizens were equally protected by the laws. It overturned black codes and ensured that blacks could make contracts and initiate lawsuits, but it did not protect black voting rights. In February 1866, Frederick Douglass and a delegation of other black leaders met with Johnson to try to convince him of the importance of black suffrage, but without success.

Tensions between the stubborn and increasingly isolated Johnson and an energetic Congress escalated over the **Fourteenth Amendment**, which Congress quickly proposed and sent to the states for ratification in 1866. Ratified in 1868, this amendment affirmed the Civil Rights Act's definition of citizenship and guarantee of "equal protection of the laws" to all citizens. Declaring that "all persons born or naturalized in the United States" are "citizens of the United States and of the State wherein they reside," it reversed the *Dred Scott* decision of 1857, which had ruled that blacks could not be citizens. To protect citizens against civil rights violations by the states, the amendment also declared that "no State shall make or enforce any law which shall abridge the privileges and immunities of citizens of the United States; nor shall any State deprive any person of life, liberty, or property without due process of law; nor deny to any person within its jurisdiction the equal protection of the laws." This clause would ultimately shape the black freedom struggle, but not before states found ways to craft racially discriminatory laws in the areas in which states were sovereign, such as public education.

Outmaneuvered, Johnson took his case to the people, embarking on an unprecedented presidential speaking tour, which proved disastrous. In the midterm elections of 1866, the Radical Republicans captured two-thirds of both houses of Congress, and the next year they moved quickly to take charge of Reconstruction by passing several Reconstruction Acts. The first **Reconstruction Act of 1867**, passed on March 2, 1867,

Freedmen's Bureau Cartoon

This vicious Democratic Party broadside from 1866 slanders the Freedmen's Bureau as well as freedpeople. Central to the party's widespread effort to get rid of the Freedmen's Bureau specifically and of Reconstruction in its entirety was a racist, vitriolic, and highly calculated public campaign against both. This broadside is a chilling representation of the discredited view that Reconstruction was a tragic mistake because it did too much too soon for the inferior and uncivilized freedpeople, who were incapable of shouldering the responsibilities of freedom. *Library of Congress, Rare Book and Special Collections Division, Washington, D.C., LC-USZ62-40764.*

dissolved state governments in the former Confederacy (except for Tennessee) and divided the old Confederacy into five military districts subject to martial law, each with a military governor. To reenter the Union, a state was required to call a constitutional convention, which would be elected by universal male suffrage (including black male suffrage); to write a new state constitution that guaranteed black suffrage; and to ratify the Fourteenth Amendment. The other three Reconstruction Acts passed in 1867 and early 1868 empowered the military commander of each district to ensure that the process of reconstruction in each state went forward, in spite of strong ex-Confederate opposition.

On March 2, 1867, Congress also passed — and later passed again, over Johnson's veto — the Tenure of Office Act, which prohibited the president from removing any cabinet member from office without the Senate's approval. The act was designed to protect Secretary of War Edwin M. Stanton, a Radical Republican who was openly critical of the president. When Johnson dismissed Stanton in February 1868, the House of Representatives impeached Johnson for this violation of the act and other charges. The Senate failed to convict him, but thereafter the president was politically sidelined, and Congress assumed primary responsibility for Reconstruction.

Black Reconstruction

Meanwhile, the military Reconstruction of the South was already under way. Many former Confederates were ineligible to vote in elections for delegates to state constitutional conventions, and up to 30 percent of whites refused to participate in elections in which black men could vote. Thus in some states, black voters were in the majority. Of the slightly more than 1,000 delegates elected to write new state constitutions, 268 were black. In South Carolina and Louisiana, blacks formed the majority of delegates. Black delegates advocated the interests of freedpeople specifically and of the American people generally, and they argued for curtailing the interests of caste and property. In South Carolina, for example, delegate Robert Smalls proposed that the state sponsor a public school system that was open to all.

The state constitutional conventions initiated a new phase of Reconstruction. Decades later, the black scholar and activist W. E. B. Du Bois called it "Black Reconstruction" in a book by that title. His subtitle, "An Essay toward a History of the Part Which Black Folk Played in the Attempt to Reconstruct Democracy in America," suggests a transformative yet short-lived revolutionary moment during which African Americans participated in southern political life. The constitutions these conventions drafted provided for a range of "firsts" for the South: universal male suffrage, public schools, progressive taxes, improved court and judicial systems, commissions to promote industrial development, state aid for railroad development, and social welfare institutions such as hospitals and asylums for orphans and the mentally ill. In many ways, these were among the most progressive state constitutions and state governments the nation ever had, and they are why Du Bois called Reconstruction a "splendid failure"[28] — splendid for what could have been.

Du Bois also argued that Black Reconstruction was splendid because it did not fail due to alleged black incompetence and inferiority, as many whites expected. Instead, Black Reconstruction clearly demonstrated African American competence and equality. From the first, white southerners who did not participate in the conventions denigrated the black delegates as incompetent and the white delegates as "carpetbaggers" and "scalawags." Carpetbaggers were northern whites who were stereotyped as having come to the South with their belongings in travel bags made from carpet and with the aim of making money off plantation, railroad, and industrial interests as well as the freedpeople themselves. Scalawags were southern whites who had turned on their fellow white southerners and tied their fortunes to the Republican Party. Such charges were overstated. While Black Reconstruction politicians ranged from liberal to conservative, they were more centrist than radical, more committed to reintegrating former Confederates into the new state governments than punishing them for having waged war against the United States, and more than competent.

During Black Reconstruction, some 2,000 blacks served as officeholders at the various levels of government in the South.[29] Although a little over half for whom information is available had been slaves, they were now literate, and they were committed. Among them were artisans, laborers, businessmen, carpenters, barbers, ministers, teachers, editors, publishers, storekeepers, and merchants. They served as sheriffs, police officers, justices of the peace, registrars, city council members, county commissioners, members of boards of education, tax collectors, land office clerks, and postmasters. Wherever they served, they sought to balance the interests of black and white southerners. In a political era marked by graft and corruption, black politicians proved to be more ethical than their white counterparts.

A few black Republicans achieved high state office. In Louisiana, Mississippi, and South Carolina, blacks served as lieutenant governor. Some were superintendents of education, a post with considerable power. More than six hundred state legislators were black, including Robert Smalls, who served in the South Carolina House of Representatives and Senate (Map 8.1). In 1874, Smalls was elected to the U.S. House of Representatives. Thirteen other black men served in the U.S. House during this era, and two served in the Senate. Like their colleagues in local and state positions in the South, these black senators and congressmen were moderate politicians who tried hard to balance the often irreconcilable concerns of freedpeople and southern whites. Hiram R. Revels (1870–1871) and Blanche K. Bruce (1875–1881) were both senators from Mississippi. A minister in the AME Church, Revels was known for his oratorical ability and his amnesty program for disfranchised former Confederates, which would have allowed them to vote and hold office with limited penalties. Bruce, a skilled Mississippi delta politician and planter, proved to be a far more vigorous champion of black civil rights and an unyielding opponent of white resistance to black political participation.

The widespread political involvement of blacks, many of whom were former slaves who had never before had any political rights, was unprecedented in the United States and unique among nineteenth-century post-emancipation societies, including Jamaica, Cuba, and Brazil. In the United States, blacks' service in office, as well as the wide range of political activities of thousands of other black men and women, amounted to a political revolution. Black politics then and since has included innumerable local, grassroots, and community-based activities outside the realm of formal politics, activities

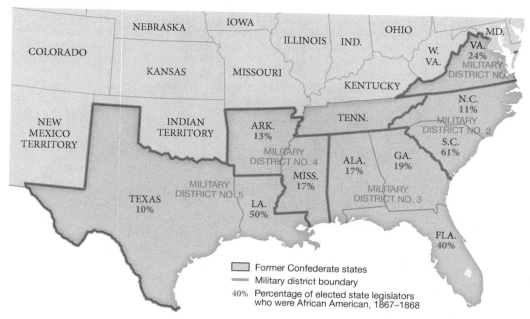

MAP 8.1   Black Political Participation in the Reconstruction South, 1867–1868

During the overlapping years of Congressional Reconstruction and Black Reconstruction, the states of the former Confederacy were reorganized into five military districts under the first Reconstruction Act of 1867. Within these districts, for the first time ever, thousands of newly enfranchised blacks participated in politics, voted, and held elected offices at all levels of the government. As this map illustrates, the percentages of African Americans elected to the first state legislatures as a result of the four Reconstruction Acts were significant: A full half of Louisiana's elected state legislators were black, and in South Carolina, black legislators comprised a 61 percent majority. DATA SOURCE: *The Atlas of African-American History and Politics: From the Slave Trade to Modern Times,* by Arwin Smallwood and Jeffrey Elliot. Copyright © 1998 The McGraw-Hill Companies, Inc.

aimed at enhancing black influence and control. Still, for the black community, political participation and the vote during Reconstruction represented key expressions of citizenship and national belonging. (See Document Project: The Vote, pp. 331–39.) When black men voted, they cast a family vote — a choice that reflected the collective aspirations of their wives, children, relatives, and extended kin, as well as those of their neighbors and communities.

Freedpeople allied themselves with the Republican Party, the party of emancipation and Abraham Lincoln. They were actively recruited by the **Union League**, which had been created in the North in 1862 to build support for the Republican Party and sent representatives to the South after the war. Along with the Freedmen's Bureau, southern branches of the Union League mobilized black support for the Republican Party and helped blacks understand their political rights and responsibilities as citizens.

African Americans viewed the right to vote as the most important of all civil rights and the one on which all other civil rights depended. The vote made economic, social,

The First Colored Senator and Representatives, 1872
This dignified group portrait represents the first black men to serve in Congress as statesmen as well as pioneering black political leaders. In the back row, from left to right, are Robert C. De Large (South Carolina) and Jefferson F. Long (Georgia). In the front row are Hiram R. Revels (Mississippi), Benjamin S. Turner (Alabama), Josiah T. Walls (Florida), Joseph H. Rainey (South Carolina), and Robert Brown Elliott (South Carolina). Except for Revels, who served in the Senate (1870–1871), all of these men served in the House of Representatives during the Forty-First (1869–1871) and/or Forty-Second Congress (1871–1873). *Library of Congress, Prints and Photographs Division, Washington, D.C., LC-DIG-ppmsca-17564.*

and political liberties possible and helped protect blacks. To ensure this right, the overwhelmingly Republican U.S. Congress proposed the **Fifteenth Amendment** in 1869, and it was ratified the next year. It declared, "The right of citizens of the United States to vote shall not be denied or abridged by the United States or by any State on account of race, color, or previous condition of servitude." With this amendment, many — including the prominent white abolitionist William Lloyd Garrison — believed that the federal government's constitutional incorporation of blacks into the Union was complete and its formal responsibility to the former slaves fulfilled.

Enforcement of the amendment was a separate issue, however, and to help clarify what equality meant, Senator Charles Sumner introduced one more civil rights bill. When passed after his death and partly in his memory, the **Civil Rights Act of 1875** required equal treatment in public accommodations and on public conveyances regardless of race. By this time, however, most Americans thought the freedpeople should be on their own and feared that further government efforts on their behalf would only undermine their self-reliance and make them wards of the state. Blacks, too, believed that they were responsible for their own future. Yet they knew all too well that the persistence of antiblack prejudice and discrimination, as well as the enduring legacy of slavery, required federal action. Only the federal government could ensure their freedom and their rights in the face of widespread and hostile white opposition.

The Defeat of Reconstruction

While northern whites thought that the Fifteenth Amendment completed Reconstruction, southern whites found black political involvement intolerable; they were shocked and outraged that their world had been turned upside down. For them, black political participation represented a "base conspiracy against human nature."[30] Even as many white southerners withdrew from the system, they immediately initiated a counterrevolution that would restore white rule and sought what they called "redemption" through the all-white Democratic Party.

White opposition movements proceeded differently in each state, but by the late 1860s they had begun to succeed. As soon as they gained sufficient leverage, southern whites ousted blacks from political office in an effort to bring back what they called "home rule" under the reinvigorated ideology of states' rights. Home rule and states' rights served as euphemisms for white domination of land, black labor, and state and local government. Under the guise of restoring fiscal conservatism — trimming taxes and cutting state government functions and budgets — southern Democrats scaled back and ended programs that assisted freedpeople, including ending South Carolina's land reform commission.

An essential element of white "redemption" was the intimidation of blacks through terror, violence, and even murder. White supremacist and vigilante organizations formed throughout the South. While the Ku Klux Klan (KKK), organized in Tennessee in 1865, was the most notable group, others were the '76 Association, the Knights of the White Camelia, the White Brotherhood, and the Pale Faces. Members of the KKK, called night riders because they conducted their raids at night, wore white robes and hoods to hide their identity. People from all sectors of southern white society joined these groups.

The targets of white attacks were often successful and economically independent black landowners, storeowners, and small entrepreneurs. Black schools, churches, homes, lodges, business buildings, livestock, barns, and fences were destroyed. Blacks were beaten, raped, murdered, and lynched. So widespread were these vicious attacks in the late 1860s and early 1870s that Congress held hearings to investigate the causes of this widespread lawlessness. "The object of it is to kill out the leading men of the republican party . . . men who have taken a prominent stand," testified Emanuel Fortune, a delegate to Florida's constitutional convention and member of the state

The Birth of a Nation, *1915*
D. W. Griffith's silent cinematic masterpiece *The Birth of a Nation* was the best movie of its time. Unfortunately, it offered a lurid treatment of southern whites' racist and erroneous rationale for overthrowing Black Reconstruction. According to this pervasive myth, widespread black misrule, abetted by corrupt and vindictive Republicans, wrought so much suffering on the defeated white South that a heroic Ku Klux Klan finally rose to take charge and restore order and white supremacy. Note the stereotypical and horrific black male presented in this scene from the movie: He is beastly, bug-eyed, and a threat to white patriarchy. While whites largely embraced Griffith's film, blacks rejected it precisely because of its racism and historical misrepresentations. *Epoch/The Kobal Collection at Art Resource, NY.*

house of representatives who had been forced from his home and county by the KKK. In other testimony, Congress learned that Jack Dupree of Monroe County, Mississippi, the strong-willed president of a local Republican club, had been lynched by the KKK in front of his wife and newborn twins.[31]

To restore order, Congress passed two **Force Acts**, in 1870 and 1871, to protect the civil rights of blacks as defined in the Fourteenth and Fifteenth Amendments.

Federal troops rather than state militias were authorized to put down the widespread lawlessness, and those who conspired to deprive black people of their civil rights were to be tried in federal rather than state or local courts.

Nevertheless, the violence continued. In Colfax, Louisiana, a disputed election in 1873 prompted whites to use cannon and rifle fire to disband a group of armed freedmen, commanded by black militia and veterans, who were attempting to maintain Republican control of the town. On Easter Sunday, in the bloodiest racial massacre of the era, more than 280 blacks were killed, including 50 who had surrendered. The Colfax Massacre demonstrated the limits of armed black self-defense and the lengths to which whites would go to secure white dominance. A similar white attack occurred in 1876 in Hamburg, South Carolina, where skirmishes between black militiamen, armed by the state, and whites, acting on their own authority, escalated into a shootout. Six black men died at the hands of the white mob. The Hamburg Massacre routed local black political authority and strengthened white resolve to "redeem" South Carolina.

In the end, the Republican Party, the federal government, and northern whites all accepted the return of white ex-Confederates to political and economic power. With the death of Thaddeus Stevens in 1868 and Charles Sumner in 1874, blacks lost their most effective spokesmen in Congress. Growing numbers of Republicans had wearied of the party's crusade on behalf of blacks and were happy to turn what they called the "Negro problem" over to southern whites, who were presumed to know best how to handle it. Republicans were confident that the Fifteenth Amendment had secured their black voting base in the South. As the party gathered strength in the Midwest and West, recruiting black Republicans — and securing a southern base for the Republican Party — became less important to the party. Instead, it turned its attention to economic issues, such as support for railroads and industry. Especially after the panic of 1873 set off a deep four-year depression, black Republicans in the South, and black civil rights in general, became expendable.

One indication of the federal government's abandonment of the freedpeople was its failure to back the Freedman's Savings and Trust Company, which collapsed during the depression. Chartered by Congress in 1865 to promote thrift and savings among freedpeople, it had many small savings accounts averaging less than $50 each. Its last president was Frederick Douglass, who deposited $10,000 of his own money to bolster the institution. When the bank failed in 1874, thousands of African Americans lost all they had. Eventually, half of the account holders received reimbursements of about 60 percent of their deposits. The other half received nothing.

By 1877, southern whites had retaken political control of all the southern states. That same year, in a political deal that resolved the disputed 1876 presidential election between the Democrat Samuel Tilden and the Republican Rutherford B. Hayes, Black Reconstruction officially ended. In return for a Hayes victory, Republicans agreed to remove federal troops from the South. In April 1877, when the troops withdrew, southern blacks were left without federal protection.

The U.S. Supreme Court further undermined black civil rights. In the 1873 **Slaughterhouse Cases**, the Court, distinguishing between national citizenship and state citizenship, ruled that the Fourteenth Amendment guaranteed only a narrow class of national citizenship rights and did not encompass the array of civil rights pertaining to state citizenship. A decade later, in the **Civil Rights Cases** (1883), the Court overturned the Civil Rights Act of 1875, declaring that Congress did not have the authority to protect against the discriminatory conduct of individuals and private groups. As a result, private companies and businesses, such as hotels, restaurants, and theaters, could refuse to serve black people, and they did. The Court thus legitimized the power of states and private individuals and institutions to discriminate against black citizens and practically canceled the power of the federal government to intervene. AME bishop Henry McNeal Turner expressed pervasive black feelings of both outrage and despair. The decision, he proclaimed, "absolves the Negro's allegiance to the general government, makes the American flag to him a rag of contempt instead of a symbol of liberty."[32]

Opportunities and Limits outside the South

During the Civil War, roughly 100,000 blacks left the South permanently, relocating in the North, Midwest, and West, especially in areas bordering on the former Confederacy (Map 8.2).[33] During Reconstruction, the migration continued, as many African Americans believed they had to leave the South to improve their lives. Wherever they went, however, they encountered well-established patterns of antiblack prejudice and discrimination. Often new patterns developed as well. White military officials, factory owners, and union leaders limited black opportunities for dignified work and fair wages, further circumscribing black lives. By the mid-1880s, national indifference to the plight of blacks meant that wherever they lived, they knew that they themselves, not the states or the federal government, had to protect their rights and liberties.

Autonomy in the West

For African Americans, as for all Americans, the West beckoned as a land of opportunity. Some who envisioned a better future for themselves in the West were young men who joined the army. The U.S. Colored Troops were disbanded after the war, but new black units (again with white officers) were authorized. Between 1866 and 1917, 25,000 black men — some former Civil War soldiers and others with no prior military experience — served in the Ninth and Tenth Cavalry Regiments and the Twenty-Fourth and Twenty-Fifth Infantry Regiments (established in 1866), all assigned to military posts in the West. There they fought in the Indian wars that tragically dispossessed Native Americans of their land and removed them onto reservations. Native Americans called these black soldiers **buffalo soldiers**, apparently in reference to their fierce fighting abilities and their dark curly hair, which resembled a buffalo's mane.

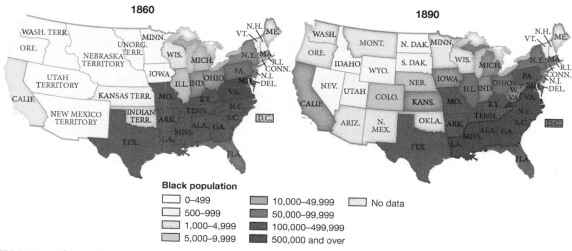

MAP 8.2   **African American Population Distribution, 1860 and 1890**

In the years following the Civil War, the black population grew significantly and began to spread across the nation. Nevertheless, the vast majority of blacks remained wedded to the South. The states that witnessed the largest and most striking growth in their black populations from 1860 onward, and those with the largest total numbers of blacks in 1890, were those of the former Confederacy — the so-called black belt states of the antebellum and postbellum South — and the states bordering them.

Thirteen enlisted men and six officers received the Congressional Medal of Honor for their service in the Indian wars. Private Henry McCombs of the Tenth Calvary bragged, "We made the West," having "defeated the hostile tribes of Indians; and made the country safe to live in."[34]

Buffalo soldiers led a rough life on remote military posts. Most were single, although over time, as camp life improved, some married or brought wives and children to join them. Unlike white soldiers, who rotated out of service in the West to posts in the South and East, buffalo soldiers remained in the West, where the army expected they would encounter less racial hostility. But tensions were evident between buffalo soldiers on one hand and whites, Native Americans, and Latinos on the other, particularly in Kansas and in Texas along the Mexican border. Sometimes these tensions erupted into violence, as when a black soldier was lynched in Sturgis, Dakota Territory, in 1885. In response, twenty men from the Twenty-Fifth Infantry shot up two saloons, killing one white civilian.

A few black men became officers, but not without enduring discrimination both within the ranks and from white officers. Henry O. Flipper is one example. Appointed to West Point by a Reconstruction Republican from Georgia, Flipper became the first black to graduate from the military academy in 1877. As a second lieutenant in the Tenth Cavalry Regiment, he was often assigned to manual labor instead of command positions. Nevertheless, he served with distinction in the Apache War of 1880. Two years later, however, he was dismissed from the army on a controversial charge of embezzlement. For the rest of his life, he fought to be exonerated and reinstated.

Other African Americans went west as families. An especially notable migration took place from Tennessee and Kentucky to Kansas, where African Americans hoped to claim cheap public land available under the Homestead Act of 1862. In 1876, the Hartwell family of Pulaski, Tennessee, in 1866 the birthplace of the KKK, migrated to Kansas because Tennessee was "no place for colored people."[35] In Kansas, black migrants built all-black towns that promised freedom from white persecution and an opportunity for self-government. Nicodemus, incorporated in 1877, was the most famous of these towns. "Nicodemus is the most harmonious place on earth," proclaimed one of the town's newspapers in 1887. "Everybody works for the interest of the town and all pull together."[36] It grew out of a development proposal by W. J. Niles, a black businessman, and a white land developer named W. R. Hill. The first black settlers came from Lexington, Kentucky, and by 1880 the thriving town, which serviced a growing county, had almost 260 black and almost 60 white residents, a bank, general stores, hotels, a pharmacy, a millinery, a livery, and a barbershop.[37] One resident was Edward P. McCabe, a talented and ambitious New Yorker and an active Republican who, upon moving to Nicodemus, became a farmer, attorney, and land agent. During the years he served as state auditor (1883–1887), he was the highest-ranking black officeholder in the country.

Benjamin "Pap" Singleton, who detested sharecropping and promoted black land-ownership as the most viable basis for black self-improvement, became the most important proponent of the black migration to Kansas. Operating out of Edgefield, Tennessee, his Edgefield Real Estate and Homestead Association spread word of available land and a hospitable environment for blacks in Kansas. Black newspapers, mass meetings, circulars, and letters home from migrants also inspired "emigration fever." Singleton became known as "the Moses of the Colored Exodus." In the spring and summer of 1879, more than 6,000 blacks from Texas, Louisiana, and Mississippi — called **Exodusters** — migrated to Kansas, where they were able to settle on land that became theirs. John Solomon Lewis of Louisiana described the feeling: "When I landed on the soil, I looked on the ground and I says this is free ground. Then I looked on the heavens, and I says them is free and beautiful heavens. Then I looked within my heart, and I says to myself I wonder why I never was free before?"[38]

Landownership made the difference, and the Exodusters established four all-black farming communities that grew into towns with businesses, churches, and schools. Most Exodusters decided for themselves to take a chance on the West, although grassroots leaders such as Singleton and Henry Adams from Shreveport, Louisiana, helped inspire them. Adams's activities in politics and black labor organizing were indicative of a growing grassroots black nationalism. Involved in a variety of regional networks along the Mississippi River, Adams promoted migration to Kansas and also supported the Colonization Council, which sought federal funds for black migration to Liberia.

Black Homesteaders

Nicodemus, Kansas, founded in 1877, is among the oldest and most famous of the black towns founded in the late nineteenth century. In these settlements, black migrants such as the men and women shown here left behind the racial restrictions and horrors of the South for the promise of a new start: a viable homestead in the West. While some whites lived in Nicodemus, the town's population was mostly black. Nicodemus peaked in the early 1880s before beginning to decline late in the decade. A few hundred people still live there today. This late-nineteenth-century photo of two well-dressed black couples in Nicodemus reflects a striking sense of frontier commitment and rough-hewn refinement. These couples vividly illustrate the sense of hope and possibility projected by the boosters of Nicodemus at its height. *Library of Congress, Prints and Photographs Division, Washington, D.C., HABS KANS, 33-NICO, 1-6, 069503p/.*

Between 1865 and 1920, more than sixty all-black towns were created in the West, some fifty of them in Oklahoma, where new settlements of southern freedmen joined with former slaves owned by Native Americans were established in what had been designated Indian Territory. Tullahassee, for example, which began as a Creek settlement in 1850, had become mostly African American by 1881, as the Creeks moved elsewhere. In the late 1880s, when Indian land in Oklahoma was opened up for settlement, all-black towns boomed. They offered a freedom unknown elsewhere. But the five- to ten-acre plots on which most black migrants settled were too small for independent farms, and many ended up working for nearby ranches and larger farms owned by whites.[39] Eventually, most of the black boomtowns died out.

The Right to Work for Fair Wages

Like Jourdon Anderson, some former slaves left the South as soon as they were free, moving north in expectation of fair wages for their labor and a good education for their children. Many gravitated to cities, where the hope of better jobs soon faltered. Black newcomers ran into the prejudice and discrimination in hiring and wages that had long hobbled black workers there. Managers were reluctant to hire them, and white workers, who saw them as competition, were hostile, especially since blacks were often hired as strikebreakers. White labor unions characteristically excluded blacks.

Some individuals were able to set out on their own. In 1865, when white caulkers in the Baltimore shipyards went on strike to force the firing of more than a hundred black caulkers and longshoremen, Isaac Myers, a highly skilled black caulker, joined with other black labor activists and a small group of supportive whites to create the black-owned and cooperatively run Chesapeake Marine Railway and Dry Dock Company. It was a strong center of black union activism, and in 1869 Myers helped found the Colored National Labor Union to advance the cause of black workers. Myers was also a proponent of interracial labor solidarity. Yet his efforts were short-lived. By the mid-1870s, the Colored National Labor Union had dissolved due to internal dissension and the economic depression that followed the panic of 1873. By the mid-1880s, the company Myers had founded also had collapsed.

The idea of interracial labor solidarity was taken up by the Knights of Labor, a broad-based union founded in 1869 that welcomed both skilled and unskilled workers and eventually African Americans and women. With the rise of industry in the North during and after the war, the Knights believed that only a united and inclusive labor movement could stand up to the growing power of industrialists, who, said the Knights, built profits through "wage slavery." The organization's motto was "An injury to one is the concern of all." At its height in 1886, the Knights had more than 700,000 members. Despite the fact that its assemblies in the South were segregated by race, the Knights' commitment to interracial unionism drew African American support. Black workers fully embraced the Knights' major goals: the eight-hour workday, the abolition of child and convict labor, equal pay for equal work, and worker-owned and worker-managed cooperatives. By 1886, two-thirds of Richmond, Virginia's 5,000 tobacco workers — many of them black — belonged to the organization. But the Knights of Labor's quick decline followed its quick rise to prominence. Failed strikes and disputes between skilled and unskilled workers weakened it internally, and the 1886 Haymarket bombing — a deadly confrontation between striking workers and police in Chicago — damaged its reputation. In Richmond, the demise of the Knights doomed prospects for interracial unionism for decades.

The Struggle for Equal Rights

In the North and West, the fight for dignified work and equal labor rights took place in concert with a growing civil rights struggle that was part of a larger black freedom struggle that had begun before the war. The National Equal Rights League (see chapter 7) continued to promote full legal and political equality, land acquisition as a basis for economic independence, education, frugality, and moral rectitude. Local, state, and national meetings kept the tradition of vigorous agitation alive, while petition campaigns and lobbying kept the pressure on the Republican Party to pass legislation and amendments guaranteeing black civil rights and suffrage.

On the local level, black campaigns against segregated seating in public conveyances continued, many of them having been initiated by women. In Philadelphia, Frances Ellen Watkins Harper and Harriet Tubman were among those who protested their forcible ejections from streetcars. The long campaign led by Octavius Catto, a teacher at the Institute for Colored Youth, and William Still, the best-known "agent" on the underground railroad, finally succeeded in getting a desegregation law passed in 1867. Three days later, when a conductor told school principal Caroline Le Count that she could not board a streetcar, she lodged a complaint, and the conductor was fined. Thereafter, Philadelphia's streetcar companies abided by the new law, reversing decades of custom.[40] A similar protest in which Sojourner Truth played a role had ended streetcar segregation in Washington, D.C., in 1865.

Segregated schools were the norm in the North, and as in the South many blacks preferred all-black schools with black teachers who took the interests of black students to heart. Catto argued for this position. He also pointed out that white teachers assigned to black schools were likely to be those not qualified for positions in white schools, and thus "inferior."[41] In other communities, black fathers initiated suits so that their children could attend white schools. Cases in Iowa in 1875 and 1876 brought court rulings in the plaintiffs' favor, but local whites blocked their enforcement. In Indiana, despite an 1869 law permitting localities to provide schools for black children, communities with few black residents did not do so, and black children all too often went without an education. The same situation pertained in Illinois and California.[42]

During Black Reconstruction, educational opportunities for black children may have been more plentiful in the South than in the North, and opportunities for black voting were better in the South, too. In 1865, black men in the North could vote without restriction only in Maine, New Hampshire, Vermont, Massachusetts, and Rhode Island. Together these states accounted for just 7 percent of the northern black population. Some northern states actually took action to deny black men the vote — Minnesota, Kansas, and Ohio in 1867, and Michigan and New York in 1868. Most northern whites viewed the vote as a white male prerogative. Even where blacks could vote, they were often intimidated and subjected to violence. In 1871, Octavius Catto was murdered on his way to the polls.

Thus, in 1869 and 1870, ratification of the Fifteenth Amendment proved to be as contentious in the North and West as it was in the South. The former slave states of Delaware, Kentucky, Maryland, and Tennessee rejected the amendment, but so did California and New Jersey; New York rescinded its ratification; and Ohio waffled, first rejecting and then ratifying the amendment. Reasons for the opposition varied. Californians, for example, wanted to ensure that the amendment did not enfranchise Chinese residents. The debate in states that eventually ratified the amendment varied. Massachusetts and Connecticut had literacy requirements that they hoped would remain unaffected. Rhode Island wanted to retain its requirement that foreign-born citizens had to own property worth at least $134 to be eligible to vote. These restrictions narrowed the electorate in the North and West by making it difficult for poor and illiterate whites, as well as blacks, to vote. After the end of Reconstruction, some of the same and similar techniques would be used by southern states to disfranchise blacks.

Yet the Fifteenth Amendment proved most contentious among many northern women for what it did *not* do: It did not extend the vote to women. Many woman suffrage supporters, especially white women, felt betrayed that black men would get the vote before women. Abolitionists and feminists had long been allied in the struggle for equal rights, and women had actively worked for abolition, emancipation, and the Thirteenth Amendment. In 1866, to present a united front in support of universal suffrage, women's rights leaders Lucy Stone, Susan B. Anthony, and Elizabeth Cady Stanton joined with Frederick Douglass to found the American Equal Rights Association. But it soon became apparent that members of this organization did not all share the same priorities. (See Document Project: The Vote, pp. 331–39.) Douglass and Stone believed that the organization should work to secure the black male vote first and then seek woman suffrage. Stanton and Anthony detested the idea that the rights of women would take a backseat to those of black men. Stanton even resorted to using the racist epithet "Sambo" in reference to black men.[43] Black feminists such as Sojourner Truth and Frances Ellen Watkins Harper took Stanton to task for ignoring the reality of black women's lives. "You white women speak here of rights," Harper protested. "I speak of wrongs."[44]

Dissension over the Fifteenth Amendment divided old allies, destroyed friendships, and split the American Equal Rights Association (AERA) — and ultimately the women's movement itself. In 1869, in the wake of the AERA's fracturing, Anthony and Stanton organized the National Woman Suffrage Association, which focused on securing voting rights for women at the national level. That same year, Stone organized the rival American Woman Suffrage Association, which included among its members Harper, Truth, and Douglass and developed a state-by-state approach to woman suffrage. The bitter fight over the Fifteenth Amendment revealed deeper divisions in American politics and society over the rights and status of African Americans that would undercut their opportunities for decades to come.

CONCLUSION

Revolutions and Reversals

The end of slavery in the United States was revolutionary. For former slaves, now free, lives and livelihoods had to be remade. Foremost on the minds of many was reuniting with family members separated by slave sales and war. New black communities were built and old ones were renewed, centering on independent black churches, schools, and enterprises. Freedpeople knew that to live independently, they had to be literate, and they placed great faith in education. They learned eagerly, and within a decade dozens of black colleges were giving students a formal and expanded education, including the opportunity to acquire job skills, such as teacher training. Former slaves remade themselves, their families, and their communities, but their hopes for economic independence faded as the reality of emancipation, which had made them free but had not provided them with land, set in. Impoverished and pressed into labor patterns that resembled slavery, most became tenant farmers or sharecroppers, dependent on white landowners, and many became trapped in a cycle of debt.

When the Radical Republicans in Congress took control of Reconstruction in 1867, their efforts to guarantee civil rights for former slaves effected a political revolution in the South that had the potential for an economic and social revolution, too. With black votes and officeholding, southern states wrote new constitutions that created state aid for economic development, progressive tax and judicial systems, much-needed social welfare institutions, and the region's first public school systems. But this so-called Black Reconstruction proved short-lived. Southern white opposition was unrelenting and often violent. By 1877, whites had regained control of state and local governments in the South. As the Republican Party, now weary of the campaign for black rights, increasingly turned its attention to economic development, southern blacks in particular were left with shockingly little protection and dwindling numbers of effective white advocates of equal rights for blacks. "When you turned us loose," Frederick Douglass chastised the Republican National Convention in 1876, "you gave us no acres: you turned us loose to the sky, to the storm, to the whirlwind, and, worst of all, you turned us loose to the wrath of our infuriated masters."[45]

Some southern blacks went west to build new communities or to serve in army units that fought the Indian wars. Others sought work in the expanding factories of the North. But wherever they went, they encountered prejudice and discrimination. Although campaigns for desegregating transportation and schools resulted in the passage of civil rights laws, those laws often went unenforced. U.S. Supreme Court rulings limited the impact of well-intentioned laws and constitutional amendments passed during Black Reconstruction. In 1883, a revived National Equal Rights League, meeting in Louisville, Kentucky, conceded "that many of the laws intended to secure us our rights as citizens are nothing more than dead letters."[46]

Abandoned by the government as they sought to carve out meaningful lives within an increasingly white supremacist nation, African Americans understood more clearly now than ever before what they had always known in their hearts: They were responsible for their own uplift (see chapter 9). Thus freedom's first generations turned inward, practiced self-reliance, and focused even more intently on self-elevation and the building of strong communities that would sustain them going forward.

CHAPTER 8 **REVIEW**

KEY TERMS

historically black colleges and universities p. 305

sharecropping p. 307

crop lien p. 307

convict lease p. 307

black codes p. 307

Black Reconstruction p. 312

Civil Rights Act of 1866 p. 313

Fourteenth Amendment (ratified 1868) p. 313

Reconstruction Act of 1867 (first) p. 313

Union League p. 317

Fifteenth Amendment (ratified 1870) p. 318

Civil Rights Act of 1875 p. 318

Force Acts (1870, 1871) p. 320

Slaughterhouse Cases **(1873)** p. 322

Civil Rights Cases **(1883)** p. 322

buffalo soldiers p. 322

Exodusters p. 324

REVIEW QUESTIONS

1. What practices, institutions, and organizations did former slaves develop to facilitate their transition to freedom? How successful were they, and what challenges did they face?

2. What factors resulted in the defeat of Reconstruction? Was it inevitable, or might things have turned out differently had any of these circumstances been different? Explain.

3. What kinds of opportunities did former slaves seek in the North and West? How did they attempt to realize their dreams? What obstacles did they have to overcome?

4. Should we judge Reconstruction on its initial promise or its ultimate failure? What is your assessment of this period?

The Vote

After the Thirteenth Amendment ended slavery in 1865, the Fourteenth Amendment, proposed in June 1866, sought to secure black civil rights by defining citizenship and guaranteeing the equal protection of the laws. In establishing the means by which representation in Congress would be apportioned, this amendment used the word *male* for the first time in the Constitution. Supporters of woman suffrage were dismayed, for they had hoped for universal suffrage — the right of every adult to vote without regard to race or sex. In August 1866, a group of women joined with Frederick Douglass to found the American Equal Rights Association (AERA), in an effort to create a united front for advancing the causes of black and women's rights. When it became evident that the Fifteenth Amendment, proposed in February 1869, would secure black male suffrage but not woman suffrage, the AERA split.

Some AERA members, led by Douglass, believed that black male suffrage was the most immediate need. Others, including Susan B. Anthony and Elizabeth Cady Stanton, gave priority to woman suffrage. But what did black women think? Did they ally themselves with black men or white women? In the following documents, black women voice their opinions on suffrage, an issue that went to the core of their identities.

Contemporary visual representations of Black Reconstruction, notably those depicting black male voters and politicians, reveal the historical moment and the political, racial, and cultural as well as the aesthetic aims of the artists. In the late 1860s, the Radical Republicans were still in their ascendancy, but by 1874 their heyday was over. Within the party and throughout the nation, support for freedpeople and their cause had diminished.

Sojourner Truth | *Equal Voting Rights, 1867*

SOJOURNER TRUTH (1797–1883) was nearly seventy years old when she spoke at the second meeting of the American Equal Rights Association in New York City in May 1867. She had begun life as a slave in New York and become one of the most famous African Americans of the nineteenth century. An abolitionist and a supporter of women's rights, Truth electrified audiences with her candor and forthright manner of expression.

I feel that if I have to answer for the deeds done in my body just as much as a man, I have a right to have just as much as a man. There is a great stir about colored men getting their rights, but not a word about the colored women; and if colored men get their rights, and not colored women theirs, you see the colored men will be masters over the women, and it will be just as bad as it was before. So I am for keeping the thing going while things are stirring; because if we wait till it is still, it will take a great while to get it going again. White women are a great deal smarter, and know more than colored women, while colored women do not know scarcely anything. They go

SOURCE: Philip S. Foner and Robert James Branham, eds., *Lift Every Voice: African American Oratory, 1787–1900* (Tuscaloosa: University of Alabama Press, 1998), 464–65.

out washing, which is about as high as a colored woman gets, and their men go about idle, strutting up and down; and when the women come home, they ask for their money and take it all, and then scold because there is no food. I want you to consider on that, chil'n. I call you chil'n; you are somebody's chil'n, and I am old enough to be mother of all that is here. I want women to have their rights. In the courts women have no right, no voice; nobody speaks for them. I wish woman to have her voice there among the pettifoggers.° If it is not a fit place for women, it is unfit for men to be there.

I am above eighty years old;° it is about time for me to be going. I have been forty years a slave and forty years free, and would be here forty years more to have equal rights for all. I suppose I am kept here because something remains for me to do; I suppose I am yet to help to break the chain. I have done a great deal of work; as much as a man, but did not get so much pay. I used to work in the field and bind grain, keeping up with the cradler;°

° Tricksters.
° She was actually about seventy.
° A machine for binding and bunching grain.

but men doing no more, got twice as much pay; so with the German women. They work in the field and do as much work, but do not get the pay. We do as much, we eat as much, we want as much. I suppose I am about the only colored woman that goes about to speak for the rights of the colored women. I want to keep the thing stirring, now that the ice is cracked. What we want is a little money. You men know that you get as much again as women when you write, or for what you do. When we get our rights we shall not have to come to you for money, for then we shall have money enough in our own pockets; and may be you will ask us for money. But help us now until we get it. It is a good consolation to know that when we have got this battle once fought we shall not be coming to you any more. You have been having our rights so long, that you think, like a slave-holder, that you own us. I know that it is hard for one who has held the reins for so long to give up; it cuts like a knife. It will feel all the better when it closes up again. I have been in Washington about three years, seeing about these colored people. Now colored men have [will soon attain] the right to vote. There ought to be equal rights now more than ever, since colored people have got their freedom.

Proceedings of the American Equal Rights Association | A Debate: Negro Male Suffrage vs. Woman Suffrage, 1869

The May 12, 1869, meeting of the AMERICAN EQUAL RIGHTS ASSOCIATION was its last. By this time, tensions between those who prioritized black male suffrage and those who prioritized woman suffrage had torn the association apart. In this excerpt from the meeting's proceedings, we hear from Frederick Douglass and Frances Ellen Watkins Harper, two of the most important African American leaders of the day and key advocates for abolition, African American rights, and women's rights. Susan B. Anthony, Lucy Stone, Pauline W. Davis, Julia Ward Howe, and Elizabeth Cady Stanton were key white advocates for both abolition and women's rights and, to differing extents, supporters of African American rights.

MR. DOUGLASS: I come here more as a listener than to speak and I have listened with a great deal of pleasure. . . . There is no name greater than that of Elizabeth Cady Stanton in the matter of woman's rights and equal rights, but my sentiments are tinged a little against [her remarks in] *The Revolution* [a magazine]. There was in the address to which I allude the employment of certain names, such as "Sambo," and the gardener, and the bootblack, and the daughters of Jefferson and Washington and other daughters. (Laughter.) I must say that I asked what difference there is between the daughters of Jefferson and Washington and other daughters. (Laughter.) I must say that I do not see how any one can pretend that there is the same urgency in giving the ballot to woman as to the negro. With us, the matter is a question of life and death, at least, in fifteen States of the Union. When women, because they are women, are hunted down through the cities of New York and New Orleans; when they are dragged from their houses and hung upon lamp-posts; when their children are torn from their arms, and their brains dashed out upon the pavement; when they are objects of insult and outrage at every turn; when they are in danger of having their homes burnt down over their heads; when their children are not allowed to enter schools; then they will have an urgency to obtain the ballot equal to our own. (Great applause.)

A VOICE: — Is that not all true about black women?

MR. DOUGLASS: — Yes, yes, yes; it is true of the black woman, but not because she is a woman, but because she is black. (Applause.) Julia Ward Howe at the conclusion of her great speech delivered at the convention in Boston last year said: "I am willing that the negro shall get the ballot before me." (Applause.) Woman! why, she has 10,000 modes of grappling with her difficulties. I believe that all the virtue of the world can take care of all the evil. I believe that all the intelligence can take care of all the ignorance. (Applause.) I am in favor of woman's suffrage in order that we shall have all the virtue and vice confronted. Let me tell you that when there were few houses in which the black man could have put his head, this wooly head of mine found a refuge in the house of Mrs. Elizabeth Cady Stanton, and if I had been blacker than sixteen midnights, without a single star, it would have been the same. (Applause.)

MISS [Susan B.] ANTHONY: — The old anti-slavery school says women must stand back and wait until the negroes shall be recognized. But we say, if you will not give the whole loaf of suffrage to the entire people, give it to the most intelligent first. (Applause.) If intelligence, justice, and morality are to have precedence in the Government, let the question of woman be brought up first and that of the negro last. (Applause.) While I was canvassing the State with petitions and had them filled with names for our cause to the Legislature, a man dared to say to me that the freedom of women was all a theory and not a practical thing. (Applause.) When Mr. Douglass mentioned the black man first and the woman last, if he had noticed he would have seen that it was the men that clapped and not the women. There is not the woman born who desires to eat the bread of dependence, no matter whether it be from the hand of father, husband, or brother; for any one who does so eat her bread places herself in the power of the person from whom she takes it. (Applause.) Mr. Douglass talks about the wrongs of the negro; but with all the outrages that he to-day suffers, he would not exchange his sex and take the place of Elizabeth Cady Stanton. (Laughter and applause.)

MR. DOUGLASS: I want to know if granting you the right of suffrage will change the nature of our sexes? (Great laughter.)

MISS ANTHONY: It will change the pecuniary position of woman; it will place her where she can earn her own bread. (Loud applause.)

SOURCE: Philip S. Foner, ed., *Frederick Douglass on Women's Rights* (New York: Da Capo Press, 1992), 86–89.

She will not then be driven to such employments only as man chooses for her. . . .

MRS. LUCY STONE: — Mrs. Stanton will, of course, advocate the precedence for her sex, and Mr. Douglass will strive for the first position for his, and both are perhaps right. If it be true that the government derives its authority from the consent of the governed, we are safe in trusting that principle to the uttermost. If one has a right to say that you can not read and therefore can not vote, then it may be said that you are a woman and therefore can not vote. We are lost if we turn away from the middle principle and argue for one class. . . . The gentleman who addressed you claimed that the negroes had the first right to the suffrage, and drew a picture which only his great word-power can do. He again in Massachusetts, when it had cast a majority in favor of Grant and negro suffrage, stood upon the platform and said that woman had better wait for the negro; that is, that both could not be carried, and that the negro had better be the one. But I freely forgave him because he felt as he spoke. But woman suffrage is more imperative than his own; and I want to remind the audience that when he says what the Ku-Kluxes did all over the South, the Ku-Kluxes here in the North in the shape of men, take away the children from the mother, and separate them as completely as if done on the block of the auctioneer. . . . Woman has an ocean of wrongs too deep for any plummet, and the negro, too, has an ocean of wrongs that can not be fathomed. There are two great oceans; in the one is the black man, and in the other is the woman. But I thank God for that XV. Amendment, and hope it will be adopted in every State. I will be thankful in my soul if *any* body can get out of the terrible pit. But I believe that the safety of the government would be more promoted by the admission of woman as an element of restoration and harmony than the negro. I believe that the influence of woman will save the country before every other power. (Applause.) I see the signs of times pointing to this consummation, and I believe that in some parts of the country women will vote for the President of the United States in 1872. . . .

MRS. PAULINE W. DAVIS said she would not be altogether satisfied to have the XVth Amendment passed without the XVIth, for woman would have a race of tyrants raised above her in the South, and the black women of that country would also receive worse treatment than if the Amendment was not passed. Take any class that have been slaves, and you will find that they are the worst when free, and become the hardest masters. The colored women of the South say they do not want to get married to the negro, as their husbands can take their children away from them, and also appropriate their earnings. The black women are more intelligent than the men, because they have learned something from their mistresses. She then related incidents showing how black men whip and abuse their wives in the South. One of her sister's servants whipped his wife every Sunday regularly. (Laughter.) She thought that sort of men should not have the making of the laws for the government of the women throughout the land. (Applause.)

MR. DOUGLASS said that all disinterested spectators would concede that this Equal Rights meeting had been pre-eminently a Woman's Rights meeting. (Applause.) They had just heard an argument with which he could not agree — that the suffrage to the black men should be postponed to that of the women. . . . "I do not believe the story that the slaves who are enfranchised become the worst of tyrants. (A voice, 'Neither do I.' Applause.) I know how this theory came about. When a slave was made a driver, he made himself more officious than the white driver, so that his master might not suspect that he was favoring those under him. But we do not intend to have any master over us. (Applause.)"

THE PRESIDENT (MRS. STANTON) argued that not another man should be enfranchised until enough women are admitted to the polls to outweigh those already there. (Applause.) She did not believe in allowing ignorant negroes and foreigners to make laws for her to obey. (Applause.)

MRS. [Frances Ellen Watkins] HARPER (colored) said that when it was a question of race, she let the lesser question of sex go. But the white women all go for sex, letting race occupy a minor position. She liked the idea of work-women, but she would like to know if it was broad enough to take colored women.

MISS ANTHONY and several others: Yes, yes.

MRS. HARPER said that when she was at Boston there were sixty women who left work because one colored woman went to gain a livelihood in their midst. (Applause.) If the nation could only handle one question, she would not have the black woman put a single straw in the way, if only the men of the race could obtain what they wanted. (Great applause.)

Mary Ann Shadd Cary | *Woman's Right to Vote, early 1870s*

MARY ANN SHADD CARY (1823–1893) was an educator, a journalist, and a reformer who was deeply committed to both black and women's rights. In the 1850s, she was also a proponent of emigration to Canada. Following the split of the AERA, she sided with Elizabeth Cady Stanton and Susan B. Anthony in founding the National Woman Suffrage Association. At the time she gave this speech, Cary was teaching in Washington, D.C. The speech captures the substance of remarks she made before the Judiciary Committee of the House of Representatives in support of a petition on behalf of enfranchising women in Washington, D.C. In 1883, Cary received her law degree from Howard University.

By the provisions of the 14th & 15th amendments to the Constitution of the United States, — a logical sequence of which is the representation by colored men of time-honored commonwealths in both houses of Congress, — millions of colored *women*, to-day, share with colored men the responsibilities of freedom from chattel slavery. From the introduction of ~~freedom~~° African slavery to its extinction, a period of more than two hundred years, *they* ~~shared~~ *equally* with fathers, brothers, denied the right to vote. This fact of their investiture with the privileges of free women of the same time and by the same amendments which disentralled their kinsmen and conferred upon the latter the right of franchise, without so endowing themselves is one of the anomalies of a measure of legislation otherwise grand in conception and consequences beyond comparison. The colored women of this country though heretofore silent, in great measure upon this question of the right to vote by the women of the [copy missing], so long and ardently the cry of the noblest of the land, have neither been indifferent to their own just claims under the amendments, in common with colored men, nor to the demand for political recognition so justly made every where ~~within its borders~~ throughout the land.

The strength and glory of a free nation, is *not so much* in the size and equipments of its armies, as in the *loyal hearts* and willing hands of its *men* and *women*; And this fact has been illustrated in an eminent degree by well-known events in the history of the United States. To the ~~white~~ women of the nation conjointly with the men, it is indebted for arduous and dangerous personal service, and generous expenditure of time, wealth and counsel, so indispensable to success in its hour of danger. The colored *women* though humble in sphere, and unendowed with worldly goods, yet, led as by inspiration, — not only fed, and sheltered, and guided in *safety* the prisoner soldiers of the Union when escaping from the enemy, or the soldier who was compelled to risk

---

° The strikethroughs throughout are part of the original document.

SOURCE: Philip S. Foner and Robert James Branham, eds., *Lift Every Voice: African American Oratory, 1787–1900* (Tuscaloosa: University of Alabama Press, 1998), 516–17.

life *itself* in the struggle to break the back-bone of rebellion, but gave their *sons* and brothers to the armies of the nation and their prayers to high Heaven for the success of the Right.

The surges of fratricidal war have passed we hope never to return; the premonitions of the future, are peace and good will; these blessings, so greatly to be desired, can only be made permanent, in responsible governments, — based as you affirm upon the consent of the governed, — by giving to both sexes practically the equal powers conferred in the provisions of the Constitution as amended. In the District of Columbia over which Congress has exclusive jurisdiction the women in common with the women of the states and territories, feel keenly the discrimination against them in the retention of the word *male* in the organic act for the same, and as by reason of its retention, all the evils incident to partial legislation are endured by them, they sincerely, hope that the word *male* may be stricken out by Congress on your recommendation without delay. Taxed, and governed in other respects, without their consent, they respectfully demand, that the principles of the *founders* of the government may *not* be disregarded in their case: but, as there are *laws* by which they are tried, with penalties attached thereto, that they may be invested with the right to vote as do men, that thus as in all Republics *indeed*, they may in future, be governed by their own consent.

A. R. Waud | *The First Vote, 1867*

This image by A. R. WAUD, which appeared in *Harper's Weekly*, evokes the revolutionary importance of African Americans' first opportunity to vote. The range of facial expressions, dress, status, and life experiences represented in the line of black male voters suggests the various meanings and expectations attached to the event. The black voters are humanized and individualized — a poor laborer, a well-dressed city man, a soldier. This all-male image captures the reality of the vote as a privilege of manhood. The flag overhead, as well as the serious expression of the white man overseeing the voting, reflects the profound political transformation represented by this very special moment.

Library of Congress, Prints and Photographs Division, Washington, D.C., LC-DIG-ppmsca-31598.

Thomas Nast | *The Ignorant Vote, 1876*

In December 1876, just after the presidential election, THOMAS NAST's *The Ignorant Vote* appeared on the cover of *Harper's Weekly*. Nast, the political cartoonist for *Harper's Weekly*, had previously created work that was more sympathetic to blacks. This cartoon, however, presents a very different and negative view in which the black voter is a dehumanized stereotype. It conveys the idea that the ignorant voters in the North, represented by a belligerent, apish Irishman, are evened out by the ignorant voters in the South, represented by a smiling, apish black man.

Library of Congress, Prints and Photographs Division, Washington, D.C., LC-USZ62-57340.

Thomas Nast | *Colored Rule in a Reconstructed(?) State, 1874*

Thomas Nast's *Colored Rule in a Reconstructed(?) State* appeared on the cover of the March 14, 1874, issue of *Harper's Weekly*. This drawing argues that Black Reconstruction was a tragic mistake owing to black inferiority and incapacity. The caption reads, "The members call each other thieves, liars, rascals, and cowards." Columbia, the goddess at the podium under the banner that says "Let us have peace," is reprimanding the legislators: "You are Aping the lowest Whites. If you disgrace your Race in this way you had better take Back Seats." Compare this view of black South Carolina legislators with the images of dignified black men and women in this chapter. Which image or images make the most powerful impression?

Library of Congress, Prints and Photographs Division, Washington, D.C., LC-USZ62-102256.

QUESTIONS FOR ANALYSIS

1. What economic arguments do Sojourner Truth and Susan B. Anthony present on behalf of women's rights?

2. What are the political arguments of Elizabeth Cady Stanton and Mary Ann Shadd Cary? How does Frederick Douglass counter such arguments? Does he take them seriously, or does he demean them?

3. Is Frances Ellen Watkins Harper a pragmatist? Why do you think she took the position she did?

4. Would you have argued that black men should get the vote first, then women, as Douglass did? Or would you have argued for universal suffrage? Why? What if you thought a universal suffrage amendment would likely fail, thus leaving both blacks and women disfranchised? Would arguing for black male suffrage be more strategic?

5. How do the images presented here reinforce racial stereotypes? Evaluate how the visual documents compare to the reality of black participation in politics in the Reconstruction-era South. Give specific examples.

NOTES

1. Jourdon Anderson to Colonel P. H. Anderson, 7 August 1865, quoted in Leon F. Litwack, *Been in the Storm So Long: The Aftermath of Slavery* (New York: Knopf, 1979), 333–35.

2. Quoted ibid., 230.

3. Provost Marshal at Sedalia, Missouri, to the Superintendent of the Organization of Missouri Black Troops, 21 March 1864, in *Freedom: A Documentary History of Emancipation, 1861–1867*, ed. Ira Berlin et al., 1st ser., vol. 1, *The Destruction of Slavery* (New York: Cambridge University Press, 1985), 481–82; Clarissa Burdett, affidavit filed before J. M. Kelley, March 27, 1865, Camp Nelson, Kentucky, in ibid., 615, 616.

4. Litwack, *Been in the Storm So Long*, 230.

5. Ibid., 229.

6. Tera Hunter, *To 'Joy My Freedom: Southern Black Women's Lives and Labors after the Civil War* (Cambridge: Harvard University Press, 1997), 39.

7. Quoted in Henry L. Swint, ed., *Dear Ones at Home: Letters from Contraband Camps* (Nashville: Vanderbilt University Press, 1966), 242–43.

8. Interview, in *The American Slave: A Composite Autobiography, North Carolina Narratives*, ed. George P. Rawick, vol. 14, part 1 (Westport, CT: Greenwood Press, 1972–1973), 248–52.

9. Interview, in *The American Slave: A Composite Autobiography, Unwritten History of Slavery*, ed. George P. Rawick, vol. 18 (Westport, CT: Greenwood Press, 1972), 124.

10. Interview, in *The American Slave: A Composite Autobiography, Arkansas Narratives*, ed. George P. Rawick, vol. 8, part 2 (Westport, CT: Greenwood Press, 1972), 52.

11. Matthew Gilbert, "Colored Churches: An Experiment," quoted in William E. Montgomery, *Under Their Own Vine and Fig Tree: The African-American Church in the South, 1865–1900* (Baton Rouge: LSU Press, 1993), 54.

12. C. Eric Lincoln and Lawrence H. Mamiya, *The Black Church in the African American Experience* (Durham, NC: Duke University Press, 1990), 25, 66.

13. Leslie A. Schwalm, *Emancipation's Diaspora: Race and Reconstruction in the Upper Midwest* (Chapel Hill: University of North Carolina Press, 2009), 144.

14. Quoted in Carter G. Woodson, *The History of the Negro Church* (Washington, DC: Associated Publishers, 1921), 225.

15. Quoted in Reginald F. Hildebrand, *The Times Were Strange and Stirring: Methodist Preachers and the Crisis of Emancipation* (Durham, NC: Duke University Press, 1995), 65.

16. Quoted in Steven Hahn et al., eds., *Freedom: A Documentary History of Emancipation, 1861–1867*, 3rd ser., vol. 1, *Land and Labor, 1865* (Chapel Hill: University of North Carolina Press, 2008), 396.

17. Quoted in Manuel Gottlieb, "The Land Question in Georgia during Reconstruction," *Science & Society* 3, no. 3 (1939): 364.

18. Quoted in Hahn, *Freedom*, 51–52.

19. Quoted in Litwack, *Been in the Storm So Long*, 366.

20. *The 2003 National Assessment of Adult Literacy*, Institute of Education Sciences, National Center for Education Statistics, U.S. Department of Education.

21. Quoted in Adam Fairclough, *A Class of Their Own: Black Teachers in the Segregated South* (Cambridge: Belknap Press of Harvard University Press, 2007), 42.

22. Quoted in Clarence E. Walker, *A Rock in a Weary Land: The African Methodist Episcopal Church during the Civil War and Reconstruction* (Baton Rouge: LSU Press, 1982), 51.

23. Quoted in Fairclough, *A Class of Their Own*, 69.

24. Quoted in "Fisk's Storied Past," Fisk University, http://www.fisk.edu/AboutFisk/HistoryOfFisk.aspx.

25. Quoted in "History," Hampton University, http://www.hamptonu.edu/about/history.cfm.

26. *Louisianian*, May 10, 1879, quoted in James D. Anderson, *The Education of Blacks in the South, 1860–1935* (Chapel Hill: University of North Carolina Press, 1988), 64.

27. Samuel Thomas to O. O. Howard, 6 September 1865, quoted in Eric Foner, *Reconstruction: America's Unfinished Revolution, 1863–1877* (New York: Harper & Row, 1988), 150.

28. W. E. B. Du Bois, *Black Reconstruction in America: An Essay toward a History of the Part Which Black Folk Played in the Attempt to Reconstruct Democracy in America, 1860–1880* (1935; repr., New York: Atheneum, 1970), 708. See also W. E. B. Du Bois, "Reconstruction and Its Benefits," *American Historical Review* 15, no. 4 (July 1910): 781–99.

29. Eric Foner, *Freedom's Lawmakers: A Directory of Black Officeholders during Reconstruction*, rev. ed. (Baton Rouge: LSU Press, 1993), xi. This book includes entries for the 1,500 officials for whom Foner found documentation. The number of black officeholders cited in the text includes those for whom documentation was lacking.

30. Quoted in James M. McPherson, *Ordeal by Fire: The Civil War and Reconstruction* (New York: Knopf, 1982), 536.

31. Emanuel Fortune, quoted in Foner, *Reconstruction*, 426; Jack Dupree story, cited ibid., 426.

32. *Christian Recorder*, November 8, 1883, quoted in Henry M. Turner, "The Barbarous Decision of the Supreme Court," in *Respect Black: The Writings and Speeches of Henry McNeal Turner*, ed. Edwin Redkey (New York: Arno Press, 1971), 60.

33. Schwalm, *Emancipation's Diaspora*, 46.

34. Quoted in Quintard Taylor, *In Search of the Racial Frontier: African Americans in the American West, 1528–1990* (New York: Norton, 1998), 164.

35. Quoted in Nell Irvin Painter, *Exodusters: Black Migration to Kansas after Reconstruction* (New York: Knopf, 1977), 158.

36. *Nicodemus Western Cyclone*, March 24, 1887, quoted in Taylor, *In Search of the Racial Frontier*, 140.

37. "Go to Kansas": History and Culture, Nicodemus National Historic Site, National Park Service, http://www.nps.gov/nico/index.htm.

38. Quoted in Painter, *Exodusters*, 4.

39. Taylor, *In Search of the Racial Frontier*, 138.

40. "Caroline Le Count," *Pennsylvania Civil War 150*, http://www.pacivilwar150.com/people/africanamericans/Story.aspx?id=1.
41. Quoted in Hugh Davis, *"We Will Be Satisfied with Nothing Less": The African American Struggle for Equal Rights in the North during Reconstruction* (Ithaca, NY: Cornell University Press, 2011), 78.
42. Davis, *"We Will Be Satisfied,"* 95.
43. Foner, *Reconstruction*, 448.
44. Frances Ellen Watkins Harper, "We Are All Bound Up Together," speech, Eleventh National Women's Rights Convention, New York, May 1866, http://www.blackpast.org/?q=1866-frances-ellen-watkins-harper-we-are-all-bound-together-0. In this speech, Harper goes on to describe her humiliation at not being allowed to ride Philadelphia's streetcars.
45. Frederick Douglass, *Proceedings of the Republican National Convention, Held at Cincinnati, Ohio . . . June 14, 15, and 16, 1876*, http://quod.lib.umich.edu/cgi/t/text/text-idx?c=moa&cc=moa&q1=republican%20national%20convention&view=text&rgn=main&idno=AEW7097.0001.001.
46. Quoted in August Meier, *Negro Thought in America, 1880–1915: Racial Ideologies in the Age of Booker T. Washington* (Ann Arbor: University of Michigan Press, 1963), 69.

SUGGESTED REFERENCES

A Social Revolution

Anderson, James D. *The Education of Blacks in the South, 1860–1935*. Chapel Hill: University of North Carolina Press, 1988.

Berlin, Ira, and Leslie S. Rowland, eds. *Families and Freedom: A Documentary History of African-American Kinship in the Civil War Era*. New York: New Press, 1997.

Fairclough, Adam. *A Class of Their Own: Black Teachers in the Segregated South*. Cambridge: Belknap Press of Harvard University Press, 2007.

Hunter, Tera. *To 'Joy My Freedom: Southern Black Women's Lives and Labors after the Civil War*. Cambridge: Harvard University Press, 1997.

Litwack, Leon F. *Been in the Storm So Long: The Aftermath of Slavery*. New York: Knopf, 1979.

Montgomery, William E. *Under Their Own Vine and Fig Tree: The African-American Church in the South, 1865–1900*. Baton Rouge: LSU Press, 1993.

Rachleff, Peter J. *Black Labor in the South: Richmond, Virginia, 1865–1890*. Philadelphia: Temple University Press, 1984.

Saville, Julie. *The Work of Reconstruction: From Slave to Wage Laborer in South Carolina, 1860–1870*. New York: Cambridge University Press, 1994.

Schwalm, Leslie A. *A Hard Fight for We: Women's Transition from Slavery to Freedom in South Carolina*. Urbana: University of Illinois Press, 1997.

Williams, Heather Andrea. *Self-Taught: African American Education in Slavery and Freedom*. Chapel Hill: University of North Carolina Press, 2005.

A Short-Lived Political Revolution

Benedict, Michael Les. *A Compromise of Principle: Congressional Republicans and Reconstruction, 1863–1869*. New York: Norton, 1974.

Du Bois, W. E. B. *Black Reconstruction in America: An Essay toward a History of the Part Which Black Folk Played in the Attempt to Reconstruct Democracy in America, 1860–1880*. 1935. Reprint, New York: Atheneum, 1970.

Foner, Eric. *Freedom's Lawmakers: A Directory of Black Officeholders during Reconstruction*. Rev. ed. Baton Rouge: LSU Press, 1993.

———. *Reconstruction: America's Unfinished Revolution, 1863–1877*. New York: Harper & Row, 1988.

Gillette, William. *Retreat from Reconstruction, 1869–1879*. Baton Rouge: LSU Press, 1979.

Hahn, Steven. *A Nation under Our Feet: Black Political Struggles in the Rural South from Slavery to the Great Migration*. Cambridge: Belknap Press of Harvard University Press, 2003.

McKitrick, Eric L. *Andrew Johnson and Reconstruction*. Chicago: University of Chicago Press, 1960.

Rabinowitz, Howard N., ed. *Southern Black Leaders of the Reconstruction Era*. Urbana: University of Illinois Press, 1982.

Opportunities and Limits outside the South

Athearn, Robert G. *In Search of Canaan: Black Migration to Kansas, 1879–80*. Lawrence: Regents Press of KS, 1978.

Davis, Hugh. *"We Will Be Satisfied with Nothing Less": The African American Struggle for Equal Rights in the North during Reconstruction*. Ithaca, NY: Cornell University Press, 2011.

Painter, Nell Irvin. *Exodusters: Black Migration to Kansas after Reconstruction*. New York: Knopf, 1977.

Richardson, Heather Cox. *The Death of Reconstruction: Race, Labor, and Politics in the Post–Civil War North, 1865–1901*. Cambridge: Harvard University Press, 2001.

Schwalm, Leslie A. *Emancipation's Diaspora: Race and Reconstruction in the Upper Midwest*. Chapel Hill: University of North Carolina Press, 2009.

Taylor, Quintard. *In Search of the Racial Frontier: African Americans in the American West, 1528–1990*. New York: Norton, 1998.

Black Life and Culture during the Nadir

1880–1915

CHRONOLOGY *Events specific to African American history are in purple. General United States history events are in black.*

1881	Tuskegee Institute founded
1886	Colored Farmers' Alliance founded
1890	*Louisville, New Orleans and Texas Railway v. Mississippi* rules segregation on common carriers lawful
	Land-Grant College Act
	Mississippi's new state constitution provides model for black disfranchisement
1892	Ida B. Wells launches antilynching campaign
1893	Blacks boycott Chicago World's Fair
1895	Wells's *A Red Record* published
	Booker T. Washington delivers Atlanta Compromise speech
1896	Paul Laurence Dunbar's *Lyrics of Lowly Life* published
	Plessy v. Ferguson establishes separate but equal doctrine
	National Association of Colored Women founded
	Populist Party dissolves
1897	Alexander Crummell founds American Negro Academy
1898	*Williams v. Mississippi* upholds voting requirements used to disfranchise blacks
	United States annexes Hawaii
	Wilmington Insurrection
	Spanish-American War
1900	Brothers James Weldon Johnson and John Rosamond Johnson create "Lift Every Voice and Sing"
	W. E. B. Du Bois addresses Pan-African Congress
	National Negro Business League founded

1901	Booker T. Washington's *Up from Slavery* published
	Charles Chesnutt's *The Marrow of Tradition* published
1903	Maggie L. Walker establishes St. Luke Penny Savings Bank
	Du Bois's *The Souls of Black Folk* published
1904	St. Louis World's Fair puts Africans, Filipinos, and Native Americans on display
	Mary McLeod Bethune founds Daytona Normal and Industrial Institute for Negro Girls
1905	Niagara movement founded
1906	Following riot in Brownsville, Texas, 167 black soldiers discharged without honor
1909	National Negro Committee founded; renamed National Association for the Advancement of Colored People in 1910
1910	African American boxer Jack Johnson's defense of world heavyweight title seen as victory for race
	National Urban League founded
	The *Crisis*, NAACP's journal, begins publication
1911	*Bailey v. Alabama* overturns Alabama law holding laborers criminally liable for taking money in advance for work not performed
1914	W. C. Handy's "St. Louis Blues"
	United States v. Reynolds outlaws criminal surety laws
1915	NAACP protests screenings of *The Birth of a Nation*
	Guinn v. United States overturns Oklahoma's grandfather clause
	Booker T. Washington dies at age fifty-nine

Ida B. Wells: Creating Hope and Community amid Extreme Repression

Seated in the ladies' car on the train from Memphis, Tennessee, to Holly Springs, Mississippi, in 1883, the twenty-one-year-old African American schoolteacher Ida B. Wells settled in for her trip home. When the conductor demanded that she move to the smoking car, she refused. She had paid for a first-class ticket and did not want to sit in the dirty, smelly smoker, where rowdy white men often insulted black women. When the conductor tried to pry her from her seat, she fought back, biting his hand. Then, as she later described it, "I braced my feet against the seat in front and was holding to the back,"[1] so that the conductor had to call for assistance. It took three white men, including the conductor, to wrench the diminutive Wells, who was less than five feet tall, from her seat. The white ladies in the car applauded the conductor and his crew.

Outraged, Wells filed suit against the Chesapeake, Ohio and Southwestern Railroad, charging the company with discrimination and assault. In spite of the violent attack — "the sleeves of my linen duster had been torn out and I had been pretty roughly handled" — she later recalled, "I had not been hurt physically."[2] Before the suit was settled, Wells filed another for a similar incident. But after an initial victory in a lower court in the first case, the Tennessee Supreme Court ruled against her in both cases in 1887, claiming that the smoker and the ladies' car were comparable and that Wells had sued only to harass the railroad.

Wells wrote about her violent expulsion from the ladies' car for Memphis's black Baptist newspaper *Living Way*. Other black newspapers reprinted her story, and she began to write regularly for the black press. In 1889, she bought a one-third interest in the *Memphis Free Speech and Headlight* and turned it into a regional voice for African American concerns. As editor, she protested conditions in the city's black schools and clauses in Mississippi's new constitution that would effectively prevent black men from voting.[3] When she denounced white Memphians for the lynching of three friends in 1892, a mob destroyed her newspaper's offices. Wells left Memphis forever, but she had found her life's purpose. As an investigative journalist, she researched and analyzed lynching, and through publications, lectures, and connections with black leaders and organizations, she helped launch a national and international antilynching crusade that made her one of the most powerful black activists of her era.

Supporting Wells's efforts were black leaders from earlier generations, such as Frederick Douglass, and from her own generation, including prominent newspaper editors and middle-class women committed to addressing the issues that defined their era. Black women and men who, like Wells, had been born in slavery but grew up in freedom, along with the first generation actually born after emancipation, constituted freedom's first generation. Black teachers, editors, preachers, and entrepreneurs contributed to a growing black middle class that helped reshape the South. They were role models for what could be achieved and also advocates for improving the lives of all African Americans. Their actions helped prepare the way for the founding of powerful organizations that would lead the black freedom struggle well into the twentieth century.

The trajectory of Wells's life illustrates what blacks did for themselves and also what they endured between the mid-1880s and 1915. New laws that required segregation in schools and public places demeaned them and circumscribed their participation in the economic, social, and political life of the South. Not only laws but also terror and violence, particularly lynching (as Wells's campaign publicized), enforced segregation. Nevertheless, despite constraints all around, black men and women created rich lives for themselves and viable, self-sufficient communities. They founded businesses that served black neighborhoods. They built schools dedicated to vocational training, teacher training, and academic curricula. They formed organizations that promoted self-help and racial advancement through black solidarity. They found new means of self-expression through theater, dance, music, and literature. Performers, musicians, and writers explored the nature of the black experience and discovered deep sources of inspiration and hope. Freedom's first generation fought hard to create viable lives and careers in the hostile context of white supremacy that emerged in this low point, or nadir, at the end of the nineteenth century. Their persistence and ingenuity fostered a powerful culture of struggle and affirmation that in the first decades of the twentieth century renewed collective protest against inequality.

Racism and Black Challenges

Negotiations between Republicans and Democrats over the contested presidential election of 1876 produced a compromise that restored white rule in the South and ended federal protections for the rights of African Americans (see chapter 8). What followed was continued intimidation, violence, and murder aimed at keeping blacks submissive to whites. New laws required segregation of the races in public places, and new voting requirements disfranchised black men. Violations, or any behavior that could be interpreted as nonsubmissive, could mean death at the hands of a white mob. Such laws and practices were embedded in a political and social culture built on views of racial hierarchy that were promoted as scientific and used to justify white dominance of peoples of color.

Racial Segregation

Black men and women had long protested discrimination by streetcar companies that required them to ride in separate cars or in the backs of cars. Stories of forced removal from public conveyances were told in many autobiographies, including those by Frederick Douglass and Harriet Jacobs, and protests were equally numerous. Before the Civil War, Elizabeth Jennings's suit against a New York City streetcar company had desegregated transportation in that city, and more recent campaigns had ended streetcar discrimination in Washington, D.C., in 1865 and in Philadelphia in 1867 (see chapter 8). But in the South, a different scenario was unfolding.

Custom had long excluded blacks from public places where whites were likely to be. During Black Reconstruction, however, the new state constitutions that black men helped write affirmed equal rights, and state laws required equal treatment of whites and blacks. Louisiana's 1869 civil rights act, for example, specifically forbade segregation on public carriers (transportation). Thus in 1872, when Josephine DeCuir was refused a ladies' stateroom on a Mississippi steamboat, she sued. The state court awarded her damages, but in 1878, in *Hall v. DeCuir*, the U.S. Supreme Court overturned the Louisiana statute, reasoning that Louisiana could not prohibit racial segregation on common carriers because matters relating to interstate commerce came under federal jurisdiction. States, according to this logic, could legally segregate intrastate but not interstate passengers. In the *Civil Rights Cases* (1883), the U.S. Supreme Court overturned the Civil Rights Act of 1875, stating that Congress had no authority to bar discrimination by private individuals and businesses (see chapter 8). In *Louisville, New Orleans and Texas Railway v. Mississippi* (1890), the Court ruled that it was actually lawful for states to require racial segregation on common carriers. In the late nineteenth century, this expanding system of spatial and physical racial separation in public transportation and elsewhere came to be called **Jim Crow**, after a popular minstrel show character that ridiculed black people.

Many streetcar and railroad companies actually opposed Jim Crow because of the extra expense involved in maintaining separate cars, the fear of losing black customers, and the difficulty of enforcement. But white-dominated southern state legislatures moved to make segregation mandatory. In 1890, Louisiana passed a law stating that "all railway companies carrying passengers in their coaches in this State, shall provide equal but separate accommodations for the white and colored races."[4] Opposition to this Separate Car Act was particularly intense among the light-complexioned African American elite of New Orleans, who in 1891 formed a committee to challenge it. They planned a highly orchestrated act of civil disobedience: A black citizen would violate the law, be arrested, and initiate a case they intended to take all the way to the U.S. Supreme Court.

On June 7, 1892, Homer Plessy, a local shoemaker who was seven-eighths white, purchased a first-class ticket and took a seat for a short trip to Covington, just north of New Orleans. When the conductor demanded that he go to the "colored car," Plessy refused and was arrested for violating the Separate Car Act. In court, Plessy maintained that this law violated the Fourteenth Amendment, and after appeals the Supreme Court agreed to hear the case.

In *Plessy v. Ferguson* (1896), the Court declared Louisiana's Separate Car Act constitutional and established the **separate but equal** legal doctrine that would protect segregation for more than half a century. The justices reasoned that the racially separate but allegedly equal railroad cars did not violate the Fourteenth Amendment's guarantee of equal protection of the laws. Furthermore, they maintained that the Separate Car Act specifically, and Jim Crow segregation generally, respected custom and did not stigmatize African Americans as inferior. They pointed to "the establishment of separate schools for white and colored children" as "a valid exercise of the legislative power" and claimed that state legislatures were "at liberty to act with reference to the established usages, customs, and tradition of the people, and with a view to the promotion of their comfort, and the preservation of the public peace and good order."[5]

The *Plessy* decision not only legalized long-standing custom and state-sanctioned discrimination against black people; it also prompted the passage of new and more comprehensive Jim Crow laws. By 1910, all southern states mandated segregated railroad cars, streetcars, and waiting rooms (Map 9.1). Despite the theory of "separate but equal," actual accommodations for black people were strikingly unequal, and blacks protested in mass meetings, sermons, editorials, petitions, and lobbying efforts. Between 1900 and 1906, they organized streetcar boycotts in more than twenty-five southern cities. But wherever blacks protested and boycotted — and despite concessions to blacks in some places — white elites marshaled their resources to pass more restrictive laws, or they resorted to intimidation and violence to enforce black submission.

Throughout the South, stores, restaurants, and hotels displayed signs designating "Colored Only" or "Whites Only" sections. Separate entrances, waiting rooms, water fountains, toilets, service counters, and ticket windows became standard. Theater balconies were reserved for "Colored Only." Public parks and recreational facilities might have a special Negro day, but generally blacks were excluded from them, and from public libraries as well. In courtrooms and city hall buildings, signs directed traffic so as to minimize interracial contact. Work sites were segregated; hospitals, clinics, asylums, and prisons were racially exclusive. In city neighborhoods where black populations were concentrated, blacks established their own parks, hospitals, and clinics.

Essential to Jim Crow was a system of racial etiquette that reinforced patterns of black subordination. Whenever blacks came into contact with whites, blacks were expected to defer. In towns, they had to surrender the sidewalk to whites, with black men expected to remove their hats and bow their heads. When spoken to by whites, blacks diverted their gaze so as not to look at whites directly. Blacks had to refer to whites as "Mr.," "Miss," or "Mrs.," proper titles of deference, while whites addressed blacks with belittling terms such as "auntie," "uncle," "boy," and "girl." Family members taught black children racial etiquette, often using "trickster tales" that traced back to West African and slave culture to show how to survive by one's wits. The children might laugh when clever Brer Rabbit outsmarted an authority figure, but they also understood the story's message about the limits of outward resistance and protest in a Jim Crow world.

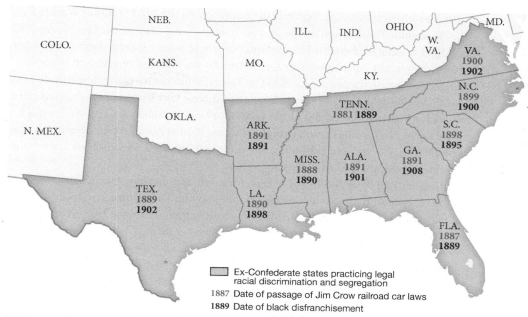

MAP 9.1 Jim Crow and Disfranchisement in Former Confederate States

As shown in this map, each state of the former Confederacy passed laws segregating railroad cars, a critical marker in the evolution of Jim Crow. Each of these states also disfranchised its black citizens, generally a short time after railroad-car segregation had taken place. Setting these developments against one another illustrates the links between Jim Crow and disfranchisement. The *Plessy v. Ferguson* decision in 1896 paved the way for the creation and enforcement of new and ever more restrictive Jim Crow laws, further circumscribing black life in the South.

Ideologies of White Supremacy

Southern-style Jim Crow and nationwide customs that subordinated African Americans showcased widely accepted ideas regarding race in both popular and academic thinking in the late nineteenth and early twentieth centuries. These ideas were prevalent not just in the United States but throughout the Western world. Notions of white supremacy justified **imperialism**, as European nations built vast colonial empires in Africa and Asia to gain raw materials and markets for their industrial products. In 1898, the United States extended its imperial reach after it took control of Puerto Rico, Guam, and the Philippines following the Spanish-American War. Hawaii had already been annexed that year, and the United States continued to expand its influence in the Caribbean and Latin America. Though motivated by trade and profit, imperialists also asserted it was the "white man's burden" to bring the benefits of civilization, including Christianity, to inferior peoples of color around the world.

Whites regarded nonwhites as primitives, even as curiosities to be displayed as spectacles, as was vividly evident at contemporary world's fairs. The 1900 Paris World's Fair, called the Exposition Universelle, presented human zoos, or "Negro Villages," with caged Africans in their "natural" surroundings. At the 1904 St. Louis World's Fair, the "Philippine Reservation" re-created the habitat and lifestyle of the Igorot people to highlight the alleged benefits U.S. governance would bring. Also on display at this fair were the defeated Apache warrior Geronimo, now a prisoner of war, and other conquered Apaches in a tepee village, and Ota Benga, a diminutive Congolese Mbuti, who would later be exhibited in the monkey house at New York's Bronx Zoo. Protests from black clergy closed the exhibit at the zoo. "Our race, we think, is depressed enough," wrote James H. Gordon, chairman of the Colored Baptist Ministers' Conference, in the *New York Times*, "without exhibiting one of us with the apes. We think we are worthy of being considered human beings, with souls."[6]

The zoo's backers and board of directors included distinguished anthropologists and zoologists who promoted theories of race and human evolution that drew on craniology studies and Charles Darwin's ideas about natural selection. The view that categorized human populations hierarchically by race, embraced white supremacy, and contended that races evolved unequally is today known as **scientific racism**. In the late nineteenth and early twentieth centuries, the academic establishment supported this pseudoscience. Anthropologists studying so-called primitives concluded that Anglo-Saxons (those most often doing the classifying) were the most advanced humans, while Negroes were at the bottom of the evolutionary scale. Sociologists, psychologists, and pathologists attributed inherent mental and moral characteristics to each race. Again, Anglo-Saxons were mentally and physically superior, while Negroes were believed to have limited intelligence, a tendency toward criminality, and a vulnerability to disease.

Pseudoscientific theories of racial evolution reinforced notions of white supremacy. Through natural selection, or "the survival of the fittest," Caucasians had risen to the top, according to the scientific establishment. As the most advanced and civilized race, their economic and political dominance of the world was both inevitable and justified. This view, known as **Social Darwinism**, also supported the economic and social order, in which blacks were deemed fit only for field work, hard labor, and domestic service. Welfare or assistance to black people, or to the poor generally, was in this view misguided, because those who resided at the bottom of the social hierarchy were fulfilling their natural destiny and thus deserved no better. Wealth and power would naturally go to the fittest, and neither government nor society should interfere.

But according to this view, government could and should keep the races from mixing, lest the strength of the white race be diluted by inferior races. Jim Crow laws were, of course, one way to do this. To further ensure against racial mixing, a majority of states, not only southern ones, passed antimiscegenation laws prohibiting interracial sex and marriage. In addition, these states sought to police what was called "racial integrity" by determining who was white and who was black. Older categorizations had defined race by fractions: A "quadroon" was one-quarter black (had one black grandparent); an "octoroon," such as Homer Plessy, was one-eighth black. Now states adopted the one-drop rule: One drop of black blood made a person black. To prevent "black blood" from polluting the white race, state registrars of vital statistics kept track of lineage, and birth

White Supremacy

This potent ad graphically illustrates the role of racist intimidation and terrorization in the 1890 campaign to disfranchise blacks in Mississippi and throughout the South. This kind of campaign was a pillar of the highly orchestrated, formal restoration of white rule in the post-Reconstruction South and the institutionalization of Jim Crow domination. *The Granger Collection, New York.*

WHITE SUPREMACY!

Attention, White Men!

Grand Torch-Light Procession

At JACKSON,

On the Night of the

Fourth of January, 1890.

The Final Settlement of Democratic Rule and White Supremacy in Mississippi.

GRAND PYROTECHNIC DISPLAY!
Transparencies and Torches Free for all.

All in Sympathy with the Grand Cause are Cordially and Earnestly Invited to be on hand, to aid in the Final Overthrow of Radical Rule in our State.

Come on foot or on horse-back; come any way, but be sure to get there.
Brass Bands, Cannon, Flambeau Torches, Transparencies, Sky-rockets, Etc.

A GRAND DISPLAY FOR A GRAND CAUSE.

records were required to state whether a newborn was white or black. Marriages were also regulated. South Carolina's 1895 law forbade anyone with one black great-grandparent to marry a white person. Because state laws differed, moving from one state to another could delegitimize a marriage and the couple's children.

This line of reasoning braced racist public policies and practices, such as those justifying segregated schools throughout the country, and helped shape white attitudes and practices toward other domestic peoples of color. The widespread and virulent idea of white supremacy led to the Chinese Exclusion Act of 1882, which barred immigration from China.

Disfranchisement and Political Activism

In politics, new voting regulations and practices that disfranchised black men demonstrated the deep-seated commitment to white supremacy. Many of these new policies also disfranchised large numbers of poor white men, seen by white elites as ignorant and unsuited to political participation. Elite white men viewed politics as their special racial and class preserve. In the South, the Democratic Party dominated, and it sought to prevent black male voters from becoming a voting bloc that might be exploited by one white faction against another. State legislatures also drew district lines to minimize black voting strength. The myth of the corrupt black voter — a persistent charge that had been used to undermine black political participation during Reconstruction — justified disfranchisement. So did

progressivism—a reform movement that sought to cleanse politics of corruption and bring efficiency to American political life. In the North, progressives tried to break the power of big-city political bosses. In the South, white progressives targeted black politicians and voters. The ideology of the New South, which promoted the region as forward-looking, industrializing, urbanizing, and modernizing, meshed with the ideologies of progressivism and white supremacy.

Wherever violence, intimidation, and coercion did not prevent black men from exercising the franchise, southern white chicanery—including moving polling places, stuffing ballot boxes, buying and manipulating black voters, and destroying black ballots—undermined the black vote. South Carolina's notorious 1882 "eight box law" demanded that voters put separate ballots for each particular issue or candidate in a specially marked box. Many voters, black and white, had their entire ballots disqualified for failing to follow the rules. Black and many poor white voters were excluded from the Democratic Party when it incorporated itself as a private club that permitted only members to vote in primary elections. In what soon came to be known as a **white primary**—a primary election that effectively excluded blacks—southern Democrats selected the white candidates who would run on their slate in the general election. Then, because the Democratic Party completely dominated southern politics, whoever won its primary inevitably won the election, too.

Other strategies for disfranchising black voters were written into law. Poll taxes—payments required to vote—were so high as to discourage voting, especially by the poor, and abuses such as shifting payment locations and times further burdened black voters. Literacy tests required reading and writing sections of the state constitution, and "understanding clauses" demanded that potential voters explain the meaning of often technical constitutional clauses. The fact that white registrars decided who passed these tests and who did not meant that potential black voters were almost always disqualified. Grandfather clauses limited the right to vote to males who could vote before 1867 and to their sons and grandsons, thus effectively eliminating black men.

In 1890, Mississippi's new constitution included a poll tax, a literacy test, and an understanding clause, a disfranchisement model the U.S. Supreme Court upheld in *Williams v. Mississippi* (1898). A decade later, similar voting laws were in place throughout the South, and their effect was dramatic. Before Louisiana's disfranchisement statutes were passed in 1897 and 1898, the state had more than 130,000 black voters; after the laws were in place, only a little more than 1,300 black voters remained. Before disfranchisement, black voters constituted a majority in twenty-six Louisiana parishes; after disfranchisement, they formed a majority in none. Black protest against these discriminatory measures proved unsuccessful.

This effective removal of southern black men from politics came just as agrarian protest movements in the South and Midwest appeared poised to bring black and white farmers together in a challenge to powerful railroad, financial, and corporate interests. All farmers had been affected by declining crop and commodity prices, especially those for cotton, and by escalating indebtedness. To outmaneuver corporate monopolies through cooperative purchasing and marketing arrangements, farmers established

Farmers' Alliances, and some dreamed of a farm-labor coalition that would be inclusive in its call for unified action. But internal divisions were apparent. The Southern Farmers' Alliance (SFA) did not admit blacks, for example, and in 1886 the Colored Farmers' Alliance (CFA) was organized in response. By 1891, the CFA had more than one million members, most of them landless farmers or day laborers, who had a different perspective from that of the white farmers who owned land and hired laborers.

Yet racial divisions persisted when both Alliances supported the Populist Party, which grew rapidly in the early 1890s by advocating federal price supports for crops as well as a fairer banking system, currency reform, and railroad regulation. In the 1896 presidential election, the Populists nominated the Democratic candidate, William Jennings Bryan, and when he lost to Republican William McKinley, the Populist Party dissolved.

In North Carolina, however, black and white Populists had united with Republicans to send the black lawyer George Henry White to the U.S. House of Representatives and win some local and state contests. But the specter of black and white cooperation threatened southern white elites, and by 1898 the Democrats had beaten back collaborative interracial politics everywhere in the state except Wilmington. A small city that was more than two-thirds black, Wilmington had a vibrant black community and a growing black professional class. In 1898, a white insurrection there took back white rule after Alexander Manly, editor of the *Daily Record* and a Hampton Institute graduate, outraged whites with an editorial arguing that interracial relationships between poor white women and poor black men were often consensual. In what became known as the **Wilmington Insurrection**, whites killed scores of blacks and destroyed black property, including the premises of the *Daily Record*. Enough blacks were driven out of the city to end their demographic majority. The white insurrectionists overthrew the local government and replaced it with their handpicked leaders.

Lynching and the Campaign against It

The Wilmington Insurrection shows how far whites were willing to go to subordinate blacks, especially to suppress their rights. When legal means did not suffice, they used intimidation and violence, even murder. Perhaps the most horrific form of violence was **lynching**, the public murder, often a hanging, of an individual by a mob acting outside the law. (See Document Project: Agency and Constraint, pp. 378–87.) "Lynching," stated the white investigative journalist Ray Stannard Baker in an article in *McClure's Magazine* in January 1905, "is not a Southern Crime, nor a Western crime, nor a Northern crime: it is an American crime."[7] But a disproportionate number of lynchings took place in the South, and a disproportionate number of the victims were black (Tables 9.1 and 9.2). In 1908, Baker published lynching statistics, concluding that "Mississippi, Alabama, Louisiana and Georgia — the black belt states — are thus seen to have the worst records."[8] For southern whites, lynching of blacks was a violent form of social control that had far less to do with punishing black crimes than with terrorizing blacks into subordination (Table 9.3).

TABLE 9.1   Lynchings by State and Race, 1882–1968

State	White	Black	Total	State	White	Black	Total
Alabama	48	299	347	Nevada	6	0	6
Arizona	31	0	31	New Jersey	1	1	2
Arkansas	58	226	284	New Mexico	33	3	36
California	41	2	43	New York	1	1	2
Colorado	65	3	68	North Carolina	15	86	101
Delaware	0	1	1	North Dakota	13	3	16
Florida	25	257	282	Ohio	10	16	26
Georgia	39	492	531	Oklahoma	82	40	122
Idaho	20	0	20	Oregon	20	1	21
Illinois	15	19	34	Pennsylvania	2	6	8
Indiana	33	14	47	South Carolina	4	156	160
Iowa	17	2	19	South Dakota	27	0	27
Kansas	35	19	54	Tennessee	47	204	251
Kentucky	63	142	205	Texas	141	352	493
Louisiana	56	335	391	Utah	6	2	8
Maine	1	0	1	Vermont	1	0	1
Maryland	2	27	29	Virginia	17	83	100
Michigan	7	1	8	Washington	25	1	26
Minnesota	5	4	9	West Virginia	20	28	48
Mississippi	42	539	581	Wisconsin	6	0	6
Missouri	53	69	122	Wyoming	30	5	35
Montana	82	2	84	**Total**	**1,297**	**3,446**	**4,743**
Nebraska	52	5	57				

SOURCE: University of Missouri–Kansas City School of Law, http://law2.umkc.edu/faculty/projects /ftrials/shipp/lynchingsstate.html.

NOTE: The statistics reported here are from the archives at Tuskegee Institute. Lynching statistics prior to 1882 scarcely exist, and even those available after 1892, when Ida B. Wells began investigating lynching and Tuskegee Institute started collecting and tabulating data, are not necessarily accurate. Innumerable lynchings were never reported to the authorities; many lynchings went unreported in newspapers, which were the sources of Wells's and Tuskegee's statistics; and there was no consistent definition of what constituted a lynching. After the NAACP began keeping lynching statistics in 1912, its numbers differed from Tuskegee's. Nevertheless, the patterns that emerged are starkly clear: More blacks than whites were lynched, lynchings occurred much more often in the South than elsewhere in the United States, and after peaking in 1892, the number of lynchings very slowly declined. For more lynching statistics, see Robert A. Gibson, "The Negro Holocaust: Lynching and Race Riots in the United States, 1880–1950," Yale–New Haven Teachers Institute, http://www.yale.edu/ynhti/curriculum/units/1979/2/79.02.04.x.html.

TABLE 9.2   Lynchings by Year and Race, 1882–1968

Year	White	Black	Total	Year	White	Black	Total
1882	64	49	113	1918	4	60	64
1883	77	53	130	1919	7	76	83
1884	160	51	211	1920	8	53	61
1885	110	74	184	1921	5	59	64
1886	64	74	138	1922	6	51	57
1887	50	70	120	1923	4	29	33
1888	68	69	137	1924	0	16	16
1889	76	94	170	1925	0	17	17
1890	11	85	96	1926	7	23	30
1891	71	113	184	1927	0	16	16
1892	69	161	230	1928	1	10	11
1893	34	118	152	1929	3	7	10
1894	58	134	192	1930	1	20	21
1895	66	113	179	1931	1	12	13
1896	45	78	123	1932	2	6	8
1897	35	123	158	1933	2	24	26
1898	19	101	120	1934	0	15	15
1899	21	85	106	1935	2	18	20
1900	9	106	115	1936	0	8	8
1901	25	105	130	1937	0	8	8
1902	7	85	92	1938	0	6	6
1903	15	84	99	1939	1	2	3
1904	7	76	83	1940	1	4	5
1905	5	57	62	1941	0	4	4
1906	3	62	65	1942	0	6	6
1907	3	58	61	1943	0	3	3
1908	8	89	97	1944	0	2	2
1909	13	69	82	1945	0	1	1
1910	9	67	76	1946	0	6	6
1911	7	60	67	1947	0	1	1
1912	2	62	64	1948	1	1	2
1913	1	51	52	1949	0	3	3
1914	4	51	55	1950	1	1	2
1915	13	56	69	1951	0	1	1
1916	4	50	54	1952	0	0	0
1917	2	36	38	1953	0	0	0

Continued

Continued

Year	White	Black	Total	Year	White	Black	Total
1954	0	0	0	1962	0	0	0
1955	0	3	3	1963	0	1	1
1956	0	0	0	1964	2	1	3
1957	1	0	1	1965	0	0	0
1958	0	0	0	1966	0	0	0
1959	0	1	1	1967	0	0	0
1960	0	0	0	1968	0	0	0
1961	0	1	1	Total	1,297	3,445°	4,742°

SOURCE: University of Missouri–Kansas City School of Law, http://law2.umkc.edu/faculty/projects /ftrials/shipp/lynchingyear.html.
° The difference of one among the tables is statistically insignificant.

TABLE 9.3 Lynchings by [Alleged] Cause, 1882–1968

Cause	Number	Percent	Cause	Number	Percent
Homicide	1,937	40.84	Robbery and theft	232	4.89
Felonious assault	205	4.32	Insult to white person	85	1.79
Rape	912	19.22	All other causes	1,084	22.85
Attempted rape	288	6.07	Total	4,743	100

SOURCE: University of Missouri–Kansas City School of Law, http://law2.umkc.edu/faculty/projects /ftrials/shipp/Lynchcauses.html.

For Ida B. Wells, lynching assumed a profoundly personal meaning after three of her friends — Thomas Moss, Calvin McDowell, and William Stewart — were lynched. The episode began in the black community on the outskirts of Memphis, where the black People's Grocery Company competed with a white grocery store. Feuds and street fights escalated into armed attacks, and when whites were injured, dozens of blacks were jailed. On March 9, 1892, a white mob broke into the jail; dragged Moss, McDowell, and Stewart from their cells; took them to a field outside the city; and shot them. Afterward, they gouged out McDowell's eyes.[9]

In the *Memphis Free Speech and Headlight*, the newspaper she co-owned, Wells lashed out against the lynching and criticized Memphis officials for not identifying the lynchers. She also revealed findings from research into alleged causes of lynchings: Although victims were most often thought to have raped a white woman, these charges were usually false. Wells's articles enraged the white Memphis establishment, but they came to the attention of the black editor T. Thomas Fortune, who reprinted them in his newspaper, the *New York Age*. Fortune soon hired Wells to write for his paper and helped her publish her research in a pamphlet titled *Southern Horrors: Lynch Law in All Its Phases* (1892).

Ida B. Wells

In an era perhaps best known for a Booker T. Washington–style accommodationism, Ida B. Wells was among those contemporary African American leaders who offered a militant alternative. This fiery journalist, leader, and activist helped spearhead the campaign against lynching, fought for women's rights and civil rights, and became a strong community leader in Chicago. *Private Collection/Prismatic Pictures/Bridgeman Images.*

With Fortune's help and the support of black women, Wells's campaign against lynching received national and international attention. Frederick Douglass helped arrange a European lecture tour for Wells. In 1894, she helped found the British Anti-Lynching Committee. Douglass also collaborated with Wells on a pamphlet explaining the black boycott of the 1893 Chicago World's Fair, where white officials rebuffed efforts to include an exhibit on black progress since emancipation but embraced an ethnographic African village featuring Dahomeyans.[10] In 1895, Wells published *A Red Record*, a more formal study of lynching statistics and the alleged causes of lynchings. Her approach was like that of white progressive reformers who sought to end corruption and lawlessness by exposing the facts. In this, she was disappointed, but her efforts, like those of her black contemporaries — especially W. E. B. Du Bois and *Boston Guardian* editor William Monroe Trotter — kept the black protest tradition alive.

Wells's analysis of lynching refuted the reasons defenders used to rationalize the practice: to crush black rebellion, to remove corrupt black voters and officials, and, most important, to protect white women from black male rapists. In each case, as Wells showed, the alleged defense was false. Most especially, she argued that the rape of a white woman by a black man was rare. In fact, it was black women's virtue that needed to be protected, notably from white men. Her analysis also demonstrated that, contrary to common belief, lynchings often targeted successful blacks, not misfits and criminals, and occurred not in out-of-the-way settings with weak police and court systems but in places where such systems were strong. In short, the police and courts that did almost nothing to protect blacks were often complicit in these murders.

Freedom's First Generation

The network of black activists Wells drew on to support her antilynching campaign was much like the network of black activists who, before and during the Civil War, mobilized to end slavery and work for equal rights. New black voices, particularly from the South, now enriched that network, and as in the old antebellum crusade, many activists were women. With an emphasis on racial solidarity, they committed themselves to racial advancement. Often part of an emerging southern black middle class, they worked with business leaders, newspaper editors, and preachers to strengthen black families and build independent communities. Members of freedom's first generation saw themselves as standing on the shoulders of those who had gone before and committed themselves to making life better for future generations. At the beginning of the twentieth century, a flowering of black cultural expressions, some new, testified to the creativity unleashed by freedom.

Black Women and Men in the Era of Jim Crow

Wells's candid analysis of the causes of lynching specifically, and her uncompromising activism generally, drew both admirers and critics. One critic was a prominent white Missouri journalist who, in a private letter to one of Wells's British supporters, slandered the morality of black women, characterizing them as prostitutes. Passed along to Josephine St. Pierre Ruffin, editor of the *Woman's Era*, the nation's first black women's newspaper, the letter caused an uproar. Ruffin circulated it among her elite black women friends throughout the North. The result was a call for a national meeting. "There was a time when our mothers and sisters could not protect themselves from such beasts," wrote one who attended the meeting in Boston in 1895, "but a new era has begun and we propose to defend ourselves."[11] Led by Margaret Murray Washington, the wife of Booker T. Washington, the attendees established the National Federation of Afro-American Women, which the next year merged with the National League of Colored Women to form the **National Association of Colored Women (NACW)**. One delegate to the NACW's inaugural meeting in July 1896, in Washington, D.C., was Harriet Tubman, the seventy-five-year-old heroine of the underground railroad. The poet Frances Ellen Watkins Harper, then in her early seventies, was also a founding member. The organization's leaders were, however, members of a new generation of women who were determined not only to defend the honor of black women but also to advance the cause of their race.

Mary Church Terrell, an Oberlin graduate and a teacher of Latin at Washington's highly regarded M Street High School, was elected NACW president. Like many of her generation, she was the child of former slaves, but her parents were freed by the time she was born and were successful in business. Thus she grew up in an elite Memphis family that stressed education and achievement. With confidence gained through education and organizing skills honed in church work, she and other prominent women assumed new leadership roles in the era of Jim Crow discrimination and disfranchisement that undercut black male leadership. They dedicated themselves to **uplift** — the notion that blacks themselves must take primary responsibility for black progress.

The NACW epitomized the increasing emphasis placed by blacks of the era on the "politics of respectability": the notion that striving for and achieving respectability promoted the cause of their race.[12] The NACW and other club organizations dedicated themselves to programs of self-help and, in the words of Fannie Barrier Williams, to the "social reconstruction" of "the great masses of the colored women in this country." These less fortunate "sisters" of black club women needed training and time "to complete the work of emancipation," explained Williams, a leader of the black women's club movement who also did social welfare work in Chicago. She recalled the motivations behind the movement: "Better homes, better schools, better protection for girls of scant home training, better sanitary conditions, better opportunities for competent young women to gain employment, and the need of being better known to the American people appealed to the conscience of progressive colored women from many communities."[13]

A key impetus for the formation of the NACW was the agitation surrounding Wells's research on lynching, but the abolishment of lynching was only one of the organization's objectives. Taking as its motto "Lifting as We Climb," the NACW developed a broad range of programs for advancing black education through fund-raising, scholarships, and grants, and for offering community-based assistance to black women in areas such as jobs, child care, temperance, health, and hygiene. The federation also supported woman suffrage and fought discriminatory Jim Crow laws and practices, including the convict lease system (see chapter 8). At its height, around 1920, it had 100,000 members.

Although Wells was a founding member of the NACW, she was not an active member. Her lawsuits and outspokenness, especially her frank statements about women's virtue, made her a little too radical for many of the elite club women of the era, who preferred not to address matters of sexuality so openly. These women worried that behavior perceived to be unladylike might undermine their cause.[14] But the NACW was fully committed to service and self-respect through the kind of leadership advocated — and modeled — by Anna Julia Cooper, another Oberlin graduate teaching Latin at the M Street High School, who had been a speaker at both the Boston and the Washington organizational meetings.

The lives of elite black women — a new class in southern society — were distinct from the lives of those they sought to elevate. Overwhelmingly, black women in the South had little time or energy for clubs. Those who lived in towns and cities worked outside the home for wages, which were usually about $2 a week. Most often they worked in white women's homes — as cooks, maids, nannies, and nurses. They might have several jobs, sewing for others or taking in laundry on the side. As many as one-fourth of them were widows, and almost 30 percent were heads of households. Black women typically outlived black men, and in southern cities the ratio of black men to black women was 87:100. The years between 1880 and 1900 saw the fertility rate of urban black women decline. Discrimination and violence against black men, who seldom made enough money on their own to support families, undermined urban black family life. In towns and cities, black men performed low-paying, unskilled, dirty, and physically demanding jobs such as hauling, loading and unloading goods, and cleaning streets, yards, gardens, buildings, and factories. Hard labor compromised their health and shortened their lives. Thus black women typically had to help sustain their families financially.

In Atlanta, there were enough black washerwomen to constitute a labor network with potential for collective action, and in early July 1881, twenty washerwomen met in a church to form the Washing Society and demand higher wages. They called for a strike on July 19, and with the support of black churches, mutual aid societies, and fraternal organizations, three thousand workers joined in. Despite arrests and threats of tax increases and license fees, the washerwomen did not budge. In the end, they got their raise, and their collective action inspired cooks, maids, and nurses to make similar demands.

Black women in rural areas lacked such opportunities for collective action. The wives and daughters of sharecroppers and tenant farmers worked around the clock. In the early morning, they prepared a typical breakfast of salt pork, molasses, and corn bread, which they would sometimes have to deliver to the fields, where family members were already at work. At noon, the same meal was carried to the fields. During planting season, women might join their husbands and children in the fields. Throughout the day and evening, women sewed, mended, washed, and cleaned; older women cared for children, and mothers nursed babies. They tended small plots, where they grew vegetables and fruits, or raised chickens and hogs to feed their families or supplement their income. According to the wife of one Mississippi farmer, many women did double duty — "a man's share in the field, and a woman's part at home."[15] As Rosina Hoard of North Carolina explained, "I had my house work and de cookin' to do and to look after de chillun, but I'd go out and still pick my two hunnert pounds ob cotton a day."[16]

For southern black men toiling in the fields, work was also nonstop. They were responsible for the cash crop — cotton, tobacco, rice, or sugar, depending on the region — and they supplemented their families' diets by hunting and fishing. No matter how hard they worked, however, they rarely got ahead. "Dem sharecroppuhs is jes like slaves," observed the former Virginia slave Archie Booker. "Dey don' know slavery is ovuh."[17] Another black man summed it up this way: "White man sit down whole year; Nigger work day and night and make crop; Nigger hardly gits bread and meat; white man sittin' down gits all. *It's wrong.*"[18]

Increasingly, blacks in the rural South were ensnared in a system of cyclical indebtedness to the landowners whose fields they worked as sharecroppers and to the storeowners from whom they bought supplies. All too often the landowner and the storeowner were the same person. Added to the array of laws and customs that worked against their economic independence was a condition known as **debt peonage**, an

Rural Women Washing
Doing the laundry was an extremely labor-intensive task for rural black women. Although this photograph, from around 1900, shows others helping out, black women all too often had to combine several jobs at once, such as looking after children and doing the laundry for their own family and for white families. This image also conveys a tension between the dignity of such work and its harshness. *The Granger Collection, New York.*

entanglement from which they almost never escaped. In this system, those who owed fines and faced prison sentences for infractions of labor contracts or vagrancy laws sold their labor to a third party in exchange for payment of their debts. (See Document Project: Agency and Constraint, pp. 378–87.) Ending debt peonage was another cause advocated by racial uplift organizations like the NACW.

Black Communities in the Cities of the New South

When twenty-one-year-old Ida B. Wells moved to Memphis in 1883, she chose city life over that of Holly Springs, Mississippi, the small town where she had been raised. She was not alone. Between 1880 and 1910, an increasing number of southern black women, men, and families moved to the cities of the New South, where white progressives were promoting growth and industry. Black women and men helped meet the labor and service needs of urban growth, but they had much to gain as well. For them, cities such as Richmond, Nashville, Atlanta, and Washington, D.C., offered better lives, especially better opportunities for education and employment, as well as the rich array of social, cultural, and intellectual activities that concentrations of black residents made possible. Between 1880 and 1890, Nashville's black population grew from 16,337 to more than 29,400, and Atlanta's from 16,330 to roughly 28,100.

These burgeoning black urban communities were what W. E. B. Du Bois described as a "group economy" — "a closed economic circle, largely independent of surrounding whites." He reflected, "There used to be Negro business men in Northern cities and a few even in Southern cities, but they catered to white trade; the Negro business man to-day caters to colored trade. . . . In every city in the United States which has considerable Negro population, the colored group is serving itself in religion, medical care, legal advice and often educating its children. In growing degree also it is serving itself in insurance, houses, books, amusements."[19]

Richmond offers one example. The black population of the former Confederate capital grew from 27,800 to 46,700 between 1880 and 1910. The city had begun to industrialize before the Civil War, and after the war black workers in the construction trades helped rebuild the city as a rail and industrial center. Blacks also worked in the city's long-standing tobacco industry. African Americans lived primarily in Jackson Ward, a neighborhood a mile northwest of the state capitol. Residents liked to think of it as "the Black Wall Street of America." A 1907 publication called *Souvenir Views: Negro Enterprises and Residences* listed four large insurance companies, four banks, four drugstores, five weekly newspapers, fourteen physicians, four dentists, two real estate agents, eight lawyers, ten large barbershops, four butchers, two ice dealers, five paperhangers, three confectionery stores and ice cream manufacturers, two "electric power" shoe repairers, one machinist, more than fifty dressmakers, five transfer companies (short-distance transportation companies), ninety public school teachers, six paint contractors, five building contractors, two brick contractors, two photographers, three "first-class tailors," one grocery, two fish and game stores, one liquor store, one wood and coal yard, one jeweler, one tinner, two upholsterers, two steam laundries, two first-class hotels, two hospitals, one cigar factory, one shoe store, one clothing and gents' "furnishing" store, one dry goods and millinery store, five funeral directors and embalmers, two colleges, one business college, seventeen printers, one automobile company, and four "first-class clubs."[20] This was indeed a lively and self-sufficient city within a city.

Of the five black newspapers, the best known was the *Richmond Planet*, a weekly founded in 1883 and edited by John Mitchell Jr. Like so many in freedom's first generation, Mitchell was born in slavery — in 1863 outside Richmond. In the city, he became a teacher and then an editor, and in the pages of the *Planet* he addressed the issues of the day, investigating lynchings and fighting against black disfranchisement in Virginia. In 1898, he voiced opposition to the Spanish-American War, warning that U.S. control of the Philippines would subject Filipinos to the same kind of racial repression that dominated the South.

Of the four banks, one was the Mechanics Savings Bank, founded by Mitchell in 1902. Another was the St. Luke Penny Savings Bank (later the Consolidated Bank and Trust Company), chartered by Maggie L. Walker in 1903. The nation's first black woman bank president, Walker was born to former slaves in 1867. Like so many black women of her generation, she was a teacher — a graduate of the Richmond Colored Normal School. But she also took classes in sales and accounting, and with her keen business sense, she revitalized the Richmond branch of the Independent Order of St. Luke, which had been founded in 1867 as a women's sickness and death benefit association. Led by Walker, this branch was a springboard for an array of enterprises, including a women's insurance company, a department store, a newspaper called the *St. Luke Herald*, a youth educational loan program, and a delinquent girls' school. A vice president of the NACW, Walker was committed to racial uplift and progressive reform. Her good friend Mary McLeod Bethune often visited her in Richmond. Bethune, who had founded the Daytona Normal and Industrial Institute for Negro Girls in Florida in 1904, was also an NACW officer.

Another bank was the True Reformers Bank, founded in 1888 by the Reverend William Washington Browne, a Georgia slave who escaped to serve in the Union army. A temperance advocate, Browne first established a temperance society in Richmond that offered members life insurance. Expanding to a bank, the True Reformers provided loans and banking services, and its three-story building, built in 1891, had meeting rooms and a concert hall for lectures and entertainment. In 1893, the True Reformers started a newspaper. When Browne died in 1897, the Reverend William Lee Taylor became president of the bank and affiliated enterprises, which included a real estate agency and a retirement home. Unfortunately, owing largely to mismanagement and scandal, the bank closed in 1910.

There were thirty-one churches in Jackson Ward in 1907, twenty-three of them Baptist. The Sixth Mount Zion Baptist Church had been founded in 1867 by the slave preacher John Jasper, who later became famous for his "De Sun Do Move" sermon, which he delivered more than 250 times, once before the Virginia General Assembly. Like so many black churches, Sixth Mount Zion provided community services to the elderly and destitute. The needs of the poor were also looked after by the Richmond Neighborhood Association and the Richmond Welfare League, founded in 1913 and 1914, respectively. They later joined with other organizations to affiliate with the National Urban League, which had been founded in New York in 1910.

The Freedmen's Bureau established the Richmond Colored Normal School (later Armstrong High School) in 1865; the school became part of the Richmond school system in 1876. In 1865, the American Baptist Home Mission Society founded Virginia Union (later Virginia Union University) in Richmond with a grant from the Freedmen's Bureau. Created in 1882 in nearby Chesterfield County, the Virginia Normal and Collegiate (later Industrial) Institute became Virginia State College for Negroes in 1930, and Virginia State University in 1979. It was funded by the State of Virginia until designated a land-grant college under the Land-Grant College Act of 1890, which required states to open land-grant colleges to all races or establish separate black colleges emphasizing agriculture and the "mechanic arts." Nearby, too, was the Virginia Industrial School for Colored Girls, set up in 1915 by Janie Porter Barrett. As president of the Virginia State Federation of Colored Women's Clubs, Barrett had raised funds for this home for delinquent girls, which taught self-direction and basic job skills.

On April 8, 1905, the *Richmond Planet* reported on that year's Emancipation Day celebration in Richmond: "The colored people of this city celebrated the fortieth year of their emancipation on last Monday with a large parade. Excursionists from other cities swelled the crowd and five bands of music mustered into service." Speeches at the Broad Street Baseball Park followed the parade, and in the evening, a banquet and a performance by a "colored" opera company delighted attendees. "The affair was a success," the *Planet* reported, "and the best of good-feeling prevailed."[21]

Good feelings did not always prevail in Richmond, however. Just one year earlier, after the Virginia Passenger and Power Company announced that it would segregate seating on its electric streetcars, the black community organized a streetcar boycott.

Emancipation Day Parade
Excitement and joviality characterized Emancipation Day parades in Richmond, Virginia, and in black communities throughout the United States. These parades, which drew participants and onlookers from miles around, featured marching bands, dignitaries, and local groups. Related activities included formal speeches, cultural performances, picnics, and parties. Celebrations of this sort fostered a sense of racial solidarity and pride.
Library of Congress, Prints and Photographs Division, Washington, D.C., LC-D401-18421.

John Mitchell Jr. in the *Planet* and Maggie Walker in the *St. Luke Herald* urged readers to join the boycott. For more than a year, the black men and women of Richmond stayed off the city's streetcars, but the streetcar company did not cave in. Instead, the Virginia General Assembly, which in 1904 allowed but did not require streetcar segregation, made the practice mandatory in 1906.

Nevertheless, for the black people of Richmond, the power of cooperative action had been demonstrated. Black workers in the city's tobacco industry had long joined together in trade unions that recognized the common interests of workers and sought to elevate the dignity of work. But possibilities for interracial unionism had died with the demise of the Knights of Labor in the late 1880s (see chapter 8), and black locals were not affiliated with the National Tobacco Workers' Union of America, an affiliate of the American Federation of Labor, which excluded blacks. Like so much in the Jim Crow era, the shared interests of the working class did not cross the color line.

In July 1910, black Richmond united with all of black America in celebrating the victory of world heavyweight boxing champion Jack Johnson over his white opponent, Jim Jeffries, in Reno, Nevada, in what was billed as the "fight of the century." "Jack Johnson Travels in Style," boasted the *Richmond Planet* on July 16; "Was Offered over $300,000 to Fake the Fight — Wouldn't Give Up the Desire of a Life-time."[22] Johnson's defense of his title against Jeffries had been hyped by both the white and black press as a contest for racial supremacy. In 1908, with his commanding victory over the reigning champion, the Australian boxer Tommy Burns, Johnson had delivered a resounding blow against the notion of white supremacy. Simultaneously, he became the first black to hold the title of world heavyweight boxing champion — an achievement symbolic of global masculine supremacy. Indeed, whenever the hard-hitting and flamboyant Johnson, who was champion from 1908 to 1915, defeated a white opponent, black Americans proclaimed a victory for their race. In the *Planet*, Lucille Watkins described her feelings in a poem: "Jack Johnson, we have waited long for you / To grow our prayers in this single blow."[23] White response to the Johnson-Jeffries match was swift. Immediately after the fight, a wave of antiblack violence swept over the country that left thirteen blacks dead and hundreds injured.

Black Richmond exemplified the thriving economic, social, and religious life that African Americans created in the cities of the New South despite the constraints of Jim Crow. W. E. B. Du Bois found the same spirit animating Durham, North Carolina, and in a 1912 essay titled "The Upbuilding of Black Durham," he praised black Durham's progress since emancipation. Attributing the city's success to the "vision, knowledge, thrift, and efficiency" of its leaders, he singled out "a minister with college training, a physician with professional training, and a barber who saved his money," along with "a bright hustling young graduate of the public schools."[24] Throughout the cities of the South, the new black middle class — including business people, entrepreneurs, editors, preachers, and teachers — dedicated themselves to moral reform, literary and cultural affairs, civic improvements, economic development, and mutual welfare. Black civic leaders built networks within their communities and with other communities.

They worked with whites to secure concessions, such as jobs and government support for black schools and services for black neighborhoods, but they knew that the most productive strategies for sustaining black community life remained self-help and self-sufficiency.

New Cultural Expressions

In 1914, Jackson Ward's new Hippodrome Theater provided an elegant setting for black entertainment. Among the illustrious performers who graced its stage was Richmond native Bill Robinson, known to the world as Bojangles. Born in the city in 1878 and soon orphaned, he ran away as a child to Washington, D.C., where minstrel shows fascinated him. He quickly learned the routines, and incorporating juba and other dances into a rhythmic tap-dancing style, he became famous on the vaudeville circuit and later in films. His development of a unique stage character rooted in tap dance was only one of the new creative expressions that emerged as freedom's first generation established a rich social and cultural life.

In San Francisco, street performers George Walker and Bert Williams combined their talents to become black musical theater's best-known song-and-dance team. Mixing songs, jokes, pantomime, and dance, they took their show to New York, where, in white theaters with balcony seating for blacks, funnyman Williams performed in blackface opposite straight man Walker. Their musical *The Gold Bug* (1896) popularized the cakewalk, a slave parody of white balls and social pretensions in which elegantly attired black women and men, arm in arm, leaned way back and grandly strutted across the stage. Soon the cakewalk was a nationwide staple of dance and entertainment, and cakewalk contests were all the rage. Other Williams and Walker shows included *In Dahomey* (1903) and *Abyssinia* (1906), both composed by Will Marion Cook. Cook also composed *Clorindy, or The Origin of the Cakewalk* (1898) and *Jes Lak White Folks* (1899). Another composer for the black musical stage was Bob Cole, known for *A Trip to Coontown* (1898) and for collaborations with the brothers James Weldon Johnson and John Rosamond Johnson, including *The Shoo-Fly Regiment* (1907).

Despite the racist constraints of American culture and the white-controlled theater world, black artists of the musical stage fought hard to endow with depth and dignity the limited range of characters available to them. As Walker observed in 1909, "We want our folks, the Negroes, to like us. Over and above the money and the prestige is a love for the race. We feel that in a degree we represent the race and every hair's breadth of achievement we make is to its credit."[25] Many black musical artists were college educated and classically trained, and committed to the ideology of uplift. The Johnson brothers expressed this ideology in "Lift Every Voice and Sing," created in 1900 when John Rosamond Johnson set his brother James Weldon Johnson's poem to music: "Sing a song full of the faith that the dark past has taught us, / Sing a song full of the hope that the present has brought us; / Facing the rising sun / Of our new day begun, / Let us march on till victory is won."[26] The song was soon performed in black

***Bert Williams and George Walker in** In Dahomey*
Bert Williams was a pantomime and comic extraordinaire and a vaudeville superstar.
Williams's blackface character, which drew upon the entertainment tradition of blacks
doing blackface minstrelsy, both epitomized and slyly undermined the clownish character
he played. Between 1893 and 1909, Williams (second from right) performed in a series of
pioneering and popular musical theater shows with partner George Walker (second from
left), whose black dandy character contrasted perfectly with Williams's oafish character.
Williams's successful solo career, which included films as well as stints with the *Ziegfeld
Follies* on Broadway, solidified his widespread fame. *Photofest.*

churches and schools and at events around the nation, and in 1919 the NAACP adopted
it as the Negro National Anthem (see Appendix).

In Memphis, cornet player and minstrel troupe leader William Christopher
"W. C." Handy took a special interest in the mixed ballads (a combination of African
American folk music and Anglo-American ballad often centered on a heroic figure like
John Henry), field hollers, work songs, moans, and chants he heard in the cotton fields.
The music that Handy heard and popularized was the blues, a rich and expressive musical genre dating back to the late nineteenth century and created largely by ordinary
black folk that explores the ups and downs of everyday life. "Southern Negroes sang
about everything," Handy later wrote. "Trains, steamboats, steam whistles, sledge hammers, fast women, mean bosses, stubborn mules — all become subjects for their
songs. . . . From these materials, they set the mood for what we now call blues."[27] The
self-styled "Father of the Blues," Handy reworked this extraordinary vein of black folk
music into his own compositions, such as "St. Louis Blues" (1914), which made him
and the blues famous.

Notable for a twelve-bar, three-line structure in which the second line repeats the first, and the third line responds to the first two lines, blues songs were performed solo yet engaged the audience in a traditional call-and-response pattern. Ma Rainey, "the Mother of the Blues," was the biggest star on the tent-show circuit, which appealed largely to working-class and poor blacks. With an earthy, riveting voice, she mesmerized audiences with songs such as "Moonshine Blues." The extraordinary impact of the blues on American music can be heard today in genres as diverse as country, rhythm and blues, rock 'n' roll, gospel, jazz, and soul.

Jazz primarily took shape in turn-of-the-century New Orleans, where a distinctive musical culture showcased African roots: rhythmic complexity, improvisation, call and response, and the separation of melody and beat, or swing. African American musicians such as cornetist and bandleader Charles "Buddy" Bolden used European brass horns to combine European harmonies with African polyrhythms in dance band music and drum ensembles. Bolden gave New Orleans jazz a strong blues grounding. Jazz pianist, composer, and arranger Jelly Roll Morton helped popularize jazz, especially in the 1920s. He was also a pioneer player of ragtime, a syncopated piano music that was made famous by Scott Joplin, the "King of Ragtime," who was born near Texarkana, Texas, and that was commonly associated with Sedalia and St. Louis, Missouri. Joplin's "Maple Leaf Rag" (1899) was one of the most influential and popular ragtime tunes.

Issues of racial identification and race struggle characterized the work of important black writers of the period. Paul Laurence Dunbar contributed his writing talent to a number of musical stage shows, notably *Clorindy* and *In Dahomey*. But he made a name for himself, and a career, as a poet and writer of fiction. His poems in black dialect catered to white tastes and stereotypes of happy slaves, and they garnered a national following. But black readers were more likely to favor the currents of protest found in his antilynching poem "The Haunted Oak" and in the poem for which he is best remembered today, "We Wear the Mask" (from his 1896 book *Lyrics of Lowly Life*), which deftly explores the realities behind the public faces put on by blacks in their efforts to endure and rise above the racist constraints of the era.

Charles Chesnutt likewise attracted support from the white literary establishment, even though his works forthrightly portrayed the lives of southern blacks. His book *The Marrow of Tradition* (1901) sparked controversy. The setting of the novel was the 1898 Wilmington Insurrection, which some of his relatives had survived, and among the themes it explored were mixed-race identity and racial justice. Like Chesnutt's final novel, *The Colonel's Dream* (1905), *The Marrow of Tradition* generated limited sales, dashing his hopes for a full-time literary career. Chesnutt shifted gears, focusing instead on his legal stenography business in Cleveland, his family, and less ambitious writing projects.

Painter Henry Ossawa Tanner, perhaps best known for *The Banjo Lesson* (1893), discovered as an art student that the racism of the American art establishment made it impossible to sustain a career in his native land. He settled instead in Paris, where he had a successful career that included painting biblical subjects.

The Banjo Lesson, 1893

Henry Ossawa Tanner's representation of an attentive male elder (perhaps a doting grandfather) lovingly teaching a young boy how to play the banjo offered a radical alternative to the common racist stereotypes of black musicians, notably banjo players, as comic, even buffoonish, characters. This popular painting also debunked the myth of innate black musicality by showing that black musical talent required training and practice. Despite this warm and deeply humane portrayal of black sociocultural life, some critics have lamented that most of Tanner's work was nonracial. *The Banjo Lesson, by Henry Ossawa Tanner, 1893, oil on canvas, 49 in. x 35½ in./Hampton University Museum Collection, Hampton University, Hampton, Virginia.*

Migration, Accommodation, and Protest

Despite Jim Crow, many black southerners built satisfying personal lives and successful communities by emphasizing self-reliance and separatism. Some chose to leave the South, moving west to the freer environments of Oklahoma's black towns and joining the black army units stationed at western forts. Others went to West Africa, where they hoped to build new lives in an all-black environment. Concurrently, two black leaders articulated competing uplift strategies. Booker T. Washington advocated that blacks accommodate to life in the segregated South while gaining the industrial and vocational training that could bring economic independence. This approach, he argued, would ultimately yield interrracial as well as intraracial progress. W. E. B. Du Bois promoted economic self-sufficiency as well as agitation for civil and political rights. Together these strategies would eventually advance the causes of civil and political equality as well as the cause of economic justice. Du Bois also asserted that the most talented of his race, notably future black leaders, must avail themselves of the best academic training to achieve at the highest levels, uplift the race, and challenge white supremacy.

Migration Hopes and Disappointments

In 1892, immediately following the lynching of her friends in Memphis, Ida B. Wells wrote in the *Free Speech and Headlight*, "There is . . . only one thing left that we can do; save our money and leave a town which will neither protect our lives and property, nor give us a fair trial in the courts."[28] Many heeded such advice, and soon Wells, too, left Memphis, one of some 250,000 southern blacks who left the South between the end of the Civil War and 1910.

Although migration to Kansas subsided after the initial Exoduster movement (see chapter 8), it never stopped, and eventually 25,000 blacks left Arkansas, Alabama, Mississippi, Louisiana, and Texas for Kansas. Black migration to Oklahoma, however, accelerated, and between 1890 and 1910 more than 100,000 blacks settled there, largely in all-black towns. The most famous of these towns was Boley, which had more than 1,000 residents in 1907 and some 2,000 black farm families in its vicinity. Like black communities everywhere, Boley featured a range of institutions, including a school, churches, restaurants, fraternal orders, and women's clubs.

In addition to farming, black men in the West worked as cowboys, among other occupations. The 1890 U.S. census reported 1,600 western cowboys of color. The dangers of the western cattle ranges induced blacks and whites to work together. But for blacks in the U.S. army, discrimination was ever present. When the four black units serving in western forts moved to Florida in preparation for deployment to Cuba in the Spanish-American War, these buffalo soldiers encountered Jim Crow. After racial violence flared in Lakeland and Tampa, Florida, Chaplain George Prioleau of the Ninth Cavalry wrote a letter to the editor of the *Cleveland Gazette*, a prominent black newspaper: "Why sir, the Negro of this country is freeman and yet a slave. Talk about fighting and freeing poor Cuba and of Spain's brutality: . . . Is America any better than Spain?"[29] The irony of ostensibly fighting to free Cubans and Filipinos from Spanish oppression was not lost on the soldiers, and Lewis Douglass, son of Frederick Douglass, warned that "injustice to dark races" prevailed wherever the United States took control.[30]

In 1906, an incident in Brownsville, Texas, where the Twenty-Fifth Infantry Regiment was stationed, captured national attention. When an exchange of gunfire left a white man dead and a policeman injured, townspeople immediately blamed the black soldiers at Fort Brown. In spite of a lack of evidence and the absence of a trial or even formal charges, President Theodore Roosevelt discharged all 167 soldiers without honor. Widespread black protest, including that of the NACW and the black press, as well as a private message from Booker T. Washington, could not convince Roosevelt to change his mind.

Some southern blacks left the United States altogether, settling in Liberia, the West African colony founded by the American Colonization Society (ACS) in 1821 for the resettlement of free African Americans. In the late nineteenth century, the Back to Africa Movement revived, and roughly 3,800 blacks, or about 238 annually, emigrated to Liberia, mostly under the auspices of the ACS, which still acted as a trustee. African Methodist Episcopal bishop Henry McNeal Turner, one of the era's most prominent black supporters of black emigration, became an honorary vice president of the ACS in 1876. Believing that blacks would never receive fair treatment in the United States, he also advocated the civilizing and Christianizing mission of African American resettlement and the pride of race a black nation in Africa could bring. But the two groups of emigrants his International Migration Society sponsored in 1895 and 1896 did not fare well. In Liberia, the new settlers suffered from a lack of jobs, high rates of illness and death, and cultural and political clashes with indigenous Liberians. Dissent among them also reduced their enthusiasm, and many returned to the United States.

Alexander Crummell, a school companion of Henry Highland Garnet, had fought to be ordained in the Episcopal Church, and under the church's auspices he had gone to Liberia as a missionary. During two decades in Liberia, he and his associate Edward Blyden, who had been born in the West Indies, advanced ideas of black unity and nationalism. But their efforts were unsuccessful, and in 1871 political strife caused Crummell to return to the United States. In addition to leading an Episcopal congregation in Washington, D.C., he wrote and spoke extensively, building an impressive scholarly reputation. In 1897, he founded the American Negro Academy, dedicated to advancing black scholarship and black intellectual life.

West Indian blacks like Blyden also sought relief from oppression by immigrating to the cities of the North, where they contributed significantly to the development of communities such as Harlem. In 1900, there were roughly 5,000 foreign-born blacks in New York City, and by 1910 almost 12,000 were living there. Most were from the British Caribbean, notably Jamaica and Barbados, where there was limited economic opportunity. Caribbean immigrant Harold Ellis observed, "You were never able to come out of the class in which you were born down there," while in the United States, "there was prejudice . . . but it was better than having no hope."[31]

The Age of Booker T. Washington

The preeminent African American spokesman between 1895 and 1915 was Booker T. Washington, head of Tuskegee Institute in Alabama, which he helped found. Emphasizing economic nationalism, race pride, racial solidarity, and interracial goodwill, Washington formulated an uplift program that reflected the spirit of the times. He was the era's most powerful race leader because of his ability to voice black people's concerns and to work with influential whites by preaching racial conciliation.

From his slave beginnings, Washington's rise to greatness is a classic American success story, carefully recounted in his 1901 autobiography, *Up from Slavery*. Born in 1856 to a slave cook and an unknown white father in Franklin County, Virginia, he was eager to succeed, and his mother supported his desire for an education. The family moved to West Virginia after the Civil War, and there nine-year-old Booker got up early to work in the salt mines so that later in the day he could attend a few hours of school. At age sixteen, he walked five hundred miles to enroll in Hampton Institute, where he took a job as a janitor to pay his room and board. He worked hard to impress those in authority, especially whites, with his moral character, work ethic, ambition, and intelligence.

At Hampton, Washington came under the influence of Samuel Chapman Armstrong, the school's president and a leading promoter of industrial and agricultural education for blacks. In 1881, after Washington had graduated and returned to Hampton as a teacher, Armstrong arranged for his protégé to head what was being organized as Tuskegee Institute for Negroes in rural southeastern Alabama. Washington first held classes in an AME Zion church. His students, learning bricklaying, literally built the school on the site of an abandoned plantation. Washington's fund-raising and public relations efforts helped achieve not only solvency but also fame for the school. By 1915, when he died, Tuskegee was enrolling 1,500 students a year and had a campus of 3,500 acres and some 100 buildings.

Washington worked hard to secure state funding and the support of northern white philanthropists, who were attracted by the Hampton-Tuskegee model of vocational education for black youths because it promoted individual and collective advancement within the confines of Jim Crow. Both Andrew Carnegie and John D. Rockefeller, men who had made their fortunes from steel and oil, respectively, contributed to Tuskegee. Julius Rosenwald, part owner of Sears, Roebuck, piloted a program with Washington that ultimately led to the creation of 5,000 rural schools for black children in the South.

With Tuskegee as a base of operations, Washington emerged as an increasingly influential black educator and spokesman. In 1900, he founded the National Negro Business League, a network of black business and professional men that encouraged the development of black-owned and black-operated enterprises. Washington cultivated loyalists within black business, church, education, and press circles. His stature allowed him to exercise great power, which he used to sustain his friends and supporters and ruthlessly cut off those who crossed him. His network became known as the Tuskegee Machine, and the era he dominated as the Age of Booker T. Washington.

In 1895, Washington delivered a speech at the Cotton States and International Exposition in Atlanta that gave classic expression to themes he had refined for more than a decade. Speaking to a largely white audience, he argued that economic uplift, especially through business development and industrial education, was the best course for black advancement. Portraying black southerners as loyal and patient, he encouraged them to begin "at the bottom of life" and not "permit our grievances to overshadow our opportunities." "Cast down your bucket where you are," he urged his listeners; black people should seek to better their condition within the South, and white employers should hire African Americans rather than foreign laborers. Finally, he called black agitation for social equality "the extremest folly." He concluded, "In all things that are purely social we can be as separate as the fingers, yet one as the hand in all things essential to mutual progress."[32]

Washington's **Atlanta Compromise speech** proved masterful precisely because its multiple messages allowed different audiences to hear what they wanted. Most important for black people were the elements of hope and possibility for a brighter future. The emphasis on self-help, solidarity, economic uplift, and making the most of life within the confines of segregation hit widely popular notes. Most important for whites was **accommodationism**, or working within the racial status quo, including segregation — an approach that Washington publicly urged.

Frederick Douglass had died earlier that year, and whites now looked to Washington as the heir apparent: the lead voice of African Americans. Philanthropists relied on his advice regarding which black institutions and causes to support, and Presidents Theodore Roosevelt and William Howard Taft consulted him before dispensing political patronage positions available to blacks. But Roosevelt incurred much criticism in 1901 when he invited Washington to dine at the White House, a breach of custom that offended many whites, especially in the South. Nevertheless, Washington continued his public efforts to promote interracial harmony by squaring black uplift with white goodwill. Privately, he spent large sums of money to defeat Jim Crow legislation and mount legal challenges, secretly retaining lawyers and working through intermediaries. These efforts were unknown to all but a few highly trusted contemporaries.

The Emergence of W. E. B. Du Bois

Numerous aspects of Washington's leadership — notably his accommodationism, his educational philosophy, and his dictatorial methods — drew increasing black criticism, especially from northern-based leaders such as William Monroe Trotter. The brilliant and radical Harvard-educated Trotter edited the *Boston Guardian*, one of the most uncompromising black newspapers of its day. Trotter viewed accommodationism as a betrayal of black people and made it a mission of his paper to challenge Washington. When, in 1903, Washington tried to deliver a speech at a black church in Boston, opponents led by Trotter heckled him. Washington was further incensed when a fight broke out, and he took Trotter to court over what came to be called the Boston Riot. Trotter was fined $500 and sent to jail for a month for his role in the affair.

Soon, W. E. B. Du Bois also became a vocal critic of Washington's accommodationism, but the two black leaders were not polar opposites. Du Bois's racial uplift ideology in many ways mirrored that of Washington and mainstream black thought. In light of Du Bois's own emphasis on racial solidarity, economic advancement, and hard work, he initially found much to admire in Washington's program. Also like Washington, Du Bois at times stressed blacks' responsibilities and duties more than their grievances and rights. Initially, he even praised Washington's Atlanta Compromise speech as a hopeful and viable program for racial progress.

Booker T. Washington and W. E. B. Du Bois
Washington (left) and Du Bois (right), brilliant and ambitious men who were zealously dedicated to their people's elevation, were the preeminent African American leaders of their day. These photographs capture their common seriousness of purpose, unwavering commitment, and laserlike intensity. Despite their differences in philosophy — particularly Washington's accommodationism versus Du Bois's militancy — and the rift that developed between them, they agreed on the ultimate goal for African Americans: full freedom and equality. *Left: Library of Congress, Prints and Photographs Division, Washington, D.C., LC-ppmsca-23961; right: Library of Congress, Prints and Photographs Division, Washington, D.C., LC-USZ62-16767.*

Yet the two men's lives had been very different. Du Bois had been born in 1868 to a family that had been free for generations. Reared largely by his mother in a small black community within essentially white Great Barrington, Massachusetts, he was a precocious child and brilliant student. He was also enormously ambitious and disciplined. His stellar academic credentials included an undergraduate degree from Fisk in 1889 and undergraduate and graduate degrees from Harvard, including a Ph.D. in 1895. Trained as a historian, he also did pioneering work in the emerging field of sociology. In the early 1900s, Du Bois taught at Atlanta University, where he conducted a series of pathbreaking studies of black life.

Du Bois was always far more outspoken than Washington about black rights and the need for the vote. Their differences grew as Jim Crow laws and black disfranchisement intensified. Du Bois also placed far more emphasis on the need for liberal arts and advanced scientific and technical education for blacks. His vision reflected an elitist, top-down leadership style. Advocating the most advanced college curricula for the academically talented, Du Bois thus hoped to prepare what he called the "talented tenth" for the rigors of race leadership.

The bitter break between Du Bois and Washington owed directly to Washington's use of his Tuskegee Machine and the lengths to which he would go to punish opponents, especially Trotter. In *The Souls of Black Folk* (1903), Du Bois spelled out his objections to accommodationism: "Mr. Washington distinctly asks that black people give up, at least for the present, three things, — First, political power, Second, insistence on civil rights, Third, higher education of Negro youth, — and concentrate all their energies on industrial education, and accumulation of wealth, and the conciliation of the South." Yet this approach, Du Bois pointed out, produced only disfranchisement, "civil inferiority," and a "withdrawal of aid from institutions for the higher training of the Negro." Moreover, Washington's approach "has tended to make the whites, North and South, shift the burden of the Negro problem to the Negro's shoulders . . . when in fact the burden belongs to the nation, and the hands of none of us are clean if we bend not our energies to righting these great wrongs."[33] The program Du Bois announced in *The Souls of Black Folk* guided his actions for the rest of his life.

Du Bois's race leadership linked national and international developments. He helped assemble an exhibit for the 1900 Paris World's Fair that summarized African American achievements since emancipation. That summer, he also led the African American delegation, which included Anna Julia Cooper, to the first **Pan-African Congress**, in London. The Trinidadian lawyer Henry Sylvester Williams, who called the meeting, promoted the concept of **Pan-Africanism** — the notion, held by those both within and outside the African continent, of a shared global sense of African identity as well as an abiding concern for the welfare of Africans everywhere. Delegates from Great Britain, the United States, the West Indies, and Africa condemned the partition of Africa into European colonies. African American leaders such as Alexander Crummell and Edward Blyden, as well as Martin R. Delany and Henry M. Turner, had not protested the European colonization of Africa because they saw in it a civilizing influence. But Du Bois was among those who clearly perceived its liabilities. In his address to the congress, he warned, "The problem of the twentieth century is the problem of the color line, the question as to how far differences of race, which show themselves chiefly in the color of the skin and the texture of the hair, are going to be made, hereafter, the basis of denying to over half the world the right of sharing to their utmost ability the opportunities and privileges of modern civilization."[34]

In 1905, Du Bois helped launch the **Niagara movement**, a militant protest organization of black intellectuals and professionals that, in opposition to Washington's program, tried to revitalize a national black civil rights agenda. Local actions by National Equal Rights League auxiliaries, particularly challenges to unequal educational opportunities for blacks (Map 9.2), had continued in northern states

Segregated schools and/or
racially discriminatory
educational practices are

- ● prohibited by law
- ○ made possible but not
  mandated by law
- ◐ mandated by law

ALASKA
○ **1905:** Statute provides for the education of white children and "children of mixed blood who lead a civilized life." Unclear whether full-blooded black children would be able to attend.

ARIZONA
○ **1909:** Statute (passed over governor's veto) gives school district trustees the authority to segregate black and white schoolchildren in districts with more than 8 black pupils.
◐ **1927:** Statute mandates that in areas with 25 or more black high-school students, an election will determine whether to segregate these students.

CALIFORNIA
◐ **1870:** Statute mandates that if 10 white children's parents provide a written request, African and Indian children will be required to attend a separate school.
● **1880:** Statute bans school segregation, mandating that children of any race or nationality can attend public schools.
○ **1902:** Statute repeals 1880 law, prohibiting black, Chinese, and Japanese children from attending schools designated for whites.

COLORADO
● **1876:** State constitution prohibits classification of students in public schools by race.

CONNECTICUT
○ **1933:** Statute permits the establishment of separate schools for black students if the authorities believe that such separation is necessary or proper.

DELAWARE
◐ **1877:** Statute levies a separate tax on blacks to fund black schools.
◐ **1915:** State code requires that schools be segregated by race.

IDAHO
● **1889:** State constitution prohibits school segregation.

ILLINOIS
● **1874:** Statute prohibits boards of education from excluding children from public school on account of color, establishing a fine of between $5 and $100 for those who exclude children and a fine of up to $25 for those who threaten to exclude them.
● **1896:** Statute prohibits school officers from excluding children from public schools on account of color, establishing a fine of between $5 and $100 for offenders.

INDIANA
◐ **1869:** Statute mandates the establishment of separate schools for black children. If there are not enough black students for this purpose, trustees are directed to find other means of educating black children.

○ **1877:** Statute decrees that black children shall be admitted to white schools if separate schools cannot be provided for them, or if they advance to a higher grade than is offered by black schools.

KANSAS
◐ **1868:** Statute mandates the establishment of separate schools for black or mixed-race students in cities with more than 150,000 people.
○ **1905:** Statute allows Kansas City to organize and maintain separate black and white schools, including high schools, but orders that "no discrimination on account of color shall be made in high schools, except as provided herein."

MASSACHUSETTS
● **1894:** Statute prohibits students' exclusion from public school on account of race, color, or religion.

MICHIGAN
● **1871:** Statute prohibits separate schools or departments based on race or color.

MINNESOTA
● **1877:** Statute prohibits segregated schools, establishing a $50 penalty per offense and mandating that the offending school district would lose funds.
● **1905:** Statute prohibits school districts from classifying students according to race or color, including by the establishment of separate schools; mandates that the offending school district would lose funds.

MONTANA
○ **1871:** Statute establishes separate schools for black children.
● **1895:** Statute declares all public schools open to all children (without express reference to separate schools or black children).

NEVADA
◐ **1865:** Statute prohibits black, Asian, and Indian students from attending public schools, empowering any district's Board of Trustees to establish separate schools for these students.

NEW JERSEY
● **1881:** Statute decrees that no child between the ages of 5 and 18 may be excluded from public school on account of religion, nationality, or color.
● **1903:** Statute decrees that no child between the ages of 5 and 18 may be excluded from public school on account of religion, nationality, or color, stipulating punishment with a misdemeanor charge, fine between $50 and $250, and/or imprisonment in a county jail, workhouse, or penitentiary.
○ **1929:** Statute authorizes segregated schools.

NEW MEXICO
◐ **1907:** Statute mandates separate rooms for the teaching of black children, noting that when "said rooms are so provided, such pupils may not be admitted to the school rooms occupied and used by pupils of Caucasian or other descent."
○ **1911:** State constitution establishes free public schools open to all school-aged children, regardless of race.

NEW YORK
● **1900:** Statute repeals an 1864 law establishing segregated schools, making it unlawful to refuse admission to any public school in New York on account of race or color.
● **1910:** Statute prohibits the exclusion of students from public schools on account of race or color.
○ **1930:** Statute endows school district trustees with the authority to establish separate schools.

OHIO
○ **1878:** Statute allows school districts to organize separate schools if "in their judgment it may be for the advantage of the district to do so."
● **1887:** Statute prohibits school segregation.

OKLAHOMA
◐ **1904:** Statute orders a fine for instructors teaching in unsegregated schools: "Any instructor who shall teach in any school, college or institution where members of the white and colored race are received and enrolled as pupils for instruction shall be deemed guilty of a misdemeanor, and upon conviction thereof, shall be fined in any sum not less than $10 nor more than $50 for each offense."

PENNSYLVANIA
◐ **1869:** Statute prohibits black children from attending Pittsburgh schools.
● **1872:** Statute repeals 1869 Pittsburgh school segregation order.
● **1881:** Statute prohibits any teacher or school administrator from discriminating against students based on race or color.
● **1911:** Statute bans school segregation.

RHODE ISLAND
● **1882:** Statute prohibits students' exclusion from school on account of race or color.

UTAH
● **1895:** State constitution prohibits school segregation.

WYOMING
○ **1887:** Statute establishes that separate schools may be provided for black children in school districts with 15 or more black children.

MAP 9.2 School Segregation in the North and West

School segregation laws and practices varied from state to state, within states, and across time. In some states and localities, segregated schools were required by law (de jure segregation); in others, they were the result of custom (de facto segregation). The absence of school segregation laws in a few states, often those with few blacks or influential black and tolerant white populations, actually fostered limited integration. This map offers a sampling of laws from the northern, midwestern, and western states that mandated, allowed, and prohibited segregated schools. As shown here, these laws at times changed, typically owing to shifting public opinion within these states.

into the 1880s. T. Thomas Fortune led two efforts to resurrect a national civil rights movement, but both foundered. The National Afro-American League lasted from 1889 to 1893 and the National Afro-American Council from 1898 to 1908 (Fortune left the latter organization in 1904).

When Du Bois, Trotter, and their colleagues met on the Canadian side of Niagara Falls to write a declaration of principles for the Niagara movement, they expressed goals similar to those of the National Afro-American League and the National Afro-American Council: voting rights, equal educational opportunities, and an end to segregation. But Fortune, a Washington supporter, was notably absent, as was Washington himself. The energetic "Niagaraites" stressed "persistent manly agitation," not accommodation, as "the way to liberty."[35]

Ida B. Wells initially maintained connections with both the National Afro-American Council and the Niagara movement. Early on she headed the council's anti-lynching bureau and served as convention secretary for three years. In June 1895, she married Ferdinand L. Barnett, founder of the *Conservator*, Chicago's first black newspaper, becoming Ida B. Wells-Barnett. She and her husband were strong supporters of the Niagara movement. But undermined by money woes, infighting, and Washington's powerful opposition, the movement achieved few tangible results.

In September 1906, Du Bois witnessed firsthand a vicious race riot in Atlanta. Five days of lawlessness devastated black areas of the city and left ten blacks and one white dead. Two years later, a race riot in Springfield, Illinois, the hometown of Abraham Lincoln, grabbed the nation's attention. A white woman's false rape accusation against a black man led rampaging whites to lynch two innocent black men and wreak havoc on the black community.

The Springfield race riot made it clear that racial tensions were a national, not just a southern, problem. In the wake of this riot, a distinguished roster of black and white progressives issued a call for an interracial organization to end racial discrimination and inequality. Those signing the call and attending the 1909 meeting to establish the National Negro Committee included Du Bois, Wells-Barnett, Mary Church Terrell, and Josephine St. Pierre Ruffin, as well as prominent white reformers such as journalists Mary White Ovington, Oswald Garrison Villard (grandson of William Lloyd Garrison), and Ray Stannard Baker, and social workers Jane Addams and Lillian Wald. At its 1910 meeting, the organization became the **National Association for the Advancement of Colored People (NAACP)**.

With a home office in New York City and branch offices in Baltimore, Boston, Detroit, Kansas City, St. Louis, and Washington, D.C., the NAACP quickly became the nation's leading African American civil rights organization, with notable early successes in spite of very limited funds. Filing a brief in *Guinn v. United States* (1915), it helped overturn Oklahoma's grandfather clause, which had contributed to black disfranchisement. Protesting *The Birth of a Nation* (see chapter 8), the 1915 film that glorified the role of the Ku Klux Klan in the overthrow of Black Reconstruction, the NAACP shut down showings in some cities and forced offensive scenes to be edited out. From its beginnings, the NAACP was vital to national efforts to end lynching. As director of publicity and research, Du Bois founded and edited the organization's journal, the *Crisis*, in which he published lynching reports and statistics together with wide-ranging news coverage and opinion pieces on issues important to African Americans. Under his direction, the journal's circulation grew from 1,000 for the first issue in November 1910 to 100,000 nine years later. When Washington died in 1915, Du Bois had already emerged as the nation's preeminent black spokesman for a comprehensive civil rights agenda and a well-supported program of organized protest.

CONCLUSION

Racial Uplift in the Nadir

"If you want to lift yourself up, lift up someone else." This saying, attributed to Booker T. Washington, exemplifies how black Americans kept hope alive in the decades between 1885 and 1915, sometimes described as the lowest moment, or nadir, in African American history. After Reconstruction, blacks lost ground in crucial areas. Without land, they struggled for economic independence. Southern states imposed segregation laws and legalized Jim Crow practices that relegated blacks to second-rate public facilities and branded them as racial inferiors. Disfranchisement, peonage, and lynching structured powerful systems of racial oppression, which kept African Americans at the bottom of every hierarchy in American politics, law, and society.

But many blacks and the institutions they built avoided these traps, subverted these realities, and surmounted these obstacles. Turning inward, freedom's first generation intensified their emphasis on racial solidarity, self-help, and economic nationalism. They strengthened their communities, seeing the building of robust African American communities as the best way to endure and even thrive in the increasingly restrictive world of Jim Crow. A powerful network of black institutions — churches, schools, businesses, mutual aid societies, and newspapers — blossomed. A new culture of freedom unleashed new forms of creativity in music, literature, and the arts. Ultimately, black leaders joined with white progressives to form a new civil rights organization that mobilized against racial injustice. Freedom's first generation thus opened the way for the New Negro of the twentieth century to forge new and even more productive paths of resistance and achievement.

CHAPTER 9 **REVIEW**

KEY TERMS

Jim Crow p. 345

Plessy v. Ferguson **(1896)** p. 346

separate but equal p. 346

imperialism p. 347

scientific racism p. 348

Social Darwinism p. 348

progressivism p. 350

white primary p. 350

Wilmington Insurrection (1898) p. 351

lynching p. 351

National Association of Colored Women (NACW) p. 356

uplift p. 357

debt peonage p. 358

Atlanta Compromise speech (1895) p. 371

accommodationism p. 371

Pan-African Congress (1900) p. 373

Pan-Africanism p. 373

Niagara movement (1905) p. 373

National Association for the Advancement of Colored People (NAACP) p. 375

REVIEW QUESTIONS

1. What connections can be drawn between the growth of Jim Crow laws, the concept of scientific racism, and American and European imperialism abroad? What underlying philosophies informed these developments?

2. How did Jim Crow laws and lynchings function as a means of social control in the South?

3. In what ways did communities of African Americans focus on racial solidarity and advancement during these years? How did this focus manifest itself socially, culturally, and economically? Consider Jackson Ward, the main black neighborhood in Richmond, Virginia, as an example. To what would you attribute the post-Reconstruction development of this "city within a city"?

4. Consider the various strains of black thought surrounding accommodationism and protest. Which individuals and organizations supported which philosophies? In what ways were these different ideas connected to and divergent from one another?

Agency and Constraint

According to one historical axiom, humans throughout history have lived their lives within the limits imposed by the specific contexts they experience. They can and do exercise agency, or purposeful action, in the struggle against the bounds of the worlds within which they operate. Even though the tension between agency and constraint shapes historical experience, ultimately constraints limit agency. African American history in particular, especially the realities of African American freedom after emancipation, vividly illustrates this dynamic tension. While African Americans, notably freedpeople, made remarkable progress at the turn of the twentieth century, it was also one of the worst periods in African American freedom, in which white supremacy tragically impeded black progress and devastated incalculable numbers of black lives.

Still, for African Americans specifically and for oppressed peoples generally, it is essential to emphasize the complexity of their historical agency — in particular, what they themselves have done historically and what they continue to do individually and collectively to advance their liberation and alleviate racist oppression. In other words, to understand what has happened and continues to happen to African Americans is not enough: We also must understand what African Americans have done and continue to do for themselves, paying special attention to the small and large ways as well as the complex and simple ways they have fought for freedom and resisted white supremacy.

Lynching functioned as a key mechanism in the violent repression of African Americans in the decades after Reconstruction. Vigilante justice, in which people took the law into their own hands and murdered individuals accused of crimes, had been practiced by mobs in America since colonial times, and during Reconstruction the Ku Klux Klan and similar groups lynched blacks as part of their terrorist campaigns. Those who perpetrated lynchings said that the victims were criminals who got what they deserved. Especially if the charge was a black man's assault on a white woman, lynching was said to be necessary to spare the woman from the ordeal of giving courtroom testimony. In the late nineteenth century, lynching reached epidemic proportions, averaging two or three recorded episodes per week. They were often public spectacles, drawing crowds of onlookers as well as participants. The setting was sometimes a desolate, secluded place, but it was just as likely to be a public square, in front of the local courthouse, with the sheriff and officers of the law among the crowd. Victims were often tortured while alive, and after death their bodies were mutilated. Bystanders took souvenirs and photographs of the event. Such photographs, affixed to postcards, were often sent to friends and relatives until Congress forbade the mailing of such materials in 1908.

The NAACP made a nationwide campaign against lynching a priority. In 1919, it published an analysis of the dire situation titled *Thirty Years of Lynching in the United States*. With each new report of a lynching, NAACP staff hung a banner out the window of its New York City headquarters stating, "A man was lynched yesterday." In 1901, George

Henry White — the last black southerner of the slave-born generation to serve in Congress — introduced a bill that would have made lynching a federal crime. It failed to pass. In 1918, with NAACP backing, Congressman Leonidas Dyer of St. Louis introduced a bill with the same intent. Neither the Dyer Anti-Lynching Bill, reintroduced numerous times, nor any other antilynching bill ever passed Congress.

Like lynching, peonage helped structure the white supremacist regime of the era. Peonage was a notoriously vicious element in the South's repressive labor regime that impoverished black agricultural workers while enriching white planters and merchants. Defined as a "condition of compulsory service, based on the indebtedness of the peon to the master,"[36] it resulted when an agricultural worker signed a contract for her or his labor but either failed to fulfill one or more requirements of the contract or, as was all too often the case, was alleged to have done so. Especially if the individual had received an advance on the promise of his or her labor, state laws made the worker liable to arrest, fine, and imprisonment for charges of contract fraud. Vagrancy and other ill-defined allegations also fed the chicanery that characterized this unjust system. The worker might avoid imprisonment and have her or his fine paid by a third party through a private labor agreement in which the worker agreed to work until the debt was paid off. The problem was that the debt persisted. Often through technicalities and trickery, the person who held the debt manipulated a set of practices ensuring control over the labor of the debtor for as long as possible. It is no wonder that to debt peons, their life and work felt like slavery. In fact, some historians have called it neoslavery.[37] In addition to prison farms, which tended to operate outside public view, a common form of highly visible convict labor that evoked slavery and ensnared many blacks was chain gangs, in which prisoners shackled together by ankle chains did hard public labor, like clearing land and building roads under strict armed surveillance. Work gangs did similar kinds of labor under comparable surveillance, but without the ankle chains.

In *Clyatt v. United States* (1905), the first case challenging debt peonage, the U.S. Supreme Court ruled that the Peonage Abolition Act (1867) was constitutional. More important, in *Bailey v. Alabama* (1911), a case that received secret support from Booker T. Washington, the Court overturned an Alabama law that held a laborer criminally liable for taking money in advance for work not performed. This law, said the Court, was in violation of both the Thirteenth Amendment, which outlawed slavery, and the Fourteenth Amendment, which ensured equal protection of the laws. Finally, in *United States v. Reynolds* (1914), the Court outlawed the criminal surety laws that had allowed debtors to avoid prison by selling their labor to an employer who agreed to pay their debts and fines.

As you examine the written and visual documents that follow, consider the environment in which lynching and peonage were practiced. What did participants and observers think of these events and systems? What role if any did gender play in limiting African Americans' agency?

The Lynching of Charles Mitchell, 1897

In June 1897, CHARLES MITCHELL, a twenty-three-year-old black hotel porter, was accused of robbery by a prominent white woman in Urbana, Ohio; next she accused him of rape. While he was in jail, a white mob gathered. The sheriff called up the militia, which fired into the crowd, killing several men and wounding others. The militia then withdrew, evidently expecting the Ohio National Guard to arrive, but the mayor had advised the guard to stay away. At that point, the mob broke into the jail, and the sheriff handed over the keys to Mitchell's cell. A noose was placed around Mitchell's neck, and he was hanged from a tree limb in the courthouse yard as shown below. Later his corpse was displayed in a coffin under the lynching tree. Amid threats of burning the body, it was removed, but not before relic hunters had "nearly cut the coat off the dead man. Every button was gone, and even his shoes and stockings were taken off and carried away." The *New York Times* reported that the "wounding of the jail assailants arouses more local indignation than the murder of the Negro."[38]

Silver gelatin print, American Photographer (nineteenth century)/Fogg Art Museum, Harvard University Art Museums, USA/On deposit from the Carpenter Center for the Visual Arts/Bridgeman Images.

The Lynching of Virgil Jones, Robert Jones, Thomas Jones, and Joseph Riley, 1908

This postcard depicts the July 31, 1908, lynching of VIRGIL JONES, ROBERT JONES, THOMAS JONES, and JOSEPH RILEY in Logan County, Kentucky. The message from the sender reads, "This happened while I was in Kentucky in a little town just a short distance from where I was stopping. The government won't allow the cards sent out [the sender placed the postcard in an envelope to conceal its contents]. A little nigger shot a farmer & his wife and started the trouble. I was right in the heat of the excitement." In reality, the men were probably lynched because they had publicly criticized the legal system. The message on the postcard (left) documents an effort to circumvent the federal ban on the mailing of lynching photographs. These materials violated standards of public decency and damaged the public image of the South and the nation. The image on the right is an enlarged detail from the postcard.

Without Sanctuary, National Center for Civil and Human Rights, Atlanta, GA, USA.

A Georgia Negro Peon | *The New Slavery in the South, 1904*

This narrative first appeared in February 1904 in the New York magazine the *Independent*. It was told to a representative of the magazine, who then prepared it for publication. The narrative begins with a sharecropper and a storekeeper settling their account, which, not surprisingly, comes out in the storekeeper's favor. Look for ways that peonage operated as a system, paying particular attention to the ways it affected black men and women differently.

I am a negro and was born some time during the war in Elbert County, Ga., and I reckon by this time I must be a little over forty years old. . . .

. . . The storekeeper took us one by one and read to us statements of our accounts. According to the books there was no man of us who owed the Senator less than $100; some of us were put down for as much as $200. I owed $165, according to the bookkeeper. These debts were not accumulated during one year, but ran back for three and four years, so we were told — in spite of the fact that we understood that we had had a full settlement at the end of each year. But no one of us would have dared to dispute a white man's word — oh, no; not in those days. Besides, we fellows didn't care anything about the amounts — we were after getting away; and we had been told that we might go, if we signed the acknowledgements. We would have signed anything, just to get away. So we stepped up, we did, and made our marks. That same night we were rounded up by a constable and ten or twelve white men, who aided him, and we were locked up, every one of us, in one of the Senator's stockades. The next morning it was explained to us by the two guards appointed to watch us that, in the papers we had signed the day before, we had not only made acknowledgement of our indebtedness, but that we had also agreed to work for the Senator until the debts were paid by hard labor. And from that day forward we were treated just like convicts.

Really we had made ourselves lifetime slaves, or peons, as the laws called us. But call it slavery, peonage, or what not, the truth is we lived in a hell on earth what time we spent in the Senator's peon camp.

I lived in that camp, as a peon, for nearly three years. My wife fared better than I did, as did the wives of some of the other Negroes, because the white men about the camp used these unfortunate creatures as their mistresses. When I was first put in the stockade my wife was still kept for a while in the "Big House," but my little boy, who was only nine years old, was given away to a Negro family across the river in South Carolina, and I never saw or heard of him after that. When I left the camp my wife had had two children by some one of the white bosses, and she was living in a fairly good shape in a little house off to herself. But the poor Negro women who were not in the class with my wife fared about as bad as the helpless Negro men. Most of the time the women who were peons or convicts were compelled to wear men's clothes. Sometimes, when I have seen them dressed like men, and plowing or hoeing or hauling logs or working at the blacksmith's trade, just the same as men, my heart would bleed and my blood would boil, but I was powerless to raise a hand. It would have meant death on the spot to have said a word. Of the first six women brought to the camp, two of them gave birth to children after they had been there more than twelve months — and the babies had white men for their fathers!

The stockades in which we slept, were, I believe, the filthiest places in the world. They

SOURCE: Herbert Aptheker, ed., *A Documentary History of the Negro People in the United States*, vol. 2, *From the Reconstruction Era to 1910*, 5th ed. (New York: Citadel Press, 1970), 832, 835–38.

were cesspools of nastiness. During the thirteen [*sic*] years that I was there I am willing to swear that a mattress was never moved after it had been brought there, except to turn it over once or twice a month. No sheets were used, only dark-colored blankets. Most of the men slept every night in the clothing that they had worked in all day. Some of the worst characters were made to sleep in chairs. The doors were locked and barred, each night, and tallow-candles were the only lights allowed. Really the stockades were but little more than cow sheds, horse stables or hog pens. Strange to say, not a great number of these people died while I was there, though a great many came away maimed and bruised and, in some cases, disabled for life. As far as I can remember only about ten died during the last ten years that I was there, two of these being killed outright by the guards for trivial offenses.

It was a hard school that peon camp was, but I learned more there in a few short months by contact with those poor fellows from the outside world than ever I had known before. Most of what I learned was evil, and I now know that I should have been better off without the knowledge, but much of what I learned was helpful to me. Barring two or three severe and brutal whippings which I received, I got along very well, all things considered; but the system is damnable. A favorite way of whipping a man was to strap him down to a log, flat on his back, and spank him fifty or sixty times on his bare feet with a shingle or a huge piece of plank. When the men [*sic*] would get up with sore and blistered feet and an aching body, if he could not then keep up with the other men at work he would be strapped to the log again, this time face downward, and would be lashed with a buggy trace on his bare back. When a woman had to be whipped it was usually done in private, though they would be compelled to fall down across a barrel or something of the kind and receive the licks on their backsides.

The working day on a peon farm begins with sunrise and ends when the sun goes down; or, in other words, the average peon works from ten to twelve hours each day, with one hour (from 12 o'clock to 1 o'clock) for dinner. Hot or cold, sun or rain, this is the rule. As to their meals, the laborers are divided up into squads or companies, just the same as soldiers in a great military camp would be. . . . Each peon is provided with a great big tin cup, a flat tin pan and two big tin spoons. No knives or forks are ever seen, except those used by the cooks. At meal time the peons pass in single file before the cooks, and hold out their pans and cups to receive their allowances. Cow peas (red or white, which when boiled turn black), fat bacon and old-fashioned Georgia cornbread, baked in pones from one to two and three inches thick, made up the chief articles of food. Black coffee, black molasses and brown sugar are also used abundantly. . . .

Today, I am told, there are six or seven of these private camps in Georgia — that is to say, camps where most of the convicts are leased from the State of Georgia. But there are hundreds and hundreds of farms all over the State where Negroes, and in some cases poor white folks, are held in bondage on the ground that they are working out debts, or where the contract which they have made holds them in a kind of perpetual bondage, because, under those contracts, they may not quit one employer and hire out to another except by and with the knowledge and consent of the former employer.

One of the usual ways to secure laborers for a large peonage camp is for the proprietor to send out an agent to the little courts in the towns and villages, and where a man charged with some petty offense has no friends or money the agent will urge him to plead guilty, with the understanding that the agent will pay his fine, and in that way save him from the disgrace of being sent to jail or the chain-gang! For this high favor the man must sign beforehand a paper signifying his willingness to go to the farm and work out the amount of the fine imposed. When he reaches the farm he has to be fed and clothed, to be sure, and these things are charged up to his account.

By the time he has worked out his first debt another is hanging over his head, and so on and so on, by a sort of endless chain, for an indefinite period, as in every case the indebtedness is arbitrarily arranged by the employer. In many cases it is very evident that the court officials are in collusion with the proprietors or agents, and that they divide the "graft" among themselves. . . .

But I didn't tell you how I got out. I didn't get out — they put me out. When I had served as a peon for nearly three years — and you remember that they claimed I owed them only $165 — when I had served for nearly three years one of the bosses came to me and said that my time was up. He happened to be the one who was said to be living with my wife. He gave me a new suit of overalls, which cost about seventy-five cents, took me in a buggy and carried me across the Broad River into South Carolina, set me down and told me to "git." I didn't have a cent of money, and I wasn't feeling well, but somehow I managed to get a move on me. I begged my way to Columbia. In two or three days I ran across a man looking for laborers to carry to Birmingham, and I joined his gang. I have been here in the Birmingham district since they released me, and I reckon I'll die either in a coal mine or an iron furnace. It don't make much difference which. Either is better than a Georgia peon camp. And a Georgia peon camp is hell itself!

W. E. B. Du Bois | *Along the Color Line, 1910*

W. E. B. DU BOIS (1868–1963), a founder of the NAACP and editor of its journal, the *Crisis*, wrote this editorial on *Bailey v. Alabama* in the journal's second issue, in December 1910. At the time, the case was making its way through the courts. Notice the position of the U.S. Department of Justice in relation to Alabama's contract labor law. The Supreme Court ruling, issued in 1911, declared Alabama's peonage law unconstitutional.

Several Southern laws, which have reduced Negro farm hands to virtual peonage, are to be tested before the United States Supreme Court. The case is the appeal of an Alabama Negro convicted of violating the contract law, upheld by the State Supreme Court, under which he was sentenced to a fine equivalent to 126 days' hard labor for the county. The Federal Department of Justice believes that the law imposes compulsory service in satisfaction of debt, reducing the Negroes to actual slavery.

The law provides that in contracts of service entered into by a laborer, where money was advanced, and the contract broken without just cause, and the money not refunded, the laborer is guilty, and may be sentenced to hard labor until the fine is worked out. The Federal Department contends that the purpose and effect of the law is not to stop fraudulent practices so much as to impose compulsory service upon the Negroes who constitute the bulk of the farm labor of the State. The point that will be attacked most vigorously is the Alabama rule of evidence in such cases, which, in practice, assumes the Negro accused was guilty of intent to defraud, "contrary to the axiomatic and elementary principle of presumption of innocence in a criminal procedure."

The reports of the abuses existing under this contract system in the South have aroused widespread indignation as they have appeared from time to time when some exceptionally flagrant case was forced into publicity. Now that the Department of Justice has become interested, and the issue is to be placed before the supreme tribunal, a definite pronouncement may be expected.

SOURCE: Herbert Aptheker, ed., *A Documentary History of the Negro People in the United States*, vol. 3, *1910–1932* (New York: Citadel Press, 1977), 31–32.

Letter to the Editor | *From the South, 1911*

In August 1911, W. E. B. Du Bois published this letter sent to him as editor of the *Crisis*. It provides details about the peonage system and life in the Jim Crow South. Notice what the writer has to say about the *Crisis* itself.

Kind Sir:

I am not an educated man. I will give you the peonage system as it is practised here in the name of the law.

If a colored man is arrested here and hasn't any money, whether he is guilty or not, he has to pay just the same. A man of color is never tried in this country. It is simply a farce. Everything is fixed before he enters the courtroom. I will try to give you an illustration of how it is done:

I am brought in a prisoner, go through the farce of being tried. The whole of my fine may amount to fifty dollars. A kindly appearing man will come up and pay my fine and take me to his farm to allow me to work it out. At the end of a month I find that I owe him more than I did when I went there. The debt is increased year in and year out. You would ask, "How is that?" It is simply that he is charging you more for your board, lodging and washing than they allow you for your work, and you can't help yourself either, nor can anyone else help you, because you are still a prisoner and never get your fine worked out. If you do as they say and be a good Negro, you are allowed to marry, provided you can get someone to have you, and of course the debt still increases. This is in the United States, where it is supposed that every man has equal rights before the law, and we are held in bondage by this same outfit.

Of course we can't prove anything. Our word is nothing. If we state things as they are, the powers that be make a different statement, and that sets ours aside at Washington and, I suppose, in Heaven, too.

Now, I have tried to tell you how we are made servants here according to law. I will tell you in my next letter how the lawmakers keep the colored children out of schools, how that pressure is brought to bear on their parents in such a manner they cannot help themselves. The cheapest way we can borrow money here is at the rate of twenty-five cents on the dollar per year.

Your paper is the best I have read of the kind. I never dreamed there was such a paper in the world. I will subscribe soon. I think there are a great many here that will take your paper. I haven't had the chance to show your paper to any yet, but will as soon as I can. You know we have to be careful with such literature as this in this country.

What I have told you is strictly confidential. If you publish it, don't put my name to it. I would be dead in a short time after the news reached here.

One word more about the peonage. The court and the man you work for are always partners. One makes the fine and the other one works you and holds you, and if you leave you are tracked up with bloodhounds and brought back.

Source: Herbert Aptheker, ed., *A Documentary History of the Negro People in the United States*, vol. 3, *1910–1932* (New York: Citadel Press, 1977), 31–32.

Chain Gang

Convict labor in the South assumed two major forms: prison farms and chain gangs. The latter in particular were a feature of southern urban and rural life between the late nineteenth century, when southern states instituted the use of chain gangs, and the 1950s, when these states formally abolished the practice. This photograph of members of a southern black chain gang reveals both their humanity and their dehumanization. The image invites the viewer's attention and concern because the subjects are looking directly yet nonthreateningly at the camera. Their youth is signaled by their lack of facial hair; and the chains, striped uniforms, and work axes clearly convey their criminalization.

Library of Congress, Prints and Photographs Division, Washington, D.C., LC-D401-16155.

QUESTIONS FOR ANALYSIS

1. Describe how black peonage and black chain gangs fit into the South's economic, legal, and criminal systems in this era. Whose interests did peonage and chain gangs serve? How did the conditions of peonage and the chain gang compare with the conditions of slavery?

2. What role did black people play in seeking to end peonage? What role did the federal government play?

3. Discuss lynching as both a spectacle and a symbol. What were the lessons to be learned from lynching for blacks? For whites?

4. After 1892, the number of lynchings declined (see Tables 9.1, 9.2, and 9.3). Speculate about the reasons for this decline. Could a lynching happen today? Why or why not?

5. How do peonage, lynching, the chain gang, and the campaigns to abolish them illustrate the tension between constraint and agency, between oppression and resistance?

NOTES

1. Ida B. Wells, *Crusade for Justice: The Autobiography of Ida B. Wells*, ed. Alfreda Duster (Chicago: University of Chicago Press, 1970), 19.

2. Wells, *Crusade for Justice*, 19.

3. Mia Bay, *To Tell the Truth Freely: The Life of Ida B. Wells* (New York: Hill and Wang, 2009), 76, 79.

4. Quoted in *Plessy v. Ferguson: A Brief History with Documents*, ed. Brook Thomas (Boston: Bedford/St. Martin's, 1997), 41.

5. Plessy v. Ferguson, 163 U.S. 537 (1896), 3, 7.

6. Quoted in Phillips Verner Bradford and Harvey Blume, *Ota Benga: The Pygmy in the Zoo* (New York: St. Martin's Press, 1992), 183.

7. Quoted in Christopher Waldrep, ed., *Lynching in America: A History in Documents* (New York: New York University Press, 2006), 186.

8. Ray Stannard Baker, *Following the Color Line: American Negro Citizenship in the Progressive Era* (1908; repr., New York: Harper & Row, 1964), 175–76.

9. Wells, *Crusade for Justice*, 47–52; Bay, *To Tell the Truth Freely*, 82–85.

10. The pamphlet was titled *The Reason Why the Colored American Is Not in the World's Columbian Exposition*, available online at http://digital.library.upenn.edu/women /wells/exposition/exposition.html. See also Bay, *To Tell the Truth Freely*, 151–68.

11. Quoted in Bay, *To Tell the Truth Freely*, 222.

12. Evelyn Brooks Higginbotham, *Righteous Discontent: The Women's Movement in the Black Baptist Church, 1880–1920* (Cambridge: Harvard University Press, 1993), 186–87.

13. Fannie Barrier Williams, "The Club Movement among Colored Women of America" (1904), in Jane Dailey, *The Age of Jim Crow* (New York: Norton, 2009), 106, 107. On uplift generally, see Kevin K. Gaines, *Uplifting the Race: Black Leadership, Politics, and Culture in the Twentieth Century* (Chapel Hill: University of North Carolina Press, 1996).

14. Bay, *To Tell the Truth Freely*, 48–49.

15. Martha Robb Montgomery, quoted in Neil R. McMillen, *Dark Journey: Black Mississippians in the Age of Jim Crow* (Urbana: University of Illinois Press, 1989), 129.

16. Quoted in Leon Litwack, *Trouble in Mind: Black Southerners in the Age of Jim Crow* (New York: Knopf, 1998), 126.

17. Quoted in Charles L. Perdue Jr., Thomas E. Barden, and Robert K. Phillips, eds., *Weevils in the Wheat: Interviews with Virginia Ex-slaves* (Charlottesville: University of Virginia Press, 1976), 53.

18. Quoted in W. E. B. Du Bois, *The Souls of Black Folk*, in *Three Negro Classics* (1903; repr., New York: Avon, 1965), 312.

19. W. E. B. Du Bois, "The Economic Revolution in the South," in *The Negro in the South: His Economic Progress in Relation to His Moral and Religious Development* (1907; repr., New York: Citadel Press, 1970), 99, 100.

20. *Souvenir Views: Negro Enterprises and Residences, Richmond, Va.* (Richmond: D. A. Ferguson, 1907), available online at American Memory, Library of Congress, http://memory .loc.gov/cgi-bin/query/h?ammem/lhbcbbib:@field (NUMBER+@band(lhbcb+82181)).

21. *Richmond Planet*, April 8, 1905, available online at Rarely Seen Richmond, VCU Libraries' Online Exhibits, http:// www.library.vcu.edu/jbc/speccoll/vbha/freedom.html.

22. *Richmond Planet*, July 16, 1910.

23. Quoted in Geoffrey C. Ward, *Unforgivable Blackness: The Rise and Fall of Jack Johnson* (New York: Vintage, 2006), 235.

24. W. E. B. Du Bois, "The Upbuilding of Black Durham: The Success of the Negroes and Their Value to a Tolerant and Helpful Southern City," *World's Work*, January 1912.

25. Quoted in Karen Sotiropoulos, *Staging Race: Black Performers in Turn of the Century America* (Cambridge: Harvard University Press, 2006), 42.

26. John Rosamond Johnson and James Weldon Johnson, "Lift Every Voice and Sing," in *Negro Year Book: An Annual Encyclopedia of the Negro, 1918–1919*, ed. Monroe N. Work (Tuskegee Institute, AL: Negro Year Book Publishing Company, 1919).

27. William Christopher Handy, *Father of the Blues: An Autobiography*, ed. Arna Bontemps (1955; repr., New York: Da Capo Press, 1991), 75.

28. Wells, *Crusade for Justice*, 53.

29. Quoted in Willard B. Gatewood Jr., comp., *"Smoked Yankees" and the Struggle for Empire: Letters from Negro Soldiers, 1898–1902* (Fayetteville: University of Arkansas Press, 1987), 28. See also "Black Americans in the U.S. Military from the American Revolution to the Korean War: The Spanish American War and the Philippine Insurgency," New York State Military Museum and Veterans Research Center, New York State Division of Military and Naval Affairs, http://dmna.ny.gov/historic/articles/blacksMilitary /BlacksMilitarySpanAm.htm.

30. Quoted in Willard B. Gatewood Jr., *Black Americans and the White Man's Burden, 1898–1903* (Urbana: University of Illinois Press, 1975), 212.

31. Quoted in Marcy Sacks, *Before Harlem: The Black Experience in New York City before World War I* (Philadelphia: University of Pennsylvania Press, 2006), 19–20.

32. Booker T. Washington, *Up from Slavery: An Autobiography*, ed. William L. Andrews (New York: Norton, 1996), 100, 99–100, 100, 101.

33. W. E. B. Du Bois, *The Souls of Black Folk*, ed. David W. Blight and Robert Gooding-Williams (Boston: Bedford/ St.Martin's, 1997), 67, 68, 72.

34. W. E. B. Du Bois, "To the Nations of the World," in *W. E. B. Du Bois: A Reader*, ed. David Levering Lewis (New York: Henry Holt, 1995), 639.

35. "Declaration of Principles," in *Black Protest Thought in the Twentieth Century*, ed. August Meier, Elliott Rudwick, and Francis L. Broderick, 2nd ed. (Indianapolis: Bobbs-Merrill, 1971), 62.

36. Clyatt v. United States, 197 U.S. 207 (1905).

37. See, for example, Douglas A. Blackmon, *Slavery by Another Name: The Re-enslavement of Black Americans from the Civil War to World War II* (New York: Anchor Books, 2009).

38. "The Lynching at Urbana," *New York Times*, June 6, 1897.

SUGGESTED REFERENCES

Racism and Black Challenges

Allen, James. *Without Sanctuary: Lynching Photography in America*. Santa Fe, NM: Twin Palms, 2000.

Baker, Ray Stannard. *Following the Color Line: American Negro Citizenship in the Progressive Era*. 1908. Reprint, New York: Harper & Row, 1964.

Bay, Mia. *To Tell the Truth Freely: The Life of Ida B. Wells*. New York: Hill and Wang, 2009.

Brundage, W. Fitzhugh. *Lynching in the New South: Georgia and Virginia, 1880–1930*. Urbana: University of Illinois Press, 1993.

Cash, Wilbur J. *The Mind of the South*. 1941. Reprint, New York: Vintage, 1991.

Fredrickson, George M. *Racism: A Short History*. Princeton, NJ: Princeton University Press, 2002.

Gilmore, Glenda Elizabeth. *Gender and Jim Crow: Women and the Politics of White Supremacy in North Carolina, 1896–1920*. Chapel Hill: University of North Carolina Press, 1996.

Gould, Stephen Jay. *The Mismeasure of Man*. New York: Norton, 1996.

Hale, Grace Elizabeth. *Making Whiteness: The Culture of Segregation in the South, 1890–1940*. New York: Pantheon, 1998.

Freedom's First Generation

Anderson, James D. *The Education of Blacks in the South, 1860–1935*. Chapel Hill: University of North Carolina Press, 1988.

Brown, Elsa Barkley. "Womanist Consciousness: Maggie Lena Walker and the Independent Order of Saint Luke," *Signs: Journal of Women in Culture and Society* 14, no. 3 (Spring 1989): 610–33.

Brundage, W. Fitzhugh, ed. *Beyond Blackface: African Americans and the Creation of American Popular Culture, 1890–1930*. Chapel Hill: University of North Carolina Press, 2011.

Daniel, Pete. *The Shadow of Slavery: Peonage in the South, 1901–1969*. Urbana: University of Illinois Press, 1972.

Higginbotham, Evelyn Brooks. *Righteous Discontent: The Women's Movement in the Black Baptist Church, 1880–1920*. Cambridge: Harvard University Press, 1993.

Hunter, Tera. *To 'Joy My Freedom: Southern Black Women's Lives and Labors after the Civil War*. Cambridge: Harvard University Press, 1997.

Litwack, Leon. *Trouble in Mind: Black Southerners in the Age of Jim Crow*. New York: Knopf, 1998.

Montgomery, William E. *Under Their Own Vine and Fig Tree: The African-American Church in the South, 1865–1900*. Baton Rouge: LSU Press, 1993.

Shaw, Stephanie J. *What a Woman Ought to Be and to Do: Black Professional Women Workers during the Jim Crow Era*. Chicago: University of Chicago Press, 1996.

Sotiropoulos, Karen. *Staging Race: Black Performers in Turn of the Century America*. Cambridge: Harvard University Press, 2006.

Migration, Accommodation, and Protest

Berlin, Ira. *The Making of African America: The Four Great Migrations*. New York: Viking, 2010.

Gaines, Kevin K. *Uplifting the Race: Black Leadership, Politics, and Culture in the Twentieth Century*. Chapel Hill: University of North Carolina Press, 1996.

Hahn, Steven. *A Nation under Our Feet: Black Political Struggles in the Rural South from Slavery to the Great Migration*. Cambridge: Belknap Press of Harvard University Press, 2003.

Harlan, Louis R. *Booker T. Washington: The Making of a Black Leader, 1856–1901*. New York: Oxford University Press, 1972.

Lewis, David Levering. *W. E. B. Du Bois: Biography of a Race*. Vol. 1, *1868–1919*. New York: Henry Holt, 1993.

Meier, August. *Negro Thought in America, 1880–1915: Racial Ideologies in the Age of Booker T. Washington*. Ann Arbor: University of Michigan Press, 1963.

Norrell, Robert J. *Up from History: The Life of Booker T. Washington*. Cambridge: Belknap Press of Harvard University Press, 2009.

Painter, Nell Irvin. *Exodusters: Black Migration to Kansas after Reconstruction*. New York: Knopf, 1977.

Taylor, Quintard. *In Search of the Racial Frontier: African Americans in the American West, 1528–1990*. New York: Norton, 1998.

The New Negro Comes of Age

1915–1940

CHRONOLOGY *Events specific to African American history are in purple. General United States history events are in black.*

1915	Carter G. Woodson establishes Association for the Study of Negro Life and History	**1933**	*Continued*
			Paul Robeson stars in film version of *The Emperor Jones*
1916	Woodson begins publishing *Journal of Negro History*	**1934**	W. E. B. Du Bois resigns as editor of the *Crisis*
	Marcus Garvey moves headquarters of Universal Negro Improvement Association to Harlem		Aaron Douglas finishes murals for Harlem branch of New York Public Library
1917	United States enters World War I		Republican Oscar De Priest loses U.S. House seat to Democrat Arthur Mitchell
	Race riot erupts in East St. Louis, Illinois	**1935**	American Federation of Labor recognizes Brotherhood of Sleeping Car Porters and Maids
	Silent march along New York's Fifth Avenue		
	Buchanan v. Warley overturns city ordinances mandating where blacks can live		National Labor Relations Act, also called Wagner Act, passed
1918	World War I ends		Committee for Industrial Organization founded (becomes Congress of Industrial Organizations in 1938)
1919	Red Summer race riots		
1920	Negro National League founded		Mary McLeod Bethune establishes National Council of Negro Women
	Nineteenth Amendment guarantees woman suffrage	**1936**	National Negro Congress founded
	James Weldon Johnson becomes first black executive secretary of NAACP		Bethune appointed head of Division of Negro Affairs of National Youth Administration (becomes official division director in 1939)
1921	*Shuffle Along*, first all-black music and dance revue, opens on Broadway		Track star Jesse Owens wins four gold medals at Berlin Olympics
1923	Charles S. Johnson founds *Opportunity*, National Urban League's journal	**1937**	Joe Louis becomes world heavyweight champion
1925	A. Philip Randolph becomes president of Brotherhood of Sleeping Car Porters and Maids		Japan invades China, igniting World War II in Pacific
	Alain Locke's *The New Negro* published		Zora Neale Hurston's *Their Eyes Were Watching God* published
1926	Woodson establishes Negro History Week (expanded to Black History Month in 1976)	**1938**	*Missouri ex rel. Gaines v. Canada* requires Missouri to admit qualified black candidates to state law school
1927	Duke Ellington and his band become regulars at Harlem's Cotton Club		
1928	Oscar De Priest elected to U.S. House of Representatives	**1939**	Marian Anderson performs at Lincoln Memorial
1929	Stock market crashes; Great Depression begins		Germany invades Poland, igniting World War II in Europe
1931	Scottsboro Boys trials begin	**1940**	Richard Wright's *Native Son* published
1933	Franklin D. Roosevelt becomes president and initiates New Deal	**1940–1941**	Jacob Lawrence paints *The Migration of the Negro*

Zora Neale Hurston and the Advancement of the Black Freedom Struggle

In 1925, Zora Neale Hurston stood on the street corners of Harlem conducting social science research. A student at Barnard College, she was taking skull measurements, and she needed to convince African Americans to allow her to place her calipers around their heads. Audacious and persuasive, Hurston succeeded in her data collection. She turned these data over to Franz Boas, a leading anthropologist at Columbia University, who used them to demonstrate that craniology was a false science. Skull measurements, which had been used for a century to argue that blacks had smaller cranial capacities than other races and thus were intellectually inferior, actually demonstrated nothing more than the biases of the analyst. Boas challenged the entire anthropology establishment with his theories of cultural relativism, overturning the notion that societies could be ranked along an evolutionary scale. He also argued that individual capabilities were determined more by environment than by race. Hurston studied with Boas after she graduated from Barnard, but by that time she had already embarked on a writing career. Everything she wrote, however, was informed by anthropology and by the core belief in equality that she admired in the social science approach of her mentor.

Hurston burst onto the African American literary scene in Harlem with short stories and plays that revealed a dazzling new talent. Her fiction drew on her memories of growing up in the all-black town of Eatonville, Florida, where her father was the mayor and her mother encouraged her inquisitiveness. Young Hurston absorbed her surroundings and delighted in the storytelling she heard on neighbors' front porches. For her, African American culture was vibrant, healthy, and the equal of other cultures. Rejecting the dominant white view of African Americans as inferior and the African American experience as tragic, Hurston presented that experience as she knew and understood it: as a life-affirming twist on the resiliency and complexity of the human condition.

Hurston's move from Florida to New York City paralleled the migration of more than a million African Americans from the rural and urban South to the metropolises of the North between 1915 and 1940. This migration changed their lives, giving many of them new jobs in industry and new visibility and power as they changed the racial composition of northern cities. Hurston's self-confidence exemplifies the increasingly affirmative spirit of African Americans. Veterans returning from the battlefields of World War I were not inclined to accept anything less than equality at home. This growing defiance characterized black mass organizations, which advanced the protest tradition. Black studies in the social sciences broadened understanding of African American lives, the nature of prejudice, and the causes of

racial conflict even as new expressions in literature, such as Hurston's, explored black heritage
and identity. The Great Depression of the 1930s
devastated African American lives and communities, but it also led to new and intensified forms
of economic and political struggle. As black
urban masses created black voting blocs and
black protest grew, the federal government began
responding to African Americans' concerns. For
the first time since Reconstruction, blacks could
look to the federal government for support.
Within the government, black political appointees lobbied for fairness. As African American
writers, artists, musicians, and sports heroes got
respectful attention from mass audiences, their
cultural achievements helped advance the spirit
animating the black freedom struggle.

The Great Migration and the Great War

Since the beginning of the Civil War, black people in the South had been on the move.
During the war, they fled to Union lines and freedom; after the war they went in search
of families and new lives. During and after Reconstruction, some moved to the New
South's growing cities; others moved to new towns in Kansas and Oklahoma; and a
small but steady number went north, seeking better jobs and educational opportunities. But starting in the decade of the 1910s, the number moving north grew exponentially, changing the demographic makeup of the nation. These northern migrants also
transformed African American identity and national race relations. Initially, they
sought jobs in industry, which were increasingly available after the start of World War I
in 1914. Moving into "Negro districts" in the North's large cities, they helped create
vibrant and self-sufficient communities. In 1917, following the U.S. entry into the war,
black men served in all-black regiments overseas. When they returned, many were
aggressive, even militant, and determined to achieve the equality so long denied them
and their people.

Origins and Patterns of Migration

"The peoples is leaving here by the thousands," wrote a black man from Atlanta to the
Chicago Defender on May 2, 1917, as he asked about jobs in Chicago.[1] From Biloxi,
Mississippi, a "willen workin woman" explained to the newspaper on April 27, 1917,
that she yearned to escape "this land of sufring."[2] From Charleston, South Carolina, on
February 10, 1917, came the report that "the times in the south is very hard and one can
scarcely live."[3] One resident of Vicksburg, Mississippi, explained on May 7, 1917, "We
are working here at starvation wages and some of us are virtually without employment
willing to accept any kind of work such as cooking, laundering, or as domestics."[4] A
hopeful man from Houston, Texas, declared on April 20, 1917, "I dont Care where
[I go] so long as I Go where a man is a man."[5]

The huge numbers of black people who decided to leave the Jim Crow South constituted one of the largest grassroots migrations in U.S. history. Today that shift in population is called the **great migration**. In 1910, 90 percent of African Africans lived in the South; by 1940, the figure was 77 percent. Between 1915 and 1940, over 1.5 million blacks moved north, mostly to cities. While many migrants came from southern cities, many also came from plantations and farms, so this was also a rural-to-urban migration, from sharecropping and tenant farming to urban wage work.

Asked why they left, migrants described both "push" and "pull" factors. Some, like the woman from Biloxi, were desperate to get away from the South, with its poverty and peonage, its repression and lynchings, its stagnant wages, and the daily violence and indignities of Jim Crow. Also pushing blacks out of the South were a series of natural disasters. The boll weevil, a cotton-eating beetle that spread from Mexico to Texas in the 1890s and then throughout the South, devastated the cotton crop. Floods in the Mississippi valley during the winter of 1916 and in North Carolina the following

The Great Migration
This 1918 photograph captures a well-dressed family that made the journey from the South to the North during World War I. Their dress reflects the importance of both the act of migration as well as the act of visually recording the moment. The fact that so many African Americans migrated as individuals or in non-kin-based groups only heightens the importance of these kinds of family migration photographs. *Chicago History Museum/Getty Images.*

summer caused extensive damage. The region was in an economic depression, due in part to the decline of the overseas cotton market following the outbreak of war in Europe. At the same time, the war was creating job opportunities in the North. War industries were expanding just as the immigrant labor pool was shrinking dramatically. In 1914, more than 1 million Europeans came to the United States, but in 1915, after the outbreak of war, fewer than 200,000 arrived. Northern industries, in desperate need of labor, dispatched agents to recruit black workers in the South. For black southerners, the pull of better jobs proved decisive, as men who had been earning 75 cents a day could earn up to $5 a day in the meatpacking, iron, steel, and auto industries.

Men often migrated first, setting up a household base for others to follow. A **chain migration** pattern emerged, in which family members, friends, and neighbors joined the first migrants, who reported their satisfaction with their new lives in the North. Through letters home, southern blacks learned of jobs with higher salaries, good schools for children, and opportunities for political involvement as well as social and cultural activities. Earlier migrants returning south for a visit made a big impression with their city clothes, new cars, and cash. Black sleeping car porters and maids were important information sources, as they traveled throughout the country and could make comparisons. They often brought with them copies of the *Chicago Defender*, a black newspaper that vigorously promoted migration, to distribute.

In Robert Horton's barbershop in Hattiesburg, Mississippi, migration was the topic of conversation as copies of the *Defender* were passed around. When Horton decided to move to Chicago, he did so as part of a migration club that he helped create, drawing on family, church, and barbershop connections. Soon forty black migrants from Hattiesburg were encouraging friends and family to join them and helping new-comers find places to stay.[6] Their experience was common, as clubs, neighborhood groups, and whole churches pooled resources to travel north together. Railroads offered special group rates, and migrations followed the rail lines. Blacks from Florida, Georgia, and the Carolinas traveled East Coast railroads to Philadelphia, Newark, New York, Buffalo, and other cities. Those from Alabama, Louisiana, Mississippi, Arkansas, and Tennessee took trains to cities such as St. Louis, Chicago, Detroit, Cleveland, and Pittsburgh (Map 10.1). As wave upon wave of newcomers arrived, they transformed the cities of the North.

Yet most blacks—six million, in fact—remained in the South; not until the 1960s would a majority of African Americans live elsewhere. Significant numbers of blacks opposed migration. Some blacks believed that the South was the historic and natural home of their people, often citing the advantages of the known against the dis-advantages of the unknown. Black business people and professionals in the South opposed migration because they did not want to lose their customer base. They pointed out the cold weather and hostile social environment that newcomers would encounter—the threat of unemployment, exclusion by labor unions, overcrowding and exorbitant rents, and race riots. Economic self-interest also drove southern white opposition to black migration, especially the fear of losing the black labor pool. Some

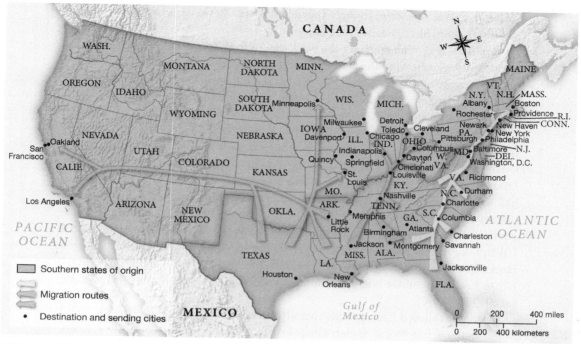

MAP 10.1 **The Great Migration, 1910–1929**

This map shows the major railroad routes used by black migrants to travel from the South to the cities of the North and, to a lesser extent, the West. It also shows the increasing national spread of the African American population. (See also Map 11.1.) DATA SOURCE: *The Atlas of African-American History and Politics: From the Slave Trade to Modern Times* by Arwin Smallwood and Jeffrey Elliot. Copyright © 1998 The McGraw-Hill Companies, Inc.

towns enforced hastily created vagrancy and labor laws to prevent blacks from leaving. Others criminalized the recruitment activities of northern employment agents.

Black Communities in the Metropolises of the North

Southern blacks wrote to the *Chicago Defender* about their hopes for migration not just because the newspaper promoted life in the North but also because it was familiar. Two-thirds of the *Defender*'s circulation — 230,000 by 1915 — was outside the paper's Chicago base. Passed from one person to another, read aloud in beauty parlors, barbershops, and churches, the *Defender* enjoyed an actual circulation that was several times the official figure. "The Mouthpiece of 14 Million People," proclaimed its masthead. Robert Abbott, who founded the paper in 1905 as a one-man operation, gave it a national presence by taking a militant stance on many race issues of the day. The paper not only promoted migration but also listed jobs and train schedules. "Ride for a day and a night to freedom," proclaimed Abbott. "You tip your hat to no white man. . . . You are a man and are expected to carry yourself as such."[7] Between 1916 and 1920, some 50,000 southern blacks headed for Chicago.

For them and other migrants, the black exodus took on biblical proportions. They saw themselves as leaving the land of persecution for the promised land, where they hoped to create new lives. Indeed, they had to rebuild households, develop new work routines, settle their children in school, make new friends, become part of new neighborhoods, establish new church homes, and join new social clubs and organizations. The benevolent societies and established black churches in the North offered help. In Chicago, the Phyllis Wheatley Home gave young women a safe place to live while they looked for work. Opened in 1908 by the Phyllis Wheatley Club, which Elizabeth Lindsay Davis, a teacher and member of the National Association of Colored Women, had founded in 1896, the home was one branch of a network of black **settlement houses** modeled on Jane Addams's Hull House, also in Chicago, which helped immigrant women from Europe adjust to life in America. The Chicago branch of the National Urban League, established in 1916, offered similar services for newly arrived southern blacks. Its social workers helped with jobs and housing, while at its "stranger meetings," Urban League members instructed newcomers in the dress and conduct appropriate for city life.

Long-established Chicago churches also smoothed the transition from the rural South to the urban North. Quinn Chapel African Methodist Episcopal Church, the city's oldest black church, attracted new members with outreach efforts. More astonishing was the growth of Olivet Baptist Church, whose members met new arrivals at the railroad station and helped them get settled in new homes. In addition to an employment bureau and home locator service, Olivet provided women's groups to aid homemakers and single women, boys' and girls' clubs, a day nursery and kindergarten for working mothers, a workingmen's home, and a food pantry with a dining room. Not surprisingly, the church's membership doubled in just four years, from 4,200 in 1916 to 8,500 in 1919.

This swift increase did not come without controversy, however, as established church members objected to the emotionalism of southern black Christians, and southerners felt out of place in sedate worship services. One newcomer confessed that she "couldn't understand the pastor and the words he used" at Olivet and she "couldn't sing their way."[8] The differences were not just a matter of worship style. There was a class divide between middle-class Chicago natives, many of whom were descendants of free blacks, and the poorer newcomers from the South. But as newcomers began to outnumber natives in Chicago's established churches, they infused worship with a "folk" religiosity and a southern preaching style. Their spirituals and rhythmic hymn singing merged with blues and secular music to create a new genre called gospel.

Many Chicago natives viewed with suspicion the storefront churches that southern Pentecostals established and the religious groups that had emerged from the breakaway holiness movement within the Methodist Church. Seeking a personal and life-changing experience of grace, rural blacks in states along the Mississippi River had been drawn to the holiness movement in the late nineteenth century. One of them, William Seymour, preached that the gift of the Holy Spirit was manifested by speaking in tongues. His Azusa Street Revival, which began in Los Angeles in 1906, is credited with launching the spread of **Pentecostalism**, but by then the Pentecostal Church of God in Christ was already strong in Tennessee and Mississippi. Migrants from this region brought their religion with them, founding twenty storefront churches in Chicago by 1919 and launching a five-year building project for Roberts Temple Church of God in Christ in 1922.

Another point of contention between the newcomers and black Chicago natives was union membership. Southerners often felt too vulnerable to join unions, especially as white workers and trade unions affiliated with the American Federation of Labor did not welcome them. The Stockyards Labor Council tried to organize Chicago's butchering and meatpacking workers in an interracial union, but only Chicago natives joined, not southern newcomers. In 1921, these newcomers, eager for work, took jobs in the stockyards vacated by striking workers, thus helping packinghouses to break the strike and exacerbating tensions in Chicago's black neighborhoods.

The most serious tensions between blacks and whites, however, were over housing. Because patterns of residential segregation circumscribed northern black neighborhoods, their populations soon exceeded what the existing housing stock could handle. Between 1910 and 1920, as Chicago's South Side population tripled, the neighborhood deteriorated. Like the overcrowded Negro districts in other cities in the North, the South Side of Chicago suffered from inferior sewage control, lighting, and police protection. Because housing was scarce, rents were higher than in nearby white neighborhoods, and groceries were more expensive. But when blacks attempted to move beyond what was called "the black belt," white homeowners' associations resisted with both legal obstacles and violence. Fifty-eight "race bombings" of black residences took place in Chicago between July 1, 1917, and March 1, 1921.[9]

In the North, racial segregation was enforced by long-standing custom (de facto) rather than by law (de jure), as in the South. Yet, as in southern cities, black communities in the North were largely distinct and separate from the white neighborhoods that surrounded and excluded them. And also like their southern counterparts, northern Negro districts were lively and self-sufficient, with businesses, churches, and social clubs and organizations owned or operated by blacks for blacks. In Chicago, for example, black doctors and civic activists established Provident Hospital, where black physicians could practice and black nurses could train. Because white funeral homes would not handle black bodies, black funeral directors catered to an exclusively black clientele. They arranged the emotion-rich "homegoing" ceremonies that southerners wanted or helped them plan for the deceased to be buried in the South. Self-contained enterprises such as Chicago's Metropolitan Funeral Home Association encompassed black funeral homes, casket makers, chemical suppliers, and insurance agents. Chicagoans led the National Negro Funeral Directors Association. Funeral directors were respected community leaders, often members of the National Negro Business

League and supporters of local NAACP and National Urban League chapters. They frequently opened their funeral parlors for community meetings and family gatherings.

As in the South, segregated funeral homes, beauty parlors, and barbershops were safe places where blacks could talk freely. Unlike in the South, however, blacks voted and organized politically in the North. Because black voting was not legally obstructed, concentrations of northern black neighborhoods created voting blocs able to put black politicians in office. In 1915, blacks on Chicago's South Side elected Oscar De Priest, a Republican, as alderman for the Second Ward. In 1928, they sent him to the U.S. House of Representatives, making him the first African American to serve in Congress since North Carolina's George Henry White completed his final term in 1901. A new factor in the black vote was the women's vote, after the Nineteenth Amendment to the U.S. Constitution granted woman suffrage in 1920.

But black women in Chicago had been politically active long before they could vote. The city was the home of Ida B. Wells and Fannie Barrier Williams, who in 1924 was the first black woman on Chicago's Library Board. Even before this decade, beauty parlors proliferated and, like barbershops, created vital spaces for frank discussions. With their hair-straightening processes and products, they offered black women, especially southern newcomers, new styles to signal their urban identity. Black women's evolving beauty culture gave them a sense of dignity and self-worth. It also provided opportunities for jobs and activism. Maggie Wilson, a Chicago sales agent for Madam C. J. Walker's hair products, explained that these jobs "made it possible for thousands of women to give up the washtub, the cook kitchen, the scrub work and that drudgery that was the only way for them to make a living."[10] Meanwhile, Madam C. J. Walker created a nationwide enterprise. Her Hair Culturists Union of America took stands on current issues, and her Walker Clubs for sales agents did community work. She also established schools that taught black beauty methods and donated much of her considerable fortune to black institutions.

African Americans and the Great War

In April 1917, when the United States entered World War I on the side of the Allies (chiefly France and Great Britain) against the Central powers (chiefly Germany and Austria-Hungary), the African American response was mixed. Most blacks rallied patriotically to the cause and supported President Woodrow Wilson's effort to "make the world safe for democracy" by enlisting in the armed forces, buying war bonds, and contributing to the American Red Cross. In the *Crisis*, W. E. B. Du Bois urged blacks to "forget our special grievances and close our ranks shoulder to shoulder with our own white fellow citizens and the allied nations that are fighting for democracy."[11] However, an influential group on the black radical left objected. Chandler Owen and A. Philip Randolph, editors of the *Messenger*, a socialist magazine, criticized the war as nothing but an effort to advance capitalist interests. In a public letter to President Wilson, they argued, "Lynching, Jim Crow, segregation, discrimination in the armed forces and out, disfranchisement of millions of black souls in the South — all these things make your cry of making the world safe for democracy a sham, a mockery, a rape on decency and a travesty on common justice."[12]

Although blacks were 10 percent of the U.S. population, they made up more than 13 percent of the draftees. More than 2.3 million black men registered for the draft; 380,000 actually served. Only 42,000 black men, however, about 3 percent of U.S. combat forces, saw actual combat. Most black servicemen worked in support units that loaded and unloaded supplies, dug trenches, and buried the dead. Army units continued to be segregated; the navy and the coast guard allowed blacks to serve only in menial positions; and the marines and nursing units excluded blacks altogether.

The four long-standing black regiments (see chapter 8) were not given overseas combat assignments, but under pressure from the NAACP and militant newspapers such as the *Chicago Defender*, the army established two black combat divisions and began training black officers at a segregated camp in Des Moines, Iowa. One thousand African Americans received commissions, but few actually commanded troops. Those who were commissioned served only in the lower ranks and led only black troops. White soldiers refused to salute them, and they were excluded from officers' clubs. Provisions and training for black troops were also unequal. Many had to train with picks and shovels instead of guns, and their camps lacked bathroom facilities and even blankets in winter. Black soldiers traveled to and from the European war front in the bottom holds of poorly ventilated, segregated ships. U.S. army camps in Europe also were segregated. Black troops faced hostility from their own white officers as well as from white soldiers.

Nevertheless, when sent into combat, black units performed ably. The most famous unit was the 369th Infantry Regiment, known as the **Hell Fighters**, from Harlem's Fifteenth New York National Guard. The Hell Fighters served a record 191 days at the front, fighting alongside the French, who outfitted, armed, and fed them. France awarded the entire unit the Croix de Guerre, the French command's highest military honor. Two other black regiments also received the Croix de Guerre. No black soldier in World War I received a medal from the United States until Corporal Freddie Stowers of Company C of the 371st Regiment received the Congressional Medal of Honor posthumously in 1991. Stowers died while courageously rallying his comrades in a September 1918 battle. The 368th of the 92nd Division became embroiled in controversy when it failed in its mission during another battle in late 1918. The white press and white officials laid the blame squarely on black soldiers, while the black press and black officials pointed to fatigue, lack of preparation, and inept white leadership as key reasons for the regiment's failure.

The people of France appreciated both the valor of black soldiers and their distinctive African American culture. Black soldiers introduced the French to jazz and ragtime. Directing the 369th's regimental band was James Reese Europe, a New York bandleader who played the music of black composers. While touring in France, the band delighted French audiences with "St. Louis Blues" and other W. C. Handy hits (see chapter 9). When the regiment returned to the United States, though, it was not permitted to march in New York City's victory parade. Instead, on February 17, 1919, the 369th held a separate parade on Fifth Avenue, its band led by Europe and drum major Bill "Bojangles" Robinson (see chapter 9). The soldiers marched north to Harlem, where cheering crowds eagerly welcomed them home.

Almost two years earlier, a black parade of a different kind had marched down Fifth Avenue. On July 28, 1917, the NAACP and New York religious leaders organized a **silent march** to protest a race riot in East St. Louis, Illinois. It was the first African American mass protest of its kind. To muffled drums, roughly 10,000 blacks — young and old, women and men, boys and girls, all dressed in white — walked quietly down Fifth Avenue in a funeral-like procession. Typical protest banners read, "Mr. President, why not make America safe for democracy?" and "We have fought in six wars, our reward was East St. Louis."[13]

Silent March, July 28, 1917
An overwhelmingly black crowd estimated at 20,000 people observed the stunning protest march of some 10,000 blacks, all dressed in white, as they silently moved down New York City's Fifth Avenue on a Saturday afternoon in 1917. Organized and led by the NAACP, the marchers were protesting the shocking spectacle of antiblack violence in America, particularly the horror of the recent East St. Louis race riot. One young marcher's sign read, "Color, blood and suffering have made us one." *Library of Congress, Prints and Photographs Division, Washington, D.C., LC-DIG-ds-00894.*

East St. Louis, an industrial city of 60,000 (including 6,000 blacks) across the Mississippi River from St. Louis, Missouri, had suffered several episodes of racial violence. Trouble exploded in February of 1917 when the Aluminum Ore Company hired 470 black workers to replace striking white workers who belonged to the American Federation of Labor local, which excluded blacks. On May 28, thousands of outraged white workers mercilessly attacked blacks in the downtown area. After several weeks of relative calm, on July 2 a car of white males shot into a group of blacks in a black neighborhood. When two white plainclothes policemen passed by in a car, the crowd mistook them for the original attackers and fired on the policemen, killing them. Roving white mobs responded savagely. When authorities finally restored order, 125 black men, women, and children had been tortured and killed; black homes had been destroyed; hundreds had been left homeless; and property damage had amounted to $400,000. Following the East St. Louis race riot, antiblack violence swept over the home front and continued through the summer of 1919. James Weldon Johnson, field secretary for the NAACP, referred to it as the **Red Summer**.

Wars typically accelerate economic and social change, and as blacks moved to northern cities to take jobs in war industries, altering the composition of neighborhoods and workplaces, white backlash occurred. Black troop encampments also raised tensions among white residents. A month after East St. Louis, a riot erupted in Houston, Texas, where the black Twenty-Fourth Infantry Regiment was stationed. Thirteen black soldiers were tried for mutiny, convicted, and hanged. The number of lynchings in the country rose as well, from 36 in 1917 to 60 in 1918 and 76 in 1919. At least 10 veterans in uniform were killed. In Birmingham, Alabama, Sergeant Major Joe Green was shot to death by a white streetcar conductor who became enraged when Green asked for his change. Private Wilbur Little, who wore his army uniform because he owned no other clothes, was murdered in Blakely, Georgia, by whites who demanded that he wear civilian clothes.

Returning veterans, who expected that their sacrifices would be rewarded with respect, were increasingly impatient with discrimination and white hostility. W. E. B. Du Bois, who had earlier counseled cooperation, now demanded action. Tensions rose during the postwar economic readjustment period as competition for scarce housing and jobs grew, and a political atmosphere of fear spread in the wake of the Communist revolution in Russia. In what was known as the Red scare, the U.S. Justice Department, determined to stamp out communism and labor radicalism, carried out mass arrests and deported aliens. A revived Ku Klux Klan now menaced immigrants, Communists, and Jews, although African Americans remained their primary targets. In the Red Summer of 1919, racial violence reached the point of national crisis as riots erupted in cities such as Charleston, South Carolina; Omaha, Nebraska; Knoxville, Tennessee; Washington, D.C.; Longview, Texas; and Elaine, Arkansas — twenty-five places in all.

The worst rioting took place in Chicago, where five days of street fights, shootings, beatings, and fires took the lives of twenty-three blacks and fifteen whites. The trouble began on July 27, when a black teenager floating on a railroad tie in Lake Michigan unwittingly drifted into the whites-only area. In the North, there were often no signs designating "Whites Only" or "Colored Only," but the boundaries were understood. Whites threw stones at the teenager, who drowned. When a white policeman refused to arrest the perpetrators, a fight broke out and then escalated and spread. City police could not stop the violence; only heavy rain and the Illinois National Guard finally restored order. More than five hundred people, most of them black, suffered serious injuries. At least a thousand black homes were destroyed.

Walter White, assistant executive secretary of the NAACP, was assigned to report on the riot for the *Crisis* and offered eight reasons for the violence: race prejudice, economic competition, political corruption, police inefficiency, newspaper lies about black crime, unpunished crimes against blacks, housing competition, and postwar racial anxieties. He concluded by observing that living in the neighborhood where the fighting took place were more than 9,000 men who had registered for the draft and 1,850 who had been in training camps. "These men," he stated, "with their new outlook on life, injected the same spirit of independence into their companions," surprising whites by fighting back.[14] In Harlem, the young Jamaican-born writer Claude McKay expressed the same thought in a poem. Titling his militant sonnet "If We Must Die," he called for defiance:

> Like men we'll face the murderous, cowardly pack,
> Pressed to the wall, dying, but fighting back![15]

The New Negro Arrives

The increasingly assertive spirit of African Americans expressed itself in many ways, including a continuing migration out of the South. An estimated 500,000 moved north during the war years; another 700,000 migrated in the 1920s. In northern metropolises, they constituted an increasingly large segment of the population, and they were vocal in demanding their rights. National mass organizations with a wide range of programs, some in service to the welfare of the newcomers and some expanding a research base that propelled black scholars to the forefront of their fields, strengthened individual and collective efforts. In black communities such as New York's Harlem, fresh forms of expression in literature, the visual arts, dance, and music affirmed black identity and culture and gained recognition for black creativity in American culture. The activism of black scholars, writers, and performers had a ripple effect, helping position African Americans as a force to be reckoned with and inspiring them to take pride in their heritage, their accomplishments, and their black identity.

Institutional Bases for Social Science and Historical Studies

The term **New Negro** had been around at least since the late nineteenth century. Booker T. Washington had used it in the title of a collection of essays he edited with Fannie Barrier Williams, *A New Negro for a New Century* (1900). But after the beginning of the great migration and the end of the Great War, the label was increasingly appropriated by blacks, mostly those based in northern cities, who rejected Washington's accommodationism. In the *Messenger*, Owen and Randolph defined the New Negro: In politics, he "cannot be lulled into a false sense of security with political spoils and patronage" but demands political equality and universal suffrage; in economics, he "demands the full product of his toil," the ability "to buy in the market, commodities at the lowest possible price," and the right to join labor unions; and in society, "he stands for absolute and unequivocal *'social equality.'* "[16] Not all black spokespersons were militant, but throughout northern cities especially, a renewed self-confidence gave rise to new and energetic challenges to discrimination.

During the Chicago riot of 1919, the city's Urban League opened its headquarters as an emergency center, and after the fighting subsided, its executive secretary, T. Arnold Hill, was instrumental in establishing the Chicago Commission on Race Relations to investigate the causes of interracial violence. Researching and writing much of the commission's report was Charles S. Johnson, who, as a graduate student in sociology at the University of Chicago, had witnessed the riot firsthand. Under Johnson's supervision, *The Negro in Chicago: A Study of Race Relations and a Race Riot* (1922) became a classic of sociological analysis. This massive 672-page social science study of the conditions of black life in Chicago and of relations between blacks and whites built on a wide range of sources, including interviews, charts, photographs, and maps. This work showcased what came to be known as the Chicago School: a famous and influential sociological approach to understanding cities, or urban sociology, developed at the University of Chicago. The School emphasized environmental and structural factors over genetics to explain urban phenomena, such as how blacks adapted to northern urban life. Another intent of the Chicago School was to inform in order to generate understanding and bring about reform. Like Du Bois, who had written a pioneering study titled *The Philadelphia Negro* in 1899, the Chicago School practitioner Charles Johnson believed that facts would dispel prejudice and advance the race.

In 1921, Johnson was appointed director of research for the National Urban League. Moving to the organization's New York headquarters, he founded the journal *Opportunity* in 1923, naming it for the league's slogan, "Not Alms but Opportunity." As editor of the journal, he published both social science research and contributions by black writers and poets. Hill, promoted to director of industrial relations, developed vocational training and programs for improving race relations in the workplace. Leading the Urban League in the 1920s, its golden era, was executive secretary Eugene K. Jones, another social scientist who, like Johnson and Hill, was a graduate of Virginia Union University in Richmond. The Urban League organized boycotts of businesses that refused to hire blacks and pressured city schools to provide training for workers. With affiliates in more than thirty cities, including some in the South, the Urban League's efforts to eliminate barriers to employment, ensure fair treatment for workers, and improve housing and sanitation had a lasting effect on individual lives and race relations. Like the NAACP, also headquartered in New York City, the Urban

League was reformist and progressive, but unlike the NAACP, it did not seek to become a mass-membership organization.

The NAACP increased its membership significantly during these years under the leadership of James Weldon Johnson, who in 1920 became its first black executive secretary. Johnson initiated a nationwide campaign to sign up new members at $1 a year. As a result, the organization became overwhelmingly black, while remaining committed to interracial cooperation. Throughout the 1920s, the NAACP claimed 100,000 members in more than 300 chapters nationwide. Johnson was particularly successful in the dangerous work of establishing chapters in the deep South, although these were subject to antiblack violence, and some had to close or go underground.

The NAACP looked to the courts to end housing discrimination and to Congress to end lynching. In 1917, in *Buchanan v. Warley*, it convinced the U.S. Supreme Court to overturn city ordinances mandating where blacks could live, and in 1926 it successfully defended the black physician Ossian Sweet from murder charges stemming from an attack on his home in Detroit. The NAACP was less successful in Congress. The Dyer Anti-Lynching Bill (see chapter 9), which the NAACP backed and which would have made lynching a federal crime, was introduced year after year but never passed, owing primarily to the opposition of southern white congressmen.

Both the Urban League and the NAACP drew together broad constituencies of blacks and sympathetic whites who wanted to end racial violence and discrimination. With Johnson and Du Bois directing research and publications for their respective organizations, sociological studies of black life became a growing part of a reformist program that had racial equality and integration as its goals — what Johnson in *The Negro in Chicago* called "adjusted neighborhoods," as opposed to "non-adjusted neighborhoods." Chicago School–trained black sociologists built a strong base of scholarship on urban and social problems. Most notable was E. Franklin Frazier, whose Ph.D. dissertation was published as *The Negro Family in Chicago* in 1932. Culminating years of sociological research on Chicago was *Black Metropolis: A Study of Negro Life in a Northern City* (1945) by St. Clair Drake and Horace R. Cayton, considered a masterpiece. The academic establishment had largely ignored Du Bois's early work, but these studies coming out of Chicago commanded acclaim, and both Johnson and Frazier later became officers in the American Sociological Association.

In 1928, Charles Johnson left the Urban League to chair Fisk University's social sciences department, where he trained a new generation of sociologists and turned his attention to the lives and conditions of rural blacks in the South. He published two important works, *Shadow of the Plantation* (1934) and *Growing Up in the Black Belt* (1941). In 1930, James Weldon Johnson joined Charles Johnson at Fisk, accepting a chair of creative writing and literature. While executive secretary of the NAACP, he had published collections of Negro spirituals and written *Black Manhattan* (1930), which hailed Harlem as "the Negro metropolis." He wrote, "The Negro's situation in Harlem is without precedent in all his history in New York; never before has he been so securely anchored, never before has he owned the land, never before has he had so well established a community life."[17] Du Bois left the NAACP in 1934 to return to Atlanta University, where he produced his landmark work *Black Reconstruction* (1935) and a history of African peoples titled *Black Folk, Then and Now* (1939).

More than any other individual, Carter G. Woodson promoted the serious study of African American history and culture. An educator who received a Ph.D. in history from Harvard in 1912, Woodson taught at the M Street High School (renamed for Paul Laurence Dunbar in 1916) and Howard University in Washington, D.C. In 1915, he established the Association for the Study of Negro Life and History, the foremost organization promoting African American history among the lay public as well as within black institutions. In 1916, he founded the *Journal of Negro History*, the major scholarly journal in its field. His *Negro History Bulletin*, which began publication in 1937, made black history accessible to educators, students, and general readers. Woodson wrote many scholarly books and articles on black history, including studies of education, the church, migration, the family, and the professions. His textbook *The Negro in Our History* (1922) was widely used for many years.

To further promote the study of black history, in 1926 Woodson created Negro History Week, a week in February (the week of Frederick Douglass's and Abraham Lincoln's birthdays) during which African American contributions could be highlighted in schools and organizations. In 1976, the annual celebration was extended to all of February as **Black History Month** and is now widely observed. Woodson donated his large collection of black history materials to the Library of Congress. For his many accomplishments, he received the NAACP's prestigious Spingarn Medal in 1926 and is remembered as "the Father of Negro History."

Another major archive of black history was the lifework of Arthur Schomburg, a historian, bibliophile, and activist who collected 5,000 books, documents, and other materials. "The American Negro must remake his past in order to make his future," Schomburg argued. "History must restore what slavery took away."[18] Schomburg's collection became the basis for a research center at the Harlem branch of the New York Public Library. Today the Schomburg Center for Research in Black Culture is one of the foremost research centers for black history in the world.

The Universal Negro Improvement Association

Of all the new organizations and fresh approaches to black elevation, Marcus Garvey's **Universal Negro Improvement Association (UNIA)** was the largest and most militant. Founded in Kingston, Jamaica, in 1914, it surged after 1916, when Garvey relocated its headquarters to Harlem. By 1919, the UNIA claimed two million members in thirty chapters in the United States and the West Indies. By 1921, the number had grown to four million members worldwide.

The UNIA's astonishing growth owed not only to Garvey's vision and oratorical skills but also to the brutal racism of the wartime and postwar era. Garvey emphasized race pride and racial unity at a time when these messages resonated deeply with blacks.

Carter G. Woodson
Carter G. Woodson became known as "the Father of Negro History" for his pioneering and immeasurable contributions to the study and recognition of African American history. These contributions include founding the *Journal of Negro History* in 1915 and, in 1926, creating Negro History Week, which was expanded to Black History Month in 1976.
The Granger Collection, New York.

He reinvigorated black nationalism, and even black separatism, and ignited a grassroots movement, with UNIA chapters forming in rural and urban areas in every part of the country. Some local units focused on practical matters, such as voter registration, health clinics, and adult night schools. Unique to the UNIA, however, was the message of African redemption, the restoration of African independence and greatness, and Pan-Africanism — the essential oneness of all African peoples, wherever they lived. Garveyism helped African Americans to recognize both the American and African components of their identity, to see themselves in an international context, and to feel that they were part of a global black movement. Unlike the uplift and reformist organizations established in the late nineteenth and early twentieth centuries (such as the NAACP), which were integrationist in ideology, the UNIA was separatist. It emphasized black self-determination — independent black nation building — rather than fighting for civil and political rights in the United States.

Born in St. Ann's Bay, Jamaica, in 1887, Garvey was a printer, journalist, and labor organizer in the Caribbean and Central and South America, where he witnessed the crushing oppression of peasants on plantations. He spent a formative period in London, where African nationalists and anticolonial activists such as Duse Muhammed Ali, editor of the *African Times and Orient Review*, strongly influenced him. Garvey was also influenced by Booker T. Washington's autobiography, *Up from Slavery*, and upon his return to Jamaica in 1912 he tried to set up an industrial training school on the Tuskegee model. He initially came to the United States to seek Washington's advice, but Washington died in 1915 before the two could meet. Garvey refocused his vision on prospects for the UNIA in the United States. Excited by what he saw and heard as he traveled among black communities throughout the country, he returned to his Harlem base to build the organization.

Garvey effectively wielded the rituals and symbols of prestige and power. He captivated followers with inspirational rhetoric, sharp dress, and proud self-presentation. The UNIA had a complex leadership hierarchy, grand titles and military orders, uniforms, and strong women's auxiliaries. It held huge mass meetings and parades and provided many opportunities for organizing and mobilizing. Its militant weekly newspaper, the *Negro World*, began in 1918 with a circulation of around 3,000. Within a year, it had 50,000 readers, and in its heyday in the early 1920s it claimed more than 200,000 readers. Amy Jacques Garvey, Marcus Garvey's second wife, edited the popular women's page, which spoke to the particular concerns of black women through the prism of Garveyism.

Everywhere Garvey went he electrified audiences as he roared maxims such as "Up, you mighty race! You can accomplish what you will!"[19] and thundered the

Garveyites
In their full regalia, these Garveyites, individually and collectively, radiate race pride, confidence, self-reliance, and unity. In particular, the men in their military-style uniforms evoke a sense of proud black manhood. Garvey and his followers imparted a comforting sense of belonging to a powerful and important organization and being part of a defining historical moment for African people everywhere. *The Granger Collection, New York.*

UNIA's motto: "One God! One Aim! One Destiny!" Along the crowded Harlem parade route to the 1920 UNIA convention at Madison Square Garden, parading Garveyites carried a striking range of banners, including those proclaiming "We Want a Black Civilization" and "Africa Must Be Free." The lead banner of the Woman's Auxiliary read, "God Give Us Real Men!"[20] At the convention Garvey was crowned the "Provisional President of the African Republic." The convention adopted the Declaration of the Rights of the Negro Peoples of the World, which asserted the right of Africans everywhere to self-definition and self-determination. In his speech, Garvey proclaimed: "We shall raise the banner of democracy in Africa, or 400,000,000 of us will report to God the reason why."[21] Under the UNIA's red, black, and green flag, the themes of race pride, racial unity, and African regeneration were proclaimed.

For many, Garveyism functioned like a religion. Garvey relied heavily on support from black ministers, who provided an organizational and recruitment network. In 1924, the African Orthodox Church, an independent black denomination with a black nationalist message, became the UNIA's official church.

At the heart of Garvey's efforts, however, was economic nationalism. Compellingly representing a dominant black position, he argued that a separate black economy and independent black enterprises were central to racial advancement. The UNIA established hotels, restaurants, and stores under the Negro Factories Corporation, whose goal was black business development. One subsidiary manufactured dolls in various shades of brown, from dark to mulatto. For Garveyites, economic enterprise was a matter of race pride.

The Black Star Line steamship company, created with much fanfare in 1919, was the movement's centerpiece, intended to unite African peoples in the Old and New Worlds spiritually, socially, politically, and economically. By undermining Western colonial rule, it would, claimed Garvey, redeem Africa. This grand promotion of commercial and travel links across the Atlantic excited not only Garveyites but also many blacks outside the movement, who were attracted by Garvey's Pan-African–related "Africa for Africans" idea — the notion that Africans themselves must rule their own nations and continent. Thus inspired, they bought stock in the company at $5 a share. The Black Star Line was to be a key instrument of black self-determination and black separatism.

As a self-identified full-blooded black who opposed racial mixing, Garvey roundly condemned integration. His call for racial purity was not unlike that of the resurgent Ku Klux Klan, and he stirred great controversy when he met with Klan leaders. Du Bois called Garvey "the most dangerous enemy of the Negro race in America and in the world," denouncing him as "either a lunatic or a traitor,"[22] while Garvey distrusted and harshly criticized light-skinned leaders such as Du Bois. Du Bois was not the only black leader alarmed by Garvey. Many criticized the Back to Africa fever as hysterical and cultlike, and they feared that Garvey was exploiting the hopes and fears of the black masses. By early 1922, the Black Star Line had sold more than 150,000 shares of stock, but the three ships it purchased and outfitted proved unseaworthy. To many, the project seemed like an ill-conceived scheme to defraud poor black stockholders. The U.S. Justice Department was also suspicious of Garvey, a foreign national who seemed to be advocating disloyalty on the part of American blacks at a time when all foreign radicals — as well as American Communists, socialists, and left-wing progressives — were viewed as dangerous.

The immediate pretext for the UNIA's swift fall was evidence of financial impropriety in the Black Star Line. Although Garvey himself was innocent of the charges, in 1923 he was convicted of mail fraud for selling bogus stock in the venture through the mail. In 1925, he began serving a five-year prison sentence, and two years later he was deported as an "undesirable alien." The UNIA soon faded, but Garveyism as an ideology persisted. The UNIA was the most important mass black movement before the modern civil rights movement.

The Harlem Renaissance

So much of the New Negro spirit, so many of the organizations that represented the New Negro, and so many New Negro leaders and celebrities were centered in Harlem that it was, declared Alain Locke, a "race capital."[23] Two of the preeminent black newspapers of the era — the *Amsterdam News* and the *New York Age* — were located in Harlem. Many of the black elite lived on Striver's Row and in Sugar Hill (Map 10.2). Locke, a Rhodes scholar with a Harvard Ph.D. in philosophy, taught literature and philosophy at Howard University in Washington, D.C., but he encouraged one of his most talented students, Zora Neale Hurston, to move to New York to study anthropology at Columbia and to write. Locke became both spokesman and promoter for a constellation of writers whose remarkable outpouring of poetry and fiction, often allied with the visual arts, dance, and music, defined a new black cultural movement. Best known as the **Harlem Renaissance**, this New Negro arts movement encompassed the ferment of black life in the metropolis and flourished in other places as well, such as Chicago and Washington, D.C.

Like Woodson and Schomburg, the writers and artists of the Harlem Renaissance sought to present authentic versions of the African American experience. Like the UNIA, they affirmed the value of blackness and the African heritage. But unlike the UNIA, they were typically integrationist, not separatist, often relying on white patrons and appealing to white audiences. Collectively, they refashioned the black image. Du Bois, as editor of the *Crisis*, and Johnson, as editor of *Opportunity*, provided a publication base for their writings and enthusiastically promoted their efforts.

In 1925, Locke edited a special issue of the *Survey Graphic*, a social science and cultural journal. In the issue, entitled "Harlem: Mecca of the New Negro," he reflected on Harlem's significance. It was not the center of black education, industry, or finance, "yet here . . . are the forces that make a group known and felt in the world. The reformers, the fighting advocates, the inner spokesmen, the poets, artists and social prophets are here," he asserted,[24] and the issue proved his point. Included were studies in history

MAP 10.2 Cultural Harlem

This map provides a geographical and neighborhood layout and tour of Harlem. It pinpoints some of the important sites where the vibrant social, cultural, intellectual, religious, and political life of the Harlem Renaissance played out. The churches, newspaper offices, theaters, and organization headquarters mapped here were places where blacks created the Renaissance. It was not unusual for whites to frequent a number of Harlem's entertainment venues. Indeed, some Harlem spots, like the Cotton Club, catered to whites-only audiences. Also shown are the residences of some of the era's central figures who served as spokespeople for the New Negro through their careers and activism. DATA SOURCE: Jeffrey Brown Ferguson, *The Harlem Renaissance: A Brief History with Documents* (Boston: Bedford/St. Martin's, 2008), 9.

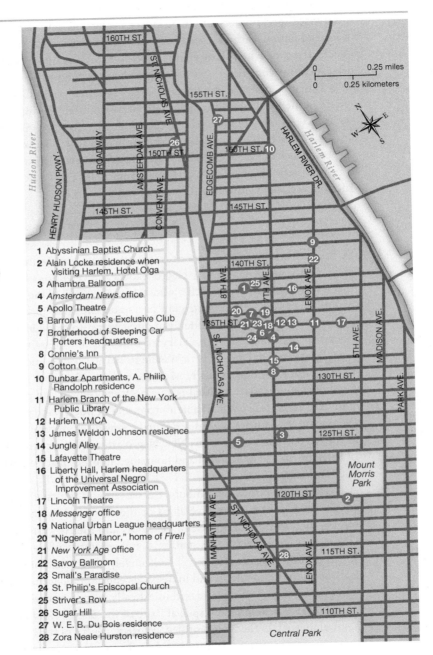

1 Abyssinian Baptist Church
2 Alain Locke residence when visiting Harlem, Hotel Olga
3 Alhambra Ballroom
4 *Amsterdam News* office
5 Apollo Theatre
6 Barron Wilkins's Exclusive Club
7 Brotherhood of Sleeping Car Porters headquarters
8 Connie's Inn
9 Cotton Club
10 Dunbar Apartments, A. Philip Randolph residence
11 Harlem Branch of the New York Public Library
12 Harlem YMCA
13 James Weldon Johnson residence
14 Jungle Alley
15 Lafayette Theatre
16 Liberty Hall, Harlem headquarters of the Universal Negro Improvement Association
17 Lincoln Theatre
18 *Messenger* office
19 National Urban League headquarters
20 "Niggerati Manor," home of *Fire!!*
21 *New York Age* office
22 Savoy Ballroom
23 Small's Paradise
24 St. Philip's Episcopal Church
25 Striver's Row
26 Sugar Hill
27 W. E. B. Du Bois residence
28 Zora Neale Hurston residence

and sociology by James Weldon Johnson, Arthur Schomburg, and Charles S. Johnson; essays on jazz and art; a reflection on color lines by Walter White; and poems by Claude McKay, Countee Cullen, Jean Toomer, and Langston Hughes. McKay, a socialist, wrote poems of disillusionment; Cullen's textured sonnets were rich with literary allusions. Like so many Harlem Renaissance writers, they expressed black themes and explored issues in black identity. Toomer is best known for *Cane* (1923), a haunting prose poem that examines the effect of the past and the present — of slavery, spiritual and material impoverishment, stunted rural and urban environments — on African American identities. Toomer's interest in the rhythms of black speech reflected a current running throughout Harlem Renaissance work, notably in the poems of Hughes and Sterling Brown.

Locke's next effort was even more spectacular. For the book *The New Negro* (1925), he wrote what might be regarded as the manifesto of the New Negro arts movement and collected an even wider array of writers and poets, including Gwendolyn Bennett and Zora Neale Hurston. Essays addressed Negro spirituals, dance, and folk literature, including Brer Rabbit tales. Supplying drawings and decorative designs was the young artist Aaron Douglas, who had moved from Kansas City to Harlem after the *Survey Graphic*'s Harlem issue convinced him that Harlem was the place to be. Douglas's distinctive style, drawing on Egyptian and West African sources as well as cubism and art deco, captured the attention of Du Bois and Johnson, who asked Douglas to illustrate their journals and draw covers for books by black authors. Douglas's race-conscious visual art explored themes in African American history and culture, especially folk culture, and connections between African Americans and Africa. Considered the father of modern African American visual art, he is also remembered as a muralist and is known especially for his murals at the Harlem branch of the New York Public Library and at Fisk University, where he founded the art department.

The short-lived *Fire!!* (1926), a magazine subtitled *Devoted to Younger Negro Artists*, was indicative of the excitement and creativity of the Harlem Renaissance. Hurston and Hughes, along with Wallace Thurman, the editor of *Fire!!*, led these younger artists, who chafed at artistic visions that aimed to attract white audiences and serve a political purpose. Du Bois had insisted that "all Art is propaganda," by which he meant that art should deal with subjects that would advance the black freedom struggle.[25] Locke offered a middle position: While rejecting art as propaganda, he called for a race-conscious art of the highest order. The writers for *Fire!!* called instead for a more complete freedom of artistic expression. Their art would embrace the lower classes and the gritty realities confronting blacks, not just genteel, middle-class concerns. Rejecting art that would "pour racial individuality into the mold of American standardization," Hughes spoke for his colleagues: "We younger Negro artists who create now intend to express our individual dark-skinned selves without fear or shame. If white people are pleased we are glad. If they are not, it doesn't matter. We know we are beautiful. And ugly too."[26]

Innovative literature and art were only part of what was happening during the Harlem Renaissance. On Broadway and in Harlem, dance revues with tap dancers such

Song of the Towers, *1934*

Aaron Douglas — painter, graphic artist, and muralist — was the pre-eminent artist of the Harlem Renaissance. His signature work, *Song of the Towers*, was the final installment of *Aspects of Negro Life*, a four-panel mural series that Douglas created in 1934 under the auspices of the Works Progress Administration for the 135th Street branch of the New York Public Library in Harlem, which became the Schomburg Center for Research in Black Culture in 1972. *Song of the Towers* boldly captures Douglas's abiding interest in African American history and culture. Aspects of Negro Life: Song of the Towers, *1934, by Aaron Douglas (1899–1979). Oil on canvas, 9' x 9'. Photo: Manu Sassoonian/Schomburg Center for Research in Black Culture, The New York Public Library, New York, NY, USA/Art Resource, NY.*

as Bojangles were wildly popular, especially after the success of *Shuffle Along* (1921), the first Broadway musical created, produced, and performed by blacks. The Chicago-based comedy team of Flournoy Miller and Aubrey Lyles wrote the script, while the musical team of Noble Sissle and Eubie Blake created hit tunes such as "I'm Just Wild about Harry." *Shuffle Along*'s famous chorus line helped launch the entertainment careers of Florence Mills and Josephine Baker. Mills combined innocence with an edgy sensuality to become the biggest black musical theater star of the era. Baker achieved her greatest stardom in Paris, where she thrilled audiences with outrageous costumes and exuberant performances of popular dances such as the Charleston and the Black

Bottom. In the late 1920s, the Alhambra Ballroom and the Savoy Ballroom became the most popular dance halls in Harlem.

Blues singers long popular on the black tent circuit now drew huge crowds to the cabarets and nightclubs of Harlem, where whites and blacks had a good time and illegal booze flowed. Jungle Alley, an area along 133rd Street between Lenox and 7th Avenues, was dotted with nightclubs and cabarets. North of Jungle Alley, many of the best-known black entertainers of the era, such as Bessie Smith and Duke Ellington, performed at the Cotton Club, the most famous Harlem venue. Like Connie's Inn and Barron Wilkins's Exclusive Club, the Cotton Club catered to all-white audiences.

Harlem blacks especially enjoyed Small's Paradise and lesser-known clubs like Tillie's Chicken Shack, which featured down-home entertainment, including raucous blues. The Lafayette Theatre and the Lincoln Theatre were highly popular black entertainment venues, and after 1934 the Apollo Theatre became the most important performance venue for black entertainers in the United States.

The music of the Harlem Renaissance, particularly jazz and blues, constituted the most original and innovative artistic developments of the 1920s. Especially noteworthy was the powerful work of blues singers such as Ma Rainey, "the Mother of the Blues" (see chapter 9), and Bessie Smith, "the Empress of the Blues." The work of these and other classic blues divas dealt profoundly with life's ups and downs and featured women's points of view, notably those of working-class and struggling women.

The New Orleans–born cornetist and trumpeter Louis "Satchmo" Armstrong pioneered several innovative and fresh developments in jazz. As shown in his classic tune "West End Blues" (1928), Armstrong's stunning technical virtuosity, improvisational skill, and vocal and compositional originality enabled him to help create the instrumental jazz solo and the vocal jazz solo. He also introduced scat singing, in which the singer mimics a musical instrument in a striking call-and-response pattern.

Duke Ellington and his jazz band were key innovators of orchestral, big band, or what is sometimes called swing, jazz. They shot to fame at the Cotton Club, where they were regulars after 1927. Over a long career, Ellington was recognized as a preeminent American composer. Swank whites-only cabarets like the Cotton Club (there was also one in Chicago), which featured jazz bands, blues singers, and black dancers, contributed to the mainstream acceptance of jazz and the blues, as did radio performances and recordings on "race labels" that allowed millions who would never see these black musical stars in person to hear and appreciate their fresh and thrilling music.

The glitter of the Harlem Renaissance crashed along with the stock market and the onset of the Great Depression, although its artists and writers continued to produce important work. In later years, certain limits of the movement came into clearer focus: its social distance from the working-class black communities it sought to energize, and its overreliance on European artistic standards and white patrons. Most important, however, the empowering change in black identity and expression that it fostered became permanent. Not only did the Harlem Renaissance promote a more accurate and affirmative understanding of African American history and culture; it also demonstrated the beauty and power of race-conscious art and enriched American culture immeasurably.

The Great Depression and the New Deal

When the stock market crashed in 1929, the national economic crisis was part of an escalating global depression. For African Americans, whether they were sharecropping in the South or working for wages in the North, the downturn hit with blunt force. Interventions by the federal government offered some immediate relief and long-term hope, but African Americans also understood that they had to take action on their own. As black organizing became increasingly political, intent on dismantling segregation in unions and the workplace, in schools, and even in stores, white politicians found it increasingly difficult to ignore the growing black vote and black economic power. The president began consulting black leaders more frequently, and blacks were increasingly placed in federal agencies to help oversee black interests. The Communist Party's successful defense of blacks in several high-profile southern court cases brought heightened attention to southern racial injustice, as well as to the party's important antiracist work. The NAACP initiated a deliberate strategy for dismantling segregation. Meanwhile, writers and artists, many overtly political and some working for federal programs, depicted African American life with a realism that increased understanding of race and class conflict and expanded the audience for African American culture.

Economic Crisis and the Roosevelt Presidency

The stock market crash of October 1929 precipitated but did not cause the Great Depression. The depression resulted from a variety of factors: unchecked financial speculation, a severe contraction of cash and credit, declining demand, weakness in the agricultural sector, corporate debt, widespread greed, and gross economic inequality. As businesses and banks failed and factories closed, national income plummeted from $81 billion in 1929 to $40 billion in 1932. By October 1930, four million Americans were unemployed. Within a year, the number increased to seven million, and then to eleven million. By 1932, 25 percent of Americans were out of work. Foreclosures skyrocketed, and millions were rendered homeless.

While many Americans had prospered in the 1920s, most black Americans had not, and the depression made their lives much more difficult. In the rural South, overproduction of cotton and the loss of overseas markets had kept the price of cotton low all through the twenties; then it collapsed, plummeting from 18 cents per pound in 1929 to 6 cents in 1933. At the same time, the gradual mechanization of southern agriculture put thousands of black tenant farmers and sharecroppers out of work. The Great Mississippi Flood of 1927 also displaced African Americans, who headed for cities such as Memphis, New Orleans, and Jackson, Mississippi; but there were no jobs.

"Negro jobs," such as garbage collection and domestic service, were now going to whites, who were desperate as well.

By 1931, two years after the depression's official beginning, black unemployment in the South stood at 33 percent; a year later it was 50 percent. Black unemployment always outpaced the national average, as blacks were the last hired and the first fired, and unions, which continued to discriminate, offered little protection. In 1932, the black unemployment rate in Harlem was 50 percent; in Philadelphia it was 56 percent. Jobless blacks were evicted from apartments, and the numbers of drifting homeless and beggars increased.

The Republican president Herbert Hoover's failure to stem the economic disaster swept the Democrat Franklin D. Roosevelt into office in the election of 1932. Hoover had taken a hands-off approach to the economy, believing it would self-correct and rebound. But the crisis of the depression proved so severe that extraordinary government intervention was necessary. Roosevelt responded by instituting a series of novel federal programs that he called the New Deal.

Thirteen-Year-Old Sharecropper
This 1937 photograph of a thirteen-year-old sharecropper near Americus, Georgia, was taken as part of the efforts of the New Deal's Farm Security Administration to publicize and ameliorate the plight of suffering Great Depression–era farmworkers. The boy's youth intensifies the photograph's emotional power. *Dorothea Lange photograph for the U.S. Farm Security Administration, 1937. Library of Congress, Prints and Photographs Division, Washington, D.C., LC-USF34-017915-C.*

A massive and unprecedented expansion of federal power, Roosevelt's First New Deal aimed to provide relief and revive the ailing economy. Emphasizing jobs over direct handouts, programs such as the Federal Emergency Relief Administration (FERA; 1933) and the Civilian Conservation Corps (CCC; 1933) helped many families make it through the worst of times. The Securities and Exchange Commission (SEC; 1934) regulated the stock market. Between 1935 and 1938, Roosevelt advanced the more aggressive Second New Deal, financed to a far greater extent by deficit spending. This plan aimed to alleviate poverty, expand jobs over relief programs, and create a social safety net. In 1935, however, the U.S. Supreme Court ruled unconstitutional the National Recovery Administration (NRA; 1933), which had sought to stabilize industry by setting prices, wages, and working hours.

Bolstered by his landslide reelection the next year, Roosevelt unsuccessfully challenged the Court by seeking to "pack" it with additional justices sympathetic to his goals. Congress balked, and the president lost some support. The Court, however, reversed course in 1937 and declared constitutional both the Social Security Act (1935), which provided old-age pensions and disability benefits, and the National Labor Relations Act (1935), known as the Wagner Act, which recognized the right of labor unions to organize, bargain collectively, and strike. That same year, Roosevelt cut back on deficit spending and contracted the New Deal, contributing to a second stock market crash and a serious recession. It took the economic expansion resulting from World War II for the economy to recover fully. Nevertheless, both the First and Second New Deals greatly expanded federal control over American society and the economy.

The racial discrimination that permeated America was evident in New Deal programs. Some called the New Deal a "raw deal" for African Americans. Where programs were administered locally, especially in the South, blacks did not benefit at the same rate as whites. The Agricultural Adjustment Administration poured millions of dollars into helping farmers, but almost none of the money benefited black sharecroppers or tenant farmers or the dwindling number of independent black farmers. The Federal Housing Administration forbade mortgage loans in integrated areas, backing loans only to blacks who lived in all-black neighborhoods. The Social Security Act excluded participation by those working in agriculture, domestic service, or day labor, the types of jobs held by most black men and women. Agricultural and domestic workers were also excluded from the Wagner Act and from the Fair Labor Standards Act, which established maximum working hours and minimum wages.

Efforts by the National Urban League and the NAACP to insert nondiscrimination clauses into New Deal legislation proved unsuccessful. However, these organizations kept the pressure on the federal government to pay attention to black concerns, as did a lobbying effort led by the black lawyer John P. Davis and the black economist Robert C. Weaver, both Harvard graduates. Black organizations had new political leverage with an administration concerned about the plight of the poor. President Roosevelt connected with all Americans through his fireside chats, radio broadcasts in which he explained the New Deal in language everyone could understand. Even more important to African Americans was the growing support of First Lady Eleanor Roosevelt. She spoke out on behalf of black concerns, built connections with black leaders and groups, and lobbied her husband, New Dealers, and other influential officials on behalf of African Americans.

One result was an increasing number of blacks entering the civil service — growing from 50,000 in 1933 to more than 150,000 by 1941 — and receiving political appointments to government agencies. Particularly visible was Mary McLeod Bethune, whose 1936 appointment to head the Division of Negro Affairs of the National Youth Administration evolved into her appointment to official division director in 1939. In this capacity, she launched opportunities for vocational training and jobs in both the private sector and government for thousands of unemployed black youths between the ages of sixteen and twenty-four. Bethune, an active member of the NAACP, had served as president of the National Association of Colored Women in the 1920s, and in 1935 she had established the National Council of Negro Women, an alliance of black women's organizations.

The black journalist Roi Ottley called Bethune "the First Lady of the Struggle." She used her influence to get the federal government to sponsor conferences highlighting black problems and devising federal solutions. Perhaps most important, in 1937 Bethune organized the Federal Council on Negro Affairs, informally known as the **Black Cabinet**, a group of influential black policy advisers who met at her home to discuss civil rights and help shape the New Deal's response to black concerns. Among them were Robert C. Weaver, Eugene K. Jones from the Commerce Department, William H. Hastie from the Interior Department, A. Philip Randolph, T. Arnold Hill, and Walter White, who, like Bethune, was a personal friend of Eleanor Roosevelt.

For the first time since Reconstruction, black people got support from the federal government, and they were drawn to the Democratic Party, for Republicans had taken black voters for granted. In 1932, the editor of the *Pittsburgh Courier*, an influential black newspaper, called on black voters to exercise their political muscle: "My friends, go turn Lincoln's picture to the wall. That debt has been paid in full."[27] In 1936, 75 percent of African Americans voted for Roosevelt, and since that time they have been an important component of the Democratic Party. Indicative of the trend, Republican Oscar De Priest lost his seat in the U.S. House of Representatives in 1934 to Democrat Arthur Mitchell, a black politician who had switched parties.

African American Politics

Throughout the latter half of the 1930s, Mitchell was the only African American in Congress, but in northern metropolises blacks increasingly constituted a voting bloc that commanded the attention of white politicians. In previous decades, black concerns had been almost completely ignored. Now Roosevelt had to balance federal efforts on behalf of black Americans against the prospect of losing the support of white Democrats from the South. As African Americans gained political power, their activism took an increasingly political turn. As was so often the case in the African American experience, this activism was particularly evident in black churches.

With the onset of the depression, black churches expanded aid for the desperately poor. Harlem's Abyssinian Baptist Church, led by the Reverend Adam Clayton Powell Sr., fed 2,000 people daily in its soup kitchen and handed out clothing and fuel. Powell Sr. had helped organize the silent march of 1917, and his son, Adam Clayton Powell Jr., who succeeded him in the pulpit in 1937, was an outspoken advocate for civil rights, organizing a "Don't buy where you can't work" campaign to pressure New York stores to hire black employees. In 1941, he was elected city councilman, and in 1944 he was elected as a Democrat to the U.S. House of Representatives. The Powells' activism was an early sign of increasing political involvement by black religious leaders.

Even more notable was the rise of independent religious movements that aimed to provide political direction along with spiritual nourishment and material relief. Both Charles Emmanuel Grace, known as "Sweet Daddy Grace" or just "Daddy Grace," and George Baker, known as "Father Divine," projected a sense of their own divinity and preached righteous living and positive thinking. Both had huge interracial followings, and their movements, with subsidiary businesses and investments, amassed great wealth, increasing their influence. Daddy Grace's United House of Prayer for All People drew on the flamboyant personality of its leader, with his crown, shoulder-length hair, purple robes, and extra-long red, white, and blue fingernails. Daddy Grace was a highly dramatic preacher and faith healer who fed the hungry in church cafeterias and housed the homeless in his apartment buildings.

Father Divine's Peace Mission movement was even more extensive. At its height, it had more than 160 mission centers in the United States, Canada, and Europe, where meals were lavish affairs, not just soup and bread. Run mostly by women secretaries, the movement preached against smoking and drinking and advocated sexual abstinence. Father Divine's progressive political agenda included support for minimum-wage legislation, curbs on corporate profits, a federal antilynching law, and the abolition of capital punishment. His emphasis on political education contributed to the era's growing black awareness and political action.

Outside the church, black activism found expression in rent strikes, boycotts, and consumer cooperatives, often organized by women. Housewives Leagues in both northern and southern cities coordinated "Don't buy where you can't work" boycotts. These were often related to "Double Duty Dollar" campaigns, which advocated patronizing black businesses because their profits would get reinvested in black neighborhoods. In Harlem, the Domestic Workers Union formed to demand fair pay and hours and to try to end street corner "slave markets," where unemployed black women gathered each morning in hopes that white women might drive by and hire them for the day or at least a few hours.

Building on the Wagner Act, in spite of its failure to bar racial discrimination in unions, A. Philip Randolph sought to leverage the power of black wageworkers. He had long advocated interracial unionism, joining the Socialist Party as a young man because of its views on labor. His first efforts to organize black workers — elevator operators and stevedores — were undermined by the American Federation of Labor (AFL). In 1925, he was elected president of the newly formed Brotherhood of Sleeping Car Porters and Maids, commonly referred to as the Brotherhood of Sleeping Car Porters. Jobs as railroad porters and maids were highly coveted, though they involved long hours and low pay. Randolph used the union as an organizational base for promoting both the rights of blacks and the rights of labor. In 1935, the AFL recognized the union, which won its first contract in 1937.

Interracial unionism gained a significant foothold in the 1930s in spite of persistent antiblack racism within the labor movement. Crucial to this advance was the Committee for Industrial Organization, which was created in 1935 as part of the AFL and became the independent **Congress of Industrial Organizations (CIO)** in 1938. The CIO promoted mass industrial unionism: the organization of all industrial workers, whether unskilled, semiskilled, or skilled, and without regard to race or ethnicity. In spite of the CIO's inclusive aims, however, black union members and their white allies, notably socialists and Communists, battled racial discrimination within CIO unions, and in time, thousands of blacks joined interracial labor unions.

The Socialist Party that Randolph joined in 1916 advocated fairness for workers and social equality, but it did not have a large black following in part because of racism within its ranks. After the 1917 revolution in Russia and the establishment of the Soviet Union, international communism broadcast a similar message and gained some black followers, notably among Harlem activists and intellectuals. Although blacks largely rejected the Communist Party's revolutionary ideology, its critique of capitalism aided their understanding of the depression, and its commitment to equality had enormous appeal.

The Communist Party's successful defense in the **Scottsboro Boys case** enhanced its reputation with blacks. In March 1931, nine young black men had hopped a freight train in Chattanooga, Tennessee, headed south. Also on board were two young white women, who, when the train stopped at Paint Rock, Alabama, falsely accused the black teenagers of rape. The nine young men were arrested and jailed, but as fears of a lynching grew, authorities moved them to nearby Scottsboro. After an all-white jury and a white judge sentenced the teens, who came to be known as the Scottsboro Boys, to death, the Communist Party publicly condemned what it called a "legal lynching" and set in motion a defense that eventually saved the lives of the defendants in a series of trials over many years. Two cases went to the U.S. Supreme Court, which overturned the teens' convictions on constitutional grounds. In *Powell v. Alabama* (1932), the Court ruled that defendants in capital trials have a right to counsel, and in *Norris v. Alabama* (1935) it ruled that potential jurors may not be excluded from juries on the basis of race. By then the Scottsboro Boys had become well known, as the Communist Party mobilized world opinion on their behalf through marches, fund-raisers, concerts, speeches, posters, and buttons. The success of this campaign impressed African Americans, many of whom participated in these party-led activities.

The Scottsboro Boys
This photograph of the nine Scottsboro Boys was taken while they were being held in the Jefferson County Jail in Birmingham, Alabama, on false charges that they had raped two young white women, Victoria Price and Ruby Bates, on a freight train in March 1931. An international effort to free them, led by the Communist Party's International Labor Defense, eventually helped secure their release. Standing, left to right, are Clarence Norris, age 19; Ozie Powell, 18; Haywood Patterson, 19; Roy Wright, 15; Charlie Weems, 20; and Eugene Williams, 16. Sitting, left to right, are Andrew Wright, 19; Olen Montgomery, 17; and Willie Roberson, 19. *CSU Archives/Everett Collection.*

The Communist Party also led efforts to organize the Alabama Sharecroppers Union, intended as a biracial union but eventually led by blacks, who joined because of its commitment to raising prices and wages and ending discrimination in New Deal agricultural programs. In another court case, the party successfully defended one of its organizers, Angelo Herndon, who in 1932 had been sent to prison for leading a biracial demonstration of unemployed workers. In 1937, the U.S. Supreme Court overturned Herndon's conviction, declaring Georgia's nineteenth-century anti-insurrection statute unconstitutional. More than any other largely white political organization, the Communist Party took action to end racial oppression. Although it did not have many black members, it had many black sympathizers and admirers. (See Document Project: Communist Radicalism and Everyday Realities, pp. 428–35.)

Thus when John P. Davis and other black leaders called for a nationwide black front of civil rights organizations in 1935, the Communist Party responded. The need for such a front had been reinforced by a riot in Harlem in 1935 that had targeted white-owned property. This signaled a new pattern in racial violence, which formerly had been instigated mostly by white mobs attacking black victims. More than 800 delegates representing almost 500 organizations — with the notable exception of the NAACP — met in Chicago in 1936 to found the **National Negro Congress**. Participants included intellectuals such as Alain Locke and Ralph Bunche of Howard University, civil rights leaders (including dissident NAACP members), black religious groups, white and black labor activists, and Communists. Elected its president, A. Philip Randolph committed the congress to interracial labor organizing and action.

Though hamstrung by a lack of money, the National Negro Congress went on the offensive. On the local level, almost seventy chapters pushed for fair hiring, housing, and relief. On the national level, however, as Communists and labor activists gained influence and the congress became more militant and secular, black religious groups withdrew their support. Ultimately, the radicals alienated those who believed that working-class concerns were obstructing the interests of black business. Randolph resigned in 1940, charging that Communists had infiltrated and overrun the organization. By then, it had already begun its descent.

Meanwhile, the NAACP, which denounced the Communist Party and was increasingly critical of racism within the labor movement, was itself criticized for overlooking the needs of black workers. W. E. B. Du Bois had resigned from the *Crisis* in 1934, and the organization was increasingly considered middle-class and middle-of-the-road. Its membership had declined as more activist black organizations arose, but beginning in 1934 a new initiative to overturn segregation, led by special legal counsel Charles Hamilton Houston, reenergized the group. Houston, as dean of Howard University Law School, had pioneered the field of civil rights law and trained a cadre of black lawyers, among them future U.S. Supreme Court justice Thurgood Marshall. In 1939, Houston helped create a legal division within the NAACP called the Legal Defense and Educational Fund.

Houston's plan was to demonstrate that the separate but equal doctrine established in 1896 by *Plessy v. Ferguson* (see chapter 9) denied blacks their Fourteenth Amendment rights to due process and equal protection under the laws. He started with a series of suits demanding that all separate black schools be made equal to white schools and that black teacher salaries be made the same as white teacher salaries. The purpose of this short-term strategy of equalization was twofold: to show states and localities that they could not afford dual educational systems and to lay the groundwork for a direct challenge to segregation's constitutionality. NAACP lawyers targeted the common southern state practice of paying the out-of-state tuition for blacks who agreed to attend graduate and professional schools in other states. In *Pearson v. Murray* (1936), the Maryland Court of Appeals ruled that the University of Maryland's refusal to admit Donald Murray, an Amherst College graduate, to its law school violated Murray's citizenship rights. In another important NAACP legal victory, *Missouri ex rel. Gaines v. Canada* (1938), the U.S. Supreme Court ruled that Lloyd Gaines, a Missouri resident, had to be admitted to Missouri's all-white law school because the state failed to provide an equal legal education for blacks. These were the first steps in a campaign that would culminate with the overturning of *Plessy* in *Brown v. Board of Education of Topeka* (1954), argued before the Supreme Court by Thurgood Marshall.

Black Culture in Hard Times

One New Deal program with direct benefits for individual African Americans was the Works Progress Administration (WPA), established in 1935 to pump federal money into public works projects that hired people who needed jobs. The WPA not only built roads, bridges, and parks; it also sponsored programs, such as the Federal Writers' Project, that employed writers, artists, musicians, and actors. In turn, the WPA brightened the grim decade of the Great Depression. For some it was a lifeline. Zora Neale Hurston, for example, was hired by the WPA to collect folklore from Florida's back roads and turpentine camps, where highly exploited black workers extracting turpentine from pine trees lived and labored, often reduced to peonage. The study to which she contributed, "The Florida Negro," ultimately included slave narratives. Today transcripts of WPA interviews with more than two thousand former slaves, all of whom were then at least in their seventies, are a rich documentary resource (see chapter 8). The work that Hurston did for the WPA paralleled her research interests, and in the 1930s she published two collections of African American folklore, *Mules and Men* (1935) and *Tell My Horse* (1938). Her most acclaimed work of fiction, *Their Eyes Were Watching God* (1937), is also grounded in African American folk culture, centering on the maturation of Janie, its protagonist, who finds within herself the means to triumph over poverty, sexism, and racism.

Richard Wright, a young black author who also worked for the WPA, criticized Hurston's fiction for its lack of social protest. In "Blueprint for Negro Writing" (1937), he rejected the "humble novels, poems, and plays" of the Harlem Renaissance writers, whom he characterized as pandering to the interests of white audiences. Wright announced a new agenda: "Today the question is: Shall Negro writing be for the Negro masses, moulding the lives and consciousness of those masses toward new goals, or shall it continue begging the question of the Negroes' humanity?"[28] Wright was a strong and angry new voice for naturalism and art with a political purpose. He joined the Communist Party in Chicago before moving to New York, where he influenced another young black writer working for the WPA, Ralph Ellison. Wright's early fiction reflected a Marxist conception of art by showing how economic forces shaped African American destiny. His 1938 collection of short stories, *Uncle Tom's Children*, probed the racial conflict and violence of the Jim Crow South, and his novel *Native Son* (1940) exhibited the same forces at work in the Chicago ghetto. Selected by the

Book-of-the-Month Club for nationwide distribution, *Native Son* was a huge commercial success, evidence that there was now a broad audience for works by black writers that did not stay within the limits of white expectations. Within a few years, Wright publicly repudiated the Communist Party, but he soon repudiated the United States as well, moving to Paris, where he lived for the rest of his life. Paris was the home of Négritude, a cultural movement allied with Pan-Africanism. Both Négritude and Pan-Africanism promoted black self-affirmation. Négritude was led by writers from French colonies, notably Léopold Sédar Senghor of Senegal, Aimé Césaire of Martinique, and Léon Damas of Guiana. The movement called for a common black identity among Africans dispersed throughout the world, opposed French colonialism, and generally favored Marxism.

Many African American visual artists of the period studied in Paris, where they found support and encouragement, but their subjects and themes often remained African American. Archibald Motley, best known for *The Picnic* (1936), painted many scenes of black Chicago and was hired by the WPA to paint murals on school walls. WPA public works projects were often enhanced by murals, including those that Aaron Douglas painted at the Harlem branch of the New York Public Library in 1934. Palmer Hayden, returning from study in Paris, worked on WPA art projects while painting scenes of African American life. His *Midsummer Night in Harlem* (1938) invoked a folk style to convey the festive atmosphere of neighbors escaping the heat of airless tenements. Also in Harlem, the sculptor Augusta Savage supervised a WPA art center, where she nurtured the talent of African Americans such as the painter Jacob Lawrence, whose *The Migration of the Negro* (1940–1941), a series of narrative panel paintings, recorded the recent black past. Asked to create a sculpture for the 1939 New York World's Fair, Savage presented *Lift Every Voice and Sing*, inspired by the Negro National Anthem, to honor African American musical contributions to the arts.

Nearly fifty years earlier, at the 1893 Chicago World's Fair, a display by African Americans had been rejected (see chapter 9). That an African American was now commissioned to exhibit her work is indicative of the status that was accorded black creativity in the 1930s. Recognition for achievement in the arts and in sports did not translate to civil equality, however. White Americans enjoyed black music, and in the clubs of Harlem they applauded when jazz vocalist Billie Holiday sang "Strange Fruit," her haunting signature song protesting lynching. Yet during the 1930s, more than one hundred blacks were lynched. White audiences sold out performances by Paul Robeson — a concert singer and actor with a magnificent bass voice — but his talents were all too often fenced in by stereotypes. Still, Robeson excelled at singing spirituals, folk songs from around the world, and European concert music. He met with wide acclaim in performing the role of Othello and the title role in the film version of Eugene O'Neill's *The Emperor Jones* (1933). His rendition of "Ol' Man River" in the movie *Show Boat* (1936) made him famous. But he felt constrained by American expectations that he should play only "Negro roles" and found attractive the relative absence of race and class prejudice that he personally experienced in the Soviet Union. An ardent internationalist and anticolonialist, Robeson, increasingly a global citizen, did innumerable benefits for freedom struggles and left-wing causes around the world.

Movies and radio were popular pastimes in the 1930s, offering an escape from the decade's hard times. But while they popularized black culture, they also perpetuated stereotypes. Even baseball, the most American of pastimes, was segregated. Banned from the major leagues in 1887, black baseball players got a chance to play ball after Andrew "Rube" Foster founded the Negro National League in 1920. It had an eight-team circuit: the Cuban Stars and seven city-based teams from St. Louis, Kansas City, Indianapolis, Dayton, Detroit, and Chicago (which had two teams). Games were played after folks got off work, with Sunday doubleheaders drawing crowds up to 10,000. The depression and Foster's death in 1930 sent the league into a tailspin, but it was revived in 1934, and by 1937 a second league, the Negro American League, had been founded. The giants of the Negro baseball leagues, such as pitcher Satchel Paige and catcher Josh Gibson, were wildly popular.

While all Americans cheered for track-and-field star Jesse Owens when he won four gold medals at the Berlin Olympics in 1936, his fellow African Americans cheered especially loudly. His outstanding performances included tying the world record in the 100-meter sprint and setting world records in the long jump, 200-meter sprint, and 400-meter relay. For black Americans, Owens's success was a strong refutation of the myth of Aryan supremacy so crucial to Nazism and the totalitarian regime of Adolf Hitler, who had intended that the Berlin games would showcase his racial theories.

Boxing was deeply political. When Joe Louis, "the Brown Bomber," knocked out the Italian heavyweight boxer Primo Carnera in 1935, his victory was seen as a blow to fascist Italy. For black Americans, it had a special meaning after Italy invaded Ethiopia, an independent African nation that had resisted colonial rule. The invasion was widely denounced in the black press, and black Americans supported the Ethiopians with financial contributions, medical supplies, and a hospital for the wounded. The event strengthened African American internationalism even as it signaled the dangers of totalitarian aggression.

Each major achievement by an African American seemed to be not only an individual success but also a step forward in the black freedom struggle. When Joe Louis defeated Jim Braddock in June 1937 with an eighth-round knockout for the world heavyweight boxing title, blacks glued to their radios erupted in joy. The next year, when Louis defeated Max Schmeling to avenge an earlier loss to the German boxer, the victory was another repudiation of white supremacy. "The Brown Bomber" was embraced as a national hero, but among blacks pride in his achievement felt personal. "He belongs to us," noted the popular black entertainer Lena Horne.[29]

On a cold and windy Easter Sunday in 1939, 75,000 Americans, black and white, gathered at the Lincoln Memorial to hear the great African American contralto

Marian Anderson sing. The concert had been arranged with the help of First Lady Eleanor Roosevelt after the Daughters of the American Revolution, of which Roosevelt was a member, had refused to allow Anderson to perform in its Constitution Hall. Roosevelt resigned from the organization, and as a member of the NAACP, she worked with Walter White to enlist the support of the U.S. secretary of the interior for an outdoor concert in a meaningful public venue. The Lincoln Memorial concert was a strong national protest against discrimination, a vivid demonstration of the increasing influence of the African American freedom struggle, and a resounding success. Standing in front of microphones that broadcast the concert to millions, Anderson opened with the patriotic anthem "America," which begins with the words "My country, 'tis of thee."

Marian Anderson at the Lincoln Memorial
This striking image of the crowd assembled to hear the great African American contralto Marian Anderson sing on Easter Sunday, April 9, 1939, captures a transformative moment in African American protest history. As an opera and concert star, Anderson had marvelously represented her country around the world. That fact made the refusal of the Daughters of the American Revolution to permit her to perform at Constitution Hall all the more galling. This mass protest was among the first to use the sacred national space of the Lincoln Memorial to make a powerful statement on behalf of racial equality. *Courtesy Everett Collection.*

CONCLUSION

Mass Movements and Mass Culture

Marian Anderson closed that epic concert with the Negro spiritual "Nobody Knows the Trouble I've Seen." All who heard Anderson knew of the "troubles" that had long confronted her and other African Americans. Black culture, however, had entered mass culture and changed American culture. Since 1915, African Americans had become both more visible and more powerful. Waves of migrants from the South swelled the metropolises of the North, changing their demographics and the nature of urban life. Black Americans who had served loyally in World War I returned ready to make America pay attention to the New Negro and live up to the promise of democracy.

As black organizations became mass organizations, black protest, lobbying, and litigation broadened and strengthened. Some groups welcomed white support and cooperation; others rejected it. All of these organizations and the publications they sponsored provided an institutional base for research into the conditions of black life that generated a new, nationwide awareness of the New Negro and a new understanding of prejudice and racial conflict. With concentrations of black voters in Negro districts and black workers in certain industries, the black presence could no longer be ignored. Two of this era's developments stand out: the rise and fall of Marcus Garvey's Universal Negro Improvement Association and the spectacular flourishing of the writers, artists, and musicians of what came to be called the Harlem Renaissance. Even as African American artists debated the character of the New Negro and the nature of their own black identity, their creativity intrigued white Americans, who increasingly reacted with admiration and respect for this bold black cultural assertiveness.

As the nation plunged into the Great Depression, individual and collective black struggle and broad-based black activism deepened. Intensifying African American demands pushed the federal government to respond increasingly to black concerns for the first time since Reconstruction. Black leaders within the federal government increasingly looked out for the welfare of their race. Despite the hard times of the 1930s, black culture flourished within the confines of racial expectations and also broke through them, constituting a cultural front in the larger black freedom struggle. Toward the end of the decade, as totalitarian regimes in Germany, Italy, and Japan embarked on conquests that would soon bring on a second world war, black Americans were positioned to demand democracy at home as never before.

CHAPTER 10 **REVIEW**

KEY TERMS

REVIEW QUESTIONS

1. Describe the tensions — between blacks and whites and between newer and more established northern blacks — brought about by the great migration. What challenges did the newcomers face, and how did they seek to address these challenges?

2. How did World War I bring about social change both for African Americans who fought in the war and for those who remained on the home front?

3. Consider the various intellectual, political, social, and cultural developments that accompanied the rise of the New Negro. What did the efforts of the black social scientists, scholars, artists, writers, and activists who pioneered this movement have in common? What were their goals?

4. How did black politicians, activists, wageworkers, authors, and artists seek to address the specific problems that the depression and the New Deal posed for African Americans? What were the results of their efforts?

Communist Radicalism and Everyday Realities

Founded in 1919, the Communist Party of the United States (CPUSA) pursued an aggressive program for organizing the country's laboring masses while maintaining vital connections to international communism. Despite Red scare repression, when all labor radicalism was equated with communism and socialism, the CPUSA soon committed itself to large and inclusive labor unions. Between 1928 and 1935, the party developed a plan for recruiting African Americans, especially those in the South, whom it viewed as a minority with the right of self-determination and the potential for constituting an all-black forty-ninth state. Between 1935 and 1939, the party shifted dramatically to a Popular Front platform that sought to unite progressive elements, including the black freedom struggle, the labor movement, and left-wing organizations, under the slogan "Communism is twentieth-century Americanism." After initially throwing its support behind the Soviet Union and opposing the United States' entry into World War II, the party shifted its position in 1941 to all-out support for the U.S. war effort.

Black support for the CPUSA grew during the Great Depression primarily because of the party's anti-imperialist, anticolonialist, and, most important, antiracist work. The party's strong support for interracial unions, keen opposition to Jim Crow, and striking encouragement of black culture were crucial to building its small yet committed base of black members. Communist theories of anticapitalist social and economic organization appealed to many blacks, including those such as Richard Wright who were party members at one time or another, as well as innumerable supporters and "fellow travelers" (known for their sympathy with Communist views) who never joined the party.

But it was the party's call for worker solidarity and social equality that appealed to black sharecroppers and workers, as Angelo Herndon's experience attests. In addition, the party's successful defense of Herndon and the Scottsboro Boys through its legal arm, the International Labor Defense, indicated not only a compelling commitment to racial equality but also an inspiring willingness to defend blacks charged with criminal offenses at a time when other groups shied away from such involvement.

The racial egalitarian or antiracist politics of the CPUSA reflected a broader and increasingly powerful current among the era's progressives. The ongoing crisis of the Great Depression brought together the cultural and political struggles of marginalized groups such as African Americans, who used artistic expressions to promote racial and economic justice. The three photographs included here are representative of the large body of progressive cultural work that emerged during this period. These photographs are part of a collection of 60,000 photographs taken for the Resettlement Administration (RA) and the Farm Security Administration (FSA) between 1935 and 1942, almost exclusively in rural and small-town America, by a stellar array of white documentary photographers, including Walker Evans, Dorothea Lange, Ben Shahn, and Marion Post Wolcott. The soon-to-be-famous black photographer and filmmaker Gordon Parks began taking photographs for the FSA in 1942. Two key aims of these photographs in particular and of the massive photo-documentary project in general were to expose problems that the FSA needed to address and to showcase the agency's efforts to address those problems. What social and economic issues are represented in these photographs? How might these photographs be used to support an antiracist agenda?

Communism's appeal for African Americans did not last. Herndon and Wright repudiated the party in the 1940s, and in the face of a second Red scare in the 1950s and 1960s, many other blacks took care to distance themselves from the CPUSA, which its enemies saw as fomenting revolution in the United States, sometimes in conspiracy with the evolving modern civil rights movement. The following documents, however, reveal much about the party's appeal for a growing number of blacks at a time when rampant economic inequality, racial injustice, and the Great Depression emboldened black criticism of capitalism, leading some to reject it altogether in favor of communism.

W. E. B. Du Bois | *Negro Editors on Communism: A Symposium of the American Negro Press, 1932*

In 1932, amid the worsening Great Depression, W. E. B. DU BOIS (1868–1963) asked African American newspaper editors to comment on communism for the *Crisis*. Two responses follow. None of the editors who contributed their thoughts were members of the Communist Party, but they clearly understood the appeal of its efforts to bridge the racial divide.

Carl Murphy |
Baltimore Afro-American

The Communists appear to be the only party going our way. They are as radical as the N.A.A.C.P. were twenty years ago.

Since the abolitionists passed off the scene, no white group of national prominence has openly advocated the economic, political and social equality of black folks.

Mr. Clarence Darrow° speaking in Washington recently declared that we should not care what

political candidates think of prohibition, the League of Nations, the tariff or any other general issue. What we should demand, Mr. Darrow said, is candidates who are right on all questions affecting the colored people. I agree with him.

Communism would appeal to Mr. Darrow if he were in my place.

Communists in Maryland saved Orphan Jones° from a legal lynching. They secured a change of venue from the mob-ridden Easton [Eastern] Shore.

° Clarence Darrow (1857–1938), the most prominent lawyer of his day, was known for defending the underdog. He successfully argued the case of Ossian Sweet for the NAACP but is best remembered for defending John T. Scopes in a 1925 trial in Tennessee involving the teaching of evolution in schools.

SOURCE: Bedford St. Martin's wishes to thank the Crisis Publishing Co., Inc., the publisher of the magazine of the National Association of the Advancement of Colored People, for the use of this material first published in the April and May 1932 issue of *Crisis* magazine.

° Euel Lee (1873–1933), known as "Orphan Jones," was accused of murdering a white family in Taylorsville, Maryland, in October 1931. Bernard Ades, a member of a Communist group that was active in racial justice issues, took on Lee's defense and arranged a change of venue for the trial, to Towson, outside Baltimore, where it was heard in the court of Judge Frank I. Duncan. Lee was convicted and, following several unsuccessful appeals, was hanged in October 1933.

They fought the exclusion of colored men from the jury, and on that ground financed an appeal of the case to Maryland's highest court. They compelled estimable Judge Duncan of Towson, Maryland, to testify that he had never considered colored people in picking jurors in his court for twenty-six years.

The Communists are going our way, for which Allah be praised.

W. P. Dabney | *Cincinnati Union*

It is as hard for people who are prosperous to visualize the great growth of Communism among American Citizens, as it is for them to realize the suffering that drives folk into its folds.

The Negro has, for many reasons, been considered immune to participation in such movement. His good humor and adaptability to vicissitudes of fortune are proverbial. His vast faith in the beatitudes of Eternity that gave birth to this song, "You may have all the world but give me Jesus." Last but not least, the class or caste of white Communists. From the earliest days of slavery, the Negro was taught by his owners to hate the "Po white man," for they knew the value of keeping the enemy divided.

That hatred, almost venomous in its intensity, was so sincerely reciprocated, that though sixty-six years have fled since [Confederate general Robert E.] Lee bowed his head in defeat, caste in the South has lost neither spite nor opportunity for its indulgence. But, "the age of miracles" has not passed! "The unexpected has happened!" Thousands of Colored Citizens have joined the Communists, and far more thousands leniently look in that direction. Poor Negroes now gather in parks and halls. They have lost their humor and their God. "If One exists," they say, "He is the friend of the rich, a patron of preachers, those fatted parasites who should be exterminated."

They argue that they have all to gain, nothing to lose. That better to die fighting like men than starve or fall victims to lynchers, as have thousands of their innocent brethren. "*Equal rights,*" the goal for which they strive. *They are sick,* of the U.S. Constitution with its impotent laws, political parties reeking with hypocrisy, philanthropists whose gold-fed institutions emasculate our intelligentsia and blind the pathetically small number of white friends to "Color" Segregation, that most cruel of all castes.

The Communists came, not bringing charity but brotherhood, not bringing words but deeds! What matters motive? When a man is drowning does he demand reasons for the helping hand? "'Tis an ill wind that blows nobody good." The world is beginning to see the tragedy that rocks and shocks "The Souls of Black Folk." Driven to desperation, they are thinking! Why should they be barred, segregated, deprived of opportunity because of circumstances beyond their control? Is it any wonder that thousands are yielding to Communism's appeal?

There will be no Black Communists in America when fair play rules, merit is recognized, race prejudice ostracised. Will Pharaoh Heed?

Angelo Herndon | *You Cannot Kill the Working Class, 1934*

ANGELO HERNDON (1913–1997), the son of an Ohio miner, began working in the mines at age thirteen. By age seventeen, he was in Birmingham, Alabama, working for the Tennessee Coal, Iron and Railroad Company. In this passage from his autobiographical pamphlet, which he wrote in 1934 with the assistance of the International Labor Defense (ILD), the Communist Party's legal defense arm, he describes his introduction to the Communist Party and his reasons for joining. He wrote the pamphlet, titled *You Cannot Kill the Working Class*, while in jail for allegedly inciting an insurrection, a conviction the ILD succeeded in getting the U.S. Supreme Court to overturn in 1937. The pamphlet depicts the hope the party offered to workers who felt they had nowhere to turn during the Great Depression.

One day in June, 1930, walking home from work, I came across some handbills put out by the Unemployment Council in Birmingham. They said: "Would you rather fight — or starve?" They called on the workers to come to a mass meeting at 3 o'clock.

Somehow I never thought of missing that meeting. I said to myself over and over: "It's war! It's war! And I might as well get into it right now!" I got to the meeting while a white fellow was speaking. I didn't get everything he said, but this much hit me and stuck with me: that the workers could only get things by fighting for them, and that the Negro and white workers had to stick together to get results. The speaker described the conditions of the Negroes in Birmingham, and I kept saying to myself: "That's it." Then a Negro spoke from the same platform, and somehow I knew that this was what I'd been looking for all my life.

At the end of the meeting I went up and gave my name. From that day to this, every minute of my life has been tied up with the workers' movement.

I joined the Unemployment Council, and some weeks later the Communist Party. I read all the literature of the movement that I could get my hands on, and began to see my way more clearly.

I had some mighty funny ideas at first, but I guess that was only natural. For instance, I thought that we ought to start by getting all the big Negro leaders like De Priest and Du Bois and Walter White into the Communist Party, and then we would have all the support we needed. I didn't know then that De Priest and the rest of

the leaders of that type are on the side of the bosses, and fight as hard as they can against the workers. They don't believe in fighting against the system that produces Jim-Crowism. They stand up for that system, and try to preserve it, and so they are really on the side of Jim-Crowism and inequality. I got rid of all these ideas after I heard Oscar Adams and others like him speak in Birmingham. . . .

I look back over what I've written about those days since I picked up the leaflet of the Unemployment Council, and wonder if I've really said what I mean. I don't know if I can get across to you the feeling that came over me whenever I went to a meeting of the Council, or of the Communist Party, and heard their speakers and read their leaflets. All my life I'd been sweated and stepped on and Jim-Crowed. I lay on my belly in the mines for a few dollars a week, and saw my pay stolen and slashed, and my buddies killed. I lived in the worst section of town, and rode behind the "Colored" signs on streetcars, as though there was something disgusting about me. I heard myself called "nigger" and "darky," and I had to say "Yes, sir" to every white man, whether he had my respect or not.

I had always detested it, but I had never known that anything could be done about it. And here, all of a sudden, I had found organizations in which Negroes and whites sat together, and worked together, and knew no difference of race or color. Here were organizations that weren't scared to come out for equality for the Negro people, and for the rights of the workers. The Jim-Crow system, the wage-slave system, weren't everlasting after all! It was like all of a sudden turning a corner on a dirty, old street and finding yourself facing a broad, shining highway. . . .

SOURCE: August Meier, Elliott Rudwick, and Francis L. Broderick, eds., *Black Protest Thought in the Twentieth Century*, 2nd ed. (Indianapolis: Bobbs-Merrill, 1971), 138–41.

In June, 1930, I was elected a delegate to the National Unemployment Convention in Chicago. . . .

In Chicago, I got my first broad view of the revolutionary workers' movement. I met workers from almost every state in the union, and I heard about the work of the same kind of organizations in other countries, and it first dawned on me how strong and powerful the working-class was. There wasn't only me and a few others in Birmingham. There were hundreds, thousands, millions of us!

Richard Wright | 12 Million Black Voices, 1941

RICHARD WRIGHT (1908–1960), the brilliant and ambitious son of impoverished Mississippians, left home as a teenager and arrived in Chicago in 1927. There he worked at various jobs, including mail sorter for the post office, until the Great Depression left him jobless, forcing him to scuffle and even go on relief at one point. An aspiring writer and a keen observer of worker despair, he joined the Communist Party in 1933. Disillusioned, he left the party in 1942. In the 1930s, his literary aspirations flowered, encouraged by an impressive group of fellow black writers, including Margaret Walker and Frank Marshall Davis; Communist colleagues; and Works Progress Administration support. His 1940 novel *Native Son* was a sensation, and Viking Press asked him to write the text for a book of photographs of black life taken for the Farm Security Administration. The result was *12 Million Black Voices: A Folk History of the Negro in the United States*, from which the following passage is excerpted. Look for Wright's depiction of the impersonal forces shaping black life and his ideas about labor.

We are the children of the black sharecroppers, the first-born of the city tenements. . . .

We are a folk born of cultural devastation, slavery, physical suffering, unrequited longing, abrupt emancipation, migration, disillusionment, bewilderment, joblessness, and insecurity — all enacted within a *short* space of historical time! . . .

The general dislocation of life during the depression caused many white workers to learn through chronic privation that they could not protect their standards of living so long as we blacks were excluded from their unions. Many hundreds of thousands of them found that they could not fight successfully for increased wages and union recognition unless we stood shoulder to shoulder with them. As a consequence, many of us have recently become members of steel, auto, packing, and tobacco unions.

In 1929, when millions of us black folk were jobless, many unemployed white workers joined with us on a national scale to urge relief measures and adequate housing. The influence of this united effort spread even into the South where black and white sharecroppers were caught in the throes of futile conflict. . . .

. . . We found that many white workers were eager to have us in their organizations, and we were proud to feel that at last our strength was sufficient to awaken in others a desire to work with us. . . . In this way we encountered for the first time in our lives the full effect of those forces that tended to reshape our folk consciousness, and a few of us stepped forth and accepted within the confines of our personalities the death of our old folk lives, an acceptance of a death that

SOURCE: *12 Million Black Voices*, by Richard Wright. Copyright © 1941 by Richard Wright. Reprinted by permission of John Hawkins & Associates, Inc. and the Estate of Richard Wright.

enabled us to cross class and racial lines, a death that made us free. . . .

. . . In many large cities there were sturdy minorities of us, both black and white, who banded together in disciplined, class-conscious groups and created new organs of action and expression. We were able to seize nine black boys in a jail in Scottsboro, Alabama, lift them so high in our collective hands, focus such a battery of comment and interpretation upon them, that they became symbols to all the world of the plight of black folk in America.

If we had been allowed to participate in the vital processes of America's national growth, what would have been the texture of our lives, the pattern of our traditions, the routine of our customs, the state of our arts, the code of our laws, the function of our government! Whatever others may say, we black folk say that America would have been stronger and greater!

Russell Lee | *Negro Drinking at "Colored" Water Cooler in Streetcar Terminal, Oklahoma City, Oklahoma, 1939*

The well-dressed young black man in this photograph must have been thirsty. He drinks from a disposable cup at a primitive water cooler that is neither inviting nor particularly clean. The state of the floor and walls reinforces the overall impression of uncleanliness. Interestingly, to his left are bathrooms for "white" and "colored" women, and on the other side are bathrooms for "white" and "colored" men. The photograph, however, does not show what we assume are racially separate bathrooms around each corner.

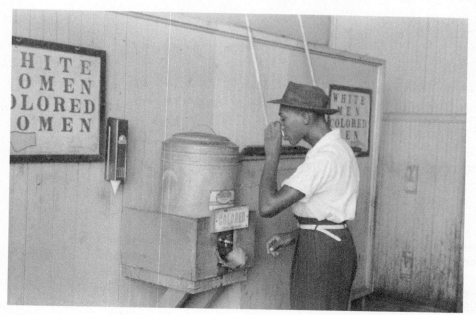

1939 photo by Russell Lee/Library of Congress, Farm Security Administration Office/Office of War Information Photograph Collection, LC-DIG-fas-8a26761.

Arthur Rothstein | *Girl at Gee's Bend, 1937*

The most arresting aspect of this photograph is the expression on the young girl's face. How are we to interpret her expression? What does that expression suggest she might be thinking about? Also noteworthy are the image's class politics as well as its racial politics, especially the stinging critique of racial and class privilege that is clearly represented in the biting juxtaposition of the harshly unjust world of black childhood poverty with the more carefree world of the middle-class white woman visible in the tattered newspaper covering the window.

Also titled "Artella Bendolph," 1937 photo by Arthur Rothstein/Library of Congress, Farm Security Administration Office/Office of War Information Photograph Collection, LC-DIG-fsa-8b35942.

Marion Post Wolcott | *Negroes Jitterbugging in a Juke Joint on Saturday Afternoon, Clarksdale, Mississippi Delta, 1939*

The well-dressed young black people having a good time in the following photograph are a prime example of the social solidarity among youth, the working class, and ordinary folks. For many, work was too often a site of oppression, sorrow, and pain, so they welcomed the opportunity to let loose and enjoy each other's company. That the photo features a woman doing fancy dance moves highlights the fact that the need and desire for pleasure are not gendered but human. The presence of the white policeman signifies the omnipresent white surveillance of black lives under Jim Crow.

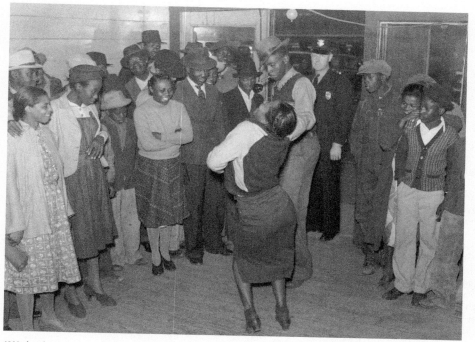

1939 photo by Marion Post Wolcott/Library of Congress, Farm Security Administration Office/Office of War Information Photograph Collection, LC-DIG-fsa-8c10917.

QUESTIONS FOR ANALYSIS

1. Why did communism appeal to an increasing number of African Americans in the 1930s?

2. Like the Socialist Party, the Communist Party sought to unite workers along class lines and across race lines. What was the black response to this effort?

3. Consider the ways in which the different political parties responded to the concerns of African Americans. What were the responses of the Democratic and Republican Parties? How did these compare with the response of the Communist Party?

4. How do the perspectives shown in the FSA photographs influence how you perceive African American life during the Great Depression? How do the artists' choices, such as camera angle and photographic subject, influence your view of African Americans of this time?

5. Compare and contrast the racial politics of the Communist Party with the racial politics of ordinary black life represented in these documents. How were these politics alike? How did they differ?

6. How do these two kinds of racial politics illustrate the cultural politics, or dynamic interaction between culture and politics, of this era?

NOTES

1. "Additional Letters of Negro Migrants of 1916–1918," comp. Emmett J. Scott, *Journal of Negro History* 4, no. 4 (October 1919): 447.

2. "Letters of Negro Migrants of 1916–1918," comp. Emmett J. Scott, *Journal of Negro History* 4, no. 3 (July 1919): 318.

3. Ibid., 295.

4. Ibid., 319.

5. Ibid., 298.

6. James Grossman, "Chicago and the 'Great Migration,'" *Migration*, Illinois Periodicals Online (IPO) Project, Northern Illinois University Libraries, http://www.lib.niu.edu/1996/iht329633.html.

7. Quoted in Eric Arnesen, "Introduction: The Great American Protest," in *Black Protest and the Great Migration: A Brief History with Documents* (Boston: Bedford/St. Martin's, 2003), 11.

8. Quoted in James R. Grossman, *Land of Hope: Chicago, Black Southerners, and the Great Migration* (Chicago: University of Chicago Press, 1989), 157.

9. Chicago Commission on Race Relations, *The Negro in Chicago: A Study of Race Relations and a Race Riot* (Chicago: University of Chicago Press, 1922), 122.

10. Quoted in Davarian L. Baldwin, *Chicago's New Negroes: Modernity, the Great Migration, and Black Urban Life* (Chapel Hill: University of North Carolina Press, 2007), 64.

11. "Close Ranks," *Crisis* 16, no. 3 (July 1918): 111.

12. Quoted in Arnesen, *Black Protest and the Great Migration*, 20–21.

13. Ibid., 86.

14. Walter White, "Chicago and Its Eight Reasons," *Crisis* 18, no. 6 (1919): 297.

15. Claude McKay, "If We Must Die," in *The Norton Anthology of African American Literature*, ed. Henry Louis Gates Jr. and Nellie Y. McKay (New York: Norton, 1997), 984.

16. A. Philip Randolph and Chandler Owen, "The New Negro — What Is He?" *Messenger* 2 (August 1920): 73–74, in Jeffrey B. Ferguson, *The Harlem Renaissance: A Brief History with Documents* (Boston: Bedford/St. Martin's, 2008), 40–41.

17. James Weldon Johnson, *Black Manhattan* (New York: Knopf, 1930), in Ferguson, *The Harlem Renaissance*, 46, 54.

18. Arthur A. Schomburg, "The Negro Digs Up His Past" (1925), in Gates and McKay, *The Norton Anthology of African American Literature*, 937.

19. Quoted in Claude McKay, *Harlem: Negro Metropolis* (New York: Dutton, 1940), 154, cited in E. David Cronon, ed., *Great Lives Observed: Marcus Garvey* (Englewood Cliffs, NJ: Prentice-Hall, 1973), 5.

20. Lawrence W. Levine, "Marcus Garvey and the Politics of Revitalization," in *Black Leaders of the Twentieth Century*, ed. John Hope Franklin and August Meier (Urbana: University of Illinois Press, 1982), 121.

21. Cited in A. Jacques Garvey, *Garvey and Garveyism* (Kingston, Jamaica: United Printers, 1963), 50.

22. W. E. B. Du Bois, "Opinion of W. E. B. Du Bois," *Crisis* 28, no. 1 (May 1924): 8.

23. Alain Locke, "Harlem," *Survey Graphic* 6 (March 1925), reprinted in Ferguson, *The Harlem Renaissance*, 79.

24. Ibid., 80.

25. W. E. B. Du Bois, "Criteria of Negro Art" (1926), in Ferguson, *The Harlem Renaissance*, 167.

26. Langston Hughes, "The Negro Artist and the Racial Mountain" (1926), in Ferguson, *The Harlem Renaissance*, 149, 154.

27. "The Patriot and the Partisan," *Pittsburgh Courier*, September 17, 1932.

28. Richard Wright, "Blueprint for Negro Writing" (1937), in Ferguson, *The Harlem Renaissance*, 172, 175.

29. Quoted in Lawrence W. Levine, *Black Culture and Black Consciousness: Afro-American Folk Thought from Slavery to Freedom* (New York: Oxford University Press, 1977), 434.

SUGGESTED REFERENCES

The Great Migration and the Great War

Arnesen, Eric. *Black Protest and the Great Migration: A Brief History with Documents*. Boston: Bedford/St. Martin's, 2003.

Baldwin, Davarian L. *Chicago's New Negroes: Modernity, the Great Migration, and Black Urban Life*. Chapel Hill: University of North Carolina Press, 2007.

Gottlieb, Peter. *Making Their Own Way: Southern Blacks' Migration to Pittsburgh, 1916–30*. Urbana: University of Illinois Press, 1987.

Gregory, James N. *The Southern Diaspora: How the Great Migrations of Black and White Southerners Transformed America*. Chapel Hill: University of North Carolina Press, 2005.

Grossman, James R. *Land of Hope: Chicago, Black Southerners, and the Great Migration*. Chicago: University of Chicago Press, 1989.

Phillips, Kimberley L. *AlabamaNorth: African-American Migrants, Community, and Working-Class Activism in Cleveland, 1915–45*. Urbana: University of Illinois Press, 1999.

Schneider, Mark Robert. *"We Return Fighting": The Civil Rights Movement in the Jazz Age*. Boston: Northeastern University Press, 2002.

Thomas, Richard W. *Life for Us Is What We Make It: Building Black Community in Detroit, 1915–1945*. Bloomington: Indiana University Press, 1992.

Trotter, Joe William, Jr. *Black Milwaukee: The Making of an Industrial Proletariat, 1915–45*. Urbana: University of Illinois Press, 1985.

Williams, Chad L. *Torchbearers of Democracy: African American Soldiers in the World War I Era*. Chapel Hill: University of North Carolina Press, 2010.

The New Negro Arrives

Goggin, Jacqueline. *Carter G. Woodson: A Life in Black History.* Baton Rouge: LSU Press, 1993.

Harold, Claudrena. *The Rise and Fall of the Garvey Movement in the Urban South, 1918–1942.* New York: Routledge, 2007.

Harris, William H. *Keeping the Faith: A. Philip Randolph, Milton P. Webster, and the Brotherhood of Sleeping Car Porters, 1925–37.* Urbana: University of Illinois Press, 1977.

Hill, Robert A., ed. *The Marcus Garvey and Universal Negro Improvement Association Papers.* 10 vols. Berkeley: University of California Press, 1983–2006.

Huggins, Nathan Irvin. *Harlem Renaissance.* New York: Oxford University Press, 1971.

Hutchinson, George T. *The Harlem Renaissance in Black and White.* Cambridge: Belknap Press of Harvard University Press, 1995.

Lewis, David Levering. *When Harlem Was in Vogue.* New York: Vintage, 1982.

Rolinson, Mary G. *Grassroots Garveyism: The Universal Negro Improvement Association in the Rural South, 1920–1927.* Chapel Hill: University of North Carolina Press, 2007.

Stein, Judith. *The World of Marcus Garvey: Race and Class in Modern Society.* Baton Rouge: LSU Press, 1991.

Wall, Cheryl A. *Women of the Harlem Renaissance.* Bloomington: Indiana University Press, 1995.

The Great Depression and the New Deal

Bates, Beth Tompkins. *Pullman Porters and the Rise of Protest Politics in Black America, 1925–1945.* Chapel Hill: University of North Carolina Press, 2001.

Cripps, Thomas. *Slow Fade to Black: The Negro in American Film, 1900–1942.* New York: Oxford University Press, 1977.

Goodman, James. *Stories of Scottsboro.* New York: Pantheon, 1994.

Kelley, Robin D. G. *Hammer and Hoe: Alabama Communists during the Great Depression.* Chapel Hill: University of North Carolina Press, 1990.

Kirby, John B. *Black Americans in the Roosevelt Era: Liberalism and Race.* Knoxville: University of Tennessee Press, 1980.

Naison, Mark. *Communists in Harlem during the Depression.* Urbana: University of Illinois Press, 1983.

Sammons, Jeffrey T. *Beyond the Ring: The Role of Boxing in American Society.* Urbana: University of Illinois Press, 1988.

Sitkoff, Harvard. *A New Deal for Blacks: The Emergence of Civil Rights as a National Issue.* Vol. 1., *The Depression Decade.* New York: Oxford University Press, 1978.

Sullivan, Patricia. *Days of Hope: Race and Democracy in the New Deal Era.* Chapel Hill: University of North Carolina Press, 1996.

Wolters, Raymond. *Negroes and the Great Depression: The Problem of Economic Recovery.* Westport, CT: Greenwood, 1970.

Fighting for a Double Victory in the World War II Era

1939–1948

CHRONOLOGY *Events specific to African American history are in purple. General United States history events are in black.*

1938	Charles Houston writes *New York Times* article protesting discrimination in armed forces
1940s	More than 1.5 million African Americans migrate out of South
1940	Frederick O'Neal and Abram Hill found American Negro Theatre in Harlem
	Walter White, A. Philip Randolph, and T. Arnold Hill demand elimination of segregation and discrimination in armed services
	First peacetime draft instituted
1940–1941	Thirteen lynchings reported in South
1941	President Franklin D. Roosevelt delivers Four Freedoms speech
	Randolph oversees March on Washington Movement
	Body of Private Felix Hall found hanging from tree at Fort Benning, Georgia
	Roosevelt issues Executive Order 8802
	Roosevelt and Winston Churchill sign Atlantic Charter
	Two hundred fifty white workers stage sit-down strike at Detroit's Packard Motor Car Company to protest promotion of two black workers
	United Service Organizations (USO) founded
	Japanese bomb Pearl Harbor
	United States declares war on Japan and Germany
1942	*Pittsburgh Courier* launches Double V campaign
	Roosevelt authorizes relocation and internment of 110,000 Japanese and Japanese Americans
	Twenty thousand white workers walk off job at Packard Motor Car Company to protest promotion of three black workers
	Three hundred fifty white workers shut down Dodge plant in Detroit to protest promotion of twenty-three black workers
	Congress of Racial Equality (CORE) founded
1943	William Hastie resigns as adviser to Secretary of War Henry Stimson
	By year's end, 242 racial battles have taken place in 47 cities
1944	Black regiments of Second Cavalry Division assigned to noncombat jobs in North Africa
	Smith v. Allwright declares all-white Texas Democratic primary illegal
	Servicemen's Readjustment Act, known as GI Bill, passed
	U.S. navy admits black women to WAVES
	Roosevelt reelected to fourth presidential term
1945	Roosevelt, Churchill, and Joseph Stalin meet at Yalta
	Roosevelt dies
	Germany surrenders
	United States drops atomic bombs on Hiroshima and Nagasaki
	Japan surrenders
1946	Columbia, Tennessee, race riot
	Morgan v. Virginia declares segregation in interstate bus travel illegal
1947	Jackie Robinson becomes first black major league baseball player
	Eight blacks and eight whites from CORE test *Morgan v. Virginia*
	President's Committee on Civil Rights issues report, *To Secure These Rights*
1948	President Harry S. Truman issues Executive Order 9981
1950	Althea Gibson becomes first African American to compete in U.S. National Tennis Championship
	National Basketball Association drafts its first black player, Charles "Chuck" Cooper

James Tillman and Evelyn Bates Mobilize for War

In 1941, twenty-one-year-old James Tillman of Pittsburgh signed up for what he thought would be a noncombat truck-driving job in the U.S. army. He ended up in the Ninety-Second Infantry Division, the only black unit to see ground combat in Europe in World War II. After joining the army, Tillman, like many other northern black men, was sent south to train. From Maryland, he traveled to the Louisiana swamps to prepare for action in the South Pacific. Then he found himself at Fort Huachuca, Arizona, training for desert fighting in Africa. A year and a half later, Tillman was still training, this time in northern Arizona for combat in the mountains of Italy. Most army units trained for three to six months, but not the "buffalo soldiers" of the Ninety-Second Infantry. Although their nickname came from the nineteenth-century black troops who fought courageously in the Indian wars and the Spanish-American War (see chapter 8), U.S. officials doubted their courage and abilities and were reluctant to send them into combat.

Tillman knew that black politicians were fighting for the Ninety-Second Infantry to see combat, however. As he put it, they wanted black soldiers to "get recognition," so that the prestige of fighting on the front line would not go only to white men.[1] Tillman and his division finally saw combat in Italy, where Tillman

manned the heavy guns that pushed the Germans back from Rome to Florence to Milan. Although many black men died in the battles that eventually forced the German surrender, neither Tillman nor the Ninety-Second Infantry got the recognition they deserved.

When Tillman landed in Norfolk, Virginia, after the war, his unit was unceremoniously left on the docks for hours with no way to get to camp. While other returning troops were cheered and paraded, Tillman's unit was subjected to the strange looks of whites who treated them as if they were convicts and to the anxious gazes of blacks who wondered if they would be lynched. As a sergeant, Tillman wouldn't let his men walk through town with their heads down; he had them march proudly, with their shoulders back and their heads held high.

Afraid that local whites would instigate a violent confrontation, the army sent the soldiers home without fanfare the following day. Tillman returned to Pittsburgh, where he could not find a job. Still, he thought his unit had accomplished much. He explained, "We were fighting . . . for our people . . . we had to prove that blacks would fight. . . . If we failed, the whole black race would fail. We were fighting for the flag and for our rights. We knew that this would be the beginning of breaking down segregation."[2]

While Tillman fought in Italy, Evelyn Bates waged her own battle at home. A native of Memphis, Tennessee, Bates took advantage of the wartime industrial expansion and got a job at the Firestone Tire and Rubber Company in her hometown. In the absence of men, Firestone, like most other factories, had to rely on women for both domestic and war production. Bates was one of the few black women to land one of these jobs, but like Tillman, she had to fight entrenched ideas about blacks in general and black women in particular.

Unlike white women, black women were thought to be suited for the same heavy labor as men. Bates initially found herself working in a field full of wasps and snakes, sorting and cutting tires. Many of her friends quit because the work was so hard, and Bates almost joined them when she had to stand outside in the cold and sweep nearly frozen water. "In that factory, the attitude was bad," she recalled. When she complained, she was reassigned to a job lifting slabs of rubber weighing up to 125 pounds onto trays that rolled along a nonstop conveyor belt. As Bates recollected, "They had mens doing it before they hired black womens. Didn't any women do it but black womens."[3]

But Bates persevered, despite the eight-hour-a-day, seven-day-a-week grind, because her weekly salary of $25 was much higher than the pittance she had made doing domestic work. At war's end, Firestone fired most of the black women it had hired in order to rehire the white men who had gone off to war. Although Bates felt fortunate to get a job sweeping the floor of the room where she had once hauled rubber, she resented the fact that white women workers were not summarily dismissed as well. Firestone had begun hiring white women five years before black women, and in typical "last hired, first fired" fashion, the company laid off the black women first. Some, like Bates, were kept on as maids because, as Bates said, "white women didn't want to sweep, she didn't want to clean up no restroom, so that was a black woman's job."[4]

Still, the war had pried open factory doors for African Americans. Bates joined the union and, with seniority, was able to apply for jobs typically reserved for white women. Although she took much abuse from white supervisors, she endured and over time attained better-paying, less demanding, and more rewarding positions.

The war spurred changes in the lives of Tillman, Bates, and millions of other African Americans who enlisted in the armed forces or sought work in the expanded war industries. World War II, black leaders maintained, would not be like World War I. Black people would not just "close ranks" with white Americans and forget their special grievances. Instead, they would fight, announced the *Pittsburgh Courier* in February 1942, for a "Double Victory" against fascism abroad and racism at home. As the experiences of Tillman and Bates made clear, achieving the "Double V" would not be easy for African Americans. But their wartime challenges prepared them for the postwar civil rights movement, which would prove to be the most important social and economic justice movement the United States had ever experienced.

The Crisis of World War II

World War I — the Great War, as it was termed — did not end all wars, as so many had hoped. Just twenty years later, German armies, now under the command of Adolf Hitler, again tore across Europe, conquering nations and subduing people. As it had in World War I, the United States entered the conflict belatedly, this time after an attack by Germany's ally Japan. At home, the war spotlighted issues of democracy and racial prejudice that could not be ignored. America thus faced a dual crisis: It had to help its allies stop German and Japanese aggression abroad, and it needed to make its own ideology of democracy and equality a reality at home.

America Enters the War and States Its Goals

December 7, 1941 — the day the Japanese bombed the U.S. naval base at Pearl Harbor, Hawaii — marked the entry of the United States into World War II. But it did not mark the beginning of that war or America's involvement in it. Europe had been fully embroiled in war since Hitler invaded Poland in September 1939. By the time the United States declared war on Japan, the **Axis powers** of Japan, Germany, and Italy had formed a military alliance. Hitler had annexed Austria and overrun most of Europe and was attempting to defeat Britain and the Soviet Union, the two nations that along with the United States would become the **Allies**. In Asia, Japan had invaded China and Indochina. Hitler's aggression had emboldened the Japanese, who wanted to expel Europeans from Asia and become the dominant power in the region. From Japan's perspective, only the United States stood in its way. Yet Japan depended on American raw materials, and when the United States placed an embargo on oil and steel, the Japanese attacked.

President Franklin D. Roosevelt and the U.S. Congress had not stood idly by as the world had devolved into chaos. Although they knew that most Americans wanted to stay out of the war and that only a direct attack on the country would convince Americans that the United States should join the conflict, they did everything they could to support Britain in its fight to save Western Europe and to prepare the nation for war. In September 1940, the first peacetime draft was instituted, compelling all men between the ages of twenty-one and thirty-five to register with local draft boards and mobilizing an army of 900,000. Congress appropriated money for American industries to produce arms and prepare military forces, and it gave Roosevelt the power to lease arms and lend ships to Britain and the Soviet Union.

American leaders also began the very careful process of explaining to the public what was at stake. The principles that America upheld were outlined in Roosevelt's **Four Freedoms** speech, delivered in January 1941, and in the **Atlantic Charter**, a document signed in August of that year by Roosevelt and British prime minister Winston Churchill. In his January speech, Roosevelt argued that people everywhere ought to have freedom of speech, freedom of religion, and freedom from want and fear. The

Atlantic Charter reiterated these freedoms and also stated that people had the right to economic advancement, to social security, and to choose the form of government they would live under. It also denounced **Nazism**, the racist totalitarian ideology expounded by the German chancellor, Adolf Hitler. Nazism proclaimed Germans to be a superior people destined to lead the world. The only thing standing in their way, Nazis said, was the Jewish people. Roosevelt's signature on the Atlantic Charter made American opposition to racism and totalitarianism official goals of the war.

African Americans Respond to the War

African Americans had been fighting racism and fascist-like southern governments since the days of slavery. As a people who had been brutalized, enslaved, raped, lynched, robbed of their property, and segregated in the workplace and society, African Americans could identify with European Jews. For centuries, European nations had terrorized and discriminated against Jews. Hitler had now gone further and stripped them of their citizenship rights, corralled them into ghettos and concentration camps, and murdered them outright, all in the name of racial supremacy. African Americans heard in Roosevelt's goals a call to end racism and fascism not only abroad but in America as well.

Early on, they protested discrimination in the armed forces. In 1938, Charles Hamilton Houston — a former army officer in World War I and now special legal counsel to the NAACP — wrote a letter to the editor of the *New York Times* warning that if the army's general staff "thinks that Negroes in the next war are going to be content with peeling potatoes and washing dishes," they had badly misread the minds of African Americans.[5] Knowing that Roosevelt needed the northern black vote to win reelection, black leaders pressured the administration for concessions. In September 1940, NAACP executive secretary Walter White, head of the Brotherhood of Sleeping Car Porters A. Philip Randolph, and T. Arnold Hill, adviser on Negro affairs for the National Youth Administration, met with Secretary of the Navy Frank Knox and Assistant Secretary of War Robert P. Patterson to push their demands for the elimination of segregation and discrimination in the armed services.

For the most part, President Roosevelt's response was disappointing. His press secretary noted that he refused "to intermingle the colored and white enlisted personnel in the same regimental organizations." According to Roosevelt, separate units "had proven satisfactory over a long period of years, and to make changes now would produce a situation destructive to morale and detrimental to the preparation for national defense." In addition to this disappointing news, black leaders were frustrated by the directive that black units would have no black officers other than medics and chaplains. Colonel Benjamin O. Davis Sr., the senior black officer in the nation's armed forces, was promoted to brigadier general, and Judge William H. Hastie, the dean of Howard University Law School, was appointed as civilian aide on Negro affairs to Secretary of War Henry L. Stimson. But the administration held fast to the idea that black men could not lead and would serve best under the direction of white men, especially southern white men.[6]

African Americans did not accept these decisions without protest. "We asked Mr. Roosevelt to change the rules of the game and he countered by giving us some new uniforms," complained the *Baltimore Afro-American*. The American Red Cross's separation of black and white blood prompted Charles Drew, the African American physician who developed the process of storing and shipping blood plasma to be used in blood banks, to resign from that organization. The navy's announcement in 1940 that it would accept blacks only as mess attendants, cooks, and stewards inspired protest and an angry NAACP editorial asking how blacks were supposed to feel about "what our white fellow citizens declare to be the 'vast difference' between American Democracy and Hitlerism." When the Army Air Corps refused the application of a Howard University student named Yancey Williams, the NAACP initiated a lawsuit on his behalf.[7]

Mass protests replaced unorganized actions when black leaders, guided by Randolph, created the **March on Washington Movement**. In January 1941, Randolph called for a gathering of 50,000 to 100,000 black Americans in the nation's capital on July 1 to demand equal opportunity for blacks in defense industries and an end to "their humiliation in the armed services."[8] The president, fearing international embarrassment, lobbied hard to get Randolph to call off the increasingly popular march, but Randolph held firm to his demands. Just five days before the scheduled march, Roosevelt issued **Executive Order 8802**, which banned racial discrimination in defense industries and created the Fair Employment Practices Commission (FEPC) to ensure compliance.

Randolph did call off the march, but the contradictions inherent in America's international and national postures remained. It seemed hypocritical to fight racism abroad with a segregated army and terribly unfair to ask African Americans to fight for democracy and citizenship rights overseas when they were accorded only second-class citizenship at home. African Americans debated these issues and tried to resolve them so that neither they nor the nation would be cheated.

Behind the debates were bitter memories of the way black Americans had been treated during and after World War I. Some blacks were so angry that they supported and admired the Japanese, if only because Japan was a nonwhite nation challenging white supremacy and Japanese Americans also confronted discrimination. Some believed that a Japanese victory "would be the first step in the darker races coming back into their own."[9] Even black Americans who opposed Japan could not bring themselves to support the United States uncritically. Some African Americans argued that it was American racism that had made the country vulnerable to the Japanese. According to the black activist and writer George Schuyler, "Race prejudice and only race prejudice caused our complacence toward Japan."[10]

These sentiments made many African American leaders nervous. Once the United States declared war on Japan in 1941, African American dissent could easily be interpreted as disloyalty, and protest could be seen as sedition. The Japanese had launched an intensive propaganda campaign to gain black Americans' support, and the Federal Bureau of Investigation and the U.S. army's Military Intelligence Division were keeping a close watch on African American leaders and newspapers for evidence of treason. If the U.S. government thought that black people posed a threat of internal subversion,

they might curtail black civil liberties. The detainment of many German Americans and Italian Americans, as well as the internment of Japanese Americans beginning in 1942, served as vivid examples of what could happen to those deemed security risks.[11]

The **Double V campaign** provided a masterful way to fight racism without endangering civil liberties. Even before its official declaration by the *Pittsburgh Courier* in February 1942, black leaders insisted that African Americans could simultaneously be patriotic and fight for black rights. A. Philip Randolph wrote an article two weeks after Pearl Harbor reminding African Americans that the principles of democracy were at stake both at home and abroad. The fight to defeat the Axis powers involved "the obligation, responsibility, and task for the Negro people to fight with all their might for their constitutional, democratic rights and freedoms here in America." The Jamaican American historian and journalist J. A. Rogers acknowledged that World War I had left blacks with lukewarm loyalty, but he urged them to "enter the fight with all the zest, thrill and patriotism of every other American group, at the same time preparing ourselves mentally and otherwise, to demand, and if necessary to seize, our rights as citizens during the conflict, and especially after it."[12]

Racial Violence and Discrimination in the Military

Fighting on two fronts would not be easy, not least because the U.S. military would not let blacks fight. Despite black leaders' best efforts, for most of the war segregation persisted in the armed forces. Few blacks were appointed to selective service boards, and blacks did not receive a proportionate share of deferments. Throughout the draft's early years, blacks were largely passed over until white soldiers began to complain that they should not be the only ones forced to sacrifice. During the last years of the war, the number of black inductees steadily increased, but 50 to 75 percent of them were assigned to noncombat and unskilled work. Only three black divisions, among them James Tillman's Ninety-Second Infantry, saw combat. Even highly trained black pilots were discriminated against. The Army Air Corps initially would not let **Tuskegee Airmen** — named for Tuskegee Institute (see chapter 9) and trained as separate units apart from white pilots — fly combat missions and only belatedly allowed them to engage in air-to-air combat, for which they were trained. Although the fighter and bomber units earned distinguished service citations, and individual airmen were decorated with the highest medals, it was not until the beginning of 1944 that the Army Air Corps deployed them in a meaningful way. (See Document Project: African Americans and the Tuskegee Experiments, pp. 467–76.)

Black officers were similarly mistreated. The army integrated its twenty officer training camps, and by the end of the war in August 1945, almost 8,000 black officers had been commissioned. Still, as of March 1945, their number represented only 1 percent of black servicemen — compared to 11 percent of white servicemen receiving a commission. Army policy did not allow a black officer to outrank a white officer in his unit, severely limiting black officers' opportunities. They could not use the white officers' clubs to which they paid dues. Even enemy prisoners of war were treated better than black soldiers and officers. In one instance, black officers stationed in Italy were required to sit in the back of an army theater where the seats in front were reserved for white officers and Italian prisoners.[13]

This humiliating treatment was something that black soldiers grappled with. Captain Luther Smith was taken prisoner of war by the Germans and later remembered being confronted by a German officer who said, "You are black American. You volunteered to fight for a country that lynches your people." Smith recalled that he was "floored" by this comment, saying that his first thought was, "You are absolutely correct. . . . Yes, I had volunteered to fight for a country that lynched my people." But Smith retorted with the kind of optimism expressed by James Tillman: "I am black American. It is my home. I will fight for it because I have no other home, and by fighting for it I can make America better."[14]

For men like Smith, conditions got worse before they got better. Not until early 1944 did the navy change its employment policy and consider individual performance rather than race in recruitment, assignments, and promotions. By the end of the war, of the nearly 168,000 black men employed in the navy, 90 percent were still messmen and only a handful had been assigned crew positions. The U.S. Marine Corps accepted no blacks until August 1942, when it set up a separate training facility for them in North Carolina.

Black women fared no better in the military. Four thousand black women volunteered for the Women's Army Corps (WAC), but most found themselves doing service work that required none of the skills for which they had been trained. At Fort Breckinridge, Kentucky, white Wacs did clerical and technical work, while blacks swept warehouse floors, served food, or endured the heat and humidity of the laundry. Of the 50,000 women who served as nurses in the wartime army, only about 500 were black. At first, army policy was to have black nurses care only for black soldiers.

But since few blacks saw combat and the need for nurses escalated precipitously as the war wore on, the army revised this policy in 1944.

As for the navy, the Roosevelt administration banned black women from its volunteer female unit, Women Accepted for Volunteer Emergency Service (WAVES), until Republican presidential candidate Thomas Dewey made the ban a campaign issue in 1944. Still, the administration's policies were so distasteful to black women that few volunteered, and at war's end, there were just 2 black female officers and 72 black enlisted women in the navy. Of the almost 11,000 navy nurses, only 4 were black.[15]

Black women who volunteered for the United Service Organizations (USO) met with similar discrimination. When the USO was founded in 1941 to provide wholesome recreation for soldiers in their off-duty hours, no thought was given to the needs of black soldiers or to the community of women who wanted to boost their morale. African American women often had to create separate USOs because blacks were prohibited from entering white facilities.

In addition to the official policies limiting their opportunities, black soldiers were subjected to an endless array of insults and indignities. At Fort Bragg, North Carolina,

Army Nurses
Although the need for nurses escalated during the war, black nurses who enlisted in the army were not allowed to treat white soldiers until 1944. Here African American nurses wait to disembark in Greenport, Scotland, in August 1944. *National Archives and Records Administration Still Pictures Record Section, Special Media Archives Services Division, identifier #531204.*

black troops could not board white buses; they had to wait for the infrequent buses marked "Colored Troops." White civilian bus drivers would often not transport them, and train agents would not sell them tickets. Black soldiers on leave sometimes had to wait for days to reach their destinations, and while waiting, they could not eat at the station restaurants or use facilities that even German prisoners of war could use.[16] When black soldiers left base, local whites often shouted racial slurs and epithets at them. In conflicts involving white civilians, black troops were usually presumed to be at fault and in many cases were jailed, court-martialed, or dishonorably discharged.[17]

The racism black soldiers experienced extended beyond verbal abuse and segregation. Although racial violence was by no means restricted to the South, southern towns and police officers were the most belligerent toward black soldiers. Countless examples of violence exist. In March 1941, the body of Private Felix Hall of Montgomery, Alabama, was found hanging from a tree at Fort Benning, Georgia. The War Department would not rule out suicide, even though Hall's hands and feet were bound.[18] In 1942, a white bus driver killed a black soldier in Mobile, Alabama; a white policeman clubbed and shot a black soldier in Beaumont, Texas; and a black army nurse in Montgomery was brutally beaten and jailed for defying the Jim Crow seating arrangements on a bus. In 1943, a white policeman in Little Rock, Arkansas, killed a black sergeant, and the white sheriff of Centreville, Mississippi, shot a black soldier at point-blank range. The sheriff was heard to ask a white military policeman after the shooting, "Any more niggers you want killed?"[19] According to the black writer and activist James Baldwin, northern black families experienced "a peculiar kind of relief when they knew that their boys were being shipped out of the south, to do battle overseas. It was, perhaps, like feeling that the most dangerous part of a dangerous journey had been passed and that now, even if death should come, it would come with honor and without the complicity of their countrymen."[20]

When provoked by racism, black soldiers either bolted the army or fought back. In Alexandria, Louisiana, the attempted arrest of a drunken black soldier led to a race riot that resulted in the shooting of 28 blacks and the arrest of nearly 3,000. In Prescott, Arizona, 43 black soldiers went absent without leave (AWOL) to escape being terrorized by whites. Numerous military bases reported race riots and incidents of black soldiers fighting white soldiers and police. To counter black retaliation, the governor of Mississippi asked the War Department to move black regiments out of his state and requested that the army remove the firing pins from black soldiers' rifles. Even the War Department was forced to admit it had a problem. In 1942, at the end of a particularly violent summer, it issued a memorandum instructing white officers to treat blacks with care and diplomacy.[21]

The War Department's ineffectiveness in addressing racial violence and discrimination was just one factor in William Hastie's decision to resign his post as adviser on Negro affairs to Secretary of War Henry Stimson in January 1943. Hastie was disgusted with the overall treatment of blacks in the military, which included the Army Air Corps' refusal to deploy the Ninety-Ninth Pursuit Squadron, the first all-black flying unit trained at Tuskegee Army Air Field, and the employment of other black aviators as trash collectors and groundskeepers.[22] (See Document Project: African Americans and the Tuskegee Experiments, pp. 467–76.) He condemned Stimson's well-publicized comments on black inferiority and the War Department's adoption of what he called "the traditional mores of the South." At his resignation press conference, he said, "It is difficult to see how a Negro in this position, with all his superiors maintaining or inaugurating racial segregation, can accomplish anything of value."[23]

A year later, it came as no surprise when, after two years of combat training, black regiments of the Second Cavalry Division — who had been shipped to North Africa because of an urgent need for combat troops — were instead assigned to jobs unloading ships, repairing roads, and driving trucks. One black soldier reasoned that black soldiers were denied the right to fight so that "after the war is over demands couldn't be so great." Whites would be able to say, "Didn't his white brother (?) die on the front line, while he was comparatively safe in the rear echelon?"[24] Indeed, when the military's segregation policy was under review after the war, South Carolina senator Burnet R. Maybank invoked that argument. "The wars of this country have been won by white soldiers," he said. "Negro soldiers have rendered their greatest service as cooks, drivers, maintenance men, mechanics and such positions for which they are well qualified."[25]

Black soldiers, however, saw their service to their country as the beginning of the end of segregation. One discharged army corporal said, "I spent four years in the army to free a bunch of Dutchmen and Frenchmen, and I'm hanged if I'm going to let the Alabama version of the Germans kick me around when I get home. No sirree-bob! I went into the Army a nigger; I'm comin' out a man."[26]

Despite all that they endured, more than 2.5 million African Americans served in the military during World War II. From the beginning, they knew theirs was a double fight: Their fight for freedom would be for both their nation and their race. They faced not only the weapons of the Germans, Italians, and Japanese but also the belligerence of their own compatriots. Still they fought, confident that American racism would sooner or later give way.

African Americans on the Home Front

World War II brought the decadelong Great Depression to a halt. As factories retooled in preparation for war, millions of the unemployed returned to work, and many who had been fortunate enough to be employed during the depression found new work that was more fulfilling, more interesting, and better paying. For African Americans who had been bound to agricultural labor and service work, the war opened up new employment opportunities. Generally shut out of jobs in the South, they migrated to the North, Midwest, and West Coast for work. Like Evelyn Bates, they met resistance at every turn. For those who worked in the war industries making munitions; building aircraft, boats, and armored vehicles; sewing uniforms; and meeting the various needs of a nation at war, the Double Victory meant not only producing the goods that allowed America to triumph overseas but also fighting for economic rights at home.[27]

New Jobs, Wartime Migration, and Race Riots

During the 1940s, more than 1.5 million African Americans migrated out of the South. Another million moved from rural to urban areas within the South, transforming a predominantly rural people into an urban population almost overnight (Map 11.1). Those who moved did so because of limited work opportunities. Blacks throughout the South were relegated to low-wage agricultural and forestry work. Ultimately, whether it was in the shipyards of Mobile, Alabama, the aircraft plants of Oakland, California, or the automobile factories of Detroit, blacks had to fight for the chance to work — especially at high-paying skilled jobs.[28]

With few exceptions, southern governors and white laborers worked together to maintain a segregated labor force that kept blacks as a continual source of cheap labor. Despite the country's war needs, they resisted federal encroachment that threatened to topple this labor hierarchy. Nothing demonstrated this fact better than the antimigration and "work or jail" laws passed by several states. Texas legislator Rogers Kelly, for

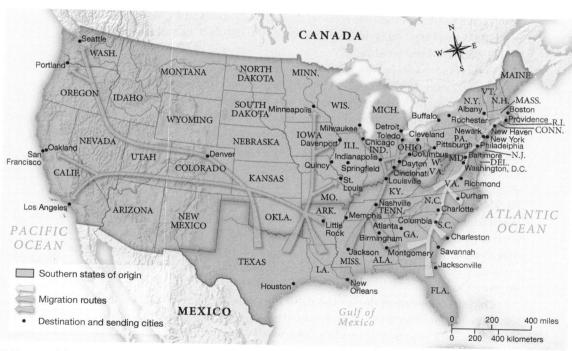

MAP 11.1   African American Migration, 1940–1970

During World War II, African Americans began a mass migration from the South to the North, Midwest, and West Coast in search of employment and other opportunities. Some stayed in the South but moved from rural to urban areas. This trend continued in the decades following the war, transplanting more than five million blacks over the course of thirty years and turning African Americans into a predominantly urban population. The wartime migration prompted an increase in racial tensions in the North and West, where newly arrived blacks competed with whites for jobs and put a strain on the housing market.

example, drafted a state law prohibiting recruiting agents to talk to black laborers about moving north to Michigan for work. In 1942, to ensure the sugarcane harvest, New Orleans ordered police to arrest vagrants. These included blacks looking for meaningful employment outside agricultural work, who were compelled to either work in the fields or go to jail. Similarly, in 1943, sheriffs in Macon, Georgia, rounded up black women and men and forced them to do farm and domestic work. If they objected, they were arrested as vagrants and jailed. A *Louisiana Weekly* editorial titled "Slavery 1942" described these laws as an attempt to "maintain control of the vast Southern reservoir of cheap labor." Southerners, the editorial charged, "don't want to lose their black labor."[29]

But the South did lose much of its cheap black labor. In 1940, 77 percent of the total U.S. black population lived in the South, with more than 49 percent in rural areas; two out of five blacks worked as farmers, sharecroppers, or farm laborers. By 1950, only 68 percent of the total black population remained in the South, a percentage that continued to drop through 1970. In what some have called a jobs movement, at least 1 million black workers entered the industrial labor force during World War II, swelling their numbers from a meager 3 percent of defense workers in 1942 to 8.3 percent in 1944. Twenty-five percent of these laborers worked in foundries, and 12 percent worked in shipbuilding and steel mills. In 1943, 55,000 of the 450,000 members of the Detroit United Auto Workers were black.[30]

Some of those who left the South had been trained by New Deal and war agencies. In 1942, for example, the War Manpower Commission (the federal agency that balanced labor needs across industries) began placing graduates from Xavier University of Louisiana's welding program in shipyards outside Louisiana. Before the war, local black activist Paul Dixon's demands that blacks be given a chance at nonagricultural work fell on deaf ears. But shortly after the war began, the U.S. Employment Service used Dixon's referrals to supply skilled workers to plants outside the South. Southerners' worst fears were realized when war needs forced government agencies to team with black activist organizations to fill skilled jobs throughout the nation. From the Florida War Training Center in Jacksonville, black workers were placed in shipyards and airports in places such as Chester, Pennsylvania, and Bridgeport, Connecticut. By May 1944, the Houston Works Progress Administration had trained close to eight hundred black shipyard workers. Only a few found work in the South; the rest migrated to the West Coast.[31]

The main route out of the South led due north to Chicago, Detroit, and other midwestern cities, but World War II also opened new routes west, giving the region its first significant black population outside Los Angeles. Western migrants hailed mostly from Texas, Louisiana, and Arkansas, but East Coast southerners also found their way west. As the sociologist Charles S. Johnson explained, "To the romantic appeal of the west, has been added the real and actual opportunity for gainful employment, setting in motion a war-time migration of huge proportions."[32] In fact, during the 1940s the West Coast's black population grew by 443,000 (33 percent). Most migrants settled in five major metropolitan areas: Seattle-Tacoma and Portland-Vancouver in the Pacific

Northwest, and the San Francisco Bay area, the Los Angeles–Long Beach area, and San Diego in California. Initially, representatives of the shipbuilding and aircraft industries recruited these workers, but African Americans soon made their way west on their own. The region's mild climate, greater freedom, and high wages promised a future that could not be realized in the South.[33]

Both skilled and unskilled workers left the South for a better life elsewhere. In what was fast becoming a civil rights issue, black Americans protested "work or jail" orders and exercised their right to move. They tapped into what became known as the "underground railroad," a network of black activists, union representatives, and northern and western recruiting agents who helped place black farmworkers in industries. For example, with the help of the United Cannery, Agricultural, Packing, and Allied Workers of America, Campbell's soup plants in New Jersey arranged contracts for, and paid the transportation of, farmworkers from Florida, Arkansas, and Tennessee.[34]

Women were among the first to leave the South. Of the 1 million or so blacks who entered defense employment during the war years, 60 percent were women. For them, factory work meant an escape from domestic work in white homes, where the pay was low and the threat of sexual assault ever present. Factory worker Lyn Childs asked, "Do you think that if you did domestic work all of your life, where you'd clean somebody's toilets and did all the cooking for some lazy characters who were sitting on top, and you finally got a chance where you can get a dignified job, you wouldn't fly through the door?"[35] Fanny Christina Hill felt the same way. The 60 cents an hour she made during her training at North American Aviation was more than she had ever made doing domestic work. As her salary increased, she gained economic security and bought a home, something she said she would never have been able to do had the war not transformed her circumstances. Quoting her sister, she reflected, "Hitler was the one that got us out of the white folks' kitchen."[36]

During the war, as a result of the new competition for jobs and tensions over migration, riots erupted in cities large and small. Several cities were racked by violence pitting white sailors and civilians against African Americans and Hispanics. In Los Angeles, the conflict was called the **zoot suit riots**, after the "zoot suits" — broad felt hats, pegged trousers, and gold chains — worn by black and Latino men there. San Diego, Long Beach, Chicago, Detroit, and Philadelphia also saw conflict. In 1943, a particularly volatile year, there were 242 racial battles in 47 cities.[37]

One of the worst riots started on June 16 in Beaumont, Texas, when between 2,000 and 3,000 white workers, mostly from the Pennsylvania Shipyards there, beat and robbed black pedestrians, overturned cars, and burned black homes. While the immediate cause was a rumor that a black man had raped a white woman, the underlying cause was tensions sparked by the migration of more than 30,000 whites and blacks who competed for the limited available housing and recreational space in Beaumont.[38]

Detroit presented a similar situation. White workers held massive strikes to prevent the promotion of black workers and resisted black housing in white neighborhoods. They excluded black residents from two new federal housing projects, one of which was

Black Women in War Industries

The war gave African American women the opportunity to trade in domestic work for higher-paying, more interesting jobs. Among the growing West Coast black population was Ann Bland, pictured here, who worked as a burner (a worker who cut metal with a torch) on the second U.S. navy ship named for an African American, the SS *George Washington Carver*. She was among the 6,000 African Americans employed at the Kaiser Shipyards in Richmond, California. *Schomburg Center, NYPL/Art Resource, NY.*

named for the black abolitionist and feminist Sojourner Truth. Tempers flared in the summer of 1943 when a fight broke out between a white man and a black man on the Belle Isle Bridge. Fighting spread as rumors circulated among blacks that whites had killed a black woman and her baby, and among whites that a black man had raped and killed a white woman. It took 6,000 federal troops to restore peace after three days of rioting, 34 deaths, 675 injuries, 1,900 arrests, and $2 million in property damage. Although white storeowners suffered property damage, of the 34 people who died, 25 were African American. Most of those who were injured and/or arrested also were black. Not long afterward, a riot erupted in Harlem after police shot a black soldier. The result was 6 deaths, 500 injuries, hundreds of arrests, and property damage totaling $5 million.

Thus, as the war created opportunities for African Americans, it also spawned racial conflict. The nation needed workers to build weapons, tanks, boats, and airplanes. It needed to feed and clothe its more than 16 million troops. African Americans took advantage of these opportunities, picking up and leaving the South despite the best efforts of legislators, governors, and the police to stop them. Although African Americans welcomed the chance to serve their country on the home front, not all Americans were welcoming toward them.

Organizing for Economic Opportunity

Getting a job was one thing. Being treated fairly, paid equitably, and given room to advance was another. African Americans had to organize in order to gain the economic rights that white Americans often took for granted. As Fanny Christina Hill discovered, getting a job was just the beginning of an uphill struggle. Although Hill worked in California, her experiences were similar to those of Evelyn Bates, who stayed in the

Racial Tensions in the North

Riots erupted as whites and blacks moved into cities where defense plants were located and competed with one another for jobs, housing, and recreational space. As in turn-of-the-century race riots and those of the post–World War I era, African Americans were attacked by vengeful whites and suffered most of the injuries and deaths. This scene from a 1943 riot in Detroit is typical of the violence blacks encountered. *© Bettmann/Corbis.*

South. Hill trained with white workers, but once she arrived on the factory floor, she, like Bates, faced misconceptions about black women's abilities. As she recalled, "All the Negroes went to Department 17 because there was nothing but shooting and bucking rivets. You stood on one side of the panel and your partner stood on this side, and he would shoot the rivets with a gun and you'd buck them with the bar."[39] She found that "white girls . . . went to better departments where the work was not as strenuous." Hill remembered that in some departments at North American Aviation, "they didn't even allow a black person to walk through there let alone work in there."[40]

Across America, conflict and violence erupted as white workers sought to maintain their privileged work status. Herbert Ward recalled that at the Lockheed-Vega aircraft factory in Burbank, California, white men made racial slurs in the restrooms "to scare you if possible, or to embarrass you to such an extent that you wouldn't want to stay." He said that fights were not uncommon.[41] In Mobile, Alabama, federal troops had to quell the rioting of 20,000 white men who took to the streets in 1943 to protest the promotion of black welders at the Alabama Dry Dock and Shipbuilding Company.[42] When one black man, John Gutter — a graduate of Xavier University of Louisiana's welding program — was promoted at the Todd-Johnson Dry Docks in New Orleans, more than 3,000 white workers walked off the job.

In the industrial powerhouse of Detroit, tensions between black and white workers were palpable. In September 1941, 250 whites staged a sit-down strike at the Packard Motor Car Company to protest the promotion of 2 blacks from polishing work to assembly work. In May 1942, 20,000 white workers at Packard walked off the job and stopped production for almost a week to protest the promotion of 3 blacks. Shortly after that, 350 white workers shut down the Dodge plant after 23 African Americans were promoted from unskilled to skilled jobs. When 2 blacks were promoted from janitorial work to machine operators at the Hudson Naval Ordnance Plant, white workers staged a work stoppage, and the black workers were demoted. An Office of War Information investigation found that white workers resented the economic gains being made by blacks and felt that "the Negro must be kept in his place."[43]

But African Americans had other ideas. During the 1941 March on Washington negotiations with President Roosevelt, A. Philip Randolph was explicit in his requests that blacks be considered for jobs in defense industries. "Our people," he said, "are being turned away at factory gates because they are colored."[44] Although Roosevelt's Executive Order 8802 established the Fair Employment Practices Commission (FEPC) to investigate complaints of discrimination and address grievances, Roosevelt crippled the agency from the start by providing no enforcement apparatus, a very limited budget, and some leaders who were less than sympathetic to African American complaints. A 1943 editorial titled "Open Letter to the President" in the NAACP's journal, the *Crisis*, noted what African Americans knew all too well: "Executive Order 8802 is being defied and sabotaged by management and labor alike."[45]

The ineffectiveness of the FEPC was a setback for African American workers but not a fatal blow. Throughout the war, blacks turned to unions, especially the new unions of the Congress of Industrial Organizations (CIO) (see chapter 10) (founded in 1935 as the Committee for Industrial Organization), for support. Because CIO unions were organized by industry, they tended to be more inclusive than the American Federation of Labor unions that organized workers on the basis of skill. The National Maritime Union; International Longshore and Warehouse Union; United Cannery, Agricultural, Packing, and Allied Workers of America; and United Packinghouse Workers of America were generally helpful in finding work for blacks, moving them between cities, and fighting for better positions for them. Often union representatives worked in coordination with regional FEPCs, African American organizations, and government agencies to advance economic equality.

Nevertheless, regional customs, politics, and the ideological leanings of union leadership determined how helpful a union would or could be. Depending on the region, for example, the United Automobile Workers (UAW) could be a help or a hindrance to black workers. On one hand, despite the white "hate strikes" at the Packard Motor Car Company in 1942, union officials continued to support black upgrades. The predominantly African American UAW Local 600 in Detroit allied with the Detroit NAACP and put civil rights at the top of its agenda.[46] On the other hand, blacks at North American Aviation in Dallas were reluctant to take their grievances to the union. According to the union representative, "Here in Texas there shall be no social equality. . . . No one is going to tell us that we will have to accept our Negroes as equals."[47] This feeling prevailed in most UAW locals in the South and Southwest.

Blacks confronted similar union policies on the West Coast, where a huge obstacle to fair employment was the International Brotherhood of Boilermakers (IBB), the umbrella union that organized shipyard workers. Before 1937, the IBB had excluded black workers from its unions. When it changed this policy, it created all-black "auxiliary" unions denying blacks full insurance rights, employment opportunities, seniority protection, and equal participation in labor guarantees and privileges. In 1943, African Americans protested these Jim Crow unions. In response, the IBB forced shipyard employers to fire black workers. Hundreds were fired in California and Oregon, including Joseph James, president of the San Francisco chapter of the NAACP. With the support of the CIO and the NAACP, James initiated a lawsuit against the Marinship shipyards in Sausalito, California. In 1944, the California Supreme Court ruled in his favor and ordered the IBB to dismantle its auxiliary structure.[48]

Throughout the country, black organizations such as the NAACP and the National Urban League worked unceasingly — not just for civil rights but also for economic justice. NAACP branches organized protests against discrimination in defense plants nationwide. In the South, the Urban League pushed for African American training, teaming up wherever possible with the War Manpower Commission, local FEPCs, and the U.S. Employment Service to place skilled and unskilled black workers in industrial jobs. Progress was always relative. In some places, especially in the South, negotiations ended with black workers accepting equal pay but segregated employment. In other places, negotiated settlements resulted in integrated unions fighting for across-the-board improvements for black and white workers alike.

To further their efforts, African Americans increasingly joined unions and other types of organizations in the 1940s. Those who could took the Urban League's advice to "get into somebody's union and stay there."[49] By 1943, some 400,000 black workers had joined CIO unions and, as members, gained access to collective bargaining, seniority rights, grievance systems to appeal violations of their rights, and national representation. Many of them also joined the NAACP. From 355 branches and a membership of about 55,000 in 1940, the NAACP grew to 1,073 branches and more than 450,000 members in 1946.[50] As its membership increased, its infrastructure grew more sophisticated. With new local branches linked to statewide networks, the NAACP could mount political campaigns and stage local protests. In 1942, a new organization, the Congress of Racial Equality (CORE), was founded for the purpose of mounting civil disobedience or direct-action campaigns to end segregation. CORE staged the first sit-down strikes to end segregation in northern restaurants and other public and private places.

The black press emerged as one of the most important institutions in the black urban community. Newspapers increased their circulation by 40 percent, becoming the main channel for expressing black protest and building community. Called **soldiers without swords** for their role on the front lines of the Double V campaign, black journalists facilitated the flow of information relevant to African Americans. For example, the *Pittsburgh Courier* provided a detailed analysis of Nazism and racism by comparing Germany and Georgia. Foreign correspondents for the *Pittsburgh Courier, Baltimore Afro-American, Chicago Defender,* and *Norfolk (Virginia) Journal and Guide* covered the deployment and treatment of black troops. The National Newspaper Publishers

Association and the Associated Negro Press reported on issues ranging from blacks in the military to employment at home. As African Americans in one part of the country learned about and were inspired by those in another part, solidarity grew.[51] Being black extended beyond one's racial identity; black people thought of themselves as a nation within a nation. During the war years, blacks became what the poet LeRoi Jones (later Amiri Baraka) would refer to as "a country."

The Struggle for Citizenship Rights

The more African Americans thought of themselves as a nation within a nation, the more they considered themselves worthy of the consideration and respect accorded to countries around the world. In July 1941, President Roosevelt and Winston Churchill wrote the Atlantic Charter, which was signed by all the Allies in January 1942. This document pledged the Allies to "respect the right of all peoples to choose the form of government under which they will live." It stated that Allied nations had to work for "improved labour standards, economic advancement, and social security," as well as to see "sovereign rights and self-government restored to those who have been forcibly deprived of them." These principles sparked revolutions in Africa and Asia, as colonial subjects asserted their right to be independent of colonial rulers.

As a people who had consistently been "forcibly deprived" of their constitutional rights, African Americans also used the war as an opportunity to assert their right to self-determination and liberty. This meant not only the right to fight for their country and to work without discrimination but also fundamental citizenship rights such as voting, holding office, and serving on juries. In addition, it meant the right to participate in the social and cultural life of America as free and equal human beings.

Fighting and Dying for the Right to Vote

Unlike the millions of African Americans who gained the right to vote when they moved north or west, those who stayed in the South remained under the political and economic domination of southern whites, who used legal tactics such as the white primary, literacy tests, poll taxes, grandfather clauses, and outright terror to keep blacks disfranchised (see chapter 9). But southern blacks understood the importance of electoral politics and knew that to fight for the right to vote meant challenging a regional culture built on black dependence and subordination. The international crisis provided the philosophical and ideological foundation for an all-out fight for the franchise. Begun during World War II, it was a fight that would continue long after that conflict ended.

Southern whites and blacks thought differently about the black vote. One southern white cotton gin owner told a *New York Times* reporter, "The niggers would take over the county if they could vote in full numbers. They'd stick together and vote blacks into every office in the county. Why you'd have a nigger judge, nigger sheriff, a nigger tax assessor—think what the black SOB's would do to you."[52] Mississippi

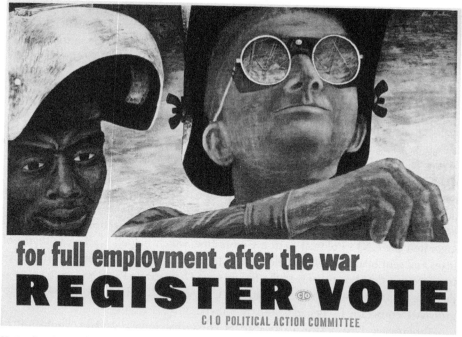

for full employment after the war
REGISTER ⋅ VOTE
C I O POLITICAL ACTION COMMITTEE

Voter Registration Poster
Most African Americans did not separate civil rights from economic justice. They believed that the right to vote and the right to earn a fair wage were rights they were entitled to as U.S. citizens. Not all CIO unions worked with blacks to achieve equality on both fronts, but many did. This 1944 CIO Political Action Committee poster is an example of CIO efforts to help blacks achieve full economic and political rights. *The Granger Collection, New York.*

senator Theodore Bilbo openly invited white registrars to illegally prevent blacks from voting: "You know and I know what's the best way to keep the nigger from voting. You do it the night before the election. I don't have to tell you any more than that. Red-blooded men know what I mean."[53] African Americans believed that the vote would allow them to oust the anti-union and antiblack officials who dominated southern politics and would help them secure economic rights. "Politics IS food, clothes, and housing," preached some black activists.[54]

Just as nations such as Britain and France were slow to realize that the days when they could subjugate the people of India, Africa, and Southeast Asia were coming to a close, southern whites were slow to understand African Americans' determination to gain the vote. Blacks were better organized than before the war and had gained many white allies, including some CIO union leaders and Washington insiders such as the president's influential wife, Eleanor Roosevelt. The First Lady supported efforts to eliminate voting barriers and rid the nation of the poll tax, which unfairly kept blacks and poor whites from voting. Many others agreed, such as Florida senator Claude

Pepper, who thought it was time for the "wave of democracy" to touch America's shores. Likewise, Senate Majority Leader Alben Barkley of Kentucky said that he could think of "no more opportune time to try to spread democracy in our country than at a time when we are trying to spread it in other countries and throughout the world."[55]

Spreading democracy in the United States turned out to be a long, drawn-out fight, especially in the South. But with unions, white liberals, and a newly invigorated NAACP on their side, African Americans made a lot of headway during the war, especially after *Smith v. Allwright* (1944), in which the U.S. Supreme Court declared the all-white Texas Democratic primary illegal. That case, said the black activist Luther Porter Jackson, "was the beginning of a complete revolution in our thinking on the right of suffrage."[56] Two weeks after the ruling, thirty-six black delegates representing every southern state met to establish the National Progressive Voters League, which aimed to help southern blacks register and vote and to coordinate the efforts of black voters throughout the United States. Just in time for the 1944 election, the ruling reinvigorated the CIO's Political Action Committee, which helped blacks pay their poll taxes and sent black and white fieldworkers into black areas to get out the vote. Activists in South Carolina organized the Progressive Democratic Party and sent a slate of delegates to the 1944 Democratic National Convention. By the end of 1944, the Progressive Democratic Party had 45,000 members.

Progressive Democratic Party leaders knew that their delegates would not be seated at the convention, but they wanted to bring attention to increasingly unacceptable contradictions in American society. One was the fact that blacks were fighting for democracy abroad yet could not participate fully in democracy at home. Another was that the Democratic Party, political home of liberal Americans and President Roosevelt, also comprised the most rabid segregationists in the nation. From the black perspective, this unholy alliance, which had persisted since the end of Reconstruction, had to go. But southern whites were of the same mind as South Carolina senator Burnet Maybank, who said, "As a Southern Democrat, I do not propose to be run out of my Party by . . . the Negroes . . . it will be my purpose to see that our Party stands where it always has — [for] states rights and white supremacy."[57]

In small towns and on city streets, blacks and their white allies met resistance from a revived Ku Klux Klan and other white terrorist organizations. In 1940–1941, there were thirteen reported lynchings in the South. Some were political in nature. For instance, Elbert Williams, the founder of the Brownsville, Tennessee, chapter of the NAACP, was murdered shortly after he launched a voter registration campaign in 1940.

Soldiers especially were targeted. Having acquired a level of self-esteem that made accepting second-class citizenship intolerable, they were among the first to register to vote when they returned home from the war. Segregationists feared their assertiveness, and the Ku Klux Klan thought they were "getting out of their place." In 1946, shortly after he returned from the war to Wrightsville, Georgia, veteran Isaac Newton was shot dead when he went to register to vote. In February 1946, a race riot in Columbia, Tennessee, pitted black veterans and their community against the police and the National Guard. When the dust settled, two black men were dead, four white policemen were wounded, and more than one hundred blacks had been arrested. The two months following the 1946 southern primary elections saw nine lynchings. Veteran Macio Snipes, the only black from his district to vote in the Georgia primary, was shot the next day while sitting on his porch. A week later, a white mob killed two black veterans and their wives in Monroe, Georgia (Map 11.2).

Segregationists killed African Americans who sought the vote, but they could not kill African Americans' determination to vote. Many more would die before Congress finally passed voting rights legislation. However, as law-abiding, taxpaying citizens of the United States, black people understood the folly of fighting and dying abroad so that others could enjoy rights that they could not enjoy at home.

New Beginnings in Political and Cultural Life

World War II marked a turning point for African Americans. Those who had migrated and found meaningful and satisfying work, as well as those who had visited foreign countries where they were not demeaned, were unwilling to return to their prewar oppression. A defense worker named Margaret Wright captured the hope of the era when she noted that after the war, "a lot of blacks that were share cropping, doing menial work and stuff, got into the army and saw how other things were and how things could be. They decided they did not want to go back to what they were doing before. They did not want to walk behind a plow, they wouldn't get on the back of the bus anymore."[58] Despite the conflict, violence, and bloodshed, the period was also marked by an exuberance and optimism expressed in black political, social, and cultural life.

Following the Allied victory in 1945, blacks rejected second-class citizenship more than they had during the war. The "new consciousness" that Wright noticed was nourished by the courageous examples set by individual African Americans. This was especially evident in the South, where usually acquiescent blacks turned out in increasing numbers to register and vote despite white terrorism. The number of blacks who voted tripled to 600,000 between the 1940 election and the 1946 Democratic primaries. When Mississippi's segregationist senator Theodore Bilbo's 1946 campaign was investigated, 200 blacks from across the state appeared for the hearings, and 68 black men and women testified to the tactics the senator had used to keep blacks from voting.

African Americans also grew more assertive in society. When Irene Morgan refused to give up her seat to a white passenger during a bus ride from Gloucester County, Virginia, to Baltimore, she was arrested, found guilty, and fined. Defiantly, she took her case to NAACP attorneys Thurgood Marshall and William Hastie, who argued it before the U.S. Supreme Court. In **Morgan v. Virginia** (1946), the Court declared segregation in interstate bus travel illegal. Blacks could no longer be made to sit in the back of the bus behind whites. In 1947, eight blacks and eight whites from the Congress of Racial Equality (CORE) tested the case in the first of many nonviolent direct-action campaigns to end segregation. In what they called the Journey of Reconciliation, they rode Greyhound and Trailways buses from Washington, D.C., through Virginia, North Carolina, and Kentucky, with the blacks sitting in front of the whites.

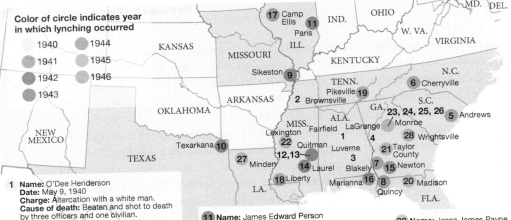

Color of circle indicates year in which lynching occurred

- 1940
- 1941
- 1942
- 1943
- 1944
- 1945
- 1946

1 Name: O'Dee Henderson **Date:** May 9, 1940
Charge: Altercation with a white man.
Cause of death: Beaten and shot to death by three officers and one civilian.

2 Name: Elbert Williams **Date:** June 22, 1940
Charge: Attempting to qualify to vote, and showing an "interest in Negro affairs."
Cause of death: Murdered; body thrown into the Hatchie River.

3 Name: Jesse Thornton **Date:** June 22, 1940
Charge: Failure to refer to a white man as "Mr."
Cause of death: Shot to death; body thrown into the Pataylogga River.

4 Name: Austin Callaway **Date:** Sept. 8, 1940
Charge: Attempted attack on a white woman.
Cause of death: Taken from jail and shot to death by band of masked men.

5 Name: Bruce Tisdale **Date:** Feb. 15, 1941
Charge: Working on a job from which whites had been discharged.
Cause of death: Head wounds; five men held responsible.

6 Name: Robert Melker **Date:** Apr. 18, 1941
Charge: Altercation with a white man.
Cause of death: Shot to death in his home by four men.

7 Name: Robert Sapp **Date:** May 6, 1941
Charge: Suspected of stealing from his employer.
Cause of death: Flogged with a club and a piece of machine belting.

8 Name: A. C. Williams **Date:** May 13, 1941
Charge: Attempted rape.
Cause of death: First taken from jail by a group of armed men, shot, and left for dead. Discovered later at a black residence, severely wounded. Placed in an ambulance for transfer to a nearby hospital. A masked band stopped the unguarded ambulance. Williams's body was found the next day on a creek bridge.

9 Name: Cleo Wright **Date:** Jan. 25, 1942
Charge: Attempted criminal assault.
Cause of death: Dragged through the streets behind an automobile; body burned.

10 Name: Willie Vinson **Date:** July 13, 1942
Charge: Suspected of attempted rape.
Cause of death: Body dragged through the streets behind a speeding automobile; hanged from a cotton gin winch.

11 Name: James Edward Person **Date:** June 22, 1940
Charge: Having "molested" people in the community.
Cause of death: Shot.

12 Name: Charlie Land **Date:** Oct. 12, 1942
Charge: Attempted rape.
Cause of death: Hung from river bridge with Ernest Green; victim was 14 years old.

13 Name: Ernest Green **Date:** Oct. 12, 1942
Charge: Attempted rape.
Cause of death: Hung from river bridge with Charlie Land; victim was 14 years old.

14 Name: Howard Wash **Date:** Oct. 17, 1942
Charge: Had been sentenced automatically to life in prison when jury failed to agree upon the punishment for a murder charge.
Cause of death: Taken from jail and hanged.

15 Name: Robert Hall **Date:** Jan. 30, 1943
Charge: Resisting arrest on charge of theft of truck tire.
Cause of death: Severely beaten by a county policeman who was also a deputy sheriff; died the following day.

16 Name: Cellos Harrison **Date:** June 16, 1943
Charge: Killing a white filling station operator in a 1940 robbery attempt.
Cause of death: Taken from jail by four masked men; clubbed to death.

17 Name: Private Holley Willis (soldier) **Date:** Nov. 7, 1943
Charge: Insulting white women over the telephone.
Cause of death: Shot to death as he tried to escape.

18 Name: Rev. Isaac Simmons **Date:** Mar. 26, 1944
Charge: Hiring a lawyer to safeguard his title to his debt-free farm, through which there was a possibility that an oil vein ran.
Cause of death: Taken from his home; shot to death by a mob.

19 Name: James Scales **Date:** Nov. 23, 1944
Charge: Murdering wife and daughter of the superintendent of the reformatory in which he was confined.
Cause of death: Taken from jail; shot to death by a mob.

20 Name: Jesse James Payne **Date:** Oct. 12, 1945
Charge: Assault with intent to rape.
Cause of death: Captured by a posse and wounded after accusation. Taken to a state prison for safekeeping. Indicted, then placed in the county jail for arraignment. Ultimately, removed from the jail and shot to death by a mob, which apparently entered with a key.

21 Name: Macio Snipes **Date:** July 18, 1946
Charge: Was the only African American from his district to vote in the Georgia primary.
Cause of death: Shot while sitting on his porch.

22 Name: Leon McTatie **Date:** July 22, 1946
Charge: Stealing a saddle.
Cause of death: Flogged to death.

23 Name: Roger Malcolm **Date:** July 25, 1946
Charge: Stabbing his former employer. Killed with wife Dorothy, their unborn child, and another couple, George and Mae H. Dorsey. The other persons were innocent of any charge, except the fact that one of the women recognized a member of the mob who came to lynch Roger Malcolm.
Cause of death: Shot.

24 Name: Dorothy Malcolm (and unborn child) **Date:** July 25, 1946
Charge: None.
Cause of death: Shot; one of the assailants then cut her unborn child out of her body.

25 Name: George Dorsey **Date:** July 25, 1946
Charge: None.
Cause of death: Shot.

26 Name: Mae H. Dorsey **Date:** July 25, 1946
Charge: None.
Cause of death: Shot.

27 Name: John C. Jones **Date:** Aug. 8, 1946
Charge: Attempting to break into a white woman's house.
Cause of death: Tortured and beaten to death.

28 Name: Isaac Newton **Date:** 1946 (exact date unknown)
Charge: Registering to vote.
Cause of death: Shot.

MAP 11.2 The Persistence of Lynching, 1940–1946

Lynching persisted in the South throughout the war years. Often its victims were African Americans who had fought for their country or asserted other citizenship rights, such as voting. Statistics on lynching are not exact, in part because experts disagree on its definition and in part because many lynchings went unreported or suspected murders were not investigated. In 1947, the President's Committee on Civil Rights proposed a host of ameliorative measures to Congress, including an antilynching law that was not enacted. DATA SOURCE: "Lynching — Crime," *Negro Year Book: A Review of Events Affecting Negro Life, 1944–1946*, by Jessie P. Guzman and W. Hardin Hughes, National Humanities Center Resource Toolbox, *The Making of African American Identity: Volume 3, 1917–1968* (http://tinyurl.com/86n69yp).

Several of them were arrested, and more than once they were dragged from the bus by angry whites. Although their protest did not end interstate segregation, it did become a model for the Freedom Rides of the 1960s (see chapter 12).[59]

African Americans also fought to end segregation in national professional organizations. Mabel Staupers, the executive secretary of the National Association of Colored Graduate Nurses, led a successful letter-writing campaign to end discrimination in the army and navy nursing corps. When both branches accepted black nurses on an equal basis with whites in January 1945, Staupers continued her crusade for full integration of black nurses into the profession at large. Her lobbying efforts paid off in 1948, when the American Nurses Association eliminated the color bar and allowed black nurses to become members.[60]

Perhaps nothing symbolized the hope of the era more than the desegregation of baseball, America's favorite pastime. Until 1945, talented African Americans could play professionally only on Negro league ball clubs. Although future Hall of Famers such as Josh Gibson and Satchel Paige were revered for their skills in black America, where regional leagues were a major source of entertainment, black ballplayers wanted a chance to compete with white players and earn similar salaries. In 1945, the Brooklyn Dodgers signed Jackie Robinson, who played for the Kansas City Monarchs in the Negro American League. After proving himself able to withstand malicious heckling from segregationists, Jim Crow accommodations during spring training, and the ever-present threats on his life, Robinson took the field on opening day in 1947 to the cheers of black and white Americans who hoped that this was the first step in the desegregation of all sports. Robinson was soon followed by other black baseball players, most notably Willie Mays of the New York Giants, Ernie Banks of the Chicago Cubs, and Hank Aaron of the Milwaukee Braves.

In tennis, Althea Gibson in 1950 became the first African American to compete in the U.S. National Tennis Championship. In 1951, she became the first black tennis player to play at Wimbledon, the sport's premier tournament. In 1950, the National Basketball Association drafted its first black player, Charles "Chuck" Cooper. Barriers in football fell, too. By 1946, six teams in what would become the American Football League had signed eight black players, but it took the National Football League until 1949 to draft a black player and until the mid-1960s to regularly play signed players. Black boxers had long dominated prizefighting. Joe Louis thrilled black and white crowds alike, especially in 1938, when his defeat of the German heavyweight boxer Max Schmeling made him the pride not only of black Americans but also of the nation as a whole (see chapter 10).

Cities nurtured black culture and made black talent visible. In 1940, the writer Frederick O'Neal and the actor Abram Hill founded the American Negro Theatre (ANT) in Harlem as a way to expand the limited opportunities available to black entertainers and the entertainment available to black audiences. In Hollywood films, for example, black actors were restricted to stereotypical roles. Most were not allowed to play anything but handkerchief-headed mammies or sluggish, pop-eyed, superstitious

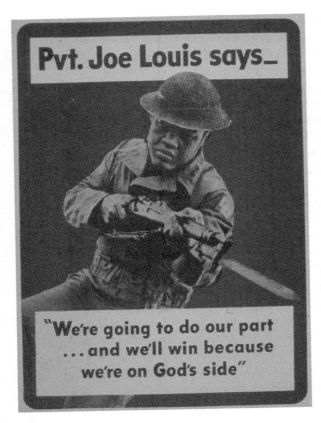

Pvt. Joe Louis Says . . . , 1942

Joe Louis was not just a black hero; he was an American hero. As a black heavyweight boxer who had achieved fame, fortune, and respect, he embodied the hopes and dreams of African Americans. As an American who had defeated the Italian fighter Primo Carnera in 1935 and the German boxer Max Schmeling in 1938 (avenging a loss to Schmeling two years earlier), he embodied the American desire to defeat the Axis powers. Before Louis's second bout with Schmeling in front of 80,000 fans in Yankee Stadium, President Roosevelt told Louis to "prove that *we* can beat Germany."[61] During World War II, the U.S. government produced this poster encouraging both black and white citizens to buy war bonds to help finance the war effort. *National Archives and Records Administration, Still Pictures Division, NWDNS-44-PA-87.*

buffoons. Black actors who rejected these parts found little or no work. The light-skinned Lena Horne was the exception that proved the rule, landing small roles in the 1943 films *Cabin in the Sky* and *Stormy Weather*. She was mostly allowed only to sing, and then with the understanding that her scenes would be cut when the films were shown in states that forbade the presence of nonstereotypical black actors on the screen. Though advised to pass for white or Hispanic in order to get more roles, Horne never did so, focusing instead on her singing career.

Besides producing plays written by black authors and featuring black actors, the ANT offered classes in acting, voice, speech, and many aspects of theater production. From 1940 to 1949, more than 50,000 people attended ANT productions in which black actors played the parts of fully developed, complicated human beings. The most successful production by far was the 1944 play *Anna Lucasta*, written by the white playwright Philip Yordan about a Polish American family. The ANT revised the play and made it suitable for a black cast. It was an immediate success, moving to Broadway after five weeks and subsequently touring to Chicago and London. *Anna Lucasta* offered an opportunity to showcase the array of untapped talent in black America.

At the center of black migrant culture was black music. Full of the expectations characteristic of the war era, this music reflected an African America that was on the move both physically and emotionally. The lyrics to jazz tune "Take the 'A' Train" told people that if they rode the New York subway uptown, they would get to "Sugar Hill in Harlem." A metaphor for a people who became mostly urban during the 1940s, the song suggested that a sweeter life awaited them if they would just "Hurry, get on now." Bebop, a new form of jazz, also reflected a people on the road to independence and in the process of breaking the mold sculpted by white America. In contrast to the big band music it grew out of, bebop featured small groups and improvisational soloists. The sound was irregular and frenetic. More suitable for listening than for dancing, it was featured in the many small nightclubs that dotted the urban landscape. Trumpeter Dizzy Gillespie and saxophonist Charlie Parker pioneered bebop, which also featured trumpeter Miles Davis, pianist Thelonious Monk, and many others.

Blacks, therefore, did not give up their fight for victory at the end of World War II. They continued to press for the domestic "V" in the Double V campaign launched at the beginning of the war. From voting to bebop, everything signaled a new beginning. Once the Allies had defeated the Axis powers, African Americans were determined to defeat injustice at home.

Desegregating the Army and the GI Bill

One glaring injustice was the continued poor treatment of African Americans in the armed forces. Their anger reached the boiling point in 1946 when Sergeant Isaac Woodard, while still in uniform, was beaten and blinded by a white sheriff, on his way home from Fort Gordon, Georgia. The sheriff claimed that Woodard—whom he said was drunk, but who was actually a teetotaler—took too long to use the "colored rest room" at a stop in South Carolina. The sheriff, who gouged out Woodard's eyes and left him overnight in a cell without medical treatment, was subsequently acquitted by an all-white jury. Other violent incidents involving black veterans had elicited anger and outrage, but the outpouring of sympathy, shock, and fury over Woodard's beating was exceptional, in part because the NAACP made sure it received widespread publicity. Even President Harry S. Truman expressed outrage. "My God," Truman told NAACP executive secretary Walter White, "I had no idea it was as terrible as that. We've got to do something."[62]

No doubt thinking about how blacks would vote in the 1948 election, Truman established the President's Committee on Civil Rights in 1946. It was made up of two blacks—Sadie T. M. Alexander, an attorney, and Channing H. Tobias, the director of a philanthropic organization—and several prominent whites. In October 1947, the committee issued its report, *To Secure These Rights*, in which it endorsed, among other things, a permanent Fair Employment Practices Commission, an antilynching law, and an end to segregation and discrimination in the military. Over the objections of high-level military officers, Truman issued **Executive Order 9981** in 1948. "It is hereby declared," the order read, "that there shall be equality of treatment and opportunity for all persons in the armed services without regard to race, color, religion, or national origin." When asked if the order foretold the end of segregation, the president answered unequivocally, "Yes."[63] Nevertheless, it would take several years for Truman's order to be fully implemented, and discrimination in the armed services would not disappear completely as long as racism remained endemic in American society.

Even as the military opened doors, other avenues of opportunity remained closed. The most significant and far-reaching example of continuing discrimination was the way the Servicemen's Readjustment Act, commonly known as the **GI Bill**, was applied to African Americans. Passed by Congress in 1944, the GI Bill was designed to help returning veterans reenter American society as productive citizens. It allowed them to complete a college education at the government's expense, take out low-interest home loans, and collect unemployment compensation. The GI Bill transformed the nature of higher education in the United States. Before the war, few working-class or even middle-class Americans attended college. As millions of returning veterans entered college classrooms, higher education ceased to be the preserve of the rich. The GI Bill also transformed the housing market, making home ownership more commonplace. As white veterans bought homes with government loans, they facilitated America's suburbanization and the rise of the white middle class.[64]

Black Americans experienced no such boon. The bill itself did not discriminate, but its administration both stifled black advancement and widened the economic gap between black and white Americans. Black soldiers, for example, received a disproportionate share of dishonorable and Section VIII, or "blue," discharges (a blue discharge was neither honorable nor dishonorable but was widely presumed to be less than honorable). Usually issued without provocation, these blue discharges not only disqualified black veterans from receiving GI Bill benefits but also stigmatized them in the job market and in the society at large. A 1946 congressional investigation found that the blue discharge "procedure lends itself to dismissals based on prejudice and antagonism," but this finding did not undo the damage done by such discriminatory policies.[65]

The GI Bill's insidious administration by the Veterans Administration (VA) placed even black veterans with honorable discharges at a severe disadvantage. The VA granted low-interest home loans to black veterans only if they purchased homes in black neighborhoods, and such homes were few in number. It forced black veterans to take service jobs by refusing to pay unemployment benefits to those who declined unskilled jobs while looking for something less dead-end. Furthermore, because most white colleges in the North and South held fast to segregation and accepted few African Americans, blacks were effectively shut out of the educational benefits of the GI Bill. Out of the 9,000 students enrolled at the University of Pennsylvania in 1946, only 46 were black. Segregation policies forced blacks to seek admission primarily to historically black colleges and universities, which quickly became overcrowded. Limited facilities forced black colleges to turn away an estimated 20,000 veterans. Meanwhile, the VA consistently refused to pay the tuition of the few blacks who were accepted by white colleges.[66]

In the end, African American soldiers were catastrophically shortchanged by the administration of the GI Bill. By contrast, whites who received VA home loans and/or college tuition payments obtained a boost to their earnings and status that they and their offspring benefited from. With the equity they built up in their homes, they were able to put the next generation through college, start businesses, and otherwise invest for the future.[67]

Although black Americans achieved a shining victory with the postwar desegregation of the armed forces, they nevertheless suffered gravely in the postwar era from the VA's poor treatment of them. In many ways, it was more disabling than the acts of violence perpetrated by individual racists because its financial effects would be felt for generations.

CONCLUSION

A Partial Victory

In May 1945, Germany surrendered to the Allies. Three months later, in August, after the United States dropped atomic bombs on Hiroshima and Nagasaki, Japan surrendered as well. Although African Americans had played a crucial role in winning the war, they could declare only a partial victory. In 1942, they had vowed to fight for victory both abroad and at home, and although the government and war industries had limited their contributions, they had given all that the nation would allow them to. At war's end, despite a few hard-won advances, they had yet to win the fight against injustice in America.

Throughout the war, despite the violence they encountered, African Americans had persisted in their fight for domestic victory. Millions had left the South, and in the next two decades, millions more would leave the region. Like immigrants from abroad, they sought out new places in the North and Midwest, and for the first time they became a significant presence on the West Coast. Though discriminated against in the workforce, black Americans expanded their work experience and were often successful in their attempt to join unions. Even so, they met resistance at every turn. White workers went on strike when blacks entered the workplace, when they were promoted out of unskilled jobs, or when they joined unions. Hate crimes, violent reprisals, and even riots followed when blacks moved into decent neighborhoods or when they wore the uniform of their country, which they had fought for the same as other Americans.

Despite the challenges and setbacks, World War II opened doors, and blacks were determined not to let those doors close again. They wanted first-class citizenship. They wanted to vote, to serve on juries, and to be elected to public office. They wanted jobs for which they were qualified. They wanted to compete in sports against white athletes, and they wanted to be portrayed in movies as real human beings. World War II had given African Americans a peek at what life could be like, and it had raised their expectations of equal opportunity. The challenge for them would be to make those expectations a reality.

Some progress was made during and immediately after the war. The U.S. Supreme Court ruled against the white primary and prohibited segregation in interstate travel. Some black pilots got a chance to distinguish themselves in battle, and some black soldiers were actually allowed to fight for their country. Although blacks were cheated out of GI Bill benefits, the armed services were finally desegregated after the war. Yet the end of combat with the Axis powers marked the beginning of a different kind of war to preserve democracy. The Cold War against communism began even before World War II ended. In this war, loyalty would be tested not on the battlefield or in war industries, but in the way Americans lived their everyday lives.

The domestic "V" in the Double V campaign would continue to be as much a challenge for the nation as a whole as it was for blacks in particular. It would be hard for white Americans to redefine democracy and freedom around the world when second-class citizenship for blacks was part of their definition of democracy and freedom at home. The challenge before the U.S. government and white Americans, therefore, was to include black people in the model of freedom the United States held up to the rest of the world — and to do it in the climate of a new Red scare.

CHAPTER 11 REVIEW

KEY TERMS

Axis powers p. 441

Allies p. 441

Four Freedoms p. 441

Atlantic Charter (1941) p. 441

Nazism p. 442

March on Washington Movement (1941) p. 443

Executive Order 8802 (1941) p. 443

Double V campaign p. 444

Tuskegee Airmen p. 445

zoot suit riots p. 451

soldiers without swords p. 455

Morgan v. Virginia (1946) p. 459

Executive Order 9981 (1948) p. 463

GI Bill (1944) p. 464

REVIEW QUESTIONS

1. Describe the strategy behind the Double V campaign. How did it enable African Americans to protest their circumstances without risking accusations of disloyalty?

2. How did wartime conditions, both in the service and on the home front, shed light on the injustices and restrictions African Americans faced? How did black individuals and organizations address these challenges?

3. What factors during the war promoted black solidarity? How did this bring about the sense of blacks becoming a nation within a nation?

4. How did African Americans use the war to advance themselves politically, socially, and culturally? What were the results of their efforts?

African Americans and the Tuskegee Experiments

Tuskegee Institute was founded in 1881 as a school for blacks in Macon County, Alabama. During the Great Depression and World War II, it was chosen as the site of two disparate experiments. One, the infamous Tuskegee Syphilis Study, represented how expendable black lives were perceived to be. The other, the launching of the famed Tuskegee Airmen, demonstrated how much blacks could achieve if given the opportunity.

The syphilis experiment began in 1932. The American medical community had long been convinced that syphilis, a contagious disease transmitted through sexual inter-course and from mother to fetus, affected whites and blacks differently. It was thought that whites, by dint of their more highly developed brains, suffered more neurological symptoms in the later stages of the disease, while blacks, ruled more by their bodies, suffered more cardiovascular complications. The Study of Untreated Syphilis in the Male Negro, sponsored by the Public Health Service (PHS), presented researchers with a chance to test their theories.

The subjects were desperately poor, uneducated sharecroppers scattered through-out rural Macon County. Most had never visited a doctor or received any kind of medical care before the experiment. Among those who recruited the men were black doctors, local pastors and teachers, and community leaders. A black public health nurse named Eunice Rivers became an invaluable liaison between the men and the doctors conducting the study.

The true nature of the experiment was revealed when, in the 1940s, penicillin became the standard treatment for syphilis. Instead of treating all of the syphilitic participants and closing the study, or splitting off a control group for testing with penicillin, PHS scientists withheld medication and information about it from patients. Even as the PHS itself began administering penicillin as the standard treatment in its clinics across the nation, the Tuskegee men were kept in the dark so that the study could reach its end point — the death and autopsy of all participants. In the late 1960s, Peter Buxtun, a PHS venereal disease investigator in San Francisco, raised questions about the study's morality. The story broke on July 26, 1972, and quickly became front-page news. The study was terminated shortly thereafter. Congressional hearings followed, and in 1974 the NAACP filed a class action suit on behalf of the study victims.

Even as the syphilis study was being conducted in Macon County, decisions were being made in Washington that would bring another, more fortunate group of African American men to the area. In 1939, in response to civil rights leaders' protests against the exclusion of blacks from military pilot training programs, Congress passed an appropria-tions bill designating funds for training African American pilots. Opposed to this idea, the War Department diverted the money into funding civilian flight schools willing to train blacks. One such school was inaugurated at Tuskegee Institute. Two years later, in 1941, when Congress passed legislation forcing the Army Air Corps to form an all-black unit, the Tuskegee Airmen, as they would come to be called, were ready. Admissions requirements for the all-black units were high, requiring flight experience or a college degree — criteria intended to exclude most applicants. Instead, the Army Air Corps was flooded with qualified applicants. The men accepted constituted an elite, highly educated group. They completed both their basic training and their flight training at the newly christened Tuskegee Army Air Field.

Despite the pitfalls of continuing segregation and discrimination, the Tuskegee Airmen went on to win 3 Distinguished Unit Citations by war's end and various individual awards, including at least 1 Silver Star, an estimated 150 Distinguished Flying Crosses, 14 Bronze Stars, and 8 Purple Hearts. When President Harry Truman finally ended segregation in the military in 1948, the veteran Tuskegee Airmen found themselves in high demand throughout the newly formed U.S. air force. Benjamin O. Davis Jr., the African American commander of the 99th and 332nd Fighter Groups, helped draft the air force plan for implementing integration and later became the first African American air force general. (He was the son of Brigadier General Benjamin O. Davis Sr. — see p. 442.) The air force was the first armed service to fully integrate in the postwar period.

Interview with a Tuskegee Syphilis Study Participant, 1972

In these notes, an interviewer records a study participant's experiences after the close of the study. As the interviewer notes, participants were told they were being treated for "bad blood," a local term used to describe several illnesses. The men were offered free medical exams, meals, and burial insurance. To allay any fears, the study employed many Macon County, Alabama, residents, including the black public health nurse Eunice Rivers, mentioned in this interview. Her public health background persuaded her that partial health care for this impoverished community was better than none at all.

Subject was asked what the study meant to the people involved, how it started, etc.

SUBJECT: Started with a blood test. Clinic met at Shiloh Church. They gave us shots. Nurse (Rivers) came out and took us in (to John Andrews Hospital). One time I had a spinal puncture — had to stay in bed for 10 days afterward. Had headaches from that. Several others did too (and stayed in bed awhile). I wore a rubber belt for a long time afterward. Had ointment to run in under the belt.

Doctors came every year or so. After 25 years they gave everyone in the study $25.00 and a certificate. They told him he was in pretty good health.

At the beginning he thought he had "bad blood." They said that was syphilis. (He) just thought it was an "incurable disease." He was booked for Birmingham for "606" shots° but "nurse stopped it." Some other doctor took blood that time and he was signed up to go to Birmingham. Nurse Rivers said he wasn't due to take the shots . . . he went to get on the bus to Birmingham and they turned him down. This was some time between 1942–1947.

SOURCE: U.S. Department of Health, Education, and Welfare, "Interview Notes, 11/01/1972," Tuskegee Syphilis Study Administrative Records, Records of the Centers for Disease Control and Prevention, 1921–2006, NARA's Southeast Region (Atlanta), Morrow, GA.

° Arsphenamine, or compound 606, a drug containing arsenic that was used to treat syphilis prior to the use of penicillin.

DOCUMENT PROJECT

He did not know he was sick before 1932. They gave them a bunch of shots — about once a month. Then they did a spinal. Nurse would notify them about the blood tests and bring them down.

He had not talked to any of the other participants lately.

He had the shots in his arm. In 1961 he had a growth removed from his bladder. (He is 66.) Health insurance paid for it. He paid his bill and his insurance paid back all but $20.

QUESTION: Could all the people in the group afford hospitalization? What would others have done?

SUBJECT: I don't know. I asked the (government) doctors about it (the growth) and they sent me to my family doctor. The government people didn't know I had insurance.

He didn't know of any others in the study who had been in the hospital although one man had become blind after awhile. He hadn't thought much about whether his disease had been cured. The doctor was seeing him every year, and he was feeling pretty good. He was not told what the disease might do to him. He stayed in the program because they asked him to. Nurse came and got him. He thought they all had the same disease. The blind man had been blind nearly 20 years — had worn glasses awhile, then had become blind.

QUESTION: Did anyone do anything about the blind man's eyes?

SUBJECT: I think he told nurse. They talked one time about sending him somewhere. Wasn't treated that he knew of. He (the blind man) never went anywhere and he (subject) didn't know the details. The blind man is about 75 now.

Nurse Rivers

Much has been written about the public health nurse EUNICE RIVERS, or Nurse Rivers, as she was known in the Tuskegee community. She has been called a race traitor because she continued with the syphilis project years after the penicillin cure had been found. She has also been accused of betraying the nursing profession because she did harm to the men in her care. Those who are more sympathetic argue that Rivers was caught between the mostly white male public health doctors and officials and the black male doctors and administration officials at Tuskegee and therefore had no agency. One historian has described her as being "neither a victim nor a villain."[68] Does this photo speak to Rivers's complicated situation? Rivers was the liaison between the Public Health Service, Tuskegee Institute, and the study participants. Why do you think she gained the trust of those involved in the project?

National Archives at Atlanta, Tuskegee Syphilis Study Administrative Records, 1929–1972, ARC Identifier 824615, Agency-Assigned Identifier 18853.

Tuskegee Study Participants

The Tuskegee Syphilis Study began in the early years of the depression, a period marked by the poverty of most Americans and the desperate poverty of African Americans. In Macon County, Alabama, as in most of the South, black sharecroppers were pushed off the land as the government paid landowners not to plant cotton and other crops. Tenants who still worked the land received low wages, and those who still sharecropped got little cash for their crops. Many were caught in a cycle of debt that amounted to peonage. Their houses mostly resembled shacks and lacked running water or indoor toilets. Medical care was almost nonexistent, and many whites believed that black people did not need medical care. In fact, the attitude of Dr. John Heller, the director of venereal diseases at the Public Health Service from 1943 to 1948, toward the study participants was that they were "subjects, not patients; clinical material, not sick people."[69] Examine this picture of the study participants. Why would Heller describe them so? What demeanor do the men project?

National Archives at Atlanta, Tuskegee Syphilis Study Administrative Records, 1929–1972, ARC Identifier 956097, Agency-Assigned Identifier 18868.

Alexander Jefferson | *Interview with a Tuskegee Airman, 2006*

LIEUTENANT COLONEL ALEXANDER JEFFERSON (b. 1921), a Tuskegee Airman who served in the Ninety-Ninth Fighter Squadron of the U.S. Army Air Corps during World War II, gave an interview in 2006 describing his experiences. In it, he described his training, the experience of being shot down and taken prisoner of war by the Germans, his observations of Europe, and his return home. During the war the white commander of Jefferson's unit, General William W. Momyer, claimed that the Ninety-Ninth "failed to display the aggressiveness and desire for combat that are necessary for a first-class fighting organization." How do Jefferson's recollections compare with General Momyer's account of the Tuskegee Airmen's capabilities?

This is June 1944. The Americans have just liberated Rome. Our job is to escort these bombers. It's B17s and B24s, [they're] going to Germany. They're 21,000/22,000 feet up to the target.

[And by that time, more than likely, we would have to turn them loose and come] back and another group would take over and bring them back home.

I was trying to explain to someone, if you look up at 12 o'clock to the horizon [to see contrails, to look behind you at six o'clock to the horizon to see] contrails of bombers going to Germany. And fighters all over the sky. Bombers in front of you, bombers behind you. It was unbelievable.

Sometimes we'd take the B17s to the target. You look up ahead, there's a big black cloud over the target.

The black cloud would extend from 15,000 feet to 25,000 feet, round like a hockey puck — flak [anti-aircraft fire]. And the bombers would fly straight into that black cloud and sometimes we got caught in that flak.

Where it was so close so they would actually hit the plane and actually knock the plane out of control. It sounds like somebody would take pebbles and throw it on a tin roof.

If you're that close and those things hit your plane, blowing holes, knocking holes in your wings and in your fuselage, you were too darn close.

Many times, we'd see the bombers go into the flak, [and out] the bottom of the cloud would come a bomber, half on fire, wing blown off. You'd hear the radio: bail out, damn it. Bail out. Bail out.

And out of this plane would come one cloud, one chute — you'd see a guy come out. And another guy came out. And all of a sudden, boosh(ph), explode.

First time was realization — I saw eight men die. I got sick. I'm sitting up there at 24,000 feet. And I got sick inside that oxygen mask. I puked and vomited. First time I ever got sick in an airplane.

[August the 12th, 1944: they simply said, some big towers and some buildings, you go over] and use your 50-calibers and shoot it up and destroy it. That's what we did.

The guys went in, down on the deck, 400 miles an hour. The first 12 guys got through okay. The side of the cliff was lighted up with anti-aircraft fire. We got down within a thousand yards, 1,500 yards, 800 yards, 600 yards. I got hits on the target and I went across the top of the target at treetop height.

Something says, boom — I looked up and there's a hole on top of the canopy. And I pulled up off of the deck and fire came out of the floor, because the shell had come up through the floor in front of the stick.

Out of the nine months of training, we never had one minute on training on how to get out [of] an airplane. I remember the tail going by and I pulled the D-ring on a parachute. Ordinarily, they'd say count one, two, three, pull it. No, I pulled that son of a gun, bang, right then. When the parachute popped, I'm in the trees and quite naturally the guys who shot me down were sitting over there about 200 or 300 yards away.

The German interrogator came down and said 332nd Fighter Group, Negroes, red tails. I looked at his book and said what the heck. He opened it up and thumbed through it, had all the pictures of all the classes that had graduated before me. They had all my marks at Clark University. They had my high school marks at Chadsey High School in Detroit. They knew how much taxes my dad paid on his house in Detroit. They knew more about me than I knew about myself.

When I got to Stalag Luft III, which is 80 miles east of Berlin, I was treated as a POW with all the rights and privileges of an American officer. No segregation, no discrimination. I was only there four months or five months when the Russians started coming west and the Germans put us out on the road and we walked 80 kilometers, temperature — 20 below zero.

Further west we wound up at Stalag 7A. I was there for about four months until April where Patton's Third Army liberated the camp I was in.

The next day after that, somebody said, hey Jeff, there's a place down there with a lot of dead people. I said what are you talking about? He said man, they've gotten people down there stacked up like cordwood. So we got a jeep and we went down to see this place, Dachau.

The ovens were still warm. The odor of human flesh is something I'll never forget. A table, 20 or 30-feet long covered with amalgam and gold teeth where they cut off the hair for seat cushions.

Man's inhumanity to man.

Coming down the gangplank by boat from London — a boat across from Le Havre to London. When you walked — [Unintelligible] down the gangplank in New York City, a big sign in front of you says: whites to the right, colored to the left. And a white soldier down at the bottom indicated whites to the right and niggers to the left. Coming back home — racist segregation.

Malcolm [X], Martin Luther King, Rosa Parks — I am part of the Civil Rights Movement. America — United States: best country in the world. You don't like it? Leave it. The only obligation, make it better. It ain't perfect but it's home.

Tuskegee Airmen

When the military established the flight training program at Tuskegee, they expected it to fail. The top brass held the belief, expressed in a 1925 report by the U.S. Army War College, that African Americans were cowards, that they lacked initiative and would not accept responsibility, that leadership qualities and intelligence were beyond them.[70] The Tuskegee Airmen, both pilots and ground support units, worked hard to show the higher-ups just how wrong they were. Black airmen came to Tuskegee from all parts of the country, but especially from New York City, Washington, Los Angeles, Chicago,

Philadelphia, and Detroit. Most had at least some college education, and many had college degrees. They trained the same way white pilots trained and took the same courses and tests in operations, meteorology, intelligence, engineering, medicine, and other officer fields. Enlisted members were trained to be aircraft and engine mechanics, armament specialists, radio repairmen, parachute riggers, control tower operators, policemen, or administrative clerks — all the skills needed so that they could fully function as an Army Air Corps flying squadron or ground support unit.[71] Look at this picture and think about the Army War College report and about the other documents in this Document Project. How does this picture demonstrate the way Tuskegee Airmen represented their race?

Afro Newspaper/Gado/Archive Photos/Getty Images.

William H. Hastie and George E. Stratemeyer | *Resignation Memo and Response, 1943*

When WILLIAM H. HASTIE (1904–1976) resigned his post as civilian aide to Secretary of War Henry L. Stimson (1867–1950), he explained his reasons in a detailed memo dated January 5, 1943. Among those reasons were "segregation within Army theatres, the blood plasma issue and the unvarying pattern of separate Negro units."

He was especially disturbed by the Army Air Corps' policies at Tuskegee. MAJOR GENERAL GEORGE E. STRATEMEYER (1890–1969), U.S. army chief of the air staff, responded to Hastie's memo on January 12, 1943. Following are excerpts from their correspondence.

WILLIAM H. HASTIE: As you know, I have believed for some time that my presence in the War Department is no longer essential to the maintenance of the several substantial gains made during the past two years in the handling of racial issues and particular problems of Negro military and civilian personnel. At the same time I have believed that there remain areas in which changes of racial policy should be made but will not be made in response to advocacy within the Department but only as a result of strong and manifest public opinion. . . .

Compelling new considerations have now arisen. In one very important branch of the Army, the Air Forces, where the handling of racial issues has been reactionary and unsatisfactory from the outset, further retrogression is now so apparent and recent occurrences are so objectionable and inexcusable that I have no alternative but to resign in protest and to give public expression to my views. This ultimate decision has been forced upon me by . . . the humiliating and morale shattering mistreatment which, with at least the tacit approval of the Air Command, continues to be imposed upon Negro military personnel at the Tuskegee Air Base. . . .

. . . The Negro program began with the organization of several so-called Aviation Squadrons (Separate). Of these units . . . it is sufficient to say, that they were organized to serve no specific military need . . . and that . . . their characteristic assignment has been the performance of such odd jobs of common labor as may arise from time to time at air fields. . . .

SOURCE: Morris J. MacGregor and Bernard C. Nalty, eds., *Blacks in the United States Armed Forces: Basic Documents*, vol. 5, *Black Soldiers in World War II* (Wilmington, DE: Scholarly Resources, 1977), 178–81, 183–85.

. . . Two Negro officers were sent by the Ground Forces to the Air Forces school for Aerial Observers. They successfully completed their course. But such information as I have been able to get reveals no plans for their utilization and no intention of training additional Negro officers in Aerial Observation. . . .

. . . To date no application of a Negro for appointment as an army service pilot has been accepted. . . .

. . . The racial impositions upon Negro personnel at Tuskegee have become so severe and demoralizing that, in my judgment, they jeopardize the entire future of the Negro in combat aviation.

GEORGE E. STRATEMEYER: I have caused an analysis to be made of the statements contained in the memorandum to the Secretary of War . . . from Judge William H. Hastie. . . .

. . . Judge Hastie's statement that Aviation Squadrons (Separate) would never have existed except for the necessity of making some provision for Negro enlisted men in the Air Forces is bluntly true. Judge Hastie, however, fails to analyze or recognize the necessity for the creation of these units. . . . Fifty-four per cent of white selectees scored 100 or better on the Army General Classification Test; 8.5% of the Negroes attained that score. Forty-eight per cent of white selectees scored 100 or better on the Mechanical Aptitude Test; 7.1% of the Negroes attained that score. Experience has shown that the soldier who fails to meet the standard of 100 or better on both these tests has difficulty in absorbing instruction at technical schools. . . . The white soldier in the lower intelligence brackets, while not assigned to Aviation Squadrons (Separate), finds himself detailed to "the performance of odd jobs of common labor as may arise from time to time at air fields." These facts clearly indicate that Judge Hastie's position with reference to Aviation Squadrons (Separate) is not well taken.

. . . The school at Tuskegee was established after most careful study and conferences with officials of Tuskegee Institute. These same officials urged the establishment of the Army Air Forces School at that location to include a Negro Contract Primary Flying School. . . . Although certain white contractors objected . . . , the program has been carried through with excellent results. . . .

. . . The two Negro officers who received training as Aerial Observers were returned to the Ground Forces for duty in consonance with current policy as were white officers simi-

larly detailed for this training. The War Department policy with reference to the assignment of Negro officers to white units precludes the training of Negro Observers for duty with the Air Forces inasmuch as there are no Negro Observation Units. . . .

. . . The statement of Judge Hastie that racial impositions upon Negro personnel at Tuskegee are so severe and demoralizing as to jeopardize the future of the Negro in combat aviation does not appear to be borne out by fact. The report of the Inspector General . . . and the statement by the Commanding General . . . that the 99th Fighter Squadron is in a superior state of training, indicates that the mission of the Army Air Forces installation at Tuskegee is being successfully accomplished.

QUESTIONS FOR ANALYSIS

1. Why do you think Tuskegee Institute was chosen as the site of these two "experiments"?

2. Integral to the success of the Tuskegee Syphilis Study was the participation of Tuskegee Institute and hundreds of black doctors, nurses, local pastors, and community leaders, including Eunice Rivers, who defended her role in the study even after it was exposed and denounced. Why do you think all of these people agreed to participate at the study's inception and continued with it throughout its forty-year life span? Examine the photo of Eunice Rivers. What kind of image does she project?

3. How do you think William Hastie reacted to George Stratemeyer's response? How do we reconcile Stratemeyer's statistics on the aptitude of black men with the superlative performance of the Tuskegee Airmen?

4. Alexander Jefferson, Hastie, and Stratemeyer paint differing pictures of the Tuskegee Airmen and the circumstances under which they were trained. Compare and contrast their descriptions.

5. Alexander Jefferson compares his treatment in a Nazi POW camp with the treatment he received on returning to the United States. What feelings must his homecoming have engendered? How might his experiences abroad as a pilot and as a POW have changed him?

6. Compare the photos of the Tuskegee Syphilis Study participants and the Tuskegee Airmen. What differences do you notice between the two groups of men? What is similar about them?

7. In 2007, President George W. Bush honored the Tuskegee Airmen with the Congressional Gold Medal, saying, "I would like to offer a gesture to help atone for all the unreturned

salutes and unforgivable indignities." Ten years earlier, President Bill Clinton had issued an apology to the Tuskegee Syphilis Study participants, saying, "We can look at you in the eye and finally say on behalf of the American people, what the United States government did was shameful, and I am sorry." Why was each apology issued so long after the fact? What is the significance of these two individuals' and/or the nation's acceptance of responsibility for these historical transgressions? Imagine that you were a Tuskegee Airman or syphilis study subject. How would you have received the president's apology?

NOTES

1. Quoted in Yvonne Latty, *We Were There: Voices of African American Veterans, from World War II to the War in Iraq* (New York: Amistad, 2004), 40.
2. Ibid., 41.
3. Quoted in Michael Keith Honey, *Black Workers Remember: An Oral History of Segregation, Unionism, and the Freedom Struggle* (Berkeley: University of California Press, 1999), 101.
4. Ibid., 105.
5. Quoted in Robert B. Edgerton, *Hidden Heroism: Black Soldiers in America's Wars* (Boulder, CO: Westview Press, 2001), 128.
6. Both quoted in Bernard C. Nalty, *Strength for the Fight: A History of Black Americans in the Military* (New York: Free Press, 1986), 139.
7. All quoted in Jack D. Foner, *Blacks and the Military in American History* (New York: Praeger, 1974), 133–38.
8. Ibid., 141.
9. Quoted in Marc Gallicchio, *The African American Encounter with Japan and China: Black Internationalism in Asia, 1895–1945* (Chapel Hill: University of North Carolina Press, 2000), 119.
10. Ibid., 118.
11. Ibid., 122–38.
12. Ibid., 116–17.
13. Foner, *Blacks and the Military*, 148–54.
14. Quoted in Latty, *We Were There*, 20.
15. Nalty, *Strength for the Fight*, 191–92.
16. Edgerton, *Hidden Heroism*, 135–38.
17. Foner, *Blacks and the Military*, 149.
18. Patricia Sullivan, *Days of Hope: Race and Democracy in the New Deal Era* (Chapel Hill: University of North Carolina Press, 1996), 136.
19. Quoted in Foner, *Blacks and the Military*, 154.
20. Quoted in Sullivan, *Days of Hope*, 137.
21. Harvard Sitkoff, "Racial Militancy and Interracial Violence in the Second World War," *Journal of American History* 58, no. 3 (1971): 668–69.
22. Edgerton, *Hidden Heroism*, 134.
23. Foner, *Blacks and the Military*, 157–59.
24. Joanna Bourke, *An Intimate History of Killing: Face-to-Face Killing in Twentieth-Century Warfare* (New York: Basic Books, 1999), 119.
25. Quoted in Edgerton, *Hidden Heroism*, 163.
26. Quoted in Vincent Harding, Robin D. G. Kelley, and Earl Lewis, *We Changed the World: African Americans, 1945–1970* (New York: Oxford University Press, 1997), 28.
27. Ronald Takaki, *Double Victory: A Multicultural History of America in World War II* (Boston: Little, Brown, 2000), 40.
28. Charles D. Chamberlain, *Victory at Home: Manpower and Race in the American South during World War II* (Athens: University of Georgia Press, 2003), 26, 56.
29. Chamberlain, *Victory at Home*, 80–81, 62.
30. Takaki, *Double Victory*, 42–43.
31. Chamberlain, *Victory at Home*, 63–67.
32. Quoted in Donna Jean Murch, *Living for the City: Migration, Education, and the Rise of the Black Panther Party in Oakland, California* (Chapel Hill: University of North Carolina Press, 2010), 15–16.
33. Quintard Taylor, "African American Men in the American West, 1528–1990," *Annals of the American Academy of Political and Social Science* 569 (May 2000): 111–12.
34. Chamberlain, *Victory at Home*, 85–86.
35. Quoted in Takaki, *Double Victory*, 45.
36. Ibid., 45–46.
37. Sitkoff, "Racial Militancy and Interracial Violence," 671.
38. Marilynn Johnson, "Gender, Race, and Rumors," *Gender and History* 10, no. 2 (1998): 256–60.
39. Quoted in Harriet Sigerman, ed., *The Columbia Documentary History of American Women since 1941* (New York: Columbia University Press, 2003), 36.
40. Quoted in Chamberlain, *Victory at Home*, 124.
41. Quoted ibid., 122–23.
42. Sullivan, *Days of Hope*, 162.
43. Quoted in Takaki, *Double Victory*, 51.
44. Nicholson Baker, *Human Smoke: The Beginnings of World War II, the End of Civilization* (New York: Simon & Schuster, 2008), 343.
45. *Crisis* 50, no. 1 (January 1943): 8.
46. Takaki, *Double Victory*, 51.
47. Chamberlain, *Victory at Home*, 138–39.
48. Ibid., 110–14.
49. Quoted in Nancy MacLean, *Freedom Is Not Enough: The Opening of the American Workplace* (Cambridge: Harvard University Press, 2006), 25.
50. Richard M. Dalfiume, "The 'Forgotten Years' of the Negro Revolution," *Journal of American History* 55, no. 1 (1968): 100.
51. *The Black Press: Soldiers without Swords* (South Burlington, VT: California Newsreel, 1998), DVD.
52. Quoted in Steven F. Lawson, *Black Ballots: Voting Rights in the South, 1944–1969* (Lanham, MD: Lexington Books, 1999), 130.
53. Quoted in Harding, Kelley, and Lewis, *We Changed the World*, 26–27.
54. Quoted in Robert Korstad and Nelson Lichtenstein, "Opportunities Found and Lost: Labor, Radicals, and the Early Civil Rights Movement," *Journal of American History* 75, no. 3 (1988): 793.
55. Quoted in Sullivan, *Days of Hope*, 119.
56. Quoted in Patricia Sullivan, "Movement Building during the World War II Era: The NAACP's Legal Insurgency in the South," in *Fog of War: The Second World War and the Civil Rights Movement*, ed. Kevin M. Kruse and Stephen Tuck (New York: Oxford University Press, 2012), 75.
57. Sullivan, *Days of Hope*, 170.
58. Quoted in Takaki, *Double Victory*, 50.
59. Sullivan, *Days of Hope*, 218–19.
60. Darlene Clark Hine, *Black Women in White: Racial Conflict and Cooperation in the Nursing Profession, 1890–1950* (Bloomington: Indiana University Press, 1989), 183–86.

61. Quoted in Edgerton, *Hidden Heroism*, 127.

62. Quoted in Nalty, *Strength for the Fight*, 205.

63. Both quoted ibid., 242.

64. Karen Brodkin Sacks, "How Did Jews Become White Folks?," in *Race*, ed. Steven Gregory and Roger Sanjek (New Brunswick, NJ: Rutgers University Press, 1994), 89–99.

65. Associated Press, "House Committee Urges Army Quit Use of 'Blue' Discharges," *Sarasota Herald Tribune*, January 30, 1946.

66. Hilary Herbold, "Never a Level Playing Field: Blacks and the GI Bill," *Journal of Blacks in Higher Education* 6 (Winter 1994–1995): 104–8.

67. Ira Katznelson, *When Affirmative Action Was White: An Untold History of Racial Inequality in Twentieth-Century America* (New York: Norton, 2005), 113–41.

68. Susan L. Smith, "Neither Victim nor Villain: Eunice Rivers and Public Health Work," in *Tuskegee's Truths: Rethinking the Tuskegee Syphilis Study*, ed. Susan M. Reverby (Chapel Hill: University of North Carolina Press, 2000), 349.

69. James H. Jones, *Bad Blood: The Tuskegee Syphilis Experiment* (New York: Free Press, 1981), 179.

70. U.S. Army War College, "The Army War College Studies Black Soldiers," HERB: Resources for Teachers, American Social History Project/Center for Media and Learning, accessed August 22, 2015, http://herb.ashp.cuny.edu/items/show/808.

71. "Who Were They?," Tuskegee Airmen National Historical Museum, accessed August 22, 2015, http://www.tuskegeemuseum.org/who-were-they/.

SUGGESTED REFERENCES

The Crisis of World War II

Edgerton, Robert B. *Hidden Heroism: Black Soldiers in America's Wars*. Boulder, CO: Westview Press, 2001.

Foner, Jack D. *Blacks and the Military in American History*. New York: Praeger, 1974.

Gallicchio, Marc. *The African American Encounter with Japan and China: Black Internationalism in Asia, 1895–1945*. Chapel Hill: University of North Carolina Press, 2000.

Honey, Michael Keith. *Black Workers Remember: An Oral History of Segregation, Unionism, and the Freedom Struggle*. Berkeley: University of California Press, 1999.

Latty, Yvonne. *We Were There: Voices of African American Veterans, from World War II to the War in Iraq*. New York: Amistad, 2004.

Miller, Richard E. *The Messman Chronicles: African Americans in the U.S. Navy, 1932–1943*. Annapolis, MD: Naval Institute Press, 2004.

Nalty, Bernard C. *Strength for the Fight: A History of Black Americans in the Military*. New York: Free Press, 1986.

Sitkoff, Harvard. "Racial Militancy and Interracial Violence in the Second World War." *Journal of American History* 58, no. 3 (1971): 661–81.

Sullivan, Patricia. *Days of Hope: Race and Democracy in the New Deal Era*. Chapel Hill: University of North Carolina Press, 1996.

African Americans on the Home Front

The Black Press: Soldiers without Swords. DVD. South Burlington, VT: California Newsreel, 1998.

Chamberlain, Charles D. *Victory at Home: Manpower and Race in the American South during World War II*. Athens: University of Georgia Press, 2003.

Dalfiume, Richard M. "The 'Forgotten Years' of the Negro Revolution." *Journal of American History* 55, no. 1 (1968): 90–106.

Gregory, James N. *The Southern Diaspora: How the Great Migrations of Black and White Southerners Transformed America*. Chapel Hill: University of North Carolina Press, 2005.

Harding, Vincent, Robin D. G. Kelley, and Earl Lewis. *We Changed the World: African Americans, 1945–1970*. New York: Oxford University Press, 1997.

Johnson, Marilynn. "Gender, Race, and Rumors." *Gender and History* 10, no. 2 (1998): 252–77.

MacLean, Nancy. *Freedom Is Not Enough: The Opening of the American Workplace*. Cambridge: Harvard University Press, 2006.

Murch, Donna Jean. *Living for the City: Migration, Education, and the Rise of the Black Panther Party in Oakland, California*. Chapel Hill: University of North Carolina Press, 2010.

Savage, Barbara Dianne. *Broadcasting Freedom: Radio, War, and the Politics of Race, 1938–1948*. Chapel Hill: University of North Carolina Press, 1999.

Takaki, Ronald. *Double Victory: A Multicultural History of America in World War II*. Boston: Little, Brown, 2000.

Taylor, Quintard. "African American Men in the American West, 1528–1990." *Annals of the American Academy of Political and Social Science* 569 (May 2000): 102–19.

The Struggle for Citizenship Rights

Bullock, Henry Allen. *A History of Negro Education in the South: From 1619 to the Present*. Cambridge: Harvard University Press, 1967.

Herbold, Hilary. "Never a Level Playing Field: Blacks and the GI Bill." *Journal of Blacks in Higher Education* 6 (Winter 1994–1995): 104–8.

Hine, Darlene Clark. *Black Women in White: Racial Conflict and Cooperation in the Nursing Profession, 1890–1950*. Bloomington: Indiana University Press, 1989.

Katznelson, Ira. *When Affirmative Action Was White: An Untold History of Racial Inequality in Twentieth-Century America*. New York: Norton, 2005.

Korstad, Robert, and Nelson Lichtenstein. "Opportunities Found and Lost: Labor, Radicals, and the Early Civil Rights Movement." *Journal of American History* 75, no. 3 (1988): 786–811.

McGuire, Phillip, ed. *Taps for a Jim Crow Army: Letters from Black Soldiers in World War II*. Lexington: University Press of Kentucky, 1993.

Sacks, Karen Brodkin. "How Did Jews Become White Folks?" In *Race*, edited by Steven Gregory and Roger Sanjek, 78–102. New Brunswick, NJ: Rutgers University Press, 1994.

Turner, Sarah, and John Bound. "Closing the Gap or Widening the Divide: The Effects of the G.I. Bill and World War II on the Educational Outcomes of Black Americans." Working Paper 9044, National Bureau of Economic Research, Cambridge, MA, 2002.

Washburn, Patrick S. *A Question of Sedition: The Federal Government's Investigation of the Black Press during World War II.* New York: Oxford University Press, 1986.

Document Project: African Americans and the Tuskegee Experiments

Jones, James H. *Bad Blood: The Tuskegee Syphilis Experiment.* New York: Free Press, 1981.

Moye, J. Todd. *Freedom Flyers: The Tuskegee Airmen of World War II.* New York: Oxford University Press, 2010.

Reverby, Susan M. *Examining Tuskegee: The Infamous Syphilis Study and Its Legacy.* Chapel Hill: University of North Carolina Press, 2009.

Smith, Susan L. "Neither Victim nor Villain: Eunice Rivers and Public Health Work." In *Tuskegee's Truths: Rethinking the Tuskegee Syphilis Study*, edited by Susan M. Reverby, 348–64. Chapel Hill: University of North Carolina Press, 2000.

The Early Civil Rights Movement

1945–1963

CHRONOLOGY *Events specific to African American history are in purple. General United States history events are in black.*

1945 Tensions between United States and Soviet Union begin to escalate in early stages of Cold War

1947 President Harry S. Truman institutes loyalty program for federal employees

House Un-American Activities Committee (HUAC) begins investigations

1948 Truman inserts civil rights plank into Democratic Party platform

States' Rights Party (Dixiecrats) runs segregationist Strom Thurmond for president

Shelley v. Kraemer rules against restrictive covenants

Truman elected for second term

1949 North Atlantic Treaty Organization (NATO) founded

Soviet Union detonates atomic bomb

1950–1953 Korean War

1950 NAACP passes loyalty resolution

McCarran Internal Security Act establishes loyalty review boards in executive branch

1951 NAACP files class action suit, *Brown v. Board of Education of Topeka*, challenging educational segregation

1952 Dwight D. Eisenhower elected president

1954 *Brown v. Board of Education of Topeka* declares separate public educational facilities unconstitutional

1955 Fourteen-year-old Emmett Till murdered in Mississippi

Montgomery bus boycott begins when Rosa Parks refuses to relinquish her seat to a white passenger

1956 *Browder v. Gayle* declares segregated buses illegal; Montgomery bus boycott ends

1957 Southern Christian Leadership Conference (SCLC) founded in Atlanta; Martin Luther King Jr. becomes first president

Governor Orval Faubus orders Arkansas National Guard to block entrance of nine black students to Little Rock Central High School; Eisenhower federalizes National Guard and mobilizes U.S. army to protect students

Soviet Union launches *Sputnik*, sparking Cold War "space race" with United States

1958 Black elected officials in Los Angeles produce state Fair Employment Practices Commission to address job discrimination

1960 Four students inaugurate sit-in movement at Woolworth's lunch counter in Greensboro, North Carolina

Student Nonviolent Coordinating Committee (SNCC) founded

John F. Kennedy elected president

1961 Congress of Racial Equality (CORE) organizes Freedom Rides

1962 Students for a Democratic Society (SDS) founded

Kennedy sends troops to Oxford, Mississippi, to quell riots after James Meredith wins right to attend University of Mississippi

1963 SCLC and Alabama Christian Movement for Human Rights attempt to desegregate Birmingham's public facilities and open civil service jobs

King writes "Letter from Birmingham City Jail"

Eugene "Bull" Connor, Birmingham's police commissioner, jails more than 600 adults and children and orders attacks on civil rights marchers

Mississippi NAACP leader Medgar Evers killed

March on Washington for Jobs and Freedom

Paul Robeson: A Cold War Civil Rights Warrior

On June 12, 1956, a weary Paul Robeson took a seat before the House Un-American Activities Committee (HUAC). Robeson, a prominent civil rights activist, had been subpoenaed to testify two weeks earlier, but his doctors had claimed he was too ill to do so. Actually, Robeson was depressed. Throughout the 1930s and during World War II, he, like so many other African Americans, had been an outspoken critic of the United States, speaking in favor of the Double V campaign and the rights of trade unions, and against colonialism and imperialism. But now, in the context of the Cold War with the Soviet Union, his remarks were denounced by blacks and whites alike. A speech he made at a 1949 peace conference in Paris, which declared that blacks would not make war on the Soviet Union, had ignited massive controversy. Blacklisted at home and prevented from going abroad when the government revoked his passport in 1950, a dispirited Robeson had reason to be distressed.

He remained defiant, however, in the face of his House interrogation. When asked, "Are you now a member of the Communist Party?" Robeson replied, "I am not being tried for whether I am a Communist. I am being tried for fighting for the rights of my people, who are still second class citizens in this U.S. of America." During his testimony, Robeson repeated his claim that blacks would not take up arms against the Soviet Union. When this drew scoffs, he reiterated that the 900 million colored people of the world would not go to war in defense of Western imperialism.[1]

Robeson's activist sentiments were born many years before the Cold War. Although he graduated from Columbia Law School in 1923, he turned to acting and concert singing (see chapter 10) when racial discrimination forced him out of a New York law firm. His wide travels allowed him to experience different cultures and political systems, and he was especially taken with the Soviet Union: "When I first entered the Soviet Union I said to myself, 'I am a human being. I don't have to worry about my color.'"[2] He reminded people that Communists had defended the Scottsboro Boys (see chapter 10). For Robeson, the Congress of Industrial Organizations (CIO) held the key to economic justice, and he was mindful that Communists had helped bring blacks into that labor organization. Robeson was also a longtime Pan-Africanist, believing that the fate of all blacks in the Western Hemisphere was linked to that of black Africa, and in 1937 he helped found the International Committee on African Affairs, which served as a clearinghouse to disseminate accurate information about Africa to uninformed Americans. He also fought against racism and lynching, which led him to found the American Crusade against Lynching in 1946.

Robeson's lifetime struggle against racism and his persecution during the 1950s offer insight into the challenges African Americans faced in the postwar era. Though critical of their country during World War II, blacks had served loyally on the battlefield and in war industries. Despite attempts to prove their disloyalty, even government operatives had been forced to admit that America, not its black citizens, needed to change. Robeson's hearing before HUAC evidenced a significant shift. During the war, black people had demanded that the government remain true to the ideals expressed in the Four Freedoms (see chapter 11). Now, with the advent of the Cold War, America demanded that blacks prove their commitment to those freedoms by denouncing communism; the Soviet Union and its leader, Joseph Stalin; and any activities undertaken by Communists in the United States and abroad.

Many African Americans would find this difficult to do. Stalin was unquestionably a tyrant, and even though Robeson refused to denounce him, most blacks did. But rank-and-file Communists and other left-leaning activists had, as Robeson indicated, been active in the black freedom struggle. Many had been instrumental in the fight for jobs and black workers' rights. Moreover, anticommunism gave segregationists a lethal weapon in their resistance to the black freedom struggle. Robeson's enemies, for example, not only crippled his acting and singing career but also stifled his activism against racial injustice. How would African Americans meet this new assault on their struggle for

freedom? Like Robeson, they remained defiant as they maneuvered in the new postwar environment. But their movement, which during World War II had emerged as an international movement for both civil and economic rights, would be irrevocably altered by the climate of fear in which those who spoke against America's inequalities were branded Communists and punished.

The anti-Communist hysteria both helped and hindered African Americans' struggle for freedom. It helped by enabling blacks to spotlight how few rights they had, demonstrating the contrast between American ideology and practice. For this tactic to work, however, the movement had to focus on demonstrable inequalities — segregation and disfranchisement — which could be altered by legislation and litigation. Less visible injustices — such as the systemic prejudices that drove housing and employment discrimination — had to be de-emphasized. The first phase of the postwar freedom struggle, therefore, used nonviolent direct-action protest — boycotts, sit-ins, Freedom Rides, and marches — to fight legalized discrimination and to enforce desegregation laws and court decisions. This new strategy was accompanied by new leaders and new organizations. Although the strategy was successful on many fronts, the persistence of virulent white resistance and the continued inequities in employment and housing caused many to question the movement's direction.

Anticommunism and the Postwar Black Freedom Struggle

Robeson was not the first African American to be investigated by HUAC. Beginning in 1947, many well-known civil rights activists, including W. E. B. Du Bois, Mary McLeod Bethune, Adam Clayton Powell Jr., and Langston Hughes, were investigated or called on to prove that their activism was unconnected to Communist activities in the United States. This period — known as the second Red scare or the McCarthy era, after Wisconsin senator Joseph McCarthy, perhaps the most outspoken anti-Communist in the nation — wreaked havoc on the black freedom struggle. The fear it generated forced civil rights and labor organizations to purge many of their most earnest and productive leaders and ultimately forced those organizations to shift direction and modify their goals.

African Americans, the Cold War, and President Truman's Loyalty Program

Ironically, it was Harry S. Truman, the same president who desegregated the armed services, who undermined the progress being made for economic and political justice. In March 1947, soon after he appointed the first President's Committee on Civil Rights (see chapter 11), Truman issued an executive order establishing a **loyalty program** to confirm the loyalty of federal employees. Passed by Congress the following August and expanded in the McCarran Internal Security Act of 1950 — an act so extreme that even Truman vetoed it, unsuccessfully — the program established loyalty review boards in every department and agency of the executive branch. It also allowed the federal government to use any means necessary to investigate any person or organization, and it allowed the government to regulate, fine, imprison, and/or deport anyone deemed disloyal. Disloyalty was defined broadly as belonging to or being in sympathy with a "foreign or domestic organization, association, movement, or group or combination of persons, designated by the Attorney General as totalitarian, fascist, communist, or subversive."[3]

The rationale for the order was the perceived threat of Communist infiltration of government agencies. In the years following World War II, tension mounted between the Soviet Union and its former allies as Moscow extended its influence throughout Eastern Europe and the Middle East. U.S. leaders feared that communism would spread in America the way it had in Poland, Czechoslovakia, Hungary, East Germany, and Greece. To protect itself, the United States joined Britain, France, Canada, and eight other nations in the North Atlantic Treaty Organization (NATO), a peacetime military pact signed in 1949 that promised mutual aid in the event of an armed attack. At home, leaders cautioned Americans to beware of subversives who wanted to destroy the country from within. During the "hot" war with Germany and Japan, the enemy was visible, and its military and weaponry could be defended against and attacked. But this new "cold" war with the Soviet Union was as much a battle to win the hearts and minds of Americans as it was a fight to gain strategic geographic advantage in the world. Every American citizen needed to be vigilant lest the new forces of evil steal government secrets, undermine America's productivity, and eventually destroy American democracy and subject American citizens to the kind of totalitarianism the Soviet Union was spreading. In actuality, few Communists infiltrated American institutions, but at midcentury the threat seemed very real.

The loyalty program and subsequent anti-Communist hysteria made it very difficult to conduct a movement for black political and economic justice. Racists and political conservatives fought hard for their right to discriminate — a right they believed was protected by the Constitution and America's free-enterprise system, which championed the rights of private property owners. Both Communists and socialists, however, were against private property, believing that the few owners of stores, companies, and land exploited the masses of workers. Communists thought that a state-directed economy was superior to a free market economy because the state would protect everyone, and the inequality between owners and workers would disappear. The black freedom struggle involved not only challenging property owners' right to discriminate but also fighting for equal employment, education, health care, and housing at a time when programs that addressed equal opportunity could be interpreted as a communistic or socialistic attempt at leveling. Worse yet, support for such programs could be taken as advocacy for state interference in private enterprise.

For activists who had spent a lifetime fighting for civil rights and economic justice, adjusting to the new reality was difficult. When W. E. B. Du Bois was called before Congress to demonstrate his loyalty in 1949, the scholar and longtime activist publicly pondered how a country that "hate[s] niggers and darkies propose[s] to control a world full of colored people."[4] Comments like these had been unwelcome during the war, but black people who had made them were nevertheless protected under the First Amendment. The loyalty program signaled a change. When Du Bois became chairman of the Peace Information Center in 1950, an organization that advocated general disarmament, the U.S. State Department indicted him as "an unregistered agent" of a foreign power. Though acquitted of the charges, Du Bois, like Robeson, had his passport revoked for eight years.[5] Other activists were deported, and cultural critics like Langston Hughes were subjected to humiliating appearances before HUAC. In 1954, even Ralph Bunche, the first black person to hold a high-level position in the State Department and the first to win the Nobel Peace Prize, for his role in Middle East peace negotiations between Arabs and Jews, was forced to appear before a civil service loyalty board. His twelve-hour, two-day grilling made it clear that tough times were ahead for civil rights advocates.[6]

African American protests that racism, not communism or socialism, posed the real threat to American democracy garnered little sympathy. In fact, many white liberals — people who, though not Communists or socialists, nevertheless believed that blacks were unjustly treated and needed government help to remedy discrimination — joined racists in calling for African Americans to demonstrate their loyalty by ending

Annie Lee Moss

In 1954, Annie Lee Moss, a Pentagon communications clerk in the Army Signal Corps, was called before Senator Joseph McCarthy's House Un-American Activities Committee to prove that she was not a Communist spy. Neither a Communist nor a spy, Moss was a tenant farmer's daughter who had migrated to Washington, D.C., in the 1940s to take advantage of the government jobs newly opened to blacks. She came to the attention of loyalty officers because of her brief membership in the United Public Workers of America, a left-leaning union of government employees that promoted workers' rights and racial equality. Moss's demure, even sickly, demeanor during her testimony at the hearing helped expose McCarthy as a bully and a despot. *Associated Press/AP Images.*

their protests. The fear of communism soon became a weapon against the black freedom struggle. In Santa Monica, California, a well-organized protest against discriminatory hiring practices at Sears, Roebuck had to be called off when its leader was effectively **Red-baited**, or accused of being a Communist.[7] The director of the Chicago Housing Authority, Elizabeth Wood, was repeatedly charged with "communistic connections" for her efforts to desegregate public housing.[8] On the entertainment front, Hazel Scott, the first black entertainer to host a television show, joined Robeson as a blacklisted artist. Her crimes: She had opposed segregated baseball; she had supported the election of Communist New York City councilman Ben Davis; and during the war, when the Soviet Union and United States were allies, she had entertained Soviet as well as American troops. Red-baiting also snared Judge Hubert T. Delany of New York, who was not reappointed because of his unequivocal support of black civil rights. "I'm sick of hearing about the rights Russians don't have," Delany said. "I'm concerned about the rights we don't have right here in this country."[9]

The Cold War also brought new challenges for labor unions, whose worker advocacy was branded as communistic. The conservative turn of the CIO was a setback for black activists. During the war, many of its unions had adopted civil rights agendas and had been leaders in the quest for equal employment opportunities, fair housing, and equal political representation for blacks. In 1947, however, business owners and management took advantage of the Cold War climate and lobbied in favor of inserting loyalty oaths into the Taft-Hartley Bill then making its way through Congress. Passed later that year, the Taft-Hartley Act, which mandated that union officers sign affidavits of non-Communist affiliation, weakened the bargaining power of unions. Rather than resist the loyalty requirements, the CIO purged members and whole unions that had been associated with behavior that could be labeled socialistic or communistic. The effect was to abandon the African American struggle for economic justice as well.

Nationwide, this had devastating consequences for black workers. In New York City, the CIO ousted the United Public Workers of America, one of the most integrated unions (by race and sex) and one that had persistently fought to create a federal Fair Employment Practices Commission. When loyalty requirements destroyed Local 22 of the Food, Tobacco, Agricultural, and Allied Workers of America, located in Winston-Salem, North Carolina, they destroyed the organization that had revitalized the NAACP, registered thousands of voters, and spearheaded the election of the first black alderman since the turn of the century. Black members of the National Maritime Workers Union were similarly hard hit. Sailors and longshoremen had joined the union as a way to improve working conditions, raise wages, and eradicate racial barriers to promotion. As they had in other CIO unions, Communists and left-wing radicals had helped maritime workers to achieve these goals. During the Red scare, blacks paid a price for this success, as an estimated 80 percent of those labeled "security risks" were black, and from 50 to 70 percent of the fired maritime workers were black or foreign-born; thus a generation of black labor activists was effectively purged from the nation's docks.[10]

Loyalty Programs Force New Strategies

Black civil rights organizations were also put on the defensive, and they were forced to adopt new strategies to survive in the changed political climate. Shortly after Truman issued his 1947 loyalty order, the U.S. attorney general presented a list of seventy-eight "subversive" organizations. Nine of these were civil rights organizations, including the National Negro Congress, the Negro Labor Victory Committee, the United Negro and Allied Veterans of America, the Southern Negro Youth Congress, and Robeson's organization, the Council on African Affairs.

To escape the Communist label and resulting Red-baiting, some black organizations, such as the NAACP, followed the CIO's lead and took it upon themselves to purge Communists and left-leaning radicals. Rather than support W. E. B. Du Bois when he was accused of being a Communist in 1950, NAACP leaders dismissed him from his post as director of special research projects and did not help him during his trial. Robeson was similarly denounced as someone who had abandoned his people for a foreign cause. To prove its membership's Americanism and stave off suspicions that the Communist Party was, as one liberal accuser described the situation, "sinking its tentacles into the NAACP,"[11] the NAACP at its 1950 national convention passed its own loyalty resolution. It called for an investigation of the "ideological composition and trends of the membership," instructing its board "to take the necessary action to suspend and reorganize, or lift the charter and expel any branch . . . coming under Communist . . . domination."[12]

In initiating their own anti-Communist programs, the NAACP and other civil rights organizations gambled that they could turn Cold War politics to their advantage. If America was in fact freer than the Soviet Union, they dared America to demonstrate it. If America cared more about colonial subjects in Asia and Africa, they dared America to show it. If America wanted to showcase its democracy, they challenged America to reverse its discriminatory policies. In short, they dared America to change or risk being shamed by the gross inconsistency between its rhetoric of freedom and its practice of giving black people second-class citizenship.

It was a risky business, with benefits and drawbacks. Civil rights groups that adopted this tactic ensured their survival, were able to use the political climate as an effective tool, and made strides in dismantling the visible signs of segregation and enabling black citizens to vote. But other rights had to be de-emphasized as a result. Issues associated with economic justice, such as inequities in employment, housing, and education, were more difficult to establish than disfranchisement, for example, which had ample evidence to support it and could be more readily addressed by law. Moreover, those seeking to prove these other types of discrimination, which presumed to challenge the rights of employers and property owners, opened themselves up to accusations of communism. Thus, although they had not been eliminated, issues that had their roots in systemic racism, or the less visible **de facto segregation**, had to take a backseat to integration and suffrage.

Some of the strengths and weaknesses of this strategy were revealed during the election of 1948, when former vice president Henry Wallace and President Harry Truman vied for Democratic votes. Wallace, Roosevelt's third-term vice president (1941–1945), ran for president on a third-party ticket. As the standard-bearer of the Progressive Party, Wallace opposed the federal loyalty program and Truman's policy of making the Soviet Union America's enemy. He correctly predicted that reactionaries would use anticommunism to reinforce racial inequalities and economic injustices. Wallace called for the elimination of racism "from our unions, our business organizations, our educational institutions and our employment practices."[13] Believing that

America had to lead the world by demonstrating its commitment to the common person, Wallace favored aggressive government policies like those initiated during the New Deal to bring about equal access and opportunity for all Americans.

Although Truman did not think Wallace could beat him on a third-party ticket, he did worry that Wallace would take enough votes away from him to allow the Republican candidate, Thomas Dewey, to win. To counter that possibility, Truman and his supporters inserted a civil rights plank into the Democratic Party platform that endorsed the findings of the President's Committee on Civil Rights. While Truman went on record as supporting antilynching legislation, desegregation of the armed forces, legislation to prevent discrimination in voter registration, and abolition of the poll tax, he stopped short when it came to measures that endorsed fair housing, employment, and education. Despite these shortcomings, African Americans and many civil rights organizations saw the inclusion of the civil rights plank in the party's platform as a victory, especially when southern segregationists bolted from the Democratic National Convention and ran their own segregationist candidate for president, Senator Strom Thurmond of South Carolina, under the newly formed States' Rights Party, also known as the Dixiecrats. Although Wallace's programs were more expansive than Truman's, he had no chance of winning, and across the country his candidacy was greeted with placards reading "Send Wallace Back to Russia." In Truman, civil rights advocates at least had someone who could take action; with Wallace, they faced more blacklists and censures.

The 1948 election seemed to validate the decision to support Truman over Wallace, especially when, just before the election, Truman issued his order to desegregate the armed services. Truman won two-thirds of the black vote, with black support in California, Illinois, and Ohio ensuring his election.

For African Americans, then, the die was cast. They would adopt more moderate platforms and keep more radical possibilities at arm's length. Although civil rights organizations did not abandon issues of economic justice, their leaders reasoned that the anti-Communist climate made it easier to dismantle segregation and fight for voting rights than to restructure employment. It was a gamble, but African Americans had a century of determined struggle for justice on their side.

The Transformation of the Southern Civil Rights Movement

Remarkably, although anticommunism shook the black freedom movement to its core, it did not destroy the movement. While African Americans lost ground in their push for jobs and housing, they mounted an assault against legalized segregation and disfranchisement, or **de jure segregation**, which kept blacks vulnerable to daily insults, substandard education, and a pervasive lack of political representation.

Many factors played into African Americans' dogged persistence. First, ordinary people's expectations had risen in the wake of World War II. Many had decided that the war was the point of no return, and they were not going to accept second-class citizenship anymore. New, effective leaders also emerged, especially Martin Luther King Jr., who appealed to both black and white Americans by expressing African American aspirations in the Cold War language of freedom and democracy. The church assumed a new role during this period and facilitated the movement by espousing a philosophy of nonviolence. Finally, America's racial injustice proved an embarrassment on the international stage, and black leaders were able to capitalize on this shame to pressure a reluctant federal government for support.

Triumphs and Tragedies in the Early Years, 1951–1956

When the NAACP turned its attention to the fight against segregation, it had a foundation to build on. The U.S. Supreme Court had already declared segregation on interstate transportation illegal, and the Congress of Racial Equality (CORE) had already sent interracial teams through the South on a mission prefiguring the Freedom Rides of 1961. In 1951, the NAACP combined five legal cases against educational segregation into one class action suit known generally as ***Brown v. Board of Education of Topeka***. Although this U.S. Supreme Court case took aim at black children's generally substandard education, it was designed to strike at the entire system of segregation. NAACP lawyers Thurgood Marshall, George E. C. Hayes, and James Nabrit argued that because segregation violated the equal protection clause of the Fourteenth Amendment (see chapter 8), the 1896 *Plessy v. Ferguson* decision that established segregation was unconstitutional (see Appendix).

While the Court did not strike down the entire 1896 decision, it did rule that segregation solely on the basis of race violated black children's Fourteenth Amendment rights. In the Court's unanimous May 1954 decision, Chief Justice Earl Warren argued that separate facilities, even when identical, were inherently unequal, because black children who were siphoned off to separate facilities suffered a psychological impairment that could stay with them the rest of their lives.

Though not the first Supreme Court decision against segregation, *Brown* galvanized black America more than earlier Court rulings did. Robert Williams, a young North Carolina marine, compared his feelings after *Brown* to what he imagined slaves felt when they heard about the Emancipation Proclamation: "Elation took hold of me so strongly that I found it very difficult to refrain from yielding to an urge of jubilation. . . . I was sure that this was the beginning of a new era of American democracy."[14]

That jubilation was short-lived, however. A year later, news of the murder of the Reverend George Lee, a grocery store owner and NAACP fieldworker in Belzoni, Mississippi, shook black America. Lee was shot at close range while driving, after trying to vote. Then came the news that Lamar Smith had been shot in broad daylight, after voting and before witnesses, in front of the Brookhaven, Mississippi, courthouse. The most shocking news of all came when fourteen-year-old Emmett Till's bloated, mutilated body was pulled from the Tallahatchie River in Mississippi on August 31, 1955.

All of these murders seemed to make a mockery of the *Brown* decision, but Till's left an imprint unlike any other. A Chicago teenager who had gone to Mississippi to visit his cousin, Till was murdered by two white men, Roy Bryant and J. W. Milam, because, they claimed, he had whistled at Bryant's wife. Mamie Till Bradley, Till's mother, was beside herself with grief. Determined to wring something meaningful from her son's senseless death, she made the fateful decision to hold an open-coffin funeral and let the world view his grotesquely battered body. She wanted black people, the American people, to do something.

The condition of Till's body enraged blacks and whites alike. More than 50,000 people filed past his coffin in Chicago, and both the black newspaper the *Chicago Defender* and the black weekly magazine *Jet* published photographs of Till's corpse, spreading the image to countless readers. Young blacks were especially affected. The author Anne Moody, then a fifteen-year-old Mississippian, dated her hatred of whites and blacks to the Till murder. She hated whites who killed blacks, and she hated blacks, particularly black men, "for not standing up and doing something about the murders."[15] (See Document Project: We Are Not Afraid, pp. 515–21.)

Emmett Till
On August 21, 1955, fourteen-year-old Emmett Till arrived in Mississippi from Chicago to visit his cousin. Less than two weeks later, his grief-stricken mother unlocked his wooden casket to view his bloated, mutilated body. Her decision to hold an open-coffin funeral so that the world could see what two murderers (who were subsequently acquitted) had done to her son sparked protests that led to the modern civil rights movement. *Till in 1954: Courtesy Everett Collection; Till in 1955: Courtesy of the* Chicago Defender.

Till's death, and especially the pictures of his mutilated body, helped fuel a movement that was beginning to shake America. Already in Montgomery, Alabama, the Women's Political Council, a black middle-class women's organization under the leadership of Jo Ann Robinson, was making plans to boycott the city's buses. Women were particularly bothered by the bus company's policies, because they — more than men, who customarily traveled by car — depended on public transportation. Bus drivers sometimes did not stop for black patrons or, after taking their money, told them to exit the front door and reenter through the rear, then departed before they could get back on. This threatened the livelihoods of black maids and washerwomen, who relied on the buses to get to work. Having to sit in the back of the bus was galling enough, but being forced to give up their seat to a white person if the white section was full was even more humiliating.

All the Women's Political Council needed was an aggrieved person whom Montgomery's black population could rally around. First there was Claudette Colvin, a fifteen-year-old, who in March 1955 refused to give up her seat to a white person when ordered to do so by a Montgomery bus driver. Although Colvin was dragged from the bus and arrested by police, hers did not become the iconic face of the civil rights movement that was about to begin. That honor fell to forty-two-year-old Rosa Parks, whom Montgomery's civil rights leaders considered to be more mature and more representative of the city's blacks. Parks, secretary of her NAACP chapter, was a veteran civil rights worker who had trained in social justice advocacy at the Highlander Folk School, a leadership training school in Tennessee. On December 1, 1955, when she was forced from a Montgomery bus after refusing to relinquish her seat, the Women's Political Council joined forces with other civil rights organizations to launch the planned boycott.

The **Montgomery bus boycott** lasted nearly thirteen months. Black locals traveled on foot or via makeshift taxis and carpool networks set up by a new organization, the Montgomery Improvement Association. The city's attempts to shut down these resources did not get blacks back on the buses; neither did the verbal and physical assaults directed at walkers by belligerent whites. Blacks walked even after their churches and homes were bombed and crosses were burned on their properties. The boycott forced the bus company to lay off drivers, cut its operations, and raise fares, but the company still would not change its policies. Its fierce resistance convinced the Montgomery Improvement Association that more pressure was needed. In February 1956, attorney Fred Gray filed the federal district court case of *Browder v. Gayle* on behalf of four plaintiffs, one of whom was Claudette Colvin. The court declared segregated buses illegal under the equal protection clause of the Fourteenth Amendment, and the boycott ended. On December 21, 1956, 381 days after it began, African Americans boarded Montgomery's buses — and sat wherever they wanted to.

The *Brown* decision, Emmett Till's death, and especially the Montgomery bus boycott turned the black civil rights struggle in a new direction and established some of its fundamentals. One was the importance of national attention. Once publicized, local issues became part of a national movement for a democracy that could withstand the criticism of the totalitarian Soviet Union. National attention also created bonds between hitherto separate black communities. Across the nation, black people in churches, beauty shops, unions, and fraternal and social organizations took up collections for the Montgomery boycott. Most sent money, but others sent shoes and warm clothes. Pacifist groups such as the Fellowship of Reconciliation and the Quakers took up collections, as did Jewish groups, which contributed money and lawyers to the NAACP. News coverage in the *New York Times* and *New York Herald Tribune* turned the local boycott into a national and international event. As the actions of local black people were broadcast across the country, others, both black and white, came to their assistance.

New Leadership for a New Movement

The emergence of the church as the guiding force in the black freedom struggle was signaled when the sanctuary of the Holt Street Baptist Church became the nerve center of the Montgomery bus boycott. The preeminent leader of the boycott, the Reverend Martin Luther King Jr., also became the iconic figure of the entire freedom struggle. On the first night of the boycott, he wedded religion to the movement when he said, "We believe in the Christian religion. We believe in the teachings of Jesus. The only weapon that we have in our hands this evening is the weapon of protest."[16]

The bus boycott, like so much of the movement that followed in its wake, depended on black women as foot soldiers, organizers, and fund-raisers. But with the centrality of the church came black patriarchal authority. King became president of the Montgomery Improvement Association, and the Reverend Ralph Abernathy became vice president. Five of the nine officers of the Montgomery Improvement Association were ministers, and despite the important roles played by the Women's Political Council, Rosa Parks, and the four female plaintiffs in *Browder v. Gayle*, it followed that the boycott, like the black church, would put men in the most visible formal leadership roles. Reflecting on this gender imbalance, Thelma Glass of the Women's Political Council seemed resigned: "It looks like . . . a male-dominated world. . . . Somehow the male comes up and gets the attention. Others seem to just respect male leadership more. I think the men have always had the edge."[17] With some important exceptions, Glass's perception would hold. The black struggle was publicly led by men but would not have been possible without the work done by women.

The choice of one man in particular, Martin Luther King Jr., was more fateful than anyone could have known. Fresh from Boston, where he had received his doctorate in theology, King was reluctant to take on the leadership role thrust upon him because he had been in Montgomery for only a little over a year before the boycott began. However, King's newness and relative youth were seen as pluses by older freedom fighters. At twenty-six, King, like Abernathy, brought a new kind of energy. It was an energy born of his belief that World War II had given black Americans a new sense of self-respect and that suffering not only was redemptive but also could be used as a powerful weapon of coercion against southern segregationists. King believed that suffering born of nonviolent passive resistance — tactics that utilized peaceful protest, noncooperation, and civil disobedience — would force white America to change. He believed that a person had the right to disobey unjust laws in order to achieve social and political goals. He also understood the ravages wrought by anticommunism and the necessity to stress black patriotism while highlighting the un-Americanism of white racism.[18]

On the eve of the boycott, King gave a speech tying together Christianity, anticommunism, and black patriotism. First, he defended himself against the inevitable charges of communism by proclaiming protest to be an American tradition. "This is the glory of our democracy," he declared. "If we were incarcerated behind the iron curtains of a Communistic nation we couldn't do this. If we were trapped in the dungeon of a totalitarian regime we couldn't do this." Instead, while denouncing the anti-Americanism of racists, he declared blacks to be patriots: "There will be nobody among us who will stand up and defy the Constitution of this nation." Finally, he wrapped himself and the bus boycott in both the American and Christian traditions: "If we are wrong, then the Supreme Court of this nation is wrong. . . . The Constitution of the United States is wrong. . . . God Almighty is wrong. If we are wrong, Jesus of Nazareth was merely a utopian dreamer and never came down to earth."[19]

Dr. Martin Luther King Jr. and the Montgomery Bus Boycott

Though only twenty-six years old when the Montgomery bus boycott began, Dr. Martin Luther King Jr., a Baptist minister, rose to prominence as a result of his leading role in the boycott. He assumed that role reluctantly, since he had only recently arrived in the city. President of the Montgomery Improvement Association and later a founder and the first president of the Southern Christian Leadership Conference (SCLC), King espoused a philosophy of nonviolence that became the foundation of the early phase of the modern black freedom struggle. This photo was taken in December 1956, shortly after the bus boycott ended. *Photo by Dan Cravens/The LIFE Images Collection/Getty Images.*

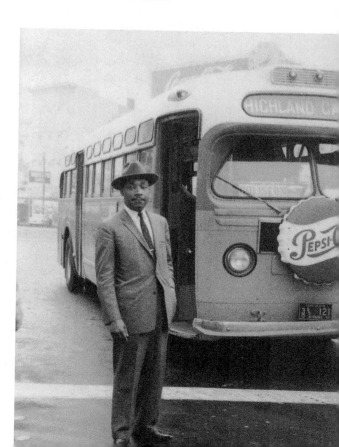

King was not the only black leader who was able to turn the black freedom struggle into a religious crusade, or, as one historian has argued, to make the civil rights movement *move*.[20] He was, however, among the first to fuse the passive resistance tactics of Mohandas Gandhi, leader of the movement for Indian independence, with the New Testament theology of Christian love to come up with what another minister, the Reverend Fred Shuttlesworth, called "the fight between light and darkness, right and wrong, good and evil, fair play and tyranny."[21] When the black struggle was defined this way, it was hard to doubt the "rightness" of the cause or the inevitable victory that lay ahead.

Demonstrators Kneeling in Prayer in Albany, Georgia, 1962
Albany, Georgia, was the scene of one of the first nonviolent direct-action protest movements conducted by civil rights organizations. The Albany protests, which lasted over a year, aimed to register blacks to vote and to desegregate schools and public places. The city's notorious police chief, Laurie Pritchett, jailed hundreds of demonstrators, including women and children. The demonstrations achieved no immediate change in Albany's racial structure, but a year after they ended, all segregation statutes were eliminated from Albany's books, and the city's black voters mobilized as a force to be reckoned with. The demonstration pictured here, in which men, women, and children kneel in prayer on an Albany sidewalk, is characteristic of the nonviolent direct-action protests that took place throughout the South. © *Bettmann/Corbis.*

The Watershed Years of the Southern Movement

The years from 1957 to 1963 were watershed years. As the world watched, African Americans and their white allies mounted a multipronged attack that eventually triumphed over segregation and disfranchisement. One of the first tasks was to harness the energy generated by the successful Montgomery bus boycott. On January 10, 1957, the Southern Christian Leadership Conference (SCLC), a church-based organization, was founded in Atlanta. King became its first president. The church had not always taken the lead in the black freedom struggle; in fact, most ministers were fearful of white reprisals and advised their impatient congregations to go slowly. But many saw great potential in an organization that took advantage of the tremendous networks of black churches, which would be able to withstand Red-baiting and accusations of communistic atheism better than unions or civil rights organizations. The SCLC became the "political arm of the black church."[22] Voting rights became the SCLC's number one goal.[23]

From the SCLC's inception, segregationists declared war on the organization, church based or not. They bombed the home of Ralph Abernathy, a founder of the SCLC, the first night the group convened. His wife and child managed to escape, but while he was on the phone talking to them, other churches in Montgomery were bombed, as was the home of Robert S. Graetz, a supportive white Lutheran minister.

If churches were not exempt from the wrath of segregationists, neither were black children. Although the 1954 *Brown* decision had made segregation illegal, there was no directive on how to desegregate schools. The U.S. Supreme Court itself did not set a timetable, but rather vaguely instructed schools to desegregate "with all deliberate speed." In practice, this meant that throughout the South, black schoolchildren bore the burden of desegregation. In some places, especially in the Upper South (Maryland, Delaware, West Virginia, and Washington, D.C.), they met little resistance. But even in these areas, most black students continued to attend segregated schools. Some school districts, such as that in Prince Edward County, Virginia, closed their schools rather than integrate. In other places, black children showed up for school to face violence and anger.

In September 1957, when the federal district court ordered the whites-only Central High School in Little Rock, Arkansas, to admit nine black students, the new enrollees confronted screaming, cursing, and threatening white men, women, and children. Governor Orval Faubus also attempted to block the students, ordering the Arkansas National Guard to surround the school. When fifteen-year-old Elizabeth Eckford arrived at Central High on September 4, she was met by angry crowds shouting, "Lynch her! Lynch her! . . . Let's take care of that nigger." When she tried to follow white students into the school, guards raised their bayonets to block her. (See Document Project: We Are Not Afraid, pp. 515–21.)

Eckford and the other students could barely count on help from Republican president Dwight D. Eisenhower, who, though sworn to uphold the laws of the country and enforce the Constitution, personally opposed federally imposed integration. Eisenhower, reluctant to interfere with the South's customs, had denounced *Brown* as a measure that "set back progress in the South at least fifteen years."[24] Only after international headlines made Little Rock a national embarrassment, and after it was clear that the Soviet Union was using the incident to demonstrate the contradictions between American practice and the nation's professed democratic ideals, did Eisenhower act. He not only called out the army but also federalized the Arkansas National Guard, ordering both to protect the **Little Rock Nine**, as these brave pioneers became known. In a speech to the country, Eisenhower linked anticommunism to civil rights, and in the process he demonstrated the potential efficacy of the new civil rights strategy: "At a time when we face grave situations abroad because of the hatred that Communism bears toward a system of government based on human rights, it would be difficult to exaggerate the harm that is being done to the prestige and influence, and indeed to the safety, of our nation and the world."[25] Eisenhower's successor, John F. Kennedy, who was elected in 1960, repeatedly made similar statements.

On February 1, 1960, four young black men from the historically black North Carolina Agricultural and Technical College challenged the segregation ordinances in Greensboro, North Carolina, by sitting down at a Woolworth's lunch counter and requesting service. Later known as the **Greensboro Four**, the men were denied service, but they returned every day with more black and white supporters, despite being bullied, spat on, and jailed and having ketchup emptied on their heads and cigarette butts ground into their skin. Black and white students from colleges across the nation soon staged similar protests, sitting in at a host of segregated lunch counters, beaches, churches, libraries, movie theaters, and skating rinks. That month saw fifty-four sit-ins in at least nine states and fifteen cities. In every instance, well-disciplined, peaceful demonstrators were met with fierce attacks by whites, who, try as they might, could not stop the students. "We had the confidence . . . of a Mack truck," said Franklin McCain, one of the original Greensboro Four.[26] Protestors sometimes prayed or sang together, which not only distracted them from the chaos and danger of their situation but also served to emphasize the contrast between their peaceful tactics and the violence being perpetrated against them.

Like the black church, students — especially black students — were an untapped source of energy, and it was important for activists to organize them. The ideal person to do this was Ella Baker. The first full-time staff member of the SCLC and later its interim director, Baker left that organization in 1960 after having grown disenchanted with King's top-down leadership style and the SCLC's male-centeredness. She had faith in young people's ability to chart their own paths, and although she lent all of her talent to help students organize the Student Nonviolent Coordinating Committee (SNCC) (pronounced "snick") in April 1960, she did not try to impose an agenda on them. She challenged adults to listen to their children, who, she said, "are asking us to forget our laziness and doubt and fear and follow our dedication to the truth to the bitter end."[27] SNCC debated everything. After deliberating over whether to focus on

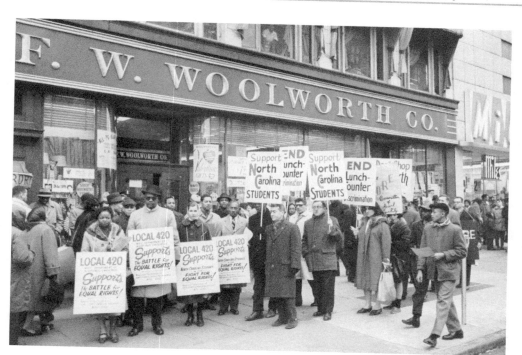

A Woolworth's Protest in New York, 1960
Within days of the Greensboro, North Carolina, lunch counter sit-in, sympathizers around the nation launched protests at their local Woolworth's. Here protesters in New York City picket the store on 125th Street, Harlem's main commercial thoroughfare. Noticeably present are representatives from Local 420, a union of nonprofessional hospital workers who, with the help of James Farmer, a founder and leader of CORE, had organized for better pay and working conditions. © *Bettmann/Corbis.*

desegregation or voting rights, SNCC decided to do both. Similarly, after debating the role of white supporters in the movement, the organization decided that the "movement should not be considered one for Negroes but one for people who consider this a movement against injustice. This would include members of all races."[28]

In the spring of 1961, CORE showed how effective interracial student activism could be. Just as the U.S. Supreme Court had ordered school desegregation in 1954 without mandating how to achieve it, in a series of cases dating from 1946, the Court had ordered an end to segregation on interstate transportation and other facilities but had not provided for enforcement.[29] To force the issue, CORE organized interracial teams of activists to ride together on buses traveling from Washington, D.C., to New Orleans in what came to be called the **Freedom Rides** (Map 12.1). Along the way, the Freedom Riders also planned to integrate bus terminal facilities, including restrooms, lunch counters, and waiting rooms. The first group made it only as far as Alabama. Outside Anniston, one bus was firebombed, and in Anniston and Birmingham mobs

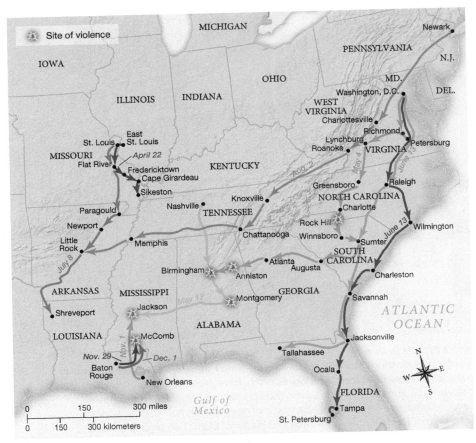

MAP 12.1   The Routes of the Freedom Rides, 1961

In the spring of 1961, the Congress of Racial Equality (CORE) organized interracial groups to ride south together by bus, integrating buses and bus terminal facilities along the way. As the activists entered the South, they were confronted by white mobs and deadly weapons, such as firebombs, and could not rely on protection from unsympathetic local officials. This map illustrates the origins and destinations of the rides, which cities the Freedom Riders passed through, and the places where violence occurred.

attacked the Freedom Riders. Interviewed on television from his hospital bed, rider James Zwerg told the world, "We will continue the Freedom Ride. . . . We'll take hitting, we'll take beating. We're willing to accept death."[30]

Although President Kennedy announced that he had directed the Interstate Commerce Commission (ICC) to outlaw segregation in facilities under its jurisdiction, the Freedom Rides continued through November, when the ban took effect. Hundreds of students rode buses from the North to Mississippi, where they were corralled in local jails; some were sent to the infamous Parchman Farm prison, where inmates were treated like slaves and subjected to unrestrained brutality. The ICC ban was evidence to many that nonviolent protest worked. Others, however, were not so sure.

White Resistance and Presidential Sluggishness

All who participated in the civil rights movement understood that their efforts could get them killed (Map 12.2). In September 1961, a Mississippi state legislator shot Herbert Lee to death in broad daylight for helping SNCC organize voter registration drives. Louis Allen, a black man who had witnessed the crime, was murdered three years later. Captain Roman Ducksworth, a military police officer on leave in Mississippi to visit his sick wife, was ordered off the bus he was traveling on and shot by a police officer for allegedly trying to integrate the bus. Paul Guihard, a white reporter for a French news service, was shot while covering the desegregation of the University of Mississippi in September 1962. In April 1963, William Lewis Moore, a white postman from Baltimore, undertook a one-man walk against segregation from Chattanooga, Tennessee, to Jackson, Mississippi. He got no farther than Collbran, Alabama, where he was shot dead by a white supremacist who was never arrested for the crime.

In 1963, Birmingham, Alabama, was one of the most dangerous cities in America. Some blacks had nicknamed it "Bombingham,"[31] knowing that blacks who stepped outside their "place" were likely to have their homes blown up. Others called it "the Johannesburg of America,"[32] comparing conditions there to those under South Africa's system of racial apartheid. In April 1963, the SCLC and another Christian group, the Alabama Christian Movement for Human Rights, led by the Reverend Fred Shuttlesworth, launched a movement to desegregate the city's public facilities and open civil service jobs to African Americans. White resistance seemed ensured: During his inaugural speech earlier that year, the newly sworn-in governor, George C. Wallace, had pledged, "Segregation now! Segregation tomorrow! Segregation forever!" Eugene "Bull" Connor, Birmingham's police commissioner, had a reputation for being tough on blacks, and he wasted no time in arresting both King and Abernathy shortly after the SCLC arrived in Birmingham.

Despite the predictability of white resistance, no one was prepared for the hostility that rained down on the activists, whose number included elementary and high school children. On May 2, Connor imprisoned more than 600 adults and children. The following day, he turned fire hoses on marchers, set attack dogs on them, and ordered police to beat them back with billy clubs. With the U.S. Information Agency reporting that the Soviet Union had "stepped up its propaganda on Birmingham . . . devoting about one-fifth of its radio output to the subject," President Kennedy was forced to act. He dispatched the assistant attorney general of the United States, Burke Marshall, to help civil rights demonstrators, city officials, and local business people work out an agreement that desegregated public accommodations and addressed employment issues.[33]

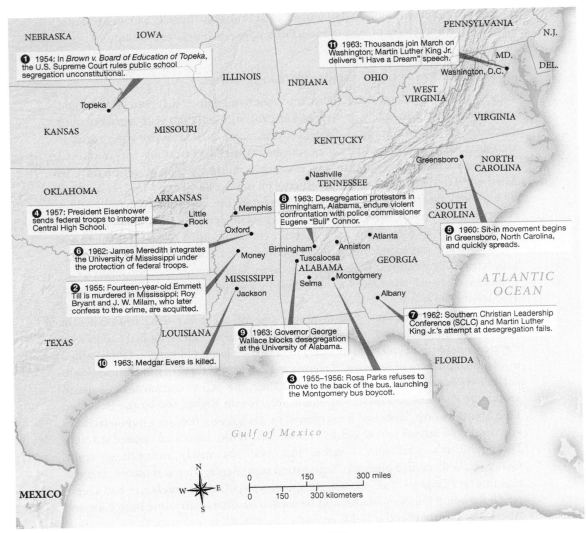

MAP 12.2   Key Southern Civil Rights Battlegrounds, 1954–1963

The civil rights movement comprised a wide variety of individual and collective actions, from major marches and U.S. Supreme Court decisions to local sit-ins and individual acts of resistance. This map shows the sites where some of the movement's most significant events took place and illustrates that the civil rights movement was truly national in scope. Although a great deal of vital movement activity took place in the South, major events also occurred in states as far-flung as New York, California, Illinois, and Kansas.

Like Eisenhower, Kennedy moved cautiously and slowly in civil rights matters. He and his brother Robert, the U.S. attorney general, favored negotiated mediation behind closed doors over direct-action demonstrations. Rather than protecting the federal rights of the civil rights protesters, the president expressed anger at their actions. Only reluctantly did he send troops to Oxford, Mississippi, in October 1962 to quell the deadly riots that ensued after James Meredith, a black student, won the right in court to attend the previously segregated University of Mississippi. Kennedy's inaction stemmed in part from Cold War concerns: Engaged in talks with Soviet premier Nikita Khrushchev about human rights in Soviet spheres, Kennedy did not want to have to explain embarrassing human rights violations at home. The attacks on civil rights activists were "exactly the kind of thing the Communists used to make the United States look bad around the world," he told his civil rights adviser.[34] Additionally, most white supremacists were Democrats, and Kennedy needed their support.

The president's inaction weighed heavily on civil rights leaders' minds. King's frustration was clear in his poignant "Letter from Birmingham City Jail," which he wrote while imprisoned during the Birmingham demonstrations. In it, King chastised white moderates, who he felt were more obstructionist than "the White Citizen's Counciler or the Ku Klux Klanner." The white moderate, King argued, was "more devoted to 'order' than to justice." The moderate perennially counseled black people to "wait" and "paternalistically" felt that he could "set the timetable for another man's freedom." King argued that blacks had waited for more than 340 years for constitutional rights that were their birthright and warned that if the repressed frustrations of black people did not come out in nonviolent ways, they would "come out in ominous expressions of violence." "This is not a threat," he wrote. "It is a fact of history."

It had been nine years since the landmark *Brown* decision, and the movement was taking a psychological toll on organizers and activists. Segregation still held fast, and blacks in the South still could not vote or hold office despite the national and international attention that nonviolent direct-action demonstrations drew. They still could not get decent jobs or live where they wanted to. They were still the targets of relentless white violence, and the perpetrators of that violence continued to escape even the slightest reprimand from federal and state governments. Although many demonstrators expressed a sense of self-respect at having put their lives on the line for such an important cause, others found the constant danger, the uncertainty about their future, and the steady demand for a high level of physical energy draining. Many began to suffer from what is now recognized as post-traumatic stress disorder. "I was totally washed out, burned out," one student activist recalled.[35]

Moreover, although passive resistance required incredible group and individual strength, participants did not always feel empowered by it; many black men found it emasculating. In fact, passive resistance went against what had become a black tradition of self-protection. "All of our parents had guns in the house," noted Joyce Ladner, a civil rights worker at this time, "and they were not only for hunting rabbits and squirrels, but out of self-defense."[36] Robert Williams, the ex-marine who had been so exhilarated by *Brown* in 1954, became so disenchanted by the late 1950s that he turned his local NAACP chapter into an armed paramilitary group and vowed to "meet lynching with lynching."[37] "Nowhere in the annals of history does the record show a people delivered from bondage by patience alone," Williams wrote.[38] The NAACP denounced him, and the government forced him into exile in Cuba. But there were many more like

American Racism in the International Press

Presidents Dwight D. Eisenhower and John F. Kennedy feared the impact of the negative publicity generated by American racism. Convincing the world that America's system of government was superior to the Soviet Union's was hard when black Americans were being attacked and murdered for demanding their rights. In this cartoon, published in the Soviet magazine *Krokodil*, a policeman prevents a black student from entering a university. The signs in the background read: "Nigger Go Away," "Lynch Him," "We Want Segregation," and "Put the Colored on Their Knees." *© Bettmann/Corbis.*

Williams. They were the ones Martin Luther King Jr. had on his mind when he warned of violence ahead.

It was only a matter of time before the "fact of history" that King spoke of in his letter revealed itself. The Birmingham demonstrations energized the civil rights movement. National and international coverage sparked sympathy marches across the country, and negative publicity threatened to cripple Birmingham's businesses. The U.S. assistant attorney general was able to negotiate an agreement that ended segregation in the city and promised to open more jobs to blacks. But even these modest gains did not sit well with some segregationists. They bombed the home of A. D. King, Martin Luther King Jr.'s brother, and the motel where they thought Martin was staying. As some outraged African Americans finally abandoned nonviolence and poured into the streets, throwing rocks and bottles, the nation held its breath.

Civil Rights: A National Movement

Although the most dramatic confrontations between civil rights workers and violent whites occurred in the South, black northerners and westerners — many of whom were recent migrants from the South — also fought persistently against discrimination in all facets of life. Their struggle was different, but not because the North and West were more egalitarian. These regions were, in fact, more segregated than the South.[39] Inequality in the North and West, however, grew from systemic, or institutional, practices rather than legal mandates, making it in some ways more difficult to rectify than southern inequality. In August 1963, when the March on Washington for Jobs and Freedom brought black and white citizens to the National Mall in Washington, D.C., people from all over the country gathered not just in support of southern blacks, but in support of civil rights across the nation.

Racism and Inequality in the North and West

Beaches, parks, public swimming pools, skating rinks, theaters, and restaurants in the North and West did not usually post "Whites Only" signs, but in the 1950s they were, nevertheless, only for white people. In Los Angeles, for example, most restaurants did not serve blacks. In Pasadena, California, blacks were not allowed to attend citywide dances.[40] In Cleveland, blacks could not go to the Skateland roller rink, and in Cincinnati, the Coney Island amusement park was off-limits. In downtown St. Louis, blacks found the major department stores — Woolworth's and Sears, Roebuck — the Greyhound bus terminal, and the Fox Theatre inaccessible. In New Jersey, African Americans could not swim in the pool at Palisades Amusement Park. Across the country, recent black migrants as well as longtime residents wondered whether they had gained much by living outside the South. Los Angeles civil rights worker Don Wheeldin recalled, "There were limits to what [blacks] could do with what they made because they couldn't buy houses anywhere, and they couldn't enjoy themselves, in terms of theaters and other things. . . . They couldn't use that money for purposes of themselves or their families."[41]

Despite the hardships, blacks throughout the country fought against discrimination and unequal treatment. The Louisiana migrant Andrew Murray and his friends staged a sit-in at the Witch's Stand drive-in restaurant in Los Angeles, and Wheeldin and his friends integrated the dances in Pasadena.[42] Across the North and West, local branches of CORE and the NAACP staged boycotts, sit-ins, stand-ins, and picket lines to desegregate public accommodations, private department stores, and recreation facilities. By the early 1960s, they had made substantial gains in these areas.

The same was not true of housing, school desegregation, and fair hiring practices, where white resistance proved that racism was a national, not just a southern, problem. The housing picture was particularly bleak. The postwar era witnessed a phenomenal housing boom underwritten by the federal government, as the Federal Housing Administration (FHA) and the Veterans Administration (VA) issued low-interest loans with minimal down payments. However, the VA, and subsequently the FHA, would issue loans to blacks only if they moved into black neighborhoods (see chapter 11). Moreover, although in *Shelley v. Kraemer* (1948) the U.S. Supreme Court had ruled against **restrictive covenants** — clauses in deeds that prohibited an owner from selling to a person or family of a particular racial or religious group — the FHA proved unwilling to challenge racist real estate practices. In some areas, it actually recommended or required restrictive covenants and would not guarantee government-secured loans without them. In other areas, such as Chicago, the FHA even refused to insure mortgages in black areas, thereby forcing blacks to buy homes "on contract" from shady speculators who sold homes at exploitative prices. If a family missed a payment, the speculator, who in fact owned the home, would evict them and resell it to another unsuspecting family, all the while pocketing the down payment and all the monthly installments.[43]

Real estate companies compounded the problem by redlining (denying loans to an area inhabited by racial minorities), steering (directing minority buyers solely to homes in minority neighborhoods), and blockbusting (playing on white fears to encourage whites to sell their homes at low prices to real estate companies, which could resell them to minorities at higher prices).[44] Both the government and real estate companies turned black people into pariahs, who everyone feared would usher in mayhem and drive down home values. When combined with the billions of dollars the government invested in building a highway system linking suburbs to urban areas, these practices allowed the government and real estate companies effectively to pin blacks in inner cities while they built white suburbs and financed white flight to them.

This was the case all over America. The *Los Angeles Sentinel*, a black newspaper, reported in 1947 that "banks won't lend money and title companies won't guarantee titles [to blacks] in what they regard as white communities even when no valid restrictions exist." A white resident of Hawthorne, California, claimed to represent the feeling of "99% of the people" when he argued that blacks "should be placed in their own all-Negro communities . . . with their own churches, their own schools and recreational facilities." That, he said, "would certainly be one of the finest things that could happen to this region."[45]

Many whites tried to make that happen. The developer William Levitt built thousands of mass-produced homes in what became known as Levittowns in Pennsylvania, New York, and New Jersey, but his settlements were only for "members of the Caucasian Race."[46] As in the South, whites used intimidation and violence to keep blacks out of places they considered their own. In 1959, in Pacoima, California, the Holmes family returned home one day to find their driveway spattered with paint, their windows broken by rocks, and a spray-painted sign that read, "Black Cancer here. Don't let it spread!" Another black family in California had a twelve-foot cross burned on the lot adjacent to their home. The citizens' group that put it there included a policeman, members of the chamber of commerce, the president of the local Kiwanis club, and a local real estate agent.[47] Just as southerners had formed White Citizens' Councils to resist black advances, white homeowners in Detroit formed more than 190 associations designed to prevent blacks from moving into their neighborhoods. In 1955, the family of Easby Wilson bought a home in one of Detroit's white neighborhoods, but before the Wilsons moved in, they found the walls and floors ruined, the drains stopped up, water damage from running faucets, and black paint everywhere. They moved in despite the warnings but were continually harassed by threatening phone calls, snakes thrown in their basement, rock-throwing incidents, and mobs of up to four hundred people, who yelled, jeered, and shouted obscenities.

Across the country, the National Urban League, the NAACP, and other civil rights groups called for fair housing policies. They fought for city ordinances to outlaw real estate practices that preyed on white fears, pressured the FHA to issue loans to blacks and let them buy foreclosed homes in white areas, and lobbied state agencies to revoke the licenses of real estate agents who steered, redlined, or blockbusted. Success was slow or nonexistent.

Black people met the same resistance even when they tried to move into public housing. In Cincinnati, a proposal to build an integrated housing project triggered the formation of a white homeowners' association that asked white residents in the surrounding area, "Do you want Niggers in your backyard?"[48] In Detroit, despite the fact that most public housing had white residents, white associations linked it negatively to both socialized housing and the presence of blacks. In Chicago's Trumbull Park community, Donald and Betty Howard were greeted by more than fifty white teenagers shouting racial epithets and throwing stones and bricks. During the decade that they and other black families lived in the mostly white public housing project, they endured bombings and physical attacks and were barely able to leave their homes without a police escort. When the head of the Chicago Housing Authority defended the rights of blacks to live in Trumbull Park, she was fired. In 1955, civil rights groups held marches at City Hall to protest years of violence at Trumbull Park, meeting with Mayor Richard J. Daley to protest police failure to stop the violence.[49] In 1966, when the SCLC marched for fair housing in a neighboring community, white citizens' violent reactions forced even Martin Luther King Jr. to retreat. "I've never seen anything like it," King reported. "I've been in many demonstrations all across the South, but I can say that I have never seen — even in Mississippi and Alabama — mobs as hostile and as hate-filled as I've seen in Chicago."[50]

Police not only failed to stop the violence but also contributed to it. To most African Americans, white police forces in the North and West seemed no better than the Bull Connors of the South. In New York City in 1950, when two white police officers shot and killed an unarmed black Korean War veteran named John Derrick, the outspoken Harlem congressman Adam Clayton Powell Jr., one of only two black congressmen (the other was Chicagoan William Levi Dawson), labeled it a lynching. "We don't call them that, but we do have lynchings right here in the north," Powell said. In 1952, New York City police beat a man and his wife, Jacob and Geneva Jackson, and a friend with whom they were driving, so badly that they needed hospitalization. In light of evidence that the police department had negotiated an agreement with U.S. Justice Department officials making the police exempt from prosecutions involving African Americans, outraged civil rights groups lobbied, unsuccessfully, for a civilian complaint review board. The depth of the problem they were up against was revealed when New York City police commissioner George P. Monaghan told the FBI that civil rights laws did not apply up north, only "south of the Mason Dixon line."[51]

This attitude prevailed throughout the North and West. Black people who migrated to these areas to find freedom instead found white authorities who were determined to restrict their movement. When asked in the 1950s about accusations of racial profiling, Los Angeles police chief William Parker said, "Any time that a person is in a place other than his place of residence or where he is conducting business, . . . it might be a cause for inquiry."[52] In Los Angeles, as elsewhere, police made race-based inquiries. When blacks protested harassment and vicious police beatings, the police chief expressed sympathy — for the police. An early 1950s survey of residents of Watts, a black neighborhood in Los Angeles, revealed that nearly half of them had been harassed, lined up on the sidewalk, frisked for no apparent reason, or slapped and kicked by the police.[53]

Farther north in Oakland, California, police harassment was equally blatant. The black migrant community had grown exponentially, and whites depended on police to keep it contained. In 1957, Oakland police established the Associated Agencies, an elaborate surveillance operation to control black youths. It connected the city's schools, social service agencies, and recreational programs to the police and the dreaded California Youth Authority, a statewide incarceration and detention center, so that those deemed potential delinquents could be identified and contained. Try as they might, the Urban League, the NAACP, and CORE could not change this prevailing culture.

Fighting Back: The Snail's Pace of Change

One way to counter police brutality was to change the political climate of urban centers. This began to happen in the 1950s as African Americans continued to migrate out of the South. Up north and out west, black people could vote and develop political alliances that yielded influence unavailable to them in the South. In cities where blacks held the balance of power, they leveraged it for political offices and political power by voting as a bloc. Change, however, was slow — much too slow for many.

Events in New York City illustrate this well. In 1950, the year after American Labor Party candidate Ewart Guinier marshaled 38 percent of the vote in a losing battle for Manhattan borough president, blacks were able to pressure the Democratic Party to nominate a black candidate, Harold Stevens, to New York City's highest court. Stevens won that election, and two years later black leaders used the threat of a third-party candidate to force the Democratic Party to nominate Julius Archibald, who became New York's first black state senator. He was one of about fifty blacks elected to office across the nation in 1952. Further maneuvering and grassroots organizing between 1953 and 1954 resulted in the election of two more African Americans, including the first black woman, Bessie Buchanan, to the New York State Assembly. Remarkably, the 1953 contest for Manhattan borough president devolved into a contest between five black candidates.

In New York City and elsewhere, black candidates ran on platforms that included calls for full employment, an end to police brutality and housing discrimination, and more schools, hospitals, and libraries in black areas.[54] In Los Angeles, for example, with the help of white allies, black elected officials were able to lobby successfully for a state Fair Employment Practices Commission in 1958 to address job discrimination, and a state fair housing act in 1963 that prohibited racial discrimination by real estate brokers. On the community level, black city council members improved neighborhood street lighting and other basic city services.[55]

Though impressive for the times, black political advances proceeded at a snail's pace. An "intense struggle for small gains" was the way one activist remembered "progress" in New York City, where blacks accounted for more than 1 million of the 14 million residents. In 1954, only 10 of 189 city judges were black; the state supreme court was all white; only 1 of 58 state senators and 5 of 150 state assembly members were black; and there was only 1 African American on the 25-member city council and 1 in the 43-member congressional delegation.[56] Like victories in the fight for equal access to jobs, education, housing, and other basic human rights, the few steps forward in gaining political office fueled expectations of more reforms, which, to the frustration of most African Americans, hardly ever materialized.

As they observed the sit-ins, marches, and demonstrations in the South, blacks in the North and West had reason to believe that changes in their regions were occurring even more slowly. Schools, for example, were not desegregating. In St. Louis, Kansas

City, Cleveland, Los Angeles, Chicago, Boston, New York, and Milwaukee, civil rights activists encountered intransigent public officials and hostile whites determined to keep blacks from receiving the same education offered to whites. Progress in employment also was slow. In an effort to end discriminatory practices in the labor movement, corporate personnel offices, and the larger institutional structure of the North and West, the NAACP and CORE targeted the employment practices of Bank of America, Bell Telephone, Western Electric, and the building and construction trades in cities such as Philadelphia, New York, San Francisco, and Newark. They also launched protests against Sheraton hotels; Howard Johnson's restaurants; Safeway; Sears, Roebuck; beer manufacturers; dealerships selling cars made by Mercury and Chrysler; and commercial advertising companies. Gains were so minimal that many wondered whether there was really any meaningful difference between the North and West and the South. Los Angeles "wasn't that much different from Oklahoma," remembered one disappointed migrant. "In Oklahoma, you knew. You was raised up that way and you didn't expect anything else. But out here, it was supposed to be different."[57]

By the time African Americans in the North and West saw pictures of the 1963 Birmingham demonstrations, they had begun to doubt the effectiveness of nonviolent direct-action protests and were beginning to look for other solutions. An idea about black power was beginning to take hold. It inclined toward more militancy rather than continued passive resistance, and it expressed an urgency that could not abide patience.

President Kennedy seemed to sense this new mood and took action. In 1963, he followed up on his commitment to the Birmingham settlement with support for a new civil rights bill. Then, when Alabama governor George C. Wallace stood in a University of Alabama doorway to block two black students from entering, Kennedy federalized the Alabama National Guard and ordered guardsmen to protect the students. On June 11, 1963, he went on national television to reiterate his support for black civil and voting rights and for desegregation. In a stirring speech, he proclaimed that the nation would not be free until all citizens were free. "Who among us would be content with the counsels of patience and delay?" he asked. Sensing the explosive state of affairs, Kennedy proclaimed that racism was "not a sectional issue"; rather, "the fires of frustration and discord are burning in every city, North and South."[58] African Americans were pleased with Kennedy's speech. Finally, he seemed to move away from segregationists and join their side.

The mood did not change in Mississippi, however. Within a few hours of the president's speech, Mississippi NAACP leader Medgar Evers was ambushed and shot dead in his driveway in Jackson.

The March on Washington and the Aftermath

On August 28, 1963, more than 250,000 black and white Americans gathered on the National Mall for the historic **March on Washington for Jobs and Freedom**. It marked the culmination of nonviolent direct-action efforts to end segregation in every segment of American life and achieve economic justice for black Americans. Although the march was peaceful, President Kennedy had readied National Guard units in case of violence. The juxtaposition of peaceful demonstrators and riot-ready troopers was in many ways symbolic of the tensions that prevailed during the latter part of 1963. In retrospect, the march proved to be one of the last gasps of what historians now call the "classic" civil rights movement — that part of the postwar freedom struggle when non-violent direct action was most potent and effective.

A huge march on Washington seemed to be the right move for civil rights organizations in 1963. President Kennedy, embarrassed internationally by the racial violence in Birmingham and fearful of more violence, seemed ready to support the demands of marchers. Moreover, since progress on black rights was moving so slowly and blacks were more insistent on change, the time seemed right to pressure Congress to support Kennedy's civil rights bill. Just as A. Philip Randolph had organized the March on Washington Movement during World War II to force President Franklin Roosevelt's hand (see chapter 11), civil rights activists in 1963 believed that the Cold War presented a similar opportunity to press for black rights.

Organizing such a march was no small matter, not least because of the tensions that had been building within the movement itself. Each civil rights organization had its own perspective on the march, and each wanted the march organized its own way. But it was A. Philip Randolph who conceived of the march and Bayard Rustin, a longtime adviser of Martin Luther King Jr., who organized it. As a union organizer, Randolph had always believed that political advancement was useless without economic gains, but to get King's participation the march had to emphasize civil rights. Once it was decided that the march would be about civil rights *and* jobs and King was brought on board, a decision had to be made about the use of civil disobedience. King wanted the gathering to include sit-ins and marches at the Capitol and the White House, but Roy Wilkins and Whitney Young, the respective heads of the NAACP and Urban League, vetoed this idea. More conservative than King and the SCLC, Wilkins and Young did not want to embarrass Kennedy or endanger the passage of the new bill. They also considered the SCLC and other new civil rights organizations to be Johnny-come-latelies and resented King's prominence. This decision outraged the younger, more radical SNCC members, who wanted to apply the utmost pressure on Washington and regarded the compromise as a sellout. They did, however, accept the leadership role of Rustin, which Wilkins rejected. Wilkins feared that Rustin's leftist past and homosexuality would be used to smear the march.[59]

A compromise was reached here, too, but male leaders incurred the wrath of black women when not one woman was invited to participate in the planning of the march or to give a major speech. Pauli Murray, a civil rights lawyer and member of the newly created (1961) President's Commission on the Status of Women, expressed the anger of many women when she complained to Randolph that "'tokenism' is as offensive when applied to women as when applied to Negroes."[60] She had not devoted the greater part of her adult life to civil rights advocacy to condone any policy that was not inclusive.

Perhaps the greatest and most lasting controversy was over the degree of militancy speakers could express. John Lewis, the chairman of SNCC, had written a speech seething with anger and outrage. He denounced the civil rights bill as "too little and too late" because it did not protect blacks against police brutality or help them to vote. At Randolph's request, Lewis toned down his speech, leaving King to give the most memorable and inspiring presentation to the hundreds of thousands who waited on the Mall, across the nation, and around the world.

Though not as scathing as Lewis's original speech, King's majestically made some of the same points. King cautioned the nation against returning to business as usual, noting that black people were just beginning to fight for their rights. "It would be fatal for the nation to overlook the urgency of the moment and to underestimate the determination of the Negro," he said. There would be "neither rest nor tranquility in America until the Negro is granted his citizenship rights," King warned, and "the whirlwinds of revolt will continue to shake the foundations of our nation until . . . justice emerges." Mindful of the housing problems blacks faced, King told his audience that blacks would not be content "as long as the Negro's basic mobility is from a smaller ghetto to a larger one." Linking the southern and northern struggles, he added that there would be no satisfaction "as long as a Negro in Mississippi cannot vote and a Negro in New York believes he has nothing for which to vote."

Although Lewis had paid lip service in his original speech to nonviolence, King, as he so often did, emphasized it because it was one of his core Christian beliefs. "Unearned suffering is redemptive," he proclaimed as he cautioned against meeting violence with violence. He paid homage to those who had come "fresh from narrow cells . . . from areas where your quest for freedom left you battered by the storms of persecution and staggered by the winds of police brutality." African Americans had to meet "physical force with soul force," reject bitterness and hatred, and embrace whites who had "come to realize that their destiny is tied up with our destiny . . . [and] that their freedom is inextricably bound to our freedom." His voice reached a crescendo as he sketched out his dream and hopes for his children, for black people, and for America. One line in particular stood out: "I have a dream that my four little children will one day live in a nation where they will not be judged by the color of their skin but by the content of their character."[61]

The March on Washington had worldwide impact. Some American citizens in Paris signed a petition supporting the march. Sympathy marches and demonstrations were held in Jamaica, Ghana, Burundi, Amsterdam, Tel Aviv, Oslo, and Munich. Newspapers across Africa and Europe and in India heralded the march with headlines that cast both aspersions and praise on America. The *Ghanaian Times* criticized the United States, claiming that American racism "casts much slur on Western civilization." But Rotterdam's *Algemeen Dagblad* praised America, asking readers to "imagine what would have happened had such a demonstration been planned in East Berlin."[62]

Martin Luther King Jr. at the March on Washington for Jobs and Freedom, 1963
The major television networks (CBS, ABC, and NBC) sent more than five hundred cameramen, technicians, and correspondents to cover the March on Washington. All three networks led their evening newscasts with the march, and it appeared on the front page of every major newspaper the following day. This iconic photograph captures the dignity, strength, and massiveness of the march, which, despite the dedication and work of hundreds of men and women, would forever be associated with Martin Luther King Jr. and his "I Have a Dream" speech. © Hulton-Deutsch Collection/Corbis.

On September 15, just as the State Department was about to play up and capitalize on the latter sentiment, a bomb exploded in Birmingham's Sixteenth Street Baptist Church, which had been the organizing center of the city's civil rights demonstrations. The shock waves from the bomb shook world opinion and rocked the civil rights movement. Both King and Lewis had stressed nonviolence in their speeches, but a violent reaction could not be contained after news spread that the bomb had killed four black girls, ranging in age from eleven to fourteen, during Sunday school. Black anger erupted into Birmingham's city streets, and during the disturbances two black male teenagers

The Bombing of the Sixteenth Street Baptist Church

In the aftermath of the March on Washington for Jobs and Freedom, these four girls were killed when the Sixteenth Street Baptist Church in Birmingham, Alabama, was bombed. In the top row are (left) Denise McNair, age eleven, and (right) Carole Robertson, age fourteen. In the bottom row are (left) Addie Mae Collins, age fourteen, and (right) Cynthia Wesley, age fourteen. When Cynthia's friend Carolyn McKinstry found out that the girls had been killed, she recalled, "I was sick inside; I was afraid. And then I was just numb. . . . I always had the sense of being protected. Now, all of a sudden, I wasn't."[63] *Associated Press/AP Images.*

were shot and killed by police. The fires of African American outrage were further fanned by FBI director J. Edgar Hoover's decision to block the prosecution of the three white men implicated in the bombing. It was the twenty-first bombing in Birmingham in eight years; none of these crimes had been solved. Black people wanted justice, and in its absence many resolved to fight back.

CONCLUSION

The Evolution of the Black American Freedom Struggle

The struggle for freedom changed substantially between 1945 and 1963. African Americans emerged from World War II determined, as defense worker Margaret Wright had said, not to "go back to what they were doing before." A consequence of that determination was the civil rights movement — a nationwide crusade to make America live up to its creed as a land of opportunity for everyone. The struggle was significantly affected, however, by the Cold War and the anti-Communist hysteria that accompanied it. To avoid being branded as Communists, African Americans had to convince the world that America, not blacks, had violated the American creed.

Blacks and their white allies used nonviolent direct-action protests to this end. They sat in at segregated facilities, integrated segregated buses, marched in protest, and tried to register to vote. In doing so, they successfully exposed to the nation and the world the brutality and injustice that blacks faced in every region of the country. However, nonviolent direct action took its toll on the freedom fighters. To be effective, it had to provoke the intense hostility and extreme, sometimes deadly, violence used to subordinate blacks. This meant that countless demonstrators had to endure untold traumas to their person and psyche. These tactics also forced activists to de-emphasize economic issues, such as employment and housing discrimination, and tackle only the problems that could be proved and addressed through legal methods.

The March on Washington for Jobs and Freedom proved to be a watershed event. It was the highlight of the nonviolent, interracial phase of the classic civil rights movement, which had been effective in broadcasting American racism and embarrassing the nation to the point of forcing Presidents Eisenhower and Kennedy to do something. But that something seemed to be not nearly enough.

After a decade of lackluster commitment from the federal government and unremitting, terroristic resistance from both white citizens and local authorities, many freedom fighters — those who had come of age in the movement as well as new recruits — were ready for a change. Their search for new leaders, new tactics, and new ideologies brought about another transformation in the black freedom struggle, as the philosophy of black power and the quest to address long-ignored economic injustices came to the fore.

CHAPTER 12 **REVIEW**

KEY TERMS

loyalty program p. 483

Red-baited p. 485

de facto segregation p. 487

de jure segregation p. 488

***Brown v. Board of Education of
Topeka* (1954)** p. 489

**Montgomery bus boycott
(1955–1956)** p. 491

Little Rock Nine p. 496

Greensboro Four p. 496

Freedom Rides p. 497

restrictive covenants p. 504

**March on Washington for Jobs and
Freedom (1963)** p. 508

REVIEW QUESTIONS

1. What impact did the Cold War have on the black freedom movement? How did black organizations adapt to postwar changes? What were the outcomes, both negative and positive, for the movement and its direction?

2. Given the triumphs and tragedies of the southern movement's early years, how would you assess the strategy of nonviolent direct-action protest? How effective was it? What were its benefits and drawbacks?

3. How did the civil rights movement force the hands of Presidents Eisenhower and Kennedy? What impelled them to move to protect demonstrators even when they disagreed with the movement's tactics or goals?

4. How would you compare the degrees and types of segregation and institutional racism that characterized the South, North, and West in this era? In what ways was progress in the North and West even slower than that in the South?

5. How was the 1963 March on Washington for Jobs and Freedom both the height of the classic civil rights movement and an indicator of the tensions that had been building within it?

We Are Not Afraid

The signature song of the early civil rights movement — the song sung before, during, and after meetings, demonstrations, and sit-ins — was titled "We Shall Overcome." Some have called it African Americans' gift to the world, because freedom fighters around the globe have adopted it as their anthem.[64] One verse of the song, "We are not afraid," is very telling. It was one thing for African Americans to proclaim, "We're not going to take it anymore," but quite another for them to conquer the paralyzing fear and feelings of hopelessness that white terrorism and violence were designed to provoke. For African Americans to overcome the tribulations of second-class citizenship, they first had to overcome their own fear.

This was far easier said than done in an era when lynchings, beatings, and bombings increased and were sanctioned by local and national law enforcement agencies. African Americans could not call on the police or the FBI for protection, for these organizations were often aligned with the perpetrators of terror. So, too, were the National Guard forces mustered by segregationist governors.

The following documents deal with terror and fear. They are firsthand accounts of movement activists' early encounters with violent racism. Recorded later in life, they tell us a good deal about how terrorism functions as a means of control and why young people were in the vanguard of the freedom movement.

Anne Moody | *Coming of Age in Mississippi*, 1968

The African American author ANNE MOODY (1940–2015), named Essie Mae Moody at birth, grew up in Mississippi. While attending Tougaloo College on a scholarship, she became active in the civil rights movement, participating in lunch counter sit-ins and voter registration drives. Her autobiography, *Coming of Age in Mississippi*, is a poignant account of rural Mississippi poverty and the way racism functioned to oppress African Americans. As you read this excerpt, consider how all-consuming white terrorism was. What kind of person did one have to be to not be paralyzed by it?

Not only did I enter high school with a new name, but also with a completely new insight into the life of Negroes in Mississippi. I was now working for one of the meanest white women in town, and a week before school started Emmett Till was killed.

Up until his death, I had heard of Negroes found floating in a river or dead somewhere with their bodies riddled with bullets. But I didn't know the mystery behind these killings then. I remember once when I was only seven I heard Mama and one of my aunts talking about some Negro who had been beaten to death. "Just like them low-down skunks killed him they will do the same to us," Mama had said. When I asked her who killed the man and why, she said,

"An Evil Spirit killed him. You gotta be a good girl or it will kill you too." So since I was seven, I had lived in fear of that "Evil Spirit." It took me eight years to learn what that spirit was. . . .

[Anne arrived home after hearing some fellow students discussing Till's murder.]

"Mama, did you hear about that fourteen-year-old Negro boy who was killed a little over a week ago by some white men?" I asked her.

"Where did you hear that?" she said angrily.

"Boy, everybody really thinks I am dumb or deaf or something. I heard Eddie them talking about it this evening coming from school."

"Eddie them better watch how they go around here talking. These white folks git a hold of it they gonna be in trouble," she said.

"What are they gonna be in trouble about, Mama? People got a right to talk, ain't they?"

"You go on to work before you is late. And don't you let on like you know nothing about that boy being killed before Miss Burke them. Just do your work like you don't know nothing," she said. "That boy's a lot better off in heaven than he is here," she continued, and then started singing again.

On my way to Mrs. Burke's that evening, Mama's words kept running through my mind. "Just do your work like you don't know nothing." . . .

[Anne went to work at the Burkes' home, where she served dinner and cleaned up the kitchen.]

When they had finished and gone into the living room as usual to watch TV, Mrs. Burke called me to eat. I took a clean plate out of the cabinet and sat down. Just as I was putting the first forkful of food in my mouth, Mrs. Burke entered the kitchen.

"Essie, did you hear about that fourteen-year-old boy who was killed in Greenwood?" she asked me, sitting down in one of the chairs opposite me.

"No, I didn't hear that," I answered, almost choking on the food.

"Do you know why he was killed?" she asked and I didn't answer.

"He was killed because he got out of his place with a white woman. A boy from Mississippi would have known better than that. This boy was from Chicago. Negroes up North have no respect for people. They think they can get away with anything. He just came to Mississippi and put a whole lot of notions in the boys' heads here and stirred up a lot of trouble," she said passionately.

"How old are you, Essie?" she asked me after a pause.

"Fourteen. I will soon be fifteen though," I said.

"See, that boy was just fourteen too. It's a shame he had to die so soon." She was so red in the face, she looked as if she was on fire.

When she left the kitchen I sat there with my mouth open and my food untouched. I couldn't have eaten now if I were starving. "Just do your work like you don't know nothing" ran through my mind again and I began washing the dishes.

I went home shaking like a leaf on a tree. For the first time out of all her trying, Mrs. Burke had made me feel like rotten garbage. Many times she had tried to instill fear within me and subdue me and had given up. But when she talked about Emmett Till there was something in her voice that sent chills and fear all over me.

Before Emmett Till's murder, I had known the fear of hunger, hell, and the Devil. But now there was a new fear known to me — the fear of being killed just because I was black. This was the worst of my fears. I knew once I got food, the fear of starving to death would leave. I also was told that if I were a good girl, I wouldn't have to fear the Devil or hell. But I didn't know what one had to do or not do as a Negro not to be killed. Probably just being a Negro period was enough, I thought.

Cleveland Sellers | *The River of No Return, 1973*

CLEVELAND SELLERS (b. 1944) was born and raised in Denmark, South Carolina, where he organized lunch counter sit-ins in 1961. While a student at Howard University, he became a member of the Student Nonviolent Coordinating Committee (SNCC) and worked with that organization on voter registration in Mississippi. Like Anne Moody, Sellers was deeply affected by Emmett Till's murder. As a young male, how might his concerns have been different than Moody's? How were they the same?

The adults, my parents included, were always afraid that we young people would take white racism too lightly. They were always urging us to "be careful." They realized that we were different from them, less afraid.

Although we did not possess the same amount of fear as our parents, we did understand what white racism was and what it could do. We learned these things from a number of sources, the most important one being the grapevine: an informal, black communications network connecting state to state, town to town, group to group and person to person.

Some of the most important pieces of information passed along the grapevine were accounts of atrocities. They contained valuable survival tips for those wise enough to heed them. I can remember hearing and reflecting on such accounts from the time I was a very young boy. They almost invariably dealt with situations where black people, usually black men, were brutalized by whites. . . .

The atrocity that affected me the most was Emmett Till's lynching. . . .

. . . Blacks across the country were outraged, but powerless to do anything.

Emmett Till was only three years older than me and I identified with him. I tried to put myself in his place and imagine what he was thinking when those white men took him from his home that night. I wondered how I would have handled the situation. I read and reread the newspaper and magazine accounts. I couldn't get over the fact that the men who were accused of killing him had not been punished at all.

There was something about the cold-blooded callousness of Emmett Till's lynching that touched everyone in the community. We had all heard atrocity accounts before, but there was something special about this one. For weeks after it happened, people continued to discuss it. It was impossible to go into a barber shop or corner grocery without hearing someone deploring Emmett Till's lynching.

We even discussed it in school. Our teachers were just as upset as we were. They did not try to distort the truth by telling us that Emmett Till's murder was an isolated event that could only have taken place in Mississippi or Alabama. Although they did not come right out and say it, we understood that our teachers held the South's racist legal system in the same low regard as we did. That's one of the good things about an all-black school. We were free to discuss many events that would have been taboo in an integrated school.

SOURCE: Cleveland Sellers with Robert Terrell, *The River of No Return: The Autobiography of a Black Militant and the Life and Death of SNCC.* Copyright © 1973 by Cleveland Sellers and Robert L. Terrell. Reprinted by permission of HarperCollins Publishers.

Elizabeth Eckford | *The First Day: Little Rock, 1957*

Children and teenagers were in the vanguard of the civil rights movement. Coming of age in a new era, and with less life experience than their parents and grandparents, they had shallower reservoirs of fear. Moreover, the desegregation of schools fell squarely on their shoulders. ELIZABETH ECKFORD (b. 1941) was one of the Little Rock Nine who desegregated Little Rock Central High School in Arkansas in 1957. On the morning of the first day of school, the other eight black students gathered with parents and civil rights workers at a designated place, but Eckford did not know that she was not to go directly to the school. There she encountered an angry white mob.

Before I left home Mother called us into the living room. She said we should have a word of prayer. Then I caught the bus and got off a block from the school. I saw a large crowd of people standing across the street from the soldiers guarding Central. As I walked on, the crowd suddenly got very quiet. Superintendent [Virgil] Blossom told us to enter by the front door. I looked at all the people and thought, "Maybe I will be safer if I walk down the block to the front entrance behind the guards."

At the corner I tried to pass through the long line of guards around the school so as to enter the grounds behind them. One of the guards pointed across the street. So I pointed in the same direction and asked whether he meant for me to cross the street and walk down. He nodded "yes." So, I walked across the street conscious of the crowd that stood there, but they moved away from me.

For a moment all I could hear was the shuffling of their feet. Then someone shouted, "Here she comes, get ready!" I moved away from the crowd on the sidewalk and into the street. If the mob came at me I could then cross back over so the guards could protect me.

The crowd moved in closer and then began to follow me, calling me names. I still wasn't afraid. Just a little bit nervous. Then my knees started to shake all of a sudden and I wondered whether I could make it to the center entrance a block away. It was the longest block I ever walked in my whole life.

Even so, I still wasn't too scared because all the time I kept thinking that the guards would protect me.

When I got in front of the school, I went up to a guard again. But this time he just looked straight ahead and didn't move to let me pass him. I didn't know what to do. Then I looked and saw that the path leading to the front entrance was a little further ahead. So I walked until I was right in front of the path to the front door.

I stood looking at the school—it looked so big! Just then the guards let some white students through.

The crowd was quiet. I guess they were waiting to see what was going to happen. When I was able to steady my knees, I walked up to the guard who had let the white students in. He too didn't move. When I tried to squeeze past him, he raised his bayonet and then the other guards moved in and they raised their bayonets.

They glared at me with a mean look and I was very frightened and didn't know what to do. I turned around and the crowd came toward me.

They moved closer and closer. Somebody started yelling, "Lynch her! Lynch her!"

I tried to see a friendly face somewhere in the mob—someone who maybe would help.

SOURCE: Daisy Bates, *The Long Shadow of Little Rock*. Copyright © 1962, 1986 by Daisy Bates. Reprinted with the permission of The Permissions Company, Inc., on behalf of the University of Arkansas Press, www.uapress.com.

I looked into the face of an old woman and it seemed a kind face, but when I looked at her again she spat on me.

They came closer, shouting, "No nigger bitch is going to get in our school! Get out of here!"

I turned back to the guards but their faces told me I wouldn't get any help from them. Then I looked down the block and saw a bench at the bus stop. I thought, "If I can only get there I will be safe." I don't know why the bench seemed a safe place to me, but I started walking toward it. I tried to close my mind to what they were shouting, and kept saying to myself, "If I can only make it to the bench I will be safe."

When I finally got there, I don't think I could have gone another step. I sat down and the mob crowded up and began shouting all over again. Someone hollered, "Drag her over to this tree! Let's take care of that nigger." Just then a white man sat down beside me, put his arm around me and patted my shoulder. He raised my chin and said, "Don't let them see you cry."

Images of Protest and Terror

As the following photographs demonstrate, the violence of the civil rights movement was very real, and the terror palpable. Somehow, demonstrators who were mostly teenagers and young adults found the strength and the will to carry out nonviolent protests despite fire hoses, attack dogs, bombs, and mean-spirited hecklers. Every demonstration, be it a march, freedom ride, sit-in, pray-in, or voter registration drive, brought the possibility of death. Many participated in protests for over ten years. How do you think they managed their fear?

John R. Salter, Joan Trumpauer, and Anne Moody Sit In at Woolworth's in Jackson, Mississippi, 1963   © Bettmann/Corbis.

Freedom Riders beside Their Burned Bus, 1961   © *Bettmann/Corbis.*

Birmingham Demonstrators Being Sprayed with Fire Hoses, 1963   *Bill Hudson/Associated Press/AP Images.*

Elizabeth Eckford Walking toward Little Rock Central High School, 1957 © *Bettmann/Corbis.*

QUESTIONS FOR ANALYSIS

1. Describe the feelings that Anne Moody and Cleveland Sellers had to overcome. How did they respond to the pervasiveness of fear in their respective communities? How did Emmett Till's murder affect each of them? How would you have felt, and what would you have done in their environment?

2. Imagine that you are Elizabeth Eckford. Would you have been able to keep walking through the angry mob? Why did the man who sat down next to Eckford tell her not to let the crowd see her cry? Would you have been able to hold back the tears?

3. In the first two documents, the local black community — the "grapevine," as Cleveland Sellers calls it — plays an important role. How did the grapevine function in each of these situations? Why was it so vital?

4. Terrorism, as a means of controlling by fear, had long been used to keep African Americans subordinate to whites. It seems not to have worked on the authors of these documents, who grew up to be activists, or on the demonstrators in the photographs. What clues can you find in the written accounts and in the photographs to suggest how these individuals were able to conquer their fear?

5. What impact do you think the photographs of besieged protesters had on the civil rights movement?

6. In the 1950s and 1960s, television was the latest and most revolutionary technology, much like the Internet is today. Every evening Americans viewed scenes like the ones in this Document Project on the nightly news. Imagine what coverage of the civil rights movement would look like in our current media climate, with the plethora of television news outlets, news blogs, and social networking Web sites now available. How do you think these images and accounts would be portrayed today?

NOTES

1. Martin B. Duberman, *Paul Robeson: A Biography* (New York: New Press, 1989), 440–41.
2. Quoted in Roberta Yancy Dent, ed., *Paul Robeson Tributes and Selected Writings* (New York: Paul Robeson Archives, 1976), 65.
3. Quoted in Legal Information Institute of Cornell University Law School at www.law.cornell.edu, CFR, Title 5, Chapter V, Part 1501, Section 1501.8.
4. Quoted in Nikhil Pal Singh, *Black Is a Country: Race and the Unfinished Struggle for Democracy* (Cambridge: Harvard University Press, 2004), 163.
5. Singh, *Black Is a Country*, 164.
6. Robert Harris, "Ralph Bunche and Afro-American Participation in Decolonization," in *The African American Voice in U.S. Foreign Policy since World War II*, ed. Michael Krenn (New York: Garland, 1998), 163–80.
7. Josh Sides, *L.A. City Limits: African American Los Angeles from the Great Depression to the Present* (Berkeley: University of California Press, 2003), 147.
8. Singh, *Black Is a Country*, 165.
9. Quoted in Martha Biondi, *To Stand and Fight: The Struggle for Civil Rights in Postwar New York City* (Cambridge: Harvard University Press, 2003), 179.
10. Biondi, *To Stand and Fight*, 151.
11. Quoted in Patricia Sullivan, *Lift Every Voice: The NAACP and the Making of the Civil Rights Movement* (New York: New Press, 2009), 349.
12. Quoted in Biondi, *To Stand and Fight*, 167.
13. Quoted in Patricia Sullivan, *Days of Hope: Race and Democracy in the New Deal Era* (Chapel Hill: University of North Carolina Press, 1996), 227.
14. Quoted in Vincent Harding, Robin D. G. Kelley, and Earl Lewis, *We Changed the World: African Americans, 1945–1970* (New York: Oxford University Press, 1997), 36.
15. Anne Moody, *Coming of Age in Mississippi* (New York: Dell, 1968), 129.
16. Quoted in Clayborne Carson et al., eds., *The Eyes on the Prize Civil Rights Reader: Documents, Speeches, and Firsthand Accounts from the Black Freedom Struggle* (New York: Viking, 1991), 49.
17. Quoted in Belinda Robnett, *How Long? How Long? African-American Women in the Struggle for Civil Rights* (New York: Oxford University Press, 1997), 59.
18. David L. Chappell, *A Stone of Hope: Prophetic Religion and the Death of Jim Crow* (Chapel Hill: University of North Carolina Press, 2004), 44–104.
19. Quoted in Carson et al., *Eyes on the Prize Civil Rights Reader*, 49–50.
20. Chappell, *A Stone of Hope*, 44–66.
21. Quoted ibid., 88.
22. Aldon Morris, quoted in Barbara Ransby, *Ella Baker and the Black Freedom Movement: A Radical Democratic Vision* (Chapel Hill: University of North Carolina Press, 2003), 175.
23. Ibid., 175–77.
24. Quoted in Harding, Kelley, and Lewis, *We Changed the World*, 67.
25. Quoted in Mary L. Dudziak, *Cold War Civil Rights: Race and the Image of American Democracy* (Princeton, NJ: Princeton University Press, 2000), 133.
26. Interview with Franklin McCain, in Howell Raines, *My Soul Is Rested: The Story of the Civil Rights Movement in the Deep South* (New York: Penguin Books, 1983), 75–82.
27. Quoted in Harding, Kelley, and Lewis, *We Changed the World*, 96.
28. Quoted ibid., 97.
29. Abraham L. Davis and Barbara Luck Graham, *The Supreme Court, Race, and Civil Rights* (Thousand Oaks, CA: Sage, 1995), 81–83.
30. Quoted in Dudziak, *Cold War Civil Rights*, 157–58.
31. Harding, Kelley, and Lewis, *We Changed the World*, 121.
32. Thomas Borstelmann, *The Cold War and the Color Line: American Race Relations in the Global Arena* (Cambridge: Harvard University Press, 2001), 160.
33. Dudziak, *Cold War Civil Rights*, 169–71.
34. Quoted ibid., 158–59.
35. Quoted in Cynthia Griggs Fleming, *Soon We Will Not Cry: The Liberation of Ruby Doris Smith Robinson* (New York: Rowman & Littlefield, 1998), 67.
36. Ibid., 112.
37. Quoted in Harding, Kelley, and Lewis, *We Changed the World*, 72.
38. Quoted in Timothy Tyson, *Radio Free Dixie: Robert F. Williams and the Roots of Black Power* (Chapel Hill: University of North Carolina Press, 1999), 215.
39. Biondi, *To Stand and Fight*, 223.
40. Sides, *L.A. City Limits*, 133.
41. Quoted in Sides, *L.A. City Limits*, 132.
42. Ibid., 133.
43. Beryl Satter, *Family Properties: How the Struggle over Race and Real Estate Transformed Chicago and Urban America* (New York: Metropolitan, 2009), 36–64.
44. George Lipsitz, *The Possessive Investment in Whiteness: How White People Profit from Identity Politics* (Philadelphia: Temple University Press, 1998), 26.
45. Both quoted in Sides, *L.A. City Limits*, 106.
46. Quoted in Biondi, *To Stand and Fight*, 230.
47. Sides, *L.A. City Limits*, 105–7.
48. Joe William Trotter Jr., *River Jordan: African American Urban Life in the Ohio Valley* (Lexington: University Press of Kentucky, 1998), 157.
49. Arnold Hirsch, "Massive Resistance in the Urban North: Trumbull Park, Chicago, 1953–1966," *Journal of American History* 82, no. 2 (September 1995): 522–50.
50. Quoted in Philip A. Klinkner and Rogers M. Smith, *The Unsteady March: The Rise and Decline of Racial Equality in America* (Chicago: University of Chicago Press, 2002), 280.
51. Both quoted in Biondi, *To Stand and Fight*, 193, 204.

52. Quoted in Sides, *L.A. City Limits*, 135.
53. Sides, *L.A. City Limits*, 136.
54. Biondi, *To Stand and Fight*, 208–22.
55. Sides, *L.A. City Limits*, 151–58.
56. Biondi, *To Stand and Fight*, 218–19.
57. Quoted in Sides, *L.A. City Limits*, 200.
58. Quoted in Lance Hill, *The Deacons for Defense: Armed Resistance and the Civil Rights Movement* (Chapel Hill: University of North Carolina Press, 2004), 263.
59. Jervis Anderson, *Bayard Rustin: Troubles I've Seen: A Biography* (New York: HarperCollins, 1997), 239–59.
60. Quoted in Sarah Azaransky, *The Dream Is Freedom: Pauli Murray and American Democratic Faith* (New York: Oxford University Press, 2011), 62.
61. All quoted in Peter Levy, *Let Freedom Ring: A Documentary History of the Modern Civil Rights Movement* (Westport, CT: Praeger, 1992), 123.
62. Both quoted in Dudziak, *Cold War Civil Rights*, 194, 197–200.
63. Quoted in Charles E. Cobb Jr., *On the Road to Freedom: A Guided Tour of the Civil Rights Trail* (Chapel Hill: Algonquin Books, 2008), 257.
64. For two versions of this song, see "We Shall Overcome," on *Voices of the Civil Rights Movement: Black American Freedom Songs, 1960–1966*, Smithsonian Folkways Recordings SF 40084, 1997, compact disc.

SUGGESTED REFERENCES

Anticommunism and the Postwar Black Freedom Struggle

Borstelmann, Thomas. *The Cold War and the Color Line: American Race Relations in the Global Arena*. Cambridge: Harvard University Press, 2001.

Duberman, Martin B. *Paul Robeson: A Biography*. New York: New Press, 1989.

Dudziak, Mary L. *Cold War Civil Rights: Race and the Image of American Democracy*. Princeton, NJ: Princeton University Press, 2000.

Harris, Robert. "Ralph Bunche and Afro-American Participation in Decolonization." In *The African American Voice in U.S. Foreign Policy since World War II*, edited by Michael Krenn, 163–80. New York: Garland, 1998.

Korstad, Robert Rodgers. *Civil Rights Unionism: Tobacco Workers and the Struggle for Democracy in the Mid-Twentieth-Century South*. Chapel Hill: University of North Carolina Press, 2003.

Singh, Nikhil Pal. *Black Is a Country: Race and the Unfinished Struggle for Democracy*. Cambridge: Harvard University Press, 2004.

Sullivan, Patricia. *Lift Every Voice: The NAACP and the Making of the Civil Rights Movement*. New York: New Press, 2009.

The Transformation of the Southern Civil Rights Movement

Carson, Clayborne. *In Struggle: SNCC and the Black Awakening of the 1960s*. Cambridge: Harvard University Press, 1981.

Carson, Clayborne, David J. Garrow, Gerald Gill, Vincent Harding, and Darlene Clark Hine, eds. *The Eyes on the Prize Civil Rights Reader: Documents, Speeches, and Firsthand Accounts from the Black Freedom Struggle*. New York: Viking, 1991.

Chappell, David L. *A Stone of Hope: Prophetic Religion and the Death of Jim Crow*. Chapel Hill: University of North Carolina Press, 2004.

Davis, Abraham L., and Barbara Luck Graham. *The Supreme Court, Race, and Civil Rights*. Thousand Oaks, CA: Sage, 1995.

Fleming, Cynthia Griggs. *Soon We Will Not Cry: The Liberation of Ruby Doris Smith Robinson*. New York: Rowman & Littlefield, 1998.

Harding, Vincent, Robin D. G. Kelley, and Earl Lewis. *We Changed the World: African Americans, 1945–1970*. New York: Oxford University Press, 1997.

Lawson, Steven F. *Civil Rights Crossroads: Nation, Community, and the Black Freedom Struggle*. Lexington: University Press of Kentucky, 2003.

Ransby, Barbara. *Ella Baker and the Black Freedom Movement: A Radical Democratic Vision*. Chapel Hill: University of North Carolina Press, 2003.

Robnett, Belinda. *How Long? How Long? African-American Women in the Struggle for Civil Rights*. New York: Oxford University Press, 1997.

Sitkoff, Harvard. *King: Pilgrimage to the Mountaintop*. New York: Hill and Wang, 2008.

Civil Rights: A National Movement

Anderson, Jervis. *Bayard Rustin: Troubles I've Seen: A Biography*. New York: HarperCollins, 1997.

Biondi, Martha. *To Stand and Fight: The Struggle for Civil Rights in Postwar New York City*. Cambridge: Harvard University Press, 2003.

Hirsch, Arnold. "Massive Resistance in the Urban North: Trumbull Park, Chicago, 1953–1966." *Journal of American History* 82, no. 2 (September 1995): 522–50.

Jones, William P. *The March on Washington: Jobs, Freedom, and the Forgotten History of Civil Rights*. New York: Norton, 2013.

Lipsitz, George. *The Possessive Investment in Whiteness: How White People Profit from Identity Politics*. Philadelphia: Temple University Press, 1998.

Self, Robert O. *American Babylon: Race and the Struggle for Postwar Oakland*. Princeton, NJ: Princeton University Press, 2003.

Sides, Josh. *L.A. City Limits: African American Los Angeles from the Great Depression to the Present*. Berkeley: University of California Press, 2003.

Sugrue, Thomas J. *Sweet Land of Liberty: The Forgotten Struggle for Civil Rights in the North*. New York: Random House, 2008.

Sullivan, Patricia. *Days of Hope: Race and Democracy in the New Deal Era*. Chapel Hill: University of North Carolina Press, 1996.

Tyson, Timothy. *Radio Free Dixie: Robert F. Williams and the Roots of Black Power*. Chapel Hill: University of North Carolina Press, 1999.

Multiple Meanings of Freedom: The Movement Broadens

1961–1976

Stokely Carmichael and the Meaning of Black Power

"Wasteland, terra incognita . . . nothing, nada, squat."[1] That is how SNCC organizer Stokely Carmichael described Lowndes County, Alabama, in 1965. Situated between Selma and Montgomery, Lowndes seemed the most unlikely birthplace of the first Black Panther Party. The county was overwhelmingly rural, with about eighty white families owning 90 percent of the land, and although blacks numbered 12,000 of the 15,000 inhabitants — 80 percent of the population — all of them were impoverished, and none of them could vote. The largest town in the county, Fort Deposit, was a Ku Klux Klan stronghold, and in Hayneville, the county seat, juries refused to convict the confessed murderers of Viola Liuzzo and Jonathan Daniels, two white civil rights workers who in separate incidents were killed for their work on behalf of black civil and voting rights. In Lowndes County, blacks lived in fear.[2] According to John Hulett, the man who would help Carmichael turn black share-croppers into an effective political force, before SNCC arrived young black men often ran and hid in the bushes if they saw car headlights on the road at night. Hulett said, "They thought the sheriff was coming by and maybe would do something to them."[3]

As bad as life was in this county, Carmichael thought he could "turn a negative into a positive."[4] Hidden behind the apparent black subservience was a history of militancy. In the 1930s, for example, there had been a black sharecroppers' union in the county that had a tradition of armed self-defense. In fact, most of the older black men and women in the county carried guns to protect themselves and their families. "You turn the other cheek, and you'll get handed half of what you're sitting on," said one local leader who had met stiff white resistance when he had tried to register to vote.[5] Carmichael also liked the fact that although the two counties bordering Lowndes had been the scenes of well-publicized civil rights marches and violent reprisals, Lowndes was, as Carmichael described it, "virgin territory." No organizations were vying for attention or loyalty. SNCC could apply its grassroots tactics of quietly meeting with families and community leaders, helping them organize and lead their own rebellion. Carmichael also saw promise in a little-used law enabling any group to become a political party on the county level if it held a convention, nominated a slate of candidates, and received 20 percent of the primary vote. The law had been nearly forgotten, because white Democrats had ruled Alabama with no Republican opposition to speak of since the 1880s. In Lowndes, all the voters were white, and they all belonged to the Alabama Democratic Party. Its slogan was "White Supremacy for the Right," and its symbol, a rooster, caused blacks to derisively nickname it the "white cock party."[6]

When Carmichael first broached the idea of an independent black political party in Lowndes, he met stiff resistance from both blacks and whites. Most blacks wanted access to the Democratic Party. Proponents of a separate party, however, said that black people needed more than simple party membership. "What would it profit a man to have the vote and not be able to control it?" asked Courtland Cox, a SNCC strategist. "When you have a situation where the community is 80 percent black, why complain about police brutality when you can be the sheriff yourself? Why complain about substandard education when you could be the Board of Education? Why complain about the courthouse when you could move to take it over yourself? . . . Why protest when you can exercise power?"[7] As the idea evolved, locals grew excited about having a party that truly represented the county majority. Hulett described the party's chosen symbol, a black panther, as "an animal that when it is pressured it moves back until it is cornered, then it comes out fighting for life or death." Blacks in Lowndes thought they had been pushed long enough. They formed the Lowndes County Freedom Organization (LCFO), and resolved, as Hulett put it, to "come out and take over."[8]

For their part, white Democrats fired African American workers who tried to vote, forced them off white-owned land, and shot at blacks who sought refuge in the tent city that SNCC set up for those who found themselves homeless as a result of these and other measures. In one particularly vicious incident, the sheriff arrested Carmichael and other civil rights workers who had come to help blacks register to vote, only to release them to a lynch mob that shot and killed one white man, Jonathan Daniels, and left another, Father Richard Morrisroe, a priest, with a bullet in his back. Undeterred, blacks continued to register, and the party sustained itself in the primary. It became the representative party of blacks in Lowndes. Five years later, the same people who had ducked into the bushes when the white sheriff passed used their vote to make John Hulett the sheriff and another black man, Charles Smith, the county commissioner.[9]

The tactics used in Lowndes represented an alternative to the nonviolent direct-action protest strategy used by mainstream civil rights organizations such as CORE and the SCLC. Lowndes showed what could happen when black people controlled their own communities from an independent base of black political strength. Lowndes also demonstrated the pitfalls of white participation in the black freedom struggle and the importance of black self-confidence. Daniels and Morrisroe were targeted by the lynch mob because they were white, convincing some black organizers that the dangerous work of grassroots organizing did not need to be made more dangerous by the presence of white volunteers. Moreover, Carmichael and other SNCC workers believed that for their own self-esteem, Lowndes County blacks needed a more positive black consciousness. Carmichael observed, "They oppress us because we are black and we are going to use that blackness to get out of the trick bag they put us in."[10]

The 1960s and 1970s were turbulent years. There were assassinations, urban rebellions, and a foreign war. The freedom struggle, though a cause of some of this turbulence, was also affected by it. Throughout this period, blacks sought new approaches for realizing economic justice and political liberty. As time wore on and white resistance persisted, African Americans became more comfortable with a black power strategy, which made blacks less dependent on white acceptance and participation. Although this strategy still exposed blacks to white retaliatory violence, it instilled race pride and self-respect and demonstrated new ways of using black political power.

The Emergence of Black Power

Many had long abandoned the notion that black citizens should walk the world unarmed. Both individual activists and organizations — such as the Nation of Islam (NOI), a black Muslim group founded in the early 1930s — had been advocating black political and economic control of their own communities for some time. Even where blacks composed the majority, white political power and police brutality were suffocating. Direct-action campaigns to integrate public schools and facilities only scratched the surface of the larger problems of widespread unemployment and underemployment and economic injustice. After ten years of boycotts, demonstrations, sit-ins, and Freedom Rides, African Americans still felt like a colonized people who, as evidenced by the treatment of men such as Ralph Bunche, Paul Robeson, and W. E. B. Du Bois (see chapter 12), were hardly free to speak their mind in the nation that was supposedly the freest on earth.

After the Sixteenth Street Baptist Church bombing in Birmingham and other events of the early 1960s, black power gained resonance and, more important, a platform. Malcolm X, a new young leader headquartered in New York City, emerged as its chief proponent. Early in 1964, he asked black men if they could "sit around and read where they bomb a church and murder in cold blood, not some grownups, but four little girls while they were praying," and not do anything about it. Malcolm X challenged black people, and black men in particular, arguing that if "the government has proven itself either unwilling or unable to defend the lives and the property of Negroes, it's time for Negroes to defend themselves."[11] New organizations advanced this idea, developing more militant philosophies that promoted black independence, self-defense, self-sufficiency, and race pride.

Expanding the Struggle beyond Civil Rights

The philosophy of black power was not new; indeed, some of these ideas had made their way into the first draft of John Lewis's March on Washington speech in 1963. But the events of the early 1960s provided the right context for black power to flourish. The emergence of forty new nation-states between 1945 and 1960 in the former colonial world had a dramatic effect on black consciousness. No longer were whites, even liberal whites, the sole point of reference, or even the only possible allies of American blacks. The black writer James Baldwin made this point as early as 1960, when he identified what he called a "new mood" among African Americans. "The American Negro," he proclaimed, "can no longer, nor will he ever again be controlled by white America's image of him. This fact has everything to do with the rise of Africa in world affairs."[12]

At home, a tumultuous start to the decade also fostered new ways of thinking. The bombing in Birmingham, and the subsequent violent street uprisings during which two black teenagers were killed, were only a harbinger of the tragedies to come. Two months later, on Friday, November 22, 1963, President John F. Kennedy was assassinated. The entire nation went into mourning. African Americans were particularly aggrieved. Kennedy's support of black civil rights had been halting, but the direct-action civil rights campaign had convinced him of the necessity of the civil rights bill that was stalled in Congress. Blacks were not confident that the new president, former vice president Lyndon Johnson, would see things the same way. During his twelve years as a senator from Texas, he had obstructed the passage and enforcement of civil rights laws. Spirits rose when Johnson announced, before a joint session of Congress, that "no memorial or eulogy could more eloquently honor President Kennedy's memory than the earliest possible passage of the civil rights bill for which he fought."[13] Johnson then proceeded to use all of his considerable influence to break a record-setting 534-hour filibuster in the Senate and get the bill passed in early July the following year.

The **Civil Rights Act of 1964** was the most important and extensive civil rights law passed in the United States since Reconstruction. It prohibited discrimination in places of public accommodation, outlawed bias in federally funded programs, authorized the U.S. Justice Department to initiate desegregation lawsuits, and provided technical and financial aid to communities desegregating their schools. The most contentious part of the act, and one that would prove the most far-reaching, was **Title VII**. It banned discrimination in employment on the basis of race, color, religion, sex, or national origin and created the **Equal Employment Opportunity Commission (EEOC)** to investigate and litigate cases of job discrimination.

As significant as the act was, however, many agreed with John Lewis's earlier assessment of the bill that it was "too little and too late." It did nothing to curb the violence directed at black people, and it did not address the Justice Department's finding that in the eighteen-month period from January 1958 to June 1960, some 34 percent of all reported victims of police brutality were black.[14] Furthermore, the act did nothing to protect black voting rights, and with the black unemployment rate double that of whites, the long and cumbersome legal process the law established to bring about equity in employment opportunities was not promising. The compromises civil rights organizations had made in the 1950s to silence anti-Communist critics had paid some dividends, but there had been no economic or political justice for African Americans. Moreover, segregation was still alive and well. By 1964, the systematic exclusion of blacks from favorable housing areas was so complete that in both northern and southern cities, blacks were the most isolated of all ethnic minorities. The failure of the Civil Rights Act to address these issues fueled new, more militant ideas about America's problems and how black people should respond.[15]

Early Black Power Organizations

Radical organizations approached the black freedom struggle differently than did mainstream organizations such as the NAACP and SCLC. They were not all the same, but they shared three important ideas. One was that more aggressive measures were needed to tackle the problems black Americans faced. Another was that blacks had, within their own communities, the resources to effect change. The third was that African Americans needed to be proud to be black.

One of the earliest black power organizations was an Ohio-based student group called the Revolutionary Action Movement (RAM). Founded in 1962 by Maxwell Stanford, RAM was greatly influenced by Robert Williams, an activist and a vocal proponent of armed self-defense, for which the NAACP denounced him. Members of RAM supported the national liberation movements in Africa, Asia, and Latin America, connecting their own plight to those of colonial subjects abroad by arguing that police patrols turned black communities into "occupied zones" or "internal colonies." They saw themselves as engaged in an anticolonial war with the American nation-state and believed their first duty was to defend themselves and monitor police activity in their neighborhoods. RAM developed a twelve-point program calling for independent black schools, national black student organizations, rifle clubs, a guerrilla army made up of young people and the unemployed, and black farmer cooperatives that fostered economic self-sufficiency. RAM's philosophy, termed **black nationalism**, was founded on the idea that black people constituted a nation within a nation, where survival depended on the exercise of power — black power.[16]

In Oakland, California, young black college students were also searching for alternative strategies. Founded in 1961 by Donald Warden, the Afro-American Association laid the intellectual groundwork for the black power movement. The group's members, who had met as students at the University of California, Berkeley, emphasized the importance of Africa and decolonization movements to the African American freedom struggle. Other groups developed strategies that were politically focused. At the March on Washington for Jobs and Freedom, the activist William Worthy distributed leaflets announcing the Freedom Now Party, an independent black political party. Although it never cohered as a national organization, it showed modest strength in local and state elections, especially in Michigan. These new organizations were joined by established groups that abandoned the moderate philosophy of nonviolence. For example, when Floyd McKissick assumed the leadership of CORE in 1966, he announced that CORE was "tired of condemning our own people when they start to fight back. . . . There is no possible return to non-violence."[17]

A variety of periodicals began to disseminate new ideas about blacks being a proud people, a nation within a nation that needed to exercise more control over its economic well-being and to be more militant in the exercise of political power. These publications included *Soulbook, Liberator, Negro Digest, Freedomways,* and the Nation of Islam newspaper, *Muhammad Speaks.*[18]

Black music, paintings, plays, and novels reified the message. In what would become known as the **Black Arts Movement**, defined by one of its founders as the "spiritual sister of the Black Power Concept,"[19] artists used their art to project the beauty and power of black culture. Echoing the varying philosophies of the black freedom movement, black artists of the 1960s and 1970s were not of one mind about what black art should be, but they had in common a notion that black art was (or should be) different from white art, with unique roots, characteristics, and goals. How this idea was interpreted depended on the artist and his or her medium, politics, and influences. Like everything else about being black during this period, art was contested, and artists were challenged to find their place on the continuum.

One thing that was not often contested among black power activists and black nationalists was a common philosophy on gender. Black power became synonymous with the liberation of black men from the emasculating effects of racism. One of activists' most enduring criticisms of nonviolent direct action was that real men did not allow *their* women to be brutalized by white segregationists. White men, activists argued, had for centuries kept the black man unemployed or underemployed in order to control the black family and keep black men from protecting black women. Whites had caricatured black men as effeminate in order to deprive the black male of his manhood, thereby keeping the race subservient. Black activists argued that the race would be free only when black men were free to assume their full patriarchal rights. When the militant Floyd McKissick assumed the leadership of CORE, he said, "The year 1966 shall be remembered as the year we left our imposed status as Negroes and became Black men." Stokely Carmichael had a similar outlook. He predicted a race war in which blacks would "stand on our feet and die like men. . . . If that's our only act of manhood, then Goddamnit we're going to die."[20]

Women had not been able to use all of their talents and play leadership roles in the direct-action phase of the movement, and the pressure on women to accept secondary roles became more pronounced as black nationalist ideas took hold. Although it was Jo Ann Robinson who mobilized the Montgomery bus boycott; Ella Baker who became the first full-time staff member of the SCLC, and later its interim director, and who helped to found SNCC; and Fannie Lou Hamer who was the principal organizer of and spokesperson for the Mississippi Freedom Democratic Party, in most black power organizations, women were bombarded with demands to stop competing with men for jobs and to stay home and have babies "for the revolution." More often than not, they were expected to do menial chores such as make coffee and clean up after the men. If they objected, they were accused of allying with whites or emasculating black men. As the activist Angela Davis noted, the late sixties and early seventies were "a period in which one of the unfortunate hallmarks of some nationalist groups was their

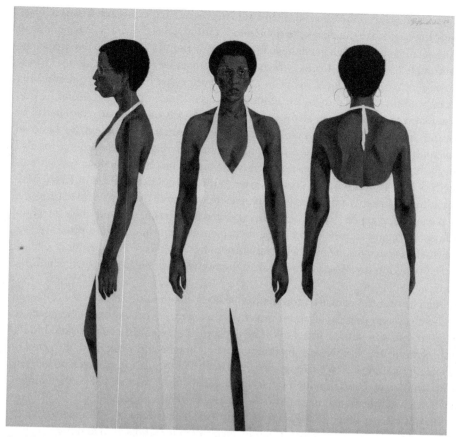

Barkley Hendricks, October's Gone . . . Goodnight, *1973*
Barkley Hendricks's *October's Gone . . . Goodnight* is one in a series of paintings Hendricks calls *Birth of the Cool.* All of the paintings are life-size and depict African Americans in realistic proud poses. In this six-by-six-foot painting, a dark-skinned black woman stands in regal elegance, unbowed. Though there is nothing flamboyant about her, her dignity and self-possession project the kind of image that was celebrated by many of the era's black writers, poets, and actors. *Oil and acrylic on linen canvas, 72 x 72 inches.*
© Barkley L. Hendricks. Courtesy of the artist and the Jack Shainman Gallery, New York.

determination to push women into the background. The brothers opposing us leaned heavily on the male supremacist trends which were winding their way through the movement."[21]

Malcolm X

The most eloquent and influential proponent of black power, including its gender politics, was Malcolm X. He had long maintained that the civil rights struggle needed a new and broader interpretation, and his was black nationalism. He expanded the civil rights struggle to the level of human rights, and argued that as a nation within a nation, black Americans could take their cause to the United Nations, where Africans, Asians, and all people of color could weigh in on their side. Attending the 1964 Cairo Conference of the Organization of African Unity, which brought together the heads of the newly independent African nations, Malcolm told a reporter that he sought "to remind the African heads of state that there are 22 million of us in America who are also of African descent, and to remind them also that we are the victims of America's colonialism or American imperialism, and that our problem is not an American problem, it's a human problem. It's not a Negro problem, it's a problem of humanity. It's not a problem of civil rights, but a problem of human rights."[22] Malcolm X's black nationalism was an outgrowth of his Muslim religion. As a minister in the nonpolitical Nation of Islam, Malcolm adhered strictly to the group's principles of economic uplift, puritan values, and race pride. He preached that if black people pooled their resources; built their own hospitals, schools, and factories; and made their own neighborhoods good places to live, they wouldn't have to integrate white establishments. This could happen only if black people learned to love themselves, protect themselves, and build their own economic system.

Articulating the gendered foundation of black nationalism, Malcolm X believed that "while a man must at all times respect his woman, at the same time he needs to understand that he must control her if he expects to get her respect." He noted in his autobiography that women are "by their nature . . . fragile and weak" and "attracted to the male in whom they see strength."[23] In Malcolm's formulation of black power, the strength and protection provided to black women by black men would be the foundation of black families and communities — indeed, the black nation.

Malcolm's insistence that "black is beautiful" had special significance for black women, who had long been negatively impacted by white standards of feminine beauty, but it resonated with both genders. He counseled blacks to embrace themselves as black people and not as "Negroes," a word that he believed whites had invented to separate blacks from their African and Asian brothers. The word *Negro* made black people hate themselves, he argued, because it was associated with slavery and docility. Malcolm agreed with the black nationalist George Grant, who in 1926 argued for the voluntary embrace of the word *black* as a way to "dispel the fallacious ideas of white purity, white beauty, and white superiority."[24]

Malcolm X's ideas stood in stark contrast to Martin Luther King Jr.'s philosophy of nonviolence and strategy of direct-action protest. Malcolm derided civil rights leaders as sellouts who were handpicked by white liberals to keep blacks in check. Black people needed land, power, and freedom, not desegregation, he argued. Desegregation did not address police brutality, substandard education, poverty, and unemployment, and from his perspective African Americans would get nowhere by loving their oppressors. "Revolution," he said, "is never based on begging somebody for an integrated cup of coffee. Revolutions are never fought by turning the other cheek. . . . And revolutions are never waged singing 'We Shall Overcome.'" Instead, he argued, "Revolutions are

Malcolm X

Shown here with his young daughter Ilyasah, Malcolm X emerged as black power's most influential advocate. Combining a philosophy of black nationalism with his role as a minister in the Nation of Islam, Malcolm portrayed the freedom struggle as an issue of human rights and encouraged the use of revolutionary tactics. In 1964, he broke with the Nation of Islam and created the secular Organization of Afro-American Unity to address black economic issues and encourage black participation in mainstream politics. Less than a year later, members of the Nation of Islam assassinated Malcolm as he addressed his new organization. © *SZ Photo/The Image Works.*

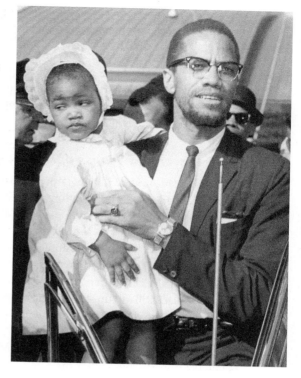

based upon bloodshed. . . . Revolutions overturn systems."[25]

Early in 1964, Malcolm X moved to make his revolutionary vision a reality. He broke his ties with Elijah Muhammad, the leader of the Nation of Islam, and resigned his ministry. For some time, he had chafed under the organization's restriction against political activity and Elijah Muhammad's seeming jealousy of his national renown. He was also disturbed by rumors regarding Elijah Muhammad's indiscretions with women and the Nation of Islam's finances. Concerned that differences over religion were preventing a united front against white racism, he established the secular Organization of Afro-American Unity (OAAU), modeled on the Organization of African Unity created by the newly independent African states. Malcolm planned to use the organization not only to build independent black institutions that would address black economic issues but also to support black participation in mainstream politics and to represent African Americans on the world stage, particularly at the United Nations.

Neither Malcolm X nor the organization survived long enough to put this plan into effect. On February 21, 1965, Malcolm was assassinated by Nation of Islam members who presumably were angered by his very public defection. But Malcolm's ideas spread like wildfire even after his death. Members of SNCC and CORE who had heard him speak circulated his philosophies. His ideas and tactics were debated and compared with those of King and other prominent civil rights leaders. Their acceptance among blacks grew in direct proportion to the growth of white resistance to black equality.[26]

The Struggle Transforms

At the end of 1963, black power and nonviolent political protest coexisted within the black freedom struggle. After 1965, however, the philosophies of black power and black nationalism became the dominant ideology. How and why that happened had to do with the intransigence of racism and the deepening determination of African Americans to resist its effects. It also had to do with some unpopular decisions and public missteps made by prominent civil rights leaders.

Black Power and Mississippi Politics

Black power ideas were floating around Mississippi in the summer of 1964 when the Council of Federated Organizations (COFO), a coalition of civil rights groups, conducted its **Mississippi Freedom Summer Project**, a massive education and voter registration campaign. During the months of June, July, and August, more than a thousand volunteers descended on Mississippi. They founded freedom schools that taught black youngsters, teenagers, and adults voter literacy and political organization skills. In alliance with local black leaders, they canvassed blacks and got them to register to vote. Although blacks made up 45 percent of Mississippi's population, only 5 percent of voting-age blacks voted. Their votes would prove pivotal in the upcoming presidential election.

It did not take much to convince black Mississippians — 86 percent of whom lived below the poverty line — that their impoverishment was directly related to their disfranchisement. They had demonstrated their voting strength in November 1963, when they had participated in a mock vote held by civil rights organizations. Unable to cast a vote in the official election, nearly 100,000 blacks had voted for the Freedom Ballot, a campaign designed to demonstrate blacks' voting strength and desire to participate in Mississippi politics. In August 1964, Mississippi blacks planned to take a separate delegation to the Democratic National Convention in Atlantic City, New Jersey, to challenge the party's all-white segregationist slate.

A tragedy during Freedom Summer highlighted black southerners' plight and caused many blacks to question the value of integrated civil rights activism. In early June, three civil rights workers — James Chaney, a native black Mississippian, and Andrew Goodman and Michael Schwerner, two white northerners — disappeared in Mississippi. They were found murdered in early August. The media attention that began after their initial disappearance, and the arrival of about 150 FBI agents and more than 200 members of the U.S. navy to search for the missing men, brought more to light than the murders. To many blacks, it seemed that America's leaders only became interested in black people's plight when white deaths were involved. As John Lewis observed, "It is a shame that national concern is aroused only after two white boys are missing."[27]

Although African Americans appreciated the work and sacrifices of the white volunteers who made up three-quarters of the Freedom Summer workers, many began to wonder whether they did more harm than good. Their middle-class background and education made them removed from most southern blacks' daily realities. For some blacks, especially those attuned to black power rhetoric, the presence of whites of greater wealth and superior education seemed to reinforce traditional patterns of racial dependence. Moreover, many understood that the presence of white women increased the wrath of segregationists, who were already convinced that the civil rights movement was a cover for interracial sexual relationships between black men and white women. The activist Fannie Lou Hamer, who carried a gun for self-defense, summed up the feeling that black men would be scapegoated when she warned, "If some whites laid hands on one of those young girls, every Negro man in Ruleville would be in trouble. That kind of trouble kills people in Mississippi."[28]

Despite these apprehensions, however, some blacks had misgivings about a blacks-only movement. As Hamer argued, "If we're trying to break down this barrier of segregation, we can't segregate ourselves." Like veteran civil rights worker Bob Moses, who argued that whites working alongside blacks changed the calculus from blacks against whites to "a question of rational people against irrational people," Hamer believed that whites had been in the movement from the beginning and had an important role to play.[29] Hamer's own accomplishments, including a food and clothing drive she had run under SNCC's auspices and an unsuccessful run for a seat in Congress, had been facilitated by interracial efforts. Experience had also taught her that middle-class blacks could harm the black freedom movement as much as, if not more than, whites.

Hamer's experience with the **Mississippi Freedom Democratic Party (MFDP)** made her suspicious of both white liberals and middle-class blacks. Black and white locals, aided by SNCC and COFO, had established the independent, nondiscriminatory political party on April 26, 1964, to represent black Mississippians. Hamer was elected vice chair of the sixty-eight-person delegation that the party planned to send to the Democratic National Convention in August. During Freedom Summer, the blacks and whites organizing the party caucuses, county assemblies, and convention that were necessary to send MFDP delegates to the national convention faced unrelenting terror. Hamer knew that people had died and lost jobs and homes for the cause; Hamer herself had lost the sight in one eye during a near-fatal beating in a Mississippi jail. But she and other activists persevered, because the last thing she and other black Mississippians wanted was for the white liberals who controlled the Democratic convention to seat the delegation that had been elected by the all-white Mississippi Democratic Party. That all-white segregationist delegation had no intention of backing Lyndon Johnson, whose support of the Civil Rights Act had antagonized them, and they were even more hostile toward the liberal Hubert Humphrey, Johnson's pick for vice president.

But during the convention, the unthinkable happened. After intense negotiation and political wrangling, national black civil rights leaders — along with Johnson, Humphrey, liberal white congressmen, and other white liberals such as Walter Reuther, head of the United Auto Workers — compromised with and even appeased the segregationist delegates. The MFDP was offered only two at-large seats on the floor of the convention, which would not allow them to participate officially. The MFDP, as well

Fannie Lou Hamer and the Mississippi Freedom Democratic Party
With the assistance of SNCC and COFO, Mississippi blacks established the Mississippi Freedom Democratic Party (MFDP) in 1964. Fannie Lou Hamer was elected vice chair of the party's sixty-eight delegates, who planned to challenge their state's all-white segregationist delegation at the Democratic National Convention that summer. During the convention, however, national black civil rights leaders and white liberals compromised with Mississippi Democratic Party delegates, and the MFDP was offered only two at-large seats on the convention floor, preventing their official participation in the convention. Here Fannie Lou Hamer, standing at center, is surrounded by other notable civil rights activists, including (from left) Emory Harris, Stokely Carmichael (wearing a straw hat), Sam Block, Eleanor Holmes Norton, and Ella Baker. © *George Ballis/Take Stock/The Image Works.*

as the SNCC staff that had supported them, rejected what they considered a "back of the bus" offer. Hamer agreed with Bob Moses, who argued that the MFDP belonged to "Mississippi and its own hopes and desires" — not to white liberals, or even to Martin Luther King Jr. and the other black civil rights leaders who characterized Hamer and other MFDP leaders as wrongheaded and ignorant.[30]

Hamer and her supporters came away from the Democratic National Convention empty-handed, but much more was lost than the right of the MFDP to represent black Mississippians. Those who backed the compromise might have thought they were being politically astute. King, for example, thought that any concession from the Democrats was better than nothing, and many liberals wanted to spare Johnson the political embarrassment of having southern white Democrats bolt from the convention. But the compromise left the strategy of nonviolent political protest impotent. According to Hamer, "We followed all the laws that the white people themselves made. . . . But we learned the hard way that even though we had all the laws and all the righteousness on our side — that white man is not going to give up his power to us."[31]

Exhausted after a summer of dodging white terrorists, John Lewis considered the MFDP defeat a turning point in the civil rights movement. "We had played by the rules, done everything we were supposed to do, had played the game exactly as required, had arrived at the doorstep and found the door slammed in our face," he argued.[32] Many felt that white liberals had double-crossed blacks, and even Bob Moses, who had long endorsed an integrated movement, left Atlantic City vowing, according to Lewis, that he would never again speak to a white man. Like Hamer, who concluded that power was something "we have to take for ourselves,"[33] Moses suggested that blacks should "set up our own [state] government . . . [and] declare the other one no good. And say the federal government should recognize us."[34] To say the least, black power scored a victory at the 1964 Democratic National Convention.

Bloody Encounters

A month before the convention, black power had also emerged victorious on the streets of New York. While search teams scoured the Mississippi countryside for the three missing civil rights workers, two black New York City communities, Harlem and Bedford-Stuyvesant, erupted in violence in response to the fatal shooting of James Powell, a slightly built fifteen-year-old black boy. "Is Harlem Mississippi?" one organization asked, issuing a call for "100 skilled revolutionaries who are ready to die."[35] African Americans threw bricks and bottles at police, looted white-owned stores, broke windows, set fires with Molotov cocktails, and booed the civil rights leaders who called for calm. In subsequent years, most cities saw similar unrest and violence. Conservatives blamed Communists, as well as black criminality and backwardness. Social scientists blamed overcrowded and deteriorating housing, poor heath, dilapidated schools, and police brutality. Black nationalists blamed white power and black powerlessness, which they vowed to change.[36]

The events following the summer of 1964 worked to the advantage of black power advocates. Lyndon Johnson won the November election, but without the support of southern Democrats. Their defection to the Republican Party candidate, archconservative Barry Goldwater, proved to many that Johnson had needlessly humiliated, and sacrificed the support of, the MFDP. Then, in 1965, Martin Luther King Jr. made a series of decisions that further destabilized the nonviolent direct-action sector of the black freedom struggle. The first occurred in March, in Selma, Alabama, where SNCC organizer Jimmie Lee Jackson had been shot and killed while protecting his mother from a police attack. Although doing so went against the organization's grassroots organizing tactics, SNCC answered King's call to participate in a protest march from Selma to Montgomery that both commemorated Jackson and supported voting rights. President

Johnson and Attorney General Nicholas Katzenbach urged King to call off the march, concerned that the publicity it would generate would adversely affect the voting rights bill that was proceeding slowly through Congress. King conceded and was nowhere in sight on March 7, a day that subsequently became known as **Bloody Sunday**. Led by SNCC head John Lewis, marchers were met at the Edmund Pettus Bridge by local police and Alabama state troopers armed with billy clubs and tear gas. The marchers stopped and knelt in prayer, which seemed only to gall the officers, who charged and clubbed their way forward, beating Lewis unconscious. The marchers retreated but reassembled three days later, again at King's urging. Once again, however, King disappointed them. This time, although he led the march, when he got to the bridge he stopped, knelt in prayer, and then asked the marchers to retreat. Angered by what they perceived as weakness on King's part, the marchers reluctantly turned back, ironically singing "Ain't Gonna Let Nobody Turn Me 'Round."[37]

King's compromises proved to be a double-edged sword. On one hand, the vicious police and trooper attacks proved that black people needed a voting rights act if only to have a voice in electing those who held policing power, and King's concessions enabled President Johnson to push the measure through Congress by August. The 1965 **Voting Rights Act** prohibited states from imposing literacy requirements and poll taxes and sent federal election examiners south to protect blacks' rights to register and vote. The impact was indisputable. Between 1964 and 1969, the percentage of blacks registered to vote in Alabama increased from 19.3 percent to 61.3 percent. The percentage of registered voters among blacks in Georgia increased by 33 percent, and in Mississippi it increased by a spectacular 60 percent (Map 13.1).

On the other hand, the brutal beatings took their toll, and King's reputation and strategy suffered a setback. John Lewis, who had his skull fractured on Bloody Sunday, noted, "We're only flesh. I could understand people not wanting to be beaten anymore. . . . Black capacity to believe [that a white person] would really open his heart, open his life to nonviolent appeal was running out." African Americans were also left to reflect on why the death of James Reeb, a white minister who was attacked shortly after the abortive demonstration, drew national publicity, while Jimmie Lee Jackson's death — the event that sparked the Selma-to-Montgomery march in the first place — garnered almost none. The outspoken young SNCC organizer Stokely Carmichael spoke for many when he complained about the outpouring of sympathy for Reeb: "I'm not saying we shouldn't pay tribute to Rev. Reeb. What I'm saying is that if we're going to pay tribute to one, we should also pay tribute to the other. And I think we have to analyze why [Johnson] sent flowers to Mrs. Reeb, and not to Mrs. Jackson."[38]

Black Power Ascends

Martin Luther King Jr. won the Nobel Peace Prize in 1964, but nonviolent, interracial protest was fast becoming a thing of the past. By the end of the Alabama demonstrations, even the moderate head of SNCC, James Forman, was proclaiming that "if we

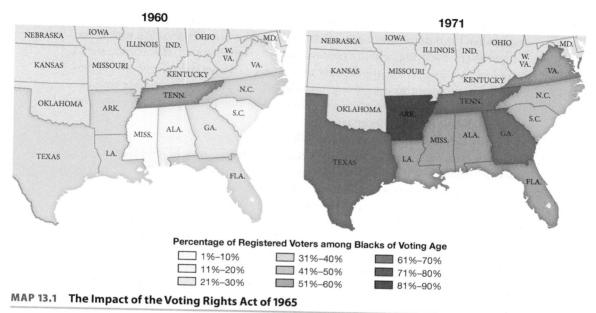

MAP 13.1   The Impact of the Voting Rights Act of 1965

Among its other provisions, the Voting Rights Act prohibited the literacy requirements and poll taxes that southern states had frequently used to prevent blacks from voting. The act also sent federal election examiners to the South to enable blacks to register and vote safely. As indicated in this map, black voter registration skyrocketed as a result of the legislation.

can't sit at the table of democracy, then we'll knock the fucking legs off."[39] Increasingly, activists believed that political work of the kind Carmichael was doing in Lowndes County paid more dividends than marches and beatings. Malcolm X's black nationalism resonated more deeply with them, as did the tactics of a new group of militants called the Deacons for Defense and Justice, an armed group that organized in Mississippi and Louisiana in 1964 to protect black people against increased Ku Klux Klan activity. Throughout 1965–1967, SNCC and CORE activists debated whether the black freedom struggle was better off with blacks-only organizations, and increasingly there were calls for whites to leave black organizations and organize their own groups to support black causes. In 1967, SNCC passed a resolution expelling whites. By that time, the leadership of SNCC had passed from the moderate John Lewis to the black power advocate Stokely Carmichael. Similarly, the leadership of CORE had passed from the moderate James Farmer to the militant community organizer Floyd McKissick.

McKissick was present in June 1966 when Carmichael made his memorable public pronouncements on black power. That summer, James Meredith — the student who had integrated the University of Mississippi — announced that he would march alone from Memphis to Jackson in what he called a march against fear. Two days into the march, Meredith was shot in the neck, back, and legs by an avowed racist named

Aubrey James Norvell. Civil rights leaders, including King, and black power advocates alike rushed to continue the march in Meredith's honor, but they marched with different mind-sets. For King, who by now was leading the old guard, the march offered proponents an unexpected opportunity to argue for new civil rights legislation and to force the government to accept responsibility for the safety of civil rights workers. Black power advocates, however, saw it as an opportunity to broadcast the perspective that black people had to be more assertive.

To insiders, the split was apparent. When marching civil rights workers shouted "Freedom," black nationalists shouted "Uhuru," the Swahili word for freedom. Black power marchers welcomed the protection of the Deacons for Defense and Justice, while civil rights workers only reluctantly accepted their support. And on the night of June 16, 1966, when Carmichael stood up and made public this advancing trend in African American thought, black power advocates cheered what civil rights workers bemoaned. "This is the twenty-seventh time that I've been arrested," said the just-released Carmichael. "I ain't going to jail no more." He proclaimed, "The only way we gonna stop them white men from whuppin' us is to take over. What we gonna start saying now is Black Power." To Carmichael's resounding question "What do we want?" came the enthusiastic reply, "Black Power!"[40]

Four months later, two students at Merritt College in Oakland, California, responded to this cry. Huey Newton and Bobby Seale had been working with the Soul Students Advisory Council, a student organization that successfully lobbied the California State Board of Education to establish a black studies department at Merritt College and to make black studies credits transferable from junior to senior colleges. The council also was pressing for the appointment of a black president at Merritt. In 1966, Seale and Newton broke with the council, believing that its emphasis on the glorification of black culture and an African past — what Newton and Seale called reactionary nationalism — would not liberate black people. They moved off campus and began organizing the poor people who lived in the area surrounding the campus. Seale and Newton then created the Black Panther Party for Self-Defense (BPPSD), making resistance to police repression its central mission. Clad in black leather jackets and black berets, the Black Panthers projected a hyper-masculine identity meant to reclaim a "manhood" that, they argued, white America had robbed them of for centuries. To resist police harassment and brutality, they carried unconcealed weapons and adopted the policy of following and monitoring the police.

Although chapters of the Black Panther Party emerged in numerous cities — including Chicago; Indianapolis; Detroit; Des Moines; Paterson, New Jersey; and Wichita, Kansas — Oakland's BPPSD was the most influential. Its "Ten Point Program" encapsulated many of the principles that black power and black nationalism had, by the mid-1960s, come to represent.[41] Included among them were self-determination for black people, full employment, decent housing and education, an end to police brutality, and exemption from military service.

The Black Panthers

Bobby Seale (left) and Huey Newton (right) created the Black Panther Party for Self-Defense (BPPSD) in Oakland, California, in 1966. Panthers made themselves recognizable by wearing black leather jackets and black berets, and they carried loaded, unconcealed weapons while patrolling black neighborhoods and monitoring the activities of local police. Their revolutionary philosophy motivated many activists and signaled a shift in the black freedom movement. For many activists, the Panthers also symbolized a reclamation of black manhood. San Francisco Examiner/Associated Press/AP Images.

The emergence of the Oakland Black Panthers revealed not only the divide between black nationalists and civil rights activists but also the many different expressions of black power. Although it was technically legal to carry unconcealed weapons in California until 1966, other black power groups thought the Oakland patrols a suicidal tactic that would provoke government retaliation, and they rejected it. When the Soul Students Advisory Council, the Revolutionary Action Movement, and the Republic of New Africa — all of which advocated some form of black power — objected to Seale and Newton's approach, their leaders were ridiculed by Seale and Newton followers as "intellectuals" whose black separatism and glorification of Africa obscured the structural inequalities hidden behind American racism.[42]

This emphasis on structural inequalities allowed the Panthers to work with radical groups that prioritized class, regardless of race, which in practical terms permitted their alliance with white organizations. Structural inequality was important to all black power organizations, but cultural nationalists believed that black powerlessness was rooted in a deficient culture that kept African Americans estranged from Africa. Stokely Carmichael, who was convinced that the black freedom struggle had to be international in scope and exclusively black, argued, "We are an African people with an African ideology."[43] Maulana Karenga, organizer of a Los Angeles group called US — as opposed to "THEM" — promoted cultural reconstruction through *Kawaida*, a "total way of life" based on African principles. US members adopted Swahili names, dressed in traditional West African clothes, and engaged in African rituals. Karenga and US invented and first observed **Kwanzaa**, an African American holiday that celebrates the

Seven Principles of Nguzo Saba, a black value system stressing unity, self-determination, self-love, and cooperative economics.

Differences between cultural naturalists and structuralists deepened divisions and made the entire freedom movement vulnerable to external attacks. While the Panthers called SNCC members and other black power organizations "armchair revolution-aries" or, worse, "pork chop revolutionaries," most black power activists derided civil rights activists as "sellouts," "chumps," "Oreos" (denoting persons who were black on the outside but white on the inside), and "Uncle Tom Negroes" (an epithet drawn from the antebellum novel *Uncle Tom's Cabin*, denoting black men who behaved subservi-ently toward whites). The word *Negro* itself became a derisive reference to a black person who slavishly embraced white culture. Black power activists adopted the terms *black* and *Afro* or *African American* to demonstrate their love of self and race and to symbolize their psychological emancipation from white oppressors.

Ultimately, the many expressions of black militancy, especially carrying weapons, increased police harassment. Law enforcement officials were also incensed by the epi-thets used by militants to describe the police and members of America's political hier-archy. Made popular by the Black Panthers' newspaper, the term *pig* — described as "a low natured beast that has no regard for law, justice, or the rights of the people; a crea-ture that bites the hand that feeds it; a foul depraved traducer, usually found masquer-ading as the victim of an unprovoked attack"[44] — was adopted by most left-wing radical groups of the era. Police retaliated by tearing down black power posters and stepping up their harassment of activists. The search and seizure of activists' cars and homes became a regular activity. Panthers and other black militants were arrested on flimsy charges and were even killed by local police and the FBI. (See Document Project: Black Power: Expression and Repression, pp. 557–66.)

Economic Justice and Affirmative Action

Black power was not the only response to the slow pace of change. Civil rights activists also adopted a new approach — or, more properly, returned to tried-and-true strate-gies for attaining economic and political justice. They did not endorse self-defense or the displays of militancy that were the hallmark of the most radical black power organi-zations. Instead, they worked through established institutions and in the process focused the nation's attention on a new concept called **affirmative action**, a set of ideas and programs aimed at compensating African Americans for past discrimination by giving them preferential treatment in hiring and school admissions.

Politics and the Fight for Jobs

Lyndon Johnson and his administration deplored the black freedom movement's turn to black nationalism. From their perspective, progress on civil rights had been unprec-edented. Johnson believed that his dedication to racial change and his effort to reduce the national poverty rate through what he called the War on Poverty were making a difference. Although he had known that the Civil Rights Act of 1964 would alienate southern Democrats, he had nevertheless forced the bill through Congress. Similar calculations were involved when he signed the Voting Rights Act in 1965. But Johnson also agreed with Martin Luther King Jr., who had, since Birmingham, urged "some compensatory consideration for the handicaps" blacks had "inherited from the past."[45]

With this argument, King demonstrated that he, like the black nationalists, was familiar with the dire economic state of black America and that he was not content with the slow pace of change. Like most other civil rights leaders, he had de-emphasized economic concerns to minimize Cold War accusations of communism. He had never abandoned the goal of economic equality, however, and he traced urban violence directly to the economic disabilities racism produced. "We must get better jobs in order to help our children to better education and housing, and in order to enjoy some of the entertainment and eating facilities that are now open to us," King told the SCLC in 1962. Other leaders agreed. "Economics is part of our struggle," said activist Bayard Rustin. James Farmer of CORE concurred: "It will be a hollow victory, indeed, if we win the important rights to spend our money in places of public accommodation, on buses, or what have you, without also winning the even more vital right to earn money."[46]

When it came to earning money, African Americans had clearly fallen behind. Despite gains brought about by civil rights activism, black unemployment was at the recession level of 10.2 percent, compared with the white rate of 4.9 percent. For black male breadwinners, unemployment in 1963 was three times higher than it was for whites. On average, employed blacks earned only 55 percent of what whites earned. The income gap between black and white women had almost closed, but this was because black women worked in greater numbers and for longer hours than white women. Among the young, black teenagers suffered joblessness at twice the rate of white teenagers.[47]

The issue was rendered more intractable by most whites' belief that their advantage resulted from their natural superiority to blacks. Surveys showed that even as they admitted that "their own employers do not open up certain types of jobs" to blacks, most whites maintained that "companies give Negroes a good break [in hiring]." Similarly, most white employers, even those who hired blacks, consistently maintained that "Negroes were not suited for any but production jobs."[48]

While liberals and conservatives differed in their views on economic injustice, the results were often the same. Conservatives were apt to believe in black incapacity: As one Milwaukee man editorialized in a conservative magazine, blacks "make themselves the way they are by being lazy, uneducated, sick, [and] undependable. . . . They cannot or *will not* compete."[49] Liberals were more likely to admit that blacks were profoundly wronged, but they nevertheless were apt to resist government action to redress those wrongs if it meant eliminating white privilege. For African Americans, then, the distinction between liberal and conservative was fast becoming irrelevant.

Urban Dilemmas: Deindustrialization, Globalization, and White Flight

At the same time that record numbers of blacks were migrating out of the South in search of more secure, higher-paying work, deindustrialization — the decline of manufacturing, especially in the auto, steel, and consumer goods industries — was decreasing the number of jobs, especially in the unskilled and semiskilled industrial sector. Detroit lost 140,000 manufacturing jobs between 1947 and 1963, while New York lost 70,000 garment industry jobs. Chicago's meatpacking industry shrank, and longshoreman, shipbuilding, and warehouse jobs in port cities such as Oakland, Newark, Philadelphia, and Baltimore disappeared as fewer ships were built and the use of industrial shipping containers reduced the need for large numbers of dockworkers.[50] In one of the most bitter ironies of African American history, unskilled southern blacks were moving north and west to escape insecure, low-paying, non-union jobs at the very time that northern and western companies were moving south and overseas in search of non-unionized, cheap labor and to suburbs in search of highly skilled professional labor.

Thus black people arrived in northern and western cities just as these cities were declining. The first generation of black migrants found the education in urban schools to be better than that in the schools they had left behind, but as companies relocated and whites, with the help of federally subsidized low-interest loans and prompted by discrimination against blacks, left cities for racially exclusive suburban neighborhoods — a phenomenon generally termed **white flight** — education became just as separate and unequal in the North and West as it was in the South. Suburban shopping malls thrived at the expense of downtown urban areas, and the highways that facilitated whites' travel to and from the cities in which they no longer lived often destroyed the black neighborhoods that they cut through. Urban renewal projects designed to reinvigorate decaying cities had much the same effect. New York destroyed Manhattan's San Juan Hill, a black and Puerto Rican neighborhood, to make way for the Lincoln Center for the Performing Arts, which housed the Metropolitan Opera. Philadelphia bulldozed its Black Bottom neighborhood to make way for a science and research center attached to the University of Pennsylvania. Chicago's Bronzeville neighborhood was cut off on one side by an expressway and on the other side by high-rise public housing.[51]

Long a source of black-white competition, public housing presented special problems for African Americans. When whites moved out of the city, making public housing more accessible to blacks, it only added to the isolating concentration of black poverty. Public housing was usually built in already impoverished black neighborhoods or on marginal land, such as garbage dumps or toxic wetlands. Chicago's Robert Taylor Homes and Stateway Gardens, Boston's Columbia Point, and Philadelphia's Passyunk Homes were all built on sites that developers could use for nothing else.[52]

Discrimination in employment and housing helped bring to light a new idea, **institutional racism**, that would inform activists' attempts to tackle economic

The Urban Crisis

Deindustrialization triggered the decline of many northern and western cities, which lost thousands of jobs just as African American migrants poured in seeking work. As jobs disappeared and white flight expanded the developing suburbs, the infrastructure of these cities began to decay. Urban renewal projects — many of which, ironically, focused on the development of public housing — often exacerbated these problems, decimating black neighborhoods. In this 1963 photograph, a major public housing complex under construction in Chicago is visible behind tenements of the sort it has displaced. The residents of the new building would have higher incomes than the residents of these older homes.
Charles E. Knoblock/Associated Press/AP Images.

injustice. In the 1950s and early 1960s, racism was still thought of as something practiced by individuals or mandated by law. Later in the decade, the idea that institutions could and did operate as unfairly as individuals began to take hold. By this logic, corporations and unions based their hiring, promotion, and firing decisions on the accepted premise that black workers were inferior to white workers in ability, reinforcing this assumption in the process. Housing discrimination was based on the same premise of black incapacity, and thus also reinforced ideas of black inferiority. Similarly, activists began to argue that the legal and criminal justice systems were discriminatory because the systems themselves grew from customs steeped in centuries of racism.

Tackling Economic Injustice

Laws that promoted black civil and voting rights could not and did not change the institutional racism that handicapped blacks in the workforce, real estate market, and legal system. "Freedom is not enough," President Johnson said in a 1965 commencement speech at Howard University. In what was to become part of the philosophical foundation of the policy of affirmative action, Johnson declared, "You do not wipe away the scars of centuries by saying: Now you are free to go where you want, and do as you desire, and choose the leaders you please. You do not take a person who, for years, has been hobbled by chains and liberate him, bring him up to the starting line of a race and then say, 'you are free to compete with all the others,' and still justly believe that you have been completely fair."[53] In 1964, as part of his War on Poverty, Johnson signed the **Economic Opportunity Act**. It established the Job Corps, to create employment opportunities for the poor; Head Start, to give poor children a preschool education; the Neighborhood Youth Corps, to give inner-city youths summer jobs; and Volunteers in Service to America (VISTA), to give advantaged young people a chance to serve the less advantaged in the United States.

More important for black employment was Title VII of the 1964 Civil Rights Act, which banned employers and unions from practicing race and gender discrimination. When opponents could not beat back Johnson's support for the measure, they weakened the act by limiting the funding and abilities of the Equal Employment Opportunity Commission (EEOC), the agency charged with investigating discrimination. In particular, opponents would not allow plaintiffs to use the low number of minorities in a particular job as evidence of discrimination; neither could a group receive preferential treatment to redress the imbalance. Opponents' efforts, however, did not prevent African Americans from using the new law. From 9,000 cases in the EEOC's first year of operation, the caseload grew to 77,000 by 1975.[54]

With the help of the Office of Federal Contract Compliance (another Johnson agency), the NAACP, and the NAACP Legal Defense and Educational Fund, black workers turned the weakened legislation to their advantage. In the process, they built a body of case law covering issues such as seniority lists that locked blacks out of good jobs; discriminatory hiring and promotion procedures; biased recruiting; segregated unions; and the use of exclusionary testing and job requirements unrelated to job performance. Many cases ended unsuccessfully, especially in the northern construction trades, where black workers met with stiff resistance from whites, who engaged in hate strikes and persistently excluded blacks from apprenticeship programs. Whites took to calling the new policies "reverse racism." Some industries gave way, however. Blacks in the South successfully accessed jobs in the textile industry, where black women especially benefited. According to a textile worker named Corine Cannon, work allowed black women "to be full-fledged citizens."[55]

The impact of Title VII extended beyond the actual number of cases won or lost. Along with the War on Poverty programs, the law breathed new life into strategies combating poverty that the Cold War had forced civil rights groups to put on hold. In Chicago in 1966, for example, King's SCLC established Operation Breadbasket, which aimed to increase both black employment in urban businesses and the number of black-owned businesses. Sounding very much like his black power counterparts, King explained that "the fundamental premise of Breadbasket is a simple one: Negroes . . . need not patronize a business which denies them jobs or advancement or plain courtesy."[56] Breadbasket won jobs by boycotting Country Delight dairy products and the A&P supermarket in Chicago. But King's ideas went beyond boycotts. Along with leaders such as A. Philip Randolph, Bayard Rustin, Whitney Young, and John Lewis, he argued for "a massive program by the government of special compensatory measures." Black civil rights leaders were virtually unanimous in supporting what they called the "Freedom Budget," or a "practical, step-by-step plan for wiping out poverty in America during the next ten years" by creating federally funded jobs at a cost of $180 billion.[57]

Proponents of compensatory programs challenged the prevailing notion that property rights gave employers the right to discriminate, that unions could promote and fire on the basis of seniority rules, and that equality and color blindness were the proper basis on which to hire workers. Instead, they insisted on affirmative action — preferential treatment for blacks through the use of numerical hiring goals — arguing that white Americans had received preferential treatment for three hundred years on the basis of their color. According to Whitney Young, head of the National Urban League, "Indemnification means realistic reparations for past injuries and wrongs. . . . Industry must employ Negroes because they are Negroes."[58] Likewise, A. Philip Randolph argued that urban chaos could be avoided only by "mak[ing] work available for those in the ghettos."[59]

Griggs v. Duke Power Co. (1971) eliminated some of the barriers that kept blacks from being employed. The case was filed in 1966 by the NAACP on behalf of Willie Griggs and thirteen other black janitors whose North Carolina employer required workers to take IQ tests or present high school diplomas in order to advance to better-paying positions. These requirements disproportionately disadvantaged African Americans. Moreover, white workers who had been hired before the institution of the requirements were found to perform their jobs capably, making it clear that meeting such requirements did not predict job performance. The U.S. Supreme Court's unanimous decision declared that tests and other requirements unnecessary for the performance of a job were, by their very nature, discriminatory. Under the ruling, if employers could not demonstrate a business necessity for employment requirements, they had to eliminate the requirements.

For many civil rights advocates, this victory was as important as the *Brown* decision in 1954. Previously, it had been almost impossible to prove that a company discriminated intentionally, and plaintiffs often did not have the financial resources to pursue the case. With *Griggs*, the burden of proof shifted to the employer, as the Court finally recognized that where minorities were concerned, seemingly neutral policies could be discriminatory. As more cases were settled under *Griggs*, it became increasingly customary for companies to set numerical hiring and promotion goals for minorities — something conservative congressmen had explicitly omitted from the original Title VII legislation. These cases made a difference in the number of blacks hired. By the second half of the 1970s, economists and social scientists concluded that affirmative action had, in fact, helped black employment. "Direct pressure," concluded one economist, "does make a difference."[60]

War, Radicalism, and Turbulence

By the mid-1960s, the black freedom struggle had completely changed from what it had been just ten years before. Direct-action protest for civil rights had almost run its course, and black power was fast supplanting nonviolent civil disobedience as the philosophy of choice. Economic justice was back on the front burner, and both civil rights and black power groups were addressing issues of unemployment, housing, and poverty. Moreover, the movement had grown less interracial. Years of white resistance had bred black suspicion and anger; for their part, whites were put off by black power ideas, and poor whites looked suspiciously at affirmative action.[61] Black nationalists, meanwhile, donned African clothing, wore natural hairstyles, and heeded black soul singer James Brown's commandment to "say it loud — I'm black and I'm proud."

With the Vietnam War as the backdrop, these conditions made for an atmosphere that was divisive and explosive. Street protests by both antiwar and black activists provoked counterdemonstrations and calls from conservatives for law and order. The assassination of Martin Luther King Jr. only deepened the nation's strife.

The Vietnam War and Black Opposition

Like Presidents Eisenhower and Kennedy, Lyndon Johnson judged the Southeast Asian nation of Vietnam central to U.S. interests in the Cold War. He believed that if Vietnam fell to the Communists, the rest of Southeast Asia would follow, imperiling democracy and American interests in the region. By 1965, the forces of the Communist and nationalist leader Ho Chi Minh controlled North Vietnam. Determined to keep South Vietnam out of the hands of the Communists, Johnson increased the number of U.S. troops already sent there by his predecessors. By the end of 1966, there were more than 385,000 U.S. combat troops in Vietnam, 15 percent of whom were African American. As the number of troops increased, so did the casualties. By the end of 1966, 6,378 Americans had been killed and more than 35,393 had been wounded. Over the next two years these numbers continued to rise.[62] As they did, African Americans' initial support for the war waned, and opposition intensified.

There were many reasons for this shift in attitudes. First, blacks were drafted and inducted into the service in disproportionate numbers. Although African Americans made up only 12 percent of the population in 1966, they made up

Black Pride
This 1969 photo of sixteen-year-old Marianne Skanks wearing an African-inspired outfit designed by her mother was taken at the height of the black power phase of the freedom movement. Along with her father, sister, and cousin, Marianne danced with an African dance group named the Ebonites. Her and dress and dance reflected the movement's nationalist impulse that embodied and reified black America's African heritage.
Bob Olsen/Toronto Star/Getty Images.

13.4 percent of military inductees. Between 1965 and 1970 — the height of U.S. involvement in Vietnam — this number rose to 14.3 percent; in 1967 and 1970, it was more than 16 percent.

Black leaders placed the blame squarely on institutional racism. Middle- and upper-class whites had an advantage, since the draft exempted students, professionals, and skilled workers. African Americans were also underrepresented on local draft boards, which played an important role in determining who would be accepted into the service. Blacks accounted for only 1.3 percent of board membership in 1966, and in most deep South states, which had large black populations, there were no black board members at all. Even when the number of black board members increased, white board members so outnumbered them as to make their presence inconsequential. Furthermore, blacks did not have the necessary personal connections to get medical deferments or even to be placed in the National Guard to avoid service in Vietnam.[63]

Second, although conditions in the armed services had improved since World War II, blacks still faced relentless discrimination, and it often got them killed. The complaints were familiar: Blacks were seldom recommended for promotion; reports about them were biased; they got the most dangerous combat assignments; they were court-martialed and imprisoned at disproportionate rates; they had higher rates of dishonorable discharges than whites; and black education was so deficient that unlike many whites who scored high on military tests, and were thus qualified for technical and specialty training, blacks qualified mostly for service, supply, and combat training. For many, the proof of racism was in the casualty figures. In 1965, African Americans made up 25 percent of all U.S. soldiers killed in Vietnam. (See By the Numbers: African Americans in the Vietnam War.) Only after these numbers raised alarms did the Pentagon reduce the proportion of blacks in combat units, which in turn reduced the number of black deaths. The switch to airpower in the latter years of the war also reduced the number. Still, as a white sergeant summed up the situation to a black private, "If you're white, you're all right, but if you're soul, there ain't no hope."[64]

This was true even for blacks as renowned as Muhammad Ali, who had become the heavyweight boxing champion of the world in 1964. As a member of the Nation of Islam, Ali resisted the draft on moral grounds. His application for conscientious objector status in 1966 claimed that as a Muslim, he could not participate in any war but a holy war. After more than a year of legal battles, Ali was convicted in 1967 of draft evasion, sentenced to five years in prison, and fined $10,000. Although the U.S. Supreme Court overturned his conviction in June 1971, by that time Ali had been stripped of his heavyweight title at the height of his career.[65]

Ali became a hero to many black Americans who opposed the war. They joined a growing and increasingly vocal antiwar effort. Like many Americans, they balked at the anti-Communist arguments advanced by the Johnson administration, arguing that Vietnam did not pose an imminent threat to national security — and certainly not enough of a threat to justify the war's heavy casualties. The disproportionately high numbers of black draftees and deaths fueled black antiwar sentiment, as did black nationalist

BY THE NUMBERS   African Americans in the Vietnam War

As the averages in this figure indicate, blacks were drafted — and died — in numbers disproportionate to their representation in the population. The draft exempted students, professionals, and skilled workers, giving middle- and upper-class whites a distinct advantage. African Americans also enjoyed little or no representation on the local draft boards that helped determine who would serve. The disproportionately high numbers of black casualties led the Pentagon to reduce the number of blacks in combat units.

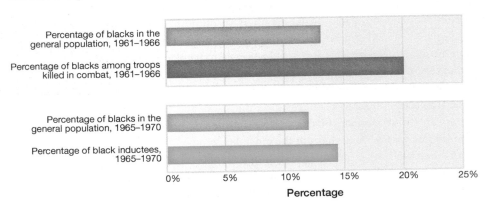

arguments that blacks should not fight other nonwhite people, especially those who were also fighting for liberation. "Why should black folks fight a war against yellow folks so that white folks can keep a land they stole from red folks?" asked Stokely Carmichael. He added, "Ain't no Vietcong ever called me nigger."[66] Most black power groups agreed with Carmichael. Drawing connections between what they called America's capitalist imperial aggression abroad and its oppression of minorities at home, the Black Panthers, SNCC, CORE, and a new group called the National Black Anti-War Anti-Draft Union helped lead the country's militant antiwar movement from its very beginning.[67]

Others, including most civil rights leaders, took a less confrontational, more cautious approach. Future secretary of state Colin Powell, for example, believed that blacks had to be involved in all national events, including those that were unpopular. Even though his father-in-law had had to arm himself to protect his home from

Black Power and the Vietnam War
In this 1968 photo, U.S. marine artillerymen pose next to their howitzer with a "Black Power Is Number One" banner and a black power salute. African Americans were drafted and inducted in disproportionate numbers throughout the Vietnam War, accounted for disproportionate numbers of the war's casualties, and faced discrimination of all kinds during their service. As the war dragged on, civil rights leaders, including Martin Luther King Jr., became more outspoken in their opposition to the conflict. *Johner/Associated Press/AP Images.*

segregationists during the Birmingham protests, Powell served two tours of duty in Vietnam and, like most civil rights leaders, believed that blacks had to fight on both fronts. Leaders of the NAACP, Urban League, and SCLC had the added worry of offending their most powerful ally, President Johnson, and therefore either supported the war or stayed silent.

However, as the draft drained black communities of their young men, and as money for the War on Poverty was reallocated to the war in Vietnam, civil rights leaders became more vocally antiwar. This was the case with Martin Luther King Jr., whose antiwar rhetoric sounded increasingly like that of black nationalists. Initially, King had quietly expressed concern that America was spending nearly $500,000 to kill each enemy soldier, but only $35 to feed each poor American.[68] But in 1967, in a public speech at Riverside Church in New York City, King spoke out passionately against the war, calling it an "enemy of the poor," both black and white. He claimed that young black men should not have to fight in Southeast Asia to guarantee liberties they could not find in southwest Georgia or East Harlem. Comparing U.S. actions in Vietnam to Hitler's genocide of Jews during World War II, King urged America to cease its bombing of Vietnamese families and villages. He also criticized capitalism, arguing for a new focus on people instead of things. "All over the globe," King pronounced, "men are revolting against old systems of exploitation and oppression, and . . . new systems of justice and equality are being born. . . . We in the West must support these revolutions."[69] America, King argued, had to once again become a force for revolutionary change. The best way to do that was to end the Vietnam War and take up an international war on poverty.

Later that year, King followed up his words with the announcement of the **Poor People's Campaign**. King's SCLC aimed to bring 1,500 protesters to Washington, D.C., in 1968 to lobby Congress and other government agencies for an "economic bill of rights." Specifically, the campaign requested a $30 billion antipoverty package that included a commitment to full employment, a guaranteed annual income measure, and increased construction of low-income housing. In what sounded like treason to President Johnson, King proclaimed that the poor people's movement had to "address itself to the question of restructuring the whole of American society." He announced that protest activities in Washington were to be supported by simultaneous demonstrations throughout the country.[70]

Urban Radicalism

Johnson had more than King to be concerned about. By the time King came out against the Vietnam War in 1967, the intensity of the black freedom struggle had been ratcheted up several notches. As radical as King had become, he remained more moderate than many black power activists. In Detroit, black workers in the Dodge, Ford, and Chrysler plants organized to prevent union and management discrimination. In 1968, the Dodge Revolutionary Union Movement conducted a series of unofficial strikes, ne of which prevented the production of three thousand cars.[71] On another front were the welfare reformers. Beginning in 1964, local welfare groups in twenty-five cities, inspired by Johnson's War on Poverty, marched on statehouses and clashed with police in protest against the administration of the government-sponsored Aid to Families with Dependent Children program. As part of a nationwide, grassroots poor people's movement, welfare rights activists, most of whom were black women, challenged eligibility requirements and insisted on better clothing and food allowances, job training programs for women, and subsidized day care. They also demanded to be employed as welfare agents since they knew best what welfare recipients needed. In 1967, under the leadership of former welfare recipient Johnnie Tillmon and college professor George Wiley, welfare activists organized the National Welfare Rights Organization. Under its aegis, welfare recipients lobbied legislators, picketed and leafleted public offices, initiated legal suits, demanded that the government guarantee an annual income, and insisted that welfare was a right.[72]

Many of the protests carried out by welfare activists were done through local **Community Action Programs (CAPs)** — programs that Johnson's War on Poverty legislation made possible by directing antipoverty agencies to recruit poor people to help solve inner-city problems. According to the logic behind the programs, community members had special insight into these problems and should participate in finding solutions. In Pittsburgh, for example, the government funded seven community offices to provide job training, child care, social services, Head Start classes, housing services, welfare consultants, legal services, and health care.[73]

The problem with CAPs was that they fed black radicalism while failing to address racism and deindustrialization, the underlying causes of black poverty. CAPs thus aroused everyone's ire. Poor people were angered by the government's failure to invest in job creation and restructure the real estate industry. City officials were angry because government-funded welfare consultants were fomenting protests that brought the wrath of recipients down on them. Community organizers were heartened by the government's newfound confidence in the power of "the people," and black nationalists hailed the unexpected endorsement of their ideology. But when government-sponsored black organizations ran anti–police brutality campaigns (as they did in New York City), or when they marched against grocery stores that overcharged blacks for mediocre goods (as they did in Los Angeles), city officials, conservatives, and urban policymakers balked at Johnson's War on Poverty and accused him of inviting race and class warfare.[74]

This was no small accusation, because cities of all sizes were erupting in violence. Some called the violence "riots" to connote spontaneous, undisciplined hoodlum activity. Others called the uprisings "rebellions," signifying conscious and deliberate political action. By any name, the violence that erupted in 300 cities contributed to the radicalism and turbulence that characterized America in the second half of the 1960s. In the Watts section of Los Angeles in 1965, 34 people died and $35 million worth of property was destroyed. In Detroit in 1967, 43 people were killed, 2,000 were wounded, and 5,000 saw their homes destroyed by fire. On February 8, 1968, the **Orangeburg Massacre** occurred near the campus of the historically black South Carolina State College when police were called to quell the violence that erupted after blacks were refused admittance to a "whites only" bowling alley. The incident was subsequently called a massacre because 3 unarmed students were killed, and another 28 students were injured; nearly all of the victims were shot in the back or side by police. All told, the urban violence of the 1960s left 250 people dead, 10,000 seriously injured, and 60,000 arrested. Fire destroyed entire neighborhoods, leaving countless blacks homeless.[75]

Subsequent studies showed that participants in the violence were mostly young, northern-born black men who were better educated than their contemporaries but had been confined to low-end jobs or were unemployed. Although most were not formal members of a radical group, they nevertheless expressed race pride and saw their burning and looting as revolutionary — and as the first step to black unity. Said one participant in recollection of the 1967 Plainfield, New Jersey, uprising, "Since the riot, we're not niggers anymore. We're black men . . . and are working together and respecting the neighborhood."[76]

Both blacks and whites struggled to make sense of the tumult. Most whites blamed the violence on black power ideology.[77] The cries heard from the street to "get whitey" or "burn, baby, burn" scared and angered many. They did not see any potential political rationale behind burning and looting, which would not end poverty, eliminate unemployment, or stop police brutality. One political scientist called the violence "outbreaks of animal spirits and of stealing by slum dwellers."[78] From many whites' perspectives, the riots, far from provoking a condemnation of police brutality, proved the necessity of police crackdowns on black youths and the imperative of imposing law and order.

Although blacks also abhorred the violence, their opinions were more varied. Many moderate civil rights leaders and organizations, including the NAACP, National Baptist Convention, National Council of Negro Women, and Prince Hall Masons, denounced the violence and the black nationalists who they believed fomented it. Calling it "black group suicide," they accused black power leaders of being no better than white segregationists.[79] Floyd McKissick, the new leader of CORE, disagreed, claiming that black people were finally fighting back. "The cup is running over in the ghetto," he argued. "It is inevitable that violence will occur."[80] Although he did not endorse the violence, Martin Luther King Jr. agreed with McKissick, arguing that "every single outbreak" had been caused by "gross unemployment, particularly among young people." He urged President Johnson to set up an agency "that shall provide a job to every person who needs work, young and old, white and Negro."[81] Still others agreed with Adam Clayton Powell Jr., the black congressman from Harlem, who repudiated revolutionary violence while supporting self-defense and the need for blacks to demand a "share of political jobs and appointments . . . equal to their proportion in the electorate."[82]

Opinions within the government also varied. The controversial **Moynihan Report**, written primarily by Assistant Secretary of Labor Daniel Patrick Moynihan, faulted the black family. According to the report, which was published in 1965, black family life was a "tangle of pathology" that poorly prepared blacks, especially black men, for useful citizenship. In 1968, Johnson's National Advisory Commission on Civil Disorders, known as the **Kerner Commission**, found that the violence could be traced to job discrimination and institutional racism rather than black power ideology or a particular organization.

Despite these official studies, the government agreed with the police: The violence was unlawful and had to be stamped out. The militancy of black nationalism and the boldness of black power organizations made them the natural targets of the nation's ire. The government thus undertook a massive campaign against radical organizations. The FBI used its substantial power to disrupt, confuse, undermine, and eliminate radicals and their organizations, using extreme methods that were often both illegal and unconstitutional. At the top of the FBI's list were the Black Panthers and the Revolutionary Action Movement, the two organizations most critical of the government's police power. But even the markedly more moderate King was targeted as someone who had to be stopped.

No one knows whether the FBI was involved in the murder of Martin Luther King Jr., but on April 4, 1968, exactly one year after King publicly positioned himself against the Vietnam War, an assassin's bullet ended his life as he stood on the balcony of a Memphis hotel. True to his renewed focus on economic justice, King had gone to Memphis to help a predominantly black sanitation workers' union gain recognition from the city. Upon news of the murder of this nonviolent icon, more than one hundred cities erupted in riots. Yet again, people died and millions of dollars' worth of property was destroyed.

CONCLUSION

Progress, Challenges, and Change

King's death marked the end of an era that many historians have called the second Reconstruction, because of the progress made by African Americans to achieve all the citizenship rights that were not conferred, or were conferred and then denied, during the period following the end of slavery. Activists in this era successfully struck down legal Jim Crow and achieved voting rights. Despite great obstacles and sometimes deadly opposition, they pried open the American workplace and forged new tactics and philosophies. In blazing their own path and demanding rights, African Americans provided a model for women, gays and lesbians, Hispanic Americans, and Native Americans to do the same. But with their struggle came sacrifice. Many leaders lost their lives, and many more lost their spirit. As a whole, the movement lost its sense of unity, which gave way as different strategies emerged to tackle the problems of American racism.

At the end of the 1960s, some civil rights supporters, especially white liberals, blamed black power for fracturing the postwar freedom struggle, but others, especially black Americans, disagreed. Most African Americans celebrated black power for the pride it instilled and for engendering intolerance of stereotypical representations of blackness. Black power linked African American struggles to nationalist struggles throughout the world, and it linked African Americans to black people in other countries. The problems faced by African Americans, many argued, were caused by whites' unwillingness to share the benefits of an ever-shrinking deindustrialized economy, and by a government willing to spend billions of dollars to fight national liberation both at home and abroad.

Although the birthday of Martin Luther King Jr. would subsequently become a national holiday and he would go down in American history as one of the nation's great freedom fighters, on the day of King's funeral, Lester Maddox, the governor of King's home state of Georgia, called him an "enemy of the country" and refused to close state offices in his honor.[83] Symbolic of the times, too, were the 120 state troopers in riot gear positioned at the entrances of the Georgia capitol to prevent the kinds of riots that erupted in Washington, D.C., and other cities.[84] As King's body was carried through the streets of Atlanta, few people understood how pivotal the 1960s legislation, court decisions, and race pride would be to black America's future. Most just wondered, "Where do we go from here?"

CHAPTER 13 **REVIEW**

KEY TERMS

REVIEW QUESTIONS

1. What conditions fostered the blossoming of the black power movement?

2. How did the various black power organizations and leaders help shape the black power ideology? What philosophies and attitudes did they promote?

3. Describe the various strains of black power that developed. How were these philosophies similar to and different from one another? In what ways did they all belong in the category "black power"?

4. What challenges did black activists confront in their fight for economic justice? What were their most significant victories in this struggle?

5. How did the conditions of the Vietnam War prompt civil rights activists to become more vocally antiwar?

6. To what different causes did various individuals and groups attribute the urban violence that erupted in the 1960s?

Black Power: Expression and Repression

Black power was not just one thing. It was at once a political, social, and economic philosophy. It was a frame of reference — a new way of being for black people and a new way of thinking. It was a consciousness. This "new mood," as James Baldwin referred to it (see p. 528), was as infectious as it was exhilarating, for at its core it presumed black control over black psyches, something that white domination had for centuries prevented and systematically crushed.

The way that black power married culture to politics is arguably what made the philosophy so intimidating to white America. It was not just the many political manifestations of black power (which were so numerous as to prevent organizing around a single agenda) that were so threatening, but the "black is beautiful" cultural concept at its root. The celebration of Africa and Africanness, of dark skin, of black dance, music, and art, prompted African Americans to abandon the term *Negro* and self-identify as black or African American — identifiers that earlier in the century would have been deemed derisive and understood as an insult. Like proponents of the Black Arts Movement, black power activists maintained that African Americans' politics, economics, and artistic expression had to work to reverse the internalized feelings of inferiority wrought by the experience of slavery and Jim Crow oppression. They believed that no civil rights laws would liberate American blacks if they did not psychologically accept the idea that black was truly beautiful. Activists, writers, musicians, visual artists, poets, playwrights, and actors were all enlisted in the project to make African Americans' views of themselves, their history, and their culture more positive.

The following documents taken from the black power movement do not represent the full scope of the movement or the resistance to it, but they demonstrate the "new mood" and the government's repressive response. As you read and examine these written and visual documents, think about the relationship between art and politics and how black power drove change. Think also about why black power provoked such a malicious governmental reaction.

Huey Newton and Bobby Seale | *October 1966 Black Panther Party Platform and Program*

HUEY NEWTON (1942–1989) and BOBBY SEALE (b. 1936) drafted the Black Panther Party Platform and Program to let the public know what their organization stood for. The Program took its form from the Nation of Islam's "Muslim Program," published each week in its newspaper, *Muhammad Speaks*, in two parts: "What the Muslims Want" and "What the Muslims Believe." Part of the Panthers' Program, however, was taken from the U.S. Constitution and the Declaration of Independence. The Panthers were one of many black power organizations. Although they did not define themselves as black nationalists, their platform incorporated many of the ideas that grounded black power.

October 1966 Black Panther Party Platform and Program
What We Want
What We Believe

1. **We want freedom. We want power to determine the destiny of our Black Community.**
   We believe that black people will not be free until we are able to determine our destiny.

2. **We want full employment for our people.**
   We believe that the federal government is responsible and obligated to give every man employment or a guaranteed income. . . .

3. **We want an end to the robbery by the white man of our Black Community.**
   We believe that this racist government has robbed us and now we are demanding the overdue debt of forty acres and two mules. Forty acres and two mules was promised 100 years ago as restitution for slave labor and mass murder of black people. . . .

4. **We want decent housing, fit for shelter of human beings.**
   We believe that if the white landlords will not give decent housing to our black community, then the housing and the land should be made into cooperatives so that our community, with government aid, can build and make decent housing for its people.

5. **We want education for our people that exposes the true nature of this decadent American society. We want education that teaches us our true history and our role in the present-day society.**
   . . . If a man does not have knowledge of himself and his position in society and the world, then he has little chance to relate to anything else.

6. **We want all black men to be exempt from military service.**
   We believe that black people should not be forced to fight in the military service to defend a racist government that does not protect us. . . .

7. **We want an immediate end to POLICE BRUTALITY and MURDER of black people.**
   . . . The Second Amendment to the Constitution of the United States gives a right to bear arms. We therefore believe that all black people should arm themselves for self-defense.

8. **We want freedom for all black men held in federal, state, county and city prisons and jails.**
   We believe that all black people should be released from the many jails and prisons because they have not received a fair and impartial trial.

9. **We want all black people when brought to trial to be tried in court by a jury of their peer group or people from their black communities, as defined by the Constitution of the United States.**
   . . . To do this the court will be forced to select a jury from the black community from which the black defendant came. We have been, and are being tried by all-white juries that have no understanding of the "average reasoning man" of the black community.

10. **We want land, bread, housing, education, clothing, justice and peace. And as our major political objective, a United Nations–supervised plebiscite to be held throughout the black colony in which only black colonial subjects will be allowed to participate, for the purpose of determining the will of black people as to their national destiny.**
    . . . We hold these truths to be self-evident, that all men are created equal; that they are endowed by their Creator with certain

SOURCE: Donna Jean Murch, *Living for the City: Migration, Education, and the Rise of the Black Panther Party in Oakland, California* (Chapel Hill: University of North Carolina Press, 128–29.

unalienable rights; that among these are life, liberty, and the pursuit of happiness. *That, to secure these rights, governments are instituted among men, deriving their just powers from the consent of the governed; that, whenever any form of government becomes destructive of these ends, it is the right of the people to alter or to abolish it, and to institute a new government, laying its foundation on such principles, and organizing its powers in such form, as to them* shall seem most likely to effect their safety and happiness. Prudence, indeed, will dictate that governments long established should not be changed for light and transient causes. . . . But, when a long train of abuses and usurpations, pursuing invariably the same object, evinces a design to reduce them under absolute despotism, it is their right, it is their duty, to throw off such government, and to provide new guards for their future security.

Loïs Mailou Jones | *Ubi Girl from Tai Region, 1972*

For artists like Larry Neal, an essayist and, with LeRoi Jones (later Amiri Baraka), cofounder of the Black Arts Repertory Theatre/School in 1965, black power involved no less than the reordering of Western aesthetics. Neal argued that black art should be underpinned by black aesthetics, "a separate symbolism, mythology, critique, and iconology." He called for "the destruction of the white thing, the destruction of white ideas, and white ways of looking at the world." Black artists had to provide a "new aesthetic . . . mostly predicated on an Ethics which asks the question: whose vision of the world is finally more meaningful, ours or the white oppressors'?"[85] To this end, many artists experimented with various materials, making art with African American hair, food, and other ephemera, and in a move inspired by African independence movements, they incorporated African art and artifacts into their work. This synthesis signaled both a desire to seek influences outside the European cultural canon and a feeling of kinship with other black arts and artists. Consider *Ubi Girl from Tai Region*, a painting by LOÏS MAILOU JONES (1905–1998). To what end does Jones use African-inspired elements? What is the spirit of the painting? What political or philosophical message does it contain?

Acrylic on canvas, 43¾ x 60 in. Museum of Fine Arts, Boston. The Hayden Collection, Charles Henry Hayden Fund. Courtesy Loïs Mailou Jones Pierre-Noël Trust.

Faith Ringgold | *The Flag Is Bleeding, 1967*

While the impetus to make black beautiful inspired most Black Arts Movement artists, for others, such as Ron (later Maulana) Karenga, black art had to do more. Karenga founded the black nationalist organization US and created Kwanzaa, a black holiday established in 1966 as a celebration of black survival and achievement. For Karenga, the real purpose of black art was to "reflect and support the Black Revolution." Black art, he noted in 1968, should be like the poems of LeRoi Jones (later Amiri Baraka), a founder of the Black Arts Movement, whose writings and cultural critiques often generated great controversy. It had to "expose the enemy," "praise the people," and be like the "poems that kill and shoot guns and 'wrassle cops into alleys taking their weapons, leaving them dead with tongues pulled out and sent to Ireland.'"[86] Does the painting *The Flag Is Bleeding* by FAITH RINGGOLD (b. 1930) achieve this goal? What political statement is the artist making with her piece? Whose blood is she depicting? What about this image might disturb white Americans? How might the FBI interpret it?

Series: American People #18, 72 x 96 in., oil on canvas. Collection of the artist/Faith Ringgold © 1967.

* * *

Given the catalytic nature of black power, it was predictable that it would generate opposition. What was not so predictable was that black liberation opponents would have the help of the FBI. The agency's involvement came to light in the 1970s, when citizens, congressional oversight committees, and some of the FBI's own agents revealed many of its illegal activities. Top-secret documents, some of which were stolen by the Citizens' Commission to Investigate the FBI and others that came to light during lawsuits filed against the FBI, showed that the bureau had been involved in antiblack repression as far back as the 1920s, when it helped orchestrate the deportation of Marcus Garvey (see chapter 10). The documents also showed that J. Edgar Hoover, head of the FBI, had opened a file on Martin Luther King Jr. in 1958 and had infiltrated the SCLC in 1960, and that by October 1962 he was planting disinformational "news stories" concerning the SCLC's alleged Communist connections. Other documents revealed that on August 25, 1967, Hoover initiated antiblack operations under the FBI's COINTELPRO (Counterintelligence Program). COINTELPRO launched systematic covert actions — infiltration, psychological warfare, legal harassment, and violence — not only against the black liberation movement but also against the American Indian Movement (AIM), the Puerto Rican independence movement, and the antiwar and student movements of the 1960s. In other words, the agency became a danger to the very democracy it was supposed to protect.

The bureau used a variety of tactics against black power organizations. Its agents forged accusatory and insulting letters and sent them to organization members to incite feuds and prevent alliances. It also printed and distributed ridiculing pamphlets and cartoons and attributed them to a particular organization or person. The FBI made efforts to pit blacks and Jews against one another and to get black street gangs to attack black political activists. It also was not above withholding or planting evidence to ensure the conviction and imprisonment of black activists. These efforts were massive. In 1967, at least 1,246 FBI agents received racial intelligence assignments each month. By 1968, the number was 1,678.

The documents that follow unveil some of the FBI's covert activities. As you read them, consider how the FBI influenced white and black America's opinion of black power.

COINTELPRO Targets Black Organizations, 1967

This 1967 FBI memo initiated COINTELPRO efforts against what it calls "black nationalist, hate-type organizations." The memo explains the purpose of this new program and directs twenty-three FBI field offices to recruit informants, continually monitor a range of groups, and look for counterintelligence opportunities to discredit them. It singles out organizations such as SNCC, CORE, the SCLC, and the Revolutionary Action Movement for special attention and identifies individuals such as SNCC leader Stokely Carmichael (1941–1998) for particular surveillance. Why might the FBI have considered these groups particular threats?

The purpose of this new counterintelligence endeavor is to expose, disrupt, misdirect, discredit, or otherwise neutralize the activities of black nationalist, hate-type organizations and groupings, their leadership, spokesmen, membership, and supporters, and to counter their propensity for violence and civil disorder. The activities of all such groups of intelligence interest to this Bureau must be followed on a continuous basis so we will be in a position to promptly take advantage of all opportunities for counterintelligence and to inspire action in instances where circumstances warrant. The pernicious background of such groups, their duplicity, and devious maneuvers must be exposed to public scrutiny where such publicity will have a neutralizing effect. Efforts of the various groups to consolidate their forces or to recruit new or youthful adherents must be frustrated. No opportunity should be missed to exploit through counterintelligence techniques the organizational and personal conflicts of the leaderships of the groups and where possible an effort should be made to capitalize upon existing conflicts between competing black nationalist organizations. . . .

Many individuals currently active in black nationalist organizations have backgrounds of immorality, subversive activity, and criminal records. Through your investigation of key agitators, you should endeavor to establish their unsavory backgrounds. Be alert to determine evidence of misappropriation of funds or other types of personal misconduct on the part of militant nationalist leaders so any practical or warranted counterintelligence may be instituted.

Intensified attention under this program should be afforded to the activities of such groups as the Student Nonviolent Coordinating Committee, the Southern Christian Leadership Conference, Revolutionary Action Movement, the Deacons for Defense and Justice, Congress of Racial Equality, and the Nation of Islam. Particular emphasis should be given to extremists who direct the activities and policies of revolutionary or militant groups such as Stokely Carmichael, H. "Rap" Brown,° Elijah Muhammad, and Maxwell Stanford.

° Activist who served as chairman of SNCC from 1967 to 1968 and in 1968 as the Minister of Justice of the Black Panthers.

SOURCE: Memorandum from FBI Director to 23 Field Offices, 25 August 1967.

FBI Uses Fake Letters to Divide the Chicago Black Panthers and the Blackstone Rangers, 1969

In this 1969 memo, the FBI authorized sending a fake anonymous letter to Jeff Fort (b. 1947), leader of the Chicago street gang the Blackstone Rangers, to stir up trouble between the Rangers and the Panthers and to thwart the Panthers' efforts to get the Rangers involved in constructive community work. Why would the FBI be opposed to the Panthers' antigang activity?

Authority is granted to mail anonymous letter to Jeff Fort, as suggested in [previous letter from an FBI agent], in care of the First Presbyterian Church, 6401 South Kimbark, Chicago, Illinois.

Utilize a commercially purchased envelope for this letter and insure that the mailing is not traced to the source. . . .

SOURCE: Memorandum from Special Agent in Charge, Chicago, to Director, 30 January 1969.

"Brother Jeff:

"I've spent some time with some Panther friends on the west side lately and I know what's been going on. The brothers that run the Panthers blame you for blocking their thing and there's supposed to be a hit out for you. I'm not a Panther, or a Ranger, just black. From what I see these Panthers are out for themselves not black people. I think you ought to know what their up to, I know what I'd do if I was you. You might hear from me again."

"A black brother you don't know"

"Special Payment" Request and Floor Plan of Fred Hampton's Apartment, 1969

On November 19, 1969, FBI informant William O'Neal gave local police a detailed inventory of arms and explosives allegedly kept in Chicago Black Panther Party leader Fred Hampton's apartment. He included a floor plan of the apartment. On December 4, police used this information in a raid that killed Hampton and fellow Panther Mark Clark. In this excerpt from a December 11 memo, the Chicago FBI agent in charge praises the vital information supplied by O'Neal and asks for a "special payment" for the unnamed informant.

Information set forth in Chicago letter and letterhead memorandum of 11/21/69, reflects legally purchased firearms in the possession of the Black Panther Party (BPP) were stored at 2337 West Monroe Street, Chicago. A detailed

SOURCE: Memorandum from Special Agent in Charge, Chicago, to Roy Martin Mitchell, 11 December 1969.

inventory of the weapons and also a detailed floor plan of the apartment were furnished to local authorities. In addition, the identities of BPP members utilizing the apartment at the above address were furnished. This information was not available from any other source and subsequently proved to be of tremendous value in that it subsequently saved injury and possible death to police officers participating in a raid at the address on the morning of 12/4/69. The raid was based on the information furnished by informant. During the resistance by the BPP members at the time of the raid, the Chairman of the Illinois Chapter, BPP, FRED HAMPTON, was killed and a BPP leader from Peoria, Illinois, was also killed. A quantity of weapons and ammunition were recovered.

It is felt that this information is of considerable value in consideration of a special payment for informant requested in re Chicago letter.

Tangible Results, 1969

In this chilling excerpt from a 1969 memo, the FBI takes credit for the decline of the Black Panther Party's Breakfast Program for impoverished children in San Diego and proudly touts what it calls "tangible results" of its attempts to incite violence and "a high degree of unrest" in the city. Why would the FBI want to disrupt positive efforts of groups such as the Black Panthers?

TANGIBLE RESULTS

The BPP Breakfast Program appears to be floundering in San Diego due to a lack of public support and unfavorable publicity concerning it. It is noted that it has presently been temporarily suspended. . . .

Shootings, beatings, and a high degree of unrest continues [*sic*] to prevail in the ghetto area of southeast San Diego. Although no specific counterintelligence action can be credited with contributing to this over-all situation, it is felt that a substantial amount of the unrest is directly attributable to this program.

SOURCE: FBI memorandum, fragment, 20 August 1969.

In view of the recent killing of BPP member SYLVESTER BELL,° a new cartoon is being considered in the hopes that it will assist in the continuance of the rift between BPP and US.°

° Sylvester Bell was a Black Panther who was shot to death in 1969 by members of the US organization. The investigation of Bell's murder traced his death to COINTELPRO tactics that created unrest between the Panthers and US.

° Maulana Karenga founded the black nationalist organization US in 1965. Unlike the Panthers, who focused on structural racism, US espoused a form of cultural nationalism that prioritized black people's African past and southern traditions.

◤ Church Committee Report, 1976

In 1975, after a series of revelations suggesting that U.S. intelligence agencies had been conducting illegal operations, the Senate created the Church Committee — named after its chairman, Idaho senator Frank Church (1924–1984) — to investigate suspected abuses of power. Among the agencies investigated were the FBI, CIA, National Security Agency, and IRS. The following year, the committee issued a series of fourteen reports on its findings, which concluded that intelligence forces had conducted concerted domestic espionage that violated the rights of U.S. citizens. The committee's recommendations were debated in Congress, and some, though not all, were eventually carried out. One tangible legacy of the committee's report was the creation of the Senate Select Committee on Intelligence to act as an oversight body for intelligence services.

IV. CONCLUSIONS AND RECOMMENDATIONS

A. Conclusions

The findings which have emerged from our investigation convince us that the Government's domestic intelligence policies and practices require fundamental reform. We have attempted to set out the basic facts; now it is time for Congress to turn its attention to legislating restraints upon intelligence activities which may endanger the constitutional rights of Americans.

SOURCE: United States Senate, *Final Report of the Select Committee to Study Governmental Operations with Respect to Intelligence Activities*, book 2, *Intelligence Activities and the Rights of Americans* (Washington, DC: Government Printing Office, 1976), 289, 290.

The Committee's fundamental conclusion is that intelligence activities have undermined the constitutional rights of citizens and that they have done so primarily because checks and balances designed by the framers of the Constitution to assure accountability have not been applied.

Before examining that conclusion, we make the following observations.

— While nearly all of our findings focus on excesses and things that went wrong, we do not question the need for lawful domestic intelligence. We recognize that certain intelligence activities serve perfectly proper and clearly necessary ends of government. Surely, catching spies and stopping crime, including acts of terrorism, is essential to insure "domestic tranquility" and to "provide for the common defense." Therefore, the power of government to conduct *proper* domestic intelligence activities under effective restraints and controls must be preserved.

— We are aware that the few earlier efforts to limit domestic intelligence activities have proven ineffectual. This pattern reinforces the need for statutory restraints coupled with much more effective oversight from all branches of the Government.

— The crescendo of improper intelligence activity in the latter part of the 1960s and the early 1970s shows what we must watch out for: In time of crisis, the Government will exercise its power to conduct domestic intelligence activities to the fullest extent. The distinction between legal dissent and criminal conduct is easily forgotten. Our job is to recommend means to help ensure that the distinction will always be observed.

— In an era where the technological capability of Government relentlessly increases, we must be wary about the drift toward "big brother government." The potential for abuse is awesome and requires special attention to fashioning restraints which not only cure past problems but anticipate and prevent the future misuse of technology. . . .

. . . Based upon our full record, and the findings which we have set forth . . . above, the Committee concludes that:

Domestic Intelligence Activity Has Threatened and Undermined The Constitutional Rights of Americans to Free Speech, Association and Privacy. It Has Done So Primarily Because The Constitutional System for Checking Abuse of Power Has Not Been Applied.

Our findings and the detailed reports which supplement this volume set forth a massive record of intelligence abuses over the years. Through a vast network of informants and through the uncontrolled or illegal use of intrusive techniques — ranging from simple theft to sophisticated electronic surveillance — the Government has collected, and then used improperly, huge amounts of information about the private lives, political beliefs and associations of numerous Americans.

QUESTIONS FOR ANALYSIS

1. Black power activists insisted that black history be taught at every educational level. How is their advocacy for black history related to the politics and art of the black power movement?

2. What political concepts are made manifest in the art shown here?

3. Was black power a threat to national security? In light of FBI activity, should we reconsider the ground on which black power has been perceived as violent?

4. Does the FBI's counterintelligence and surveillance of black power activists bear any resemblance to the counterterrorist activities undertaken by the federal government since the September 11, 2001, attack on the World Trade Center in New York? What general concerns, if any, should the American public have about government surveillance of activists deemed "un-American"?

NOTES

1. Stokely Carmichael, *Ready for Revolution: The Life and Struggles of Stokely Carmichael (Kwame Ture)*, with Ekwueme Michael Thelwell (New York: Scribner, 2003), 457.
2. Charles E. Cobb, *On the Road to Freedom: A Guided Tour of the Civil Rights Trail* (Chapel Hill: Algonquin Books, 2008), 241–45.
3. Quoted in Carmichael, *Ready for Revolution*, 461–62.
4. Quoted ibid., 458.
5. Quoted in Clayborne Carson, *In Struggle: SNCC and the Black Awakening of the 1960s* (Cambridge: Harvard University Press, 1981), 164.
6. Cobb, *On the Road to Freedom*, 244.
7. Quoted in Hasan Kwame Jeffries, *Bloody Lowndes: Civil Rights and Black Power in Alabama's Black Belt* (New York: New York University Press, 2009), 149.
8. Quoted in Carson, *In Struggle*, 166.
9. Carmichael, *Ready for Revolution*, 457–83.
10. Quoted in Jeffries, *Bloody Lowndes*, 180.
11. Both quoted in George Breitman, ed., *Malcolm X Speaks: Selected Speeches and Statements* (New York: Grove Press, 1994), 43.
12. Quoted in Nikhil Pal Singh, *Black Is a Country: Race and the Unfinished Struggle for Democracy* (Cambridge: Harvard University Press, 2004), 184–85.
13. Quoted in Vincent Harding, Robin D. G. Kelley, and Earl Lewis, *We Changed the World: African Americans, 1945–1970* (New York: Oxford University Press, 1997), 131–32.
14. Mary Frances Berry and John W. Blassingame, *Long Memory: The Black Experience in America* (New York: Oxford University Press, 1982), 242.
15. Douglas S. Massey and Nancy A. Denton, *American Apartheid: Segregation and the Making of the Underclass* (Cambridge: Harvard University Press, 1993), 42–57.
16. Thomas J. Sugrue, *Sweet Land of Liberty: The Forgotten Struggle for Civil Rights in the North* (New York: Random House, 2008), 318–23.
17. Quoted ibid., 340–41. In these pages, also note Stokely Carmichael's statement about the amorphous and uncongealed nature of black radicalism. According to Carmichael, in the North it had "no clear, solid center . . . no single accepted community of leadership and resistance you could identify" (340). It is impossible, and would be inaccurate, to impose more order on the philosophy and nature of black radicalism than actually existed.
18. Peniel E. Joseph, *Waiting 'Til the Midnight Hour: A Narrative History of Black Power in America* (New York: Henry Holt, 2006), 53.
19. Larry Neal, "The Black Arts Movement," in *Within the Circle: An Anthology of African American Literary Criticism from the Harlem Renaissance to the Present*, ed. Angelyn Mitchell (Durham: Duke University Press, 1994), 184.
20. Both quoted in Paula Giddings, *When and Where I Enter: The Impact of Black Women on Race and Sex in America* (New York: Bantam, 1984), 315.
21. Quoted ibid., 317–24.
22. "Malcolm X: A Problem of Human Rights," interview, YouTube, July 1964, http://www.youtube.com/watch?v=mzjn11OGBK8.
23. Malcolm X, *The Autobiography of Malcolm X*, with the assistance of Alex Haley (New York: Ballantine, 1992), 91, 226.
24. Berry and Blassingame, *Long Memory*, 110–12, 394.
25. Quoted ibid., 417.
26. Harding, Kelley, and Lewis, *We Changed the World*, 145.
27. Quoted in Carson, *In Struggle*, 113–15.
28. Quoted in Chana Kai Lee, *For Freedom's Sake: The Life of Fannie Lou Hamer* (Urbana: University of Illinois Press, 1999), 75.
29. Both quoted in Carson, *In Struggle*, 99.
30. Lee, *For Freedom's Sake*, 85–102.
31. Quoted ibid., 100.
32. John Lewis, *Walking with the Wind: A Memoir of the Movement*, with Michael D'Orso (New York: Simon & Schuster, 1998), 291.
33. Quoted in Lee, *For Freedom's Sake*, 100.
34. Quoted in Carson, *In Struggle*, 128.
35. Both quoted in Joseph, *Waiting 'Til the Midnight Hour*, 110.
36. Janet L. Abu-Lughod, *Race, Space, and Riots in Chicago, New York, and Los Angeles* (New York: Oxford University Press, 2007), 159–94.
37. Carson, *In Struggle*, 158–61.
38. Both quoted ibid., 161.
39. Quoted ibid., 160.
40. Quoted in Joseph, *Waiting 'Til the Midnight Hour*, 142.
41. Robert O. Self, "The Black Panther Party and the Long Civil Rights Era," in *In Search of the Black Panther Party: New Perspectives on a Revolutionary Movement*, ed. Jama Lazerow and Yohuru Williams (Durham, NC: Duke University Press, 2006), 36–38; Sugrue, *Sweet Land of Liberty*, 342–43.
42. Joseph, *Waiting 'Til the Midnight Hour*, 207–14.
43. Quoted ibid., 225.
44. United States Congress, House Comm. on Internal Security, *Gun-Barrel Politics: The Black Panther Party, 1966–1971*, rep., 92d Cong., 1st sess. (Washington, DC: Government Printing Office, 1971), 43.
45. Quoted in Nancy MacLean, *Freedom Is Not Enough: The Opening of the American Workplace* (Cambridge: Harvard University Press, 2006), 55.
46. All quoted ibid., 38, 39, 52–53.
47. Sugrue, *Sweet Land of Liberty*, 256.
48. Quoted in MacLean, *Freedom Is Not Enough*, 54–55.
49. Ibid., 54–55, 62.
50. Sugrue, *Sweet Land of Liberty*, 257–58.
51. Ibid., 259–60.
52. Ibid., 261.
53. Quoted in Ira Katznelson, *When Affirmative Action Was White: An Untold History of Racial Inequality in Twentieth-Century America* (New York: Norton, 2005), 175.
54. MacLean, *Freedom Is Not Enough*, 70–71, 76.

55. Ibid., 88, 95–103.

56. Quoted in Chester Higgins, "We Can Change Course of U.S.," *Jet*, July 1967, 23.

57. Both quoted in MacLean, *Freedom Is Not Enough*, 104–5.

58. Quoted in Sugrue, *Sweet Land of Liberty*, 273.

59. Quoted in MacLean, *Freedom Is Not Enough*, 106.

60. Ibid., 109–10.

61. Ibid., 242–43.

62. James E. Westheider, *The African American Experience in Vietnam: Brothers in Arms* (Lanham, MD: Rowman & Littlefield, 2008), 21.

63. Ibid., 23–36.

64. Ibid., 25–36, 39–62.

65. Ibid., 30–32.

66. Quoted ibid., 25.

67. Ibid., 64–65.

68. Harding, Kelley, and Lewis, *We Changed the World*, 155.

69. Martin Luther King Jr., *I Have a Dream: Writings and Speeches That Changed the World*, ed. James Melvin Washington (New York: HarperSanFrancisco, 1992), 138, 149.

70. MacLean, *Freedom Is Not Enough*, 340.

71. Martin Glaberman, "Survey: Detroit," *International Socialism*, no. 36 (April/May 1969): 8–9.

72. Sugrue, *Sweet Land of Liberty*, 384–91.

73. Ibid., 371.

74. Ibid., 367–74.

75. Harding, Kelley, and Lewis, *We Changed the World*, 147–48.

76. Quoted in Sugrue, *Sweet Land of Liberty*, 346–47.

77. Sugrue, *Sweet Land of Liberty*, 346.

78. Quoted ibid., 349.

79. Sugrue, *Sweet Land of Liberty*, 338–39.

80. Quoted ibid., 340.

81. Quoted in MacLean, *Freedom Is Not Enough*, 106.

82. Quoted in Sugrue, *Sweet Land of Liberty*, 340.

83. B. Marybeth Gasman with Louise W. Sullivan, *The Morehouse Mystique: Becoming a Doctor at the Nation's Newest African American Medical School* (Baltimore, MD: The Johns Hopkins University Press, 2012), 5.

84. Rebecca Burns, *Burial for a King: Martin Luther King Jr.'s Funeral and the Week That Transformed Atlanta and Rocked the Nation* (New York: Scribner, 2011), 137.

85. Neal, "The Black Arts Movement," 184, 186.

86. Quoted in Jerry Gafio Watts, *Amiri Baraka: The Politics and Art of a Black Intellectual* (New York: New York University Press, 2001), 194.

SUGGESTED REFERENCES

The Emergence of Black Power

Carmichael, Stokely. *Ready for Revolution: The Life and Struggles of Stokely Carmichael (Kwame Ture)*. With Ekwueme Michael Thelwell. New York: Scribner, 2003.

Giddings, Paula. *When and Where I Enter: The Impact of Black Women on Race and Sex in America*. New York: Bantam, 1984.

Griffin, Farah Jasmine. "'Ironies of the Saint': Malcolm X, Black Women, and the Price of Protection." In *Sisters in the Struggle: African American Women in the Civil Rights–Black Power Movement*, edited by Bettye Collier-Thomas and V. P. Franklin, 214–29. New York: New York University Press, 2001.

Jeffries, Hasan Kwame. *Bloody Lowndes: Civil Rights and Black Power in Alabama's Black Belt*. New York: New York University Press, 2009.

Joseph, Peniel E. *Waiting 'Til the Midnight Hour: A Narrative History of Black Power in America*. New York: Henry Holt, 2006.

Malcolm X. *The Autobiography of Malcolm X*. With the assistance of Alex Haley. New York: Ballantine, 1992.

Murch, Donna Jean. *Living for the City: Migration, Education, and the Rise of the Black Panther Party in Oakland, California*. Chapel Hill: University of North Carolina Press, 2010.

Singh, Nikhil Pal. *Black Is a Country: Race and the Unfinished Struggle for Democracy*. Cambridge: Harvard University Press, 2004.

Sugrue, Thomas J. *Sweet Land of Liberty: The Forgotten Struggle for Civil Rights in the North*. New York: Random House, 2008.

The Struggle Transforms

Abu-Lughod, Janet L. *Race, Space, and Riots in Chicago, New York, and Los Angeles*. New York: Oxford University Press, 2007.

Branch, Taylor. *At Canaan's Edge: America in the King Years, 1965–68*. New York: Simon & Schuster, 2006.

Carson, Clayborne. *In Struggle: SNCC and the Black Awakening of the 1960s*. Cambridge: Harvard University Press, 1981.

Lee, Chana Kai. *For Freedom's Sake: The Life of Fannie Lou Hamer*. Urbana: University of Illinois Press, 1999.

Lewis, John. *Walking with the Wind: A Memoir of the Movement*. With Michael D'Orso. New York: Simon & Schuster, 1998.

Miller, Jeanne-Marie A. Review of *We Walk the Way of the New World*, by Don L. Lee. *Journal of Negro History* 56, no. 2 (April 1971): 153–55.

Payne, Charles M. *I've Got the Light of Freedom: The Organizing Tradition and the Mississippi Freedom Struggle*. Berkeley: University of California Press, 2007.

Self, Robert O. "The Black Panther Party and the Long Civil Rights Era." In *In Search of the Black Panther Party: New Perspectives on a Revolutionary Movement*, edited by Jama Lazerow and Yohuru Williams, 15–55. Durham, NC: Duke University Press, 2006.

Economic Justice and Affirmative Action

Anderson, Terry H. *The Pursuit of Fairness: A History of Affirmative Action*. New York: Oxford University Press, 2004.

Graham, Hugh Davis. *Collision Course: The Strange Convergence of Affirmative Action and Immigration Policy in America*. New York: Oxford University Press, 2002.

Katznelson, Ira. *When Affirmative Action Was White: An Untold History of Racial Inequality in Twentieth-Century America*. New York: Norton, 2005.

MacLean, Nancy. *Freedom Is Not Enough: The Opening of the American Workplace*. Cambridge: Harvard University Press, 2006.

Massey, Douglas S., and Nancy A. Denton. *American Apartheid: Segregation and the Making of the Underclass*. Cambridge: Harvard University Press, 1993.

War, Radicalism, and Turbulence

Blackstock, Nelson. *Cointelpro: The FBI's Secret War on Political Freedom*. New York: Pathfinder, 1988.

Churchill, Ward, and Jim Vander Wall. *Agents of Repression: The FBI's Secret Wars against the Black Panther Party and the American Indian Movement*, 2nd ed. Cambridge, MA: South End Press, 2002.

Glaberman, Martin. "Survey: Detroit." *International Socialism*, no. 36 (April/May 1969): 8–9.

Terry, Wallace. *Bloods: Black Veterans of the Vietnam War: An Oral History*. New York: Random House, 1984.

Westheider, James E. *The African American Experience in Vietnam: Brothers in Arms*. Lanham, MD: Rowman & Littlefield, 2008.

———. *Fighting on Two Fronts: African Americans and the Vietnam War*. New York: New York University Press, 1997.

Racial Progress in an Era of Backlash and Change

1967–2000

CHRONOLOGY   *Events specific to African American history are in purple. General United States history events are in black.*

1965	Immigration and Nationality Act of 1965
1967	National Welfare Rights Organization founded
1968	Fair Housing Act
	Shirley Chisholm elected to Congress
	Richard Nixon elected president
1969	Black Panthers expel hundreds of members to weed out government agents; begin "survival programs"
	Nixon implements southern strategy
1970s	Stagflation intensifies competition in job market
1970	Ohio National Guard shoots unarmed antiwar protesters at Kent State University
	Local police shoot students during demonstrations at historically black Jackson State University
1971	Congressional Black Caucus founded
	Milliken v. Bradley mandates that Detroit public schools be merged with those in surrounding suburbs; hundreds of thousands of whites protest
1972	Chisholm makes bid for Democratic presidential nomination
	Angela Davis acquitted of charges of aiding prison inmates to escape from California courtroom
	Title IX of Education Amendments of 1972 outlaws discrimination in educational institutions receiving federal funding
1973	Black Panther Bobby Seale runs for mayor of Oakland, California; Black Panther Elaine Brown runs for city council
	Rockefeller drug laws instituted in New York
	Organization of Petroleum Exporting Countries (OPEC) declares oil embargo, prompting oil crisis in United States

1974	Supreme Court overturns lower courts' rulings in *Milliken v. Bradley*
	Nixon resigns due to Watergate scandal; Gerald Ford succeeds him as president
	Boston erupts in violence over busing
Mid-1970s	Rap music emerges on New York City streets
1976	Jimmy Carter elected president
1977	Lionel Wilson elected first black mayor of Oakland
1978	*Regents of the University of California v. Bakke* deals blow to affirmative action
1979	*United Steelworkers of America v. Weber* upholds affirmative action
1980	Ronald Reagan elected president
1982	Reagan declares war on drugs
1984	Reagan reelected president
1985	Crack cocaine appears in inner-city neighborhoods
1988	George H. W. Bush elected president
1991	Los Angeles police officers' beating of Rodney King caught on videotape
	Bush nominates Clarence Thomas to U.S. Supreme Court; law professor Anita Hill accuses Thomas of sexual harassment
1992	Los Angeles erupts in riots following acquittal of police in Rodney King case
	Bill Clinton elected president
1995	O. J. Simpson acquitted of murdering Nicole Brown Simpson and Ronald Goldman
	Million Man March in Washington, D.C.
1996	Personal Responsibility and Work Opportunity Reconciliation Act
	Clinton reelected president
1997	Million Woman March in Philadelphia

Shirley Chisholm: The First of Many Firsts

Sometime in the 1940s, Stanley Steingut, the district leader of Brooklyn's Democratic Party, gave a speech at Brooklyn College. Sophomore Shirley Anita St. Hill was in the audience. Though born in America, St. Hill had received her early education in Barbados, the birthplace of her Bajan mother, who, along with her Guyanese father, had sent St. Hill to Barbados at the age of three to live with her maternal grandmother, aunt, and uncle. Years later, Shirley Chisholm (she married Conrad Chisholm in 1949) credited Steingut's remarks as being the impetus for her career in politics. By then, Chisholm was renowned for being the first black woman in Congress, the first African American to run for president within a major party, and the first woman to make a bid for the Democratic presidential nomination. What she remembered about Steingut's speech was that although he had applauded blacks for fighting for their rights, he also had said that blacks would have to accept "one basic truth" regardless of whether they "want to or not": "Black people cannot get ahead unless they have white people." Chisholm's response? "That's what you think."[1]

Chisholm received her master's degree in early childhood education from Columbia University Teachers College in 1952 and might have stayed in that traditionally female profession had not the state assemblyman for her district in New York vacated his seat. Her landslide victory in 1964 sent her to Albany as the state representative from the mostly poor, black and West Indian Bedford-Stuyvesant neighborhood of Brooklyn. Her first few years in politics were frustrating — of the fifty bills she sponsored, only eight passed. One of the eight was a measure establishing the SEEK (Search for Education, Elevation, and Knowledge) program, which provided college funding for disadvantaged youths. Another secured unemployment insurance for domestics and day care providers, and another enabled tenured schoolteachers who took time off from work to have a baby to keep their tenure on their return to service.

Although her constituents appreciated her efforts, politics in the 1960s was still very much a male domain, and men of all stripes let the outspoken Chisholm know that she was not welcome. A founder of the National Organization for Women (NOW) and an early supporter of the National Black Feminist Organization, Chisholm always maintained that she met more resistance from men than from whites. "Men. White men, black men, Puerto Rican — men. They gave me a hard time," she remembered. "When they saw me coming, they almost dropped dead. . . . They were afraid of my mouth."[2] Her male colleagues also feared her independence and the fact that she refused to be beholden to any political machine. Machine bosses, she said, never questioned her competence or dedication. "What they said," she noted, "was always that I was 'hard to handle.'"[3]

The 1968 election that sent Chisholm, instead of veteran civil rights worker James Farmer, to Congress also demonstrated the steadfast support she received from local women, both black and white. During the election, Farmer played on black men's fears of domineering women, portraying Chisholm as "a bossy female, a would-be matriarch." At one point, she complained that television stations were favoring Farmer, who attracted attention with "sound trucks manned by young dudes with Afros, beating tom-toms: the big, black, male image." When she called one station to protest, the man she spoke to said derisively, "Who are you? A little schoolteacher who happened to go to the Assembly."[4]

That year, however, Chisholm became the schoolteacher who went to Congress. Farmer thought that being a man gave him an advantage, but in that congressional district registered female voters outnumbered male voters by more than 2 to 1. With help from women in PTAs, social groups, and civic clubs, Chisholm beat Farmer handily. As she later wrote, women "stay put, raise their families — and register to vote in greater numbers." They "are always organizing for something."[5]

Women stayed devoted to Chisholm, and she did not disappoint them. While in Congress, she authored a bill to finance child care facilities that passed both houses. President Richard Nixon, who rode into office in 1968 on a conservative wave, vetoed it. She also helped push through a bill that gave domestic workers the right to earn a minimum wage. Her staff, composed almost entirely of women, half of whom were black, helped her work on a number of bills that financed education, social services, and health care. She worked tirelessly against the seniority system in Congress, which she believed gave rise to fossilized practices and "horse and buggy thinking."[6]

Chisholm disrupted that kind of thinking during her historic run for the presidency in 1972. Her candidacy unsettled many. She met resistance from native-born African Americans — who, she recalled, often derided West Indians as "monkeys," complaining that they were "taking over everything"[7] — and even from women. The National Women's Political Caucus, which did not immediately endorse Chisholm — instead hoping to influence the Democratic platform by promising a bloc vote to candidate George McGovern — characterized her candidacy as a "quixotic joke."[8] Black men, Chisholm recalled, felt that "in this first serious effort of Blacks for high political office, it would be better if it were a man."[9] Still, those who gathered at Brooklyn's Concord Baptist Church on January 25, 1972, for the kickoff of her presidential campaign gave her a standing ovation when she proclaimed, "I am not the candidate of black America, although I am black and proud; I am not the candidate of the women's movement of this country, although I am a woman and I'm equally proud of that. I am the candidate of the people of America. And my presence before you now symbolizes a new era in American political history."[10]

Chisholm did not win the Democratic Party nomination, but her candidacy, political career, and politics marked the beginning of a new era. In the early 1970s, America was rocked not only by the black freedom movement but also by the freedom movements of Hispanics, Native Americans, women, and the lesbian, gay, bisexual, and transgender (LGBT) community. The anti–Vietnam War movement and the sexual revolution, which was changing relationships between men and women, also were in full swing. Meanwhile, deindustrialization and inflation made for a worsening economy. Chisholm's politics and candidacy symbolized all this change, proving that by virtue of the 1965 Voting Rights Act, black power could be translated into electoral victories. Chisholm represented the aspirations of black women, who insisted that their distinct issues were also race issues. As a black American of West Indian descent, she also symbolized the increasing diversity of African America and the tensions that such diversity provoked. Finally, the reaction to her liberal politics reflected the tenor of the times, which were marked by a conservative backlash and a "law and order" agenda that would continue to repress the black freedom movement.

Shirley Chisholm
In 1972, many people, including most blacks, could not imagine that a black person could be elected president of the United States. The notion that a black *woman* could be elected to the nation's highest office was even more unthinkable. However, it was not inconceivable to Shirley Chisholm, who that year became the first black major-party candidate for president. Here, with Manhattan borough president Percy Sutton by her side, she announces her candidacy. Chisholm went on to win 152 first-ballot votes at the Democratic National Convention. *Don Hogan Charles/Archive Photos/Getty Images.*

Opposition to the Black Freedom Movement

Opposition to the black freedom movement began at the movement's inception, but it reached its high point with the election of Republican president Richard Nixon in 1968. The ascendancy of the Republicans, the political party that had opposed the Civil Rights Act of 1964 and the Voting Rights Act of 1965, was a blow to African Americans. Nixon and subsequent Republican presidents legitimized and strengthened the massive political power behind white resistance, changing everything from the language of discrimination to the politics of racism. In doing so, they transformed the very nature of the Republican Party and reshaped the black struggle for racial equality.

The Emergence of the New Right

The year 1964 marked a turning point for Republicans. By that time, President Harry Truman's desegregation of the armed forces after World War II and Democratic support of the Civil Rights Acts of 1957 and 1964 (the former of which was a weak bill committing the federal government to support black voting rights) had delivered southern Democrats to the Republican Party. William Rusher, publisher and editor of the conservative *National Review*, argued that Democrats had "run with the hares down South on the race issue, while riding with the hounds up North — nominating loudly integrationist presidential candidates while calmly raking in, on locally segregationist platforms, 95 percent of all Senate and House seats . . . south of the Mason–Dixon line."[11] Republicans felt they could exploit this divide by giving segregationist Democrats and other conservatives a permanent home in the Republican Party. But they had to repackage themselves. In 1964, when Republican presidential candidate Barry Goldwater had argued that it was unconstitutional to require states to desegregate public facilities, he had come across as an extremist and a racist. After 1964, conservatives remade themselves in the image of the American mainstream.

One of their first moves was to tone down their rhetoric on race. By the late 1960s and early 1970s, most white Americans accepted token integration and rejected the ideologies of organizations such as the Ku Klux Klan. Blatant bigotry was unattractive, and Republicans now reasoned that they could garner more support if they targeted issues of social conservatism — law and order, and the drawbacks of a meddling federal government — rather than focusing overtly on race.

The birth of what became known as the **New Right** can be traced to Richard M. Nixon's 1968 campaign for the presidency. Against the backdrop of urban riots, gun-toting Black Panthers, and protests to end the Vietnam War and obtain various rights, Nixon ran on a platform of "law and order"; against the independent party bid of rabid segregationist George Wallace, Nixon ran on a platform of tolerance. He promised to speak for the "silent majority," which he defined as "the great majority of Americans, the forgotten Americans, the non-shouters, the non-demonstrators . . . those who do not break the law, people who pay their taxes and go to work, who send their children to school, who go to their churches . . . people who love this country."[12] To African Americans, however, Nixon's "silent majority" was code for the white majority.

Law and Order, the Southern Strategy, and Anti–Affirmative Action

Once in office, Nixon implemented what he called the **southern strategy** — policies aimed at moving southern whites and northern conservatives into the Republican Party. He placed staunch conservatives at the head of the Departments of Commerce and Health, Education, and Welfare. His head of the Office of Economic Opportunity, one of the agencies charged with implementing affirmative action, eliminated ten regional offices and scores of antipoverty programs before a federal court ruled the actions illegal. His attorney general, John Mitchell, opposed an extension of the 1965 Voting Rights Act, which was due to expire in 1970. To drive a wedge between black and white laborers, Nixon supported equity in the hiring of black construction workers on projects that received federal funding, then cut federal construction by 75 percent.[13] Nixon also came out against school desegregation, opposing Johnson administration guidelines that would have terminated federal funding to segregated schools. When the Supreme Court rebuffed his efforts, voting unanimously in favor of strategically busing students to integrate school systems, Nixon began the process — which subsequent Republicans would complete — of moving the federal judicial system to the right.

Moreover, Nixon gave the FBI the green light to target and destroy the Black Panthers and other black nationalist organizations. In 1969, deeply affected by government infiltration, the Panthers — now a nationwide organization with numerous chapters and substantial membership — expelled hundreds of members to "weed out provocateurs and agents." The tactics of the FBI and local police also led to interorganizational violence and several government-sanctioned assassinations (see chapter 13). In 1969, for example, members of the black nationalist US organization had a shootout with the rival Los Angeles Panthers on the UCLA campus, killing Panthers John Huggins and Alprentice "Bunchy" Carter. Subsequent documents revealed that the FBI had manipulated antagonism between the two groups to the point of violence.[14]

The sensational trials of African Americans during the period only heightened tensions among blacks and convinced whites of the need for law and order. In 1968, the trial of Huey Newton for allegedly murdering a policeman infuriated law enforcement, as black and white radicals joined forces to present Newton as a victim of political and police persecution. While the two thousand black and white demonstrators outside the courthouse thought it a travesty that Newton received a prison sentence of two to fifteen years, most Americans thought it a tragedy that the sentence was so light. Similar sentiments were aroused when Bobby Seale was charged with inciting a riot during the 1968 Democratic National Convention in Chicago, and then again in 1970 when he was charged with murdering a Panther suspected of being a government informant. In 1972, Black Panther and UCLA philosophy professor Angela Davis was tried for aiding the escape of several prison inmates from a California courtroom — an incident during which a judge was killed and a prosecutor and a juror were wounded. Although she was acquitted, the trial enraged many whites. With her signature Afro hairdo, she became an iconic image of black radicalism. For most Americans, Newton, Seale, and Davis represented all that had gone wrong with the black movement for freedom and justice.

Most Americans also supported the tough actions Nixon took against black and white student activists. On May 4, 1970, at Kent State University, four students were killed by National Guardsmen who had been called to the campus to quell demonstrations that erupted after Nixon expanded the Vietnam War by invading Cambodia. Eleven days later in Jackson, Mississippi, local police killed two black students and wounded twelve others during demonstrations at the historically black Jackson State University. Students on the campus were outraged by the war in Vietnam, the Kent State shootings, and local racial issues that pitted black students against white locals. Although the President's Commission on Campus Unrest, established in the wake of both incidents, judged the tactics of the guard and the police as extreme and unjustified, no one was convicted of a crime in either case.

Nixon supporters also attacked affirmative action. In the mid-1960s, civil rights leaders and President Lyndon Johnson had argued that government jobs and anti-poverty programs were compensatory measures needed to reverse past discrimination. Conservatives opposed affirmative action from the beginning but had to wait for a favorable political climate to mount an attack. Nixon's presidency provided that climate. So did the postindustrial economic downturn, which was in full swing by the 1970s. During this decade, factories closed and commercial enterprises abandoned cities. Every major northeastern and midwestern city lost jobs. Philadelphia, for example, lost 150,000 jobs, one-sixth of its employment base.[15] High inflation, high unemployment, and stagnant economic growth, collectively termed "stagflation," made for intense competition in the job market and led to a search for a scapegoat.

Opponents of affirmative action, including many who had been steadfast supporters of the civil rights movement against de jure segregation, derogated as quota systems the special college and professional admissions programs that aimed to increase the enrollment of minorities and women, contending that they placed unqualified people in positions that rightfully belonged to the more meritorious. "Merit alone must govern," one critic wrote.[16] When blacks and women pointed to real discrimination in the workplace and argued that race- and gender-based criteria redressed centuries of inequalities, the New Right argued that compensatory measures were un-American, squelching equal opportunity and depriving individuals of due process of law. These measures, conservatives said, were actually "reverse discrimination." They also argued that affirmative action was unfair, because instead of using "color-blind" criteria, it used race as the primary basis for awarding government contracts, hiring workers, and admitting students to colleges and professional schools. Paradoxically, opponents of affirmative action associated compensatory programs with inequality. In their rhetoric, antipoverty programs became taxpayer "handouts" for the undeserving, and race- and gender-based criteria for contracts, jobs, and education rewarded, as one conservative put it, "the dumb, lazy, and unambitious at the expense of the smart, talented, and ambitious."[17] These "reverse discrimination" and "color-blind" arguments were effective precisely because they employed the same rationale as affirmative action itself — that America was and should be a land of opportunity for everyone.

Such rhetoric appealed to many working-class whites, who believed they might lose their jobs because of affirmative action. A substantial number of labor leaders, though not all rank-and-file union members, had allied with blacks during the civil rights struggle against de jure segregation. Affirmative action, however, pitted white workers and black workers against each other as they competed for jobs in an era of high unemployment and inflation. White workers in the construction trades often walked off the job when black workers were hired under affirmative action guidelines. They hazed new black journeymen and often refused to teach black apprentices at all.[18] Besides mandating employment of black workers, affirmative action also altered the time-honored system of seniority, which in practice gave the most secure and best-paying jobs to white workers, many of whom had been hired when discrimination barred black workers from anything but janitorial work. In 1968, the Dodge Revolutionary Union Movement (DRUM) staged a two-day picket of Chrysler's main Dodge automobile plant in Hamtramck, Michigan, decrying "racism, discrimination, and intimidation, bigotry and abuse." Many white autoworkers responded by supporting segregationist George Wallace, the independent presidential candidate who charged that the government favored blacks over whites. By and large, those who did not support Wallace withdrew their support from the Democratic candidate, George McGovern, a proponent of affirmative action, and gave their votes to Nixon. Thus the black–labor alliance, which had already been strained by the CIO's McCarthy-era purging (see chapter 12), was further jeopardized.[19]

The Reagan Era

Richard Nixon resigned his presidency in 1974 as a result of the Watergate scandal, a break-in at the Democratic National Committee headquarters that his administration attempted to cover up. But his anti–affirmative action arguments gathered steam under Ronald Reagan, who, with the support of the white working class, a traditional Democratic Party constituency, gained the presidency in 1980 and subsequently underpinned the conservative rollback of federal antipoverty funding, jobs programs, and court challenges. Reagan had launched his presidential campaign in Philadelphia, Mississippi, where three civil rights workers were murdered in 1964. There he announced his conservative agenda, saying pointedly, "I believe in states' rights," and arguing that discrimination was a "myth." According to one of Reagan's favorite conservative theorists, George Gilder, if discrimination had ever existed in the United States, it had "already been effectively abolished," and if anything, there now was "discrimination in favor of blacks," a "racial spoils system" that was "odious" to "principle."[20] During his 1976 campaign for president, Reagan popularized the myth of the "welfare queen," an irresponsible, sexually promiscuous black woman who lived comfortably, even extravagantly, on the taxpayers' dime. He frequently used the fictitious example of a Chicago woman who "has 80 names, 30 addresses, 12 Social Security cards, and is collecting veterans' benefits on four non-existing deceased husbands."[21] Once he became president, Reagan, acting on the principle that welfare was a handout, cut child nutrition and job training programs — programs that both the white and black poor depended on. He also axed the Comprehensive Employment and Training Act (CETA), a program initiated by his predecessor, Jimmy Carter, that had provided more than 300,000 jobs for poor people. Ten percent of welfare recipients were cast adrift, and an additional 300,000 families had their welfare assistance reduced. Determined to please conservatives, Reagan filled the Civil Rights Commission and the Equal Employment Opportunity Commission (EEOC) with people opposed to civil rights and slashed the budgets of both the EEOC and the Office of Federal Contract Compliance (see chapter 13). He encouraged school boards to resist court-ordered **busing**, which transported both black and white children to schools in different neighborhoods in order to promote integration, and he ordered his attorney general to fight affirmative action in the courts.

One of Reagan's more onerous moves was his 1982 declaration of a "war on drugs," in which he centralized drug policy in the executive branch, cut addiction programs, and required stiff penalties for the possession of all illegal drugs regardless of type. Prior to Reagan's policy, the 1973 **Rockefeller drug laws** in New York had called for a mandatory prison sentence of fifteen years to life for the possession of just four ounces of a narcotic — about the same sentence as for second-degree murder. (The laws got their name from New York governor Nelson Rockefeller, a staunch supporter of them.) These laws seemed innocent enough because, like other conservative ideas, they appeared race neutral. But in 1982, only 2 percent of the American public viewed drugs as the most important issue facing the nation, and most Americans were unaware that crack cocaine did not make its first appearance in inner-city neighborhoods until 1985. These facts meant that when the national media turned its attention to black communities in the mid-1980s and exposed the joblessness, low-performing schools, deficient health care facilities, and decrepit housing there, Americans were led to believe that drug use — and not the lack of jobs haunting all American workers at the time — had made slums of the nation's inner cities. The extraordinarily punitive antidrug laws that imprisoned many first-time offenders but few dealers disproportionately affected African Americans.[22] (See By the Numbers: The War on Drugs, 1980–2000.) In New York State, for example, 886 people were incarcerated for drug offenses in 1980. Of these individuals, 32 percent were Caucasian, 38 percent were African American, and 29 percent were Hispanic. In 1992, the year in which the state reported the highest number of incarcerations for drug offenses, only 5 percent of those incarcerated were Caucasian, while 50 percent were African American and 44 percent were Hispanic.

BY THE NUMBERS   The War on Drugs, 1980–2000

The laws enacted during Ronald Reagan's war on drugs affected African Americans more significantly than any other group, penalizing drug offenders most harshly for their use of crack cocaine — the drug that predominated in inner cities — and mandating long prison sentences for possession. One FBI study noted that while blacks represented only 12 percent of all illegal drug users, they made up 41 percent of all those arrested on cocaine and heroin charges. As the war on drugs progressed, funding for antidrug efforts increased, and African Americans were disproportionately arrested and imprisoned for drug-related offenses. DATA SOURCE: Human Rights Watch, *Decades of Disparity*. Available online at http://www.hrw.org/print/reports/2009/03/02/decades-disparity.

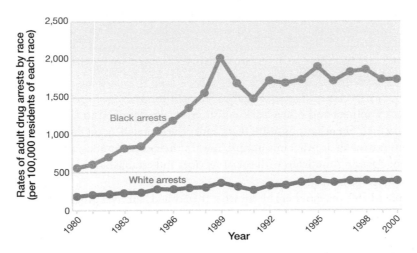

Reagan secured his war on drugs and anti–affirmative action agenda by turning the judicial branch to the right. By the time he took office, the U.S. Supreme Court had rendered two contradictory decisions on affirmative action. In *Regents of the University of California v. Bakke* (1978), the Court ruled that the university's medical school at Davis had discriminated against Allan Bakke, a white male, when it took race into account in determining admissions. In *United Steelworkers of America v. Weber* (1979), however, the Court declared that Brian Weber, a white male, had not been discriminated against by either the United Steelworkers union or the Kaiser Aluminum Corporation when they initiated a job training program to bring the proportion of blacks in the craft trades closer to their proportion in the local labor force.

Reagan and his conservative power base successfully swung the Court away from decisions like that rendered in *Weber*. During his two terms in office, Reagan appointed 368 district court and appeals court judges — nearly half of all the judges on the federal courts. Only twenty-four of these judges were minorities (seven were black, fifteen were Hispanic, and two were Asian), and twenty-nine were women. The rest were white males, most of whom were conservative. Reagan did, however, appoint the first woman, Sandra Day O'Connor, to the Supreme Court in 1981. Although she and another Reagan appointee, Anthony Kennedy, turned out to be centrists, Reagan ensured the Court's rightward swing when he elevated Nixon appointee and archconservative William Rehnquist to chief justice and named another archconservative, Antonin Scalia, to fill Rehnquist's seat.

The Persistence of the Black Freedom Struggle

The assault on the national black power movement and the conservative backlash forced African Americans to pursue equality on a more local level and to seek more diverse leadership. This shift was evident in the decline of the Black Panther Party and the new emphasis on local politics, the emergence of women's issues, and the local nature of the conflicts that occurred over open housing, school desegregation and community control, and neighborhood economic development.

The Transformation of the Black Panthers

The Black Panthers and other black power groups succumbed to law enforcement's assault on their organizations. With their leaders dead, in jail, or on the run, these organizations turned their programs inward, toward their communities, and refocused on providing African Americans with social services and establishing community control of black neighborhoods.

Late in 1969, the Panthers began what they called "survival programs." Across the country, chapters established breakfast programs for children, health clinics, clothing drives, and schools. In doing so, they reconnected with local churches, where they often conducted their community service programs. Huey Newton acknowledged the new relationship in 1971: "We will work with the church to establish a community which will satisfy most of our needs so that we can live and operate as a group."[23] Accordingly, the Oakland Black Panthers held their first breakfast program at St. Augustine's Episcopal Church.

Community service programs also served as a conduit to women's organizations that worked both within and outside the church. Until this turn toward community survival, the Panthers, like other black power organizations, had been male-oriented and sexist. Women such as Kathleen Cleaver, wife of Panther leader Eldridge Cleaver, and Angela Davis, who wanted their opinions and leadership recognized, had to either act as "masculine" as possible or appear nonthreatening to the men with whom they worked. The survival programs, however, needed community women, and so, like Shirley Chisholm in her first congressional campaign, the Panthers turned to them for help. The Panthers announced their new direction with ads in their newspaper: "The Black Panther Party is calling on all mothers, and others who want to work with this revolutionary program of making sure that our young . . . ha[ve] full stomach[s] before going to school. . . . Mothers, welfare recipients, grandmothers, guardians and others who are trying to raise children . . . LET'S DO IT NOW!"[24]

The Panthers also focused on schooling. "Why should it be that a school in East Oakland . . . should have a public school . . . [that is] poorly equipped and poorly cared for with little or no funding for extra programming? And a school in the same city, in the hills, run by the same school district would have all kinds of additional programming and funding?" they asked. The Panthers addressed this issue by setting up "liberation schools" for children ages four through eleven in cities across the country. These schools fed children breakfast and lunch and offered a first-rate education that included black history and culture classes. In Oakland, the Intercommunal Youth Institute was established in 1971 under the direction of Ericka Huggins. Later renamed the Oakland Community School, it employed accredited instructors in math, science, social science, Spanish, environmental studies, physical education, and fine arts. With a motto that revealed its focus on "learning *how* to think, not *what* to think," the school represented blacks' efforts to control education in their communities.[25]

Similarly, the Panthers' turn toward electoral politics represented African American efforts to take political control of their communities across the country. In May 1973, Bobby Seale turned in his leather jacket and black beret for a dark business suit and white shirt and announced that he was running for mayor of Oakland. Alongside him was the Panthers' new minister of information, Elaine Brown, who announced that she was running for city council. On a platform that included promises to increase taxes on the rich and use the additional revenue to improve education, transportation, street lighting, and crime fighting, Seale and Brown mobilized the black poor and middle class, as well as black and white students, into a new voting bloc to demonstrate that "voting unity . . . is Power of the People: the only means to begin implementing community control."[26] Although neither candidate won, Seale received enough votes to force a runoff election. In the process, the Panthers returned to the tactic used by the Lowndes County Freedom Organization in Alabama back in 1965 (see chapter 13). In winning 40 percent of the vote, Seale and the Panthers registered enough voters to make a difference in other municipal elections, most notably those for Oakland's antipoverty agencies. Four years later, the Panthers' efforts paid big dividends when Lionel Wilson was elected Oakland's first black mayor.

Black Women Find Their Voice

As black America refocused on local issues in the late 1960s and 1970s, black women emerged from the shadow of their male counterparts. Shirley Chisholm led the way in politics; also noteworthy was Barbara Jordan, who served as a Texas state senator from 1966 to 1972 and was elected to Congress in 1972. Black women authors such as Toni Morrison, Maya Angelou, Ntozake Shange, Toni Cade Bambara, Alice Walker, bell hooks, and Michele Wallace used novels, plays, poetry, and literary criticism to articulate black women's perspectives on just about everything. Black women had persistently argued that sexual exploitation, reproductive rights, equal pay for equal work,

Bobby Seale Campaigning
In May 1973, Black Panther Bobby Seale ran for mayor of Oakland. Seale and fellow Black Panther Elaine Brown, who ran for city council, sought to increase taxes on the wealthy and put the money collected toward improvements in education, transportation, street lighting, and crime fighting. They worked to mobilize young people and the black poor and middle class, encouraging them to take control of their communities. Here Seale is addressing riders on a city bus. *Associated Press/AP Images.*

and quality child care were issues that affected all blacks. They had marched, organized, and been imprisoned and beaten during the black freedom struggle, but it was only in the late 1960s and 1970s that they were able to make their needs, ideas, and feelings fully known.

Poor black women especially needed help. Too many were raising children without the financial support or presence of a man. These women typically had to rely on Aid to Families with Dependent Children, commonly known as welfare, to survive. As a result, they were forced to endure various indignities, including "midnight raids," in which caseworkers would barge into clients' homes in the middle of the night searching for evidence of a male presence, and welfare office interviews in which clients would be asked humiliating questions such as "When did you get pregnant? Who got you pregnant? How many men did you go with before you got pregnant?"[27] Conservatives even went so far as to call for mandatory sterilization of women on welfare, egged on by politicians such as Louisiana senator Russell Long, who referred to welfare rights leaders as "brood mares."[28] Even though the overwhelming majority of women on welfare were white, by the 1960s the stereotypical welfare recipient was a lazy, irresponsible, and immoral black woman.

Alternately treated like children or criminals, and virtually ignored by civil rights and black power organizations, poor, black, single women began organizing as early as 1962 into local welfare rights organizations. They brought these groups together into the National Welfare Rights Organization (NWRO) in 1967. They fought national and local laws prohibiting welfare recipients from having a male presence in the home and challenged the constitutionality of midnight raids. They supported women's right to reproductive freedom, which to them meant the right to have children and not be forced to undergo chemical or surgical sterilization. They also fought against forced work programs and supported job training for skilled work — work that paid enough for black mothers to be able to afford quality child care. But because they believed that a skilled job did not exist for every worker, they pressed for a guaranteed annual income based on need that would include cost-of-living increases.

Female welfare rights advocates were different from civil rights and black power advocates in that they identified their issues not just as black issues but as class and women's issues. They understood that their race, class, and gender intersected and reinforced one another. They were poor not just because they were female or because they were black, but because they were both female *and* black. They understood that white welfare recipients were not automatically stereotyped. For black women, their race intersected with their gender and class to determine the treatment meted out to them. Johnnie Tillmon, the chairwoman of the NWRO, described it this way: "I'm a woman, I'm a black woman. I'm a poor woman. I'm a fat woman. I'm a middle-aged woman. And I'm on welfare. In this country, if you're any one of those things — poor, black, fat, female, middle-aged, on welfare — you count less as a human being. If you're all those things, you don't count at all."[29]

Due to internal conflicts, the NWRO folded in 1975, but local welfare rights organizations and other black women's groups continued to articulate black women's experiences at the intersection of race, class, and gender. The Third World Women's Alliance, for example, began when a group of women within SNCC challenged the sexism of that organization. When these women split from SNCC in 1969, one of the first issues they addressed was the 1965 Moynihan Report, the government document blaming black women for the black family's decline (see chapter 13). Additionally, in establishing solidarity with Asian, Puerto Rican, Native American, and Mexican American women — other women of color — members demonstrated the interrelatedness of women's rights and international liberation struggles.[30]

Other black feminist groups were established in the late 1960s and early 1970s. The National Black Feminist Organization, the National Alliance of Black Feminists, the Combahee River Collective, and Black Women Organized for Action all emerged in response to the black freedom movement, which they felt excluded them, and the new women's rights movement, which likewise neglected their particular issues. Over and over, they reiterated the concept of double jeopardy — "the phenomenon of being Black and female, in a country that is *both* racist and sexist."[31] They argued that all black people had to fight on several fronts simultaneously, and they challenged white feminists to make racism and classism women's issues.

Black feminists tackled negative images of black women in popular culture, protesting, for example, a television show called *That's My Mama*, which featured a heavy-set black woman as a domineering mother. According to Sandra Flowers of the National Black Feminist Organization's Atlanta chapter, the show "repopularized the concept of the devious . . . black woman . . . not by implication, and not indirectly, but actively and by design."[32] Black feminists also addressed domestic violence, women's health care and reproductive rights, day care, welfare, the exploitation of women workers worldwide, and prisoners' rights.

More than any other black constituency, black feminists tackled the issue of black heterosexism and homophobia. Although the Black Panthers had allied with gays and lesbians as part of their political program to topple capitalism, feminists dealt with lesbianism on a daily basis — not only because some of the founders of black feminist organizations were lesbians but also because one of the ideological tenets of black feminism was that all women did not experience their gender the same way. Just as race determined how black and white women approached their womanhood, so too did sexuality. Black feminists were not always successful in eliminating bias against lesbians, but to their credit they introduced into the black public discussion a topic that would persist into the next century. The Third World Women's Alliance put it this way: "Whether homosexuality is societal or genetic, it exists in the third world community. The oppression and dehumanizing ostracism that homosexuals face must be rejected and their right to exist as dignified human beings must be defended."[33]

The Fight for Education

Women took the lead in the fight for quality education for their children. In cities of all sizes, African American children received a substandard education. Black children's achievement levels were consistently lower than those of white children. Their dropout rates were higher, their schools were dilapidated, their textbooks were out of date, and their often demoralized teachers were more concerned with maintaining order than with teaching. In cities as large as Chicago, New York, Detroit, and Denver, and as small as Plainfield, New Jersey, and Stamford, Connecticut, black mothers mobilized to improve the quality of their children's education. They fought for integration via busing, mostly because they believed it was the best way to address the problem quickly. White children went to well-funded, well-equipped schools that were often underpopulated. Black mothers, such as those who organized Chicago's Truth Squad or Englewood, New Jersey's Englewood Movement, sought to place these "neighborhood schools" within the reach of black children. NAACP lawyers supported them, arguing that there was no difference between school segregation that occurred as a result of a legal mandate (de jure segregation) and that which occurred as a result of state-sanctioned real estate discrimination (de facto segregation). Both types of segregation resulted in black deprivation.[34]

Black education advocates met with stiff resistance from whites, also mostly mothers, who greeted black children with racial epithets. In Plainfield, after a 1964 state order to desegregate schools, black students found the words "nigger steps" and "nigger entrance" painted on parts of Plainfield High School. In 1971, a U.S. district court mandated in *Milliken v. Bradley* that Detroit's public schools be merged with those in the surrounding suburbs; hundreds of thousands of whites organized against the decision. They rejected the district judge's finding that federal, state, and local governments had combined with private organizations to keep housing, and thereby schools, segregated. White parents claimed reverse discrimination, insisting that their right to send their children to their neighborhood schools was being violated. "Why ship the kids someplace else when we got a school right here?" one white mother asked. Whites claimed that blacks attended segregated schools out of choice, not because of a racist real estate market that kept blacks and whites segregated.[35]

White resistance forced African Americans to reconsider busing. Not only did Republicans, who had initiated the program, withdraw support, but by the 1970s whites who could do so had either moved to suburban areas that were beyond the reach of desegregation orders or sent their children to private schools. Instead of busing, black mothers demanded that more state and federal funding be directed toward black schools so that per capita spending on black and white students would be the same. They also wanted special programs to bring black students up to par with whites. And they demanded more control of their schools, reasoning that this would force principals and teachers to be more accountable to the community and therefore more sensitive, respectful, responsive, and concerned about black youths.[36]

These efforts also met with white resistance. Whites argued that their property taxes paid for their children's education and that they were not responsible for segregated housing. In addition, they believed that federal tax dollars should be distributed equally. Without extra money, however, schools in black areas could not afford the special programs that black students needed.

Community Control and Urban Ethnic Conflict

White resistance to school integration and affirmative action convinced many African Americans that their progress hinged on their ability to procure city, state, and federal resources and to dictate what happened in their communities while protecting the gains of the freedom movement. However, their efforts only increased tensions between blacks and other ethnic and racial groups that felt the same way.

One explosive issue was community control of schools. In 1967, the New York legislature made school funding contingent on local control of education. When blacks gained control of the school board in the Harlem and Ocean Hill–Brownsville sections of New York City, they fired or threatened to fire white principals and teachers. This pitted the powerful United Federation of Teachers (UFT), which was predominantly Jewish American, against advocates of community control. Tens of thousands of the city's teachers went on strike in the fall of 1968, prompting members of the black community to cry racism, while some in the Jewish community made allegations of anti-Semitism against community control proponents. Still others, including both blacks and Jews, condemned the firing of teachers and saw the issue as a dispute over labor rights and class. In the end, the city assumed control of the hiring and placement of teachers, but the traditional alliance of blacks and Jews, a relationship forged during the freedom movement, had been sorely tested.

In New York and elsewhere, the problem was not so much one of governance as one of resources.[37] Deindustrialization, globalization, and white flight had diminished urban tax bases, making public resources scarce; those who could not or would not move were left to fight among themselves — and fight they did. In 1974, Boston erupted in violence after a judge ordered the city to implement a busing program to desegregate its schools. In South Boston, a predominantly Irish American working-class neighborhood, angry white mobs shut down high schools, pelted buses with bricks and stones, and besieged city council meetings.[38] It had been twenty years since the U.S. Supreme Court had outlawed segregated schools, but the South Boston riots proved just how intractable the issue was. In addition to pitting blacks against white ethnic groups, the fight over desegregation showed how much class mattered. Those who could escape the city for quality schools in the suburbs avoided the issue completely. This was especially so after the Supreme Court overturned *Milliken v. Bradley* in 1974. Freed from the prospect of city-suburban school mergers, the affluent left the poor and middle classes to compete for shrinking city resources. By the late 1970s, middle-class blacks also were escaping the cities.

African Americans felt pressure to compete with other ethnic groups in order to keep what gains they had and to progress further. For example, the NAACP initially opposed extending coverage of the 1965 Voting Rights Act to "language minorities," including Latinos. The fear was that the addition of language provisions would under-cut the central focus on blacks and also jeopardize extension of the act. Although in 1975 Congress mandated that voting materials had to be provided for different lan-guage groups, many blacks felt that the Voting Rights Act was theirs exclusively because African Americans had fought for its passage. Protectively they thought, "What are you doing fooling around with our act?"[39] Many also coveted the money that governments allocated for bilingual education, arguing that African American children needed just as much help with English as immigrants. Their advocacy peaked in the 1990s, as educators in California pushed to get the state to recognize Ebonics, a kind of black dialect, as a language spoken in African American homes. The strategy behind the argument was to persuade legislators that black children needed enhanced instruction in Standard English in the hope that the state would then direct a portion of the bilingual education funds toward programs for African Americans. The effort failed miserably, however, as politicians and even some black leaders perceived Ebonics advocates as endorsing the dialect rather than trying to eliminate it.[40]

As demonstrated by the clashes over voting rights and bilingual education, African Americans were increasingly at odds with Latinos and other immigrant groups who, following passage of the Immigration and Nationality Act of 1965, entered the country in greater numbers than in previous years. In both New York and California, hostility characterized relations between blacks and the Koreans who owned many of the shops

Busing in Boston
Busing brought white children to predominantly black schools and black children to better-funded, often underpopulated white schools in an effort to promote integration and improve the quality of black education. In 1974, Boston exploded in violence as a result of court-ordered busing. In this photograph, students and police engage in an altercation outside of Hyde Park High School. *Paul Connell/*Boston Globe *via Getty Images.*

in their neighborhoods. A 1992 survey found that Korean shopkeepers in New York City viewed their black customers, when compared to whites, as violent and dishonest. Most believed blacks were more criminally oriented and less intelligent than whites. Almost half thought blacks were lazy, and few believed blacks were poor because of racial discrimination. By contrast, this same survey revealed that most blacks felt Koreans were dishonest, disrespectful, and violent in their dealings with blacks. They believed that Korean shopkeepers charged high prices for low-quality goods and that Koreans were concerned only about profits and added nothing of value to their communities. In Los Angeles, the distrust between blacks and Koreans manifested itself during the 1980s in the murders of nineteen Korean merchants, nearly all of which were committed by African Americans.[41] Tensions in the city came to a head in 1991 when Latasha Harlins, a fifteen-year-old black girl, was shot in the back of the head by Korean store owner Soon Ja Du. Though Du was convicted of voluntary manslaughter, an offense that carries a maximum prison sentence of sixteen years, she was only fined and sentenced to probation and community service. Harlins's murder was one of the events that precipitated the 1992 Los Angeles riots, during which Du's store was burned, along with many other Korean establishments.

Black Political Gains

Ultimately, the control of resources was a question of political economics and electoral politics. The battle to control the allocation of tax dollars was waged on every political front, from school boards, antipoverty commissions, and city councils to mayoral offices, state legislatures, and congressional chambers. African American candidates fared best in places where blacks constituted a majority, and where they did not, they joined with new immigrants, white liberals, and some working-class whites to forge political alliances. Starting in 1971, the **Congressional Black Caucus** helped get black candidates elected. Founded by Shirley Chisholm, the only black woman in Congress, and twelve black congressmen, the Congressional Black Caucus supported black candidates in local races; lobbied for reforms in job training, health care, welfare, and social service programs; and attempted to fashion a national strategy to increase black political power.

Black political efforts paid dividends. In 1970, there were only 1,469 black elected officials in the United States; by 2006 this number had increased sixfold to 9,040.[42] In 1964, there were only 4 African Americans in Congress; by 1968 there were 10, the highest number since Reconstruction, and by 1972 that number had increased to 15. Similar developments occurred on the local level. In 1970, there were only 2 African American mayors of big cities — Carl Stokes in Cleveland and Richard Hatcher in Gary, Indiana. In 1973, Tom Bradley and Maynard Jackson were elected mayor in Los Angeles and Atlanta, respectively. By 2001, there were 47 African American mayors in cities with populations greater than 50,000, and only about half of those cities had black majorities.[43] It is important to note that the largest annual increase in the percentage of black elected officials between 1969 and 2000 occurred in 1971, indicating that the impact of the black freedom movement on black electoral participation and representation was immediate.[44]

African Americans also continued to have an impact on presidential elections. Blacks voted overwhelmingly Democratic in the last three decades of the twentieth century and as part of the Democratic Party base helped elect Jimmy Carter and Bill Clinton. In 1984 and 1988, Jesse Jackson, an African American civil rights worker who had worked closely with Martin Luther King Jr., won several hundred Democratic Party delegates. In 1988, he captured close to seven million votes, winning seven primaries and four caucuses. Jackson's candidacy proved that white Americans would vote for a black man if he had the right message and could build coalitions. In 1988, Jackson brought together rural farmers, black and white urban workers, women, and environmentalists in the Rainbow Coalition with a populist message that condemned big business for exporting jobs and Reagan policies that gave tax breaks to the rich.[45]

Electoral gain was one thing, but economic power was another. As with education, political leaders had no magic wand that would make resources materialize out of thin air. Economic progress, therefore, was steady but halting. With more African Americans holding political office, however, blacks had more access to government employment. It is no accident that the largest gains in white-collar employment among blacks came in personnel offices that dealt with local, state, and federal agencies, especially those that enforced antidiscrimination laws.[46] Blacks made progress in other areas of the labor market as well. The U.S. Supreme Court's ruling in *Griggs v. Duke Power Co.* (1971) enabled African Americans to put Title VII, the antidiscrimination clause of the 1964 Civil Rights Act, to work for them (see chapter 13). In 1972, Congress passed Title IX of the Education Amendments of 1972, which outlawed discrimination in educational institutions receiving federal funding. A subsequent amendment made it unlawful to discriminate against personnel in academic institutions. These laws helped achieve what black electoral power alone could not: putting black people to work so that they had the ability to help themselves.

The Expansion of the Black Middle Class

The black middle class transformed considerably in the late 1960s and throughout the 1970s and 1980s. In the years before midcentury, the black middle and upper classes comprised blacks who served their own communities. They were morticians, barbers, beauticians, and owners of restaurants, stores, and clubs. Black middle-class professionals, from teachers to doctors, also served a community that was almost exclusively black. The black freedom movement, however, changed the very nature of black America (and, by extension, the rest of America) by opening up jobs that had previously been closed to blacks. In 1963, when the Ford Motor Company was asked to list its white-collar jobs for which blacks were welcome to apply, it mentioned valets, porters, security guards, messengers, barbers, mail clerks, and telephone operators — a list that by its narrowness explained the urgency and militancy of the struggle for jobs and education.[47] By 1980, things had changed dramatically. Nationwide, the number of black professional and managerial workers had tripled, and the number of black sales and clerical workers — about half of whom were women — had increased fivefold. Between 1970 and 1980 alone, the number of black college students doubled, increasing from 522,000 to more than 1 million. These gains were accompanied by an increase in black earnings relative to those of whites. The emergence of a substantial black middle class was a hallmark of the black struggle for economic and political justice — despite the fact that a black middle-class family was more likely than its white counterpart to depend on the income of both spouses, an indication of the fragility of its status.[48]

That fragility could also be seen in housing. In 1968, Congress passed another civil rights act. Title VIII of this act, known as the **Fair Housing Act**, prohibited discrimination based on race, color, sex, religion, and national origin in the sale or rental of housing. It also made the practices of blockbusting, steering, and redlining illegal (see chapter 12). As initially passed, however, the act excluded 80 percent of the nation's housing stock, reflecting the conservative backlash that was already under way. (A subsequent 1968 Supreme Court ruling brought all of the nation's housing under the act.) In addition, the act gave no government agency the power to identify and root out discrimination, in effect ensuring that if desegregation occurred at all, it would occur not because the government had provided strong enforcement mechanisms, but because victims, on a case-by-case basis, bore the costs of investigation and prosecution. As one political scientist noted, "What Congress did was hatch a beautiful bird without wings to fly."[49]

In practice, this meant that despite the tireless efforts of churches, civil rights organizations, and numerous open-housing groups to desegregate white suburbs, the same discriminatory housing policies used in the 1950s and 1960s by private homeowners, real estate agents, mortgage brokers, and FHA and VA administrators continued to be used for the remainder of the twentieth century. Increasingly, class-based bias was used to keep blacks out of white suburbs. Some towns were rezoned so that affordable housing was disallowed or only the very wealthy could afford to move in. Towns were helped by a series of Supreme Court rulings that made such rezoning legal. In 1977, for example, the Court ruled that Arlington Heights, a suburb of Chicago, did not violate the Constitution by prohibiting a church-sponsored apartment development. In this blow to open housing, the Court ruled that even though Arlington Heights' refusal to rezone for the apartments might have discriminatory effects, the plaintiff had not demonstrated that the town's intent was discriminatory. Only regulations clearly designed "with racially discriminatory intent," the Court held, violated the Constitution. Since, as a federal appeals court warned, "clever men may easily conceal their motivation," legal reliance on racist intent provided ample cover for race bias.[50]

Many African Americans argued that the black middle class ought to stay in black neighborhoods to uplift and empower them. Some opponents of open housing asked why blacks should have to beg whites for acceptance. According to one preacher, blacks were "coming to realize that even though they must fight for 'open occupancy' or the right to live any place they choose, once this right is secured for cultural, political and economic reasons it is desirable that the great majority of black men choose to live together in separate Negro communities." For other opponents, it was a question of black power politics. One black politician noted, "If they [blacks] disperse the communities, they'll only create smaller ghettos subservient to the white middle class. If they [the communities] remain intact, they'll have some power."[51]

These arguments were not lost on members of the black middle class. But like other Americans, they wanted quiet residential neighborhoods, safe places for their children to play, supermarkets where the food was fresh, modern homes with new appliances, streets that were cleaned on a regular basis, responsive fire departments, police protection against crime, and, above all, schools where their children could get a quality education. When asked what she and her neighbors expected from their move from New York City to Long Island, one black woman said that they "wanted backyards and front yards, they wanted a garage for themselves, they wanted comfortable spaces." The Harlem businessman Percy Sutton explained, "Black people, just as white people, seek to live wherever their job opportunities are, to live . . . where educational opportunities are, so they are seeking to move into the suburbs."[52]

African Americans moved, but within the limits set by white resistance. Sometimes black inner-city neighborhoods simply expanded outward past city limits. Kept out of white areas that were distant from the city, blacks were forced to stay in older

The Black Middle Class

African Americans' ability to move to the suburbs was hindered by the discriminatory policies of private banks and real estate agencies and others in the mortgage industry, and of federal agencies such as the Federal Housing Authority and the Veterans Administration. Blacks who accomplished the move were able to experience a lifestyle that had been common to middle-class whites for decades. © *Hub Willson/ClassicStock/The Image Works.*

inner-ring areas that were just beyond city boundaries. Residents of these inner-ring suburbs usually had the same problems as their inner-city counterparts — inferior municipal services, unresponsive political leaders, poor schools, high crime rates, and high property taxes. Blacks who moved to integrated suburbs usually found that the suburb remained integrated for only a short time. Once a black family moved in, real estate agents scared or steered white families away, causing a racial turnover in as little as a year. Once turnover occurred, municipal services declined, reproducing patterns of racial segregation and neighborhood deterioration. A few suburbs, such as Oak Park, Illinois, had open-housing committees that valued integration and worked to prevent resegregation. Blacks who moved to these suburbs enjoyed the kind of life they had imagined. So, too, did those who lived in all-black, upscale, upper-middle-class communities. Generally, however, African Americans did not reap the same gains as whites when they moved to the suburbs. The few who moved to predominantly white suburbs — a phenomenon that occurred with greater frequency toward the end of the century — paid for their benefits with greater social isolation.[53]

By the year 2000, one-third of all African Americans lived in suburbs. In the last two decades of the twentieth century, as many moved there as had moved in the first seventy years.[54] That most black suburbanites lived in black suburbs and that most

African Americans still lived mostly in all-black neighborhoods, city or otherwise, testified to the persistence of racism and the resistance to integration. And yet the fact that the fight for equality continued in the face of overwhelming white power is testimony to the strength of African Americans' commitment to full inclusion in American society.

The Different Faces of Black America

In 1998, the Harvard University professor Henry Louis Gates Jr. hosted an episode of the PBS series *Frontline* titled "The Two Nations of Black America." At issue was the question of class, or, more specifically, the emergence of a black America that was possibly more divided by class than it was united by race. Gates, a distinguished African American scholar, put the question front and center in an essay he wrote in conjunction with the program: "How have we reached this point, where we have both the largest black middle class and the largest black underclass in our history?"[55]

One of the many points brought to light by "The Two Nations of Black America" was the fact that by 1990, a new generation of African Americans had emerged that reflected all of the advances and setbacks of the past forty years. Although most African Americans still had a profound sense that what happened to them as a group affected them as individuals — what political scientists call "linked fate"[56] — more blacks than ever before approached life first as individuals and only secondarily as African Americans.

African America was also marked by gender, ethnic, sexual, and generational diversity. By the end of the twentieth century, black immigrants from other parts of the world were changing the meaning of African American culture, and a new generation of young African Americans were spurning their parents' way of thinking and were remaking blackness.

The Class Divide

African Americans had never been a monolithic people. Nevertheless, by 1998 class differences had become a more defining feature of this group. Although there was debate over the precise percentage of blacks in each class, it was accepted as fact that one portion of black America had advanced into the middle and upper classes, while another was mired in poverty.

The use of the term *underclass* to describe the impoverished was new in the 1990s. It referenced a whole set of conditions, ranging from the factual conditions of poverty, such as unemployment and low income, to the culture of poverty that these conditions gave rise to. Some preferred the term *truly disadvantaged* over *underclass*. Both terms, however, referred almost exclusively to African Americans who, for any number of reasons, were trapped in declining cities, unable to find employment in the new postindustrial economy that demanded skills they did not possess and could not obtain.[57]

As a group, African Americans had the highest rate of poverty in the nation. More than one-third lived in poverty, and the unemployment rate for young black males reached 50 percent in the 1990s. (See By the Numbers: Black Poverty and Unemployment, 1980–1998.) The firearm homicide rate for black males was two to four times higher than that for any other socioeconomic census group, accounting for 42 percent of all young black male deaths. And although African Americans made up only 11.4 percent of the total U.S. population, African American males accounted for almost 31 percent of all prison inmates. By 1990, there were more black males between the ages of eighteen and twenty-two in jail than in college. With so many men in prison, two-thirds of black women of marriageable age were left unmarried. By 1990, half of all African American children lived in single-parent, female-headed households, and almost 50 percent of them were born into poverty.[58]

The use of crack cocaine in American cities during the 1980s was both cause and effect of the devastation these statistics represent. Caught in a downward spiral of unemployment and poverty, many urban blacks turned to this highly addictive, inexpensive drug in an attempt to escape their misery. Others used the crack trade as a source of employment. As one scholar explained, many African Americans, particularly young men, were excluded from both the service and high-tech industries that developed in the postindustrial Los Angeles area. Unable to find blue-collar work in the new economy — the kind of work that had fueled migration and sustained black families during World War II — African Americans found the crack trade an attractive alternative to the abject poverty they otherwise faced.[59] And yet this trade increased black-on-black crime and illicit sex. The crack trade also gave law enforcement a new reason to investigate and incarcerate black Americans. While it sanctified material trappings of wealth — cars, jewelry, and high fashion — it also decimated family and community relations.[60]

The government was no help. The laws against drug use enacted in the 1970s and 1980s hit African Americans particularly hard because of the ratios used in determining sentencing: Possession of crack cocaine, as opposed to powdered cocaine, was counted at a 100:1 ratio. Five ounces of crack, which was cheaper and thus more common among poor people, was considered equal to 500 ounces of powdered cocaine, the drug used by the more affluent. As a result, African Americans were disproportionately arrested and given long prison sentences. Not only did this criminalize a public health problem, but it also criminalized African Americans, who were more likely to be arrested than whites. An FBI study noted that while blacks represented only 12 percent of all illegal drug users, they were 41 percent of all those arrested on cocaine and heroin charges.[61]

Black men and women were also disproportionately harmed by the AIDS epidemic and the government's response to the crisis. Under President Reagan, little government funding was directed toward researching and fighting the disease. By 1990, HIV/AIDS was the sixth leading cause of death for African Americans, and it was fast becoming the leading cause of death for African American women between the ages of twenty-five and thirty-four.[62] Although the number of Americans who died from AIDS declined toward the end of the century, blacks failed to benefit from new treatments in the same proportion as whites, because they lacked the resources to pay for the more expensive

BY THE NUMBERS   Black Poverty and Unemployment, 1980–1998

African Americans had the highest rate of poverty in the nation over the last two decades of the twentieth century. More than a third of African Americans lived in poverty, as this figure illustrates, and the unemployment rate for young black men reached 50 percent in the 1990s. Clinton's signing of the 1996 Personal Responsibility and Work Opportunity Reconciliation Act ended sixty years of guaranteed federal aid to the country's poorest citizens, mandating that poor families could receive aid for only two consecutive years and for five years total.

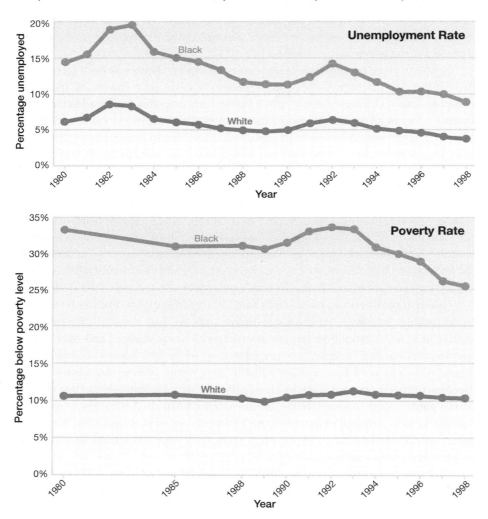

drugs and because they were, as one historian put it, "invisible as objects of public concern." At the end of 2006, there were an estimated 1.1 million people living with HIV in the United States, of which almost half (46 percent) were African American.[63]

Although Democrat Bill Clinton, who held office from 1993 to 2001, was popular among African Americans, his policies did not narrow the gap between the black poor and the middle and working classes. Unlike Reagan, Clinton lent his support to health and education programs to help the disadvantaged. His support for the earned income tax credit, an increased minimum wage, and funding for civil rights enforcement benefited all working blacks. His 1997 race initiative, which involved colleges and universities, cities, and states in a national dialogue on the issue of race, earned him black support. Yet his appointments, 14 percent of which went to blacks, immediately impacted only the black middle and upper classes.

Clinton's fear of a conservative backlash made him careful not to appear too sympathetic to the black poor. This was illustrated by the case of Lani Guinier, a black woman whom Clinton nominated as a candidate for assistant attorney general for civil rights. When her opinion on cumulative voting and proportionate interest representation (European-style voting that ensures that minorities are always represented) was characterized by conservatives as a "quota" voting system, conservatives began calling her the "quota queen," reminiscent of the "welfare queen" label they had attached to black female welfare recipients, and Clinton withdrew the nomination.

The administration's priorities were confirmed when Clinton, who campaigned on the pledge to "end welfare as we know it," signed the 1996 Personal Responsibility and Work Opportunity Reconciliation Act, ending sixty years of guaranteed federal aid to the country's poorest citizens. Although the act replaced the much-maligned Aid to Families with Dependent Children, federal aid to the poor was frozen at 1996 levels, and in 2003 the House voted to continue the freeze through 2008. America's poor families could receive aid for only two consecutive years and for five years total. States received bonuses for sharply cutting their public assistance rolls and could be penalized if they did not force recipients to work a minimum of twenty hours a week.[64]

A sign of the times was the lack of outrage in response to this act on the part of the black middle and working classes, who, like most Americans, stereotyped welfare recipients as black female profligates. Few social service agencies lobbied on behalf of welfare recipients, and the bill passed through Congress with almost no resistance from the Congressional Black Caucus. The estrangement between the black poor and the black middle class continued into the twenty-first century. This was evident in 2004 when comedian and educator Bill Cosby publicly proclaimed that "the lower economic and lower middle economic people are [not] holding their end in this deal. In the neighborhood that most of us grew up in, parenting is not going on."[65] Said eleven years before his credibility plummeted because of his arrest on charges of sexual assault, Cosby's comments were applauded by much of middle-class black America. At that time he was admired for articulating what many thought but were reluctant to say.

Hip-Hop, Violence, and the Emergence of a New Generation

The withdrawal of government support for black equality, the hostility and equivocation of national and local leaders who were former allies of the black freedom struggle, and the staggering poverty and disruption of black inner-city neighborhoods affected African Americans in a variety of ways. One of the most profound developments was the emergence of the hip-hop counterculture and **rap music** among younger African Americans. Originating on the streets of Harlem and the South Bronx in the early to mid-1970s, rap music began as pure showmanship at block parties, recreation centers, and parks, where disc jockeys, or DJs (also called emcees), competed with one another by layering in beats at the turntable, rhyming while friends battled it out on the break-dancing floor. Very quickly, however, the music emerged as a way for young people to deal with the violence and poverty of their neighborhoods. On one hand, young DJs used rap lyrics to critique poverty, police surveillance, drug addiction, black-on-black crime, and unemployment. On the other hand, stage competitions often replaced gang rivalries. Rap music allowed for the expression and release of frustrations, and as an industry it also functioned as an avenue to escape the poverty that produced it. Rap artists such as Notorious B.I.G. and Tupac Shakur became millionaires seemingly over-night, and black record labels such as Death Row Records were similarly successful. But as hip-hop moved into the mainstream, it became, in the minds of older black and white Americans, a symbol of everything that was wrong with the underclass, and that thinking had a negative effect on all of black America.

Some of the animosity stemmed from discomfort with lyrics that offered explicit descriptions of ghetto life, were graphically sexual and violent, and denigrated women while glorifying "gangstas." More discomfort grew from the unabashed use of profanity and the word *nigga*, which hip-hop artists claimed defanged the historically pejorative reference to black people. Even greater anxiety arose when rap music was embraced wholeheartedly by white and black youths who rejected America's mainstream middle-class culture.

Like black nationalists before them, rappers targeted the police, who again were likened to an occupying army. From the time of the 1970s block parties, the police, armed with the new drug laws, had gone after artists for their appropriation of public spaces. As rappers' lyrics became more incendiary and violence accompanied rap con-certs, the opinion that rap not only expressed but also caused violence was reinforced.[66] When one act, N.W.A. (Niggaz with Attitude), penned an anthem unapologetically titled "Fuck tha Police," the FBI issued a warning to the group.[67] The drive-by shootings that killed Tupac Shakur and Notorious B.I.G. in 1996 and 1997, respectively, con-vinced both white and black Americans of the danger of hip-hop.

White Americans had difficulty disassociating the violence and antisocial behav-ior of hip-hop from other violent events that occurred in the 1990s. In 1991, the public repeatedly viewed a bystander's videotape of the arrest of a black man named Rodney King by white Los Angeles police officers. It showed King lying on the ground while police beat him with batons. Although the officers argued that King's violent resistance required the use of force, many, including most African Americans, saw it as police brutality and proof of the general mistreatment of blacks by law enforcement. When the assault case against the officers was moved out of racially diverse Los Angeles to the predominantly white suburb of Simi Valley and a mostly white jury returned a not guilty verdict in 1992, Los Angeles, still simmering over the murder of Latasha Harlins,

Still from the Movie* Beat Street, *1984
The movie *Beat Street* featured break-dancing contests and a new DJ technique subsequently labeled turntablism (whereby the DJ simultaneously plays two records on separate turntables and mixes them by holding and scratching them in a particular sequence). The film introduced to America and the world the fantastically athletic and rhythmic moves that would forever marry hip-hop and break dancing to the young. Here a lead character demonstrates one of the vigorous moves that are the hallmark of break dancing. *© Orion Pictures Corporation/Orion Pictures/Photofest.*

erupted in riots that left 55 people dead and 2,300 injured. The verdict also ignited violence in Atlanta, Birmingham, Chicago, and Seattle. Underlying the violence were the poverty and unemployment caused by the postindustrial economy. But for African Americans, the whole King incident, from arrest through trial, symbolized the continuation of the unmitigated extralegal justice that followed blacks, particularly black men, wherever they went.

For this reason, a majority of African Americans sided with former football superstar O. J. Simpson in 1994 when he was arrested for killing his white ex-wife, Nicole Brown Simpson, and her white friend Ronald Goldman. After nine months of sensational televised hearings that featured the best defense lawyers money could buy, and a defense that effectively put the Los Angeles Police Department and the criminal justice system on trial for racism, Simpson was acquitted in 1995 by a mostly black and female jury. As evidence of just how far apart blacks and whites were on issues of race, blacks overwhelmingly approved of the verdict, while most whites thought Simpson was guilty.[68]

Gender and Sexuality

Other changes in black America could be seen in the Clarence Thomas Supreme Court hearings. President George H. W. Bush's 1991 nomination of the black jurist to replace the venerable Thurgood Marshall highlighted the emergence of a relatively small but significant population of black conservatives. Marshall, the first African American to serve on the U.S. Supreme Court, had earned his liberal credentials arguing civil rights cases, most notably *Brown v. Board of Education of Topeka* (1954). By contrast, Thomas had opposed affirmative action as a federal judge and as head of the Equal Employment Opportunity Commission (EEOC). Thomas's record on race earned him the rebuke of leading civil rights organizations, and his conservative credentials made him anathema to pro-choice women, who correctly predicted that Thomas would add his weight to the growing antiabortion contingent on the Supreme Court.

Women grew even more opposed to Thomas after the African American law professor Anita Hill testified before the Senate that Thomas had sexually harassed her when she worked for him at the EEOC. The vicious Senate battle that ensued, after which Thomas was narrowly approved by a vote of 52 to 48, reverberated throughout black America. Not only did black liberals oppose black conservatives, but black men and women also found themselves in an unprecedented public debate about the significance of sexual harassment — indeed, sexism in general — in black America. The televised Senate hearings, which featured the testimony of the most educated and privileged African Americans, also revealed the depth of the class divisions in black America. Never before had the schisms been so deep and so public.

In addition to the ideological, gender, and class differences exposed during the hearings, African Americans were torn between debating Thomas's record and presenting a united racial front. When Hill and her supporters were accused of racial treason, they retorted that Thomas's supporters had committed racial suicide by supporting a nominee opposed to affirmative action. Black men accused black women of emasculating Thomas, and black women returned with the charge of sexism. So intense was the dispute that some African Americans saw the conflagration as the end of racial solidarity. Nobel laureate Toni Morrison noted, "In matters of race and gender, it is now possible and necessary, as it seemed never to have been before, to speak about these matters without the barriers, the silences, the embarrassing gaps in discourse. . . . The time for undiscriminating racial unity has passed."[69]

Several years later, African Americans did what Morrison suggested. In October 1995, African American men gathered on the National Mall in Washington, D.C., for the **Million Man March**. Depending on who was reporting, from 400,000 to 2 million black men were present to address America's criminalization of black men

Clarence Thomas and Anita Hill
In 1991, President George H. W. Bush's nomination of the conservative black jurist Clarence Thomas to the U.S. Supreme Court was challenged when the African American law professor Anita Hill testified before the Senate that Thomas had sexually harassed her when she worked for him at the EEOC. The televised hearings that followed revealed fissures in the black community that set liberals against conservatives, and men against women, as they chose sides in the very public debate. Hill's accusations also brought the issues of sexism and sexual harassment firmly to the fore, a significant and lasting development for women of all races.
Thomas: Doug Mills/Associated Press/AP Images; Hill: © Mark Reinstein/The Image Works.

and what black men needed to do to improve themselves and their communities. Women were specifically asked not to attend. At the march, black men pledged to atone for their neglect and abuse of African American women, black families, and communities. They vowed to dedicate their lives to spiritual, moral, mental, social, political, and economic improvement. Two years later, in October 1997, African American women gathered on the Benjamin Franklin Parkway in Philadelphia for the **Million Woman March**. They called for "Repentance, Restoration, and Resurrection": repentance for the pain black women caused one another, and restoration and resurrection of the bonds of family and community in African American life. Though organized in the name of racial unity, these marches, which ironically found black men and women addressing their gender issues in separate forums, reflected the divisions in black America that had intensified since the late 1960s.

That the black LGBT community insisted on representation in these marches also showed how much black America had changed since 1963, when Bayard Rustin had had to hide his homosexuality for fear of hurting the black cause (see chapter 12).

In the 1990s, black LGBTs openly protested the heterosexual construction of black identity. They marched to counter the idea that sexual difference was inherently abnormal, undesirable, shameful, and "un-black." As one gay marcher observed, the Million Man March offered a "unique opportunity to empower black gay men and lesbians and black gay youth" by providing "positive images of open, courageous, proud and diverse black gay people."[70]

All Africa's Children

Nothing more clearly illustrates black America's diversity at the end of the twentieth century than the different ethnic groups that defined themselves as black. As a result of the Immigration and Nationality Act of 1965, which abolished a quota system established in 1924 that had limited immigration by country of origin, one million people came to the United States from Africa — more than were brought here during the transatlantic slave trade. According to 2010 census figures, 1.5 million blacks in the United States claim Caribbean ancestry. In fact, scholars note that the United States is the only place in the world where all of Africa's children — native-born Africans, Afro-Caribbeans, Afro-Hispanics, Afro-Europeans, and African Americans — are represented.

The diverse ethnic backgrounds of black Americans showed the many faces of blackness. (See Document Project: Redefining Community, pp. 603–11.) By the end of the century, immigrants were changing black culture, introducing their foods, their music, their traditional dress, and even their religion into their adopted communities. An exchange between a British man and an African American female journalist named Ytasha L. Womack illustrates this point. In discussing the terms *black* and *African American*, the British man asked Womack, "What's the difference?" Womack replied, "Some people feel 'African American' has more of a cultural identity. . . . It can also refer to blacks with longtime roots in America, versus if your roots are elsewhere. . . . For example, if you're talking about African American culture, that term refers to maybe the experiences of slavery and the culture that emerged afterward. . . . Versus, if you just immigrated from, say, Nigeria. If you're Nigerian, obviously you're African American in that you're black and live in this country, but culturally, well, at first you may have very strong ties to Nigeria and prefer 'Nigerian American.'" When the British man argued that the Nigerian was still black, Womack continued, "Well, yeah, but the culture they emerged from is different. . . . If you're talking about soul food and blues, you're talking about African American culture. If you're talking about reggae and salt fish, you're talking about Jamaican culture. Of course, you have Jamaicans in America. You have people whose grandparents were Jamaican, and they eat Jamaican food and partake in Jamaican culture, but they're African American."[71]

Ethnic differences made for a vibrant black America, but they also provoked tensions. Many black immigrants were reluctant to identify with native-born African Americans, who in turn often resented having to compete against immigrants in the job market. According to sociologists, many West Indians believed that they worked harder than native-born blacks, had stronger family ties, and were less likely to be criminals. By contrast, native-born blacks attributed West Indians' attitude to arrogance and resented their tendency to distance themselves from blacks born in America.[72]

Because black immigrants tended to be better educated than their native-born counterparts, they accentuated the class divide in black America. Africans, for example, were among the most educated immigrant groups in the United States, with some 50 percent holding a bachelor's degree. According to the 2000 census, African immigrants were more educated than any native-born ethnic group, including white Americans, holding twice as many degrees as white Americans and four times as many as native-born black Americans.

The growing numbers of black immigrants made for a very different African American population at the end of the twentieth century than existed at midcentury, when the civil rights movement was just beginning. Unlike their midcentury forebears, fewer blacks at the turn of the millennium had experienced the American South, Jim Crow, or the civil rights movement, either because they were born in a later era or because these were not part of their heritage. Less likely to understand the structural dimensions of American racism, many were also less likely to see the need for affirmative action and more disposed to see race as one of many identity variables, rather than as the most defining one.

CONCLUSION

Black Americans on the Eve of the New Millennium

The last three decades of the twentieth century marked the close of the black freedom movement and the rise of a black America that was more diverse than ever before. Both phenomena had as much to do with the success of the movement as with the rise of a politically based national backlash to restore what was euphemistically referred to as a "color-blind" society based on "law and order." Despite the conservative resurgence, however, America looked very different at the end of the century than it had at the beginning. Legal segregation was gone, and the door to the American workplace had been pried open. The American political system had slowly but surely adapted to the new realities that multiplied the number of black elected officials and laid the political foundation for the election of America's first black president. The black freedom movement had given birth to a substantial middle class and allowed millions of African Americans to do what had once been only a pipe dream: to prioritize something besides surviving racism.

At the turn of the millennium, black America faced new challenges. While black men searched for more satisfying ways to express their manhood, black women formed new organizations to fight racism and sexism. Insisting on inclusion in the black community, black lesbians, gays, bisexuals, and transgenders asserted their black identity. Meanwhile, black immigrants, in larger numbers than ever before, were changing the culture and politics of black America. In essence, at the turn of the millennium the very definition of *African American* was changing. And young people were making that change palpable. Their hip-hop culture was an in-your-face assertion of their presence. Like the young generations that had made it possible for blacks to travel comfortably on buses that traversed interstate highways, staged sit-ins at lunch counters, and braved racist mobs who opposed their presence in all-white public schools, the hip-hop generation conducted their own countercultural revolution. For many people, all this change was welcome, a just reward for more than a century of struggle. For others, it was foreboding, for it seemed to signal the end of a unified black America.

In 1903, the historian and activist W. E. B. Du Bois prophetically proclaimed that the problem of the twentieth century was "the problem of the color-line."[73] He probably would have been overjoyed, yet troubled, on the eve of the twenty-first century. For even though the visible lines of apartheid had disappeared, invisible markers — such as high rates of imprisonment, segregated housing and schooling, employment discrimination, and the criminalization of black spaces — remained. At the beginning of the new century, black America could look back on the previous century and see progress against racism. Looking ahead to continued progress in the future, however, was a bit more of a challenge.

CHAPTER 14 **REVIEW**

KEY TERMS

New Right p. 574

southern strategy p. 575

busing p. 578

Rockefeller drug laws (1973) p. 578

Regents of the University of California v. Bakke **(1978)** p. 579

United Steelworkers of America v. Weber **(1979)** p. 579

Congressional Black Caucus p. 588

Fair Housing Act (1968) p. 589

rap music p. 596

Million Man March (1995) p. 598

Million Woman March (1997) p. 599

REVIEW QUESTIONS

1. Describe the tactics of Richard Nixon and the New Right. What strategies did they pursue in their opposition to the black freedom movement and affirmative action?

2. How did Ronald Reagan build on Nixon's policies?

3. What new tactics did black activists adopt to counter the New Right? How successful were they?

4. What roles did black women play in the evolving black freedom struggle? Why were their efforts so significant?

5. How did the fight for jobs and resources affect previous political alliances?

6. Describe the many divisions that came to characterize black America in the decades following the civil rights and black power movements. In what ways did these changes undermine racial unity? In what ways did they enhance solidarity?

Redefining Community

When *Washington Post* journalist Courtland Milloy wrote about the 1995 Million Man March, he stated his hope that the march would bring back the days when "we were all just black" and not separated by "income, skin tone and hair texture."[74] Milloy was echoing the feelings of many who attended the Million Man March and the 1997 Million Woman March. That each event was organized around the goal of achieving racial unity reflected the increasing diversity of black America. But why was this end-of-century diversity so different from that which existed in previous eras?

Contrary to Milloy's belief, African Americans had never been monolithic. Black America had always divided over color and class. There had always been differences between light-, brown-, and dark-skinned blacks, and between elite, middle-class, working-class, and lower-class blacks. For example, the Brown Fellowship Society, founded in 1790 in Charleston, South Carolina, was restricted to free men with light skin. Paying the society's $50 membership fee plus its monthly dues required considerable means. Founded in the same city more than a hundred years later (1843) was the Humane Brotherhood, whose members were also wealthy but dark-skinned.[75] In the late nineteenth and twentieth centuries, some fraternities and sororities accepted only those prospective pledges who could pass the notorious "paper bag test," named thus because one's skin had to be lighter than the color of a brown paper bag.[76] While working- and middle-class blacks without college degrees joined fraternal and sororal societies like the Masons, the Elks, and the Eastern Star, college-educated African Americans joined black Greek organizations.

Blacks had divided along other lines as well. African Methodist Episcopalians did not take tea with Baptists, for example, while black Episcopalians, Presbyterians, and Catholics shunned both black Baptists and AME church members for being overly emotional.[77] Even when it came to politics, African Americans were never of one mind. Although the differences between the followers of Booker T. Washington and those of W. E. B. Du Bois were never as stark as they are often depicted as being, there was no consensus within the African American community about whether the best strategy for fighting segregation and discrimination was to accommodate racism by turning inward and focusing on community and individual development, or to fight openly for civil and political rights. The diversity of black opinion persisted into the midcentury freedom movement, as various organizations — NOI, CORE, the SCLC, SNCC, the NAACP, COFO, the OAAU, the MFDP, the BPPSD, RAM, and US,° to name a few — espoused a wide array of tactics, including nonviolent direct action, legal action through the courts, grassroots political organizing, armed self-defense, nationalist economic community development, or various combinations thereof. Similarly, men and women had fought for black rights, but often in separate organizations and in conflict with each other. For example, the

---

° The Nation of Islam, the Congress of Racial Equality, the Southern Christian Leadership Conference, the Student Nonviolent Coordinating Committee, the National Association for the Advancement of Colored People, the Council of Federated Organizations, the Organization of Afro-American Unity, the Mississippi Freedom Democratic Party, the Black Panther Party for Self-Defense, the Revolutionary Action Movement, and the US organization.

late-nineteenth-century founders of the National Association of Colored Women (see chapter 9) held fast to the idea expressed by Anna Julia Cooper in 1892 that women rather than men were the best representatives of the race because they molded the homes and communities from which the black nation grew. In addition, the invisibility of black lesbians, gays, bisexuals, and transgender individuals within the larger African American community did not translate into nonexistence, so on this score, too, African Americans had been far more diverse, and even oppositional with one another, than Courtland Milloy imagined.

The following documents reveal the diversity of black America on the eve of the twenty-first century. As you read them, see whether you can discern the source of Milloy's anxiety. Imagine the ways that black America could redefine community.

Combahee River Collective | *The Combahee River Collective Statement, 1977*

The COMBAHEE RIVER COLLECTIVE was a Boston-based black lesbian feminist group named after a Civil War expedition led by Harriet Tubman on the Combahee River in South Carolina. That 1863 raid freed hundreds of slaves and disrupted Confederate supply lines. Written in the freedom-fighting spirit that was Tubman's trademark, this statement is an example of black feminist ideas about systems of racism, classism, sexism, and homophobia. It represents the thinking of many black women who opposed the 1991 Supreme Court nomination of Clarence Thomas, and of those who objected to the exclusion of women from the Million Man March in 1995.

We are a collective of Black feminists who have been meeting together since 1974. . . . We are actively committed to struggling against racial, sexual, heterosexual, and class oppression, and see as our particular task the development of integrated analysis and practice based upon the fact that the major systems of oppression are interlocking. . . .

1. THE GENESIS OF CONTEMPORARY BLACK FEMINISM

. . . A Black feminist presence has evolved most obviously in connection with the second wave of

the American women's movement beginning in the late 1960s. . . .

Black feminist politics also have an obvious connection to movements for Black liberation, particularly those of the 1960s and 1970s. . . . It was our experience and disillusionment within these liberation movements, as well as experience on the periphery of the white male left, that led to the need to develop a politics that was anti-racist, unlike those of white women, and anti-sexist, unlike those of Black and white men. . . .

2. WHAT WE BELIEVE

Above all else, our politics initially sprang from the shared belief that Black women are inherently

SOURCE: *Capitalist Patriarchy and the Case for Socialist Feminism,* edited by Zillah Eisenstein, Monthly Review Press, 1978. Used by permission of Zillah Eisenstein.

valuable. . . . Merely naming the pejorative stereotypes attributed to Black women (e.g., mammy, matriarch, Sapphire, whore, bulldagger), let alone cataloguing the cruel, often murderous, treatment we receive, indicates how little value has been placed upon our lives. . . .

. . . We know that there is such a thing as racial-sexual oppression which is neither solely racial nor solely sexual, e.g., the history of rape of Black women by white men as a weapon of political repression.

Although we are feminists and Lesbians, we feel solidarity with progressive Black men. . . . Our situation as Black people necessitates that we have solidarity around the fact of race. . . .

3. PROBLEMS IN ORGANIZING BLACK FEMINISTS

. . . We have found that it is very difficult to organize around Black feminist issues, difficult even to announce in certain contexts that we *are* Black feminists. . . .

. . . We do not have racial, sexual, heterosexual, or class privilege to rely upon, nor do we have even the minimal access to resources and power that groups who possess any one of these types of privilege have. . . .

The reaction of Black men to feminism has been notoriously negative. . . . They realize that they might not only lose valuable and hardworking allies in their struggles but that they might also be forced to change their habitually sexist ways of interacting with and oppressing Black women. Accusations that Black feminism divides the Black struggle are powerful deterrents to the growth of an autonomous Black women's movement. . . .

. . . We feel that it is absolutely essential to demonstrate the reality of our politics to other Black women and believe that we can do this through writing and distributing our work. . . .

4. BLACK FEMINIST ISSUES AND PROJECTS

. . . The inclusiveness of our politics makes us concerned with any situation that impinges upon the lives of women, Third World and working people. . . . We might, for example, become involved in workplace organizing at a factory that employs Third World women or picket a hospital that is cutting back on already inadequate health care to a Third World community, or set up a rape crisis center in a Black neighborhood. . . .

. . . Eliminating racism in the white women's movement is by definition work for white women to do, but we will continue to speak to and demand accountability on this issue.

Cleo Manago | *Manhood—Who Claims? Who Does It Claim?*, 1995

CLEO MANAGO (b. 1963) is the founder and CEO of AmASSI (African, American Advocacy, Support-Services & Survival Institute) and the Black Men's Xchange, organizations that foster African American mental, sexual, and community health. Manago prefers to be referred to as "same gender loving" (SGL) and is often credited with coining the term, which denotes homosexuals of African descent. According to Manago, unlike the term *gay, SGL* connotes pride in being both black and homosexual. An outspoken critic of racism in the gay community, Manago also believes that *SGL* signifies that same gender loving men and women have to contend with both racism and homophobia. Manago argues that black men, especially SGL, bisexual, and transgender males, need health

DOCUMENT PROJECT

care and a social environment that take black culture and circumstance into account. Although he was asked to speak at the 1995 Million Man March, at the last minute he was pulled from the program because of time constraints. Unwilling to be silenced, he published his speech in *Alternatives*, an SGL magazine. The speech also appeared in the journal *The Black Scholar*. As you read Manago's speech, imagine what black America would be like if it followed Manago's guidelines.

Much of our experience in this country, our "manhood" has been subject to the whims of another culture, "our" manhood defined for us, not by us. . . .

Who is defining us, defining blackness, manhood, male responsibility? Who created the model? Does the model work? And work for whom? Why do we want to be men? Why don't some of us want to be *black* men? Why are we all here today? Might it be because the model, wherever it came from, doesn't work — for the black community?

Manhood, what is it? What difference does it make and why? Is it important enough to address? Yes, we are called black men, African-American men, but are we African? Does what determines black maleness or manhood originate in us, in Africa? Which part? Africa is a huge continent, one more diverse in expression than we are here today. Most of us can't fathom the diversity of black people, black expression in America, let alone Africa. Some of us today

believe being a strong black man means being Africentric (whatever that means), being hard, strong, masculine, heterosexual, responsible. . . . How does one, a male, take responsibility for something he has no frame of reference for, or affirmation of?

Even in skin that is called black, we are as diverse as the fish, flowers, the elements of the universe. So which one of us as black men have the market on manhood? . . . What is a man?

We as black men, as black people have been snatched from under our essence, are now distracted by an unnatural fight to know and love ourselves. I, as a black man who loves men, who falls in love with black men, lovingly challenge you to embrace the diversity of black men, a diversity as vast and as old as time. Black men are and have always varied in size, shape, sensibility, demeanor, and purpose. I'm in attendance at this march, with the blessings of the community, of same-gender loving Sisters and Brothers who love black people. . . . We do this as same-gender loving people, no less oppressed, or endangered than any of you my Brothers. Peace out!

SOURCE: Cleo Manago, "Manhood — Who Claims? Who Does It Claim?," *The Black Scholar*, 1996. Reprinted by permission of the publisher, Taylor & Francis, LTD. www.tandfonline.com.

Douglas S. Massey, Margarita Mooney, Kimberly C. Torres, and Camille Z. Charles | *Black Immigrants and Black Natives Attending Selective Colleges and Universities in the United States, 2007*

In 2004, black intellectuals Lani Guinier and Henry Louis Gates Jr. noted that because almost two-thirds of Harvard's black undergraduates were of African or West Indian descent, African Americans whose roots were anchored in American slavery were being denied opportunity.° Although most elite schools reported similar statistics, and black students were engaged in heated debate over the issue, college administrators generally avoided the sensitive subject. Several scholars decided to tackle the issue and provide hard evidence for the debate. The conclusion of their study, which is backed by thorough statistical analysis, is presented here. Consider the nature of this document: How is it both a primary and a secondary source? How is it similar to or different from other documents you have examined? And what does the document tell us about the twenty-first-century African American community? About black diversity?

° See Sara Rimer and Karen W. Arenson, "Top Colleges Take More Blacks, but Which Ones?," *New York Times*, June 24, 2004.

In recent years, observers have increasingly recognized the overrepresentation of the children of immigrants among African Americans attending selective colleges and universities in the United States, and this fact has become the focus of a vigorous debate about the purposes of affirmative action in higher education and whether blacks of immigrant origins are appropriate beneficiaries. The debate so far, however, has transpired largely in the absence of information about the phenomenon, and in this article we have drawn upon data from the National Longitudinal Survey of Freshmen to provide an empirical foundation for future discussions.

The NLSF surveyed the cohort of freshmen entering 28 selective colleges and universities in the fall of 1999. . . . In general, we found the overrepresentation of immigrants to be greater in private than in public institutions and within more rather than less selective schools. . . . Within the Ivy League, perhaps the most exclusive segment of American higher education, students of immigrant origin made up 41 percent of entering black freshmen.

Given that first- and second-generation immigrants make up just 13 percent of the African

American population, the overrepresentation of immigrant origins is substantial within all segments of elite academia. Nonetheless, data from the NLSF suggest relatively few and generally modest differences in the social origins between black students of immigrant and native origins. In terms of most indicators — income, wealth, parental employment, parental child-rearing practices, peer support, perceptions of social distance, academic preparation, and academic achievement — the two groups are virtually identical. Demographically, students of immigrant origin are . . . somewhat more likely to come from two-parent families.

Perhaps the most critical difference, however, is that black immigrant fathers were far more likely to have graduated from college and to hold advanced degrees than native fathers. Possibly as a result of this difference, immigrant children were more likely to attend private school, and in this setting they experienced a lower exposure to violence than the children of native blacks and modestly more exposure to members of other groups. Black immigrant students were more likely to have grown up within integrated neighborhoods and thus to have more nonblack friends and to have emerged from high school with a low susceptibility to peer influence. . . .

Although the NLSF data do not permit a direct assessment of the mechanism by which immigrant-origin students came to be overrepresented at elite colleges and universities, the fact that most indicators of socioeconomic status, social preparation, psychological readiness, and especially academic preparation are identical for immigrants and natives suggests that immigrant origins per se are not favored in the admissions process but, for whatever reason, children from immigrant families have come to exhibit the set of traits and characteristics valued by admissions committees, both those that are readily observable (grade point average, quality of high school, and advanced placement courses taken) and those that are more difficult to observe directly (self-esteem, self-efficacy, and social distance from whites).

The fact that immigrant parents are much better educated than native parents is consistent with an immigrant population that is highly selected for human capital and the drive to attain it, traits that are passed on to children to put them into a superior position for admission to a selective college or university. Once on campus, however, immigrant- and native-origin African Americans perform roughly at the same academic level. . . . Evidence of the high motivation and determination of immigrant-origin black students is that the process of college

grade achievement appears to be considerably more arduous for them relative to their native counterparts. Once on campus, the advantages of high parental education appear to be erased, as immigrant blacks are less able than natives to translate parental education into high grades and are less able to convert advanced placement courses and self-confidence into academic achievement.

Ultimately, the data we have presented cannot answer the question of whether the children of black immigrants are worthy beneficiaries of affirmative action, for the answer rests largely on a moral judgment about whether the policy is a form of restitution for past racial injustice or a mechanism to ensure that selective schools continue to reflect the racial and ethnic diversity of a nation that is being transformed by immigration. All we can say is that, with several notable exceptions, black immigrants and natives display similar traits and characteristics and, more important, evince equal levels of academic preparation. Whatever processes are operating on college campuses to depress black academic performance below that of whites with similar characteristics, they function for immigrants as well as natives.

* * *

Born on the streets of Harlem and the South Bronx in the late 1970s and early 1980s, hip-hop first became an artistic outlet for young people without access to expensive instruments, art materials, or formal dance classes. Soon, however, it became a metaphor for a generation. As you examine the photographs that follow, imagine how hip-hop challenged the civil rights generation's notions of blackness.

A Graffiti Artist in Long Island City, Queens, New York, 2009

At first perceived to be a form of vandalism, graffiti soon became recognized as art that could decorate rather than destroy cities. Graffiti artists needed only spray paint and blank walls or subway cars to create their supersized works. From city locations graffiti art moved to galleries, and worldwide came to represent the art of the hip-hop generation.

© *Frances Roberts/Alamy Stock Photo.*

Run-DMC, 1987

By the late 1980s, hip-hop music, with its infectious beats and rhyming poetry, had broken out of the inner city and found a huge fan base among restless youths in rural and suburban America. The radio play of groups such as Run-DMC, shown at the top of page 610, introduced hip-hop culture to the nation. The athletic clothing and brand-name sneakers worn by dancers, and the stocking caps and large gold jewelry worn by rap artists and DJs, became iconic. "Street" morphed into an ethos — an identity that could be purchased or assumed by those who had never been to a block party or called a housing project home.

© Laura Levine/Corbis.

Salt-N-Pepa, 1994

African American women also found a place behind the mic in hip-hop. In songs that dealt with black women's issues, such as domestic violence, harassment on the streets, and relationship problems, they carved out a place for themselves and changed the look and sound of hip-hop in the process. The all-female rap group Salt-N-Pepa found power in their sexuality. Bucking the trend toward the baggy athletic clothing favored by hip-hop men, Salt-N-Pepa preferred scanty, sexy clothing that revealed, rather than disguised, their bodies.

© Neal Preston/Corbis.

QUESTIONS FOR ANALYSIS

1. What role has racial unity played in the black experience in America? Does journalist Courtland Milloy have reason to worry about the future of black unity?

2. Is the black diversity evident at the turn of the millennium different from that which came before? If so, will it change the way black people define their community?

3. The Combahee River Collective believed that "if Black Women were free, it would mean that everyone else would have to be free since our freedom would necessitate the destruction of all the systems of oppression." What was the rationale behind this statement?

4. How does Cleo Manago's speech both reflect and differ from black power rhetoric? If his vision of blackness and masculinity were realized, how would black America change?

5. What trends are uncovered by the study of black immigrants, and what are the possible political, social, and economic implications? Can inferences be drawn about the future of black unity?

6. What about hip-hop culture might be troubling to some black people, and how might the hip-hop generation's ideas about black unity and community be different from those of previous generations?

NOTES

1. "Shirley Chisholm: Men in My Political Career," interview, YouTube video, 4:01, posted by "visionaryproject," April 26, 2010, http://www.youtube.com/watch?v=Hubaho0vX2U&feature=related.
2. Ibid.
3. Shirley Chisholm, *Unbought and Unbossed* (Boston: Houghton Mifflin, 1970), 67.
4. Ibid., 71, 74.
5. Ibid., 75.
6. Ibid., 103.
7. Ibid., 76.
8. Quoted in Paula Giddings, *When and Where I Enter: The Impact of Black Women on Race and Sex in America* (New York: Bantam, 1984), 337–38.
9. Quoted ibid., 339.
10. "Chisholm '72 Unbought & Unbossed Women Make Movies Clip," YouTube video, 3:09, from the documentary film *Chisholm '72 — Unbought and Unbossed* by Shola Lynch, posted by Women Make Movies, January 22, 2010, http://www.youtube.com/watch?v=vU0jtxf7-vo.
11. Quoted in Sara Diamond, *Roads to Dominion: Right-Wing Movements and Political Power in the United States* (New York: Guilford Press, 1995), 63.
12. Quoted in William H. Chafe, *The Unfinished Journey: America since World War II*, 5th ed. (New York: Oxford University Press, 2003), 364.
13. Nancy MacLean, *Freedom Is Not Enough: The Opening of the American Workplace* (Cambridge: Harvard University Press, 2006), 100.
14. Peniel E. Joseph, *Waiting 'Til the Midnight Hour: A Narrative History of Black Power in America* (New York: Henry Holt, 2006), 242.
15. Thomas J. Sugrue, *Sweet Land of Liberty: The Forgotten Struggle for Civil Rights in the North* (New York: Random House, 2008), 518.
16. Quoted in MacLean, *Freedom Is Not Enough*, 208.
17. Ibid., 233.
18. David Goldberg and Trevor Griffey, eds., *Black Power at Work: Community Control, Affirmative Action, and the Construction Industry* (Ithaca, NY: ILR Press/Cornell University Press, 2010), 135.
19. Kevin Boyle, *The UAW and the Heyday of American Liberalism, 1945–1968* (Ithaca, NY: Cornell University Press, 1998), 252–53.
20. MacLean, *Freedom Is Not Enough*, 303–4.
21. Quoted in Sugrue, *Sweet Land of Liberty*, 518–19.
22. Michelle Alexander, *The New Jim Crow: Mass Incarceration in the Age of Colorblindness* (New York: New Press, 2010), 40–57.
23. Quoted in Donna Jean Murch, *Living for the City: Migration, Education, and the Rise of the Black Panther Party in Oakland, California* (Chapel Hill: University of North Carolina Press, 2010), 173.
24. Ibid., 172.
25. Ibid., 178, 181–83.
26. Ibid., 203.
27. Annelise Orleck, *Storming Caesar's Palace: How Black Mothers Fought Their Own War on Poverty* (Boston: Beacon Press, 2005), 107.

28. Quoted in Deborah Gray White, *Too Heavy a Load: Black Women in Defense of Themselves, 1894–1994* (New York: Norton, 1999), 235.
29. Quoted ibid., 234.
30. Kimberly Springer, *Living for the Revolution: Black Feminist Organizations, 1968–1980* (Durham, NC: Duke University Press, 2005), 47–50.
31. Ibid., 186.
32. Quoted in White, *Too Heavy a Load*, 245.
33. Quoted in Springer, *Living for the Revolution*, 132–33.
34. Sugrue, *Sweet Land of Liberty*, 449–92.
35. Ibid., 465–83.
36. Ibid., 464.
37. Ibid., 476.
38. Ibid., 488.
39. Ari Berman, "The Lost Promise of the Voting Rights Act," *Atlantic*, August 5, 2015, http://www.theatlantic.com/politics /archive/2015/08/give-us-the-ballot-expanding-the -voting-rights-act/399128/.
40. DeBray "Fly Benzo" Carpenter, "Bilingual Education as It Relates to African-Americans: The Ebonics Debate," *San Francisco Bay View*, March 9, 2012, http://sfbayview .com/2012/03/bilingual-education-as-it-relates-to-african -americans-the-ebonics-debate/.
41. Brenda Stevenson, *The Contested Murder of Latasha Harlins: Justice, Gender, and the Origins of the LA Riots* (New York: Oxford University Press, 2013), 75–77.
42. David A. Bositis, *Black Elected Officials: A Statistical Summary* (Washington, DC: Joint Center for Political and Economic Studies, 1998–2009), 5.
43. Ibid., 26.
44. Ibid., 17.
45. See Frank Clemente, ed., *Keep Hope Alive: Jesse Jackson's 1988 Presidential Campaign* (Boston: South End Press, 1989).
46. Sugrue, *Sweet Land of Liberty*, 537.
47. Ibid.
48. Andrew Wiese, *Places of Their Own: African American Suburbanization in the Twentieth Century* (Chicago: University of Chicago Press, 2004), 2, 124–25, 217–18, 259, 285.
49. Quoted in Douglas S. Massey and Nancy A. Denton, *American Apartheid: Segregation and the Making of the Underclass* (Cambridge: Harvard University Press, 1993), 195–96.
50. Both quoted in Wiese, *Places of Their Own*, 228.
51. Both quoted in Sugrue, *Sweet Land of Liberty*, 425.
52. Both quoted in Wiese, *Places of Their Own*, 231.
53. Wiese, *Places of Their Own*, 254.
54. Ibid., 255.
55. Henry Louis Gates Jr., "Are We Better Off?" *Frontline*, PBS .org, 1998, http://www.pbs.org/wgbh/pages/frontline/shows /race/etc/gates.html.
56. Michael C. Dawson, *Behind the Mule: Race and Class in African-American Politics* (Princeton, NJ: Princeton University Press, 1994), 80–84.
57. See William Julius Wilson, *The Truly Disadvantaged: The Inner City, the Underclass, and Public Policy* (Chicago: University of Chicago Press, 1987), 6–8, 112–18.
58. Patricia Hill Collins, *Black Sexual Politics: African Americans, Gender, and the New Racism* (New York: Routledge, 2004), 80–81.
59. Mark Anthony Neal, "Postindustrial Soul: Black Popular Music at the Crossroads," in *That's the Joint: The Hip-Hop Studies Reader*, ed. Murray Forman and Mark Anthony Neal (New York: Routledge, 2004), 368.
60. Clarence Lusane, *Pipe Dream Blues: Racism and the War on Drugs* (Boston: South End Press, 1991), 22–25, 44–47, 62–63.
61. Ibid., 3.
62. Ibid., 55–66.
63. Chafe, *The Unfinished Journey*, 522.
64. Orleck, *Storming Caesar's Palace*, 305.
65. "Dr. Bill Cosby Speaks at the 50th Anniversary Commemoration of the *Brown vs. Topeka Board of Education* Supreme Court Decision," May 17, 2004, transcript, Eight Cities Media and Publications, http://www.eightcitiesmap.com /transcript_bc.htm.
66. Michael Eric Dyson, "The Culture of Hip-Hop," in Forman and Neal, *That's the Joint*, 62.
67. Neal, "Postindustrial Soul," 378.
68. Chafe, *The Unfinished Journey*, 518–19.
69. Toni Morrison, "Introduction: Friday on the Potomac," in *Race-ing Justice, En-Gendering Power: Essays on Anita Hill, Clarence Thomas, and the Construction of Social Reality*, ed. Toni Morrison (New York: Pantheon, 1992), xxx.
70. Quoted in Darren Lenard Hutchinson, "'Claiming' and 'Speaking' Who We Are: Black Gays and Lesbians, Racial Politics, and the Million Man March," in *Black Men on Race, Gender, and Sexuality: A Critical Reader*, ed. Devon W. Carbado (New York: New York University Press, 1999), 28.
71. Ytasha L. Womack, *Post Black: How a New Generation Is Redefining African American Identity* (Chicago: Lawrence Hill, 2010), 50–51.
72. Mary C. Waters, *Black Identities: West Indian Immigrant Dreams and American Realities* (Cambridge: Harvard University Press, 1999), 64–76.
73. W. E. Burghardt Du Bois, *The Souls of Black Folk: Essays and Sketches* (Chicago: A. C. McClurg, 1907), vii.
74. Courtland Milloy, "Awakened by Spirits of Change," *Washington Post*, October 18, 1995, Metro section, D1.
75. Deborah Gray White, *Let My People Go: African Americans, 1804–1860* (New York: Oxford University Press, 1996), 94–95.
76. Audrey Elisa Kerr, *The Paper Bag Principle: Class, Colorism, and Rumor and the Case of Black Washington, D.C.* (Knoxville: University of Tennessee Press, 2006).
77. White, *Too Heavy a Load*, 72.

SUGGESTED REFERENCES

Opposition to the Black Freedom Movement

Black, Earl, and Merle Black. *The Rise of Southern Republicans*. Cambridge: Belknap Press of Harvard University Press, 2002.

Diamond, Sara. *Roads to Dominion: Right-Wing Movements and Political Power in the United States.* New York: Guilford Press, 1995.

Ferguson, Thomas, and Joel Rogers, eds. *The Hidden Election: Politics and Economics in the 1980 Presidential Campaign.* New York: Pantheon, 1981.

———. *Right Turn: The Decline of the Democrats and the Future of American Politics.* New York: Hill and Wang, 1986.

Guinier, Lani, and Gerald Torres. *The Miner's Canary: Enlisting Race, Resisting Power, Transforming Democracy.* Cambridge: Harvard University Press, 2002.

Hancock, Ange-Marie. *The Politics of Disgust: The Public Identity of the Welfare Queen.* New York: New York University Press, 2004.

MacLean, Nancy. *Freedom Is Not Enough: The Opening of the American Workplace.* Cambridge: Harvard University Press, 2006.

McGirr, Lisa. *Suburban Warriors: The Origins of the New American Right.* Princeton, NJ: Princeton University Press, 2001.

The Persistence of the Black Freedom Struggle

Bositis, David A. *Black Elected Officials: A Statistical Summary.* Washington, DC: Joint Center for Political and Economic Studies, 1998–2009.

Dawson, Michael C. *Behind the Mule: Race and Class in African-American Politics.* Princeton, NJ: Princeton University Press, 1994.

Formisano, Ronald P. *Boston against Busing: Race, Class, and Ethnicity in the 1960s and 1970s.* 2nd rev. ed. Chapel Hill: University of North Carolina Press, 2004.

Goldberg, David, and Trevor Griffey, eds. *Black Power at Work: Community Control, Affirmative Action, and the Construction Industry.* Ithaca, NY: ILR Press/Cornell University Press, 2010.

Hero, Rodney E., and Robert R. Preuhs. *Black-Latino Relations in U.S. National Politics: Beyond Conflict or Cooperation.* New York: Cambridge University Press, 2013.

Horne, Gerald. *Fire This Time: The Watts Uprising and the 1960s.* New York: Da Capo Press, 1997.

Massey, Douglas S., and Nancy A. Denton. *American Apartheid: Segregation and the Making of the Underclass.* Cambridge: Harvard University Press, 1993.

Murch, Donna Jean. *Living for the City: Migration, Education, and the Rise of the Black Panther Party in Oakland, California.* Chapel Hill: University of North Carolina Press, 2010.

Orleck, Annelise. *Storming Caesar's Palace: How Black Mothers Fought Their Own War on Poverty.* Boston: Beacon Press, 2005.

Podair, Jerald E. *The Strike That Changed New York: Blacks, Whites, and the Ocean Hill–Brownsville Crisis.* New Haven, CT: Yale University Press, 2008.

Springer, Kimberly. *Living for the Revolution: Black Feminist Organizations, 1968–1980.* Durham, NC: Duke University Press, 2005.

Stevenson, Brenda. *The Contested Murder of Latasha Harlins: Justice, Gender, and the Origins of the LA Riots.* New York: Oxford University Press, 2013.

Sugrue, Thomas J. *Sweet Land of Liberty: The Forgotten Struggle for Civil Rights in the North.* New York: Random House, 2008.

White, Deborah Gray. *Too Heavy a Load: Black Women in Defense of Themselves, 1894–1994.* New York: Norton, 1999.

Wiese, Andrew. *Places of Their Own: African American Suburbanization in the Twentieth Century.* Chicago: University of Chicago Press, 2004.

The Different Faces of Black America

Alexander, Michelle. *The New Jim Crow: Mass Incarceration in the Age of Colorblindness.* New York: New Press, 2010.

Chisholm, Shirley. *The Good Fight.* New York: Harper & Row, 1973.

———. *Unbought and Unbossed.* Boston: Houghton Mifflin, 1970.

Collins, Patricia Hill. *Black Sexual Politics: African Americans, Gender, and the New Racism.* New York: Routledge, 2004.

Forman, Murray, and Mark Anthony Neal, eds. *That's the Joint: The Hip-Hop Studies Reader.* New York: Routledge, 2004.

Giddings, Paula. *When and Where I Enter: The Impact of Black Women on Race and Sex in America.* New York: Bantam, 1984.

Johnson, E. Patrick, and Mae G. Henderson, eds. *Black Queer Studies: A Critical Anthology.* Durham, NC: Duke University Press, 2005.

Lusane, Clarence. *Pipe Dream Blues: Racism and the War on Drugs.* Boston: South End Press, 1991.

Morrison, Toni, ed. *Race-ing Justice, En-Gendering Power: Essays on Anita Hill, Clarence Thomas, and the Construction of Social Reality.* New York: Pantheon, 1992.

Waters, Mary C. *Black Identities: West Indian Immigrant Dreams and American Realities.* Cambridge: Harvard University Press, 1999.

Wilson, William Julius. *The Truly Disadvantaged: The Inner City, the Underclass, and Public Policy.* Chicago: University of Chicago Press, 1987.

Womack, Ytasha L. *Post Black: How a New Generation Is Redefining African American Identity.* Chicago: Lawrence Hill, 2010.

African Americans and the New Century

2000–Present

CHRONOLOGY *Events specific to African American history are in purple. General United States history events are in black.*

2000	Barack Obama loses bid for House of Representatives to former Black Panther Bobby Rush
	George W. Bush elected president
2001	*Freestyle* exhibition debuts post-black art in Harlem
	Al Qaeda terrorists crash hijacked planes into World Trade Center, Pentagon, and field in Pennsylvania
	Afghanistan War begins
2003–2011	Iraq War
2004	Bill Cosby delivers Pound Cake speech
	Bush reelected president
	Obama elected to U.S. Senate
2005	Hurricane Katrina devastates Gulf coast
2006	Democrats retake control of both houses of Congress
	Six black teenagers charged with attempted murder in Jena Six case
2007	*Washington Post* reporter Eugene Robinson declares end to monolithic black America
2008	Obama delivers historic speech on race, "A More Perfect Union"
	Global financial crisis begins
	Obama elected first African American president
2009	Michael Steele becomes head of Republican National Committee
	Eric Holder becomes first African American attorney general of the United States
	American Recovery and Reinvestment Act (ARRA)
	Henry Louis Gates Jr. arrested at his home in Cambridge, Massachusetts
	Obama wins Nobel Peace Prize

2010	Obama signs health care reform bill
	Republicans gain seats in U.S. Senate, win majority of seats in House of Representatives
2011	Osama bin Laden, head of Al Qaeda, killed by U.S. forces
	Obama certifies that gays and lesbians can serve openly in military
2012	Black teenager Trayvon Martin fatally shot by George Zimmerman in Sanford, Florida
	Obama announces that his views have evolved such that he endorses same-sex marriage
	Obama issues executive order preventing deportation of some young immigrants
	Obama reelected president
2013	#BlackLivesMatter founded after acquittal of George Zimmerman
2014	Obama launches My Brother's Keeper
	Eric Garner dies after being choked by New York police officer Daniel Pantaleo
	Black teenager Michael Brown fatally shot by Ferguson, Missouri, police officer Darren Wilson
2015	Loretta Lynch becomes first African American woman to hold position of attorney general of the United States
	Obama announces that American troops will stay in Afghanistan until 2017
	Obama establishes diplomatic relations with Cuba
2016	Hillary Clinton becomes the first woman to be nominated by a major party for president

Barack Hussein Obama, America's Forty-Fourth President

By the time Barack Obama left his high-paying job at a Manhattan consulting firm to become a community organizer, the national civil rights and black power movements of the 1960s and early 1970s were a fading memory. It was 1983, and although the future president was unsure about what a community organizer did, he was certain that change needed to occur on the local level. With few exceptions, those around him greeted his aspirations with disappointment and skepticism. Ike, a black security guard who worked in Obama's office building, advised, "Organizing? . . . Why you wanna do something like that? . . . Forget about this organizing business and do something that's gonna make you some money. . . . Young man like you, got a nice voice — hell, you could be one a them announcers on TV. Or sales. . . . That's what we need, see. Not more folks running around here, all rhymes and jive. You can't help folks that ain't gonna make it nohow, and they won't appreciate you trying. Folks that wanna make it, they gonna find a way to do it on they own."[1]

Ike's blunt but well-meaning advice grew from his having seen the workplace open for black people. Jobs that had once been the exclusive reserve of white men were, by the mid-1980s, available to minorities and women. Millions of people of color were in higher occupational categories than they had been twenty years earlier.[2] The better-off black working and middle classes had narrowed the gap in earnings that had once existed between college-educated blacks and whites. There were advances in politics as well: In 1965, there were only about 100 black elected officials in the nation. Ten years later, there were 3,500. As blacks became the mayors of major cities, African Americans gained greater access to municipal services and employment opportunities. The number of black businesses likewise increased. In 1960, black-owned businesses numbered approximately 32,000; by 1977 that number had grown to 231,000. Given all the opportunities that seemed to be opening up, Ike had good reason to advise the aspiring young Obama to shoot for the moon.

Obama was mindful of these gains, but he thought they could be sustained only by people committed to organizing the poor at the grassroots level. In 1985, his commitment took him to Altgeld Gardens, a public housing project on Chicago's South Side, where 5,300 African Americans eked out an existence amid an abandoned steel mill, a toxic landfill, and a rancid sewage plant. Altgeld Gardens presented the kinds of problems Obama wanted to address. By the 1980s, it had been abandoned not only by whites who had left the city for the suburbs but also by blacks who had left the inner city for the inner suburbs.

Like other urban centers, Chicago had sworn in its first black mayor, Harold Washington, two years before Obama arrived. Washington, however, faced the same problems as other inner-city mayors. Chicago had lost a good portion of its middle- and upper-class residents, as well as its industrial plants. Consequently, its tax base had shrunk, leaving Washington with limited resources to address the poverty, homelessness, single-parent households, crime, drug addiction, and deteriorating health conditions that plagued the city's poor. Even if the mostly female residents of Altgeld Gardens could get Washington's attention — a big if — it was unlikely that the mayor could fix even a small part of this ailing South Side community.

Obama worked among the residents of Altgeld Gardens for three years before deciding that he would be more effective with a law degree. After graduating from Harvard Law School in 1991 and beginning a political career, he lost his 2000 bid for the U.S. House of Representatives to the Democratic incumbent, Bobby Rush, a former Black Panther who beat Obama decisively in an election nicknamed "the Black Panther against the professor." The

A Young Barack Obama with His Grandparents
Of biracial descent, Obama was born in Hawaii and raised mostly by his maternal grandparents, Stanley and Madelyn Dunham. His Ivy League education, political acumen, and charismatic personality identified him as someone who transcended race even before he became the first black president of the United States in 2009. *Reuters/Landov.*

election epitomized the tensions in black America at the turn of the millennium. Generational tensions were clear as Rush, by now part of the old guard, defended his turf against the younger newcomer, who had the kind of education that most people of Rush's generation could only dream of. Class tensions also surfaced, as did the perennial issue of race, which in 2000 presented itself differently than it had before. Obama, a lecturer at the University of Chicago who lived in the posh Hyde Park section of the South Side, connected with his district's white constituency but failed to do so with the black working-class residents of the predominantly black community. "Is Obama really black? Is he black enough?" These questions reverberated throughout millennial elections in places where a new, well-educated black leadership class was emerging. They reflected the new reality of black Americans — a reality that was representative of both the advances that had occurred and the divisiveness that flowed from them.

The choices Obama had available to him, the dilemmas he faced, the world he knew — these were familiar to turn-of-the-twenty-first-century African Americans. It was a period marked by the expansion of a middle class that could take advantage of the opportunities Ike, the security guard, had alluded to. Yet this period was also marked by widespread surveillance that gave rise to the highest incarceration rates black America had ever experienced. It also was marked by the irony exposed when black citizens in New Orleans and the Gulf coast region were abandoned during Hurricane Katrina by a government whose secretary of state was African American. It was a period that saw those who came of age during the civil rights and black power movements — movements built on black unity and communalism — hand over leadership and culture to a new generation that venerated individualism and diversity. In sum, this period reflected the hope that fueled Obama's successful run for president in 2008 but also the harsh realities that made "change" the enduring slogan of his campaign.

Diversity and Racial Belonging

In October 2007, the *Washington Post* reporter and columnist Eugene Robinson wrote an op-ed piece proclaiming that "if there ever was a monolithic 'black America' — absolutely and uniformly deprived and aggrieved, with invariant values and attitudes — there certainly isn't one now." Robinson, an African American, called for "a new language, a new vocabulary and syntax," because, he claimed, "'black America' is an increasingly meaningless concept."[3] One month later, the Pew Research Center, an independent, nonpartisan public opinion research organization, found that 37 percent of African Americans agreed with Robinson, believing that "because of the diversity within their community, blacks can no longer be thought of as a single race."[4] The following year, the award-winning black novelist, screenwriter, and scholar Charles Johnson published an article provocatively titled "The End of the Black American Narrative." In it, Johnson argued that the narrative of victimization—of slavery, segregation, and legal disfranchisement—needed revision. "In the 21st century," Johnson stated, "we need new and better stories, new concepts, and new vocabularies and grammar based not on the past but on the dangerous, exciting, and unexplored present." Johnson argued that for better or worse, this was what Martin Luther King Jr. had dreamed of when he hoped a day would come when men and women were judged not by the color of their skin, but by their individual deeds and the content of their character. Johnson was pleased that the new stories would be "narratives of individuals, not groups."[5]

Although African America had always been diverse, seldom had its internal divisions been as public as they were at the start of the twenty-first century. Its diversity had never before prevented African Americans from defining themselves as a "community," bound by a heritage of oppression and united by their need for self-defense. Things were changing at the turn of the millennium. As black people became more secure about their freedom, they were more willing to think and speak publicly about their nonracial identities and to question the need for racial solidarity. In short, a growing number of black people were beginning to construct new ideas about racial belonging.

New Categories of Difference

Turn-of-the-century black America had come to be characterized by class, gender, sexuality, and generational diversity (see chapter 14). There was, however, another way to characterize difference in black America: namely, by the way various groups related to American institutions. Similar in many respects to the twentieth-century categories delineating the middle and working classes and the underclass or truly disadvantaged, this new categorization spoke also to black America's perception of racial progress and its sense of racial and national belonging.[6]

Middle- and working-class African Americans entered the new century more confident about their American citizenship than were previous generations. To be sure, however, at no time during the first decade of the twenty-first century did this group of mainstream blacks reach equality with whites. In 2006, for example, the black median household income was just 61 percent of the white median household income, and in 2010 the National Urban League calculated the equality index—the relative status of blacks versus whites in American society—at 71.8 percent.[7] Nevertheless, by 2010 almost half of all African American families, or about six million households, had become wealthy enough to own their homes, and a fourth of black adults worked in management or professional jobs. Seventeen percent of African American households, or 2.4 million, had an annual income of $75,000 or more, and although these mainstreamers suffered a setback in the 2008 financial collapse, if they constituted a sovereign nation, it would have the seventeenth-largest economy in the world—larger than that of Turkey, Saudi Arabia, or South Africa.[8]

These African Americans were characteristically optimistic about America and their place in the nation. Previous generations of affluent and middle- and working-class

African Americans had achieved much, but they had been subject to pogroms, disfranchisement, lynching, and Jim Crow segregation. Despite the fact that twenty-first-century African Americans still paid what was termed the **black tax** — meaning that they needed to work twice as hard as whites to achieve the same outcomes and were held responsible for the negative actions of other blacks — middle- and working-class blacks nevertheless felt freer, and were in fact freer, than any previous generation of African Americans. More of them than ever before accepted the advice of the black cultural critic Debra Dickerson, who told them to "surrender themselves to America" and "give themselves permission to be happy Yanks and well-adjusted Westerners."[9]

The less advantaged were not receptive to this advice. Living at or below the poverty line, which at the turn of the century was about $8,000 in annual income for one person and roughly $17,000 for a family of four, about one-quarter of the African American population felt abandoned. "They really don't care too much," said a welfare recipient when asked what she thought Congress felt about women on welfare.[10] Since almost half (48 percent) of all black families were single-parent, female-headed households, an astonishingly large proportion of those below the poverty line were women and children. Without stable employment (the unemployment rate for African Americans in 2010 was 15.4 percent, compared to 8.6 percent for whites), there was no way for these lower-class blacks to live the American dream of home ownership. The victims of the most intense police surveillance, poor blacks attended the worst schools in the nation, lived in the most dilapidated housing, had the least access to hospitals, were the most likely victims of crimes, and were the most likely to be exposed to the illicit drug and sex trade economy. Many felt unworthy. Describing how poverty generated feelings of shame within many in the black community, a mother of an incarcerated teenager lamented, "We hate ourselves. . . . We have been programmed that it's something that's wrong with us."[11] The nation was also programmed to think this way. Featured as deviants on the evening news each night, the black poor were held in disdain by many whites who took them as representative of all blacks, and by many middle- and working-class blacks who held them responsible for the continued discrimination they faced.

A few blacks, called the "Transcendent" by Eugene Robinson, managed to escape racial identification altogether. Although wealth was not their only asset — education and talent were important, too — the color green influenced their lives more than their brown skin did. According to Robinson, Oprah Winfrey belonged in this group, as did sports stars such as Michael Jordan and Tiger Woods, actors such as Will Smith, media moguls such as Robert L. Johnson of Black Entertainment Television, and CEOs such as Ursula M. Burns at Xerox and Kenneth Chenault at American Express. In 2010, for example, Oprah Winfrey's entertainment and lifestyle empire was estimated at $2 billion. The seven million viewers who watched Oprah's daily talk show did not associate her with Reagan's welfare queen (see chapter 14) or the poor woman heading up a single-parent household. For all practical purposes, Winfrey and these other African Americans transcended race. More numerous than at any other time in history, this group, having achieved fame, prosperity, and power, were not just black Americans who had done well; they were quintessentially American and recognized as such at home and abroad.[12]

These people seemed to have escaped blackness, but there were others who were still striving to sidestep their black identity. In 2007, one in four black people in New York, Massachusetts, and Minnesota was foreign-born, and immigrants made up one-fifth of the black population in Florida and Washington State. They came to this country to take advantage of its economic opportunities and political and social freedoms and to be upwardly mobile — not part of a disparaged minority. In 2009, researchers found that compared to native-born blacks, more black immigrants went to college, and they were also more likely to come from households where both parents were highly educated (Map 15.1). Before the early 2000s, segregation had made it difficult for black immigrants to distance themselves from African America, and in fact many, such as the Jamaican immigrant Marcus Garvey (see chapter 10), became outspoken leaders for African American rights. In the last decade, however, the sheer numbers of black immigrants have enabled the creation of distinct communities apart from African Americans. As black immigrants move up the socioeconomic ladder and into integrated middle-class communities, they can, if they so choose, escape native-born African Americans altogether.

Children with one black parent and one white parent also viewed themselves as apart from the category of "black" or "African American." According to the 2000 census, the first census that let respondents self-identify as belonging to more than one race, 785,000 — or about 11 percent — claimed to be half black and half white. The number of biracials is actually estimated to be larger than that because, historically, a person with any "black blood" was defined as black, and biracials — especially those with discernible black pigmentation or features — typically checked only the "black" box on the census. Because biracials often had a white parent who protected and provided for them, they disproportionately became leaders of black America. Now there is the potential for biracials to become a separate group.

Though accounting for only a small percentage of the population in 2000, biracials were on the rise as more blacks and whites expressed favorable views of interracial marriage. In 2008, for example, 22 percent of black male newlyweds and 9 percent of black female newlyweds married outside their race. By 2013, the percentages had increased to 25 and 12 percent for black males and females, respectively. Like most immigrants, whatever their race or ethnicity, many biracials wanted to be American more than they wanted to be black or white. Whether torn between two countries, two races, or two ethnicities, this ever-growing group did not want to have to choose.[13]

Solidarity, Culture, and the Meaning of Blackness

Throughout most of the twentieth century, black solidarity could be counted on to challenge the economic and political injustices caused by racism. But twenty-first-century diversity has the potential to undermine this staple of black self-defense.

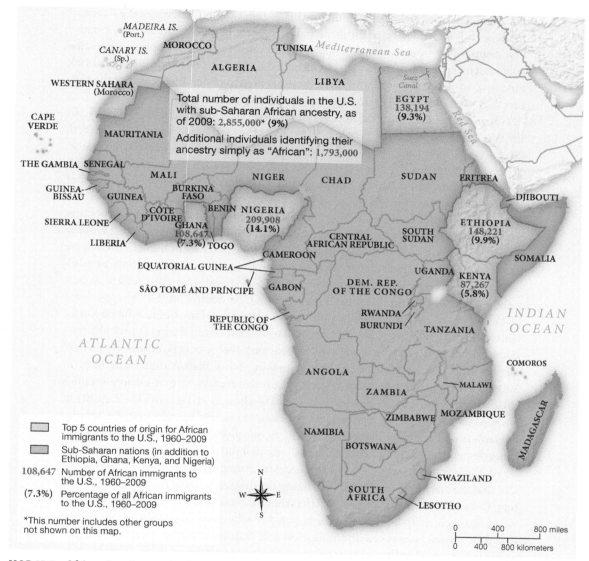

Total number of individuals in the U.S. with sub-Saharan African ancestry, as of 2009: 2,855,000* (9%)

Additional individuals identifying their ancestry simply as "African": 1,793,000

EGYPT 138,194 (9.3%)

NIGERIA 209,908 (14.1%)

GHANA 108,647 (7.3%)

ETHIOPIA 148,221 (9.9%)

KENYA 87,267 (5.8%)

Map legend:

- Top 5 countries of origin for African immigrants to the U.S., 1960–2009
- Sub-Saharan nations (in addition to Ethiopia, Ghana, Kenya, and Nigeria)

108,647 Number of African immigrants to the U.S., 1960–2009

(7.3%) Percentage of all African immigrants to the U.S., 1960–2009

*This number includes other groups not shown on this map.

0   400   800 miles
0   400   800 kilometers

MAP 15.1   African Immigrants in the Twentieth and Twenty-First Centuries

Recent black immigrants, whose top five countries of origin are shown here, have become an increasingly numerous and significant portion of America's black population. Such immigrants often do not see themselves as racially, ethnically, or culturally related to African Americans. Nevertheless, millions of nonimmigrant black Americans view themselves as sharing a common ethnic heritage with these more recent arrivals.

For example, in the twentieth century the black upper class — known as the "talented tenth" — was depended on to speak for, indeed represent, the race. In the early twenty-first century, the best-educated, wealthiest, and most prominent African Americans could not be counted on to do that. For most of the twentieth century, even when black men and women saw issues differently, they marched together. By the end of the century, however, they found themselves marching separately.

This is suggested by the passionate discussion of "blackness" and who is "black." In the twentieth century, black people debated what they wanted to be *called* — colored, Negro, Afro-American, African American, black — but not who was actually black. When the professional golfer Tiger Woods called himself a "Cablinasian" in recognition of his white, black, American Indian, and Asian ancestry, he set off a firestorm of debate. Online news forums lit up with commentary: Some argued that Woods was not black but biracial. Others believed that he had earned his black credentials because he had experienced racism, with one commentator arguing that "before he [Woods] was famous, there were golf clubs in the U.S. that wouldn't let him play." There were those who held the opinion that "African-American isn't [as] much of a race as it is a culture, so him being black is an incorrect term." And there were many who were outright angry about his transcendent status: "F him if he doesn't want to be considered black. When his fame has ended and white people turn on him, because he no longer benefits them, he'll want to be black."[14] Similar issues emerged during Barack Obama's 2008 presidential campaign, with many believing that Obama's midwestern white mother and Kenyan father made him something other than African American. In 2006, the novelist and columnist Stanley Crouch proclaimed that Obama was not "black like me" because he "did not — does not — share a heritage with the majority of black Americans, who are descendants of plantation slaves."[15] Said Debra Dickerson, the author of *The End of Blackness*, " 'Black,' in our political and social reality, means those descended from West African slaves," and that did not include Obama.[16]

Although there was never a time in African American history when it could be said that "all black people think alike," during the first ten years of the twenty-first century, researchers found a "values gap" that showed racial unity on important issues to be on the decline. To be sure, when compared to whites, black people on average felt that they experienced more discrimination and that the criminal justice system was unfair to blacks. More blacks than whites said that poor schools, high dropout rates, unwed motherhood, and poor housing were real problems in their communities. Yet in 2007 and 2010, slightly more than half of all black people believed that "blacks who cannot get ahead in this country are mainly responsible for their own situation." Only about a third (34 percent) said that racial discrimination was the reason blacks did not advance. This was an astounding change from 1994, when a majority felt that racial discrimination held blacks back. Economics and generation made the difference. More affluent and better-educated African Americans were not only less concerned about job discrimination, unwed motherhood, and crime, but, along with younger blacks, they were also more likely to believe that blacks and whites had a lot in common and that the black middle class and poor were growing apart. This, too, had changed over time. In 1986, there was less divergence between the black poor and middle class on these issues.[17]

These changes were reflected in black culture. The Black Arts Movement (see chapter 13) had been founded on the ideas that black art had to mirror the black experience, advance the politics of freedom, and boost the psychological morale of African Americans, and it emphasized the notion that black and white art were fundamentally different. The *Freestyle* exhibition, which debuted at the Studio Museum in Harlem in 2001, announced a new direction for black art. According to Thelma Golden, the museum's chief curator, the exhibition embodied a new **post-black** art in that it "was characterized by artists who were adamant about not being labeled as 'black' artists, though their work was steeped, in fact deeply interested, in redefining complex notions of blackness."[18] As explained by Golden and some of the exhibition's artists, blackness had new meaning in the twenty-first century. There were so many ways to be black that "black" had lost its meaning as a signifier of identity. Ironically, the unifying force of this exhibition was "individuality," which gave birth to the title *Freestyle*. Like the improvisational musician, who "finds the groove and goes all out in a relentless and unbridled expression of the self," Golden believed that black artists and black people needed to free themselves from old ideas about blackness and be whoever they could and wanted to be.[19]

Throughout the first decade of the twenty-first century, the idea of post-blackness stirred up intense debate among artists, writers, social critics, and scholars. Many agreed with museum curator Thelma Golden and sided with art historian Michael Harris, who argued that "an African American artist needs a cultural rootedness as a foundation."[20] But the Harvard scholar Henry Louis Gates Jr. doubted the utility of such a foundation. There were "forty million ways" to be black, he argued. The writer and cultural critic Touré concurs, "There is no dogmatically narrow, authentic Blackness because the possibilities for Black identity are infinite."[21] The San Francisco–based artist John Bankston thought post-blackness was impossible, because work by black artists will always be interpreted in terms of race and work by white artists will always be characterized by the absence of race.[22] The black British novelist Zadie Smith countered that race itself had gained new meaning. "The reality of race has diversified," she said. White people did not speak with one voice, and neither did black people. While she understood the utility of black unity, Smith also thought that unity had "confined and restricted" blackness, making it "a sort of prison cell, two feet by five," in which no black person could live comfortably.[23]

Diversity in Politics and Religion

That black people in the early 2000s did not speak with one voice was evident in the political realm. A small minority of African Americans self-identified as conservatives, believing that blacks who had not advanced should blame it on their own inability to compete, deficient values, and victimization mentality. They endorsed the belief that

***Rashid Johnson,* China Gates, 2008**
Post-black art such as Rashid Johnson's *China Gates*, a freestanding steel sculpture, is not immediately recognizable as "black art." Artists of this genre emphasize the diversity of the black experience and the individuality of the artist, and the art they produce is often conceptual and enigmatic in nature. They depart from the tradition of the Black Arts Movement in that they feel they do not have to directly represent black people as a group. *Rashid Johnson, China Gates, 2008. Steel, brass, shea butter, and incense. 66 x 48 x 18 in. (67.64 x 121.92 x 45.72 cm.). Inv# RJ 09.054. Courtesy of David Kordansky Gallery, Los Angeles, California.*

affirmative action was harmful because its beneficiaries could never be fully confident that their success stemmed from their talent and because it engendered a backlash. On welfare, conservatives felt that the single parenthood and crime found in black communities could be traced to social welfare programs that fostered a debilitating dependency and irresponsible behavior. Welfare is "a license not to develop," argued the prominent black conservative Shelby Steele in 2001. Steele felt that welfare "all but mandated inner-city inertia, . . . destroyed the normal human relationship to work and family, and . . . turned the values of hard work, sacrifice, and delayed gratification into a fool's game."[24]

Although the number of African Americans who self-identified as conservative was small, a much larger number of blacks held conservative opinions on a wide variety of issues. Again, welfare is a good example. When researchers asked Americans whether or not they agreed with the statement "Many people today think they can get ahead without working hard and making sacrifices," there were only modest differences between whites and African Americans: Sixty-one percent of whites and 56 percent of African Americans agreed. When researchers presented the statement "Poor people have become too dependent on government assistance programs," the responses from blacks and whites again differed only slightly. Blacks still believed that affirmative action programs were necessary, but a majority agreed with Shelby Steele, who advocated self-help and argued that "a group is no stronger than its individuals; when individuals transform themselves they transform the group; the freer the individual, the stronger the group; social responsibility begins in individual responsibility."[25] Ike, the security guard who encouraged Barack Obama, put it differently: "Folks that wanna make it, they gonna find a way to do it on they own."

Black diversity also spawned new attitudes about black leadership. For most of the twentieth century, when a black leader spoke for the race, he or she spoke for most black people. As journalist Eugene Robinson wrote, "What was good for poor people was good for black people, since so many black people were poor. Conversely, what was good for rich people was bad for black people, since so few black people were rich." Similarly, "what was good for the established order was bad for black people, who didn't belong to the Establishment."[26] In the twenty-first century, a variety of leaders emerged to represent different segments of black America and the American population in general, and fewer race men and women — blacks who dedicated their lives to working for and representing African Americans — took up the cause of civil rights. According to National Football League Hall of Famer Lynn Swann, who in 2006 ran for governor of Pennsylvania on the Republican ticket, "We as African-Americans are as diversified as any group. . . . I don't think we have real freedom unless we have real choices." Although most African Americans are Democrats, other black Republicans running for office in 2006 included Maryland's lieutenant governor, Michael Steele, who ran for the U.S. Senate, and Ohio's secretary of state, Ken Blackwell, who ran for governor. "African Americans don't have monolithic thought," said Deval Patrick, a black Democrat who was elected governor of Massachusetts in 2006. "It's a new day and a new way," said Charles Steele, head of the Southern Christian Leadership Conference from 2004 to 2009, touting the veteran civil rights organization's new slogan.[27]

The new day and new way gave rise to a new kind of black politician and a politics that reified black diversity. Mayors such as Cory Booker of Newark, New Jersey, and Adrian Fenty of Washington, D.C., and congressmen such as Harold Ford of Tennessee and Artur Davis of Alabama were heirs to privileges that the civil rights generation fought for and won. According to the Stanford-educated Booker, "The civil rights generation . . . had tremendous challenges; and because of their successes, they opened up doors."[28] Unlike the politicians of the 1970s and 1980s, who emerged out of the civil rights struggle and served a constituency that was overwhelmingly African American, early-twenty-first-century black politicians represented diverse communities. Like Barack Obama, whose Hyde Park district was 35 percent white when he first ran for Congress, new black politicians had to appeal to a wider constituency and also satisfy the demands of the business people and financiers who backed them. "We're not trying to integrate lunch counters so much," said Michigan state senator Bert Johnson during his 2012 bid to unseat civil rights worker and founding Congressional Black Caucus member John Conyers Jr.[29] Some, like Booker, minimized the differences between the old and new guard. "It's just a different set of challenges," said Booker. He added, "Our community needs everyone. We need not start separating a people and talking about disconnects. We need a full team on the field."[30] Others were not so sure. When asked about the relevance of people such as the Reverend Jesse Jackson — the veteran head of the Chicago-based Rainbow PUSH (People United to Serve Humanity) Coalition who was trained and mentored by Martin Luther King Jr. — a young African American minister suggested that younger blacks faced different problems and needed their own set of

T. D. Jakes
The Reverend T. D. Jakes, pastor of the nondenominational Potter's House in Dallas, Texas, delivers mesmerizing sermons, writes compelling moralizing novels, and produces movies centered on the pressures of modern family life. His 30,000-member congregation exemplifies the new black megachurches, where ministers resemble corporate CEOs as much as they do the Pentecostal preachers of the past. *John Bazemore/Associated Press/AP Images.*

leaders: "The reality is most of our traditional civil rights leaders don't have a clue about the hip-hop community. It's not a part of their understanding."[31]

The new generation of African Americans also had a different understanding of the **black church**. Just as the late twentieth and early twenty-first centuries marked a transformation in black diversity, these years saw a change in the makeup and leadership of churches with predominantly black congregations. In its size and theology, the twenty-first-century black megachurch was different from the denominationally based neighborhood congregations of the twentieth century. Since most black churches have traditionally been congregational, or not bound to follow the dictates of an overarching governing body, there has always been great diversity in and among black congregations. But in general, the 1950s saw most black churches prioritize issues of social justice. Pastors such as Martin Luther King Jr. and Ralph Abernathy preached the gospel but also became leaders of the civil rights struggle. Churches such as the Holt Street Baptist Church, where the Montgomery bus boycott was organized (see chapter 12), or St. Augustine's Episcopal Church, where the Oakland Black Panthers operated their breakfast program (see chapter 14), were both places of worship and centers of cooperative social justice movements. The new black megachurch departed from the social justice model. Like the *Freestyle* art exhibition that premiered post-black art, most black megachurches encouraged individual internal reflection and promoted an individualistic theology of self-empowerment. Additionally, unlike old guard churches that served people who lived relatively close by, these congregations numbered upwards of 2,000 members. Though grounded in the African American emotional and musical heritage, especially the Pentecostal tradition, they were often nondenominational, led by pastors with college and advanced degrees, and located in suburbs inaccessible by public transportation.

Pastored by T. D. Jakes, the 30,000-member, nondenominational Potter's House was representative of the new black church. In many ways, this Dallas, Texas, megachurch, founded in 1996, resembled a corporation, and Jakes a chief executive officer. TDJ Enterprises produced television and radio shows, films, and records. Like Oprah Winfrey, Jakes appealed not just to black Americans but, through his various media outlets, to all Americans. He was even favorably compared to the white evangelist the Reverend Billy Graham, who for years was known as "America's Preacher."[32] Unapologetic about his wealth and lavish lifestyle, Jakes, like most megachurch leaders, appealed to middle- and working-class blacks, who also increasingly believed that personal autonomy was the best counter to racism and that those who accepted personal responsibility for their actions would reap God's reward of grace and a comfortable life.[33]

Thus the new century found black America facing new challenges. Black people were relating to the nation, to themselves, and to one another differently. There was a new culture, a new politics, a new church life, and a new theology. As the first decade of this new century progressed, these changes would play out not in a vacuum, but on a transformative stage filled with both tragedy and joy.

Trying Times

The first years of the new millennium were trying ones in many ways. Black Americans had to work through their issues with diversity while responding to a nation that had, since the black freedom struggle, moved consistently to the right. Just how difficult this would be was suggested by a 2001 U.S. Civil Rights Commission investigation that found that officials in Florida had effectively disfranchised large numbers of traditionally Democratic African American voters, thus giving George W. Bush a victory in the 2000 presidential election.

African Americans also had to reconcile racial loyalty with a diverse black leadership. Black officeholders, like their white counterparts, could be corrupt and ineffective. They could champion the causes of the black middle class over the lower classes, or they could bypass racial issues altogether and prioritize their individual needs or the needs of their political party. With no movement and fewer leaders to champion the cause of civil rights, African Americans had to navigate the twenty-first-century terrain without an ancestral road map to guide them. The continued rise of the carceral state, the wars in Afghanistan and Iraq, and the disaster in the aftermath of Hurricane Katrina showed how bumpy the terrain had become.

The Carceral State, or "the New Jim Crow"

African Americans watched the rightward turn of the judicial system with dismay. Each election that brought a Republican president to the helm brought fears that the accomplishments of the freedom struggle would be transformed, if not actually undone, by a judicial system that endorsed the conservative ideas of reverse discrimination and color blindness. African Americans, especially those of the middle and working classes, focused their attention on affirmative action cases, where the Supreme Court increasingly narrowed the circumstances under which racial preferences could be used. They saw the policy officially disappear in California, Washington, Michigan, Nebraska, and Texas when those states passed propositions and legislation banning any kind of affirmative action.

While the black middle and working classes focused on these judicial and legislative setbacks, laws that imprisoned hundreds of thousands of African Americans for drug possession were making life for all African Americans more difficult. In 1972, fewer than 350,000 people were being held in prisons and jails nationwide; that number had risen to more than 2 million by 2010. Drug possession accounted for the astronomical increase, and black men were disproportionately imprisoned. (See By the Numbers: Black Male Incarceration Rates, 2000–2009.) Despite the fact that the National Institute on Drug Abuse and the National Household Survey on Drug Abuse reported in 2000 that "white students use cocaine at seven times the rate of black students, use crack cocaine at eight times the rate of black students, and use heroin at seven times the rate of black students," and that whites between the ages of twelve and seventeen were "more than a third more likely to have sold illegal drugs than African American youth," black juveniles were punished more severely than white juveniles. Although the majority of illegal drug users and dealers nationwide were white, three-fourths of all people imprisoned for drug offenses were black or Hispanic. Young black offenders were more likely to be transferred to adult courts and to receive longer sentences. Whereas white juveniles were more likely to be sentenced to serve time in jails, small local lockups that could be easily visited by family and friends, blacks were more likely to be sent to prisons, large facilities far from home.[34]

These disproportionate incarceration rates can be traced, in general, back to the "law and order" agenda that conservatives adopted in the wake of the black freedom movement, and specifically to the Reagan administration's war on drugs (see chapter 14). State and federal laws criminalized the possession of small amounts of drugs and condemned not only those individuals who possessed drugs but also anyone who was in the company of someone with drugs. These laws and court decisions eliminated protection against unreasonable searches and seizures and allowed police to use traffic violations, however minor, to conduct drug searches. They also gave police permission to stop and frisk anyone who looked suspicious. **Mandatory sentencing laws**, which stipulated minimum sentences for certain crimes and disallowed discretionary sentencing by judges and juries who could weigh the facts of a case when imposing penalties, and mandatory three-strikes laws, which could and did condemn nonviolent offenders to extremely long and sometimes life sentences, also accounted for the high imprisonment rate.[35]

The effects of these "zero tolerance" measures on African Americans were, and continue to be, devastating. One scholar has called the mass incarceration of blacks "the new Jim Crow" because, like legal segregation, it is a system of racialized social control that maintains the racial hierarchy and "locks a huge percentage of the African

BY THE NUMBERS Black Male Incarceration Rates, 2000–2009

As this figure illustrates, at the end of the twentieth century and beginning of the twenty-first, African American men were incarcerated at rates entirely out of proportion with their numbers in the general population. Black men have always been subject to stricter police surveillance, but harsh new drug laws imposing stiffer penalties and mandatory minimum sentences disproportionately affected African Americans and compounded the problem significantly. Additionally, when convicted, black offenders were more likely than white offenders to be sentenced to time in large prisons rather than local jails.

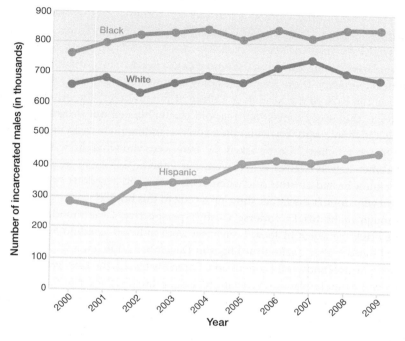

American community out of the mainstream society and economy."[36] Others use the term **carceral state** to indicate the extensive surveillance and penalties employed to restrict the movement of black people and control their behavior. Incarcerated blacks have no social mobility, not just because they are locked behind bars but also because once they have served their time and are released, they are burdened with disabilities that make it impossible for them to be contributing members of any community and make it probable that they will be reimprisoned. Drug felons, even those convicted for minor infractions, are barred by law from public housing, discriminated against by private landlords, ineligible for food stamps, and forced to disclose their felony status on employment applications. They are denied licenses for a wide range of professions, subject to regular surveillance by police and parole personnel, and denied basic citizenship rights such as voting or serving on juries. Making the analogy to Jim Crow lynching, one felon said, "They don't have to call you a nigger anymore. They just say you're a felon. . . . Today's lynching is a felony charge. Today's lynching is incarceration. Today's lynch mobs are professionals. They have a badge; they have a law degree. A felony is a modern way of saying, 'I'm going to hang you up and burn you.' "[37]

Unlike the 1960s, when police brutality and incarceration were civil rights issues against which blacks presented a united front, early-twenty-first-century incarceration can divide or unite black Americans. While most bemoan the systemic or legislative inequities that unjustly target black America, significant numbers of the black middle and working classes find fault with black people. "The lower economic and lower middle economic people are [not] holding their end in this deal," said the renowned comedian Bill Cosby, in a 2004 speech commemorating the fiftieth anniversary of the *Brown v. Board of Education of Topeka* Supreme Court decision (see chapter 12).

In what has become known as the **Pound Cake speech**, Cosby quipped, "These are not political criminals. These are people going around stealing Coca Cola. People getting shot in the back of the head over a piece of pound cake!" Exposing the generational divide, the nearly sixty-seven-year-old Cosby blamed not drug laws but poor parenting. Of people who "cry when their son is standing there in an orange suit [the color of prison fatigues]," Cosby asked, "Where were you when he was two? Where were you when he was twelve? Where were you when he was eighteen, and how come you don't know he had a pistol? And where is his father, and why don't you know where he is? And why doesn't the father show up to talk to this boy?"[38]

Although many blacks endorse Cosby's perspective, large numbers cried foul when six black teenagers in Jena, Louisiana, were indicted as adults on a charge of attempted murder after a schoolyard fight in December 2006 left a white teen, Justin Barker, with bruises and a mild concussion. For many blacks, the **Jena Six case** exposed the unequal treatment blacks receive in the justice system. Earlier in the school year, three white students at Jena High School had been recommended for suspension by the principal when school officials found them guilty of hanging nooses from a tree they wanted reserved for whites only, but the school board overruled him, claiming the nooses were just a childish prank. Although the nationwide outcry subsequently resulted in one of the Jena Six, Mychal Bell, serving time for battery and the other defendants being fined $500 and given seven days of probation, the case exposed the differential punishment often meted out to blacks and whites. What was unfair, said Charles Ogletree, a black Harvard law professor who testified before Congress on the matter, was that the white students who hung nooses committed a hate crime as defined by federal and Louisiana statutes, but neither the federal nor the state government chose to prosecute the white students because they were juveniles. By contrast, the black juveniles were indicted for attempted murder and subject to up to twenty years in prison for what some believed was no more than a schoolyard fight. Ogletree asked, "Why is it that one set of conduct which violates the law was prosecuted and another set was handled within the school system? It's a disparity, it's based on race, and it's hard to justify under these circumstances."[39]

9/11 and the Wars in Afghanistan and Iraq

On the morning of September 11, 2001, the twin towers of the World Trade Center in New York were attacked by Al Qaeda terrorists, who piloted two hijacked planes into the skyscrapers. Before the shock of that attack could sink in, hijackers flew another plane into the Pentagon in Washington, D.C. Yet another hijacked airliner crashed in a field in Pennsylvania when some passengers attempted to regain control of the plane. Americans watched in horror as the twin towers collapsed and people in New York and Washington ran for their lives. Close to 3,000 people were killed in the attacks. President George W. Bush and Congress declared a war on terror, first invading Afghanistan, which was thought to be harboring Al Qaeda leaders such as Osama bin Laden, and then, two years later, invading Iraq, whose leader, Saddam Hussein, was thought to have weapons of mass destruction.

Like all Americans, blacks were saddened and outraged by the 9/11 attacks, but while they supported the war on terror and the war in Afghanistan, an overwhelming majority of blacks opposed the war in Iraq. One poll showed a 40 percent differential between black and white support for the Iraq War, although white support for the war eventually dwindled.[40] That the African American secretary of state, the four-star general Colin Powell, and the African American national security adviser, Condoleezza Rice, supported the war was proof that blacks were getting used to expressing a diversity of political opinion.

Reflecting African American opposition to the war, black enrollment in America's now all-volunteer army fell from 23 percent in 2001 to 12.4 percent in 2006. Having previously enrolled in the military in larger numbers than their proportion in the general population because poor schooling and discrimination limited their opportunities, African Americans were loath to fight a war that appeared to benefit the exclusionary military defense industry and oil companies. As one black soldier put it, "This is not a black people's war. This is not a poor people's war. This is an oilman's war."[41] African American opposition deepened as the war wore on and Iraqi weapons of mass destruction never materialized. Derrick Jackson, an African American columnist for the *Boston Globe*, expressed black opinion well: "A White House that is not committed to opportunity in Illinois must be questioned about Iraq. An America that remains comfortable with discrimination in Baltimore must be questioned as to how discriminating it will be in bombing Baghdad. An America that has not been true to black patriotism might want to question just how true the White House is to them."[42]

Hurricane Katrina

When the winds of Hurricane Katrina roared through the Gulf coast states of Mississippi, Alabama, and Louisiana in the early morning of Monday, August 29, 2005, black America came to believe that the White House was not true at all. Katrina devastated the Gulf coast states, but the historic below-sea-level city of New Orleans

Colin Powell and Condoleezza Rice
The Republican Party was the first to give African Americans top leadership positions in the executive branch. General Colin Powell and Condoleezza Rice both served as national security adviser before going on to become secretary of state. The highest-ranking black executive branch appointees in history, these two politicians helped blaze the trail for Barack Obama. *Stephen Jaffe/AFP/Getty Images.*

sustained the most damage. That damage came not so much from Katrina's high winds and heavy rains but from the broken levees and failed pumps that could not keep the waters of the Mississippi River and Lake Pontchartrain from flooding the city streets. By the time the hurricane departed, more than 85 percent of New Orleans was under water that was, in some places, twenty feet deep. Although both the mayor of the city, African American Ray Nagin, and white Louisiana governor Kathleen Blanco issued evacuation orders and established emergency procedures days before Katrina hit, upwards of 2,000 people lost their lives, and many more had to be rescued with boats and helicopters. (The number of deaths has never been confirmed. Estimates run as high as 4,000 and as low as 1,000.) Countless people lost all their earthly possessions.

Although whites, blacks, and Hispanics were all victims of the storm, Katrina put the issue of racism front and center. In part this was because most of the people who were stranded for days with no food, clean water, or police or fire protection were black

Man Clinging to a Vehicle after Hurricane Katrina
Hurricane Katrina wreaked havoc on the Gulf coast region and caused terrible human suffering. Many New Orleans residents barely escaped the rushing waters, and some who did left their homes with only the clothes on their backs. Those who survived faced additional hardships in the days and weeks following the crisis. They had to find shelter and food and keep themselves and their families, friends, and neighbors safe. Images like this one shocked the nation. *Robert Galbraith/Reuters/Landov.*

and poor. Without cars, money, or out-of-town friends, they could not escape the hurricane. Ordinarily these people were invisible, but Katrina exposed their poverty. When significant federal and state aid failed to arrive in a timely fashion, many took it as a sign of the nation's neglect of and insensitivity to poor blacks. African American political leaders charged that the response would have been far quicker had the hurricane hit a predominantly white city such as Palm Beach or Boca Raton, Florida. The rap artist Kanye West said what many African Americans believed: "George Bush doesn't care about black people." When reports (which subsequently proved to be erroneous) revealed a preponderance of looting, critics noted that if whites had been forced to break into stores for food and water, they would have been lauded for their survival skills rather than attacked for their criminal behavior. When whites in Algiers Point, an upland area that had escaped the brunt of the storm and was designated an official evacuation zone, barricaded the neighborhood and shot at blacks trying to take refuge there, many wondered why the perpetrators were not arrested for their actions.

The finger-pointing that occurred after the hurricane raised more questions than it answered. Some blamed Mayor Nagin for not evacuating the city earlier, not anticipating the problems poor people would have in evacuating, and not using city funds to strengthen the levees. He and others blamed the federal government and the Army Corps of Engineers for the poor design and maintenance of the levees. The government, they argued, had been slow to respond, and when it did, the response was ineffectual and led by incompetent officials. Others blamed the wars in Iraq and Afghanistan. Funds for strengthening the levees had been diverted to the war, as had high-water vehicles, Humvees, generators, and refuelers that could have been used to aid Katrina's victims. The Katrina relief effort needed manpower, but 35 percent of the Louisiana National Guard and 40 percent of the Mississippi National Guard were serving in Iraq. So were Louisiana's 256th Infantry Brigade and Mississippi's 155th Armored Brigade, both of which included engineering and support battalions that specialized in disaster relief.

On the issue of Katrina, blacks and whites were as far apart as they had been almost fifteen years earlier when America's racial pulse had been taken by the Rodney King beating and the O. J. Simpson murder trial verdict (see chapter 14). When polled on whether race affected the government's response (or lack thereof), whites generally proclaimed that race did not matter, while blacks believed it was the only thing that mattered.[43] Almost a year and a half after the hurricane, the levees had not been rebuilt, and neighborhoods, including the predominantly black Ninth Ward, were still in shambles. Although tourist areas were up and running, victims of the storm were still living in cheaply built government trailers that were revealed to emit toxic levels of formaldehyde gas, and no one person had been appointed to oversee the recovery operation. Again, blacks felt that race figured in the process, and whites felt that it did not. According to Melissa Harris-Perry, a political science professor at the University of Chicago who conducted a study on racial attitudes regarding the recovery effort, "I think that what we have here is a real question around issues of citizenship." While whites supported less government spending to rebuild, "African-Americans understand this as a question of citizens and homeowners displaced through no fault of their own who deserve the support of a government into which they have paid all these years."[44]

Change Comes to America

Katrina put a dent in the optimism that had been on the rise in black America, but it did not destroy the new feeling of national belonging. The sense of citizenship that allowed blacks to feel entitled to government help extended into politics, where Barack Obama's nomination for president in 2008 symbolized change on many levels. It was not just that, for the first time in history, a black man would run on a major party ticket for the highest office in the land on a platform that made "change" its signature slogan. Obama was a self-identified African American who had no black ancestor born on American soil, and who in previous centuries might have been advantaged by his biracial heritage but would never have been perceived as transcending race. For all the doubts and anxiety raised by what some called post-blackness, here was a sign that the changes that had occurred in the era following the black freedom movement might have a positive outcome. Here was a change that Americans of all races were being asked to endorse.

Obama's Forerunners, Campaign, and Victory

Barack Obama was not the first African American presidential candidate to be taken seriously. Congresswoman Shirley Chisholm saw herself as a pathfinder when she launched her campaign for the Democratic Party nomination in 1972 (see chapter 14). "What I hope most," she said, "is there will be others who will feel themselves as capable of running for high political office as any wealthy, good-looking white male."[45] Many blacks ran for president on lesser-known third- and fourth-party tickets, and Jesse Jackson made a serious run for the Democratic Party nomination in 1984 and 1988 (see chapter 14). Other African Americans also blazed the trail for Obama. General Colin Powell, a Republican, served as national security adviser under President Ronald Reagan before becoming the first, and so far the only, African American chairman of the Joint Chiefs of Staff. In 2001, he became the sixty-fifth U.S. secretary of state, appointed by President George W. Bush, and the first African American to serve in that position. Four years later, he was succeeded by another African American, Condoleezza Rice, who was only the second woman (after Madeleine Albright) to be appointed to the post. Like Powell, Rice had previously served as national security adviser, another first for African American women.

A combination of factors made it possible for Obama to win the 2008 election, not the least of which was his compelling personal story. Born in 1961 to a white mother from Kansas and a black father from Kenya, he was raised in Hawaii mostly by his white grandparents, although he also spent some years in Indonesia with his mother and her second husband. Only in America, he would later proclaim, could such improbable circumstances not prevent one from becoming president of the United States.

Obama's personal story embodied his campaign theme of "change." On the eve of the election, the nation was bogged down in two wars, with no victory in sight. Bush's economic policies of tax cuts, deficit spending to finance the wars, and deregulation of the financial markets blew up in America's face in the summer and fall of 2008. Banks folded, the credit market froze, and industry laid off workers. All Americans suffered in what became the worst financial disaster since the Great Depression of the 1930s. African Americans were disproportionately hurt by mortgage foreclosures, losing a reported $71 billion to $122 billion in housing assets.[46] Obama promised to end the war in Iraq and to rescue the American middle class. These and other ideas resonated with many Americans, including most blacks.

Still, Obama's road to the White House was not easy. His principal rival was New York senator Hillary Clinton, the former First Lady and wife of former president Bill Clinton, who was very popular with African Americans. Obama's early win in the Iowa caucuses established him as a serious contender, but over the next two months Obama and Clinton traded primary victories. In March, the Obama campaign suffered a setback when ABC News aired inflammatory remarks made by Obama's pastor, the Reverend Jeremiah Wright, including Wright's contention that the 9/11 attacks proved that "America's chickens are coming home to roost."[47] As his polling numbers slipped,

Obama took the opportunity to speak publicly about race, a subject he had thus far avoided addressing directly.

In his speech, called "A More Perfect Union," Obama put the issue front and center (see Appendix). He explained how the history of slavery contradicted the principles outlined in the U.S. Constitution and noted that slavery's end, and the end of Jim Crow, was made possible by the Constitution, which promised liberty and justice for all. He lauded America's quest for a "more perfect union" and pledged to continue to bring the nation's promise closer to reality. Obama then narrated his own American story, stating that "in no other country on Earth is my story even possible." But he challenged all races to focus on mutual understanding and a path to unity. White Americans needed to realize that black Americans did not simply imagine injustice: They did, in fact, experience discrimination that resulted in widespread poverty, high incarceration rates, disruption of the family, and inferior schools and health care. "The anger is real; it is powerful; and to simply wish it away, to condemn it without understanding its roots, only serves to widen the chasm of misunderstanding that exists between the races," Obama said. But he also told black Americans that they did not have a lock on suffering. White Americans, too, were hurting: "Most working- and middle-class white Americans don't feel that they have been particularly privileged by their race. Their experience is the immigrant experience — as far as they're concerned, no one's handed them anything, they've built it from scratch. They've worked hard all their lives, many times only to see their jobs shipped overseas or their pension dumped after a lifetime of labor." Black and white Americans, he said, could either focus on the things that divided them or find the things that united them. Americans of all races had to go forward, united in their dedication to create the most perfect union possible.

Obama's speech was lauded as "historic" and "honest." Shortly afterward, he won the endorsement of former presidential candidate and New Mexico governor Bill Richardson, a Hispanic who stated that the speech had bolstered his decision: "Senator Barack Obama addressed the issue of race with the eloquence and sincerity and decency and optimism we have come to expect of him. . . . He did not seek to evade tough issues or to soothe us with comforting half-truths."[48] Jon Stewart of *The Daily Show*, in a rare moment of straight-faced sincerity, finished his otherwise satirical coverage of the speech by calmly stating, "And so, at eleven o'clock a.m. on a Tuesday, a prominent politician spoke to Americans about race as though they were adults."[49]

When Hillary Clinton conceded the Democratic nomination on June 7, Obama turned his full attention to his Republican rival, Senator John McCain. In many ways, the prolonged primary struggle benefited Obama. He entered the general election with a battle-tested organization, field offices in nearly every state, and an unequaled fundraising operation and Internet and social media presence. He also had been forced to hone his message of change, which served him well against McCain, who chose little-known Alaska governor Sarah Palin as his running mate. Palin immediately went on the attack, calling into question Obama's patriotism and background. She seized on an association between Obama and Bill Ayers, a former leader of the radical leftist organization the Weather Underground in the 1970s. Investigations by the *New York Times*, CNN, and other news organizations concluded that Obama did not have a close relationship with Ayers, but Palin returned to the issue repeatedly in her stump speeches, using it to portray Obama as "not like us" — language many pundits identified as thinly veiled racism.[50]

In the last months of the campaign, it was the economy that weighed most heavily on voters' minds. In the fall of 2008, news sources reported that the economy was in its worst shape since the Great Depression. Nevertheless, after the collapse of Lehman Brothers, a giant financial services firm, McCain announced that "the fundamentals of our economy are strong."[51] McCain's position on the economy was one reason the Republican former secretary of state Colin Powell endorsed Obama. McCain "didn't have a complete grasp of the economic problems," Powell said. Citing other issues such as the rightward movement of Republicans and McCain's choice of the inexperienced Palin for vice president, Powell lauded Obama as a "transformational figure." According to Powell, America needed someone who could convey "a new image of American leadership, a new image of America's role in the world."[52]

On November 4, 2008, Obama won the election, early and big. He took several states that had previously been staunchly Republican, including the southern states of Virginia and North Carolina, and lost by only a small margin in Georgia. He won the swing states of Florida, Ohio, and Pennsylvania, as well as the entire Northeast, by a comfortable margin and captured the Great Lakes states of Michigan, Wisconsin, and Minnesota by double digits. By 11 p.m. on election night, news organizations had declared Obama the winner. When all the votes were tallied, he was victorious in the electoral college by a margin of 365 to 173 and had received over 8 million more popular votes than McCain. Most African Americans were especially jubilant. Oprah Winfrey, an early supporter of Obama, wept as she stood in Chicago's Grant Park to witness his victory speech. "It feels like hope won. It feels like there's a shift in consciousness. It feels like something really big and bold has happened here," she exclaimed.[53] Jesse Jackson shed his own tears of joy, invoking slain civil rights leaders Medgar Evers and Martin Luther King Jr.: "I thought about who was not there, . . . the martyrs and the murdered whose blood made last night possible. I could not help but think this was their night."[54]

The excitement was not limited to America. Following Obama's speech, spontaneous street parties broke out in cities around the world, including London, Berlin, Rio de Janeiro, and Nairobi. "What an inspiration. He is the first truly global U.S. president the world has ever had," said the twenty-nine-year-old Thai student Pracha Kanjananont to an interviewer in Bangkok.[55] "By choosing you," President Nicolas Sarkozy of France wrote in a letter to Obama, "the American people have chosen change, openness and optimism. At a time when all of us must face huge challenges together, your election raises great hope in France, in Europe and elsewhere in the world."[56]

The New Obama Administration

Through the inauguration and the first one hundred days of the Obama administration, the president's approval ratings reached 82 percent, according to the *Los Angeles Times*. At age forty-seven, Obama was the fifth-youngest president to take office, and reporters could hardly resist drawing comparisons with John F. Kennedy, who was only forty-three upon his inauguration. Both men were strikingly handsome and married to an attractive, stylish wife. After Kennedy was assassinated, his administration was often referred to as Camelot, an allusion to its idealism, and with Obama's election, there were references to a "Black Camelot." Similarly, the Princeton- and Harvard-educated Michelle Obama was compared favorably with her counterpart, Jacqueline Kennedy. And the public seemed pleased that Obama, like Kennedy, brought young children to the White House. When Malia and Sasha posed with their parents for a White House family photo, they composed a portrait few could have imagined would ever carry the caption "First Family."

In keeping with Obama's campaign pledge to roll back many Bush-era policies, the new administration outlawed the torture of prisoners detained in the war on terror, lifted restrictions on federal funding for stem cell research, and ended the ban on federal grants to international groups that provide abortion services or counseling. Obama also was true to his promises regarding the wars in Afghanistan and Iraq. On October 21, 2011, he announced the end of the Iraq War, and by the end of the year, most American troops had returned home. Obama also ordered Operation Neptune Spear, which successfully located and murdered Osama bin Laden, the Al Qaeda leader behind the 9/11 attacks. Obama began the withdrawal of troops from Afghanistan in 2011 as well, at one point affirming plans to complete the drawdown of troops by the end of 2014, but in 2015 he announced that U.S. troops would remain in Afghanistan until at least 2017. Obama's early efforts to replace American armed intervention abroad with diplomacy earned him the 2009 Nobel Peace Prize. When asked whether Obama deserved the prize so early in his tenure as president, the Nobel Committee cited the hope that he had inspired around the world and the deep changes occurring because of his promise to reduce nuclear weapons and ease U.S. tensions with Muslim nations.[57]

Of the legislation enacted in Obama's first one hundred days, perhaps the most controversial was the **American Recovery and Reinvestment Act (ARRA)**. Passed on February 13, 2009, the $787 billion stimulus package was intended to bolster the faltering economy and included tax incentives, expansion of unemployment benefits, aid to low-income workers and retirees, and money for infrastructure improvements. The vote was largely partisan, with no Republican support for the legislation in the House and only three moderate Republicans voting for it in the Senate. Reacting to the immense price tag, conservatives across the country organized protests against what they termed Obama's "obesity" spending. The protests increased in March and April when Obama directed the U.S. Department of the Treasury to make loans to General

Obama Family Portrait, 2015

One of the things that made Barack Obama appealing to Americans, especially African Americans, was the traditional image his family projected. Before Barack became president, Michelle Obama had been a working mom, and the two of them had had to balance the pressures of work and home life while raising well-adjusted children and paying back student loans. Given how social scientists and policymakers had pathologized African American family life, blacks took particular delight in celebrating this two-parent family who were visibly dark-skinned. *Pete Souza/Photoshot/Newscom.*

Motors and Chrysler, allowing those companies to restructure so they would not close down and throw hundreds of thousands of people out of work. Over the following months, and especially when Obama and congressional Democrats introduced plans to revamp health care in July, opposition to government spending coalesced into the Tea Party movement, a loose affiliation of national and local groups. Sarah Palin reemerged as the unofficial leader of the movement, which over the summer of 2009 disrupted town hall meetings convened nationwide to inform the public about the proposed health care reform bill.

After a long divisive battle, the two bills comprising Obama's health care program passed Congress in March 2010. Supporters of the Patient Protection and Affordable Care Act and the Health Care and Education Reconciliation Act praised the provisions, which, broadly summarized, guaranteed medical coverage to everyone, including the poor, and prevented insurance companies from raising premiums on the sick, denying claims based on preexisting conditions, or establishing coverage caps. The Tea Party derisively labeled the legislation "Obamacare" and vowed to repeal it. They and other opponents charged that the provisions providing government subsidies to help the poor purchase insurance would swell the federal budget and give the government license to interfere in what ought to be a private concern. They also argued that the provision requiring everyone to purchase insurance violated Americans' right to freedom of choice and was unconstitutional. In June 2012, the Supreme Court ruled against Obama's opponents. In a five-to-four decision that upheld the new health care law, the Supreme Court ruled that the government's power to tax gave it the power to require everyone to purchase health insurance.

Some Tea Party supporters objected as much to Obama himself as to his policies, sponsoring Web sites questioning his U.S. citizenship and displaying placards with patently racist language and images at rallies. Former president Jimmy Carter spoke out against the extreme rhetoric, saying that "when a radical fringe element of demonstrators and others begin to attack the president of the United States as an animal or as a reincarnation of Adolf Hitler or when they wave signs in the air that said we should have buried Obama with Kennedy, those kinds of things are beyond the bounds."[58] Carter drew fire from Republican leaders, whom he also took to task for not condemning the attacks as racist and dangerous. A sign of the diversity of opinion that now characterized black America was the response that came from Michael Steele, who had become the first African American head of the Republican National Committee in early 2009. "President Carter is flat-out wrong," he said. "This isn't about race. It is about policy."[59]

Racism Confronts Obama in His First Term

Ironically, although America had its first black president, race as a policy issue became off-limits. For many Americans, Obama's election signaled the end of race as a problem. The country, they argued, had entered a **post-racial** era, in which Martin Luther

King Jr.'s dream of people being judged by the content of their character rather than the color of their skin was finally a reality. Those who pointed to the disparity between white and black incomes, education, wealth, and incarceration were called unpatriotic and accused of being divisive. Saying that America had entered a new age, Sarah Palin asked, "Isn't it time we put aside the divisive politics of the past once and for all and celebrate the fact that neither race nor gender is any longer a barrier to achieving success in America — even in achieving the highest office in the land?"[60]

During his campaign, Obama gave the memorable speech on race that was celebrated as the most significant in years, but during his administration he had to walk a fine line. When he spoke his mind about racial disparity, he was accused of being a black partisan, unrepresentative of all Americans. When he did not address racial issues, either in speeches or in policy initiatives, he was criticized for being so transcendent as to have forgotten how hard it was to be black in America. In 2011, with black unemployment levels near 16 percent, the black scholar Cornel West attacked Obama's policies on racial grounds. "It's understandable," West said in reference to policies he thought too favorable to monied interests. "As a young brother who grows up in a white context, brilliant African father, he's always had to fear being a white man with black skin. All he has known culturally is white. He is just as human as I am, but that is his cultural formation."[61]

Obama's comments regarding two racially charged incidents show just how difficult the issue was for him. In July 2009, the Harvard professor Henry Louis Gates Jr. was arrested at his home in Cambridge, Massachusetts, for disorderly conduct. Police had arrived at the professor's residence after receiving calls that someone was burglarizing the home. It turned out that the reported "burglar" was Gates himself, trying to unjam his front door, but the police demanded proof that Gates was the owner of the house and that he was who he claimed to be. After Gates showed police his driver's license and Harvard identification, an altercation ensued. Gates was angry at what he took to be an incident of **racial profiling** — the use of race, rather than specific evidence, to determine how a person should be treated. A white man, he believed, would not have been treated so disrespectfully in his own home and would not have been mistaken for a burglar in the first place. For his part, the arresting officer, Sergeant James Crowley, believed that Gates had treated him disrespectfully. He claimed that he and his fellow officers had followed police protocol and should not have been subjected to Gates's invective.

Some black Americans showed little sympathy for Gates. The poet and social critic Ishmael Reed claimed that Gates had "gotten a tiny taste of what 'the underclass' undergo each day" and pondered whether Gates would now stop his Cosby-like, blaming-the-victim criticism of the black poor. "If a black man in an inner city neighborhood had hesitated to identify himself, or given the police some lip," Reed argued, "the police would have called SWAT [the special weapons and tactics unit]."[62]

Obama's impromptu comments about the incident, made at the end of a news conference on health care reform, intensified a debate that had been passionate from

Henry Louis Gates's Arrest
In July 2009, the Harvard professor, social critic, and television personality Henry Louis Gates Jr. was arrested for disorderly conduct at his home when he was mistaken for a burglar and questioned by police. Many felt that the case was an example of the racial profiling that blacks — especially blacks of a lesser social or economic standing than Gates — regularly endure. This candid photograph of a handcuffed Gates, snapped by a neighbor, appeared in myriad news outlets following the incident. *B. Carter/Demotix Images/Associated Press/ AP Images.*

the start. Not having witnessed the event personally, Obama at first hesitated to answer a question about the role race might have played in Gates's arrest. Yet he did note the "long history in this country of African Americans and Latinos being stopped by law enforcement disproportionately." After joking that he would get shot if he tried to unjam the door to his home, the White House, Obama said that the "police acted stupidly" when there was already proof that Gates was in his own house.[63] Obama's comments set off a firestorm of criticism. The Cambridge police commissioner said that the president should not have weighed in on a local matter about which he did not have all the facts, calling his officers "pained" by the comment. When Obama tried to refocus the nation's attention on health care reform, saying it was more important than the Gates matter, conservative commentators such as Rush Limbaugh and Glenn Beck called Obama a racist. Limbaugh argued that Obama is "angry at this country, he's not proud of it,"[64] and Beck said that Obama "has a deep-seated hatred for white people or the white culture."[65] Obama's response was to make the incident what he called a "teachable moment." He invited Gates and Crowley to the White House, where he and Vice President Joe Biden sat down with them to work out their differences in what was colloquially called the "beer summit." If the incident proved anything, it was that race still mattered in America and the post-racial ideal had not yet been achieved.

In 2012, the Trayvon Martin case similarly demonstrated the dilemma that race posed for Obama and the nation. On February 26, Martin, a black teenager in Sanford, Florida, who was on his way home from buying candy and an iced tea, was shot and killed by a neighborhood watch volunteer named George Zimmerman. Interracial protests erupted nationwide when Zimmerman was not arrested for the killing. Critics of the police claimed that Martin had been a victim of racial profiling. When Obama was asked about the case, he said, "When I think about this boy, I think about my own kids, and I think every parent in America should be able to understand why it is absolutely imperative that we investigate every aspect of this and that everybody pulls together . . . to figure out exactly how this tragedy happened. . . . If I had a son, he'd look like Trayvon, and I think they [his parents] are right to expect that all of us as Americans are going to take this with the seriousness it deserves and that we're going to get to the bottom of exactly what happened."[66] Republican presidential hopeful Newt Gingrich called Obama's comments "disgraceful" and "appalling." He claimed that Obama's comment that a son of his would look like Trayvon was "dividing this country up."[67] Although Obama's aides reiterated the president's feeling that the incident was a tragedy for the country, the controversy nevertheless illustrated how difficult the subject of race was for a black president governing a country that many believed no longer had to grapple with race.

The 2012 Election

In the midterm elections of 2010, Democrats lost six seats in the U.S. Senate and sixty-three seats in the House of Representatives. The big winners were the Tea Party candidates. Even Republican incumbents lost seats to the new right wing of their party. Obama attributed the losses to the fact that not enough Americans were feeling the effects of the economic recovery.

The influence of the far-right wing of the Republican Party was evident as the 2012 presidential primary season began in earnest. Several Tea Party activists, including African American business executive and early front-runner Herman Cain, joined the Republican lineup advocating tax cuts, reductions in the size and spending of the federal government, and an end to entitlement programs. After months of debates, Mitt Romney, former Massachusetts governor and cofounder of the investment firm Bain Capital, emerged as the leader, outspending his main opponent, Pennsylvania senator Rick Santorum, by nearly 5 to 1.

At the Republican National Convention, held during the week of August 27 in Tampa, Florida, Romney was confirmed as his party's standard-bearer. Many Republicans initially considered him too moderate: While serving as governor, he had supported abortion and gay rights and instituted a health care reform act in Massachusetts that became the model for the national health care reform passed under Obama. Faced with uniting his party, Romney began a steady move to the right, choosing Wisconsin congressman and Tea Party favorite Paul Ryan as his running mate and disavowing many of his earlier, more moderate stances on issues. The Romney/Ryan ticket advocated tax cuts that would reduce taxes for corporations and wealthy Americans; across-the-board deregulation; increased military spending; and dramatic cuts in federal spending for programs like Medicaid, subsidies for low-income housing, food stamps, and financial aid for college students. The ticket also opposed abortion — Ryan opposed it even in cases of rape and incest — and same-sex marriage. Although the economy had steadily improved since Obama took office, Republicans pointed to the slow rate of recovery and argued that the country needed an experienced businessman like Romney. In their focus on entitlement programs, Republicans also argued that President Obama and the Democrats fostered government dependency and opposed individual responsibility.

For his part, Obama championed the middle class and Democratic principles. In campaign speeches, he argued that America could not afford to return to the policies that had resulted in the worst economic downturn since the Great Depression. Deregulation of corporations and banking had hurt the middle class, as had a Republican tax policy that benefited the extremely wealthy. Obama and his vice president, Joe Biden, touted their health care program, their bailout of the automobile industry, their opposition to shipping jobs abroad, their commitment to manufacturing jobs — especially clean energy jobs — and their support for a woman's right to equal pay for equal work. Obama also ran on his foreign policy record. He had ended the war in Iraq and brought the troops home. In Afghanistan, he had crippled Al Qaeda by finding and killing Osama bin Laden and other top officials responsible for the attack on the World Trade Center, and he had made plans for withdrawing American troops by 2014. On social issues, Obama and the Democrats stood firmly for abortion rights. They supported the repeal of President Clinton's contentious "don't ask, don't tell" policy, which had forced gays, lesbians, and bisexuals in the military to hide their sexual orientation, and the adoption of a policy that allowed them to serve openly. Democrats also lauded Obama's support of same-sex marriage, something he announced just months before the election. Another change that came late in the election cycle had to do with the nation's immigration policy. Throughout his first years in office, Obama had called on Congress to pass the Democratic-backed Dream Act, a legislative proposal to give immigrants who had entered the country before the age of sixteen and who had been here for five years a path to citizenship. As the 2012 election approached, Obama, who had come under criticism for deporting close to 400,000 illegal immigrants annually since he became president, used his executive power to sign into law a measure that allowed this same cohort to remain in the United States and work without fear of deportation for at least two years.

As both candidates crisscrossed the nation, delivering their platforms to voters, campaign financing and voter fraud emerged as issues. In some states, Republican lawmakers tried to institute measures limiting early voting periods, requiring government-issued photo IDs at the polls, and excluding felons from the voter rolls. Advocates of these laws insisted that such measures bolstered the integrity of the voting process, but voting rights activists believed that they disproportionately impacted African American, Latino, young, disabled, elderly, and homeless voters, for whom, for example, photo IDs were not always easily attainable. As the election drew nearer, many of the restrictive voting laws were struck down in the courts. The election was also notable for the amount of money spent: According to the Federal Election Commission, candidates, parties, and outside groups spent an astronomical $7 billion on the 2012 campaign, making it the most expensive election on record. This spending spree was partly attributable to the Supreme Court's decision in the 2010 *Citizens United* case, in which the Court ruled that corporations and unions could spend as much as they wanted to support or oppose political candidates.

The presidential race appeared to be tight until the very end. President Obama's poor showing in the first of three presidential debates resulted in a bounce for Romney, but as the campaign entered its final weeks, Obama enjoyed a slight lead in the polls. Ultimately, the race was not as close as predicted. African Americans, Asians, gays, Hispanics, women, and young people voted in record numbers for Obama, who emerged victorious with a nearly five-million-vote margin over Romney in the popular vote and an electoral college victory of 332 to 206. Obama's victory made him only the fourth Democratic president — Woodrow Wilson, Franklin D. Roosevelt, and Bill Clinton were the others — to be elected to a second term since the beginning of the twentieth century.

Moving Forward

From the outset, Republicans made it clear that they would be no more cooperative during Obama's second term than they had been during his first. Gridlock came to characterize relations between the White House and Congress, especially after the 2014 midterm elections gave Republicans a majority in both the Senate and the House of Representatives. Nevertheless, Obama used his victory as a mandate to do as his campaign slogan had promised: Press "forward." The president worked with Congress when possible; otherwise, he used the powers of the executive branch to push his agenda. The Democratic losses in the midterm elections paradoxically seemed to embolden Obama, as he continued to use executive orders to bypass a defiant Congress in both foreign and domestic policy. And despite congressional complaint — and to the delight of African Americans — Obama became more vocal about race and racism in America.

Obama's Second Term

Both in foreign policy and in domestic policy, Obama undertook new initiatives while maintaining focus on old problems. The war in Afghanistan, for example, still waged. During his 2012 campaign, Obama had pledged to bring the war to a close by the end of 2014, and he reaffirmed this promise in his 2013 State of the Union address. However, the spread of Al Qaeda and the rise of a new terrorist group — the Islamic State, or ISIS — forced the Obama administration to rethink those plans, and in October 2015, Obama announced that around five thousand U.S. troops would remain in Afghanistan until after his term ended in 2017. Changes in policy toward Iran and Cuba marked Obama's new initiatives. In July 2015, the Obama administration announced a deal with Iran in which the economic sanctions that had been imposed and enhanced since 1979 would be withdrawn in exchange for Iran agreeing to severe restrictions on its nuclear weapons program. The deal raised objections from many in Congress who were wary of any promises made by Iran, a nation that for decades has denied the right of Israel, America's ally, to exist. Congress failed to block the deal within its allotted sixty-day review period, and in October 2015 Iran and the United States began taking steps to put the deal into effect. On another front, Obama used his executive powers to reestablish diplomatic relations with Cuba, opening the door to lifting the more than fifty-year-old economic embargo on the island nation ninety miles south of Florida. Reasoning that America would exert a more positive influence on these nations through open contact than it would through isolating punitive measures, Obama said, "The progress that we mark today is yet another demonstration that we don't have to be imprisoned by the past."[68]

On the domestic front, two Supreme Court decisions greatly impacted African Americans. In June 2013, the Court struck down the heart of the 1965 Voting Rights Act when it declared that states and counties with a previous history of discrimination did not need federal approval to change voting laws. Despite Attorney General Eric Holder's argument that federal oversight had ensured minority voting rights, the Court held that because the laws that defined what was and was not discriminatory had not been updated, it was impossible to determine whether voting municipalities were in fact violating the law. Clarence Thomas, the only African American justice, voted with the majority in the five-to-four decision. The ruling effectively kills the Voting Rights Act until Congress passes legislation explicitly delineating discriminatory behavior, something that a Republican-dominated Congress is unlikely to do in the near future. Without federal oversight, states are freer to pass voter ID laws and other measures that have been shown to hinder minority voting.

African Americans fared better in the Supreme Court's June 2015 decision in *King v. Burwell* upholding Obamacare. In the first five years immediately following enactment of the health care legislation in 2010, congressional Republicans held more than fifty votes trying to weaken or repeal the Patient Protection and Affordable Care Act, which provides federal subsidies to millions who would otherwise be unable to afford medical insurance. The *King* decision resolved a dispute over language in the bill that allowed federal coverage in state plans. It was the second major defeat on this issue for the Court's conservative contingent, which again included Justice Thomas. Speaking of his administration's victory in the case, Obama predicted that "the Affordable Care Act is here to stay"[69] — a statement that expressed more optimism than fact since the president's signature domestic achievement almost certainly faces future challenges in both Congress and the Supreme Court.

Nevertheless, the decision boded well for Obama's relationship with African Americans, many of whom were critical of the president for failing to explicitly address black issues, despite his receiving 96 percent of the African American vote in 2008 and 93 percent of it in 2012. In his second term, Obama gave more public attention to racial inequality. One fact he emphasized was that the Affordable Care Act enabled more African Americans than ever before to obtain medical insurance. According to the Office of the Assistant Secretary for Planning and Evaluation, during Obama's second term the uninsured rate among blacks declined from 22.4 percent to 12.1 percent with an additional 2.6 million adults gaining coverage.

Obama also turned his attention to the criminal justice system. In 2013, Attorney General Eric Holder directed the Justice Department to drop the federal mandatory minimum sentencing requirements that had sent so many African Americans to jail for long periods of time for minor drug offenses. The policy change decriminalized some drug offenses and allowed judges and prosecutors to be more lenient in punishing others. In addition, Obama commuted the sentences of ninety inmates who had been sent to prison in the 1980s for drug offenses that he believed did not merit the long sentences mandated by the era's drug laws. To underscore his commitment to criminal justice reform, Obama toured the El Reno federal prison in Oklahoma in July 2015 and met with inmates there. This dramatic move made him the first sitting president to visit a penitentiary. In another first, Obama appointed Loretta Lynch to the position of U.S. attorney general after Eric Holder stepped down. The appointment, which came after Senate Republicans had blocked the nomination for five months, made Lynch the first African American woman to serve in that role.

Refusing to capitulate to truculent Republicans in the House and Senate, Obama went before the NAACP at its annual convention in July 2015 and called on Congress to pass laws reducing mandatory sentencing and preventing employers from asking job applicants about their criminal history. He also announced that he had asked the attorney general to conduct a review of the use of solitary confinement in federal prisons. This was in response to the suicide of Kalief Browder a month earlier. Browder was sixteen when he was arrested for stealing a backpack in the spring of 2010. Unable to raise the $3,000 bail, Browder awaited trial in prison for three years, spending much of that time in solitary confinement. Although the charges were ultimately dismissed, the ordeal took its toll on Browder. "I'm not all right. I'm messed up," he told a journalist in the fall of 2014.[70] In June 2015, two years after his release from prison, he committed suicide.

My Brother's Keeper (MBK), a $200 million initiative launched by the Obama administration in February 2014, was designed to help young men like Browder. In a White House report on the economic costs of keeping black boys undereducated, jobless, and exposed to the criminal justice system, Obama outlined the MBK program, which works to get business, church, and civic leaders engaged in establishing and financing mentoring programs for boys and young men of color. My Brother's Keeper aims to ensure that, among other things, boys learn how to read by the third grade; graduate from high school, and receive education and training beyond that; become gainfully employed; and stay safe from violent crime. In practice, MBK involves private businesses like the National Basketball Association, the Citi Foundation, and the College Board in projects that break down stereotypes and develop career readiness skills.

Despite Obama's insistence that he would do more if he had a cooperative Congress, critics complained that Obama's approach was not extensive enough. Many wanted sweeping legislation to reform the criminal justice system; others wanted a comprehensive jobs program. They pointed to the black unemployment rate, which in July 2014 was 12.2 percent, compared to 5.6 percent for whites. The unemployment rate disparity between black and white teenagers was even starker: In July 2014, white

President Obama Launches My Brother's Keeper
African Americans applauded Obama's effort on behalf of black boys, for whom he is an important role model. But they also thought it was long overdue. While many criticized his failure to sponsor a government-funded jobs program to address the chronic unemployment of black youth, others derided his exclusion of girls from the My Brother's Keeper initiative. *Kevin Lamarque/Reuters/Corbis.*

youths between sixteen and nineteen years old had an 18.9 percent unemployment rate, compared to a whopping 36.8 percent for black teens. Obama also took a lot of criticism for not including girls within the scope of the My Brother's Keeper initiative. Law professor Kimberlé Williams Crenshaw spoke for many black women when she argued that Obama's focus on males amounted to "an abandonment of women of color, who have been among his most loyal supporters." Crenshaw pointed out that black girls grew up in the same impoverished households, attended the same underfunded schools, and were just as exposed to violence as black boys, and they were more likely than other females to be victims of sex trafficking and domestic violence. And black women's income, argued Crenshaw, was less than that of either white or black men.[71] Although many shared Crenshaw's frustration over the exclusion of black females from My Brother's Keeper, others noted that the program fell short of making the kind of institutional changes that would alter the racism that structured education and employment in America.

While critics debated the merits of Obama's initiatives, Obama himself became more vocal about racism. In July 2013, a few days after George Zimmerman was acquitted of murder charges in the death of Trayvon Martin, Obama addressed the American people as a black man in America. Speaking for and about African Americans, he told the nation that, before he became a senator, he had been racially profiled while shopping and knew what it felt like to have people fearfully lock their car doors as he walked down the street. He asked white Americans to consider the context of black peer violence and to understand that African Americans were not dismissive of it. He also asked them to consider whether Trayvon Martin had the right to defend himself against a threatening, armed assailant. Making it clear that America had not entered a post-racial era, Obama called for programs to help black male youth (the genesis of My Brother's Keeper), and he called on Attorney General Eric Holder to review federal incarceration guidelines (the genesis of Holder's changes to federal minimum sentencing requirements).

Obama made more impassioned remarks on race in his eulogy for the Reverend Clementa Pinckney, a pastor and state senator who was killed along with eight other African Americans after a white gunman opened fire at a Bible study inside the Emanuel AME Church in Charleston, South Carolina, in June 2015. The shooter reportedly made racist statements before and during the attack, and he had previously set up a Web site on which he posted a photo of himself holding a Confederate flag. At Pinckney's funeral, Obama once again spoke not just as the nation's president but as an African American. He talked about the black church and how it had historically nourished African Americans and the American principles of liberty and equality. He argued for the removal of the Confederate flag from the state capitol of South Carolina and asserted that the flag was not just a symbol of a proud southern heritage but a painful reminder of slavery and Jim Crow. And he urged Americans to recognize that racism did not manifest itself only in racial slurs but also in the "impulse to call Johnny back for a job interview but not Jamal," a reference to job discrimination. Rejecting the idea that

America needed to have a conversation about race — "we don't need more talk" — or that symbolic gestures like removing the Confederate flag would suffice (though the flag was eventually removed), Obama called on people to roll up their sleeves and do the hard work of eradicating racism.[72]

African Americans and Law Enforcement

The way police patrol African American neighborhoods directly relates to the issue of mass incarceration. An inordinate number of African Americans are imprisoned for minor offenses because they are more likely than whites to be arrested. Many urban police departments have adopted the **broken windows theory** of policing, which holds that if minor crimes are kept to a minimum, then major crimes are unlikely to occur. This approach has manifested itself in **"stop and frisk"** programs, in which citizens are stopped and patted down for weapons and other contraband. According to the New York Civil Liberties Union, in New York City, where police must record all stop-and-frisk encounters, pedestrians were stopped by the police 191,558 times in 2013, and 88 percent of those stopped were completely innocent. Moreover, 56 percent of those stopped were black, and 29 percent were Latino, while only 11 percent were white.

African American complaints that broken windows practices and stop-and-frisk policies resulted in police harassment and civil rights violations sparked a debate that led to the reduction of such stops in New York and other cities, but concerns arose over another, more distressing phenomenon: the number of African Americans killed each year by police officers. When eighteen-year-old Michael Brown was killed in August 2014 by a policeman in Ferguson, Missouri, protest against the shooting sparked a nationwide movement against police brutality. "#BlackLivesMatter," the movement's moniker, compelled the nation to take a candid look at the number of African Americans murdered by police each year. (See Document Project: #BlackLivesMatter, pp. 653–68.) Although local police departments were woefully negligent in keeping officer shooting statistics, the numbers that were available were startling, as were the individual cases that made it onto nightly news broadcasts. For example, a *Washington Post* study revealed that in the first five months of 2015, 385 people were shot and killed by the police nationwide, with blacks killed at three times the rate of whites.

Although police claim the number of killings cited by African Americans is exaggerated, the socioeconomic factors exposed by investigations into the killings are disturbing. Like the disaster that followed in the wake of Hurricane Katrina, the peaceful and violent protests that followed the killing of Michael Brown exposed the neglect, exploitation, and unequal distribution of resources experienced by African Americans, not just in Ferguson but all around the country. When investigators from the Department of Justice and other agencies and organizations looked behind the violence in Ferguson, they found much that was disturbing but not atypical. Ferguson had once been 80 percent white, but when black families moved to Ferguson, whites fled.

In 2014, Ferguson's population was 69 percent black, but the mayor and police chief were both white, as were five of six city council members (though in April 2015 two African Americans were elected to the Ferguson City Council, including its first African American woman). Blacks were not represented on the city's school board because few owned enough property to induce them to establish political roots. Of the fifty-three officers in the Ferguson Police Department, only three were black; on the other hand, according to statistics kept by the state attorney general's office, blacks accounted for 86 percent of traffic stops in the city and 93 percent of the arrests resulting from those stops. Economic indicators were equally startling. In the St. Louis metro area, which includes Ferguson, the unemployment rate for young African American men between the ages of sixteen and twenty-four was 47 percent in 2012, compared to 16 percent for young white men; the poverty rate between 2007 and 2012 was consistently two to three times higher for blacks than for whites. According to a Brookings Institution study, "As dramatic as the growth in economic disadvantage has been in this community, Ferguson is not alone."[73] That blacks living in suburban neighborhoods outside of a hundred other large metropolitan areas experience some of the same economic disadvantages as blacks in Ferguson is demonstrable proof that, despite the two-time victory of Barack Obama, America has not yet become post-racial.

CONCLUSION

The Promise or Illusion of the New Century

African Americans began the new century with new opportunities but also with old problems. Times had changed because the midcentury freedom movement had borne fruit. The workplace had been integrated, as had higher education — not nearly to the extent black people desired, but enough to make a difference in the ways significant numbers of African Americans related to the nation and their racial community. Race mattered, but so did gender, sexuality, class, and ethnicity. At the beginning of the twenty-first century, blacks could and did take advantage of the many different ways there were to be black.

Although opportunity presented itself to some, the police killings and the economic indicators brought to light in their wake reveal that, for others, it was a pipe dream and an illusion. Poverty, surveillance, and incarceration circumscribe too many African Americans' lives, and consequently many are unwilling to let go of the nurturing racial community and culture that gave their lives coherence. For them, the politics of color blindness and post-racialism is the most corrosive and dangerous because structural racism is a reality they experience every day.

Obama symbolized change, and the national and worldwide jubilation witnessed upon his election demonstrated the hope that he brought to America and the world. But the irony of being the first black president in an age proclaimed by many to be color-blind was obvious. Obama is black, and despite his biracial heritage, he is a living reminder both of America's history of enslavement, disfranchisement, and violence toward African Americans and of black Americans' fierce determination to overcome racism and become American on their own terms.

Obama's mixed heritage calls to mind the codependent relationship Frederick Douglass identified on the eve of the Civil War. In reference to the future of the nation, Douglass tied the liberty and freedom of black people to America's fate. He claimed that "the destiny of the colored man is bound up with that of the white people of this country. . . . *We are here*, and here we are likely to be. . . . We shall neither die out, nor be driven out; but shall go with this people, either as a testimony against them, or as an evidence in their favor throughout their generations."[74] Although discrimination and racism persist, the twenty-first century has brought changes that Douglass could hardly have predicted. Yet the verdict is still out on which testimony about America and its black citizens will ultimately prevail.

CHAPTER 15 **REVIEW**

KEY TERMS

black tax p. 619

post-black p. 623

black church p. 626

mandatory sentencing laws p. 628

carceral state p. 629

Pound Cake speech (2004) p. 630

Jena Six case (2006) p. 630

American Recovery and Reinvestment Act (ARRA) (2009) p. 638

post-racial p. 640

racial profiling p. 641

broken windows theory p. 650

"stop and frisk" p. 650

REVIEW QUESTIONS

1. How would you describe the differences that had come to characterize black America by the first decade of the twenty-first century? How were these differences made manifest in politics, culture, and religion?

2. How did the challenges of the new century — the rise of the carceral state, the war in Iraq, Hurricane Katrina — reveal the changes that had taken place in post–civil rights black America?

3. In what ways was the Obama presidency — and the president himself — emblematic of the changing times?

4. What is meant by a post-racial era? Has the nation entered such a period? What evidence can you provide for your argument?

5. If you had to give Obama a grade (A, B, C, D, or F) for his performance as president, what grade would you give him? How would you support your grade?

#BlackLivesMatter

On August 9, 2014, in Ferguson, Missouri, eighteen-year-old Michael Brown was shot and killed by Darren Wilson, a twenty-eight-year-old police officer. The details of this encounter that left a black male dead, lying facedown in the street, and a white officer proclaiming that he was only doing his job were disputed, but the effects were clear and immediate. A day after Brown's death, protests erupted in Ferguson and continued for several days. Demonstrations started peacefully, with marchers holding their hands high and shouting, "Hands up, don't shoot," a chant born of their belief that Brown had been shot while surrendering to Wilson. Though Brown's intent in raising his hands was one of the many disputed facts of the case, that gesture stuck, and around the country protesters against police brutality chanted the phrase as they marched with their hands in the air. In Ferguson and other cities, the mostly peaceful demonstrations sometimes took a violent turn, as angry marchers looted and burned residences and stores. The demonstrations became only more intense in November after the prosecutor decided not to indict Officer Wilson in the shooting — a frequent outcome in such cases — and again in March 2015, when the United States Department of Justice announced that, because it could not disprove Wilson's claim that in his encounter with Brown he feared for his life, it would not charge Wilson for violating federal criminal civil rights law.

The marches and demonstrations surrounding Michael Brown's death formed the foundation of a national movement whose genesis lay in the February 2012 killing of Trayvon Martin, a seventeen-year-old black teenager, by George Zimmerman, a neighborhood watch volunteer in Sanford, Florida. Alicia Garza, Patrisse Cullors, and Opal Tometi founded the social media hashtag #BlackLivesMatter to protest all the ways that racism destroys black lives, including the state-sanctioned killing of black men and women by the police and the mass incarceration of people of African descent.[75] With the death of Michael Brown, their call to action moved beyond social media and into the streets. Along with the chants of "Hands up, don't shoot," protesters could also be heard shouting, "Black lives matter!"

The movement grew quickly. One reason for this had to do with African Americans' long and persistent fight against police brutality. Members of the baby boom generation remembered the police action taken against blacks who tried to vote prior to passage of the 1965 Voting Rights Act. Others recalled how Birmingham police commissioner Eugene "Bull" Connor had set police dogs and fire hoses on demonstrators during the 1963 civil rights demonstrations (see chapter 12). Still others remembered how police authorities harassed young, black urban migrants, how they collaborated with the FBI's COINTELPRO to kill Black Panthers and destroy the Panthers' organization, and how, in city after city, calls for civilian review boards were repeatedly rejected. For those who did not reach back into history, the many high-profile deaths of young African Americans at the hands of police in 2014 and 2015 — one research agency reported that 336 blacks were shot and killed by police in 2015 alone — were enough to keep protesters marching.[76] Because text messaging and communication social platforms like Twitter made it easy to spread news of police confrontations almost instantaneously, activists were able to mobilize and organize dissent quickly, making it difficult for police assaults and killings to go unreported. One of the most publicized cases occurred in Staten Island, New York, in July 2014: In a violent encounter captured by several bystanders on their camera phones, police officer Daniel Pantaleo held forty-three-year-old Eric Garner around his neck and did not release him despite Garner's pleas of "I can't breathe." Garner was pronounced dead an hour after the incident, and the coroner subsequently ruled the death a homicide. Though the New York City Police Department officially prohibits chokeholds, a grand jury failed to indict Pantaleo. In the wake of that decision, peaceful protests were held around the country, and even in London, England.[77] To the chants "Hands up, don't shoot" and "Black lives matter," protesters added "I can't breathe" and "No justice, no peace."

The protests against police brutality, which coalesced under the banner "#Black LivesMatter," were too widespread for police departments and the Department of Justice (DOJ) to ignore. Investigations by the DOJ and by various organizations revealed appalling patterns of police harassment and abuse of power. The Justice Department's investigation of the police department and court system in Ferguson, for example, revealed that, although 69 percent of Ferguson's population was black, almost 90 percent of the documented uses of force by police officers were against African Americans, and in every police canine bite incident, the person bitten was black. The report also showed how the police and the courts worked together to use traffic arrests and the imprisonment of African Americans to raise revenue for the city, often in violation of the Fourth and Fourteenth Amendments. Such practices, said the DOJ, had destroyed the black community's trust in the police and city government.[78] A May 2015 report by the President's Task Force on 21st Century Policing found that this lack of trust existed in black communities throughout the nation. One of the task force's many recommendations was for law enforcement agencies to "minimize the appearance of a military operation and avoid using provocative tactics and equipment that undermine civilian trust,"[79] a reference to the militarization of local police agencies that had occurred after the war on drugs was declared in 1982, and which was stepped up after the terrorist attack on the World Trade Center in 2001. The report noted that the tactics used in the war against terrorism should not be used against citizens, whose right to protest peacefully is protected by the First Amendment.

The following documents and photographs relate to law enforcement and to #BlackLivesMatter. As you review them, consider the different points of view that are represented.

Alicia Garza | A Herstory of the #BlackLivesMatter Movement, 2014

Although #BlackLivesMatter was created by ALICIA GARZA (b. 1981), PATRISSE CULLORS (b. 1984), and OPAL TOMETI (b. 1984) after George Zimmerman was acquitted of murder charges in the death of Trayvon Martin, it moved to the streets and became a protest movement only after eighteen-year-old Michael Brown was killed in Ferguson,

Missouri. While it coalesced and gathered steam around the issues of police shootings and black incarceration, it was founded with the broad intention of calling attention to the way institutional racism and state violence systematically destroy black lives — not only black male lives but also black female lives, as well as the lives of queer, disabled, and poor blacks. The creators of #BlackLivesMatter are careful to note that they believe that all lives matter, but their focus on blacks has to do with America's long history of oppression in which blacks were excluded from Thomas Jefferson's dictum that "all men are created equal." "When Black people get free, everybody gets free," says Alicia Garza, who argues that all blacks — whether straight or queer, rich or poor, male or female, able-bodied or disabled — suffer so disproportionately from state oppression that the far-reaching benefits of their freedom, once it is obtained, will transform the whole of American society. "We're not saying Black lives are more important than other lives, or that other lives are not criminalized and oppressed in various ways. We remain in active solidarity with all oppressed people who are fighting for their liberation and we know that our destinies are intertwined." In the following essay by Garza, how does she characterize #BlackLivesMatter? What is her sense of its place in history?

I created #BlackLivesMatter with Patrisse Cullors and Opal Tometi, two of my sisters, as a call to action for Black people after 17-year-old Trayvon Martin was posthumously placed on trial for his own murder and the killer, George Zimmerman, was not held accountable for the crime he committed. It was a response to the anti-Black racism that permeates our society and also, unfortunately, our movements.

Black Lives Matter is an ideological and political intervention in a world where Black lives are systematically and intentionally targeted for demise. It is an affirmation of Black folks' contributions to this society, our humanity, and our resilience in the face of deadly oppression.

We were humbled when cultural workers, artists, designers, and techies offered their labor and love to expand #BlackLivesMatter beyond a social media hashtag. Opal, Patrisse, and I created the infrastructure for this movement project — moving the hashtag from social media to the streets. Our team grew through a very successful Black Lives Matter ride, led and designed by Patrisse Cullors and Darnell L. Moore, organized to support the movement that is growing

in St. Louis, MO, after 18-year-old Mike Brown was killed at the hands of Ferguson Police Officer Darren Wilson. We've hosted national conference calls focused on issues of critical importance to Black people working hard for the liberation of our people. We've connected people across the country working to end the various forms of injustice impacting our people. We've created space for the celebration and humanization of Black lives.

THE THEFT OF BLACK QUEER WOMEN'S WORK

As people took the #BlackLivesMatter demand into the streets, mainstream media and corporations also took up the call; #BlackLivesMatter appeared in an episode of *Law & Order: SVU* in a mash up containing the Paula Deen racism scandal and the tragedy of the murder of Trayvon Martin.

Suddenly, we began to come across varied adaptations of our work — all lives matter, brown lives matter, migrant lives matter, women's lives matter, and on and on. While imitation is said to be the highest form of flattery, I was surprised when an organization called to ask if they could use "Black Lives Matter" in one of their campaigns. We agreed to it, with the caveat that a) as

SOURCE: "A Herstory of the #BlackLivesMatter Movement by Alicia Garza," The Feminist Wire, October 7, 2014, http://www.thefeministwire.com/2014/10/blacklivesmatter-2.

a team, we preferred that we not use the meme to celebrate the imprisonment of any individual and b) that it was important to us they acknowledged the genesis of #BlackLivesMatter. I was surprised when they did exactly the opposite and then justified their actions by saying they hadn't used the "exact" slogan and, therefore, they deemed it okay to take our work, use it as their own, fail to credit where it came from, and then use it to applaud incarceration.

I was surprised when a community institution wrote asking us to provide materials and action steps for an art show they were curating, entitled "Our Lives Matter." When questioned about who was involved and why they felt the need to change the very specific call and demand around Black lives to "our lives," I was told the artists decided it needed to be more inclusive of all people of color. I was even more surprised when, in the promotion of their event, one of the artists conducted an interview that completely erased the origins of their work — rooted in the labor and love of queer Black women.

When you design an event/campaign/et cetera based on the work of queer Black women, don't invite them to participate in shaping it, but ask them to provide materials and ideas for next steps for said event, that is racism in practice. It's also hetero-patriarchal. Straight men, unintentionally or intentionally, have taken the work of queer Black women and erased our contributions. Perhaps if we were the charismatic Black men many are rallying around these days, it would have been a different story, but being Black queer women in this society (and apparently within these movements) tends to equal invisibility and non-relevancy.

We completely expect those who benefit directly and improperly from White supremacy to try and erase our existence. We fight that every day. But when it happens amongst our allies, we are baffled, we are saddened, and we are enraged. And it's time to have the political conversation about why that's not okay.

We are grateful to our allies who have stepped up to the call that Black lives matter, and taken it as an opportunity to not just stand in solidarity with us, but to investigate the ways in which anti-Black racism is perpetuated in their own communities. We are also grateful to those allies who were willing to engage in critical dialogue with us about this unfortunate and problematic dynamic. And for those who we have not yet had the opportunity to engage with around the adaptations of the Black Lives Matter call, please consider the following points.

BROADENING THE CONVERSATION TO INCLUDE BLACK LIFE

Black Lives Matter is a unique contribution that goes beyond extrajudicial killings of Black people by police and vigilantes. It goes beyond the narrow nationalism that can be prevalent within some Black communities, which merely call on Black people to love Black, live Black, and buy Black, keeping straight cis Black men in the front of the movement while our sisters, queer and trans and disabled folk take up roles in the background or not at all. Black Lives Matter affirms the lives of Black queer and trans folks, disabled folks, Black-undocumented folks, folks with records, women, and all Black lives along the gender spectrum. It centers those that have been marginalized within Black liberation movements. It is a tactic to (re)build the Black liberation movement.

When we say Black Lives Matter, we are talking about the ways in which Black people are deprived of our basic human rights and dignity. It is an acknowledgment [that] Black poverty and genocide is state violence. It is an acknowledgment that 1 million Black people are locked in cages in this country — one half of all people in prisons or jails — [that] is an act of state violence. It is an acknowledgment that Black women continue to bear the burden of a relentless assault on our children and our families and that assault is an act of state violence. Black queer and trans folks bearing a unique burden in a hetero-patriarchal society that disposes of us like garbage and simultaneously fetishizes us and profits off of us is state violence; the fact that 500,000 Black people in the US are undocumented immigrants and relegated to the shadows is state violence; the fact that Black girls are used as negotiating chips during times of conflict and war is state violence; Black folks living with disabilities and different abilities [bearing] the burden of state-sponsored Darwinian experiments that attempt to squeeze us into boxes of normality defined by White supremacy is state violence. And the fact that the lives of Black people — not ALL people — exist within these conditions [a] is consequence of state violence.

When Black people get free, everybody gets free.

#BlackLivesMatter doesn't mean your life isn't important — it means that Black lives, which are seen as without value within White supremacy, are important to your liberation. Given the disproportionate impact state violence has on Black lives, we understand that when Black people in this country get free, the benefits will be wide reaching and transformative for society as a whole. When we are able to end hyper-criminalization and sexualization of Black people and end the poverty, control, and surveillance of Black people, every single person in this world has a better shot at getting and staying free. When Black people get free, everybody gets free. This is why we call on Black people and our allies to take up the call that Black lives matter. We're not saying Black lives are more important than other lives, or that other lives are not criminalized and oppressed in various ways. We remain in active solidarity with all oppressed people who are fighting for their liberation and we know that our destinies are intertwined.

And, to keep it real — it is appropriate and necessary to have strategy and action centered around Blackness without other non-Black communities of color, or White folks for that matter, needing to find a place and a way to center themselves within it. It is appropriate and necessary for us to acknowledge the critical role that Black lives and struggles for Black liberation have played in inspiring and anchoring, through practice and theory, social movements for the liberation of all people. The women's movement, the Chicano liberation movement, queer movements, and many more have adopted the strategies, tactics, and theory of the Black liberation movement. And if we are committed to a world where all lives matter, we are called to support the very movement that inspired and activated so many more. That means supporting and acknowledging Black lives.

Progressive movements in the United States have made some unfortunate errors when they push for unity at the expense of really understanding the concrete differences in context, experience, and oppression. In other words, some want unity without struggle. As people who have our minds stayed on freedom, we can learn to fight anti-Black racism by examining the ways in which we participate in it, even unintentionally, instead of the worn out and sloppy practice of drawing lazy parallels of unity between peoples with vastly different experiences and histories.

When we deploy "All Lives Matter" as to correct an intervention specifically created to address anti-blackness, we lose the ways in which the state apparatus has built a program of genocide and repression mostly on the backs of Black people — beginning with the theft of millions of people for free labor — and then adapted it to control, murder, and profit off of other communities of color and immigrant communities. We perpetuate a level of White supremacist domination by reproducing a tired trope that we are all the same, rather than acknowledging that non-Black oppressed people in this country are both impacted by racism and domination, and, simultaneously, BENEFIT from anti-black racism.

When you drop "Black" from the equation of whose lives matter, and then fail to acknowledge it came from somewhere, you further a legacy of erasing Black lives and Black contributions from our movement legacy. And consider whether or not when dropping the Black you are, intentionally or unintentionally, erasing Black folks from the conversation or homogenizing very different experiences. The legacy and prevalence of anti-Black racism and hetero-patriarchy is a lynch pin holding together this unsustainable economy. And that's not an accidental analogy.

In 2014, hetero-patriarchy and anti-Black racism within our movement is real and felt. It's killing us and it's killing our potential to build power for transformative social change. When you adopt the work of queer women of color, don't name or recognize it, and promote it as if it has no history of its own such actions are problematic. When I use Assata's powerful demand in my organizing work, I always begin by sharing where it comes from, sharing about Assata's significance to the Black Liberation Movement, what it's political purpose and message is, and why it's important in our context.

When you adopt Black Lives Matter and transform it into something else (if you feel you really need to do that — see above for the arguments not to), it's appropriate politically to credit the lineage from which your adapted work derived. It's important that we work together to build and acknowledge the legacy of Black contributions to the struggle for human rights. If you adapt Black Lives Matter, use the opportunity to talk about its inception and political framing. Lift up Black lives as an opportunity to connect struggles across race, class, gender, nationality, sexuality, and disability.

And, perhaps more importantly, when Black people cry out in defense of our lives, which are uniquely, systematically, and savagely targeted by the state, we are asking you, our family, to stand with us in affirming Black lives. Not just all lives. Black lives. Please do not change the conversation by talking about how your life matters, too. It does, but we need less watered down unity and more active solidarities with us, Black people, unwaveringly, in defense of our humanity. Our collective futures depend on it.

Protesting the Killing of Unarmed Black Men

According to a study by the *Washington Post* and Bowling Green State University, there have been thousands of fatal shootings at the hands of the police since 2005, but as of April 2015 only fifty-four officers had been charged. The majority of the charged officers in those cases that had already been resolved by the time of the study were cleared or acquitted, and those officers who were convicted or who pled guilty tended to spend little time in jail — four years on average, and sometimes only weeks.[80] In the Michael Brown and Eric Garner cases, the officers responsible for their deaths were never charged, much less put on trial. For African Americans, this was additional proof that black lives did not matter, and they marched to say the opposite. The protest pictured on the next page took place in New York City shortly after a grand jury failed to indict Officer Daniel Pantaleo in Eric Garner's homicide. What does this photo tell you about the protesters? What do their placards say? Why do you think so few policemen are charged in cases in which unarmed civilians are killed?

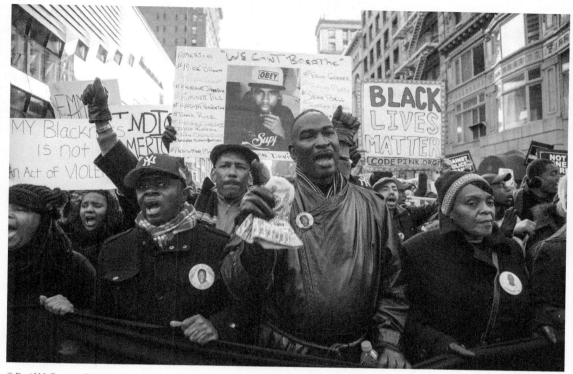

© *David M. Grossman/Image Works.*

Citizen-Police Confrontation in Ferguson

As shown in the following photo, demonstrators who gathered in Ferguson, Missouri, on August 11, 2014, to protest Michael Brown's killing were confronted by police who wore Kevlar vests, helmets, and camouflage and who, armed with pistols, shotguns, and automatic rifles, used rubber bullets and tear gas to disperse the protesters.[81] The show of such overwhelming force against citizens exercising their First Amendment right to free speech and protest prompted many to question how and why a relatively small city like Ferguson had acquired weapons normally found on the battlefields of Iraq and Afghanistan. Researchers traced the militarization of police departments back to Ronald Reagan's war on drugs, when federal money and military equipment began to flow into state and local law enforcement agencies. Even before the Bush administration's war on terror began after the September 11, 2001, attacks, the Pentagon regularly gave millions of dollars in firepower to local law enforcement agencies around the country, which they used in setting up special weapons and tactics (SWAT) teams for narcotics enforcement. In 1997 alone, the Pentagon handed over more than 1.2 million pieces of military equipment to local police departments. A retired police chief in New Haven, Connecticut, told the *New York Times*, "I was offered tanks, bazookas, anything I wanted."[82] After 9/11 federal funding for tools of combat only increased as towns and cities prepared themselves for possible attack; and as the wars in Iraq and Afghanistan wind down, the military's surplus tools of combat have been transferred to local law enforcement. It is not uncommon for small towns like Ferguson to own M-16 rifles, grenade launchers, and armored personnel carriers and helicopters and to use these weapons of war to carry out community policing. Critics of police militarization argue that communities are not war zones and that police should be trained to protect citizens and their right to be presumed innocent until proven guilty. Police, they argue, are not soldiers, who are trained to kill the enemy. Supporters of militarization, however, argue that communities must be prepared, even for something that may never happen. Moreover, they say, the equipment keeps police safe and allows them to keep up with criminals, who are arming themselves more heavily.[83] How does this photo speak to the issue of police militarization?

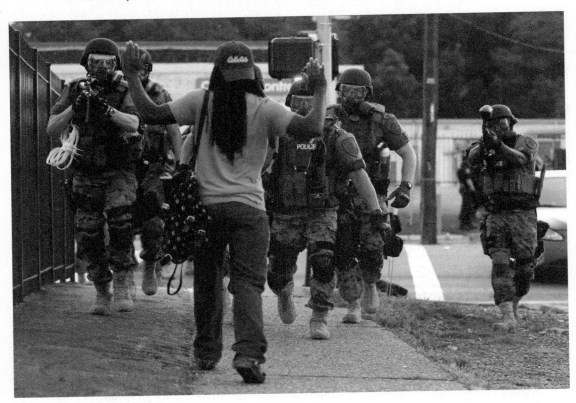

Jeff Roberson/Associated Press/AP Images.

"We Can't Breathe" Headline

Eric Garner was choked to death by Officer Daniel Pantaleo on July 17, 2014, several weeks before Michael Brown was shot by Ferguson police. Protest erupted immediately after Garner was killed, but it reached fever pitch five months later when a Long Island grand jury failed to indict Pantaleo, even though the coroner had ruled the death a homicide. The following image shows the December 4, 2014, cover of the *Daily News*, a popular New York tabloid. How do you think New Yorkers reacted to this cover? Is it more favorable to the police or to Garner sympathizers? Both Eric Garner and Michael Brown were large males, and in both cases the white officers involved alleged that they felt threatened. Does this picture of Garner, moments before his death, speak to the fear expressed by many police officers who encounter black men? Does it say anything at all about the countless black women killed in police encounters? Eric Garner was recorded saying "I can't breathe." What do you make of the headline "We Can't Breathe"?

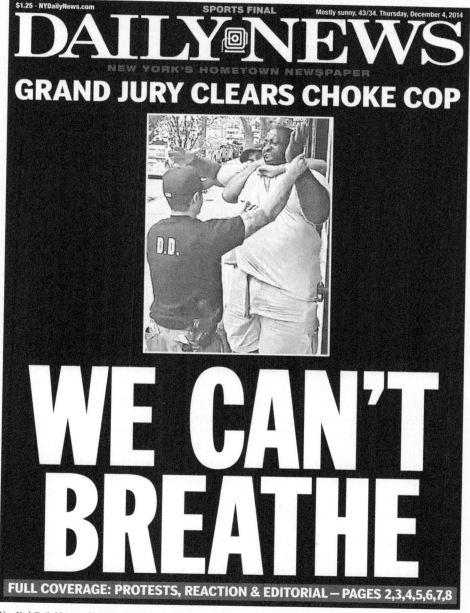

The Police See It Differently

Michael Brown's killing has not only prompted inquiries into police militarization but has also led to scrutiny of general community policing, particularly police use of firearms. In the wake of statistics that reveal the high number of African Americans killed in civilian-police encounters, and criticism that police departments are inherently racist, the police have countered with arguments that repudiate their portrayal as gun-toting vigilantes. They argue that a high number of police shootings occur in black neighborhoods because that is where the most crimes occur, and that their presence in these neighborhoods is needed and *requested* by residents who daily are the victims of black crime. Their priority is the safety of both themselves and the citizens they protect, and race, they maintain, is irrelevant. They argue that they are the first line of defense against society's social, economic, and psychological problems, problems that they have no part in creating. They express regret that some suspects are harmed in their custody, but suspects, they say, always complain that the police are hurting them when they are handcuffed or otherwise detained, because they do not want to go to the police station or jail. Guns are everywhere, police argue, and officers need to be skeptical and vigilant in doing their job lest they be the victim of a gun crime.[84]

In making their rebuttal, law enforcement officials point to police shot in the line of duty. The December 2014 murder of Wenjian Liu and Rafael Ramos, two minority police officers in New York City, by Ismaaiyl Brinsley, a black man with a history of mental illness, provided proof of the dangers cops face every day. Brinsley was seeking revenge for the deaths of Michael Brown and Eric Garner and shot Liu and Ramos as they sat in full uniform in their patrol car; they were killed for no reason other than that they were police officers. Law enforcement officials argue that the danger that they face, day in and day out, goes unrecognized and unappreciated, not only by the minority communities they serve but also by city, state, and federal officials, who, they say, too often side with antipolice activists. Indeed, at the funeral of Officer Ramos, many of the thousands of police officers who had come from around the country to pay their respects turned their backs on New York City mayor Bill de Blasio because they believed he did not support the New York City Police Department. Earlier in the month, after the grand jury's decision not to issue an indictment in the death of Eric Garner but before Liu and Ramos were killed, de Blasio had told the press that he and his black wife had for years schooled their biracial son on "how to take special care in any encounters he has with the police officers who are there to protect him." The mayor also stated that "we are dealing with centuries of racism that have brought us to this day. . . . One chapter has closed with the decision of this grand jury. There are more chapters to come."[85] From the point of view of the police, de Blasio seemed to side with black leaders such as the National Action Network's Reverend Al Sharpton, whose antipolice rhetoric, they believed, contributed to the murder of Officers Liu and Ramos.

The following two documents reflect police sentiment. The first is a press release issued by the Phoenix Law Enforcement Association (PLEA) after Rumain Brisbon, a thirty-four-year-old black man, was shot and killed by Mark Rine, a white police officer, on December 2, 2014. At the time of this press release, the events surrounding Brisbon's death were in dispute. What was known, however, was that Brisbon was unarmed and that Rine, who was investigating a drug deal, felt threatened after he saw Brisbon reach for something. Some community activists saw parallels to the killings of Michael Brown and Eric Garner. As this press release from PLEA demonstrates, the police saw the shooting differently. As you read PLEA's side of things, consider Rine's fears and what he confronted on December 2. Does race appear to have been a factor in Brisbon's killing? Could things have been done differently, by Brisbon and the police?

The second document is a letter written to President Obama and Attorney General Eric Holder by Thomas J. Nee, the president of the Boston Police Patrolmen's Association, after the funeral of Patrolman Rafael Ramos. Like PLEA's press release, the letter expresses the sentiment common among law enforcement officials that police officers risk their lives daily and that lack of support from the nation's top officials makes their work even riskier. Do you agree with Nee?

Phoenix Law Enforcement Association
The Professional Association of Phoenix Police Officers since 1975

Date: December 15, 2014
To: All Valley Media
Subject: Recent Phoenix Police Officer
             Involved Shooting

The recent officer involved shooting that occurred on December 2, 2014, involving Phoenix Officer Mark Rine and criminal suspect Rumain Brisbon that occurred at an apartment complex near 25th Avenue and Greenway Road was an unfortunate incident that did not have to end the way it did.

The Phoenix Law Enforcement Association believes it is important for the media and public to view this case from a perspective of examining the facts rather than emotion devoid of fact. It is important for the media and public to understand a few things about this incident:

First, it is truly unfortunate when anyone, be it citizen or officer, is injured or killed as a result of a police contact. Contrary to what many may believe, our officers do not relish the thought of conflict with the citizens we serve.

Officer Rine is an exemplary, decorated employee with seven years of police service. The incident on December 2nd was the first shooting incident he has been involved in.

Officer Rine did not start his shift on December 2nd with the intent of shooting someone, let alone with the intent of targeting someone because of their race. Officer Rine initiated contact with Rumain Brisbon after he [Brisbon] and the vehicle he was in had been previously identified to him by two different citizens in the span of approximately 10–15 minutes as possibly being involved in the sale of drugs. The first citizen even provided a license plate number which matched the description of the vehicle Brisbon was in.

It was only after the second citizen pointed out Brisbon's vehicle and identified Brisbon as a person selling drugs from the vehicle that Officer Rine attempted to surveil Brisbon and his vehicle until backup officers could arrive to render assistance. Prior to arrival of backup, Mr. Brisbon exited the vehicle and began walking towards nearby apartments. Officer Rine had a decision to make and elected to make contact with Mr. Brisbon before he could get inside an apartment.

Mr. Brisbon failed to follow instructions given him by a uniformed sworn peace officer and acted in a threatening manner by reaching for an object concealed in his waistband. In the ensuing altercation, Officer Rine, while attempting to physically detain Mr. Brisbon, believed him to be in possession of a concealed handgun. Mr. Brisbon's

SOURCE: Phoenix Law Enforcement Association, "Recent Phoenix Police Officer Involved Shooting," news release, December 15, 2014.

continued refusal to submit to lawful authority, obey verbal commands, and let go of the object in his waistband while fighting with Officer Rine ultimately culminated in him being shot.

The media has already published details of the backgrounds of Officer Rine and Rumain Brisbon. Suffice it to say that Mr. Brisbon is no stranger to police contact and the legal and prison systems. Mr. Brisbon had the choice to live that evening. Mr. Brisbon knew he was engaged in illegal activity and likely knew he would stand a good chance of returning to prison if arrested. It was Mr. Brisbon who elected to disobey repeated commands, run from the police, fight with police, resist any efforts to detain him, and engage in further behavior leading the officer to believe he was armed. Had Rumain Brisbon simply submitted to lawful authority there would have been no arguments, no physical altercation, and most importantly, the situation would not have escalated to the point where lethal force would have been needed to control the situation.

Some in the media and in the community have expressed concerns that Mr. Brisbon was ultimately found to be unarmed after the shooting. There are certain fallacies that need to be exposed here.

- Any time a police officer is involved in a close-quarter physical fight with a suspect there is always a weapon available — the officer's. Suspects who engage in fights with officers are often successful in gaining control of the officer's gun. This scenario is a very real concern for everyone in law enforcement and justifiably so, as every year in America, police officers are killed by suspects who gain control of their side arms. This is why the rule of thumb, on the wear of body armor, is that it be able to stop the caliber of the handgun carried by the officer.
- Police officers are trained to always keep in the back of their minds that persons they come in contact with are possibly armed. This is not to say officers pull guns on everyone they come in contact with, but

that they are extra vigilant and look for tell-tale cues and indicators that could spell danger. These cues can include things such as conspicuous ignoring, failure to follow verbal commands, sudden or furtive movements, intentionally turning away, putting hands in pockets or the front or rear waistband, belligerent attitude and profane language, and squaring off in a fighting stance, many of which are often a prelude to a fight.

- **"They shot an unarmed person!"** There are numerous accounts from across the nation where police officers have justifiably shot unarmed subjects and not been prosecuted or faced internal discipline from their departments. Police use of force is judged based on Supreme Court case law, relevant state statutes governing the justification for use of deadly force, and police department policies. Most states, including Arizona, have statutes that allow police officers to use lethal force as long as they can reasonably articulate fear of imminent serious injury or death to themselves or another. The law does not require an officer to see a handgun or a muzzle flash before shooting. The law looks at whether or not a reasonable officer on scene would have believed the suspect to be armed and would have perceived a lethal threat given the totality of the circumstances.
- **"Why didn't the officer use a Taser?"** Tasers, while effective in many instances, are not a cure-all. They are a less lethal force option and are applied only in certain scenarios. Phoenix officers are generally trained not to deploy a Taser unless lethal backup is available. Officers involved in lethal force encounters, particularly in a one-on-one setting, are not trained to respond with lesser force options such as a Taser, pepper spray, baton, or fist strikes.

- **Police are only 50% of the equation.** The vast majority of police contacts are concluded peacefully and without harm because citizens comply and yield to lawful authority. They follow directions, keep their hands in plain view, don't engage in argumentative or abusive language, and don't attempt to make furtive moves or elude officers. The place to butt heads and engage in disagreement is not in the street but in the legal arena of a courtroom.

As a final note, the Phoenix Law Enforcement Association is always open to improving how we do business and how we interact with all segments of the community we serve. It is our belief that we should always strive to have open dialogue and communication.

However, issues confronting the community at large cannot be constructively addressed when self-anointed "civil rights leaders" such as the Reverend Jared Maupin are out in public trying their best to turn Phoenix into another Ferguson. At a recent protest filmed by ABC News 15, Maupin was heard making the following statements:

- "Just remember that a lot of these officers are ni - - er killers."
- "The PPD tried to make Rumain look like a ni - - er criminal."
- "The officers themselves were ni - - er killers."
- In another statement Maupin states: "and if all of us showed up on 24th Street and Camelback and pointed out every two-bit cracker in an Escalade and said there were drug dealers . . ." Referring to white people with the racist label of "two-bit crackers."

The Phoenix Law Enforcement Association has tried in the past to have constructive dialog with Reverend Maupin. We can no longer have a relationship with a person that spews unfounded, hate-filled, racist statements such as the ones enumerated above. Our members pay a heavy price to serve the community and baseless allegations such as these only serve to further inflame and aggravate an already tense situation.

As far as the Phoenix Law Enforcement Association is concerned, our first obligation is the care of the members of our organization. We protect those who protect the citizens, and we will not tolerate individuals or groups who attack our Officers in the furtherance of their own selfish agendas.

DOCUMENT PROJECT

National Association of Police Organizations, Inc.
Representing America's Finest

December 29, 2014

The President
The White House
1600 Pennsylvania Avenue, N.W.
Washington, D.C. 20500

The Attorney General
United States Department of Justice
Constitution Avenue and Tenth Street, N.W.
Washington, D.C. 20530

Dear Mr. President and Mr. Attorney General,

American police officers are, quite literally, bleeding to death. In the entirely predictable fulfillment of well-publicized threats, killers are stalking and murdering our officers. They are cloaking themselves in the rhetoric of protest and "justice." But their very public actions are those of violence and bloodshed. American officers are not just "putting their lives on the line," they are dying.

Rightly or wrongly, these violent killers are reading the inaction of your administration as a tacit concession that their goals have merit. They hear your words of sympathy for violent protestors as conferring legitimacy upon their cause. The firebrands and provocateurs among them are only too willing to fill the void left by your absence of condemnation of their crimes and riots with chants of "What do we want? Dead cops! When do we want them? Now!" And now, completely predictably, the continued lack of any meaningful response whatsoever by your administration has allowed an atmosphere of hatred against police officers to grow, to fester and to finally burst forth in murderous gunfire, hatchet attacks and vehicular run-downs of officers across our nation. The mere fact that you permit the likes of Al Sharpton to sit by your side and have a place in the White House is a clear shot across the bow of the law enforcement community.

The time for standing by and offering weak platitudes about peaceful protest has passed. These are no peaceful protests and they never were. Both "Burn this bitch down!" and "What do we want? Dead cops!" have proved to be open notices of exactly what was going to be done. Some 750,000 sworn officers go to work each day, risking their own safety to uphold our freedoms and constitutional liberty, yet the violent anarchists have made it dangerous merely to wear our uniforms in public.

Unless and until you reverse course and *take action* against these killers and the violent and lawless mobs that support them, unless and until you are just as swift in effectively protecting our police as you have proved to be in doubting them, here will be more officers killed. Both of you men have attended many of our group's meetings and have always pledged your strong support for law enforcement. Now more than ever our men and women in uniform need that support to be shown in a very open way. As Vice President Biden put it at Officer Ramos's funeral this weekend, "When an assassin's bullet targeted two officers, it targeted this city and it touched the soul of the entire nation." Our nation and our nation's police need your public support. More than that, they deserve it.

Sincerely,
Thomas J. Nee

SOURCE: Thomas J. Nee, letter to President Barack Obama and Attorney General Eric Holder, 29 December 2014, National Association of Police Organizations, Inc., www.napo.org.

Sybrina Fulton | *Letter to Michael Brown's Family, 2014*

Before Michael Brown's killing, the death of Trayvon Martin at the hands of neighborhood watch coordinator George Zimmerman garnered national and international attention and inspired the founding of #BlackLivesMatter. The two cases were different in many respects but similar in others. Both Michael Brown and Trayvon Martin were black teenagers killed by white men — Brown by a police officer and Martin by a civilian. Both white men claimed to be threatened by the unarmed youth they shot. Moreover, the shootings sparked federal investigations and national protests that drew attention to, among other things, how the killing of African Americans by the police and their surrogates has so often gone unquestioned by most Americans and the news media. When Zimmerman was acquitted for killing Martin, whose only crime, many believed, was walking in a white neighborhood on a rainy night while wearing a hoodie, #BlackLivesMatter asked, along with President Obama, if Martin and other slain blacks had rights that anyone was bound to respect. While the nation debated this question, and while civilians and law enforcement agencies sparred over police tactics, those close to the victims grieved. Their distress was personal and heartrending, and the national conversations regarding their loved ones only added to their pain. Trayvon Martin's mother, SYBRINA FULTON (b. 1966), wrote the following letter to Michael Brown's family. In what ways are Fulton's concerns different from and even indifferent to those expressed by the general population? Notice that she speaks of gun violence as a general concern and not just in reference to her son. Why do you think she does this? Some scholars argue that "the personal is political." What do you think this means? Does it hold true for Sybrina Fulton?

To the Brown Family,

I wish I had a word of automatic comfort but I don't. I wish I could say that it will be alright on a certain or specific day but I can't. I wish that all of the pain that I have endured could possibly ease some of yours but it won't. What I can do for you is what has been done for me: pray for you then share my continuing journey as you begin yours.

I hate that you and your family must join this exclusive yet growing group of parents and relatives who have lost loved ones to senseless gun violence. Of particular concern is that so many of these gun violence cases involve children far too young. But Michael is much more than a police/gun violence case; Michael is your son. A son that barely had a chance to live. Our children are our future so whenever any of our children — black, white, brown, yellow, or red — are taken from us unnecessarily, it causes a never-ending pain that is unlike anything I could have imagined experiencing.

Further complicating the pain and loss in this tragedy is the fact that the killer of your son is alive, known, and currently free. In fact, he is on paid administrative leave. Your own feelings will bounce between sorrow and anger. Even when you don't want to think about it because it is so much to bear, you will be forced to by merely turning on your television or answering your cell phone. You may find yourselves pulled in many different directions by strangers who may be well-wishers or detractors. Your circle will necessarily close tighter because the trust you once, if ever,

SOURCE: Sybrina Fulton, "Trayvon Martin's Mom: 'If They Refuse to Hear Us, We Will Make Them Feel Us,'" *Time*, August 18, 2014, http://time.com/3136685/trayvon-sybrina-fulton-ferguson/.

had in "the system" and their agents [is] forever changed. Your lives are forever changed.

However, with those changes come new challenges and opportunities. You will experience a swell of support from all corners of the world. Many will express their sympathies and encourage you to keep fighting for Michael. You will also, unfortunately, hear character assassinations about Michael, which I am certain you already have. This will incense and insult you. All of this will happen before and continue long after you have had the chance to lay your son to rest.

I know this because I lived and continue to live this. I have devoted my life to the comprehensive missions of The Trayvon Martin Foundation — including providing support to families that have lost a young child to senseless gun violence regardless of race, ethnicity, or gender. I will support you and your efforts to seek justice for your Michael and the countless other Michaels & Trayvons of our country. The 20 Sandy Hook children. Jordan Davis. Oscar Grant. Kendrick Johnson. Sean Bell. Hadya Pendleton. The Aurora shooting victims. The list is too numerous to adequately mention them all. According to The Children's Defense Fund, gun violence is the second leading cause of death for children ages 1–19. That is a horrible fact.

Facts, myths, and flat-out lies are already out there in Michael's case. Theories, regardless of how ridiculous, are being pondered by the pundits. My advice is to surround yourselves with proven and trusted support. Through it all, I never let go of my faith, my family, or my friends. Long after the overwhelming media attention is gone, you will need those three entities to find your "new normal." Honor your son and his life, not the circumstances of his alleged transgressions. I have always said that Trayvon was not perfect. But no one will ever convince me that my son deserved to be stalked and murdered. No one can convince you that Michael deserved to be executed.

But know this: neither of their lives shall be in vain. The galvanizations of our communities must be continued beyond the tragedies. While we fight injustice, we will also hold ourselves to an appropriate level of intelligent advocacy. If they refuse to hear us, we will make them feel us. Some will mistake that last statement as being negatively provocative. But feeling us means feeling our pain; imagining our plight as parents of slain children. We will no longer be ignored. We will bond, continue our fights for justice, and make them remember our children in an appropriate light. I would hate to think that our lawmakers and leaders would need to lose a child before protecting the rest of them and making the necessary changes NOW . . .

With Heartfelt Support,
Sybrina D. Fulton

QUESTIONS FOR ANALYSIS

1. African Americans and the police seem to be very far apart on the issue of police shootings and community policing in general. Is there any room for reconciliation? If you were a mediator, where would you begin the process of bringing black communities and the police together?

2. How do the police shootings relate to issues surrounding hip-hop, the carceral state, post-blackness, and post-racialism?

3. What role should the president of the United States play, if any, in local issues surrounding the police? Is President Obama's role necessarily different from that of other presidents because he is an African American?

4. Much of this chapter has dealt with the evolving diversity of African America and the watershed moment of President Barack Obama's election. What lessons, if any, do the police shootings and the #BlackLivesMatter movement have for students of African American history?

NOTES

1. Quoted in Barack Obama, *Dreams from My Father: A Story of Race and Inheritance* (New York: Random House, 1995), 135–36.

2. Nancy MacLean, *Freedom Is Not Enough: The Opening of the American Workplace* (Cambridge: Harvard University Press, 2006), 317–18.

3. Eugene Robinson, "Which Black America?," *Washington Post*, October 9, 2007.

4. Pew Research Center, "Optimism about Black Progress Declines: Blacks See Growing Values Gap between Poor and Middle Class," results of survey conducted in association with National Public Radio, November 13, 2007, 1, http://pewsocialtrends.org/files/2010/10/Race-2007.pdf.

5. Charles Johnson, "The End of the Black American Narrative," *American Scholar* 77, no. 3 (Summer 2008): 42.

6. This discussion parallels Eugene Robinson's exploration of black diversity in *Disintegration: The Splintering of Black America* (New York: Doubleday, 2010). He describes four categories of difference: Mainstream, Abandoned, Transcendent, and Emergent.

7. Pew Research Center, "Optimism about Black Progress Declines," 4; National Urban League, "The State of Black America, 2010; Jobs: Responding to the Crisis, with the 2010 Equality Index," executive summary, http://www.nul.org/sites/default/files/EXECUTIVE%20SUMMARY%20SOBA.pdf. The 2010 equality index is based on five categories: economics, health, education, social justice, and civic engagement.

8. Robinson, *Disintegration*, 91–93.

9. Debra J. Dickerson, *The End of Blackness: Returning the Souls of Black Folk to Their Rightful Owners* (New York: Pantheon, 2004), 25.

10. Quoted in Ange-Marie Hancock, *The Politics of Disgust: The Public Identity of the Welfare Queen* (New York: New York University Press, 2004), 121.

11. Quoted in Michelle Alexander, *The New Jim Crow: Mass Incarceration in the Age of Colorblindness* (New York: New Press, 2010), 163.

12. Robinson, *Disintegration*, 139–62.

13. This is a very simplified and reductive description of biracial identity, which intersects with other identity delineators such as gender and sexuality. For more on this topic, see Signithia Fordham, "Passin' for Black: Race, Identity, and Bone Memory in Postracial America," *Harvard Educational Review* 80, no. 1 (Spring 2010): 4–29 [especially 13–23].

14. "Tiger Woods—Is He Now Black?," online forum, Topix, http://www.topix.com/forum/afam/TTU198070JT01AEQH.

15. Stanley Crouch, "What Obama Isn't: Black like Me on Race," *New York Daily News*, November 2, 2006, http://www.nydailynews.com/archives/opinions/obama-isn-black-race-article-1.585922.

16. Debra J. Dickerson, "Colorblind," *Salon*, January 22, 2007, http://www.salon.com/2007/01/22/obama_161/.

17. Pew Research Center, "Optimism about Black Progress Declines," 19–29; Pew Research Center, "A Year after Obama's Election: Blacks Upbeat about Black Progress, Prospects," results of survey conducted in association with National Public Radio, January 12, 2010, 5, http://pewsocialtrends.org/files/2010/10/blacks-upbeat-about-black-progress-prospects.pdf.

18. Thelma Golden, introduction to *Freestyle: The Studio Museum in Harlem*, exhibition catalog (New York: Studio Museum in Harlem, 2001), 14.

19. Ibid., 15.

20. Catherine Fox, "National Black Arts Festival: Role of Race in Black Art Debated," *Atlanta Journal Constitution*, July 25, 2003, Features section, 4F.

21. Touré, *Who's Afraid of Post-Blackness? What It Means to Be Black Now* (New York: Free Press, 2011), 5.

22. Cathy Byrd, "Is There a 'Post-Black' Art? Investigating the Legacy of the 'Freestyle' Show," *Art Papers* 26, no. 6 (November 2002): 37.

23. Zadie Smith, "Speaking in Tongues," *New York Review of Books*, February 26, 2009.

24. Shelby Steele, "The Double Bind of Race and Guilt," *Hoover Digest*, no. 1 (2001).

25. Shelby Steele, "The Age of White Guilt: And the Disappearance of the Black Individual," *Harper's Magazine*, November 2002, 34.

26. Robinson, *Disintegration*, 229.

27. All quoted in Joy Bennett Kinnon, "Election 2006: The New Black Power," *Ebony*, November 2006, 166.

28. Cory Booker, interview by Ed Gordon, "Cory Booker Wins Newark's 'Street Fight,'" *News and Notes*, NPR, June 2, 2006, transcript, http://www.npr.org/templates/transcript/transcript.php?storyId55446231.

29. Quoted in Norman Merchant, "New Generation Challenging Old Guard Blacks in Congress," *Washington Times*, May 14, 2012.

30. Booker interview, "Cory Booker Wins Newark's 'Street Fight.'"

31. Quoted in Sylvester Monroe, "Does the Rev. Jesse Jackson Still Matter?," *Ebony*, November 2006, 176.

32. David Van Biema, "Spirit Raiser," *Time*, September 17, 2001.

33. For an extensive review of the black megachurch, see Sharon E. Moore, ed., "African American Megachurches and Community Empowerment: Fostering Life in Dry Places," special issue, *Journal of African American Studies* 15, no. 2 (June 2011).

34. Heather Ann Thompson, "Why Mass Incarceration Matters: Rethinking Crisis, Decline, and Transformation in Postwar American History," *Journal of American History* 97, no. 3 (December 2010): 707–14.

35. Alexander, *The New Jim Crow*, 8, 58–98.

36. Ibid., 12–13.

37. Quoted ibid., 159.

38. "Dr. Bill Cosby Speaks at the 50th Anniversary Commemoration of the *Brown vs. Topeka Board of Education* Supreme Court Decision," May 17, 2004, transcript, Eight Cities Media and Publications, http://www.eightcitiesmap.com/transcript_bc.htm.

39. Charles Ogletree, interview by Neal Conan, "Congress Questions 'Jena 6' Lawyers," *Talk of the Nation*, NPR, October 16, 2007, http://www.npr.org/templates/story/story.php?storyId515340680.

40. Derrick Z. Jackson, "Blacks Have Good Cause to Oppose War in Iraq," *Boston Globe*, February 26, 2003.

41. Quoted in Derrick Z. Jackson, "For African-Americans, Folly of This War Hits Home," *Boston Globe*, May 9, 2007.

42. Jackson, "Blacks Have Good Cause."

43. Stephen Zunes, "Hurricane Katrina and the War in Iraq," CommonDreams.org, September 3, 2005.

44. Melissa Harris-Lacewell (later Harris-Perry), interview by Ed Gordon, "Study on Race and Rebuilding New Orleans," *News and Notes*, NPR, January 23, 2006, http://www.npr.org/templates/story/story.php?storyId55168014.

45. Quoted in Harriet Sigerman, ed., *The Columbia Documentary History of American Women since 1941* (New York: Columbia University Press, 2003), 219.

46. Christina Kasica, "Subprime Crisis Causing Huge Loss of African-American Wealth," *San Francisco Bay View*, New America Media, January 23, 2008, http://news.newamericamedia.org/news/view_article.html?article_id5b121910bf335fc737295ea33b0fadedb.

47. Quoted in Brian Ross and Rehab el-Buri, "Obama's Pastor: God Damn America, U.S. to Blame for 9/11," *The Blotter*, ABC News, March 13, 2008.

48. Quoted in Jeff Zeleny, "Richardson Endorses Obama," *New York Times*, March 21, 2008.

49. Jon Stewart, "Barack's Wright Response," *The Daily Show with Jon Stewart*, March 18, 2008, http://www.thedailyshow.com/watch/tue-march-18-2008/barack-s-wright-response.

50. See, for example, Douglass K. Daniel, "AP: Palin's Ayers Attack 'Racially Tinged,'" *Huffington Post*, October 5, 2008, http://www.huffingtonpost.com/2008/10/05/ap-palins-ayers-attack-ra_n_132008.html.

51. Quoted in John Bentley, "McCain Says Taxpayers Should Not Bail Out Wall Street, Criticizes Obama for 'Nasty' Campaign," *CBSNews.com*, September 15, 2008, http://www.cbsnews.com/8301-502443_162-4449233-502443.html.

52. Colin Powell, interview by Tom Brokaw, *Meet the Press*, NBC, October 19, 2008, transcript, http://www.clipsandcomment.com/2008/10/19/transcript-colin-powell-on-meet-the-press-endorses-barack-obama-october-19/.

53. Quoted in Kate Stroup, "Oprah on Obama's Election: 'It Feels Like Hope Won,'" *People*, November 5, 2008.

54. Quoted in Michel Martin, "Civil Rights Leaders React to Obama's Win," *Tell Me More*, NPR, November 5, 2008, http://www.npr.org/templates/story/story.php?storyId596645057.

55. Quoted in "Obama Victory Sparks Cheers around the Globe," *Baltimore Sun*, November 5, 2008, http://www.baltimoresun.com/news/nation-world/bal-world1105-story.html.

56. Quoted in "U.S. Election Reaction," BBC News, November 5, 2008, http://news.bbc.co.uk/2/hi/americas/us_elections_2008/7710020.stm.

57. "Obama Wins Nobel Peace Prize," *Huffington Post*, October 9, 2009, http://www.huffingtonpost.com/2009/10/09/obama-wins-nobel-peace-pr_n_314907.html.

58. Quoted in "Carter Again Cites Racism as Factor in Obama's Treatment," CNN.com, September 15, 2009, http://articles.cnn.com/2009-09-15/politics/carter.obama_1_president-jimmy-carter-president-obama-health-care-plan?_s5PM:POLITICS.

59. Ibid.

60. "The Charge of Racism: It's Time to Bury the Divisive Politics of the Past," Sarah Palin's Facebook page, July 13, 2010, http://www.facebook.com/note.php?note_id5408166998434.

61. Quoted in Krissah Thompson, "Cornel West's Criticism of Obama Sparks Debate among African Americans," *Washington Post*, May 18, 2011.

62. Ishmael Reed, "Post-Race Scholar Yells Racism," *Counterpunch*, July 27, 2009, http://www.counterpunch.org/2009/07/27/post-race-scholar-yells-racism/.

63. Barack Obama, White House press conference, YouTube video, July 23, 2009, http://www.youtube.com/watch?v5wOIsJzk0sUU.

64. Rush Limbaugh, interview by Greta Van Susteren, Fox News, YouTube video, July 23, 2009, http://www.youtube.com/watch?v5Q2EQKUQkG7M.

65. Quoted in Janet Shan, "Glenn Beck Calls President Barack Obama a Racist over His Comments about Henry Louis Gates' Arrest by White Officer," *Hinterland Gazette*, July 28, 2009, http://hinterlandgazette.com/2009/07/glenn-beck-calls-president-barack-obama.html.

66. Barack Obama, White House press conference, YouTube video, March 23, 2012, http://www.youtube.com/watch?v5ueWsjzbwOxQ.

67. Newt Gingrich, interview by Sean Hannity, *The Sean Hannity Show*, YouTube video, March 23, 2012, http://www.youtube.com/watch?v5Oa_pb6dXqK4.

68. The White House, Office of the Press Secretary, "Statement by the President on the Re-Establishment of Diplomatic Relations with Cuba," https://www.whitehouse.gov/the-press-office/2015/07/01/statement-president-re-establishment-diplomatic-relations-cuba.

69. See Ariane de Vogue and Jeremy Diamond, "Supreme Court Saves Obamacare," CNN.com, June 25, 2015, http://www.cnn.com/2015/06/25/politics/supreme-court-ruling-obamacare/.

70. Jennifer Gonnerman, "Before the Law," *New Yorker*, October 6, 2014, http://www.newyorker.com/magazine/2014/10/06/before-the-law.

71. Kimberlé Williams Crenshaw, "The Girls Obama Forgot," *New York Times*, July 29, 2014.

72. "Remarks by the President in Eulogy for the Honorable Reverend Clementa Pinckney," whitehouse.gov, June 26, 2015, https://www.whitehouse.gov/the-press-office/2015/06/26/remarks-president-eulogy-honorable-reverend-clementa-pinckney.

73. Elizabeth Kneebone, "Ferguson, Mo. Emblematic of Growing Suburban Poverty," *The Avenue/Rethinking Metropolitan America*, Brookings Institution, August 15, 2014, http://www.brookings.edu/blogs/the-avenue/posts/2014/08/15-ferguson-suburban-poverty.

74. Quoted in Derrick Bell, *Faces at the Bottom of the Well: The Permanence of Racism* (New York: Basic Books, 1992), 40.

75. "About the Black Lives Matter Network," Black Lives Matter, accessed August 22, 2015, http://blacklivesmatter.com/about/.

76. Mapping Police Violence, home page, last modified January 1, 2016, http://mappingpoliceviolence.org/.

77. "Eric Garner Death: 76 Arrested at London Westfield Demo," BBC News, December 11, 2014, http://www.bbc.com/news/uk-england-london-30424338.

78. U.S. Department of Justice, Civil Rights Division, *Investigation of the Ferguson Police Department*, March 4, 2015, http://www.justice.gov/sites/default/files/opa/press-releases/attachments/2015/03/04/ferguson_police_department_report.pdf.

79. President's Task Force on 21st Century Policing, *Final Report of the President's Task Force on 21st Century Policing* (Washington, DC: Office of Community Oriented Policing Services, 2015), 25.

80. Kimberly Kindy and Kimbriell Kelly, "Thousands Dead, Few Prosecuted," *Washington Post*, April 11, 2015.

81. Alex Kane, "Not Just Ferguson: 11 Eye-Opening Facts about America's Militarized Police Forces," Moyers & Company, August 13, 2014, http://billmoyers.com/2014/08/13/not-just-ferguson-11-eye-opening-facts-about-americas-militarized-police-forces/14.

82. Quoted in Alexander, *The New Jim Crow*, 72–73.

83. Matt Apuzzo, "War Gear Flows to Police Departments," *New York Times*, June 8, 2014, http://www.nytimes.com/2014/06/09/us/war-gear-flows-to-police-departments.html?_r=0.

84. Ira Glass, "547: Cops See It Differently, Part One," *This American Life*, podcast audio, February 6, 2015, http://www.thisamericanlife.org/radio-archives/episode/547/transcript; Ira Glass, "548: Cops See It Differently, Part Two," *This American Life*, podcast audio, February 13, 2015, http://www.thisamericanlife.org/radio-archives/episode/548/transcript.

85. Erin Durkin, "De Blasio Talks of Worries for Son Dante after Grand Jury Declines to Indict Cop in Eric Garner Death," *New York Daily News*, December 3, 2014, http://www.nydailynews.com/new-york/nyc-crime/de-blasio-talks-biracial-son-eric-garner-grand-jury-article-1.2032253.

SUGGESTED REFERENCES

Diversity and Racial Belonging

Dickerson, Debra J. *The End of Blackness: Returning the Souls of Black Folk to Their Rightful Owners.* New York: Pantheon, 2004.

Golden, Thelma. *Freestyle: The Studio Museum in Harlem.* New York: Studio Museum in Harlem, 2001. Exhibition catalog.

Hancock, Ange-Marie. *The Politics of Disgust: The Public Identity of the Welfare Queen.* New York: New York University Press, 2004.

Johnson, Charles. "The End of the Black American Narrative." *American Scholar* 77, no. 3 (Summer 2008): 32–42.

Moore, Sharon E., ed. "African American Megachurches and Community Empowerment: Fostering Life in Dry Places." Special issue, *Journal of African American Studies* 15, no. 2 (June 2011).

Obama, Barack. *Dreams from My Father: A Story of Race and Inheritance.* New York: Random House, 1995.

Robinson, Eugene. *Disintegration: The Splintering of Black America.* New York: Doubleday, 2010.

Touré. *Who's Afraid of Post-Blackness? What It Means to Be Black Now.* New York: Free Press, 2011.

Trying Times

Alexander, Michelle. *The New Jim Crow: Mass Incarceration in the Age of Colorblindness.* New York: New Press, 2010.

Latty, Yvonne. *We Were There: Voices of African American Veterans, from World War II to the War in Iraq.* New York: Amistad, 2004.

Manza, Jeff, and Christopher Uggen. *Locked Out: Felon Disenfranchisement and American Democracy.* New York: Oxford University Press, 2006.

Marable, Manning, and Kristen Clarke, eds. *Seeking Higher Ground: The Hurricane Katrina Crisis, Race, and Public Policy Reader.* New York: Palgrave Macmillan, 2008.

Phillips, Kimberly. *War! What Is It Good For? Black Freedom Struggles and the U.S. Military from World War II to Iraq.* Chapel Hill: University of North Carolina Press, 2012.

Thompson, Heather Ann. "Why Mass Incarceration Matters: Rethinking Crisis, Decline, and Transformation in Postwar American History." *Journal of American History* 97, no. 3 (December 2010): 703–34.

Wailoo, Keith, Karen M. O'Neill, Jeffrey Dowd, and Roland Anglin, eds. *Katrina's Imprint: Race and Vulnerability in America.* New Brunswick, NJ: Rutgers University Press, 2010.

Change Comes to America

Bonilla-Silva, Eduardo. *Racism without Racists: Color-Blind Racism and the Persistence of Racial Inequality in the United States.* 2nd ed. Lanham, MD: Rowman & Littlefield, 2006.

Lusane, Clarence. *Pipe Dream Blues: Racism and the War on Drugs.* Boston: South End Press, 1991.

———. *Race in the Global Era: African Americans at the Millennium.* Boston: South End Press, 1997.

Ogletree, Charles. *The Presumption of Guilt: The Arrest of Henry Louis Gates Jr. and Race, Class, and Crime in America.* New York: Palgrave Macmillan, 2010.

Sugrue, Thomas J. *Not Even Past: Barack Obama and the Burden of Race.* Princeton, NJ: Princeton University Press, 2010.

Wise, Tim. *Colorblind: The Rise of Post-Racial Politics and the Retreat from Racial Equity.* San Francisco: City Lights, 2010.

The Declaration of Independence

IN CONGRESS, JULY 4, 1776, THE UNANIMOUS DECLARATION OF THE THIRTEEN UNITED STATES OF AMERICA

When in the Course of human events, it becomes necessary for one people to dissolve the political bands which have connected them with another, and to assume among the Powers of the earth, the separate and equal station to which the Laws of Nature and of Nature's God entitle them, a decent respect to the opinions of mankind requires that they should declare the causes which impel them to the separation.

We hold these truths to be self-evident, that all men are created equal, that they are endowed by their Creator with certain unalienable rights, that among these are Life, Liberty, and the pursuit of Happiness. That to secure these rights, Governments are instituted among Men, deriving their just powers from the consent of the governed. That whenever any Form of Government becomes destructive of these ends, it is the Right of the People to alter or to abolish it, and to institute new Government, laying its foundation on such principles and organizing its powers in such form, as to them shall seem most likely to effect their Safety and Happiness. Prudence, indeed, will dictate that Governments long established should not be changed for light and transient causes; and accordingly all experience hath shown, that mankind are more disposed to suffer, while evils are sufferable, than to right themselves by abolishing the forms to which they are accustomed. But when a long train of abuses and usurpations, pursuing invariably the same Object evinces a design to reduce them under absolute Despotism, it is their right, it is their duty, to throw off such Government, and to provide new Guards for their future security. — Such has been the patient sufferance of these Colonies; and such is now the necessity which constrains them to alter their former Systems of Government. The history of the present King of Great Britain is a history of repeated injuries and usurpations, all having in direct object the establishment of an absolute Tyranny over these States. To prove this, let Facts be submitted to a candid world.

He has refused his Assent to Laws, the most wholesome and necessary for the public good.

He has forbidden his Governors to pass Laws of immediate and pressing importance, unless suspended in their operation till his Assent should be obtained; and, when so suspended, he has utterly neglected to attend to them.

He has refused to pass other Laws for the accommodation of large districts of people, unless those people would relinquish the right of Representation in the Legislature, a right inestimable to them and formidable to tyrants only.

He has called together legislative bodies at places unusual, uncomfortable, and distant from the depository of their public Records, for the sole purpose of fatiguing them into compliance with his measures.

He has dissolved Representative Houses repeatedly, for opposing with manly firmness his invasions on the rights of the people.

He has refused for a long time, after such dissolutions, to cause others to be elected; whereby the Legislative powers, incapable of Annihilation, have returned to the People at large for their exercise; the State remaining in the mean time exposed to all the dangers of invasion from without and convulsions within.

He has endeavoured to prevent the population of these States; for that purpose obstructing the Laws of Naturalization of Foreigners; refusing to pass others to encourage their migrations hither, and raising the conditions of new Appropriations of Lands.

He has obstructed the Administration of Justice, by refusing his Assent to Laws for establishing Judiciary powers.

He has made Judges dependent on his Will alone, for the tenure of their offices, and the amount and payment of their salaries.

He has erected a multitude of New Offices, and sent hither swarms of Officers to harass our People, and eat out their substance.

He has kept among us, in times of peace, Standing Armies without the Consent of our legislature.

He has combined with others to subject us to a jurisdiction foreign to our constitution, and unacknowledged by our laws; giving his Assent to their Acts of pretended Legislation:

For quartering large bodies of armed troops among us:

For protecting them, by a mock Trial, from Punishment for any Murders which they should commit on the Inhabitants of these States:

For cutting off our Trade with all parts of the world:

For imposing taxes on us without our Consent:

For depriving us, in many cases, of the benefits of Trial by jury:

For transporting us beyond Seas to be tried for pretended offences:

For abolishing the free System of English Laws in a neighbouring Province, establishing therein an Arbitrary government, and enlarging its Boundaries so as to render it at once an example and fit instrument for introducing the same absolute rule into these Colonies:

For taking away our Charters, abolishing our most valuable Laws, and altering fundamentally the Forms of our Governments:

For suspending our own Legislatures, and declaring themselves invested with Power to legislate for us in all cases whatsoever.

He has abdicated Government here, by declaring us out of his Protection and waging War against us.

He has plundered our seas, ravaged our Coasts, burnt our towns, and destroyed the lives of our people.

He is at this time transporting large armies of foreign mercenaries to compleat the works of death, desolation, and tyranny, already begun with circumstances of Cruelty & perfidy scarcely paralleled in the most barbarous ages, and totally unworthy the Head of a civilized nation.

He has constrained our fellow Citizens taken Captive on the high Seas to bear Arms against their Country, to become the executioners of their friends and Brethren, or to fall themselves by their Hands.

He has excited domestic insurrections amongst us, and has endeavoured to bring on the inhabitants of our frontiers, the merciless Indian Savages, whose known rule of warfare, is an undistinguished destruction of all ages, sexes, and conditions.

In every stage of these Oppressions We have Petitioned for Redress in the most humble terms: Our repeated Petitions have been answered only by repeated injury. A Prince, whose character is thus marked by every act which may define a Tyrant, is unfit to be the ruler of a free people.

Nor have We been wanting in attention to our British brethren. We have warned them from time to time of attempts by their legislature to extend an unwarrantable jurisdiction over us. We have reminded them of the circumstances of our emigration and settlement here. We have appealed to their native justice and magnanimity, and we have conjured them by the ties of our common kindred to disavow these usurpations, which would inevitably interrupt our connections and correspondence. They too have been deaf to the voice of justice and of consanguinity. We must, therefore, acquiesce in the necessity, which denounces our Separation, and hold them, as we hold the rest of mankind, Enemies in War, in Peace Friends.

We, therefore, the Representatives of the United States of America, in General Congress, Assembled, appealing to the Supreme Judge of the world for the rectitude of our intentions, do, in the Name, and by Authority of the good People of these Colonies, solemnly publish and declare, That these United Colonies are, and of Right ought to be FREE AND INDEPENDENT STATES; that they are Absolved from all Allegiance to the British Crown, and that all political connection between them and the State of Great Britain, is and ought to be totally dissolved; and that as Free and Independent States, they have full Power to levy War, conclude Peace, contract Alliances, establish Commerce, and to do all other Acts and Things which Independent States may of right do. And for the support of this Declaration, with a firm reliance on the Protection of Divine Providence, we mutually pledge to each other our Lives, our Fortunes, and our sacred Honor.

John Hancock

Button Gwinnett	George Wythe	James Wilson	Josiah Bartlett
Lyman Hall	Richard Henry Lee	Geo. Ross	Wm. Whipple
Geo. Walton	Th. Jefferson	Caesar Rodney	Matthew Thornton
Wm. Hooper	Benja. Harrison	Geo. Read	Saml. Adams
Joseph Hewes	Thos. Nelson, Jr.	Thos. M'Kean	John Adams
John Penn	Francis Lightfoot Lee	Wm. Floyd	Robt. Treat Paine
Edward Rutledge	Carter Braxton	Phil. Livingston	Elbridge Gerry
Thos. Heyward, Junr.	Robt. Morris	Frans. Lewis	Step. Hopkins
Thomas Lynch, Junr.	Benjamin Rush	Lewis Morris	William Ellery
Arthur Middleton	Benja. Franklin	Richd. Stockton	Roger Sherman
Samuel Chase	John Morton	John Witherspoon	Sam'el Huntington
Wm. Paca	Geo. Clymer	Fras. Hopkinson	Wm. Williams
Thos. Stone	Jas. Smith	John Hart	Oliver Wolcott
Charles Carroll of Carrollton	Geo. Taylor	Abra. Clark	

The Constitution of the United States of America

AGREED TO BY PHILADELPHIA CONVENTION, SEPTEMBER 17, 1787
IMPLEMENTED MARCH 4, 1789

We the People of the United States, in Order to form a more perfect Union, establish Justice, insure domestic Tranquility, provide for the common defence, promote the general Welfare, and secure the Blessings of Liberty to ourselves and our Posterity, do ordain and establish this Constitution for the United States of America.

ARTICLE I

SECTION 1. All legislative Powers herein granted shall be vested in a Congress of the United States, which shall consist of a Senate and a House of Representatives.

SECTION 2. The House of Representatives shall be composed of Members chosen every second Year by the People of the several States, and the Electors in each State shall have the Qualifications requisite for Electors of the most numerous Branch of the State Legislature.

No Person shall be a Representative who shall not have attained to the Age of twenty-five Years, and been seven Years a Citizen of the United States, and who shall not, when elected, be an Inhabitant of that State in which he shall be chosen.

Representatives and direct Taxes shall be apportioned among the several States which may be included within this Union, according to their respective Numbers, *which shall be determined by adding to the whole Number of free Persons, including those bound to Service for a Term of Years, and excluding Indians not taxed, three fifths of all other Persons.*[1]

The actual Enumeration shall be made within three Years after the first Meeting of the Congress of the United States, and within every subsequent Term of ten Years, in such Manner as they shall by Law direct. The Number of Representatives shall not exceed one for every thirty Thousand, but each State shall have at Least one Representative; and *until such enumeration shall be made, the State of New Hampshire shall be entitled to chuse three, Massachusetts eight, Rhode Island and Providence Plantations one, Connecticut five, New-York six, New Jersey four, Pennsylvania eight, Delaware one, Maryland six, Virginia ten, North Carolina five, South Carolina five, and Georgia three.*

Note: The Constitution became effective March 4, 1789. Provisions in italics are no longer relevant or have been changed by constitutional amendment. Copy highlighted in yellow pertains to African Americans.

---

1. Changed by Section 2 of the Fourteenth Amendment.

When vacancies happen in the Representation from any State, the Executive Authority thereof shall issue Writs of Election to fill such Vacancies.

The House of Representatives shall chuse their Speaker and other Officers; and shall have the sole Power of Impeachment.

SECTION 3. The Senate of the United States shall be composed of two Senators from each State, *chosen by the Legislature thereof,*[2] for six Years; and each Senator shall have one Vote.

Immediately after they shall be assembled in Consequence of the first Election, they shall be divided as equally as may be into three Classes. The Seats of the Senators of the first Class shall be vacated at the Expiration of the second Year, of the second Class at the Expiration of the fourth Year, and of the third Class at the Expiration of the sixth Year, so that one-third may be chosen every second Year; and if Vacancies happen by Resignation, or otherwise, during the Recess of the Legislature of any State, the Executive thereof may make temporary Appointments until the next Meeting of the Legislature, which shall then fill such Vacancies.[3]

No person shall be a Senator who shall not have attained to the Age of thirty Years, and been nine Years a Citizen of the United States, and who shall not, when elected, be an Inhabitant of that State for which he shall be chosen.

The Vice President of the United States shall be President of the Senate, but shall have no Vote, unless they be equally divided.

The Senate shall chuse their other Officers, and also a President pro tempore, in the absence of the Vice President, or when he shall exercise the Office of President of the United States.

The Senate shall have the sole Power to try all Impeachments. When sitting for that Purpose, they shall be on Oath or Affirmation. When the President of the United States is tried, the Chief Justice shall preside: And no Person shall be convicted without the Concurrence of two thirds of the Members present.

Judgment in Cases of Impeachment shall not extend further than to removal from Office, and disqualification to hold and enjoy any Office of honor, Trust or Profit under the United States: but the Party convicted shall nevertheless be liable and subject to Indictment, Trial, Judgment and Punishment, according to Law.

SECTION 4. The Times, Places and Manner of holding Elections for Senators and Representatives, shall be prescribed in each State by the Legislature thereof; but the Congress may at any time by Law make or alter such Regulations, except as to the Places of Chusing Senators.

The Congress shall assemble at least once in every Year, and such Meeting *shall be on the first Monday in December, unless they shall by Law appoint a different Day.*[4]

SECTION 5. Each House shall be the Judge of the Elections, Returns and Qualifications of its own Members, and a Majority of each shall constitute a Quorum to do Business; but a smaller number may adjourn from day to day, and may be authorized to compel the Attendance of absent Members, in such Manner, and under such Penalties, as each House may provide.

Each House may determine the Rules of its Proceedings, punish its Members for disorderly Behavior, and, with the Concurrence of two thirds, expel a Member.

Each House shall keep a Journal of its Proceedings, and from time to time publish the same, excepting such Parts as may in their Judgment require Secrecy; and the Yeas and Nays of the Members of either House on any question shall, at the Desire of one-fifth of those Present, be entered on the Journal.

Neither House, during the Session of Congress, shall, without the Consent of the other, adjourn for more than three days, nor to any other Place than that in which the two Houses shall be sitting.

SECTION 6. The Senators and Representatives shall receive a Compensation for their Services, to be ascertained by Law, and paid out of the Treasury of the United States. They shall in all Cases, except Treason, Felony and Breach of the Peace, be privileged from Arrest during their Attendance at the Session of their respective Houses, and in going to and returning from the same; and for any Speech or Debate in either House, they shall not be questioned in any other Place.

No Senator or Representative shall, during the Time for which he was elected, be appointed to any

---

2. Changed by Section 1 of the Seventeenth Amendment.
3. Changed by Clause 2 of the Seventeenth Amendment.

4. Changed by Section 2 of the Twentieth Amendment.

civil Office under the Authority of the United States, which shall have been created, or the Emoluments whereof shall have been increased, during such time; and no Person holding any Office under the United States, shall be a Member of either House during his Continuance in Office.

SECTION 7. All Bills for raising Revenue shall originate in the House of Representatives; but the Senate may propose or concur with Amendments as on other Bills.

Every Bill which shall have passed the House of Representatives and the Senate, shall, before it becomes a Law, be presented to the President of the United States; If he approve he shall sign it, but if not he shall return it, with his Objections to that House in which it shall have originated, who shall enter the Objections at large on their Journal, and proceed to reconsider it. If after such Reconsideration two thirds of that House shall agree to pass the Bill, it shall be sent, together with the Objections, to the other House, by which it shall likewise be reconsidered, and if approved by two thirds of that House, it shall become a Law. But in all such Cases the Votes of both Houses shall be determined by Yeas and Nays, and the Names of the Persons voting for and against the Bill shall be entered on the Journal of each House respectively. If any Bill shall not be returned by the President within ten Days (Sundays excepted) after it shall have been presented to him, the Same shall be a Law, in like Manner as if he had signed it, unless the Congress by their Adjournment prevent its Return, in which Case it shall not be a Law.

Every Order, Resolution, or Vote to which the Concurrence of the Senate and the House of Representatives may be necessary (except on a question of Adjournment) shall be presented to the President of the United States; and before the Same shall take Effect, shall be approved by him, or being disapproved by him, shall be repassed by two thirds of the Senate and House of Representatives, according to the Rules and Limitations prescribed in the Case of a Bill.

SECTION 8. The Congress shall have Power to lay and collect Taxes, Duties, Imposts and Excises, to pay the Debts and provide for the common Defence and general Welfare of the United States; but all Duties, Imposts and Excises shall be uniform throughout the United States;

To borrow money on the credit of the United States;

To regulate Commerce with foreign Nations, and among the several States, and with the Indian Tribes;

To establish an uniform Rule of Naturalization, and uniform Laws on the subject of Bankruptcies throughout the United States;

To coin Money, regulate the Value thereof, and of foreign Coin, and fix the Standard of Weights and Measures;

To provide for the Punishment of counterfeiting the Securities and current Coin of the United States;

To establish Post Offices and post Roads;

To promote the Progress of Science and useful Arts, by securing for limited Times to Authors and Inventors the exclusive Right to their respective Writings and Discoveries;

To constitute Tribunals inferior to the supreme Court;

To define and punish Piracies and Felonies committed on the high Seas, and Offenses against the Law of Nations;

To declare War, grant Letters of Marque and Reprisal, and make Rules concerning Captures on Land and Water;

To raise and support Armies, but no Appropriation of Money to that Use shall be for a longer Term than two Years;

To provide and maintain a Navy;

To make Rules for the Government and Regulation of the land and naval Forces;

To provide for calling forth the Militia to execute the Laws of the Union, suppress Insurrections and repel Invasions;

To provide for organizing, arming, and disciplining the Militia, and for governing such Part of them as may be employed in the Service of the United States, reserving to the States respectively, the Appointment of the Officers, and the Authority of training the Militia according to the discipline prescribed by Congress;

To exercise exclusive Legislation in all Cases whatsoever, over such District (not exceeding ten Miles square) as may, by Cession of particular States, and the acceptance of Congress, become the Seat of Government of the United States, and to exercise like Authority over all Places purchased by the Consent of the Legislature of the State in which the Same shall be, for the Erection of Forts, Magazines, Arsenals, dock-Yards, and other needful Buildings; — And

To make all Laws which shall be necessary and proper for carrying into Execution the foregoing Powers, and all other Powers vested by this Constitution in the Government of the United States, or in any Department or Officer thereof.

SECTION 9. *The Migration or Importation of such Persons as any of the States now existing shall think proper to admit, shall not be prohibited by the Congress prior to the Year one thousand eight hundred and eight but a tax or duty may be imposed on such Importation, not exceeding ten dollars for each Person.*

The privilege of the Writ of Habeas Corpus shall not be suspended, unless when in Cases of Rebellion or Invasion the public Safety may require it.

No Bill of Attainder or ex post facto Law shall be passed.

No capitation, or other direct, Tax shall be laid, unless in Proportion to the Census or Enumeration herein before directed to be taken.[5]

No Tax or Duty shall be laid on Articles exported from any State.

No Preference shall be given by any Regulation of Commerce or Revenue to the Ports of one State over those of another: nor shall Vessels bound to, or from, one State, be obliged to enter, clear, or pay Duties in another.

No Money shall be drawn from the Treasury, but in Consequence of Appropriations made by law; and a regular Statement and Account of the Receipts and Expenditures of all public Money shall be published from time to time.

No Title of Nobility shall be granted by the United States: And no Person holding any Office of Profit or Trust under them, shall, without the Consent of the Congress, accept of any present, Emolument, Office, or Title, of any kind whatever, from any King, Prince, or foreign State.

SECTION 10. No State shall enter into any Treaty, Alliance, or Confederation; grant Letters of Marque and Reprisal; coin Money; emit Bills of Credit; make

any Thing but gold and silver Coin a Tender in Payment of Debts; pass any Bill of Attainder, ex post facto Law, or Law impairing the Obligation of Contracts, or grant any Title of Nobility.

No State shall, without the Consent of the Congress, lay any Imposts or Duties on Imports or Exports, except what may be absolutely necessary for executing its inspection Laws: and the net Produce of all Duties and Imposts, laid by any State on Imports or Exports, shall be for the Use of the Treasury of the United States; and all such Laws shall be subject to the Revision and Control of the Congress.

No State shall, without the Consent of the Congress, lay any duty of Tonnage, keep Troops, or Ships of War in time of Peace, enter into any Agreement or Compact with another State, or with a foreign Power, or engage in War, unless actually invaded, or in such imminent Danger as will not admit of delay.

ARTICLE II

SECTION 1. The executive Power shall be vested in a President of the United States of America. He shall hold his Office during the Term of four Years, and, together with the Vice President, chosen for the same Term, be elected, as follows:

Each State shall appoint, in such Manner as the Legislature thereof may direct, a Number of Electors, equal to the whole Number of Senators and Representatives to which the State may be entitled in the Congress; but no Senator or Representative, or Person holding an Office of Trust or Profit under the United States, shall be appointed an Elector.

The Electors shall meet in their respective States, and vote by Ballot for two Persons, of whom one at least shall not be an Inhabitant of the same State with themselves. And they shall make a List of all the Persons voted for, and of the Number of Votes for each; which List they shall sign and certify, and transmit sealed to the Seat of the Government of the United States, directed to the President of the Senate. The President of the Senate shall, in the Presence of the Senate and House of Representatives, open all the Certificates, and the Votes shall then be counted. The Person having the greatest Number of Votes shall be the President, if such Number be a Majority of the whole Number of Electors appointed; and if there be more than one who have such Majority, and have an equal Number of Votes, then the

---

5. Changed by the Sixteenth Amendment.

House of Representatives shall immediately chuse by Ballot one of them for President; and if no Person have a Majority, then from the five highest on the List the said House shall in like Manner chuse the President. But in chusing the President, the Votes shall be taken by States, the Representation from each State having one Vote; a quorum for this Purpose shall consist of a Member or Members from two thirds of the States, and a Majority of all the States shall be necessary to a Choice. In every Case, after the Choice of the President, the Person having the greatest Number of Votes of the Electors shall be the Vice President. But if there should remain two or more who have equal Votes, the Senate shall chuse from them by Ballot the Vice President.[6]

The Congress may determine the Time of chusing the Electors, and the Day on which they shall give their Votes; which Day shall be the same throughout the United States.

No Person except a natural born Citizen, or a Citizen of the United States, at the time of the Adoption of this Constitution, shall be eligible to the Office of President; neither shall any Person be eligible to that Office who shall not have attained to the Age of thirty five Years, and been fourteen Years a Resident within the United States.

In Case of the Removal of the President from Office, or of his Death, Resignation, or Inability to discharge the Powers and Duties of the said Office, the same shall devolve on the Vice President, *and the Congress may by Law provide for the Case of Removal, Death, Resignation, or Inability, both of the President and Vice President, declaring what Officer shall then act as President, and such Officer shall act accordingly, until the Disability be removed, or a President shall be elected.*[7]

The President shall, at stated Times, receive for his Services a Compensation, which shall neither be increased nor diminished during the Period for which he shall have been elected, and he shall not receive within that Period any other Emolument from the United States, or any of them.

Before he enter on the Execution of his Office, he shall take the following Oath or Affirmation: — "I do solemnly swear (or affirm) that I will faithfully execute the Office of President of the United States, and will to the best of my Ability, preserve, protect and defend the Constitution of the United States."

SECTION 2. The President shall be Commander in Chief of the Army and Navy of the United States, and of the Militia of the several States, when called into the actual Service of the United States; he may require the Opinion, in writing, of the principal Officer in each of the executive Departments, upon any Subject relating to the Duties of their respective Offices, and he shall have Power to Grant Reprieves and Pardons for Offences against the United States, except in Cases of Impeachment.

He shall have Power, by and with the Advice and Consent of the Senate, to make Treaties, provided two thirds of the Senators present concur; and he shall nominate, and by and with the Advice and Consent of the Senate, shall appoint Ambassadors, other public Ministers and Consuls, Judges of the supreme Court, and all other Officers of the United States, whose Appointments are not herein otherwise provided for, and which shall be established by Law: but the Congress may by Law vest the Appointment of such inferior Officers, as they think proper, in the President alone, in the Courts of Law, or in the Heads of Departments.

The President shall have Power to fill up all Vacancies that may happen during the Recess of the Senate, by granting Commissions which shall expire at the End of their next Session.

SECTION 3. He shall from time to time give to the Congress Information of the State of the Union, and recommend to their Consideration such Measures as he shall judge necessary and expedient; he may, on extraordinary Occasions, convene both Houses, or either of them, and in Case of Disagreement between them, with Respect to the Time of Adjournment, he may adjourn them to such Time as he shall think proper; he shall receive Ambassadors and other public Ministers; he shall take Care that the Laws be faithfully executed, and shall Commission all the Officers of the United States.

SECTION 4. The President, Vice President and all civil Officers of the United States, shall be removed from Office on Impeachment for, and Conviction of, Treason, Bribery, or other high Crimes and Misdemeanors.

---

6. Superseded by the Twelfth Amendment.
7. Modified by the Twenty-Fifth Amendment.

ARTICLE III

SECTION 1. The judicial Power of the United States, shall be vested in one supreme Court, and in such inferior Courts as the Congress may from time to time ordain and establish. The Judges, both of the supreme and inferior Courts, shall hold their Offices during good Behaviour, and shall, at stated Times, receive for their Services a Compensation, which shall not be diminished during their Continuance in Office.

SECTION 2. The judicial Power shall extend to all Cases, in Law and Equity, arising under this Constitution, the Laws of the United States, and Treaties made, or which shall be made, under their Authority; — to all Cases affecting Ambassadors, other public Ministers and Consuls; — to all Cases of admiralty and maritime Jurisdiction; — to Controversies to which the United States shall be a Party; — to Controversies between two or more States; — *between a State and Citizens of another State;*[8] — between Citizens of different States; — between Citizens of the same State claiming Lands under Grants of different States, and between a State, or the Citizens thereof, and foreign States, Citizens or Subjects.

In all Cases affecting Ambassadors, other public Ministers and Consuls, and those in which a State shall be Party, the supreme Court shall have original Jurisdiction. In all the other Cases before mentioned, the supreme Court shall have appellate Jurisdiction, both as to Law and Fact, with such Exceptions, and under such Regulations as the Congress shall make.

The trial of all Crimes, except in Cases of Impeachment, shall be by Jury; and such Trial shall be held in the State where said Crimes shall have been committed; but when not committed within any State, the Trial shall be at such Place or Places as the Congress may by Law have directed.

SECTION 3. Treason against the United States, shall consist only in levying War against them, or in adhering to their Enemies, giving them Aid and Comfort. No Person shall be convicted of Treason unless on the Testimony of two Witnesses to the same overt Act, or on Confession in open Court.

The Congress shall have Power to declare the Punishment of Treason, but no Attainder of Treason shall work Corruption of Blood, or Forfeiture except during the Life of the Person attainted.

ARTICLE IV

SECTION 1. Full Faith and Credit shall be given in each State to the public Acts, Records, and judicial Proceedings of every other State. And the Congress may by general Laws prescribe the Manner in which such Acts, Records, and Proceedings shall be proved, and the Effect thereof.

SECTION 2. The Citizens of each State shall be entitled to all Privileges and Immunities of Citizens in the several States.

A Person charged in any State with Treason, Felony, or other Crime, who shall flee from Justice, and be found in another State, shall on demand of the executive Authority of the State from which he fled, be delivered up, to be removed to the State having Jurisdiction of the Crime.

No Person held to Service or Labour in one State, under the Laws thereof, escaping into another, shall, in Consequence of any Law or Regulation therein, be discharged from such Service or Labour, but shall be delivered up on Claim of the Party to whom such Service or Labour may be due.[9]

SECTION 3. New States may be admitted by the Congress into this Union; but no new State shall be formed or erected within the Jurisdiction of any other State; nor any State be formed by the Junction of two or more States, or parts of States, without the Consent of the Legislatures of the States concerned as well as of the Congress.

The Congress shall have Power to dispose of and make all needful Rules and Regulations respecting the Territory or other Property belonging to the United States; and nothing in this Constitution shall be so construed as to Prejudice any Claims of the United States, or of any particular State.

SECTION 4. The United States shall guarantee to every State in this Union a Republican Form of Government, and shall protect each of them against Invasion; and on Application of the Legislature, or of the Executive (when the Legislature cannot be convened) against domestic Violence.

---

8. Restricted by the Eleventh Amendment.

9. Superseded by the Thirteenth Amendment.

ARTICLE V

The Congress, whenever two thirds of both Houses shall deem it necessary, shall propose Amendments to this Constitution, or, on the Application of the Legislatures of two thirds of the several States, shall call a Convention for proposing Amendments, which, in either Case, shall be valid to all Intents and Purposes, as Part of this Constitution, when ratified by the Legislatures of three fourths of the several States, or by Conventions in three fourths thereof, as the one or the other Mode of Ratification may be proposed by the Congress; Provided that no Amendment which may be made prior to the Year One thousand eight hundred and eight shall in any Manner affect the first and fourth Clauses in the Ninth Section of the first Article; and that no State, without its Consent, shall be deprived of its equal Suffrage in the Senate.

ARTICLE VI

All Debts contracted and Engagements entered into, before the Adoption of this Constitution, shall be as valid against the United States under this Constitution, as under the Confederation.

This Constitution, and the Laws of the United States which shall be made in Pursuance thereof; and all Treaties made, or which shall be made, under the Authority of the United States, shall be the supreme Law of the Land; and the Judges in every State shall be bound thereby, any Thing in the Constitution or Laws of any State to the Contrary notwithstanding.

The Senators and Representatives before mentioned, and the Members of the several State Legislatures, and all executive and judicial Officers, both of the United States and of the several States, shall be bound by Oath or Affirmation, to support this Constitution; but no religious Test shall ever be required as a Qualification to any Office or public Trust under the United States.

ARTICLE VII

The Ratification of the Conventions of nine States shall be sufficient for the Establishment of this Constitution between the States so ratifying the Same.

Done in Convention by the Unanimous Consent of the States present the Seventeenth Day of September in the Year of our Lord one thousand seven hundred and Eighty seven and of the Independence of the United States of America the Twelfth. In Witness whereof We have hereunto subscribed our Names.

Go. Washington
President and deputy from Virginia

New Hampshire
John Langdon
Nicholas Gilman

Massachusetts
Nathaniel Gorham
Rufus King

Connecticut
Wm. Saml. Johnson
Roger Sherman

New York
Alexander Hamilton

New Jersey
Wil. Livingston
David Brearley
Wm. Paterson
Jona. Dayton

Pennsylvania
B. Franklin
Thomas Mifflin
Robt. Morris
Geo. Clymer
Thos. FitzSimons
Jared Ingersoll
James Wilson
Gouv. Morris

Delaware
Geo. Read
Gunning Bedford jun
John Dickinson
Richard Bassett
Jaco. Broom

Maryland
James McHenry
Dan. of St. Thos. Jenifer
Danl. Carroll

Virginia
John Blair
James Madison, Jr.

North Carolina
Wm. Blount
Richd. Dobbs Spaight
Hu Williamson

South Carolina
J. Rutledge
Charles Cotesworth
     Pinckney
Charles Pinckney
Pierce Butler

Georgia
William Few
Abr. Baldwin

Amendments to the Constitution

AMENDMENT I [1791][1]

Congress shall make no law respecting an establishment of religion, or prohibiting the free exercise thereof; or abridging the freedom of speech, or of the press; or the right of the people peaceably to assemble, and to petition the government for a redress of grievances.

AMENDMENT II [1791]

A well-regulated militia being necessary to the security of a free State, the right of the people to keep and bear arms shall not be infringed.

AMENDMENT III [1791]

No soldier shall, in time of peace, be quartered in any house without the consent of the owner, nor in time of war, but in a manner to be prescribed by law.

AMENDMENT IV [1791]

The right of the people to be secure in their persons, houses, papers, and effects, against unreasonable searches and seizures, shall not be violated, and no warrants shall issue but upon probable cause, supported by oath or affirmation, and particularly describing the place to be searched, and the persons or things to be seized.

AMENDMENT V [1791]

No person shall be held to answer for a capital, or otherwise infamous crime, unless on a presentment or indictment of a grand jury, except in cases arising in the land or naval forces, or in the militia, when in actual service in time of war or public danger; nor shall any person be subject for the same offence to be twice put in jeopardy of life or limb; nor shall be compelled in any criminal case to be a witness against himself, nor be deprived of life, liberty, or property, without due process of law; nor shall private property be taken for public use without just compensation.

AMENDMENT VI [1791]

In all criminal prosecutions, the accused shall enjoy the right to a speedy and public trial, by an impartial jury of the State and district wherein the crime shall have been committed, which district shall have been previously ascertained by law, and to be informed of the nature and cause of the accusation; to be confronted with the witnesses against him; to have compulsory process for obtaining witnesses in his favor, and to have the assistance of counsel for his defence.

AMENDMENT VII [1791]

In suits at common law, where the value in controversy shall exceed twenty dollars, the right of trial by jury shall be preserved, and no fact tried by a jury shall be otherwise reexamined in any court of the United States, than according to the rules of the common law.

AMENDMENT VIII [1791]

Excessive bail shall not be required, nor excessive fines imposed, nor cruel and unusual punishments inflicted.

AMENDMENT IX [1791]

The enumeration in the Constitution, of certain rights, shall not be construed to deny or disparage others retained by the people.

AMENDMENT X [1791]

The powers not delegated to the United States by the Constitution, nor prohibited by it to the States, are reserved to the States respectively, or to the people.

AMENDMENT XI [1798]

The judicial power of the United States shall not be construed to extend to any suit in law or equity, commenced or prosecuted against one of the United States by citizens of another State, or by citizens or subjects of any foreign state.

AMENDMENT XII [1804]

The electors shall meet in their respective States, and vote by ballot for President and Vice-President, one of whom, at least, shall not be an inhabitant of the same State with themselves; they shall name in their ballots the person voted for as President, and in

---

1. The date in brackets indicates when the amendment was ratified.

distinct ballots the person voted for as Vice-President, and they shall make distinct lists of all persons voted for as President, and of all persons voted for as Vice-President, and of the number of votes for each, which lists they shall sign and certify, and transmit sealed to the seat of government of the United States, directed to the President of the Senate; — the President of the Senate shall, in the presence of the Senate and House of Representatives, open all the certificates and the votes shall then be counted; — the person having the greatest number of votes for President shall be the President, if such number be a majority of the whole number of electors appointed; and if no person have such majority, then from the persons having the highest numbers not exceeding three on the list of those voted for as President, the House of Representatives shall choose immediately, by ballot, the President. But in choosing the President, the votes shall be taken by States, the representation from each State having one vote; a quorum for this purpose shall consist of a member or members from two-thirds of the States, and a majority of all the States shall be necessary to a choice. And if the House of Representatives shall not choose a President whenever the right of choice shall devolve upon them, before *the fourth day of March* next following, then the Vice-President shall act as President, as in the case of the death or other constitutional disability of the President.[2]

The person having the greatest number of votes as Vice-President shall be the Vice-President, if such number be a majority of the whole number of electors appointed; and if no person have a majority, then from the two highest numbers on the list the Senate shall choose the Vice-President; a quorum for the purpose shall consist of two-thirds of the whole number of Senators, and a majority of the whole number shall be necessary to a choice. But no person constitutionally ineligible to the office of President shall be eligible to that of Vice-President of the United States.

AMENDMENT XIII [1865]

SECTION 1. Neither slavery nor involuntary servitude, except as a punishment for crime whereof the party shall have been duly convicted, shall exist

within the United States, or any place subject to their jurisdiction.

SECTION 2. Congress shall have power to enforce this article by appropriate legislation.

AMENDMENT XIV [1868]

SECTION 1. All persons born or naturalized in the United States, and subject to the jurisdiction thereof, are citizens of the United States and of the State wherein they reside. No State shall make or enforce any law which shall abridge the privileges or immunities of citizens of the United States; nor shall any State deprive any person of life, liberty, or property, without due process of law; nor deny to any person within its jurisdiction the equal protection of the laws.

SECTION 2. Representatives shall be appointed among the several States according to their respective numbers, counting the whole number of persons in each State, excluding Indians not taxed. But when the right to vote at any election for the choice of electors for President and Vice-President of the United States, Representatives in Congress, the executive and judicial officers of a State, or the members of the legislature thereof, is denied to any of the male inhabitants of such State, being twenty-one years of age and citizens of the United States, or in any way abridged, except for participation in rebellion, or other crime, the basis of representation therein shall be reduced in the proportion which the number of such male citizens shall bear to the whole number of male citizens twenty-one years of age in such State.

SECTION 3. No person shall be a Senator or Representative in Congress, or Elector of President and Vice-President, or hold any office, civil or military, under the United States, or under any State, who, having previously taken an oath, as a member of Congress, or as an officer of the United States, or as a member of any State legislature, or as an executive or judicial officer of any State, to support the Constitution of the United States, shall have engaged in insurrection or rebellion against the same, or given aid or comfort to the enemies thereof. Congress may, by a vote of two-thirds of each house, remove such disability.

SECTION 4. The validity of the public debt of the United States, authorized by law, including debts incurred for payment of pensions and bounties for

---

2. Superseded by Section 3 of the Twentieth Amendment.

services in suppressing insurrection or rebellion, shall not be questioned. But neither the United States nor any State shall assume or pay any debt or obligation incurred in aid of insurrection or rebellion against the United States, or any claim for the loss or emancipation of any slave; but all such debts, obligations, and claims shall be held illegal and void.

SECTION 5. The Congress shall have power to enforce, by appropriate legislation, the provisions of this article.

AMENDMENT XV [1870]

SECTION 1. The right of citizens of the United States to vote shall not be denied or abridged by the United States or by any State on account of race, color, or previous condition of servitude.

SECTION 2. The Congress shall have power to enforce this article by appropriate legislation.

AMENDMENT XVI [1913]

The Congress shall have power to lay and collect taxes on incomes, from whatever source derived, without apportionment among the several States, and without regard to any census or enumeration.

AMENDMENT XVII [1913]

SECTION 1. The Senate of the United States shall be composed of two Senators from each State, elected by the people thereof, for six years; and each Senator shall have one vote. The electors in each State shall have the qualifications requisite for electors of [voters for] the most numerous branch of the State legislatures.

SECTION 2. When vacancies happen in the representation of any State in the Senate, the executive authority of such State shall issue writs of election to fill such vacancies: Provided, that the Legislature of any State may empower the executive thereof to make temporary appointments until the people fill the vacancies by election as the Legislature may direct.

SECTION 3. This amendment shall not be so construed as to affect the election or term of any Senator chosen before it becomes valid as part of the Constitution.

AMENDMENT XVIII [1919; Repealed 1933 by Amendment XXI]

SECTION 1. After one year from the ratification of this article the manufacture, sale, or transportation of intoxicating liquors within, the importation thereof into, or the exportation thereof from the United States and all territory subject to the jurisdiction thereof, for beverage purposes, is hereby prohibited.

SECTION 2. The Congress and the several States shall have concurrent power to enforce this article by appropriate legislation.

SECTION 3. This article shall be inoperative unless it shall have been ratified as an amendment to the Constitution by the legislatures of the several States, as provided by the Constitution, within seven years from the date of the submission thereof to the States by the Congress.

AMENDMENT XIX [1920]

SECTION 1. The right of citizens of the United States to vote shall not be denied or abridged by the United States or by any State on account of sex.

SECTION 2. Congress shall have the power to enforce this article by appropriate legislation.

AMENDMENT XX [1933]

SECTION 1. The terms of the President and Vice-President shall end at noon on the twentieth day of January, and the terms of Senators and Representatives at noon on the third day of January, of the years in which such terms would have ended if this article had not been ratified; and the terms of their successors shall then begin.

SECTION 2. The Congress shall assemble at least once in every year, and such meeting shall begin at noon on the third day of January, unless they shall by law appoint a different day.

SECTION 3. If, at the time fixed for the beginning of the term of the President, the President-elect shall have died, the Vice-President-elect shall become President. If a President shall not have been chosen before the time fixed for the beginning of his term, or if the President-elect shall have failed to qualify, then the Vice-President-elect shall act as President until a President shall have qualified; and the Congress may by law provide for the case wherein neither a

President-elect nor a Vice-President-elect shall have qualified, declaring who shall then act as President, or the manner in which one who is to act shall be selected, and such person shall act accordingly until a President or Vice-President shall have qualified.

SECTION 4. The Congress may by law provide for the case of the death of any of the persons from whom the House of Representatives may choose a President whenever the right of choice shall have devolved upon them, and for the case of the death of any of the persons from whom the Senate may choose a Vice-President whenever the right of choice shall have devolved upon them.

SECTION 5. Sections 1 and 2 shall take effect on the 15th day of October following the ratification of this article.

SECTION 6. This article shall be inoperative unless it shall have been ratified as an amendment to the Constitution by the Legislatures of three-fourths of the several States within seven years from the date of its submission.

AMENDMENT XXI [1933]

SECTION 1. The eighteenth article of amendment to the Constitution of the United States is hereby repealed.

SECTION 2. The transportation or importation into any State, Territory, or Possession of the United States for delivery or use therein of intoxicating liquors, in violation of the laws thereof, is hereby prohibited.

SECTION 3. This article shall be inoperative unless it shall have been ratified as an amendment to the Constitution by conventions in the several States, as provided in the Constitution, within seven years from the date of the submission thereof to the States by the Congress.

AMENDMENT XXII [1951]

SECTION 1. No person shall be elected to the office of the President more than twice, and no person who has held the office of President, or acted as President, for more than two years of a term to which some other person was elected President shall be elected to the office of President more than once. But this article shall not apply to any person holding the office of President when this Article was proposed by the Congress, and

shall not prevent any person who may be holding the office of President, or acting as President, during the term within which this Article becomes operative from holding the office of President or acting as President during the remainder of such term.

SECTION 2. This article shall be inoperative unless it shall have been ratified as an amendment to the Constitution by the legislatures of three-fourths of the several States within seven years from the date of its submission to the States by the Congress.

AMENDMENT XXIII [1961]

SECTION 1. The District constituting the seat of Government of the United States shall appoint in such manner as the Congress may direct: A number of electors of President and Vice-President equal to the whole number of Senators and Representatives in Congress to which the District would be entitled if it were a State, but in no event more than the least populous State; they shall be in addition to those appointed by the States, but they shall be considered for the purposes of the election of President and Vice-President, to be electors appointed by a State; and they shall meet in the District and perform such duties as provided by the twelfth article of amendment.

SECTION 2. The Congress shall have the power to enforce this article by appropriate legislation.

AMENDMENT XXIV [1964]

SECTION 1. The right of citizens of the United States to vote in any primary or other election for President or Vice-President, for electors for President or Vice-President, or for Senator or Representative in Congress, shall not be denied or abridged by the United States or any State by reason of failure to pay any poll tax or other tax.

SECTION 2. The Congress shall have the power to enforce this article by appropriate legislation.

AMENDMENT XXV [1967]

SECTION 1. In case of the removal of the President from office or of his death or resignation, the Vice-President shall become President.

SECTION 2. Whenever there is a vacancy in the office of the Vice-President, the President shall nominate a

Vice-President who shall take office upon confirmation by a majority vote of both Houses of Congress.

SECTION 3. Whenever the President transmits to the President pro tempore of the Senate and the Speaker of the House of Representatives his written declaration that he is unable to discharge the powers and duties of his office, and until he transmits to them a written declaration to the contrary, such powers and duties shall be discharged by the Vice-President as Acting President.

SECTION 4. Whenever the Vice-President and a majority of either the principal officers of the executive departments or of such other body as Congress may by law provide, transmit to the President pro tempore of the Senate and the Speaker of the House of Representatives their written declaration that the President is unable to discharge the powers and duties of his office, the Vice-President shall immediately assume the powers and duties of the office as Acting President.

Thereafter, when the President transmits to the President pro tempore of the Senate and the Speaker of the House of Representatives his written declaration that no inability exists, he shall resume the powers and duties of his office unless the Vice-President and a majority of either the principal officers of the executive department[s] or of such other body as Congress may by law provide, transmit within four days to the President pro tempore of the Senate and the Speaker of the House of Representatives their written declaration that the President is unable to discharge the powers and duties of his office. Thereupon Congress shall decide the issue, assembling within forty-eight hours for that purpose if not in session. If the Congress, within twenty-one days after receipt of the latter written declaration, or, if Congress is not in session, within twenty-one days after Congress is required to assemble, determines by two-thirds vote of both Houses that the President is unable to discharge the powers and duties of his office, the Vice-President shall continue to discharge the same as Acting President; otherwise, the President shall resume the powers and duties of his office.

AMENDMENT XXVI [1971]

SECTION 1. The right of citizens of the United States, who are eighteen years of age or older, to vote shall not be denied or abridged by the United States or by any State on account of age.

SECTION 2. The Congress shall have power to enforce this article by appropriate legislation.

AMENDMENT XXVII [1992]

No law, varying the compensation for the services of the Senators and Representatives, shall take effect, until an election of Representatives shall have intervened.

The Emancipation Proclamation [1863]

BY THE PRESIDENT OF THE UNITED STATES OF AMERICA:
A PROCLAMATION.

Whereas, on the twenty-second day of September, in the year of our Lord one thousand eight hundred and sixty-two, a proclamation was issued by the President of the United States, containing, among other things, the following, to wit:

"That on the first day of January, in the year of our Lord one thousand eight hundred and sixty-three, all persons held as slaves within any State or designated part of a State, the people whereof shall then be in rebellion against the United States, shall be then, thenceforward, and forever free; and the Executive Government of the United States, including the military and naval authority thereof, will recognize and maintain the freedom of such persons, and will do no act or acts to repress such persons, or any of them, in any efforts they may make for their actual freedom.

"That the Executive will, on the first day of January aforesaid, by proclamation, designate the States and parts of States, if any, in which the people thereof, respectively, shall then be in rebellion against the United States;

and the fact that any State, or the people thereof, shall on that day be, in good faith, represented in the Congress of the United States by members chosen thereto at elections wherein a majority of the qualified voters of such State shall have participated, shall, in the absence of strong countervailing testimony, be deemed conclusive evidence that such State, and the people thereof, are not then in rebellion against the United States."

Now, therefore I, Abraham Lincoln, President of the United States, by virtue of the power in me vested as Commander-in-Chief, of the Army and Navy of the United States in time of actual armed rebellion against the authority and government of the United States, and as a fit and necessary war measure for suppressing said rebellion, do, on this first day of January, in the year of our Lord one thousand eight hundred and sixty-three, and in accordance with my purpose so to do publicly proclaimed for the full period of one hundred days, from the day first above mentioned, order and designate as the States and parts of States wherein the people thereof respectively, are this day in rebellion against the United States, the following, to wit:

Arkansas, Texas, Louisiana, (except the Parishes of St. Bernard, Plaquemines, Jefferson, St. John, St. Charles, St. James Ascension, Assumption, Terrebonne, Lafourche, St. Mary, St. Martin, and Orleans, including the City of New Orleans) Mississippi, Alabama, Florida, Georgia, South Carolina, North Carolina, and Virginia, (except the forty-eight counties designated as West Virginia, and also the counties of Berkley, Accomac, Northampton, Elizabeth City, York, Princess Ann, and Norfolk, including the cities of Norfolk and Portsmouth[)], and which excepted parts, are for the present, left precisely as if this proclamation were not issued.

And by virtue of the power, and for the purpose aforesaid, I do order and declare that all persons held as slaves within said designated States, and parts of States, are, and henceforward shall be free; and that the Executive government of the United States, including the military and naval authorities thereof, will recognize and maintain the freedom of said persons.

And I hereby enjoin upon the people so declared to be free to abstain from all violence, unless in necessary self-defence; and I recommend to them that, in all cases when allowed, they labor faithfully for reasonable wages.

And I further declare and make known, that such persons of suitable condition, will be received into the armed service of the United States to garrison forts, positions, stations, and other places, and to man vessels of all sorts in said service.

And upon this act, sincerely believed to be an act of justice, warranted by the Constitution, upon military necessity, I invoke the considerate judgment of mankind, and the gracious favor of Almighty God.

In witness whereof, I have hereunto set my hand and caused the seal of the United States to be affixed.

Done at the City of Washington, this first day of January, in the year of our Lord one thousand eight hundred and sixty three, and of the Independence of the United States of America the eighty-seventh.

By the President: ABRAHAM LINCOLN
WILLIAM H. SEWARD, Secretary of State.

Presidents of the United States

Years in Office	President	Party
1789–1797	George Washington	No party designation
1797–1801	John Adams	Federalist
1801–1809	Thomas Jefferson	Democratic-Republican
1809–1817	James Madison	Democratic-Republican
1817–1825	James Monroe	Democratic-Republican
1825–1829	John Quincy Adams	Democratic-Republican
1829–1837	Andrew Jackson	Democratic
1837–1841	Martin Van Buren	Democratic
1841	William H. Harrison	Whig
1841–1845	John Tyler	Whig
1845–1849	James K. Polk	Democratic
1849–1850	Zachary Taylor	Whig
1850–1853	Millard Fillmore	Whig
1853–1857	Franklin Pierce	Democratic
1857–1861	James Buchanan	Democratic
1861–1865	Abraham Lincoln	Republican
1865–1869	Andrew Johnson	Republican
1869–1877	Ulysses S. Grant	Republican
1877–1881	Rutherford B. Hayes	Republican
1881	James A. Garfield	Republican
1881–1885	Chester A. Arthur	Republican
1885–1889	Grover Cleveland	Democratic
1889–1893	Benjamin Harrison	Republican
1893–1897	Grover Cleveland	Democratic
1897–1901	William McKinley	Republican
1901–1909	Theodore Roosevelt	Republican
1909–1913	William H. Taft	Republican
1913–1921	Woodrow Wilson	Democratic
1921–1923	Warren G. Harding	Republican
1923–1929	Calvin Coolidge	Republican
1929–1933	Herbert C. Hoover	Republican
1933–1945	Franklin D. Roosevelt	Democratic
1945–1953	Harry S. Truman	Democratic
1953–1961	Dwight D. Eisenhower	Republican
1961–1963	John F. Kennedy	Democratic
1963–1969	Lyndon B. Johnson	Democratic
1969–1974	Richard M. Nixon	Republican
1974–1977	Gerald R. Ford	Republican
1977–1981	Jimmy Carter	Democratic
1981–1989	Ronald W. Reagan	Republican
1989–1993	George H. W. Bush	Republican
1993–2001	William Jefferson Clinton	Democratic
2001–2009	George W. Bush	Republican
2009–2017	Barack Obama	Democratic

Selected Legislative Acts

The following four pieces of legislation touched myriad aspects of African American life: unjust employment practices, discrimination in public facilities, black voter disfranchisement, and the ability of blacks to immigrate to the United States from elsewhere in the world. From opening new work opportunities and spurring black voter participation to paving the way for one million new black immigrants, these acts had profound consequences for African Americans. The brief excerpts that follow provide some of the key provisions of the acts. As you read them, consider the specific impact these words had on the lives of African Americans — both individually and as a group.

The Civil Rights Act of 1875

The Civil Rights Act of 1875, introduced by Senator Charles Sumner and passed after his death, stipulated that all individuals were to receive equal treatment in public facilities — such as hotels, trains, and places of public amusement — regardless of race. The act made discrimination in such facilities a criminal offense and established monetary damages for those who were victims of discrimination. The law was not well enforced, however. It was finally struck down altogether in the 1883 *Civil Rights Cases,* in which the Supreme Court ruled that Congress lacked the authority to outlaw discriminatory practices by private individuals and businesses.

Whereas it is essential to just government we recognize the equality of all men before the law, and hold that it is the duty of government in its dealings with the people to mete out equal and exact justice to all, of whatever nativity, race, color, or persuasion, religious or political; and it being the appropriate object of legislation to enact great fundamental principles into law: Therefore,

Be it enacted, That all persons within the jurisdiction of the United States shall be entitled to the full and equal enjoyment of the accommodations, advantages, facilities, and privileges of inns, public conveyances on land or water, theaters, and other places of public amusement; subject only to the conditions and limitations established by law, and applicable alike to citizens of every race and color, regardless of any previous condition of servitude.

SECTION 2. That any person who shall violate the foregoing section . . . shall, for every offense, forfeit and pay the sum of five hundred dollars to the person aggrieved thereby, to be recovered in an action of debt, with full costs; and shall also, for every such offense, be deemed guilty of a misdemeanor, and, upon conviction thereof, shall be fined not less than five hundred nor more than one thousand dollars, or shall be imprisoned not less than thirty days nor more than one year. . . .

SECTION 3. That the district and circuit courts of the United States shall have . . . cognizance of all crimes and offenses against, and violations of, the provisions of this act; and actions for the penalty given by the preceding section may be prosecuted in the territorial, district, or circuit courts of the United States wherever the defendant may be found, without regard to the other party; and the district attorneys, marshals, and deputy marshals of the United States, and commissioners appointed by the circuit and territorial courts of the United States . . . are hereby specially authorized and required to institute proceedings against every person who shall violate the provisions of this act, and cause him to be arrested and imprisoned or bailed, as the case may be, for trial before such court of the United States, or territorial court, as by law has cognizance of the offense, except in respect of the right of action accruing to the person aggrieved; and such district attorneys shall cause such proceedings to be prosecuted to their termination as in other cases . . . and any district attorney who shall willfully fail to institute and prosecute the proceedings herein required, shall, for every such offense, forfeit and pay the sum of five hundred dollars to the person aggrieved thereby, to be recovered by an action of debt, with full costs, and shall, on conviction thereof, be deemed guilty of a misdemeanor, and be fined not less than one thousand nor more than five thousand dollars. . . .

SECTION 4. That no citizen possessing all other qualifications which are or may be prescribed by law shall be disqualified for service as grand or petit juror in any court of the United States, or of any State, on account of race, color, or previous condition of servitude; and any officer or other person charged with any duty in the selection or summoning of jurors who shall exclude or fail to summon any citizen for the cause aforesaid shall, on conviction thereof, be deemed guilty of a misdemeanor, and be fined not more than five thousand dollars.

The Civil Rights Act of 1964

The Civil Rights Act of 1964 was a watershed for both African Americans and women. It prohibited discrimination on the basis of race, color, religion, sex, or national origin in employment and voting practices, federally assisted programs, public education, and places of public accommodation; authorized the Justice Department to institute desegregation suits; and provided technical and financial aid to assist communities in the desegregation of their schools. The act's fundamental Title VII, which dealt with discrimination in the workplace, established the Equal Employment Opportunity Commission to investigate cases of job discrimination.

AN ACT

To enforce the constitutional right to vote, to confer jurisdiction upon the district courts of the United States to provide injunctive relief against discrimination in public accommodations, to authorize the Attorney General to institute suits to protect constitutional rights in public facilities and public education, to extend the Commission on Civil Rights, to prevent discrimination in federally assisted programs, to establish a Commission on Equal Employment Opportunity, and for other purposes. . . .

TITLE I — VOTING RIGHTS

. . .

"(2) No person acting under color of law shall —

"(A) in determining whether any individual is qualified under State law or laws to vote in any Federal election, apply any standard, practice, or procedure different from the standards, practices, or procedures applied under such law or laws to other individuals . . . who have been found by State officials to be qualified to vote;

"(B) deny the right of any individual to vote in any Federal election because of an error or omission on any record or paper relating to any application, registration, or other act requisite to voting, if such error or omission is not material in determining whether such individual is qualified under State law to vote in such election; or

"(C) employ any literacy test as a qualification for voting in any Federal election unless (i) such test is administered to each individual and is conducted wholly in writing, and (ii) a certified copy of the test and of the answers given by the individual is furnished to him within twenty-five days of the submission of his request. . . ."

TITLE II — INJUNCTIVE RELIEF AGAINST DISCRIMINATION IN PLACES OF PUBLIC ACCOMMODATION

. . . (a) All persons shall be entitled to the full and equal enjoyment of the goods, services, facilities, and privileges, advantages, and accommodations of any place of public accommodation, as defined in this section, without discrimination or segregation on the ground of race, color, religion, or national origin.

(b) Each of the following establishments which serves the public is a place of public accommodation within the meaning of this title if its operations affect commerce, or if discrimination or segregation by it is supported by State action:

(1) any inn, hotel, motel, or other establishment which provides lodging to transient guests, other than an establishment located within a building which contains not more than five rooms for rent or hire and which is actually occupied by the proprietor of such establishment as his residence;

(2) any restaurant, cafeteria, lunchroom, lunch counter, soda fountain, or other facility principally engaged in selling food for consumption on the premises. . . .

(3) any motion picture house, theater, concert hall, sports arena, stadium or other place of exhibition or entertainment; and

(4) any establishment (A)(i) which is physically located within the premises of any establishment otherwise covered by this subsection, or (ii) within the premises of which is physically located any such covered establishment, and (B) which holds itself out as serving patrons of such covered establishment. . . .

(d) Discrimination or segregation by an establishment is supported by State action within the meaning of this title if such discrimination or segregation (1) is carried on under color of any law, statute, ordinance, or regulation; or (2) is carried on under color of any custom or usage required or enforced by officials of the State or political subdivision thereof; or (3) is required by action of the State or political subdivision thereof.

(e) The provisions of this title shall not apply to a private club or other establishment not in fact open to the public, except to the extent that the facilities of such establishment are made available to the customers or patrons of an establishment within the scope of subsection (b). . . .

TITLE III — DESEGREGATION OF PUBLIC FACILITIES

SECTION 301. (a) Whenever the Attorney General receives a complaint in writing signed by an individual to the effect that he is being deprived of or threatened with the loss of his right to the equal protection of the laws, on account of his race, color, religion, or national origin . . . the Attorney General is authorized to institute for or in the name of the United States a civil action in any appropriate district court of the United States against such parties and for such relief as may be appropriate. . . .

TITLE IV — DESEGREGATION OF PUBLIC EDUCATION . . .

Survey and Report of Educational Opportunities

SECTION 402. The Commissioner shall conduct a survey and make a report to the President and the Congress, within two years of the enactment of this title, concerning the lack of availability of equal educational opportunities for individuals by reason of race, color, religion, or national origin in public educational institutions at all levels in the United States,

its territories and possessions, and the District of Columbia.

Technical Assistance

SECTION 403. The Commissioner is authorized, upon the application of any school board, State, municipality, school district, or other governmental unit legally responsible for operating a public school or schools, to render technical assistance to such applicant in the preparation, adoption, and implementation of plans for the desegregation of public schools. Such technical assistance may, among other activities, include making available to such agencies information regarding effective methods of coping with special educational problems occasioned by desegregation, and making available to such agencies personnel of the Office of Education or other persons specially equipped to advise and assist them in coping with such problems. . . .

TITLE V — COMMISSION ON CIVIL RIGHTS . . .

"**SECTION 104.** (a) The Commission shall —

"(1) investigate allegations . . . that certain citizens of the United States are being deprived of their right to vote and have that vote counted by reason of their color, race, religion, or national origin; . . .

"(2) study and collect information concerning legal developments constituting a denial of equal protection of the laws under the Constitution because of race, color, religion or national origin or in the administration of justice;

"(3) appraise the laws and policies of the Federal Government with respect to denials of equal protection of the laws under the Constitution because of race, color, religion or national origin or in the administration of justice;

"(4) serve as a national clearinghouse for information in respect to denials of equal protection of the laws because of race, color, religion or national origin, including but not limited to the fields of voting, education, housing, employment, the use of public facilities, and transportation, or in the administration of justice;

"(5) investigate allegations . . . that citizens of the United States are unlawfully being accorded or denied the right to vote, or to have their votes properly counted, in any election. . . ."

TITLE VI — NONDISCRIMINATION IN FEDERALLY ASSISTED PROGRAMS

SECTION 601. No person in the United States shall, on the ground of race, color, or national origin, be excluded from participation in, be denied the benefits of, or be subjected to discrimination under any program or activity receiving Federal financial assistance. . . .

TITLE VII — EQUAL EMPLOYMENT OPPORTUNITY . . .

Discrimination Because of Race, Color, Religion, Sex, or National Origin

SECTION 703. (a) It shall be an unlawful employment practice for an employer —

(1) to fail or refuse to hire or to discharge any individual, or otherwise to discriminate against any individual with respect to his compensation, terms, conditions, or privileges of employment, because of such individual's race, color, religion, sex, or national origin; or

(2) to limit, segregate, or classify his employees in any way which would deprive or tend to deprive any individual of employment opportunities or otherwise adversely affect his status as an employee, because of such individual's race, color, religion, sex, or national origin.

(b) It shall be an unlawful employment practice for an employment agency to fail or refuse to refer for employment, or otherwise to discriminate against, any individual because of his race, color, religion, sex, or national origin, or to classify or refer for employment any individual on the basis of his race, color, religion, sex, or national origin.

(c) It shall be an unlawful employment practice for a labor organization —

(1) to exclude or to expel from its membership, or otherwise to discriminate against, any individual because of his race, color, religion, sex, or national origin;

(2) to limit, segregate, or classify its membership, or to classify or fail or refuse to refer for employment any individual, in any way which would deprive or tend to deprive any individual of employment opportunities, or would limit such employment opportunities or otherwise adversely affect his status as an employee or as an applicant for employment, because of such individual's race, color, religion, sex, or national origin; or

(3) to cause or attempt to cause an employer to discriminate against an individual in violation of this section.

(d) It shall be an unlawful employment practice for any employer, labor organization, or joint labor-management committee controlling apprenticeship or other training or retraining, including on-the-job training programs to discriminate against any individual because of his race, color, religion, sex, or national origin in admission to, or employment in, any program established to provide apprenticeship or other training.

(e) Notwithstanding any other provision of this title, (1) it shall not be an unlawful employment practice for an employer to hire and employ employees, for an employment agency to classify, or refer for employment any individual, for a labor organization to classify its membership or to classify or refer for employment any individual, or for an employer, labor organization, or joint labor-management committee controlling apprenticeship or other training or retraining programs to admit or employ any individual in any such program, on the basis of his religion, sex, or national origin in those certain instances where religion, sex, or national origin is a bona fide occupational qualification reasonably necessary to the normal operation of that particular business or enterprise, and (2) it shall not be an unlawful employment practice for a school, college, university, or other educational institution or institution of learning to hire and employ employees of a particular religion if such school, college, university, or other educational institution or institution of learning is, in whole or in substantial part, owned, supported, controlled, or managed by a particular religion or by a particular religious corporation, association, or society, or if the curriculum of such school, college, university, or other educational institution or institution of learning is directed toward the propagation of a particular religion. . . .

Equal Employment Opportunity Commission

SECTION 705. (a) There is hereby created a Commission to be known as the Equal Employment Opportunity Commission, which shall be composed of five members, not more than three of whom shall be members of the same political party, who shall be appointed by the President by and with the advice and consent of the Senate. . . .

(g) The Commission shall have power —

(1) to cooperate with and, with their consent, utilize regional, State, local, and other agencies, both public and private, and individuals;

(2) to pay to witnesses whose depositions are taken or who are summoned before the Commission or any of its agents the same witness and mileage fees as are paid to witnesses in the courts of the United States;

(3) to furnish to persons subject to this title such technical assistance as they may request to further their compliance with this title or an order issued thereunder;

(4) upon the request of (i) any employer, whose employees or some of them, or (ii) any labor organization, whose members or some of them, refuse or threaten to refuse to cooperate in effectuating the provisions of this title, to assist in such effectuation by conciliation or such other remedial action as is provided by this title;

(5) to make such technical studies as are appropriate to effectuate the purposes and policies of this title and to make the results of such studies available to the public;

(6) to refer matters to the Attorney General with recommendations for intervention in a civil action brought by an aggrieved party under section 706, or for the institution of a civil action by the Attorney General under section 707, and to advise, consult, and assist the Attorney General on such matters. . . .

TITLE VIII — REGISTRATION AND VOTING STATISTICS

SECTION 801. The Secretary of Commerce shall promptly conduct a survey to compile registration and voting statistics in such geographic areas as may be recommended by the Commission on Civil Rights.

The Voting Rights Act of 1965

The 1965 Voting Rights Act eliminated the practices responsible for the widespread disfranchisement of blacks in the South, such as poll taxes and literacy tests. It also established a strict system of enforcement, providing federal oversight for the administration of elections — particularly in states that had consistently engaged in discriminatory voting practices. The impact of the act was tremendous: Blacks registered in droves, and black voter participation skyrocketed throughout the South.

SECTION 2. No voting qualification or prerequisite to voting, or standard, practice, or procedure shall be imposed or applied by any State or political subdivision to deny or abridge the right of any citizen of the United States to vote on account of race or color.

SECTION 3. (a) Whenever the Attorney General institutes a proceeding under any statute to enforce the guarantees of the fifteenth amendment in any State or political subdivision the court shall authorize the appointment of Federal examiners by the United States Civil Service Commission . . . to serve for such period of time and for such political subdivisions as the court shall determine is appropriate to enforce the guarantees of the fifteenth amendment. . . .

(b) If in a proceeding instituted by the Attorney General under any statute to enforce the guarantees of the fifteenth amendment in any State or political subdivision the court finds that a test or device has been used for the purpose or with the effect of denying or abridging the right of any citizen of the United States to vote on account of race or color, it shall suspend the use of tests and devices in such State or political subdivisions as the court shall determine is appropriate and for such period as it deems necessary. . . .

SECTION 4. (a) To assure that the right of citizens of the United States to vote is not denied or abridged on account of race or color, no citizen shall be denied the right to vote in any Federal, State, or local election because of his failure to comply with any test or device in any State. . . .

SECTION 7. (a) The examiners for each political subdivision shall, at such places as the Civil Service Commission shall by regulation designate, examine applicants concerning their qualifications for voting. An application to an examiner shall be in such form as the Commission may require and shall contain allegations that the applicant is not otherwise registered to vote.

(b) Any person whom the examiner finds, in accordance with instructions received under section 9(b), to have the qualifications prescribed by State law not inconsistent with the Constitution and laws of the United States shall promptly be placed on a list of eligible voters. . . . The examiner shall certify and transmit such list, and any supplements as appropriate, at least once a month, to the offices of the appropriate election officials, with copies to the Attorney General and the attorney general of the State, and any such lists and supplements thereto transmitted during the month shall be available for public inspection on the last business day of the month and, in any event, not later than the forty-fifth day prior to any election. The appropriate State or local election official shall place such names on the official voting list. Any person whose name appears on the examiner's list shall be entitled and allowed to vote in the election district of his residence unless and until the appropriate election officials shall have been notified that such person has been removed from such list. . . .

(c) The examiner shall issue to each person whose name appears on such a list a certificate evidencing his eligibility to vote. . . .

SECTION 8. Whenever an examiner is serving under this Act in any political subdivision, the Civil Service Commission may assign, at the request of the Attorney General, one or more persons, who may be officers of the United States, (1) to enter and attend at any place for holding an election in such subdivision for the purpose of observing whether persons who are entitled to vote are being permitted to vote, and (2) to enter and attend at any place for tabulating the votes cast at any election held in such subdivision for the purpose of observing whether votes cast by persons entitled to vote are being properly tabulated. . . .

SECTION 9. (a) Any challenge to a listing on an eligibility list prepared by an examiner shall be heard and determined by a hearing officer appointed by and responsible to the Civil Service Commission and under such rules as the Commission shall by regulation prescribe. . . .

SECTION 10. (a) The Congress finds that the requirement of the payment of a poll tax as a precondition to voting (i) precludes persons of limited means from voting or imposes unreasonable financial hardship upon such persons as a precondition to their exercise of the franchise, (ii) does not bear a reasonable relationship to any legitimate State interest in the conduct of elections, and (iii) in some areas has the purpose or effect of denying persons the right to vote because of race or color. Upon the basis of these findings, Congress declares that the constitutional right of citizens to vote is denied or abridged in some areas by the requirement of the payment of a poll tax as a precondition to voting. . . .

SECTION 11. (a) No person acting under color of law shall fail or refuse to permit any person to vote who is entitled to vote under any provision of this Act or is otherwise qualified to vote, or willfully fail or refuse to tabulate, count, and report such person's vote.

The Immigration and Nationality Act of 1965

Also known as the Hart-Celler Act, the Immigration and Nationality Act of 1965 was a substantial revision of the immigration policy that had prevailed in the United States since 1924, when a quota system was established that limited immigration by nation of origin. The new system used different criteria to determine eligibility, such as immigrants' skills, family connections within the United States, and potential benefit to the national economy. As a result of the act, immigration surged, bringing one million immigrants from Africa — as well as large numbers from Asia and Latin America — to the United States.

"(1) Visas shall be first made available, in a number not to exceed 20 per centum of the number specified in section 201(a)(ii), to qualified immigrants who are the unmarried sons or daughters of citizens of the United States.

"(2) Visas shall next be made available, in a number not to exceed 20 per centum of the number specified in section 201(a)(ii), plus any visas not required for the classes specified in paragraph (1), to qualified immigrants who are the spouses, unmarried sons or unmarried daughters of an alien lawfully admitted for permanent residence.

"(3) Visas shall next be made available, in a number not to exceed 10 per centum of the number specified in section 201(a)(ii), to qualified immigrants who are members of the professions, or who because of their exceptional ability in the sciences or the arts will substantially benefit prospectively the national economy, cultural interests, or welfare of the United States.

"(4) Visas shall next be made available, in a number not to exceed 10 per centum of the number specified in section 201(a)(ii), plus any visas not required for the classes specified in paragraphs (1) through (3), to qualified immigrants who are the married sons or the married daughters of citizens of the United States.

"(5) Visas shall next be made available, in a number not to exceed 24 per centum of the number specified in section 201(a)(ii), plus any visas not required for the classes specified in paragraphs (1) through (4), to qualified immigrants who are the brothers or sisters of citizens of the United States.

"(6) Visas shall next be made available, in a number not to exceed 10 per centum of the number specified in section 201(a)(ii), to qualified immigrants who are capable of performing specified skilled or unskilled labor, not of a temporary or seasonal nature, for which a shortage of employable and willing persons exists in the United States.

"(7) Conditional entries shall next be made available by the Attorney General, pursuant to such regulations as he may prescribe and in a number not to exceed 6 per centum of the number specified in section 201(a)(ii), to aliens who satisfy an Immigration and Naturalization Service officer at an examination in any non-Communist or non-Communist-dominated country, (A) that (i) because of persecution or fear of persecution on account of race, religion, or political opinion they have fled (I) from any Communist or Communist-dominated country or area, or (II) from any country within the general area of the Middle East, and (ii) are unable or unwilling to return to such country or area on account of race, religion, or political opinion, and (iii) are not nationals of the countries or areas in which their application for conditional entry is made; or (B) that they are persons uprooted by catastrophic natural calamity as defined by the President who are unable to return to their usual place of abode. For the purpose of the foregoing the term 'general area of the Middle East' means the area between and including (1) Libya on the west, (2) Turkey on the north, (3) Pakistan on the east, and (4) Saudi Arabia and Ethiopia on the south: *Provided*, That immigrant visas in a number not exceeding one-half the number specified in this paragraph may be made available, in lieu of conditional entries of a like number, to such aliens who have been continuously physically present in the United States for a period of at least two years prior to application for adjustment of status."

Selected Supreme Court Decisions

The cases that follow were landmarks in African American legal history, bringing about both immediate and long-term change and establishing vital precedents for future cases. Grappling with issues as diverse as the right of Congress to limit slavery, the citizenship status of slaves, the permissibility of state-sanctioned segregation, discrimination in the workplace, and the constitutionality of affirmative action, these cases exerted a tremendous impact on both black citizens and the nation as a whole. The following brief excerpts have been carefully selected from the full opinions of the U.S. Supreme Court. As you read them, consider how they are reflective of the specific historical and social contexts in which they were written.

Dred Scott v. Sandford [1857]

In 1846, the Missouri slave couple Dred and Harriet Scott sued for their freedom, claiming that their temporary residence with their master on free soil had rendered them free. Eleven years later, in *Dred Scott v. Sandford*, the Supreme Court ruled that the Scotts were to remain enslaved. In its decision, the Court harked back to the original intent of the writers of the Declaration of Independence and the U.S. Constitution, arguing that this was of paramount importance in interpreting the meaning of those documents for slaves and others of African descent. The Court argued that neither Scott nor any other person of African descent was entitled to U.S. citizenship and thus could not legitimately bring suit in court. Further, the Court asserted that slaves were property and emphasized that Congress lacked the authority to deny slaveholders their property. With this decision, the Court made it clear that Congress could not prevent slaveholding anywhere, rendering all laws that forbade slavery in the territories — including the Missouri Compromise of 1820 — unconstitutional.

The question is simply this: Can a negro whose ancestors were imported into this country, and sold as slaves, become a member of the political community formed and brought into existence by the Constitution of the United States, and as such become entitled to all the rights and privileges and immunities guaranteed to the citizen? One of which rights is the privilege of suing in a court of the United States in the cases specified in the Constitution. . . .

In the opinion of the court, the legislation and histories of the times, and the language used in the Declaration of Independence, show, that neither the class of persons who had been imported as slaves, nor their descendants, whether they had become free or not, were then acknowledged as a part of the people, nor intended to be included in the general words used in that memorable instrument.

It is difficult at this day to realize the state of public opinion in relation to that unfortunate race, which prevailed in the civilized and enlightened portions of the world at the time of the Declaration of Independence, and when the Constitution of the United States was framed and adopted. But the public history of every European nation displays it in a manner too plain to be mistaken.

They had for more than a century before been regarded as beings of an inferior order, and altogether unfit to associate with the white race, either in social or political relations; and so far inferior, that they had no rights which the white man was bound to respect; and that the negro might justly and lawfully be reduced to slavery for his benefit. He was bought and sold, and treated as an ordinary article of merchandise and traffic, whenever a profit could be made by it. This opinion was at that time fixed and universal in the civilized portion of the white race. It was regarded as an axiom in morals as well as in politics, which no one thought of disputing. . . .

The language of the Declaration of Independence . . . would seem to embrace the whole human family, and if [these words] were used in a similar instrument at this day would be so understood. But it is too clear for dispute, that the enslaved African race were not intended to be included, and formed no part of the people who framed and adopted this declaration. . . .

. . . The right of property in a slave is distinctly and expressly affirmed in the Constitution. . . .

Upon these considerations, it is the opinion of the court that the act of Congress which prohibited a citizen from holding and owning property of this kind in the territory of the United States north of the line therein mentioned, is not warranted by the Constitution, and is therefore void; and that neither Dred Scott himself, nor any of his family, were made free by being carried into this territory; even if they had been carried there by the owner, with the intention of becoming a permanent resident.

Plessy v. Ferguson [1896]

In this landmark case, a shoemaker named Homer Plessy, who was seven-eighths white, argued that he had been denied equal protection under the Fourteenth Amendment when a Louisiana train conductor forced him to ride in the "colored car" rather than in the first-class car for which he had purchased a ticket. Plessy was arrested and charged with violating Louisiana's Separate Car Act. The Court found the act to be constitutional, arguing that separate facilities did not violate one's right to equal protection under the laws or imply the inferiority of blacks. In protecting local custom and state-sanctioned discrimination and establishing the legal doctrine of separate but equal, the decision effectively legitimized and legalized Jim Crow, paving the way for new and ever more sweeping laws. In 1954, the Court would take up the issue once again in *Brown v. Board of Education of Topeka*, this time with a very different outcome.

A statute which implies merely a legal distinction between the white and colored races — a distinction which is founded in the color of the two races, and which must always exist so long as white men are distinguished from the other race by color — has no tendency to destroy the legal equality of the two races, or re-establish a state of involuntary servitude. . . .

. . . The object of the [fourteenth] amendment was undoubtedly to enforce the absolute equality of the two races before the law, but, in the nature of things, it could not have been intended to abolish distinctions based upon color, or to enforce social, as distinguished from political, equality, or a commingling of the two races upon terms unsatisfactory to either. Laws permitting, and even requiring, their separation, in places where they are liable to be brought into contact, do not necessarily imply the inferiority of either race to the other, and have been generally, if not universally, recognized as within the competency of the state legislatures in the exercise of their police power. . . .

We consider the underlying fallacy of the plaintiff's argument to consist in the assumption that the enforced separation of the two races stamps the colored race with a badge of inferiority. If this be so, it is not by reason of anything found in the act, but solely because the colored race chooses to put that construction upon it. The argument necessarily assumes that if, as has been more than once the case, and is not unlikely to be so again, the colored race should become the dominant power in the state legislature, and should enact a law in precisely similar terms, it would thereby relegate the white race to an inferior position. We imagine that the white race, at least, would not acquiesce in this assumption. The argument also assumes that social prejudices may be overcome by legislation, and that equal rights cannot be secured to the negro except by an enforced commingling of the two races. We cannot accept this proposition. If the two races are to meet upon terms of social equality, it must be the result of natural affinities, a mutual appreciation of each other's merits, and a voluntary consent of individuals. . . . Legislation is powerless to eradicate racial instincts, or to abolish distinctions based upon physical differences, and the attempt to do so can only result in accentuating the difficulties of the present situation. If the civil and political rights of both races be equal, one cannot be inferior to the other civilly or politically.

Brown v. Board of Education of Topeka [1954]

In the 1954 *Brown v. Board of Education of Topeka* decision, the Supreme Court unanimously declared the establishment of separate public schools for black and white children unconstitutional, thereby reversing its 1896 ruling in *Plessy v. Ferguson*. While the case dealt specifically with education, it was designed to have larger repercussions for the system of segregation as a whole. The NAACP lawyer Thurgood Marshall, who served as lead counsel on the case — and later became the first African American Supreme Court justice — argued successfully that segregation violated the equal protection clause of the Fourteenth Amendment, rendering *Plessy v. Ferguson* unconstitutional. The Court did not strike down the entire 1896 decision, but it did rule that race-based segregated facilities were inherently unequal in their psychological effects on black children.

Today, education is perhaps the most important function of state and local governments. . . . It is the very foundation of good citizenship. Today it is a principal instrument in awakening the child to cultural values, in preparing him for later professional training, and in helping him to adjust normally to his environment. In these days, it is doubtful that any child may reasonably be expected to succeed in life if he is denied the opportunity of an education. Such an opportunity, where the state has undertaken to provide it, is a right which must be made available to all on equal terms.

We come then to the question presented: Does segregation of children in public schools solely on the basis of race, even though the physical facilities and other "tangible" factors may be equal, deprive the children of the minority group of equal educational opportunities? We believe that it does. . . .

. . . To separate them from others of similar age and qualifications solely because of their race generates a feeling of inferiority as to their status in the community that may affect their hearts and minds in a way unlikely ever to be undone. The effect of this separation on their educational opportunities was well stated by a finding . . . by a court which nevertheless felt compelled to rule against the Negro plaintiffs:

["]Segregation of white and colored children in public schools has a detrimental effect upon the colored children. The impact is greater when it has the sanction of the law, for the policy of separating the races is usually interpreted as denoting the inferiority of the negro group. A sense of inferiority affects the motivation of a child to learn. Segregation with the sanction of law, therefore, has a tendency to [retard] the educational and mental development of negro children and to deprive them of some of the benefits they would receive in a racial[ly] integrated school system.["]

Whatever may have been the extent of psychological knowledge at the time of *Plessy v. Ferguson*, this finding is amply supported by modern authority. Any language in *Plessy v. Ferguson* contrary to this finding is rejected.

We conclude that, in the field of public education, the doctrine of "separate but equal" has no place. Separate educational facilities are inherently unequal. Therefore, we hold that the plaintiffs and others similarly situated for whom the actions have been brought are, by reason of the segregation complained of, deprived of the equal protection of the laws guaranteed by the Fourteenth Amendment.

Griggs v. Duke Power Co. [1971]

In *Griggs v. Duke Power Co.*, an employment discrimination case, the Supreme Court decided unanimously that under Title VII of the Civil Rights Act of 1964, intelligence and other tests that did not measure one's ability to perform a job were discriminatory. The NAACP filed the case on behalf of Willie Griggs and thirteen other black janitors whose employer had begun to require IQ tests or high school diplomas as prerequisites for promotion. These requirements affected African Americans disproportionately, and the able performance of workers hired before the institution of the requirements made it clear that the tests were unnecessary to perform the work. In its verdict, the Court placed the burden of proof on the employer: Unless intelligence or other tests were "demonstrably a reasonable measure of job performance," employers could not require them under Title VII.

The objective of Congress in the enactment of Title VII is plain from the language of the statute. It was to achieve equality of employment opportunities and remove barriers that have operated in the past to favor an identifiable group of white employees over other employees. Under the Act, practices, procedures, or tests neutral on their face, and even neutral in terms of intent, cannot be maintained if they operate to "freeze" the *status quo* of prior discriminatory employment practices.

The Court of Appeals' opinion, and the partial dissent, agreed that, on the record in the present case, "whites register far better on the Company's alternative requirements" than Negroes. . . . This consequence would appear to be directly traceable to race. Basic intelligence must have the means of articulation to manifest itself fairly in a testing process. Because they are Negroes, petitioners have long received inferior education in segregated schools. . . . Congress did not intend by Title VII, however, to guarantee a job to every person regardless of qualifications. In short, the Act does not command that any person be hired simply because he was formerly the subject of discrimination, or because he is a member of a minority group. Discriminatory preference for any group, minority or majority, is precisely and only what Congress has proscribed. What is required by Congress is the removal of artificial, arbitrary, and unnecessary barriers to employment when the barriers operate invidiously to discriminate on the basis of racial or other impermissible classification.

. . . The Act proscribes not only overt discrimination, but also practices that are fair in form, but discriminatory in operation. The touchstone is business necessity. If an employment practice which operates to exclude Negroes cannot be shown to be related to job performance, the practice is prohibited. . . .

The Court of Appeals held that the Company had adopted the diploma and test requirements without any "intention to discriminate against Negro employees." . . . We do not suggest that either the District Court or the Court of Appeals erred in examining the employer's intent; but good intent or absence of discriminatory intent does not redeem employment procedures or testing mechanisms that operate as "built-in headwinds" for minority groups and are unrelated to measuring job capability. . . .

Nothing in the Act precludes the use of testing or measuring procedures; obviously they are useful. What Congress has forbidden is giving these devices and mechanisms controlling force unless they are demonstrably a reasonable measure of job performance. Congress has not commanded that the less qualified be preferred over the better qualified simply because of minority origins. Far from disparaging job qualifications as such, Congress has made such qualifications the controlling factor, so that race, religion, nationality, and sex become irrelevant. What Congress has commanded is that any tests used must measure the person for the job, and not the person in the abstract.

Regents of the University of California v. Bakke [1978]

In this case, the Supreme Court ruled that the medical school of the University of California, Davis, had discriminated against Allan Bakke, a white prospective student, when it denied him admission. Bakke believed he was the victim of reverse discrimination. The school maintained an admissions quota, overseen by a special committee, in which sixteen out of one hundred seats in each entering class were reserved for racial minorities. The justices were divided over the case. Ultimately, in a 5–4 decision, the Court argued that a system of racial "quotas" was unconstitutional, whereas a more flexible policy of affirmative action — with educational diversity as its goal — could, under some circumstances, be constitutional. The Court believed that the medical school's system did not meet the requirements for constitutionality and thus ordered Bakke's admission.

Racial and ethnic classifications of any sort are inherently suspect and call for the most exacting judicial scrutiny. While the goal of achieving a diverse student body is sufficiently compelling to justify consideration of race in admissions decisions under some circumstances, petitioner's special admissions program, which forecloses consideration to persons like respondent, is unnecessary to the achievement of this compelling goal, and therefore invalid under the Equal Protection Clause. . . .

The concept of "discrimination," like the phrase "equal protection of the laws," is susceptible of varying interpretations, for as Mr. Justice Holmes declared, "[a] word is not a crystal, transparent and unchanged, it is the skin of a living thought and may vary greatly in color and content according to the circumstances and the time in which it is used." . . .

. . . The parties fight a sharp preliminary action over the proper characterization of the special admissions program. Petitioner prefers to view it as establishing a "goal" of minority representation in the Medical School. Respondent, echoing the courts below, labels it a racial quota.

This semantic distinction is beside the point: The special admissions program is undeniably a classification based on race and ethnic background. To the extent that there existed a pool of at least minimally qualified minority applicants to fill the 16 special admissions seats, white applicants could compete only for 84 seats in the entering class, rather than the 100 open to minority applicants. Whether this limitation is described as a quota or a goal, it is a line drawn on the basis of race and ethnic status.

Selected Documents

These documents, penned by two of history's most influential African Americans, are revealing of the state of black America at key points in the nation's history. In each document, the author lays out the circumstances as he sees them and provides his thoughts on how best to address the situation. As you read these documents, consider how they would have been received by their audiences and what they have to tell us about the evolution of race relations in the nineteenth and twenty-first centuries.

Booker T. Washington, *The Atlanta Compromise Speech* [1895]

When Booker T. Washington delivered the following speech at the Cotton States and International Exposition in Atlanta, he managed to speak to multiple audiences. Washington urged that blacks remain in the South, start at the bottom, and advance within the confines of the prevailing system. White employers, he argued, should do their part by recognizing blacks' contributions and hiring them rather than foreign laborers. Washington's emphasis on black self-help and economic uplift as the keys to race advancement proved a hopeful message for many blacks. Whites, however, focused on Washington's accommodationism and acceptance of the racial status quo, drawing encouragement from his admonition that blacks should struggle for their own economic prosperity rather than agitate for social equality.

Mr. President and Gentlemen of the Board of Directors and Citizens.

One-third of the population of the South is of the Negro race. No enterprise seeking the material, civil, or moral welfare of this section can disregard this element of our population and reach the highest success. I but convey to you, Mr. President and Directors, the sentiment of the masses of my race when I say that in no way have the value and manhood of the American Negro been more fittingly and generously recognized than by the managers of this magnificent Exposition at every stage of its progress. It is a recognition that will do more to cement the friendship of the two races than any occurrence since the dawn of our freedom.

SOURCE: Booker T. Washington, *Up from Slavery: An Autobiography* (New York: Doubleday, Page, 1907), 218–25.

Not only this, but the opportunity here afforded will awaken among us a new era of industrial progress. Ignorant and inexperienced, it is not strange that in the first years of our new life we began at the top instead of at the bottom; that a seat in Congress or the state legislature was more sought than real estate or industrial skill; that the political convention or stump speaking had more attractions than starting a dairy farm or truck garden.

A ship lost at sea for many days suddenly sighted a friendly vessel. From the mast of the unfortunate vessel was seen a signal, "Water, water; we die of thirst!" The answer from the friendly vessel at once came back, "Cast down your bucket where you are." A second time the signal, "Water, water; send us water!" ran up from the distressed vessel, and was answered, "Cast down your bucket where you are." And a third and fourth signal for water was answered, "Cast down your bucket where you are." The captain of the distressed vessel, at last heeding the injunction, cast down his bucket, and it came up full of fresh, sparkling water from the mouth of the Amazon River. To those of my race who depend on bettering their condition in a foreign land or who underestimate the importance of cultivating friendly relations with the Southern white man, who is their next-door neighbour, I would say: "Cast down your bucket where you are" — cast it down in making friends in every manly way of the people of all races by whom we are surrounded.

Cast it down in agriculture, mechanics, in commerce, in domestic service, and in the professions. And in this connection it is well to bear in mind that whatever other sins the South may be called to bear, when it comes to business, pure and simple, it is in the South that the Negro is given a man's chance in the commercial world, and in nothing is this Exposition more eloquent than in emphasizing this chance. Our greatest danger is that in the great leap from slavery to freedom we may overlook the fact that the masses of us are to live by the productions of our hands, and fail to keep in mind that we shall prosper in proportion as we learn to dignify and glorify common labour and put brains and skill into the common occupations of life; shall prosper in proportion as we learn to draw the line between the superficial and the substantial, the ornamental gewgaws of life and the useful. No race can prosper till it learns that there is as much dignity in tilling a field as in writing a poem. It is at the bottom of life we must begin, and not at the top. Nor should we permit our grievances to overshadow our opportunities.

To those of the white race who look to the incoming of those of foreign birth and strange tongue and habits for the prosperity of the South, were I permitted I would repeat what I say to my own race, "Cast down your bucket where you are." Cast it down among the eight millions of Negroes whose habits you know, whose fidelity and love you have tested in days when to have proved treacherous meant the ruin of your firesides. Cast down your bucket among these people who have, without strikes and labour wars, tilled your fields, cleared your forests, builded your railroads and cities, and brought forth treasures from the bowels of the earth, and helped make possible this magnificent representation of the progress of the South. Casting down your bucket among my people, helping and encouraging them as you are doing on these grounds, and to education of head, hand, and heart, you will find that they will buy your surplus land, make blossom the waste places in your fields, and run your factories. While doing this, you can be sure in the future, as in the past, that you and your families will be surrounded by the most patient, faithful, law-abiding, and unresentful people that the world has seen. As we have proved our loyalty to you in the past, in nursing your children, watching by the sick-bed of your mothers and fathers, and often following them with tear-dimmed eyes to their graves, so in the future, in our humble way, we shall stand by you with a devotion that no foreigner can approach, ready to lay down our lives, if need be, in defence of yours, interlacing our industrial, commercial, civil, and religious life with yours in a way that shall make the interests of both races one. In all things that are purely social we can be as separate as the fingers, yet one as the hand in all things essential to mutual progress.

There is no defence or security for any of us except in the highest intelligence and development of all. If anywhere there are efforts tending to curtail the fullest growth of the Negro, let these efforts be turned into stimulating, encouraging, and making him the most useful and intelligent citizen. Effort or means so invested will pay a thousand per cent interest. These efforts will be twice blessed — "blessing him that gives and him that takes."

There is no escape through law of man or God from the inevitable: —

> The laws of changeless justice bind
> Oppressor with oppressed;
> And close as sin and suffering joined
> We march to fate abreast.

Nearly sixteen millions of hands will aid you in pulling the load upward, or they will pull against you the load downward. We shall constitute one-third and more of the ignorance and crime of the South, or one-third its intelligence and progress; we shall contribute one-third to the business and industrial prosperity of the South, or we shall prove a veritable body of death, stagnating, depressing, retarding every effort to advance the body politic.

Gentlemen of the Exposition, as we present to you our humble effort at an exhibition of our progress, you must not expect overmuch. Starting thirty years ago with ownership here and there in a few quilts and pumpkins and chickens (gathered from miscellaneous sources), remember the path that has led from these to the inventions and production of agricultural implements, buggies, steam-engines, newspapers, books, statuary, carving, paintings, the management of drugstores and banks, has not been trodden without contact with thorns and thistles. While we take pride in what we exhibit as a result of our independent efforts, we do not for a moment forget that our part in this exhibition would fall far short of your expectations but for the constant help that has come to our educational life, not only from the Southern states, but especially from Northern philanthropists, who have made their gifts a constant stream of blessing and encouragement.

The wisest among my race understand that the agitation of questions of social equality is the extremest folly, and that progress in the enjoyment of all the privileges that will come to us must be the result of severe and constant struggle rather than of artificial forcing. No race that has anything to contribute to the markets of the world is long in any degree ostracized.

It is important and right that all privileges of the law be ours, but it is vastly more important that we be prepared for the exercise of these privileges. The opportunity to earn a dollar in a factory just now is worth infinitely more than the opportunity to spend a dollar in an opera-house.

In conclusion, may I repeat that nothing in thirty years has given us more hope and encouragement, and drawn us so near to you of the white race, as this opportunity offered by the Exposition; and here bending, as it were, over the altar that represents the results of the struggles of your race and mine, both starting practically empty-handed three decades ago, I pledge that in your effort to work out the great and intricate problem which God has laid at the doors of the South, you shall have at all times the patient, sympathetic help of my race; only let this be constantly in mind, that, while from representations in these buildings of the product of field, of forest, of mine, of factory, letters, and art, much good will come, yet far above and beyond material benefits will be that higher good, that, let us pray God, will come, in a blotting out of sectional differences and racial animosities and suspicions, in a determination to administer absolute justice, in a willing obedience among all classes to the mandates of law. This, this, coupled with our material prosperity, will bring into our beloved South a new heaven and a new earth.

Barack Obama, *A More Perfect Union* [2008]

In March 2008, during the presidential primaries, presidential hopeful Senator Barack Obama delivered the following speech. He addressed the issue of race head-on, partially in response to public concern over controversial statements made by his former pastor, the Reverend Jeremiah Wright. Quoting the preamble of the Constitution, Obama laid out the lingering problems and divisions that characterized both black and white America. Americans could either focus on divisiveness, he said, or they could move forward by addressing their shared concerns in a unified way. This, Obama argued, would be the first step toward improving the American lot and creating as perfect a union as possible.

"We the people, in order to form a more perfect union."

Two hundred and twenty-one years ago, in a hall that still stands across the street, a group of men gathered and, with these simple words, launched America's improbable experiment in democracy. Farmers and scholars; statesmen and patriots who had traveled across an ocean to escape tyranny and persecution finally made real their declaration of independence at a Philadelphia convention that lasted through the spring of 1787.

The document they produced was eventually signed but ultimately unfinished. It was stained by this nation's original sin of slavery, a question that divided the colonies and brought the convention to a stalemate until the founders chose to allow the slave trade to continue for at least twenty more years, and to leave any final resolution to future generations.

Of course, the answer to the slavery question was already embedded within our Constitution—a Constitution that had at its very core the ideal of equal citizenship under the law; a Constitution that promised its people liberty, and justice, and a union that could be and should be perfected over time.

And yet words on a parchment would not be enough to deliver slaves from bondage, or provide men and women of every color and creed their full rights and obligations as citizens of the United States. What would be needed were Americans in successive generations who were willing to do their part—through protests and struggle, on the streets and in the courts, through a civil war and civil disobedience and always at great risk—to narrow that gap between the promise of our ideals and the reality of their time.

This was one of the tasks we set forth at the beginning of this campaign—to continue the long march of those who came before us, a march for a more just, more equal, more free, more caring and more prosperous America. I chose to run for the presidency at this moment in history because I believe deeply that we cannot solve the challenges of our time unless we solve them together—unless we perfect our union by understanding that we may have different stories, but we hold common hopes; that we may not look the same and we may not have come from the same place, but we all want to move in the same direction—towards a better future for our children and our grandchildren.

This belief comes from my unyielding faith in the decency and generosity of the American people. But it also comes from my own American story.

I am the son of a black man from Kenya and a white woman from Kansas. I was raised with the help of a white grandfather who survived a Depression to serve in Patton's Army during World War II and a white grandmother who worked on a bomber assembly line at Fort Leavenworth while he was overseas. I've gone to some of the best schools in America and lived in one of the world's poorest nations. I am married to a black American who carries within her the blood of slaves and slaveowners — an inheritance we pass on to our two precious daughters. I have brothers, sisters, nieces, nephews, uncles and cousins, of every race and every hue, scattered across three continents, and for as long as I live, I will never forget that in no other country on Earth is my story even possible.

It's a story that hasn't made me the most conventional candidate. But it is a story that has seared into my genetic makeup the idea that this nation is more than the sum of its parts — that out of many, we are truly one.

Throughout the first year of this campaign, against all predictions to the contrary, we saw how hungry the American people were for this message of unity. Despite the temptation to view my candidacy through a purely racial lens, we won commanding victories in states with some of the whitest populations in the country. In South Carolina, where the Confederate Flag still flies, we built a powerful coalition of African Americans and white Americans.

This is not to say that race has not been an issue in the campaign. At various stages in the campaign, some commentators have deemed me either "too black" or "not black enough." We saw racial tensions bubble to the surface during the week before the South Carolina primary. The press has scoured every exit poll for the latest evidence of racial polarization, not just in terms of white and black, but black and brown as well.

And yet, it has only been in the last couple of weeks that the discussion of race in this campaign has taken a particularly divisive turn.

On one end of the spectrum, we've heard the implication that my candidacy is somehow an exercise in affirmative action; that it's based solely on the desire of wide-eyed liberals to purchase racial reconciliation on the cheap. On the other end, we've heard

my former pastor, Reverend Jeremiah Wright, use incendiary language to express views that have the potential not only to widen the racial divide, but views that denigrate both the greatness and the goodness of our nation; that rightly offend white and black alike.

I have already condemned, in unequivocal terms, the statements of Reverend Wright that have caused such controversy. For some, nagging questions remain. Did I know him to be an occasionally fierce critic of American domestic and foreign policy? Of course. Did I ever hear him make remarks that could be considered controversial while I sat in church? Yes. Did I strongly disagree with many of his political views? Absolutely — just as I'm sure many of you have heard remarks from your pastors, priests, or rabbis with which you strongly disagreed.

But the remarks that have caused this recent firestorm weren't simply controversial. They weren't simply a religious leader's effort to speak out against perceived injustice. Instead, they expressed a profoundly distorted view of this country — a view that sees white racism as endemic, and that elevates what is wrong with America above all that we know is right with America; a view that sees the conflicts in the Middle East as rooted primarily in the actions of stalwart allies like Israel, instead of emanating from the perverse and hateful ideologies of radical Islam.

As such, Reverend Wright's comments were not only wrong but divisive, divisive at a time when we need unity; racially charged at a time when we need to come together to solve a set of monumental problems — two wars, a terrorist threat, a falling economy, a chronic health care crisis and potentially devastating climate change; problems that are neither black or white or Latino or Asian, but rather problems that confront us all.

Given my background, my politics, and my professed values and ideals, there will no doubt be those for whom my statements of condemnation are not enough. Why associate myself with Reverend Wright in the first place, they may ask? Why not join another church? And I confess that if all that I knew of Reverend Wright were the snippets of those sermons that have run in an endless loop on the television and YouTube, or if Trinity United Church of Christ conformed to the caricatures being peddled by some commentators, there is no doubt that I would react in much the same way.

But the truth is, that isn't all that I know of the man. The man I met more than twenty years ago is a man who helped introduce me to my Christian faith, a man who spoke to me about our obligations to love one another; to care for the sick and lift up the poor. He is a man who served his country as a U.S. Marine; who has studied and lectured at some of the finest universities and seminaries in the country, and who for over thirty years led a church that serves the community by doing God's work here on Earth — by housing the homeless, ministering to the needy, providing day care services and scholarships and prison ministries, and reaching out to those suffering from HIV/AIDS.

In my first book, *Dreams from My Father*, I described the experience of my first service at Trinity:

"People began to shout, to rise from their seats and clap and cry out, a forceful wind carrying the reverend's voice up into the rafters. . . . And in that single note — hope! — I heard something else; at the foot of that cross, inside the thousands of churches across the city, I imagined the stories of ordinary black people merging with the stories of David and Goliath, Moses and Pharaoh, the Christians in the lion's den, Ezekiel's field of dry bones. Those stories — of survival, and freedom, and hope — became our story, my story; the blood that had spilled was our blood, the tears our tears; until this black church, on this bright day, seemed once more a vessel carrying the story of a people into future generations and into a larger world. Our trials and triumphs became at once unique and universal, black and more than black; in chronicling our journey, the stories and songs gave us a means to reclaim memories that we didn't need to feel shame about . . . memories that all people might study and cherish — and with which we could start to rebuild."

That has been my experience at Trinity. Like other predominantly black churches across the country, Trinity embodies the black community in its entirety — the doctor and the welfare mom, the model student and the former gang-banger. Like other black churches, Trinity's services are full of raucous laughter and sometimes bawdy humor. They are full of dancing, clapping, screaming and shouting that may seem jarring to the untrained ear. The church contains in full the kindness and cruelty, the fierce intelligence and the shocking ignorance, the struggles and successes, the love and yes, the bitterness and bias that make up the black experience in America.

And this helps explain, perhaps, my relationship with Reverend Wright. As imperfect as he may be, he has been like family to me. He strengthened my faith, officiated my wedding, and baptized my children. Not once in my conversations with him have I heard him talk about any ethnic group in derogatory terms, or treat whites with whom he interacted with anything but courtesy and respect. He contains within him the contradictions — the good and the bad — of the community that he has served diligently for so many years.

I can no more disown him than I can disown the black community. I can no more disown him than I can my white grandmother — a woman who helped raise me, a woman who sacrificed again and again for me, a woman who loves me as much as she loves anything in this world, but a woman who once confessed her fear of black men who passed by her on the street, and who on more than one occasion has uttered racial or ethnic stereotypes that made me cringe.

These people are a part of me. And they are a part of America, this country that I love.

Some will see this as an attempt to justify or excuse comments that are simply inexcusable. I can assure you it is not. I suppose the politically safe thing would be to move on from this episode and just hope that it fades into the woodwork. We can dismiss Reverend Wright as a crank or a demagogue, just as some have dismissed Geraldine Ferraro, in the aftermath of her recent statements, as harboring some deep-seated racial bias.

But race is an issue that I believe this nation cannot afford to ignore right now. We would be making the same mistake that Reverend Wright made in his offending sermons about America — to simplify and stereotype and amplify the negative to the point that it distorts reality.

The fact is that the comments that have been made and the issues that have surfaced over the last few weeks reflect the complexities of race in this country that we've never really worked through — a part of our union that we have yet to perfect. And if we walk away now, if we simply retreat into our respective corners, we will never be able to come together and solve challenges like health care, or education, or the need to find good jobs for every American.

Understanding this reality requires a reminder of how we arrived at this point. As William Faulkner once wrote, "The past isn't dead and buried. In fact, it isn't even past." We do not need to recite here the history of racial injustice in this country. But we do need to remind ourselves that so many of the disparities that exist in the African American community today can be directly traced to inequalities passed on from an earlier generation that suffered under the brutal legacy of slavery and Jim Crow.

Segregated schools were, and are, inferior schools; we still haven't fixed them, fifty years after *Brown v. Board of Education*, and the inferior education they provided, then and now, helps explain the pervasive achievement gap between today's black and white students.

Legalized discrimination — where blacks were prevented, often through violence, from owning property, or loans were not granted to African American business owners, or black homeowners could not access FHA mortgages, or blacks were excluded from unions, or the police force, or fire departments — meant that black families could not amass any meaningful wealth to bequeath to future generations. That history helps explain the wealth and income gap between black and white, and the concentrated pockets of poverty that persist in so many of today's urban and rural communities.

A lack of economic opportunity among black men, and the shame and frustration that came from not being able to provide for one's family, contributed to the erosion of black families — a problem that welfare policies for many years may have worsened. And the lack of basic services in so many urban black neighborhoods — parks for kids to play in, police walking the beat, regular garbage pick-up and building code enforcement — all helped create a cycle of violence, blight and neglect that continues to haunt us.

This is the reality in which Reverend Wright and other African Americans of his generation grew up. They came of age in the late fifties and early sixties, a time when segregation was still the law of the land and opportunity was systematically constricted. What's remarkable is not how many failed in the face of discrimination, but rather how many men and women overcame the odds; how many were able to make a way out of no way for those like me who would come after them.

But for all those who scratched and clawed their way to get a piece of the American Dream, there were many who didn't make it — those who were ultimately defeated, in one way or another, by discrimination. That legacy of defeat was passed on to future generations — those young men and increasingly young women who we see standing on street corners or languishing in our prisons, without hope or prospects for the future. Even for those blacks who did make it, questions of race, and racism, continue to define their worldview in fundamental ways. For the men and women of Reverend Wright's generation, the memories of humiliation and doubt and fear have not gone away; nor has the anger and the bitterness of those years. That anger may not get expressed in public, in front of white coworkers or white friends. But it does find voice in the barbershop or around the kitchen table. At times, that anger is exploited by politicians, to gin up votes along racial lines, or to make up for a politician's own failings.

And occasionally it finds voice in the church on Sunday morning, in the pulpit and in the pews. The fact that so many people are surprised to hear that anger in some of Reverend Wright's sermons simply reminds us of the old truism that the most segregated hour in American life occurs on Sunday morning. That anger is not always productive; indeed, all too often it distracts attention from solving real problems; it keeps us from squarely facing our own complicity in our condition, and prevents the African American community from forging the alliances it needs to bring about real change. But the anger is real; it is powerful; and to simply wish it away, to condemn it without understanding its roots, only serves to widen the chasm of misunderstanding that exists between the races.

In fact, a similar anger exists within segments of the white community. Most working- and middle-class white Americans don't feel that they have been particularly privileged by their race. Their experience is the immigrant experience — as far as they're concerned, no one's handed them anything, they've built it from scratch. They've worked hard all their lives, many times only to see their jobs shipped overseas or their pension dumped after a lifetime of labor. They are anxious about their futures, and feel their dreams slipping away; in an era of stagnant wages and global competition, opportunity comes to be seen as a zero sum game, in which your dreams come at my expense. So when they are told to bus their children to a school across town; when they hear that an African American is getting an advantage in landing a good job or a spot in a good college because of an injustice that they themselves never committed; when they're told that their fears about crime in urban neighborhoods are somehow prejudiced, resentment builds over time.

Like the anger within the black community, these resentments aren't always expressed in polite company. But they have helped shape the political landscape for at least a generation. Anger over welfare and affirmative action helped forge the Reagan Coalition. Politicians routinely exploited fears of crime for their own electoral ends. Talk show hosts and conservative commentators built entire careers unmasking bogus claims of racism while dismissing legitimate discussions of racial injustice and inequality as mere political correctness or reverse racism.

Just as black anger often proved counterproductive, so have these white resentments distracted attention from the real culprits of the middle class squeeze — a corporate culture rife with inside dealing, questionable accounting practices, and short-term greed; a Washington dominated by lobbyists and special interests; economic policies that favor the few over the many. And yet, to wish away the resentments of white Americans, to label them as misguided or even racist, without recognizing they are grounded in legitimate concerns — this too widens the racial divide, and blocks the path to understanding.

This is where we are right now. It's a racial stalemate we've been stuck in for years. Contrary to the claims of some of my critics, black and white, I have never been so naive as to believe that we can get beyond our racial divisions in a single election cycle, or with a single candidacy — particularly a candidacy as imperfect as my own.

But I have asserted a firm conviction — a conviction rooted in my faith in God and my faith in the American people — that working together we can move beyond some of our old racial wounds, and that in fact we have no choice if we are to continue on the path of a more perfect union.

For the African American community, that path means embracing the burdens of our past without becoming victims of our past. It means continuing to insist on a full measure of justice in every aspect of American life. But it also means binding our particular grievances — for better health care, and better schools, and better jobs — to the larger aspirations of all Americans — the white woman struggling to break the glass ceiling, the white man who's been laid off, the immigrant trying to feed his family. And it means taking full responsibility for own lives — by demanding more from our fathers, and spending more time with our children, and reading to them, and teaching them that while they may face challenges and discrimination in their own lives, they must never succumb to despair or cynicism; they must always believe that they can write their own destiny.

Ironically, this quintessentially American — and yes, conservative — notion of self-help found frequent expression in Reverend Wright's sermons. But what my former pastor too often failed to understand is that embarking on a program of self-help also requires a belief that society can change.

The profound mistake of Reverend Wright's sermons is not that he spoke about racism in our society. It's that he spoke as if our society was static; as if no progress has been made; as if this country — a country that has made it possible for one of his own members to run for the highest office in the land and build a coalition of white and black; Latino and Asian, rich and poor, young and old — is still irrevocably bound to a tragic past. But what we know — what we have seen — is that America can change. That is [the] true genius of this nation. What we have already achieved gives us hope — the audacity to hope — for what we can and must achieve tomorrow.

In the white community, the path to a more perfect union means acknowledging that what ails the African American community does not just exist in the minds of black people; that the legacy of discrimination — and current incidents of discrimination, while less overt than in the past — are real and must be addressed. Not just with words, but with deeds — by investing in our schools and our communities; by enforcing our civil rights laws and ensuring fairness in our criminal justice system; by providing this generation with ladders of opportunity that were unavailable for previous generations. It requires all Americans to realize that your dreams do not have to come at the expense of my dreams; that investing in the health, welfare, and education of black and brown and white children will ultimately help all of America prosper.

In the end, then, what is called for is nothing more, and nothing less, than what all the world's great religions demand — that we do unto others as we would have them do unto us. Let us be our brother's keeper, Scripture tells us. Let us be our sister's keeper. Let us find that common stake we all have in one another, and let our politics reflect that spirit as well.

For we have a choice in this country. We can accept a politics that breeds division, and conflict, and cynicism. We can tackle race only as spectacle — as we did in the OJ trial — or in the wake of tragedy, as we did in the aftermath of Katrina — or as fodder for the nightly news. We can play Reverend Wright's sermons on every channel, every day and talk about them from now until the election, and make the only question in this campaign whether or not the American people think that I somehow believe or sympathize with his most offensive words. We can pounce on some gaffe by a Hillary supporter as evidence that she's playing the race card, or we can speculate on whether white men will all flock to John McCain in the general election regardless of his policies.

We can do that.

But if we do, I can tell you that in the next election, we'll be talking about some other distraction. And then another one. And then another one. And nothing will change.

That is one option. Or, at this moment, in this election, we can come together and say, "Not this time." This time we want to talk about the crumbling schools that are stealing the future of black children and white children and Asian children and Hispanic children and Native American children. This time we want to reject the cynicism that tells us that these kids can't learn; that those kids who don't look like us are somebody else's problem. The children of America are not those kids, they are our kids, and we will not let them fall behind in a 21st century economy. Not this time.

This time we want to talk about how the lines in the Emergency Room are filled with whites and blacks and Hispanics who do not have health care; who don't have the power on their own to overcome the special interests in Washington, but who can take them on if we do it together.

This time we want to talk about the shuttered mills that once provided a decent life for men and women of every race, and the homes for sale that once belonged to Americans from every religion, every region, every walk of life. This time we want to talk about the fact that the real problem is not that someone who doesn't look like you might take your job; it's that the corporation you work for will ship it overseas for nothing more than a profit.

This time we want to talk about the men and women of every color and creed who serve together, and fight together, and bleed together under the same proud flag. We want to talk about how to bring them home from a war that never should've been authorized and never should've been waged, and we want to talk about how we'll show our patriotism by caring for them, and their families, and giving them the benefits they have earned.

I would not be running for President if I didn't believe with all my heart that this is what the vast majority of Americans want for this country. This union may never be perfect, but generation after generation has shown that it can always be perfected. And today, whenever I find myself feeling doubtful or cynical about this possibility, what gives me the most hope is the next generation — the young people whose attitudes and beliefs and openness to change have already made history in this election.

There is one story in particular that I'd like to leave you with today — a story I told when I had the great honor of speaking on Dr. King's birthday at his home church, Ebenezer Baptist, in Atlanta.

There is a young, twenty-three-year-old white woman named Ashley Baia who organized for our campaign in Florence, South Carolina. She had been working to organize a mostly African American community since the beginning of this campaign, and one day she was at a roundtable discussion where everyone went around telling their story and why they were there.

And Ashley said that when she was nine years old, her mother got cancer. And because she had to miss days of work, she was let go and lost her health care. They had to file for bankruptcy, and that's when Ashley decided that she had to do something to help her mom.

She knew that food was one of their most expensive costs, and so Ashley convinced her mother that what she really liked and really wanted to eat more than anything else was mustard and relish sandwiches. Because that was the cheapest way to eat.

She did this for a year until her mom got better, and she told everyone at the roundtable that the reason she joined our campaign was so that she could help the millions of other children in the country who want and need to help their parents too.

Now Ashley might have made a different choice. Perhaps somebody told her along the way that the source of her mother's problems were blacks who were on welfare and too lazy to work, or Hispanics who were coming into the country illegally. But she didn't. She sought out allies in her fight against injustice.

Anyway, Ashley finishes her story and then goes around the room and asks everyone else why they're supporting the campaign. They all have different stories and reasons. Many bring up a specific issue. And finally they come to this elderly black man who's been sitting there quietly the entire time. And Ashley asks him why he's there. And he does not bring up a specific issue. He does not say health care or the economy. He does not say education or the war. He does not say that he was there because of Barack Obama. He simply says to everyone in the room, "I am here because of Ashley."

"I'm here because of Ashley." By itself, that single moment of recognition between that young white girl and that old black man is not enough. It is not enough to give health care to the sick, or jobs to the jobless, or education to our children.

But it is where we start. It is where our union grows stronger. And as so many generations have come to realize over the course of the two hundred and twenty-one years since a band of patriots signed that document in Philadelphia, that is where the perfection begins.

James Weldon Johnson and John Rosamond Johnson, *Lift Every Voice and Sing* [1900]

Also known as the Negro National Anthem, "Lift Every Voice and Sing" was written by James Weldon Johnson and set to music by his brother John Rosamond Johnson. Black schools and churches across the country took up the anthem, which is still sung by students and choirs today. James Weldon Johnson noted a feeling of special joy at hearing his song sung by black children.

1

Lift ev'ry voice and sing
Till earth and heaven ring,
    Ring with the harmonies of Liberty;
Let our rejoicing rise
High as the list'ning skies,
Let it resound loud as the rolling seas;
Sing a song full of the faith that the dark past has
    taught us,
Sing a song full of the hope that the present has
    brought us;
Facing the rising sun
Of our new day begun,
Let us march on till victory is won.

2

Stony the road we trod,
Bitter the chast'ning rod
Felt in the days when hope had died;
Yet, with a steady beat,
Have not our weary feet
        Come to the place for which our fathers sighed,
We have come over a way that with tears has been
    watered,
We have come, treading our path thro' the blood of the
    slaughtered,
Out from the gloomy past,
Till now we stand at last
Where the white gleam of our bright star
    is cast.

3

God of our weary years,
God of our silent tears,
        Thou who hast brought us thus far on the way;
Thou who hast by Thy might,
Led us into the light,
Keep us forever in the path, we pray,
Lest our feet stray from the places, our God, where we
    met Thee,
Lest, our hearts drunk with the wine of the world, we
    forget Thee,
Shadowed beneath Thy hand,
May we forever stand,
True to our God, true to our Native Land.

SOURCE: Tuskegee Institute Department of Records and Research, Monroe N. Work, ed., *Negro Year Book: An Annual Encyclopedia of the Negro, 1918–1919* (Tuskegee, AL: Negro Year Book, 1919).

African American Population of the United States, 1790–2010

Year	Black Population	Percentage of Total Population	Number of Slaves	Percentage of Blacks Who Were Enslaved
1790	757,208	19.3	697,681	92
1800	1,002,037	18.9	893,602	89
1810	1,377,808	19.0	1,191,362	86
1820	1,771,656	18.4	1,538,022	87
1830	2,328,642	18.1	2,009,043	86
1840	2,873,648	16.1	2,487,355	87
1850	3,638,808	15.7	3,204,287	88
1860	4,441,830	14.1	3,953,731	89
1870	4,880,009	12.7	—	—
1880	6,580,793	13.1	—	—
1890	7,488,788	11.9	—	—
1900	8,833,994	11.6	—	—
1910	9,827,763	10.7	—	—
1920	10,463,131	9.9	—	—
1930	11,891,143	9.7	—	—
1940	12,865,518	9.8	—	—
1950	15,044,937	10.0	—	—
1960	18,871,931	10.6	—	—
1970	22,580,289	11.1	—	—
1980	26,482,349	11.8	—	—
1990	29,986,060	12.0	—	—
2000	34,658,190	12.3	—	—
2010	38,929,319	12.6	—	—

SOURCES: U.S. Census Bureau, *Historical Statistics of the United States, Colonial Times to 1970* (1975); *Statistical Abstract of the United States,* 2010.

Unemployment Rates in the United States by Race and Hispanic Origin, 2005–2010

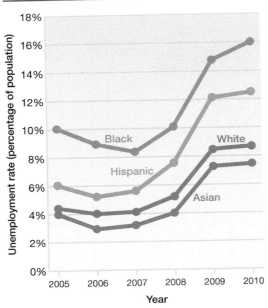

SOURCE: U.S. Bureau of Labor Statistics, "Employment and Earnings Online," January 2011 issue, March 2011, http://www.bls.gov/opub/ee/home.htm and http://www.bls.gov/cps/home.htm.

African American Educational Attainment in the United States, 2011

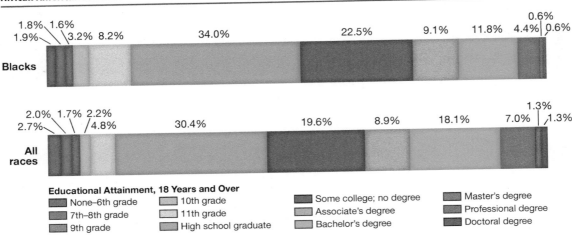

SOURCE: U.S. Census Bureau, Current Population Survey, 2011 Annual Social and Economic Supplement.

Educational Attainment in the United States, 1960–2010

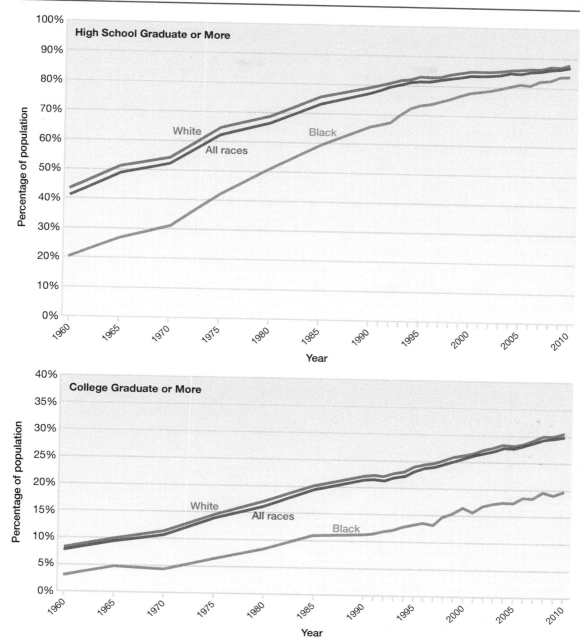

Sources: U.S. Census Bureau, U.S. Census of Population, 1960, 1970, and 1980, Summary File 3; Current Population reports and "Educational Attainment."

Historically Black Colleges and Universities, 1865–Present

College/University and Location	Year Founded	Principal Funding Source
Alabama A&M University, Normal, Alabama	1875	Alabama
Alabama State University, Montgomery, Alabama	1867	Alabama
Albany State University, Albany, Georgia	1903	Georgia
Alcorn State University, Lorman, Mississippi	1871	Mississippi
Allen University, Columbia, South Carolina*	1870	African Methodist Episcopal
Arkansas Baptist College, Little Rock, Arkansas	1884	Baptist
Barber-Scotia College, Concord, North Carolina	1867	Presbyterian
Benedict College, Columbia, South Carolina*	1870	Baptist
Bennett College, Greensboro, North Carolina*	1873	United Methodist
Bethune-Cookman College, Daytona Beach, Florida*	1904	United Methodist
Bluefield State College, Bluefield, West Virginia	1895	West Virginia
Bowie State University, Bowie, Maryland	1865	Maryland
Central State University, Wilberforce, Ohio	1887	Ohio
Cheyney University, Cheyney, Pennsylvania	1837	Quaker
Claflin College, Orangeburg, South Carolina*	1869	United Methodist
Clark Atlanta University, Atlanta, Georgia*	1988	United Methodist
Concordia College, Selma, Alabama	1922	Lutheran
Coppin State University, Baltimore, Maryland	1900	Maryland
Delaware State University, Dover, Delaware	1891	Delaware
Dillard University, New Orleans, Louisiana*	1869	United Church of Christ and United Methodist
Edward Waters College, Jacksonville, Florida*	1866	African Methodist Episcopal
Elizabeth City State University, Elizabeth City, North Carolina	1891	North Carolina
Fayetteville State University, Fayetteville, North Carolina	1867	North Carolina
Fisk University, Nashville, Tennessee*	1866	United Church of Christ
Florida A&M University, Tallahassee, Florida	1887	Florida
Florida Memorial College, Miami, Florida*	1879	Baptist Church
Fort Valley State College, Fort Valley, Georgia	1895	Georgia
Grambling State University, Grambling, Louisiana	1901	Louisiana
Hampton University, Hampton, Virginia	1868	American Missionary Association and Freedmen's Bureau
Harris-Stowe State College, St. Louis, Missouri	1857	Missouri
Howard University, Washington, D.C.	1867	Federal
Huston-Tillotson University, Austin, Texas*	1877	United Church of Christ
Jackson State University, Jackson, Mississippi	1877	Mississippi

* United Negro College Fund member college

Continued

Continued

College/University and Location	Year Founded	Principal Funding Source
Jarvis Christian College, Hawkins, Texas*	1913	Christian Church (Disciples of Christ)
Johnson C. Smith University, Charlotte, North Carolina*	1867	Presbyterian Church
Kentucky State University, Frankfort, Kentucky	1886	Kentucky
Knoxville College, Knoxville, Tennessee	1875	Presbyterian Church
Lane College, Jackson, Tennessee*	1882	Christian Methodist Episcopal Church
Langston University, Langston, Oklahoma	1897	Oklahoma
LeMoyne-Owen College, Memphis, Tennessee*	1871	United Church of Christ
Lincoln University, Jefferson City, Missouri	1866	Missouri
Lincoln University, Lincoln, Pennsylvania	1854	Pennsylvania
Livingstone College, Salisbury, North Carolina*	1879	African Methodist Episcopal Zion
Miles College, Birmingham, Alabama*	1908	Christian Methodist Episcopal
Mississippi Valley State University, Itta Bena, Mississippi	1946	Mississippi
Morehouse College, Atlanta, Georgia*	1867	Baptist
Morgan State University, Baltimore, Maryland	1867	Maryland
Morris Brown College, Atlanta, Georgia	1881	African Methodist Episcopal
Morris College, Sumter, South Carolina*	1908	Baptist
Norfolk State University, Norfolk, Virginia	1935	Virginia
North Carolina A&T State University, Greensboro, North Carolina	1892	North Carolina
North Carolina Central University, Durham, North Carolina	1909	North Carolina
Oakwood College, Huntsville, Alabama*	1896	Seventh-day Adventist
Paine College, Augusta, Georgia*	1882	United Methodist Church and Christian Methodist Episcopal
Paul Quinn College, Dallas, Texas	1872	African Methodist Episcopal
Philander Smith College, Little Rock, Arkansas*	1877	United Methodist
Prairie View A&M University, Prairie View, Texas	1878	Texas
Rust College, Holly Springs, Mississippi*	1866	United Methodist
Saint Augustine's University, Raleigh, North Carolina*	1867	Episcopal
Saint Paul's College, Lawrenceville, Virginia	1888	Episcopal
Savannah State University, Savannah, Georgia	1890	Georgia
Selma University, Selma, Alabama	1878	Baptist
Shaw University, Raleigh, North Carolina*	1865	American Baptist Home Mission Society and Freedmen's Bureau
Simmons College, Louisville, Kentucky	1879	Baptist
South Carolina State University, Orangeburg, South Carolina	1896	South Carolina

* United Negro College Fund member college

Continued

Continued

College/University and Location	Year Founded	Principal Funding Source
Southern University and A&M College, Baton Rouge, Louisiana	1880	Louisiana
Southern University at New Orleans, New Orleans, Louisiana	1956	Louisiana
Southwestern Christian College, Terrell, Texas	1949	Church of Christ
Spelman College, Atlanta, Georgia*	1881	Presbyterian
Stillman College, Tuscaloosa, Alabama*	1876	Presbyterian
Talladega College, Talladega, Alabama*	1867	United Church of Christ
Tennessee State University, Nashville, Tennessee	1912	Tennessee
Texas College, Tyler, Texas*	1894	Christian Methodist Episcopal
Texas Southern University, Houston, Texas	1947	Texas
Tougaloo College, Tougaloo, Mississippi*	1869	United Church of Christ
Tuskegee University, Tuskegee, Alabama*	1881	Alabama
University of Arkansas at Pine Bluff, Pine Bluff, Arkansas	1873	Arkansas
University of Maryland Eastern Shore, Princess Anne, Maryland	1886	Maryland
University of the District of Columbia, Washington, D.C.	1977	D.C./Federal
University of the Virgin Islands, St. Thomas, United States Virgin Islands	1962	U.S. Virgin Islands
Virginia State University, Petersburg, Virginia	1882	Virginia
Virginia Union University, Richmond, Virginia*	1865	Baptist
Virginia University of Lynchburg, Lynchburg, Virginia	1886	Baptist
Voorhees College, Denmark, South Carolina*	1897	Episcopal
West Virginia State University, Institute, West Virginia	1891	West Virginia
Wilberforce University, Wilberforce, Ohio*	1856	Methodist Episcopal
Wiley College, Marshall, Texas*	1873	Methodist Episcopal
Winston-Salem State University, Winston-Salem, North Carolina	1892	North Carolina
Xavier University of Louisiana, New Orleans, Louisiana*	1925	Catholic

* United Negro College Fund member college

African American Occupational Distribution, 1900 and 2010

1900

Occupation/Industry	Percentage of African American Laborers	Occupation/Industry	Percentage of African American Laborers
Agricultural laborers	33.7	Nurses and midwives	0.5
Farmers, planters, and overseers	19.0	Clergymen	0.4
Unspecified laborers	13.7	Tobacco and cigar factory operatives	0.4
Servants and waiters	11.7	Hostlers[2]	0.4
Launderers	5.5	Bricklayers and stonemasons	0.4
Draymen, hackmen, and teamsters[1]	1.7	Dressmakers	0.3
Steam railroad employees	1.4	Iron- and steelworkers	0.3
Miners and quarrymen	0.9	Seamstresses	0.3
Sawmill and planing mill employees	0.8	Janitors and sextons[3]	0.3
Porters and helpers (in stores etc.)	0.7	Housekeepers and stewards	0.3
Teachers and professors	0.5	Fishermen	0.3
Carpenters and joiners	0.5	Engineers and firemen	0.2
Turpentine farmers and laborers	0.5	Blacksmiths	0.2
Barbers and hairdressers	0.5	Other occupations	4.6

1. Drivers of horses, cabs, and trucks.   2. Those who look after horses or service vehicles.   3. Those who maintain graveyards.

2010

Occupation/Industry	Percentage of African American Laborers	Occupation/Industry	Percentage of African American Laborers
Educational and health services	30.1	Financial activities	5.6
Retail trade	11.2	Other services	4.1
Leisure and hospitality	8.9	Construction	3.3
Manufacturing	8.4	Information	2.3
Transportation and utilities	7.6	Wholesale trade	1.9
Government	7.2	Agriculture and related industries	0.4
Professional and business services	5.7	Mining	0.2

SOURCES FOR BOTH TABLES: U.S. Census Bureau, 1900 Census of Population and Housing, Bulletin 8: Negroes in the United States, table LXII; U.S. Bureau of Labor Statistics, "Employment and Earnings Online," January 2011 issue, March 2011, http://www.bls.gov/opub /ee/home.htm and http://www.bls.gov/cps/home.htm.

African American Regional Distribution, 1850–2010

| Year | Percentage of Total Population | | | |
	Northeast	Midwest	South	West
1850	1.7	2.5	37.3	0.7
1860	1.5	2.0	36.8	0.7
1870	1.5	2.1	36.0	0.6
1880	1.6	2.2	36.0	0.7
1890	1.6	1.9	33.8	0.9
1900	1.8	1.9	32.3	0.7
1910	1.9	1.8	29.8	0.7
1920	2.3	2.3	26.9	0.9
1930	3.3	3.3	24.7	1.0
1940	3.8	3.5	23.8	1.2
1950	5.1	5.0	21.7	2.9
1960	6.8	6.7	20.6	3.9
1970	8.9	8.1	19.1	4.9
1980	9.9	9.1	18.6	5.2
1990	11.0	9.6	18.5	5.4
2000	11.4	10.1	18.9	4.9
2010	11.8	10.4	19.2	4.8

SOURCES: U.S. Census Bureau; U.S. Census Bureau, *Census 2000 Redistricting Data (Public Law 94-171) Summary File*, table PL1; U.S. Census Bureau, *2010 Census Redistricting Data (Public Law 94-171) Summary File*, table P1; U.S. Census Bureau, *Census 2000 Redistricting Data (Public Law 94-171)* Population Characteristics (1990 CP-1).

Glossary of Key Terms

This Glossary of Key Terms contains definitions of words and ideas that are central to your understanding of the material covered in this textbook. Each term in the Glossary is in boldface purple in the text when it is first defined. We have included the page number(s) on which the full discussion of the term appears so that you can easily locate the complete explanation. We have also included the page numbers for documents that appear in the first Appendix.

For words not defined here, two additional resources may be useful: the Index, which will direct you to many more topics discussed in the text, and a good dictionary.

abolitionist movement (232): A loose coalition of organizations with black and white members that worked in various ways to end slavery immediately.

abroad marriages (202): Marriages between slaves who belonged to different owners and lived on different plantations.

accommodationism (371): A strategy, popularized by Booker T. Washington, for achieving black progress through vocational/industrial training and an acceptance of the racial status quo, including segregation.

affirmative action (542): A set of ideas and programs aimed at compensating African Americans for past discrimination by giving them preferential treatment in hiring and school admissions.

Allies (441): The nations that fought against the Axis powers in World War II. Among the Allies were the United States, Canada, France, Great Britain, Mexico, and the Soviet Union.

American Missionary Association (235): A Protestant missionary organization resulting from the merger of black and white missionary societies in 1846 to promote abolition and black education.

American Recovery and Reinvestment Act (ARRA) (2009) (638): A measure intended to boost the economy that included tax incentives, expansion of unemployment benefits, aid to low-income workers and retirees, and money for infrastructure improvements.

Amistad **case** (190): An 1839 slave insurrection aboard the *Amistad*, a Spanish ship, in international waters near Cuba. The case became a widely publicized abolitionist cause and ultimately reached the U.S. Supreme Court, which freed the rebels in 1841.

asiento (18): A contract or trade agreement created by the Spanish crown.

Atlanta Compromise speech (1895) (371, A-28–A-30): Booker T. Washington's classic statement of racial conciliation and accommodationism.

Atlantic Charter (1941) (441): A document signed by President Franklin Roosevelt and British prime minister Winston Churchill in August 1941. Among other things, it declared that all people had the right to economic advancement, to social security, and to choose their own form of government.

Axis powers (441): The nations that fought against the United States and the other Allies in World War II. The principal Axis powers were Germany, Italy, and Japan.

barracoons (22): Barracks or sheds where some slaves were confined before boarding the slave ships.

bilboes (27): Iron hand and leg cuffs used to shackle slaves.

Black Arts Movement (530): The cultural side of black power, in which black musicians, artists, dancers, playwrights, and novelists in the 1960s and 1970s used their talent to demonstrate black pride and nationhood.

Black Cabinet (417): The informal name of the Federal Council on Negro Affairs, a group of black New Deal political advisers organized by Mary McLeod Bethune in 1937.

black church (626): A term often used to indicate the centrality of black religious congregations in African American life. Traditionally, the church served as an educational, social, and civil rights center as well as a place of worship. This does not, however, indicate that all black people attend the same church or belong to the same denomination.

black codes (307): Laws regulating the labor and behavior of freedpeople passed by southern states in the immediate aftermath of emancipation. These laws were overturned by the Civil Rights Act of 1866.

black convention movement (227): A series of national, regional, and local conventions, starting in 1830, where black leaders addressed the concerns of free and enslaved blacks.

Black History Month (405): A celebration of African American history and culture that began in 1926 as Negro History Week, established by Carter G. Woodson. It became Black History Month in 1976.

black laws (148): Laws adopted in some midwestern states requiring all free black residents to supply legal proof of their free status and post a cash bond of up to $1,000 to guarantee their good behavior.

black nationalism (244, 529): A diffuse ideology founded on the idea that black people constituted a nation within a nation. It fostered black pride and encouraged black people to control the economy of their communities.

Black Reconstruction (312): The revolutionary political period from 1867 to 1877 when, for the first time ever, black men actively participated in the mainstream politics of the reconstructed southern states and, in turn, transformed the nation's political life.

black tax (619): A colloquial reference to the extra work African Americans must do to achieve the same goals as whites. Many also use the term to indicate that black people, regardless of individual achievements, are held responsible for the behavior of black people collectively.

Bloody Sunday (1965) (538): A confrontation on March 7, 1965, between black voting rights advocates and Alabama state troopers on the Edmund Pettus Bridge in Selma, Alabama.

Bobalition (156): A rendition of the word *abolition*, based on what whites heard as a mispronunciation by blacks. It was used on broadsides and in newspapers to mock free black celebrations of abolition.

bozales (16): A term used by the Spanish for recently imported African captives.

broken windows theory (650): A criminology theory that holds that if small crimes are left unaddressed, bigger, more serious crimes are sure to follow. For example, if the windows of a building are not repaired, vandals will break more windows, and soon the building itself will be burglarized. Cities that adopt the broken windows method of policing closely monitor behavior such as loitering and public alcohol and drug consumption in order to prevent crimes like larceny and murder.

Brown v. Board of Education of Topeka (1954) (489, A-25–A-26): A landmark U.S. Supreme Court case that overturned *Plessy v. Ferguson* (1896) by declaring that segregated public schools were inherently unequal.

buffalo soldiers (322): Black soldiers who served in U.S. army units in the West.

busing (578): A strategy to promote integration by transporting black children to predominantly white schools and white children to predominantly black schools.

carceral state (629): The extensive surveillance and criminalization of public spaces that results in restricted mobility and control of people's behavior.

carracks/caravels (11): Small sailing ships used by the Portuguese to explore Africa and the Atlantic world. Lightweight, fast, and easy to maneuver, they generally had two or three masts.

cash crops (25, 76, 133, 175): Readily salable crops grown for commercial sale and export rather than local use.

chain migration (394): A migration pattern in which initial migrants prepare the way for family members and friends to follow, creating migrant clusters from specific locales in their new settings.

chattel slavery (52): A system by which slaves were considered portable property and denied all rights or legal authority over themselves or their children.

civil disobedience (238): The refusal to obey a law that one believes is unjust.

Civil Rights Act of 1866 (313): An act defining U.S. citizenship and protecting the civil rights of freedpeople.

Civil Rights Act of 1875 (318, A-17–A-18): An act requiring equal treatment regardless of race in public accommodations and on public conveyances.

Civil Rights Act of 1964 (528, A-18–A-21): A law prohibiting discrimination in places of public accommodation, outlawing bias in federally funded programs, authorizing the U.S. Justice Department to initiate desegregation lawsuits, and providing technical and financial aid to communities desegregating their schools. President Lyndon Johnson used his considerable influence to break a record-setting 534-hour filibuster in the Senate.

Civil Rights Cases (1883) (322): The U.S. Supreme Court ruling overturning the Civil Rights Act of 1875.

Code Noir (71): The slave code used in France's New World colonies.

coffle (22): A group of animals, prisoners, or slaves chained together in a line.

colonization (158): The idea that blacks should be sent back to Africa or moved to another territory outside the United States.

Community Action Programs (**CAPs**) (553): Programs initiated and financed by President Lyndon Johnson's War on Poverty that directed antipoverty agencies to involve poor people in solving the problems of their own communities.

Compromise of 1850 (237): A compromise aimed at reducing sectional tensions by admitting California as a free state; permitting the question of slavery to be settled by popular sovereignty in New Mexico and Utah Territories; abolishing the slave trade in the District of Columbia; resolving the Texas debt issue; and enacting a new fugitive slave law.

Confederate States of America (263): The eleven southern states that seceded from the United States in 1860 and 1861, precipitating the Civil War.

Congressional Black Caucus (588): An organization of black representatives that became an official presence in Congress in 1971. It supported black candidates, lobbied for social reforms, and attempted to fashion a national strategy to increase black political power.

Congress of Industrial Organizations (**CIO**) (419): An association of unions based on industry rather than skill. African Americans joined CIO unions in record numbers during World War II.

conjure (94): Traditional African folk magic in which men and women called conjurers draw on the powers of the spirit world to influence human affairs.

contraband (267): A refugee slave seeking protection behind Union lines. This designation recognized slaves' status as human property and paved the way for their emancipation.

convict lease (307): A penal system in which convict labor is hired out to landowners or businesses to generate income for the state.

country marks (59): Facial scars indicating particular African origins.

creole (57): A language that originated as a combination of other languages; the term *creole* can also refer to people who are racially or culturally mixed.

Creole insurrection (190): An 1841 slave insurrection aboard the *Creole*, a ship carrying 135 slaves from Hampton Roads, Virginia, to New Orleans, Louisiana.

crop lien (307): An agricultural system in which a farmer borrows against his anticipated crop for the seed and supplies he needs and settles his debt after the crop is harvested.

debt peonage (358): A system of forced labor requiring servitude in exchange for payment of one's debts. This system trapped thousands of black agricultural workers in the South in conditions not unlike those of slavery.

de facto segregation (487): Racial separation that occurs in practice — as a result of housing patterns or social custom, for example — but is not based on law. Though caused by particular practices, these causes are less visible than the causes of de jure segregation and often appear to be the result of unintentional or natural circumstances.

de jure segregation (488): Racial separation mandated by law.

diaspora (4): The dispersion of a people from their homeland. Applied to Africans, this term usually describes the mass movement of Africans and their descendants to the Americas during the slave trade.

Double V campaign (444): Nickname for the "Double Victory" campaign, a World War II strategy committing African Americans to fight for liberty both at home and abroad.

Dred Scott v. Sandford (1857) (243, A-24): The controversial U.S. Supreme Court decision ruling that Scott, a slave, was not entitled to sue in the Missouri courts and was not free even though he had been taken into a free territory; that no person of African descent could be a citizen; that slaves were property; and that Congress had no authority to regulate slavery in the territories.

driver (59): A slave assigned to oversee the work of other slaves.

Economic Opportunity Act (1964) (546): Part of President Lyndon Johnson's War on Poverty, this act established the Job Corps, Head Start, the Neighborhood Youth Corps, and Volunteers in Service to America (VISTA).

Elmina Castle (18): A fortress in present-day Ghana, built by the Portuguese as a trading post in 1482 and used as a major slave trading center by the Dutch from 1637 to 1814.

Emancipation Proclamation (1863) (271, A-14–A-15): A presidential proclamation, issued by Abraham Lincoln, freeing all slaves under Confederate control and authorizing the use of black troops in the Civil War.

encomienda (14): A labor system used by the Spanish in their colonization of the Americas. Under this system, the crown granted colonists control over a specified number of Native Americans from whom they could extract labor.

Equal Employment Opportunity Commission (EEOC) (528, A-20–A-21): The agency charged, under Title VII of the 1964 Civil Rights Act, with investigating and litigating cases of employment discrimination.

Executive Order 8802 (1941) (443): President Franklin Roosevelt's response to the March on Washington Movement. It banned racial discrimination in defense industries and created the Fair Employment Practices Commission (FEPC).

Executive Order 9981 (1948) (463): Issued by President Harry Truman, this order called for "equality of treatment and opportunity for all persons in the armed services without regard to race, color, religion, or national origin."

Exodusters (324): Black migrants who left the South to settle on federal land in Kansas.

Fair Housing Act (1968) (589): A law prohibiting discrimination based on race, color, religion, or national origin in the sale or rental of housing, and making the practices of blockbusting, steering, and redlining (see chapter 12) illegal. Subsequent amendments prohibited discrimination based on sex, familial status, and disability.

fictive kin (203): People regarded as family even though they were not related by blood or marriage.

Fifteenth Amendment (ratified 1870) (318, A-12): The constitutional amendment that enfranchised black men.

First Confiscation Act (1861) (267): A congressional act authorizing the confiscation of Confederate property, including slaves employed in the rebellion, who were then considered free.

Force Acts (1870, 1871) (320): Two laws providing federal protection of blacks' civil rights in the face of white terroristic activities.

Four Freedoms (441): The four essential human rights that, in January 1941, President Franklin Roosevelt proclaimed people everywhere ought to have. These included freedom of speech and religion and freedom from want and fear.

Fourteenth Amendment (ratified 1868) (313, A-11–A-12): The constitutional amendment that defined U.S. citizenship to include blacks and guaranteed citizens due process and equal protection of the laws.

Freedmen's Bureau (1865–1869) (283): The federal agency created to aid freedpeople in their transition to freedom.

Freedom Rides (497): An organized effort in 1961 to desegregate interstate travel by having white and black students ride buses through the South and use "whites only" facilities.

freedom suits (102): Legal actions by which slaves sought to achieve freedom in British and American courts.

Fugitive Slave Act (1850) (237): Part of the Compromise of 1850, this law strengthened federal authority over fugitive slaves.

fugitive slave clause (135): The constitutional clause permitting slave owners of any state to retrieve their fugitive slaves from any other state.

gag rule (190): A series of congressional resolutions passed by the House of Representatives between 1836 and 1840 that tabled, without discussion, petitions regarding slavery; the gag rule was instituted to silence dissent over slavery. It was repealed in 1844.

GI Bill (1944) (464): The popular name of the Servicemen's Readjustment Act, providing returning soldiers with educational benefits, low-interest home loans, and unemployment benefits. African Americans were disproportionately denied these benefits.

Great Awakening (96): A multidenominational series of evangelical revivals that took place in North America between the 1730s and the 1780s.

great migration (393): The migration of 1.5 million African Americans from the South to the metropolises of the North in the years 1915 to 1940.

Greensboro Four (496): The four black college students who, by sitting down at a segregated lunch counter in Greensboro, North Carolina, and requesting service in February 1960, initiated the nationwide sit-in movement.

Griggs v. Duke Power Co. (1971) (547, A-27–A-28): The U.S. Supreme Court ruling that held that IQ tests, high school diplomas, and other requirements that were not necessary for the performance of a job were by their very nature discriminatory and had to be eliminated.

Guanches (12): The aboriginal inhabitants of the Canary Islands.

Gullah (96): A creole language composed of a blend of West African languages and English.

habeas corpus (103): A feature of English common law that protects prisoners from being detained without trial. Translated literally, the Latin phrase means "you should have the body."

half-freedom (65): A status allotted primarily to Dutch-owned slaves who helped defend New Netherland against Indian attacks. Half-freedom liberated adult slaves but not their children.

Harlem Renaissance (409): The New Negro arts movement, a flourishing of African American art and culture rooted in Harlem in the 1920s.

Hell Fighters (399): The 369th Infantry Regiment, formed from the Fifteenth New York National Guard in Harlem, one of the most highly decorated fighting units of World War I.

hiring out (144): The practice of owners contracting out their slaves to work for other employers.

historically black colleges and universities (305, A-40–A-42): Separate institutions of higher learning for African Americans. Most of them were founded in the post-emancipation era.

imperialism (347): The late-nineteenth-century European and U.S. extension of political and economic power over nations in Africa, Asia, and the Americas.

indentured servants (52): White laborers who came to the English North American colonies under contract to work for a specified amount of time, usually four to seven years.

Indian Removal Act (1830) (178): An act signed into law by President Andrew Jackson forcing Indians living east of the Mississippi River to relocate to Indian Territory (present-day Oklahoma).

institutional racism (544): Discrimination practiced by corporations and governments.

invisible church (196): A term used to describe groups of African American slaves who met in secret for Christian worship.

Jena Six case (2006) (630): The arrest and indictment as adults of six black teenagers in Jena, Louisiana, for attempted murder after a schoolyard fight sent a white youth to the hospital.

Jim Crow (345): A system of laws and customs that enforced segregation, the spatial and physical separation of the races.

John Brown's raid (1859) (245): An unsuccessful attempt by the white abolitionist John Brown to seize the federal arsenal at Harpers Ferry, Virginia, and incite a slave insurrection.

Kansas-Nebraska Act (1854) (240): A law that allowed the residents of Kansas and Nebraska Territories to decide whether slavery should be allowed.

Kerner Commission (554): Officially, the National Advisory Commission on Civil Disorders. In 1968, it found that the violence plaguing inner cities could be traced to job discrimination and institutional racism rather than black power ideology or a particular organization.

Kwanzaa (541): An African American holiday first celebrated during the winter of 1966–67. Invented by Dr. Maulana Karenga, founder of the black power organization US, it is organized around the Nguzo Saba, or Seven Principles: Unity, Self-Determination, Collective Work and Responsibility, Cooperative Economics, Purpose, Creativity, and Faith.

ladinos (16): Latinized blacks who were born or raised in Spain, Portugal, or these nations' Atlantic or American colonies and who spoke fluent Spanish or Portuguese.

Little Rock Nine (496): The nine black students who, in 1957, tested *Brown v. Board of Education of Topeka* (1954) by enrolling in Little Rock Central High School in Little Rock, Arkansas.

living out (144): The practice of allowing slaves who were hired out in urban areas to keep part of their wages to pay for their rented lodgings.

Lord Dunmore's Proclamation (1775) (108): A document issued by Virginia's royal governor John Murray, the Earl of Dunmore, in November 1775, offering freedom to "rebel" colonists' slaves who joined his forces.

Louisiana Purchase (1803) (141): The federal government's purchase of Louisiana from France, which doubled the size of the United States and fostered the spread of slavery.

loyalists (108): Colonists who remained loyal to Britain during the American Revolution.

loyalty program (483): The program instituted by President Harry Truman in 1947 requiring federal employees to swear that they were not Communists or Communist affiliates. Many unions and several civil rights organizations adopted similar programs thereafter.

lying out (191): A form of resistance in which slaves hid near their home plantations, often to escape undesirable work assignments or abusive treatment by their owners.

lynching (351): The public murder, by a lawless mob, of an individual alleged to have committed a crime or a breach of social custom.

mandatory sentencing laws (628): Laws that require a judge to impose a specified sentence regardless of the circumstances of a crime.

March on Washington for Jobs and Freedom (1963) (508): A gathering of more than 250,000 Americans on August 28, 1963, to protest discrimination in all facets of American life. Martin Luther King Jr. delivered his "I Have a Dream" speech during the event.

March on Washington Movement (1941) (443): A. Philip Randolph's call for 50,000 to 100,000 black Americans to gather in Washington, D.C., on July 1, 1941, to demand equal opportunity for blacks in defense industries and the armed services.

maroons (49): Members of runaway slave communities; also known as cimarrons, from the Spanish *cimarrón*.

Million Man March (1995) (598): A gathering of mostly African American men on the National Mall in Washington, D.C. The men gathered to affirm their commitment to black women, children, and communities and to dedicate their lives to improving themselves and their communities.

Million Woman March (1997) (599): A gathering of mostly African American women on the Benjamin Franklin Parkway in Philadelphia. The women came together to affirm their commitment to one another and the black family and community.

Mississippi Freedom Democratic Party (**MFDP**) (535): An independent, nondiscriminatory political party established to represent black Mississippians at the 1964 Democratic National Convention.

Mississippi Freedom Summer Project (534): A massive education and voter registration campaign conducted in the summer of 1964.

Missouri Compromise (1820) (178): An agreement balancing the admission of Missouri as a slave state with the admission of Maine as a free state and prohibiting slavery north of latitude 36°30′ in any state except Missouri.

Montgomery bus boycott (1955–1956) (491): A thirteen-month boycott begun on December 1, 1955, when Rosa Parks refused to give up her seat to a white person on an Alabama bus. The boycott resulted in significant economic losses for the bus company.

moral suasion (230): A primary strategy in the abolitionist movement that relied on vigorous appeals to the nation's moral and Christian conscience.

Morgan v. Virginia (1946) (459): The U.S. Supreme Court ruling that declared the practice of making blacks sit in the back of the bus behind whites in interstate bus travel illegal.

Moynihan Report (554): The controversial 1965 report written primarily by Assistant Secretary of Labor Daniel Patrick Moynihan that labeled the black family dysfunctional and set off a storm of protest within black America.

mulatto (57): A person with mixed white and African ancestry.

mutual aid society (151): An organization or voluntary association in which members agreed to assist one another in securing benefits such as insurance.

National Association for the Advancement of Colored People (**NAACP**) (375): Founded in 1909, the leading advocacy group for black civil rights up to the present.

National Association of Colored Women (**NACW**) (356): A federation of black women's clubs founded in 1896 to promote the interrelated uplift of black women and black people.

National Equal Rights League (285): An organization established by black leaders in 1864 to promote emancipation, legal equality, and black male suffrage.

National Negro Congress (421): An umbrella organization of black organizations whose first national meeting in 1936 expressed a commitment to radical politics and militant labor organization and activism.

Naturalization Act of 1790 (148): The nation's first immigration law, which instituted a two-year residency requirement for immigrants who wished to become U.S. citizens and limited naturalization to free white people.

Nazism (442): A racist totalitarian ideology proclaiming Germans to be a superior race destined to rule the world.

Negro Election Day (93): An annual New England celebration in which black communities elected their own kings and governors in elaborate ceremonies that included royal processions, political parades, and inaugural parties.

New Lights (96): Protestant ministers who, during the Great Awakening, challenged traditional religious practices by delivering emotional sermons that urged listeners to repent and find salvation in Christ.

New Negro (402): A term used increasingly after World War I to describe a growing assertiveness animating African Americans, especially those associated with Marcus Garvey's Universal Negro Improvement Association and the Harlem Renaissance.

New Right (574): An ideology introduced in the late 1960s meant to broaden the conservative base of the Republican Party. Proponents added the politics of law and order and a meritocratic color-blind ideal to an ideology that had previously been centered on anticommunism, limited government, and racialism.

New York City draft riots (1863) (278): Antiblack riots sparked by white working-class opposition to the Union's military draft.

Niagara movement (1905) (373): A militant protest organization committed to revitalizing a national black civil rights agenda in opposition to Booker T. Washington's accommodationist program.

North Star (194): A star, also known as Polaris, that always points north and was used by escaped slaves to navigate their way to freedom.

Northwest Ordinance (1787) (134): An act of the Confederation Congress organizing the region known as the Old Northwest, which included U.S. territories north of the Ohio River and east of the Mississippi River. Slavery was banned in these territories.

Orangeburg Massacre (553): An incident that occurred on February 8, 1968, in Orangeburg, South Carolina, near the campus of the historically black South Carolina State College. Police were called to quell the violence that erupted after blacks were refused admittance to a "whites only" bowling alley. This incident is called a massacre because twenty-eight students were injured, and three unarmed students were shot in the back or side by police.

Pan-African Congress (1900) (373): An international meeting in London to address the welfare of Africans around the world and to argue for an end to European colonization of Africa.

Pan-Africanism (373): The notion, held by those both within and outside the African continent, of a shared global sense of African identity as well as an abiding concern for the welfare of Africans everywhere.

Pentecostalism (397): A religious movement that emphasized a personal and life-changing experience of grace and promoted the belief that the presence of the Holy Spirit is manifested by speaking in tongues.

personal liberty laws (237): A series of state laws in the North aimed at preventing the return of fugitive slaves to the South.

Plessy v. Ferguson (1896) (346, A-24–A-25): The U.S. Supreme Court decision upholding the constitutionality of state laws mandating racial segregation in public facilities.

political action (232): A primary strategy in the abolitionist movement that relied on working through political channels to force changes in the law and political practices.

Poor People's Campaign (552): A movement spearheaded in 1967–1968 by Martin Luther King Jr. and the Southern Christian Leadership Conference (SCLC) demanding a $30 billion antipoverty package from the U.S. government. The desired package would include a commitment to full employment, a guaranteed annual income measure, and increased construction of low-income housing.

popular sovereignty (237): An approach to resolving the question of whether to allow slavery in new states by letting residents of the territories decide.

Port Royal Experiment (269): An attempt by government officials and civilian volunteers to assist Sea Island slaves, who had been abandoned by their owners, in their transition to freedom.

post-black (623): A controversial term differentiating black identity at the end of the twentieth century from that during other periods in American history. Not to be confused with *post-racial*, this term emphasizes the individuality and diversity of black Americans.

post-racial (640): A controversial term used to indicate that racism no longer inhibits the life chances of minorities in America. Not to be confused with *post-black*, this term is often used by conservative blacks and whites.

Pound Cake speech (2004) (630): A widely debated speech in which the black comedian Bill Cosby castigated lower-class blacks for their behavior.

preliminary Emancipation Proclamation (1862) (271): A presidential proclamation giving the Confederacy one hundred days to cease the rebellion. If it did not, all its slaves would be freed.

Proclamation of Amnesty and Reconstruction (1863) (279): Lincoln's proposal for the reorganization and readmission into the Union of the defeated Confederate states.

progressivism (350): A wide-ranging reform movement that sought to eliminate corruption, bring efficiency to American political and economic life, and improve society.

Quaker (68): A member of the Religious Society of Friends, a pacifist Protestant sect known for its commitment to social justice.

racial profiling (641): Using race, rather than specific evidence, to determine how a person should be treated.

rap music (596): Type of music developed in the early to mid-1970s critiquing poverty, police surveillance, drug addiction, black-on-black crime, and unemployment.

Reconstruction Act of 1867 (first) (313): An act dividing the South into military districts and requiring the former Confederate states to write new constitutions at conventions with delegates elected by universal male suffrage.

Red-baited (485): Accused of being a Communist. Red-baiting was used to discredit individuals during the Red scare beginning in 1947 in order to undermine their politics.

Red Summer (1919) (401): The summer of 1919, in the aftermath of World War I, during which a series of more than two dozen race riots, many in northern cities, took place.

Regents of the University of California v. Bakke (1978) (579, A-27): The U.S. Supreme Court decision ruling that the university's medical school at Davis had discriminated against Allan Bakke, a white male, when it took race into account in determining admissions.

restrictive covenants (504): Discriminatory clauses in deeds that prohibited owners from selling their property to a person or family of a particular racial or religious group.

ring shout (197): A religious ritual developed by slaves in the West Indies and North America that involved forming a circle and shuffling counterclockwise while singing and praying.

Rockefeller drug laws (1973) (578): New York State laws imposing a mandatory sentence of fifteen years to life for possession of four ounces of a narcotic.

scientific racism (348): Pseudoscientific yet powerful notions of white superiority endorsed by most of the academic and scientific establishment until well into the twentieth century.

Scottsboro Boys case (1931) (419): A highly publicized series of trials of black youths in Scottsboro, Alabama, who were falsely accused of rape and successfully defended by lawyers paid for by the Communist Party.

Second Confiscation Act (1862) (269): A congressional act declaring freedom for all slaves employed in the rebellion and for refugee slaves able to make it to Union-controlled territory.

Second Great Awakening (189): A Christian revival movement that took place during the first half of the nineteenth century.

separate but equal (346): The legal doctrine established in *Plessy v. Ferguson* (1896) stating that as long as they were deemed equal to those of whites, separate (Jim Crow) facilities and accommodations for blacks did not violate the Fourteenth Amendment's equal protection clause.

settlement houses (396): Urban institutions created by progressive women reformers to house migrant women and help them adjust to urban life.

sharecropping (307): An agricultural system that emerged during Reconstruction in which a landowner contracts with a farmer to work a parcel of land in return for a share of the crop.

silent march (1917) (400): A mass march orchestrated by the NAACP down New York City's Fifth Avenue on July 28, 1917, to protest the horrific East St. Louis, Illinois, race riot of July 2.

Slaughterhouse Cases (1873) (322): The U.S. Supreme Court ruling limiting the authority of the Fourteenth Amendment. The ruling expanded the scope of state-level citizenship at the expense of U.S. citizenship.

Social Darwinism (348): The idea that the evolutionary notion of the survival of the fittest applies to society and the economy, used to justify white domination of both.

soldiers without swords (455): The name given to African American journalists because of their relentless reporting of the injustices blacks suffered during World War II.

Somerset case (1772) (103): A British legal case that freed an American slave named James Somerset and inspired other slaves to sue for their freedom.

southern strategy (112, 575): 1. An unsuccessful British military plan, adopted in late 1778, that was designed to defeat the patriots by recapturing the American South. 2. Policies adopted by President Richard Nixon in 1969 aimed at moving southern whites, who were traditionally Democrats, into the Republican Party.

Special Field Order 15 (1865) (282): A military order by Union general William T. Sherman distributing confiscated and abandoned Confederate land to freedmen.

Stono rebellion (1739) (75): A slave rebellion that took place near South Carolina's Stono River in 1739. It was led by slaves who hoped to find freedom in Spanish Florida. The rebels killed about twenty whites before they were captured and subdued.

"stop and frisk" (650): Otherwise known as a "Terry stop"—after a 1968 Supreme Court decision that upheld the constitutionality of such stops—stop and frisk is the practice by which the police detain and search anyone who appears to be engaged in suspicious activity. While some blacks and police argue that stop-and-frisk laws, which are used in tandem with broken windows policing, are necessary to keep a community and the police safe, most blacks and Latinos complain that stop and frisk amounts to police harassment of mostly innocent people. They believe that people of color are more likely than whites to be detained and patted down, which they say is unfair.

Taino Indians (14): One of the indigenous peoples of the Caribbean.

task system (59): A system of slave labor in which enslaved workers were assigned daily tasks and permitted to work unsupervised as long as they completed their tasks.

Thirteenth Amendment (1865) (283, A-11): The constitutional amendment that officially outlawed slavery everywhere in the Union.

Three-Fifths Compromise (135): A compromise between the northern and southern states, reached during the Constitutional Convention, establishing that three-fifths of each state's slave population would be counted in determining federal taxes and representation in the House of Representatives.

tight packing (27): Crowding the human cargo carried on slave ships to maximize profits. By contrast, "loose packing" involved carrying fewer slaves in better conditions in an effort to keep mortality rates low.

Title VII (528, A-20–A-21): The most contentious part of the Civil Rights Act of 1964, it banned discrimination in employment on the basis of race, color, religion, sex, or national origin and created the Equal Employment Opportunity Commission to investigate and litigate cases of job discrimination.

triangle trade (18): The trade system that propelled the transatlantic slave trade, in which European merchants exchanged manufactured goods for enslaved Africans, whom they shipped to the Americas to exchange for New World commodities, which they then shipped back to European markets.

truant (191): A slave who ran away for a limited period of time to visit loved ones; attend religious meetings or other social events; or escape punishment, abusive treatment, or undesirable work assignments.

Tuskegee Airmen (445): Black pilots trained by the Army Air Corps at Tuskegee Institute during World War II. The pilots earned distinction despite efforts to disband and malign them.

Uncle Tom's Cabin (1852) (240): A best-selling novel by Harriet Beecher Stowe that portrayed the horrors of slavery, boosted the abolitionist cause, and angered the proslavery South.

underground railroad (194): A network of antislavery activists who helped fugitive slaves escape to the North and Canada.

Union League (317): An organization founded in 1862 to promote the Republican Party. During Reconstruction, the league recruited freedpeople into the party and advanced their political education.

United Steelworkers of America v. Weber (579): The 1979 case in which the Supreme Court ruled that Brian Weber, a white male, had not been discriminated against by either the United Steelworkers union or the Kaiser Aluminum Corporation when they initiated a job training program to bring the proportion of blacks in the craft trades closer to their proportion in the local labor force. The decision was considered a victory for affirmative action.

Universal Negro Improvement Association (UNIA) (405): The global organization founded by Marcus Garvey in Jamaica in 1914 that promoted race pride, racial unity, black separatism, and African redemption.

uplift (221, 357): The idea that racial progress demands autonomous black efforts; especially seen as the responsibility of the more fortunate of the race to help lift up the less fortunate.

U.S. Colored Troops (273): The official designation for the division of black units that joined the U.S. army beginning in 1863.

vigilance committees (238): Groups led by free blacks and their allies in the North to assist fugitive slaves.

Voting Rights Act (1965) (538, A-21–A-22): An act outlawing literacy requirements and poll taxes and sending federal election examiners south to protect blacks' rights to register and vote.

Wade-Davis Bill (1864) (281): A congressional proposal for the reorganization and readmission into the Union of the defeated Confederate states. Lincoln refused to sign the bill.

white flight (544): The movement of whites out of urban areas to racially exclusive suburbs. It was facilitated by federal highway construction, federally subsidized low-interest loans, and discrimination against blacks.

white primary (350): A state primary election in the Democratic Party–controlled South in which the party functioned as a private club that determined its own membership and was thus able to exclude blacks. This practice was outlawed by *Smith v. Allwright* in 1944.

Wilmington Insurrection (1898) (351): A race riot in Wilmington, North Carolina, that restored white political power in the city and signaled the end of biracial politics in the city and state.

Wilmot Proviso (1846) (236): A controversial congressional proposal that sought to prohibit slavery in the new territories gained as a result of the Mexican-American War. Although it did not pass the Senate, it sparked angry debate between the North and South.

zoot suit riots (451): World War II riots in Los Angeles pitting white sailors and civilians against African American and Hispanic men. So called because of the blacks' and Latinos' broad felt hats, pegged trousers, and gold chains, which were popularly referred to as zoot suits.

Index

Mia Bay,
Waldo E. Martin Jr.,
and Deborah Gray White
(Copyright 2013 Macmillan, Photo by Denise Wydra)

About the Authors

Deborah Gray White (Ph.D., University of Illinois at Chicago) is Board of Governors Professor of History at Rutgers University. She is the author of many works including *Too Heavy a Load: Black Women in Defense of Themselves, 1894–1994*; *Ar'n't I a Woman? Female Slaves in the Plantation South*; the forthcoming *Lost in the USA: Marching for Identity at the Turn of Millennium*; and the edited volume *Telling Histories: Black Women Historians in the Ivory Tower*. She is a recipient of the John Simon Guggenheim Fellowship and the Woodrow Wilson International Center Fellowship.

Mia Bay (Ph.D., Yale University) is professor of history at Rutgers University and the director of the Rutgers Center for Race and Ethnicity. Her publications include *To Tell the Truth Freely: The Life of Ida B. Wells* and *The White Image in the Black Mind: African-American Ideas about White People, 1830–1925*. She is a recipient of the Alphonse Fletcher Sr. Fellowship and the National Humanities Center Fellowship. Currently, she is at work on a book examining the social history of segregated transportation and a study of African American views on Thomas Jefferson.

Waldo E. Martin Jr. (Ph.D., University of California, Berkeley) is the Alexander F. and May T. Morrison Professor of American History and Citizenship at the University of California, Berkeley. He is the author of *No Coward Soldiers: Black Cultural Politics in Postwar America*; *Brown v. Board of Education: A Brief History with Documents*; *The Mind of Frederick Douglass*; and, with Joshua Bloom, the coauthor of *Black against Empire: The History and Politics of the Black Panther Party*. With Patricia A. Sullivan, he serves as coeditor of the John Hope Franklin Series in African American History and Culture. Current projects include a forthcoming book on the impact of black cultural politics on the modern black freedom struggle.

Key to the Cover Images

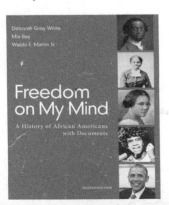

Top to bottom:

Olaudah Equiano

Harriet Tubman

Madame C. J. Walker

Shirley Chisholm

Barack Obama

Cover images (top to bottom): Royal Albert Memorial Museum, Exeter, Devon, UK/Bridgeman Images; Retrieved from the Library of Congress, https://www.loc.gov/item/2003674596; Granger, NYC; © Everett Collection Historical/Alamy Stock Photo; Andrew Harrer/Bloomberg via Getty Images